THE NEMESIS OF POWER

NEMESIS OF POWER
Unconditional Surrender, Rheims, May 7, 1945

THE
NEMESIS OF POWER

The German Army in Politics
1918–1945

JOHN W. WHEELER-BENNETT
K.C.V.O., C.M.G., O.B.E.

Second Edition

LONDON
MACMILLAN & CO LTD
NEW YORK · ST MARTIN'S PRESS
1964

MACMILLAN AND COMPANY LIMITED
St Martin's Street London WC2
also Bombay Calcutta Madras Melbourne

THE MACMILLAN COMPANY OF CANADA LIMITED
Toronto

ST MARTIN'S PRESS INC
New York

PRINTED IN GREAT BRITAIN

FOREWORD

IN the writing of this book I have been the fortunate recipient of much help and criticism from a number of friends to whom I would express my most sincere gratitude.

To my friends : Mr. James Joll of St. Antony's College ; Mr. Alan Bullock, the Censor of St. Catherine's Society ; Mr. James Passant, Mr. Brian Melland and the Hon. Margaret Lambert, all of whom have read the typescript of the book, I am immensely grateful for much stimulating and helpful comment and advice, to which both I and my book owe much. It is also with warm gratitude that I acknowledge my debt to Professor Sir Lewis Namier, whose wisdom, criticism and counsel have ever been to me a source of pleasure and improvement.

I am also greatly in the debt of many, both in England and in Germany, who have assisted me in the compilation and checking of facts, or in other ways. I would mention, with particular gratitude : the Bishop of Chichester, Dr. George Bell ; the Warden of Wadham College, Sir Maurice Bowra ; the Warden of St. Antony's College, Mr. F. W. D. Deakin ; Dr. K. T. Parker, Keeper of the Ashmolean Museum ; Sir George Ogilvie Forbes ; Sir Nevile Bland ; Major-General Sir Kenneth Strong ; Mr. Ian Colvin and others.

I must also gratefully acknowledge the very considerable obligation which I have incurred for the generous, kindly, efficient and indispensable aid which I have constantly received from Miss A. C. Johnston and her staff in the Documents Section of the Foreign Office Library, and from Dr. Alfred Wiener and his staff of the Wiener Library, 19 Manchester Square, W.1.

In the field of technical help, my most sincere thanks are due to Miss Elizabeth Wilson for the excellence of her translations, and to her and Mrs. P. E. Baker for their indefatigable and meticulous checking and correction of the proofs ; to my secretaries, Miss Juliet Heaton and Miss Dorothy Bonnaire, who between them have laboured through the typing of the whole MS. ; and to my wife for her invaluable assistance in the compilation of the bibliography.

J. W. W.-B.

v

The Germans have no taste for peace; renown is easier won among perils, and you cannot maintain a large body of companions except by violence and war. The companions are prodigal in their demands on the generosity of their chiefs. It is always 'give me that war-horse' or 'give me that bloody and victorious spear'. As for meals with their plentiful, if homely, fare, they count simply as pay. Such open-handedness must have war and plunder to feed it. You will find it harder to persuade a German to plough the land and to await its annual produce with patience than to challenge a foe and earn the prize of wounds. He thinks it spiritless and slack to gain by sweat what he can buy with blood.

TACITUS, *Germania*, 14 (trans. H. Mattingly)

The German nation is sick of principles and doctrines, literary existence and theoretical greatness. What it wants is Power, Power, Power! And whoever gives it Power, to him will it give honour, more honour than he can ever imagine.

JULIUS FROEBEL, in 1859
Quoted by Heinrich, Ritter von Srbik in
Deutsche Einheit, III, p. 5

PREFACE TO THE SECOND EDITION

SINCE this book was written the German Army has been reborn. It might perhaps be more correct to say two German Armies, because the Soviet Union and the Western Powers have vied with one another in rearming their German allies. The Federal German Army (*Bundeswehr*) was formally created on November 12, 1955, and we have had the opportunity to observe its impact on German politics during the last eight years. The position of the so-called ' People's Army ' in East Germany is of less importance. Despite its apparent regard for old traditions — even down to the goose-step — it is, like other institutions in that sad satellite, the product of an alien régime which can be expected to wither at the root the moment Soviet protection is removed from it.

At the end of this book I pose the question : ' *Is* there a new spirit abroad in Germany or is this merely " where we came in " in the repetitive history of the German Army in politics ? ' It is no part of my purpose here to estimate the influence of the *Bundeswehr* in Federal German politics to-day. Nevertheless the events of the past few years have not suggested that this issue is an unimportant one. Nor does it seem to me that we can afford to ignore the lessons of the past when making an assessment of Germany's armed forces, or when taking decisions about our future attitude towards them.

I am thankfully aware that in many respects, as Mr. Allemann has told us, Bonn is not Weimar. The *Bundeswehr* has not been able to maintain unbroken the tradition of the Prussian/German Army and its Officer Corps as was done after the First World War. The relative positions of the new Republic and the new Army are very different from those which pertained in 1919. Then a nation in political confusion was forced to rely on the army as a pillar of support against anarchy. By skill and evasion the Officer Corps avoided committing itself to a whole-hearted defence of the Republic and escaped responsibility for Germany's defeat and her subsequent hardships. In 1955 the situation was quite different. Monarchism was out of date and the Nazi movement had lost its prestige after leading the Germans into an unparalleled disaster. In the form of the Federal Republic Western Germany had been transformed with remarkable rapidity from an abjectly defeated nation to a Sovereign

State allied to three of her erstwhile victors. Economically the country was flourishing, and it has continued to be so. The Army was the creation of the Republic and not an unreliable ally capable of maintaining a dangerous autonomy. The law regulating the new army (the *Soldatengesetz*) was framed with conscious attention to the problem of associating the German Army with a democratic state system, and the Federal German Parliament has established a standing committee to consider military affairs. Lastly, those optimistic about the future of Germany's armed forces can point to the fact that all her troops are integrated into NATO and come under the control of the Allied Supreme Commander.

One hopes that the grounds for such optimism are not misplaced. The position which the Federal Defence Ministry has obtained in Federal politics during the last eight years must warn us against taking the Army's rôle too lightly. In a country where military questions are of such importance, the Army and its political leadership are bound to form a very influential part of the administration. Revelations during the ministerial crisis which led to the resignation of the Defence Minister, Herr Franz-Josef Strauss, in November 1962 did not reassure the public that the Defence Ministry would always use its executive powers in the most scrupulous fashion.

Although the *Bundeswehr* is a new creation it has by no means turned its back on the traditions of its predecessor, and its leading personnel form a physical link with the older organization. An unfortunate result of cold war tensions has been a tendency to gloss over the less attractive features of Germany's military history, a tendency which is eagerly exploited by those who wish to see the old German Army rehabilitated. Even assuming that anti-democratic forces in German political life have for the moment been eclipsed, one is justified in asking how far the nation's attitude towards its military past has really altered since the war. The myth of the unpolitical soldier dies hard. When discussing the recruitment of volunteer cadres for the foundation of the new army in June 1955, Herr Blank told the Federal Parliament that: 'The German soldier did his duty loyally and obediently. He believed himself to be doing it for his Fatherland. He was misused by a criminal leadership. Therein lies his tragedy.' It might fairly be remarked that the German soldier's refusal to question where his duty lay was a tragedy for his fellow countrymen and for the rest of the world.

During the last few years a great deal of work has been done, both in Germany and elsewhere, on recent German history, with especial emphasis on the failure of the Weimar Republic and the tragedy of the German opposition to Hitler. I have found much that is interesting in these accounts, but I have had no cause to alter my interpretations of either the Army in German politics between the two world wars or of the rôle played by the military in the opposition to Hitler.

So far as the earlier period is concerned I adhere to my view that the *Reichswehr* owed its extraordinarily independent position in the Weimar Republic to von Seeckt, and that it had cause to regret the machinations of von Schleicher. By keeping the Officer Corps out of politics von Seeckt managed to preserve its integrity and traditions. Had it not been for him the Army would have found it difficult to maintain its old character in a republican era. This may well have been a tragedy for Germany; nobody can deny von Seeckt's rôle in carrying it through. It is true that he had political aspirations and even dreamed of becoming *Reich* President, but he was cautious enough to know his own limitations and the *Reichswehr* benefited from his shrewdness. I find the apologists for von Schleicher less impressive. He was undeniably intelligent and a patriot after his own fashion. Yet none of the publications which have appeared since this book first went to press has convinced me that his plans and intrigues were other than disastrous for Germany, disastrous because they were based neither on sound political principles nor on the wisdom which comes from long experience in a responsible public office.

To turn to the later period, there has been considerable disagreement about the extent to which the German General Staff can be held responsible for the outbreak of war in 1939, and for the manner in which the war was waged. In particular it has been denied that the military leaders knew how Hitler intended to behave towards his victims in Eastern Europe. Interest has centred on the meeting at the Berghof on August 22, 1939, at which the *Führer* explained his decision to attack Poland. It has been claimed that some accounts of this meeting are misleading, and that Hitler did no more than discuss the possibility of war with his generals, giving them no inkling of his projected brutality towards the Polish population. I have already explained the difficulties involved in assessing the evidence about this meeting in my footnote on page 447. Hitler's address was long and confusion has arisen because some accounts refer to only one part of it. Nor is it surprising that some reports should be more colourful than others, but the similarities between all of them are striking and I remain convinced of their general validity. This is, of course, a matter of interpretation, but I think that the reader who consults even one of the more reserved accounts — such as that given in Halder's recently published *Kriegstagebuch* (vol. 1, pp. 23-6) — will be left in little doubt that Hitler had given his generals a good idea of what sort of war he intended to wage in Poland.

Lastly, a word on the German opposition to Hitler. Some distinguished Germans — Dr. Gerhard Ritter, for example — have been angered by my suggestion that a victory for the German opposition in 1938 or 1944 might not have been an unmixed blessing for the Germans and for Europe. I think we should ask ourselves two questions when considering this problem. First, could the conspirators have provided Germany with a system of government suitable for a modern industrial society? Second, were the opposition circles capable of building a Germany which would be able to take its place in the community of nations without provoking international conflict? So far as internal policy is concerned I do not feel that very many of the opposition showed themselves able to come to terms with the twentieth century. Dr. Ritter himself remarks that German political parties and trade unions owed their reappearance after 1945 largely to the influence of the occupying powers — striking tribute, one would think, to the allied policy of re-education upon which so much contempt has been lavished. As to the international question, one can hardly do better than turn to Dr. Ritter's own excellent biography of that most intelligent and courageous conspirator, Carl Goerdeler. What Dr. Ritter has to tell us about Goerdeler's European schemes does not leave an impression of acute statesmanship. It is worth remembering that when Goerdeler approached Vansittart in the spring of 1938 with proposals for a European settlement he included as a matter of course the cession of the Sudetenland to Germany — a demand which had not at that time been made by the Nazi government — and that in 1939 he took a similarly generous view of Germany's Polish frontiers. Nobody would deny that the present situation in Europe is less than satisfactory. But would the world have been much more secure if, instead of the present power balance, a situation had existed in which a large and fully armed German state dominated Central Europe? It is an experiment which few of us would care to see attempted.

In this new edition I have listed in my bibliography what I consider to be the most important recent publications. Where possible I have amended the text if it seemed to me that my version had been proved inadequate. Responsibility for the views expressed is naturally still my own. Owing to the method of photographic reproduction used in this edition it has been impossible to conduct a wholesale revision, but I am satisfied that the text as it stands represents a fair interpretation of the German Army in politics from 1918 to 1945, and that this area of the past still deserves careful study by both the Germans and their allies.

In this work of revision I must once again acknowledge with gratitude the invaluable help of my friend Brian Melland.

Throughout the work I have been aided in a very major degree by Mr. Anthony Nicholls, a Research Fellow of St. Antony's College, Oxford. To his great ability and indefatigable effort, and to the meticulous accuracy of his research, I am deeply indebted. I am also most grateful to him for the pleasure which I have derived from our association in this project.

JOHN W. WHEELER-BENNETT

GARSINGTON MANOR,
    OXON.
  July 1963

INTRODUCTION

I T is little more than a hundred and sixty years ago that the Comte de Mirabeau, returning to Paris from an unsuccessful mission to Berlin, recorded two prophetic dictà on the country of his recent sojourn. *'La Prusse n'est pas un pays qui a une armée, c'est une armée qui a un pays'*, he wrote in 1788, and added, *'La guerre est l'industrie nationale de la Prusse'*.

In support of this view it must be recorded, without prejudice, that since it was expressed by Mirabeau, Prussia, or Germany, has become involved in no less than seven wars, of which four — those of 1813–15, 1864, 1866, and 1870–71 — have resulted in outstanding victories, but three have ended in disasters even more resounding. No country has been so roundly and truly defeated as Prussia at Jena and Germany at the close of the First and Second World Wars. No country has displayed a more phenomenal capacity for military resilience or for beating ploughshares into swords.

On the occasion of each of these pronounced defeats, the victor sought by every means and device known in his age, by restriction and supervision and compulsion, to destroy the German potential for war, physically, morally, and spiritually. All three attempts were to prove futile. The united and surreptitious genius of Scharnhorst and Gneisenau evaded the confining provisions of the Convention of Königsberg with the same staggering success that Hans von Seeckt's clandestine brilliance circumvented the disarmament clauses of the Treaty of Versailles, thus creating the framework for the military expansion effected with such speed and proficiency by Adolf Hitler. In each case the victors were outwitted to their subsequent detriment.

At the conclusion of the Second World War it did seem that the aim of the ages might be achieved and the spirit of German militarism laid to rest. The armed forces of the Reich, by the instruments of Unconditional Surrender, had become, one and all, prisoners of war. The High Command of those forces had made public acceptance of the responsibility for that Unconditional Surrender. The great German General Staff and the Officer Corps had for the second time in a quarter of a century been officially declared dissolved and

xiii

their re-creation pronounced a crime. The full force of Allied Occupation propaganda in Germany was turned against the spirit of militarism and toward the liquidation of the profession of arms as heretofore practised in Germany. The trials of war criminals resulted in the conviction, imprisonment or, in some cases, the execution of some of the outstanding personalities in Germany's politico-military leadership.

Germans were, in accordance with the agreement reached between the four Allied Powers on September 20, 1945,[1] and by subsequent rulings of the Allied Control Council,[2] prohibited from military organization in any form, and when the Western German Federal Republic was established in 1949, particular care was taken to safeguard the permanency of these provisions.[3] If ever provision was made for the permanent suppression and exorcism of German militarism it was during the years 1945–50.

And, who knows? It might have succeeded had not Fate, with one of those malevolent twists which have frequently changed the course of history, decided otherwise. Between 1950 and the present day there has occurred a complete transmogrification of the German scene. In a far shorter period than was the case after the First World War, German rearmament is now in operation, not, however, in secret contravention of treaty provisions but with the open and avid approval and the material assistance of the Western Allied Powers themselves. Provision for an army of some 12 divisions, comprising between 300,000 and 400,000 men to be raised by selective conscription,[4] and for an air-force of fighter squadrons with a complement of some 75,000 men, is already afoot. The register of the Officer Corps has already been re-established. The ex-Soldiers' Leagues are already in the field. The legends of the 'stab in the back' are already in circulation. Moreover, the

[1] Text in *The Axis in Defeat* (U.S. Department of State, publication 2423), pp. 7-81.
[2] *E.g.* OMGUS, Law No. 154, *Elimination and Prohibition of Military Training,* July 14, 1945 ; Control Council Order No. 4, *Confiscation of Literature and Material of a Nazi and Militarist Nature,* May 13, 1946 ; Control Council Law No. 8, *Elimination and Prohibition of Military Training,* November 30, 1946 ; Control Council Law No. 23, *Prohibition of Military Construction in Germany,* April 10, 1946 ; Control Council Directive No. 18, *Disbandment and Dissolution of the German Armed Forces,* November 12, 1945.
[3] Article 139 of the Bonn Constitution reads as follows : 'The legal provisions enacted for the liberation of the German people from National Socialism and militarism shall not be affected by the provisions of this Basic Law'.
[4] Radio statement by Herr Theodor Blank at Bonn, January 20, 1952 (*The Times,* January 21, 1952).

apologists for the German militarists are already active in our own country.

The cause and reason for this amazing shift in policy has been the progressive change of the Soviet Union from the status of respected ally, which she enjoyed in 1945, to that of suspect aggressor and saboteur of peace. So complete has been this transformation that the Western Continental Powers, backed by the United States and Great Britain, have been constrained to take extraordinary precautions for the protection of their security and independence against threatened Soviet aggression. This has involved, willy-nilly, a reversal of the policy universally accepted for Germany at the close of the war. It has entailed the readmission of the principle of an armed Germany — albeit fenced about with restrictions and limitations.[1] It has necessitated the formation of the North Atlantic Treaty Organization (NATO) and the European Defence Community (E.D.C.), into the latter of which the new German *Wehrmacht* is to be integrated.

Let it be said at once that the policy pursued by successive British Governments, in collaboration with their allies, is essentially the only one to follow under the exigencies of present conditions. The defence of Western Europe demands a contribution of strength from Western Germany; there can be no doubt of this. The courageous doctrine preached long ago by Mr. Churchill and which has now become the fundamental of the policy of H.M. Government, whether it be conducted by Conservatives or Socialists — the doctrine of opposing aggression and tyranny, from whatever quarter they may come, with steadfastness and courage, and, in addition, of taking first things first — makes it imperative that we should pocket our scruples at the prospect of accepting the Germans as allies and should subordinate to the requirements of the greater danger such apprehensions as one may entertain at the spectacle of a rearmed Germany.

But we should be doing less than our duty — and even a positive disservice to posterity — if, in our anxiety to make secure the future, we were to forget or ignore the lessons of the past. In a Press

---

[1] These decisions were taken at meetings of the Conference of the Three Foreign Ministers and of the North Atlantic Council in New York in September 1950, and of the Council of the Brussels Treaty Powers, at Brussels, in the following December, and were finally confirmed at the Lisbon meeting of the North Atlantic Council in February 1952. It should, however, be remembered that a revival of militarism had already begun considerably earlier in Eastern Germany under direct Russian supervision.

conference at Ottawa in January 1952, Mr. Churchill, who could never be accused of not being a realist in politics, is reported to have said of the projected European Army that its marching songs would doubtless be the *Sambre et Meuse* and the *Wacht am Rhein* — and added meaningly, 'Let us hope that it will not become *Deutschland über alles*'.[1] The warning is both salutary and necessary.

It is against this kaleidoscopic background of men and events, of the changes and permutations of policies and objectives, that this book has been written. It is not a history of the German Army as a military force, nor of the Weimar Republic, nor of Opposition and Resistance to Hitler before and during the Second World War, though all these factors have their natural bearing on the central theme — the German Army in Politics. This book attempts to tell the story of how the German Army survived the circumstances of its hitherto most disastrous defeat in November 1918; of how, having survived, it proceeded to dominate the political life of the German Republic; of how, by its very withdrawal from the active arena of politics, it exercised an amazing degree of power and influence, in the furtherance of which, be it remembered, the Army did not hesitate to collaborate with Soviet Russia; and of how, when it was mistaken enough to come down into the arena and to play politics instead of controlling them, it began a descent which only ended in abject defeat — militarily, politically and spiritually. It has also been my aim to show the extent of the responsibility of the Army for bringing the Nazis to power, for tolerating the infamies of that régime once it had attained power, and for not taking the measures — at a time when only the Army could have taken them — to remove that regime from power.

It is, in fact, the story of how the German Army, having achieved supreme power within the State, threw away the substance for the shadow and became a victim to the Nemesis of this action.

It is also, in some respects, a moral tale. It may be, with the disappearance of Prussia from the map of Germany, with the Reich dichotomized by an Iron Curtain, that Mirabeau's foreboding will be stilled, that the German Army will cease to possess the German State, that the 'national industry of Prussia' will be productive only as and when desired internationally, and that the infection of the virus of the *furor Teutonicus* may be at last eradicated from the body politic of Germany. All these things may come to pass, and it is to be devoutly and sincerely hoped that they will. But they will

[1] *Daily Telegraph*, January 8, 1952.

certainly fail to do so unless the rulers of Germany — and indeed the rulers of Germany's new allies — keep constantly before them the precept and warning of yet another Frenchman : '*L'état social et politique d'une nation est toujours en rapport avec la nature et la composition de ses armées*'.[1]

[1] Fustel de Coulange (1830–89), *La Cité antique*, p. 327.

JOHN W. WHEELER-BENNETT

GARSINGTON MANOR,
OXON.
July 1949–*June* 1952

CONTENTS

APPENDICES

LIST OF ILLUSTRATIONS

xxi

PART I

THE ARMY AND THE REICH
(1918–1926)

'We shall wait in vain for the awakening in our country of
that public spirit which the British and the French and
other peoples possess, if we do not imitate them in setting
for our military leaders certain bounds and limitations
which they must not disregard.'—FREIHERR VOM STEIN.

CHAPTER I

FROM SPA TO KAPP

(November 1918–March 1920)

(i)

VERY early in the morning of November 10, 1918, a little group of weary and saddened men stood to attention as a special train, whose splendours of cream and gold passed unnoticed in the darkness, glided quietly from its siding at the little Belgian station of Spa and vanished towards the Dutch frontier. The two red lamps on the rear carriage signified to those few who remained behind that the last of the German Emperors was passing into exile.

The departure of Wilhelm II from Spa came as the climax of a period of ever-increasing tension and dramatic incident.[1] On the previous day the Kaiser had heard from the lips of his First Quartermaster-General, Wilhelm Gröner, the bitter and historic words: *'Der Fahneneid ist jetzt nur eine Idee'*,[2] and, thus convinced at last that he no longer commanded the loyalty of his troops or his subjects, he had released his officers from their oaths of fealty and departed into exile, there to abdicate as German Emperor and King of Prussia.[3] His going marked the end of an epoch both for the German Reich and for the German Army, for it left the one without a Kaiser and the other without a War Lord.

For an Englishman, accustomed to the legal maxim that a soldier, at any rate in time of peace, 'is only a civilian armed in a

---

[1] A brilliant account of these events has been written by Professor Maurice Baumont, of the University of Paris, entitled *L'Abdication de Guillaume II* (Paris, 1930), of which an English translation, *The Fall of the Kaiser*, was published in New York in 1931. See also Kuno Graf von Westarp, *Das Ende der Monarchie am 9. November 1918* (Berlin, 1952), and J. W. Wheeler-Bennett, *Hindenburg: the Wooden Titan* (London, 1936), pp. 183-205.

[2] Literally translated these words mean 'The oath on the colours is now but a fiction', but their meaning is more clearly conveyed by: 'To-day oaths are but words'.

[3] Wilhelm II's original intention was to abdicate only as German Emperor and to retain his rights as King of Prussia; however, under pressure from Berlin, he signed on November 28, 1918, at Amerongen an unequivocal abdication both as King and Emperor.

3

particular manner'[1] and as much subject to jurisdiction of the civil courts as a civilian, it is particularly difficult to comprehend the predicament in which the abdication of Wilhelm II placed the Officer Corps of the German Army. Hitherto this exclusive group of persons had constituted a military caste bound only by the 'unconditional obedience' sworn to their Emperor, an obedience which had 'no legal limits' (keine rechtlichen Grenzen). They were thus, in the most literal sense of the phrase, a law unto themselves, for no civil court could touch them — and they behaved accordingly.

Indeed there is no parallel to the status which the Army occupied in Prussia and in Germany. In France, at the time of the Dreyfus Affair, considerable political pressure was brought to bear by the General Staff; and in Japan, during the decade which preceded the attack on Pearl Harbour, the military leaders exercised exceptional influence in the formulation of national policy. But in neither case is there any comparison with the circumstances and the extraordinary position of ascendancy which the military caste maintained in the Kingdom of Prussia and in the German Reich for very little short of a century and a half.

Born of the bitterness and humiliation which followed Napoleon's victories over Prussian arms at Jena and Auerstädt, the new military machine, which was to replace that bequeathed in moribund rigidity and obsolescence by Frederick the Great to his successors, was the brain-child of the twin genius of Scharnhorst and Gneisenau, and it is somewhat ironical that the creators of the new Prussian Officer Corps and of the Prussian General Staff were neither of them Prussians.[2]

The Prussian military reforms of 1808 aimed primarily at the breaking down of the exclusively aristocratic character of the Officer Corps as established by the Great Frederick[3] and its replacement

---

[1] A dictum of Lord Justice Bowen's in the case of Rex v. Gilliam, quoted by Brigadier-General J. H. Morgan, K.C., in Assize of Arms (London, 1945), i, 95 and 104. The position of the British civil courts vis-à-vis the military authorities was emphasized by Sir Leonard Costello when presiding at the Devon Quarter Sessions at Exeter on October 1, 1951. 'We can tolerate no interference with our orders either by the military authorities or any one else', he declared. 'We conceive it to be a fundamental principle of the British Constitution that the civil courts are paramount, at any rate, in time of peace' (Daily Telegraph, October 2, 1951).

[2] Gerhard Johann David von Scharnhorst (1755-1813) was born of a Hanoverian smallholder family, while August Wilhelm Anton, Graf Neithardt von Gneisenau (1760-1831), was the son of a Saxon officer.

[3] Frederick II had laid down his views on this point in an appendix to the Army Regulations of 1779 : 'It is much more requisite than is generally believed, in the choice of officers, to keep to the nobility, because nobles generally possess a sense of honour. It cannot, however, be denied that merit and talent are sometimes

by the formula evolved by Scharnhorst that 'in times of peace, knowledge and education only, and in times of war, outstanding bravery and the capacity of comprehensive understanding, shall constitute claims for the position of officers'.[1]

This was indeed a laudable basis of reorganization, but at the same time that it was enunciated it was accompanied by two additional principles, namely the introduction of the system whereby the members of the Officer Corps, who had hitherto been nominated by the royal prerogative of the King, were now elected by the Corps itself, and the innovation of the military Court of Honour, the *Ehrengericht*, with extensive authority over the members of the Corps, who came to regard themselves — and to be regarded — as less and less subject to the jurisdiction of civilian courts of justice. Contrary to the intentions of Scharnhorst and of Gneisenau, the result of their reforms was to sustain and strengthen, rather than to weaken, the concept of the Officer Corps as 'a hierarchical group so rigidly organized that it became a caste',[2] and whose members considered themselves as the knightly servants of the monarch and not of the nation.

The creation of the Prussian General Staff was an event in military science comparable in importance to the innovation of the ironclad and of aerial and mechanized warfare. Napoleon had revolutionized the science of war, but, though he had possessed a brilliant *Chef-d'état majeur* in Berthier, he lacked a highly trained General Staff which could interpret and exploit his genius, and it was to this fact — that his Marshals did not, or could not, enter into his ideas — that von Schlieffen[3] attributed the ultimate cause of the Emperor's defeat.

The essential basis of the General Staff as conceived by Gneisenau was to adapt the Napoleonic military heritage to modern methods and to combine and assimilate it with the tradition of

found also with people of no birth ; but it happens only rarely and in this case it is quite right to retain and advance such.' According, however, to Treitschke, Frederick, 'less friendly to the commoner than his father, thought that only an aristocrat had honour in his body. He removed the non-aristocratic officers from most of the troops, and in the aristocratic Officer Corps there developed a junker-spirit which was to become even more detestable than the coarse arrogance of former times.'

[1] Scharnhorst's *Fundamental Order of the Day*, August 3, 1808.

[2] Christian W. Gässler, *Offizier und Offizierkorps der alten Armee in Deutschland als Voraussetzung einer Untersuchung über die Transformation der militärischen Hierarchie* (Mannheim, 1930), p. 68.

[3] Alfred, Graf von Schlieffen (1833–1913), Chief of the Great German General Staff, 1891–1906 ; author of the famous 'Schlieffen Plan' for the attack on France by way of the invasion of Belgium.

Prussian military discipline and with the scientific thoroughness of the German universities. To this end the Prussian War Academy was founded by Clausewitz [1] in 1810. Here were enrolled picked members of the Officer Corps, who experienced the first stages of a process of rigorous intellectual selection, entailing intense physical strain; those who survived emerged in due course as trained experts in operational strategy. The members of the General Staff Corps, a *corps d'élite* within the military caste, were men of high individual ability and an amazing homogeneity of outlook. Governed by an ascetic self-discipline, their strength and power lay in their complete self-effacement to the point of anonymity, in favour of the transcending national and political ideal, while at the same time they retained the most complete freedom of expression within the caste on all service matters.

Actuated by an exceptional *esprit de corps*, these officers owed a caste loyalty to their leader, the Chief of the General Staff; a loyalty parallel with, and sometimes transcending, that which was claimed by their own unit commander. From this double loyalty grew up that peculiar institution characteristic of the Prusso-German direction of operations, the dual command. The Chief of Staff of a corps was no longer a subordinate executive but a junior partner with a right to notify to a higher quarter any objection which he might wish to record, if his advice were disregarded on a major issue. Ideally, however, the Chief of Staff was supposed to form with his commander a composite entity rather than two distinct or conflicting personalities; a complementary and supplementary combination capable of composing such differences as might arise, and making no clear distinction in the contribution which each made to the common good. Such 'happy marriages' are exemplified in the relationships between Blücher and Gneisenau during the War of Liberation, and between Hindenburg and Ludendorff, a hundred years later, where, in both cases, a blending of personalities and genius was effectively achieved. In some cases, however, the Chief of Staff came to occupy a position altogether more important than his superior, as, for example, General Max Hoffmann when serving as Chief of Staff to Prince Leopold of Bavaria, the German Commander-in-Chief on the Eastern Front in the years 1916–18.[2]

This renovation of the Prussian military machine by Scharnhorst

---

[1] Karl von Clausewitz (1780–1831), a Prussian General of Polish descent, whose masterpiece, *Vom Kriege*, published posthumously by his widow (1832–34), dominated the military strategy of the nineteenth century.

[2] This relationship is brilliantly discussed by General von Seeckt in his book, *Thoughts of a Soldier* (London, 1930), pp. 108-19.

and Gneisenau was but part of the very considerable reforms in machinery of government which had been inaugurated on the civil side by Freiherr vom Stein and Prince Hardenberg. The genius and cunning of the generals had outwitted Napoleon's intelligence service and had evaded the crippling military provisions of the Convention of Königsberg;[1] just as, little more than a hundred years later, the genius and cunning of Hans von Seeckt was successfully to evade the even more severe disarmament clauses of the Treaty of Versailles.[2] Moreover, as a result of the Convention of Tauroggen, concluded by Yorck von Wartenburg with the Russians, the Prussian Corps of the Grand Army had changed sides after Napoleon's retreat from Moscow.[3] The tradition of the new Prussian Army, therefore, was based on the principle of strictest patriotic fervour — a fervour which recognized devotion only to the greater glory of Prussia and of the Army itself; a loyalty transcending all other oaths of allegiance.

Nevertheless, when the War of Liberation had ended in the final overthrow of Napoleon, Blücher and Gneisenau — Scharnhorst had fallen at Leipzig — though holding different views on foreign policy, loyally supported Stein and Hardenberg in their policy of reform, and, with them, fought the opposition of that vacillating monarch, Frederick William III. Yet Stein, wise and foreseeing, was aware of the danger to the Monarchy and to the Government if the control of the military machine should at some future time fall into less scrupulous hands than those of his colleagues. 'We shall wait in vain', he wrote 'for the awakening in our country of that public spirit which the British and the French and other peoples possess, if we do not imitate them in setting for

---

[1] By a secret clause to the Convention of Königsberg, signed between France and Prussia on September 8, 1808, the King of Prussia undertook to reduce his army to 42,000 and not to increase it again for ten years. These restrictions were partially evaded by Scharnhorst's famous *Krümper* system of reserve training. Though this scheme had not been specifically designed to thwart Napoleon, it is a fact that by 1813 the Prussian Army and its trained reserves numbered more than 65,000 officers and men. (See Gordon Craig, *The Politics of the Prussian Army, 1640–1945* (Oxford, 1955), pp. 49–50.)

[2] See below, pp. 92–102.

[3] On December 30, 1812, Graf Hans Yorck von Wartenburg (1759–1830) concluded with Alexander I of Russia the Convention of Tauroggen, whereby the Prussian corps declared its temporary neutrality and the Russian forces were permitted to occupy unopposed the territory between Memel and Königsberg. Frederick William III of Prussia repudiated the Convention but vom Stein summoned the estates of East Prussia to meet at Königsberg and opened the Prussian harbours to the Russians and Swedes. Russia and Prussia signed a Treaty of Alliance at Kalish on February 28, 1813, and Prussia declared war on Napoleon on March 16.

our military leaders certain bounds and limitations which they must not disregard.'[1] No more prescient prophecy of the future of Germany could have been uttered, and it is a tragic irony of history that the man who succeeded in confining the German military leaders within bounds and limitations was Adolf Hitler — and for a very different purpose than that visualized by Freiherr vom Stein.

Step by step the military hierarchy created by Scharnhorst and Gneisenau came to assume that fateful position in Prusso-German state life which Stein had so clearly foreseen. A dominant school of thought arose convinced that true patriotism, and even the workings of Divine Providence, could only be expressed through the medium of militarism.[2] Under Bismarck, Moltke, and Roon,[3] this school of thought raised Prussia from a state of subservience to Austria to the controlling position of Imperial power.[4] As a result the Officer Corps became god-like in its attributes, and the General Staff Corps the elect of Olympus.

If during this period the military system had any outstanding virtues they were due in large measure to the fact that the Emperor Wilhelm I kept himself in the background and was content to be borne upward on the successes of his armies. Very different was the attitude of his grandson. Wilhelm II delighted in military display, gave full rein to the martial ambitions of his generals, and regarded with favour the tendency of his Officer Corps to look upon themselves as his knightly paladins and upon him as their sovereign and war lord to whose authority alone they owed loyalty, obedience and discipline.

Under the last of the Kaisers the Officer Corps became the spear-head of Prussian hegemony throughout the Reich. As War Lord of the German Armies, the Kaiser commanded the uncondi-tional obedience not only of his own Prussian officers but of those of

---

[1] Cited by Jakob Hegemann, *Entlarvte Geschichte* (Leipzig, 1933), p. 210.

[2] In a letter of December 11, 1880, to the great Swiss jurist, Johann Kaspar Bluntschli, Field-Marshal Graf Helmuth von Moltke (1800–91), the first Chief of the Great German General Staff (1870–88), wrote as follows : 'Eternal peace is a dream and not even a beautiful one. War is a link in God's order of the world. In war, the noblest virtues of man develop : courage and renunciation, devotion to duty and readiness for sacrifice, even at the risk of one's life. Without war the world would sink into materialism.'

[3] Field-Marshal Graf Albrecht Theodor Emil von Roon (1803–79), Prussian Minister of War, 1859–73.

[4] Though the combination of civil and military forces worked smoothly as a general rule, it should be remembered that the Chancellor Bismarck himself was not allowed to sit at the meetings of the Supreme Council of War lest 'this civilian might betray the secrets of State', and that Moltke's successor as Chief of the Great German General Staff, Count von Waldersee, took an active part in the final struggle to unseat the Iron Chancellor in 1890.

the States of Bavaria, Saxony and Württemberg also. The officers of these lesser armies did indeed bind themselves by their military oath to be faithful (*getreulich*) to their respective sovereigns, but by the same oath they also swore unconditional obedience to the King of Prussia as German Emperor. There can be no doubt to which of these two obligations the average non-Prussian officer would give priority, since the King of Prussia as *Deutscher Kriegsherr*, could transfer any officer, even against that officer's will, from any of the three Contingent armies to his own, and no officer in any of these Contingents could be promoted to the rank of General except with the consent of the German Emperor.[1]

Thus the Officer Corps stood to the Kaiser in the relation of the Praetorian Guards to the Roman Emperors of old, and, in one respect at least, the Emperor openly acknowledged the Corps as such, since he regarded it, in the last resort, as the basis of his sovereign power.[2] If at any time he wished to create a military dictatorship — and this idea did flit periodically through that volatile imperial mind — or if he chose to think that the public security of the Reich were threatened, whether by strikes or civil disturbance, or by the merest street brawl in the working-class districts of Berlin, Wilhelm II could, by Proclamation, declare 'a state of siege' (*Belagerungszustand*) throughout the Reich. From that moment all civil authority passed into the hands of the military, and all laws, whether Federal or State, relating to the liberty of the subject were suspended by military decree. The executive authority of the local commanding officer became the law of the land. He might hang or shoot anyone out of hand during the period of the 'State of Siege' and could rest assured that no proceedings of enquiry would be instituted after the emergency was over.[3]

[1] Article 64 of the Reich Constitution of 1871 reads as follows :

'All German troops are obliged to obey unconditionally the commands of the Emperor. This obligation is to be incorporated in the military oath. The highest commander of a Contingent and also all officers who command troops exceeding a Contingent, and all fortress commanders, are appointed by the Emperor. The officers appointed by him render to him the military oath. In the case of generals and officers discharging generalships with a Contingent the appointment is to be made dependent on the approval of the Emperor in each instance.

'The Emperor is authorized, for the purpose of transfer, with or without promotion, to elect officers from all the Contingents of the Imperial Army for the places to be filled by him in the Imperial service, whether in the Prussian Army or in other Contingents.'

[2] Cf. Ludendorff's statement that 'No one should forget that in times of danger, the guardianship of the State devolves upon the officer supported by the N.C.O. This explains the exclusiveness of the Officer Corps and their holding aloof from political life' (*My War Memories* (London, 1919), i, 28).

[3] See Article 68 of the Reich Constitution of 1871.

That Wilhelm II took seriously the great powers with which he was invested may be judged from his address to the officers of the Emperor Alexander Regiment on the dedication of their new barracks. The occasion took place on March 28, 1901, in the midst of his battle with the Social Democratic Party, who, he believed, were capable of raising the people of Berlin against him as they had risen against his great-uncle in 1848.[1] In addressing the assembled officers, and also the citizens who thronged the outskirts of the barrack square, he said : 'The Emperor Alexander Regiment is called upon in a sense to stand ready as bodyguard by night and by day, if necessary, to risk its life and its blood for the King and his House ; and if ever again the city should presume to rise up against its master, then I have no doubt that the regiment will repress with the bayonet the impertinence (*Frechheit*) of the people toward their King'.[2]

It may be easily imagined that, with so marked an approbation from so august a source, the members of the Officer Corps considered themselves as demi-gods elect above men, and as far removed from the 'bloody civilian' as was the orthodox Jew from the Samaritan.

Jealously they guarded their cherished privileges of election to the Corps and the right of appeal to Courts of Honour. The first they asserted even against the Kaiser himself, who would never have dared to sign the commission of an officer-candidate who had not previously received the imprimatur of his regimental comrades' approval.[3] The Emperor, on the other hand, could with confidence rely upon the regimental choice in respect of the social and political desirability of the candidate.[4]

---

[1] Wilhelm II had been struck in the face by a piece of iron hurled at him by an irresponsible youth, named Weiland, in the streets of Bremen on March 6, 1901. Though there was no evidence to connect Weiland with the Social Democratic Party, it was in all probability this incident, together with the increasing strength of the SPD in the country, that put the possibility of a rising into the Emperor's mind.

[2] Christian Gauss, *The German Emperor as shown in his Public Utterances* (New York, 1915), p. 172.

[3] The only two ways of becoming eligible for election as an officer in the German Army were either through membership of a cadet school or by the nomination by the Regimental Commanding Officer of a 'volunteer' (*Fahnenjunker*), as distinct from a conscript, who, having served in the ranks for a few weeks, was declared to be an 'aspirant'.

[4] Cf. the statement of the unusually frank and disillusioned former General Staff Officer, Major Franz Carl Endres, who, after the First World War retired to Switzerland and renounced German nationality, that 'no man who was a Social Democrat could ever hope to become a German officer' (*Reichswehr und Demokratie* (Leipzig, 1919), p. 39).

Though immune from the jurisdiction of the civil courts and the public police, members of the Officer Corps stood in awe and respect of their own Court of Honour. For breaches of military regulations the punishment was fortress detention, but for offence against the code of honour of an officer and a gentleman — and these offences included failure to assert the superiority of the Corps over mere civilians [1] — the ultimate and most dreaded punishment was to degrade the offender to civilian status. This indeed was to afflict him with social leprosy. 'Stripped of his commission, despoiled of all his prerogatives as an officer, deprived of his right to wear uniform, he was an outcast. The places that had known him, knew him no more. As a soldier he was dead or worse than dead, for in Germany it was not better to be a living dog than a dead lion. The only course open to him, if he wished to avoid a life-long disgrace, was to shoot himself. He usually did.'[2]

Such in 1914 was the Officer Corps, which Clausewitz had described a hundred years before as 'a kind of guild, with its own laws, ordinances, and customs'. It was in many ways akin to a medieval Order of Knighthood (but without its chivalry), and was so recognized by at least one military writer, General von Rabenau, who admitted that the Corps might well be called *ein Anachronismus*, but added that this was 'a good thing for both the Army and the people' since it succeeded in maintaining the immunity of the Army from parliamentary control.[3]

Thus, at the outbreak of the First World War, the relationship of the Kaiser to his Army rested on the basis of a unique personal bond. Through his Military Cabinet Wilhelm II exercised his rights of nominations, appointments, pensions, promotions, and all other military favours. The Chief of the Great General Staff, together with all corps commanders and all inspectors-general, had the right of direct access to him, and the reports of the military and naval attachés from the diplomatic posts abroad went directly to him and not to his Ministers. There was indeed every precaution against the War Minister's interposing between the King of Prussia and his Army, and yet this unfortunate individual had to represent both the Chief of the Military Cabinet and the Chief of the General

---

[1]. General Morgan points out (p. 97) that it was a definite offence for an officer not to punish on the spot any slight which he might fancy had been put upon him by a civilian.

[2] Morgan, p. 97.

[3] Lieutenant-General Friedrich von Rabenau, *Seeckt, aus seinem Leben* (Leipzig, 1940), p. 6. General von Rabenau was *Chef der Reichsarchiv* and was executed after the *Putsch* of July 20, 1944.

B

Staff before the Prussian Parliament.[1] No Roman Emperor exercised more martial authority than Wilhelm II when he went to war, but little by little the War Lord became the prisoner of his paladins and the control of German destinies passed ever more completely into the hands of those enigmatic and anonymous figures who wore the coveted wine-red trouser stripe of the General Staff.[2]

The fiction of Wilhelm II as Supreme War Lord did not long survive the crisis at Imperial Headquarters which followed the defeats suffered by the German armies on the Marne and the Aisne in the summer of 1914. The last appointment to be made by the Kaiser of his own unfettered will was that of General Erich von Falkenhayn,[3] the Prussian Minister of War, to succeed the unhappy and unfortunate Helmuth von Moltke [4] as Chief of the Great General Staff in September 1914. From thenceforward the Kaiser's personal influence and imperial prestige alike dwindled, for there had arisen on the Eastern Front that great military constellation of Hindenburg and Ludendorff, and before the brilliance of these luminaries even the star of the Hohenzollerns waned and paled.

The victories of Tannenberg and the Masurian Lakes, outstanding as they were and exaggerated as they had been in order to offset the defeats which the German armies had suffered on the

---

[1] Although the Kaiser exercised his authority as War Lord by virtue of his position as German Emperor there was no Reich Ministry of War. Prussia, Bavaria, Saxony and Württemberg each had independent Ministers, but for practical purposes the Prussian Ministry was the only one of any importance. Similarly the Kingdom of Bavaria had its own General Staff, but in time of war this was subordinated to the Great German General Staff. It is worth notice, however, that, even before the First World War broke out, the influence of the Military Cabinet was already under attack (see K. Schmidt-Bückeburg, *Das Militär-Kabinett* (Berlin, 1933), chap. iv).

[2] The growth of the influence of the Great General Staff, even in time of peace, greatly impressed Lord Haldane during his visit to Germany in 1906. To his observation it appeared to be 'a body before whose injunctions even the Emperor always has bowed' (Viscount Haldane, *Before the War* (London, 1920), p. 26).

[3] Lieutenant-General Erich von Falkenhayn (1861–1922), Prussian Minister for War, 1912–15 ; Chief of the Great General Staff, 1914–16. He published in 1919 a book, entitled *General Headquarters 1914–1916 and its Critical Decisions*, in defence of his strategic theories.

[4] Colonel-General Graf Helmuth Johannes Ludwig von Moltke (1848–1916), Chief of the Great General Staff, 1905–14. The nephew of the great Field-Marshal, he succeeded General Graf von Schlieffen as the head of the General Staff, but lacked both the judgment and the resolution to carry out the grand designs of his predecessor. Unhappy in his high position, he earned the nickname of *Feldherr wider Willen*, under which title General Gröner wrote a book (Berlin, 1931), criticizing his strategy in the early days of the war. In 1922, von Moltke's widow published, in Stuttgart, his collected papers under the title of *Erinnerungen, Briefe und Dokumente, 1877–1916*.

Western Front, had brought Hindenburg, and, to a lesser degree, Ludendorff, to a peak of popular adulation which none but Bismarck and the great Moltke had previously attained. The German people had come to look upon them as figures of superhuman grandeur and to expect from them feats of legendary proportions. Nor was this attitude confined to the mere rank and file of the population. Already in 1915 there had arisen in Germany a growing dissatisfaction with the conduct of the war on land and sea, and the inevitable search for a scapegoat was in process. The usual victim was the Imperial Chancellor, but in this case the malcontents were not satisfied with such a sacrifice. For the first time there came whispers that the Supreme War Lord should, if not abdicate, at least relinquish the conduct of the war and of internal policies to the direction of the Chiefs of the Armed Forces. In March and April 1915 Grand-Admiral von Tirpitz [1] was advocating a plan, for which he claimed the approval and support of the Kaiserin and the German Crown Prince, whereby the Emperor should dismiss both Bethmann Hollweg and Falkenhayn, and then go into temporary retirement, having called Hindenburg to the position of Dictator of the Reich, a rôle which would combine the office of Chancellor and Commander-in-Chief on land and sea.[2] This drastic solution for Germany's war-time political problems never progressed beyond the stage of discussion, but that such a thing could have been thus bruited and canvassed in the highest circles indicated clearly that around Wilhelm II 'the divinity that doth hedge a king' had already lost much of its mystic qualities and that the Supreme War Lord was rapidly deteriorating into an item of excess impedimenta at Imperial Headquarters.

This, however, was but a beginning. Though the Tirpitz plan never materialized in the form in which the Grand-Admiral had originally envisaged it, its essential provisions were realized before eighteen months had passed. Court intrigue, political pressure and the clamour of the populace all beat upon the Kaiser to call Hindenburg to the supreme position at the war council. It appeared that this gigantic figure, unknown in Germany two years before, was now, under God, the sole agent of victory. In August 1916 Wilhelm II

[1] Grand-Admiral Alfred von Tirpitz (1849–1930), Secretary of State for the Admiralty, 1897–1916, and 'Father of the German Navy'. After the First World War he published his memoirs, which form a trenchant analysis of pre-war Germany, and sat in the *Reichstag* as a member of the Nationalist Party from 1924–28. His daughter Ilse married Ulrich von Hassell, later Ambassador in Rome, who was among those executed after the abortive *Putsch* of July 20, 1944.

[2] Tirpitz, *My Memoirs* (London and New York, 1919), ii, 314-16, 317, 320, 322, 343-4.

bowed before the storm and, dismissing Falkenhayn, summoned Hindenburg from the Eastern Front to the Imperial Headquarters at Pless, as Chief of the Great General Staff. With him came Erich Ludendorff, the flame of whose brilliant, unstable genius cast so lurid a light.

For the next two years Germany, and indeed the Quadruple Alliance, was ruled and governed by the Condominium of the Supreme Command and the world was treated to an experiment in government by the Great General Staff. Rarely in modern times had military dictatorship achieved more unfettered licence. In the course of their rule Hindenburg and Ludendorff dragooned into submission the Kaiser, the Imperial Chancellor, the Cabinet and the *Reichstag*, the party chieftains, the captains of industry, and the leaders of the trade unions. They caused two Chancellors [1] and a Foreign Minister [2] to be dismissed from office and they humbled 'the Hydra', the hitherto all-powerful heads of the Kaiser's private cabinets. The Chief of the Military Cabinet [3] trembled before them; the Chief of the Civil Cabinet [4] they forced to resign; the Chief of the Naval Cabinet [5] identified himself with their policies.

And what did their policies achieve? In the field of foreign affairs the Supreme Command insisted upon the introduction of unrestricted U-boat warfare and thereby made inevitable the entry

[1] Theobald von Bethmann Hollweg (1856–1921) succeeded Prince von Bülow as Imperial Chancellor in 1909. He was dismissed by Wilhelm II at the behest of Hindenburg and Ludendorff in 1917 and was succeeded by their candidate, Georg Michaelis (1857–1936), a Prussian civil servant, who only retained their confidence for a hundred days, July-October 1917. On the recommendation of the Supreme Command Graf Georg von Hertling (1843–1919), the Bavarian Prime Minister, was then appointed Chancellor and continued in office for the remainder of the period of Condominium. Both Bethmann Hollweg and Michaelis have left records of their Chancellorships, *Betrachtungen zum Weltkriege* (Berlin, 1919–21, 2 vols.) and *Für Staat und Volk* (Berlin, 1922). Count Hertling's son published an account of his father's term of office entitled *Ein Jahr in der Reichskanzlei* (Freiburg-im-Breisgau, 1919).

[2] Richard von Kühlmann (1873–1949), a Bavarian diplomat, appointed German State Secretary for Foreign Affairs in 1917. Having opposed the policy of the Supreme Command during the negotiations with the Bolsheviks at Brest-Litovsk, he was dismissed in July 1918, to be succeeded by Admiral von Hintze. His memoirs were published shortly before his death, *Erinnerungen* (Heidelberg,1948).

[3] Colonel-General Freiherr Moritz von Lyncker (1853–1932), Chief of the Imperial Military Cabinet, 1908–18.

[4] Graf Rudolf von Valentini (1855–1924), Chief of the Imperial Civil Cabinet, 1908–18. His memoirs, *Kaiser und Kabinettschef*, edited by Bernard Schwertfeger, were published posthumously (Oldenburg, 1931).

[5] Admiral Georg Alexander von Müller (1854–1940), Chief of the Imperial Naval Cabinet, 1906–18.

of America into the war on the side of the Allies. They demanded
the establishment of a Kingdom of Poland and thereby destroyed
all hopes of a separate peace with Tsarist Russia. The predatory
nature of their demands upon France and Belgium ruined what
chances of success may have attended the Papal peace proposals
of 1917. It was they who were responsible for the return of Lenin
and his colleagues from Switzerland to Russia in the famous 'sealed
train', and the rapacity of the terms which they subsequently enforced upon the Bolsheviks at Brest-Litovsk not only defeated their
own ends but branded before the world those who initiated them
as naked annexationists.

Moreover, the Condominium of the Supreme Command did
not win the war for Germany. The gruelling sacrifices for which
they called upon the German people were in vain; the mighty
offensive which they launched against the West in March 1918 did
not end in victory, and from August 8, 'the Black Day in the history
of the German Army', their defeat at the hands of the Allies was
assured. No 'stab in the back' had brought about the discomfiture
of the German armies in the West. They were well and truly
beaten in the field and they knew it. The break-down of October
and November was in a sense a general strike of a hopelessly defeated
army against the madness of its leaders.

Hindenburg and Ludendorff were not entirely insensible to the
course of events. Once they had realized, late in September 1918,
that the tide of war had turned irrevocably against them, they sought
to take such measures as they deemed necessary to safeguard the
Reich from invasion, and to preserve the Monarchy. But the
measures which they proposed were not only born of panic but
were utterly inadequate to meet the exigencies of the situation.
They were both too little and too late.

To meet the growing clamour of the masses the Condominium
demanded the immediate opening of negotiations for an armistice,
and a 'Revolution from above'. In the minds of Hindenburg and
Ludendorff both these proposals were designed to mitigate the
severity of the terms of peace which might be forthcoming from the
Allies. The Fourteen Points, which President Wilson had pro-
pounded in January of that year, were considered by the Supreme
Command as a basis of negotiation, not of surrender. Similarly
the proposed constitutional reforms were advocated for the dual
purpose of consolidating the morale of the country behind the
Emperor and the Army and of impressing the Allies with the 'progressive' character of the 'New Germany'. In both cases the Army
would appear in the rôle of saviour. It was never dreamed by the

Condominium that the action which they now urged so imperatively would terminate in a military capitulation, which would reduce the German Army to impotence, and in a political revolution, which would sweep the Kaiser from his throne.

Yet this, in effect, is what occurred. The world was undeceived by the transparently deceptive strategy of the Supreme Command. Once negotiations for the cessation of hostilities had begun it became swiftly and abundantly clear that no armistice could be concluded until military dictatorship and imperial authority alike had been replaced in Germany by a form of government which President Wilson could recognize as democratic; while, within the Reich itself, once the flood-gates had been opened to reforms long overdue, there was no stemming the torrent. In their efforts to safeguard the imperial throne and the position of the military caste, the Supreme Command had ensured the downfall of both.[1]

It is, however, true — and here again is irony — that the constitutional reforms introduced in October 1918, at the behest of Hindenburg and Ludendorff, were more sweeping than any which had before occurred in Germany, and that the establishment of parliamentary government in the Reich, and of universal suffrage in Prussia, were due to the initiative of the Supreme Command.[2]

The immediate results of these reforms were the ignominious

---

[1] Interesting, though not entirely impartial, studies of the relation of Wilhelm II with the Supreme Command and of the final events at Imperial Headquarters in the summer and autumn of 1918 are to be found in the works of Alfred Niemann, *Kaiser und Revolution* (Berlin, 1928) and *Kaiser und Heer* (Berlin, 1929). The author served as personal representative of the Supreme Command with the Kaiser.

[2] The constitutional reforms of October 1918 came as the tardy conclusion of a gradual process of development, which had begun ten years earlier with Prince von Bülow's assurance to the *Reichstag*, after the *Daily Telegraph* affair of 1908, that the Kaiser would cultivate greater reserve in future. A Constitutional Commission (*Verfassungsausschuss*) had been set up in 1917 for the discussion of post-war reforms, but any substantial progress had been prevented by the intransigent attitude of the Conservatives. The chief innovation of the 1918 reforms was the amendment to Article 15 of the Constitution whereby the Chancellor required the confidence of the *Reichstag* for the conduct of business and, together with his colleagues, became responsible to the *Reichstag* and the *Bundesrat*, and not to the Emperor as heretofore. The Chancellor was also made responsible for all acts of political importance which the Emperor committed by virtue of his constitutional competence. A further amendment of Article 64 made the appointment by the Emperor of all military commanders dependent upon the counter-signature of the Chancellor, and it was under this provision that the dismissal of Ludendorff was obtained by Prince Max of Baden. (See Arthur Rosenberg, *The Birth of the German Republic* (London, 1931), pp. 246-50; Johannes Mattern, *The Constitutional Jurisprudence of the German Republic* (Baltimore, 1928), pp. 59-64; and Herbert Kraus, *The Crisis of German Democracy, a Study of the Spirit of the Constitution of Weimar* (Princeton, 1932), pp. 37-9).

flight to Sweden of Ludendorff, disguised in blue spectacles and false whiskers, and the more dignified departure of Wilhelm II for Holland. Only Hindenburg remained, to whom the Kaiser had, as a final act, entrusted the supreme command of the German Army.

(ii)

Of the greatest importance to subsequent history is the fact that the events of November 9, 1918, in Spa and in Berlin were almost entirely the results of outside interference. It is true that on the Western Front the growing war-weariness of the defeated German armies gradually produced a mass-gesture of lack of confidence in the High Command. It is also true that on the Home Front the ever-increasing privations, the heavy casualties, and the general hopelessness of the situation had provided a 'confederate season' for the propaganda of the enemies of the Monarchy and the established order. But the event which rang the death-knell of Imperial and military domination and authority was the announcement by President Wilson on October 23, that if the Allies had to treat with 'the military authorities and the monarchical autocrats of Germany . . . they must demand not negotiations for peace but surrender'.

From that moment the Spartakists of Liebknecht and Rosa Luxemburg and Haase's Independent Socialists did not cease to reiterate that the Kaiser and the Generals alone stood between Germany and a just peace. More sober and responsible minds sought desperately to preserve the Monarchy but could find no other means of so doing than to effect the abdication of the Kaiser and the Crown Prince in order to clear the way for a regency. The Social Democrats, viewing with the gravest apprehension the ever more rapid approach of the day when they, who had enjoyed for nearly fifty years the privileged position of critical opponents of the Imperial régime, would themselves have to shoulder the burden of office and responsibility, now made frantic efforts to shore up that very imperial structure which they had hitherto so persistently undermined.

But the German Social Democrats had, in the progress of their parliamentary experience, put off much of their revolutionary ardour. Like their comrades in England and France, they had contented themselves with 'evolution', and indeed 'gradualism'. It was one thing to rail against an existing régime as an opposition party with no chance of assuming the responsibility of office, and quite another thing to be suddenly burdened with the onus of that responsibility. The Social Democrats crossed their Rubicon with profound reluctance. 'There might be something of exaltation in waking up famous like Byron', wrote Theodor Wolff of Fritz Ebert, 'but it was less pleasant to find oneself in the morning the Supreme Commander of the Revolution after going to bed as a member of the respectable middle class.' [1]

This critical situation, of which the seeds had long been sown, was precipitated by Mr. Wilson's declaration. The efforts to preserve the Monarchy at the expense of the monarch were frustrated by the obstinate refusal of Wilhelm II to abandon his throne. Had he abdicated in the last week of October 1918 he would almost certainly have preserved the monarchical form of government in Germany, for all conservative, liberal, and bourgeois forces within the Reich were united in the belief that herein lay the best way of combating the threat of Communism.[2]

The Kaiser, entrenched among his paladins at Spa, whither he had departed from Berlin on October 30, would listen to none of the pleadings of Prince Max of Baden nor of the envoys whom the harassed Chancellor despatched to the Imperial Headquarters. He would not abdicate. Whereupon Prince Max, faced with a mounting wave of revolution, announced the abdication on the afternoon of November 9 in a last effort to save the throne. The gesture came too late. Already Karl Liebknecht was announcing the establishment of a Soviet régime from the steps of the Imperial Palace. The Social Democrats, very much *malgré eux*, were forced into 'making a revolutionary gesture in order to forestall a revolution', and, in a moment of mingled exultation and panic, Philip Scheidemann [3]

[1] At the Munich 'stab in the back' trial in October-December 1925, Scheidemann testified that he and his colleagues had neither wanted nor planned a revolution. They would indeed have willingly accepted Prince Max of Baden as Regent of the Empire, and even Prince August-Wilhelm, the Kaiser's youngest surviving son (afterwards a prominent Nazi) as Regent in Prussia. The maximum demand made by the Social Democrats in their ultimatum of November 8 to the Chancellor was the abdication of the Kaiser and the Crown Prince. (Cf. *Memoirs of Prince Max of Baden* (New York, 1928), ii, 240-42 ; Theodor Wolff, *Through Two Decades* (London, 1936), pp. 118 et seq.)

[2] 'If the Kaiser abdicates, the back of the Republican movement will be broken', said Edward David, one of the SPD Under-Secretaries in the Cabinet, to a friend on October 31 (*Memoirs of Prince Max of Baden*, ii, 225).

[3] Philip Scheidemann (1865-1939), a Majority Socialist leader of some prominence. He joined Prince Max of Baden's Cabinet in October 1918 as a State Secretary without portfolio, was a member of Ebert's Provisional Government (November 1918-February 1919) and became the First Chancellor of the Weimar Republic on February 13, 1919. His Cabinet resigned in June of the same year as a protest against the Allied peace terms. He never took office again but remained a member of the *Reichstag* until the election of 1930. He was proscribed by the Nazis in 1933 and retired to Denmark, where he died on November 29,

proclaimed the German Republic from the window of the *Reichstag* building.

Such were the circumstances of the birth of republican Germany. The change of régime did not come as a result of any long-planned revolutionary movement. It did not represent any basic change of heart on the part of the German people themselves. It was brought about without any great deep-seated conviction or willingness on the part of its progenitors, who would certainly at the time have preferred to retain the Monarchy. It occurred, in very great measure, because those in power believed that by this means alone could Germany comply with President Wilson's preliminary pre-requisite for peace, and partly because of the fear of Bolshevism; both courses being the result of pressure from outside rather than from within Germany.

But if those who assumed power in Germany on the afternoon of November 9, 1918, were reluctant to do so, they were even more incompetent to wield their new-found authority. The group of six to whom Prince Max of Baden handed over the Government of the Reich was composed of three Majority Socialists and three Independents.[1] Over this group, who called themselves indifferently the 'Peoples Commissaries' or the 'Imperial Government', Fritz Ebert [2] the Majority Socialist leader presided, retaining somewhat

1939. A vain and somewhat stupid man, he did little to enhance the reputation of his party or of himself. After the war he published *Der Zusammenbruch* (Berlin, 1921), an account of the German collapse of 1918 from the point of view of the Social Democrats, and later there appeared his *Erinnerungen* (Berlin, 1928), an outspoken volume of memoirs.

[1] The German Provisional Government of November 9, 1918, comprised Ebert, Scheidemann and Landsberg (Majority Socialists), and Haase, Dittmann and Barth (Independents). The terms 'Majority' and 'Independent' Socialists derive from the schism in the SPD which occurred in 1916, when Haase and his followers, calling themselves 'Minority' or 'Independent' Socialists, broke away from the Party line established in 1914 by which the Social Democrats supported the policy of the Imperial Government and voted war-credits. From 1916 onwards Haase and his group voted against the Government in the *Reichstag*, notably in opposition to war-credits and to the ratification of the Treaties of Brest-Litovsk and Bucharest.

[2] Friedrich Ebert (1871–1925) was born at Heidelberg, the son of a tailor. He became a saddler first in Hanover and later in Bremen, in which place he also kept a small beer *Lokal*. He became a member of the SPD at an early age and from 1905 onwards played an important part in the direction of its policies. Elected to the *Reichstag* in 1912, he became Chairman of the Parliamentary Party a year later and was largely responsible for the decision of the Social Democrats to vote for war-credits in August 1914. He was successively the last Chancellor of Imperial Germany, President of the Provisional Government, and first President of the German Republic. He died in office on February 28, 1925, after repeated attacks of appendicitis, for which he refused to be operated on. He was distinguished not so much for political genius as for political

anomalously the title of *Reichskanzler*.[1]

From the very first, however — even in the negotiations which preceded the formation of this Coalition — it was apparent that there was no real basis of agreement between the Majority Socialists and the Independents. Ebert and his followers were fundamentally opposed to any compromise with extremism. In their attitude was all the fear and hatred of the bourgeois for the Communist, that bitter doctrinal cleavage which subsequently separated the Second International from the Third. Haase and his colleagues were infinitely nearer in spirit to the Spartakists. Though far from being whole-hearted Communists, they were, in effect, the earliest form of 'fellow-travellers'. They wished to see the Soldiers' and Workers' Councils, at that moment springing into existence all over Germany as a result of the break-down of the Imperial régime, in some way integrated with the National Constituent Assembly which it was proposed to call at Weimar, thereby establishing a form of Soviet system parallel with the governmental machinery of the State.

To Ebert the parallel with events in Russia — then only a year old — was too clear, too terrifying. Already the Spartakists were in the streets. Seated in the Chancellor's Palace in the Wilhelmstrasse, he could hear their demonstrations as they advanced down Unter den Linden from their stronghold in the Imperial Palace. Compromise now might place him and his comrades in the fatal position of Kerensky, for, with little encouragement, the Spartakists could win control of the Councils and confront the Government with a *fait accompli*. It would mean Bolshevism and in such an event he could not count on the support of the Independents.

Thus, on that fatal night of November 9, confronted with the spectre of civil war, Ebert cast about desperately for the means to buttress his flimsy authority. On whom could he depend? What of the Officer Corps?

The answer came with dramatic suddenness. On the Chancellor's table stood a telephone connecting him by a private and

common sense and integrity. Passionately devoted to the ideas and ideals which he held to be right, Ebert combined organizing vitality and sober suavity. Above all, he could command the complete trust and loyalty of his followers. In 1925 Ebert's collected public papers were published by his son, Friedrich junior (who, after having been imprisoned by the Nazis in 1933, became in 1947 the political puppet of the Russians as Lord Mayor of the Soviet Sector of Berlin), under the title of *Friedrich Ebert: Schriften, Aufzeichnungen, Reden*, and a year later a further volume appeared under the same editorship, *Friedrich Ebert: Kämpfe und Ziele aus seinem Nachlasse*.

[1] The term *Reich* (as in *Reichsregierung, Reichskanzler*), which had hitherto stood for 'Empire' in German history, was retained by the Weimar Republic with the somewhat equivocal translation of 'Realm'.

secret line with the headquarters at Spa. Over this line the unhappy
Max of Baden had made his last despairing efforts to persuade the
Kaiser to sacrifice himself for the sake of the throne, and had failed ;
now to Prince Max's successor over this same line came a message
of hope. Ebert was alone. The windows were closed, the curtains
drawn. But through them came the discordant cries of the demonstrations in the street. Suddenly the ringing of a bell transcended
all other sounds. Ebert picked up the receiver with a hand that
trembled. Then he almost wept with joy.

'Gröner speaking.'

Was the Government willing to protect Germany from anarchy
and to restore order ? enquired the crisp military voice from Spa.
Yes, said Ebert, it was. 'Then the High Command will maintain
discipline in the Army and bring it peacefully home', Gröner replied.
What was the attitude of the High Command towards the Soldiers'
Councils ? Ebert asked. Orders had been given to deal with them
in a friendly spirit, was the reply. 'What do you expect from us ?'
enquired the Chancellor. 'The High Command expects the Government to co-operate with the Officer Corps in the suppression of
Bolshevism, and in the maintenance of discipline in the Army. It
also asks that the provisioning of the Army shall be ensured and all
disturbance of transport communications prevented.' He added
that Hindenburg would remain at the head of the Army.

Thus, in half a dozen sentences over a telephone line, a pact
was concluded between a defeated army and a tottering semi-
revolutionary régime ; a pact destined to save both parties from the
extreme elements of revolution but, as a result of which, the Weimar
Republic was doomed at birth.

(iii)

What indeed had prompted Gröner [1] to make this *démarche*
to Berlin ? Certainly his motives were mixed, and among them

---

[1] Wilhelm Gröner (1867-1939), the son of a non-commissioned officer in the
Württemberg Army, himself entered the Army at the age of eighteen and eventually
became a brilliant Staff officer. Throughout his military career he was the rival
of Erich Ludendorff, who only secured the coveted position of Chief of the
Operations Section of the General Staff, for which both were candidates, because
he, and not Gröner, was of the military caste. As Chief of Field-Railway Transport
in 1914-16 Gröner solved with unqualified success the gigantic problems of
logistics presented for the first time by modern warfare. Later, from 1916 to 1917,
he was in charge of the so-called 'Hindenburg Programme' for the economic
intensification of war production, in which position he effected a remarkable
degree of co-operation between the leaders of capital and labour. In the spring
of 1918 he endeavoured, as Chief of Staff to the Commander-in-Chief of the

were, undoubtedly, a deep sense of patriotism, a strong desire to
safeguard the unity and the integrity of the Reich, and a determination to preserve the prestige, the authority, and the reputation
of the German Army and the Officer Corps. Gröner saw more
clearly than many of his colleagues in the Supreme Command —
and certainly more clearly than Hindenburg — the implications of
the events of November 9. He was far more uninhibited by tradition and romantic mysticism than those Prussian soldiers and
courtiers who had to the last refused to tell the truth to Wilhelm II,
or to admit it even to themselves. To Gröner, a Swabian, had fallen
the unhappy duty of informing the Supreme War Lord of Germany
that he no longer commanded the loyalty of his troops, and he had
done so with courage and determination, well knowing what it might
mean to him in the future.[1] His duty as he saw it now was not to
sovereigns and dynasties but to Germany and the Army, and he
faced the situation accordingly.

The situation was indeed a unique one. For the first time in
German history the Army was without a Commander-in-Chief and
the Officer Corps without a Sovereign. The mystic ties which had
bound the military paladins of Germany to their Emperor and King
had been abruptly severed when Wilhelm II had released his officers
from their oaths of fealty. The foundation of rigid obedience of
all ranks to their Supreme War Lord, and, under him, to the Great
General Staff, had been shattered, and though, as a parting act, the
Kaiser had confided the command of the Army to Hindenburg,
this in no way filled the vacuum created by his abdication. The
Imperial and Prussian Army, the backbone of the Reich, was confronted with the spectre of disintegration.

It was, moreover, an unescapable fact that the Revolution which
had occurred was primarily a military mutiny, and that the Soldiers'
Councils which had come into being in every unit, were the revolutionary expression of the Army's dissatisfaction with its leaders.

German Army of Occupation, to implement the economic advantages which had
theoretically been gained by Germany and Austria-Hungary from Russia under
the Treaty of Brest-Litovsk, but his efforts were defeated, largely through the
refusal of the Ukrainian peasantry to co-operate with the Occupation Authorities.
When Ludendorff was dismissed in October 1918, Gröner succeeded him as First
Quartermaster-General, and it was in this capacity that he took part in the events
at Spa of November 9. His subsequent record will be found in the following pages.

[1] 'Gröner was right, but he should have said to the Marshal [Hindenburg]:
"Find a Prussian to say these things"', was the comment of King William of
Württemberg in his diary on Gröner's announcement to the Kaiser : 'Der Fahneneid ist jetzt nur eine Idee'. The Prussian military caste never forgave Gröner for
this incident, even after a Court of Honour in 1922 had declared him to have
been prompted by the highest motives.

Because, therefore, the Revolution was primarily the work of the Army, it was impossible to oppose it overtly.

Nor was this all. In Gröner's calculations on the night of November 9, there remained the all-important factor that for the last twenty-four hours a German delegation had been in negotiation with Marshal Foch at Compiègne for the conclusion of an armistice. In the course of the pre-Armistice exchanges the Supreme Command, though they had initiated them by their demand of September 29 that a peace offer be despatched forthwith, had sought to escape from their responsibility and had refused to have anything to do with the final appointment of the Armistice Commission. This pusillanimous attitude had been materially, if unintentionally, strengthened by the fact that President Wilson in his Note of November 5 had stated that Marshal Foch was prepared to receive properly accredited representatives *of the German Government* and to acquaint them with the Armistice conditions. Though consistent with the President's earlier statement (October 23) that the Allies could only treat with 'the military masters and the monarchical autocrats of Germany' on the basis of unconditional surrender, this insistence now upon negotiation with representatives of the German Government played directly into the hands of the Supreme Command, who were thereby relieved of all responsibility, with the result that no representative of the General Staff was included in the Armistice Commission.[1] What is, perhaps, surprising is that their

---

[1] The German Armistice Commission, of which Mathias Erzberger was president, did include one Army officer, Major-General von Winterfeldt, a former military attaché at the German Embassy in Paris, who had been hurriedly brought out of retirement. He did not participate in the subsequent negotiations for the renewal of the Armistice. When the Commission had arrived at Spa on November 7, on its way to Compiègne, there had been a moment of hideous uncertainty on the part of the High Command lest Erzberger might at the last moment refuse to go and they might, after all, have to provide a substitute. General von Gündell had actually been warned for duty in this emergency, but Hindenburg, with tears in his eyes and grasping Erzberger by the hand, besought him to undertake this terrible task for the sacred cause of his country. His vanity flattered by this personal appeal from the Marshal, Erzberger consented to serve and departed to put his signature to a document which was to prove his own death-warrant. He was assassinated by Nationalist gunmen in 1921 for his part in the Armistice negotiations (Erzberger, *Erlebnisse im Weltkrieg* (Berlin, 1920), p. 326 ; Wheeler-Bennett (*op. cit.*), pp. 188-9 ; Jacques Benoist-Méchin, *Histoire de l'armée allemande depuis l'armistice* (Paris, 1936-8), i, p. 41). M. Benoist-Méchin (b. 1902), whose book is a classic on its subject and was *couronné* by the French Academy, was nominated, after the collapse of France in 1940, Delegate-General for Prisoners of War with residence in Berlin. Later, in Vichy, he served successively as Secretary of State to Admiral Darlan and to Laval, 1941-2. Arrested after the Liberation of France, he was tried as a collaborationist before the High Court of Justice and was condemned to death on June 6, 1947 ; this sentence was later commuted by

relief was shared by the Chancellor, Prince Max of Baden.[1]

For the Army, therefore, it was all important that the onus of responsibility for accepting the Armistice conditions in all their severity — and the text had been received at Spa on the afternoon of November 9 — should remain with the Government and not with the General Staff, and for that purpose it was essential that a Government of some sort should exist in Berlin.[2]

Seated in his office in the Hôtel Britannique, the Supreme Command Headquarters at Spa, Gröner surveyed the situation with the cool detachment and balanced judgment of a Württemberger. Other Germans — Prussians for example — had displayed deep emotion. At that very moment, a few yards from where Gröner sat, that monumental Prussian, Paul von Hindenburg, was lying in the sleep of exhaustion, emotionally prostrated by the events of the day ; away in the south-east of Europe, where the German arms had been deserted by their Turkish allies, Hans von Seeckt, another Prussian, was weeping, as he subsequently confessed, for the first time in decades. Nor were these isolated instances of Prussian sentimental agitation. But Gröner, *der biedere Schwabe*, was differently constructed. His emotion, though deeply stirred, found relief neither in sleep nor tears. He knew the size of the stakes for which he was playing. The destiny of the German Army, and perhaps of the German Reich itself, was in his hand that night and he played his cards with the consummate skill of a master gambler.

The next twenty-four hours would, he knew, decide the fate of many things. Such action, therefore, as was necessary, must be taken at once. Already the troops were beginning to waver between the authority of the Soldiers' Councils and their discipline towards their officers. Further hesitation after the departure of the Emperor might mean a complete disintegration of morale and the capture of the Army by the extremist elements.

On the other hand, the group, if not in power, at least at the

President Vincent Auriol (July 30, 1947) to one of imprisonment for life with hard labour. He was later released (see *Le Procès Benoist-Méchin*, Paris, 1948).

[1] 'Our prevailing feeling was one of relief that at least the Army would not have to wait upon Foch' is Prince Max's comment on the receipt of Wilson's note (*Memoirs*, ii, 305).

[2] General Morgan (p. 168) advances the more extreme view that the Supreme Command welcomed the existence of a revolutionary Government in Berlin 'who would take the odious responsibility of negotiating and signing the Armistice and whose action both they and the Supreme War Lord, the Kaiser, could subsequently repudiate when the Allied Governments had demobilized. This, unquestionably, was why Hindenburg counselled the Kaiser to retire "temporarily" into Holland.' This view, though intriguing, is nevertheless open to question in the light of the evidence.

head of affairs in Berlin, contained one man, Fritz Ebert, with whom Gröner had worked in cordial and constructive relations during the war. A mutual confidence and respect had grown up between the tailor's son, whose destiny had now made him Chancellor of Germany, and the son of an N.C.O., who had achieved the virtual command of her armies. Gröner knew that he could trust Ebert, though this confidence did not extend to Scheidemann or Landsberg, and certainly not to Ebert's three Independent Socialist colleagues. Time, however, would take care of them, and meanwhile the group which Ebert headed represented the constituted authority of the Reich and, above all, the civilian government which must bear the responsibility of the Armistice. By allying themselves with the Provisional Government on the basis of equality — and not of subordination — the Officer Corps could preserve law and order in the Reich, suppress Bolshevism, and maintain their traditional position as the ultimate guardian of the State.

It was on this basis that Gröner made his historic telephone call to Berlin.

(iv)

The Gröner-Ebert pact of November 9, 1918, was to have the most momentous and far-reaching results for the German Reich. The objects with which it was concluded were clearly described by Gröner himself at the 'stab in the back' trial in Munich in the winter of 1925.[1] 'The aim of our alliance', he said, 'was to combat the revolution without reservation, to re-establish lawful government, to lend this government armed support, and to convene a National Assembly.' Pressed further under cross-examination, he added that both he and Ebert were also agreed on the desirability of getting rid of the Independent Socialists from the Government and of eliminating the Soldiers' and Workers' Councils from any position of influence. 'Our aim was to get the army out of the atmosphere of revolution as soon as possible.'

An important step towards achieving this latter aim was taken at once. In the telegram despatched to Spa by Ebert on behalf of the Provisional Government, in ratification of the agreement with Gröner, it was specifically stated that 'the officer's superiority in rank remains. Unqualified obedience in service is of prime importance for the success of the return home to Germany. Military

---

[1] For Gröner's statement at the Munich Trial see Beckmann, *Der Dolchstossprozess in München* (Munich, 1925), pp. 110-11. See also Reginald H. Phelps, 'Aus den Groener Dokumenten. I. Groener, Ebert, und Hindenburg', *Deutsche Rundschau*, July 1950.

discipline must therefore be maintained under all conditions.'
Officers were, moreover, permitted to retain their arms and the
insignia of their rank. The Soldiers' Councils were instructed to
support their officers, 'without reserve', in the maintenance of
discipline and order, their immediate rôle being restricted to the
exercise of 'an advisory voice' in maintaining confidence between
officers and rank and file in questions of food, leave, etc.[1]

This gave the Supreme Command exactly what it wanted.
Armed with this protection against any interference, they met the
delegates of the Councils next morning (November 10) with a calm
confidence derived from the knowledge that they held the highest
trumps. The delegates were received by Lieutenant-Colonel Faupel
of the General Staff,[2] who, having demonstrated to them before a
huge staff map the gigantic problems involved in the task of bringing
home the defeated army to Germany, asked whether they were really
prepared to complicate matters further by attempting to exercise an
untimely interference in the work of officers who were already
over-burdened with work and responsibility. Stunned by this exposition of problems of which they had previously neither knowledge
nor understanding, the delegates were struck silent. Whereupon
Faupel asked them if they were aware that the Supreme Command
had concluded an agreement with the Government in Berlin, and,
when they demanded proof, read to them the telegram addressed by
Ebert to Hindenburg and Gröner. The ground thus cut from beneath their feet, the discomfiture of the delegates was complete and
they readily fell in with Faupel's proposal — without perceiving the
irony of the suggestion — that they should set up an office with the
Supreme Command to ensure collaboration with the General Staff
and to exhort the troops to maintain discipline and obedience.[3]

Having thus gained their first peaceful victory and won the first

[1] *International Conciliation*, Documents of the American Association for
International Conciliation for 1919 (New York, 1920), i, 548 ; Benoist-Méchin,
i, 70.

[2] Lieutenant-Colonel Wilhelm Faupel later retired from the Army with the rank
of Lieutenant-General. He became head of the Ibero-American Institute in
Berlin, and in July 1936, on the recognition of General Franco's Government by
Hitler, was appointed as German diplomatic representative with the military
Junta at Burgos.

[3] Erich Otto Volkmann, *Revolution über Deutschland* (Oldenburg, 1930), pp.
69-71 ; Colonel Wilhelm Reinhard, *1918-1919, Die Wehen der Republik* (Berlin
1933), p. 26. Volkmann was formerly a major in the Army and later an official
in the *Reichsarchiv* ; his book is an important source of material for the period
from the breakdown of November 1918 to the Kapp *Putsch* of March 1920 ; it is,
however, somewhat weighted on the side of the military. Colonel Reinhard was
appointed by Noske to succeed the Majority Socialist Otto Wels as military
commandant of Berlin in December 1918.

round in their fight for rehabilitation — just twenty-four hours
after their admission of defeat — the General Staff and the Officer
Corps turned their attention to the colossal problem in logistics
which confronted them. The Armistice agreement was signed on
November 11 and came into force at five minutes before noon on
that day.[1] By this agreement the German Army was ordered to
complete the evacuation of French and Belgian territory within a
fortnight, and the withdrawal behind the bridge-heads and the
demilitarized zone of the Rhine within a month, of the date of
signature.

The march home proceeded with perfect smoothness and without incident. Though undoubtedly aided by the dry weather — it
was a St. Martin's summer — the perfect execution of the operation
redounded greatly to the credit of Gröner as the presiding genius,
the General Staff for its triumph of organization, and the Officer
Corps for the maintenance of order and discipline. For them the
retreat was a further psychological victory, since it restored their
shaken self-confidence and left them once again with the conviction
that they constituted the one super-force in Germany.

Nor was it long before this new-found confidence made itself
evident. Throughout the retreat Gröner had kept in close contact
with Ebert through Colonel von Haeften,[2] and had by this means
been enabled to smooth over various minor difficulties and mis-
understandings. Once home, the Supreme Command was installed

---

[1] Though successful to the end in avoiding a direct participation in the
Armistice negotiations, the Supreme Command could not evade the responsibility
of having given an opinion. In a telegram to General von Scheuch, the Prussian
Minister of War, Hindenburg, on November 10, proposed various amendments for
which the German Commission might be instructed to press in mitigation of the
Armistice conditions. The telegram concluded with these words : 'If it is impossible to gain these points, it would nevertheless be advisable to conclude the
agreement'. Emphasis was laid on this document in the preface to the *Vorgeschichte des Waffenstillstandes* which the German Government issued in 1919 in
an attempt to counter the propaganda of the 'stab in the back' legend then being
avidly circulated by the Nationalist Party. An English edition of this book
was published by the Carnegie Endowment for International Peace, *Preliminary
History of the Armistice* (New York, 1924). The telegram referred to appears on
pp. 148-9.

[2] Hans von Haeften, an officer of the Second Regiment of Foot Guards and a
member of the General Staff Corps, had been the representative of the Supreme
Command with the Imperial Chancellor and the Foreign Office under Michaelis,
Hertling, Prince Max of Baden, and Ebert. With the rank of Major-General he
was appointed President of the *Reichsarchiv* in 1931, but resigned in 1934 in
protest against the attempts of the Nazis to pervert history by suppressing certain
of the archives and forging others. He remained an opponent of the National
Socialist régime until his death. His two sons, Hans-Bernd and Werner, were
executed for participation in the plot of July 20, 1944.

on December 1 in its new headquarters at Cassel — in the Schloss of Wilhelmshöhe where the great Napoleon's brother, Jerome, had once held his comic-opera court as King of Westphalia, and where later the Emperor's nephew, Napoleon III, had lived as a prisoner of war after Sedan. The secret telephone line to the *Reichskanzlei* in Berlin was again installed and direct contact between Gröner and Ebert was once more established. Each night, between eleven and one, the two men in whose hands the destiny of Germany rested talked together without fear of being overheard, and, in Gröner's words, 'reviewed the situation from day to day according to developments'. Indeed this secret wire became a kind of umbilical cord which bound the infant German Republic to its progenitor and protector, the German Army.

These conversations were not always felicitous. Ebert, although he did not repent of his original pact with Gröner, was finding it more and more of a one-sided agreement. Originally it had been undertaken as an alliance of equals, now already, less than a month later, the General Staff was beginning to dictate to the Government, and Ebert, though he shared in principle many of the objectives which Gröner urged upon him, found it increasingly hard to put them into practice. The aim of the Supreme Command at Cassel was to secure the dissolution of the Soldiers' and Workers' Councils — thus disarming the Spartakists — and the ultimate elimination of the Independents from the Provisional Government. Gröner, however, was aware that the great majority of the troops who had returned to Germany wanted to be in their homes for Christmas and that, if this were not arranged officially, they would simply go home anyway. He was under no illusions as to the possibility of maintaining indefinitely the high standard of discipline which had obtained during the retreat. Once the troops were in Germany they would inevitably disperse. If, therefore, the objectives of the Supreme Command were to be achieved, if necessary with the use of armed force, there was no time to be lost, and he therefore demanded the military entry into Berlin of ten divisions under the command of General von Lequis.

Ebert was not averse to being rid of the Councils and particularly of the Spartakists, who were a perpetual menace to the stability of his Government. There undoubtedly occurred to him once again the example of the unhappy termination of the February Revolution in Russia, together with the thought that the era of Ebert-Kerensky might be succeeded by that of Liebknecht-Lenin. In this parallel, however, there was one essential difference; Gröner was no Kornilov, the Army would stand firmly behind the Government in dealing with the extremists of the Left. Ebert, however, had all the bourgeois horror of a *Bürgerkrieg*. He wished, above all else, to avoid the shedding of blood in the streets of Berlin, and he feared an armed conflict if the Army were given a free hand in the process of disarming the Spartakists. He therefore resisted both the telephonic persuasiveness of Gröner and the direct approaches of von Haeften to arrange for the military occupation of the capital.

This hesitancy on the part of the Chancellor occasioned intense annoyance at Cassel where it was realized that the sands were running out in the glass. Forthwith the Supreme Command decided to play its highest card. Hitherto there had been no formal ratification of the Gröner-Ebert pact from the side of the Army. Now on December 8 Hindenburg indited a somewhat pompous letter to Ebert which could be interpreted either as a reaffirmation of the pact or the premonitory symptom of its denunciation. 'If I address the following lines to you', wrote the Marshal condescendingly, 'I do so because I am credibly informed that you, like myself, as a true German, love your fatherland before everything, putting aside personal opinions and wishes, as I have had to do in order to help my country in its hour of need. In this spirit I have joined forces with you to rescue our people from a threatening collapse.' The demands of the Supreme Command were then put forward; first, the summoning of the National Assembly; secondly, the abolition of the Workers' and Soldiers' Councils — 'instead of them, a few representatives of the workers can collaborate with the authorities, having only a consultative voice' — thirdly, the Government must be safeguarded by the police and the army. The letter closed with the words: 'The fate of the German people has been laid in your hands. Upon your determination it will depend whether the German Reich acquires a new impetus (*noch einmal zu neuem Aufschwung gelangen wird*). I am ready, and behind me stand the whole Army, to support you unreservedly. We all know that after this lamentable upshot of the war (*diesem bedauerlichen Ausgang des Krieges*), the reconstruction of the realm can only be effected upon new foundations and in new forms.' [1]

[1] The text of Hindenburg's letter was read in open court during the Magdeburg Trial of December 1924, when Ebert, as President of the Republic, was forced to bring a libel action against certain of his Nationalist traducers who had impugned the patriotism of his actions both during and subsequent to the war (see Karl Brammer, *Der Prozess des Reichspräsidenten* (Berlin, 1925), pp. 101-2). The text of the excerpts of the letter as printed by Benoist-Méchin (i, 87) is exceedingly misleading since he quotes as *oratio recta* what is in fact a paraphrase of a passage in Volkmann (p. 126) which that author does not claim as a textual rendering of the letter.

There was little of comfort to be derived by Ebert from this patronizing epistle which merely under-scored the difficulties of his position. The responsibility for decisions was all his ; the Supreme Command were in effect telling him that they would help him to extricate himself from his dilemma on their own terms, and their terms were the assumption by the Army of the Guardianship of the State. It was, moreover, clear beyond peradventure that when Hindenburg wrote of 'new foundations and new forms' in the government of the Reich, he was not referring in any way to an alteration in the status of the Army, save in the sense of added importance. In the reformed Reich which would emerge as a result of this 'new impetus', the Army would suffer certainly not a diminution of status — 'New presbyter is but old priest writ large', as Milton wrote of English Puritanism. Nothing would be changed except for the better, and it is to be noted that the Supreme Command were already beginning to talk with Olympian detachment of the 'lamentable upshot of the war', as if they had had no part in the responsibility for the military collapse which the German armies had sustained.

Ebert was, in fact, being invited to employ the Furies of the Right to expel the Harpies of the Left. But who, he wondered, would rid him of the Furies? Machiavelli's Prince would have employed the one to destroy the other and then devised means to hamstring the destroyer ; but Ebert was no Machiavellian figure, he was only a harassed but honest and intensely patriotic German bourgeois who had lost two sons in the war and who, despite all the doctrinal influence of international socialism, still retained a deep respect for a Prussian Field-Marshal.

The receipt of Hindenburg's letter precipitated an acute crisis in the ranks of the Provisional Government. If the Army wished to disarm the civil population, the Independent Socialists wished to disarm the Army. Barth insisted that only those troops which formed the metropolitan garrison should be allowed to enter Berlin.[1] Ebert returned an equivocal reply to Cassel, which in its turn brought a forthright ultimatum from the Supreme Command conveyed in person by a figure who was destined to play a part of some notoriety in the subsequent history of Germany, Major Kurt von Schleicher.

To Ebert von Schleicher brought word that the Supreme Command at Cassel considered that the time for equivocation had ended

---

[1] Emil Barth later published his account of these events and of the revolutionary period of November 1918–March 1919 in *Aus der Werkstatt der deutschen Revolution* (Berlin, 1919).

and the moment for action had come. If the Provisional Government would not take the necessary measures to dispose of the Spartakists, the Field-Marshal would act on his own responsibility and would employ all the means at his disposal against them. Ebert asked him to repeat his message at a session of the Provisional Government — the first, but by no means the last, Cabinet council at which von Schleicher was to be present — and his arguments won the day. A compromise was reached on the vexed question of disarmament, but it was agreed that General von Lequis' divisions should enter Berlin.[1]

And so on the morning of December 11 — just a month after the conclusion of the armistice which had signified their defeat — the returning German legions marched up Unter den Linden where their fathers and grandfathers had marched in triumph after their victories over Denmark and Austria and France. Under a leaden sky the troops defiled with their standards and their music and their arms, as if they too were victors. At the Brandenburger Tor, surmounted by the quadriga of Victory, Ebert greeted them with the words : 'I salute you, who return unvanquished from the field of battle '.[2] With this sentence, intended to gratify the troops, he absolved the General Staff and condemned the Revolutionary Republic. The legend of the 'stab in the back' had been born ; the seeds of the Second World War already sown.

(v)

But the real crisis had yet to come. The General Staff and the Officer Corps had won a substantial victory, but they had yet to reckon with their deadly enemies of the Councils. The decisive moment arrived within a week of the march into Berlin. On December 16 there assembled in the hall of the Prussian Diet the first Soviet Congress of Germany composed of the delegates of the Soldiers' and Workers' Councils throughout the Reich, and which, since the Imperial *Reichstag* had dissolved itself in November 1918 and the election for the National Assembly had not yet been held,

---

[1] It is fair to point out that Ebert's government did try to create a republican militia capable of keeping order. On December 12, 1918, the Council of People's Representatives issued an order authorizing the formation of a *Volkswehr*. This attempt to organize a reliable armed force failed because the troops recruited were either politically unreliable or ineffective from a military viewpoint. (Cf. Gordon, *The Reichswehr and the German Republic, 1919–1926*, pp. 18-19.)

[2] *Friedrich Ebert: Schriften, Aufzeichnungen und Reden* (Dresden, 1926), ii, 127-130.

was the only parliamentary body then in existence in Germany. The political complexion of the Congress was predominantly Majority Socialist, so much so that, despite the frenzied efforts of Spartakists and the Independent Socialists, neither Karl Liebknecht nor Rosa Luxemburg was elected.[1] But, though divided on many points of Socialist doctrine and dogma, the Congress was unanimous and vociferous in its determination to put an end once and for all to the Officer Corps.

The attack was progressive. On the day of its opening the Congress made a formal demand for the dismissal of Hindenburg; on the 17th a resolution was adopted dissolving the military Cadet Schools which for generations had been the nurseries of the Officer Corps; and on the following day the Congress delivered what was intended to be the *coup de grâce* to the militarist caste. A seven-point resolution was put forward; the supreme command of the Army and Navy to be transferred to the Control Committee of the Councils; all insignia of rank to be abolished and the carrying of arms, other than on duty, to be prohibited; the Soldiers' Councils to be held responsible for the conduct and discipline of troops; there was to be no superiority of rank when off duty; troops should elect their own officers and only those officers who had retained the confidence of their men should be eligible for re-election; and finally, the suppression of the regular Army and the substitution of a civil guard.[2]

Ebert fought energetically against the adoption of these measures, which were closely modelled on the notorious *Prikaz No. 1* which in 1917 had begun the disintegration of the Russian Army.[3] Both on the tribune of the Congress and in the sessions of the Provisional Government, he made every effort to support his military allies at Cassel, well knowing what the result would be if the resolutions were passed. But the Chancellor fought in vain. Though supported by his Independent Socialist colleagues Haase and Dittmann, he was opposed at every point by Barth, who with Ledebour had now formed a working alliance with the Spartakists. The resolutions were adopted by a substantial majority and, though the Congress broke up in confusion, with Ebert considering his hands still free to

---

[1] A proposal to invite the Spartakist leaders to attend the sessions of the Congress as 'guests of honour' was also heavily defeated.

[2] Volkmann, p. 142.

[3] On March 14, 1917, the Petrograd Soviet promulgated 'Order No. 1', which took authority from the officers of the army and navy and gave it to the Soldiers' Committees. For text see *Izvestiya* No. 3 March 15, 1917; also Frank Alfred Golder, *Documents of Russian History, 1914–1917* (New York, 1927), pp. 386-7.

negotiate with the Supreme Command, the effect at Cassel was one
of impassioned fury.

But the position of the Supreme Command had also become
weakened. As Gröner had foreseen, the morale and discipline of
the rank-and-file of the Army had seriously deteriorated with the
approach of Christmas and demobilization. Von Lequis reported
adversely on the reliability of the majority of his troops, many of
whom had already deserted, while the remainder were fraternizing
with the civilian population and responding to Spartakist propaganda. As yet, moreover, the organization of the volunteer Free
Corps, which had already been put into operation, was by no means
complete. The crisis produced by the Congress resolutions had
therefore caught the Supreme Command at a weak moment.

Nevertheless their response was immediate. This was a matter
of life and death for the Officer Corps. To acquiesce in the provisions of the resolutions would be to surrender their last cherished
prerogatives. They would rather fight and die. 'You may tell Herr
Ebert', said the Marshal to Gröner, 'that I decline to recognize the
ruling of the Congress with regard to the executive authority of our
officers ; that I shall oppose it by every means in my power, and
that I shall not allow my epaulettes or my sword to be taken from
me. Now, as before, the Army supports the Government and
expects it to carry out its promise to preserve the Army.' At the
same time he telegraphed to all troop commanders that no change
was to be made in the Army regulations. Ebert begged the Supreme
Command to reconsider their attitude. If they persisted in it civil
war was inevitable, and at the first shot the Provisional Government
would be overthrown.

'It is not we who began the quarrel,' replied Gröner, 'and it is
not our business to end it. We have taken our decision and it is
irrevocable. For the Marshal, for the whole of the General Staff
and for myself, it is a question of life and death.'

Once again the Supreme Command's tactics of bluff and intransigence triumphed. The resolutions of the Congress were tacitly
ignored by the Provisional Government, but the relations between
Cassel and Berlin had been strained to breaking point ; only a
miracle could save them from rupture. The fates, however, were
on the side of the Army. The miracle occurred.

On the morning of December 23 Ebert and his Cabinet found
themselves besieged in the Chancellery by troops of the 'People's
Marine Division', who had been quartered in the stables of the
Imperial Palace since the early days of the Revolution. Incited
by Spartakist agitators to demand increased rates of pay, they

demonstrated in the Wilhelmstrasse, and, when their demands were refused, forced their way into the office of the Chancellor and cut all telephone wires. All but one; the secret wire to Wilhelmshöhe remained intact, and once again Ebert fell back upon his last line of defence. It was von Schleicher who answered the telephone. 'The Government is held prisoner, Major', came the agitated voice of Ebert. 'We need your support; you must act.' It was the moment for which the Supreme Command had waited with growing impatience and von Schleicher gave the immediate reply, 'I will give orders at once to General von Lequis to march from Potsdam to liberate you.'

What followed was in the nature of an anti-climax. By the time von Lequis' much heralded march from Potsdam had been accomplished, the mutinous sailors had been persuaded to withdraw from the *Reichskanzlei* to their quarters in the *Marstall* (Imperial stables) and the attempt of von Lequis' troops on Christmas Eve to dislodge them from this position was a signal failure.[1]

In other circumstances this inability to make good their boasts might well have proved a fatal set-back to the fortunes of the Supreme Command, and indeed the Officer Corps was deeply chagrined at their failure. But Gröner and von Schleicher were able to turn even this untoward event to their advantage. When it became clear that the Government was prepared to use force against the radicals in Berlin if the situation required it, the Independent Socialists resigned from the Government. While Schleicher rallied the morale of the Officer Corps Ebert took the momentous step of summoning Gustav Noske to take over responsibility for national defence.[2]

---

[1] The evacuation of the Marine Division from the *Marstall* was eventually negotiated by the Independent Socialists, notably Barth, on condition that their full demands for back pay were met by the Government.

[2] Gustav Noske (1868–1946) was born at Brandenburg-an-der-Havel, a small town outside Berlin in the heart of the Mark. His father was a basket-weaver and to this trade Noske was reluctantly apprenticed. Later he became a master-butcher, a calling the political connotation of which both he and his opponents did not hesitate to exploit — '*Einer muss der Bluthund werden*' was his own comment on his appointment as *Reichswehr* Minister, and '*Mörder Noske*' he remained to the Left throughout his political career. Noske became identified with the trade-union movement at an early age and subsequently joined the Social Democratic Party in which he soon gained local reputation and authority. In 1906 he was elected to the *Reichstag*, where he soon identified himself with the Right wing of the Party, supporting its nationalist policies in opposition to Haase, Liebknecht, and Ledebour. He applied himself to the study of military and naval affairs, becoming the recognized Party authority on these subjects, and it was for this reason that he was recommended by Ebert to Prince Max of Baden as the most suitable person to deal with the naval mutiny in Kiel in November 1918. In a week he had restored

The passage of Noske across the stage of Republican Germany, brief though it was, was fraught with significance, if for no other reason than that it marked the transitory appearance of a Majority Socialist who was prepared to defend the new Republic even to the effusion of blood and who was ready to offer implacable opposition to anarchy and disorder, be they never so carefully disguised beneath the standard of democracy and brotherhood. Square-headed and compactly built, with a physical strength and courage which belied his spectacles and straggling moustache, Noske was a believer in the necessary use of force, a natural born disciple of Nietzsche. Not endowed with great intelligence but richly indued with that *Bauernschlauheit*, that good horse-sense and cunning of the German working-man and peasant, he now appeared as the 'strong man' of the Republic.[1]

He had already given proof at Kiel of his willingness to accept responsibility and his ability to take decisions, and his shrewd yet forceful handling of the mutinous sailors on that occasion had commended him to the approbation of the High Command. Gröner approved of the appointment. He promised his support to Noske and lost no opportunity of playing upon the innate vanity of the new Minister.

For Noske, like so many of his fellow Socialists, entertained a curious love-hate complex for the Generals. While affecting to despise and condemn the General Staff they were, nevertheless, secretly flattered to acquire their commendation. Noske was no exception to the rule. He purred under the compliments of Gröner and of von Schleicher, and, before he knew where he was, he found

law, order and discipline in the fleet and had laid the foundation of his reputation as a Strong Man. He was responsible for military affairs from December 1918 until after the Kapp *Putsch* of March 1920. He was then appointed Provincial President of Hanover, in which post he continued until the Nazi Revolution of 1933, when he was dismissed, though with retention of his pension rights. During the Second World War he was arrested twice, first for a few days at its outbreak, and then on July 22, 1944, in connection with the Generals' Plot. He escaped from the Moabit Prison in April 1945 when the Russians were in the suburbs of Berlin, and died on November 30, 1946, on the eve of departure to give a lecturing tour in the United States. Of his two books, the first, *Von Kiel bis Kapp* (Berlin, 1920), gives a trenchant account of his career as a Minister. The second, his autobiography, completed in 1933 but published posthumously, *Erlebtes aus Aufstieg und Niedergang einer Demokratie* (Zürich, 1947), is disappointing, perhaps for the reason that, as he himself states in the introduction, the author cherished the illusion until 1936 that the book could be published under the Nazi régime.

[1] '*Il fait songer à ces vieux Germains dont parle Tacite*', wrote a Frenchman of Noske at this time, '*les barbares vêtus de peaux de bêtes et qui, impulsifs comme des sauvages, tranchaient tout différend par la force du poing*' (Paul Gentizon, *L'Armée allemande depuis la défaite* (Paris, 1920), pp. 34-5).

himself the centre of a group of the ablest Staff officers in the Supreme Command; von Lüttwitz, von Hammerstein, von Dohna, von Lettow-Vorbeck, von Stockhausen, men distinguished alike for their family quarterings and for their own military achievements. Between these men and their new Chief there developed a relationship which, in the ensuing months, was to have the greatest importance for the future of the German Republic.

When he entered the Cabinet on December 27, 1918, Noske was charged with a dual task; on the one hand he was entrusted by Ebert with the defence of the Republic, on the other, by Gröner with the throttling of the Revolution. To both his new masters he put the same question: with what was he to defend or throttle? The answer was not immediately apparent. The defeat of the *Marstall*, followed by the Christmas holidays, had reduced the effective regular troops at the disposal of the Supreme Command in Berlin to something in the neighbourhood of one hundred and fifty men, exclusive of officers. But the answer was forthcoming a week later when, on January 4, Ebert and Noske were invited by General von Lüttwitz to the military camp at Zossen. There, to their intense surprise they found a force of four thousand men fully equipped and disciplined, who passed in review on the snow-covered parade ground in impeccable order, according, for the first time in the history of the Prussian Army, full military honours to civilians.

These troops, assembled and equipped by General Ludwig Maercker, were among the first of those volunteer Free Corps which the Supreme Command had been urgently forming from the wreck of the old Imperial Army, and each man had given a written oath of 'loyal service to the Provisional Government of Chancellor Ebert until the National Assembly has constituted a definitive government'.[1]

Noske was delighted with this new weapon to his hand. 'Don't worry, everything's going to be all right now' (*Sei nur ruhig, es wird alles wieder gut werden*), he said to Ebert as they drove back to Berlin.[2]

And in so far as throttling the Revolution was concerned, he was right. There followed the Bloody Week of January 10–17, at the end of which the Spartakists had been crushed by the Free Corps under the direction of Noske and the command of von Lüttwitz, and their leaders, Karl Liebknecht and Rosa Luxemburg, had been lynched by the officers of the Guard Cavalry Division.[3] The result,

---

[1] General Maercker, *Vom Kaiserheer zur Reichswehr* (Leipzig, 1922), p. 53.
[2] Maercker, p. 64; Volkmann, pp. 171-2.
[3] The officer commanding the detachment which removed Rosa Luxemburg from the Hotel Eden, where she had been brought after her arrest on the night of

however, was to make the Ebert Government even more dependent on the Army than before, and when the National Assembly met at Weimar on February 6, 1919, it was under the protection of Maercker's bayonets.

(vi)

The three months which separated the Revolution of November 9, 1918, from the opening of the National Assembly on February 6, 1919, had witnessed a considerable change in the political atmosphere of Germany. The elections of January 19 had shown a superficial victory for the forces of the democratic revolution, but it was only superficial. For though the combined forces of Social Democracy — the Majority Socialists and the Independents — polled 13,700,000 votes out of the 30,000,000 cast and had between them 185 out of 421 seats in the Assembly, they were bitterly divided.[1] As a result, the Majority Socialists, on whom lay the onus of the events of the past three months, though they could command 163 votes, did not constitute a majority.

More important than the disunity of the Left was the fact that the Right had regained its courage. In November 1918 the members of the old Conservative and Liberal Parties had seen their world collapse about them and themselves confronted with circumstances which might, for all they knew, produce in Germany conditions similar to those in Russia. In those dark days Ludendorff had fled to Sweden in disguise, and others, such as Count Westarp, the veteran Conservative leader, had appealed to Ebert for protection.[2] Within three months, however, the Right had learnt to distinguish

January 15, and which was responsible for her murder, was arrested on February 20, and brought before a military tribunal which sentenced him to two years and four months in prison and dismissal from the Army. This officer, a certain Lieutenant Vogel, subsequently escaped to Holland with a forged passport and a gift of 30,000 marks from the Committee of the Association of Officers in his pocket. It was later alleged, both in the National Assembly and in the *Reichstag*, that a naval officer, who had been a member of the tribunal which had condemned Vogel, had been an accessory to his escape. The naval officer concerned was Lieutenant-Commander Wilhelm Canaris, later to figure as head of the *Abwehr* (counter-espionage organization) and a leading figure in the conspiracy which culminated in the attempted assassination of Hitler on July 20, 1944. (See E. J. Gumbel, *Les Grands Crimes politiques en Allemagne* (Paris, 1931), pp. 28-30 ; Ian Colvin, *Chief of Intelligence* (London, 1951), pp. 12-13 ; Karl Heinz Abshagen, *Canaris* (Stuttgart, 1949), pp. 61-9.)

[1] In the *Reichstag* elections of 1912 the undivided Social Democratic Party had won 4,250,000 votes out of the total of 12,208,000 cast. The increase in the electorate, notably caused by the enfranchising of women, had therefore not greatly increased the proportional representation of the Party.

[2] Theodor Wolff, p. 160.

between the varying shades of Red on the Left — the flaming
vermilion of the Spartakists, the 'near-red' of the Independents,
and the 'parlour pink' of the Majority Socialists. Moreover, they
had watched, with growing relief and satisfaction, the waxing
differences and schisms arising between their political opponents,
culminating in the liquidation of the extreme Left elements by the
Government of the Majority Socialists immediately before the
elections; and, above all, they had observed, with increasing com-
placency and gratification, the rôle which the Supreme Command
was successfully playing in national affairs.

By February 1919 Ludendorff had resumed his residence in
Germany unmolested and was writing contemptuously to his wife
of the Provisional Government : 'It would be the greatest stupidity
for the revolutionaries to allow us all to remain alive. Why, if ever
I come to power again, there will be no pardon. Then with an easy
conscience, I would have Ebert, Scheidemann and Co. hanged, and
watch them dangle.' [1]

At the National Assembly elections the Conservatives — now,
in accordance with the spirit of the day,[2] called the German National
People's Party — polled 3,200,000 votes and obtained 42 seats ;
their allies on the Right, the former National-Liberals, rechristened
the German People's Party, secured 1,200,000 votes and 22 seats.
These two groups represented the forces of reaction in the Assembly ;
the Conservatives led by Clemens von Delbrück, a former Imperial
Minister, and von Düringer, formerly chief of the Kaiser's Civil
Cabinet, and the Liberals [3] by Gustav Stresemann, who throughout
the war had constituted himself the mouthpiece of the Supreme
Command in the *Reichstag* and the arch-apostle of the Policy of
Annexation.

When the Assembly opened on February 6, under the comforting protection of Maercker's Jaegers, it was treated to a glowing
encomium of Wilhelm II from Delbrück, and a spirited defence by
the German People's Party of the policies of July 1914, of Pan-
Germanism and of the U-boat warfare. Even Hugo Preuss, the

---

[1] Margaritte Ludendorff, *Als ich Ludendorffs Frau war* (Munich, 1929), p. 209.
[2] In keeping with the prevailing *Zeitgeist*, most of the old political parties
appeared at Weimar in new and 'popular' trappings.
[3] Such Liberal thought as was to be found at Weimar existed in the Democratic
Party which was born in December 1918 of a fusion of the old Progressive Party
with the group of National-Liberals who had refused to follow Stresemann into
the *Vaterlandspartei* during the war. This new Party attracted such men as Conrad
Haussmann, Friedrich Naumann, the author of *Mittel-Europa*, Bernhard Dern-
burg and Wilhelm Solf, former Colonial Ministers, Count Bernstorff, the ex-
Ambassador, Theodor Wolff, editor of the *Berliner Tageblatt*, and Theodor Heuss.
For a time it also numbered Hjalmar Schacht amongst its members.

chief artificer of the Constitution of the Weimar Republic, urged as an additional argument in favour of its adoption that, 'if ever the monarchy is restored in Germany it will be unitary'.

In spirit the Weimar Assembly was far from being a 'revolutionary' body. The Centre described the Revolution as 'regrettable' and the Democrats, in their turn, characterized it as 'useless'. In so far as the tone of the Assembly was revolutionary at all, it was a revolution towards the Right rather than towards the Left which was achieved — though not by comparison with pre-1914 standards. Well knowing that, for the time being, nothing could be done against the will of the victors, the founders of the new Reich looked forward to a day when Germany should have regained her strength. Provided that their future possibilities were not restricted, they were prepared to resign themselves for the moment to the *fait accompli*. What they really feared — and this anxiety they shared in common with the General Staff — was the disunion and partition of the Reich. The object of their immediate and ardent desire was to recoup those territorial losses, which they knew to be inevitable, by compensating additions in the union of Austria, and possibly of the Sudetenland, with Germany, for they knew well that nothing would be irretrievably lost to them as long as a large and populous territory formed a German unitary State.

Nowhere was this more clearly demonstrated than in the articles which Friedrich Naumann was now writing in the *Berliner Tageblatt* : [1] he called for 'a strong German unity such as had been delineated on August 4, 1914', and concluded with an appeal to his 'brother Germans in Alsace, Bohemia, and Austria' to participate in this unity.[2]

It is a remarkable tribute to Bismarck — and equally a most revealing commentary on the German political character — that the German unity which he had achieved by military triumph should survive and even be strengthened by military defeat. His two guiding principles, German unity and State power, were those which inspired the large majority of the deputies to the National Assembly. What they achieved was not, like the German Empire after 1815, a

[1] *Berliner Tageblatt*, January 20-22, 1919; also Theodor Heuss, *Friedrich Naumann, der Mann, das Werk, die Zeit* (Stuttgart, 1949), pp. 484-5.
[2] In the original text of the Weimar Constitution as adopted by the National Assembly on August 11, 1919, provision was made under Article 61 for the union of German-Austria with the Reich and her representation on the *Reichsrat*. The Austrian Republic had already, on November 12, 1918, declared itself to be an integral part of the German Reich. The Allied Powers, however, annulled these provisions and by Article 80 of the Treaty of Versailles and Article 88 of the Treaty of St. Germain forbade the *Anschluss* between Germany and Austria.

Staatenbund (a federation of States), nor, like the Second Reich, a *Bundesstaat* (a federal State) ; it was a superficially decentralized unitary State,[1] and an infinitely closer approximation to Bismarck's ideal than that statesman could have ever dared to hope for.

That the victorious Allied Powers allowed these events at Weimar to go not only unchecked but largely unnoticed and unrealized is among the many tragedies of the Peace Conference of Paris. Not that warnings were lacking. Day after day Jacques Bainville and others sounded a tocsin of alarm in the French Press, but their prescient threnodies failed to dissipate the roseate visions of the wishful thinkers and the insensate optimism of the uninformed men of good-will. Bismarck had suffered from a *cauchemar* that the Reich which he had created might provoke a European Coalition which would destroy it, but, as Bainville bitterly remarked, he never envisaged a coalition sufficiently stupid to use its victory to consummate the work of German unity.[2]

Still, in 1919 the majority of the leading statesmen of the world were more afraid of Communist Russia — a new phenomenon of evil — than of a possible revival of the old Adam of German nationalism, and those who were shaping the new policies of Germany were quick to take advantage of the opportunity presented by this aberration. They themselves were genuinely alarmed at the Communist menace, but they were also well aware of the advantages to be gained by an exploitation of this fear which they shared in common with the Allies. It was, in effect, the only common ground which existed between victors and vanquished, and already at Weimar there appeared that same line of propaganda which, twenty years later, was to be used by Hitler — and, thirty years later, by Dr. Adenauer and Herr Schumacher — namely, that Germany constituted Europe's first bastion of defence against Bolshevism.[3]

It was not only the structure of government which emerged stream-lined from Weimar. The National Assembly gave to

---

[1] Godfrey Scheele, *The Weimar Republic* (London, 1946), p. 42.

[2] *Action Française*, May 9, 1919 ; Jacques Bainville, *L'Allemagne* (Paris, 1939), ii, 34.

[3] This line of argument had been used by the Germans from the earliest days of their defeat. In the course of the discussions at Réthondes two members of the German Armistice Commission, Count Oberndorff and General von Winterfeldt, both attempted to extract from General Weygand concessions in the conditions of surrender by assuring him that acceptance by Germany of the terms as they stood would inevitably drive her into the arms of Bolshevism, an event which would create a new menace for the Allies in Central Europe. General Weygand, however, refused to be impressed by this piece of psychological warfare. 'The victors have nothing to fear', was his reply (Karl Friedrich Nowak, *Versailles* (London, 1928), p. 15).

Germany, in addition to a centralized Reich, an army which, though curtailed in numbers, was more unified in organization and control than the *Kaiserheer* had ever been. For, with the disappearance of Bavaria, Saxony, and Württemberg as semi-autonomous kingdoms within the Empire, there vanished also their respective War Ministries, General Staffs, and individual contingents. For the first time in its history the German Army was organized on a permanently unified basis as distinct from the *ad hoc* unification for war purposes which had existed under the Empire.

Before, however, the Assembly had taken this momentous decision to create a unitary army, and, indeed, before it had even met at all, the Ebert Government had taken two preliminary steps towards military reorganization which were destined to have important effects upon the future of the German Army and its attitude towards the Republic. In the first place they had legalized the Free Corps by issuing an appeal (January 6, 1919) to all able-bodied men to join these military foundations for the defence of the frontiers of the Fatherland and the preservation of order in the interior. This step, which was taken two days after the review of Maercker's Jaegers at Zossen by Ebert and Noske on January 4, placed the Free Corps on an official footing; whereas they had previously existed as the independent creation of the General Staff,[1] they were now accorded official recognition by the Government, and became, in effect, almost its sole military resource.

But what the Ebert Government did not know, and what Noske's military entourage certainly did not tell him, was that there had been formed on November 28, 1918 — even before the return of the Field Army to Germany — the German Officers' Association (*Deutscher Offiziersbund*) with the avowed aim 'to keep intact the entire old Führer-class (*die Erhaltung des gesamten Standes der alten Führerschicht*) as one of the forces needed for the rebirth of the nation and as a guarantee for the education of the youth'. A fortnight later (December 16, 1918) there was also born the National Association of German Officers (*Nationalverband deutscher Offiziere*) whose purpose was to provide a 'political fighting organization and

---

[1] The Supreme Command had issued orders on November 27, 1918, for the reinforcement of the depleted Army by voluntary enlistment. This was the basis on which the Volunteer Corps (*Freiwilligenkorps*) came into being (Major Gerhardt Thomée, *Der Wiederaufstieg des deutchen Heeres 1918–1938* (Berlin, 1939), p. 14 ; Hans Ernst Fried, *The Guilt of the German Army* (New York, 1942), p. 170). For accounts of the activities of the Free Corps during the five years of their existence, see F. W. von Oertzen, *Die Deutschen Freikorps 1918–1923* (Munich, 1936), Edgar von Schmidt-Pauli, *Geschichte der Freikorps 1918–1924* (Stuttgart, 1936), and Robert G. L. Waite, *Vanguard of Nazism* (Cambridge, Mass., 1952).

"shock troop" on a Germanic national militant and monarchistic basis'.[1]

These measures had been taken secretly by the Officer Corps for the preservation of their traditions and beliefs at a moment when these appeared to be threatened with imminent extinction. Subsequent events had favoured their fortunes. Their prospects improved and the formation of the Free Corps had provided an early opportunity for advancing the aims with which these two organizations had been formed, since no recruit was accepted into the Corps who was not 'politically reliable'. The Free Corps, though nominally for the defence of the Reich within and without, became a potential weapon for the active preservation of militant and reactionary nationalism, and their formal recognition by the Government played directly into the hands of the military.

Though it may well have been inevitable for Ebert and Noske to give the approval of the Government to the Free Corps — for they were engaged simultaneously in suppressing Spartakism within the Reich and in resisting the annexationist efforts of the Poles on the Eastern frontiers — they made a further concession to the sensibilities of the General Staff when, by an ordinance of January 19, they completely transformed the character of the Soldiers' Councils, placing them, together with all military formations, under ·the authority of the Prussian Minister of War and virtually relegating them to technical and consultative functions.

Thus, when the National Assembly met on February 6, the position of the military had been greatly strengthened, both by Government action and by the enhanced prestige derived from the suppression of the Spartakists in Berlin, and the fact that the Assembly met under the protection of Maercker's Jaegers was eloquent of this new status.

Under the Constitution of 1919, the relation of the Chief of State to the Army was very different from that enjoyed by the Kaiser. Following the constitutional reforms of October 1918, the Army was, in theory, subjected to parliamentary control. The President of the Republic was the titular Supreme Commander (Article 47) but the members of the armed forces took the oath not to the President but to the Constitution (Article 176). As Supreme Commander the President had the power of appointment and dismissal of general officers (Article 46), and his acts had to be countersigned by the

---

[1] These disclosures were made in a public address by Major-General Count Rüdiger von der Goltz, President of the United Patriotic Associations of Germany, in 1929 (*Volk und Reich der Deutschen*, B. Harms, ed. (Berlin, 1929), vol. ii, 161: Fried, p. 238).

Chancellor or by a competent Minister (Article 50). Since, however, the Chancellor was not appointed by the President but elected by the *Reichstag*, and could therefore be dismissed by a vote of no confidence, an additional check was thus placed on the use of the Army.

But though the authority of the Chief of State over the Army was thus restricted by the Weimar Constitution, that of the Army itself was rather strengthened. All legislative authority was transferred from the States to the Reich (Articles 4 and 6) and the Army was organized on a uniform basis for the whole country under a national Minister of Defence (*Reichswehrminister*) who was a member of the Cabinet (Article 79), and a single General Commanding Officer.

In one respect, however, the Constitution of 1919 gave to the President an authority which had never been possessed by the German Emperor. Under the Constitution of 1871 the Prussian Army could not be used to intervene in the affairs of the Federal States except on the express request of the Government of any one State, and then only with the assent of the *Bundesrat*. But in 1919, though the spirit of the National Assembly was towards a greater degree of centralization of national government, there were certain tendencies of disunity and secession within the Reich, notably in Saxony and Bavaria, which were not in consonance with this spirit. The framers of the Constitution, therefore, saw fit to include within its provisions certain safeguards for that greater unity which they desired to create, and to this end they conferred sweeping emergency powers upon the President, under Article 48, to use the armed forces of the Reich to enforce the performance by any state of the duties and obligations imposed upon it by the Constitution.[1] The use of these powers was destined to influence materially the relation of the President with the *Reichswehr*.

The law for the provisional organization of the *Reichswehr* was introduced into the Assembly on February 25, and came under severe criticism from all parties. Its passage, however, was greatly facilitated by the course of events. On March 2 there occurred in Berlin the second Spartakist rising which was suppressed with ease and severity by Noske and the Free Corps. Before the fighting had

---

[1] Paragraphs 1 and 2 of Article 48 of the Weimar Constitution read as follows :

'If a State fails to perform the duties imposed upon it by the federal constitution or by federal law, the President of the Republic may enforce performance by the aid of the armed forces.

'If public order and security are seriously disturbed or endangered within the Reich, the President of the Republic may take all necessary steps for their restoration, intervening, if need be, with the aid of the armed forces.'

C

44   THE ARMY AND THE REICH   PT. I

ended, the *Reichswehr* bill had become law (March 6) and the
energetic efficiency displayed by Noske gained him the further
approbation of the High Command at Cassel.[1]

The provisional army law presented in many ways a striking
example of the situation then obtaining in Germany, for it was a
confused hodge-podge of democratic aspirations and reactionary
tendencies. Viewed objectively it appeared to represent an honest
attempt to realize — in the words of Noske — 'the great ideal of a
nation in arms which imposes democracy in military affairs'; an
effort to reconcile the new spirit of parliamentary supervision with
the rigid traditions of Prussian efficiency. But the very ambiguity
of the circumstances led inevitably to the victory of the military
traditions over the democratic principles.

Moreover these principles were even used as a mask for the more
sinister survivals among the traditions. For example, for the first
time in its history the German Army was made responsible to
Parliament through a Cabinet minister who could be questioned
in the *Reichstag*. It was hoped, by this means, to inaugurate parliamentary supervision, to destroy the independent status hitherto
enjoyed by the Army and to obviate the danger of abuses of policy,
both internal and foreign, by the chiefs of the Army. Excellent
though this idea was in theory, it never worked in practice.
Throughout the fifteen years of the Weimar Republic there were
but four Ministers of Defence, though there were fourteen Chancellors. Of these, the first two, Noske and Gessler, were civilians
who were so much in the hands of their military advisers that,
either as dupes or confederates, they served their masters uncomplainingly and in their turn hoodwinked their colleagues in the
Cabinet or procured their tacit consent to secret policies of the
details of which they themselves were imperfectly informed. Their
successors were both Generals, Gröner and von Schleicher, who
knew very well what was in train and kept the Cabinet informed to
just that degree which they considered desirable. Any attempt on
the part of members of the *Reichstag* to elicit information on the
activities of the Army was met with evasion, prevarication, or blank
refusal. As a result, Hitler, when he came to power, found a firm
foundation of rearmament on which to rebuild the German military
machine. So much for parliamentary control.

[1] 'The High Command', wrote Gröner to Noske on March 18, 'has confidence in the Government, limited confidence in the Ministry of War and unlimited confidence only in the Minister for National Defence' (Wheeler-Bennett,
p. 215). By the end of May 1919 the Free Corps had also overcome by force Left-
wing elements in Bremen, Brunswick, Bavaria, Central Germany, and Saxony.

The rapidity with which the *Reichswehr* had been able to reorganize itself may be judged from the fact that, whereas in December 1918 the Government had been hard put to it to equip Maercker's 4000 volunteers, in May 1919 they had at their disposal 400,000 men, trained in arms and confident in their leaders.[1] Within the six months following the military collapse of Germany the Army had preserved the unity of the Reich, overcome the menace of civil war and, above all, restored the prestige of its own leaders. By the summer of 1919 it had assumed a vitally important position in the political councils of the Reich.

It was at this moment that the Allies delivered the conditions of peace to the German delegation at Versailles.

(vii)

Since the Armistice of November 1918 the German people had been living in a fools' paradise regarding the future Peace Treaty. They had been told by their leaders that, having got rid of the Monarchy, submitted to the conditions of surrender, and established a democratic and republican form of government, they would duly receive their reward in the shape of a peace based on impartial justice — the fruits of those promises which President Wilson had made to the world in his Fourteen Points and their subsequent elaborations. The German Government professed to believe that what was called the 'pre-Armistice agreement' of October-November 1918, which had resulted in the sending of the German delegation to Compiègne, constituted a *pactum de contrahendo* between the Allied Powers and Germany which was legally binding as a basis for peace.

In 1919, as in 1945, no collective sense of war-guilt was evident among the German people. As a result of years of consistent and systematic propaganda the majority of Germans believed that the War had been forced upon them by the policies of France and Russia; and of those who considered Germany in any way contributory to a general culpability, the majority were of the opinion that her sins had been greatly mitigated by the destruction of the old order, and that the new Germany, purged of imperial despotism and military autocracy, was ready to resume at once her place in the European family of nations. Germans, as a whole, were either ignorant or unmindful of the hatreds which had been engendered against them during the war years, though they cherished their own

[1] Noske, *Von Kiel bis Kapp*, p. 167.

enmities with warmth and avidity. They were completely unprepared for the peace terms then in preparation at Paris.

The German Government had at the outset entertained hopes that at some point in the deliberations of the Peace Conference, their delegates might be called in by the Allies to discuss the terms of peace in their penultimate form. But by April these hopes had dwindled to the point of submitting counter-proposals.[1] They still clung, however, to the basis of the 'Wilson Programme' and, on April 15, a message from Ebert was read to the National Assembly in which the President declared that Germany would sign only a 'peace of understanding and conciliation'.

The German representatives were speedily disillusioned after their arrival at Versailles. On May 5 they received the irrevocable refusal of the Allies to negotiate face to face, and two days later, at the historic session at the Trianon Palace Hotel, Clemenceau's inexorable 'L'heure du lourd règlement des comptes est venue' brought them to an abrupt and stern realization of the facts of their position.

Among the conditions of peace with which the horrified and infuriated Germans found themselves confronted — conditions which included the cession of territory to Poland, France, and Belgium, the loss of all colonies, a heavy burden of reparation and restrictions in the economic life of the country — were certain terms designed by the Allies to render Germany militarily impotent (Part V, Articles 159-213). The Army was to be reduced to a total of 100,000 men, recruited for twelve years, except for 4,000 officers serving for twenty-five years. Germany might possess no military aeroplanes, tanks, or weapons of offence. The Great German General Staff must be dissolved, 'and may not be reconstituted in any form', and a similar fate awaited the War Academy and such training establishments as the Lichterfelde Cadet School. The occupied Rhineland and a strip 50 kilometres wide to the east of it were to be demilitarized, and further restrictions were placed on other fortifications. The German battle fleet, already surrendered under the terms of the Armistice, was to be replaced by a minute token force of which the heaviest armed vessel was not to exceed 10,000 tons. There were to be no U-boats.

In addition the Sovereign War Lord of Germany, Wilhelm II,

---

[1] The Instructions to the German plenipotentiaries, drawn up by the Ministry of Foreign Affairs in April 1919, opened with the statement: 'In all probability the Allies will submit a final draft of a treaty with the explanation that it can only be accepted or rejected. It is not advisable to present a comprehensive counter-draft treaty. It can only be a question of presenting single counter-proposals' (Alma Luckau, *The German Delegation at the Paris Peace Conference* (New York, 1941), p. 199).

was publicly arraigned 'for a supreme offence against international
morality and the sanctity of treaties'; both he and other German
war leaders were to be surrendered to the Allies for trial on charges
of violation of the laws of war (Part VII, Articles 227-230). Lastly,
Germany was to acknowledge and accept the responsibility for a
war imposed by the aggression of herself and her allies (Part VIII,
Article 231).

The publication of the Allied peace terms came as a stunning
shock to the German people. 'The incredible has happened',
declared Konstantin Fehrenbach, President of the National Assembly: 'Our enemies have laid before us a treaty which surpasses by
far the fears of our greatest pessimists'.[1] On May 8 the President
and Cabinet issued a statement to the German people branding
the terms as 'unbearable' and 'unrealizable', and contrary to the
promises made in the pre-Armistice agreement;[2] while on the
following day the German delegation, in a note to M. Clemenceau
declared them to be 'intolerable for any nation'.[3] From end to end
of the Reich spontaneous mass-meetings of protest were held and
all places of public entertainment were closed.

The National Assembly itself was summoned in special session
on May 12 in the great Aula of the University of Berlin — a setting
similar to that in which, a hundred years before, after an even more
crushing defeat, Johann Fichte, in his 'Addresses to the German
People', delivered in the Academy of Berlin, had called upon his
compatriots to throw off the Napoleonic yoke. The purpose of the
special session was to give formal expression to the indignation of the
German people against the conditions of peace, and never before
had the National Assembly displayed so complete a unanimity of
thought. From the extreme Right, where the aged Count Poso-
dowsky-Wehner denounced the terms as a product of 'French
revenge and English brutality', to the extreme Left, where Hugo
Haase claimed the right of protest because, alone among the parties
of the *Reichstag*, the Independent Socialists had exercised that
same right against the ratification of the Treaties of Brest-Litovsk
and Bucharest, the condemnation was general and unanimous. 'For
five hours, men and women from all sections of the German Reich,
representing parties often diametrically opposed in their views, expressed their opinion of the conditions of peace in speeches which

---

[1] Luckau, p. 94.
[2] Schulthess' *Deutscher Geschichtskalendar, Vom Waffenstillstand bis zum Frieden
von Versailles* (Leipzig, 1919), pp. 489-90.
[3] *Urkunden zum Friedensvertrag zu Versailles vom 28 Juni 1919* (Berlin, 1920-21),
i, 208-9.

were extraordinarily alike in substance, although they varied in patriotic ardour.'[1] Fehrenbach finally brought the meeting to a close with an impromptu oration in which he warned the Allies — as it turned out with prophetic accuracy — to think of their own children and grandchildren, since the concomitant hardships of the treaty would create a generation in Germany in whom 'the will to break the chains of slavery would be implanted' from their earliest childhood.[2]

But a country united in protest soon proved not to be a country united in resistance. There were many throughout the Reich who favoured rejection of the peace terms, but there were comparatively few who would face up to the inevitable sequel of the renewal of hostilities. Some there were who were prepared for this and others who advocated rejection and a passive acceptance of the consequent Allied advance into Germany. Haase and the Independents reverted to their programme of November 1918 and preached 'peace at any price' to a people whose energy and will to resist had been sapped by the hardships of four years of war and nearly five of blockade ; a people who, though with protest and bitter resentment in their hearts, were more willing to make their submission in the hope that it would bring about an end to their privations, than to accept the warnings of those such as Friedrich Naumann, that 'they would have to starve and suffer even after they accepted the Treaty, and that this peace would mean the end of Socialism'.[3]

In the summer of 1919 the German people had been temporarily deprived of their physical and moral capacity for further resistance. They could still hate, but they lacked the power to translate their hatred into active opposition. Instead they cherished it within their bosoms, warming themselves with its rancorous fire, until the day should come when it might leap again into a living flame. Thus the great storm of violent popular reaction against the treaty gradu-

---

[1] Luckau, p. 99.

[2] Fehrenbach's speech on this occasion left a deeper impression upon his hearers than that of any other speaker. 'He was inspired in that hour by God to say what was felt by the German people', wrote Stresemann. 'His words, spoken under Fichte's portrait, the final words of which merged into "*Deutschland, Deutschland über alles*", made it an unforgettably solemn hour. There was in that sense a kind of uplifting grandeur. The impression left on all was tremendous' (Gustav Stresemann, *Von der Revolution bis zum Frieden von Versailles* (Berlin, 1919), pp. 170-71.)

[3] Heuss, pp. 640-41. Dr. Theodor Heuss (b. 1884) was the disciple and biographer of Friedrich Naumann, and also an early opponent of National Socialism. His work, *Hitlers Weg*, published in 1932, was among the books publicly burned by the Nazis on their accession to power. In September 1949, Dr. Heuss was elected the first President of the new Federal German Republic.

ally subsided and in place of the strident and uncompromising cry, 'We will not sign', was heard the sullen mutter of 'We must'.

The discussions within the Reich Cabinet followed much the same course as the trend of popular opinion.[1] At first there was unanimous support for Chancellor Scheidemann's verdict of 'unacceptable' and that 'the hand should wither' which signed a treaty that placed all Germany in shackles. Instructions were accordingly sent to the delegation at Versailles to seek mitigations of the conditions by means of counter-proposals. But when the Allies refused any concession beyond the Upper Silesian plebiscite, the unity within the Cabinet began to disintegrate. The Chancellor and the Foreign Minister, Count Brockdorff-Rantzau,[2] then at Versailles, remained adamant in favour of rejection, but to them was opposed the devious mind of Mathias Erzberger, whose meretricious ability, avid ambition, and unscrupulous character rendered him, had the Allies realized it, a very dangerous opponent. The fact that he now emerged as the champion of acceptance was no indication of the sweet reasonableness with which he was credited by the British and French, nor of the treachery to his country with which he was charged by the German Nationalists, and for which he was subsequently murdered.[3]

[1] Since the official records of the discussions within the Reich Cabinet have not yet been made public, the historian is dependent upon the memoirs and personal recollections of the persons concerned. These are inevitably *ex parte* in character, but it is believed that they convey a sufficiently accurate impression of what occurred.

[2] Ulrich, Count Brockdorff-Rantzau (1869–1928) came of an ancient Holstein family which had earned fame and distinction in the service of the Kings of Denmark and of France. One of his ancestors, Count Josias Rantzau, Marshal of France, was indeed alleged to have been the father of Louis XIV, and, when questioned about this legend by one of the French officers attached to the German Peace Delegation at Versailles, Count Brockdorff-Rantzau replied coldly : 'Oh yes, in my family the Bourbons have been considered bastard Rantzaus for the past three hundred years'. The Count himself entered the German diplomatic service in 1894, and at the close of the War was Minister in Denmark. After the November Revolution he retired, and though not a member of any political party he maintained relations with the Democrats. He accepted with reluctance the position of Minister of Foreign Affairs in Scheidemann's Cabinet and led the German delegation to Versailles, where he acquired notoriety by remaining seated while making his reply to Clemenceau on the occasion of the handing over of the peace terms. He refused to sign the Treaty and resigned with the Cabinet in June 1919. Recalled again from retirement in 1922, after the Treaty of Rapallo, he was appointed the first Ambassador of the German Republic to Moscow. There his cold and autocratic bearing found a remarkable response from Chicherin, and the successful conduct of German-Soviet relations for the ensuing six years was in great measure due to his ability and statesmanship. He died in 1928 while on leave in Berlin.

[3] Matthias Erzberger (1875–1921), a Württemberger, entered the *Reichstag* in 1903 as a deputy of the Centre Party. He displayed considerable ability and

Erzberger was playing a much deeper game than many realized at that time. He had been deeply impressed by the course of events in the Russian Revolution in which the Bolsheviks had succeeded in overthrowing the Kerensky régime because it had deceived the Russian people's hopes of peace.[1] But he had equally appreciated the tactics of Lenin in accepting the Treaty of Brest-Litovsk with the full intention of sabotaging its execution by passive resistance. To preserve the unity and stability of the Reich, Germany must accept the peace terms, since to reject them would inevitably entail the dismemberment of the Reich, the overthrow of the Government by the Independents and the Spartakists and, above all, the dissolution of the *Reichswehr*. But this acceptance, he argued, would be a mere matter of form both on the part of the Allies, who, once hey had gained their point, would certainly make concessions, and on the part of Germany, who would adopt a policy of long-term evasion.

These views Erzberger submitted to his Cabinet colleagues in the form of a memorandum,[2] and when they argued in their innocence that it was dishonest to undertake obligations which they had neither the power nor the intention to fulfil, he replied : 'Who of us, if bound hand and foot and ordered at the point of a revolver

by 1914 was recognized as one of the party's leaders, though far from popular with his fellow-members. On the outbreak of war he was appointed Director of Propaganda, but his activities lay in more devious ways and he quickly became immersed in political intrigue for which he had a flair and an addiction. He supported Tirpitz in his demands for unrestricted U-boat warfare although he later criticized the way in which this policy was implemented in 1917. In July 1917 he sponsored the *Reichstag* Resolution for Peace without annexations, which, originally designed as a daring piece of psychological warfare, earned him the hatred and resentment of the extreme Nationalists of the Right. Erzberger served as a State Secretary in Prince Max of Baden's Government and as such led the Armistice Commission to Compiègne; later he was appointed a Minister without Portfolio in the Scheidemann coalition. Vain, able, and unscrupulous, he had a genius for making enemies and for evoking distrust, yet he became Vice-Chancellor in Bauer's Cabinet and successfully tided Germany over her first post-war economic crisis. Attacked for his financial policies by another former Minister of Finance and Vice-Chancellor, Karl Helfferich, Erzberger fought and lost a celebrated libel action in February 1920. He resigned from the Cabinet in March and on August 26, 1921, was murdered in the Black Forest by Nationalist gunmen. His principal assassin, a former naval officer, Heinrich Tillessen, fled to Hungary where he remained until the Nazi Revolution of 1933 when he returned to Germany and joined the Party. He was arrested in the French Zone of Germany in 1946 and tried and sentenced by a German court for the murder he had committed twenty-five years before.

[1] Otto Landsberg, in *The Germans at Versailles*, edited by Victor Schiff (London, 1930), p. 138. Landsberg was Minister of Justice at the time and also a member of the delegation at Versailles.

[2] Mathias Erzberger, *Erlebnisse im Weltkrieg* (Berlin, 1920), pp. 371-3 ; Scheidemann, *Der Zusammenbruch*, pp. 244-8.

to sign an agreement to fly to the moon in forty-eight hours, would refuse our signature ? It is exactly the same with the peace treaty. When one signs under duress there is no question of insincerity.'[1]

Erzberger's memorandum was considered at special Cabinet meetings on June 3 and 4, at the end of which its author had the satisfaction of knowing that he had shattered the unanimity among his colleagues and that, though the majority still adhered to the policy of rejection, he had initiated the movement of retreat from Scheidemann's position of intransigence.[2] With tireless energy he sought to widen the fissure he had created, and in his efforts he was to have the zealous assistance of Noske and of Gröner. Unable to reach an agreement, the Cabinet resolved on June 4 to refer the whole question to the parties of the Coalition for their decision.[3]

Ebert, in the meantime, was seeking advice and counsel from his old ally General Gröner. The President himself was in favour of rejection and had been unimpressed by Erzberger's arguments. He knew, however, that in the final analysis the last word lay with the Army and, while he waited for the return of Brockdorff-Rantzau from Versailles to strengthen the ranks of the 'rejectionists' in the Cabinet, he asked from Gröner a military appreciation of the situation.

Gröner had already made his own calculations and deductions.[4] He had been kept fully informed of the course of events at Versailles by the military member of the commission, General von Seeckt, and as soon as the nature of the peace terms had been known he had taken his soundings throughout the Reich on the possibility of armed resistance in the event of rejection. The result had been profoundly discouraging. The officers whom he had sent on this mission of investigation had reported that on no account would the war-weary people of Germany support a resumption of hostilities. Local resistance might be possible, but no general response to a *levée en masse* could be counted on. On the contrary, it was quite

---

[1] Erzberger, p. 374.

[2] Scheidemann, *The Making of New Germany* (New York, 1929), ii, 314-16 ; *Der Zusammenbruch*, p. 249 ; Heuss, p. 644 ; Landsberg, pp. 138-9.

[3] Erzberger, p. 375. Luckau writes (p. 106) :
'It was unquestionably one of the most fatal decisions the Cabinet could possibly have made, because from then on the question of signing the treaty became the subject of bitter partisan strife, whereas it had previously been the one issue on which all parties but the Communists had agreed. This resolution not only aggravated the existing differences between the eight political parties but it tended to split the ranks of the majority parties who formed the Coalition Government.' It is not known who proposed the resolution in the Cabinet.

[4] Phelps, 'Die Aussenpolitik der OHL bis zum Friedensvertrag', *Deutsche Rundschau*, August 1950.

C 2

clear that, should hostilities be resumed, the *Reichswehr* would have to contend not only with the Allied Armies but with armed opposition from within, since the Independents and the Spartakists would certainly raise the standard of revolt in 'defence of peace'.

In view of this intelligence the practical mind of Gröner did not hesitate. Little more than a year before, when confronted with the terms of Ludendorff, Lenin had told his followers that these must be accepted because Russia could no longer fight; now Ludendorff's successor returned the same answer in similar circumstances. To Ebert and to Hindenburg, Gröner counselled acceptance in the face of *force majeure*; but Ebert required something in writing and Hindenburg was still hesitant.

'Should we not appeal to the Corps of Officers and demand from a minority of the people a gesture of sacrifice in defence of our national honour?' the Marshal asked of Gröner.

'The significance of such a gesture would escape the German people', Gröner replied dryly. 'There would be a general outcry against counter-revolution and militarism. The result would only be the downfall of the Reich. The Allies, baulked of their hopes of peace, would show themselves pitiless. The Officer Corps would be destroyed and the name of Germany would disappear from the map.'

After two days of bitter mental conflict, the irrefutable logic of Gröner's reasoning triumphed over Hindenburg's traditional instincts. Yet the Marshal could not bring himself to make a complete endorsement of the policy of surrender.

'In the event of a resumption of hostilities,' he wrote to Ebert on June 17, 'we can reconquer the province of Posen and defend our frontiers in the East. In the West, however, we can scarcely count upon being able to withstand a serious offensive on the part of the enemy in view of the numerical superiority of the Entente and their ability to outflank us on both wings.

'The success of the operation as a whole is therefore very doubtful, but as a soldier I cannot help feeling that it were better to perish honourably than accept a disgraceful peace.' [1]

On the previous day (June 16) the Allies at Versailles had categorically rejected the German counter-proposals to the conditions of peace and had informed Count Brockdorff-Rantzau that if his Government had not accepted the conditions within five days (*i.e.* by June 21) [2] the Armistice agreement would be terminated and ' the Allied and Associated Powers will take such steps as they

---

[1] Benoist-Méchin, i. 384-8; Volkmann, pp. 377-82; Wheeler-Bennett, pp. 217-18.   [2] The ultimatum was later extended by two more days.

think needful to enforce their terms'.¹ The delegates left Paris that same day, but it took them two days and a night to reach Weimar, so that it was not till June 18 that the battle for or against acceptance was finally joined in the sessions of the Cabinet.

On that day Brockdorff-Rantzau made a passionate appeal for rejection in which he was supported by Scheidemann and Landsberg. Erzberger led the opposition and Noske, who had been convinced by Gröner's arguments, followed his lead. The discussion lasted for hours. Finally, at three o'clock in the morning of June 19, a vote resulted in eight voices for rejection and six for acceptance. Ebert, though his sympathies were with the majority, ruled that a majority of two was no clear mandate either to sign or to reject the treaty, and that the final decision must be with the National Assembly.²

In the meantime a similar crisis was developing among the Generals. Gröner had travelled from Kolberg ³ to Weimar on the night of June 17, taking with him his own military appreciation and Hindenburg's statement. On the morning of the 18th he had an interview with General Reinhardt, the Prussian Minister of War, whom he found a violent exponent of the doctrine of rejection and resistance, even though a dismemberment of the Reich should follow. Such a dichotomy would, in his view, be purely ephemeral. The south and west might be temporarily occupied by the enemy and even separated from the Reich, but they would be able to save the eastern provinces, the cradle of the Prussian State, and to this nucleus the *terra irredenta* would gradually be reunited. This was an argument typical of the pure Prussian military tradition which could never accept the German Reich as being anything more than an adjunct to the Kingdom of Prussia,⁴ but such parochialism made little appeal to Gröner, a Württemberger, whose whole policy since the Armistice and the Revolution had been based on preserving the unity of the Reich. Forcefully he put his views before Reinhardt, but the Minister was unmoved and countered with the wholly unexpected demand that, should the Assembly vote for acceptance of the Treaty, the High Command should withdraw its

¹ Allied Reply to the German counter-proposals, June 16, 1919 (text in *International Conciliation*, November 1919, No. 144, pp. 1341-1424).

² Landsberg, p. 140 ; Heuss, p. 642. Erzberger (p. 376) writes of an even vote of seven for and seven against.

³ The General Headquarters of the High Command had been transferred from Cassel to Kolberg in Pomerania in February 1919.

⁴ This was in consonance with the opinion held by Wilhelm I at the founding of the German Empire in 1871. 'My son is heart and soul with the new state of affairs,' the old monarch complained to Bismarck, 'whilst I don't care a jot about it. I only cling to Prussia.'

support from the Government and place itself at the head of a national insurrectionary movement in the East. To this proposal Gröner returned an indignant refusal. If the Assembly voted for acceptance the High Command would certainly take no part in any attempt to overthrow the Government. On the other hand, if the decision were for rejection, the High Command would assume the direction of military operations as an organ of the Government, even though they believed that the battle was lost before it had begun. With this declaration of loyalty the First Quartermaster-General quitted the office of the Prussian Minister of War for that of the Reich Minister of Defence, whom he found to be in greater accord with his ideas than General Reinhardt.[1]

Noske's firm support of Erzberger's thesis of acceptance in the subsequent Cabinet discussions is certainly attributable to Gröner's influence and it is a matter of interesting speculation whether either the Minister or the General appreciated the full inwardness of Erzberger's policy. Was Gröner advocating acceptance of the peace terms simply on the score of the impossibility of resistance? Or had he, even at this early stage in the game, a vision of that secret rearmament of Germany which was to be among the most outstanding achievements of the German Army?

Certain it is that, whatever his motives, Gröner fought one of the hardest and most bitter battles of his career on June 19, when, with Noske, he met the first major Council of War to be summoned since that fatal meeting of November 9, 1918. Then it had been Gröner's unhappy lot to disillusion the War Lord of Germany; now it was again his task to disillusion his fellow Generals. At the outset the great majority of those present[2] were in support of Reinhardt's advocacy of resistance in the eastern provinces — and Generals von Below and von Lossberg went so far as to repeat Reinhardt's previous threat of disloyalty in the event of an order to evacuate the territories to be ceded to Poland under the treaty. Gröner repeated once more that he had not come to attend a Council of War in order to take part in a conspiracy against the Government. He would only consider such action after the Prussian *Landtag* and the representatives of Prussia in the *Reichstag* had formally decided

---

[1] Benoist-Méchin, i, 388-9 ; Volkmann, pp. 282-3.

[2] Those present at the Council, in addition to Noske, Reinhardt, and Gröner, included all the principal Corps commanders from the central and eastern parts of the Reich, the military Governors of Bavaria, Württemberg, and Saxony, the Chief of the *Marineleitung*, Admiral von Trotha, General von Below, commanding the XVII Corps, General von Lossberg, Chief of Staff of the Army of the South, Colonel Heye, Chief of Staff of the Army of the North, General Maercker, and others.

to secede from the Reich and to proclaim an independent state. 'To think that generals can assume political direction of such a movement is absurd', said Gröner. 'In the eyes of the world and of the law you would be no better than rebels and the Entente would consider and treat you as such.'

Noske at this moment disclosed to the Council that the resignation of the Cabinet was in effect a foregone conclusion, since the Chancellor was himself bitterly opposed to acceptance. He hinted that he had already been sounded as to whether he would head a new Government in which he would also retain the Ministry of Defence, thereby having virtually dictatorial powers. He would only accept such an invitation, he said, on the understanding that he had the High Command, the General Staff, and the Officer Corps behind him.

Gröner at once pledged the support of the High Command to the Minister of Defence and in such glowing terms that the majority of those present joined in a tribute of confidence to the man who had re-formed the *Reichswehr* and had piloted the Law of March 6 through the Assembly. The incident was in fact a turning point in the history of the *Reichswehr*, for it marked a voluntary abdication of the High Command in favour of Noske.

It is indeed possible that Gröner realized that he had lost the ascendancy which he had exercised over the Army since the Revolution, and that the cleavage between himself and the Prussian traditionalists was too wide and too deep to be healed. In offering his loyalty to Noske he was providing a rallying point for Germans of all regions, and it may well be that he did this with intent. It is certainly true that from this juncture the influence of the Supreme Command · at Kolberg became a diminishing force and that the Generals turned more and more to Noske as a possible embodiment of their ideal of a military dictatorship. Here indeed was irony. Gröner had sought to strengthen the Government by securing the adherence of the Generals to Noske, but in reality he had done just the reverse, for the Generals looked to Noske to overturn the Government with their help and, if he would not co-operate with them, they would revolt.[1]

But events did not turn out quite as Noske had led the Generals to expect. Scheidemann and his Cabinet did indeed resign on the night of June 19 and Ebert was only with difficulty dissuaded from following their example.[2] For two precious days of the period of grace permitted by the Allied ultimatum the Reich was without

---

[1] Maercker, pp. 286-7 ; Benoist-Méchin, i, 389-95 ; Volkmann, p. 283-90.
[2] Landsberg, p. 140-41 ; Heuss, p. 642.

a Government, but it was not to Noske that Ebert turned for a Chancellor.

On June 22, with just twenty-four hours before the expiry of the ultimatum, the Social Democrat Gustav Bauer formed a Cabinet of the Centre and the SPD with Erzberger as Vice-Chancellor and Minister of Finance,[1] Noske as Minister of Defence, and Hermann Müller at the Foreign Ministry. After a three-hour debate the new Chancellor received a vote of confidence in the Assembly and a mandate to sign the peace treaty 'without thereby acknowledging that the German people are the responsible authors of the World War, and without accepting Articles 227-231' (the surrender and trial of war criminals). This decision was at once telegraphed to the German Delegation at the Peace Conference [2] and brought an immediate reply from the Allies demanding an unconditional signature. 'The time for discussion has passed', wrote Clemenceau.[3]

The position of Erzberger and Noske was now far from enviable. The Vice-Chancellor had led the cry for acceptance on the ground that once the Allies had received the German submission they would be charitable, but the curt reply of Clemenceau gave little support to this thesis. Noske, on the other hand, was in the position of having acquired the confidence of the Generals under somewhat false pretences and was hard put to it to devise some means of retaining their support. He had not become Chancellor as he had led them to believe that he might, and he had voted for acceptance with reservations. Now he was again upon the razor edge of uncertainty, for once more the Cabinet of the Reich were confronted with the same dilemma — to sign or not to sign.

Noske's predicament was soon brought home to him. Early on the morning of June 23 he received a telephone message from General von Lüttwitz, Group Commander of the troops in the Berlin area, in which the General pointed out that in the event of the Government accepting the treaty without conditions the bulk of the troops would not remain loyal to it. Lüttwitz said he would regret it very much if they also had to come out in opposition to the *Reichswehr* Minister. This point was pressed home by Noske's own staff officer, Major von Gilsa. He urged Noske not to desert the

---

[1] Scheidemann, ii, 316-17 ; Erzberger, pp. 377-9. Erzberger himself, who had done more than anyone else to bring down the Scheidemann Government, would have us believe that he accepted office in the new Cabinet with reluctance. 'I resisted at first', he writes, 'but all my personal repugnance vanished in the face of national necessity.'

[2] For text of German Note see David Hunter Miller, *My Diary at the Peace Conference* (privately printed, 1928), XVIII, pp. 528-32.

[3] *Ibid.* XVIII, pp. 532-3.

Reich in its hour of need, but to take over the leadership of Germany himself and thus save the honour of the nation. In such a situation he would have the *Reichswehr* and the Officer Corps squarely behind him.

Noske was evidently impressed by this appeal, although he treats the episode with great restraint in his memoirs.[1] He had certainly grasped the hopelessness of the military position, but may have felt that anything was preferable to civil war. At any rate he now came out strongly against acceptance of the Treaty, basing his arguments on the danger presented to Germany by the possibility of a military revolt.[2] Word reached Erzberger of Noske's defection. The Vice-Chancellor hastened to the Schloss and received from Noske confirmation of his intention to resign from the Cabinet. Too subtle to make a direct attempt to reverse this decision, Erzberger persuaded Noske to come before a meeting of the Centre Party deputies and make his explanation to them, confident that they would stand by their resolution to sign the treaty.

But Noske's oratory had a very different effect. Contrary to Erzberger's belief, his Party colleagues, after listening to the Minister for Defence, voted 58 to 14 in favour of rejecting the treaty. Erzberger, shocked and overwhelmed, hurried to Ebert's office there to acquaint him with the full gravity of the situation. It was near noon. In seven hours the Allied ultimatum would expire and with it the Armistice agreement. A resumption of hostilities, or even the unopposed advance of the Allied armies into Germany, could not fail to unleash the horrors of a civil war. The Government of the Reich would certainly be overthrown either from the Left by the Spartakists and the Independents, or from the Right by the rebel Generals and the Officer Corps. What was the President going to do in so appalling a situation ? [3]

In the face of this outburst of hysteria, Ebert remained calm. It may not have been entirely unwelcome to him to see the wily and sardonic Erzberger caught in his own devious snares and terrified at the spirits with which he had sought to conjure. As always in an emergency, Ebert turned to Gröner for counsel. Shortly before noon the President decided he must put through a call from his office in Weimar to the first Quartermaster-General in Kolberg.

When the call came through Hindenburg was with Gröner near the telephone, and quickly realized who was speaking. The Marshal

[1] Noske, pp. 153-4.
[2] W. Gröner, *Lebenserinnerungen* (Göttingen, 1957), pp. 506-7.
[3] Erzberger, pp. 380-2 ; Benoist-Méchin, i. 400-3 ; Volkmann, pp. 298-302.

knew that further resistance to the Entente Powers would be impossible. But he did not try to speak to Ebert. It may have been that he thought Gröner wanted to talk frankly to the President and did not wish to embarrass him by his presence. Or it may have been that the Marshal had once again made up his mind that it must not be his voice which explained unpleasant facts to the President, just as on a previous occasion it could not be he who could tell the final truth to the Emperor Wilhelm. Whatever his motives, he quietly left the room.

Ebert told Gröner that the SPD and the Centre would probably accept the peace terms, but that in view of information received from General Lüttwitz the Government feared mutiny among the soldiers in the event of the unconditional acceptance of the Versailles Treaty. The President would only agree to sign it if the High Command had come to the conclusion that there was no chance left of armed resistance. Ebert demanded that Gröner should make clear to him the attitude of the High Command towards the Allied ultimatum.

Once again Gröner was called upon to make an agonizing and humiliating decision, a decision which his superior, Hindenburg, had carefully avoided taking. Speaking to Ebert 'as a German' rather than as a Staff Officer, he told him that further resistance to the Allies offered no prospect of success. He demanded that Noske should be given political power in the Republic and should take over the responsibility for making peace. The *Reichswehr* Minister should issue an appeal to the armed forces explaining and justifying the decision to sign the Treaty, and urging all officers to stay at their posts for the good of the Fatherland. Only in this way could civil chaos and an outbreak of hostilities on the Eastern Frontier be avoided. Some time after Gröner had finished speaking Hindenburg returned. When his colleague told him what had happened he was silent for some time and then said, 'You are right. You have got to be the black sheep once again.' [1]

Meanwhile Gröner had immediately followed up his telephone call with a cabled message to Weimar in which he repeated his conclusions. Ebert was able to make good use of the Quartermaster-General's message in the cabinet meeting which was held at midday. In response to the President's direct appeal, Noske withdrew his notice of resignation and invoked the loyalty of the Army, as Gröner had suggested, with the result that a general disaffection was at any rate postponed.[2] The members of the Assembly seemed

[1] Gröner, *Lebenserinnerungen*, pp. 507-9.
[2] Noske, pp. 153-5.

almost relieved to have the responsibility taken from them by the verdict of the High Command. By a large majority they voted to sign the treaty, and as Fehrenbach, the President of the Assembly, announced the vote he added: 'We commend our unhappy country to the care of a merciful God'.[1]

The German decision to accept was transmitted by Herr von Haniel to Clemenceau just nineteen minutes before the ultimatum expired,[2] and five days later (June 28) the German signatures to the treaty were affixed in the Galerie des Glaces.

The Battle for Acceptance was over and the parties concerned drew breath to await the outcome of the victory. The light of battle had shone harshly upon much that was weak and pusillanimous and picayune and also upon some greatness. Its glare had shown the Prussian Generals to be small-minded men whose basic patriotism was that of the provincial and who would have been willing to sacrifice all the rest of Germany to preserve 'the cradle of the race'. It had disclosed Hindenburg not as a rock and a defence, not as the Wooden Titan on whom the people of Germany had lavished their praise and devotion, but as a poor thing, a thing of plaster and of *papier mâché*. For Hindenburg knew the truth of what he did and had not the courage to publish that truth abroad. It had been given to him to see further than his brother Prussians, and he had deliberately closed his eyes and had sought for one to lead him by the hand.

In contrast, the light of battle had illumined Wilhelm Gröner to his credit. This Swabian had had a greater care for and a greater loyalty to the Reich of Bismarck than had the Prussians; this son of an N.C.O. had shown a better sense of the fitness of behaviour than had the scions of the Prussian military caste. He had also displayed a broader vision of statesmanship than had the Marshal. Gröner was a German patriot, and he was fighting for certain established things in which he believed. He believed in German survival, in the essential unity of the Reich, in the continued tradition of the Officer Corps, and in the ultimate re-emergence of Germany as a great and powerful military nation, capable of avenging herself for her present humiliations. Like a good strategist he was prepared to suffer initial defeats to achieve ultimate victory and success. His genius lay in long-term planning for the future and not in rigid devotion to archaism which finds its escape in a senseless immolation and in national suicide.

With the acceptance of the peace treaty the *raison d'être* for the

---

[1] Viktor Schiff, *The Germans at Versailles*, p. 162.
[2] *Urkunden*, i. 699-700 (English text in Luckau, p. 482).

Supreme Command had ceased. Indeed its continued existence would have been illegal since the treaty had decreed the dissolution of the Great German General Staff of which the Supreme Command was the embodiment. The General Headquarters at Kolberg was dispersed. On June 25 Ebert accepted the resignation of Hindenburg and expressed to him 'the inextinguishable gratitude of the German people', and Gröner officially retired on October 1.

The treaty, designed to mark the end of Germany's military menace to the peace of the world, was signed on June 28, 1919. A week later (July 5) the German Government created a new organization, 'The Preparatory Commission for the Peace Army' (*Volkskommission für das Friedensheer*) and appointed as its president General Hans von Seeckt.

(viii)

The acceptance of the treaty at Weimar and its signature at Versailles marked the permanent passing of any real sense of unity in German politics under the Weimar Republic. For a brief moment all parties had been at one in their denunciation of the treaty, but they were not united to the point of resistance, and in the years to come the struggle for and against fulfilment of the treaty was as bitter as the battle fought for and against its acceptance.

More especially was the issue one of clear-cut hostility between the Republic on the one hand and the Conservatives and the Army on the other. At one moment it had seemed as if the Right might almost have turned the Weimar structure into a Conservative Republic, but after June 28, 1919, it became clear that between the Right and the Republic there was a great gulf fixed and that warfare, open for the time being, but later of a more guerrilla nature, was the only relation possible between them. The burden of government, therefore, rested upon the parties of the Left and Centre, whose leaders instantly became the target of Nationalist hatred, abuse — and bullets.

Within the Army the opposition to the treaty was political, traditional, and economic. The surrender of provinces to the despised and hated Poles was what cut most deeply into the national pride. The relinquishment of territory which the Great Frederick had acquired by conquest, as in the case of Silesia, and by agreement or partition, as in the case of Posen and West Prussia, was utterly unbearable to the military caste. In the first place, they regarded the Poles as an inferior race and, in the second, they feared the extension of Polish annexationist claims to other portions of the Eastern Marches, on the maintenance of which Prince von Bülow was wont to declare that 'the fate of Prussia, of the Empire, nay, of the whole German nation depends'.[1] With the restricted military force permitted under the treaty it was held doubtful whether Germany could defend herself successfully against a Polish invasion. The economic factor was also severe for the Army. At the time of signing, Germany possessed an Army of 400,000 officers and men, which, within three months of the coming into force of the treaty, must be reduced to 200,000 and, by March 3, 1920, at the latest, to the statutory figure of 100,000 (Article 163). This meant, in effect, that nearly a quarter of a million men would almost immediately be turned adrift at a time when the economic depression of the country had already caused an appreciable increase in unemployment.

The Government had lost the support of the Officer Corps, and it now reaped the harvest of its earlier appeasement of that body. The stripping of all power from the Soldiers' Councils — an action which had been taken by the Government to placate the Generals — had caused considerable resentment in the other ranks, who considered, moreover, that the part which they had played and the losses which they had sustained in the suppression of Left Wing elements within the Reich was not sufficiently appreciated by the Government and by the Assembly.[2]

The unfortunate Noske, who so recently had been the idol of the *Reichswehr*, now found himself an object of abuse from all quarters, from those who were threatened with unemployment and from those who were to remain with the colours. Gone were the days when a German General (Maercker) would say to a Social Democrat Minister: '*Für Sie, Herr Minister, lasse ich mich in Stücke hauen and meine Landesjäger auch*'.[3] Noske had lost the pre-eminent position of authority which he had once enjoyed with the Generals, who now looked for leadership to one of themselves, General Freiherr Walther von Lüttwitz (1859–1942), the senior commanding officer of the *Reichswehr*.

It would be difficult to imagine a more perfect example of military reaction than General von Lüttwitz. Born of ancient

---

[1] Prince Bernhard von Bülow, *Imperial Germany* (New York, 1915), p. 325. Prince von Bülow (1849–1929) was Imperial Chancellor from 1900, when he succeeded Prince Hohenlohe-Schillingsfürst, until 1909, when he himself gave place to Theodor von Bethmann Hollweg. His memoirs, *Denkwürdigkeiten*, published posthumously in Germany in 1930–31, and subsequently in England, evoked a storm of criticism, denial, and rejoinder on the part of certain of those mentioned therein or their descendants.

[2] Maercker, p. 318.

[3] 'For you, Sir, I would allow myself and my troops to be cut to pieces' (Noske, p. 154).

military stock, small, slight, and dapper, he was an aristocrat and monarchist to his finger-tips, and his ideas had never progressed beyond the days of Emperor Wilhelm I. Intolerant of all politics, he was completely out of tune with his epoch, and his real desire was to see Germany once again in possession of an Army like that of August 1914. He would, indeed, have been more in period in the days of Frederick the Great, for there was something essentially eighteenth century about him. His one ambition was to liberate his country by a brilliant *coup d'Yorck* (*eine Yorcktat*),[1] but as his comrade-in-arms, General Maercker, wrote of him : 'He was far from being a Yorck'.[2]

The politicians of the Right were also in a ferment. The Junkers, the die-hard Conservatives, the Industrial Barons, had learnt nothing from the lessons of the recent past and had forgotten nothing of the Germany which till November 1918 had seemed so strong. Let them but regain power and it should not, they thought, be difficult to hustle these Socialists back into the class to which they rightfully belonged and there to deal faithfully with them.

But how to gain power ? The National Assembly resolutely remained in being. With the signing of the Treaty of Peace on June 28 and the promulgation of the Constitution on August 14, the Assembly might have been held to have exhausted its mandate, since it had been elected as a constituent body. The Constitution itself called for the popular election of a President of the Reich, and the Conservatives, under the leadership of Karl Helfferich,[3] were confident that, if they could persuade Hindenburg to be their candidate, he would sweep the field. Once this staunch monarchist was elected they proposed to hold a national referendum on the future form of government, and they themselves were assured that the people of Germany were eagerly awaiting a return to Monarchy. They, therefore, embarked on a campaign of agitation for the

---

[1] See above, p. 7, footnote.   [2] Maercker, pp. 66-7.
[3] Karl Theodor Helfferich (1872-1924), a member of the Conservative Party, was, from 1915-17, State Secretary for Finance, and later Vice-Chancellor and State Secretary of Interior, under Bethmann Hollweg. As such he first violently opposed, and subsequently became an enthusiastic advocate of, the unrestricted U-boat warfare and he assisted Hindenburg and Ludendorff in their campaign to bring down the Chancellor. In July 1918 Helfferich was appointed Ambassador to Moscow in succession to Count Mirbach, who had been assassinated by the Left Social Revolutionaries as a protest against the Peace of Brest-Litovsk. He remained only a fortnight in Russia, being summoned back to Berlin in August to support the tottering régime. Helfferich sat in the *Reichstag* from 1920 to 1924, when he was killed in a railway accident in Switzerland. His war memoirs, *Der Weltkrieg* (Berlin, 1919, 3 vols.), provide caustic commentaries on men and policies.

dissolution of the Assembly and the holding of elections for the Presidency and the *Reichstag*.

Further to the Right of these men, however, there existed a group of malcontents, who, taking their lead from Ludendorff, had founded the *Nationale Vereinigung*, a political unit rather than a party, which favoured an immediate return to absolute Monarchy by means of armed force if need be. Of this group, the leaders, apart from Ludendorff who remained olympianly in the background, were Count Westarp, former Conservative leader in the *Reichstag*; Pastor Traub, who had been Court Chaplain to Wilhelm II; Colonel Walter Bauer, Ludendorff's Chief of Operations, 1916–18; the former Police President of Berlin, Traugott von Jagow; Captain Waldemar Pabst, a strange *rastaquouère* figure who, though the founder of the *Garde-Kavallerie Freikorps*, had been subsequently dismissed from the Army for indiscipline; — and Dr. Wolfgang Kapp.

Kapp, like von Lüttwitz, was a fanatical, outmoded German patriot, but of a different tradition. Whereas the ancestry of von Lüttwitz was rooted in German soil, Kapp came of a family of *Auslandsdeutsche*, his grandfather having emigrated as a political refugee after the revolution of 1848 to New York, where Wolfgang was born twenty years later. In two generations the liberalism of his ancestors had burnt out, but the fanaticism remained, and young Kapp, returning to Germany, became the most ardent of reactionary jingoes. As a civil servant he did not rise beyond the rank of head of a district agricultural finance office (*Generalland-schaftsdirektor*) in a remote part of East Prussia, but in the wider field of politics he gained some notoriety.

An ardent member of the Pan-German League, he had been a strong supporter of the annexation policies of Hindenburg and Ludendorff and of the unrestricted U-boat warfare. As such he had viciously attacked von Bethmann Hollweg in the press in 1916, characterizing him as a weakling. The Chancellor had made a sharp reply, so sharp indeed that Kapp considered that his honour and dignity had been impugned and responded with a challenge to a duel, which was contemptuously ignored. It was Kapp, however, who composed the memorandum which was the basis of the intrigue that brought down Bethmann, and having accomplished this end, he was amongst those Conservatives who fathered the foundation of the *Vaterlandsfront* which gave political support in the *Reichstag* to the territorial annexationist demands of the Supreme Command. After a brief period of retirement, he now re-emerged to play a part once more in the cause of extreme reaction, and that as a civilian he was chosen leader of a conspiracy was comparable to the selection by the Supreme Command of Georg Michaelis as Imperial Chancellor in the third year of the War.

Between the three groupings of von Lüttwitz, Helfferich and Kapp, there was clearly much in common, but although liaison certainly existed on the lower levels, and though Helfferich was in contact with both Kapp and von Lüttwitz, there is no evidence of a meeting between these latter before the late summer of 1919. This was not for want of trying on Kapp's part. He had made early efforts to reach an agreement with the military hierarchy but had been repulsed. 'We must strike now', he had written to Colonel Heye on July 5, but the Chief of Staff of the Army of the North had returned an evasive answer.[1]

The truth was that the Army Chiefs were divided amongst themselves. On July 26, von Lüttwitz had summoned his senior staff officers and troop commanders [2] to a conference, at which he had outlined a certain irreducible programme of demands on the part of the Army. These included a blank refusal either to surrender the old Army leaders as 'war-criminals' or to reduce the effectives of the *Reichswehr* in view of the Bolshevik peril; to preserve the unity of the Reich and to insist upon the exclusion of any member of the Independent Socialist Party from the Government.[3] All present were unanimous in adopting these as guiding principles of policy, but there was sharp dissension on the means to be employed in attaining them.

Von Lüttwitz himself, together with von Lettow-Vorbeck and Reinhard, favoured a rupture with the civil authorities and the establishment of a military dictatorship by force. The more moderate school, led by Maercker and von Oven, in which also was von Hammerstein, Lüttwitz's son-in-law, insisted that a resort to force was sheer folly and could only end in the defeat of all they hoped to achieve; the Army, it was urged, must keep faith with the Government of the day and endeavour to attain its aims by bringing pressure to bear on Ebert and Noske.[4]

---

[1] Elmer Luehr, *The New German Republic* (New York, 1929), p. 204; also article on the Kapp *Putsch*, by Professor Fritz Kern in the issue of *Die Grenzboten* of April 1920, quoted by Heinrich Ströbel, *The German Revolution and After* (London, n.d.), pp. 225-6.

[2] Among those present were Generals von Hoffmann, von Oven, von Heuduck, von Hülsen, Maercker, von Lettow-Vorbeck, and von der Lippe, and Colonels von Stockhausen, von Hammerstein and Reinhard.

[3] General Freiherr Walther von Lüttwitz, *Im Kampf gegen die November-Revolution* (Leipzig, 1921), p. 85.

[4] Maercker, p. 325.

Unable to win over the opposition to the use of force, von
Lüttwitz, in anger, expressed his contempt for their pusillanimous
attitude and declared his intention of devoting himself to canvassing
the troops in favour of a military *coup d'état*.[1] Later, in mid-August,
he stated, both to Ebert and to the Chancellor, Bauer, his profound
dissatisfaction with the state of affairs in the Reich, both political
and economic, and presented to them the demands formulated and
approved by the conference of officers.

The Cabinet sensed their danger. They were not yet fully alert
to the many threats which menaced them, but they were sufficiently
aware of the position to realize that unless something were done to
check the contumacious military, the situation would pass beyond
their control. They thereupon hit upon a device designed simultaneously to appease the Allied demand for surrender of war-
criminals and to put these same individuals on the defensive. On
August 20 the National Assembly passed a resolution creating a
Commission of Inquiry to investigate the responsibility for causing
the war, for not ending it sooner, for acts of disobedience or disloyalty to responsible political authorities, and for acts of cruel or
harsh conduct contrary to the laws of war. On the following day
(August 21) Friedrich Ebert took the oath to the new constitution.
The Government had decided not to risk a popular vote on the
Presidency, since they believed that this would lead to the choice of a
Right-wing candidate.

The effect of these measures was to draw together the ranks of
the opposition. The first meeting between Kapp and von Lüttwitz
occurred on August 21,[2] the day Ebert took the oath, and as a
result of it the General sent to Noske a letter on September 1,
which gave the Minister seriously to think. Von Lüttwitz, this time,
made two demands of a non-military nature, namely, the suppression
of doles to the unemployed, on the principle that those who do
not work should not eat, and the rigorous prohibition of all strikes.
If the Government were prepared to act with force and vigour, the
Army was ready to support them with all the means at its disposal;
if, however, the Government continued to pursue a policy of vacillation and surrender, they would inevitably turn the Army against
them and their component parties. 'To-day as yesterday', wrote
the General in Delphic conclusion, 'the Army remains the basis of
authority in the state.'[3]

Though the Chancellor and Erzberger were profoundly disturbed at this communication, Ebert and Noske professed an

---

[1] Lüttwitz, p. 87.   [2] *Ibid.* p. 97.   [3] *Ibid.* p. 89.

optimism and an assurance completely inconsonant with the gravity
of the situation. Nor would they permit themselves to be moved
from their sanguine view when, a few days later, Colonel Reinhard,
in an address to his troops denounced the Government as a pack
of rascals. Scheidemann, on behalf of the SPD demanded his
instant dismissal, but Ebert equivocated and excused the offender
on the grounds that he had not known that his remarks would be
reported in the Press! When Scheidemann urged the good effect
which Reinhafd's dismissal would have on all Republican officers,
the President snapped at him : 'I shall not think of doing anything
of the sort'.[1]

At about this time an event took place which, though unheard
of for years to come and unheralded at the time, was to have an
incalculably important effect upon Germany and upon the world:
in mid-September, 1919, Adolf Hitler became a member — *Parteige-
nosse* No. 7 — of the *Deutsche Arbeiter Partei* in Munich.

Ebert and his fellow wishful-thinkers were counting upon the
Commission of Enquiry to bring about the discrediting of the old
régime. The High Command, it was believed, would now be forced
into the position of accepting responsibility for the military collapse
which they had hitherto successfully evaded, and, in a broader view,
the trial of the High Command would become the trial of the Army
and of the whole military caste. The Revolution and the Republican
régime would at last be vindicated at the bar of public opinion.[2]

Alas for the realization of any such hopes — fantastic though
they may have seemed at any time. The enquiry, when it opened
on October 21, proved to be a process of unrelieved humiliation
and defeat for the Government. The first witnesses, Bernstorff,
von Bethmann Hollweg, and Admiral von Capelle, delivered themselves of long and boring statements in answer to questions from
the Committee which failed to shed any new light on what was
already known. Thereafter, on November 12, Karl Helfferich took
the stand to answer for the U-boat warfare, which he had at first
opposed and then had as warmly supported. The former Vice-
Chancellor and Nationalist leader had no intention of losing such
an opportunity as this for making a political demonstration. With

---

[1] Scheidemann, ii, 325-6.

[2] In 1806, after the military collapse of Prussia, Scharnhorst instituted a
similar investigation, an *Immediatkommission*, to enquire into the conduct of high-
ranking officers, and particularly into the circumstances of military capitulations.
As a result over 200 officers were severely punished and stripped of their commands,
among them a certain Paul von Hindenburg, an ancestor of the Field-Marshal,
who had failed to defend the fortress of Spandau (Fried, pp. 39-40). The result of
the Committee of Investigation of 1919 was very different.

brazen effrontery he ignored the questions put to him and assumed the offensive. 'Who is the cause of our ruin?' he demanded. 'I will tell you, it is Erzberger, whose name will for ever be linked with the misery and shame of Germany.' [1]

And then Hindenburg arrived in Berlin. He came not as a man indicted comes before his judges but as a conquering hero, a darling of the populace, a Father of his People. The Army had arranged his journey; a special saloon car had brought him from Hanover, and at the Friedrichstrasse Station a guard of honour was in waiting. Two regular army officers were attached to him as honorary aides-de-camp and two steel-helmeted sentries were posted outside Helfferich's villa in the Hitzigstrasse, where the Marshal was a guest. Huge crowds cheered Hindenburg at his every appearance and this provoked counter-demonstrations by the Independent Socialists, who missed no chance of depicting in flaming terms the dangers of reaction. So fierce did the factional feeling become that the Government, now thoroughly alarmed, forbade all demonstrations and the Marshal himself issued an appeal to his admirers not to disturb traffic.

For several days before his actual appearance before the Commission of Enquiry, Hindenburg was closeted with Helfferich and Ludendorff and others of the extreme Nationalist leaders. In this brief period was crystallized the legend of the 'stab-in-the-back', in justification of which many innocent Germans were to suffer when the National Socialists came to power; for in this legend was the basis of many of Adolf Hitler's charges against the Social Democrats.

Briefed and indoctrinated by his fellow reactionaries, the Marshal finally testified before the Commission on November 18, in a scene which has now become historic. It is indeed too much to say that he testified; he rather made a public appearance and, with a sublime contempt for the President of the Commission and his questionings, addressed himself to the German people. Their defeat, he told them, was not attributable to the Army but to the civilian demoralization and disunion. The irreproachable Army had received a 'stab-in-the-back' (*Dolchstoss*) from the Revolution. It was the first use of that historic phrase, and Hindenburg said airily that he was quoting the remark of a British General. Had he been asked the

---

[1] Helfferich's whole strategy was to turn the enquiry into a farce and, at the same time, a weapon against the Government. He, therefore, succeeded in making himself a martyr and hero by committing a contempt of court, for which he was fined some twenty pounds and permitted to continue with his evidence and with his obstructionist tactics. (Cf. Moritz J. Bonn, *A Wandering Scholar* (London, 1949), pp. 243-4. Dr. Bonn was one of the experts attached to the sub-committee of the Commission of Enquiry before which these scenes took place.)

name of this officer, and the authority of the statement, he might well have been nonplussed for he was not given to reading in foreign languages and was clearly repeating parrot-fashion a lesson well learned and memorized. The Commission, however, allowed this point to pass by them unchallenged. They were now mesmerized by the deep rumbling voice of the aged Field-Marshal and they waited spell-bound for his final words : 'I doubt whether you gentlemen have ever felt such a responsibility for the Fatherland as we were bound to bear, deep down in our hearts, for years'.[1]

There followed an unseemly wrangle between Ludendorff and Bernstorff on the subject of the American entry into the war in April 1917, in the course of which the General bellowed like a bull and the Ambassador remained icily unmoved, but when the session was adjourned at 2.15 in the afternoon, the Government was so disturbed at the state of public opinion that no further meeting was held for the next five months.

On the following day (November 19) Hindenburg, with exquisite correctness, informed the Government that, if they had no more questions to put to him, he would like to go home. Nothing indeed would suit the Government better, and to the enquiry of the aide-de-camp as to whether a guard of honour should be ordered for the Marshal's departure there came the answer of a harassed civil servant in the Ministry of Defence : 'Certainly give him a guard of honour. Give him two if necessary, but for God's sake get him out of Berlin.'[2]

So the Marshal left with the same pomp and ceremony with which he had arrived, but the Government were not yet to be quit of this military splendour. A month later the same pageantry was enacted when General von Seeckt gave formal welcome to his old chief, Field-Marshal von Mackensen, on the latter's homecoming to Berlin. Von Seeckt received him ceremonially at the Anhalter Station and a guard of Mackensen's own Death's Head Hussars stood between the tracks.[3] Once again the Army was trailing its coat in the face of the Independent Socialists and the workers of Wedding and Neuköln.

If Ebert and the Reich Government had really believed that they could discredit the Army and the High Command through the

---

[1] Wheeler-Bennett, pp. 235-9 ; Bonn, pp. 245-8. For text of the statements of Hindenburg and Ludendorff see *Official German Documents relating to the World War, being the Reports of the First and Second Sub-committees of the Committee appointed by the National Constituent Assembly to enquire into the responsibility for the war* (New York, 1923), ii, 849-904.

[2] Reinhard, p. 118.   [3] Rabenau, ii, 210.

instrument of the Commission of Enquiry, they were woefully mistaken. Diametrically the opposite had occurred. Thanks to the ingenuity of Helfferich, the High Command had come forth from their 'ordeal' with greatly enhanced prestige, and the story of their responsibility for the hysterical demand for an armistice was buried for ever. Erzberger and the Majority Socialists, on the other hand, had emerged be-slimed with slander and with the onus for the defeat of Germany nailed upon their shoulders in that 'stab-in-the-back' legend, to which Ebert himself had unwittingly made so great a contribution when he greeted the returning Guards Regiments at the Brandenburger Tor, with the fatal words : 'I salute you, who return unvanquished from the field of battle'.[1] They were to carry this burden until the collapse of the Republic fourteen years later, and as the years passed it weighed upon them more and more heavily.[2]

By the close of 1919 it appeared that the German Republic was doomed to inevitable and imminent destruction. Talk was general of a military coup and a restoration of the monarchy.[3] It was

---

[1] See above, p. 31. In its final Report published in 1928, the Fourth Sub-Committee of the Commission of Enquiry gave much space to the 'stab-in-the-back' legend and a whole volume is devoted to documentary material on this subject (see *Die Ursachen des Deutschen Zusammenbruches im Jahre 1918*, vol. vi (Berlin, 1928), of which a partial translation was published by the Hoover War Library of Stanford University, California, *The Causes of German Collapse in 1918* selected by Ralph Haswell Lutz (Stanford University, 1934), pp. 132-87). The *Dolchstoss* legend was also the subject of two famous libel actions at Magdeburg in 1924 and at Munich in 1925, the proceedings of which have already been cited above.

[2] The hatred engendered by the Nationalist propaganda loosed by Helfferich may be judged from the events of the next few years. In January 1920 an unsuccessful attempt was made to assassinate Erzberger, and he was finally murdered in August 1921. Walter Rathenau, the then Foreign Minister, was shot down in broad daylight in the suburbs of Berlin in June 1922, and unsuccessful attempts were made on Scheidemann in the same month and on the famous journalist, Maximilian Harden in July. Later, attempts were also made to murder Stresemann and Brüning. The perpetrators of each of these criminal acts were shown in the subsequent proceedings to be members of ultra-Nationalist and reactionary organizations. '*Est-ce qu'il faut mourir, pour prouver qu'on est sincère?*' was André Tardieu's comment in the French Chamber in 1929 on this series of outrages.

[3] 'Colonel Dosse returned to-day from Shavli with reliable information concerning the plans of a *coup d'état* — the object of which is to overthrow the existing Berlin Government, establish a Military Dictatorship and refuse to accept the Peace Treaty', reported General Turner, of the Allied Mission in the Baltic, to the British Foreign Office, on December 5, 1919. 'In general the plan is as follows : Spartakist riots will be arranged in Berlin and will be the excuse for the Iron Division in East Prussia and similar formations in Hanover and South Germany to march on Berlin. Ludendorff is quoted as one of the prime movers in the affair and is known to have visited the Iron Division at Mitau three weeks ago. Von der Goltz, who is now at Königsberg Headquarters, Hindenburg and Mack-

common knowledge that, having reluctantly decided that neither Wilhelm II nor the Crown Prince was eligible for the throne, the conspirators had agreed upon the Kaiser's second son, Prince Eitel Friedrich, as their candidate. The Government seemed paralysed and there was even some suspicion that Noske might succumb to the intensive monarchist influences to which it was known he was submitted by his Chief of Staff, von Gilsa.[1]

Into this fetid atmosphere of rancour and fear, intrigue and hatred, there fell like a bombshell the Allied Note of February 3, 1920, presenting the first list of those who, it was demanded, should be surrendered for trial as war criminals. The list comprised nearly 900 names, including almost every leader in German public life during the War. The German Crown Prince and two of his brothers figured in it, charged with common theft, and arraigned on a variety of other charges, ranging from petty larceny to the issuing of orders to take no prisoners, were four Field-Marshals — the Crown Prince of Bavaria, Duke Albrecht of Württemberg, von Hindenburg and von Mackensen — Grand Admiral von Tirpitz, Generals Ludendorff and von Falkenhayn, von Kluck, von Bülow and von Below, Admiral von Capelle, the former Chancellors von Bethmann Hollweg and Michaelis, the former Vice-Chancellor Helfferich, and Count Bernstorff. In addition there were a number of officers and non-commissioned officers of all grades. The Allied Note concluded that the list was not final.[2]

The effect of the publication of the Note in the German Press was cataclysmic. Germans of almost every kind, without restriction as to class or rank or political creed, were outraged at this demand for the surrender of men whom they regarded as national heroes and of whom a number had been publicly vindicated in the Sessions of the Commission of Enquiry. From the Majority Socialists on the Left to the Nationalists on the Right came the same reaction of fury. Only the Spartakists and the Independents dared to voice a qualified degree of approval. The vast majority of Germans shared the view of Otto Braun, the Social Democrat Prime Minister

ensen are also concerned in the movement. The date- of execution is unknown but the plan is openly discussed by officers of the Iron Division . . .' (E. L. Woodward and Rohan Butler, *Documents on British Foreign Policy 1919–1939*, First Series, iii (London, 1949), 245).

[1] Memorandum to General Neill Malcolm, Head of the British Military Mission in Berlin, from Colonel Maude, dated December 31, 1919 (Woodward and Butler, First Series, iii, 295).

[2] On receipt of this Note in Paris the German Representative, Freiherr von Lersner, had refused to transmit it to his Government and had resigned his position, whereupon M. Millerand, the French Premier, had despatched the Note to Berlin by special messenger.

of Prussia, in denouncing this 'senseless claim for the surrender of
the Kaiser and over 800 so-called "war-criminals"'.[1]

Among the Army leaders the frenzy of anger reached fever pitch.
Von Lüttwitz, in a public speech, demanded resistance at all costs,
even at the risk of war. Von Seeckt called a conference of his Staff
Officers and departmental chiefs on February 9, and told them
that if the Government was either unable or unwilling to refuse
the demands of the Allies, then the new *Reichswehr*, to whom the
tradition of the Old Army had been bequeathed as a sacred trust,
must oppose such action by every means in its power, even if such
opposition entailed the reopening of hostilities. He personally believed that the Allies would not invade the Reich in order to enforce
their demands, but, should they do so, his plan was to retire the
German troops in the West, fighting step by step, behind the Weser
and the Elbe, where defensive positions would already have been
prepared. But in the East they would move against Poland and
try to establish contacts with Soviet Russia, with whom, having
crushed the Poles, they might march against France and Britain.[2]
Von Seeckt told his officers that no further sale or destruction of
German war material would be permitted and that Noske would
sign an order to this effect. Henceforth the Army would only be
reduced on paper.[3]

The Bauer Government knew that they dared not comply with
the Allied demands. They were well aware that their bodies, and
those of any of their successors who pursued the same policy, would
be dangling from the trees of the Tiergarten and the lamp-posts of
the Wilhelmstrasse within an hour of such a decision. They therefore temporized — as it turned out, very successfully — but nothing
short of blatant defiance of the Allies could now forestall a military
coup.

All circumstances seemed to contribute to such an event. The
Allied Commission of Control had just ordered the demobilization

---

[1] '*Die unsinnige Forderung nach Auslieferung des Kaisers und über 800 sogenannter
"Kriegsverbrecher"*' (Otto Braun, *Von Weimar zu Hitler* (New York, 1940), p. 86).
[2] Though these desperate measures never materialized, they contained the
germ of that threatened 'Red Army on the Rhine' with which 'von Seeckt made
such play in future years, and, moreover, of that military liaison which existed
between Berlin and Moscow from 1922 to 1933, and which was, in its strange
way, the precursor of the Nazi-Soviet Pact of 1939.
[3] Albert Grzesinski, *Inside Germany* (New York, 1939), pp. 83-4. Wheeler-
Bennett, pp. 294-5. Grzesinski, a Social Democrat, was Under-Secretary for War
in the Prussian Government at this time. He adds that the circular order, bearing
Noske's signature, was actually despatched, and it was confirmed by members of
von Seeckt's staff that the General favoured the establishment of a military
dictatorship with possibly Noske at its head.

of two Free Corps formations, the Marine Brigade, commanded by
the former naval Captain Ehrhardt, and the Baltikum Brigade of
General Count von der Goltz which had formed a part of the Iron
Division in East Prussia. These units had been sent to the military
depot at Döberitz, outside Berlin, preparatory to dispersal, and
there, on March 1, was staged a spectacular review at which von
Lüttwitz took the salute and assured the troops that he would not
allow their disbandment to take place.

The little General would have declared there and then for a
march on Berlin but was persuaded by more temperate counsellors,
among them von Stockhausen and von Hammerstein, to delay so
precipitate an action until after every legal means had been exhausted.
An interview was then arranged between von Lüttwitz and representatives of the two political parties of the Right, Hergt [1] of the
Nationalists (Conservatives) and Heinze [2] of the German People's
Party (Liberals). At this meeting it was agreed that the two Parties
should demand from the Government the dissolution of the National
Assembly and the holding of elections for the *Reichstag* and for a
new President of the Reich. The General unwillingly consented
to postpone military action until after the result of these political
manœuvres, but he made it quite clear that he expected little to
come of them.[3]

Meanwhile the group around Kapp was busily preparing memoranda of policy, drafting proclamations to the nation and engaging
in that pastime so fascinating to amateur politicians, the drawing
up of a 'shadow Cabinet'.

On March 9 Hergt and Heinze returned to von Lüttwitz with
the news that their demands had been met with a blank refusal
from Ebert and from Bauer. The General greeted the two crest-
fallen Party leaders with sarcastic contempt. 'You see what comes
of all your political combinations', he said, 'I prefer to put my
faith in my troops'. Once again Hergt assured him that the parties
of the Right would not support him if he persisted in a recourse to
force. But von Lüttwitz would listen no longer. His mind was
made up; with a discourteous comment on the pusillanimity of
politicians, he dismissed them. '*Immer noch Kadett*' was Hergt's
comment as he left the meeting.[4]

[1] Oskar Hergt served the old Conservative Party as Prussian State Secretary for
Finance before the War and as *Reichsfinanzminister* in 1917-18.

[2] Rudolf Heinze (1865-1928) had been in Saxon politics as a Liberal before
and during the War and was Saxon Minister of Justice in 1918. After the
Revolution he joined Stresemann's German People's Party and served as Reich
Minister of Justice in the Fehrenbach Coalition Government of 1920-21.

[3] Volkmann, pp. 338-42.   [4] *Ibid.* pp, 242-3.

That night von Lüttwitz took the first step towards action. Colonel Bauer, in the course of a meeting with the Head of the British Military Mission, hinted at the possibility of a military *Putsch* in the near future and endeavoured to find out what the attitude of the British Government would be in such an event. He was left under no misapprehension. General Malcolm told him plainly and firmly that such an act would be 'sheer madness' and would not be condoned or tolerated for a moment.[1] Undeterred by this discouragement the conspirators pressed forward, not with their preparations — for they proved woefully unprepared — but with their intention to make a national insurrection at the earliest possible moment.

In these critical March days the conduct of Noske presents something of an enigma. If he knew of the coming *Putsch* in its preliminary stages, he was either very naive or very astute, or else merely very dishonest. And it is almost impossible to believe that he did not know of it. The Security Police had got wind of its proximity on March 2, one day before the interview between von Lüttwitz and the Party Leaders of the Right. Stresemann heard of it at Hamburg on March 5, and every Allied Mission and foreign journalist in Berlin had been aware of the possibility of such an event for months past. Yet the Government did nothing. The question of a monarchist *coup* had actually been raised in the National Assembly, where, on March 1, Noske had declared that, while a monarchist movement certainly existed in Germany, as indeed it did in France, the Government were confident that if the Allies were not too harsh towards the Reich, the monarchists would present no menace to the Republic.

From this it might be supposed that, if at this date the Minister of National Defence had any foreknowledge at all of a *Putsch* in the making, he was not above discounting its danger against its advantages in an attempt to blackmail the Allies into greater leniency.

Some inkling of their approaching peril appears to have penetrated to the Cabinet by the middle of the second week of March, for Noske, on March 9, that is to say, the day on which Hergt and

---

[1] Despite this categorical statement, however, the conspirators, in their later announcements, persistently declared that they had had the previous approval and connivance of the British Military Authorities in Berlin. This was due, it is believed, less to a misapprehension than to a deliberate falsehood calculated to split the ranks of the Allies in the event of opposition. France and Britain were far from seeing eye to eye on German policy at the time and the story of British approval for the *Putsch* would, and did, inevitably have the effect of arousing French suspicion of her ally. These political warfare tactics on the part of the 'putschists' were not uncommendable in skill.

Heinze had made their unsuccessful embassy, issued an order trans-
ferring Ehrhardt's Naval Brigade at Döberitz from the authority
of the General Commanding the *Gruppenkommando I* (von Lüttwitz) to that of the Head of the *Marineleitung*, Admiral von Trotha,
as a preliminary to their demobilization. It was this action which
touched off the powder train.

Von Lüttwitz, well aware that if the troops at Döberitz were
removed from his command, he would have lost his striking force,
demanded and was granted an audience of President Ebert on the
evening of March 10, but without previously consulting or informing
Kapp. He came accompanied by Generals von Oven and von
Oldershausen ; Ebert was supported by Noske. On that same day
the Cabinet had received a comprehensive report from their Police
Commissary, von Berger, on the activities of the Right.[1] They were,
therefore, not entirely unprepared for the attack of the Generals.

Von Lüttwitz began by making certain demands of Noske ; the
further disbandment of troops must be suspended ; General von
Wrisberg must replace Reinhard, as Chief of the *Heeresleitung*,
and the Ehrhardt Brigade must remain under his (von Lüttwitz's)
orders. Noske replied with categorical refusals and added that he
would immediately suspend from duty any General suspected of
disloyalty to the Republic. With rising choler, von Lüttwitz proceeded to his wider challenge. He asked of Ebert new *Reichstag*
elections, a presidential plebiscite, the appointment of a Cabinet of
Experts, who would be better qualified than politicians to deal with
the economic crisis, and a refusal to surrender the 'war-criminals'.
The President, an experienced negotiator, discussed the points
raised without assenting to them, and the General feeling himself
at sea in an atmosphere of debate, began to bluster. Whereupon
Noske took the offensive. 'Matters have gone far enough', he said
to von Lüttwitz. 'The time has come when you either obey orders
or resign. You are mistaken if you think you have the whole *Reichswehr* behind you. If you use force, we shall proclaim a general
strike.' [2]

On this note the interview concluded, the Generals withdrawing
in silence. Ebert and Noske were confident that von Lüttwitz
would send in his resignation, but when this was not forthcoming
by the following morning (March 11) Noske, with the President's
approval, took the sudden step of removing the General from his
command. At the same time warrants were issued for the arrest of
Kapp, Pabst, and Colonel Bauer, and other leaders of the conspiracy.

---

[1] Noske, pp. 204-6.
[2] *Ibid.*, pp. 207-8 ; Volkmann, pp. 346-8 ; Benoist-Méchin, ii, 84-6.

Only two, Grobowski and Schnitzler, were actually arrested. All the rest had received advanced warning, and when the police arrived at the headquarters of the *Nationale Vereinigung* they found them empty and deserted.

By the morning of March 12 it was evident that a trial of strength between the Republic and the militarists was practically unavoidable. The Press was full of rumours of an imminent *Putsch* and the Government, on receipt of reports of the concentration of the conspirators at Döberitz and that the Ehrhardt Brigade was under arms preparatory to marching the twelve miles to the capital, was at last thoroughly alarmed. Precautions were taken but Noske did not lose his fatal optimism. By that evening, even, he had no definite information of any sort of plot, and, in its absence, he hit upon the idea of sending Admiral von Trotha to Döberitz to reconnoitre the position.

This choice of an emissary could scarcely have been more unfortunate, since the Admiral, who had little sympathy with the Republic, announced his coming in advance by telephone, and in consequence, and not very surprisingly, saw nothing untoward on his arrival.[1] He returned to Berlin about ten o'clock and reported 'all quiet at Döberitz', whereupon Noske telephoned this reassuring news to the editor of *Vorwärts*, Erich Kuttner, adding that he did not regard 'a military catastrophe as imminent'.[2] An hour later the Marine Brigade was on the march. Even then the Government was not the first to receive the news. They learned of the approaching danger through a telephone call from a newspaper reporter.

At a hastily summoned Council of War in the small hours of Saturday, March 13, Noske realized too late the false foundation of his optimism. What he had said to von Lüttwitz two days before had been strictly true. The *Reichswehr* as a whole were not prepared to support the rebel General, but neither were they prepared to oppose him. Of the officers present at the meeting only two, General Reinhardt and, surprisingly enough, Noske's own Chief of Staff, Major von Gilsa, who had generally been suspected of defection, were in favour of resistance.[3] The majority shared the

---

[1] Noske, p. 208.

[2] Erich Kuttner in *Vorwärts*, April 3, 1920 ; Scheidemann, ii, 351-2 ; Ströbel, pp. 223-4.

[3] Noske, p. 209. There were present at the Council General Reinhardt, Chief of the *Heeresleitung*; General von Oven, who had succeeded von Lüttwitz as G.O.C. *Gruppenkommando* I ; General von Oldershausen, Chief of Staff G.K.I.; General von Seeckt, Chief of Staff of the *Reichswehr*; Admiral von Trotha, Chief of the *Marineleitung*, and Major von Gilsa.

D

view of von Seeckt, who bluntly told the Minister : ' There can be
no question of setting the *Reichswehr* to fight these people. Would
you force a battle at the Brandenburger Tor between troops who a
year and a half ago were fighting shoulder to shoulder against the
enemy ?' And General von Seeckt left the Council and went on
indefinite leave of absence.

This was the first instance of that which was to become von
Seeckt's fundamental policy in his subsequent reorganization of the
Reichswehr — namely, to keep it out of politics and, above all,
united. The traditional sympathies and even the aspirations of the
Army were with Kapp and von Lüttwitz, but they had no real
confidence in their chances of success. To join them overtly would
mean an open breach with the League of Republican Officers and
would render civil war inevitable, since the workers, in the course
of a general strike, would certainly meet force with force.

On the other hand, the Army had little enthusiasm for a régime
which, in accepting the peace treaty, had condoned the drastic
reduction of the Reich military establishment and was even now
reaping the whirlwind in the shape of the war-criminals controversy.
The fact that the Ebert-Bauer-Noske Cabinet represented the constitutional Government of Germany weighed little with the *Reichswehr*.
Von Seeckt had no intention of permitting his troops to fire on their
old comrades-in-arms. The Army would sit on the fence until the
issue of this trial of strength could more clearly be discerned ; it
would then descend, with force and dignity, on the side of the
winner. If this were von Lüttwitz, the status of the Army would be
restored in all its pre-revolutionary splendour, but if it were Ebert,
von Seeckt was shrewd enough to know that a republican régime
restored to power by means of a general strike would be forced
to lean heavily upon the Army in order to prevent anarchy. Whatever the outcome, therefore, the Army would retain its position
as the ultimate and basic source of sovereign power within the
Reich.

That Noske was bitterly disappointed at this attitude there can
be no doubt. In his vanity and naive optimism he had banked
upon the ephemeral devotion which the Generals had accorded him
and had counted on his ability to swing the *Reichswehr* behind the
Government. He discovered too late — this former non-commissioned officer who had been so gratified to be in control of the Generals
and so flattered by their facile praise and compliments — that from
the beginning he had been a dupe and a puppet in the hands of the
General Staff, who had used him for their own salvation and were
now prepared as ruthlessly to jettison him. 'This night has shown

the bankruptcy of all my policy', Noske cried aloud in his bitterness.
'My faith in the Officer Corps is shattered. You have all deserted
me. There is nothing left but suicide.'[1]

Abandoned by the Army and with the double-edged weapon of
a general strike as their last resort, the President, Chancellor, and
Cabinet of Republican Germany fled from Berlin in a convoy of
motor-cars at five in the morning of March 13. Less than an hour
later, in the cold light of a March dawn, with all the pomp of martial
music and the brave glory of the old Imperial colours, with the
swastika on their steel helmets, the men of the Ehrhardt and Baltikum
brigades arrived at the Brandenburger Tor. Here they were met by
Ludendorff and von Lüttwitz in uniform and by Kapp and his staff,
all of whom marched at the head of the troops to the Wilhelmstrasse,
where they occupied the Chancellor's Palace and the Government
offices. It was perhaps a fitting symbol of the enterprise that the
civilian leaders appeared in the full splendour of morning-dress,
complete with top-hats and spats.

The Kapp *Putsch* was a triumph of ineptitude, infirmity of purpose, and lack of preparedness. Though the conspiracy had been
nine months coming to birth, in the final phase events had moved
too quickly for these immature politicians. It had originally been
intended that von Lüttwitz should give Kapp a full fortnight's
warning before making the actual *coup*, during which time it was
hoped that the Nationalist and German People's Parties could be
won over for immediate political support. The decision of the
Government to comply with the Allied demand for the disbandment
of the Ehrhardt Brigade, coupled with the intolerant impetuosity of
the General, had combined to prevent this notice being given and
the final decision to march was taken by von Lüttwitz without consulting Kapp. Moreover, if the neutrality of the *Reichswehr* had
proved an embarrassment to Ebert and Noske, it had also hamstrung the *Putsch*, as von Lüttwitz himself later admitted,[2] since he
had counted on the support of the troops in the provinces.

But the most elementary preparations were uncompleted. A
Naumburg lawyer, Dr. Hermann, had been busily engaged in
drawing up new laws and a new constitution, but on March 13 these
were still unfinished. Fräulein Kapp, who was to have written the
new régime's manifesto to the nation, found on her arrival at the
Chancellery that there was no typewriter for her to use and by
the time one had been found and the work finished, it was too
late for the Sunday papers, and therefore the country was without

---

[1] Volkmann, pp. 356-9. Noske thought better of this, however. He lived till
1946. (See above, p. 34, footnote.)   [2] Lüttwitz, pp. 118-20.

official news of the *coup* and of its high intentions until Monday morning (March 15), by which time rumour and anti-climax had taken the gilt off the gingerbread.

The financial preparations were equally lacking. No plans existed for a levy or for taxation or for requisition. When the troops demanded their pay, Kapp could think of no better means of procuring money than to take it from the *Reichsbank* by force, but when he suggested this course of action to Ehrhardt, that shocked naval officer replied that he was no bank-robber.

Indeed, within twenty-four hours the political incapacity of Wolfgang Kapp was glaringly apparent. With an optimism as fatal and fallacious as Noske's he had staked all on a great popular welcome, and when confronted with blank hostility, he showed himself bewildered, weak, and helpless. This Pan-German chauvinist, who had helped to bring down von Bethmann Hollweg, disclosed, when he himself was faced with the problems of government, that he was without versatility or ingenuity. He proclaimed himself Chancellor, but let it be known that he would give up this position to anyone who could command popular support. He sought to conciliate all and succeeded in pleasing none. He blew hot and cold ; played the strong man and then revoked his own edicts, and proved himself a monumental exemplar of the military maxim : 'Order, counter-order, disorder'.

In contradistinction to the indecision of the rebels, the Republican régime acted with determination and despatch. They had first fled to Dresden, but finding General Maercker lukewarm in his support, had moved the seat of Government to Stuttgart. There they denounced Kapp and von Lüttwitz as traitors, proclaimed a general strike and convened the National Assembly (March 13–14).

The effect of these measures in Berlin was one of paralysis and chaos. The wheels of Government ceased to turn ; industry and commerce were at a standstill ; all public services — water, light, and transport — were cut off. The power of the Trade Unions, neglected in the calculations of Kapp and von Lüttwitz, manifested itself in silent hostility, and Kapp had not the courage or the ruthlessness to arrest the strike-leaders. Had he exerted the brutal energy with which the Nazis later seized power and smashed their political opponents, he might have succeeded, but he was not the man for such an emergency. Instead, he embarked on a series of actions which demonstrated his own uncertainty of mind. He dissolved the Prussian Diet on Saturday and cancelled the dissolution on Monday by negotiation with the political leaders. He arrested the Prussian Cabinet and then released them in an attempt to

secure their co-operation — in which he failed. Finally, in desperation, he ordered the shooting of all strikers, but when this order
was not carried out by the troops, he attempted to negotiate a
settlement.

By Monday, March 15, it was manifest that the tide was running heavily against the conspirators. Maercker, who had
flown to Berlin, had received certain tentative proposals for a
settlement, which were peremptorily rejected by Ebert at Stuttgart.
The President retorted with a stirring appeal to the *Reichswehr*,
which was dropped in leaflet form by plane over the barracks
and distributed to the troops by strikers. Maercker retired to
Dresden to announce his support of the old Government; his
lead was followed by the *Reichswehr* commanders in Munich and
in Munster.

That same evening a further hope of the conspirators was shattered
— if it had ever been seriously entertained. Count Brockdorff-
Rantzau conveyed to Kapp the terse comment of Lord Kilmarnock,
the British High Commissioner, that the claim of the rebels that
the British Government had promised them support was '*un sacré
mensonge*'. The Count, who had only contempt for the histrionics
of the *Putsch*, left the 'Dictator' white and trembling, a picture of
miserable indecision.[1] On the following day (March 16) General
Neill Malcolm confirmed to von Lüttwitz that Britain would never
recognize the new régime in Berlin, and thereby completed its
discomfiture.[2]

The Nationalist Party, which had given their support to the
rebels to the extent of boycotting the National Assembly and
declaring it to be unconstitutional, now urged Kapp to make a
graceful exit and the National Association of German Industries,
the organization of the powerful industrialists, which had hitherto
maintained a reserved attitude on the general strike, came out with
a formal denunciation of the Kapp régime.

The *coup de grâce* was delivered on the morning of the 17th
when the Security Police, who had so far been neutral, demanded
Kapp's resignation. Without the tacit support of this body it
would be impossible to preserve order in the capital and there
had already been clashes between the workers and the troops

---

[1] Stewart Roddie, *Peace Patrol* (New York, 1933), pp. 153-4.
[2] The conspirators did not quite abandon hope of foreign recognition even
then, for on March 19 Colonel Bauer made an appeal through the columns of
The Times to the Allied Powers for help. (See *The Times*, March 19, 1920; also
H. G. Daniels, *The Rise of the German Republic* (London, 1927), p. 142. Mr.
Daniels was *The Times* correspondent in Berlin during this period.)

which had resulted in over a hundred casualties.

A last-minute attempt to find a face-saving formula was made by certain of the Party leaders, led by Stresemann, who, though he had given no support to the *Putsch*, had not come out strongly against it.[1] As a result Kapp issued a final and completely mendacious manifesto announcing his resignation — 'having completed all my aims' — and handing over his authority to General von Lüttwitz. A taxi-cab was hastily summoned to the Chancellor's palace and the man who had entered it on Saturday morning in the elegant *tenue* of '*Zylinder und Spatzen*', with a self-imposed mission to restore the monarchy, now left it on the Wednesday evening, muffled to the eyes and with a soft hat pulled down over his brow. There was no luggage. A package of papers was thrust in after him and a sheet, tied at the four corners, containing the personal effects he had had no time to pack, was thrown up on top of the taxi. Finally, there came his daughter weeping. The cab drove rapidly away to Tempelhof, where a plane was waiting to take them to Sweden. The Kapps had made an inglorious exit. The 'Dictator's' reign had lasted exactly a hundred hours.[2]

There remained von Lüttwitz. The General was somewhat bewildered at the way in which the whole structure of the conspiracy had suddenly crumbled around him. He blamed the failure largely on the politicians, for whom his scorn was now even greater than before. Left to himself, he might have established a stern and disciplined dictatorship of a purely military kind, but he had been beguiled into being yoked with Kapp and had remained a contemptuous observer of the 'Dictator's' tergiversations and indecision. Kapp's flight had left von Lüttwitz as heir to a tottering throne and he was soon to learn that the throne was not even supported by bayonets.

Ludendorff advised the General to brazen it out and von Lüttwitz, who was as physically brave as he was politically inept, might well have done so, had it not been for the intervention of his officers. Early in the afternoon of March 17, von Lüttwitz received a

---

[1] 'The time was not yet come when Stresemann was to be ready to defend the Republic with his life', wrote Rudolf Olden. 'What power he had so far won under the Republic was very trifling, too trifling to let him have any legitimist feeling for the Republic' (*Stresemann* (London, 1930), p. 109). The other intermediaries were Hergt and Count Westarp (Nationalists), Gothein (Democrat) and Trimborn (Centre).

[2] Kapp later returned to Germany and surrendered himself to the Reich authorities. He died in jail in 1922 while awaiting trial. Under the Nazi régime a eulogistic biography was written by Ludwig Schemann, entitled *Wolfgang Kapp und das Märzunternehmen vom Jahre 1920* (Munich/Berlin, 1937).

Planet News

GENERAL OF INFANTRY ERICH LUDENDORFF

GENERAL FREIHERR WALTHER VON LÜTTWITZ

delegation of officers from the Bendlerstrasse [1] headed by Colonel Heye. Heye told von Lüttwitz that he did not enjoy the confidence of the Army and advised him to resign. Von Lüttwitz, like Wilhelm II in a similar situation, received this news with choler, threatening to put Heye under arrest for insubordination. But he had to submit. He drove to the Justice Ministry and, after consulting with some of the party leaders, including Stresemann, wrote out his resignation. Meanwhile his position was being still further undermined by a mutiny among his own local commanders. These had been summoned to a meeting in the Reich Chancellery by General von Oven, now G.O.C. *Gruppenkommando I*, to consider the situation. Most of those present agreed that it was an impossible one and that the *Putsch* should be liquidated as soon as possible.[2] The Potsdam garrison was in a state of mutiny and the regimental officers as a whole had lost faith in von Lüttwitz.

The General was furious at the insubordination of his own commanders, but he wisely rejected Ehrhardt's suggestion that they be arrested for mutiny. He followed Kapp into exile.[3] It was six o'clock in the evening. The Army had been placed under the command of Hans von Seeckt, who, ironically enough, had been the one general officer forced to resign from service under the Kapp régime. The *Putsch* was over.[4]

[1] The Ministry of Defence was situated in the Bendlerstrasse and the term 'Bendlerstrasse' was used in Germany to denote the General Staff in the same sense that the 'Wilhelmstrasse' denoted the Chancellery and the Foreign Office.

[2] Those present included Generals von Oven, Ludendorff, von der Goltz, von Hülsen, von Klewitz, von der Lippe, Colonels Bauer, Heye, von Hammerstein, and Reinhard, Captain Ehrhardt and Major Pabst.

[3] General von Lüttwitz found refuge in Hungary on the estate of Prince Lynar. He subsequently returned to Germany after the general amnesty of 1925, where he died in 1942.

[4] Of the principal conspirators, Colonel Bauer, after a period of exile in Europe, during which he wrote an account of the *Putsch*, *Der 13te März, 1920* (Berlin, n.d.), became the first of General Chiang Kai-shek's German military advisers in 1927, a post in which he was succeeded by Kriebel, von Wetzell, von Seeckt, and von Falkenhausen. Bauer died in Shanghai in 1929. Pabst fled to Austria where he was involved in various political intrigues and finally became an ardent supporter and agent of the Nazi Party. Captain Ehrhardt received permission from von Seeckt to march his troops out of Berlin after the collapse of the *Putsch* with the honours of war. As the last files were passing through the Brandenburger Tor, they turned about and fired point blank into the crowds who thronged the pavements and had hooted the troops as they marched down Unter den Linden, with the result that many were killed and wounded. The sailors then resumed their return march to Döberitz, singing as they marched that *Ehrhardt Brigade Lied*, to the tune of which, as 'Good-bye, my Bluebell', American troops had marched in Cuba in 1898 and British troops in South Africa during the Boer War. Ehrhardt later joined von Lüttwitz in Hungary, but returned to Germany and became a member of the Nazi Party. He left it later on.

The Kapp *Putsch* had one important result. It had demonstrated that German militarism had, of itself, no concrete political programme and was incapable of taking over the government of the country. Having occupied Berlin, the conspirators had literally not known what to do next, and, as a result they had done nothing.[1] It was therefore borne in upon the chiefs of the *Reichswehr* that, to achieve their aim of re-establishing Germany as a strong military power, they must work *through* and not *against* the Republic. As a result there began a new phase in the relationship between the two, a phase which marked a change in the attitude of the Army from one of sullen unreliability — part ally, part master, part servant, vacillating between grudging subservience and bitter hatred — to that of a strong supporter of legitimate and constituted authority. During this phase, which lasted for six years, the Army achieved its greatest political ascendancy and its maximum of real power in Germany. Credit for this achievement is due to the genius of one man, Hans von Seeckt.

Note. There has been some controversy about the timing of the first telephone conversation between Gröner and Ebert (see pp. 20-1). Gröner, in his memoirs written at the end of the 1930's and published in 1957, claimed that he first telephoned Ebert on the evening of November 10. This seems strange in view of the fact that at noon on that day a telegram had already been despatched from Spa containing the main terms of the pact between the High Command and the new government. (See H. Goldschmidt, H. Kaiser, H. Thimme, *Ein Jahrhundert deutscher Geschichte 1815–1919*, Nr 136. Facsimile telegram.) I cannot believe that Gröner would have waited so long to contact Ebert, when a direct telephone line was at his disposal. (Cf. Wilhelm Gröner, *Lebenserinnerungen* (Göttingen, 1957), p. 467.)

    [1] For brief accounts of the Kapp *Putsch* see Harold J. Gordon, *The Reichswehr and the German Republic, 1919–1926* (Princeton, 1957), pp. 113-29; William Halperin, *Germany tried Democracy* (New York, 1946), pp. 168-88, a pamphlet by Theodor Heuss, 'Kapp-Lüttwitz : das Verbrechen gegen die Nation' (Berlin, 1920); and Miss Alma Luckau's article in the Journal of Central European Affairs, January 1948, entitled 'Kapp Putsch — Success or Failure'.

CHAPTER 2

THE SEECKT PERIOD

(1920–1926)

(i)

THE name of Hans von Seeckt is written with those of von Moltke, von Roon, and von Schlieffen in the annals of German military fame. Like von Moltke, he fashioned anew the pattern and the mould of the military machine, starting from very small beginnings ; like von Schlieffen, he looked forward and planned and contrived for a day, the exact time of which he could not foresee, when his master plans would be put into effect for the greater glory of Germany. Like both his predecessors, he left the German Army stronger and more efficient than he found it. But, whereas both von Moltke and von Schlieffen based their calculations on the security born of victory and well-being, von Seeckt, like Scharnhorst and Gneisenau, was compelled to build upon the ashes of defeat, yet withal finding them no unsubstantial a foundation for achievement. His genius lay, not in the formation of large armies but in the creation of a military microcosm, complete within itself in every detail, yet capable at the given moment of limitless expansion.

Hans von Seeckt was born in Schleswig on April 22, 1866. His family were of ancient and noble Pomeranian lineage ; they had given to Prussia sons who had found distinction both as soldiers and as civil servants. His father, also a General, had been awarded by Wilhelm I the highest Prussian honour, the collar of a Knight of the Order of the Black Eagle. Von Seeckt himself entered the First (Emperor Alexander's) Regiment of Foot Guards as a subaltern at the age of nineteen and almost immediately became marked for rapid preferment. Not only did he display an ability to handle troops, but, to that lynx-eyed group who were continually on the watch for promising material, he disclosed himself as a born staff officer. As a result, in 1899, at the age of thirty-three, and as a mere lieutenant, he was transferred to the *élite* of the General Staff Corps. In the intervals of an exceptionally rapid career, he found time to travel widely in Europe and even to Africa and India, where, at

Delhi, he established friendly relations with Lord Kitchener. Von Seeckt's record showed him to be an outstandingly successful example of that item of German military organism, to which such great importance was attached, a Chief of Staff, and it was in this capacity that he began the War. As Chief of Staff to the Third Corps, he greatly distinguished himself in the planning of the local break-through at Soissons, and his perfection of this technique caused him to be appointed Chief of Staff to Mackensen's newly formed Eleventh Army on the Eastern Front. Here, in May 1915, he achieved one of the most spectacular victories of the War, the break-through at Gorlice which crushed the Russian front and penetrated it to a tremendous depth. Whole provinces were yielded up to the German advance, and the fortresses of Przemysl, Ivangorod, Lemberg, Warsaw and Brest-Litovsk fell into their hands.[1]

The victory of Gorlice earned for von Seeckt the coveted order *Pour le Mérite*; it also singled him out as the perfect Chief of Staff. As such he served many commanders and on numerous fronts in the ensuing years.[2] The end of the war found him in Turkey, whence he made his way home to Germany via the Black Sea, the Ukraine and Poland.

The collapse of November 1918 came as an appalling shock to von Seeckt. He has left it on record that he wept, but he never lost faith or hope. He followed the lead of Hindenburg and of Gröner, and in January 1919 he was sent by them to organize the retreat of the German armies from White Russia and the Ukraine and the protection of the frontiers of the Reich against the incursions of both Poles and Bolsheviks.[3] On the theory — which he was later to develop on a greater scale — that attack is the best means of defence, von Seeckt launched an offensive which in May resulted in the recapture of Riga. Though of minor and ephemeral import-

---

[1] The Austro-Hungarian Foreign Minister, Count Ottokar Czernin, in a defence of his policy before the Vienna Parliament immediately after the War (December 11, 1918), declared his belief that at one point only in the course of the War, namely after the battle of Gorlice, 'with the Russian Army in flight and the Russian fortresses falling like houses of cards', was it possible to have secured a peace based on 'a policy of renunciation'. The Russians, he believed, were prepared for it, but the German military party refused to consider the possibility (Czernin, *In the World War* (London, 1919), p. 329).

[2] Von Seeckt served as C.G.S. to Mackensen's composite Army Group of German, Austrian and Bulgarian troops in the Balkans, to the Archduke Karl (later the last of the Austrian Emperors) in Hungary and Rumania, and finally to the Turkish Army (December 1917).

[3] On this mission von Seeckt was accompanied by his G.S.O.1, Major Freiherr Werner von Fritsch, who was destined to be his ultimate successor as Commander-in-Chief of the *Reichswehr*.

ance this success had an important psychological effect upon both commander and troops. It confirmed von Seeckt in his belief in the military future of Germany, and it taught the men that they could still win battles. Of this new confidence were born the *Freikorps* of the Eastern Marches.[1]

Summoned home from his last victory, he was despatched by Gröner and Noske to Versailles as the military member of the German Peace Commission. His reports forewarned his Chiefs of the bitter draught which was being prepared for them in the disarmament clauses of the treaty ; they, in their turn, recognized that the one man who could carry out, and, if possible, circumvent, these conditions was von Seeckt himself, and they therefore appointed him Chairman of the Preparatory Commission of the Peace Army.

Such was the career of Hans von Seeckt, but what of his personality ?

Seeckt's is not an easy character to analyse, for he combined the best traditions of the Prussian military caste with a breadth of outlook and a political flair unusual in these circles.[2]   His travels abroad had rendered him a man of the world in the best sense of the term, shrewd in judgment and adroit in the handling of men and affairs ; his *savoir-faire* gave him a particular charm ; he was well and widely read and his keen appreciation of beauty in every form — music, art, women and nature — afforded an ampler vision than could ever have been achieved by, for example, Ludendorff.[3] To dine with him was always a pleasurable experience, for, apart from excellent food and wine, the host, himself an excellent conversationalist, so assorted his company that talk ranged from horse-breeding and military history to politics and the arts.   Von Seeckt, himself, in later years declared that vanity, a sense of beauty and the cavalier's instinct were the three outstanding traits in his character,[4] but this was an understatement.   Lord D'Abernon wrote

---

[1] It was not without irony that almost the first task which von Seeckt had to undertake after the signature of the Peace Treaty was to persuade the German forces in the East to abandon the areas which this offensive had gained.   As a result of his personal intervention, Riga was evacuated on July 11, 1919.

[2] Two such diverse but equally shrewd observers as Tsar Ferdinand of Bulgaria and Count Bernstorff have both recorded their opinion that, alone among the German Generals, von Seeckt had a clear and precise appreciation of the political aspects of the War.

[3] No such streak of aestheticism coloured Ludendorff's character. 'He was a man blind in spirit', his medical director once confessed. 'He had never seen a flower bloom, never heard a bird sing, never watched the sun set. I used to treat him for his soul' (Wheeler-Bennett, 'Ludendorff : The Soldier and the Politician', *Virginia Quarterly Review*, Spring 1938).

[4] Herbert Rosinski, *The German Army* (London, 1939), p. 177.

of him as having 'a broader mind than is expected in so tight a uniform, a wider outlook than seems appropriate to so precise, so correct, so neat an exterior',[1] and this was nearer to the mark.

A strange man, Hans von Seeckt; at first glance a typical Prussian officer, with his thin, red turkey-neck, his inscrutable face and its inevitable monocle. Just another General, one thought, as he entered a room, but that impression only remained until he took his hands from behind his back, and one was amazed at their beauty. Long, thin, sensitive, they might have belonged to Cellini or to Chopin, and, indeed, in his military genius von Seeckt combined the precision and accuracy of the soldier with the vision and imagination of the creative artist. For such he was, an artist in making bricks without straw, in beating ploughshares into swords, in fashioning a military machine which, though nominally within the restrictions of the Peace Treaty, struck admiration and awe into the heart of every General Staff in Europe.

Like many soldiers von Seeckt had an attitude of ambivalence towards war. 'The soldier, having experience of war, fears it more than the doctrinaire, who being ignorant of war talks only of peace', he wrote on one occasion before Hitler came to power. 'The figure of the sabre-rattling fire-eating general is an invention of poisoned and unscrupulous political strife.'[2] Yet after the rearmament of Germany — the foundations for which he had so ably laid — had been publicly proclaimed, he gave vent to sentiments similar to those of the elder Moltke:[3] 'War is the highest summit of human achievement; it is the natural, the final stage in the historical development of humanity.'[4] It is not impossible that the fierce and savage beauty of war, as well as the professional pride of the soldier, may have been present in his mind, for he was artist as well as warrior.

Never fundamentally converted to belief or confidence in a republican Germany, von Seeckt was prepared, unlike many of his caste, to use the Republic for his own ends; and to co-operate with it as the existing constituted authority to restore the strength and power of those two institutions to which his devotion and loyalty were deep and unswerving, the German Reich and the German

---

[1] Viscount D'Abernon, *Portraits and Appreciations* (London, 1931), pp. 158-9.

[2] *Thoughts of a Soldier* (London, 1930), p. 5.

[3] See above, p. 8, footnote, for Moltke's letter to Bluntschli. The Field-Marshal repeated these views in another letter to Dr. Lueder in which he said that 'want and misery, disease and suffering and war are all permanent elements in man's destiny and nature' and as such are to be welcomed as indispensable to his 'development' (*Entwicklung*)—(cf. Morgan, p. 247).

[4] *Militärwissenschaftliche Rundschau*, vol. i (1936), p. 2.

Army. 'The Reich!' he wrote in ecstasy, 'There is something supernatural in this word. It embraces far more and connotes something other than the conception of a State. It does not stand for the State institutions of to-day. . . . It is an organic living entity (*Lebewesen*) subject to the laws of evolution.'[1] As such it must neither become rigid nor tyrannical; it must contain, not dominate the individual. 'The starting point is the individual with his natural right to Freedom, not the State conception with its right to Might. In the same way, the ultimate end is the individual, not the State.'[2]

But within this 'living entity' von Seeckt had no doubt as to what should be the place of the Army. 'The Army should become a State within the State, but it should be merged in the State through service; in fact it should itself become the purest image of the State.'[3]

With these as his basic principles von Seeckt set himself two great objectives: first, so to organize the new *Reichswehr* within the restrictions imposed by the treaty that in due course it could be expanded into a national army, and, secondly, to preserve intact the German military traditions despite these same treaty restrictions. In later years he himself avowed that his consistent policy had been 'to neutralize the poison (*das Gift*)' contained in the disarmament clauses of the Treaty of Versailles', and that in consummating this ambition he 'owed everything to the German Officer Corps'.[4] Von Seeckt recognized, above all, the vital and essential truth that the spiritual disarmament of Germany was more important to the Allies — and consequently more dangerous to Germany — than her physical disarmament;[5] it was his mission to prevent this, and he succeeded.

(ii)

On the morrow of the Kapp *Putsch*, however, the position of the *Reichswehr* was by no means one of great strength. It was disunited within itself and was also the target of fierce attack from without. Thanks to von Seeckt's foresight, an open breach in the ranks of the Army and of the Officer Corps had been avoided, but there remained a source of bitterness between those of von Lüttwitz's officers who had sided with him and those who had opposed him, and, again, between these and the Generals who had openly supported the Ebert Government.

[1] *The Future of the German Empire* (London, 1930), p. 23.
[2] *Ibid.* p. 163.
[3] *Thoughts of a Soldier*, p. 77.
[4] *Die Reichswehr* (Leipzig, 1933), pp. 16, 30.   [5] *Ibid.* p. 13.

Moreover, the 'neutrality' of the *Reichswehr* throughout those critical March days and the fact that the *Putsch* had been defeated by the weapon of the General Strike, had intensified the hostility of the workers toward the Army, since it was well-known 'against whom' the *Reichswehr* had been 'neutral', and where their real sympathies had lain. This hostility found expression in a clamorous demand from the Parties of the Left for the most severe measures against all those who had taken part in the *Putsch*; for the purging of the Officer Corps of all reactionary elements; for the reorganization of the *Reichswehr* on the lines of a democratic national militia, the recruitment of which would be controlled by the trade unions; and, above all, for the dismissal of Noske, who was regarded as having become either the dupe or the agent of the High Command.

Such was the situation which confronted President Ebert and the Reich Government on their return to Berlin on March 18, 1920, and in certain aspects it resembled that of November 1918. For the second time in eighteen months the Army were in a position of essential weakness, and for the second time Ebert was faced with the choice of yielding to the demands of the Left and attempting to bring the Army under democratic control or of treating with it on terms of equality and thereby recognizing its claims to be 'a State within a State'.

Yet Ebert's position was not as strong as it seemed. The Republic had crushed the revolt of the militarists, but it had only done so by employing the dangerous and double-edged weapon of the General Strike. To alienate the support of the Army at this juncture might mean a surrender to the extremist elements of the Left, and this, as a Majority Socialist of the old school, Ebert feared even more than he distrusted the Army.

In face of this dilemma Ebert chose as he had chosen on the fateful evening of November 9, 1918. He appointed von Seeckt Chief of the *Heeresleitung* and renewed with him the pact which he had sealed with Hindenburg and with Gröner a year and a half before.[1]

The Army were not over exacting in their terms. They naturally rejected all idea of a 'popular' reorganization of the *Reichswehr*, but von Seeckt agreed to the retirement of a number of dissident Generals.[2] However, with the support of Gröner, who now entered the Cabinet as Minister of Transport, and of Hindenburg, he interceded with Ebert on behalf of the junior officers and troops who had taken part in the *Putsch*, urging that to let loose a witch-hunt

[1] Volkmann, p. 386.
[2] Including von Oven, Maercker, and von Lettow-Vorbeck.

throughout the Reich would serve no good purpose and would only increase the bitterness of the political cleavages already existing. Ebert gave way on this point and, while issuing warrants of arrest for the leaders of the *Putsch* — most of whom were already safely out of the country — granted a general amnesty to the rank and file of the conspirators.[1] Von Seeckt had thus avoided a purge of the Officer Corps.

Noske finally succumbed to the attacks of the Left. No one intervened for him, for it was felt by all concerned that he was unreliable both as a colleague and as a conspirator. He resigned on March 24, to be succeeded as Minister of National Defence by Otto Gessler, a bullet-headed Bavarian lawyer who, as *Bürgermeister* of Nuremberg and a member of the Democratic Party, seemed nicely balanced in his political views between the Right and the Left.[2]

There remained the problem of what to do with the *Freikorps*. Despite their dubious loyalty they were needed by Ebert and von Seeckt to carry out repressive measures against the recalcitrant workers of the Ruhr, who, having armed themselves during the *Putsch*, were now refusing to call off the General Strike or to lay down their arms. So to the Ruhr were sent the dreaded corps of Löwenfeld and von Epp and Faupel, of Rossbach and of Lützow, and there ensued some bitter fighting. No quarter was given by the Government forces; both prisoners and wounded were shot out of hand.[3] By mid-April order had been restored and the Army retired, but not before its presence in the demilitarized zone had occasioned the occupation of certain Ruhr towns by French troops.[4]

---

[1] Benoist-Méchin, ii, 112.

[2] Of Gessler, General Nollet, President of the Inter-Allied Commission of Control, wrote with some bitterness but also much perception : 'He confined himself to signing the decisions of General von Seeckt. . . . It was under the cover of his name and of his political authority that von Seeckt carried out his work of reorganization. This authority secured the General against attacks in the *Reichstag* and the Press' (Nollet, *Une Expérience de désarmement* (Paris, 1932), p. 110).

[3] 'You see,' said one of the *Freikorps* officers to Commandant Graff of the French Military Mission, 'most of these fellows are young men who, during the five years of the war have had no paternal discipline, and, as it is too late to train them, the best thing is to wipe them out' (Morgan, p. 152). 'No pardon is given', a soldier of von Epp's Corps wrote to his family on April 2, 1920. 'We shoot even the wounded. The enthusiasm is great, almost unbelievable' (Fried, p. 192).

[4] The Ruhr strikers and Spartakists had made their resistance to local authorities and police inside the demilitarized Rhineland zone, whither Germany was prohibited by the treaty from sending troops. Ebert petitioned the Allied Supreme Council for permission for troops to enter the forbidden zone for a period of twenty days, and so confident was he that the Free Corps could complete their task within that time that he offered to give France the right to occupy Frankfurt, Darmstadt and Duisburg if German troops had not evacuated the zone by the end

The Kapp *Putsch* was thus finally liquidated in the bloody suppression of the same forces which had brought about its collapse. Events had worked out exactly as von Seeckt had foreseen. The Government had had need of the Army to re-establish its authority.

But though von Seeckt had stood between the Officer Corps and the wrath of the Left, and had found a temporary solution for the problem of the *Freikorps* in the blood-letting of the Ruhr, he had no intention of being dictated to by either, and lost no time in asserting his authority over both.

In his first Order of the Day to the Officer Corps after assuming command of the *Reichswehr*,[1] he told them bluntly that he would not tolerate a repetition of the previous acts of treason to the Constitution. 'It is the tragic result of such adventures that the many who are innocent have to suffer for the faults of the few.' There was no room in the new Army for those who had committed an offence against military honour. There was much to be done for Germany. United, they could overcome all their difficulties, but united and loyal they must be. 'The decisive hour for the Officer Corps has struck', von Seeckt warned them, and then called for a return to 'the old spirit of silent self-effacing devotion in the service of the Army, which in this moment, more full of danger than ever before, does not permit anyone to withhold his services for the common weal'. Political strife within the Army was incompatible with the spirit of comradeship, detrimental to discipline and harmful to military training; therefore, said von Seeckt, political activity of every kind would be energetically excluded. 'We do not enquire into the political life of individuals, but I must assume of everyone who remains in the Army, that he loyally respects his oath and accepts, of his own free will and as an honourable soldier, the Constitution of the Reich.'

With these words, which evoked no little criticism and indignation from the old Guard of the military caste,[2] von Seeckt had shown the Corps who was to be master and had at the same time done

of that period. The Allies refused this request, whereupon the German Government sent in its troops, in defiance of the ban, on April 2. French troops occupied the three Ruhr cities by way of sanctions two days later, and though the German forces were clear of the zone by April 10, the French remained until May 17.

[1] Both Volkmann (pp. 384-5) and, consequently, Benoist-Méchin (ii, 110-11), give the date of this Order as March 18, 1920. Von Seeckt's official biographer, General von Rabenau, however, states this to be an error, and that it was delivered on April 18, on the occasion of his formal investment as *Chef der Heeresleitung* by Gessler, the Minister of Defence (Rabenau, ii, 239, footnote).

[2] This indignation was expressed by Colonel Bauer in no uncertain terms. Von Seeckt, he wrote, had 'discredited himself for ever in the eyes of those officers who preserved the cult of the true Prussian military tradition' (Bauer, p. 28).

much to appease the Left, who saw in his address only an abandonment of military adventures by the Army and an acceptance of the Constitution. These were indeed von Seeckt's immediate intentions, but his ultimate aims went much further. By a judicious amalgam of reproof and appeal he had laid the foundation of a personal loyalty of the Officer Corps to himself, on which he proposed to build a superstructure, not of personal aggrandizement, but of impersonal achievement for the future strength of Germany.

There remained the problem of the *Freikorps*. These formations with their personal devotion to individual leaders and their *Landsknecht* indiscipline, their indifference to law and order and their general political ignorance and arrogance, were manifestly an embarrassment both to the Army and to the Government. Called into being in a moment of emergency and chaos, they were symptomatic of a revolutionary period which both Ebert and von Seeckt were anxious to forget. They had served their turn with brutal efficiency, but their continued existence was a cause of anxiety to the Allied Powers who persistently demanded their disbandment, and they could find no place for themselves within the new *Reichswehr*, which was destined by its creator to be a 'State within a State'.

Von Seeckt, therefore, supported the Government in their enactment of a law for the relinquishment by individuals and formations of all arms of which they were illegally possessed, and the duty of destroying this equipment, in conformity with the orders of the Allied Control Commission, was entrusted to a special Reich Commissioner.[1] Over a period of months the various *Freikorps* were dissolved. The best elements were absorbed into the *Reichswehr*.[2] The more unruly took refuge in Bavaria, which had become the hot-bed of reaction and where the writ of the Reich Government could scarcely be said to run, and here they re-formed themselves into

---

[1] This law of August 8, 1920, was passed by the *Reichstag* on the initiative of the Fehrenbach Government, which had succeeded the Cabinet of Hermann Müller after the general elections of June 6. In these the Parties of the Left had lost heavily at the polls. The SPD achieved only 5½ million votes, having lost more than half of its adherents ; the Nationalists and the German People's Party together obtained 7,300,000 votes ; the Democrats 2,200,000, and the Centre 3½ million. The Majority Socialists left the Government and Fehrenbach formed a coalition Cabinet based on the Centre, the German People's Party and the Democrats.

[2] Many also became members of the *Stahlhelm* (Steel Helmet) Organization of ex-service men, founded on December 25, 1918, by Franz Seldte, a Magdeburg reserve officer, who, in his initial statement to his followers, declared that the association had been formed to oppose 'the spirit of the front soldier' to the 'swinish revolution'.

secret societies designed to undermine and overthrow the Republic.[1]

The High Command of the *Reichswehr* were, however, unwilling to relinquish completely all control over this superfluous source of man-power and armament, more particularly in view of the developments on Germany's eastern frontier and her manifest inability to resist an attack from this quarter. The years 1920 and 1921 were marked by a singular display of Polish chauvinism. Poland embarked upon military adventures in Upper Silesia, in the Ukraine, and in Lithuania, the results of which were largely advantageous to her. Germany, ever apprehensive of an attack from the East, developed an acute war-neurosis, partly genuine and partly fostered by the Army for its own purposes. It was impossible, von Seeckt argued, to make an adequate defence of even the eastern frontiers of the Reich with an army of 100,000 men and it was therefore necessary to supplement them by certain secret formations, which, disguised as non-military labour battalions, could be attached peripherally to the *Reichswehr*.

The task of forming these *Arbeits-Kommandos* (AK) was entrusted to a certain Major Buchrucker, a former officer of the General Staff, and the immediate supervision of this first step in the clandestine rearmament of Germany was confided to a small group in the Bendlerstrasse, who were also responsible for keeping up liaison between the *Reichswehr* and all illicit military formations in Germany. This group consisted of Kurt von Schleicher, Kurt von Hammerstein, Fedor von Bock, and Eugen Ott, all of whom were marked by destiny for future eminence.

Officially the members of the AK were volunteer civilian labourers engaged on short-term contracts, but this disguise deceived nobody. They wore military uniform and were cantoned in the barracks of the *Reichswehr*, from whom they received their rations, their training and their orders. In a comparatively short space of time, Buchrucker had raised a force of some 20,000 men, quartered east of the Fortress of Küstrin and operating within the area of *Wehrkreis III.* (Berlin-Brandenburg), of which von Bock was Chief of Staff.[2]

---

[1] Simultaneously with the Kapp *Putsch* in Berlin, the SPD Premier of Bavaria was forced to resign as the result of military pressure, and power was put into the hands of a conservative civil servant, Ritter Gustav von Kahr. Bavaria thenceforth became a centre for anti-republican movements including the notorious organization Consul, whose members were involved in the murders of Erzberger and Rathenau. A para-military home guard — the *Einwohnerwehr* — was also expanded and strengthened under von Kahr's benevolent protection.

[2] Since the funds of the *Reichswehr* were not sufficient to meet the full cost of these new formations, the main expenses were met by voluntary donations from the heavy industries and the agrarian groups, who placed the necessary sums at Buchrucker's disposal.

This revival of Scharnhorst's famous *Krümper* system,[1] of which the Prussian, if not the Reich, Government was fully cognizant,[2] might have proved more successful could it have been maintained on a purely secret military basis, but its leaders took it upon themselves to revive the horrors of the medieval *Femegerichte* (Secret Courts)[3] for the punishment of those who were suspected of denouncing their activities to the Reich Disarmament Authorities or to the Allied Control Commission. A series of brutal murders resulted in criminal trials in which the disclosures made during the proceedings attracted the most unwelcome attention of the press to the existence and exploits of what became known as the 'Black Reichswehr'.

In the course of these trials it was more than once alleged by counsel — and the allegations were taken up and repeated in the radical and pacifist press — that these hired bravoes of the 'Black Reichswehr' were really only acting under the guidance and instructions of their masters in the Bendlerstrasse, and that, as Carl von Ossietzky wrote in *Die Weltbühne* of the Schulz case, 'Lieutenant Schulz (charged with the murder of informers against the "Black Reichswehr") did nothing but carry out the orders given him, and that certainly Colonel von Bock, and probably Colonel von Schleicher

[1] See above, p. 7, footnote.

[2] A definite agreement was negotiated between von Seeckt and the Prussian Ministry of Interior for the organization of this new and secret army which was primarily designed to protect the eastern frontier of Germany against a sudden attack by Polish volunteer forces or similar groups. This agreement has been tacitly admitted, by both Otto Braun, who was Social Democrat Prussian Premier almost continuously from 1921–32 and Carl Severing, also a Social Democrat, who served as Prussian Minister of Interior from 1920–26 and 1930–32 and as Minister of Interior in the Reich Cabinet from 1928–30. When giving evidence as defence witness for Grand-Admiral Raeder before the International Military Tribunal at Nuremberg on May 21, 1946, Severing made the following statement: 'That the army of 100,000 men granted to Germany was not sufficient even for a defensive war was and is known to-day possibly to everyone in Germany concerned with politics. Germany got into a very bad situation with regard to her eastern neighbours since the establishment of the Corridor. The insular position of East Prussia forced Germany, even at that time (1920–22), to take measures which I reluctantly helped to carry out' (*Official Record of the International Military Tribunal*, xiv (Nuremberg, 1948), p. 250. See also Carl Severing, *Mein Lebensweg* (Cologne, 1950), i, 303-7, and Otto Braun, pp. 265-6).

[3] The Secret Courts — or *Femegerichte* — of which Sir Walter Scott wrote in *Anne of Geierstein*, were an important element in German criminal law in the later Middle Ages, at a time when lawlessness among the feudal barons had rendered the Imperial courts impotent. They were operated by 'holy bands' of men, sworn to the utmost secrecy, who dispensed, by means of a system of terror, a brutal but efficient form of justice. The courts became so strong, especially in Westphalia, and sought to usurp so much of the function of government that the Emperor and the petty princes took joint action for their suppression, and by the end of the sixteenth century they had largely disappeared.

and General von Seeckt, should be sitting in the dock beside him.'[1]

There was at once a clamour of denial and exculpation. In the *Reichstag*, Otto Gessler, the Defence Minister, when questioned, declared that he not only knew nothing about the activities of the 'Black Reichswehr' but that such a body had never existed, and when his interpellators seemed unsatisfied with this reply, he shouted to them, in his broad Bavarian accent, that 'he who speaks of the "Black Reichswehr" commits an act of high treason'. Whether in a fit of temper or due to genuine *naïveté*, Gessler had been betrayed into committing the indiscretion of speaking the truth. The 'Black Reichswehr' were engaged in the secret business of the rearmament of Germany : mention, let alone criticism, of their activities was, therefore, in violation of the vital interests of the State ; in fact, high treason. It was for this reason that von Bock and von Schleicher and von Hammerstein all vehemently denied in court — for they were more than once summoned as witnesses — that the Bendler-strasse had either known of, or condoned, the activities of the 'Black Reichswehr', whom they characterized as a pack of 'military Bolsheviks'.

Von Seeckt, however, was more straightforward. In a letter to the President of the Supreme Court of Berlin, which was accompanied by a request that it should be withheld from publication, he admitted the existence of the 'Black Reichswehr' but argued that a court of law could not appreciate the extraordinary circumstances which had led to its formation. It was essential in the interests of the Reich that the measures adopted for its protection be kept secret. Normal and ordinary means for combating treason could not be applied under such circumstances and '. . . the members of the *Arbeits-Kommandos* could very well have held the view that

---

[1] Carl von Ossietzky (1887–1938), a member of an aristocratic Prussian Catholic family, was married to the daughter of a British General. His experiences as an officer in the First World War rendered him a convinced and ardent pacifist, and for the remainder of his life he devoted himself to the struggle against militarism. As the editor of the leading German radical weekly, *Die Weltbühne*, he was a permanent thorn in the side of the Bendlerstrasse, who recognized in him one of their most dangerous opponents. Arrested by the Brüning Government on a charge of high treason for exposing certain of the clandestine violations of the Treaty of Versailles, he was tried before the Reich Supreme Court and condemned on November 23, 1931, to eighteen months' imprisonment. Released under the Christmas Amnesty of 1932, he refused to leave the country and was rearrested by Storm Troopers on the night of the *Reichstag* fire, February 27, 1933, when he was consigned to a concentration camp. Much to Hitler's rage, von Ossietzky was awarded the Nobel Peace Prize in 1935, with the result that all German citizens were forbidden by law to accept future Nobel awards. Worn out by maltreatment and persecution, he died in hospital in Berlin on May 4, 1938.

it was in the interests of the country to deal summarily with traitors.' [1]

The episode of the 'Black Reichswehr' was the least creditable in von Seeckt's career. To rearm the Reich illegally in defiance of the Treaty of Versailles may be explained on the grounds of patriotic motives. It was not, for example, held to be a crime within the terms of its Charter by the International Military Tribunal at Nuremberg. To arraign those who exposed such illegal rearmament before the courts on charges of high treason is possibly understandable if one accepts the patriotic motives behind such rearmament. But to condone the murder of those whose patriotic motives, though of a different calibre, were none the less sincere, is inexcusable, and it is well for the prestige and military honour of Hans von Seeckt that his reputation as a soldier rests on other and surer grounds.

(iii)

The secret of von Seeckt's political and military genius was his ability to take a long view. Like Lenin, he appreciated the technique of the strategic retreat in politics for the purpose of the ultimate achievement of the greater objective ; the seeming abandonment of an immediate and segmentary aim in deference to the desire and pursuit of the whole. Von Seeckt knew, like Alexander I at Tilsit and Lenin after Brest-Litovsk, that what his Army urgently required was a *peredyshka*, a breathing space, in which to reorganize and consolidate its own position within the Reich, to the end that it might later play the decisive rôle in the restoration of Germany as a Great Power (*Machtstaat*). For, like Scharnhorst and Gneisenau in 1807, this was the goal which von Seeckt had set for his selfless ambition, and to attain this goal he was prepared to subordinate all lesser interests, however ephemerally important they might appear.

Himself a devoted monarchist, he realized from the first that the restoration of the Monarchy was among those things which

---

[1] First-hand information on the 'Black Reichswehr' is exceedingly difficult to obtain since, on the evidence of both Buchrucker and von Bock, the relations between them were always verbal ; nothing was ever put in writing. Von Rabenau is diplomatically silent on the subject. Buchrucker, however, after his dismissal and arrest in connection with the Küstrin Mutiny of 1923 (see below, p. 111 *et seq.*) wrote a book, *Im Schatten Seeckts, die Geschichte der Schwarzen Reichswehr* (Berlin, 1928), in which he gives his side of the story. This the present writer has consulted, with such other sources as Gessler's memorandum of March 2, 1926, to the *Reichstag* Commission of Enquiry on the *Feme* Murders, and Buchrucker's counter-memorandum ; Alfred Apfel, *Behind the Scenes of German Justice, 1882–1933* (London, 1935), pp. 84-104 ; E. J. Gumbel, pp. 165-256 ; von Oertzen, pp. 458-69 ; Grzescinski, pp. 91-6 ; and Benoist-Méchin, ii, 262-78.

must be temporarily jettisoned. In the long run it was the unity
of the Reich and the restoration of German power that mattered,
not the trappings and forms of the State. Von Seeckt was no
impractical visionary, he was a stark realist; he knew that to
achieve his eventual design, he must use the tools which were
immediately to his hand. The German Reich was, at any rate for
the present, a Republic; therefore the Republic must be strong,
but strong in the sense in which von Seeckt desired. It must be
strong in the sense that within it there must be one ultimate source
of power, and only one — the Army; and to achieve this supreme
political position, the Army must be withdrawn from politics and
from the disruptive influence of political controversy.

Under the leadership of von Seeckt the Bendlerstrasse turned
its back upon sterile political ambitions, upon facile patriotic indignation and barren military adventures. The brains of the Army
were concentrated upon the all-important task of its own internal
reconstruction. Von Seeckt himself withheld his own thoughts from
all but his most trusted collaborators. To the world he presented
a front of ironic silence, which earned him the nickname of 'the
Sphinx'.[1]

'The Army serves the State; it is above party.' This was the
political basis of the new *Reichswehr*. All forms of political activity,
participation in any political organization or in any political gathering, were strictly forbidden to both officers and men. Even the
constitutional right of the soldiers to vote as citizens in parliamentary
elections was suspended during their period of service. When von
Seeckt did a thing he did it thoroughly.

On the other hand, no effort was spared to retain in veneration
and in actual practice, the ancient traditions of Prussian military
glory. As von Seeckt had written : 'The chains of Versailles which
curtailed Germany's freedom of action must not be allowed to bind
her spirit.' A dual target was presented to the *Reichswehr* by its
Chief — to achieve the highest pitch of technical efficiency within
the restrictions imposed by the Treaty of Versailles, and so to
circumvent those restrictions *in petto* that, on the dawning of
'The Day', the German Army might arise phoenix-like and fully
prepared.

Of primary concern was the conservation of the spirit and the
essence of the German General Staff, specifically and explicitly
dissolved and prohibited by the Treaty of Versailles. For without
the survival of this palladium, the brain and genius of the Army

---

[1] 'General into fox' was Lord D'Abernon's unofficial comment on von Seeckt.

would wither and atrophy.[1] This had been uppermost in von Seeckt's mind from the beginning and his aims are clearly apparent from his letter to Hindenburg of July 7, 1919, on the occasion of his succeeding the Marshal as Chief of the General Staff : 'If I succeed in preserving, not the form but the spirit, then I shall be able to see in my work something more than merely the burial of the General Staff'.[2] Very shortly thereafter, in his first Order of the Day as Chief of the General Staff, he gave the same message to his subordinates : 'The form changes, but the spirit remains as of old. It is the spirit of silent, selfless devotion to duty in the service of the Army. General Staff officers remain anonymous.'[3]

Von Seeckt's earliest activities after assuming the Presidency of the Commission for the Organization of the Peace Army had been directed toward the establishment of the *Truppenamt* of the Defence Ministry as a disguised and camouflaged form of General Staff. To this homogeneous group of anonymous toilers for the military renaissance of the Reich, von Seeckt was nominated the First Chief (July 9, 1919). From that day forward he and his successors worked unceasingly to train and prepare a cadre of Staff officers who, in the fullness of time should guide the fortunes of a greater and mighty army. The *Generalstabsoffiziermentalität* was carefully preserved and cherished. Under the very noses of the Allied Commission of Control, the training of Staff Officers proceeded in the seven *Wehrkreise* of the Reich, as well as in the Ministry of Defence. In addition, courses and tests in military science and general culture were established at the universities, in order to replace, in a hidden form, the lectures and examinations of the War Academy.

The true worth and meaning of these secret activities was disclosed when in 1935, Germany, having made unilateral denunciation of the military clauses of the Treaty of Versailles, the then head of the *Truppenamt*, General Ludwig Beck, was at once appointed Chief of the newly constituted General Staff.[4]

[1] The necessity for retaining the spirit of the General Staff *in esse* was recognized even by civilians. The famous sociologist, Max Weber, who had been a member of the German Peace Commission to Versailles and had sat as a Democrat in the National Assembly, confided to one of his pupils, shortly after the ratification of the treaty by the Assembly on July 16, 1919, that he had no further political plans, 'except to concentrate all my intellectual strength on the one problem, how to get once more for Germany a Great General Staff' (Gustav Stolper, *This Age of Fable* (London, 1943), p. 276 ; J. P. Mayer, *Max Weber and German Politics* (London, 1944), p. 82).

[2] Rabenau, ii, 188.   [3] *Ibid.* ii, 193.

[4] In 1936 Beck, in an oration at the funeral of General Wever, openly admitted that 'in the days of the old *Reichswehr*, the *Truppenamt* had filled the rôle of the Great General Staff' (Benoist-Méchin, ii, 127, footnote 2) and von Seeckt's official

As with the General Staff so with the Officer Corps. In choosing his original four thousand officers allowed to the *Reichswehr* under the treaty, von Seeckt paid meticulous attention to their selection. He had plenty of material but not all of it was of desirable quality. In his first Order of the Day [1] he had lain down the fundamental requirements which he demanded from his officers, and in the months that followed he chose accordingly. Disregarding the *Landsknecht* characters who had followed Kapp and von Lüttwitz, he singled out moderate and responsible types who were capable of adapting themselves not only to modern methods of warfare but to the modern conditions of society in which they had to live. No longer the darling of society, the officer was now forced to maintain himself in a world which had little sympathy for his calling or outlook, and he was, therefore, essentially dependent upon the real spirit of his professional tradition.

Under the treaty the period of service of officers was fixed at twenty-five years, and this provision had been deliberately aimed at preventing the rapid recruitment and expansion of an Officer Corps. Von Seeckt met this difficulty in numerous ways ; partly by training his officers in the Prussian Police Force.[2] But he was quick to take advantage of an oversight on the part of the framers of the treaty which placed no restriction on the number of N.C.O.s permitted to the *Reichswehr*. Here was an admirable opportunity to build up a masked reserve of 'officer material', and he at once seized upon it. At one moment there were 40,000 non-commissioned officers in an army limited by treaty to 96,000 'other ranks', and of these a considerable proportion, having been selected by their regimental commanders as men of proved 'National' reliability, were being trained as a cadre of 'aspirant' officers.[3] In this way, the basis of selection of officers by their regimental commanders, which had been so salient a feature of the Officer Corps in the Old Army, was carried over into the New. Particular efforts were made to attract the sons of the aristocracy and the military caste for service

---

biographer, writing during the Second World War, paid equal tribute to the work of the organization. 'It would', he said, 'have been extremely difficult to accomplish the work of 1935 to 1939 if the directive departments (*Führungsstellen*) of the Army had been maintained in proportion to its insignificant size between 1920 and 1934' (Rabenau, ii, 449).   [1] See above, p. 90.

[2] The Prussian Police were a highly efficient and semi-militarized force of some 85,000 men, equipped with armoured cars, heavy machine-guns and pistols in addition to the very effective rubber truncheon (*Gummiknüppel*). Enlisted, like the *Reichswehr*, for a period of twelve years, more than a third of its members lived in barracks and carried out collective military training. Other German Federal States had similar organizations, though in general they were less efficient.

[3] Morgan, p. 122.

as N.C.O.s, and ultimately as officers, and so successful was this policy that, of the Officer Corps of the *Reichswehr* in 1921, 23 per cent were members of the aristocracy, that is to say, 1 per cent higher than in the Imperial Army of 1913.[1]

The same scrupulous care was exercised in recruiting the rank and file. Compulsory service having been abolished, both by the provisional *Reichswehr* Law of March 6, 1919, and by the Peace Treaty, every citizen of the Reich, who was over seventeen years old and able-bodied, was, in theory, free to offer himself for voluntary enlistment, whatever his religion, his social position, his profession or his political opinion might be. In practice, however, great attention was paid to all four of these factors. Jews and those suspected of Leftist tendencies in politics were lumped together as 'Marxists' and excluded. Recruits from industrial and urban areas were also in the main discouraged. Preference was given to the sons of peasant families and of former N.C.O.s, who might reasonably be supposed to have been imbued with the proper principles of conduct and therefore free from any undesirable political taint.

This method of careful selection and subsequent pruning resulted in a rank and file which was not only politically (or 'non-politically') reliable but which also enjoyed so great an increase in its educational and social levels that an appreciable number were not inferior to their officers.[2] Moreover, with more than 60 millions as a reservoir from which to draw some 8,000 volunteers per year, it was possible to maintain the standard of bodily fitness at a very high level; only the most perfect specimens were accepted. The net result was an army with physical and intellectual criteria unachievable in any force based upon conscription.

An inevitable outcome of these new conditions was the revision of the relationship between officer and man. The days of social segregation and of brutal oppression were dead upon the fields of Flanders. The break-down of the contact between officers and their troops in the autumn of 1918 had been a hideous revelation to all and a warning to those who were prepared to learn from it. Though von Seeckt had not observed these things himself, he had heard

---

[1] Benoist-Méchin, i, 199, footnote 2. Another statistical enquiry, grouping the officers according to the social background of their fathers, shows that in 1930 95.1 per cent came from strata which before the First World War would have been considered 'eligible' and only 4.9 per cent, or some 200 in all, from social groups hitherto excluded from the officer ranks (Rosinski, p. 186).

[2] In 1930 no less than 9 per cent of the 96,000 non-commissioned officers and men in the *Reichswehr* had been to a secondary school; 3 per cent, or approximately 2,900 had reached the *Einjährige*; and 1 per cent, or nearly 1,000, had matriculated (Rosinski, p. 186).

and read the reports of his colleagues, and from the first he had been determined not to allow a similar gulf to develop in the New Army. The young officer of the *Reichswehr*, therefore, was most emphatically instructed in the necessity of gaining the confidence and comradeship of his men without forfeiting his personal authority or loosening the bonds of essential discipline.

But if von Seeckt was prepared to abolish the evil usages of the Old Army, no one was more alive than he to the value of military tradition. It was one of the fundamental bases of his reorganization. Everything was done to link the New Army ideologically with the Old in all that was inspiring and glorious. In memory of the Great War — the outcome of which was represented not as a defeat but as a betrayal — the field grey and the steel helmet of the Imperial Army were retained as the uniform of the *Reichswehr*. To each company or battery or squadron of the New Army was allocated the duty of maintaining the tradition and honour of one of the now disbanded Imperial regiments, to carry on its peculiar customs and usages, and to keep contact with its former officers, non-commissioned officers and men.

This system had two advantages, one mystical, the other practical. On the one hand, it linked the volunteers of 1920 with the tradition of glory which ran like a thread of gold from the Great Elector and the Old Fritz, through Scharnhorst, Gneisenau and Blücher, to Moltke and to Schlieffen and to Hindenburg. This was the glory which had transcended the disasters of Kolin [1] and of Jena and had overcome the humiliation of Tilsit. It was now called upon to survive an even greater disaster and to evade even more severe restrictions. This glorious heritage, the young recruit was taught, was as much his as it was the old Imperial Army's, and it must inspire him to maintain it intact and unsullied. The battle for Germany's military honour was unending.

So much for the mystical and ideological value of the *Traditionsträger* system, but it also had its material advantages. In effect, it meant that, when the Great Day dawned and von Seeckt's dreams came true — just as each senior officer of his army 'in little' could command a division and each junior officer a battalion ; just as each N.C.O. was a potential officer and each private a potential

---

[1] In June 1758 Frederick the Great was resoundingly defeated at Kolin, a town on the Elbe in eastern Bohemia, by the Austrian Army under Marshal Daun. As a result of this disaster it was widely believed in the chancelleries of Europe that the War, begun in the previous August, would now be concluded with the humiliation of Prussia. Frederick, however, retrieved his fortunes, defied the Grand Alliance and continued to wage what became the Seven Years War, from which he emerged as victor.

N.C.O. — so each unit, already a nuclear force, could expand with comparative speed and facility into the full regimental structure of which it was now but the blue-print.[1]

But von Seeckt's prophetic soul went further. Both as a military historian and a proved master of strategy, he believed implicitly in the Prussian tradition of mobility, which von Falkenhayn had allowed himself to abandon in favour of trench warfare. The planner of the 'break-through' at Soissons and of the greater 'break-through' at Gorlice held fast to the belief that decisive annihilation can only be achieved in the supremacy of the attack over the defence in rapidity and facility of movement. 'The mistake lies', he wrote, 'in opposing an immobile and almost defenceless human mass to the brutal action of material. . . . Material is superior to the living, mortal human mass, but it is not superior to the living and immortal human mind.'[2] The war of the future must be for Germany a war of movement, and on this theory von Seeckt based his strategic concepts and his tactical training. The technique of the modern mechanized army, developed later in theory by General Fuller and de Gaulle and perfected in practice by Guderian, was originally conceived by von Seeckt when in 1921 he wrote his famous memorandum on 'Basic Ideas for the Reconstruction of our Armed Forces' (*Grundlegende Gedanken für den Wiederaufbau unserer Wehrmacht*),[3] in which he stressed the necessity of attaining technical superiority by uniting modern military science with modern military preparation. 'The whole future of warfare appears to me to be in the employment of mobile armies, relatively small but of high quality, and rendered distinctly more effective by the addition of aircraft, and in the simultaneous mobilization of the whole defence force, be it to feed the attack or for home defence.'[4]

Thus, with 'quality not quantity' as his guidon, von Seeckt proceeded to organize the new German Army; an army, as he said, not of mercenaries, but of leaders (*nicht ein Söldnerheer, sondern ein Führerheer*). Conserving what was of value from the past, combining it with the exigencies of to-day and with the visions of to-morrow, he succeeded in creating, qualitatively speaking, the finest army in the world. Much of his achievement lay within the

[1] For this remarkable army of 100,000, there was a budgetary provision for 670 senior ranking officers out of the 4,000 permitted by the treaty. Of these there were 55 Generals, 3 Divisional Commanders, 9 Army Inspectors with the rank of General and 123 Colonels. In addition 300 officers were employed in the *Reichswehr* Ministry (Grzesinski, p. 93).
[2] Seeckt, *Thoughts of a Soldier*, p. 59.
[3] Rabenau, ii, 474-5.
[4] *Thoughts of a Soldier*, p. 62.

letter, if not the spirit, of the Treaty of Versailles, but much, as will be seen, was done in violation of the Treaty.[1]

The weapon which he forged fulfilled in every sense his own definition of the Army as a 'State within a State'. Its loyalty was essentially, first and foremost to the Reich and not necessarily to the Republic, which von Seeckt regarded as a transient political phenomenon destined in time to give place, if not to a restored Monarchy, at any rate to something considerably more conservative than the Weimar structure. Nevertheless, while the maintenance of the unity of the Reich demanded the defence of the Republic, he was prepared to use the *Reichswehr* to defend it, and this was clearly seen in his line of conduct during the crucial months of 1923–4.

(iv)

The year 1923 was one of testing not only for the *Reichswehr* but for the whole political structure and national unity of the Reich. At no time between the First and Second World Wars was Germany so beset simultaneously by intervention from without and dissension from within. For the better part of a year it seemed that at any moment the flimsy edifice of the Weimar Republic would disintegrate at the first breath of treason, to be replaced by a monarchy, a military junta or a Communist dictatorship. That this did not happen is largely attributable to the conduct of Hans von Seeckt, in whose hands the destinies of Germany rested for a twelvemonth and who had other designs for her than to precipitate her dismemberment and disunity on the grounds of petty political issues.

At the close of the previous year the Cabinet of Cuno [2] had come

---

[1] It must be admitted that von Seeckt's ability to create bricks without straw — or, alternatively, to provide his own straw for brick-making — was recognized by certain individuals in the Allied countries. Brigadier-General J. H. Morgan cried an unheeded warning in Britain, and in France M. Jacques Bainville, in *L'Action Française*, and M. Auguste Gauvain, in *Le Journal des Débats*, were equally Cassandra-like in their forebodings. M. Gauvain was particularly prescient. Writing on July 4, 1919, in reference to Mr. Lloyd George's defence of the decision of the Big Three to allow Germany a professicnal army of 100,000 men instead of the 200,000 short-term troops originally agreed upon, M. Gauvain said : 'We are profoundly convinced that this change was a serious blunder, and that the hundred thousand professionals will constitute the cadre of a dangerous force'.

[2] Wilhelm Cuno (1876–1933), a Catholic, a member of the German People's Party, and managing director of the Hamburg-Amerika Line, had been summoned by Ebert, on the fall of the Wirth Ministry, in November 1922, to form a non-party Cabinet not based on a parliamentary majority and responsible only to the President. In this Cabinet of experts, Friedrich Rosen, a professional diplomat, was Foreign Minister, and Helfferich the financial 'genius' behind the scenes. Cuno's great achievement was not, however, in politics but in the

forward with, in one hand, a request for a four-year moratorium on all reparation payments other than deliveries in kind, and, in the other, a proposal for an undertaking between Great Britain, France, Italy, and Germany to renounce war between themselves for a period of thirty years.[1] M. Poincaré, on behalf of France, rejected the first of these approaches as unacceptable even as a basis of discussion, and the second as 'a clever manœuvre', and demanded Allied action to enforce the Reparation Clauses of the treaty. The British Government, however, was disposed to consider a reduction of the total amount of Germany's reparation obligations, and the inevitable clash occurred at the Allied Conference in Paris on January 4. Mr. Bonar Law and the British delegation withdrew from the meeting, whereupon M. Poincaré declared that France had recovered her full freedom of action for ensuring the execution of the Peace Treaty. His opportunity to exercise this regained liberty occurred within a week, when on January 9 the Reparation Commission declared Germany to be in default in respect of her deliveries of coal and timber. Two days later French and Belgian troops entered the Ruhr.

The Cuno Government at once responded with a declaration to the world that France and Belgium had openly broken the Treaty of Versailles by their independent action. Germany, said the Chancellor, with the official approval and support of President Ebert, was unable to defend herself against an unjust use of force, but she would not submit to this breach of international law. He called for a general cessation of work throughout the Ruhr and declared that as long as the French and Belgian occupation continued, Germany would be unable to make any reparation payments or deliveries to the Powers.[2]

This declaration of 'passive resistance' resulted in a pronouncement by the Reparation Commission that Germany was now in general default [3] and in a counter-declaration by the French and Belgian Governments of their intention to remain in occupation of the Ruhr until Germany fulfilled her reparation obligations (March 14).[4]

restoration of the Hamburg-Amerika Line, and of German shipping as a whole, to the position which it had held before the First World War.

[1] Cuno's request for a moratorium was made on November 14, his offer of a peace pact followed on December 18.

[2] Text in *Belgian Grey Book, Documents diplomatiques relatifs aux Réparations* (*26 décembre 1922–27 août 1923*), No. 9, p. 16.

[3] The vote in the Reparation Commission both on January 9 and January 26 was not unanimous. The British representative, Sir John Bradbury, dissented on both occasions. (See Reparation Commission Communiqués, Nos. 186 and 191.)

[4] *Belgian Grey Book*, No. 16, p. 20.

Thus by the third month of 1923 a complete *impasse* had developed, with public opinion in both France and Germany in firm support of the action taken by their respective Governments. In Paris, Poincaré received overwhelming votes of confidence in the Chamber and enjoyed a laudatory press ; in Germany, Cuno's policy of passive resistance united the country as it had not been united since the publication of the Allied peace terms in May 1919. From Right to Left what came to be called the *Ruhrkampf* was acclaimed as a holy war ; Cuno also got his votes of confidence.

Both sides fought the *Ruhrkampf* with all means short of open hostilities. The Germans interpreted 'passive' resistance to include active sabotage, the blowing up of trains, jamming of signal-points, etc. The French responded by arresting trade-union leaders and industrial magnates alike and by shooting the *saboteurs*. In May a court martial sentenced Gustav Krupp von Bohlen und Halbach, his board of directors and his works manager, to terms of imprisonment varying from twenty years to six months, and in the same month Leo Schlageter was executed by the French military authorities for sabotage and industrial espionage.[1]

The French and Belgian Governments, moreover, seized upon the long-sought opportunity to detach the Rhineland permanently from the Reich by open support of Separatist Movements in their respective zones. The 'Rhineland Republic' was proclaimed at Aachen and the 'Autonomous Government of the Palatinate' at Speyer, and these bodies were formally recognized by Paris and Brussels and by the Rhineland High Commission, against the vote of the British representative, Lord Kilmarnock.[2]

By the summer of 1923, however, the position had reached a stalemate. The French and Belgians had found the task of 'digging coal with bayonets' to be unproductive of economic results. The

---

[1] Leo Schlageter, a young ex-officer of the Imperial Army, who had fought with the *Freikorps* in the Baltic and in Upper Silesia, was operating in the Ruhr as a member of the Heinz Organization, which was actively engaged in sabotage. His execution was seized upon by the Nationalists, and later by the Nazis, as an example of patriotic martyrdom and was the subject of plays, films and numerous books, one of which was translated into English with an introduction by Ernst von Salomon, a man implicated in the murder of Rathenau (Friedrich Glombowski, *Frontiers of Terror: The Fate of Schlageter and his Comrades* (London, 1935).

[2] These 'spontaneously' created separatist Governments, which were, in effect, completely 'Quisling' in character, did not long survive the withdrawal of French and Belgian support at the termination of the 'Ruhr Incident'. The President of the 'Autonomous Government of the Palatinate', Herr Heinz, was assassinated at Speyer on January 6, 1924, and the other Separatist leaders soon took refuge in France. One of them, Dr. Adam Dorten — 'pretty Addi' as he was nicknamed in the Rhineland — subsequently published an account of the Separatist movement, *La Tragédie rhénane* (Paris, 1945).

Germans, for their part, had lost the 'first fine careless rapture' of defiance and were faced with the hideous prospect of national bankruptcy. The mark, which on the morning of the occupation of the Ruhr (January 11) had stood at 50,000 to the pound sterling, was 250,000 at the end of January and continued to fall catastrophically. In June it was half a million to the pound; in July a million and a half; in August twenty million. Passive resistance had become a disastrously expensive form of national immolation, and it was evident that capitulation could not be long postponed. 'It comes to this', said the Foreign Minister, Rosen, to the British Ambassador, Lord D'Abernon, on August 7, 'the alternative is chaos with honour or chaos with dishonour.' He added that neither the Chancellor nor he 'would run away or give in'; they would remain at their posts and carry out their policy 'until we are cut to pieces'.[1] This final sacrifice, however, was not required of them. The Cuno Cabinet fell five days later and Ebert called upon Stresemann to form a government.

Gustav Stresemann had come a long way since the war-time period when, as the spokesman of Hindenburg and Ludendorff in the *Reichstag*, he had thundered in support of annexationist claims and jingo policies. He had even travelled far since the last days of the Kapp *Putsch* when he had sought to find a face-saving formula for the fallen and discredited 'Dictator'.[2] He was still at heart a monarchist[3] and a Conservative, but, like von Seeckt, he had realized that, if Germany was to be restored to a position of greatness and power among the nations, it must be through the existing republican structure and in collaboration with the rest of Europe. What the policy of Germany would be once she had been thus restored to the status of a *Machtstaat*, was another matter. That eventuality lay within the womb of time. What mattered immediately was the preservation of the unity of the Reich, now sorely menaced by internal dissension and economic disaster. The deadlock in the Ruhr must be broken; normal relations with the Powers must be restored, and for this a necessary prerequisite was the

---

[1] Viscount D'Abernon, *An Ambassador of Peace* (London, 1929–30), ii, 226-7.
[2] See above, p. 80.
[3] Like many Germans of the successful upper middle-class Stresemann had a certain *snobbismus* in regard to royalty. He was proud of his familiarity with the members of the royal house of Prussia and liked being referred to by them familiarly as 'Onkel Gustav'. He kept in correspondence with the German Crown Prince, whom he visited in exile at Wieringen in Holland in 1921 and to whom he was about to pay a second visit in the summer of 1923 when he was called upon to become Chancellor. With the approval of his Cabinet colleagues, including the Social Democrats, Stresemann permitted and facilitated the return of the Crown Prince in November 1923 to permanent residence at his estate near Oels in Silesia.

abandonment of passive resistance. Stresemann was ready to make this gesture — in reality, it was relieving Germany of an unendurable encumbrance — provided that the terms of surrender were honourable, and led to counter-concessions by the French in the shape of a return to the *status quo ante*. If this were forthcoming he was prepared to make a fresh start on a new basis — the basis not of Obstinate Resistance but of Fulfilment (*Erfüllung*).

Stresemann had at last realized the truth which, in the field of military policy, had been revealed to Gröner and to von Seeckt long before. If Germany was to be great again she must be strong, and to be strong she must have a period of peace and recuperation, and peace would not be forthcoming until the fears and suspicions of the Allies had been, at any rate to some extent, allayed. Both von Seeckt and Stresemann had turned their backs upon the glamorous but unattainable dreams of monarchist restoration and Conservative dictatorship. They had decided to use the democratic and republican form of government provided by the Weimar Constitution as a convincing weapon in their campaign of reassurance to the West. Though neither of them was a sincere Republican, they were both deeply sincere in their several efforts to rehabilitate and protect the Republic. What both believed in and laboured for was the future greatness and might of Germany, an aim which transcended all lesser causes and minor loyalties. The best instrument to their hand for this purpose was the Weimar Republic, and to this political organism — as representing the Reich — each gave, at least temporarily, his loyalty — even at the risk of assassination.

This is not to suggest that they were always in harmonious accord on all issues. In the early days, at any rate, Stresemann was profoundly suspicious of the *Reichswehr* in general and of von Seeckt personally, while the General was never a believer in the Stresemann policy of appeasement in the West. Von Seeckt mistrusted the efficacy of any agreement entered into with the French, who, he was convinced, desired the complete destruction of Germany. He was an 'Easterner' in foreign policy and was unmoved by the menace of Bolshevism, seeing in Russia a powerful, if unscrupulous, ally.

Nevertheless, the fact remains that when in August 1923 Stresemann reached his great decision to abandon passive resistance and to bring the *Ruhrkampf* to a close, he took the first step along the road to the Dawes and Young Plans, Locarno and the League of Nations, the Kellogg Pact and the final realization of his dream — though he did not live to see it attained — the evacuation of the Rhineland by Allied troops a full five years before the treaty date

for the end of the occupation.[1]   At each step along this road Stresemann extracted material concessions for Germany from the Western
Powers while giving very little of practical value in return.   Yet so
skilfully did he win his points that confidence and trust in Germany
were completely re-established in the financial and political circles of
Britain and the United States, from whom Stresemann successfully
contrived to keep France isolated.   And behind this diplomatic front
von Seeckt perfected his military foundation for the Greater Germany
of the future.

But in the summer of 1923 all these triumphs were unforeseen
and perhaps undreamed of.   Stresemann's momentous decision in
respect of passive resistance was fraught with danger.   Though his
views on the necessity of abandoning this policy were by this time
shared by the leaders of all parties making up his 'Grand Coalition',[2]
they were bitterly opposed by the two parties outside the Government, the Nationalists and the Communists.   These Radicals of the
Right and Left were the implacable inner enemies of the Republic
and, each with their own political ends in view, sought to utilize
the chaos, which the continuation of passive resistance would inevitably entail, to destroy the Weimar Structure and to replace it
by a reactionary junta or a dictatorship of the proletariat.   Each
Party therefore, both within the *Reichstag* and, through their allies
in other parts of Germany — the Nationalists in the Prussian and
Bavarian Diets, and the Communists in the Saxon Government —
denounced the idea of abandoning passive resistance as treasonable
to national honour, as a betrayal of the Ruhr workers, and as an
unwarranted and pusillanimous surrender to 'a half-sated irre-
concilable France'.

[1] Under Articles 428 and 429 of the Treaty of Versailles the Western Rhineland
was divided into three zones of occupation by Allied troops as a guarantee of the
execution of the treaty. If the conditions of the treaty were faithfully carried out
the first zone was to be evacuated at the end of five years (*i.e.* by January 1925),
the second by January 1930 and the third by January 1935. At the beginning of
1925 the Allies were not satisfied that Germany had complied satisfactorily with
the disarmament clauses of the treaty and evacuation of the First Zone was
therefore postponed. Stresemann, however, secured from the Western Allies
their consent to the beginning of the evacuation of this Zone being made coincident
with the signing of the Locarno Agreement in London on December 5, 1925. His
second triumph in this respect was achieved at the Hague Conference of 1929
when, by an agreement formally signed on August 31, British troops were withdrawn
from the Second Zone by the end of that year and French troops from the Third
Zone by June 1930. This document was the last international agreement to be
signed by Stresemann. He died on October 3, 1929.
[2] Stresemann's 'Cabinet of a Hundred Days' (August-November 1923) was
based on the Centre, the Social Democrats, the Democrats and the German
People's Party. He himself was Foreign Minister.

E

It was clear to Stresemann that, as and when the Government made public their decision, they must be prepared to meet the worst from their political opponents, and the worst might well mean armed resistance, attempted secession and consequent civil war. Under these circumstances they must look for support and salvation to the inevitable ultimate source of strength, the *Reichswehr*. But Stresemann was not yet wholly trustful of von Seeckt and he would not accept the assurance of Otto Gessler, his Minister of Defence, that the Army would give its unqualified support to the Republic.[1]

The Chancellor need have had no such apprehension. This was von Seeckt's great opportunity to justify his theory of an Army above politics acting as the guardian of the State, and he had no intention of missing it. Throughout the *Ruhrkampf* he had watched and waited, appreciating with his rare political intuition the advantage accruing to Germany from an obvious division between her former enemies, Britain and France, and restraining those military hot-heads who, by acts of national patriotic insanity, would have precipitated an armed conflict in which Germany must have been defeated.[2] Now, however, the situation was radically changed. The Reich — that word in which he found something 'supernatural' — was menaced by inner dissension and political disunity. In such a juncture von Seeckt had no difficulty in seeing where his duty, and that of the Army, lay. It was to prevent civil war, to enforce respect for the needs of the State and to preserve the unity of the Reich, yet, withal, maintaining its aloof status above all parties.

Once before in a meeting of the Reich Cabinet he had declared : 'Gentlemen, no one but I in Germany can make a *Putsch*, and I assure you I shall make none',[3] and now he was as good as his word. When in September 1923 the fanatical Pan-German Nationalist Heinrich Class invited him to make common cause with the Patriotic Associations and place himself at the head of a military dictatorship, he replied with vehemence : 'What you propose to me is a violation of the Constitution, an act of sedition. I tell you I will fight to the last shot against the revolutionaries of the Right as well as against those of the Left. The rôle of the *Reichswehr*

---

[1] 'Gessler's opinion of the unconditional loyalty of the *Reichswehr* to the State as at present constituted seems to me unjustified optimism in the face of the attitude of the officers and the rank and file', Stresemann had written to the German Crown Prince on July 23, 1923, shortly before taking office (Eric Sutton, *Gustav Stresemann, His Diaries, Letters and Papers* (London, 1935-40), i, 215).

[2] In the early days of the occupation of the Ruhr a wild plan had been developed by a group of officers headed by General Freiherr von Watter to execute a 'Sicilian Vespers' on the French garrison with 60,000 well-disciplined workers (Rabenau, ii, 326).   [3] *Ibid.* ii, 341.

is to maintain the unity of the Reich, and those who compromise this are its enemies, from whichever side they come.' [1] Thus repulsed, Class and his fellow radicals of the Right retired in bitter disappointment to pursue their plans without the co-operation of the Commander of the *Reichswehr*, and to plot his assassination. [2] But the destined protector of the Reich went fearlessly on his way.

The Reich Cabinet finally decided to proclaim the official cessation of passive resistance on September 26. Very early the next morning, however, news reached Berlin that the Bavarian Council of Ministers, under the presidency of Freiherr Eugen von Knilling, an ardent monarchist, who, though under the impression that he controlled the Patriotic Associations, was, in fact, their tool, had proclaimed a state of emergency, suspended the fundamental rights of the citizens and appointed as State-Commissionary for Bavaria that rabid Bavarian nationalist, Ritter von Kahr, who had become Premier at the time of the Kapp *Putsch*. [3]

A meeting of the Reich Cabinet, which von Seeckt was invited to attend, was hastily summoned in the Chancellor's library. Ebert presided and both he and Stresemann were in a state of nervous excitement. In the early light of dawn the ministers arrived in varying stages of matutinal disarray. Some were unshaved, one had forgotten his neck-tie, all were desperately anxious. The same query was in the minds of everyone. What would the Army do in such a crisis ? And still von Seeckt had not arrived. Suddenly the door of the library was thrown open and, cool and inscrutable, be-monocled and immaculate, the Commander of the *Reichswehr* entered and took his place at the table.

Without delay Ebert put the question directly to him : 'Will the Army stick to us, General ?' And in von Seeckt's answer there was all the pride of centuries of Prussian military tradition, not unmixed with something of that contempt in which Prussian officers held all civilians and politicians : 'The Army, Mr. President, will

[1] Letter of Seeckt to Class, dated September 24, 1923, quoted by Benoist-Méchin (ii, 260).

[2] In the small hours of January 15, 1924, a group of ex-officers, all members of the Patriotic Associations, and former adherents of von Lüttwitz, were arrested in Berlin on a charge of conspiring to assassinate von Seeckt that same day as he took his morning walk in the Tiergarten. During the trial, which took place from May 25–June 5, 1924, many revelations occurred. Both von Seeckt and Class appeared as witnesses, and it was in his evidence that von Seeckt made public the fact that Class had made him a treasonable proposal and that he had rejected it. One of the accused, a Dr. Gottlieb Grandel, described in some detail how, in October 1923, he had been approached by Class with a plan for von Seeckt's assassination. At a later point in the proceedings Grandel retracted this testimony and Class emerged from the trial uninculpated (Gumbel, pp. 155-161).

[3] See above, p. 92, footnote 1.

stick to me' ('*Die Reichswehr, Herr Reichspräsident, steht hinter mir*').[1]
This was possibly the proudest moment of von Seeckt's life,
certainly of his post-war career. It was the direct appeal of the
State to the Army, the acknowledgment of the *Reichswehr* as ultimate guardian of the Reich, the recognition of his claim for the
Army to be 'a State within a State'. The safety of the Reich was
in his hands. Yet his answer to Ebert was not an expression of
personal self-glorification. He was not threatening the President and
his Cabinet. He was exacting no terms, driving no bargain, as had
Gröner in November 1918. What he said was a matter of simple
fact. The Army, non-political and above party, would do what he,
its Commander-in-Chief, ordered it to do, and he, the symbol of
that aloofness from politics, was ready to do what was necessary for
the protection of the Reich.

Ebert and Stresemann recognized the position, accepted it, and
acted accordingly. Later in the day (September 27) the citizens of
the Reich read in their newspapers, side by side with the announcement of the cessation of passive resistance in the Ruhr, a proclamation declaring a State of Emergency (*Ausnahmezustand*)
throughout Germany, under Article 48 of the Constitution,[2] and
the temporary transfer of the executive functions of the Reich to
the Minister of National Defence. This meant, in actual fact, that,
for the time being, von Seeckt, as Commander of the *Reichswehr*,
became the supreme power in Germany. The Ordinance of August
11, 1920, had made him virtually independent of the Minister of
Defence in military matters by investing him with all the power of
the pre-war Military Cabinet of the Kaiser and of the pre-war Chief
of the Great General Staff,[3] and it was now tacitly understood that
the transfer of executive functions to Gessler was a pure formality
in order to conform with the provisions of the Constitution.

In effect, for half a year — for the emergency powers were not
rescinded until February 1924 — von Seeckt and the *Reichswehr*
governed Germany in all administrative as well as executive functions.
Through the Generals commanding the seven military districts
(*Wehrkreise*) the Army controlled prices, currency regulations and
labour conditions; it organized relief work for the unemployed,
and set up feeding centres. At Christmas time every garrison
arranged for the presentation of gifts to the poor and military
concerts helped to collect funds for charitable work. In these
activities von Seeckt's ideas of a new spirit of social consciousness
in the *Reichswehr* found their first expression, a spirit which sought

[1] Rabenau, ii, 342.   [2] See above, p. 43, footnote.
[3] Morgan, pp. 115-16.

to revive the old State-socialism of Prussia. Especially among the younger officers the idea developed, vague and sentimental, of a community of comradeship between soldiers and workers.[1]

In the meantime the authority of the Reich was challenged in Prussia and Saxony as well as in Bavaria, and in each instance von Seeckt dealt faithfully with the malcontents, though in one case he was for a time hard put to it to make good his boast that the *Reichswehr* would stick to him, and in another an earlier folly, the 'Black Reichswehr', now proved once more a source of embarrassment.

The reactionary extremists in Prussia and in Bavaria had planned —not very expertly and without any marked degree of co-ordination— to make common cause in crushing and overthrowing the Weimar Republic. The essential prerequisite for success in this project was the support of the Army and, whereas the Bavarian Nationalists had had some success with their local *Reichswehr* commander, the Prussians, as has been seen, had failed to elicit anything from von Seeckt save expressions of active hostility. In the face of this inhibiting disability, wiser or more efficient men might well have abandoned their plans, but as political conspirators the Germans are neither wise nor efficient. From the *Reichswehr* proper they turned to its bastard product the 'Black Reichswehr'. The plans were laid for an occupation of Berlin, *à la* Kapp-Lüttwitz, and in preparation for this, small groups were filtered into Küstrin and to Spandau. The date chosen for the *Putsch* was the night of September 29/30, the first Sunday after the abandonment of passive resistance.[2] How far, if at all, the civilian conspirators had informed Buchrucker of their failure to win the approval of the Army for their move is unknown. The leader of the 'Black Reichswehr', according to his own record, had certainly no intention of opposing the Bendlerstrasse, and was either under the impression that the plans were blessed in advance by the High Command or that the Generals were waiting for a *fait accompli* before showing their hand.

Buchrucker's first impression that all was not as he had supposed appears to have been on September 27 when, having made himself responsible for assembling some 4,500 men, he reported this fact to Colonel von Bock, his official liaison contact with the *Reichswehr*. Von Bock was furious at this disclosure, for, according to

---

[1] Scheele, pp. 122-3 ; Rosinski, pp. 182-3. The officer responsible for the organization of this 'military government' and to whom much of the credit for its successful operation was due was Kurt von Schleicher, whom von Seeckt promoted lieutenant-colonel in February 1924 in recognition of his services.

[2] Buchrucker, p. 35.

his account, Buchrucker had been strictly cautioned that the 'Black Reichswehr' were on no account to be mobilized without direct orders from the Bendlerstrasse. Von Bock told him that the Army would give him no support and he added: 'If von Seeckt knew you were here, he would screw his monocle into his eye and say: "Go for him"'.[1] He advised Buchrucker to demobilize his men as soon as possible.

Discouraged and disillusioned, Buchrucker returned to Küstrin, where he appears to have lost his head completely. On the night of September 30, with 550 men, he occupied the Forts of Gorgast, Säpzig and Tschernow, and raised the Imperial colours of black, white and red, hoping perhaps thereby to force the hand of the *Reichswehr* into declaring for a national dictatorship. If this was his intention it was conspicuously unsuccessful. Von Seeckt at once ordered the Army to repress the revolt, and after a siege of two days Buchrucker and his men surrendered at discretion. Placed on trial for high treason, he was condemned (October 25) to ten years' fortress detention and a fine of 100 milliards of marks (the equivalent of ten gold *Reichsmarks*),[2] and von Seeckt took the opportunity of finally dissolving the *Arbeits-Kommandos*, the official name of the 'Black Reichswehr'.[3]

Von Seeckt had thus won the first round for the forces of established authority and constitutional government and had given proof of the truth of his claim that the *Reichswehr* would stick to him. He had also freed himself from a discreditable incubus.

He was equally successful in the next round of the contest which took place in Saxony, where the Social Democrat Premier, Dr. Erich Zeigner, had most unwisely purchased the support of the Communist Party in the *Landtag* by permitting the establishment of a Red Militia. In protest against the Proclamation of the State of Emergency in the Reich the Communists demanded a reconstruction of the Saxon Cabinet and obtained two seats. This representation was, however, sufficient for them to exercise a substantial influence over the Premier, and, on October 5, the new Government issued a series of demands to the Government of the Reich, which included the recognition of the Red Militia and the democratization of the Army. At the same time acts of sabotage and civil disturbance, already frequent throughout Saxony, increased in violence. In fiery

---

[1] '*Wenn Seeckt erfährt, dass Sie da sind, klemmt er sich das Monokel ins Auge und sagt: "Sind anzugreifen"*' (Buchrucker, p. 41).

[2] Buchrucker was released under the general political amnesty of 1927 after having served four years in the fortress of Gollnow. It was in the following year that he published his book.

[3] Buchrucker, pp. 37-54; Gumbel, pp. 189-96; Benoit--Méchin, ii, 269-78.

COLONEL-GENERAL HANS VON SEECKT

speeches Zeigner denounced Stresemann and Gessler as reactionaries, and the Communist Ministers called for a Dictatorship of the Proletariat throughout Germany.

The reply of the Reich Government was a vigorously worded ultimatum demanding the restoration of law and order, the dissolution of the Red Militia and the dismissal of the Communist members of the Saxon Government. When these requirements were not complied with, the local *Reichswehr* commander, General Alfred Müller (*Wehrkreis IV*) proceeded to disband the Militia by force and to arrest not only the Communist Ministers but Dr. Zeigner and his Socialist colleagues as well (October 27–29). The functions of government were vested in a Reich Commissioner, for which post Stresemann selected his colleague of the German People's Party, Dr. Rudolf Heinze, who had been prominent in the negotiations with von Lüttwitz just prior to the Kapp *Putsch*.[1]

This commendable display of forceful action [2] proved, however, to be altogether too red-blooded for Stresemann's Socialist colleagues in the Reich Cabinet, to whom the crushing of a military revolt in Prussia was one thing, but the suppression of a Government in which their fellow Social Democrats were in the majority — though actually under the control of the Communists — was quite another. This they could not stomach, and in protest against the action of the *Reichswehr* they resigned from the Cabinet. Stresemann reconstructed his Government without them and proceeded, with the support of Gessler and von Seeckt, to deal with the dangerous and complex situation created by the defection of Bavaria.

The Bavarian predicament was not a straightforward issue such as the Reich Government and the Army had had to contend with in the suppression of Radicals of the Right in Prussia and of the Left in Saxony. It was complicated by a number of additional factors which were not present in these other instances. To begin with, the reactionary régime of Ritter von Kahr was not the only claimant to the authority of government in Munich ; there was also the *Kampfbund*, the political group of the National Patriotic Associations, of which on September 25 Adolf Hitler was appointed political director. However, the directing force of this body was not Hitler, but Ludendorff, who, ever since the collapse of the Kapp *Putsch*, had lived in venomous retirement in Bavaria. The active association of the former Quartermaster-General with the *Kampfbund* revived the old issue between the 'unreconstructed'

---

[1] See above, p. 72.
[2] Similar actions by the *Reichswehr* were carried out against the Communists in Hamburg and in Thuringia.

militarists who had followed Ludendorff and von Lüttwitz three years before, and the 'new thinkers' who abode by the ideas of von Seeckt and Gröner. Thus, to some extent, the affair assumed the aspect of a final struggle between the Old Army ideology and the New.

Nor was this all. Perhaps the most dangerous element in the whole situation was the fact that the commander of *Wehrkreis VII*, General Otto von Lossow, himself a Bavarian,[1] was hand in glove with von Kahr, though sharing with him a common distrust and contempt for the National Socialists of Adolf Hitler, to whom he himself had first given employment.[2]

The position was therefore that the Bavarian Government stood in defiance of Reich authority and the local *Reichswehr* were in dubious loyalty to their Commander-in-Chief. Von Seeckt's boast to the President that the *Reichswehr* would stick to him, was thus challenged for the first time and, indeed, it is difficult to see how he could have extricated himself from his dilemma had it not been for an opportune falling-out between his opponents.[3]

In an attempt to out-trump the influence of Ludendorff, Hindenburg was persuaded to send a message to the Patriotic Associations to the effect that 'Bavaria must in no circumstances, not even temporarily, separate herself from the Reich'.[4] This had no effect save to evoke a demand from Ludendorff and Hitler for a march on Berlin and an overthrow of the Weimar régime. Not to be outdone, von Kahr announced that Ebert's proclamation of a State of Emergency had no application to Bavaria whose sovereignty and

---

[1] The von Lossows, although originally of Brandenburg stock, had founded a cadet-branch at Hof in Upper Franconia, at the end of the eighteenth century, when that part of Bavaria, as a portion of the Margravate of Bayreuth, belonged to Prussia (1792–1806). This branch of the family became completely 'Bavarianized', the sons entering the Civil Service and the Officer Corps. The General's father was *Bürgermeister* of Lindau, but he himself was born at Hof in 1868. He died in Munich in 1938.

[2] For the earlier relation of the *Reichswehr* with Hitler see below, Part II, Chapter 2, 'The Army and Hitler'.

[3] A further cause of confusion of thought, at least to the outside observer, was the presence in the camp of the enemy of the wife of the Commander-in-Chief of the *Reichswehr* at the height of this politico-military conflict. Fritz Thyssen (*I paid Hitler* (New York, 1941), p. 84) clearly insinuates that the visit of Frau von Seeckt to Munich at this time — a visit from which she only returned to Berlin after the Hitler *Putsch* of November 9 had failed — was not entirely fortuitous, and that von Seeckt was preparing to 'copper his bets' as he had at the time of the Kapp-Lüttwitz adventure. General von Rabenau (ii, 344) vehemently asserts that the visit had no political significance at all and was purely a social visit to friends. This is probably true, though it was certainly unwise and indiscreet, lending itself to false interpretation.

[4] *Stresemann Diaries*, i, 126.

authority was from thenceforward vested solely in the Bavarian State Government.

The Munich press began a bitter campaign against the Reich Government, and the *Völkischer Beobachter*, which was now appearing as a Nazi daily under the editorship of Alfred Rosenberg, was particularly vitriolic against von Seeckt, a hated Prussian, and Gessler, a renegade Bavarian. Von Seeckt ordered General von Lossow to suppress the paper, but this he refused to do on the grounds that he must remain on friendly relations with von Kahr. He also described Hitler's followers as the 'best of patriots'. A second order, this time to arrest Captain Heiss, the leader of the *Reichsflagge*, one of the patriotic associations forming the *Kampfbund*, was also disobeyed, whereupon, on October 20, President Ebert, as Supreme Commander of the Armed Forces of the Reich, with the approval of Gessler and von Seeckt, dismissed von Lossow from his command and appointed General Kress von Kressenstein as his successor. Von Kahr's *riposte* was to denounce von Lossow's dismissal as 'an invasion of the police power of Bavaria' and to appoint him *Landeskommandant* of the Bavarian *Reichswehr*. At the same time he refused to have any further communication with Gessler and von Seeckt.

Von Seeckt met this crisis with courage and determination. He at once issued an order to the troops of the Bavarian Division calling on them to remain true to the oath which they had taken to the Reich, and to place themselves unconditionally at the orders of their supreme military commander.[1] This he followed up on November 4 with his memorable General Order of the Day to the whole Army.[2] After recapitulating the tasks performed by the troops in suppressing the Communist movements in Saxony, Thuringia and Hamburg — with a notable omission of any reference to the Mutiny of the 'Black Reichswehr' at Küstrin — he wrote :

> As long as I remain at my post, I shall not cease to repeat that salvation [for Germany] cannot come from one extreme or the other, neither through foreign aid nor through internal revolution — whether from the Right or from the Left — and that only by hard work, silent and persistent, can we survive. This can only be accomplished on the basis of the laws of the Constitution. To abandon this principle is to unleash civil war. Not a civil war in which one of the parties will succeed in winning, but a conflict which will only terminate in their mutual destruction, a conflict similar to that of which the Thirty Years' War has given us so ghastly an example.

---

[1] *Stresemann Diaries* i, 168.   [2] Rabenau, ii, 371.

E 2

It is the duty of the *Reichswehr* to prevent such a disaster. The task of the Commander-in-Chief is to recognize the vital interests of the State and to see that they are respected. As for the soldier, it is not for him to seek to know more or to do better than his commanders : his duty consists in obedience. A *Reichswehr* united in obedience will always be invincible and will remain the most powerful factor in the State. A *Reichswehr* into which the cancer of political discord has entered will be shattered (*zerbrochen*) in the hour of danger.

I require all Generals and all Corps Commanders to call the attention of their subordinates to the importance of this fact and to expel from the ranks any member of the Reichswehr who is concerned in political activity.

This General Order was a reaffirmation of von Seeckt's basic credo, both in respect of the State and of the Army. In it he placed once again before the officers and men the standard of ideals which he had set for them and for himself, and called upon them to maintain that standard. It was also something more. In it von Seeckt proclaimed to the Army the intention of its Commander-in-Chief to avoid civil war at all costs — even, paradoxically enough, by the use of armed force. He no longer adhered to his theory at the time of the Kapp *Putsch* that the *Reichswehr* could not be set to fight the *Reichswehr*. If von Lossow and von Kahr and their fellow Bavarians persisted in their efforts to disrupt the unity of the Reich, the Army would oppose them, and von Seeckt was already in process of drawing up plans for such an eventuality, notwithstanding that so grave a decision would create a breach in the unity of the Army.

Events, however, did not go this far. The principal pretext of von Kahr and von Lossow for the superiority of their brand of national patriotism over that of Berlin was in respect of the menace of Communism and its toleration by the Reich Government, and certainly this was the chief basis of their association with Hitler. But by the end of October the action of the Army in Saxony, Thuringia and Hamburg had largely removed this menace and had given ample evidence that the government of the Reich did not need to fear the menace of a Red dictatorship. Von Kahr and von Lossow were therefore deprived of their chief talking point. They had also been hoping for a Right-wing *coup* in Berlin in which the *Reichswehr* would support a new dictatorship, but on November 4 they learned that the prospects in North Germany were very unfavourable to this project. Bavaria was isolated and there seemed good reason to suppose that those separatist tendencies in Bavarian life, tendencies to which von Kahr and von Lossow were evidently not immune, might now become predominant.

To such fantasies Hitler was utterly inimical. He was no
separatist. He had realistic plans for a strong totalitarian Reich
with a national army, and in these plans the restoration of monarchy
played a very small part, save as bait for monarchists. He had been
aware of these separatist ideas among his allies, but he had hoped
to utilize them to effect a march on Berlin which would arouse such
a wave of nationalist feeling that 'particularism' would be effectively
and finally swamped by it.

When, therefore, it was reported to him that von Kahr and von
Lossow, with the support of the head of the state police, Colonel
von Seisser, planned to make a *Putsch* without him on November 9 —
the fifth anniversary of the proclamation of the German Republic
— Hitler determined to forestall them and, by a *coup de théâtre*, to
compel them, willy nilly, to support him. This was the basis of
the now famous scene in the Bürgerbräu Cellar on the night of
November 8, when, having compelled silence by firing a revolver
into the air, Hitler proclaimed a 'National Government' to take the
place of the 'Government of Criminals in Berlin'. Ernst Pöhner,
Police President of Munich, was declared Premier; von Kahr,
State Commissioner for Bavaria; von Lossow, Minister of National
Defence, and Ludendorff Commander-in-Chief of the National
Army. 'I propose', said Hitler modestly, 'that until the treaties
that are ruining Germany are cancelled, I should direct the policy
of this provisional National Government myself.' He added, ' To-
morrow will see either a National Government in Germany, or it
will see us dead.'

In point of fact neither of these things happened. Having
promised to give Hitler their support, von Kahr, von Lossow and
von Seisser were ill-advisedly released, whereupon they repudiated
their association with Hitler and declared him to be guilty of high
treason.

Thus it happened that, when in the early hours of November 9
the Reich Cabinet, meeting again in the Chancellor's study, was
informed that a revolt had occurred in Munich, and, without further
hesitation, placed full executive power in von Seeckt's hands, —
thereby re-enacting, to the very day,.the events of five years before
— the report was quickly followed by further news that the National-
Socialists, headed by Hitler and Ludendorff, had been dispersed by
the police under the orders of von Lossow and von Seisser. Ludendorff had been arrested and Hitler had fled.[1]

---

[1] For details of the Nazi *Putsch* and its sequel see below, Chapter III, pp. 172-6.
It may be noted here, however, that the editor of Lord D'Abernon's diaries,

In this way the Reich and the *Reichswehr* were alike delivered
from the peril of disruption by the very disunity of their opponents.
Had the Munich reactionaries been of one mind and purpose,
had von Lossow's *Feldgrauen* and Hitler's Brown Shirts marched
northwards to Berlin united under the command of Ludendorff, von
Seeckt would either have had to give them battle — or else perform
a rôle similar to that of Ney at Lons-le-Saulnier in March 1815.[1]
Almost certainly the extreme Nationalists of Prussia would have
joined forces with their allies of the south, and almost without doubt
the Republic would have collapsed.

As it was, von Seeckt was saved from this dilemma by 'a whiff
of grape-shot' — and not even his own. Hitler's *Putsch* cut short a
conflict between the Commander-in-Chief and a contumacious
subordinate. Its failure prevented a clash between von Seeckt and
Ludendorff, and permitted von Lossow to make his peace. Those
who had fallen before the bullets of von Seisser's police had been
Nazi Storm Troopers and not the venerated veteran of the Imperial
Army. Thus through this crisis, as in 1920, the unity of the *Reichswehr*, and especially of the Officer Corps, had been miraculously
preserved. Gratefully President Ebert tendered the thanks of the
Republic to its preserver, Hans von Seeckt.

This gratitude von Seeckt most justly merited, but perhaps not
entirely in the sense intended by Ebert. He had certainly deserved
well of the Republic, for by his fortitude and determination —
albeit aided not a little by the fortunate turn of events at the climax
— he had preserved it from disintegration, at the cost of the lives of
a few score Communists and Nazis. Yet, in the final analysis, it
was the *Reich*, not the *Republic*, that von Seeckt had been bent on
preserving. It was the State and not the existing form of State
government for which he had been prepared even to fight if necessary.

Professor M. A. Gerothwohl, writing in 1929, added the following footnote :
Hitler 'was arrested and subsequently tried for high treason, receiving a sentence
of five years in a fortress. He was finally released after six months and bound
over for the rest of his sentence, thereafter fading into oblivion' (D'Abernon,
ii, 51).

[1] After Napoleon's escape from Elba and landing in France, Marshal Ney,
who had plighted his loyalty to the Bourbons on the first Restoration, assured
Louis XVIII that he would capture the Emperor and bring him back to Paris
'in an iron cage'. However, on meeting Napoleon at Lons-le-Saulnier, Ney was
deserted by his troops and himself at once joined the Emperor in his triumphal
progress to the Tuileries. The possibilities of this historical parallel are infinite,
since von Seeckt and Hitler had already met for the first time in Munich (March 11,
1923) and the General, deeply moved, had set on record the view : 'We were one
in our aim ; only our paths were different' ('*Im Ziele waren wir uns einig, nur der
Weg war verschieden*') (Rabenau, ii, 347-8).

Had it seemed to him that a combination of reactionary forces in north and south Germany would have benefited the ultimate aims of the restoration and establishment of a strong Germany, he would have jettisoned the Republic without hesitation. His loyalty lay essentially to the German Reich, but while the vital interests of the Weimar Republic coincided with those of the Reich, he would protect the Republic against all comers. He had already done so, and in so doing had established beyond all challenge the position of the Army as the strongest and most powerful force within the State.

Indeed, in view of the all-too-apparent impotence of the *Reichstag* to achieve administrative reforms which would prevent future conflicts between the Reich and the Federal States, it became increasingly clear that this task could only be performed by the Army, and that, within the Reich itself, the only two pillars capable of sustaining the edifice of government were the Army and the President, who alone under the Constitution had power to take emergency measures and to bring about military intervention. Thus the alliance which Ebert had concluded with Gröner on the night of November 9, 1918, as a temporary expedient, had by November 9, 1923, become an absolute and recognized essential. The position of the Army was inseparable from that of the President ; he guaranteed its unity and it guaranteed the unity of the Reich.

(v)

But while von Seeckt was establishing the Army as the most powerful single political factor in the Reich, he was not neglecting the task of perfecting the technique of his military machine in clandestine disregard of the Treaty of Versailles. It was, as he frankly admitted, his consistent policy 'to neutralize the poison' contained in its Articles of Disarmament, and to do this he ventured into foreign fields with the same cool, calculating, shrewd ruthlessness which he had shown in his dealings with the inner enemies of the Reich. When the extreme Nationalists and the ultra-reactionaries of the Old Army were inveighing against the menace to Germany from the Soviet Union, von Seeckt did not allow his innate hostility to Communism as a disintegrating force within the Reich to blind him to the manifest possible advantages to be accrued from a *Kuhhandel* with Soviet Russia as a foreign ally.

Ever since the re-emergence of Prussia in the 'sixties as a dynamic force in Europe there had been within her counsels two warring schools : one thought of Russia as the natural ally of Prussia in the coming struggle with Austria and France; the other group thought in terms of a Greater Germany which included Austria and her traditional hostility to Russia. Bismarck, in his early years, had been no whole-hearted disciple of either of these doctrines. From 1862-71 his aim had been to put an end to the Germanic Confederation in which Prussia had had to play second fiddle to Austria; to establish Prussian predominance and to remove all French and Russian influence from Germany. Having finally attained these ends with the establishment of the German Empire, he proceeded on the policy that, of the five Great European Powers, Germany should always have two on her side, and for the next ten years he sought to unite Germany, Russia and Austria-Hungary in one combination which would be unchallengeable in Europe. This feat he ultimately accomplished in 1882 with the League of the Three Emperors (*Dreikaiserbund*), but the success was of short duration. Rivalries between Russia and Austria-Hungary in the Balkan Peninsula made it clear that a clash between them would sooner or later become inevitable. Bismarck thereupon urged upon the young Emperor Wilhelm II the absolute necessity of maintaining the *entente* with Russia, both as a counterpoise to Austrian ambitions and to prevent her from falling into the arms of France. This was exactly what Wilhelm II failed to do — with disastrous results. The pro-Austrian Greater-Germany school came into the ascendant and found its ultimate expression in the predatory Treaty of Brest-Litovsk (March 1918) by which it was intended to eliminate Russia as a political factor in European affairs.

It might well have been assumed that the Peace of Brest-Litovsk marked the final parting between Germany and Russia, and to many it did indeed appear that in no forseeable period could these two States be found together in the same camp. But one of those unpredictable *rapprochements*, which have always characterized German-Russian relations, now occurred, and for the reason which had so frequently united these States before and was to unite them again in the future — the existence of Poland. It is a curious fact, however, that, just as the over-vaulting ambition of triumphant German militarism had dictated the Peace of Brest-Litovsk, so now this same German militarism, grown humble and cunning in defeat and concerned only with its own survival, brought about the renewal of amicable relations. In the shifting of power which followed the collapse of the monarchies of Central Europe, Bismarck's tradition reasserted itself: Germany and Russia found themselves drawn together as pariahs and discovered that they had grievances as well as interests in common.

The seeds of this unlooked-for and undesirable *rapprochement* lay in the very text of the Armistice Agreement itself, by which the Germans were ordered to maintain their troops in position on the Eastern Front, in territories which, before the war, had formed part of Russia, until such time 'as the Allies shall think the moment suitable, having regard to the internal situation of these territories', for the retirement of these troops behind the line of the German frontier as of August 1, 1914. The withdrawal of German troops on the territory of Russia proper, on the other hand, was to begin at once.[1] This meant that the Allies intended to keep the German divisions in the Baltic Provinces as a bulwark against the possible advance westwards of a Bolshevik Army, for, despite General Weygand's Olympian reply to the Germans at Compiegne that 'the victors have nothing to fear' from the menace of Bolshevism,[2] they were, in effect, very exercised in their minds regarding this menace in Eastern Europe and especially in relation to the fortunes of the newly reborn and highly vital Republic of Poland.

The position in the Baltic Provinces was somewhat complicated by the presence there, in addition to the forces of the local Estonian and Latvian Governments, who, though they had declared their independence of Russia, had not yet been recognized *de jure* by the Allies, of the White Russian armies of Generals Yudenitch and Rodzianko, and of a corps, commanded by Prince Lieven, composed of Russian prisoners of war in Germany, equipped and paid by the German High Command. These forces, together with the German divisions under the command of General Count von der Goltz, were united only in their common hostility to the Bolshevik armies confronting them. For the rest, they were wonderfully divided. The Baltic peoples, though they regarded the Germans as a desirable protection against the Reds, were anxious to get rid of them as soon as was compatible with safety, and had little affection for the White Russians. Von der Goltz, on the other hand, was in no hurry to evacuate the 'Baltikum', which he regarded as a source of German power, while Yudenitch and Rodzianko sought the reunion of the Baltic Provinces in that restored and liberated Russia, then represented by a shadowy and ephemeral régime under Admiral Kolchak in Siberia. But von der Goltz and the White Russian Generals were in temporary alliance to utilize the Baltic area as a military base from which, with German reinforcements, they might recapture Petrograd and restore the House of Romanov; while in

---

[1] See Articles XII and XIII of the Armistice Agreement of November 11, 1918.
[2] See above, p. 40, footnote 2.

Berlin the National Opposition would simultaneously overthrow the republican régime and bring back the Kaiser from Holland. The two restored monarchies would then ally themselves against the Entente Powers, by whom Germany had been defeated and Russia deserted.[1]

Here was the first revival of the Bismarck tradition, but in a completely impracticable and fantastic guise. It presupposed the impossible ; the restoration of Tsardom and the *Kaiserreich*, and was a typical product of those mental processes which subsequently found expression in the activities of Kapp and von Lüttwitz and von Lossow. There existed, however, a much more subtle and sinister aspect of the same tradition which found its exponent in the shrewd, far-seeing Hans von Seeckt.

The rebirth of an independent Poland created a genuine and common bond of interest between Germany and Russia, an interest quite apart from the consideration of whatever governmental régimes existed in either State. To von Seeckt, with his strong sense of political realism, the schemes of von der Goltz were sheer fantasy. He was not averse to retaining the Baltic Provinces for Germany if that could be done, but to him, and to others of the German High Command, a matter of far greater moment was the declared intention of the Allies to restore Poland. The creation of a strong Polish State, inevitably allied with a strong France, would constitute a permanent menace to the German Reich. It would be infinitely more advantageous to Germany as a Great Power in Europe to have Russia as a contiguous neighbour, even should that country remain Bolshevik, and the hope was entertained that by offering up Poland to Russia at the outset it might be possible to preserve for Germany those Polish provinces which Prussia had acquired by the Partitions and which she would certainly be called upon to surrender to a reborn Polish State. To this end, therefore, the evacuation of the

[1] Von der Goltz, *Als politischer General im Osten 1918 und 1919* (Berlin, 1936), pp. 166-7. Benoist-Méchin points out (ii, 29, footnote) that in the earlier edition of his memoirs, published in 1920, von der Goltz did not mention the fact that he planned a march on Berlin and the overthrow of the Weimar régime ; this he only disclosed in the version published under the Third Reich. See also the volume of official documents, *Die Rückführung des Ostheeres* (Berlin, 1920), the memoirs of August Winnig, *Reichskommissar* for the Eastern Territories and one of the few Social Democrats who approved of the Baltic venture, *Das Reich als Republik, 1918-28* (Berlin, 1929), pp. 147-58, and R. H. Phelps, 'Aus den Gröner-Dokumenten : IV, Das Baltikum, 1919', *Deutsche Rundschau*, October 1950. From the Allied side, the British story of the German forces in the Baltic is told, for the first time with full documentation, in Woodward and Butler, First Series, iii, 1-307. For the French account see General Niessel, *L'Évacuation des pays baltiques par les Allemandes, contribution à l'étude de la mentalité allemande* (Paris, 1935).

German divisions from Bielorussia and from the Ukraine was deliberately carried out in such a manner as to facilitate the entry of the Bolsheviks, with the inevitable outcome of a clash between them and the Poles.[1]

This initial attempt to throttle the infant Polish State did not escape the vigilance of the Allies. Mr. Lloyd George recalled the historic peril lurking in the possibility of a German-Russian *rapprochement* and realized the danger inherent in the continued existence of a German army in the East. 'They must be cleared out,' he told the House of Commons, 'otherwise the peace of Europe is not safe',[2] and by the close of December 1919 the last German detachment was back within the frontiers of the Reich.

But the process of *rapprochement* did not cease. It was too natural a process for that. Already, in the early days of the German Revolution, Karl Radek had offered the German Government, on behalf of Lenin, a military alliance against the Entente, which Ebert and Scheidemann had wisely refused.[3] The episode was thought to have ended with the arrest of Radek after the First Spartakist rising of January 1919. But Radek gaoled was a more potent force than Radek free.[4] In his cell in the Moabit Prison he held court and was visited not only by German Communists but by high military officers, by big business men and even by a British journalist. Colonel Bauer went there, and Walter Rathenau [5] and Felix

[1] Cecil F. Melville, *The Russian Face of Germany* (London, 1932), p. 36 ; Scheele, p. 260.
[2] *House of Commons Debates*, November 17, 1919, col. 726.
[3] Daniels, p. 105.
[4] Karl Radek (b. 1885), by birth an Austrian Pole and an early disciple of Marx, began his revolutionary career at the age of fourteen and, though not an original Bolshevik, was in general a follower of Lenin, differing from him, however, on certain important points. Radek attended the Zimmerwald and Kienthal Conferences during the War and left Switzerland with Lenin in the 'sealed train'. He accompanied the Soviet Delegation to the Peace Conference of Brest-Litovsk, and after the German Revolution was sent to Berlin to organize a Communist outbreak. His failure cost him his position on both the Executive and Central Committees of the Communist Party. He joined the Trotskyist group in 1924 and was finally expelled from the CPSU three years later. On recanting, he was readmitted in 1930, but in the great purges of 1937 he was convicted of Trotskyist heresy and sentenced to ten years' penal servitude. For years he was editor of *Pravda*, in the columns of which his vitriolic humour shone and sparkled. He was a brilliant dialectician. There is still some mystery about his ultimate fate, but he is now generally presumed to be dead.
[5] Walter Rathenau (1867–1922), German-Jewish statesman, industrial leader and social theorist, succeeded his father as President of A.E.G. in 1912 and during the First World War was head of the department to supply raw materials. He opposed the surrender of 1918 and called for a *levée en masse* to resist the Allied armies ; however, under the Republic he became, first, Minister of Reconstruction and, later, of Foreign Affairs. An early believer in the Policy of Fulfilment,

Deutsch, and to them Radek, with that gift of brilliant exposition and irrefutable argumentation, mingled with the biting wit which had so enraged the German delegates at Brest-Litovsk, expounded the thesis of an alliance between Bolshevik Russia and Nationalist Germany directed against their common enemy, the victors of Versailles. Though an 'ambassador in bonds', without an official mandate and far from his home base, Radek, like St. Paul, was a powerful and efficient propagandist. His words took root in the minds of his hearers, and found echoes far beyond the confines of his cell.[1] They reached the ears of General von Seeckt in the Bendlerstrasse and of Freiherr Ago von Maltzan in the Foreign Office.

Ago von Maltzan, of whom Lord D'Abernon wrote that he was 'possibly the cleverest man who worked in the Wilhelmstrasse since the war',[2] was, in diplomacy and in politics, the pupil of Kiderlen-Waechter, who, in his turn was the pupil of Bismarck. Von Maltzan had therefore inherited and imbibed the pro-Russian doctrines of his masters, and, when he became head of the Eastern European division of the German Foreign Office, he brought to it a formidable array of diplomatic qualities and a clear and definite view of policy, based on the conception that friendship with Russia was indispensable, even if expensive, for Germany. Though a Mecklenburger by birth, there was about von Maltzan something Oriental. He was not quite European and certainly very un-Germanic. He seemed to have the detachment and century-old philosophy of the Chinese and something also of their Confucian indifference to contemporary standards; to this he added a Russian agility of mind and a Polish grace of manner. Von Maltzan had that curious type of mind whose very acuteness prefers to deal with the devious and the unreliable.

Rathenau sought to come to an understanding with both France and Russia, and signed the Treaty of Rapallo with the latter in April 1922. He was assassinated by Nationalist gunmen three months later.

[1] Edward Hallett Carr, *German-Soviet Relations between the two World Wars, 1919–1939* (Baltimore, Md., 1951), pp. 17–24.

[2] D'Abernon, *Portraits and Appreciations*, p. 161. Ago, Freiherr von Maltzan zu Wartenberg und Penzlin (1877–1927), a member of an old Mecklenburg family with Slav connections, and a professional diplomat, was appointed head of the Eastern Division of the German Foreign Office in 1919, and remained in that post, except for a brief period as Minister in Athens in 1921, until he became Ambassador in Washington in 1923. His strong pro-Russian influence resulted in the signing of the Treaty of Rapallo, but Stresemann sensed in him a formidable opponent of the Policy of Fulfilment and took an early opportunity of getting him out of Europe. Even this was not entirely successful, for von Maltzan took long spells of leave from his American exile during which he worked actively in Berlin for the strengthening of German-Russian relations. It was during one of these visits that he was killed in an aeroplane accident in Thuringia in September 1927.

Fundamentally honest himself, he neither gave the impression of being so nor looked for it in others, and, in the opinion of the British Ambassador, his personal sympathies for the Russians was strengthened by the very fact of their unreliability. During his comparatively brief reign in the Wilhelmstrasse — before being *limogé* to Washington — he exercised a major degree of influence over the formulations of German foreign policy, for, with von Seeckt, he laid the foundation of that German-Soviet *entente* which from frail beginnings in 1920 continued unbroken until after Hitler had taken over the direction of German foreign policy.

Von Maltzan was essentially a man after von Seeckt's own heart and together they constituted a powerful combination. Both saw in Poland a menace to German security, and in Russia a means both of counteracting this menace and of building up a bargaining power in the relations of Germany with the Western Powers. Neither was in any sense pro-Communist nor even a 'Fellow-traveller'; both were stark realists and, while not placing implicit trust in Russia, saw and seized the opportunity presented for strengthening the position of Germany as a Great Power. But for von Seeckt it was something more. He saw in co-operation with Russia a further possibility of circumventing the military restrictions imposed upon the *Reichswehr* by the Treaty of Versailles. Russia was not a party to the treaty and was therefore not bound by its provisions. By reaching a secret military understanding with the Red General Staff it would be possible to instruct German officers and men in those branches of military training and armament prohibited to Germany. It would also be possible to establish in Russia factories for aircraft and other types of military material for delivery to Germany. Lastly, German officers could train the Red Army and render it a mighty reservoir of man-power in support of the Reich.

The idea of an agreement with Russia had been in von Seeckt's mind ever since February 1920, when the prospect of a Russo-Polish clash began to cause concern in Germany. Von Seeckt was very emphatic in his view that German policy should not come into conflict with that of Russia, and that, although Germany should avoid hostilities which might provoke Allied intervention, a Russian victory against the Poles would be in her best interests.[1]

In April 1920 the war between Russia and Poland, long hoped for by the German General Staff, became at last a reality. Throughout Germany the radicals of the Right and the Left united in hailing the Bolsheviks as their allies and saviours — to the cynical

[1] Cf. Gerald Freund, *Unholy Alliance* (London, 1957), pp. 74-5, and F. L. Carsten, 'The Reichswehr and the Red Army', in *Survey*, October 1962.

amusement of Lenin [1] — and when in July the armies of General
Tukachevsky were sweeping towards Warsaw it seemed that German
hopes for Poland's destruction were about to be realized. Von
Seeckt was not eager to involve Germany in the conflict, even
though he did favour contacts with the Russians.[2] In any case
the Soviet Government felt itself capable of defeating the Poles
without German help.

But the sudden reversal of the fortunes of war and the foiling
of the Russian offensive by Weygand and Pilsudski rendered a
military understanding very much more attractive for the Russians.
Its conclusion was not long delayed. The defeat of the Red armies
had convinced Lenin of the necessity of reorganizing the Soviet
military machine, and who were more willing and better equipped
to aid in this task than the *Reichswehr*? Lenin also was a realist.
'I am not fond of the Germans by any means,' he told his followers,
'but at the present time it is more advantageous to use them than
to challenge them. An independent Poland is very dangerous to
Soviet Russia : it is an evil which, however, at the present time has
also its redeeming features ; for while it exists, we may safely count

[1] At the same time Paul Levi, a leader of the Spartakist Party in the *Reichstag*,
who was in communication with Radek, publicly offered civil peace in the Reich
to any German Government who would enter into alliance with Russia (Ruth
Fischer, *Stalin and German Communism* (Cambridge, Mass., 1948), p. 197). These
manifestations of sympathy from the Right and Left in Germany called forth the
comment from Lenin that 'everyone in Germany, including the blackest reactionaries and monarchists, declared that the Bolshevists would be their salvation' ; and again 'a curious type of reactionary-revolutionary has come into
existence in Germany. We find an example of him in the raw lad from East
Prussia who said that Wilhelm must be brought back because there was no law
and order in Germany, but that the Germans must march with the Bolshevists'
(speech of September 22, 1920).

[2] During his period of service in Turkey, von Seeckt had established friendly
relations with the notorious Enver Pasha who, after the Turkish collapse, fled to
Berlin. Von Seeckt facilitated his removal, in October 1919, to Moscow, whence
it was hoped that he would keep up a regular correspondence with the Bendlerstrasse. But a chapter of accidents caused Enver months of delay on his journey
to Russia, despite the new Junkers aeroplane put at his disposal by the Germans.
He finally arrived in the summer of 1920 and on August 26, after the Soviet defeat
before Warsaw, he wrote urging Seeckt, on behalf of Trotsky and certain elements
in the Red General Staff, to help the Russians with arms and intelligence reports.
In return for this the Soviet Government would be prepared to agree to the re-
establishment of the old 1914 frontier with the Reich. Von Seeckt's reaction to
these proposals is not known, but although he behaved with caution, designs such
as those adumbrated in Enver Pasha's letter undoubtedly had his sympathy.
(Freund, p. 71 ; Carsten, p. 117 ; Rabenau, ii, 307 ; Carr, pp. 36-7 ; Wipert
von Blücher, *Deutschlands Weg nach Rapallo* (Wiesbaden, 1951), pp. 129-37.) Von
Rabenau claimed that von Seeckt had drawn up operational plans for action against
the Poles similar to those used by Hitler in September 1939 (Rabenau, ii, 297).

on Germany, because the Germans hate Poland and will at any
time make common cause with us in order to strangle Poland. . . .
Everything teaches us to look upon Germany as our most reliable
ally. Germany wants revenge, and we want revolution. For the
moment our aims are the same.' But Lenin was not blind to the
future. 'When our ways part', he added, 'they [the Germans] will
be our most ferocious and our great enemies. Time will tell whether
a German hegemony or a Communist federation is to arise out of
the ruins of Europe.' [1]   Just a hundred and fifty years earlier
Frederick the Great, with cynical blasphemy, had written of Russia,
Prussia and Austria as 'taking Communion in the one Eucharistic
body which is Poland'. Now Germany and Russia were preparing
to celebrate the same rite, and twenty years later they were actually
to do so.

In the spring of 1921, after the Treaty of Riga had brought the
Russo-Polish War to an end (March 18), Lenin applied formally to
the German Government for assistance in the reorganization of the
Red Army.[2] Von Seeckt had not waited till this moment to formulate
his plans. He had already created within the Bendlerstrasse a secret
unit, *Sondergruppe R.*, at the head of which he placed the former
Chief of Military Intelligence, Colonel Nicolai; its task was the
potential co-operation with the Red General Staff. In this group
were Otto Hasse and von Hammerstein, both later Chiefs of the
Truppenamt; Colonel Oskar von Niedermayer, who during the First
World War had led a daring expedition into Persia and Afghanistan;
Colonel von Schubert, a former military attaché in Moscow; and
Major Fritz Tschunke. But the most acute mind among them all
probably belonged to Major Kurt von Schleicher. Preliminary
negotiations were carried on in Berlin with Victor Kopp, the Soviet
diplomatic agent in Germany, and through him with Trotsky.
Finally von Niedermayer, von Schubert and Tschunke were despatched on a mission to Moscow.

The first results of these contacts was the openly negotiated
German-Russian Commercial Agreement of May 6, 1921, which,
however, was concerned not only with purely economic commodities
but also with goods of war-potential character. In the following September secret negotiations were begun in von Schleicher's

---

[1] *Ost-Information* (Berlin), No. 81, December 4, 1920, quoted by Professor
A. L. P. Dennis in *The Foreign Policies of Soviet Russia* (New York, 1924), pp.
154-5.

[2] Otto Gessler, Minister of Defence, admitted this fact before the Foreign
Affairs Committee of the *Reichstag* on February 24, 1927.

apartment in Berlin for German assistance in building up the Russian arms industry.[1]

In these conversations the Soviet Commissar for Foreign Trade, Leonid Krassin, was the principal Russian negotiator. Von Seeckt participated in them from time to time, though he kept as much out of the limelight as possible, preferring to let Hasse and von Schleicher deal with the actual business of negotiation. The whole affair was carried on with the knowledge and approval of Joseph Wirth, then Chancellor and Minister of Finance, and of Walter Rathenau, the Foreign Minister, and had the active support of Ago von Maltzan.

From these talks von Seeckt's policy of *Abmachungen* (German-Russian collaboration) emerged in concrete form. A private trading concern was formed under the innocent enough name of 'Company for the promotion of industrial enterprises' (*Gesellschaft zur Förderung gewerblicher Unternehmungen*, or GEFU) with offices in Berlin and Moscow, at the disposal of which the Reich Government placed the considerable sum of RM. 75 million. General von Borries was placed in charge of the company, with Tschunke as its general manager. The chief tasks of GEFU were the establishment of a Junkers factory at Fili, near Moscow, for the yearly production of 600 all-metal aircraft and motors ;[2] the formation of a joint German-Russian Company for the manufacture at Trotsk, in the province of Samara, of poison gas and the production of 300,000 shells at factories in Tula, Leningrad and Schlüsselberg.

Parallel with these tasks assigned to GEFU, von Niedermayer maintained the purely military connection between Berlin and Moscow. This involved the establishment of tank and flying schools with German participation, and the training in them of Russian and German personnel. A mission of generals and technicians was established in Moscow and close contact was maintained

---

[1] The parallel between the events of 1921-2 and 1939 is of interest. Just as the conclusion of the German-Soviet Commercial Agreement was the forerunner of the Rapallo Treaty, so were the negotiations for an economic agreement in the summer of 1939 the cover for the early conversations which culminated in the Nazi-Soviet Non-Aggression Pact of August 23.

[2] A previous attempt to establish a Junkers factory in Russia, as early as October 1919, was brought to light by the forced landing of a plane, one of the latest Junker types, near Kovno, where the pilot, passengers and papers were taken in charge by the British Military Mission in the Baltic States. The pilot, an ex-officer of the German Air Force, said that he had been commissioned by Junkers to fly to Moscow for the purpose of exploring with Leonid Krassin the general possibilities of trade in aircraft between Russia and Germany, and for the setting up of a branch factory near Moscow. The pilot's papers confirmed his story and showed that he had embarked on his venture with the approval of the General Staff (Woodward and Butler, First Series, ii, 44-7).

between the two General Staffs, both by this channel and by visits to Russia of von Schleicher, von Hammerstein, Hasse, and later of von Blomberg, in the course of which they conferred with the Russian Generals Lebedev and Tukachevsky.

Von Niedermayer's side of the work continued until 1933, when Hitler ordered that co-operation with the Red Army should be broken off. This was done by the autumn of that year,[1] but the GEFU projects were shorter lived, and only the order for shells was completed *in toto*. This was due in part to Russian obstruction and partly to the fact that by 1925 the Army were unable to obtain from the Reich Government the necessary funds to continue their contract with Junkers. The aircraft factory at Fili was closed down, but, since all arrangements had been made in secret, the Junkers Company could not sue in court for breach of contract. It therefore issued a detailed memorandum on the matter to every *Reichstag* deputy, and this document formed the basis of the *Manchester Guardian* revelations of December 3, 1926, and of Scheidemann's speech in the *Reichstag* on December 16, as a result of which the organization of GEFU and its secret activities were brought into the open, and shortly thereafter liquidated.[2]

There can be no doubt that, though von Seeckt's policy of

---

[1] Carsten, p. 131. See also Helm Speidel, 'Reichswehr und Rote Armee', in *Vierteljahrshefte für Zeitgeschichte*, 1, 1953, p. 41.

[2] Gerald Freund, pp. 210 *et seq.*; Ruth Fischer, p. 528, footnote; F. L. Carsten, pp. 121-2.

Scheidemann's revelations of December 1926 were followed up early in 1927 by a pamphlet issued by the Social Democratic Party, entitled 'Sowjetgrenaden', largely based on interviews with German workmen at some of the factories concerned in the manufacture of shells, and this in time evoked further admissions from the *Reichswehr* Minister, Otto Gessler, before the Foreign Affairs Committee of the *Reichstag*. For his own version of the military links with Russia see Otto Gessler, *Reichswehr Politik in der Weimarer Zeit* (Stuttgart, 1958), pp. 196-202.

The story of German-Russian military and economic co-operation has been very much more clearly illuminated in the past few years, and the availability of the Seeckt papers, which are now in the *Militärgeschichtliches Forschungsamt* at Freiburg im Breisgau, West Germany, can lead us to hope for yet more clarification in the future. Although General von Rabenau drew heavily on the Seeckt papers when compiling his biography of the General (cf. Rabenau, volume ii, 305-21), it has now become clear that he did not tell the whole story. There is much interesting information concerning the work of the GEFU in a letter from Major Tschunke to General von Rabenau dated February 13, 1939, the contents of which von Rabenau did not see fit to use, but which was later published by Julius Epstein in *Der Monat* (November 1948). Much of interest is also to be found in the article by Helm Speidel, 'Reichswehr und Rote Armee', in *Vierteljahrshefte für Zeitgeschichte*, 1, 1953. See also G. Hilger and A. G. Meyer, *The Incompatible Allies* (New York, 1953); G. R. Treviranus, *Revolutions in Russia* (New York, 1944); and C. F. Melville, *The Russian Face of Germany* (London, 1932).

Abmachungen may have failed in some of its earliest aspects, it had considerable long-term advantages. The training of German officers in military aeronautics and tank warfare was of great importance, and, as Tschunke does not fail to note, 'no less important was the information we obtained from personal observation about the condition of the Red Army, its composition, armaments, training, etc.' The contacts now formed with Russian industry were also of considerable benefit to Germany. Large orders were received by German industrial concerns, which not only brought them financial profit,[1] but permitted them to expand their plants, to exploit and foster all forms of technical progress, and to maintain the army of specialized workers necessary for the secret rearmament of Germany then being carried on within the Reich.[2] 'It is doubtful', writes Tschunke to von Rabenau in 1939, 'whether, without these preliminary conditions, we should have been able to carry through such a vast rearmament programme.'

Thus the decisions which von Seeckt took in secret in 1919 had the most far-reaching repercussions on German policy. They were in fact the first links in a chain of events which led to the Nazi-Soviet Pact twenty years later. For the Fourth Partition of Poland, which was consummated by Hitler and Stalin in September 1939, was but the realization of the ambition shared by von Seeckt and Lenin in the early 'twenties. The Head of the *Reichswehr* had sketched the blue-print for the future.

In the meantime von Seeckt's influence on the German diplomatic front was also apparent — as was that of Radek. The unofficial approaches for a German-Russian *entente*, which had begun in a prison cell in Moabit with so powerful an effect in both the Bendlerstrasse and the Wilhelmstrasse, had already resulted in the launching of military and economic co-operation. Now Rathenau and von Maltzan essayed to extend the *rapprochement* created by the German-Soviet Commercial Agreement of May 1921.[3] With the approval

---

[1] According to Tschunke, in the years 1929–35 alone, Germany delivered to the U.S.S.R. machinery and other industrial products to the value of RM. 4 milliards in gold and silver, the balance being paid in essential raw materials.

[2] See below, p. 142 *et seq*.

[3] It is necessary to make a distinction between the attitudes of Rathenau and von Maltzan in this matter. Rathenau was the first of the post-war German leaders who can be described as a European in the sense that Bismarck and Stresemann were Europeans — good or bad. He was an intensely patriotic German with strong nationalistic views but, in addition, great breadth of vision. His design was to restore Germany in strength and greatness by reintegrating her together with Russia, in a United States of Europe. To this end he wooed the West, becoming the first exponent of the Policy of Fulfilment (*Erfüllung*) — which Stresemann later adopted — and also sought an understanding with Russia. He

and support of the Chancellor, Joseph Wirth, they brought their efforts to a successful conclusion a year later.[1] During the Genoa Conference, the German and Russian representatives, by a sudden *coup de théâtre*, which gravely disconcerted the other delegations at the Conference, signed on April 17, 1922, the Treaty of Rapallo, by which the diplomatic and commercial relations between the two countries, established after the Treaty of Brest-Litovsk and subsequently abrogated by both parties,[2] were formally resumed, and the German-Russian *entente*, long suspected and feared by the rest of Europe, was disclosed as an accomplished fact.[3]

The world at large believed — and, indeed, many continue to believe — that the Rapallo Treaty was accompanied by some formal secret Russo-German military agreement. This von Seeckt vehemently denied. To him the treaty presented first and foremost a very essential strengthening of German prestige in the world. He saw it as a valuable weapon of psychological warfare, in that more was suspected behind it than was actually justified — 'There exist no politico-military agreements : but this possibility is believed in', he wrote to Colonel Hasse, on May 27, 1922. 'Is it in our interests to destroy this pale halo (*diesen schwachen Nimbus zu zerstören*) ?'[4] But the possibility remained, and to this von Seeckt clung. The Treaty of Rapallo provided the suitable circumstance for the

converted Mr. Lloyd George to his views at the Chequers meeting in December 1921 and was in great degree responsible for the calling of the Genoa Conference, which he hoped would prove the realization of his dreams. It was only when, in the course of this conference, he found that Britain and France were negotiating with Russia to the exclusion of Germany, that Rathenau succumbed to the advice of von Maltzan, who, like von Seeckt, was an 'Easterner' in foreign policy, *pur et simple*, and had no time for *Erfüllung*. Disappointed at the failure of his hopes for European reconstruction and under pressure from von Maltzan, Rathenau accepted the Treaty of Peace and Friendship offered by the Russians, who had no desire to see Germany 'return to Europe'. In a final speech to the Genoa Conference on May 19, 1922, Rathenau made an impassioned plea for the restoration and preservation of the peace of Europe, ending with the cry of Petrarch : '*Pace — Pace — Pace*'. A month later he was assassinated in a suburb of Berlin by Nationalist youths who suspected his patriotism and yet grudgingly admired his courage (June 24, 1922). For the psychological outlook of his murderers, which was in many ways the forerunner of Nazi psychology, see *Die Geächteten*, Berlin, 1931 (*The Outlaws*, London, 1931), by Ernst von Salomon, who was identified with the assassination.
  [1] Indeed, as recently as January 1952, Joseph Wirth has publicly reaffirmed his belief in the Rapallo policy and has urged a return to it as beneficial to Germany.
  [2] Germany was forced to abrogate the Treaty of Brest-Litovsk under Article XV of the Armistice Agreement, and two days later (November 13, 1918) the Soviet Central Executive Committee also denounced it. The treaty was formally annulled by Article 116 of the Treaty of Versailles.
  [3] Carr, pp. 49-66 ; von Blücher, pp. 153-65. For a study of the Soviet attitude at this time see 'The Russian Road to Rapallo', an article by Lionel Kochan in *Soviet Studies* (Oxford, October 1950). [4] Rabenau, ii, 313.

advancement of that military and economic co-operation — the policy of *Abmachungen* — for which he had already laid the foundations, and this needed no more binding agreement than already existed.

Von Seeckt's policy met with a severe challenge, however. Rathenau and von Maltzan wished to follow up their success at Rapallo by sending to Moscow, as Germany's first Ambassador, her ablest diplomatist. They turned almost without hesitation to Count Brockdorff-Rantzau, believing that one who was almost pathologically anti-French in his views could not fail to be a supporter of their policy of *rapprochement* with Russia. They were therefore disagreeably surprised when, on being approached by the Chancellor, Joseph Wirth, their candidate replied with a memorandum in a very different strain.

Brockdorff-Rantzau was indeed bitterly and irreconcilably anti-French. He had never recovered from the affront to his personal vanity — and, incidentally, the humiliation to Germany — suffered in the Hall of Mirrors at Versailles on May 8, 1919. But he saw danger in a combination with Russia because it might provoke the hostility of England. For this reason he feared in the Rapallo Agreement the very aspects which to von Seeckt were assets.

Any appearance of a military alliance on our part with the East would have the most detrimental effect on our relations with the West [he wrote to the Chancellor, on August 15, 1922].[1] The weighty disadvantage of the Rapallo Agreement lies in the military fears attached to it. A German policy orientated exclusively towards the East would at the present moment be not only precipitate and dangerous, but without prospect and, therefore, a mistake. The policy is precipitate because we are, like the Russians, economically not yet in a position to risk such an experiment. It is dangerous because by agreements which bind us militarily we are giving ourselves into the power of the utterly unscrupulous Soviet Government. . . . The policy is hopeless because, in the event of Russia attacking Poland (and this is the only serious consideration) we should be almost defenceless in the West against a French invasion. . . . Even if the Russians were to succeed in overrunning Poland, we should be giving over Germany as a battle ground for the conflict between East and West, because we should never be able to protect our Western Frontier, and it is sheer utopia to assume that in the face of France's unlimited numerical and technical superiority, we could hold in the West until the arrival of the Russians, quite irrespective of the dubious pleasure of having to welcome these Red Allies within our country. They are not coming to our help in the struggle for liberation against the Entente, but to extend the frontiers of Asia to the Rhine.

[1] Gerald Freund, p. 131, footnote 2.

In view of all this, Brockdorff-Rantzau argued that to try to engage in a '*Bismarck Politik*' with Russia, as Ago von Maltzan sought to do, was 'sheer illusion'. As an alternative policy he offered the alienating of Britain from France and so to exacerbate relations between them 'that England solicits — and must solicit — an alliance with us'. A German-Russian combination, on the other hand, would eventually drive Britain and France into each other's arms, and a formal military alliance with the Russians was not only dangerous but quite unnecessary, since in the event of a war between the Allied powers and Germany, 'Russia would not stand by with folded arms but would in all probability intervene spontaneously [on the German side], banking on chaos in Germany'.

When Brockdorff-Rantzau handed this memorandum to Chancellor Wirth he declared that if the policy outlined in it was not accepted he would refuse to be Ambassador in Moscow, and he wanted assurances that von Seeckt would not be allowed to operate with the Russians behind his back. A copy of his memorandum was given to von Seeckt on September 9. Within two days his reply was ready.

No two documents could demonstrate more clearly the diverse personalities of their authors, who had but one thought in common, a hatred of France. Brockdorff-Rantzau was a survival of the diplomacy of the Edwardian era. He wrote and thought as such. His is the polished style of Hohenlohe or Bülow ; his argument is as devious as theirs, hoping by labyrinthine methods to achieve the best of all possible worlds. Von Seeckt's phraseology, on the other hand, is the classic Prussian style of Clausewitz and Moltke ; his reasoning, too, derives from them and from the *Realpolitik* of Bismarck. His conciseness of wording renders his reply a far more compelling document than that of his opponent. His memorandum is the basic concept of his whole policy of German-Russian *rapprochement*, for which he had already made preparation, and the stark and brutal realism of his thesis is not only important as a reflection of the past but as an illumination of the future, for, *mutatis mutandis*, it was Hitler's policy.

GERMANY'S ATTITUDE TO THE RUSSIAN PROBLEM [1]

Reply to a Pro Memoria from Count Br.-R. [Brockdorff-Rantzau]
to the Reich Chancellor, dated September 11, 1922

Germany must pursue a policy of action. Every State must do that. The moment it stops pursuing a forward policy it ceases to be a State.

[1] Text in Rabenau, ii, 315-18 ; also in *Der Monat*, November 1948, pp. 44-7.

An active policy must have a goal and a driving force. For carrying it out it is essential to assess one's own strength correctly and at the same time to understand the methods and aims of the other Powers.

The man who bases his political ideas on the weakness of his own country, who sees only dangers, or whose only desire is to remain stationary, is not pursuing a policy at all, and should be kept far away from the scene of activity.

The year 1814/15 saw France in complete military and political collapse, yet no one at the Congress of Vienna followed a more active policy than Talleyrand — to France's advantage. Has the world ever seen a greater catastrophe than that suffered by Russia in the last war? Yet with what vigour the Soviet Government recovered, both at home and abroad! Did not the Sick Man of Europe seem to be dead once and for all, and buried by the Treaty of Sèvres? Yet today, after the victory over Greece, he stands up to England with confidence. He followed an active Turkish policy.

Have not Germany's first stirrings in active politics, the Treaty of Rapallo, clearly brought her at last nearer to being more respected?

This treaty splits opinion into different camps when the Russian problem is considered. The main point about it is *not* its economic value, though that is by no means inconsiderable, but its political achievement. This association between Germany and Russia is the first and almost the only increase of power which we have so far obtained since peace was made. That this association should begin in the field of economics is a natural consequence of the general situation, but its strength lies in the fact that this economic *rapprochement* is preparing the way for the *possibility* of a political and thus also a military association. It is beyond doubt that such a double association would strengthen Germany — and also Russia. Now, there are German politicians who fear such an increase of power. They see in the symptoms of a political, military, and economic strengthening of Germany, and in a forward German policy, the danger of renewed and intensified counter-measures on the part of our western enemies. They are thus confronted with the question, which they prefer not to answer, of whether they should face East or West. This question, however, has in fact not arisen at all. It is best here to avoid misleading parallels with Bismarck's policy, and merely to extract from it for ourselves the principle of at all times following a German policy, that is, to examine, on the assumption that every country is pursuing a policy of egotism, how these interests of the others can be exploited for the benefit of our own people for tomorrow and the future. We shall have to see how the interests of the Western Powers stand in relation to our own. We should be quite clear as to France's attitude. She is following a policy of annihilation pure and simple, which she must follow in pursuance of the unshakable principles of her policy. The hope that economic decisions may divert French policy into another course can be discounted altogether, quite apart from the fact that it is doubtful whether in any case the economic strengthening of Germany would be in the interests of the ruling industrial circles of France. The contrary appears to be the case, and the French economic interests have the same object as the purely political, that is, the annihilation of Germany. This aim is not affected by the consideration that the debtor, already insolvent, will become even less able to pay up. France no longer expects payment, and in fact does not want it as it would upset her political plans. Nor are her objects altered by any Lubersac-Stinnes Agreement, which aims at rescuing something more from the wreck before bankruptcy officially sets in. The whole policy of reconciliation and appeasement towards France — no matter whether it is pursued by a Stinnes or by General Ludendorff — is hopeless in as far as it aims at political success. The question of orientation towards the West, as far as France is concerned, is ruled out. French policy is not quite indifferent as to whether we ally ourselves with Russia or not, for in either case the complete destruction of Germany, not yet fully brought about, remains her objective, and this aim would be more difficult to achieve if Germany were supported by Russia.

England is drifting towards another historic conflict with France, even though she does not face imminent war. That lurks in the background. A glance at the East is surely sufficient even for those who before Genoa did not wish to use their eyes and ears. The British interests in the Dardanelles, Egypt, and India are certainly infinitely more important at the moment than those on the Rhine, and an understanding between Britain and France at Germany's expense, that is, a concession by Britain in return for an immediate advantage, is by no means improbable. Yet even such an understanding would be only temporary. The moment is coming, and must come, when Britain will be looking round for allies on the continent. When that moment arrives she will prefer the mercenary who is growing in strength, and will even have to make him stronger.

A *rapprochement* between Germany and Russia would not have a decisive influence on Britain's attitude either in making a concession to France or in searching for an ally. British policy is ruled by other more compelling motives than anxiety about some far-distant threat from a Russia made strong with the help of Germany. Later on a German politician may again have to choose between East and West, Russia and England. A much more immediate question is that of choosing between England and France. The answer to that will not be difficult for Germany, as it is dictated by the attitude of France as described above. Every day comes proof that England is interested in having Germany economically stronger. Renewed world competition from Germany also comes into the class of distant dangers which England will not have to face until later. The fact that economic strengthening is inconceivable without political *and* military strengthening too will be clearer to the British than to many a German politician. Given the rupture between England and

France, England has every interest in France's neighbour becoming militarily strong, and will just have to accept the situation if Germany derives this strength from the East. Germany's attitude towards Russia, however, cannot and need not be influenced by consideration of Britain.

It can scarcely be maintained that America would be unfavourably influenced against Germany were the latter to join in an association with Russia. She is interested, though not decisively so, in the economic development of Germany, and is anything but an opponent of Russia.

We must now glance at the East and South-East. The growing *rapprochement* between Yugoslavia and Russia may escape many people's notice, but it is one of the decisive factors in Balkan politics. To all appearances Czechoslovakia is entirely dependent on France, but she is trying to rid herself of this relationship by means of other alliances. She sees herself being guided by France in a direction which is not to her advantage ; it is not in the Czech interest to be antagonistic either to Germany or Russia. In the event of war between Poland and Germany Czechoslovakia will expect to obtain territorial advantages in Silesia, though these would be as nothing compared with the great economic interests which bind her to Germany. Czechoslovakia must look to Russia for a market for her overgrown industry. Russia was Bohemia's hope when she was still part of the Habsburg Monarchy. The Czech regiments deserted to the Russians, and they still cannot be used against Russia. A *rapprochement* between Germany and Russia would carry no threat to Czechoslovakia, but would rather heighten her desire to live in peace with a Germany growing in strength. In spite of an apparent *rapprochement* Czechoslovakia stands in opposition to Poland.

With Poland we come now to the core of the Eastern problem. The existence of Poland is intolerable and incompatible with Germany's vital interests. She must disappear and will do so through her own inner weakness and through Russia — with our help. Poland is more intolerable for Russia than for ourselves ; Russia can never tolerate Poland. With Poland collapses one of the strongest pillars of the Peace of Versailles, France's advance post of power. The attainment of this objective must be one of the firmest guiding principles of German policy, as it is capable of achievement — but only through Russia or with her help.

Poland can never offer Germany any advantage, either economically, because she is incapable of development, or politically, because she is a vassal state of France. The restoration of the frontier between Russia and Germany is a necessary condition before both sides can become strong. The 1914 frontier between Russia and Germany should be the basis of any understanding between the two countries.

This attitude to Poland on the part of Germany need be no anxiously guarded secret. As far as Russia is concerned its publication can only create confidence. Poland could not be more hostile to Germany than she is now. In the long run the threat from both sides will shake the stability of Poland more and more. Above all, it is impossible to over-estimate the advantage which would accrue to Germany if Poland knew that if she joined in a war of sanctions with France against Germany she would have Russia to contend with. The mere fact that the Treaty of Rapallo made military consequences appear possible was sufficient to influence Polish policy in our favour, when its repercussions reached the eastern Border States and Finland. These matters must not be over-looked when considering a fresh strengthening of Russia with our assistance, and therefore at the same time a more active German policy.

Assuredly, he who only sees in an agreement with Russia the danger that we 'expose' ourselves to the British, and does not see that Russia needs us, rejecting every more active policy with the catch-phrase 'military experiment', cannot arrive at a correct appreciation of the position, and still less can he exploit it logically. A man who suffers from a 'uniform complex' and has not yet understood that in the last resort all political and economic activity is based on power, will not pursue a forward German policy. But he who sees in the Treaty of Rapallo mainly a political blunder, though perhaps fit to work in another place, would seem to be unfit for the post of German representative in Moscow.

In political life it is an old, but not a good, device to exaggerate the other side's intentions until they become absurd, and then to attack this absurdity. Who, then, has concluded a written military agreement, binding us unilaterally, or who intends at present to do so ? Certainly not the responsible military authorities. Where, then, is this dreaded exposure of ourselves ? That the Treaty of Rapallo has brought upon us the suspicion that we could have achieved this increase of power *without* binding ourselves is the main advantage, scarcely to be over-estimated, of this Agreement.

What, then, is our aim ? What do we want from, in, and with Russia ? Wherein lies the dreaded eastern orientation ?

We want two things. Firstly, a strong Russia, economically, politically, and therefore militarily, and thus indirectly a stronger Germany in as far as we would be strengthening a possible ally. We also want, cautiously and tentatively at first, a direct increase of strength for ourselves by helping to build up in Russia an armaments industry which in case of need would be of use to us.

Our first aim would, of course, be directly promoted by such an armaments industry. It would be carried out by private German firms who would follow our instructions. The extent of this development would depend on how the situation in Russia progressed, and on the goodwill and efficiency of German private industry. Russian requests for further military assistance could, as far as was deemed possible and beneficial, be met by supplying materials and personnel. In other military aspects contact could, on request from Russia, be established and maintained, for which purpose it would be desirable to have military representatives on both sides. Details cannot be discussed here, and in any case are matters for the future. The aim of preparing direct rearmament will be served by the same method of private industry.

In all these measures, still largely in the initial phase, participation, and even official recognition by the German Government would be absolutely out of the question. The detailed negotiations could only be conducted by military authorities. It should be taken for granted that the latter make no agreements binding on the Reich without the knowledge of the political authorities. As long as the German Government do not conduct official negotiations, the German Embassy in Moscow is not the proper place in which to negotiate. It should merely not work in opposition to the aims described, and should be inwardly in agreement with the policy pursued. The man who still lives in the days of Versailles, and maintains that Germany has permanently abjured all 'imperialist and military aims', that is, stripped of its demogogic jargon, all policy of action, is not fit to represent German interests in Russia, nor perhaps anywhere else.

I will touch on one or two more objections to the policy demanded towards Russia. Germany today is certainly not in a position to resist France. Our policy should be to prepare the means of doing so in the future. A French advance through Germany to go to the help of Poland would make nonsense from the military point of view, so long as Germany did not voluntarily cooperate. The idea springs from the notions of our 1919 diplomats, and there have been three years of work since then. War on the Rhine between France and Russia is a political bogy. Germany will not be Bolshevized, even by an understanding with Russia on external matters.

The German nation, with its Socialist majority, would be averse from a policy of action, which has to reckon with the possibility of war. It must be admitted that the spirit surrounding the Peace Delegation at Versailles has not yet disappeared, and that the stupid cry of 'No more war !' is widely echoed. It is echoed by many bourgeois-pacifist elements, but among the workers and also among the members of the official Social Democrat Party there are many who are not prepared to eat out of the hands of France and Poland. It is true that there is a widespread and understandable need for peace among the German people. The clearest heads, when considering the pros and cons of war, will be those of the military, but to pursue a policy means to take the lead. In spite of everything, the German people will follow the leader in the struggle for their existence. Our task is to prepare for this struggle, for we shall not be spared it.

If it comes to war — and that seems to be already within measurable distance — it will *not* be the duty of our leading statesmen to keep Germany out of war — that would be either impossible or suicidal — but to come in on the right side with all possible strength.

(Signed) S.

The Government of the Reich found it hard to fulfil Brockdorff-Rantzau's conditions with regard to the *Reichswehr*. The Count went, nevertheless, as Ambassador to Moscow where he later came into conflict with the policy of the German Government. He was bitterly opposed to Stresemann's policy of *Erfüllung* and to the entry of Germany into the League of Nations, preferring to champion the cause of Russo-German *rapprochement*.

Von Seeckt had, in fact, achieved his major objective. He had been able to preserve the Army's ability to maintain foreign relations without interference from the German Foreign Office. The *Reichswehr's* character of a state within a state was thus preserved. Moreover the Seeckt policy produced immediate practical results. During the *Ruhrkampf*, when Germany was fully preoccupied with France and Belgium, the Soviet Government let it be known in Warsaw that they would mobilize if Poland attempted any anti-German move such as the seizure of East Prussia.[1] To von Seeckt's clear-thinking mind this placed Germany only under an obligation to reciprocal action against Poland, which to him was the axis of Russo-German co-operation. He felt no inhibitions later in the Year of Testing at ordering the *Reichswehr* to shoot down German Communists in Saxony, Thuringia and Hamburg. The ideological factor did not enter into his calculations respecting the Soviet Government. They might be Voodooists or Sun Worshippers or adherents of the Salvation Army, for all he cared; he regarded them solely as allies who, though erratic and not to be completely relied upon, had yet something of value to contribute to the restoration of the German Army and the German Reich. The fact that they happened to be Communists influenced him not one whit in favour of their fellow Communists within Germany, who constituted an entirely separate and unrelated menace, a menace which he was prepared to suppress with ruthless vigour.

Thus at the close of 1923 von Seeckt had established himself, and, in his person, the German Army, as the recognized arbiter of the internal affairs of the Reich and, to some extent, of her foreign policy also. But as Stresemann's hands became freed of domestic problems — he ceased to be Chancellor in November — it became

---

[1] Louis Fischer, *The Soviets in World Affairs* (London, 1930), pp. 451-2. According to Mr. Fischer, who, it must be remembered, was at this time an ardent apologist for the Soviet Union, but has since recanted (see *The God that Failed*, London, 1950), the Poles made a direct approach to Moscow through Radek, offering the Bolsheviks a free hand to establish a Communist régime in Germany provided that Poland could annex East Prussia. The offer was refused and, says Mr. Fischer, 'the Bolsheviks saved the situation for Germany by keeping her eastern neighbour in inactivity'.

F

increasingly difficult for the Foreign Minister and the Commander-in-Chief of the *Reichswehr* to see eye to eye on policy.

The real position of Stresemann in all these matters is still not completely clear, although several studies have recently appeared, based on the documentary material from the German Foreign Office Archives which has been made available to private research workers in the Public Record Office in London, and the National Archives in Washington.[1] His concept of Germany's place in Europe was basically that of Rathenau, but he lacked Rathenau's romantic mysticism and Hebraic imagination. Like von Seeckt he was motivated by a strong desire to see Germany restored to a position of power, but whereas von Seeckt was prepared to bring this about in concert with Russia alone, Stresemann sought, as he said, to make Germany 'the bridge which would bring East and West together in the development of Europe'. He desired to conciliate the Western Powers in order to expedite the withdrawal of the Allied Armies of occupation from Germany. He wished Germany to enter the League of Nations because, fully alive to the possibilities presented by the public sessions of the Council and the Assembly, he proposed to air before these bodies Germany's grievances in respect of War Guilt, Disarmament, Danzig and the Saar ; matters in which, as he wrote to the German Crown Prince, 'a skilful speaker at a plenary session of the League may make it very disagreeable for the Entente'.[2] On the other hand he told Krestinsky, the Soviet Ambassador in Berlin, that Germany's presence on the Council would enable her to veto any anti-Russian moves there. Further than this, however, he would not go, and when, in 1924, in an attempt to bribe Germany not to enter the League, the Soviet Government proposed a partition of Poland and the restoration of the German-Russian frontier of 1914, Stresemann refused the offer, contenting himself with the assurance to Litvinov and Krestinsky that Germany had no intention of supporting the Entente or Poland against Russia and that this intention formed the basis of the argument with the Western Powers over Article 16 of the Covenant.[3]

[1] See p. 141, footnote 2.
[2] Letter to the Crown Prince, dated September 7, 1925 (*Stresemann Diaries*, ii, 504).
[3] Article 16 of the Covenant made it obligatory upon all members of the League to take part in financial and economic sanctions against a recalcitrant State. Further, States Members must contribute to the armed forces, as recommended by the Council, to be used for the protection of the covenants of the League, whether the State against whom action was to be taken was a member of the League or not. By a Note of December 1, 1925, the Locarno Powers other than Germany informed her that they interpreted these obligations as constituting a pledge by Members of the League to co-operate 'loyally and effectively' in resistance to

It is to be doubted whether, as some believe, the apparent triumph of Stresemann's policy of peace and reconciliation in the West only masked a policy of war and revenge in the East (*i.e.* Poland), of which the principal exponents were in the *Reichswehr* Ministry.[1] To believe this is to over-simplify. To Stresemann conciliation did not mean weakness or passivity. He knew of von Seeckt's transactions with Russia and was prepared to connive at them.[2] He certainly denied categorically to Lord D'Abernon in November 1923 the existence of the armament factories in Russia,[3] and it must, therefore, have been somewhat embarrassing for him, when, three years later, the disclosures in the *Manchester Guardian* and by Scheidemann in the *Reichstag*, coincided with the announcement from Stockholm that he had been awarded the Nobel Peace Prize (December 9, 1926). On the other hand, he removed Ago von Maltzan, the greatest exponent of German-Russian *rapprochement*, from the Foreign Office,[4] and encountered the most bitter opposition to his Locarno policy from von Seeckt and Brockdorff-Rantzau, whereas the *Reichswehr* Minister, Otto Gessler, usually a firm adherent to von Seeckt's views, supported Stresemann.[5]

Von Seeckt remained profoundly opposed to the Locarno policy. He regarded it as an unwarranted appeasement of an insatiable France, determined in the long run upon the destruction of Germany. He was also sceptical of the profit which Germany would derive from entering the League of Nations, which to him appeared as selling out to the West and a consequent weakening of the Russian connection. By accepting the terms of the Locarno Agreement

any act of aggression 'to an extent which is compatible with its military situation and takes into consideration its geographical position'. In a Note to the Soviet Government of April 24, 1926, Stresemann used this interpretation as an assurance to Russia that, should the Council of the League arrive at a decision (in which Germany could not concur) that the U.S.S.R. was an aggressor in the event of war with some other State, Germany would not consider herself bound by the obligations of Article 16.   [1] Cf. Scheele, p. 257.

[2] Hans W. Gatzke, *Stresemann and the Rearmament of Germany* (Baltimore, 1954), pp. 77 *et seq.*; Gerald Freund, pp. 169-71. Another book which makes use of new archive materials is Annalise Thimme's *G. Stresemann. Eine politische Biographie* (Hanover, 1957). See also Gatzke's articles, 'The Stresemann Papers', in *Journal of Modern History*, March 1954, and 'Von Rapallo nach Berlin : Stresemann und die deutsche Russlandspolitik', *Vierteljahrshefte für Zeitgeschichte*, 4 jhrg. January 1956.

[3] *D'Abernon Diaries*, ii, 272.

[4] 'Had he remained as Secretary of State at the Foreign Office, there would have been no Locarno', wrote Lord D'Abernon. 'He was too wedded to the Russian connection. His whole bias was to sacrifice everything to relations with Russia, which meant a certain deference to Russian desires, and Russia desired nothing less than an assured peace in the West' (*Portraits and Appreciations*, pp. 163-4).   [5] *Stresemann Diaries*, ii, 139.

and the Covenant of the League Germany assumed certain obligations to Poland, the ally of the Western Powers, and Poland was the
immediate object of Russian aversion, from which derived the
imperative need for a *rapprochement* with Germany.

Despite the strong support of the Nationalist Party, Brockdorff-
Rantzau and von Seeckt were unable to defeat the negotiation of
the Locarno Agreement, but later events played into their hands.
The fiasco of the session of the Assembly specially convened in
March 1926 to admit Germany to the League, from which Stresemann returned humiliated to Berlin, had its inevitable repercussions.
The Nationalists urged him to abandon the policy of Locarno and
Geneva and to enter into closer relations with Russia. This he
refused to do, but he was prepared to enter into a reinsurance agreement with the Soviet Union. 'I had said that I would not come
to conclude a treaty with Russia so long as our political situation in
the other direction was not cleared up', he had told Krestinsky in
the previous June, 'as I wanted to answer the question whether we
had a treaty with Russia in the negative'.[1] Now, however, the
Locarno Agreement had been initialed and signed, and the way
was clear to negotiate with Moscow not a treaty of alliance, but a
reaffirmation of the Rapallo Agreement. The German-Soviet Treaty
of Neutrality and Non-Aggression was signed in Berlin on April
24, 1926. By it both parties agreed to settle all disputes amicably,
to observe neutrality in cases of armed conflict and under no circumstances to take part in any economic or financial measures against the
other by third parties.

Thus were the Seeckt and Stresemann policies welded together
in a document which — renewed by the Brüning Government in
1931, and ratified by Hitler in 1933 — became the recognized basis
of the Nazi-Soviet Pact of 1939.[2]

(vi)

Von Seeckt's activities for the clandestine circumvention of the
restrictions imposed upon Germany by the military clauses of the
Treaty of Versailles were by no means confined to the Russian
connection. However valuable the results of this liaison with
Moscow might prove, they could never be anything but secondary

[1] *Stresemann Diaries*, ii, 472.
[2] The Preamble to the Nazi-Soviet Pact of August 23, 1939, declares the two
parties to be 'desirous of strengthening the cause of peace between Germany and
the U.S.S.R. and proceeding from the fundamental provisions of the Neutrality
Agreement concluded in April 1926'. No mention is made of the Rapallo Agreement, although this in its turn was recognized as the basis of the 1926 Treaty.

in importance to the effort which must be made within the Reich itself. The 'Army in little', which he was in process of perfecting for future military expansion, must be matched by an economic organization within Germany equally capable of expansion and designed to equip and maintain the military might of Germany once that had been restored.

The parallel planning and preparation for the total economic mobilization of the State for military purposes was as vitally important to von Seeckt as the training and reorganization of the Army itself, for he was among the first to realize and appreciate the industrial aspect of military development in the age of total war. 'There is only one way to equip masses with weapons', he wrote in 1930, 'and that is by fixing the type and at the same time arranging for mass production in case of need. The army is able, in co-operation with technical science, to establish the best type of weapon for the time being by constant study in testing shops and on practice grounds. An agreement must be made with industry to secure that this fixed type can be reproduced at once and in necessary quantities. The intensive preparations necessary for this co-operation will hardly be possible without legislative sanction.' [1]

Von Seeckt was writing not in an academic vacuum but out of his own personal experience. It was precisely this task which he set for his subordinates when, in November 1924, he formed a special and highly secret office in the Bendlerstrasse, under the direction of General Wurzbacher, with the guiding principle that 'the outcome of a War of Liberation will largely depend on the Economic General Staff'.[2] The immediate task of this office, the *Rüstamt* (short for *Rüstungsamt*), was that of preparing plans for the economic mobilization of the Reich for the equipment and maintenance of an army of 63 divisions.[3] It became their duty to ascertain the total requirements in armaments, munitions, equipment and clothing of the Army and Navy, and also of a potential Air Force, the raw materials necessary for these requirements, and also the essential transport and other services. In addition, the *Rüstamt* was instructed to explore the possibility of obtaining the co-operation of industry in the establishment of 'spear-head organizations', not only within Germany but also in such countries as Austria, Switzerland, Sweden, Spain, the Netherlands and Italy. A vast card-index was begun as

[1] *Thoughts of a Soldier*, p. 66.
[2] '*Der Ausgang eines Befreiungskampfes wird wesentlich von der Güte des wirtschaftlichen Generalstabes abhängen.*'
[3] Later, in March 1926, it was found that industry was unable to provide for so large a military establishment and the programme was accordingly scaled down to 21 divisions.

a basis for a survey of foreign raw materials and industries, and special emphasis was laid on the importance and urgency of training military officers in economic affairs. By February 1925 a *Wehrwirt-schaftsoffizier* had been appointed in each of the seven military districts of the Reich, specially selected agents of proved confidence and security, whose duty it was to concentrate on the development of economic and industrial rearmament.

The approaches of the *Rüstamt* met with warm enthusiasm in the circles of German heavy industry, many of whom had already taken their own measures to replace the plant and property demolished as a result of the orders of the Inter-Allied Commission of Control.[1] There is now ample published evidence of the co-operation which these Industrial Barons gave to the *Reichswehr* in these early days of secret rearmament.[2] They openly boasted of it during the Third Reich and some of their boastings were later used against them in evidence. It is only necessary to take one case as an illustration of what could be done inside and outside Germany in the days when the official policy of the Reich was based on the word 'Fulfilment'.

As a result of the Allied demolition order, property amounting to more than 104 million gold marks belonging to the Krupp interests was destroyed : 9,300 machines with a total weight of 60,000 tons were demolished ; 801,420 gauges, jigs, moulds and tools with an aggregate weight of nearly a thousand tons, together with 379 installations, such as hardening ovens, oil- and water-tanks, cooling plants and cranes, were smashed.

'In those days the situation seemed hopeless. It appeared even more desperate if one remained as firmly convinced as I was that "Versailles" could not represent the end', wrote Gustav Krupp von Bohlen und Halbach, the adopted head of the dynasty,[3] in proud

---

[1] Because it freed the German armament industry from the threat of rapid obsolescence, the destruction of the 1918 equipment by the Control Commission proved in the end more advantageous than not to Germany. In any case, however, in the opinion of one of the members of the Commission, its work could not be considered as having crippled the industry. 'After a most careful estimate by our experts in all the industrial districts of Germany, we found that, from the moment control is withdrawn, it would take the German authorities only one year to attain their maximum production in 1918 of guns and munitions', wrote Brigadier-General Morgan in the *Quarterly Review* for October 1924.

[2] *E.g.* Colonel T. H. Minshall, *Future Germany* (London, 1943), pp. 29-44 ; also Scheele, pp. 110-19 ; Benoist-Méchin, ii, pp. 371-81.

[3] On October 15, 1906, Gustav von Bohlen und Halbach, a somewhat obscure Westphalian aristocrat and diplomat, married Bertha, elder daughter and heiress of Friedrich Alfred Krupp, the last male descendant of Peter Friedrich Krupp (1787–1826), the founder of the family business. In order to preserve the family connection, the two names were conjoined. Indicted before the International

remembrance in 1941. 'If ever there should be a resurrection for Germany, if ever she were to shake off the chains of Versailles, then Krupps would have to be prepared. The machines were demolished ; the tools were destroyed ; but one thing remained — the men, the men at the drawing boards and in the workshops, who, in happy co-operation had brought the manufacture of guns to its last perfection. Their skill would have to be saved, their immense resources of knowledge and experience. Even though camouflaged I had to maintain Krupps as an armament factory for the distant future, in spite of all obstacles.' [1]

Thus the great armament industry was temporarily 'converted' into an arsenal of peace, devoted to the manufacture of articles which seemed to be particularly remote from the activities of the weapon-smithy. 'Even the Allied spying commission was fooled', Krupp adds proudly: 'padlocks, milk cans, cash registers, rail-mending machines, refuse carts and similar rubbish appeared really innocent, and locomotives and motor cars appeared perfectly "peaceful".'

But behind this pacific smoke-screen the genius of armament was at work devising means whereby these simple agricultural and domestic implements could be utilized for the War of Liberation. The study and development of heavy tractors paved the way for experiments in the construction of tanks, and in 1928 — just one year after the withdrawal of the Allied Control Commission — the first tanks were in production at the Grusonwerk.[2]

The men at the drawing-boards and in the workshops were not the only assets left to Krupps after the demolition. They retained patents, licences and secret processes of manufacture, which by the simple device of forming anonymous limited companies with foreign subsidiaries, could be utilized outside Germany, the blue-prints being provided by the experts in the research and experimental departments in Essen. Thus, through the Siderius A.G., Krupp controlled shipbuilding yards in Rotterdam, where a special centre for ordnance manufacture was established, staffed by the· constructional department of the Germania shipyard at Kiel, who had been moved *en bloc* to Rotterdam. Similar holding companies were established in Barcelona, Bilbao and Cadiz, so that U-boats could

Military Tribunal at Nuremberg in November 1945, as one of the twenty-four major war criminals, Gustav Krupp von Bohlen was adjudged too ill to stand his trial. He died on January 16, 1950, at the age of eighty.

[1] Chapter, entitled 'Works Leader and Armament Worker', written by Krupp in April 1941, for inclusion in a book compiled by the Todt Organization as a presentation volume to the German armament workers (*International Military Tribunal Document* D-64).

[2] Memorandum, dated February 21, 1944, on establishment of an experimental tank factory by the Grusonwerk (*IMT Document* D-96).

be, and were, built in Holland and in Spain, as well as in Turkey and Finland, under the expert guidance of the best German naval architects.[1]

Perhaps the greatest *coup* achieved by Krupp during the period of secret rearmament was the penetration of the Bofors Arms factory in Sweden, to whom Krupp proceeded to sell the most valuable of his assets in patents and secret armament processes in return for a substantial block of the company's shares. To these holdings he added by purchases on the stock exchange, the transaction being financed by a substantial grant from the Reich Government, ostensibly given for the rehabilitation of the Rheinmetall Company.[2] By December 1925 — that is to say, the month in which the Locarno Agreements were signed in London — Krupps had acquired a controlling interest in Bofors, holding six million out of nineteen million shares, and were again busily engaged in the manufacture and development of the latest patterns of heavy guns, anti-aircraft guns and tanks.[3]

Such then is an example — and one example only — of the process of secret rearmament carried out by the heavy industry of Germany in co-operation with and under the stimulus of the *Reichswehr*. The process followed the lines sketched by von Seeckt and elaborated by the *Rüstamt*; it was enthusiastically executed by those whom it would chiefly benefit.

The question inevitably arises, did Stresemann know of these illicit preparations for war at the time that he was negotiating a pact of security with the Western Powers ? There is every reason to believe that the Reich Cabinet gave their tacit consent to the clandestine operations of the *Reichswehr*. Certainly Gessler, the *Reichswehr* Minister, was informed and also the Minister of Economic Affairs, the Nationalist Dr. Albert Neuhaus, who, in April 1925, set up a special secret division in his Ministry to facilitate closer liaison with the *Rüstamt*. If Stresemann did not know it at the time, he certainly knew it later, for another of his colleagues, Carl Severing, Reich Minister of Interior, described at Nuremberg a Cabinet session of October 18, 1928, at which the heads of the

[1] *Essays on the Operational and Tactical considerations of the German Navy and the consequent measures taken for its expansion between 1919–1935.* Files of the German Admiralty (*IMT Document* D-854).

[2] According to a statement reported by the German Trans-Ocean Agency on April 15, 1943, by Dr. Waniger, the director of technical design in the Rheinmetall-Börsig Company, in association with Krupps : 'The illegal manufacture of arms began in 1921. In those days the construction of big guns was taken up most thoroughly.'

[3] Bernhard Menne, *Krupp, or the Lords of Essen* (London, 1939), pp. 364-71.

Army and Navy 'familiarized the members of the Cabinet with the details of what might be considered a concealment of the budget or violations of the Versailles Treaty'.[1]

But if Stresemann had really not had an inkling at least of what was going on at the time in the matter of secret rearmament, it was something of an achievement, for as early as January 1924, there had been an exchange of letters on the subject between Professor Ludwig Quidde and General von Seeckt. The veteran leader of German pacifism, who four years later was to follow Stresemann as the Nobel Peace Prize winner, wrote on January 3, expressing concern at the clandestine militarization, the existence of which was apparently well known outside military circles. Von Seeckt replied with perhaps understandable choler, that he could not enter into a discussion of the subjects raised by Professor Quidde. 'For a people as maltreated internationally as the Germans, ideas of international pacifism are difficult to understand in any event', he added. 'But if there are Germans who, after the experiences of the Ruhr invasion and in a time when France daily tramples the Treaty of Versailles underfoot, argue in favour of the execution of that treaty in favour of the French, then I can only call this the peak of national indignity. Incidentally, I want to draw your attention to the fact that in case the question touched on in your letter should be discussed publicly, I should immediately act against you, on the basis of emergency powers ; and this regardless of whether or not a proceeding for high treason would be instituted.'

With some courage the peace organizations, on whose behalf Professor Quidde had written, published von Seeckt's reply, which was as near an admission of their allegations as might be obtained, a full week before the emergency powers were withdrawn.[2] The Foreign Minister was fully alive to this exchange of letters because Quidde had sent him copies of the correspondence. These copies were duly filed among Stresemann's papers and are now in the archives of the German Foreign Office.[3]

From all available evidence the conclusion is inescapable that at the time of the Locarno negotiations, Stresemann was well informed of von Seeckt's policy, and either condoned it or deliberately closed his eyes and ears. Von Seeckt at least had no doubts as to his duty, which was to use the façade created by Stresemann's *Erfüllungspolitik* as a screen for completing that steady process of remilitarization which was to receive in later years the public

[1] *Nuremberg Record*, xiv, 255.
[2] *Die Weltbühne*, vol. xx, No. 6, February 7, 1924 (quoted by Fried, pp. 248-9).
[3] Hans W. Gatzke, p. 19.

F 2

commendation of the reconstituted General Staff: 'When Hitler came to power in 1933, he found all the technical preparations for rearmament ready, thanks to the *Reichswehr*'.[1]

(vii)

On February 28, 1925, Friedrich Ebert, last Imperial Chancellor and first President of the German Reich, died suddenly. With his death a perceptible change passed over the parliamentary democracy of Germany. Hitherto it had been seen at its inefficient best; thereafter it was to show at its increasingly inefficient worst, until its disappearance in a final welter of betrayal and ineptitude some eight years later.

Not perhaps a great man as judged by the world's standards, Fritz Ebert was one for whom no German need feel anything but respect. Though vilified by many of his countrymen, he had deserved well of the German Reich. Courage, no little shrewdness, a fine singleness of purpose and a deep sense of patriotism had been his salient attributes, and lesser men would have shrunk from the overwhelming responsibilities which this former saddler, joiner and café-keeper was called upon to take up at the moment of his country's downfall. A man of destiny *malgré lui*, he sought to the end to preserve the Monarchy, but when a Republic was forced upon him and he found himself rather breathlessly hustled into the position of its chief executive, he assumed this office with a dignity and a nobility of spirit that was unexpected. Though his patriotism was frequently impugned by his opponents, in reality it never wavered. His judgment may be questioned, his wisdom in forming and maintaining so close an alliance with the Army may be doubted, but his patriotism as a German, with the true sense of all that that implied, can never for a moment be gainsaid.

Even his relations with the Army appear in retrospect to have been an inevitable sequence in an inexorable fatality. Whatever the facts may have been, the imminence of a Communist *coup d'état* must have been very real to Ebert on the night of November 9, 1918, and how else could he meet the threat save in alliance with the Army? From then on, one step led to another. Successive Spartakist and Separatist crises had rendered the Republic and its President more and more dependent upon the *Reichswehr*, until latterly the feckless folly of the *Reichstag* and the political parties had left the President and the Army the sole dependable props of the structure

---

[1] Statement by Major Wurmsiedler, of the German General Staff, on the German Radio, May 26, 1941.

of government. Once one has become imprisoned in the hug of
the grizzly bear it is well-nigh impossible to break the embrace.
This Ebert had learned in his relations with the *Reichswehr*, and
the *Reichswehr* were later to learn it, in their turn and to their cost,
in their relations with the Nazi Party. But it would have taken
something stronger, subtler and more ruthless than Ebert's right-
wing Menshevism to have withstood successfully Hans von Seeckt
in his relentless pursuit of the fulfilment of his selfless anonymous
ambition.

   The choice of Ebert's successor was as vitally important to the
Army as it was to the Republic, for the President was not only the
Chief Executive of the Reich but also Supreme Commander of its
armed forces. The candidate of the *Reichswehr* was Otto Gessler,
the Minister of Defence, and for a moment it seemed as if he would
be elected without difficulty, for he was supported by a group of
parties extending from the Nationalists on the Right to the Democrats
on the Left. But the unsavoury character of German politics
asserted itself. Gessler was bitterly opposed by those same radical
elements of the Right and Left which he, together with von Seeckt,
had fought and defeated in 1923. More important than the slanders
of extremist groups was the opposition expressed by Stresemann
himself. He claimed that Gessler's election would damage Franco-
German relations because the French might think that the political
leadership of Germany was passing into the hands of the *Reichswehr*.
He said that von Hoesch, the German Ambassador in Paris, had
raised objections to Gessler on an earlier occasion. Stresemann's
influence was decisive in ruining Gessler's chances of election, with
the result that the coalition formed to support him split up into its
component parts, and that on March 29, 1925, seven major candidates
offered themselves to the electorate.[1]

   The Parties of the Right, the Nationalists and the German
People's Party, found a compromise candidate in the eminently dull
and respectable *Bürgermeister* of Duisburg, Dr. Karl Jarres; the
Social Democrats chose Otto Braun, the Minister-President of
Prussia; the Centre selected Wilhelm Marx, a former and future
Reich Chancellor; the Communists put forward their leader, Ernst
Thälmann; the Bavarian People's Party nominated Dr. Heinrich
Held, the Minister-President of Bavaria, and the Democrats Dr.
Willy Hellpach, the *Staatspräsident* of Baden. At the last moment
the situation was still further complicated by the emergence of
General Ludendorff as the standard-bearer of National Socialism,

[1] Wheeler-Bennett, *Hindenburg*, pp. 252-4 ; Gessler, pp. 333-8 and pp. 506-7.

which most people believed had been buried on the Odeonsplatz in Munich two years before.

With so wide a field it was impossible for any one candidate to obtain the absolute majority of votes cast which was necessary for election on the first ballot, and a second was announced for April 26. Both Right and Left saw the necessity for concentrating their forces. Marx was agreed upon as the candidate for all the Parties of the Left and Centre, with the exception of the Communists, who persisted in keeping Thälmann in the field, but the Right were only at one in deciding that Jarres, although he had headed the poll on the first ballot, was not a strong enough candidate to beat Marx in a straight fight. He was therefore somewhat unceremoniously bundled back to Duisburg, and the Parties of the Right cast about in vain for his successor.

The Nationalists thought, first of all, of the possibility of an Imperial Prince as their candidate, but reluctantly abandoned this course as impracticable. They then seriously considered nominating von Seeckt, but he too was discarded for the reason that, though he was indeed the hero of Gorlice and the Rumanian campaign, he had since then shed the blood of Communists in Saxony, Thuringia and Hamburg, and of Nazis in Bavaria, and that these more recent exploits would not recommend him to the electorate. They likewise rejected the suggestion of a great industrialist, such as Krupp, or Thyssen, on the grounds that the choice of a representative of Big Business, and all that that implied, would play too much into the hands of their opponents. At last they hit upon the idea of Hindenburg, and after considerable dissension among themselves, some strenuous opposition from Stresemann and the German People's Party, and a spirited display of genuine unwillingness on the part of the Old Gentleman himself, Field-Marshal Paul von Beneckendorff und Hindenburg was nominated as candidate of the *Reichsblok*, and on April 26, 1925, was elected President of the German Reich in the seventy-ninth year of his age.[1]

The election of Hindenburg to the position of first citizen of the Reich had a profound effect upon the relation of the Army to the Republic and upon the personal position of von Seeckt. The *Reichswehr* as a whole were no more wedded to the Republic than they had ever been, but they had found in its new President a

[1] Wheeler-Bennett, pp. 255-66. Stresemann was opposed to putting forward either von Seeckt or von Hindenburg as a candidate, on the grounds that the election of a soldier as President of the German Republic at this juncture would inevitably arouse suspicion in France and in Britain, and might therefore jeopardize the success of the negotiations which three months earlier he had opened in the greatest secrecy with London and Paris for the conclusion of a pact of security.

Supreme Commander to whom they could give their unswerving loyalty as a Field-Marshal. The hero of the victories of Tannenberg and the Masurian Lakes, the veteran commander who had led them back to the Fatherland in the dark days of defeat, was a very different personality to the portly, unmilitary, thoroughly bourgeois figure of Fritz Ebert. The Army, therefore, would be loyal to the Republic so long as its President and their Supreme Commander remained a Field-Marshal, and any attempt to overthrow the Republic or to change its constitution by a military *coup d'état* could therefore only succeed with the support of the President. Thus, while the election of Hindenburg increased the military influence in the Republic, the Army and the Republic were welded together in the person of the Field-Marshal, and as long as Hindenburg kept his constitutional oath the position of the Republic was unassailable. The President alone could overthrow it.

For von Seeckt, on the other hand, the election of Hindenburg meant an inevitable diminution of stature. Hitherto he had been the first soldier of the Reich and the guardian of the Constitution to whom the President had turned for support as to an equal. Now all this was changed. The Commander-in-Chief of the *Reichswehr* was very definitely the subordinate of the Supreme Commander, and the Marshal took this position as seriously as — perhaps even more seriously than — he did that of President of the Reich. Hindenburg insisted on all military questions being reserved for his personal decision, and while he offered a determined resistance to all attempts on the part of civilian politicians to interfere in military issues, he was equally strongly opposed to any independence of action on the part of his subordinate Generals.

Moreover, the personal relationship between von Seeckt and the new President was very different from that which had existed with his predecessor. With Ebert, von Seeckt had established a measure of respect and understanding, almost a degree of comradeship. With Hindenburg, there was nothing of this. Old jealousies prevailed. The Field-Marshal could never forget — or forgive — the memory that the break-through of Gorlice had been won on *his* front, and that von Seeckt had been brought by von Falkenhayn from the West to win it under the eye of the Emperor, while he, the Commander-in-Chief in the East, had been forced to stand by with Ludendorff and Hoffmann, and watch this new-comer carry off the laurels of victory.[1]

The diminution in von Seeckt's political stature and influence was not lost upon those who, for varying reasons, had found him an obstacle to their personal advancement or that of their policies.

[1] Cf. Wheeler-Bennett, pp. 55-6.

The insatiable intriguing ambition of Kurt von Schleicher now caused him to murmur against his chief. He and von Seeckt had never been on intimate terms, they were too different in character for that; von Seeckt a far-seeing planner and von Schleicher a political opportunist. Yet von Schleicher had been closely associated with his chief in that little group of trusted confidants in the Bendlerstrasse and had played an important part in the 'Black Reichswehr' affair, in the formulation of the Russian connection, and in the organization of 'military government' within the Reich during the Year of Testing. In all these episodes von Seeckt had recognized and appreciated the executive ability of his subordinate, as well as his skill in political negotiations for which the *Reichswehr* Chief himself was less well suited. But von Schleicher could never dominate von Seeckt as he could Gröner. He felt an inferiority in the presence of that ice-cold, cynical intellect. Now, with the coming of Hindenburg to the Palace of the Reich President, von Schleicher saw an opportunity for personal preferment in his friendship with the Marshal's son Oskar, a fellow officer in the Third Regiment of Foot Guards, whose shallow character and limited intelligence made him a ready tool for von Schleicher's unscrupulous ambition.

Stresemann also viewed with some satisfaction the lessening of von Seeckt's authority. He had successfully won over both Hindenburg and Gessler to the support of his Policy of Fulfilment, and he regarded von Seeckt's continued opposition to any security pact with the Western Powers as an unwarranted infringement of his control over foreign relations. Though he carried through his policy to a successful conclusion in the Locarno Agreement of October-December 1925, in spite of von Seeckt's resistance, Stresemann continued to nurse a sense of grievance and suspicion against the General.

Thus the election of Hindenburg in April 1925 marked the beginning of the end of the Seeckt period, and when, some eighteen months later, von Seeckt committed the unpardonable indiscretion of permitting the eldest son of the Crown Prince to take part in the autumn manœuvres of 1926, the period came to an abrupt termination. The fact that von Seeckt had granted this permission entirely on his own authority, without having informed either his Minister or his Supreme Commander, indicates how little he himself appears to have realized his own loss of power. Such complete disregard for ministerial responsibility and military discipline might possibly have been ignored under Ebert, but it was certain of disaster under Hindenburg. When the facts came to light in a clamour of denunciation from the press of the Left, both Gessler, the Minister concerned, and Stresemann pressed Hindenburg to call for von Seeckt's resignation, and it may be imagined that no favourable whisper in the Presidential *Umgebung* was forthcoming from Kurt von Schleicher. Von Seeckt bowed to the storm, recognizing in it the occasion rather than the cause of his fall. He resigned on October 9, 1926.

His passing marked the end of the 'non-political' *Reichswehr*. Thenceforward, under the influence of von Schleicher, it was to participate more and more in the internal political affairs of the Reich, with a marked inadequacy of appreciation of the nature and difficulties of the issues involved. The Seeckt Period had seen the German Army established as the strongest single political factor within the State, the recognized guardian of the Reich ; the Schleicher Period saw the descent of the Army into the arena of political intrigue, with a consequent besmirching of its reputation and the ultimate destruction of its authority.

PART II

THE ARMY AND HITLER

1920–1933

'The hour is coming when these untrained bands will become battalions, when the battalions will become regiments, and the regiments divisions; when the old cockade will be raised from the mire; when the old banners will once again wave before us.'—ADOLF HITLER (before the People's Court at Munich, March 27, 1924).

CHAPTER I

COURTSHIP, HONEYMOON AND SEPARATION

(1920–1926)

(i)

'WE had realized that there was a healthy kernel in the Hitler movement', General von Lossow told a crowded court-room in Munich in February 1924; 'we saw this healthy kernel in the fact that the movement possessed the power to make converts among the workers for the cause of nationalism.'[1] This statement, made in the course of the trial of Ludendorff and Hitler after their unsuccessful *coup* of November 1923, epitomizes the relationship between the *Reichswehr* in Bavaria and the Nationalist Socialist movement during the period between the collapse of Germany and the abortive Nazi *Putsch*.

To understand fully the complexity of the circumstances it is necessary to appreciate something of the peculiar position occupied by Bavaria within the Reich after the collapse and the equally peculiar position of the *Reichswehr* within Bavaria. The spearhead of the German Revolution had been in Bavaria. The naval mutiny which had broken out at Kiel on November 4, 1918, was hailed as a revolutionary movement in Munich, where, on November 7, the Bavarians deposed the Wittelsbach dynasty, whose dukes, electors and kings had reigned over them with varying degrees of eccentricity for the past eight hundred years. Within the next six months Bavaria was governed successively by the Independent Socialist Kurt Eisner — whom Count Arco-Valley assassinated on February 21, 1919 — by the Majority Socialist Hoffmann, and by a Soviet dictatorship headed at first by anarchists and later by the communist leader, Eugene Leviné. This last régime was finally overthrown by the military operations of a composite force, directed by Noske in Berlin and commanded by Generals von Epp and von Oven, consisting of two regular Guards Divisions and *Freikorps* formations from Prussia, Bavaria and Württemberg. Munich was forced into

---

[1] Quoted by Fried (p. 27) from Georg Schott, *Das Volksbuch vom Hitler* (Munich, 1928), p. 21. See also 'Der Hitlerprozess vor dem Volksgericht in München', Part I (Munich, 1924), p. 164.

surrendering on May 1, 1919, and the Hoffmann Government was re-established under the protection of the *Reichswehr* and the Free Corps.

The period had been marked by all the severities of civil war; the taking and shooting of hostages by the revolutionaries and the inevitable revenge exacted by the liberating forces of counter-revolution. When order had been restored, the Bavarians were left with a bitter hatred of all Leftist movements and a firm determination that nothing resembling a Bolshevik revolution should ever again take place within their borders. This reaction was superimposed upon their older and equally deep-seated hostility to Prussia and a consequent antagonism to the Reich Government, which was sus-pected of being at the same time under Socialist influence and of attempting to establish too great a measure of centralization. Thus the opposition of Bavaria to the Weimar constitution was grounded both on the ideological objection to Majority Socialism and on the inherent separatism of a State which disliked being in any degree subservient to Berlin.[1]

All circumstances, therefore, combined towards Munich becom-ing the centre of reaction against the Weimar System, and it was not surprising that, at the time of the Kapp-Lüttwitz *putsch* in Berlin (March 1920), the Hoffmann Government, which had maintained a precarious existence for some nine months, was replaced by a succession of more reactionary Cabinets under Ritter von Kahr, Count Lerchenfeld and Freiherr von Knilling. After the failure of the Kapp adventure and the subsequent dissolution of the Free Corps, Bavaria became the refuge and asylum for all the disgruntled political and military elements who found themselves either pro-scribed or unemployed.

The attitude of the Army in Bavaria developed along much the same lines. It was 'particularist' rather than national, it resented the predominance of the Prussian element in the *Heeresleitung* and deplored the merging of the Bavarian General Staff with the General Staff of the *Reichswehr* in Berlin. Moreover, it showed the same hostility to the Socialist Republic. Like the military leadership in Berlin before von Seeckt took over the command, it was permeated by the spirit of politics, and successive commanding Generals in Munich, from 'the Liberator', Ritter von Epp,[2] to Otto von Lossow,

---

[1] This Bavarian resentment against a centralization of government, which had been an important factor in the *Kaiserreich*, was equally in evidence in the summer of 1949 when the Land Government in Munich refused to ratify the draft federal constitution of Bonn.

[2] Lieut.-General Franz Xaver, Ritter von Epp (1868–1947), a member of a Bavarian military family, entered the Army in 1887 and served with the Allied expeditionary force in China, 1901–2, against the Hereros in German South-West

were in constant search among the many amoebic political groupings, which were feverishly forming and reforming in Bavaria, for some Party which the *Reichswehr* might use as an instrument of its own policy. It was the achievement of Adolf Hitler that he found this Party for the *Reichswehr*.

In November 1918 Corporal Adolf Hitler was discharged from the military hospital of Pasewalk, near Stettin, where he had been treated for the effects of poison gas on the lungs and eyes, and rejoined the reserve battalion of his regiment, the 16th Bavarian Infantry, at Trauenstein, in Upper Bavaria. His record as a soldier was not discreditable and he had emerged from the war with the Iron Cross, both of the First and Second Class. He moved to Munich and was there when the Soviet Republic was established in April 1919. His activities at this time are obscure, although later he claimed that he had narrowly escaped arrest by the Communists at a time when prisoners were in some danger of being shot.[1]

Whatever Hitler's part in crushing the Soviet Republic may have been — and it was certainly not at all important — he soon found that the panic-stricken political atmosphere of Munich after the suppression of the 'Red Menace' offered him a fine opportunity to better himself. The Army was looking for propagandists of the right variety to bolster morale. He was selected with others from his regiment to attend a course of lectures and discussions which had been organized by the Army Headquarters for the purposes of political indoctrination. In the course of a debate, someone present was moved to defend the Jews at some length, and this evoked from Hitler perhaps the earliest of those anti-semitic diatribes for which he was later to become world-infamous. His capacity to sway an audience and the impeccable character of his sentiments were soon recognized, and Captain Mayr, head of the Press and Propaganda Section of the Bavarian *Reichswehr*, appointed Hitler to be an 'education officer' at a camp in Lechfeld. The Army had launched him on his political career.

It was the duty of these 'education officers' to restore the political morale of the troops, to remove the psychological effects of the military collapse, and to teach them to 'think and feel nationally and patriotically again'. The young soldiers were inculcated with

Africa, 1904–7, and in the First World War. He was one of the first to raise a Free Corps, which saw action in Bavaria and in the Ruhr. As Military Commander of Munich, Epp financed the Nazi Party in its early days. Later he became a member of the *Reichstag, Statthalter* of Bavaria and Chief of the Party's Department for Colonial Policy. He was known in the Army as '*der Mutter Gottes General*'.

    [1] Alan Bullock, *Hitler, A Study in Tyranny* (Pelican ed., London, 1962), p. 64.

the 'new traditions' of the 'stab in the back' and of the slavery imposed upon Germany by the 'shackles of Versailles'. They were encouraged to look upon the Central Government in Berlin as 'the November Criminals' who had signed away the birthright of Germany. No assignment could appeal more strongly to Hitler's gifts and emotions. He became a highly effective demagogue, and he claims that, beginning with his own company, 'many hundreds, probably thousands' of his comrades were 'brought back to the Fatherland' as a result of his lectures.

The Bavarian Army leaders were convinced that civilians could no longer be trusted to maintain political stability in the country. They decided to be vigilant in politics as well as in military affairs. Mayr sent agents to spy on all political organizations in Munich so that the Army could be forewarned against those which were subversive and give discreet support to those favourable to the national cause. It was on the authority of Mayr that Hitler went to investigate the German Workers' Party (*Deutsche Arbeiter Partei*) and made contact with its leader, Anton Drexler. Drexler was impressed by Hitler's ability as a speaker, and the programme of the DAP — nationalist, patriotic, nebulous and infinitely malleable — appealed to Hitler. It was therefore as an Army agent and with the full approval of his commanding officer that Hitler joined the ranks of the DAP as party member No. 7 in September 1919. It was the second and most important step in his political career.[1]

Though Hitler may have entered the Party as an agent of the *Reichswehr*, he very soon forsook that rôle for one of ally. He was still clothed, fed, housed and paid by the Army — he was not actually demobilized until March 1920 — but his whole activity was devoted to attaining control of the Party and remoulding it to his own design. Within six months of joining he had altogether ousted Harrer, one of the co-founders, and had caused the Party programme to be rewritten. He had passed beyond the stage of a political recruit or an army 'stooge', and stood disclosed as a well-known mob-orator, a practical politician and a potential leader of men with a policy of his own.

The new Party programme, made public at a meeting in Munich on February 24, 1920, contained much that appealed warmly to the Bavarian High Command.[2] They welcomed the demands for a Greater Germany, for the abrogation of the Treaty of Versailles,

---

[1] Ernst Deuerlein, 'Hitlers Eintritt in die Politik und die Reichswehr', *Vierteljahrshefte für Zeitgeschichte*, April 1959.

[2] The programme also appealed to individual serving officers and several were soon to join the party. One of the most notorious was Captain Ernst Röhm.

for the provision of *Lebensraum* (living space), for the settlement of Germany's surplus population and, above all, for the abolition of the professional Army enforced by the Treaty and the formation of a National Army, which meant, presumably, the reintroduction of compulsory military service. In so far as they understood the remainder of the programme, with its social policy and the open profession of anti-semitism, they were either in general agreement or regarded these points as being amongst those ephemeral items in any Party pronouncement which in due course find their way into the political limbo.

What they did not understand was that in proclaiming his Twenty-five Points, Hitler was enunciating a political credo which he regarded as fundamentally immutable, and to which, one day, the Army would be required to give its unqualified assent. These Bavarian 'particularist' reactionaries, both political and military, in their enthusiasm for this new tool which they imagined was pliable in their hands, apparently overlooked the last point in the Party programme, with its potential threat for the future : 'In order that all this may be carried out, we demand the creation of a strong central authority in the State ; the unconditional control by the political central parliament over the entire Reich and its organizations in general.'

For the Army especially this final provision was fraught with menace. In Hitler's concept there were no exceptions to this central control, which was to become a personal authority. The Army was as much an 'organization of the Reich' as any other State institution, and although at this time he still entertained a considerable degree of respect for the *Reichswehr*, this did not affect his views on the ultimate form of State structure which he was planning for the German Reich. Within this structure there was no provision for a 'State within a State', such as von Seeckt envisaged. On the contrary, every institution, from the postal services to the Army, must be subject to the control of the central authority, and, though it might take him years to establish that authority, the day was to come when he would both make and break German Field-Marshals, compel them to commit suicide, and even hang one of their number on a charge of high treason.

But all this was a quarter of a century away in the gay exciting days of March 1920, when it seemed as if all the dreams of the Right were about to be fulfilled at once. With the Ebert Government of 'November Criminals' in flight to Stuttgart, with Kapp and von Kahr installed as the Generals' nominees in Berlin and in Munich, it was almost as if the 'good old days' were back already. Former officials of the Hohenzollern and Wittelsbach Courts emerged suddenly from the social retirement which they had imposed upon themselves since November 1918 and scurried, like the White Rabbit, along dark corridors. The Crown Prince Rupprecht of Bavaria was received with even greater enthusiasm on his appearances in Munich, and a series of monarchical restorations was apparently only 'just around the corner'.

This happy period of hope was, however, short-lived. From Berlin came the news that the régime of Kapp and von Lüttwitz was crumbling, but in Bavaria the forces of reaction were able to chalk up a discreet but substantial victory.[1] The *Reichswehr* commander, Arnold Ritter von Möhl, co-operated with von Kahr and the leaders of the Bavarian *Einwohnerwehr* to overthrow Hoffmann's coalition government. From this time onwards Bavaria was to be a safe haven of refuge for anti-republican conspirators.

These developments were very favourable for Hitler. The failure in Berlin made Munich more important. For the time being Hitler and his Party became the pampered darlings of the Bavarian *Reichswehr* and the spoiled children of successive nationalist governments. General von Epp provided the money to buy the *Völkischer Beobachter* as an organ for the Party, and Ritter von Kahr and, to some degree, his successors, Lerchenfeld and von Knilling, gave police protection to the Nazis for their intrigues and propaganda against the Reich.[2]

Nevertheless the attitude of both the Army and the Government towards Hitler was still that of patron to protégé. The Bavarian High Command might indeed recognize him and his followers as a 'healthy kernel' to attract recruits to the cause of nationalism, but they also regarded them as an instrument to be used at the will and discretion of the Army. This status of tutelage was anything but agreeable to Hitler. He was ready to take all the aid and succour which the Bavarian *Reichswehr* and Government could afford him, but he was prepared to give nothing in return. He had passed beyond the vassal stage. He would no longer regard himself as on any other footing than that of equality. His plans and ambitions were growing well beyond the range of leading-strings. He had already conceived himself in the rôle of the Leader of the new

---

[1] According to Heiden, p. 82, Hitler was sent to Berlin by plane to urge the Prussian Generals to hold out until help could reach them from the south. Although this mission was a failure it was an interesting indication of Hitler's increased stature among powerful reactionary groups.

[2] The Police President of Munich, Ernst Pöhner, was an early convert to National Socialism. Hitler pays glowing tribute to him in *Mein Kampf*. (*Mein Kampf* (Munich, 1938), p. 403).

German Reich and, as he was later to tell his judges : 'The man who is born to be a dictator is not compelled ; he wills ; he is not driven forward ; he drives himself forward'.[1]

By the beginning of 1921 he had renamed the Party the *National-Sozialistische deutsche Arbeiter Partei* (NSDAP) and, relegating Drexler to the obscurity of Honorary President, had become its acknowledged Leader. The first stage of his political career had ended. With the assistance of the *Reichswehr*, he had raised himself from an unknown corporal to be head of a political movement which was already beginning to make itself heard and felt outside Bavaria. The second phase of his career was about to open, and for it Hitler set himself the political targets of imposing his will first upon the State of Bavaria and then upon the Reich as a whole.

In the attainment of these goals Hitler was not entirely confident of the support of the *Reichswehr*, nor was he willing to be entirely dependent upon it. A National Movement, such as he intended the Nazi Party to become, must stand on its own feet and have its own source of power. It was with this end in view — in addition to the immediate needs of self-protection — that in November 1921 he formed the Storm Troops (SA) ; a force composed of fanatical members of the Party, trained primarily in the technique of 'strongarm' tactics and street fighting, but ultimately designed to become, not a rival to the *Reichswehr* — Hitler always conceived of the Army as the only bearers of arms within the Reich — but a paramilitary formation to be used as an auxiliary both to the Army and to the Police in enforcing the will of the Nazi State upon the German people. The subsequent rivalry which developed between the Army and the SA was entirely unwelcome to Hitler, but his methods of resolving it should have provided a warning to the Generals that drastic ruthlessness is the final resort of dictators.

At the outset, however, the *Reichswehr* welcomed the innovation of the SA as one more example of the ability of the Nazi Movement to attract recruits to the cause of nationalism, and as a possible reserve of man-power against the Day of Liberation. Along with other illegal organizations, the Storm Troopers were allowed to carry out military exercises with the regular Army and to receive instruction in tactics and the use of weapons. They were provided with side-arms and on occasion were permitted the loan of rifles from Government arsenals. Within a year of its formation the SA numbered 6,000 men and within twelve years it was to total $2\frac{1}{2}$ million. With the approval and consent of the *Reichswehr*, but for his own purposes, Hitler had created a Party Praetorian Guard.

[1] Heiden, p. 166.

It was to wax in strength and influence until the day when, like the
Praetorians of old, it tried to dictate policy. Then Hitler, at the
behest of the *Reichswehr*, but again to suit his own purposes, was to
suppress it in the ruthless and bloody massacre of June 30, 1934.

(ii)

The entry of French troops into the Ruhr on January 11, 1923,
seemed to Hitler the opportune moment for a general uprising, not
in resistance to the invader but against the Central Government
of the Reich. In a series of frenzied speeches he urged and pleaded
for the overthrow of the 'November Criminals', but his exhortations
found no echo outside Bavaria. The storm of passion which swept
through Germany in the early days of the *Ruhrkampf* was one of
patriotic unity behind Ebert and Cuno in bitter hatred of France.
The declaration of Passive Resistance had transformed the country
overnight from a land torn by political dissension to one united in
a common willingness to meet the invader with the one weapon
available. The only result of Hitler's fulminations was the interdiction of his Party formations by the Governments of Prussia,
Saxony, Thuringia, Baden and Mecklenburg.

Frustrated in his attempt to evoke a national response to his
slogan of '*Deutschland erwache*', Hitler was forced again to restrict
himself to the confines of Bavaria, where, at least, he was sure of a
consoling animosity against Berlin. But here his movement was
but one of many patriotic organizations, among which it was not
as yet recognized as being even *primus inter pares*. Here were
collected the residue of the Free Corps, the exiled and proscribed,
the disgruntled and unemployable remnants of the old Imperial
Army. Here they had formed themselves into bitter groups with
mysterious and valiant names — 'Oberland' and 'Orka', 'Reichsflagge' and 'Viking', 'Blücherbund' and 'Bayern und Reich' —
and over them brooded the wayward acrid personality of their
revered World War Commander, General Ludendorff.

To Ludendorff, Hitler, with his SA and his Party programme
containing commendably patriotic and anti-semitic sentiments, was
just one more unit in that Nationalistic Movement which regarded
him — and of which he regarded himself — as Leader. To Hitler,
Ludendorff, besides being an object of personal veneration, represented a high trump card, not only with the German people but with
the Army. He, therefore, conceived the idea of welding together
all the patriotic organizations into one fighting front, with the
veteran First Quartermaster-General as its titular head and himself

as political chieftain, which, with the support of the *Reichswehr* and the approval of the Separatist elements in Bavaria, should march on Berlin.

In the execution of this plan the personality of Ludendorff, if primarily an asset, proved also to be a liability. The General might indeed be an idol to the Patriotic Organizations, but both he and they, in the main, were North Germans and, as such, inimical to the Bavarian nationalist movements, whose affection and loyalty were pledged to their own Crown Prince Rupprecht, himself a Field-Marshal. It was well known that, both as soldier and statesman, the Bavarian Crown Prince had strongly opposed Ludendorff's war-time policies, and his rankling enmity had been increased by Ludendorff's irresponsible post-war attacks upon the Christian religion in general and the Roman Catholic Church in particular. Besides the personal antagonism, there was now the repugnance of an out-raged and devout Catholic, and behind the hostility of the Crown Prince there stood the embattled power of the Cardinal-Archbishop Faulhaber and the Papal Nuncius, Msgr. Pacelli (later to become Pope Pius XII).

The idea had been entertained by some among Prince Rupprecht's followers — and even, it was said, by the Crown Prince himself — that the time was ripe not only for the separation of Bavaria from the Reich, but for the setting up of a South-German Catholic State, of which Bavaria and Austria would be the initial members and over which the restored House of Wittelsbach would reign. Such a programme was entirely at variance with the ideas of Hitler and of Ludendorff, both of whom were adherents of the 'Greater Germany' school, and, though Hitler meditated from the first an *Anschluss* with Austria, he conceived it in terms of a union with the German Reich as a whole and not with any component part thereof.

The Bavarian Government of the day, moreover, under the inept premiership of Baron von Knilling, a vain, weak and vacillating character, was quite unfitted to deal with the emergencies with which it was called upon to contend. The Minister-President himself was a reactionary and a monarchist, who laboured under the delusion that he alone could constitute the link between the Patriotic Organizations, on the one hand, and the Bavarian 'particularists' on the other. He fondly imagined that he was in command of a situation which in reality was rapidly passing beyond his control, for the Nazi influence had already penetrated into his Cabinet. Franz Gürtner, the Minister of Justice, had become a convert to Hitler's theories and threw the full weight of his influence, with the secret support of Police President Pöhner and his chief assistant, Wilhelm

Frick, into frustrating the efforts of his colleague, the Minister of Interior, Franz Schweyer, to bring Hitler to justice as a disturber of the peace and a conspirator against both the Bavarian and Reich Governments.[1]

Even within the *Reichswehr* there were now divided opinions in regard to the Nazi Party. Hitler still retained the staunch support of such men as General von Epp and Ernst Röhm, both of whom were Party members, but General von Lossow was becoming disturbed at the degree of independence and insubordination now being manifested by the Party. The movement for which he had authorized support was becoming altogether too dictatorial in its attitude for his liking. His political objectives were those of a monarchist and conservative of an authoritarian variety. He was no sort of revolutionary, and naturally regarded Hitler's grandiose plans for a general national uprising with considerable misgivings. Moreover, among the lower ranks of officers, the majors and captains and lieutenants, von Seeckt's teachings of the value of a non-political *Reichswehr* were beginning to have their effect. Surrounded as they were in Munich by the fetid atmosphere of political intrigue, the wisdom of their Commander-in-Chief became apparent, and to these younger men there came a realization of the responsibility which the Army held as the ultimate guardian of the State and of the inevitable corollary that it must remain above Party. At a conference of officers, of whom von Lossow asked whether they would fire upon the National Socialists if ordered to do so, the General was amazed — and Epp and Röhm were appalled — at the enthusiasm with which the large majority answered in the affirmative.

In the midst of this jungle of intrigue and dissension Hitler struggled throughout the spring and summer of 1923 to attain his dual purpose of uniting the Patriotic Organizations into a single fighting unit and to secure the co-operation of the *Reichswehr* for action against Berlin. The value of the first was dependent upon the second, for the Army held both the money and the arms which were necessary, and Hitler, therefore, laid siege to von Lossow, to whom, through von Epp, he had secured direct access, using upon him the strategic technique of the Importunate Widow.[2]

---

[1] Hitler marked both these men for future reward. On the night of the *Putsch* of November 9, 1923, Schweyer was kidnapped by Hess and a party of SA men, threatened with death and only released when the news came that the *Putsch* had failed. He persisted, however, in his opposition to the Nazi movement, and in January 1933 was arrested and sent to a concentration camp. Gürtner, on the other hand, was appointed Reich Minister of Justice by Hitler, in which position he continued until his death in 1941. Frick served as Reich Minister of Interior 1933–43.   [2] St. Luke, xviii, 3-5.

He called weekly, and later daily, upon the General, lavishing upon him all the magnetic power of his eloquence and rhetoric. At first these speeches made a strong impression, but later their repetition and their length — sometimes they lasted for as long as two and a half hours! — became infinitely wearisome. To von Lossow, as he listened to these seemingly interminable harangues it became clear that Hitler lacked a sense of reality and the ability to see what was possible and what was not. He was unsuitable to lead a dictatorship, but his abilities in the propaganda field could be used in the service of a dictatorship. So thought the General. 'I was quite agreeable that Hitler should be our political drummer', he later told the court at Hitler's trial. Despite this ordeal of verbal *peine forte et dure*, he kept a firm grip on the keys of the treasury and the arsenals, and when Hitler tried to force his hand by strata-gem — as he did on the occasion of the May Day celebrations — von Lossow did not hesitate to show him that there was no velvet glove upon its steel.[1]

By the late summer of 1923 Hitler and the *Reichswehr* were definitely estranged, and the unification of the Patriotic Organizations seemed as far off as ever. And then the situation changed suddenly, almost overnight. The fall of the Cuno Government on August 13 and the succession of Stresemann as Chancellor were accompanied by the premonitory symptoms of an imminent termination of the *Ruhrkampf*; a cessation of passive resistance and a capitulation to the French. At once the smouldering political fires of Munich blazed up with fierce intensity. The partisans of a monarchist restoration, of a secession of Bavaria from the Reich, and of the overthrow of the Central Government, all, despite the diversity of their causes, saw in this moment the opportunity which they had sought so long. The result was chaos. The streets and halls of Munich re-echoed with the rival slogans of '*Auf nach Berlin*' and '*Los von Berlin*', and both parties waited for a sign from von Lossow and the *Reichswehr*. 'Which way will the grey cat jump?' was a question to which all sought the answer.

An immediate result of this political welter was the galvanizing

---

[1] On the pretext that the Socialists and Communists were to make a Marxist *Putsch* on May Day, Hitler demanded that rifles should be issued to his followers. When von Lossow refused, SA men obtained them from a regimental depot by a ruse and triumphantly paraded with them. Von Lossow ordered a cordon of troops to be thrown around the Nazi parade-ground and the rifles to be surrendered. His orders were complied with. For an account of this incident, based on the revelations made by a subsequent Committee of Investigation ordered by the Bavarian Diet, see a pamphlet, *Hitler und Kahr*, published by the Bavarian Social-Democratic Party (Munich, 1928).

of the Patriotic Organizations into unity. At a great demonstration at Nuremberg on September 2 — Sedan Day — more than a hundred thousand men, representing some half-dozen organizations, passed in review before Ludendorff who was making his first public appearance since the Kapp *Putsch*. After the parade Hitler and the leaders of the other groups entered into a formal alliance on the basis of which was founded the *Deutscher Kampfbund*, with Ludendorff as its President and Leader.

There seems to be little doubt that at this moment Hitler had in his mind the possibility and the intention of making a *coup d'état* in Germany similar to that which Mussolini had accomplished in Italy only a year before. The legions of the *Kampfbund* with their affiliations in other parts of the Reich would play the rôle of the Black Shirts, and the resistance of the Republican régime would crumble at their coming as had the opposition of the House of Savoy before the advance of the Duce. In preparation for this *coup*, Hitler launched forth into an intensified campaign of vilification of the Treaty of Versailles and the Jew-infested, Marxist-ridden régime which had signed it. In the course of the next few weeks he spoke not only daily but sometimes five or six times a day, prophesying without. cessation the downfall of the Weimar Republic. 'The régime of November nears its end ; the edifice totters ; the framework cracks', he told an audience on September 12. 'There are now only two alternatives before us : the swastika or the Soviet star ; the world despotism of the International or the Holy Empire of the Germanic nation. The first act of redress must be a march on Berlin and the installation of a national dictatorship.' [1] Impressed beyond measure and even perhaps hypnotized by Hitler's transports of eloquence and demoniac energy, his allies in the *Kampfbund* yielded him pride of place among them and, prompted by the ever-faithful Röhm, appointed him their political chief on September 25.

Nor had these latest political activities passed unnoticed by the Bavarian Cabinet, in whose ranks they had caused great perturbation. Schweyer pleaded for the legal suppression of the *Kampfbund* and its component bodies ; Gürtner urged appeasement. The Prime Minister, von Knilling, stood aghast at the genii which his own weak tolerance and tacit encouragement had allowed to escape from the bottle. The Patriotic Organizations as possible factors for the separation of Bavaria from the Reich and the restoration of the dynasty were one thing, but the Patriotic Organizations, united in a *Kampfbund*, dignified by the leadership of Ludendorff, spurred on by the frenzy of Hitler and clamouring for a March on Berlin,

[1] *Adolf Hitlers Reden* (Munich, 1933), pp. 87-93.

were altogether something else. It was quite as much against this new menace as against the Berlin Government that von Knilling finally declared a State of Emergency on September 26, and thankfully confided supreme power to von Kahr as Commissioner-General.[1]

Von Kahr took energetic measures. He banned all demonstrations by the *Kampfbund* and mobilized his own volunteer organizations which he placed under the command of another veteran of the Kapp *Putsch*, Captain Ehrhardt. Then he waited ; both sides waited with their eyes on the grey cat upon the wall.

General von Lossow was now in a position of supreme power in Bavaria. President Ebert's proclamation of September 26 had delegated the executive functions of the Reich Government to Gessler and to von Seeckt, and through them to the local *Reichswehr* commanders.[2] General von Lossow was commander of *Wehrkreis VII*, and it was beyond doubt that, in accordance with his oath to the Constitution and with all the tradition of military discipline, his duty lay in obedience to the orders of his Commander-in-Chief. Those orders were to exercise the supreme authority now vested in him for the preservation of the unity of the Reich. Never was a soldier's duty more clearly defined. Yet the General hesitated. Like most general officers of the *Reichswehr*, including von Seeckt himself, he had no love for the Weimar régime, with its bourgeois lack of respect for the armed forces of the State. But in von Lossow there was more of von Lüttwitz than of von Seeckt, and he had neither the wit nor the vision to realize, as von Seeckt had done, that, for the rehabilitation of the Army, the essential prerequisite was the restoration of Germany's strength and that this could only be accomplished by working through, and not against, the Republic ; by utilizing the Republican Government as an ally, albeit unwilling and, perhaps, unwitting, for the perfection of the *Reichswehr* within its restricted limits and for the clandestine preparation for the Day of Liberation.

The return of Ludendorff to public life and his active association with the *Kampfbund* was also an important factor in von Lossow's calculations. Hitler he frankly despised as a political leader, though he did not underrate his abilities as a demagogue, but for the veteran Quartermaster-General he had great respect, and it did not seem entirely impossible to him that Ludendorff and he could exploit Hitler and his followers in the furthering of a national revolution,

---

[1] Between the end of his premiership in 1921 and his appointment as Commissioner-General, von Kahr had served as *Regierungspräsident* of Upper Bavaria.
[2] See above, p. 110.

in which the High Command of the *Reichswehr* would undoubtedly collaborate once it was under way. Such a movement would sweep away the Republican Government in Berlin, replace it by a Conservative regime backed by the Army, and promulgate a Constitution for the Reich in which Bavaria would be restored to her old privileged position. Even the restoration of the Wittelsbachs and the Hohenzollerns would not be precluded. In view of these considerations von Lossow turned a deaf ear to his orders from Berlin and decided to await the initiative of von Kahr on one side and of Hitler on the other. The grey cat continued to sit upon the wall.

The initiatives were immediately forthcoming. Hitler resumed his frequent and wearying interviews with von Lossow, to whom on a number of occasions he offered the position of *Reichswehr* Minister in the new National Government, and von Kahr besought him to seize the opportunity of the Communist *coup* in Saxony to march upon Dresden, using the anti-Communist pretext to begin a counter-revolution. Still the General hesitated. Then two things happened. The rapid action of the *Reichswehr* in Saxony, Thuringia and Hamburg removed the Communist menace, and Hitler, himself now wearied of his fruitless importunings, decided to force the hand of the Berlin Government by so intensifying the scandalous character of his attacks as to compel them to take action against him. His press campaign against Stresemann, Gessler and von Seeckt at this time was carried on with intent to provoke precisely the result which it did provoke. On October 6 came von Seeckt's order to von Lossow to suppress the *Völkischer Beobachter*.[1]

From Hitler's point of view it was a master stroke. Von Lossow must at last take action. Von Kahr, who had gone far in his own separatist defiance of Berlin, could not now move against Hitler who was, outwardly at any rate, an ally. The grey cat could no longer sit upon the wall and, moreover, it had to perform the unusual and frankly impossible feat of coming down on both sides at once. Under pressure from von Kahr, von Lossow refused to suppress the paper and, in his reply to von Seeckt, referred to Hitler as being 'among the best of German patriots'. A second order from Berlin to arrest the leader of one of the organizations of the *Kampfbund* was also disobeyed and von Lossow was dismissed from his command on October 20.

The General had not been a big enough personality to fill the rôle which he had cast for himself. From the position of supreme authority which he had occupied as local commander of the German *Reichswehr*, he now found himself relegated to the command, on

[1] See above, p. 115.

von Kahr's appointment, of the local Bavarian *Reichswehr* ; a very different position. He had now become merely a petty conspirator, and from then on must consort with other conspirators equally petty. With von Kahr and Colonel von Seisser, the chief of the State Police, he formed a triumvirate to govern Bavaria in open defiance of Berlin.

The political temperature of Munich now rose to fever pitch. Plot and counter-plot followed one another with bewildering rapidity. Every day brought fresh rumours of an imminent *coup d'état*. Rival slogans resounded in the streets and halls and disfigured the public buildings ; the monarchist leagues and the *Kampfbund* marched and counter-marched. In some bewilderment the troops of the disinherited VII Division of the *Reichswehr* stood to arms awaiting an order from somebody. The very air seemed thick with intrigue and treachery, and the pace increased to a point of acceleration which could only end in farce or in tragedy — or, as it happened, in both.

The situation could scarcely have been more complicated. Two groups of conspirators, each mutually suspicious of the other, though, by force of circumstances and for the time being, interdependent, were racing against time and against each other to be the first to raise the standard of revolt. Would it bear the legend '*Auf nach Berlin*' or '*Los von Berlin*' ? It is difficult to say how far von Kahr, von Lossow and von Seisser, controlling between them the troops and police, that is to say, all the armed forces of the State, were influenced by 'separatist' motives in November 1923. They may have still been hoping for an authoritarian *coup* in Berlin which would enable them to restore the Wittelsbach monarchy and give back Bavaria her old rights under the Imperial Constitution. The Triumvirate was prepared to give seeming assistance to Hitler's movement for a national revolution up to the point where, having exhausted his usefulness, they could discard him. Von Kahr and von Lossow were determined that when the time came to take action against Berlin the movement should be under their control and not that of Hitler. It was a miscalculation which others were to make later on.

Hitler, for his part, was just as devious. He knew that he could not take on both the Reich and the Bavarian State authorities at the same time, and he was not prepared to launch his crusade against Berlin without the support of von Lossow's troops. By not unskilful manœuvring he had forced the Reich Government to take action which had precipitated the final defiance of Bavaria and had thereby compelled the Triumvirate to become his unwilling, untrusting — and unfaithful — allies. He was now ready to create an incident which should render the March to Berlin inescapable and, from his contacts with the 'Gentlemen of the North', he was confident of support in Berlin, Silesia, Pomerania, Westphalia and East Prussia. As for the Army, had not von Seeckt declared at the time of the Kapp *Putsch* that the *Reichswehr* could not be ordered to fire upon the *Reichswehr*? The presence of Ludendorff, the support of von Lossow and his troops, would ensure the co-operation, or at worst, the neutrality of the Army. And had not Hitler had a not entirely unsatisfactory meeting with von Seeckt in March? — an interview which had deeply stirred the Commander-in-Chief of the *Reichswehr* and had left him with the impression that he and the *Führer* were at one in their aims and were only at variance as to the means to be employed in achieving them. Hitler, therefore, busied himself with the completion of his plans, leaving the date open.

The final phase in this Masque of Treachery opened on November 6, when the Triumvirate, anxious to keep control of events in their own hands, summoned the leaders of the *Kampfbund* and forbade them to make a *Putsch* before the signal had been given by von Lossow and von Kahr. At this meeting the General finally committed himself. 'I am ready', he said, 'to take part in any *Putsch* which has fifty-one per cent probability of success.' [1]

Hitler gave the required assurance on behalf of the *Kampfbund* that they would not make a *Putsch* without the agreement of the Triumvirate and promptly went home to complete the plans for doing exactly the opposite. His impression of the meeting, as he later told his judges, was that von Kahr, von Lossow and von Seisser wanted to act but did not dare to. Very well, he would give them the signal and they must follow.

But here he underestimated the capacity of the Triumvirate for intrigue. Scarcely had he returned from the meeting when news reached him that they had planned a mass meeting at the Bürgerbräu Cellar on the night of November 8, at which von Kahr was scheduled to deliver a speech of great political importance to the leading figures in Bavarian public life. It was rumoured that a restoration of the Wittelsbachs was contemplated. Hitler certainly feared that this was a preliminary step to a Bavarian *coup* aimed at splitting the *Reich*. Incensed beyond words at being outdone in treachery, Hitler decided that this demonstration on the 8th should be the occasion for his own signal for revolt. Orders to the *Kampfbund* were given accordingly.

[1] See Hitler's opening speech before the Bavarian High Court at Munich on February 26, 1924, also *Die Memoiren des Stabschefs Röhm* (Saarbrücken, 1934), p. 120. Von Lossow himself denied before the court that he had ever used these words.

The Bürgerbräu Keller was no mere beer hall, such as the Nazis frequently used for their meetings, but a fashionable rendezvous lying on the outskirts of Munich beyond the River Isar. On the evening of November 8 nearly everybody who was anybody in Bavarian nationalist and monarchist circles was present — with the exception of the Crown Prince and the Cardinal — as well as many guests from the Parties of the Right in other parts of Germany. Almost the entire Bavarian Cabinet were there, and many officers in full uniform. Like the Kapp *Putsch* in Berlin, von Kahr's revolution was to be a *coup d'état en frac*.

The Triumvirate occupied the platform and von Kahr had begun a somewhat rambling address, when at 8.30 precisely the doors were thrown open and steel-helmeted SA men, armed with revolvers and carrying machine-guns, occupied the hall. Pandemonium ensued. Women fainted, men shouted, crockery and beermugs cascaded from overturned tables. The din was unbelievable, and von Kahr was too flabbergasted to move or speak. Leaping on a table Hitler fired two revolver shots in the air and secured quiet, then he announced that the hall was occupied and surrounded by armed men. 'The barracks of the *Reichswehr* and of the police have been occupied', shouted the hoarse, strident voice, 'the *Reichswehr* and the police have mounted the swastika'.

This last statement was entirely untrue, but it had a curiously reassuring effect on the crowd and trumped the last ace of the Triumvirate, who allowed themselves to be led away unresisting to a side room, where Hitler, having left Göring in charge of the main hall, followed them. Here in a highly excitable state, bathed in sweat and brandishing his pistol, he announced to the startled trio that he and Ludendorff had formed a new Reich Government, with the General as Commander-in-Chief of the National Army and himself in charge of political direction. Von Lossow was to be Minister of War, von Seisser Minister of Police.[1] Von Kahr and Pöhner were to divide the authority in Bavaria between them.

The Triumvirate hesitated — they were no doubt still somewhat breathless at what had happened — whereupon Ludendorff appeared like a *deus ex machinâ*, and, though his opening remark that he was just as surprised as they were at the course events had taken gave the lie to Hitler's previous statement, his presence gave reassurance to the three men, who up to that moment had been uncertain whether

---

[1] There was no federal police force in Germany at the time, police duties being reserved to the various States of the Reich. Hitler did not succeed in uniting the police under one command until 1936, when he placed them under the control of Himmler. But he had this intention from the beginning.

they were co-conspirators or prisoners. They must all go forward together, said Ludendorff, there could be no turning back now. Whereupon von Lossow, according to Hitler and to Röhm, though he himself denied it vehemently, seized the Quartermaster-General's hand and, with tears in his eyes, declared : 'Your Excellency's wishes are my command. I will organize the Army in fighting order as Your Excellency requires.'

Von Kahr, however, still had scruples. 'I can only take over the administration of Bavaria', he said, 'as the representative of the Monarchy.' Hitler at once declared that he was ready to go immediately to 'His Majesty', whereupon von Kahr took the *Führer*'s hand in both his own.

They all returned to the hall, where Hitler proclaimed the new regimes in Germany and in Bavaria and enunciated a ferocious decree declaring Ebert, Scheidemann and the other 'November Criminals' as outlaws, to be tried by a specially constituted national tribunal and, if found guilty, to be executed within three hours of the verdict.[1] Ludendorff closed the proceedings by giving the adventure his blessing and support.

At this moment Hitler was called away. There had been a hitch in the proceedings and, whereas Röhm had succeeded in occupying the Army Headquarters with the officer-cadets of the Infantry School, whom Rossbach had virtually kidnapped from under the nose of their Commandant, the other government buildings were not surrendering according to plan. The personal intervention of the *Führer* was required, and he left Ludendorff and the deposed Triumvirate in deep conversation. When he returned the Quartermaster-General was alone. Von Kahr, von Lossow and von Seisser had departed after giving him their parole, and when someone had protested, Ludendorff had frozen him with the retort : 'I forbid you to doubt the word of honour of a German officer'.

The trio retired to the barracks of the 19th Infantry Regiment, where, almost immediately, they received a visit from Prince Rupprecht's adjutant, who had arrived post-haste from Chiemsee, with the word that neither 'His Majesty' nor the Cardinal would be a party to any restoration which owed its support to General Ludendorff. 'Crush this movement at any cost' was the command of the royal messenger. 'Use the troops if necessary.'[2]

The would-be restorers of the monarchy were snubbed by the heir of the dynasty and faced formidable opposition from the

[1] Hitler's opening speech of February 26, 1924 ; see *My New Order* (Hitler's collected speeches, 1919–41), edited by Count Raoul de Roussy de Sales (New York, 1941), pp..72-81 ; Röhm, p. 122.   [2] Benoist-Méchin, ii, 300-301.

Reichswehr — both inside and outside Bavaria. Von Lossow seems to have hesitated after his retirement from the Bürgerbräu meeting. There is no very clear evidence that he had made up his mind to oppose Hitler from the moment the pact had been made between them, although this is the version of events which he produced afterwards to ease his embarrassment. The decisive factor was probably the attitude of his subordinate army commanders in Munich. By the early hours of the morning he and von Kahr had rejected the *Putsch*.

The dawn of November 9, the fifth anniversary of the 'stab in the back' — and the 124th anniversary of the *18 Brumaire* — broke dark and gloomily over the Bürgerbräu. Amidst the debris of the initial *coup* the Nazi leaders waited for their Leader's word — and it was now the Leader, not the *Reichswehr*, who was hesitating. To Hitler all, even honour, seemed lost. It had always been his intention to make his *Putsch* in co-operation with, and not against, the *Reichswehr*, but now he found the rifles levelled against him and himself proscribed where he had meant to outlaw others. Only retreat was possible, and of all lines of retreat he chose the one least likely to succeed, in seeking the mediation of the Crown Prince Rupprecht, whom he besought to intervene with von Kahr and von Lossow to procure a pardon for himself and Ludendorff.

Ludendorff, however, would have none of this. He had meant what he said, when he declared that there could be no going back now. The die was cast and the game had to go on. Moreover, Ludendorff had not yet conceded victory to the enemy. He was still assured of the influence of his personal prestige over the troops. He was still loath to believe that von Lossow had willingly broken his parole — 'I will never trust the word of a German officer again', he remarked bitterly, when the truth was finally revealed to him — and he still remained convinced that when confronted with the veteran Quartermaster-General of the First World War the *Reichswehr* would lower their rifles and fall in behind him. 'We march', he said peremptorily to Hitler, and when the *Führer* objected that they would be fired on, the General simply repeated in an inexorable voice of command, 'We march.'

And so the columns were formed and, under a grey November sky, the three thousand *Kampfbund* fighters and the officer-cadets of the Infantry School, led by Ludendorff and Hitler, moved off shortly before noon. On through the outskirts of Munich they marched ; on through the inner city, sometimes singing their war songs, sometimes grimly silent ; on towards the *Kommando Wehrkreis VII*, hard by the Feldherrn Halle, where Röhm now lay

beleaguered by the *Reichswehr*. To reach their objective they had to
cross the broad expanse of the Odeonsplatz, and to reach the Platz
they must pass through a narrow street, The Residenzstrasse, where
only a column of fours might march. Most of the approaches to
the Odeonsplatz were held by the *Reichswehr*, but this particular
entry was blocked by a cordon of von Seisser's 'Green Police'. The
column continued to advance. Ludendorff, when he saw the cordon,
did not slacken his pace; cold and expressionless he went forward.
The police levelled their rifles. A man — Ulrich Graf, Hitler's
bodyguard — sprang forward from the advancing column crying
'For God's sake don't shoot, it is His Excellency Ludendorff'.
The marching column had already passed through some less resolute
police cordons, but this one showed more determination. Commanded by a Bavarian nobleman, Freiherr von Godin, it resisted
the advance. A shot was fired from the Nazi side, and was answered
immediately by a police volley. The leaders of the column fell to
the ground, some of them killed or wounded.[1]

When the firing ceased it was seen that the leading files of the
column were in confusion, but well in front of them, erect, unscathed
and seemingly unmoved, stood Ludendorff, his hands in the pockets
of his old shooting-coat. With the crash of the volley it had suddenly been revealed to him that the magic which had once pertained
to his name had lost its spell. The incredible had happened;
German rifles had fired upon Germany's foremost veteran. He had
escaped by a miracle, and now, coldly disdainful and of such a
tremendous appearance that none dare approach him, he walked
forward with unhurried pace towards the police. That same cool
courage which had carried him up the escarpment of the fortress
of Liége to hammer on the door with the pommel of his sword, now
brought him through this, the last semi-creditable episode of his
career. He passed between the rifles of the police, on to the Odeonsplatz, and out of glory. It was the one almost redeeming feature of an
otherwise thoroughly sordid and disreputable affair. It was the last
gesture of the Old Imperial Army.

The November *Putsch* was over. The March on Berlin had failed
to reach the first milestone.

(iii)

In many respects the sequel to the Bürgerbräu *Putsch* of November 9 was of greater and more far-reaching importance than the
event itself — and more especially in regard to the relations between
the Army and the Party.

[1] Ernst Deuerlein, *Der Hitlerputsch. Bayerische Dokumente zum 9. November
1923*, pp. 330-1.

The *Putsch* had been catastrophic in every respect for Hitler. It had been imprudent in that, despite all his adroit and devious manœuvrings, he had been placed finally in the position of having seemed to oppose the *Reichswehr*, whereas he had been particularly anxious to avoid this ; it had been inglorious in that its failure had been public and complete. There could have been no more thorough example of political miscalculation and the miscarriage of plans. Moreover, Hitler's personal prestige had suffered considerably, for, though there is no reason to believe that his conduct on the morning of November 9 smacked of cowardice, it had certainly not been very conspicuously resplendent. The honours of that occasion, such as they were, had gone to Ludendorff.

But Hitler was given the chance at the trial which followed to win back all that he had lost and more besides. As the leader of an armed revolt he had been a fiasco, but as a political defendant in a court of law on a charge of high treason he was in his element, whereas Ludendorff cut a less-distinguished figure. The State authorities had no choice other than to bring the conspirators of November 9 to trial, but in so doing they afforded Hitler a platform and an opportunity for publicity far greater than he had yet obtained. He was not the man to allow such an opportunity to escape him.

Within Germany the fortunes of the Reich had taken a turn for the better in the interval between the *Putsch* and the trial. The collapse of the March on Berlin had marked the termination of any attempts at armed opposition to the authority of Ebert, Gessler and von Seeckt, whether from the Right or from the Left. The restoration of law and order coincided with the improvement of economic conditions. On the morrow of the *Putsch* (November 12) Ebert appointed the financial wizard Hjalmar Schacht as Currency Commissioner of the Reich and under his magic touch the mark was first arrested in its cataclysmic fall and then stabilized. Furthermore the opening of the New Year saw the beginnings of a new approach to the reparation problem with the first session of the Dawes Committee in Paris on January 14, and a month later Stresemann made his initial proposals — tentative and secret — to the Western Powers for a pact of security.

In Bavaria there had also been changes. The separatist movement, though not yet quite dead, lay dormant after the excitement in November. The régimes of von Kahr and von Knilling were soon to be replaced by the more moderate Government of Dr. Heinrich Held, the leader of the Bavarian People's Party, and General Freiherr Kress von Kressenstein, the hero of the German-Turkish

operations in the Suez Canal Zone and in the Caucasus during the
First World War, had succeeded von Lossow in the command of
Wehrkreis VII. Von Kressenstein was also a Bavarian, but, unlike
von Lossow, he was neither a separatist nor a fool. A personal friend
of von Seeckt, he was a firm believer in the Commander-in-Chief's
policies and had already done much to restore the morale and
discipline of the troops under his command.[1]

It was under these improved circumstances that the trial of
Hitler, Ludendorff, and eight others — including Pöhner, Röhm,
and Frick — opened before the People's Court at Munich on
February 26, 1924. The People's Courts were another Bavarian
speciality dating from the days of the revolution. They were bitterly
unpopular among Left-wing circles. There was no appeal from them,
and it was argued that they were unconstitutional. This type of
court was an advantage to Hitler, and he determined to seize every
chance to further his cause while appearing before it. He would
not, for example, repeat the conduct of those who, when brought
to trial after the failure of the Kapp *Putsch*, had solemnly declared
that they 'knew nothing, had intended nothing, and wished for
nothing'. Hitler had no such desire for exculpation. From the
first he was determined to obtain the utmost publicity for his intentions and for his political programme. His aim was to make it
abundantly clear to the world, to the German people and to the
German Army that he had on November 9 made a serious and
premeditated effort to destroy the Weimar Republic and to liberate
Germany from the rule of the 'November Criminals' and from the
tyranny of the shackles of Versailles.[2] He was at equal pains to
establish, for the benefit of the Army, that, in making this attempt,
he had at no time been in conflict with the *Reichswehr* as such, but
only with the Munich police and the units of the VII Division whose
leaders were themselves in revolt against their military superiors.

---

[1] On von Seeckt's orders, von Kressenstein had, for example, closed the
Infantry Cadet School, and returned to their commands those officer candidates
who had taken part in the *Putsch*. The school was reorganized later at Ohrdruf,
in Thuringia, where von Seeckt addressed the cadets one morning in March
1924. 'This is the first occasion', he told them, 'during my long years of service
that I have addressed mutineers. I say this with full intent; for what you did
at Munich was mutiny — no matter what your motives were. Neither consideration for yourselves nor your parents has induced me to permit you to remain in
the Army, but only the fact that on that night at Munich no officer of the School
opposed you with drawn pistol at the gate.'

[2] For the comparison with the attitude of the leaders of the Kapp *Putsch*
see Hitler's Anniversary Speech on November 9, 1934 (*Völkischer Beobachter*,
November 10, 1934).

The Court itself was of indifferent calibre. The Bavarian governmental purges had not gone farther than the upper stratum. The civil servants and the judicial authorities who had aided and protected Hitler and his Nazi movement in its early days still occupied the same positions. Some members of the court had even been present at the Bürgerbräu Keller on the night of November 8 to give their support and approval to von Kahr's measures for a monarchical restoration and secession from the Reich, and these same men were now called upon to try Hitler and his accomplices on a charge of high treason.

The irony of the situation and its possibilities for exploitation did not escape Hitler. In conducting his defence he was not only openly contemptuous of his judges, but he also essayed, in some degree successfully, to demonstrate that it was not he and his fellow defendants who should be sitting in the dock, but the star witnesses of the prosecution, von Kahr, von Lossow and von Seisser — particularly von Lossow. It was these men who had betrayed the National Revolution which he and Ludendorff had proclaimed, and he did not scruple to emphasize that by his conduct von Lossow had sought to bring about a split in the *Reichswehr*.

The main tenor of the defence — shot through though it was with casuistry, falsehood and misrepresentation — was to convince the Army that the Nazi movement was not against, but at one with it, in its aims and ideals, that all would have been well had not von Lossow and von Seisser ordered the troops and police to oppose the March on Berlin, and that henceforth the Army and the Party had a common goal in the creation of a Greater Germany. From the dock of the People's Court Hitler was making his opening bid for a future alliance with the *Reichswehr*, an alliance which he knew to be of paramount necessity to the success of his ultimate ambitions.

'When I learned that it was the "Green Police" which had fired, I had the happy feeling that at least it was not the *Reichswehr* which had besmirched itself. The *Reichswehr* remains as untarnished as before. One day the hour will come when the *Reichswehr* will stand at our side, officers and men. The Army which we have formed grows from day to day ; from hour to hour it grows more rapidly. Even now I have the proud hope that one day the hour is coming when these untrained bands will become battalions, when the battalions will become regiments, and the regiments divisions ; when the old cockade will be raised from the mire, when the old banners will once again wave before us ; and then reconciliation will come in that eternal last Court of Judgment — the Court of God —

G 2

before which we are ready to take our stand.' [1]

With these words Hitler closed his defence on March 27, and though the proceedings had effectively exposed in accusation and counter-accusation the intrigue and treachery which had preceded the *Putsch*, the *Führer* had successfully managed to keep his primary theme in the forefront and, brushing aside past events as ephemeral, kept his thoughts and words directed towards the future. His final words were destined to ring down the years and to beguile the imagination of millions of his adopted countrymen : 'That Court of Honour will not ask us "Did you commit high treason or did you not ?" That Court will judge us, the Quartermaster-General of the Old Army, his officers and his soldiers, who, as Germans, desired only the good of their people and fatherland ; who wanted to fight and to die. You may pronounce us guilty a thousand times over, but the Goddess who presides over the Eternal Court of History will with a smile tear in shreds the indictment of the Public Prosecutor and the judgment of this Court, for she declares us guiltless.'

The trial was an almost unqualified triumph for Hitler. Immense publicity was centred on the proceedings, and he took full advantage of it. The public galleries were in the main sympathetic to him, and he succeeded in casting greater discredit on von Kahr and von Lossow than the Prosecution were able to attach to him and his fellow defendants. The judges, whether willingly or by intimidation, were predisposed towards him. It was within their power to have sentenced him to a long period of imprisonment and then to deportation as an undesirable alien — for he was still an Austrian citizen and remained so until 1932 — they elected, however, to make their verdict coincide as nearly as possible with that which Hitler himself had prophesied would be handed down by 'the Goddess who presides over the Eternal Court of History'.[2]

The sentences were pronounced, appropriately enough on April

---

[1] Hitler's final speech, March 27, 1924. See *Adolf Hitlers Reden* (Munich, 1933), p. 122 ; Heiden, p. 167 ; *The Speeches of Adolf Hitler, April 1922–August 1939*, edited by Professor Norman H. Baynes (Oxford, 1942), i, 86. These words were to contribute materially toward the subsequent rivalry and hostility which developed between the Army and the SA, who interpreted them as a pledge that the para-military formations were to be included *en bloc* in the *Reichswehr* when the Party had come to power. See below, p. 204.

[2] An attempt to obtain an order for Hitler's deportation was actually made at this time by the Bavarian Secret Police through the Minister of the Interior, Dr. Schweyer. The move was, however, blocked by Franz Gürtner, the Minister of Justice. (See Robert M. W. Kempner, 'Blueprint of the Nazi Underground — Past and Future Subversive Activities', *Research Studies of the State College of Washington* (Pullman, Washington, xiii) No. 2, June 1945.)

HITLER, LUDENDORFF AND THEIR ACCOMPLICES AFTER THE MUNICH TRIAL, APRIL 1924

Fools' Day, in an atmosphere more suited to a gala social event than a court of justice. Ladies appeared wearing large rosettes of black-white-and-red ribbons, the Nationalist colours, and bouquets of flowers were presented to the accused ; officers attended in full uniform. Röhm and Frick, though formally condemned, were released at once. Hitler received the lowest penalty prescribed by the law for the crime of high treason, five years' detention in a fortress, with the understanding that the clemency of the court would be exercised in six months. Ludendorff was acquitted altogether. 'I consider my acquittal a disgrace for the uniform and the decorations that I wear', was his bitter comment on the verdict.[1]

[1] In addition to the works to which specific reference is made in footnotes, other sources for this chapter include Rudolf Olden, *Hitler* (New York, 1936) ; Kurt Ludecke, *I Knew Hitler* (New York, 1937) ; Heinz A. Heinz, *Germany's Hitler* (London, 1934) ; and Erich Ludendorff, *Auf dem Weg zur Feldherrnhalle* (Munich, 1937). More recent works include Karl Schwend, *Bayern zwischen Monarchie und Diktatur* (Munich, 1954), and H. H. Hofmann, *Der Hitlerputsch* (Munich, 1961).

CHAPTER 2

THE SCHLEICHER PERIOD

(1926-1933)

(i)

IF Hans von Seeckt was the Sorcerer of the *Reichswehr*, it was reserved for Kurt von Schleicher to play the unsavoury and tragic rôle of the Sorcerer's Apprentice. He was, indeed, the evil genius of the later Weimar Period, symbolizing in himself all the worst traits of the General in politics. Vain he was, and unscrupulous, and unfaithful ; with a passion, amounting almost to an obsession, for intrigue, and a marked preference for the devious and the disingenuous ; but his ambitions were for power rather than responsibility, for influence rather than position.

Yet, though vain, von Schleicher was not petty. He had grandiose schemes which never got beyond the stage of planning. He dreamed not only of restoring the conservative military caste in Germany but also of reviving that old spirit of comradeship between the soldier and the worker, that spirit of Prussian military-socialism which should unite the Army with the Trade Unions and thereby provide a ready reservoir of man-power upon which the military direction might draw at will. He dreamed, too, of social reforms which should reduce the corrupt abuses which had grown up under the Weimar régime and of bringing back to Germany the old Prussian austerity — 'the black broth of Sparta' — which had been preached and practised by Scharnhorst and Gneisenau, and in one of his broadcasts as Chancellor he besought the German youth to fight against what he mystically termed '*der innere Schweinehund*'.

But pre-eminently von Schleicher was a master of cross-section contacts and cabal, and the more constructive side of his character was obscured by his overweening predilection for intrigue. It is to be recorded of him that whereas no man owed more to his superiors, the path of his subsequent career was littered with the political corpses of those early patrons. With the exception of Otto Meissner,[1] no

---

[1] Otto Meissner (b. 1880), a Prussian civil servant whose early career had been in the railway administration of the *Reichsland* (Alsace-Lorraine), became State Secretary to the President of the Republic on the return of the Government to Berlin after the failure of the Kapp *Putsch* in March 1920. He continued in

one exercised more power or reigned longer behind the scenes of the Weimar Republic than did General von Schleicher; and no one made a briefer appearance before the curtain.

Kurt von Schleicher (1882–1934), the son of an old Brandenburg family, began his military career in 1900 as a subaltern in Hindenburg's old regiment, the Third Foot Guards. Here he formed the friendship with Oskar von Hindenburg which was to serve him so well in later life, and as the friend of the son he became a frequent visitor to the house of the father. Picked for service with the General Staff, von Schleicher had the good fortune to attract the attention of Gröner, then an instructor at the *Kriegsakademie*, who considered him, together with Kurt von Hammerstein-Equord, as being among his most brilliant pupils. Thus a second valuable friendship was engendered, for when Gröner was appointed Head of the Transport Section of the General Staff, he had von Schleicher transferred to his department.

Except for a brief period of service on the Eastern Front, during which he was awarded the Iron Cross, von Schleicher's record throughout the First World War was that of a *Schreibtischoffizier* (a 'chair-borne' soldier) and he discharged his duties with great efficiency. Not ill-favoured in looks, charming of manner and witty of speech, with no doubts as to his own capabilities, he let no opportunity slip — and there were many at General Headquarters — to make acquaintance with the great ones who surrounded him, and he soon became an essential figure in many important circles. Ludendorff, however, had little use for the young dandy and relegated him to the Press Department, where he was discovered and plucked forth by Gröner, who, on his appointment as Quartermaster-General in October 1918, promptly made him his personal assistant.[1]

Von Schleicher's politico-military career began from that moment, and thenceforward he was never to be far from the vital centre of events. With Gröner he was present at the momentous interview with Hindenburg on November 10, 1918, when the Marshal was persuaded to accept and support the existing Government in Berlin simply because it was a government; and he became the trusted

this office under Ebert, Hindenberg and Hitler, who promoted him to Minister of State in 1937. He exercised great influence on the two Presidents of the Reich, but under the Nazi régime his authority diminished. Placed on trial as a War Criminal in the 'Ministries Case' before a United States Military Tribunal at Nuremberg in November 1947, he was acquitted of all charges when the Tribunal finally rendered its judgment on April 14, 1949. His memoirs — *Staatssekretär unter Ebert, Hindenburg und Hitler* (Hamburg, 1950) — contribute little that was not already known of the period.

[1] H. R. Berndorff, *General zwischen Ost und West* (Hamburg, 1951); K. Caro and W. Oehme, *Schleichers Aufstieg* (Berlin, 1933); Rabenau, ii, 546-51.

envoy between the High Command at Cassel and the *Reichskanzlei* during the dark and perilous winter which followed the military collapse. He played an important part in the organization and equipping of the Free Corps, but, along with von Hammerstein, he refused to accept the orders of von Lüttwitz at the time of the Kapp *Putsch*. Both were rewarded by von Seeckt, on his appointment as Commander-in-Chief of the *Reichswehr*, by inclusion in that little band of confidants who planned and executed the more clandestine activities of the New Army. It was von Schleicher who, with von Bock, supervised the activities of the 'Black Reichswehr', and it was von Schleicher who had been largely responsible for the success of the *Reichswehr*'s experiment in 'military government' from September 1923 to February 1924. It had been in his flat that the first tentative and secret negotiations took place in September 1921 for the building up of the Soviet arms industry for the greater benefit of the German Army, and later he was one of those officers sent by von Seeckt to Moscow for confidential talks with the Red General Staff ; later still, von Seeckt, who had never liked von Schleicher personally, displayed appreciation of his political ability, by entrusting to him the delicate duties of maintaining the political contacts of the Ministry of Defence.

From the austere little room in the Bendlerstrasse, looking over the Landwehr Canal, von Schleicher began to tread that winding path of political intrigue which was to bring him to the Chancellor's Palace — and to the assassin's bullet. Not that he was an intriguer for the pure love of intrigue — he was too intelligent for that ; his plots were always directed towards some larger end which would justify them if they failed or came to be discovered prematurely. Little by little he achieved a position where his advice and opinion were sought by politicians, hostesses and journalists, and any foreign observer who visited Berlin. Outside the official circle and the growing body of his acquaintances, his name was unknown in the country at large, yet he came to know all there was to be known in the political world of Germany, and eventually perfected for his own advantage a far-reaching system of 'something which, when practised by our enemies, we call espionage'. There was to be a time when not a telephone conversation of consequence took place in Berlin but its content was reported to him ; his agents were in every Ministry and Government office, and even in the Chancellor's Palace. His reputation as a pertinacious pryer into the secrets of the official world equalled that of Holstein and was probably better earned. Never had a man so justified his name.[1]

---

[1] Schleicher's name in English means 'creeper'.

(ii)

With the advent of Hindenburg as President of the Reich in 1925 von Schleicher's influence began to manifest itself almost immediately, though it did not become of paramount importance until some four years later. While von Seeckt remained as Chief of the *Heeresleitung* von Schleicher's intrigues were largely blocked or at least kept under control, for he feared the contemptuous cold blue eye of the 'Field Grey Sphinx'. It was, therefore, with relief that von Schleicher welcomed von Seeckt's fall in October 1926. If he had no hand in bringing it about — a matter which is still open to debate — he certainly did nothing to prevent it, and he was at pains to see that the successor was a man more susceptible to his persuasion.

The successor chosen was Colonel-General Wilhelm Heye, whose melancholy duty it had been to inform first Wilhelm II and then General von Lüttwitz that they no longer enjoyed the confidence of the German Army. A good Staff officer and well grounded in the fundamental principles of his predecessor, Heye continued to pursue the von Seeckt policy in a modified form ; modified, that is to say, by the advice of von Schleicher and von Hammerstein, who now became the controlling influences in the Bendlerstrasse.

These were halcyon days for the *Reichswehr*, for, in company with the whole Reich, they were reaping the benefits of Stresemann's Policy of Fulfilment, the Dawes Plan, the Locarno Agreement, and membership of the League of Nations. In January 1927 the Allied Commission of Control was withdrawn from Germany, and its passing was marked by curious circumstances. The German application for admission to the League in March 1926 had been accompanied by the demand that all controls should be abolished, on the grounds that all the requirements of the Treaty of Versailles had been complied with. The Control Commission was therefore instructed by the British, French and Belgian Governments to make a final inspection of Germany's armaments with a view to satisfying this demand. Contrary to the expectation of London, Paris and Brussels, the Commission's report, a document of some five hundred pages, stated in essence that 'Germany had never disarmed, had never had the intention of disarming, and for seven years had done everything in her power to deceive and "counter-control" the Commission appointed to control her disarmament'.[1] So anxious, however,

[1] Brigadier-General J. H. Morgan in *The Times* of November 6, 1933. General Morgan's allegations were closely followed by those of the Belgian Senator de Dordolot to the effect that the British and French Governments had compelled the Commission to weaken both the tenor and the text of their final report (*Nation Belge*, November 10, 1933).

were the Governments concerned to place the final coping-stone upon the edifice of Locarno, so confident were they in the validity of Stresemann's pledges of Germany's peaceful intentions, that they deliberately suppressed and ignored this final report and issued a *communiqué* on December 13, 1926, that of more than a hundred questions of disarmament outstanding in June 1925 there remained now but two, that the Powers had agreed to continue negotiations on these two items and that the Commission of Control would be withdrawn on January 31, 1927.[1]

With this clean bill of health from the Western Powers in their pocket it was not surprising that both the German Government and the *Reichswehr* could meet with equanimity the disclosures which Scheidemann made in the *Reichstag* three days later (December 16, 1926) concerning German-Soviet military collaboration or that the motion of no-confidence in Gessler tabled by the Social Democratic Party on this occasion was defeated by a heavy majority. If the Governments of the Western Powers were prepared to condone the deceptions, which both sides now knew to be in practice, why should the Reich authorities be concerned?

The fruits of Stresemann's policy had other far-reaching effects. They induced in Germany a condition of prosperity which, though basically false had, nevertheless, all the semblance of actuality. Germany received loans from abroad between 1924 and 1929 to the tune of 25,000 million gold marks, whilst the total of her reparation payments under the Dawes plan for the same period was under 8,000 million marks. With the surplus she was able to re-equip her industries, to indulge in large public works and enterprises, to subsidize her agriculture and to rebuild her export trade. There followed an orgy of profligate expenditure by governmental and municipal authorities which brought in its train inevitable corruption and ultimate scandalous disclosures.[2]

---

[1] *The Times*, December 13, 1926.

[2] There were many such scandals in this period of which perhaps the most notorious was that in which a firm of tailors, the Sklarek Brothers, were alleged to have made enormous profits to the tune of some 9 million marks by means of forged or falsified order forms in connection with goods supplied to the Berlin municipality. A number of senior municipal officials had, directly or indirectly, received bribes and the Chief Burgomaster of Berlin, Herr Böss, was himself heavily involved. The Sklarek scandal, which broke in the winter of 1929, did much to discredit the Weimar system in the public mind and is said to have increased both the Communist and the Nazi vote in Berlin in the elections of September 1930. 'A "Sklarek" fur worn by the wife of the Chief Burgomaster acquired a symbolic significance in the collapse of the Weimar Republic similar to that attaching to the diamond necklace of Marie-Antoinette in the history of the French Revolution' (Arthur Rosenberg, *A History of the German Republic* (London, 1936), p. 291).

The *Reichswehr* had its share in both the extravagant expenditure and the corruption of the period. The plans for economic and industrial mobilization matured by the *Rüstamt* [1] were now pushed forward as a part of the industrial development of the country. From 1924 to 1927 the emphasis lay on the planning and the blueprinting of prototypes, but with the departure of the Control Commission there opened that second phase in German rearmament during which the centres of German industry were adapted for the mass-production of the prototypes prepared abroad. German military expenditure began to increase steadily and rapidly. From the beginning of the Dawes period in 1924 to the peak point of prosperity four years later, the *Reichswehr* Budget rose from 490 million marks to 827 million. Thereafter, due to the economic depression, it decreased slightly, but in 1932 it was still at the figure of 766 million.[2]

In addition to this direct military expenditure, the Defence Ministry also encroached on the budgets of other ministries — such as those of the Interior, for the military equipment of the State police forces, and of Transport, for the development of military aviation — in which rearmament projects were thereby camouflaged as innocent items of peaceful civilian expenditure. It is said that the amount spent on these camouflaged items during the period 1924–32 amounted to some 3,219 million marks.[3]

In addition to these inroads upon the budgets of other ministries, the *Reichswehr* also had at its disposal a number of secret funds. In earlier days these had been used for such political ventures as the equipping of the Free Corps and the 'Black Reichswehr' and in making subventions to such political movements as the National Socialist Party in Munich. Now, however, the fever for gambling and speculation which afflicted the whole world in the days of the prosperous 'twenties, infected also those officers who had charge of these secret monies. They went boldly into the world of commerce

---

[1] See above, p. 143.

[2] The annual budget of the *Reichswehr* during the period 1924–32 was as follows :

1924 .	. 490 million marks	
1925 .	. 633	,,
1926 .	. 704	,,
1927 .	. 759	,,
1928 .	. 827	,,
1929 .	. 752	,,
1930 .	. 787	,,
1931 .	. 759	,,
1932 .	. 766	,,

[3] W. M. Knight-Patterson, *Germany from Defeat to Conquest* (London, 1945), pp. 404–7.

and, with the valour of ignorance, established businesses like ordinary civilians. Their aim was not to enrich themselves personally but to increase the Army's secret funds by profitable investment. Unfortunately for them, in their business ineptitude they were unable to distinguish between investment and speculation. They became hopelessly involved in matters far beyond their ken and the result was disastrous. One particular venture, the film company 'Phoebus', failed so resoundingly that the scandal became public and the subsequent bankruptcy proceedings in the winter of 1927 resulted in disclosures not only of the secret business transactions of the *Reichswehr* but also of much of their illicit rearmament activities besides. Otto Gessler, whose tenure of office at the Bendlerstrasse had seemed to be as 'permanent' as that of Stresemann at the Wilhelmstrasse,[1] was so deeply compromised that he was forced to resign, and on January 20, 1928, von Schleicher was able to score a further personal advantage in persuading Hindenburg to appoint Gröner as Defence Minister.[2]

From both the political and the technical point of view, however, the most important undertaking of the *Reichswehr* during this period was the rebirth of the German Navy —.hitherto regarded as 'the ugly step-child of the Republic'. With her new wealth and regained prosperity it was felt that Germany could now replace the obsolete warships permitted to her under the Treaty of Versailles by an entirely new type of naval vessel which, though strictly within the prescribed limitation of the Treaty, was destined to excite the admiration and concern of the world. This was the 'pocket-battleship' of 10,000 tons displacement, which, with its 11-inch guns and its extensive cruising range, was claimed to be superior to the 10,000 ton cruisers with 8-inch guns which Britain and the United States were building under the Washington Agreement. It seemed that German naval architects had designed, in a perfectly legal manner, the perfect type of high-seas commerce raider which 'could outrun anything that could defeat it and could defeat anything that could overtake it'.[3]

In response to the arguments advanced by Gröner and the Chief of the *Marineleitung*, Admiral Zenker, President von Hindenburg

---

[1] Gessler was Minister of Defence from 1920–28, Stresemann Foreign Minister from 1923–29.

[2] For the circumstances and effect of Gröner's appointment see below, p. 194.

[3] The falsity of this claim was finally shown on December 13, 1939, when the *Admiral Graf von Spee*, the second of the 'pocket-battleships', after a running fight with the British cruisers *Ajax*, *Achilles* and *Exeter* was forced to take refuge in the Uruguayan waters of the River Plate, where she was finally scuttled on the direct orders of Hitler (December 18).

became a warm supporter of the 'pocket-battleship' programme, and it was on his instructions that the government of Chancellor Marx included in the Reich Budget for 1928 an unobtrusive item of 9·3 million marks, representing the first instalment of expenditure on the construction of *Panzerkreuzer A*.

Neither the significance nor the implication of the item, however, escaped the notice of the Social Democrats, who saw in it both an unnecessary extravagance and also the seeds of a second 'big navy policy' reminiscent of that with which Wilhelm II and von Tirpitz had saddled Germany in the beginning of the century. To vote for the first instalment meant logically to vote for the remainder and also for the building of four other such vessels, as well as a flotilla of cruisers and smaller warships which it was known were envisaged in the *Reichswehr's* naval programme.

A bitter conflict ensued, both in the Budget Committee and in the plenary session of the *Reichstag*, and in the country at large, where the whole strength of the SPD political machine was mobilized in opposition to the new naval estimates.[1] Despite the popular clamour, however, the measure was finally voted in March, but the general elections which followed in May resulted in a signal victory for the Social Democrats, who compaigned under the slogan of '*Kinderspeisung oder Panzerkreuzer*' and obtained over 9 million votes and 153 seats; their strongest representation since the elections of 1919.

A somewhat piquant situation now arose. As the head of a constitutional State, President von Hindenburg was in duty bound to call upon the leader of the strongest Party in the *Reichstag* to form a government; and thus it came about that the Marshal, who had fathered the *Panzerkreuzer* programme, was compelled to send for Hermann Müller, the man who had signed the Treaty of Versailles, and who, as leader of the SPD, had so violently opposed the naval estimates.

But the Marshal was more resolute in his stand than the leader of the Social Democrats. He made it a condition that, if Müller were to form a government, he and his SPD colleagues should retain Gröner in office and should loyally accept the naval building programme.

Müller hesitated. He could have refused and precipitated a new political crisis, but Stresemann, deeply involved in negotiations preliminary to the Kellogg-Briand Pact and the preparatory moves for the revision of the Dawes Plan, needed above all as stable a

[1] Otto Braun (*op. cit.*), pp. 250-53; Friedrich Stampfer, *Die vierzehn Jahre der ersten Deutschen Republik* (Karlsbad, 1936), pp. 480-82.

government in Germany as could be formed. He urged Müller to accept the President's terms and to base his coalition on the SPD, the German People's Party, and the Centre.

Severely torn in conscience, Müller agreed in principle and took office accordingly, but he sought to gain time, first, by making an appeal to the Powers at Geneva to hasten their tardy measures for calling the General Disarmament Conference, and secondly by making a thorough investigation of the rearmament situation within the Reich.

Neither of these procrastinatory moves was conspicuously successful. Though Müller was able to make the first tentative steps towards the evacuation of the Rhineland by the Allied armies of occupation, his speech in the League Assembly on September 7, in which he criticized the lack of progress made in Allied disarmament, was on the whole coldly received, and the Chancellor returned to Berlin a disappointed man.

The rearmament investigation was equally barren of results. The allegations on the subject of secret rearmament, which had been made by the Social Democrats with persistency since Scheidemann's opening attack in December 1926, coupled with the disclosures resulting from the 'Phoebus' scandal, rendered it no longer possible for any Cabinet of the Reich, let alone one in which Social Democrats held key positions, to close their eyes, however willingly, to these irregularities. Since entering the Cabinet in January 1928, Gröner had consistently declared his policy to be one of 'defensive pacifism', and had frankly admitted that under his predecessor there had been violations of the Peace Treaty and misrepresentations in the Defence Budgets, which he pledged himself to discontinue. The Cabinet, however, required more than this, and the Social Democrat Ministers were particularly anxious to know the full extent to which secret rearmament had progressed.

It was agreed, therefore, that the Chiefs of the Army and Navy should attend a plenary session of the Cabinet and should tell all. Heye and Raeder,[1] who had just succeeded Admiral Zenker, accord-

---

[1] Erich Raeder (1876–1960) was born in Wandsbeck near Hamburg, the son of a minor Government official. He entered the Navy in 1894, but, because of his diminutive stature, he never achieved an active command. In 1910, however, he was assigned as navigation officer on the Imperial Yacht *Hohenzollern*, where he earned the commendation of the Kaiser and formed a friendship with Franz Hipper, to whom he served as Chief of Staff at the Battle of Jutland. After the Armistice of 1918 Raeder was appointed head of the Control Department of the Admiralty, but at the time of the Kapp *Putsch* he made every effort to persuade the naval officer corps to support the new régime. As a result he was relegated to the Department of Naval Archives for two years, but was reinstated in 1922 with the rank of Rear-Admiral, a high rank in the republican Navy, as Inspector of

ingly appeared on October 18, 1928, and were cross-examined. In the words of one who was present, 'the members of the Cabinet were familiarized with the details of what might be considered a concealment of the Budget or violations of the Versailles Treaty'.[1] How accurate this survey may have been can be judged by the fact that the total amount involved was stated, and later confirmed in writing, to be not more than between $5\frac{1}{2}$-6 million marks, a statement so palpably false that the credulity of the Cabinet in accepting it is at once suspect.

Nor was this all. Heye and Raeder confirmed, both verbally and in writing, the statement of Gröner to his colleagues that the infringement of the Treaty restrictions were of a purely defensive character, involving 'only anti-aircraft guns, coastal fortifications, etc.'. The fears and suspicions of the Social Democrat Ministers withered before this apparently honest confession on the part of the military chiefs, and, with an assurance that there would be no repetition of these clandestine activities without the foreknowledge and approval of the Cabinet, the General and the Admiral withdrew. 'The impression I gained from the reports of the two *Wehrmacht* leaders was that only trifles were involved', Carl Severing later testified. 'It was this impression which caused me to assume a certain political responsibility for these things, and especially in view of the fact that we were assured that further concealment of budget items or other violations were not to occur in future.'

But even these protestations of future candour and good conduct on the part of the chiefs of the *Reichswehr* did not wholly remove the objections of Hermann Müller and his SPD colleagues to the naval estimates. They had campaigned against the *Panzerkreuzer* during the election in May as a piece of unwarranted extravagance, the money for which should either be devoted to social welfare development or the paying off of reparations, and the rank and file of the SPD were still strongly hostile to the naval building programme. Very shortly thereafter, in August, the Government of Hermann Müller had signed the Pact of Paris, by which in principle the use of war as an instrument of national policy was renounced

Training and Education and later commanded the squadron in both the North Sea and the Baltic. He succeeded Zenker as Chief of the *Marineleitung* in January 1928 and caused a minor political crisis by publicly proposing the health of the Kaiser at the first dinner given in honour of his appointment. He continued as ranking officer of the German Navy until 1943, when he was dismissed by Hitler and succeeded by Dönitz. Placed on trial at Nuremberg as a major War Criminal, Raeder was found guilty and sentenced to life imprisonment on October 1, 1946. He was released from Spandau in September 1955 and died in 1960.

[1] Evidence of Carl Severing, Reich Minister of Interior, 1928–30, before the International Military Tribunal, May 21, 1946 (*Nuremberg Record*, xiv, 252-8).

by the contracting parties, and Stresemann had made a further declaration of Germany's peaceful intentions. The Chancellor and his Foreign Minister were hoping to open the way to negotiations for the 'complete and final settlement of the reparation problem' and the evacuation of the Rhineland, but were under constant fire from the Agent-General for Reparation Payments for their profligate expenditure of public monies. From every angle, therefore, whether for reasons of Party ideology, political honesty or economic expediency, it seemed to Müller and his Socialist colleagues in the Cabinet that this was no time to pursue a policy of naval rearmament, however 'legal' it might be claimed to be. As a further consideration they were fully aware that the parliamentary fraction of their Party would inevitably move for the reduction of estimates when the *Reichstag* again debated the *Reichswehr* naval programme. The feeling within the Party, and particularly within the Trade Union element, was so strong that it was known that they would vote against their own representatives in the Cabinet, leaving the Government to be saved by the votes of the Nationalist Parties in opposition. In view of all these factors, and despite the pledge which he had given to von Hindenburg on taking office, Hermann Müller wavered.

But von Hindenburg and Gröner had dealt with Social-Democrats before, and the Minister of Defence now reverted to the tactics which he and the Marshal had frequently employed toward Ebert in the early days of the Republic. In the first week of November, 1928, on the eve of the Budget debate in the *Reichstag*, he circulated to his Cabinet colleagues a memorandum in which the arguments in favour of the 'pocket-battleships' were treated in relation to the defence and external policies of the Reich. Lest his exposition should not be in itself sufficiently convincing, Gröner added to it the threat of his own resignation if the continued construction work on *Panzerkreuzer A* was further delayed.

The memorandum is a document of considerable interest.[1] Though couched in the terms of that 'reasonable pacifism' which Gröner had declared on his first appearance before the *Reichstag*

---

[1] The memorandum, which had been destined as a Cabinet paper and for subsequent circulation to certain carefully selected members of the Budget Committee of the *Reichstag*, was made available, by some indiscretion, whether 'calculated' or otherwise, to the British Press and was published in full by Mr. Wickham Steed in the *Review of Reviews* (January 15, 1929). Amongst the Parties of the Left it was at once suggested that this leak had been engineered by certain reactionaries of the Right who, though they favoured the 'pocket battleship' policy, were hostile to Gröner personally and hoped that by revealing the contents of the memorandum they would get the best of all possible worlds, *i.e.* the acceptance of the naval estimates and the discrediting of the Minister.

would be the guiding principle of his policy, it is startling evidence of the complete cynicism with which the Kellogg-Briand Pact, just signed, was regarded in at least one quarter of the Reich Government. In its original inception the 'pocket-battleship' had been designed and promoted as a super high-seas commerce raider, and there had never been any question but that this was to be its primary office. Now, however, the argument was advanced that Germany needed these new warships to defend herself against her enemies in the Baltic. 'Poland's hunger for German territory in East Prussia and Upper Silesia, and the general aggressiveness of her policy' were adduced as reasons for increased naval rearmament. Soviet Russia was also listed as a possible opponent and a British journal, *The Naval and Military Record*, was cited as welcoming 'an efficient German fleet as a counter-weight to Russian sea-power in the Baltic'.

As a sop to the Socialist arguments against extravagant expenditure, Gröner pointed out that, on the contrary, the new naval construction programmes would actually benefit the national economy and the workers since it would ensure employment to some 3,000 workers at Kiel and it might be assumed that 'approximately 70 per cent of this expenditure, *i.e.* 56 million marks out of a total of 80 million marks, will return to the people largely in the form of wages'.

The kernel of the argument, however, is contained in three paragraphs in which the sweet reasonableness of Gröner's pacifism, his anxiety to restore and maintain Germany's *Wehrwillen* (will to defence) takes the strange form of advocating a preparedness to plunge into armed conflict if there were any chance of success.

If we do not want our neutrality to be violated and our territory made a battleground, then we must defend our neutrality by force of arms. And further, unless we wish to see the belligerent Powers ruthlessly disregarding our multifarious cultural and economic interests, which extend beyond our frontiers, then we must see to it that our interests are given weighty representations.

The possibility of conflict must be weighed very soberly. Germany will take part in armed hostilities only if she has a real chance of success. If she has no such chance, either as a result of her own position, or as the result of developments amongst the Powers concerned, then no responsible President would think of hurling the German people into senseless and bloody conflict and new chaos.

However, if the chances of success are present, then Germany would be able to make the better use of them the stronger she was.

The appealing force of Gröner's arguments, together with the threat of his resignation and, in addition, some degree of pressure from the Presidential Palace, removed or silenced the objections of the Chancellor and his fellow Social Democrats in the Cabinet. It was agreed to go forward with the naval estimates at the risk of a split in the Party.

The defence budget passed its committee stage with difficulty and the successful outcome was due in no small measure to the efforts of a brilliant young deputy of the Centre Party, Heinrich Brüning, who, having entered the *Reichstag* in the elections of 1924 was already recognized as a coming leader, and from this time became the marked favourite of Kurt von Schleicher for office.

The final word in the parliamentary battle of the 'pocket-battleship' was spoken on November 17, 1928, when a formal motion demanding that work on its construction should cease was defeated by 225 votes to 203, the Social Democrats voting against their representatives in the Cabinet.[1]

Once again the will of the *Reichswehr* was being implemented by a Social-Democratic Chancellor, even at the expense of the support of his own party.

(iii)

The succession of Wilhelm Gröner to Otto Gessler as *Reichswehr* Minister in January 1928 was an event of major importance in the history of the German Republic, in the history of the German Army — and, incidentally, in the career of Kurt von Schleicher, who played an important part in bringing it about.

Von Schleicher had known for some time of the President's desire that the Minister of Defence should be a professional soldier. He himself was well aware of the greater advantage to his own schemes which would accrue from the appointment of a general to his own liking, and who so much to his liking as Gröner? When, therefore, the 'Phoebus' scandal broke in the winter of 1927-8, though he had been fully cognizant of, and a participant in, many of the illicit activities which were disclosed, and though he owed some gratitude to Gessler for his spirited, if ill-judged, defence in the *Reichstag* of the 'Black Reichswehr', von Schleicher made no attempt to defend his ministerial chief, either openly or with the

[1] Brüning's connection with *Panzerkreuzer A* did not end here. When, as the *Deutschland*, she was launched at Kiel on May 9, 1931, Brüning, then Chancellor, accompanied President von Hindenburg to the christening ceremony. At the moment in his speech when he had reached a passage containing the words 'Disarmament . . . League of Nations', the ship was seen to be sliding prematurely down the ways into the water, leaving the President grasping an unbroken bottle of champagne and the Chancellor with his peroration in mid-air. 'Like Germany, she was so tired of phrases', commented an onlooker. The ceremony of christening was performed later from a launch.

LIEUTENANT-GENERAL WILHELM GRÖNER AND DR. OTTO GESSLER

President. On the contrary, when Gessler's resignation was demanded by the Left, von Schleicher urged von Hindenburg to agree to his dismissal.

The problem then arose of finding a successor, who must be a general acceptable both to the President and to the Social Democrats ; for the weather-wise prophets in politics could already descry the premonitory symptoms of that swing to the Left which resulted five months later in the return of the SPD as the largest single party in the *Reichstag*.

To von Schleicher the choice of a successor presented no problem at all. On all counts, in the national interest as well as his own, the finger of destiny pointed to Gröner. But there were obstacles to be overcome. The Social Democrats were opposed on principle to the Minister of Defence being a general, and the Army, though delighted at the idea, were far from united on the choice of Gröner. To many of the older members of the Officer Corps he was still a 'November Criminal'. They regarded him with disfavour and contempt as the Man of Spa and of Kolberg, who had first sent his Kaiser into exile and had later supported the acceptance by the Government of the peace terms of Versailles. Other candidates were put forward, chief among them being Count von der Schulenburg, formerly Chief of Staff of the Army Group of the German Crown Prince, and Freiherr von Willisen, the 'mystery man' of the *Reichswehr* and regarded by many, in contradistinction to von Schleicher, as its '*good* secret genius'.

Others of the Officer Corps, however, had changed their views in the course of the years. They were prepared to accept the verdict of the Court of Honour which in 1922 had cleared Gröner's conduct at Spa, albeit somewhat frigidly,[1] and to forget the 'treachery of Weimar'. Moreover, Gröner had strong partisans among the *Heeresleitung* in the Commander-in-Chief, Heye, who had served on his Staff at Spa, and in the Head of the *Truppenamt*, von Hammerstein, who had been his pupil and protégé at the War Academy. Both had followed his leadership without hesitation in 1918 and 1919, and had heeded his advice during the Kapp *Putsch* of 1920. Prompted by von Schleicher, they canvassed strenuously on Gröner's behalf and with such success that the opposition crumbled before them. Von Willisen, who had also been among Gröner's pupils and had remained a warm friend and admirer, refused point-

---

[1] In 1922 a Court of Honour had pronounced that in his conduct towards the Emperor at Spa in November 1918, Gröner had 'acted according to his conscience, holding that thus he could best serve the interest of his country' (Wheeler-Bennett, p. 221).

blank to allow himself to be considered as a competitor, while von der Schulenburg, who had been Gröner's arch-antagonist at Spa and latterly one of his principal traducers, now felt so strongly that he alone could fill the position that he telegraphed : 'We must have Gröner at all costs. We have all been mistaken about him'.[1]

With the field thus cleared of competitors, von Schleicher, Heye and von Hammerstein, with the support of Oskar von Hindenburg, urged upon the President the selection of Gröner. But here too there were difficulties. Gröner represented a link with the past which the Marshal would willingly have severed, and he did not at once give his consent. For alone of living mortals Gröner knew the whole truth of what had passed at Spa and at Kolberg when he had shouldered responsibility for decisions which should have been von Hindenburg's. In the years which had elapsed since those crucial days Gröner had remained silent in the face of the attacks and calumnies which had been levelled against him and in all this time the Marshal had said no word in his defence or had ever denied that the whole burden of responsibility for the fatal decisions rested with Gröner.

Why, a group of his friends once asked Gröner, did he make no effort to protect his name and reputation? 'Because I believed that in the interests of the New Army the myth of Hindenburg should be preserved', was his reply. 'It was necessary that one great German figure should emerge from the war free from all blame that was attached to the General Staff. That figure had to be Hindenburg.'[2]

Gröner's reticence, coupled with his own, had induced in Hindenburg a sense of embarrassment rather than of gratitude. The Swabian was cast in a nobler mould than the Prussian, and the Prussian knew it. The President was not at first anxious to renew the connection.

But von Schleicher had an answer for everything. There was no gainsaying him. With subtlety of argument and cajolery he bore down the President's objections. The welfare of the *Reichs-wehr*, he maintained, demanded that Gröner should defend its interests in the Cabinet and in the *Reichstag*. None other had so long and so complete an experience of the military machine as he, none could serve its interests better, and none would be as acceptable to the Social Democrats as this 'democratic' general. This he said to the President, while to the Socialists he recalled the services which Hindenburg and Gröner had together rendered in the past to Ebert

---

[1] Telegram from Count von der Schulenburg to Gottfried Treviranus (Wheeler-Bennett, p. 301).   [2] Wheeler-Bennett, p. 221.

and Scheidemann in making possible the establishment and the survival of the Republic.

Under the weight of such arguments the President withdrew his opposition and the Socialists swallowed their scruples, with the result that Gröner entered the Marx Cabinet at the end of January 1928 and was retained, without challenge or demur, by Hermann Müller when he formed his government after the general election, six months later.

For a man of sixty-one, hard bitten in the battles of war and peace, Gröner embarked upon his renewed political career with the confidence and enthusiasm — and also the *naïveté* — of a man much younger in years and experience. No premonition of the tragedy which was later to overwhelm him darkened the brightness of his artless and ingenuous belief in the loyalty and trust of the men with whom he was now called upon to work. When he took office in January 1928 there was no portent of the day of disillusion when he, who had told Wilhelm II : '*Der Fahneneid ist jetzt nur eine Idee*', was himself to learn that friendships plighted upon sword-hilts are equally unenduring.

With the President, Gröner was convinced, he would always be able to carry his point in the last instance because, as he told Brüning, 'he, in order to protect von Hindenburg's renown, had sacrificed his own irreproachable reputation in the interests of the nation'.[1] And, indeed, it did seem at the outset that the Marshal was not displeased at this reunion with his old Quartermaster-General, whom he greeted with cordiality. He was favourably impressed with Gröner's determined handling of the 'pocket-battleship' programme and, as a mark of his approbation, he granted him the privilege of criticizing manœuvres, a favour which he would never have conceded to any civilian Minister of Defence.[2]

As for the heads of the *Reichswehr*, Heye and von Hammerstein, they were, as Gröner happily announced, 'his friends, his old comrades, his colleagues';[3] he had no doubt that they would defer to his political judgment. And above all he leaned upon the shoulder of his young disciple and friend, the man whom he considered, and openly referred to, as his 'adopted son' — Kurt von Schleicher.

Von Schleicher was now approaching the apogee of his power.

---

[1] Heinrich Brüning, 'Ein Brief', *Deutsche Rundschau*, July 1947, p. 3.

[2] Heinz Brauweiler, *Generäle in der Deutschen Republik* (Berlin, 1932), p. 31.

[3] Letter from Gröner to Richard Bahr, May 22, 1932, quoted by Professor Gordon Craig in his brilliant study of the period, '*Reichswehr* and National Socialism ; the Policy of Wilhelm Gröner', *Political Science Quarterly* (New York, June 1948), p. 202.

With his patron as head of the Ministry and his nominees in the position of Commander-in-Chief and Head of the *Truppenamt*, he could virtually control the policy of the *Reichswehr*. But more was added unto him. Gröner, whose implicit trust in von Schleicher was equalled by his respect for the other's political intelligence, created for him a new division of the *Reichswehrministerium*, the *Ministeramt*, whose task it was to deal with all matters in which both the Army and the Navy were concerned and also to act as a liaison body between the Armed Services on the one hand and the other Reich Ministries and the political parties on the other.

In many respects this new appointment raised to an official status the functions which von Schleicher had performed during the latter days of the Seeckt Period, but it also greatly extended the scope and the influence of his activities. It was largely due to his efforts in this capacity that the passage of the naval estimates was eventually effected in the Budget Committee and in the *Reichstag* in 1929, and it was through this medium that his first official contact was formed with Heinrich Brüning.

Moreover, the political situation within the Reich was confederate to von Schleicher's ascendancy. The Chancellor, Hermann Müller, was in ill-health and was frequently away from Berlin for long periods, while Stresemann, also a sick man, was attending the protracted sessions of the Hague Conference of 1929 which brought the Young Plan into being, and with him were three other Ministers. During these absences a rump Cabinet, presided over by Gröner as Minister of Defence, endeavoured to cope with the business of government, but without conspicuous success, and as a result it became the butt of many a joke at the café tables and cabaret performances.

At this time the political structure of the Weimar System showed at its worst and weakest. Thanks to the futility inherent in proportional electoral representation, a multiplicity of political Parties were returned at each election, no one of which could of itself command a majority in the *Reichstag*, and so carry into effect a clear Governmental programme. The inevitable coalition governments were created not as an emanation of the Parties, but rather as a concession to administrative necessity. There was little sense of loyalty among the Party members to their representatives in the Cabinet and no Chancellor or Minister could ever be sure that he would not be stabbed in the back by his own followers. There was, however, strict discipline within the parties themselves where the power lay in the hands of the Party Committee, or 'machine', whose first loyalty was to the Party interests. The deputies were mere puppets in the hands of the Party bosses. The Committees became all-powerful and politics came to consist solely in their tactical manœuvrings.[1]

The result was parliamentary bankruptcy, the increasing discredit of democratic institutions, and the relapse of power into the hands of the bureaucracy. Indeed, had it not been for the integrity and ability of the Civil Service, which continued to carry on the administration of the Reich under the Republic as under the Empire, the whole machinery of government would have come to a standstill. While the politicians ranted and wrangled the bureaucrats ruled.

It was at this moment of parliamentary incompetency that von Schleicher gained access to the highest stratum of State affairs. Gröner, unused and in many ways unsuited to the position of acting Chancellor, leaned more and more heavily upon the political intelligence of his brilliant young coadjutor — 'My Cardinal in politics', as he called him — whom he used frequently as go-between in negotiation with party leaders. Von Schleicher, now a Lieutenant-General, prepared Gröner's Cabinet statements and supervised routine business, thus becoming conversant with secrets of State. Soon it became necessary for him to join the State Secretaries of the President and the Chancellor at Cabinet meetings and this was followed by the right of direct access to the President. Now, both in his official capacity and also unofficially as a friend of the Hindenburg family, he could exercise influence upon the old Marshal.

This indeed was power, and it was all the more attractive to von Schleicher since it was power without responsibility. In his use of it he could not restrain his inveterate tendency to intrigue. He saw himself as the secret arbiter of German destinies. No longer was it a matter of resisting republican influences, he was now in a position to dominate the inner political life of the country and to liberate it from the thraldom in which the political irresponsibility and inefficiency of a democratic parliamentary régime had held it for ten years. Through the implicit trust of Gröner, the respectful acquiescence of Heye, and von Hammerstein's dog-like devotion, which was only equalled by his incurable laziness,[2] von Schleicher exercised a controlling influence in the *Reichswehr*. His

---

[1] R. T. Clark, *The Fall of the German Republic* (London, 1935), pp. 127-35; Scheele, pp. 124-7.

[2] 'He [Hammerstein] follows his friend Schleicher like a well-trained hound', wrote Gröner bitterly to General von Gleich at a later date (May 22, 1932) when his eyes had been opened (quoted by Craig, p. 228). Von Hammerstein was aware of his besetting indolence and would say laughingly to his friends that the only thing which had hampered him in his career was 'a need for personal comfort (*Bequemlichkeit*)' (Ulrich von Hassell, *Vom andern Deutschland* (Zürich, 1946), p. 314).

prestige with the President was steadily gaining. All that remained was to find a Chancellor who should be acceptable to the Marshal and to the Army. Then, with a hand-picked Cabinet, they could send the *Reichstag* packing and govern the country by virtue of Article 48 of the Constitution, until such time as that instrument had been so amended as to ensure an authoritative and stable Government in Germany.

This was the plan which von Schleicher had conceived in the winter of 1929, this the project which he and his friends began subtly to adumbrate in the many circles in which he now had contacts : that the Marshal and the German Army should, by an act of daring and authority, rescue the Reich from the morass of economic chaos and political ineptitude in which she was sinking and suffocating as a result of the Great Depression and of the Weimar System. His objective was to identify the President with the Army, both as its Supreme Commander and as Chief of State. The loyalty of the Army was therefore pledged to its constitutional Chief to the exclusion of any other constitutional considerations. The President alone could save the Reich, but it was made abundantly clear that the *Reichswehr* was henceforth the sole source of the President's power and was inseparable from him.[1]

Von Schleicher's henchmen busily disseminated this thesis. 'The Revolution has taught the German Army officer to discriminate between the *provisional régime* of the State and its *permanent identity*, and to serve the latter, which is symbolized by the *Reichspräsident*, elevated above ephemeral ministries and incoherent governmental bodies', wrote von Hammerstein on July 21, 1929, in a Magdeburg paper. 'The *Reichswehr* serves the State, not the parties', was the terse injunction issued to the troops by Heye on May 9, 1930 ; and shortly thereafter, Colonel Erich Marcks, von Schleicher's public relations officer, wrote in one of the military journals : 'The President is elected by the people and represents in consequence the will of the people. His ultimate prerogative of action is to proclaim a state of emergency, for the Army is the only organism of the Reich which radiates over the whole country and which is capable of imposing the will of the Reich everywhere. This fact suffices to emphasize the importance of the *Reichswehr* in the government of the Reich and its close connection with the President, who *alone* possesses the right to take emergency measures and to invoke the intervention of the Army.'[2] This was a deliberate and deceptive perversion of von Seeckt's doctrine that 'The Army serves the

---

[1] Brauweiler, p. 76.   [2] *Wissen und Wehr*, January 1931.

State and the State alone, for it *is* the State': [1] but it served von
Schleicher's turn in the fulfilment of his Great Design.

It was in prosecution of this Design that this 'Cardinal in politics'
embarked upon a course of personal negotiations which led him
on to those later intrigues of colossal and fateful dimensions. His
choice for Chancellor was the forty-four-year-old Heinrich Brüning,
the parliamentary leader of the Centre Party, whose gallant war
record as the commander of a machine-gun company in the famous
'Winterfeldt Group' had been crowned with the decoration of the
Iron Cross (First Class) and a citation for 'unparalleled heroism'.
Brüning, however, was not easily persuaded, nor was he in the least
convinced of the efficacy of von Schleicher's dream-plan to govern
the Reich indefinitely through the *Reichswehr*. He was not averse
to the use of Article 48, if the necessity arose, but he was strongly
opposed to the violation of the constitutional provision which called
for the ratification by the *Reichstag* of the legislative decrees promulgated under that Article. In addition, he was a close and loyal
friend of Hermann Müller and rejected out of hand any scheme
which would entail his participation in an intrigue to oust the
Chancellor.

He therefore rebuffed the early advances of von Schleicher which
were made with Gröner's support and approval during the Christmas
season of 1929. But the *Feldgrau Eminenz* of the *Reichswehr* was
neither abashed nor deterred. He continued to undermine the
position of Müller with the President and to prepare Hindenburg's
mind for the reception of Brüning. So that when the inevitable
political crisis occurred in March 1930 and the last Cabinet of the
'Grand Coalition' fell, it was for Brüning that the President sent
on the insistence of Gröner, von Schleicher, his son Oskar, and the
Chiefs of the Army, and it was Brüning who formed a non-party
Cabinet. [2]

Von Schleicher had had his first experience as a breaker and
maker of Chancellors. It was not to be his last, and it had two
disastrous results. In the first place, the *Reichswehr*, in the persons
of von Schleicher and Gröner, with the support of von Hammerstein,
became the manipulator of politics in the Reich and in so doing
abdicated that high position of non-political power to which von
Seeckt had raised it. From being the guardian of the State and its
ultimate source of power, the Army descended to the status of
political broker and Party boss. Gröner saw too late the danger of

[1] Seeckt, *Thoughts of a Soldier*, p. 80.
[2] For details of the fall of the Müller Government and the appointment of
Brüning as Chancellor, see Wheeler-Bennett, pp. 328-30, 337-48.

the course they were following and tried to arrest the descent into the swamp of politics, but the web of von Schleicher's intrigues had enmeshed him too closely, and ultimately it was he who fell in a political intrigue.

The second result of von Schleicher's policy was that Brüning, who had hoped to restore and rehabilitate the prestige of democratic parliamentary government in Germany, was forced by the sequence of events and the irony of Fate into the position of introducing the thin end of the wedge of authoritarian government into the German political structure. Compelled by circumstances to invoke Article 48, he failed to secure the approval of the *Reichstag* for his decrees, and as a result of the elections of September 1930, for which Hindenburg granted him a dissolution, there appeared a new and hitherto unheeded factor in Reich politics. The Nazis, who in 1928 had secured only 12 seats in the *Reichstag* with 810,000 votes, were now supported by over 6 million voters and became a Party of 107 members, second only in size to the Social Democrats — an event which caused General von Schleicher to recast his calculations for the shape of things to come.

(iv)

When Adolf Hitler was released from the fortress of Landsberg on December 20, 1924, he came forth a wiser, if not a better, man. The expression of his political philosophy in the muddy prose of the first volume of *Mein Kampf* had not been his only occupation during his eight months' detention. He had thought deeply, and, as a result, there was added to his sense of mission and his redoubtable powers of demagogy a certain shrewd political cunning which was to serve him well in the years which lay ahead.

One vitally important decision he had taken. Never again must he and his followers confront the rifles of the *Reichswehr*. For Hitler the Way of Armed Revolt was no longer open — unless the lead be given by the *Reichswehr* itself. In future the National Revolution must be achieved by the Way of the Constitution, and the attainment of power must be made with the unquestioned support of the Army.

Hitler was no less a revolutionary than he had been in 1923, and regretted nothing of the past. He realized, however, that without the favour and backing of the *Reichswehr* he could never achieve the highest peak of his ambition, the control of the State; and, further, that the *Reichswehr* would never approve, and would certainly oppose, any repetition of such adventures as the Bürgerbräu

Putsch, or indeed any revolt against the Government, which they did not themselves initiate ; and this would never occur so long as the aged Marshal was President. Henceforward, therefore, the NSDAP should follow the Way of the Constitution, and in place of Hitler, the Rebel in Arms, there appeared 'Adolphe Légalité'.

But the situation with which Hitler found himself faced at the beginning of 1925 could hardly have been less favourable. Germany was on the road back to stability and the ultra-Nationalist cause was in chaos. The NSDAP, which had sent thirty-two deputies to the *Reichstag* elected in March 1924, saw this number dwindle to fourteen in the general elections which followed in December, and Ludendorff's fiasco as a National Socialist candidate in the first presidential ballot in March 1925 showed that there was still no popular support for extreme revolutionary nationalism. Moreover, the Party, which Hitler had left under the direction of a duumvirate composed of Rosenberg and Röhm, was rent by factions, feuds and *frondes* in consequence of the jealousies resulting from this first experiment in delegated power under the *Führerprinzip*. The relations of the NSDAP with the Nationalist Party and with the extreme reactionaries of the Right in Northern Germany, which had deteriorated since November 1923, diminished almost to vanishing point after the election of Hindenburg to the Presidency, since these elements regarded the return of the Marshal as the penultimate achievement of their hopes. In addition, the revelation of hideous homosexual scandals in the SA caused a number of peripheral supporters, among them Ludendorff and Count von Reventlow, to break altogether with the Party.

Nor were the rebuilding of the Party machine and the re-establishment of its political contacts the only problems with which Hitler had to contend in the years 1925–8. Divergences of thought arose between him and his military advisers as to the purpose and functions of the Party's para-military organizations. The *Führer* never at any time recognized military claims in the Party. He was content to see the *Reichswehr* as the one military organism within the Reich — provided it was on his side. It was part of his strategy in wooing the Army to insist upon this as an immutable principle of Nazi policy. In his concept of the SA they were primarily and essentially for purposes of intimidation, for political guerrilla warfare, for street-fighting, for the protection of Nazi mass-meetings and for breaking up the mass-meetings of others.

Adolf Hitler had an uncanny understanding of the German national psychology. He recognized, whether by instinct or study or merely by a fellow-feeling, that the German people are the most

H

inhibited in Europe, fundamentally governed by a sense of inferiority for which they over-compensate by arrogance, and altogether lacking in self-assurance and a sense of responsibility to themselves. All these symptoms Hitler read aright and used them to his own advantage. The SA, with its military formation, its ranking hierarchy, its banners and its bands, was designed to satisfy the German craving for uniforms and emblems, for that military glamour and display which the drab rule of Weimar had done its poor best to suppress. But at no time had Hitler destined his Brown Shirts as even an auxiliary, let alone a rival, to the Army.

Such, however, was not the view of the High Command of the SA. To Röhm and Rossbach and Pfeffer the Storm Troops were an essential part of the future German Army which should one day wage a victorious War of Liberation. They recalled the gesture of reconciliation to the *Reichswehr* which Hitler had made from the dock at Munich, and the vision conjured up by his words that 'one day the hour is coming when these untrained bands will become battalions, when the battalions will become regiments and the regiments divisions ; when the old cockade will be raised from the mire; when the old banners will once again wave before us'.[1] Now was the time, they urged, to make good this gesture, to approach the *Reichswehr* with an offer to hand over the whole SA as an organization to their command, and thus to create a trained reserve of man-power, impregnated with Nazi ideology, upon which the Army could draw on the dawning of 'The Day', and which would itself proselytize the Army for National Socialism.

No proposition could have been less acceptable either to Hitler or to the Army, and the *Führer* took energetic measures to scotch it at the outset. It was on these grounds — and not in disapprobation of his moral perversity — that Hitler broke with Röhm in May 1925, and the breach was to last five years.[2] He reorganized the leadership of the SA, and he also created a unit, a *corps d'élite* of the Party, the *Schutz Staffel* (SS), a hand-picked group fanatically devoted to himself, which was in later years to become the dread weapon of Heinrich Himmler. As a final check upon the military ambitions of his lieutenants, he issued emphatic orders forbidding either the SA or the SS to have any connection whatsoever with the *Reichswehr*.

---

[1] See above, p. 179.

[2] For the years of his exile from the Party Ernst Röhm retired to Bolivia, where the Army was being reorganized and trained by an unofficial military mission composed of General Kundt and a group of former officers of the Imperial German Army. Röhm served in the Bolivian Army as a Lieutenant-Colonel until 1930, when he was recalled to Germany by Hitler, who appointed him Chief of Staff of the SA.

On the part of the *Reichswehr*, a general order was issued prohibiting the acceptance of National Socialists as candidates for the Army, and even forbidding their employment as workers in arsenals and supply establishments, on the grounds that the Party had set itself the aim of overthrowing the constitutional form of the German Reich.

By 1927 the relations between the Army and the Party were virtually non-existent and Hitler seemed in no great hurry to restore them. The Army could wait ; it would come to him, he was confident, in time ; and, meanwhile, he was fully engaged in rebuilding his party organization, dragooning his followers into a new discipline, extending the sphere of his party affiliations across the Main into Northern Germany, and, most important of all, cultivating the new connections which, through his devoted followers, Otto Dietrich and the septuagenarian convert Emil Kirdorff, he had succeeded in establishing with the captains and princes of heavy industry and Big Business.

The evil leaven of Hitler's movement was working very slowly within the Reich. Conditions of prosperity were against him in the years of Stresemann's ascendancy and, when the results of the general elections of May 1928 became known, it was seen that the fourteen National Socialist deputies in the *Reichstag* had shrunk to twelve. Would the Nazis disappear altogether as a parliamentary party, was a question widely debated, and the wishful thinkers in all other parties took comfort at the possibility.

But the strength of the NSDAP was not to be measured by the size of its representation in the *Reichstag*. It was steadily on the increase. In the year 1926–7 its membership rose from 17,000 to 40,000, and thenceforward it grew rapidly. In the summer of 1929 there were 120,000 registered members of the Party, by the following spring the number had risen to a quarter of a million, and in the autumn of 1930 Hitler claimed a million followers.

The reason was not far to seek. The crucial year of 1929, that *annus terribilis* which brought down the dreams and the illusions of the Age of False Security about the heads of the dreamers, brought forth fresh hopes and new success for Adolf Hitler. The economic crisis, which had already begun in Germany in 1928, was soon driving increasing numbers of the newly unemployed into the ranks of the Party, which, with its glowing promises of work for all and the destruction of the 'shackles of Versailles' — to these all Germany's ills were attributed — gave them fresh hope for security and revenge.

It was now also that the Young Plan crisis burst upon the Reich.

In an attempt to reach 'a complete and final settlement of the reparation problem', a committee, representing creditor and debtor nations and presided over by Mr. Owen D. Young, had drawn up a New Plan to complete the work begun by the Dawes Committee of 1924. Signed by its authors in Paris in June 1929, the Plan was accepted in August with certain amendments, at a Conference of the Powers at the Hague.

From the outset the German Nationalist Party and the great industrialists had been bent upon sabotaging the negotiations. In an attempt to outmanœuvre them, Stresemann had insisted upon a representative of heavy industry being appointed as one of Germany's representatives on the Young Committee, and Dr. Albert Vögler, the steel magnate, had accordingly accompanied Schacht, the President of the Reichsbank, to Paris. But Vögler resigned rather than accept the provisions of the New Plan, and Schacht, though he signed the Plan, repudiated it after the Hague Conference and campaigned vehemently against it both in Germany and in America.

The Nationalists, having failed to thwart the adoption or the acceptance of the Plan, now concentrated their forces for a final effort to prevent its ratification by the *Reichstag*. The occasion was to be one not only of opposition to the Plan itself but for a full-scale attack upon Stresemann's policy and the whole Weimar System.

The record of the Nationalist Conservative Party in Germany during the Weimar Republic is one of deep dishonour. It epitomizes the failure of the German people as a whole to appreciate the decencies of political conduct and parliamentary behaviour. Prince von Bülow in his memoirs [1] records with some pride a scene in the Bavarian *Landtag* in which a Government front bench deputy, whom he describes as 'noble in spirit and not merely by birth', interrupted the Leader of the Opposition, first by shaking his fist, then by spitting in his face and finally by throwing a chair at him, 'at which the people in the packed public gallery broke into tumultuous cheers'.[2] This same line of conduct was pursued by the German Nationalists under the Republic. In the early days of the November Revolution they were frightened and were then grateful enough to obtain assurances of personal safety from the Republican leaders, but with the opening of the National Assembly at Weimar they displayed a culpable lack of political responsibility and, in many cases, of decent personal conduct. The vitriolic attacks of Helfferich

---

[1] Prince von Bülow, *Memoirs, 1849-1897* (London, 1932), p. 164.
[2] It is not without interest, in the light of subsequent history, that the name of this belligerent deputy was Freiherr von Stauffenberg.

and others upon their political opponents inspired the assassins of Erzberger and of Rathenau, and also encouraged those perverted characters in the Nationalist Party who found satisfaction in sending through the post the decomposed carcass of a dog to the French Ambassador and parcels containing human excrement to leaders of the Social Democrats.

The Nationalist Party deliberately shunned the burden of the responsibility of government. In only two of the nineteen parliamentary Cabinets between 1919 and 1932 did they participate,[1] and the total period of their participation over these thirteen years was twenty-seven months. Though urged by President von Hindenburg on more than one occasion, no Nationalist leader would assume the duty of forming a Government. Rather than support the Republic they preferred to watch the decline of the Republican Parties, in the hope that in the final chaos they might come to power. The Nationalists did not vote against the acceptance of the Versailles Treaty until they were certain that there was a majority in its favour and that they could therefore oppose it with impunity and subsequent advantage. They gave tacit support to Kapp and to von Lüttwitz in 1920. On the acceptance of the Dawes Plan their attitude was one of equivocal opposition, and they broke with Luther and with Stresemann over Locarno. At no time during the Weimar Republic did they make a single constructive contribution to the government of the country. Their ultimate objective was the destruction of the Republic and to the attainment of this end they subordinated all national interests, not having the wit to see that, while they worshipped and genuflected before the broken altars of dead gods, the interests of Germany were being ably served by von Seeckt and Stresemann, whom they traduced and obstructed.

Nor is it possible to excuse from blame those members of the nobility and landed gentry who shut themselves up on their estates and refused all participation in civic life. By their seclusion they deprived the Nationalist Party of its traditional leadership and allowed it to become more and more the Party of the great industrialists. The bankruptcy and the blindness of the Nationalists is epitomized in the fact that they permitted the leadership of their Party to pass into the hands of such a man as Alfred Hugenberg, the newspaper and film magnate, as borné and bigoted a character as one might expect to meet, and one who reduced the Party to a

---

[1] The Nationalists held three portfolios in the Luther Cabinet formed in January 1925, but resigned in October in protest against the Locarno Agreement. They were allotted four ministries in the fourth Marx Cabinet, which held office from January 1927 to May 1928.

mere political machine, of which he became the unchallenged boss.[1]

Had the German Conservatives reconciled themselves to the Republic — bringing to it that wealth of experience and knowledge which they had accumulated in the past, and performing those invaluable services which are always fulfilled in the government of any country by an able constitutional Opposition, ready to take office should the occasion arise — they would have conferred a considerable benefit not only upon Germany — to whom they would have given that which she had so long lacked, a genuine Conservative Party — but also upon the cause of Conservatism throughout the world. They did not do this. Under the cloak of loyalty to the Monarchy, they either held aloof or sabotaged the efforts of successive Chancellors to give a stable government to the Reich. The truth is that after 1918 many German Nationalists were more influenced by feelings of disloyalty to the Republic than of loyalty to the Kaiser, and it was this motive which led them to make their fatal contribution to bringing Hitler to power. The sequel is to be found in the long list of noble names among those executed after the *Putsch* of July 20, 1944, when many expiated upon the scaffold the sins which they or their fathers had committed a generation earlier.

[1] Alfred Hugenberg (1865–1951), a member of a family which had distinguished itself in the service of the Kings of Hanover, entered the Prussian civil service and made a fortunate marriage with the daughter of the famous *Oberbürgermeister* of Frankfurt-am-Main, Dr. Adikes. Aided by his father-in-law's considerable influence, he became a *Geheimrat*, and at an early date in his career disclosed violently anti-Polish sentiments. An active member of the Pan-German League, Hugenberg joined the board of Krupps during the First World War. After the collapse he took a leading part in organizing the Nationalist Party and directed his personal energies towards those channels which influence public opinion. By 1928 he had gained complete control of the ALA publicity firm, which exercised a virtual monopoly over all German advertising, of the Scherl publishing firm, of the UFA film combine, which both made pictures and owned cinemas, and of a chain of newspapers. In this same year Hugenberg became President of the Nationalist Party, and the pact which he made with Hitler in July 1929, and further strengthened at Harzburg in 1931, was the forerunner of his final disastrous collaboration with von Papen in bringing the Nazis to power in January 1933. In the original Cabinet of the National Revolution Hugenberg was Minister of Agriculture and Economics, but in six months he had been forced to resign all his offices, and the Nationalist Party, in common with all political parties in the Reich with the exception of the NSDAP, had been dissolved. Thereafter, though he continued nominally to be a member of the *Reichstag*, to which he had originally been elected in 1920, until the collapse of the Third Reich in 1945, he lived in retirement, a disillusioned and disappointed old man. Arrested in the British Zone in October 1946, Hugenberg was brought before a series of de-nazification trials between December 1947 and July 1950. Having first been placed in Category III (a minor offender), he was later down-graded to Category V (Exoneration). A volume entitled *Hugenbergs Ringen in deutschen Schicksalsstunden* (Detmold, 1951) gives an account of these legal processes.

The first step upon this last stage in the disastrous progress of the Nationalist Party was taken by Hugenberg in July 1929. To give expression to his agitation against the acceptance of the Young Plan, he had determined upon the utilization of a provision of the Weimar Constitution permitting the consultation of the electorate by referendum under certain circumstances (Art. 73, Section 3). It was his purpose to bring before the *Reichstag* 'A Bill against the Enslavement of the German People', whereby the acceptance of the Plan was declared to be an act of treachery, and those Ministers of the Reich who were responsible for its acceptance were charged with high treason. To be brought before the *Reichstag*, this preposterous measure required a petition by one-tenth of the qualified voters and it was in his zeal to achieve this proportion that Hugenberg turned to Hitler.

The Nationalists had everything but the masses, the Nazis had everything but the money. On this basis of mutual need a pact was concluded and both Parties flung themselves into the campaign with a fanatical zest and venomous disregard for the decencies of public life as had hitherto not been seen in German politics. The attacks upon Müller and Stresemann, and now even upon Hindenburg, who, because of his support of his Ministers, had become a target for the vitriol of the Right, exceeded all bounds. But the very frenzy of the advocates of the Bill defeated their aims. When the vote was taken on November 3 the necessary percentage was only gained by the fractional figure of 10·02, and the Bill, when it came to the *Reichstag* three weeks later, was rejected with ignominy.

The incident, however, had two important results. The debate in the *Reichstag* was the occasion of the first revolt of certain members of the Nationalist Party against the leadership of Hugenberg. Treviranus and Schlange-Schönigen [1] first abstained from voting for the Bill and subsequently seceded from the Party to form their own Conservative group in the *Reichstag*. They were joined later by Count Westarp, the parliamentary leader of the Party, and some twenty other Nationalist deputies. The revolt, however, which had been stimulated by von Schleicher in the desire to destroy Hugenberg's grip on the Party, came too late to deter him from his disastrous course, and the rebels were too weak numerically to make anything more than a moral gesture.

---

[1] Gottfried Treviranus and Hans Schlange-Schöningen both served later in Brüning's Administration, and the latter was appointed in April 1950 as the first diplomatic agent of the Western German Federal Government in London. His memoirs, *Am Tage danach* (Hamburg, 1947), are of considerable interest, and it was in answer to certain statements made therein that Dr. Brüning was moved to write his famous letter to the *Deutsche Rundschau* in July 1947.

The only people to benefit from the whole disreputable affair of the *Volksbegehren* (Referendum) were the National Socialists. Hitler used the money so liberally provided by Hugenberg and the industrialists for the re-equipment and expansion of the SA and for the furtherance of his own propaganda. The campaign expenses of the referendum he left to the Nationalists. The added publicity which he and his movement gained was all grist to his mill, and though the voting had not shown any great increase over his popular support in the elections of the previous year, he had had an opportunity of getting his ideas before the electorate 'free of charge' and also of making many new and valuable contacts in the world of business and industry. It was now abundantly clear that a major economic and political crisis overshadowed Germany, and the cause of National Socialism throve in the atmosphere of crisis. The *Führer* had no reason to be dissatisfied with an adventure which had brought him fresh allies, however dubious, for the events which might lie ahead ; for in the pact of the *Volksbegehren* lay the seeds of the National Opposition which was to bring him to the Chancellor's Palace.

In all these calculations, however, the prerequisite and, as yet, the uncertain factor, was the attitude of the Army, and it was to the consideration of this problem that Hitler now applied his attention.

(v)

Hitler's open fight to gain the support of the *Reichswehr* began in the spring of 1929 and continued until the very eve of his advent to power in January 1933. It began at a moment when, under the impact of the losses sustained by the Nazis in the general elections of May 1928, Hitler was momentarily contemplating the abandonment of the Way of the Constitution, to which he had adhered since his release from Landsberg in December 1924, and was considering the possibility of a second *Putsch* against the Reich Government, provided that he could secure the support, or at worst the neutrality, of the *Reichswehr*. A change, however, came over the conduct of the campaign after the Nazi successes in the general elections of September 1930, when Hitler realized that the Way of the Constitution offered him more certain chances of success after all, but that in order to attain power he must direct his efforts towards reassuring the *Reichswehr* in addition to seducing them from their loyalty to the State.

The opening shot of the campaign was fired at a public mass meeting in Munich on March 15, 1929, at which, in a speech of some considerable length, Hitler issued a covert challenge to the

Army to forsake its pledged loyalty to the State and to co-operate with the National Socialist movement in the overthrow of the Republic.[1] The Nazi conception of the loyalty of the Army was disclosed as being not to the State but to the people, and that the duty of the Army lay in eliminating this 'lazy and decayed State'. The *Reichswehr*, said Hitler, had a political as well as a military mission to fulfil, namely, to assist in the destruction of 'the muddle and pestilence of party politics'. Had the Army been imbued with the ideology of National Socialism and acted accordingly, 'Germany would never have found herself in this swamp of party politics and parliamentarianism'. Salvation was now to be gained solely by the establishment of a dictatorship, for by this means only could that hegemony of Europe, which was absolutely necessary for the freedom of the German people, be achieved.

Again and again Hitler extolled the example set to all armies in times of revolutionary stress and crisis by General Badoglio in October 1922, when he offered no opposition to Mussolini's March on Rome. How different had been the attitude of the *Reichswehr* in November 1923; how different was it even to-day. 'The Italian Army did not say, "Our job is to maintain peace and order". Instead they said, "It is our duty to preserve the future for the Italian people". . . . You, as officers, cannot maintain that you do not care about the fate of the nation. . . . Either you have a healthy State with a really valuable military organization, which means the destruction of Marxism, or you have a flourishing Marxist State, which means the annihilation of the military organization capable of serving the highest purposes.'

As an alternative to the National Socialist State, which would give again to the Army that pride of service which it had been so long denied, Hitler depicted the future prospects of the Army in a Germany in which 'democratic-Marxism' had triumphed. In words prophetic of what he himself was later destined to do, he warned the Officer Corps: 'You may then become hangmen of the régime and political commissars, and if you do not behave, your

---

[1] This important speech, which, curiously enough, is omitted from both the collections of Hitler's speeches compiled by Professor Baynes and Count de Roussy de Sales, was published as a special *Reichswehr* edition of the *Völkischer Beobachter* on March 26, 1929. It figured prominently in a long report submitted to the Prussian Ministry of Interior by its Secret Police Department in 1930, the object of which was to reveal the NSDAP as guilty of treason. The report was forwarded by the Prussian Authorities to the Reich Minister of Interior (Carl Severing) and to the Public Prosecutor of the Reich (*Oberreichsanwalt*) at Leipzig, but, despite all efforts, the Chief Law Officers of the Reich could not be persuaded to take legal action against the Party. (For text of Report and correspondence with Attorney-General, see Kempner, pp. 56-134.)

wife and child will be put behind bars; and if you still do not behave, you will be thrown out and perhaps stood up against a wall, for human life counts little with those who are out to destroy a people.'

The purpose and import of this speech were clearly to seduce the *Reichswehr* from their loyalty to their oath, to win them over to the ideology of National Socialism, and to secure their active co-operation against the Government of the Reich in the event of a Nazi *Putsch*. In the months that followed, the same line of attack was pursued in the columns of the *Völkischer Beobachter* — whose editor at this time, Wilhelm Weiss, was a former captain of the Imperial Army — and in articles and pamphlets published by the Party's ...ilitary periodical, *Deutscher Wehrgeist*; and there was ample evidence that this propaganda, taken in conjunction with the bitter and venomous attacks made upon the Government by the Nationalist and Nazi leaders during the campaign of the Young Plan Referendum, was having the effect of turning a number of young officers towards National Socialism as a means of escape from Germany's financial and political troubles.

It became increasingly clear to Gröner and to the senior officers of the *Reichswehr* that National Socialism was a real danger and far more of a threat to the Republic than Communism, which had hitherto been regarded as the principal menace. And there were disturbing characteristics about the Nazi movement which rendered it nearer to the purely destructive principles of Bolshevism rather than the more disciplined theories of Fascism, to which the *Reichswehr* were not altogether inimical. 'They want to destroy the present fabric of the State, but have no constructive programme with which to replace it, except a sort of mad-dog dictatorship', an officer of the Defence Ministry complained to the British Military Attaché in Berlin.[1]

To Gröner the similarity between National Socialism and Communism recalled the nightmare days of chaos in 1918, when military discipline had been undermined by the Soldiers' Councils and had only been maintained by the action of the Officer Corps. Now it was not only the rank and file but also the officers who were becoming the target and the victims of subversive propaganda, and this, together with the weakness of the Müller Government and the rapidly increasing unemployment, constituted as great a danger of disintegration of national unity as had confronted the Reich in 1923.

---

[1] Cf. a report by H.M. Military Attaché in Berlin, Colonel (later General Sir James) Marshall-Cornwall, on a conversation with Colonel Kühlenthal, of the *Reichswehr* Ministry, in May 1930 (Woodward and Butler, Second Series, i, 478).

In a warning to the Army as to where its duty lay in these grave circumstances, Gröner issued an Order of the Day on January 22, 1930,[1] which in tone and content recalls that which von Seeckt had issued in a similar situation on November 4, 1923.[2] The Nazis, Gröner told the Army, 'are to be distinguished from the Communists only by the national base on which they take their footing'. Greedy for power, 'they therefore woo the *Wehrmacht*. In order to use it for the political aims of their Party, they attempt to dazzle us . . . [with the idea that] the National Socialists alone represent the truly national idea.' But the triumph of either National Socialism or Communism in destroying the existing political system would be disastrous, for it would inevitably bring civil war in its train. It was the duty of the *Reichswehr*, wrote Gröner — as von Seeckt had written six years before — to prevent such an eventuality and to preserve the Reich from 'a catastrophe for State and economy'.

It is the sacred task of the *Wehrmacht* to prevent the cleavage between classes and parties from ever widening into suicidal civil war. In all times of need in the history of a people there is one unshakable rock in the stormy sea : the idea of the State. The *Wehrmacht* is its necessary and most characteristic expression. It has no other interest and no other task than service to the State. Therein lies the pride of the soldier and the best tradition of the past. . . . [The *Wehrmacht*] would falsify its essence and destroy itself if it descended into party conflict and itself took part. To serve the State — far from all party politics, to save and maintain it against the terrible pressure from without and the insane strife at home — is our only goal.

Thus in 1930 Gröner admonished the *Reichswehr* as von Seeckt had admonished it in 1923, but with this difference, that when von Seeckt uttered his warning there was still time to profit from it, but when Gröner cautioned the *Reichswehr* against party politics, the virus was already infecting the body of the Army. Evidence of this was forthcoming almost before the print was dry on his Order of the Day. On March 6, 1930, two young lieutenants of the 5th Regiment of Artillery, then garrisoned at Ulm, were arrested and charged with spreading National Socialist propaganda in the ranks of the Army.

The story of these two young men may have been duplicated in other garrisons and regimental depots in Germany, but it presented a very pretty example of the effects of Nazi propaganda upon younger members of the Officer Corps and the lengths to which they would go as a result of it. Richard Scheringer (26) and Hans

---

[1] *Reichswehrministerium, Erlass*, January 22, 1930 (quoted by Craig, pp. 205-6).

[2] See above, p. 115-6.

Ludin (25) both came of good middle-class families and, so far as
is known, their military records had been exemplary. They were
types of normal intelligence with perhaps somewhat more than the
average young man's interest in politics. They did not need to
know the inner secrets of the political situation in Berlin to comprehend the parlous condition into which Germany had fallen in
1929. The ever-lengthening queues of unemployed before the
Labour Exchanges and the soup kitchens was sufficient proof, and
they had but to read their daily newspapers in order to learn that the
Government and the *Reichstag* were either incapable or unwilling to
meet the emergency with the force and courage which it necessitated.

But Scheringer and Ludin read other newspapers besides the
local press of Ulm. They read the *Völkischer Beobachter* and the
Deutscher Wehrgeist, where, for example, they found the injunction
that 'the only faction with which an army of military value and
significance can maintain a spiritual relationship is that consciously
national nucleus of a people, which not merely out of tradition
thinks militarily, but which, rather out of a national love, conviction
and enthusiasm, is always ready to don the soldier's uniform in order
to protect the honour and freedom of its people'.[1]

One may believe that these two young officers were genuinely
concerned for the welfare of their country, and that they swallowed
this poisonous pabulum in good faith — or perhaps in desperation
— believing that in the realization of Nazi doctrines lay the sole
means of German salvation. But there was also in their thinking
that sense of hopeless helplessness which beset so many young
Germans at this time. To what could they look forward, these
young officers? There was no hope of promotion. There was
no hope, under the Weimar System, of a War of Liberation which
should free Germany from the shackles of Versailles and restore
to the Officer Corps that prestige which had been their proud
heritage in the past. Only the grinding monotony of garrison life
as the despised bearers of arms was their lot. Hitler offered glory,
freedom; a national resurgence and an expanded Army; there
would be promotion and hope restored; lieutenants and captains
would become colonels and generals; there would be honour
and liberation and economic security. It was therefore as willing
victims of an insidious and noxious propaganda reacting upon
hearts oppressed by hopelessness and boredom that these young
officers were prompted to violate their oath and to commit high
treason.

Scheringer and Ludin got into touch with the leader of the local

[1] *Deutscher Wehrgeist*, No. 3, p. 101 (quoted by Kempner, p. 105).

NSDAP group at Ulm, one Held, offering themselves as contact men between the Party and the Army. Held realized that an affair of this importance was outside his competence and referred the matter to headquarters, with the result that on November 1, 1929, the two lieutenants visited Munich, where, at the Brown House, they were received by Captain Weiss, the editor of the *Völkischer Beobachter*, with whom were Captain von Pfeffer and Captain Otto Wagener, respectively Chief Leader and Chief of Staff of the SA. Once the *bona fides* of the two young men had been established, the Nazi leaders talked freely of their desire to gain either the support or the neutralization of the Officer Corps in the event of a Nazi Revolution, and urged the two converts to work for the furtherance of this end. But they were told that outwardly the Party could have nothing to do with their plans. They might even be disavowed if discovered in their treason. Outwardly the Party was pledged to legality.

On their return to Ulm, Scheringer and Ludin sounded out certain of their comrades in the 5th Artillery Regiment and succeeded in converting one of them, an officer senior to themselves, First Lieutenant Hans Friedrich Wendt, who was later charged with them. For the next five months these three men employed their spare time in journeying about the Reich with the express purpose of establishing contact men in other garrisons, who should in their turn get into touch with persons designated in each case by the Party and should feel out the attitudes of both their comrades and their superiors. The ultimate goal of their plan, as Ludin subsequently testified at their trial, was that they should either be successful in winning over the whole Officer Corps or else that the majority of the young officers should refuse to fire in the event of an attempted revolution from the Right. Inevitably their activities, which were carried on in the most amateur manner, led to their detection, and on the morning of March 6, 1930, they were arrested on the barrack square at Ulm.

The arrest of Scheringer, Ludin and Wendt caused a major sensation, not only in *Reichswehr* circles but throughout Germany. It coincided with the beginning of that turn of the tide in the popular fortunes of the NSDAP which carried them first into the State Parliaments of Baden and Thuringia and later into the *Reichstag* as the second largest Party. There were those in the *Reichswehr* Ministry and High Command who urged Gröner to treat the Ulm affair as a simple matter of military discipline in order not to give it great publicity, and when the *Reichstag* was dissolved in July, and the country was once more in the grip of a general election,

these voices became the more insistent. Gröner was at first disposed to agree that this was no time to advertise unnecessarily the
fact that treason existed within the ranks of the Officer Corps. He
endeavoured to deal with the matter by means of a regular court-
martial, but the attitude and conduct of the accused made this
impossible.

From his cell Scheringer smuggled out the MS. of an article
which was subsequently published in the *Völkischer Beobachter*.
In it he disclosed himself as unrepentant and gave further publicity
to his unregenerate views. 'The actual purpose of the *Reichswehr*
as a citadel of the military idea and the basic nucleus for the future
war of liberation pales', wrote Scheringer. 'The need of earning
bread becomes all important. Soldiers turn into officials, officers
become candidates for pensions. What remains is a police troop.'
All the aching monotony of an army at peace came out in the next
sentence. 'People know nothing of the tragedy of the four words :
" Twelve years as subalterns ". . . . Let the old men be silent.
They have their lives behind them, ours are just beginning. A lost
war, an impotent State, a hopeless system, an enslavement enduring
fifty-nine years, a Reich on the brink of the abyss, that is our life —
and they are to blame. . . . Consequently, we have the right to
fight with all means for our freedom and that of our children. The
world may be sure that we are determined to do so, and we shall be
victorious just as surely as France is a dying nation.' [1]

Such sentiments could not have been bettered by Hitler himself,
and this reaffirmation of seditious notions compelled Gröner to
take action on the highest level, despite the now added complication
that, as a result of the general elections on September 14, the Nazis
had become the second strongest Party in the *Reichstag*. On September 23 the three subalterns were arraigned before the Supreme
Court of the Reich at Leipzig on a charge of high treason.

The trial at once became a *cause célèbre*. It had indeed many
aspects of both immediate and future interest. For example,
Scheringer was defended by a young Munich lawyer, Hans Frank,
and Ludin by the well-known Berlin attorney, Dr. Carl Sack, both
of whom were destined to be hanged.[2]

As the proceedings continued it became increasingly clear how

[1] Heiden, pp. 314-15.
[2] Hans Frank, who subsequently became Bavarian Minister of Justice, Reich
Minister without portfolio, and, finally, the notorious Nazi Governor-General of
Poland, was sentenced to death by the International Military Tribunal at Nurem-
berg and hanged on October 16, 1946. Dr. Sack, who later became Judge Advocate-
General of the German Army, was an active member of the Conspiracy against
Hitler. He was hanged after the abortive *Putsch* of July 20, 1944.

adverse they were for the interests of the *Reichswehr*, as witness
after witness testified to the degree of discontent which existed in
the Army.[1] Not one of the accused attempted to conceal his beliefs
or to mitigate his acts of treason. They candidly admitted that it
had been their intention to set up within the Army an organization
which would have prevented a repetition of what had occurred in
November 1923, and Scheringer frankly declared that 'the struggle
for liberation will always remain the ultimate goal of the *Reichswehr*'. A number of officers were examined by counsel and in nearly
every case the fact emerged that to some degree or other they shared
the views of the accused. One declared that 'Nationalism is equivalent to patriotism, and pacifism to treason'. Another went further
and roundly stated : 'We officers are patriotic and patriotism is the
attribute of only a very few parties'. All agreed that throughout
the Army in all ranks the Government was a constant butt of contemptuous raillery.

Of particular interest was the evidence of the colonel commanding
the 5th Artillery Regiment at Ulm. He had protested energetically
at the arrest of his three subalterns, had spoken warmly on their
behalf at the preliminary investigation, and had been greatly incensed
at the decision to try them before a civil court. At Leipzig he was
called as a character witness for Scheringer and when that misguided
young man repeated his *credo* that the duty of the Army lay in
leading the German people to a victorious war of liberation, his
colonel corroborated his sentiments with cynical casuistry. 'The
Reichswehr', said he, 'is told daily that it is an army of leaders.
What is a young officer to understand by that ?' (*es wird täglich der
Reichswehr gesagt, sie sei eine Führerarmee, was soll sich ein junger
Offizier anderes darunter vorstellen ?*).[2]

This was a deliberate perversion of the principle of a *Führerarmee*.
As enunciated by von Seeckt it had meant an 'army of leaders', in
that each man was trained to become the leader of a unit on the day
that the order for the expansion of the Army was given. But.the
cynical twist given to the words by the regimental commander was
an indication of the false interpretation which was being placed
upon the phrase in certain circles and which he for one was not
prepared to correct. It is a matter of interest that the regimental
commander was Colonel Ludwig Beck.

But though these revelations of the extent to which the German

---

[1] Gottfried Zarnow, *Gefesselte Justiz* (Munich, 1931), i, 172-82 ; F. W. von
Oertzen, *Im Namen der Geschichte!* (Hamburg, 1934), pp. 102-24 ; also R. H.
Phelps, 'Aus den Groener-Dokumenten. v. Der Fall Scheringer-Ludin-Wendt',
Deutsche Rundschau, November 1950.

[2] *Berliner Tageblatt*, September 27, 1930.

Army had been permeated and corrupted by politics and of the degree
to which National Socialist propaganda had taken hold upon at least
a considerable number of the junior officers, must have been a
source of no little satisfaction to Hitler, they were somewhat of an
embarrassment at the moment. He had just won a conspicuous
electoral success. His registered Party membership was well over a
quarter of a million; more than 6 million Germans had voted for
his Party Programme ; he was the leader of the second largest group
in the *Reichstag*, controlling 107 seats out of 577. But all this had
been accomplished behind the façade of legality, and he was now
faced with a situation in which young officers were charged with
treason on the basis of their adherence to, and their desire to further,
Nazi doctrines. Hitler knew that, even with the successes already
achieved, he could not attain ultimate power without the support
of the *Reichswehr*, it was therefore highly inconvenient that he
should be placed in the position of supporting Scheringer and
Ludin who had openly admitted their intention of disrupting the
Army in the interests of National Socialism. This, Hitler realized,
was no way to win support. He must employ the means of seduction
rather than those of intimidation or disruption. He must make the
Army realize that he was indispensable to them and that to maintain
the unity of the Reich — as well as in their own interests — they
must support and not oppose him.

Hitler therefore chose to make the Leipzig Trial the occasion
for a further gesture to the Army, not this time from the dock, as
at Munich six years before when he himself had been charged with
high treason, but from the witness-box, as the admitted Leader of
a great national movement. The Prosecution had alleged that the
NSDAP was a revolutionary Party bent upon the overthrow of the
Government of the Reich by violence, and that as a first step to this
end they had attempted to tamper with the loyalty of the armed
forces of the State. Hans Frank, for the defence, vehemently denied
these charges on behalf of the Party and, to substantiate his denial,
he obtained the permission of the Court to call the *Führer* as a
witness.

Hitler's performance at Leipzig on September 25 was a masterpiece of intellectual dishonesty ; a *tour de force* in the reconciliation
of 'legality' with 'illegality'. He spoke for hours, declaring upon
oath, 'I have always held the view that every attempt to disintegrate
the Army was madness. None of us have any interest in such disintegration. We will see to it that, when we have come to power,
out of the present *Reichswehr* shall rise the great army of the German
people.' The Army was responsible for the destiny of the people,

it must essentially be the supporter of the '*völkisch*' idea.[1] As for the SA, their sole purpose was for the protection of National Socialist propaganda. As long ago as 1925 he had given orders that they were not to carry arms, and that they should have no military character.[2]

From this Hitler passed to wider topics of policy, still juggling deftly with the terms of 'legality' and 'illegality', and keeping one eye always on the *Reichswehr*. 'Our movement does not require violence,' he declared. 'If we have two or three more elections the National Socialist movement will have the majority in the *Reichstag* and then we shall make the National Revolution.' 'By legal means, of course?' asked the President of the Court dryly. 'Of course', assented Hitler with emphasis.

'And how do you interpret the expression "German National Revolution"?' enquired the President.

'The concept of a "National Revolution" is always taken in a purely political sense', Hitler replied. 'But for National Socialists this means exclusively a rescuing of the enslaved German nation we have to-day. Germany is bound hand and foot (*geknebelt*) by the Peace Treaties. The whole German legislation to-day is nothing else than the attempt to anchor the Peace Treaties in the German people. The National Socialists do not regard these treaties as law, but as something imposed upon Germany by constraint. We do not admit that future generations who are completely innocent should be burdened by them. If we protest against them with every means in our power then we find ourselves on the path of revolution.'

'With illegal means also?' the President inquired at this point.

'I presuppose for the moment that we have won the day; then we shall fight against the treaties with every means, even, from the point of view of the world, with illegal means', was Hitler's answer.[3]

Long ago in the height of his forensic campaign against the Ruhr occupation, Hitler had promised that 'heads will roll in the sand',[4] and this remark was now recalled to him by the President of the Court. How did Hitler reconcile this promise with his pledges of legality? 'I can assure you', the *Führer* replied, 'that when the National Socialist Movement is victorious in its fight, then there will come a National Socialist Court of Justice, then November

---

[1] *Frankfurter Zeitung*, September 26, 1930 ; Baynes, i, 552.
[2] Baynes, i, 177. [3] Baynes, ii, 993.
[4] Speech of September 5, 1923, *Adolf Hitlers Reden* (Munich, 1923), p. 82 ; Baynes, i, 74.

1918 will find its retribution and then heads will roll.'[1]

The public, which consisted mainly of Nazi supporters who had packed the galleries, burst into wild applause and were reproved by the President of the Court, who had apparently taken no exception to the sentiments expressed — for he had offered no objection — but merely to the reaction which they produced. Not even the Public Prosecutor objected. This statement of Hitler's, which created a sensation in every country in the world, went unchallenged in the Supreme Court of the Reich. Only the interruption it caused was deprecated.

Some attempt was made from Berlin to counteract the effect of Hitler's demonstration. Dr. Zweigert, the State Secretary of the Reich Ministry of the Interior, flew to Leipzig to deliver a counter-blast on Hitler's 'illegality'. To a court which seemed uninterested in his statement, he declared that for years his office had passed to the Public Prosecutor the ever accumulating evidence of the treasonable activities of the Nazi Party, but all to no avail. No action had been taken ; every attempt to bring the Nazi leaders to justice had been blocked at a high level in the office of the *Oberreichsanwalt*.[2]

The Public Prosecutor did not seem to be disconcerted. The Court did not appear to be interested. Shocked and humiliated, Dr. Zweigert returned to Berlin, and at the same time Hitler was borne in triumph from the Palace of Justice to the railway station, where a special pullman car waited to take him back to Munich.

The Court returned to the case of Scheringer and Ludin, whose significance in the proceedings had somewhat diminished since their trial had been made the occasion and excuse for a public statement of policy by the *Führer*. Their actions had now been publicly disavowed by the Leader of the Party to which they had proclaimed allegiance, and their case, shorn of these higher motives, assumed a rather more sordid character. They were sentenced on October 4 to eighteen months' fortress detention for conspiracy to commit high treason. Hitler had sacrified his tools for the greater glory of his Party.[3]

---

[1] *Frankfurter Zeitung*, September 26, 1930 ; Baynes, i, 191.
[2] See above, p. 211, footnote.
[3] The subsequent careers of these two officers were very different. Scheringer in his prison cell reached the conclusion that National Socialism was not all that he had believed it to be and that the sacred principles of the National Revolution had been betrayed. In a letter to one of the Communist deputies in the *Reichstag* in March 1931, he renounced his former Nazi beliefs and declared himself a Communist. 'Only by smashing capitalism in alliance with the Soviet Union can we be freed', he wrote. When this letter was read out in the Chamber, Goebbels telegraphed to Scheringer asking whether he had indeed committed this

(vi)

The events of September 1930 were a climacteric in German post-war history. The Nazi successes at the polls and the dramatic appearance of Hitler at the Scheringer-Ludin trial had a profound effect upon all strata of society and not least in the ranks of the Officer Corps, in which a disturbing conflict of loyalties among the junior officers had been disclosed during the proceedings at Leipzig. Many senior officers, also, who had hitherto been sceptical as to the worth or worthlessness of Hitler, were impressed and reassured by his declaration that he was opposed to any undermining of the *Reichswehr*.[1] And there were also many who, though they viewed the National Socialist successes with amazement and apprehension, were now convinced that its further advance could not be stemmed. 'It is the *Jugendbewegung*', they said, 'it can't be stopped.' [2]

And indeed it was true that an inebriation, born of a nationalist and ideological craving, had seized upon the youth of Germany. Unemployment, economic insecurity and no hope of advancement on the one hand, and a failure, on the other, of the Republic to make its ideals appealing to youth, had rendered both those who had been old enough to bear arms in the First World War and those who had grown up under the debilitating effects of the Weimar System, increasingly susceptible to the insidious poison of Nazi propaganda, which offered glittering prizes to those who would but pluck them. Intoxicated, blinded, dazzled, the youth of Germany enthusiastically enrolled itself in the Storm Troops in the deluded belief that in the National Socialist movement lay the way to both national and individual salvation.

apostasy. Back came the reply : 'Hitler betrayed revolution declaration authentic reprint, Scheringer' (Heiden, p. 324). On his release Scheringer threw himself into the fight against National Socialism with all the zeal of a former believer. His name was amongst those to be liquidated on June 30, 1934, but he miraculously survived the Blood Purge and also subsequent persecutions, emerging after the conclusion of the Second World War in Munich, where he is believed still to live.

Ludin, on the other hand, remained loyal to his original beliefs. On the termination of his sentence, as an enthusiastic member of the Party, he was elected to the Reichstag in 1932 and later became both a Major-General in the SA and an SS Group Leader. In 1940 he was appointed Minister to Slovakia, where he remained until the end of the War, when he was arrested and executed by Slovak patriots.

[1] Cf. the evidence of Alfred Jodl before the International Military Tribunal on June 3, 1946 (*Nuremberg Record*, xv, 285).

[2] Cf. a memorandum by the British Military Attaché in Berlin (Colonel J. H. Marshall-Cornwall) on conversations with German officers during the autumn manœuvres about the September election results (Woodward and Butler, Second Series, i, 512, footnote 2).

222 THE ARMY AND HITLER PT. II

Just as the *Reichswehr* had, in the early days, regarded the
NSDAP as a movement possessing 'the power to make converts
among the workers for the cause of nationalism',[1] so now they recognized the capacity of Hitler to attract the youth of Germany to his
banner; not only the youth of the working class but of that dis-
possessed middle class which had suffered so severely from the
inflation and the depression. There was, however, one important
difference between the 'twenties and the 'thirties. In 1920 the
Reichswehr felt themselves strong enough to use the Nazis as a
tool; a force which they could control and utilize to their own
advantage. In 1930 the position had changed in that the Nazis had
become a power in their own right. They remained a force which
might be utilized, but they were no longer a tool, subject to direct
control. If the *Reichswehr* wished to utilize the Party, their approach
must be on the basis of negotiation with a potential ally over whom
only an indirect control could be exercised.

The Army as a whole were quick to recognize this readjustment
in their relations with the Party. Hitler's promises of a national
army, expanded and rearmed, evoked a sympathetic reception from
those whose hopes of promotion and fame in their profession had
burned low, and it was discovered that there was much in common
between that which vitally concerned the Reich, the Army and the
Party. 'The *Reichswehr* will always stand where there are the
strongest national interests. . . . It would be a pity to have to fire
on these splendid youths (the SA)', became the accepted view of
many officers.[2]

Such, however, was not the view of Gröner, who, outwardly at
least, preserved a front of unshaken optimism. 'It is a complete
mistake to ask where the *Reichswehr* stands', he replied to a friend's
enquiry about the general attitude of the Army. 'The *Reichswehr*
does what it is ordered to do, *und damit Basta.*'[3] But it became
increasingly uncertain what the *Reichswehr* would be ordered
to do.

Gröner himself had been strongly criticized by former high-
ranking officers of the Army — who had to some extent come
under the influence of Hitler's spell — on the grounds that by
bringing Scheringer and Ludin to public trial he had weakened
the spirit of comradeship and solidarity within the Officer Corps.
Among his more virulent critics were Graf von der Goltz, and,
much more surprisingly, Hans von Seeckt, who had entered upon

---

[1] See above, p. 157.
[2] Friedrich Meinecke, *Die deutsche Katastrophe* (Zürich/Wiesbaden, 1946),
pp. 69, 71.   [3] *Ibid.* p. 69.

the least creditable period of his career, that of politician.[1] Gröner
defended himself with energy and emphasized that the essence of
the Officer Corps was its discipline and its *Überparteilichkeit*. 'It
must not be party programmes', he wrote to von der Goltz, 'or resounding slogans drawn from them, that determine the manner in
which the *Reichswehr* serves the Fatherland, but the will of the
President of the Reich and those high officers appointed by him.'[2]
To the Officer Corps itself he gave warning that in future 'we should
appoint only such persons as possess the courage of their convictions
and sufficient spiritual authority to educate the youth of the present',[3]
thereby intimating that the Corps must at long last give an unequivocal sign of allegiance to the Weimar System, as represented by the
Brüning Cabinet.

   To Gröner, the Government of which he was a member was
almost ideal from the *Reichswehr* point of view. It was essentially
überparteilich, for, though it depended on the votes of the Centre and
Social Democrats for its majority in the *Reichstag*, there were no
Socialists among its members and only four representatives of the
Centre, the remainder ranging from former members of the National-
ist Party, like Treviranus and Schlange-Schöningen and Martin
Schiele,[4] to Joseph Bredt of the *Wirtschaftspartei* and Julius Curtius

---

   [1] Von Seeckt had resolved upon a political career in 1930, according to some,
with an eye to becoming President of the Reich on the death of Hindenburg. After
an unsuccessful attempt to be adopted as a candidate for the Centre Party, he was
eventually elected to the *Reichstag* in September 1930 as a member of the German
People's Party — which since the death of Stresemann had drifted considerably
farther to the Right under the leadership of Edward Dingeldey — and was re-
elected in the general elections of July and November 1932. In 1923 von Seeckt
had believed that he and Hitler had been at one in their aims and that only their
paths were different (see above, p. 118), but now even this divergency seemed
to have been removed. Gröner wrote to von Gleich on December 28, 1930, that
he would expect to see von Seeckt at any moment 'walking arm-in-arm with Herr
Goebbels' (Craig, p. 207) and in less than a year he was openly allied with Hitler
in the Harzburg Front (October 1931). In April 1932 he wrote urging his sister
to vote for Hitler in the presidential election : 'Youth is right. I am too old'
(Rabenau, ii, 665). When, however, he returned from his second visit to China
in 1935 the process of disenchantment was rapid, and, though Hitler appointed
him Colonel-in-Chief of his old regiment on his seventieth birthday (April 22,
1936), when he died in the following December von Seeckt retained no illusions.
   [2] Letter to General Graf von der Goltz, October 1930 (quoted by Craig,
p. 207).
   [3] *Reichswehrministerium, Erlass (Geheim)*, October 6, 1930 (quoted by Craig,
p. 208).
   [4] Although the secession of Treviranus and his followers from the Nationalist
Party had failed to break the power of Hugenberg — 'old Hugendabel, the key-hole
politician' as Gröner called him — they had only failed by a very slight margin.
At a fateful meeting of the Party on June 30, 1930, the decision not to support the
Brüning Cabinet in the *Reichstag* was only carried by two votes, because some of

of the German People's Party. The Brüning Cabinet had the added advantage of being united and disciplined. It was the first of the post-war governments to include former front-line fighters among its members and at least six ministers, including the Chancellor, were holders of the Iron Cross (First Class).[1] Because they were a group of men chosen by their leader for their ability and *expertise* and not as representing a coalition of parties, they enjoyed a greater freedom from the intrigues of the party caucuses than did their predecessors. Above all they were *Kanzlertreu*, loyal to their chief and untrammelled by those inner combinations and cabals which had brought more than one Weimar Cabinet to an untimely end.

Between Gröner and Brüning there was a strong mutual respect and friendship. 'His (Brüning's) attitude in parliament towards the babblers (*Quatschköpfe*) is nothing short of an aesthetic pleasure', Gröner wrote to von Gleich. 'I have concluded a firm alliance with him. . . . I have never known a statesman, chancellor, minister [or] general who combined in his head as much positive knowledge and political clarity and adaptability as Brüning.'[2] On his side, the Chancellor saw in his Defence Minister the epitome of that moral integrity and intellectual capacity inherent in the best type of German General Staff officer. '*Er ist ein fabelhafter Mann*', was his frequent comment on Gröner.[3]

Thus, at the outset of this critical period, the co-operation of the Army with the Government at the highest level could not have been stronger. The Chancellor was on terms of close personal friendship with the Minister of Defence and both at this time enjoyed the confidence and support of the Marshal-President. To strengthen the High Command, Gröner had urged Heye to retire, ostensibly on the grounds of age (he was in his sixty-second year), but actually because he lacked the necessary drive and initiative which the situation demanded. To succeed him as *Chef der Heeresleitung* Gröner advised Hindenburg to appoint von Hammerstein, whose post as head of the *Truppenamt* went to another of von Schleicher's protégés, General Wilhelm Adam.

Von Hammerstein was outspoken in his distrust and contempt

Hugenberg's opponents were absent from the meeting. Had they been present and succeeded in swinging the support of the Nationalists to Brüning instead of to Hitler, the results might have been incalculable (Meinecke, p. 93).

[1] The holders of the Iron Cross, in addition to Brüning, were Gröner, Treviranus, Bredt, Joel and Schlange-Schöningen.

[2] Letters to General von Gleich of December 28, 1930, and April 26, 1931 (quoted by Craig, p. 210).

[3] The author of this book was much in Germany at this time and was fortunate enough to be on friendly terms with both Brüning and Gröner, thus having opportunities of observing their relationship at first hand.

for the Nazis. 'The *Reichswehr* will never allow them to come to power', he assured Severing,[1] and Gröner wrote of him that he was 'the man to strike with *brutality*'.[2]   Indeed there seemed no doubt in the winter of 1930–31 that, despite the National Socialist sympathies which had been disclosed within its ranks, the *Reichswehr*, if ordered to do so by the President, would have supported the Brüning Government in an open trial of strength with the Nazis had Hitler been foolish enough to risk a *Putsch* against the established authority of the Reich.

But Hitler, of course, was not so foolish. He was still pursuing his revolution by constitutional means. He was still 'Adolphe Légalité '. However, his conception of 'legal revolution' may be summed up in the phrase of one of his subordinates, namely, that 'the NSDAP will not let the German people rest until they have obtained power'.[3]   In other words, the Party would maintain a ceaseless programme of propaganda, 'a cold war' of press attacks, inflammatory speeches and mass demonstrations, which should keep the Reich in a ferment which only their advent to power, on their own terms, would assuage.

In pressing this policy Hitler did not scruple in the choice of his allies. While keeping his hand in the till of Hugenberg and the Nationalist Party, he did not hesitate to make common cause when necessary with the Communists in order to embarrass the Government.[4]   On the other hand, it was believed by many that he aimed at provoking a Communist *Putsch* which he would then use as an excuse for a 'descent into the streets' of the SA 'in defence of law and order', thereby confronting the *Reichswehr* with simultaneous uprisings from the Right and Left. Whether he actually contemplated this line of action, or whether he merely used it as a weapon of political warfare is uncertain, but the effect was much the same in either event. For this fear of a double *Putsch* by the Nazis and the Communists became an obsession in the calculations of the *Reichswehr* — who believed that such an occurrence would be seized upon by the Poles for an invasion of Upper Silesia [5] — and materially affected their future conduct.

---

[1] Cf. the evidence of Carl Severing before the International Military Tribunal on May 21, 1946 (*Nuremberg Record*, xiv, 264).

[2] Letter to General von Gleich, January 26, 1932 (quoted by Craig, p. 210).

[3] Speech delivered in Brunswick by *Reichstag* Deputy Adolph Wagner, July 9, 1930 (quoted by Kempner, p. 97).

[4] This policy was most flagrantly illustrated in November 1932 when the Nazis and Communists combined to organize a general transport strike in Berlin for their mutual satisfaction in embarrassing the Government of Franz von Papen.

[5] Brüning, *Ein Brief*, pp. 2–3.

It was, in fact, this double fear of civil war and foreign aggression which induced Kurt von Schleicher to make his first gestures of appeasement to the Nazis. It is to be believed that von Schleicher recognized the essential harmfulness of National Socialism and that he never entertained the idea of handing over the fate of the Reich to Hitler. But this did not prevent him from endeavouring to exploit it for the benefit of the *Reichswehr*, and his natural vanity and ambition, together with his penchant for intrigue, caused him to believe that he, and he alone, could guide the German ship of State into safety and tranquillity by means of clever and devious manœuvres calculated either to beguile or to divide the enemy.

To von Schleicher may well have occurred the historical parallel of the days before the War of Liberation, when the idealistic patriotism of national resurgence engendered by the *Tugendbund* had been 'captured' and controlled by the genius of Scharnhorst and Gneisenau. The Prussian General Staff had forged from it a weapon which had thrice overthrown the military might of France at Leipzig and Waterloo and at Sedan; and had humbled the pride of the Habsburgs at Sadowa. To be sure, it had itself suffered defeat in 1918, but those fatal mistakes would not be made again, and it was clearly the mission of the *Reichswehr*, and particularly of von Schleicher, to canalize this great force of awakening youth into channels where it could do most good for Germany and for the Army. Hitler's individual power must be nipped in the bud and every means used to bring him and his movement under the influence of the *Feldgrau Eminenz*.

Thus von Schleicher dreamed and planned and sought to establish his contacts with the Party. Nothing could have better suited Hitler's book. At the end of 1930 he had recalled Ernst Röhm from his Bolivian exile, and now sent him on a reconnoitring expedition to the Bendlerstrasse. There, in the *Truppenamt*, Röhm found an old friend and comrade from Bavaria, Colonel Franz Halder, and, through him, was brought into contact with von Schleicher.[1]

A strange confidence was established between these two men, so very different in character — for von Schleicher was an accomplished ladies' man — but having in common a predilection for intrigue and, each according to his own lights, a strong desire to see the German Army reborn in power and strength. Röhm repeated Hitler's assurances of legality and his denials that he had any intention of disintegrating the *Reichswehr*. As an earnest of good faith the *Führer* intended to appoint Röhm Chief of Staff of

[1] Röhm, p. 170.

the SA and to remove from command those SA leaders who had planned acts of violence.

Von Schleicher was impressed by Röhm's sureties and persuaded Gröner — it is believed, against the latter's better judgment — that some kind of gentleman's agreement might be entered into with the SA. This was accomplished by progressive stages. On New Year's Day 1931 Röhm's appointment as Chief of Staff of the SA was gazetted by Hitler. On January 2 a *Reichswehr* ordinance announced that thenceforth National Socialists might be employed in the Army's arsenals and depots, thereby rescinding in part the general interdiction on any contact between the Army and the Party imposed by Heye in 1927.[1] This was followed by a proclamation by Hitler to the SA on February 20, ordering them to refrain from street-fighting — 'I understand your distress and your rage, but you must not bear arms'[2] — an order which provoked a mutiny among the Storm Troop detachments in Berlin, who regarded it as a betrayal of the fundamental revolutionary principles of the Party.[3] With the support of Goebbels, now *Gauleiter* of Greater Berlin, Hitler energetically quelled this revolt, and expelled the Berlin SA leader, Captain Stennes, from the Party,[4] thereby giving an added verisimilitude to his pledge to the *Reichswehr* that he would discipline those of his lieutenants who had deviated from the way of 'legality'.

The next step in this *rapprochement* took place a month later, and was one taken almost certainly without the knowledge of either Hitler or Gröner, both of whom would have been completely hostile to it for different reasons. According to Röhm, von Schleicher gave him a promise (*Zusicherung*) in March 1931 that, in the event of an emergency arising, the SA would come under the command of *Reichswehr* officers, and it was upon the basis of this promise that Röhm reorganized the SA on lines parallel to those of the Army.[5] Von Schleicher undoubtedly hoped that by this ruse he would allay the haunting fear that the *Reichswehr* would one day be confronted with simultaneous risings from the Right and Left.

---

[1] See above, p. 205. The first part of Heye's general order, that forbidding National Socialists to enter the Army, was withdrawn on January 29, 1932 (Kempner, p. 152).   [2] Heiden, pp. 322-3.

[3] It was this proclamation of Hitler to the SA which occasioned Scheringer's formal repudiation of the NSDAP (see above, p. 220, footnote).

[4] Walter Stennes continued his fight for the 'pure principles' of National Socialism outside the Party. With Otto Strasser and Buchrucker, the former leader of the 'Black Reichswehr', he formed the 'Black Front', which, with headquarters in Prague, became the spearhead of the 'Nazi *émigré*' activities against Hitler. Later he went to China, where he became commander of Chiang Kai-shek's bodyguard.   [5] Röhm, p. 107.

In the event of a Communist *Putsch*, whether accompanied or not by a Polish incursion into Silesia, the SA would now come automatically under the orders of the *Reichswehr* and the forces of disorder be thereby controlled and disrupted.

It was a scheme characteristic of von Schleicher's devious mentality, but the ultimate results were the assassination of himself and Röhm some three years later.

That Gröner was ignorant of von Schleicher's secret pact with Röhm is clear from his unceasing and outspoken hostility to the SA, which, in its new guise as a disciplined and co-ordinated body, he regarded as an increasing menace to the State. From the spring of 1931 onwards he sought for some means to bring about the dissolution of the Brown Army, but found that his path to success in achieving this ambition was beset with obstacles. For one thing, there were many officers in the Bendlerstrasse and in the Army as a whole, some of whom later testified before the International Military Tribunal at Nuremberg, who regarded a war with Poland as 'a sacred duty though a sad necessity', in order to wipe out the 'desecration' involved in the creation of the Polish Corridor and to obviate the threat of a Polish attack on East Prussia or Silesia.[1] They were therefore strongly in favour of retaining an organization which would in the event of war prove a valuable auxiliary force. These were added to those who opposed any action which should disrupt the growing friendliness between the Army and the NSDAP on the grounds that it was inevitable that Hitler would come to power sooner or later — by 'legal means', of course — and that he would then make good his promise : 'We shall create for you a great army, much larger than you yourselves imagine to-day,' and there were others again who defended the SA for its beneficial influence of discipline and training upon the youth of Germany.[2]

Though Gröner neither accepted, nor agreed with, any of these arguments he was forced to take them into consideration. It became increasingly clear that if he was to succeed in getting rid of the Storm Troops he must offer some *quid pro quo* to his critics, some alternative measure which would fulfil the aspirations and functions which they found favourable in the SA while removing its political significance and danger.

To this end Gröner developed two schemes. In order to provide a substitute for the advantages of pedagogical and physical training which were alleged to accrue from the SA and the *Hitler Jugend*,

---

[1] Cf. statements given at Nuremberg by Field-Marshal von Blomberg, dated November 7, 1945, and General von Blaskowitz, dated November 10, 1945 (*IMT Documents*, PS-3704 and PS-3706).   [2] Meinecke, p. 71.

he planned the creation of a gigantic sport organization (*Wehrsport-verband*) which should replace not only the Nazi para-military formations, but also those of the Social-Democrats and the Right. This new body would be nominally placed under the aegis of the *Stahlhelm*, with the hope that the veterans' organization might thus be wooed away from its affiliation with Hugenberg and with Hitler ; actually, however, it was to be under State control.[1]

To those who argued in favour of an auxiliary force, or, alternatively, for something which would provide for the hundreds of thousands of young Germans whom the depression had cast unemployed upon the streets, Gröner offered a more daring project. He proposed to Brüning, who gave his unqualified assent and support, that they should approach the Allied Powers at the forthcoming Disarmament Conference with a proposal for the concession to Germany of a measure of rearmament, together with the right to increase the existing *Reichswehr* by a national militia made up, on the basis of universal military service, from new recruits and men with six months' training, to a strength of some two hundred thousand.[2] This expansion of the *Reichswehr*, by which it was expected to attract into the ranks of the Army members of both the *Stahlhelm* and the SA, was to be followed by the placing of a formal ban upon the wearing of political uniforms. This, it was anticipated, would not only satisfy the numerical demands of the Bendlerstrasse but would attract the youth of the country to the Army rather than to the Party. Hitler would thus suffer both in popular support and also by the successful trumping of his rearmament programme which he regarded as one of the strongest cards in his hand.[3]

So hardy a scheme commended itself to Brüning, who, as a result of his visits to the capitals of Europe in the fateful summer of 1931, had reached the conclusion that, in order both to stem the rising flood of the Nazi movement and to save the German economic position from complete collapse, daring and drastic action must be taken at home and abroad. In a desperate race against time and fate the Chancellor planned with boldness and imagination. He sought to accomplish no less than an extensive revision of the peace settlement of Versailles and the reshaping of the constitution of the German Reich. His formula for success in both instances was based upon his firm belief in the monarchic principle.

[1] Meinecke, p. 100.
[2] Meinecke, pp. 72-3 ; Wheeler-Bennett, p. 382.
[3] Craig, p. 214. It was in practical application of these principles that Gröner, with Brüning's approval, issued an order on January 29, 1932, permitting the acceptance of Nazi recruits into the Army, and followed it up with the dissolution of the SA and SS on April 14.

Brüning knew that no such sweeping programme of treaty amendment as he envisaged would have the remotest chance of success if put forward by the German Government, and he therefore sought to find a sponsor for his plan who should at once be above suspicion of being under German influence and should command respect in the world at large. In his travels he had met most of the leading statesmen of Europe and had failed to find among them one who could or would give the lead. He therefore turned to the one remaining figure of outstanding and compelling dignity, the *roi-chevalier*, Albert of Belgium, and through the agency of friends he placed before the King, who viewed the plan with favour, a comprehensive proposal both for the treaty revision, including the termination of reparations and a qualified form of rearmament, and for the economic stabilization of Europe.[1]

In the internal situation of Germany Brüning's considerations were governed by the fact that in the spring of 1932 Hindenburg's seven-year period of office as President of the Reich would come to an end. If the Marshal refused to stand again, the election of a Nazi — most probably of Hitler himself — was a foregone conclusion. On the other hand, Hindenburg was all but eighty-five years old and hence could not, in the natural course of events, be expected to live out a further period of seven years. If possible an election should be avoided, to preserve both the Old Gentleman and the country from the strain and turmoil of a campaign, and this could be constitutionally accomplished by a two-thirds majority in the *Reichstag* and *Reichsrat* voting to extend the Marshal's period of office. If this were not forthcoming and an election proved inevitable, Brüning was confident that Hindenburg would win it, even though Hitler gained heavily in popular support. In either case, the *coup* which he planned must take place immediately after Hindenburg had once more become President of the Reich. At that moment Brüning proposed to have the restoration of the Monarchy proclaimed by a vote of both Chambers with the Marshal as *Reichsverweser* (Regent) for his lifetime, at the end of which one of the sons of the Crown Prince should succeed to the throne.

This was a return in part to the desperate last-minute recourse of November 1918.[2] Then, Gröner and Ebert had tried to maintain the Monarchy, with Prince Max of Baden as Regent, in order to save Germany from Communism; now, Gröner and Brüning sought to restore the Monarchy, with Marshal von Hindenburg as Regent, in order to preserve Germany from National Socialism.

Nor was the plan as fantastic as it at first appeared. In the

[1] Wheeler-Bennett, pp. 379-80.   [2] See above, p. 18.

first place, Brüning had already gained for it the reluctant support of certain of the Social Democrat and Trade Union leaders, who saw therein the only practical alternative to an ultimate Nazi dictatorship ; in the second, it would have caused serious dissension within the forces of the Right, since neither Hugenberg and the Nationalists, nor Seldte and the *Stahlhelm*, could have come out in opposition to a monarchist restoration. Even the ranks of the Nazis themselves would have been split, Brüning confidently believed, for that conservative element of Hitler's supporters — officers of the Old Army, East Prussian landowners, industrial magnates, former Government officials and the like, who had joined the NSDAP out of despair, or as the only means of realizing their political ambitions — would desert the *Hakenkreuz* and revert to their old loyalty once the standard of the Hohenzollerns was unfurled. Above all, the restoration of the Monarchy, together with an increase, however small, in the military establishment of the Reich, would, the Chancellor thought, rivet the *Reichswehr* to the forces opposed to National Socialism, and would arrest the canker which had already begun to eat at the heart of its loyalty.[1]

By such drastic action, at home and abroad, did Brüning essay to hamstring the Hitler movement, by first isolating it and then stealing its thunder, thereby rendering it so diminished in influence that it might well be summoned to undergo the sobering effect of sharing the responsibilities of office. Alas, however, for his schemes and dreaming. He was pitted against forces either too powerful or too evil to be overcome — the waywardness of fate, the incalculable variations in the tempo of events, the untrustworthiness of others. Brüning, in his calculations and his planning, had overestimated the

[1] Wheeler-Bennett, pp. 354-8. Hitler also was not unaware of the value of the Monarchy as a political bargaining factor, but he never seriously considered it as anything else than a means to dupe some and attract others, just as he had temporarily won the support of von Kahr in November 1923. (See above, p. 174.) He made frequent promises of restoration in the right quarters, and thereby succeeded in winning the enlistment of one of the Kaiser's sons, Prince August Wilhelm, as a member of the Nazi Party, and the support of another, the Crown Prince, for his campaign for the presidency in the spring of 1932. In the autumn of that same year Göring spent a week as the guest of the Kaiser at Doorn, and even after the advent of the Nazis to power Hitler continued to give guarded encouragement to the idea of a restoration until the death of Hindenburg and his own succession to supreme power. The final sequel came, according to Schacht, one day during the war when Göring, on Hitler's instructions, summoned one of the former Social Democrat Ministers for the purpose of informing him that the *Führer* had discovered from his historical researches that the SPD had done Germany the historic service of deliberately and permanently abolishing the Monarchy, and that, in his view, special thanks were due to them on that account. (See Thyssen, pp. 110-11. Hjalmar Schacht, *Account Settled* (London, 1949), pp. 209-10.)

ability of the Western Powers to comprehend the intricacies of the
German internal situation, and had underestimated the capacity
of Hitler for ruthless infamy and nefarious intrigue. Moreover, he
had not sufficiently taken into account the growing senility of the
Marshal, with its consequently alternating obstinacy and variance,
and above all, he, like Gröner, but perhaps not to the same extent,
had trusted Kurt von Schleicher.

Von Schleicher's conduct, from the summer of 1931 until his
dismissal from office as Chancellor some eighteen months later,
became increasingly devious and also increasingly difficult to follow.
It is to be believed that to the end he did not wish to see the Nazis
in a position of supreme power, but he was convinced that he alone
could prevent this from coming to pass, and under the influence
of this monomaniacal obsession he was prepared to intrigue with
all parties concerned and to betray them with equally unscrupulous
impartiality. As a result the influence of the *Reichswehr* was
divided and uncertain. The Minister of Defence stood firmly behind
the Chancellor in his efforts to combat and to frustrate, by all means
under the Constitution, the rise of National Socialism, while the
Head of the *Ministeramt*, who led the G.O.C. of the *Reichswehr*
by the nose, was sometimes working with, sometimes against, his
superiors, but was always in secret treaty with the Nazis to a degree
unsuspected by either Brüning or Gröner. Over and above them
all loomed the titanic figure of the Supreme Commander, the
President of the Republic, Marshal von Hindenburg, who with the
growing befuddlement of age was rapidly degenerating into that
state of senility in which he was a prey to the advice of whomsoever
had last spoken with him. Such were the forces which defied
National Socialism.

Brüning, Gröner, von Schleicher and von Hammerstein were
at one, however, in the late summer of 1931, in agreeing that,
however senile the Marshal might be, the one chance of defeating
Hitler in the presidential election which fell due in the following
spring, lay either in obtaining the prolongation of Hindenburg's
term of office or, failing this, in persuading him to stand again and to
risk the stress and strain of an election campaign upon his physical
constitution and mental faculties. They were also in agreement that,
until one or other of these aims had been assured, there should be
no change in the Government.

Brüning's first attempt in September at negotiation with Hugenberg and Hitler for the retention of Hindenburg in the Presidency
failed completely, and the situation was further complicated at this
moment by the fact that the Marshal suffered a complete mental

break-down for some ten days — a fact which had to be kept a deathly secret — during which time he developed an almost violent antipathy to the personality, and the continuance in office, of his Chancellor, with whom, hitherto, he had been on terms of paternal friendship and amiability. From this dilemma Brüning was rescued by the direct intervention of the heads of the *Reichswehr*. Gröner, von Schleicher and von Hammerstein, acting together, succeeded, with great difficulty, in making it clear to the President that, if he desired a change in the Government, he must either find a Chancellor who would include the Nazis in his Cabinet or suppress the National Socialists by force, which might entail a civil war.

Recoiling from either of these alternatives, Hindenburg, under the pressure of the Generals, at length declared himself ready to continue to support Brüning and his policy on condition that two ministers particularly obnoxious to him, Curtius and Wirth, were dropped from the Government. Brüning accepted the bargain. He took over the Ministry of Foreign Affairs himself and persuaded Gröner, whose health was already failing, to add the burden of the Ministry of Interior to that of the Ministry of Defence.[1]

He did more ; he assented to the importunings of von Schleicher to arrange for Hitler to be received by Hindenburg. Röhm had long been urging that the President and the *Führer* should meet, confident that Hitler would impress the Marshal with his personality. Von Schleicher had suggested it more than once to Brüning, who had demurred. Now he did so no longer, and the interview took place in Berlin on October 10.

It was not a happy meeting. Hitler's frenzied eloquence produced a far from favourable impression upon the Marshal, who had not the patience of von Lossow in listening to prolonged harangues, and the *Führer* was equally disillusioned by the lack of receptivity to his arguments. He departed in dudgeon to the little Brunswick spa of Bad Harzburg, where on the following day, he formed with Hugenberg the National Opposition.

The Harzburg Rally of October 11, 1931, was the formal declaration of war by the parties of the Right against the Brüning Government — a concentration of all the forces of reaction, both past and present, in one great demonstration of hostility to the Weimar System. The Brown legions of the SA, the field-grey formations of the *Stahlhelm* veterans, the green-shirted units of the Bismarck

---

[1] Brüning, *Ein Brief*, pp. 7-8. It was Gröner's desire at this time that von Schleicher should become *Reichswehr* Minister. Brüning would not have opposed the appointment but von Schleicher would not consider it. His time had not yet come.

Youth, defiled in a seemingly endless parade before their political chiefs, Hitler and Seldte and Hugenberg, who addressed them in words of flame, inciting them to fight and die for the liberation of Germany at home and abroad. But, in addition to these three leaders, there were also present figures which evoked many memories of the past twelve years. Schacht was there, making his first public appearance in support of Hitler, and, surprisingly enough, General von Seeckt was found on the same platform with General von Lüttwitz, whom he had refused either to support or oppose in 1920, and with *Justizrat* Dr. Class, who had been accused of inciting the assassination of von Seeckt in 1923. All personal enmities seemed now to have been forgotten, all hatchets buried, and on the grave there was reared a great memorial to the hatred of the Right for Weimar.

In effect, however, the Harzburg Front was but a façade of defiance, behind which there was little love lost between the chief protagonists. It was Hugenberg's day rather than Hitler's and the latter resented this, marking his displeasure by issuing an independent declaration of policy from that of the Nationalist leader, and by refusing to wait while Seldte's *Stahlhelm* passed the saluting base. Thus, the concluding passage of Hugenberg's address: 'Anyone who breaks our line will be considered an outlaw', was somewhat anti-climactic, since the line, never a strong one, was already breaking as he spoke. It was Hugenberg's last appearance as the leader of the National Opposition. Henceforth it danced to Hitler's piping.

The shift of power in the leadership of the Opposition was not lost upon von Schleicher. He was deeply disturbed by the events at Harzburg and his anxiety increased with the intensification of the new attack which Hitler now launched against the *Reichswehr*. Gröner's combination of Minister of Defence and Interior had been the signal for the *Völkischer Beobachter* to begin a campaign of psychological warfare against a 'veiled military dictatorship',[1] and on October 14 Hitler began a full-scale offensive when, in an open letter to the Chancellor, he dilated upon 'the true task of the Army of the Reich'.[2]

Deploring the more and more frequent descents of the *Reichswehr* into domestic politics and civil strife, Hitler wrote that 'the victory of our ideas will give to the entire nation a political mode of thought, an outlook on the world, which will bring the Army in

---

[1] Craig, p. 215.
[2] Hitler's *Auseinandersetzung mit Brüning* (Munich, 1932), pp. 35-6 ; Baynes, i, 552-3.

spirit into truly intimate relation with the whole people, and will thus free it from the melancholy fact of being an alien body within its own people. The success of your view, *Herr Reichskanzler*, will mean the obligation on the' part of the Army to maintain a political system which in its tradition and in its essential views is in deadly opposition to the spirit of an army. And this in its final result, whether the result is intended or not, must set upon the Army the stamp of a police-troop, designed more or less for domestic purposes.'

This repetition by Hitler of the charges against the *Reichswehr* which he had originally made in his Munich speech of March 1929 [1] was not the only criticism which Gröner had to withstand in his new dual capacity. The governments of the *Länder* were making more insistent demands that action be taken by the Reich Government against the SA, and the Social Democrats, upon whose support the Brüning Government was dependent in the *Reichstag*, made no secret of their suspicion that Gröner's continued delay in taking such action was conclusive proof that the *Reichswehr* was determined to shield and protect the Nazi movement.

This suspicion, in so far as von Schleicher was concerned, was not entirely without foundation. The General, at this moment, was as antagonistic to the Social Democrats as he was to the Nazis and was of the belief that the latter must be used as a counter-weight to the former — 'If there were no Nazis it would be necessary to invent them', he wrote to Gröner. [2] But he was also engaged in one of those many and futile attempts in which he indulged to bend the Nazis to his will and if possible to create a split within their inner councils.

Von Schleicher believed that, through his negotiations with Röhm and with Gregor Strasser, he had overcome Hitler's refusal to support the plan of the Government for the prolongation of Hindenburg's period of office, and when Brüning reopened the negotiations for this purpose in January 1932, both he and Gröner were assured by von Schleicher that Hitler's assent would be forth-coming without much difficulty. But what von Schleicher did not know was that, within the Party conclave, while Strasser had favoured a temporary truce and an accommodation with the Government, Röhm had betrayed his military ally and had so demolished Strasser's arguments that the meeting had adopted a policy of rejection by a large majority. Von Schleicher's stratagem had

---

[1] See above, p. 210 *et seq.*

[2] Von Schleicher to Gröner, March 23, 1932 (quoted by Craig, p. 217, footnote).

I

failed and, to his personal chagrin and the disappointment of Gröner and Brüning, both Hitler and Hugenberg returned unqualified negative replies to the Government proposals.

This refusal of the Parties of the Right to support his re-election by parliamentary means greatly annoyed the Marshal, and had the effect of removing his last reluctance to contest an election. His pride and his anger were aroused and he agreed to fight. But his resentment was not only directed against the Right but also against the man, who, he began to feel in his tired old brain, was really responsible for forcing him into an open conflict with his old supporters of 1925. Brüning, he felt, had somehow mismanaged the whole thing, and there grew up a coldness between the Marshal and the man whom he had once described enthusiastically as 'the best Chancellor since Bismarck'.

To von Schleicher too it appeared that he had been wrong in his choice of Brüning as the one who should tame the Nazis and give a strong government to Germany, and he began to canvass the field for a suitable successor. He had now reverted to his original scheme that the *Reichstag* must be dissolved and not be reconvened until the Constitution had been suitably amended, and that in the interval the Marshal must rule by decree with the support of the *Reichswehr*. But before that could be done Hindenburg must be re-elected and von Schleicher was forced to admit that the one man who could accomplish this feat was Brüning. It was not, therefore, politic to remove the Chancellor until after the President was secure in his new term of office, and to this end he gave a two-faced support to Brüning, while planning to replace both him, and, if necessary, Gröner, as soon as they had served their turn in re-electing Hindenburg.[1]

Yet while Kurt von Schleicher was weaving his web of intrigue, Goebbels was writing in his diary (February 4, 1932): 'To put the thing in a nutshell: Gröner must go — followed by Brüning and Schleicher, otherwise we shall never attain full power.'[2] The astute General was himself a dupe. He was doing the work of the Nazis for them and at the same time preparing the snare for his own feet.

On April 10, 1932, Field-Marshal von Hindenburg was re-elected President of the German Reich, decisively defeating his Nazi and Communist opponents, Adolf Hitler and Ernst Thälmann. A second ballot had been necessary and in it Hindenburg had

---

[1] Wheeler-Bennett, pp. 361-5 ; von Papen's evidence, June 14, 1946 (*Nuremberg Record*, xvi, 243).

[2] Joseph Goebbels, *My Part in Germany's Fight* (London, 1935), p. 37.

achieved more than 19 million votes, as against Hitler's 13 million and Thälmann's 3 million. The contest had been hard-fought and bitter, and in it all traditional affinities had been swept aside. Behind Hindenburg, the devout Protestant Prussian Monarchist, had stood the embattled forces of the Catholic Centre, Social Democracy, the Trade Unions and the Jews ; while to the standard of Hitler, the nominally Catholic, Austrian-born, quasi-Socialist,[1] had rallied the upper classes of the Protestant North, the German Crown Prince, the great industrialists of the Rhineland and the Ruhr, and the Conservative agrarian magnates of East Elbia.[2] All the elements which had been opposed to Hindenburg at his first election now voted for him ; all his former supporters turned to Hitler and vilified the name of Germany's greatest veteran. Hindenburg's victory was a resounding one, but the 13 million votes cast for Hitler were also eloquent evidence that National Socialism was not to be gainsaid much longer.

And now von Schleicher began preparing his *coup de grâce*. Brüning had exhausted his usefulness ; as Müller had gone, so must he go, to make place for some other Chancellor who would adhere more obediently to the political ideas of General von Schleicher. The campaign to remove him opened on general lines. Von Schleicher took care to do nothing to diminish the sense of resentment which the tired and aged President now entertained for his Chancellor. To the Old Gentleman Brüning was represented as the man whose tactics had exposed Hindenburg to unnecessary humiliations and had identified the spirit of Tannenberg and the Hindenburg Legend with the abhorrent doctrines of Social Democracy. Brüning had made the Marshal cheap in the eyes of the world, said von Schleicher, and it had all been quite unnecessary. Had his advice been followed, it need never have happened. It needed a strong man to handle these Nazis ; a strong man and a closed *Reichstag*.[3]

[1] Hitler only became a German citizen on February 26, 1932, by virtue of his appointment as a Government official by Dietrich Klagges, then a National Socialist Minister in the Brunswick Government.

[2] Hugenberg put up an independent Nationalist candidate in the first ballot, in the person of Colonel Theodor Düsterberg, the Second Leader of the *Stahlhelm*, who only secured 2½ million votes and was withdrawn in order to concentrate the forces of the Right in support of Hitler in the second ballot.

[3] Von Schleicher was becoming more and more obsessed with the belief that salvation for Germany lay only in the hands of 'a strong man'. One evening in the spring of 1932 the author of this book was dining with a group of friends at the Königin Restaurant on the Kurfürstendamm in Berlin, when von Schleicher's party arrived at the next table. The general was resplendent in full uniform and in excellent spirits. His bald head gleamed in the harsh light and he laughed a good deal. Suddenly the dance-band stopped with the abruptness of syncopation and von Schleicher, whose voice had been raised to be heard by his friends above

To the Nazis von Schleicher was equally equivocal. Brüning's days were numbered, he now told Röhm, with whom he had become reconciled, and it was no good negotiating with him. But the Chancellor who would succeed Brüning, as to whose identity the General was mysteriously discreet, would be a man of a different timbre and calibre, and with him it might be worth coming to terms. Let them but be patient.

The tempo and nature of events now combined to hasten the tragic end of the Weimar régime, a régime which, though pitiably weak and vacillating, was still immeasurably better than that which was to follow. The stars in their courses fought against Brüning and against Gröner. The ruthless, untiring determination of Hitler allied to the nefarious duplicity of von Schleicher were too strong a coalition to be defied.

Even before the Presidential election Brüning had determined to risk all on his ability to achieve a spectacular success in foreign policy. In January he had publicly declared that Germany would not, or could not, resume reparation payments after the termination of the Hoover Moratorium,[1] and the Creditor Powers had agreed to reconsider the situation at a conference to be held in February. At the Chancellor's suggestion the experts in the *Reichswehr* Ministry had prepared detailed proposals embodying the plans which Brüning and Gröner had matured for the token rearmament of Germany and the creation of national militia,[2] and these proposals Brüning intended to lay before the statesmen of America, Britain, France and Italy when he attended the Disarmament Conference in April.

If he could succeed in gaining a virtual cancellation of reparation payments and a substantial concession in the matter of rearmament, the Chancellor believed that the position of his Government would be so strengthened in the country, and that of the Nazis correspondingly weakened, that he could afford to take decisive measures against them and suppress the para-military formations of the Party.

The first check to Brüning's strategic planning came with the postponement of the proposed reparation conference from February to July. The second check was when the Reich Government was

the music, was overheard declaiming : 'What Germany needs to-day is a strong man' ; and he tapped himself significantly upon the breast.

[1] In an attempt to stem the course of the economic depression in Europe, and especially its effects in Germany, President Hoover proposed on June 20, 1931, a moratorium for one year on all reparation and inter-allied debt payments. Final agreement accepting the President's proposal was reached on July 6.

[2] See above, p. 229.

forced to take action — as Brüning subsequently thought, prematurely [1] — against the SA and SS.

Both these formations had been fully mobilized throughout the Reich on the night preceding the first ballot in the Presidential election (March 12/13) and a cordon of the SA had been thrown around Berlin. Though Röhm had informed von Schleicher that these were purely 'precautionary measures',[2] it was more than evident that they constituted preparation by the Party to seize power in all its aspects should Hitler be elected President the following day. Hitler's failure at the polls postponed the committing of any overt act, but the latent threat remained. Nor was this all. Plans for taking over the control of the State, and draft decrees establishing the death penalty for enemies of the Party, which the police of Hesse had seized at the local NSDAP headquarters at Boxheim in the previous November,[3] and this, together with the further discovery by the Prussian Secret Police in Silesia of orders by the local SA leaders that, in the event of a sudden Polish attack upon Germany, the Storm Troops should not take part in the defence of their country,[4] was conclusive proof that the Nazis were bent upon high treason both within and without the Reich and that the menace could no longer be met by passive resistance.

Thoroughly alarmed and determined to brook no further dalliance, the representatives of the *Länder* governments at a meeting with Gröner on April 5 confronted him with a virtual ultimatum. They demanded immediate action against the SA, and if the Reich Government would not take it, they would take it themselves. Brüning was absent from Berlin, engaged in the heat of the campaign for the second electoral ballot, but Gröner realized that the representatives of the *Länder* meant what they said and that such independent action as they threatened would not only severely damage the prestige of the Reich Government but would dangerously weaken the political structure of the Reich itself. Moreover, any further delay in taking action might jeopardize the continued support of the Social Democrats in the *Reichstag*. On the basis of *Staatsräson*, therefore, Gröner declared for extreme measures and gave his assurance to the representatives of the *Länder* that he would urge upon the President and the Chancellor the suppression of the SA and SS by decree immediately after the conclusion of the elections, that was to say, in five days' time.[5]

---

[1] Brüning, *Ein Brief*, p. 4.   [2] Heiden, *Der Führer*, p. 353.
[3] Konrad Heiden, *A History of National Socialism* (London, 1934), p. 155.
[4] Heiden, *Der Führer*, p. 353.
[5] For sources of the following account of the suppression of the Nazi formations see R. H. Phelps, 'Aus den Groener-Dokumenten. vii. Das SA Verbot und der

The active chiefs of the *Reichswehr* warmly endorsed the decision of their Minister. Von Hammerstein was uncompromising in his support and enthusiasm, and von Schleicher boasted that Gröner had taken the decision on his suggestion and that, whereas hitherto he had counselled delay, he was now convinced that this was the psychological moment to act. This was Kurt von Schleicher's attitude on April 8. On the following day Gröner had a preliminary discussion with the President and received the impression that Hindenburg was generally in agreement with the proposed dissolution. But now there was a change in von Schleicher's attitude. Would it not be wiser, he argued, to send an ultimatum to Hitler insisting that he make his organizations conform to a given set of regulations and conditions within a specified time ? This would avoid giving the *Führer* any opportunity of posing as a martyr as he might do if the SA and SS were suppressed without warning.

Though personally dubious of the cogency of von Schleicher's argument, Gröner agreed that it should be given a hearing when they met with the Chancellor on Brüning's return to Berlin the following day (April 10). At this meeting all present were opposed to von Schleicher's suggestion — a fact which the General received with an ill grace — and Gröner's decision was accepted by Brüning. It was agreed that the Chancellor and Gröner should present the matter to the Marshal next morning, when they brought him the formal congratulations of the Cabinet on his re-election, and Meissner, the President's State Secretary, assured them that no difficulty would be encountered in obtaining Hindenburg's signature to the decree.

And so at first it seemed. On the morning of April 11, the President promised his signature. Later, however, after a talk with his son Oskar, who had previously seen von Schleicher, he reversed his decision and declared himself against dissolution. Wearily, on the following morning, Brüning and Gröner recapitulated their arguments and eventually regained their lost ground, but only after Gröner had promised to take full responsibility for the action before the *Reichstag* and before the country. Once again, for the third and last time, Gröner was made the scapegoat for Hindenburg. His confidence in the Marshal's gratitude, in which he had so warmly believed, had been terribly misplaced.

The decree, which was approved by the Cabinet on April 13 and signed by the President on the same day, was promulgated on

Sturz des Kabinetts Brüning', *Deutsche Rundschau*, January 1951 ; Craig, pp. 219-26 ; Wheeler-Bennett, pp. 374-7.

E. Bieber

COLONEL-GENERAL FREIHERR KURT
VON HAMMERSTEIN

E. Bieber

LIEUTENANT-GENERAL KURT VON SCHLEICHER

the 14th, and at once a storm of obloquy broke over the devoted head of the Minister of Defence. Nor did it come from Nazi sources only. The German Crown Prince wrote an angry letter, and this was accompanied by bitter reproaches from former military leaders of the Reich. These attacks Gröner could sustain with fortitude, but what followed caused him deep personal and professional anguish.

Immediately after his defeat at the meeting of April 10 von Schleicher had confidentially informed the commanders of the seven military districts of the Reich that in the pending issue both he and von Hammerstein were in dissent from the views of the Government, and no sooner had the decree of dissolution been promulgated than he informed Gröner that the *Reichswehr* deeply resented the action taken against the Nazi formations. It was also clear that neither he nor von Hammerstein were prepared to stamp out this disaffection, which, he warned, was so strong that he had grave doubts whether Gröner would be able to continue as Defence Minister.[1]

Deeply hurt at this treatment from one whom he had trusted and cherished as a son, Gröner was to have further proofs of von Schleicher's disloyalty and ingratitude. On April 16 he received a cantankerous letter from Hindenburg, complaining of the suspicious and possibly treasonable activities of the *Reichsbanner*, the uniformed but unarmed formation of the Social Democrats, and indicating that it too should be suppressed. The letter was published simultaneously in the papers of the Right and was accompanied by certain evidence of a palpably flimsy character. So flimsy was it that Gröner made investigation as to its source. He found that it emanated from the files of the *Wehrmachtabteilung* of the Defence Ministry, a section headed by Eugen Ott, over which von Schleicher had immediate charge, and furthermore, that, contrary to all regulations and procedure, it had been transmitted to the President by von Hammerstein. With difficulty and with a heavy heart, Gröner succeeded in convincing Hindenburg that nothing could be proved against the *Reichsbanner* and that the allegations which he had publicly made were baseless.

[1] Von Hammerstein was playing a deep game at this moment and was at some pains to give an outward semblance of loyalty to Gröner. In this he succeeded, in any case in so far as the British Military Attaché, Colonel (now General Sir Andrew) Thorne was concerned. This officer reported on April 19 to his Ambassador, Sir Horace Rumbold, who repeated the information to the Foreign Office : 'For some time the Defence Minister has become more unpopular among the officers of the Army who are inclined to look upon him as a "traitor" to their cause ; General von Hammerstein alone showing no sign of any such bias' (Woodward and Butler, Second Series, iii, 118).

Still not fully willing to believe the worst of von Schleicher, Gröner, in the weeks that followed, was confronted with irrefutable evidence of his protégé's cabal against him. A malicious 'smear campaign' was carried on in the very *coulisses* of the Defence Ministry. He was said to have sold out to the Social Democrats, to have become a convert to the teachings of Professor Quidde and the pacifists, and much ribald capital was made over his second marriage and the premature birth of his child. With profound reluctance Gröner was compelled to recognize that these malicious whisperings could come only from von Schleicher and von Hammerstein. His only recourse was to dismiss them, and this he refused to do for fear that such an open breach within the senior hierarchy of the Army would lead to the weakening, and possibly the overthrow, of Brüning's Cabinet. Silently, grimly, he held on, waiting for events to take their course.

And events were moving rapidly towards a climax. Von Schleicher was now in treaty not only with Röhm but with Count Helldorf, the SA leader of Berlin, and other Nazi chieftains, whom he assured on April 22 that he had always disapproved of the decree of dissolution. Three days later he told Helldorf that he was ready 'to change his course', and on April 28 he had a conversation with Hitler himself, of which Goebbels records that 'the conference went off well'.[1] The purport of these meetings was made clear by Hitler to his lieutenants immediately after he had met with Oskar von Hindenburg, Meissner, and von Schleicher at the latter's home (May 8). Here the whole plan was laid before the *Führer* in all the Machiavellian deviation in which von Schleicher had contrived it. The Brüning Government was to fall piecemeal; first Gröner, then the Chancellor. It was to be replaced by a Presidential Cabinet. The *Reichstag* would be dissolved and the decrees against the paramilitary formations rescinded. 'How odd it seems', wrote Goebbels that evening, 'that nobody as yet has the slightest prevision; least of all Brüning himself'.[2]

The first blow was struck two days later when the *Reichstag* reassembled on May 10. Gröner explained the Government's action against the SA and SS. He was scathingly attacked by Göring, who openly appealed to the *Reichswehr* against its civilian chief, and, perhaps because he was both ailing physically and sick at heart, Gröner allowed himself to be provoked into an unprepared reply. He was interrupted at every sentence by a howl of invective from the Nazi benches. He was overwhelmed with abuse and his voice drowned in cat-calls and strident laughter.[3] Enraged and humili-

[1] Goebbels, pp. 80, 83, 84.   [2] *Ibid.*, p. 88.   [3] *Ibid.*, p. 90.

ated he left the Chamber, to be greeted by von Schleicher with a bland suggestion that he take sick leave. This Gröner refused to do and his refusal forced von Schleicher into the open. With cold brutality he informed Gröner that he 'no longer enjoyed the confidence of the Army' — that same dread formula which had previously eliminated, each in his turn, Wilhelm II, von Lüttwitz and Gessler — and that he must resign immediately.[1]

Woefully disillusioned, borne down by treachery, Gröner bowed to the inevitable and, after a vain appeal to Hindenburg, who 'regretted that he could do nothing in the matter', he resigned on May 13. 'We have news from General von Schleicher', Goebbels recorded jubilantly ; 'everything is progressing according to plan.'[2]

Neither Gröner nor Brüning spared von Schleicher in expressing their opinions of his conduct. 'Scorn and rage boil within me,' wrote Gröner, 'because I have been deceived in you, my old friend, disciple, adopted son ; my hope for people and Fatherland.'[3] The Chancellor tried, unsuccessfully, to shame von Schleicher into taking over the Ministry of Defence himself, since he had undermined the confidence of the Army in Gröner. 'I will, but not in your Government', was the General's retort.

And he was right. On the morning of May 30 — two months after Hindenburg's re-election and seventeen days after Gröner's

---

[1] Craig, pp. 225-6. Wheeler-Bennett, pp. 384-5. Not till years later did the Army leaders realize that von Schleicher had duped and lied to them in his representation of the case against Gröner. Many of them, including von Hammerstein, subsequently sought out Gröner in his retirement and explained sadly that, had they been fully and accurately informed of the facts, they would never have thus deserted him. One crumb of comfort reached Gröner. By devious ways there came to him a remark which the Kaiser had made to a member of his suite at Doorn : 'Tell Gröner', the Emperor said, 'that he has my full sympathy. I always expected that this would happen.' Wilhelm II had not forgotten the November days at Spa, but he knew now where the responsibility lay and that it was not with Gröner.   [2] Goebbels, p. 92.

[3] Letter from Gröner to von Schleicher, November 29, 1932 (quoted by Craig, p. 226). These sentiments are curiously at variance with those which Gröner expressed for the consumption of foreign diplomats. 'A lifelong and intimate friend' of the General, in conversation with a member of the British Embassy in May 1932, quoted Gröner as saying that 'It was Schleicher's duty in any event to inform the Government and the President of the state of feeling in the *Reichswehr*. It would be quite misleading to talk of a camarilla or of an intrigue on Schleicher's part. We are friends of long standing.' (See a despatch from Mr. B. C. Newton, British Chargé d'Affaires in Berlin, May 26, 1932, to Sir J. Simon (Woodward and Butler, Second Series, iii, 140-43).) The German Army had its own code of honour and conduct. Outwardly it preserved the *convenances*, did not wash its dirty linen in public and maintained a united front (see also above, p. 241, footnote). An interesting commentary is herein presented on the difficulties confronting diplomats in foreign countries in their efforts to provide their home governments with accurate information.

fall — von Schleicher, by methods which can only be described as worthy of one who bore the name of 'Creeper', brought about the final consummation of his plan to destroy the Brüning Government. The Chancellor was dismissed with scant courtesy and without a hearing.[1]

Two days later von Schleicher presented Hindenburg with the new Chancellor of his choice, the man who, under his guidance and with the support of the *Reichswehr* which he, Kurt von Schleicher, would control as Minister of Defence, should save Germany both from the Nazi menace and from the Weimar Constitution; the 'strong' man who should take Hitler captive and make him the hostage-helot of the Right.

The name of this snake-charming lion tamer was Franz von Papen. 'Everyone is overjoyed', wrote Goebbels in his diary.[2]

(vii)

What was in the mind of Kurt von Schleicher when he so wantonly destroyed the Brüning Government in the early summer of 1932 ? Was there behind this seemingly impenetrable twilight of machinations and treachery some higher motive which might mitigate his otherwise damnable conduct; or even some master plan which should bring to fruition and success the Machiavellian intrigues which he had employed with such persistent falsity and cunning ?

As to his motives, von Schleicher was impelled by the same basic incitement which since November 1918 had stimulated every German general — whether von Seeckt, or von Lüttwitz, or Gröner — the greater glory of the German Army ; but he had not von Seeckt's patience and vision, nor von Lüttwitz's singleness of purpose, nor Gröner's honesty. Von Schleicher's fundamental error was in abandoning that *Überparteilichkeit* on which von Seeckt had set such store for the Army, in dragging the *Reichswehr* into the arena of politics, in using it, not for the defence or the maintenance of the unity of the Reich, but as a political weapon, a Praetorian Guard, for the making and unmaking of Chancellors and Ministers, and in employing its political influence in the devious game of 'cut-throat' which he was playing with the Nazis.

What von Schleicher did not realize, for he was too caught up in the web of his own spinning to see thus far, was that, by the attitude which he had adopted in the matter of the suppression of the SA and his subsequent undermining of Gröner's authority

---

[1] For details see Wheeler-Bennett, pp. 386-95.   [2] Goebbels, p. 99.

with the Army, he had not only damaged the prestige and the discipline of the Officer Corps but had destroyed his own jealously guarded position as the only soldier who could negotiate with the Nazis. Encouraged by his example, such men as von Blomberg, von Reichenau and Keitel, who had long been 'crypto-Nazis' at heart, now began to dabble in politics and to negotiate with Hitler, but — also following von Schleicher's example — without informing the chiefs of the *Reichswehr*.

Thus the day of Nemesis was already dawning for Kurt von Schleicher at the very moment when his schemes seemed nearest to success. For in May 1932 he was at the height of his power and of his influence with Hindenburg. Oskar and Meissner were his allies, and, having removed Brüning, he had a clear field both as to policy and to the nomination of a successor.

The policy which he envisaged was the same which he had more than once urged upon Brüning without success ; the elimination of the Social Democrats as a political force, the indefinite proroguing of the *Reichstag* pending a new Constitution, and the government of the country by the President and the *Reichswehr*, with a Chancellor and a Cabinet of 'the President's friends'. To accomplish this dangerous design he was prepared to gamble on the support of the forces of reaction, the Nationalists and the Nazis. When they had served his purpose, von Schleicher trusted to his own astuteness to hamstring the Nazis at a later date, partly by dividing their inner political councils by taking the more conservative elements into the government, and partly by seducing the SA from its allegiance to the *Führer* by incorporating it with the Army. As an ultimate goal he may have dreamed of persuading the President to restore the Monarchy, for he was in lively correspondence with the Crown Prince.[1] That wily customer, however, was sceptical of the chances of success for such a project, and warned the General against placing implicit trust in Hindenburg. The Hohenzollerns, at least, knew the worth of the Marshal's word.

Such was the Grand Design of von Schleicher to which he had won the assent of the President. 'Now I can have a Cabinet of my friends', Hindenburg muttered as Brüning parted from him for the last time.[2] But where were these friends to be found ? With Meissner and von Schleicher, the Marshal spent considerable time in canvassing the various possibilities for Chancellor.[3] Their first choice was Count Westarp, the leader of the Independent Con-

[1] Craig, p. 227.   [2] Wheeler-Bennett, p. 395.
[3] Affidavit sworn by Otto Meissner at Oberursel, November 28, 1945, (*IMT Document*, PS-3309).

servative group, which, on von Schleicher's instigation, had seceded from the Nationalists in 1929.[1] It was hoped by this means to retain Brüning in the Cabinet as Foreign Minister, and also Treviranus, who was nominally a follower of Westarp.[2]

This idea had been proposed to Brüning, at his penultimate interview with Hindenburg on May 29,[3] and in rejecting it he had made the counter-proposal that his successor should be Carl Goerdeler, the former *Oberbürgermeister* of Leipzig, who had been serving for some time as Price Controller in the Brüning administration, a man who was later to serve Hitler in the same capacity and ultimately to be a leader of the conspiracy against him.[4] Hindenburg refused to consider this suggestion and also rejected the name of Hugenberg, whose insults in the past he had not forgotten and whom he termed 'the Sergeant', just as he later called Hitler 'the Corporal'.

In the meantime von Schleicher had bethought him of a name which he submitted to Hindenburg and to Hitler as a suitable choice, and gradually, by persistent lobbying, he gained the approval of both of them.[5] The selection of the fifty-three-year-old Franz von Papen had little at first sight to recommend it. 'No one but smiled or tittered or laughed', wrote the French Ambassador in Berlin, 'because von Papen enjoyed the peculiarity of being taken seriously by neither his friends nor his enemies. He gave the impression of an incorrigible levity of which he was never able to rid himself. . . . He was reputed to be superficial, blundering, untrue, ambitious, vain, crafty and an intriguer.' [6]

This is not an unfair description. Von Papen was certainly not above fifth-rate — though he was clever enough to keep himself from being murdered by Hitler for thirteen years, and to talk his way out of a prison sentence at Nuremberg in 1946. A dashing cavalryman

---

[1] See above, p. 209.

[2] Memorandum entitled *Schleicher, Hammerstein and the Seizure of Power*, written for the author by Dr. Kunrath von Hammerstein, son of the General, based upon his father's notes and diaries.

[3] Wheeler-Bennett, p. 392. Still anxious to retain the undoubted value of Brüning's influence and prestige abroad, Hindenburg and von Schleicher later pressed him to become Ambassador in London. This too was refused.

[4] Brüning, *Ein Brief*, p. 10.

[5] It is uncertain at what date von Schleicher had actually decided upon von Papen as his candidate. Goebbels (p. 95) records on May 24 that his appointment 'is more or less settled', yet this must apparently have been without the knowledge of von Papen himself, who in his evidence at Nuremberg stated that he was first approached on May 26, when von Schleicher telephoned to him to come to Berlin for consultation (*Nuremberg Record*, xvi, 243).

[6] André François-Poncet, *Souvenirs d'une ambassade à Berlin, septembre 1931–octobre 1938* (Paris, 1946), pp. 42-3.

and famous as a gentleman-rider, he was best known to the world at large for the unsavoury nature of his exit from the United States during the First World War, whence he had been expelled as military attaché on a charge of sabotage. A fervent Catholic, he had subsequently sat in the Prussian *Landtag* as one of the extreme right wing of the Centre Party, in whose Party organ, *Germania*, he was a large shareholder, but he had never succeeded in being elected to the *Reichstag*.[1] A member of a family of the Westphalian aristocracy, he had acquired considerable wealth and influence by marriage with Martha von Boch, the daughter of one of the leading industrialists of the Saar.

Despite his seemingly overwhelming disqualifications in character and temperament, von Papen possessed certain attributes which von Schleicher had descried and which he was confident could be utilized to advantage. Von Papen was an ardent conservative, yet he did not belong to Hugenberg's followers and was therefore not included in the general anathema which the Marshal had pronounced against the Nationalists. His desire to effect reactionary amendments to the constitution of the Reich and to the State Law of Prussia was well known, and he was an avowed enemy of Social-Democracy, having for years endeavoured to break up the alliance which had existed between the SPD and the Centre during the Chancellorships of Müller and of Brüning.

These qualities, thought von Schleicher, would certainly endear his candidate to the President, and in addition, the General counted upon von Papen's wit and *panache* — that air of a gay and dashing captain of Uhlans which he had succeeded in carrying into the middle fifties — to charm the Marshal and to lift him out of the depressing atmosphere of politics. The earnest sincerity of the machine-gun subaltern Brüning was to be replaced by the shallow frivolity of the cavalryman von Papen. Brüning had been too genuine to play the courtier, but it was second nature to his successor.

All turned out as von Schleicher had hoped and planned. In the afternoon of May 30 Hindenburg received Hitler and repeated the terms which von Schleicher had outlined on the 8th :[2] a Presidential Cabinet ; the lifting of the ban on the SA and the prohibition of Party uniforms ; and the dissolution of the *Reichstag*. And in return asked from the *Führer* an undertaking to support the

---

[1] An attempt had once been made by von Papen's friends to have him nominated as a candidate for the *Reichstag*, but the proposal met with the uncompromising opposition of Carl Herold (1848–1931), the veteran Honorary President of the Centre Party, and himself a Westphalian. On being asked why he objected so strongly, Herold replied : ' I am too old to have to give reasons, but I will not have Franz von Papen in the *Reichstag* '.   [2] See above, p. 242.

new Government.[1] This assurance Hitler gave in an equivocal form which, in his own mind if not in the President's, left him complete freedom of action after the election.

Well pleased with the result of the interview, Hindenburg received von Papen that same afternoon, and was delighted with him. 'I have called you', he said, 'because I want a Cabinet of independent men.' And when von Papen made polite demurrance, the Old Gentleman reminded him of his duty to the Fatherland and added pathetically — just as two years before he had said to Brüning — 'I am an old solider. You cannot leave me in the lurch when I need you', whereupon von Papen accepted.[2]

The President at once set about forming 'the Cabinet of his Friends', and he would brook no denial or objection. He ordered von Schleicher, as a German officer on duty, to become Minister of Defence; to Freiherr von Neurath, then Ambassador in London, he appealed on his knightly oath as a Württemberg nobleman to take charge of the Foreign Office; while to Graf Schwerin von Krosigk, a career civil servant who doubted his ability to assume Cabinet responsibilities, the President gave six hours in which to decide whether he would accept promotion or dismissal.

As a result of these tactics the new Government was announced to an astonished world on June 1. Within six weeks of his election by over 19 million votes of the Left and Centre, Hindenburg had appointed a Cabinet of which seven out of nine ministers were of the old nobility with definitely Rightish affiliations, and in which, for the first time since 1918, there was no representative of organized labour.[3]

Such was the Government which von Schleicher regarded as ideal from the point of view of the *Reichswehr* and in which he as Minister of Defence was the dominant force. It had no support in

[1] Goebbels, p. 99.

[2] Evidence of von Papen before the International Military Tribunal, June 14, 1946 (*Nuremberg Record*, xvi, 244). Von Papen denied at Nuremberg that he had given any pledge to Hitler on the matter of the dissolution of the *Reichstag* before becoming Chancellor, and this was strictly true since the pledge had been given by von Schleicher and Hindenburg before his appointment. However, von Papen further stated that he met Hitler for the first time in his life five or six days after the dissolution had been announced on June 4, whereas Goebbels (p. 100) records a meeting between the Chancellor and the *Führer* on May 31, at which the question of the dissolution was discussed but not definitely settled.

[3] The members of the von Papen Government were : Freiherr von Neurath (Foreign Office) ; Freiherr von Gayl (Interior) ; General von Schleicher (Defence) ; Freiherr von Braun (Food and Agriculture) ; Professor Warmbold (Economics) ; Graf Schwerin von Krosigk (Finance) ; Dr. Gürtner (Justice) ; Freiherr von Eltz-Rubenach (Communications). The Ministry of Labour was administered by the State Secretary, Dr. Dietrich Syrup.

the *Reichstag* apart from the thirty odd votes of the disgruntled Nationalist Party. The Left were solidly hostile, believing that this 'Cabinet of Barons' was clearly destined to destroy democratic institutions ; the Centre had remained loyal to Brüning and had unanimously expelled von Papen from its midst, and the German People's Party maintained an attitude of reserved detachment. The new Government was dependent upon the good-will of the President, the support of the armed forces of the State and the unreliable backing of the National Socialists, whose promise of 'toleration' was as ephemeral as the wind. Yet this was the very foundation on which von Schleicher had built this strange political structure. The breathing space gained by Nazi 'toleration' must be used by the Government to bring about its reforms, after which they would deal with the Nazis. Whereas Brüning had failed either to control, placate or destroy the Nazi Party, von Schleicher had promised the President that the new Government would certainly achieve either the first or the last. To do either, however, it was necessary to follow the middle course in the earlier stages, otherwise they might be confronted with an attempt by the Nazis to seize power by force, an eventuality which must be avoided at all costs.

It was upon this vitally important issue of how to handle the Nazis that the Cabinet showed its first signs of disunity. The President, buoyed up by von Schleicher's optimism, was of the opinion that the strength and popular support of the National Socialist Party was only ephemeral and would disappear with improved economic conditions, and for this reason he was unwilling to entrust the Nazis with even a share of the government of the country. In this view he was supported at the outset by the Chancellor and von Gayl, the Minister of Interior. There was, however, a group of ministers headed by Gürtner, Hitler's former protector in Munich in the 'twenties and now Minister of Justice, and by Graf Schwerin von Krosigk, a former Rhodes Scholar of proven ability as a civil servant but little capacity for politics,[1] who favoured taking certain of the more moderate elements among the Nazi leadership into the Government. Von Schleicher himself wavered

---

[1] Gürtner, who was retained at the Ministry of Justice by both von Schleicher and Hitler, died in 1941. Schwerin von Krosigk remained uninterruptedly in office from 1932–45, and served in Admiral Doenitz's transitory administration at Flensburg as Nazi Germany's last Foreign Minister. Placed on trial at Nuremberg, before the United States Tribunal No. IV, in the 'Ministries Case', he was sentenced on April 14, 1949, to ten years' imprisonment on charges of War Crimes and Crimes against Humanity. Released on February 3, 1951, he subsequently published an entertaining collection of pen-portraits of leading German characters entitled *Es geschah in Deutschland* (Tübingen/Stuttgart, 1951).

between these two groups ; anxious to keep his hands free, if soiled, and his policy pliant, he would not declare himself definitely as a supporter of either,[1] and of all the ministers he alone kept up continuous contact with the Nazis, a record of which Goebbels kept faithfully in his diary.

Nor were the Nazis greatly deceived by von Schleicher's repeated tergiversations. They had dealt with the General for some time now and they knew what to expect of him. 'Any Chancellor who has Herr von Schleicher on his side must expect sooner or later to be sunk by the Schleicher torpedo', wrote Göring ; 'there was a joke current in political circles — "General von Schleicher ought really to have been an Admiral, for his military genius lies in shooting under water at his political friends".'[2]

To Hitler, however, at this time, the General was a not unvaluable asset. All that the *Führer* desired was a dissolution of the *Reichstag*, for he was confident that in the election which would follow he would not only increase his parliamentary representation beyond its existing 107 seats, but would even add to the popular vote of 13 millions which he had gained at the second presidential ballot in April. Once, therefore, the decree of dissolution had been promulgated on June 4, the NSDAP concentrated all its efforts on the electoral campaign, during which they became more and more critical of the Government they had agreed to 'tolerate'. They remained unimpressed by the undoubted diplomatic success which von Papen achieved in the cancellation of reparation payments at Lausanne, or by the unilateral repudiation of the War-guilt Clause of the Treaty of Versailles with which the Chancellor followed it,[3] or by the truculent attitude assumed by the German delegation at the Disarmament Conference at Geneva.[4] Their only concern was

---

[1] Meissner Affidavit (*IMT Document* PS-3309).

[2] Hermann Göring, *Germany Reborn* (London, 1934), p. 102.

[3] Reaping the harvest which Brüning had sown but had not been permitted to garner, von Papen reached an agreement with the Creditor Powers at Lausanne on July 9, 1932, whereby except for a token sum of three milliard RM., which everyone tacitly admitted would never be paid, Germany was released from all further reparation obligations. Von Papen at once (July 11) declared that this cancellation constituted a formal abrogation of Part VII of the Treaty of Versailles together with its hated War-guilt Clause (Article 231). This view remained unconfirmed in either London or Paris.

[4] As a result of Germany's failure to secure the assent of the Western Powers to her moral equality in the matter of armaments and also her right to some measure of rearmament, the German Government withdrew from the Disarmament Conference on July 23, 1932. An attempt by von Neurath and von Schleicher to reach an agreement with the French by direct negotiation also failed, but on December 11 the Powers and Germany concurred on the formula of 'equality of rights within a system of security for all nations', and on this basis Germany returned to the Conference.

the more sinister sequence of events which occurred within the Reich.

Here it was clear to all, except perhaps the Chancellor, that the Nazis were headed for a very substantial victory. On June 5 they overwhelmed their political opponents in the Mecklenburg elections, securing 29 seats in the local Diet, or as many as all the other Parties combined. Ten days later, after considerable pressure from Hitler, the President signed the decree rescinding the ban on the Storm Troops and at once a wave of political violence and assault swept through the country. Nazis and Communists responded with avid enthusiasm to the provocation which each offered to the other, and bloody disputes ensued in all parts of the Reich. Nor did the Nazis confine their assaults to the Communists. They were equally violent against the Social Democrats, breaking up their election meetings and the parades of the *Reichsbanner*, and attacking the editorial offices of *Vorwärts*.

The ordinary law-abiding German citizen went in terror of his life under this 'Government of the President's Friends' which von Schleicher and the *Reichswehr* had brought into being. Not only were the streets rendered unsafe by frequent conflicts between armed hoodlums of the Right and Left, but the criminal class did not hesitate to exploit the situation created by the political extremists, and among the outrages were many cases of burglary with assault, highway robbery and the settling of private feuds.

This state of virtual civil war reached its climax in the Altona riots of July 17, when, in a working-class suburb of Hamburg, a clash between SA men and Red Front Fighters resulted in fifteen dead and fifty seriously injured.[1] All Parties now demanded action by the Government to terminate this deplorable condition of lawlessness. The Army were themselves alarmed by the reappearance of the ancient bogy of their being called upon to quell simultaneous risings from the Right and Left. In his first proclamation to the Army as Minister of Defence, on June 2, von Schleicher had announced his intention of 'making the *Reichswehr* capable of defending Germany's frontiers and of insuring national security. I shall further see to it', he added, 'that those spiritual and physical forces in our people, which form the indispensable foundation of our country's defence, are strengthened.' It now seemed as if these

---

[1] It should be remembered, however, that political violence had been steadily on the increase in Germany for the past few years. In 1929 there were 42 deaths ; in 1930, 50 ; while, in the first half of 1931, the figure rose to well over 100. For example, there were 15 deaths, 200 serious casualties and over 1,000 minor casualties during the months of April and May alone in that year (*Berliner Tageblatt*, June 1, 1931).

foundations were to be cemented in the blood of German citizens.

In response to the general demand, the Government reimposed the ban on political parades and demonstrations, but the Chancellor and his Minister of Defence essayed to turn the trick to their own advantage by taking an action which should have the multiple gain of placating the Nazis and stealing their anti-Marxist thunder, while at the same time furthering the plans of the Cabinet for a new and more centralized Government for Germany and for disposing of their political opponents of the Left. Whatever difference there may have been between von Papen and von Schleicher on the issue of how to deal with the Nazis, they were at one in their views on the suitable treatment for Social Democrats.

The opportunity for this all-embracing master-stroke was presented by the political situation of Prussia, where almost without interruption since 1919 a Social-Democrat Prime Minister had led some form of coalition government. In the elections for the Prussian Diet on April 24, 1932, however, this combination had been destroyed by the return of the Nazis with 162 out of 420. But, though the largest Party, they were unable, even with the support of the Nationalists, to command a majority of the Right, and the Socialist-Centre group was also in a minority.[1] The only possible combination of forces on 'which a Government could be built was a coalition of the Nazis with the Centre; and negotiations to this end had been in desultory progress for the past three months. At one moment, when it seemed as if the Nazi demands were weakening, von Schleicher had deliberately sabotaged the discussions as a part of his general plan to bring down the Brüning Government.[2] Meantime the Braun-Severing Cabinet, which had formally resigned on May 19, still remained a Government *ad interim*.

To end the deadlock, Brüning had considered a return to the convention which had existed under the Imperial régime, whereby the offices of Imperial Chancellor and Minister-President of Prussia were vested in the same individual, and Braun had expressed his willingness to resign the premiership to Brüning if such an identifi-

---

[1] The Prussian elections of April 24, 1932, resulted in the following state of the Parties : Nazis, 162 ; Nationalist, 31 ; Social Democrats, 93 ; Centre, 67 ; Communists, 57 ; German People's Party, 7 ; State Party, 2.

[2] On this occasion, when the question of a coalition with the Centre was being debated in the Nazi Party conclave, Gregor Strasser made an eloquent appeal for accepting the conditions offered. He was answered by Röhm, who displayed such vehemence and such an uncanny insight into the insecure position of the Brüning Cabinet, that Strasser's motion was defeated. As the meeting closed, Strasser, passing behind the chair in which Röhm had been sitting, saw that he had left his notes on the table, and, on looking closer, observed that they were written on the headed stationery of the Ministry of Defence (Wheeler-Bennett, pp. 373-4).

cation of offices would constitute an added bulwark against the rising tide of National Socialism. Brüning, however, had delayed taking a final decision ; but, before he himself was swept away in the whirlwind, he had gone to the length of having a decree prepared for the President's signature.

It was this draft measure which von Papen and von Schleicher now proposed to put into effect, but by force, not by consent.

The dismissal of the Prussian *ad interim* Government and its replacement by a Reich Commissioner had been a subject of discussion between the Nazi leaders and von Papen's Government almost from the time that the latter took office. The Nazi Press became more and more insistent that a solution of the Prussian Problem be speedily found and one which should sweep away the taint of Marxism, more particularly in the police department.[1] But the psychological moment for action for which the Chancellor sought did not arise until the Bloody Sunday at Altona (July 17) had brought the civil unrest to a hideous climax and had roused all voices in the country to a pitch of protest.

On the following morning von Schleicher triumphantly produced for his puppet-chief evidence from the Prussian Ministry of Interior, where he presumably had one of his many 'men of confidence', to the effect that the police department had not only been grossly lax in its dealing with the Communists in their clashes and demonstrations, but that they were on all too intimate terms with the Communist Party as a whole. The time for action had at last arrived.[2]

Von Papen and von Schleicher hurried with their evidence to the President at Neudeck. Hindenburg approved their proposed course of action, and they returned to Berlin to perfect their plans. The Commanding Officer of *Wehrkreis III* (Berlin-Brandenburg), General Gert von Rundstedt, was warned to hold his troops in readiness for immediate action, and the Chancellor called a meeting of the Prussian Cabinet at the Reich Chancellery for the afternoon of July 20. This, however, was merely to lull his victims into a sense of false security. Von Papen's real intentions were disclosed when he suddenly summoned the Prussian Minister of Interior, Carl Severing — Otto Braun was absent from Berlin on sick leave

---

[1] 'We consider it intolerable that the greatest State in Germany should still be governed by Social Democrats and their allies during the elections set for July 31', Goebbels wrote in *Der Angriff* on June 11, and three days later in the same paper he demanded the dismissal of the Police President, Grzesinski, and his second-in-command (see also Goebbels, pp. 104, 112).

[2] Von Papen's evidence before the International Military Tribunal, *Nuremberg Record*, xvi, 250 ; von Papen's testimony under interrogation at Nuremberg, September 19, 1945.

—and two of his colleagues to the Chancellery early in the morning of the 20th, and informed them, in the presence of von Schleicher and von Gayl, the Reich Minister of Interior, that the President had decided to remove the Braun Government from office and to install in their place a Reich Commissioner. He then requested the Ministers to sign a protocol recognizing their dismissal 'by mutual consent'.

Severing was incensed. He protested vigorously against the charge that the Prussian police had been either lax or incompetent in the handling of their very difficult and critical tasks of maintaining law and order, and denied emphatically that they had been in any way partial to the Communists. He declared that he would yield up his office only if compelled to do so by force, and with his colleagues he left the Chancellery.

The necessary force was in readiness. The Reich Government at once proclaimed a state of martial law in the city of Berlin and the Mark of Brandenburg, and placed full powers in the hands of General von Rundstedt. Simultaneously a decree was published, under Article 48 of the Constitution, signed by Hindenburg, appointing von Papen as Reich Commissioner and authorizing him to dismiss the Prussian ministers.[1] The notification of their dismissal was made known to them by General von Rundstedt over the telephone. Their physical ejection was performed by squads of police officers under new commanders. In no case was resistance encountered. By evening the whole operation had been completed. A revolution of the Right had been accomplished in Prussia without bloodshed and virtually without opposition.[2]

Nearly a quarter of a century before, von Oldenburg-Januschau, the Agrarian leader, whom Prince von Bülow eulogistically described as 'one of the best types of Junker', had made his notorious statement that the Kaiser should never allow the *Reichstag* to become so strong that he could not send a lieutenant and ten men of the Prussian Guards to close it at any moment.[3] It had not taken even

---

[1] A new Prussian Government was at once appointed in which the Minister of Interior was Dr. Franz Bracht, formerly Chief *Bürgermeister* of Essen, who also served as von Papen's Deputy and discharged the functions of Minister-President.

[2] Severing's evidence before the International Military Tribunal (*Nuremberg Record*, xiv, 271); *Mein Lebensweg*, ii, 348-52; Braun, pp. 403-7; Grzescinski, pp. 156-60.

[3] Bülow, *Memoirs 1903–1909*, p. 481; Graf Robert Zedlitz-Treutschler, *Zwölf Jahre am deutschen Kaiserhof* (Berlin, 1923), p. 231.

Elard von Oldenburg-Januschau (1855-1937) was a veteran leader of the Agrarian reactionaries, and a member of the Conservative, and later of the German Nationalist, Party. A devoted follower of Ernst von Heydebrand, he made a vehement defence of Wilhelm II's policy at the time of the *Daily Telegraph* crisis

this force to evict the Government of Prussia. A police captain and five constables had been sufficient.

But, because von Papen and von Schleicher had the support of the *Reichswehr*, they had succeeded where Kapp and von Lüttwitz had failed. They had taken a gigantic stride towards that form of authoritarian government favoured by the 'Cabinet of the President's Friends'. The Social Democrats had lost their last stronghold, and they had lost it without a struggle. In 1920 the Left had proclaimed a general strike, now they contented themselves with ineffectual verbal protests and recourse to legal formulae. This was due partly to the general lessening of vitality and dynamic purpose which all political Parties — with the exception of the Nazis and the Communists — had suffered over the past twelve years, and partly to the insidious assurances with which General von Schleicher had paralysed the Trade Union movement.

The General had always been on good terms with the Trade Union leaders, for he regarded their organizations as reserves of man-power on which almost unlimited drafts could be made. But, like most of von Schleicher's friends, they suffered from his duplicity. In the days when he was secretly plotting the downfall of Brüning, he had assured them that though his real aim was to get rid of the *Reichstag*, he planned to replace it by a form of corporative parliament based largely upon the Trade Unions. It was too late to save the political parties. They were doomed by their own ineptitude. But their place must be taken by the great guilds of organized labour.[1]

With these will-o'-the-wisp promises, von Schleicher had successfully divided the forces of the Left. For, whereas the Social Democrats were frankly distrustful, rightly descrying in him one of their bitterest opponents, the Trade Union leaders were beguiled by his words, and the spell even lasted after the Rape of Prussia. The Social Democrats were prepared to call a general strike immediately, to meet force with force, even at the risk of precipitating a civil war, but the Trade Union leaders, still trusting blindly in the word of von Schleicher, prevailed upon their members to wait for the promised millennium.

And what was to be the nature of this millennium towards which

in 1908, and his famous remark with regard to the *Reichstag* was made two years later. An uncompromising opponent of the Weimar régime, he played an important part in sustaining the hostility of Hindenburg against the republican elements, and it was also due to his initiative that the estate of Neudeck in East Prussia was bought by national subscription and presented to the Marshal on his eightieth birthday — with disastrous consequences (Wheeler-Bennett, pp. 311-15).

[1] Wheeler-Bennett, pp. 404-5.

von Papen and von Schleicher and von Gayl were, in their own imagination, herding the German people ? They were quite determined that the new Constitution should perpetuate the authoritarian rule which they had established, yet they were anxious to allay as much suspicion of their intentions as possible. On July 23, at a meeting with the Premiers of the German States at Stuttgart, at which the Bavarian Prime Minister, Dr. Held, threatened to arrest any Reich Commissioner who might be appointed for Bavaria, 'as soon as he dared to step on Bavarian soil', the Chancellor gave solemn assurances that the action taken in Prussia was to be regarded neither as a permanent step nor a precedent for relations between the Government of the Reich and other German States. Three days later martial law was withdrawn and von Schleicher, in a radio broadcast to the nation, declared that he would never permit the *Reichswehr* to deviate from its impartial attitude and from the idea that it must serve only the nation as a whole ; 'a Government supported by bayonets alone must end in failure'. Questioned on the same day (July 26) in the *Reichstag* Committee of Elders as to whether the *Reichswehr* would also act against the Nazis if they attempted to seize power, the Minister of Defence replied, 'Of course'.

So much for the protestations of General von Schleicher and the Government which he had brought into being. It remained, however, for that ancient die-hard, Herr von Oldenburg-Januschau, once again to give the clue to their intentions, when he promised a meeting of the Nationalist Party that he and his friends 'would brand the German people with a new Constitution that would take away their sight and hearing'.

What was actually envisaged appears to have been a virtual return, *mutatis mutandis*, to the constitutional position existing before the panic-stricken 'Revolution from Above', which Ludendorff had demanded and Prince Max von Baden had accomplished in October 1918.[1] The President and the *Reichstag* were to be elected by popular vote, for which the electoral age was to be raised from twenty to twenty-five and all ex-soldiers and the heads of families were to have a double suffrage. Neither the President nor his Cabinet were to be responsible either to the *Reichstag*, which was to be subject to repeated dissolution, or to the new second chamber, a kind of Senate, comprising the existing *Reichsrat*, representing the Federal States, together with representatives of various social and professional strata and of other distinguished persons appointed for life by the President. This body was to exercise a certain right of veto. In addition a structural reform was planned

[1] See above, p. 15 *et seq.*

FIELD-MARSHAL GERD VON RUNDSTEDT

whereby the three South German States — Bavaria, Württemberg and Baden — were to be merged with the Reich, thus further strengthening the Central Government.[1]

It was with these ambitions that the Papen-Schleicher Government sailed into its first election on July 31, 1932 — and with disastrous results or, rather, results which would have been considered disastrous for any Government dependent upon the support of a parliamentary majority. The Nazis emerged as the largest Party in the *Reichstag*, their representation increasing from 107 to 230. The Social Democrats, though they held their second place, paid the price of having failed to resist the Rape of Prussia ; their numbers fell to 133, a loss of ten seats. The Catholic bloc (the Centre and the Bavarian People's Party) rose by 10, from 87 to 97 ; and the Communists, increasing their popular vote by nearly 2 million, gained 89 seats as against 77 in 1930. The outstanding losses, apart from the Social Democrats, were sustained by the 'splinter parties', which were virtually wiped out, and by the only two Parties upon whom the Government might rely in the *Reichstag*, the Nationalists and the German People's Party, who, in a House of 608, could only muster 44 seats between them. Though sharply divided upon the issue of what they *did* want, the German electorate had made it clear beyond peradventure that they did *not* want the 'Cabinet of the President's Friends'.

In these results the influence of Kurt von Schleicher may be clearly descried. It was his policy which had brought about the election in the first place, thereby giving the Nazis the opportunity which they had so ardently desired. It was his policy which had split the forces of the Left at the moment of the Rape of Prussia, thereby driving many shocked and disgruntled Social Democrats into support of the Communists. It was his treatment of Brüning which had whipped the Catholic vote into righteous wrath and had thereby increased their representation. Finally, it was he who had in great part actuated the Government in following a policy which had so signally failed to win the support of the electorate. This 'chair-borne' General, now the civilian head of the *Reichswehr*, had set his mark indelibly upon the course of German politics and was to grave it even deeper before his career was ended by the assassin's bullet.

It was indeed a matter of high tragedy for Germany that, at this fateful moment in her history, the disposition of her destiny should have been at the mercy of the capricious rivalry of two such men

[1] Edgar Ansell Mowrer, *Germany Puts the Clock Back* (London, 1933), pp. 318-19.

as Franz von Papen and Kurt von Schleicher; between the gay, crafty irresponsibility of the Uhlan captain and the cunning, devious Byzantinism of the General Staff Officer. Never had the national interests of the Reich been so ill served as at this time when political ineptitude went hand-in-hand with personal rancour.

For, for the next six months, the two men who exercised the greatest influence in the direction of events were to pursue policies which were not only conflicting but which in course of time were to become completely contrary and reversed, and the only inevitable beneficiary from these tergiversations was Adolf Hitler.

Von Papen's reaction to the election results was that of the imperturbable equanimity of the *Herrenreiter*. He was prepared to remain at the head of the Government, take the Nazis into camp and proceed with his structural reorganization of the Reich. 'The National Socialists have to be given responsibility,' he said publicly, 'and, when that has been done, we have to bring about a reform of the Constitution.' [1]

Hitler, however, had no intention of being thus 'fobbed off' with second place. Flushed with his electoral success, he was for demanding his right, as the leader of the largest Party in the *Reichstag*, to be entrusted with the Chancellorship and the formation of a government, and to achieve this he sought the assistance of von Schleicher, who, alone among the Cabinet of the President's Friends', had been conspicuously immune from Nazi insults during the election campaign.

The two men met on August 5 at the Fürstenberg Barracks outside Berlin. There the *Führer* outlined to the General his future plans: the Chancellorship for himself, and for his followers the Premiership of Prussia, the Reich and Prussian Ministries of Interior and the Ministry of Justice. Von Schleicher was to remain as Minister of Defence and there was some talk of the Vice-Chancellorship. The name of von Papen was not mentioned in the 'Shadow Cabinet'. Hitler expressed his confidence that he could wring a majority from the *Reichstag* as Mussolini had done from the Italian parliament in 1922, and that an Enabling Act must then be passed. If the *Reichstag* refused to pass it, the *Reichstag* must be dissolved.

To this course von Schleicher was entirely favourable. If Hitler was able to command a majority, he said, no one would, or could, prevent him from governing. And the *Führer* was so delighted with this reply, which he interpreted as a promise to make him Chancellor, that he proposed that a memorial tablet should be let into the wall of the building in which they had met, bearing the

[1] Interview with the Associated Press, August 3, 1932.

inscription : 'Here the memorable conference between General von Schleicher and Adolf Hitler took place'.[1] Yet in less than two years' time he had accepted responsibility for von Schleicher's murder.

But when the General went to lay his solution before the President, he found Hindenburg entirely averse to any such course of action. The Marshal was gravely concerned for the internal security of the Reich, where every hour brought new tidings of bloody clashes between the SA and the Communist 'Iron Front', and of murders committed by both sides. In an attempt to combat this state of lawlessness, the Government again declared martial law throughout Prussia on August 9, providing summary justice and the death penalty for acts of violence.[2] This was no time, said the Marshal, to confide the government of the Reich to the 'Bohemian Corporal'. Moreover, both Hindenburg and his son Oskar were completely under the spell of von Papen's charm, and the President was determined to retain him at all costs. Von Schleicher's decoy duck had turned out to be a cuckoo and had supplanted him in the affections of the Hindenburgs, pere et fils.

Thus, when summoned to Berlin to confer with the President, Hitler proceeded from Berchtesgaden in the firm belief that von Schleicher had made good his promises. He was speedily undeceived. In his interviews with the leaders of the Government, both von Papen and von Schleicher, who had now changed his tune, refused to consider any proposal other than the Vice-Chancellorship for Hitler himself and the Prussian Ministry of Interior for one of his lieutenants. Moreover, in the famous interview of August 13 with Hindenburg, in the presence of Meissner,[3] Hitler received what was probably the roughest handling he ever suffered in his political career. With extraordinary vehemence and clarity for one who only ten months before had suffered a complete mental breakdown,[4] the Marshal first fought his opponent to a standstill and then proceeded to demolish him with a 'dressing-down' of considerable severity. In concluding his curtain lecture on constitutional government, in which he clearly and definitely refused to

---

[1] Heiden, Der Führer, p. 377 ; A History of National Socialism, pp. 176-7 ; Goebbels, pp. 132-3.

[2] On this same night of August 9 five Nazis murdered a Communist in the Upper Silesian village of Potempa. The strong measures which the Government had just enacted, and which were designed primarily for use against the Communists, had therefore in the first instance to be employed against the National Socialists. The five murderers, with whom Hitler at once proclaimed a 'blood-brotherhood', were tried and condemned to death, but their execution was indefinitely delayed. The incident was an important factor in exacerbating the relations between Hitler and von Papen.

[3] Meissner Affidavit, IMT Document, PS-3309.   [4] See above, pp. 232-233.

appoint Hitler to the Chancellorship or to give him supreme power, the Marshal recommended his infuriated listener to exercise greater chivalry in his future political campaigns.

This spirited performance of the President in support of his Chancellor was of but temporary advantage. It was of no real benefit to von Papen, who, having now completely alienated the Nazi Party, was defeated at the first vote of confidence in the *Reichstag*, which, with the President's authority, he promptly dissolved.

The Government conducted the ensuing general election on the slogan of 'Support our ideas or we shall continue to govern alone until you do'. Bu. ⁺he results on November 6, though they proved a considerable set-back to the Nazis,[1] were again eloquent of the fact that the German people would not support the Presidential Cabinet. Ninety per cent of the votes were cast against the Government, and it became clear at last, even to von Papen, that if he were to continue in office, his sole support, apart from the 62 votes of the Nationalist and German People's Parties, would be the bayonets of the *Reichswehr*.

It was also apparent that the *Reichswehr* would only support the Government if ordered to do so by their Supreme Commander, the President. They had no great respect for von Papen personally, despite his record as a cavalryman and his membership of the Officer Corps. Their commander, von Hammerstein, on the other hand, was a devoted friend of von Schleicher, and the issue resolved itself into which of these two paladins, the Chancellor or the Minister of Defence, could exercise the greater influence upon the Marshal.

Both men recognized that in the election results of November 6 the Nazis had suffered a reverse which had gravely weakened their bargaining power with the President and with the Government. Moreover, the decline in the popular vote of the NSDAP was very encouraging to the Chancellor and his General, though their satisfaction was tempered by the fact that most of the votes lost by the Nazis appeared to have been gained by the Communists.

[1] The comparative results of the general elections of July 31 and November 6, 1932, were as follows :

	July	November
Total membership of the *Reichstag* (all Parties)	608	584
National Socialists	230	196
Communists	89	100
Social Democrats	133	121
Centre and Bavarian People's Party	97	90
Nationalists	37	52
German People's Party	7	11
Democratic Party	4	2
Other Groups	11	12

The Nazi popular vote fell from 1 ⸱,745,000 in July to 11,700,000 in November.

In the Chancellor's opinion, there were two courses open to the Cabinet; first, to discover whether there was any basis for co-operation with the other political Parties in order to obtain a parliamentary majority in the *Reichstag*, and, secondly, if the first should fail of success, the President must summon Hitler and offer him, as on August 13, the Vice-Chancellorship and the Prussian Ministry of Interior, or insist that he form a Government with a parliamentary majority. This he could only do by making a coalition with the Nationalists and the Centre. If Hitler could, or would, do neither of these things — and von Papen rightly assumed that the *Führer* would not withdraw from his demands for supreme power — then some extraordinary, and, if necessary, unconstitutional, measures must be applied by a new Presidential Government under von Papen, but the important thing was first to confront Hitler with the choice of impossible alternatives.

Von Papen found little difficulty in obtaining the approval of Hindenburg for his programme of action, and it was tacitly understood between them that a new Papen Cabinet would not be long in coming to life. The consent of the Cabinet to the Chancellor's proposals was forthcoming at the first meeting after the elections (November 9), but von Papen was misguided — or over-confident — enough to agree that von Schleicher should undertake secret negotiations with Hitler, parallel to his own official *pourparlers*.[1]

The Chancellor should have known better than to have thus exposed his flank to von Schleicher. That astute warrior had discerned in the weakened position of the Nazis an opportunity to destroy his political opponents of the Right as effectively as he had disposed of those on the Left, and by the same tactics, those of 'divide and conquer'. To him it seemed that the effect of the electoral set-back upon the Party counsels had been to strengthen those elements represented by Gregor Strasser which favoured a temporary truce with the Government and were prepared to enter a Cabinet, provided it were not led by von Papen.[2]

The fine flower of von Schleicher's friendship with Hitler, which had apparently bloomed so luxuriantly at the Fürstenberg Barracks, had withered under the icy blast of Hindenburg's rebuke of August 13. Yet the General had continued to avoid an open breach with the Party — a fact which was not overlooked by Joseph Goebbels:

[1] Schwerin von Krosigk's diary entry for November 13, 1932.

[2] The Nationalist Party was meanwhile hard at work to persuade Hindenburg to retain von Papen as Chancellor and to strengthen the Nationalist character of the Government by substituting Hugenberg for Warmbold, and General Otto von Stülpnagel for von Schleicher (cf. Schwerin von Krosigk's diary entry, November 5, 1932).

'General von Schleicher does his best to avoid burning his bridges. That quite fits into his character'[1] — and he did not yet despair of finding that magic formula which would effect the political miracle that he had so long sought to have performed. But it was slowly dawning upon him that he might have to take a direct hand in the performance; that he, Kurt von Schleicher, who had hitherto never sought office and had been content to work in the dusk behind the throne, might now have to emerge — albeit with genuine reluctance — as *deus ex machinâ*, to the greater glory of Germany and the *Reichswehr*.

The first prerequisite for success was the elimination of von Papen; and who was better skilled in such technique than the 'Cardinal in Politics'? While seeming to fall in with the Chancellor's plan of campaign, he undermined the Chancellor's position within the Cabinet by playing upon the anxieties of his colleagues, among the majority of whom there was no little apprehension as to where their volatile leader was taking them, and also considerable speculation as to whether he knew himself. 'If "Fränzchen" remains Chancellor, we shall have civil war', was the burden of the 'Cardinal's' whispered warnings to his friends.

A few days sufficed to make it crystal clear that no Party in the *Reichstag*, and indeed no responsible statesman in Germany, would support or enter the Papen Government. The Chancellor thereupon resorted to his second course. He and his Cabinet resigned on November 17, in order to facilitate the President's consultations with Party leaders, and thereafter all followed seemingly according to plan. Hitler was summoned by the Marshal and informed that he could either be Vice-Chancellor under von Papen or Chancellor of a Cabinet which could command a parliamentary majority. Perforce the *Führer* rejected both alternatives and, after a fruitless exchange of letters with Meissner, retired baffled to Weimar (November 27). An attempt by the leaders of the Centre Party to form a coalition was equally unsuccessful, and by the close of the month the situation appeared to be exactly that which von Papen had foreseen and desired.

Both he and the General were called to a conference with the President at six o'clock in the evening of December 1, and remained with him for two hours. Von Papen proposed that he should be entrusted with the formation of a second Presidential Cabinet and that the *Reichstag* should be prorogued indefinitely, pending the preparation of a constitutional reform bill which would be submitted to a newly elected national assembly. He also recommended the

[1] Goebbels, p. 139.

dissolution of all political parties, trade unions and industrial and agricultural associations, if necessary, with the help of the *Reichswehr* and the police. These measures, the Chancellor admitted, would constitute a flagrant breach of the Constitution, but he urged that the President might salve his conscience in the matter of his constitutional oath by reason of the extraordinary exigencies of circumstances.

This was the opportunity for the launching of one of the famous 'Schleicher torpedoes'. The General was well aware of Hindenburg's earnest desire to remain faithful, at least in form, to his oath, and he made this the basis of his attack. What von Papen had suggested was indeed a flagrant breach of the Constitution — though it was precisely what von Schleicher had himself urged successive Chancellors to do since 1929, when he had first taken a hand in Cabinet-making. He now advanced a plan which, he claimed, would not only provide a solution for the difficult situation in which they found themselves but would make it unnecessary for the President to violate his pledged word. He was, he said, confident that a Government could be formed, if not by von Papen then by someone else, which could command a parliamentary majority in the *Reichstag* by splitting the National Socialist Party. There were forces within the Party already ripe for revolt, and he suggested that the negotiations with these disgruntled elements should be left in his hands.[1]

This change of front took both the President and von Papen by surprise ; but the nicely timed attack was not immediately successful. Hindenburg, though torn between his anxiety to keep within the terms of the Constitution and his desire to keep his 'Fränzchen' as Chancellor, was shrewd enough to doubt the ability of von Schleicher to make good his promises of success. His confidence in von Papen was still abundant, and it seemed clear to him that if Hitler would not enter a coalition himself he was certainly strong enough within his own Party to prevent any schism such as von Schleicher envisaged. He therefore rejected the General's proposal and confided the task of forming a government to von Papen with instructions to follow the course of action which he had prescribed.[2]

The 'Field-Grey Eminence' was not, however, defeated. He fell back upon that all-powerful argument of the confidence of the

---

[1] In his evidence at Nuremberg, von Papen stated that von Schleicher made a definite offer to form a Government (*Nuremberg Record*, xvi, 259). This assertion was not made in von Papen's testimony under interrogation on September 3, 1945, and is unsupported by any other of the contemporary authorities ; *e.g.* Meissner, Schwerin von Krosigk, *et al.*

[2] Von Papen's evidence (*Nuremberg Record*, xvi, 257-9) ; von Papen's Interrogation ; Meissner's Affidavit.

Army which had removed alike the Kaiser and von Lüttwitz, and
with which he himself had eliminated, each in turn, Gessler, Gröner
and Brüning. He also, at the suggestion of Göring, sent an officer
of his staff as envoy to the *Führer* at Weimar.[1]

On the following morning (December 2) at a meeting of the
interim Cabinet, the Minister of Defence came out into open
opposition. He, who had formerly urged energetic action against
the Nazis — even if this meant using the police and the Army —
now reversed his position and declared himself for an understanding
with Hitler. The reasons he adduced were the refusal of all parties
to support, or even tolerate, a second Papen Cabinet and the fear of
a simultaneous insurrection by the Nazis and the Communists in
the event of von Papen's policy being put into operation. There
was also the additional risk of a general strike being called by
organized labour. The result would undoubtedly be civil war and
the united forces of the *Reichswehr* and the police, untrained in
this type of fighting, would not be equal to quelling a large-scale
revolt on two fronts, even if supported by voluntary civilian formations. The forces of the Reich would be disrupted; they had
already been undermined by propaganda. The outcome of such a
conflict would be at best uncertain, and, in any case, hideous in the
extreme. Moreover, it was scarcely possible that Poland would
ignore so golden an opportunity to make her long-dreaded descent
upon East Prussia.

Von Schleicher assured his colleagues that he did not speak
unadvisedly or without consideration. On his orders the Ministry
of Defence had made a *Kriegsspiel* (war-plan) under the theoretical
conditions foreseen and the officer who had been in charge of this
operation was in waiting to give his report to the Cabinet. The
officer, Colonel Eugen Ott, the Head of the *Wehrmachtabteilung* of
the Ministry, was admitted and corroborated in detail the opinion of
his friend and chief. In the emergency envisaged, the *Reichswehr*
could not guarantee the maintenance of law and order in the country,
nor the inviolability of her frontiers.[2]

[1] Goebbels, pp. 200-201.
[2] Von Papen's evidence (*Nuremberg Record*, xvi, 260-61); von Papen's
Interrogation; Meissner's Affidavit; Schwerin von Krosigk's diary entry for
December 2, 1932. The text of Ott's report to the Cabinet is to be found in an
admirable article by Monsieur G. Castellan in the first issue of *Cahiers d'histoire
de la guerre* (Paris, January 1949), entitled 'Von Schleicher, von Papen, et
l'avènement de Hitler'. On the basis of reports from the French Military Attachés
in Berlin, on letters written by von Papen to M. François-Poncet after the war,
and on correspondence between himself and von Papen's son, M. Castellan has
provided a valuable study of the period in which certain new facts and aspects
appear for the first time. An excellent and detailed report on the crisis is contained

Here was an inglorious confession of weakness. In 1923 von Seeckt had not hesitated to say that the *Reichswehr* 'would stick to him' in suppressing insurrection from whatever source it might come. Nine years later — nine years in which the dominant force in the Army had been Kurt von Schleicher — this was no longer true. In 1932 the *Reichswehr* which von Seeckt, and after him Gröner, had sought so diligently to keep free from the canker of politics, had become so infected with this corrosive blight, that it was forced to admit its own impotence to meet armed revolt within the Reich, or, rather, its unwillingness to fire on the youth of Germany as represented by the SA.

If this were true, the major portion of the responsibility lay with Kurt von Schleicher, who by his intrigues and machinations, his underminings of the authority of his superiors and his coquetting with the Nazi leaders and with the Storm Troops, had plunged the Army into the muck-heap of politics. But was it true ? At least once before, in the previous May, von Schleicher had deliberately misled his fellow-generals into withdrawing their confidence from Gröner, their civilian chief. The heads of the *Reichswehr* — von Hammerstein, the Commander-in-Chief; Adam, Head of the *Truppenamt* ; von Bredow, who had succeeded von Schleicher in the *Ministeramt* ; and Ott himself — were blindly devoted to him, and his influence was no less strong with the district commanders in December 1932 than it had been in May. Had they listened once again unquestioningly to his seductive arguments ? And were they not almost the same arguments ? [1]

Certainly von Schleicher's objective was the same in both instances — the withdrawal of the confidence of the Army from the individual whom at the moment he wished to eliminate from the political scene — and certainly he was as successful in the case of von Papen as he had been in that of Gröner. Appalled at the situation which the Defence Minister depicted, the Cabinet voted to a man against the adoption of von Papen's policy, and in favour of von Schleicher's thesis of 'divide and conquer'; and among a majority of them the view was held that, for better or for worse, the General must himself assume the office of Chancellor.

Faced with a situation in which both the Army and his own Cabinet colleagues had declared their lack of confidence in von

in the despatch of the British Ambassador, Sir Horace Rumbold, dated December 7, 1932 (Woodward and Butler, Second Series, iv, 92-9).
[1] See above, p. 241. It should also be remembered that it was Ott who, as Head of the *Wehrmachtabteilung*, had produced the evidence upon the basis of which Hindenburg had ordered Gröner to suppress the *Reichsbanner*.

Papen, Hindenburg was forced to resign himself to the loss of his 'Fränzchen'. By the evening Kurt von Schleicher had been appointed Chancellor — the only General to hold that office except von Caprivi.[1] But his duplicity was neither forgiven nor forgotten by the President or by von Papen, to whom Hindenburg sent his photograph inscribed : '*Ich hatt' einen Kameraden*'.

(viii)

The Reich Government which took office on December 2, 1932, marked the apogee of power of the Army — and of Kurt von Schleicher — in German politics. In influence the Army had undoubtedly been stronger under von Seeckt, who had established and maintained it as the detached and final arbiter of fate within the Reich. This influence, however, had been only oblique and indirect — and for that very reason it had been all the stronger — but in December 1932 the Army and the military caste had the highest offices of State concentrated in their hands.

At the head stood the Field-Marshal, President of the Reich and Supreme Commander, to whom the armed forces of the State were unswerving in their loyalty and veneration. Beneath him was General von Schleicher, who, as Chancellor, directed the policy of State, as Reich Commissioner for Prussia controlled the largest police force in Germany, and, as Minister of Defence, enjoyed the personal friendship and devotion of the chiefs of the *Reichswehr*. For the first time since the Seeckt Period the Army stood squarely and truly behind the Chancellor. No longer were the Wilhelmstrasse and the Bendlerstrasse pursuing rival and conflicting policies ; no longer was the Chancellor in constant danger of the fell sentence that he 'no longer enjoyed the confidence of the Army'. In December 1932 those who a dozen years before had been von Seeckt's 'young men' — von Schleicher, von Hammerstein, Adam, Ott, von Bock and von Bredow — were in the saddle ; the reins of power were in their hands. And yet, from this same moment, when the Army leadership seemed to be adorned with all the trappings of political, as well as military, authority, there began that decline and fall, that infirmity of purpose and lack of decision, that final descent into Avernus, where military reputations would be made and destroyed at the whim of the 'Bohemian Corporal', and a German Field-Marshal was destined for slow strangulation upon a meat-hook.

---

[1] General Count Georg Leo von Caprivi de Caprara de Montecuccoli (1831–99) was appointed Imperial Chancellor by Wilhelm II on Bismarck's dismissal in 1890. He continued in office, without notable achievement, until 1894, when he was succeeded by Prince Hohenlohe-Schillingsfürst.

For all the seeming strength of its position the Schleicher Cabinet was one of the weakest and most inept, and also the briefest in duration, which ever took office under the Weimar Republic, and not least because of the personality of its Chancellor.

To do him justice, Kurt von Schleicher had not sought this position. His intrigues had never at any time been directed towards personal advancement to the seats of the mighty. His ambition was for power without responsibility and he was shrewd enough to know well that the source and control of power lies more often behind the throne than upon it. Twice before, Brüning had urged him to become Minister of Defence — once in October 1931 when Gröner had become Minister of Interior and again in May 1932 after Gröner's fall — and each time von Schleicher had refused. It was only with great reluctance and in response to a direct order from the Marshal that he had accepted this position in the Papen Cabinet. Nor had he designs upon the Chancellorship, preferring to put forward others whom he thought he could influence and manipulate.[1]

But in December 1932 these days of crepuscular security were ended. The friends and enemies of Kurt von Schleicher combined with fate to thrust him forward slowly but surely, forward and upward, step by step, to the giddy and lonely pinnacle of responsible power, where he was to experience that solitariness and frustration, that ultimate defeat by intrigue, which he had forced so many others to endure.

Brüning, whom von Schleicher, with a certain shamelessness, did not hesitate to consult through an intermediary after the November elections, returned the advice that the General could no longer continue to act as *régisseur* behind the scenes but must now take the leading rôle himself.[2] The German Crown Prince gave him similar counsel but warned him not to place his trust in Hindenburg.[3] After the famous Cabinet meeting of December 2, at which the fate of the Papen Cabinet was sealed, friend and foe alike among his colleagues, though from different motives, assured the General that he, and he only, could be the next Chancellor.[4]

Von Schleicher struggled ineffectively against his fate. He recommended Schacht to the President as a successor to von Papen,

---

[1]. 'What is one to make of a man who will not become Chancellor?' Gröner wrote in bewilderment to von Gleich on May 22, 1932 (quoted by Craig, p. 227). According to von Hammerstein, von Schleicher told Arthur Zarden, the State Secretary of the Reich Finance Ministry, on December 1, 1932, that he did not desire the Chancellorship for himself but that he had an eye to the Presidency of the Reich later on (*Hammerstein Memorandum*).

[2] Brüning, *Ein Brief*, p. 14.   [3] *Hammerstein Memorandum*.

[4] Schwerin von Krosigk's diary entry for December 4, 1932.

K

and, when this suggestion was refused, looked for others who might serve in place of himself. 'I am the last horse in your stable and would rather be kept dark', he told the President ; but Hindenburg was as relentless as the others. He caught the General by his sword-knot of honour and, with a mixture of senile pathos and military peremptoriness, compelled him to take office.[1]

And now the General himself experienced those torments which he had so often inflicted upon others : insecurity of high office, the wavering loyalty of the President, the machination of the Palace *camarilla*, for Oskar, Meissner and von Papen were all against him. Too late he realized that in the seat of supreme authority he was far more isolated than in that little room in the Bendlerstrasse overlooking the Landwehr Canal, which had been the scene of his early intrigues and triumphs. The rats knew how near his ship was to sinking. His agents deserted him ; the marionettes no longer responded to his touch. Though he was in control of all the armed forces of the State, he found that they could avail him nothing, and his mentality, attuned to intrigue rather than leadership, was barren of constructive statesmanship. In his political armoury he had but one weapon, that of attempting to divide the Parties by intrigue from within. He had used it unsuccessfully in the case of the Nationalists in 1929, when he had persuaded Westarp and Treviranus to secede from Hugenberg, and successfully three years later, when at the time of the Rape of Prussia, he had divided the Trade Unions from the SPD. It was this weapon which he was now to employ against the Nazis.

The essential weakness of von Schleicher's position was that he had pledged himself to find a parliamentary majority in the *Reichstag*, ranging from the moderate Nazis on the Right to the moderate Social Democrats on the Left, and though, after his official installation as Chancellor, he told von Hammerstein that the President had promised him authority to dissolve parliament in case he failed in this effort,[2] it is extremely doubtful whether this was true. Von Schleicher either deluded himself into the belief that this promise had been made to him or else he deliberately invented it in order to bolster up his position.

Two factors alone were in the Chancellor's favour : the trough of ill-fortune in which the Nazis were wallowing, and the keen desire of all political Parties to avoid further repetition of the general elections which had already convulsed the country four times in less

---

[1] *Hammerstein Memorandum.*
[2] *Ibid.* See also Hermann Foertsch, *Schuld und Verhängnis* (Stuttgart 1951), pp. 24 *et seq.*

than a year,[1] and from which, it was generally realized, the Communists alone stood to gain. Indeed it was to this disinclination for further elections that the Schleicher Government owed the brief span of existence that it achieved ; for, by common consent, it was agreed that the Chancellor should not meet the *Reichstag* until after the Christmas recess which ended on January 31, 1933.

Von Schleicher at once began his manœuvres to split the Nazi Party. On December 3 he offered Gregor Strasser the Vice-Chancellorship and the Premiership of Prussia, adding the threat that, if the Nazis refused him their support when the *Reichstag* reconvened in February, he would unhesitatingly seek a dissolution. Strasser wavered. In the Party conclaves he urged a policy of toleration to the new Government, indicating that if this was not forthcoming he would create a schism in the Party by submitting his own list of candidates at the next election. There followed, on December 6, the election in Thuringia in which the Nazis lost 40 per cent of the popular vote they had gained in July. Strasser, thinking that he read correctly the writing on the wall, raised the standard of revolt, resigned all his Party offices and pressed forward his negotiations with von Schleicher.

But he had reckoned without the demonic dynamism of the *Führer*. Hitler met the revolt with drastic action. He rallied the Party leadership about him with a threat of suicide, and in twenty-four hours had smashed the powerful political machine in Berlin which Strasser had for so long ruled with semi-independence. By December 9 Strasser had been completely isolated and stripped of power.[2] The Chancellor found himself negotiating with a political corpse. The Schleicher Torpedo, launched in the hope of disrupting the Nazi Party, had fatally misfired, and the name of Gregor Strasser was added to the list of those, among whom were many of von Schleicher's former associates, who were destined for murder.

But Hitler did not remain on the defensive. Though the fortunes of the Nazi Party were at their lowest ebb, so that there not only occurred schisms in the hierarchy but actual mutiny in the ranks of the *Führer's* own bodyguard, Hitler never wavered in his confidence that success, though withheld from him for the moment, was in reality only 'just around the corner', and this belief not only accounted for his intransigence of attitude towards the government but also coloured all his political manœuvrings of the time.

---

[1] The two presidential ballots in March and April, and the *Reichstag* elections of July and November. In addition the general election in Prussia had involved nearly a third of the Reich and other elections had taken place in smaller states.

[2] Goebbels, pp. 203-9.

To von Schleicher's threat to dissolve the *Reichstag*, Hitler replied by making the initial moves in a project which he had been maturing ever since his rebuff at the hands of Hindenburg on August 13 ; a project which had for its objective no less than the impeachment and removal from office of the President of the Reich on a charge of the unconstitutional use of Article 48 of the Constitution. The motion for impeachment required, under Article 59 of the Constitution, a vote of 100 members of the *Reichstag*, and the Nazis held 196 seats. The removal of the President from office, however, required a two-thirds majority of the *Reichstag* (Article 43), but Hitler was confident of obtaining these requisite 290 votes, for, in addition to his own 196, he could safely count on the co-operation of the 100 Communists on an issue of this kind, and even on the support of a section of the 121 Social Democrats, who thirsted to revenge the Rape of Prussia.[1]

There was, however, one preliminary obstacle to be removed. Under Article 51 of the Constitution, in the event of a vacancy in the Presidency, whether occasioned by death or other causes, the functions of the Chief of State devolved temporarily upon the Chancellor until a successor had been elected. It was no part of Hitler's planning to replace Hindenburg by von Schleicher, and, to obviate such an eventuality, the *Führer* caused the Nazi Party to introduce legislation substituting the President of the Supreme Court for the Chancellor. The Bill became law on December 9, being passed by 404 votes to 127. Hitler had thus made a display of force to cover the actual weakness of his position, and was now free to use his threat of impeachment as a weapon of blackmail in any future negotiation with the President or with the Government.

Thus, within ten days of von Schleicher's appointment as Chancellor, the whole basis on which he had taken office had dropped to pieces. By December 10 it was clear that he could neither divide the Nazi Party nor secure their toleration or support. The Centre would have none of him, and his subsequent negotiations with the Left were to prove equally abortive. The net of failure was closing about the General's feet, but he could not, or would not, recognize it. A fantastic and fatal optimism, whether real or assumed, seemed to permeate his thought and action, and he even succeeded in transmitting it to the President. For, deceived by the false tranquillity of the Christmas vacation, the Old Gentleman greeted his Chancellor on the morning of December 25 with the words : 'Christmas was never so peaceful before. I have to thank you for that, my young friend.'[2]

---

[1] Brüning, *Ein Brief*, pp. 13-14.   [2] *Hammerstein Memorandum.*

No lull before the breaking of a cyclone could have been more deceptive, for the atmosphere of Berlin at the close of 1932 was heavy and fetid with intrigue, and the President could not have been entirely ignorant of what was afoot. Franz von Papen was laying the first stones upon which the Third Reich was to be built. A curious freak of fate assisted him. Repairs in the President's Palace in the Wilhelmstrasse had been begun under von Papen's Chancellorship and he had temporarily placed his apartment in the *Reichskanzlei* at the disposal of the President and his son, while he himself moved a few houses down to the vacant lodgings of the Prussian Minister of Interior, where, by special permission of the President, he was allowed to remain after his resignation. Von Schleicher lived in the official residence of the Minister of Defence in the Bendlerstrasse, whence he transacted most of the business of government. He was thus separated from the President by about half a mile, whereas von Papen could walk through the gardens of the Wilhelmstrasse in a matter of minutes. It was a walk he often took, for the President and Oskar loved their 'Fränzchen' and, even after he had ceased to be Chancellor, they welcomed his gay and frivolous incursions into the deplorably dreary atmosphere of their Prussian household. Von Papen took full advantage of his opportunities and saw to it that certain items of political importance were intermixed with his gaiety.

His colossal vanity and the itch of ambition, which had been greatly excited during his six months as Chancellor, made his continued absence from the public eye intolerable, and there was also a lust to revenge himself upon von Schleicher.[1] Moreover, he now confidently believed, as did many others, that the political and financial fortunes of the NSDAP were so low as to preclude the possibility of complete recovery. Bankrupt the Nazi Party was, in every sense of the word, at the beginning of 1933. Funds they must have; if von Papen could provide these, he would be entitled to do so on his own terms. Thus at one stroke von Schleicher would be eliminated and Hitler brought into camp as the captive of the Right.

On December 10, therefore — the day after the 'dragooning' of Strasser and the failure of von Schleicher to divide the Nazi Party — von Papen made his first advances for a meeting with Hitler. They were made to the great Cologne banker, Freiherr von Schröder, through the good offices of Freiherr von Lersner, that German

---

[1] 'Herr von Papen had developed an intense hatred of General von Schleicher, whom he planned to eliminate as Chancellor of the Reich', writes Fritz Thyssen of this period (*I Paid Hitler*, p. 109).

diplomat who, in February 1920, had refused to transmit to Berlin the Allied Note demanding the surrender for trial of the first list War Criminals.[1] Von Schröder had already been approached by Wilhelm Keppler [2] with a similar request on the part of Hitler.[3]

The historic meeting took place at von Schröder's home at Cologne on January 4, 1933. Hitler was accompanied by Hess, Himmler and Keppler, but the vital discussions, which began at 11.30 and lasted for two hours, were carried on à deux, in the presence of von Schröder as a silent witness.

What was actually said at this meeting is the subject of lively controversy between the two surviving participants. According to von Schröder, von Papen proposed a concentration of all the forces of the Right, the Nazis, the Nationalists and the Stahlhelm in one Cabinet to be headed co-equally by Hitler and himself. Hitler countered with the claim for the Chancellorship for himself, but conceded that von Papen's friends could enter the Government as ministers provided they accepted his, Hitler's policy, and agreed to the necessary changes which he intended to make. Among these changes he included the elimination of all Social Democrats, Jews and Communists from leading positions in public life and the restoration of law and order. 'Von Papen and Hitler reached an agreement in principle so that many of the points which had brought them into conflict could be eliminated and they could find a way to get together.' [4]

Though the meeting was intended to be kept secret, the fact that it had occurred became common property almost immediately and the version of what had been said tallied in all essential respects with that of von Schröder. Yet von Papen had the effrontery to maintain, under cross-examination at Nuremberg by Sir David Maxwell Fyfe, that all he had urged Hitler to do on this occasion

[1] See above, p. 70, footnote 2.

[2] Wilhelm Keppler (born 1882) was an industrialist and an early member of the NSDAP, in which he served as Hitler's chief economic adviser. He was appointed Commissioner for Economic Affairs in the Reich Chancellery in July 1933, and personal adviser to Göring on the Four-Year Plan in 1936. Through personal contacts with Seyss-Inquart he prepared the way for the Anschluss of Austria and was Reich Commissioner in Vienna from March to June 1938. From 1938 to 1945 he served as a State Secretary for special duties in the Ministry of Foreign Affairs. Indicted as a War Criminal in the 'Ministries Trial' in November 1947, Keppler was, on April 14, 1949, sentenced to ten years' imprisonment.

[3] Affidavit sworn by von Schröder at Nuremberg, December 5, 1945 ; affidavit sworn by Keppler at Nuremberg, November 26, 1945. Von Papen, under cross-examination at Nuremberg on June 18, 1946, denied that he had made the first advances for the meeting with Hitler, stating that these had come from Hitler himself (Nuremberg Record, xvi, 345).

[4] Von Schröder's Affidavit.

was to enter the Cabinet of General von Schleicher.[1] This may well have been what he told to the Chancellor at their meeting on January 9, after which an amicable *communiqué* was issued,[2] but the vehemence of the denials which both Hitler and von Papen issued at the time that their conversation had been in any way directed against the von Schleicher Government,[3] are eloquent only of the fact that that which had been said at a supposedly secret meeting had unaccountably become known, and are reminiscent of Bismarck's celebrated remark that 'no story is worth believing until it has been officially denied'.

An equally important result of the Cologne meeting was the material change in the financial fortunes of the Nazi Party. Bankrupt in December 1932, the NSDAP by the middle of January 1933 was once again in the Big Money by reason of the fact that Rhenish-Westphalian industrial magnates had assumed responsibility for the Party deficit. These leaders of West German finance and industry had petitioned Hindenburg after the November elections to appoint Hitler Chancellor of a Nazi-Nationalist coalition, 'because not only the Black-White-Red Party and its related groups, but the NSDAP as well, are fundamentally opposed to the former parliamentary party régime', and that by 'entrusting the leader of the largest national group with the responsible leadership of a Presidential Cabinet which contains the best technical and personal forces in the country, the blemishes and errors which afflict any mass movement will be perforce eliminated'.[4]

In the November of 1932 these views of Big Business and Heavy Industry had been the complete antithesis of Chancellor von Papen's, and he had sharply rebuked the signers of the letter for their heresy. Now, in January 1933, the would-be Chancellor von Papen had himself lapsed from orthodoxy and was espousing the very heresy which he had previously anathematized. In return for certain 'promises to pay' on the part of Hitler, as, if and when he came to power, the Rhenish-Westphalian magnates were persuaded. to shoulder the burden of the Party's debts and to put the NSDAP back into the political arena as a fighting force.[5] Without the

---

[1] *Nuremberg Record*, xvi, 349.

[2] *Kölnische Volkszeitung und Handelsblatt*, January 10, 1933.

[3] *NSDAP Korrespondenz*, January 6, 1933.

[4] *IMT Document*, PS-3901. The thirty-eight signers of this letter included Schacht, Thyssen, Krupp, Siemens, Bosch; Springorum, the Steel King; the former Chancellor Cuno, the heads of the Hamburg-Amerika and North German-Lloyd Shipping Lines, and Freiherr von Schröder.

[5] Hitler, on coming to power, was meticulous in fulfilling his promises, which included the elimination of the Communists, the abolition of trade unions, no nationalization of industry and rearmament on a grand scale. 'Heavy industry

formidable assistance of the industrialists, the Nazi Party would have foundered on the rocks of bankruptcy. Herr von Papen has always steadfastly denied that he was in any way responsible for the negotiation of this arrangement between the industrialists and the Party — though there are many who believe to the contrary. The fact, however, remains that the miraculous salvation of the NSDAP from financial ruin dates from the second week in January 1933 ; that is to say, immediately after the Cologne meeting.

Meantime, in Berlin, von Schleicher continued in the fatal myopic optimism, and the fantastic political ineptitude, which characterized his whole chancellorship. With inexplicable political necrophilia, he resumed negotiations with Gregor Strasser, whom he actually persuaded Hindenburg to receive on January 4, the very day of the Cologne Meeting. He also made advances towards the Left. In his 'fireside chat' to the German people on December 15 he had assumed a certain detachment towards both capital and labour. 'For me', he had said, 'concepts such as private economy or planned economy have lost their terrors.' But having nothing original to contribute he had fallen back upon one of Brüning's most unpopular projects, and had come out strongly in favour of the land settlement of the peasants, promising them eight hundred thousand acres from the bankrupt estates in the eastern areas of the Reich.

This statement had merely had the effect of antagonizing the Right. It had certainly not deceived the Left. Now, when the Chancellor invited the Trade Unionist leader Theodor Leipart to discuss with him the collaboration of organized labour, hoping once more to divide the Trade Unions from the SPD, he found that the Left had learned its lesson. Organized labour was no longer deceived by the General's blandishments as it had been at the time of the Rape of Prussia. Leipart consulted the Social Democratic leaders and with them concerted an attitude of intransigent opposition to the Government (January 6).[1]

The reaction of the Right was even more devastating. Nicely timed to follow the announcement of the Hitler-Papen meeting at Cologne, the *Landbund* (the Agrarian Association) launched a direct attack upon the Government on January 12, and its President, Count von Kalkreuth, called in person upon Hindenburg to protest against the Chancellor's projected confiscation of a part of the bankrupt estates in Eastern Germany and the settling on them of

simply followed the man who promised the extra farthing per ton of iron', was the succinct comment of State Secretary Zarden.

[1] Gustav Noske, *Erlebtes aus Aufstieg und Niedergang einer Demokratie*, p. 311 ; Braun, pp. 435-9 ; Stampfer, p. 611.

peasant farmers. Here was a strange irony, since this same bogy of *Agrarbolschewismus* had been among the arguments which von Schleicher had himself employed six months earlier to undermine the position of Brüning with the President.

Thus, having failed to divide the Nazis or to woo the support of the Trade Unions, von Schleicher had now added to the ranks of his political opponents the powerful *Landbund*, whose influence with Hindenburg was the more puissant since, by the national gift of the manor of Neudeck, he had been made, in every sense, 'one of them'.

The Chancellor's reply to the challenge of the landlords was one which displayed more courage than sagacity. His answer to the Junkers was a threat to publish the report of the *Reichstag* enquiry into the *Osthilfe* loans of 1927–8, with which the great estates of East Prussia had been kept alive. The investigation had disclosed scandals of which the stench reeked to high heaven and of which the mud splashed even to the steps of the President's Palace.[1] Here indeed was a Pandora's box which, when opened, poured forth a flood of loathsome crawling things. There stood disclosed the example of a landowner, bankrupt through his own ineptitude, whose estates had been 'reconstructed' three times, and, after a fourth breakdown, had been ceded, under the *Osthilfe*, to a daughter who was still a minor. There were absentee landlords also, who, with the money loaned them by the Government to reconstruct their estates, had bought motor-cars and levanted to the Riviera, leaving banks and tradesmen, who had trustfully given them credit, to whistle for their money. There were also those, in the inexorable report of the Government investigation, who had squandered public relief funds on 'wine and women', and had yet received further grants in aid because their names had been for centuries coupled with their estates. The scandals affected not only the average landowner, but struck at the titled leaders of the *Landbund*; none was spared.[2]

By the threat of these disclosures von Schleicher hoped to cow the Junkers and bring them to heel. Utilizing the only weapon of which he was possessed, that of 'divide and conquer', he thought

---

[1] When in 1927 the family estate of Neudeck had been bought by national subscription and presented to Hindenburg on his eightieth birthday, the title deeds had been made out in Oskar's name in order to evade the payment of death duties. This illegality was customary among Junker families at this time, but, though it had no direct connection with the *Osthilfe* scandal, Oldenburg-Januschau at once warned Oskar that von Schleicher would certainly publish the affairs of the tax evasion along with the *Osthilfe* Report.

[2] Wheeler-Bennett, pp. 423-4.

to split the forces of the Right by pitting the Nazis against the Nationalists, since he was certain of National Socialist support on an issue which would undoubtedly be popular with the masses. The General had never realized the truth of Lassalle's dictum that it might cost a man his head to be too clever in great affairs. He could not see that he was sawing off the branch on which he was sitting. At one stroke he had destroyed the union of two forces from which he might have secured support. For two hundred years the Officer Corps and the Junkers had been inseparably united by a bond of common interest. Von Schleicher had broken that bond. In entering upon his battle with the *Landbund* he had underestimated the strength of the political and economic vested interests which he was attacking, and he was too superficial to sense the power of a tradition which for hundreds of years had centred in one caste.

Thus, while representatives of the thirteen thousand Junker families thronged the ante-rooms of the President and clamoured for the Chancellor's dismissal, while every indication from the provinces showed that the decline of Nazi fortunes had ceased and that they were once again in the ascendant, von Schleicher remained urbanely and obstinately optimistic. At the many social functions which he still found time to attend, he professed the utmost confidence in the security of his position, saying that Hindenburg had promised him full support and von Papen had pledged himself not to intrigue further against the Government. And it appears that he really believed what he was saying. Herr Hitler was no longer a problem, he assured Kurt von Schuschnigg, when the future Austrian Chancellor called upon him in Berlin; the Nazi movement had ceased to be a political danger, the whole problem had been solved, it was a thing of the past.[1] This remarkable assurance was given on January 15, on which day in the elections in Lippe the Nazis gained 20 per cent on the November poll. Both participants in the conversation later learned, to their cost, the falsity of the Chancellor's judgment.

But even von Schleicher's bland imperturbability was to some degree shaken when on January 20, the Nationalist Party, in an open declaration of war, withdrew its support from the Government. The General had now successfully alienated the respect and confidence of every Party in the *Reichstag*, from the extreme Right to the extreme Left. No vestige of hope remained — if indeed a hope had ever existed — for even the remote chance of fulfilment of that mandate with which von Schleicher had been entrusted by Hindenburg little more than six weeks ago — the forming of a Government

[1] Kurt von Schuschnigg, *Farewell Austria* (London, 1938), pp. 165-6.

with a parliamentary majority. He who had promised that he would either reach an agreement with Hitler or split the Nazi Party, had signally failed to do either. He had made himself the bugbear of every political group in the *Reichstag*, and his statement on January 20 that he no longer attached any importance to a parliamentary majority was but a recognition of a situation which had existed for some time.

What then should be the next step of this 'military Cardinal in Politics'? At this moment there arrived in the Bendlerstrasse the self-appointed agent of the Crown Prince Rupprecht, Freiherr zu Guttenberg, who sought to induce the Chancellor to countenance a royalist *coup d'état* in Bavaria in order to forestall the Nazis' rise to power. But even von Schleicher's proclivity for intrigue was proof against this folly. A monarchist *Putsch* in Munich might well be the signal for that simultaneous rising from the Left and Right with which, he had assured his Cabinet colleagues on December 2, the armed forces of the Reich were not strong enough to contend. The disappointed envoy of the Wittelsbachs returned empty-handed.[1]

Von Schleicher now asked counsel of the German Crown Prince, who advised him either to establish a military dictatorship or, as a very generous gesture, to hand over the Government to Hitler. Above all, he urged his friend Kurt not to trust in the word of Hindenburg.[2]

The position was now precisely the same as it had been on December 2, save for two important factors : the political fortunes of the Nazis had appreciably improved and the rôles of von Papen and von Schleicher had become completely reversed. At that time von Papen had urged strong measures to meet the emergency and von Schleicher had opposed him ; now the General was himself ready to fight the Nazis and he came to Hindenburg with the identical policy which von Papen had advocated in December ; the indefinite suspension of the *Reichstag* and the establishment of a military dictatorship under Article 48.

But the President was not prepared to give to the General the powers which he had been willing to give to his predecessor. Old, tired, and bewildered, he had reverted to his rigid adherence to his constitutional oath. Moreover, he was weary of this constant change of front on the part of the volatile General, and he had a strong desire to have 'Fränzchen' back in the Chancellery. He therefore received von Schleicher coldly, refused him the decree of dissolution

---

[1] For his share in this curious incident the name of Georg Enoch Freiherr zu Guttenberg figured in the list of those arrested on June 30, 1934. By good fortune he escaped with his life.   [2] *Hammerstein Memorandum.*

and ordered him back to his hopeless task of finding a parliamentary majority.[1]

This was the moment for which Franz von Papen had been waiting. Von Schleicher was now politically a dead man and it only remained to bury him. Von Papen's walks through the snowy gardens behind the Wilhelmstrasse to the temporary Presidential quarters in the *Reichskanzlei* became more frequent and the gay frivolity of his conversation was carefully interlarded with shrewd insinuations and denigration of his rival. Now for the first time he informed Hindenburg of the purport of his meeting with Hitler at Cologne, hinting at the possibility of a grand concentration of conservative forces, which, though possibly headed by the *Führer* as Chancellor, would be directed in all essentials of policy by himself.

Yet this was not the only solution evolved by von Papen's mercurial mentality. He was also toying with the idea of resuming the Chancellorship himself in an alliance with Hugenberg and the Nationalists. Such a Cabinet would have no backing in the country or in the *Reichstag*, but he was fully prepared to send this body packing and he was very confident that the President would not refuse *him* the decree of dissolution if he asked for it. Such a solution, moreover, would certainly be more acceptable to Hindenburg, who was still averse to having Hitler as Chancellor, and to Oskar, who, having quarrelled with his old comrade-in-arms, von Schleicher, had consistently urged his father to reappoint von Papen.

With that uncanny psychological insight which Hitler so frequently displayed in personal relations, he struck unerringly at the weakest link. On January 22 he invited Oskar to meet him at the home of Ribbentrop in the fashionable Berlin suburb of Dahlem.[2] Oskar took Meissner with him and on arrival found a large company assembled, among whom were Göring and Frick. Somewhat to Meissner's surprise — for Oskar had made a special point of his being present at any conversation with Hitler — the *Führer* and the President's son disappeared into a smaller room, where they remained closeted for about an hour.

Of what passed between them 'under four eyes' no record exists, but it is not difficult to imagine the arguments which Hitler would have adduced. In fine, they most probably were these: If Hitler

---

[1] Meissner Affidavit.

[2] In his entry in the 1935 edition of *Wer Ist's* (the German *Who's Who*) Ribbentrop claims that 'Through his intermediation . . . at this time . . . the Hitler Government was formed ; the decisive meetings took place in his [Ribbentrop's] Berlin-Dahlem house'.

were not made Chancellor with full powers, the Nazis would proceed
with their threat of impeachment of the President and would disclose
the scandal of his son's tax evasion in respect of the Neudeck estate.
If, on the other hand, Oskar would use his influence with his father
in Hitler's interests, the *Führer* would loyally support the Marshal
as Chief of State, Oskar would receive military promotion and, in
addition, the Neudeck estate might well benefit.

This is, of course, essentially surmise, but, whatever the burden
of the conversation had been, Oskar was very silent as they drove
back to the Wilhelmstrasse. He made only one remark. 'It cannot
be helped', he said, sighing heavily, 'the Nazis must be taken into
the government.' [1]

In this last week of January 1933 the political world of Berlin
hummed like an overturned hive. Rumours, often fantastic and
contradictory, followed one another thick and fast. In the house of
the President, in Ribbentrop's luxurious Dahlem villa, in the headquarters of the *Landbund*, in the premises of the *Herrenklub*, and
in the Hotel Kaiserhof, the leaders of the Nazis and the Nationalists
met, sometimes together, sometimes severally, in a series of complicated conspiracies and cabals, which, though often antagonistic
in design, had at least one *leitmotif* in common, the elimination of
Kurt von Schleicher.

Alone and isolated, the Chancellor in these days rarely left the
Bendlerstrasse, where in the consoling company of his fellow-
generals, he awaited the final stroke of fate. He was disillusioned
now. His confidence, his optimism and his bland self-assurance
had deserted him. Since his interview with the President on the
20th he had known that the dismissal of his Cabinet could be but a
matter of days and he was now chiefly concerned as to what should
follow him.

Both he and von Hammerstein were now agreed that the appointment of a Papen-Hugenberg Cabinet would almost inevitably result
in a civil war, in which the sympathies of the *Reichswehr* would
certainly not be with the Government of Herr von Papen. It would
be opposed by over 90 per cent of the German people, and the
opportunity for a Nazi-Communist revolt would be irresistible. A
week earlier von Schleicher had asked for the establishment of a
military dictatorship which would, on his own showing in December,

---

[1] Meissner Affidavit. It is a matter of record that in August 1933, seven
months after Hitler had become Chancellor, a further 5,000 acres were added,
tax free, to the Neudeck estate and that a year later, when Hitler became Supreme
Commander of the *Wehrmacht* on the death of the Marshal, Oskar von Hindenburg
was promoted to the rank of Major-General.

have had precisely the same effect, but now, with the prospect of the return of his Nationalist enemies to power, he had veered round to a preference for what he conceived to be the lesser of two evils, Adolf Hitler.

After consultation with Meissner, it was agreed that von Hammerstein should put the views of the *Heeresleitung* before Hindenburg. The Marshal received him on January 26 and it was soon apparent that he deeply resented this incursion of the *Reichswehr* into what he regarded as a purely political matter. If he had been cold to von Schleicher, he was glacial to von Hammerstein, refusing at first to discuss the political situation at all, merely criticizing the General's leadership at the recent manœuvres, and recommending him to study the directions which Waldersee had issued forty years before.[1] At parting, however, the Marshal gave vent to an irritable remark which showed that he remained unconverted. 'I have no intention whatever', he said, 'of making that Austrian Corporal either Minister of Defence or Chancellor of the Reich.'[2] His worst fears confirmed, von Schleicher met his Cabinet on the morning of the 28th, and a unanimous decision was taken to resign if the decree for the dissolution were not forthcoming.

Von Schleicher went to the President. How often had he stood in that gigantic presence and destroyed by his wiles, his cajolery and his specious arguments the confidence of Hindenburg in other Chancellors ? Did not the shades of his former victims pass between him and the Marshal, like the procession of the kings in Macbeth — von Seeckt and Gessler, Müller, Gröner and Brüning, and lastly von Papen, with his vulpine grin of a silver fox ? Now his own turn had come, and though he strove with all the eloquence at his command to warn the President against handing over the Chancellorship to von Papen, it was as if he had spoken to a stone wall. The Marshal would not listen to him and merely ground out a short set speech, which he had clearly learned by heart, accepting the resignation. At the close he relented for a moment. 'I have already one foot in the grave, and I am not sure that I shall not regret this action in Heaven later on', he said. 'After this breach of trust, Sir, I am not sure that you will go to Heaven', was von Schleicher's rejoinder.[3]

The reactions of the General's former victims to von Schleicher's fall were characteristic of the men themselves. One of his first

---

[1] Schwerin von Krosigk's diary entry for February 5, 1933.
[2] *Hammerstein Memorandum.*
[3] *Ibid.* 'Haven't I always told you that you can rely absolutely on the Old Gentleman's proverbial faithlessness ?' the German Crown Prince wrote to the fallen General.

messages of condolence was from Brüning.[1] Gröner expressed himself ready for a reconciliation. Von Seeckt remained bitterly triumphant. 'I am personally pleased at the dismissal of the Reich Chancellor,' he wrote to his wife, 'which I consider to be a sign of a certain inherent justice.'[2]

(ix)

'I shall not allow myself to be plucked to pieces', was von Schleicher's comment to von Hammerstein on his return at noon to the Bendlerstrasse from his visit of resignation to the President.[3] He was fuming with anger and humiliation over the circumstance of his final interview and referred with persistent bitterness to 'the gratitude of the House of Hindenburg'. There is no bitterness like to that of the intriguer who is at length caught in the toils of his own intrigues.

To the Generals it seemed that now, if ever, it was the duty of the *Reichswehr* to protect Germany against the planning of her rulers. The Army had always regarded itself as the ultimate source of power and security within the Reich. Now was the time to prove this, even at the risk of seeming disloyalty. Both von Schleicher and von Hammerstein were convinced also, after their recent interviews, that the old Marshal was no longer in possession of his mental powers. God alone knew into what paths of folly he might be guided now that Franz von Papen was back at his elbow.

The political scene was hopelessly obscured. On January 26 von Papen was still hesitating between a 'great solution' of a Hitler-Papen-Hugenberg coalition and a 'small solution' of a Papen-Hugenberg Cabinet. On that day Hindenburg had assured von Hammerstein that he would never make 'the Austrian Corporal' Chancellor of the Reich, and on January 27 the Nazi leaders themselves believed that the 'small solution' was the more likely, but that von Papen would be quickly overthrown.[4] On the 28th, the day on which the Schleicher Cabinet had resigned, von Papen was still hesitant. Conflicting desires to be Chancellor himself or to bring Hitler into a grand alliance as a junior partner, were battling

---

[1] Schwerin von Krosigk's diary entry for February 5, 1933. To do von Schleicher justice, it is only fair to recall that, immediately after his own fall from power, he sought out Brüning on his sick-bed in the St. Hedwig's hospital and there, admitting his past errors, he sought to expiate his conduct. 'Your dismissal was a hard one', he said to Brüning, 'but, believe me, it was pleasant compared to mine.'

[2] Letter to Frau von Seeckt, dated February 1, 1933 (Rabenau, ii, 675).

[3] *Hammerstein Memorandum.*   [4] Goebbels, p. 233.

within him. He sounded his former colleagues who were still Ministers *ad interim* of the Schleicher Cabinet and found that, faced with a choice between what von Hammerstein termed 'the hopelessly stupid German Nationalists and the shameless National Socialists',[1] the majority preferred the latter.[2] By the evening it seemed that Hindenburg alone was adamantly opposed to the appointment of Hitler as Chancellor and in favour of a Papen-Hugenberg régime.

On the morning of Sunday, January 29, the position was still unresolved. The air was thick with rumours, all of which were reported to the Bendlerstrasse, and from there it seemed to von Schleicher and von Hammerstein that the Papen-Hugenberg solution was a distinct probability.[3] They decided to make another approach to Hindenburg and despatched Major Erich Marcks, von Schleicher's Chief Press Officer, to the President in an attempt to persuade him to appoint Hitler Chancellor. But Marcks, who had formerly been in high favour with the Marshal, also encountered a stone wall. He too returned empty-handed.[4]

In the meantime, von Schleicher had been seeking the advice of his friends both within Berlin and outside. Amongst those to whom he telephoned was Otto Wolff, the steel king of Cologne, from whom he learned a startling piece of news. Without the knowledge or consent of the Minister of Defence or the General Commanding the Army, General von Blomberg, chief military delegate at the Disarmament Conference, had been ordered to report forthwith to the President. He was to leave Geneva at once. Otto Wolff advised von Schleicher to make use, for immediate action, of the powers which still remained to him as interim Chancellor and Minister of Defence. He should proclaim a state of emergency, declare martial law and establish a military dictatorship for a limited period. This being done, he should transport the Hindenburgs, *père et fils*, under 'honourable detention' to Neudeck, and have von Blomberg arrested as soon as he crossed the Swiss frontier.[5]

Both Generals were furious at this recalling of von Blomberg behind their backs, and von Schleicher at once telephoned to

---

[1] *Hammerstein Memorandum.*

[2] Schwerin von Krosigk's diary entry or January 29, 1933.

[3] In reality, at this moment von Papen had virtually abandoned the idea of the 'small solution' and was negotiating with Göring for the formation of a Hitler-Papen-Hugenberg-Seldte government, in which the President should appoint the Ministers of Defence and Foreign Affairs (von Blomberg and von Neurath) and von Papen as Vice-Chancellor should be the liaison between the Chancellor and the President. The outstanding obstacle remained whether or not the new Cabinet should be given the immediate power to dissolve the *Reichstag*, upon which the Nazis insisted.

[4] *Hammerstein Memorandum.*   [5] *Ibid.*

Meissner with bitter protests and reproaches.[1] But he hesitated before taking the forceful measures advised by Otto Wolff. Instead he sent von Hammerstein to Hitler. Their meeting took place at Charlottenburg, in the house of Carl Bechstein, the piano manufacturer. To the *Führer* the Head of the *Reichswehr* told his fears, and asked whether the negotiations with von Papen for the appointment of Hitler as Chancellor could be considered as serious, or whether they might not all wake up one morning to find a Papen-Hugenberg Cabinet a *fait accompli*. If there was any danger of this latter eventuality, von Hammerstein undertook 'to influence the position'. It was then four o'clock in the afternoon, and Hitler still did not know whether or not Göring's negotiations with von Papen were being used as a screen for some *coup de théâtre*. He promised to let the General know as soon as he had any definite news,[2] and added an assurance of his willingness, in the event of his becoming Chancellor, to retain von Schleicher at the Ministry of Defence. Shortly thereafter Göring arrived with the glad tidings that all was settled and that the *Führer* would be installed as Chancellor on the morrow; only the question of the dissolution remained outstanding.[3] But no telephone message reached von Hammerstein.

There was held that evening in Berlin the great riding tournament in the Ausstellungshallen, an annual event of some importance at which the Head of the *Reichswehr* was always present. Von Hammerstein attended it with a heavy heart. Between nine and ten o'clock he was back at the Bendlerstrasse, anxiously enquiring of von Schleicher for news of the crisis. The 'Cardinal in Politics' knew nothing. He who had once had his ear to every keyhole in Berlin, from whom no telephone conversation of any importance had remained a secret, was now isolated and uninformed. The man who was still, for the moment, Chancellor of Germany and Minister of Defence confronted the Commander-in-Chief of the Army in silent and bewildered ignorance.[4]

To them now entered Freiherr Werner von Alvensleben, a leading light of the *Herrenklub* and formerly one of von Schleicher's chief liaison men with the Nazis. He too knew nothing, but he agreed to go to Hitler at Goebbels' home in the Reichskanzlerplatz and seek

---

[1] Schwerin von Krosigk's diary entry for February 5, 1933.
[2] *Hammerstein Memorandum.*   [3] Goebbels, p. 234.
[4] Von Schleicher's henchmen had been kept so entirely in the dark that on the morning of January 30, his State Secretary at the Chancellery, Erwin Planck, telephoned to Schwerin von Krosigk that the negotiations with Hitler had completely broken down and that the *Führer* had left Berlin for Munich. Two hours later Hitler was Chancellor of the Reich (Schwerin von Krosigk's diary entry for February 5, 1933).

information. There he found qualified jubilation. Hitler was still adamant in his demand for an immediate dissolution, and it was not yet entirely certain that the President would give way on this point.[1] In a moment of excitement, in which he allowed zeal to outrun discretion, von Alvensleben said to Hitler : 'If the Palace crowd are only playing with you, the *Reichswehr* Minister and the Chief of the *Heeresleitung* will have to turn out the Potsdam garrison and clean out the whole pig-sty from the Wilhelmstrasse'.[2]

Such a remark, uttered in so highly charged an atmosphere, was like a spark to powder. The wildest panic at once spread through the Government quarter of Berlin. Meissner, called from his bed at two o'clock on the morning of the 30th, was informed that General von Hammerstein was preparing to transport the President and Oskar to Neudeck 'in a lead-lined cattle-truck', and that he himself, von Papen and Hugenberg were also to be arrested.[3]

A few hours later, on his arrival at the Anhalter Bahnhof, General von Blomberg was met on the platform by Oskar von Hindenburg, and also by Major von Kuntzen, von Hammerstein's adjutant. He received conflicting commands ; the one ordering him to report at once to the President, the other to go at once to the Bendlerstrasse. Von Blomberg went to Hindenburg ; at nine o'clock in the morning he was appointed Minister of Defence in a so far otherwise non-existent Cabinet, and warned not to go to his Ministry lest he too should be arrested.[4]

Two hours later, with the last obstacles removed, the last objections silenced, Adolf Hitler had been sworn in as Chancellor. The Third Reich was a thing in being. The Day of Dupes was over.

Nothing could have been more inglorious and inept than the record of the Army in this whole period. After two months of the most amateurish political 'finagling', the General-Chancellor, who had engaged himself either to disrupt the Nazi régime or to bring it into submission, supported by the Commander-in-Chief, who had declared with vehemence that the *Reichswehr* would never allow the Nazis to come to power, was so bankrupt of resources that he was driven to contemplate a military *Putsch* to ensure the appointment of Hitler as Chancellor, in order to protect Germany from the danger of National Socialism ! The planning of von Schleicher and von Hammerstein was identical with that of von Papen in that it suffered

---

[1] Hindenburg's opposition on this point was not actually overcome until the morning of January 30, shortly before the swearing-in of the new Cabinet.
[2] *Hammerstein Memorandum.*
[3] *Ibid.* ; Schwerin von Krosigk's diary entry for February 5, 1933.
[4] *Ibid.* ; von Papen's Interrogation of September 19, 1945.

from the delusion that Hitler could be made a captive. It differed in that von Papen sought to make him the captive of the Conservative Right, whereas the Generals saw him as the captive of the Army. Both parties displayed, thereby, a lamentable ignorance of the psychology, the ability, and the ruthlessness of the man with whom they were dealing, since both were confident not only of their competence to outmanœuvre the *Führer*, but that, once fettered with the responsibility of government, his strength, and that of his movement, would decline and wither.

The irony of the situation lies in the fact that what Hindenburg and his advisers undoubtedly believed on the night of January 29, namely that the Generals were planning a *Putsch* in order to keep the Nazis *out*, was never contemplated by the leaders of the *Reichswehr*, either before or after the appointment of Hitler as Chancellor.[1] It does not appear to have occurred to them to take the President into protective custody in order to protect him from the Nazis, though they could certainly have done this, if they had the power to make a *Putsch* at all. Determined action at that moment, even at the risk of precipitating a civil war, would certainly have been justified in motive, and even by success ; for eight months later Hitler was himself to declare publicly : 'We all know well that if, in the days of the Revolution, the Army had not stood on our side, then we should not be standing here to-day '.[2]

The truth is that even that part of the Army leadership, as represented by von Schleicher and von Hammerstein, which was allegedly anti-Nazi, was not 100 per cent so. They wished to secure, for the benefit of the *Reichswehr*, all that could be gained to advantage from the Nazi movement, while dominating and controlling it in policy. They were still dreaming in their blindness of a martial State in which the masses, galvanized and inspired by modified National Socialism, would be directed and disciplined by the Army. They may well have had it in their power in those fateful January

---

[1] On January 30 Carl Severing asked for an interview with von Hammerstein in order to discuss joint action between the Army and organized labour in opposition to Hitler. The General replied that, while he was in principle prepared to grant an interview, he did not think the moment propitious. The meeting never took place (*Hammerstein Memorandum* ; Severing's evidence on May 21, 1946, *Nuremberg Record*, xiv, 264). See also an article by General Freiherr Erich von dem Bussche (in 1933 head of the *Heerespersonalamt*) entitled 'Hammerstein und Hindenburg' in the *Frankfurter Allgemeine Zeitung* for February 5, 1952. Hitler himself appears to have been uncertain of the true intentions of the *Reichswehr* and took certain precautions against a possible anti-Nazi *Putsch* (see Henry Picker, *Hitlers Tischgespräche im Führerhauptquartier 1941–1942* (Bonn, 1951), pp. 427–30).

[2] Speech on *Stahlhelm* Day, September 23, 1933 (*Frankfurter Zeitung*, September 24, 1933 ; Baynes, ii, 556).

days to combat successfully the final consummation of that National
Socialist rise to power, which they, by their own equivocal policy,
had helped to promote ; but they did not wish to do so.

Years later, on the eve of yet another military *Putsch*, when the
Army had learned to its cost the fatal errors of its past record,
Goerdeler said to Kunrath von Hammerstein : 'In those days your
father stood at the helm of world history'.[1] Unfortunately the
General was no navigator, and the helm was quickly grasped by
other and more determined hands.

[1] *Hammerstein Memorandum.* In the writing of the latter part of this chapter
the present writer has been greatly indebted to a memorandum entitled 'The
Birth of the Third Reich' (London, 1950), specially written for him by Dr. Dietrich
Mende, a former senior civil servant in the Prussian Ministry of Finance, a close
friend of the Minister Johannes Popitz, and a member of the 'Schleicher Ring'.

PART III

HITLER AND THE ARMY

1933–1945

'Armies for the preparation of peace do not exist; they exist for triumphant exertion in war.'—ADOLF HITLER, 1930.

CHAPTER I

FROM THE SEIZURE OF POWER TO
THE DEATH OF HINDENBURG

(January 1933–August 1934)

(i)

ADOLF HITLER, when he became Chancellor in January 1933, had a pronounced complex against Generals. From the earliest days of the National Socialist movement every successive attempt to achieve power had been prevented by a General; at the end of every avenue there had appeared a bemonocled figure in field grey, and claret-coloured trouser stripes, with uplifted hand, crying 'Halt!'.

For, though Hitler and the NSDAP had owed their early survival and development to the secret aid and succour of the *Reichswehr*, this assistance had always been given for the advantage of the Army and not for the benefit of the Party. Whenever Hitler had attempted to depart from his rôle, first of satellite, and, later, of junior partner, he had found the Generals ranged against him.

It was a General, von Lossow, who had first patronized, then betrayed, and finally fired upon Hitler at Munich. It was a General, von Seeckt, who had steadfastly opposed the March on Berlin. It was a General, Gröner, who had suppressed the para-military organizations of the Party; and though another General, von Schleicher, had coquetted with the Party, had negotiated with Hitler and, in the chaotic fantasy of the last days of January 1933, had even contemplated a *coup d'état* to make the *Führer* Chancellor, Hitler remembered the earlier attempts of this General to split the Party, and recognized full well the fundamental hostility which von Schleicher and von Hammerstein entertained toward National Socialism. Hitler had not been deceived by the manœuvres of January 29. He appreciated fully the motives which had inspired the projected *Putsch* — the desire for revenge upon the Hindenburgs and von Papen, and the intention of bringing the Nazis to power as the captives of the Army rather than of the Conservative Right — and was well aware that his own *beaux yeux* did not figure among them. He knew also that the General, von Blomberg, who had been introduced into his Cabinet as Minister of Defence, had been placed there as a protective custodian rather than as a responsive colleague. And, above all, Hitler recognized the inimical attitude of the veteran Field-Marshal, the President of the Reich, with whom he must now work as Chancellor.

But Hitler's complex against the Generals was rooted in apprehension as well as antipathy. The *Führer* had a profound respect for the Army, he had great designs for it and its rôle bulked largely in the dreams of his ambition. 'It is impossible to build up an Army and give it a sense of worth if the object of its existence is not the preparation for battle', he had written as early as 1930. 'Armies for the preparation of peace do not exist; they exist for triumphant exertion in war.'[1] Yet, though this was Hitler's basic concept of the *raison d'être* of the Army which he purposed to create, he feared that the Generals, once the arms and man-power were made available to them, would either use them to replace the régime which had provided them by a military junta or a restored monarchy, or would 'jump the gun' and involve Germany in war before the *Führer* was ready for it.

Before he became Chancellor, Hitler's idea of a German General was that of a fire-eating dragon, and of the General Staff 'a mastiff which had to be held by the collar because it threatened all and sundry'.[2] It was, therefore, with an admixture of both trepidation and aversion that he contemplated this future relationship. Nevertheless, he was shrewd enough to know that, come what might, he must keep the Army on his side at the outset, until he had become so firmly established, and they so closely wedded to the new régime, that the partnership could be dissolved only of his volition. To achieve this, he was prepared to yield them pride of place on every public occasion, to make open profession of his desire to restore the *Wehrhoheit* (Military Sovereignty) of Germany, and to set in motion immediate planning towards the realization of this ambition by increasing both the scope and the tempo of German secret rearmament. The Army, in the early days of the Third Reich, was treated as the petted favourite and respected ally of the new régime. No

---

[1] *National-Sozialistische Monatshefte*, No. 3, 1930, p. 101.

[2] Hitler admitted this fact in bitter petulance before a Staff conference at Field-Marshal von Bock's Headquarters (Army Group Centre) at Borisow on the Eastern Front in the summer of 1941. 'Before I became Chancellor', he complained, 'I thought the General Staff was like a mastiff which had to be held tight by the collar because it threatened all and sundry. Since then I have had to recognize that the General Staff is anything but that. It has consistently tried to impede every action that I have thought necessary. . . . It is I who have always had to goad on this mastiff.' (Fabian von Schlabrendorff, *Offiziere gegen Hitler* (Zürich, 1946), pp. 47-48. See also *Halder's Diary* for August 4, 1941.)

effort was spared to enlist and retain its support and to obviate any cause or reason for suspicion or animosity.

Still, Hitler's first contact with the Army was, perhaps, not one of the happiest or the best calculated to harmonize his relations with the Generals. Early on the morning of January 31, not twenty-four hours after his appointment as Chancellor, the *Führer* arrived without warning at the barracks of the Berlin Garrison and there made a vigorous address to the *Truppen* on the spirit of the new Germany. Von Hammerstein, as Commander-in-Chief of the *Reichswehr*, was shocked at this unorthodox approach to the rank and file over the heads of their officers — a proceeding which recalled all too vividly the *Stimmung* of 1918. A few days later Hitler dined in von Hammerstein's flat with leading personalities of the Army and the Navy. Whether the host had hoped to impress Hitler with the combined galaxy of Generals and Admirals, or to expose the Chancellor and his turgid eloquence to the secret ridicule of the armed services, is unknown, but the result of the meeting must have been somewhat of a shock to him. In a speech lasting more than two hours, the *Führer* made a complete and detailed *exposé* of his general policies, particularly emphasizing that he was taking over the direction of domestic and foreign politics and that the Army and Navy would thenceforth be free to work, entirely unhindered, on training and development for the defence of the Reich. It was a daring and well-calculated manœuvre, and it not only succeeded in removing much of the suspicion occasioned by his direct approach to the troops but in dispelling in the minds of many of his hearers those more deep-seated misgivings which had hitherto been harboured as to the wider objectives of the new régime. Hitler made many converts that evening and, though some present still adhered to their original views on the 'Bohemian Corporal', the attitude of the majority was summed up in the remark of one of them, overheard on leaving: 'At any rate no Chancellor has ever expressed himself so warmly in favour of defence'.[1]

Hitler had won his first skirmish with the Generals. Thereafter he was careful to consolidate and maintain the ground gained before making further advances. The opposition was not as great as he had expected. The die-hards he could not hope to win to his standard, but for every die-hard there were ten or so who, for reasons of present ambition or past frustration, were prepared to co-operate,

---

[1] Grand-Admiral Erich Raeder, *My Relationship with Adolf Hitler and the Party*, a study written in Moscow after his capture by the Soviet Army in Potsdam-Babelsberg on May 16, 1945, and before his return to face trial before the International Military Tribunal at Nuremberg. See also Rosinski, p. 215.

and the die-hards could always be replaced. 'It will be up to the
Generals to see that the Army does not in the end kiss Herr
Schicklgruber's¹ hands like hysterical women', Gröner had written
a few months earlier.² The Generals proved neither competent nor
willing to prevent this feast of osculation. Indeed they led the way,
and at the solemn ceremony at the grave of Frederick the Great
in the Garrison Church at Potsdam on March 21, 1933 — an event
astutely exploited to the full by the egregious Joseph Goebbels —
the Old Army and the New, the ancient Prussian order and the
National Revolution, were united in unholy wedlock as the forty-four-
year-old Corporal grasped the hand of the octogenarian Field-
Marshal in all the simulation of respectful humility.³

Why, indeed, it may be asked, did the Army first sanction,
and later abet, the National Socialist Movement in its progress
towards seizure of complete power in Germany? The reasons
are varied, and in some cases pitiful. In the first place, the Army
had been ordered to co-operate by its Supreme Commander, the
Field-Marshal-President of the Republic, and this, for many, was a
sufficiently satisfying answer to any scruples which may have arisen
as to the wisdom or rectitude of the order. That which the Field-
Marshal had countenanced, that which he had himself condoned,
must be of over-riding consideration with that type of officer — and
there were many — who did not wish to think for himself and who
used the Seeckt formula of 'Überparteilichkeit' as a buckler behind
which to shelter from all the inner blows of conscience and, indeed,
from anything calculated to unsettle men's minds.

A second reason, and one which motivated another numerous
group in the Officer Corps, was the design to find, in collaboration
with the National Socialists, the necessary cover for the degree of
secret rearmament which was now regarded as essential, and also to
achieve that national unity, so lacking under the Weimar Republic,
which the Army hoped to transform into a military dictatorship as a
preliminary to a restored monarchy. Those who held these views
were guilty of the same errors of judgment as were von Papen and

¹ Schicklgruber was the name of Adolf Hitler's paternal grandmother. Hitler's
father, Alois, bore this name until 1877, when in his fortieth year, he changed to
Hitler, the name of his putative father.
² Letter to General Gleich, dated May 22, 1932 (quoted by Craig, p. 229).
³   'Orgelspiel und Hitlermärsche,
            alte Weltkriegsgenerale
            beugen ihre harten Arsche
            preisen Gott im Dankchorale',
wrote Horst Lommer in 'Tag von Potsdam, 21. Marz 1933' (Das tausendjährige
Reich (Berlin, 1947), pp. 15-16).

VON HINDENBURG WITH HITLER AND GÖRING, TANNENBERG, 1933

Keystone

Hugenberg. Both persisted in regarding the Nazis as turbulent but useful allies, who, if handled with cynical 'realism', could be utilized to the greater glory of the German Army or of the cause of German Conservative reaction. The alliance with the Nazis appeared to many Generals, and also to many Conservative leaders, as an inspired means of eliminating any danger of revolution from the extreme Right. Patronized and controlled by the Army and the Conservative Right, the NSDAP seemed an appropriate instrument for the creation of national unity, for it had already demonstrated its masterly technique in dealing with the masses, and had achieved a popular following such as no other national group had succeeded in obtaining. For a considerable period of time there were Conservative leaders, such as von Papen; Generals, such as von Fritsch; and public men, such as Schacht, who aided and abetted Hitler because they believed that he could be controlled by the groups and interests which they represented. Not until they had riveted the fetters upon their own wrists did they realize who indeed was captive and who captor. The self-delusion manifested in 1933 by men who could and should have known better, is something of which only Germans are capable.[1]

There was a third group in the Officer Corps who were constrained to sanction and co-operate with the new régime because, in the words of so indisputably an anti-Fascist as the Swiss theologian Karl Barth, '. . . . in the first period of its power National Socialism really had the character of a political experiment like others. . . . It was right and proper for the time being to give the political experiment of National Socialism a trial.'[2] This attitude was one widely held by Germans of all political complexions and callings. They welcomed the possibility of salvation by means of a new will and a new approach. This was particularly true of foreign policy and rearmament. The Social Democrats, for example, who alone had voted against the passage of the Enabling Act in the *Reichstag* on March 23, 1933, voted, in common with all other political parties, on May 17, in support of Hitler after his *exposé* of the alternatives of general disarmament or German rearmament; and this was after the Trade Unions had been dissolved on May 2 and after the Party Funds of the SPD had been confiscated on May 10. Even later, when, in the summer of 1933, the political parties went into 'voluntary liquidation', they did not do so in a spirit of 'hara-kiri',

[1] Hermann Rauschning, *Germany's Revolution of Destruction* (London, 1939), pp. 131-68; Rosinski, pp. 216-17.
[2] Karl Barth, *Eine Schweizer Stimme, 1938-1945* (Zollikon/Zürich, 1945), pp. 80-81.

but of support for the new régime. They assured Hitler that their former members would loyally collaborate with the Nazi State and they called upon these former members to do so.[1]

If this was true of political circles it was even truer in certain military circles, where rearmament, for instance, was not only a national but a personal ambition, since it involved hopes of promotion. That which the sterile rule of Weimar had failed to accomplish, might well be achieved by this new political experiment, which, if it 'paid dividends', would be more than justified.

Finally, there was among the Corps of Officers a further group who espoused the cause and precepts of National Socialism with a warmth and avidity born of that brutal ruthlessness which had characterized the *Landsknechte* of the Middle Ages and the Free Corps Officers of the 1920s. It was from these men — professionally brilliant, boundlessly ambitious, unscrupulous mercenaries, soldiers who were soldiers before and above all else, and concerned only with their own career and power and influence — that Hitler drew his chief, and most dangerous, support. They would follow any man who would give them high command, the opportunity of personal aggrandizement and the chance of military adventure. Reckless advocates of a policy of force and strength, to them rearmament and the inevitable concomitant of war were but the framework of their own careers. Neither republican nor monarchist — and certainly not Nazi — they were without political convictions or scruples, and would have abandoned National Socialism as speedily as they had adopted it, had there been opportunities of further personal advancement in so doing. But Hitler saw to it that their bread was always buttered.

Thus, for one reason or another, the *Reichswehr* stood by during that first fateful twelve months of the Third Reich and watched the Nazi régime establish, consolidate and tighten its grip upon the machinery of the German State. Toward the unveiled horrors of the Brown Terror, the destruction of the Trade Unions, the dissolution of the political parties, the forced incorporation of the *Stahlhelm* with the Storm Troops, and the rapid elimination of the Conservatives from the Cabinet, the Army preserved an impervious equanimity, which sprang from the deluded conviction that they were still undisputed masters of the situation. Their contempt for the Conservative leaders, who, like the leaders of the Army, had been the victims of self-delusion, was only equalled by their derision

---

[1] Cf. the closing speech of Dr. Egon Kubuschok, Defence Counsel for the Reich Government, before the International Military Tribunal at Nuremberg, August 28, 1946 (*Nuremberg Record*, xxii, 104).

for the German people for their readiness to tolerate such a reign of terror. Haughtily confident that nothing of the sort could occur in their own domain, they retained the assurance that they could put an end to the whole 'experiment', as soon as it suited their book to do so.

The Generals thought themselves very astute in their handling of the national problem. 'It was a point of honour with the Prussian officer to be correct; it is a duty of the German officer to be crafty', boasted von Blomberg on one occasion. But the German officer did not realize that in craft and guile he was but a child — a new-born babe — as compared with the cunning and deceit of those pitted against him. For the hour it suited Hitler to defer to the Army in all things; it was indeed vital to the success of his plans and ambitions that he should do so. The Army accepted the deference as nothing more than their rightful due; they were more than satisfied with the promises of rearmament made so lavishly and with the evidence that those promises were to be fulfilled. Deceived as much by their own vanity as by Hitler's blandishments, the Generals watched the internal position of Germany deteriorate to the point at which the Army alone could have overthrown the Nazi régime, and to the Army it appeared manifest that it was not in their interest to do so. The price of this error, which was the misery, suffering and death of millions, was paid in blood after the 20th of July 1944.

(ii)

The personality of Werner von Blomberg, Minister of Defence in Hitler's Cabinet from 1933–8, will ever remain something of an enigma. He was no field-grey sphinx — whether, like von Seeckt, *with* a secret, or, like von Fritsch, *without* one — but there remains about him an air of mystery which is heightened, if anything, by the very frankness of his seeming *naïveté*.

Magnificent in physical appearance, tall, blond and Wagnerian, a veritable Siegfried — if one can conceive of Siegfried with a monocle — von Blomberg was fifty-four when, in January 1933, he was called upon to play a rôle of destiny. His military career had been one of considerable ability, and from 1927–9 he had been head of the *Truppenamt*, or virtual Chief of the General Staff, though perhaps not among the more dangerously clear thinkers who had held this post. It was during these years, however, that under the Seeckt plan, which still continued to function well after the departure of its progenitor from active service, von Blomberg made the visit to Russia which was to prove a turning-point in his career.

There he saw for the first time the enhanced position of power and respect which the Army enjoyed — at least superficially — under a totalitarian régime. There was no civil service red tape and no difficulty about the budget. What the armed services asked for they got, and no questions asked; and the attitude of the people, also, seemed to him very different from that of the German masses; in Russia the proletariat was enthusiastic about the defence forces of the State; there was no grumbling over conscription or the hardships of barrack life. Every proletarian seemed proud of the army and regarded it with a personal interest.

Such was the picture with which von Blomberg returned to Germany, with dreams of a resurgent Prussian military Socialism revolving in his mind. Had it then been possible for a German General to espouse Communism for purely opportunist purposes, he might conceivably have done so — as did Paulus and von Seydlitz and others some fifteen years later. 'I was not far short of coming home a complete Bolshevist', he himself confessed.

But it was to the other extreme of political revolution that Fate directed von Blomberg, ripe as he was for authoritarian rule. Appointed to the command of *Wehrkreis I* (East Prussia) with headquarters at Königsberg, he found in his senior Lutheran chaplain, Ludwig Müller, a devoted follower of National Socialism, and from him the General imbibed the heady wine of the new German totalitarianism.[1] It was the summer of 1930, a period of tension and alarm in East Prussia, where one of the Polish crises had produced an atmosphere of momentarily expected invasion. All eyes were turned to the new saviour of Germany, Adolf Hitler, who, on his visit to Königsberg in August during the general election campaign, was greeted with prayers and hailed with the title of 'German Margrave'. Von Blomberg was deeply impressed with the *Führer* and even more with his doctrines. Here was a man who could do for Germany and the German Army that which the Soviet régime had done for the Red Army; who could evoke a spirit of national pride in the masses which would be reflected in a new approach to the *Reichswehr*, a readiness to accept conscription and rearmament; who could identify the people with the Army, making the *Reichswehr* a truly popular body and not merely a show-piece or a 'State within a State'.

Thenceforward, Werner von Blomberg was firmly persuaded of the political advantage which a National Socialist régime could

---

[1] It was this same Ludwig Müller who later, as leader of the German Christian Movement, was imposed by Hitler upon the Evangelical Church as its 'Reich Bishop'.

confer upon the German armed forces. He was not a convinced National Socialist, any more than he would have been a convinced Communist, but he was a convinced believer in Adolf Hitler and was one of the very few in the higher brackets of the military hierarchy who was prepared to make public profession of his belief that the *Führer* would, and should, come to power. His nickname among his fellows — which had hitherto been the 'Rubber Lion' (*Gummi-löwe*) from his mild manner — now became 'Hitler Junge Quex', from the film of that name which portrayed the devotion of a Hitler Youth member to the cause and precepts of his *Führer*.

When, during an official visit to the United States, von Blomberg proceeded to preach not only the inevitability but also the desirability of a Nazi Government, he began to be regarded as a menace by the authorities at home, and, taking advantage of a severe riding accident sustained in 1931 the effect of which appeared to increase the patient's nervous and mental instability, Brüning asked Gröner to remove von Blomberg from active command. But the means chosen to *limoger* him could not have been more unfortunate. The General was appointed chief military delegate to the Disarmament Conference at Geneva, a position which he used not only as a sounding-board for his pro-Nazi manifestations, but also as a means of direct access to the President as Supreme Commander, and it was his adverse reports on Brüning's armament policy which materially contributed to that Chancellor's downfall.[1]

By a curious concatenation of circumstances, therefore, it came about that the only active General officer whom the Nazis wished to have as Minister for Defence happened to be a man who enjoyed the personal liking and regard of Field-Marshal von Hindenburg, and this regard was not minimized by the manifest antipathy of von Blomberg for von Schleicher and von Hammerstein.

The task which the new *Reichswehr* Minister conceived to have been allotted to him was to co-operate with the Nazis up to the point beyond which the interests of the Army would be compromised or imperilled, to take with both hands all that the Nazis were prepared to give in the way of rearmament and military development, to encourage them to give more, and to take the *Reichswehr* out of politics in the sense in which it had been involved under the Schleicher régime. To this end he proceeded to sweep out the Schleicher *Umgebung* from the Bendlerstrasse and to replace them with men whom he believed would be more amenable to the new rôle which the *Reichswehr* must play in the New Germany.

[1] Brüning, *Ein Brief*, p. 18.

In the place of von Bredow he appointed, as head of the *Ministeramt*, Walter von Reichenau, who had been his Chief of Staff in Königsberg. Von Reichenau was a colder and more calculating personality than his chief. He was also a considerably abler soldier, having been master pupil of the great Max Hoffmann, whom many believe to have been the brains behind Hindenburg and Ludendorff on the Eastern Front from 1914-16. A gunner and a scientist, von Reichenau had none of von Blomberg's *Schwärmen* for Hitler, but his keen political sense was fully awake to the advantages which would accrue, both personally and to the Army as a whole, from co-operation with the régime. He had imbibed much of the military thought of National Socialism in regard to the idea of a *Volksheer*, and had himself so far broken with the Prussian military tradition as to make personal contact with the troops under his command, not only in the line of duty but in participating in the cross-country runs and physical training courses which he inaugurated for the betterment of their stamina and morale. A fine athlete, he had, as a member of the German Olympic Committee, travelled more widely than many of his fellow-officers, and, though less cultured than von Blomberg, he had a more penetrating and analytical intelligence.[1] His lack of orthodoxy and scruple, and his eminent ability had earned him the suspicion, dislike and jealousy of many of his comrades.

The substitution of von Reichenau for von Bredow was carried out immediately by von Blomberg, but by October he had effected a further important change in the hierarchy; Wilhelm Adam had given place to Ludwig Beck as head of the *Truppenamt*. Beck's appointment to the key post in the *Reichswehr* was undoubtedly due primarily to his record as a soldier, which was outstanding, but was also not unconnected with his appearance at the Supreme Court at Leipzig in September 1930, at the trial of Scheringer and Ludin.[2] On that occasion, as the commanding officer of the two accused officers, Beck had given evidence of a nature which indicated that, though by no means a Nazi, he was to be numbered among those who would welcome the advent of National Socialism as a political experiment because of the manifest benefits which, if its doctrines meant anything at all, it must confer upon the Army. Beck was above all else a man of high honour, matchless integrity

---

[1] The author of this book was, in retrospect, impressed with von Reichenau's farsightedness as demonstrated in a conversation which took place in April 1934. In answer to a question as to what part he thought Italy would play in the next war, the General replied : 'Mark my words, it does not matter on which side Italy begins the war, for at its close she will be found playing her historic rôle as "the Whore of Europe".'

See above, p. 217.

and great moral courage. He was the epitome of the virtues of the German General Staff, but he also suffered from their *borné* approach to life, their inability to see beyond the interests of their own calling. He was typical of those who believed that the Army might tolerate the National Socialist 'experiment' with impunity since it could always bring about its abrupt termination, if and when it had extracted all the advantages of rearmament that were forthcoming. It is to his credit that he was among the very few of his caste who, when — alas, too late — they discovered the shocking error of judgment which they had committed, did endeavour, albeit fruitlessly, to do something to rectify that error, and it may be said of him that nothing became him so much in this world as his leaving it.

But it must also be admitted that, at the outset, Beck was prepared to serve as a military opportunist, trafficking with National Socialism as a means of restoring Germany to a position of predominant power among the nations. Like many of his fellow Generals, he did not regard war as the primary rôle of the soldier, but believed that Germany's armaments should be of such a degree that they would lessen rather than increase the danger of war by making it impossible for Germany to be attacked or gainsaid with impunity. If, on the other hand, despite all, war should ensue, a well-armed Reich would be in a position to create the most favourable conditions for peace by a war as short and as successful as possible. Herein lay the fundamental difference of view between the professional soldier, such as Beck, who regarded war as a last resource in the game of international politics, to be undertaken only under the most favourable strategic conditions, and Hitler, who looked upon war as something to be threatened, and, if necessary carried on, under conditions of purely political advantage, without giving sufficient concern to strategy or other military considerations; and it was this issue, rather than any more moral controversy, that caused the final split between Beck and his *Führer*.

The final replacement in the upper ranks of the *Heeresleitung* was that of Eugen Ott, who, relieved of his post as head of the *Wehramt*, was despatched on a tour of liaison duty with the Japanese Army and a few months later was confirmed as military attaché in Tokyo.[1] He was succeeded by Fritz Fromm, whose equivocal

---

[1] Ott never had another military command, though, after the elimination of von Blomberg and the creation of OKW, the Army High Command intervened on his behalf more than once with Keitel. Ott's intimacy with and loyalty to von Schleicher, was, however, apparently considered an overruling disqualification even after the latter's murder, but it was on the initiative of Keitel with Hitler and Ribbentrop that Ott was appointed Ambassador to Japan in April 1938, a

conduct on the 20th of July 1944 stood out in marked distinction to that of Beck, but failed to save him from the firing squad.

All von Schleicher's intimates were thus accounted for except von Hammerstein, and his case demanded greater circumspection. The Commander-in-Chief of the *Reichswehr* had not resigned, despite his antipathy to von Blomberg, because he had continued to hope that he might yet successfully influence the President to take action against the régime. This depended, however, upon his ability to effect a reconciliation with the Hindenburgs, in whom von Schleicher's allegedly threatened *Putsch* of January 29 and the fatal mention of 'a lead-lined cattle-truck' had bred deep resentment. Von Blomberg therefore concentrated on maintaining this cleavage and on preventing the Commander-in-Chief from resuming the old footing of intimacy which he had enjoyed in the Presidential Palace and at Neudeck. He, the Defence Minister, was the new military favourite now, and for all his mild manner the 'Rubber Lion' proved as ruthless as von Schleicher in undermining the position of his rivals. By the end of June, von Hammerstein was completely isolated and was only able to obtain access to the Field-Marshal on matters of a strictly military nature.[1] He remained at his post for a further six months, but resigned in January 1934. The man who had once stood at 'the helm of world history' disappeared into the twilight of conspiracy.

(iii)

Meantime, while von Blomberg was setting his own house in order, the *Führer*, in addition to consolidating his hold upon the governmental structure of the Reich, was not forgetful of the promises which he had made to the Army for the restoration of their own privileges and status, and of the *Wehrhoheit* of Germany. One of the first acts of the Government was to take a decision on April 4, 1933, to create a Reich Defence Council which should be charged with the co-ordination and direction of the secret rearmament in continuation of the work carried on by the *Rüstungsamt* under the Seeckt régime.[2] Three months later, on July 20 (a fateful day in the history of the *Reichswehr*) the new Army Law was promulgated, whereby, *inter alia*, the jurisdiction of the civil courts over the military was abolished, as was the system of elected representation of the rank and file, the military and naval chambers, and the last

post which he retained until December 1942. (See a letter from Keitel to Ribbentrop dated March 17, 1938, *Documents on German Foreign Policy*, Series D, i (London, 1949), p. 851.)

[1] Brüning, *Ein Brief*, pp. 18-19.   [2] See above, p. 143.

meagre remnants of the powers of the individual German States over their local armed forces. It also decreed that 'in the event of any public emergency or any threat to public order' the *Reichswehr* was bound to give to the Government of the Reich any assistance they might demand, and this provision was to many Germans a source of relief, since what body, save alone the SA, could cause a public emergency or constitute a threat to public order ?

The New Year, however, brought fresh developments. The resignation of von Hammerstein, in January 1934, precipitated the first trial of strength between the new forces and the old within the Army. Von Blomberg, with Hitler's approval, put forward to Hindenburg the name of von Reichenau as the new Commander-in-Chief, but the conservative elements within the Officer Corps would have none of it. Von Reichenau was regarded as a military radical, who had openly set at nought many of the traditional taboos of the military caste. A General who talked unashamedly of a *Volksheer*, who fraternized with his troops and actually led them in runs across country, was altogether too revolutionary a character for Chief of the *Heeresleitung*, and the reactionaries urged upon Hindenburg the appointment of their own candidate, Freiherr Werner von Fritsch, who was the 'very model of a German Colonel-General'.

Born in 1880, Werner von Fritsch had entered the Army at the age of eighteen, as a gunner, and had, at an early stage in his career, displayed those qualities for which the lynx-eyed 'talent scouts' of the General Staff were on the watch. In 1907, when only twenty-seven years old, he was transferred to the War Academy, where with von Hammerstein, von Schleicher and von Willisen he became a pupil of Gröner, and in 1911, while still a first lieutenant, he obtained the coveted appointment to the General Staff Corps. By the out-break of the First World War von Fritsch's reputation within the inner circle of the Great General Staff was assured and he spent the war years in a succession of Staff duties of increasing importance. Sacrificing professional preferment to the accumulation of vital knowledge as a Staff officer, he became an assiduous pupil of Colonel Max Bauer, Ludendorff's *alter ego*, and though at the conclusion of hostilities he was still only a major, he was among that esoteric group of Staff officers who had become fully and deeply initiated into the political influences governing the general direction of the German armed forces and their objectives. As such he was appointed Chief of Staff to General Count von der Goltz during that military adventurer's expedition to the Baltic,[1] where both his ability and his failings impressed the head of the Inter-Allied Commission,

[1] See above, p. 121.

General Niessel. 'Major von Fritsch is young, arrogant and extremely self-confident', wrote the French General. 'It seems he
has no qualms about playing hide-and-seek with truth or evading
uncomfortable issues. He has all the professional advantages and
all the faults of character of the Prussian General Staff officer, who
frequently considers himself superior — and rightly too — to the
ordinary mortal.' [1]

It was these very capabilities — wide knowledge and quick resourcefulness, patience and concentration, a marked shrewdness and
a profound belief in the thesis that the end justified the means —
which commended von Fritsch to von Seeckt in his moulding of the
Reichswehr in 1920. In this forty-year-old, round-faced and inevitably bemonocled officer, the new Commander-in-Chief descried
one of that small group of soldier-politicians whom he needed at the
head of his 'non-political' Army. In military and political thought
von Fritsch became the reflection, and, on occasion, the illumination,
of his Chief. He was an ardent devotee of the liaison with Russia, a
bitter hater of Poland and an untiring worker for the advancement
of the secret rearmament of Germany, and it was largely due to his
cool nerve and ruthless use of cajolery and admonition, coupled with
the *suaviter-in-modo* of von Schleicher, that Gessler and Heye found
safe passage through the shoals and rocks of the crisis which attended
the secret rearmament disclosures in the *Reichstag* during the winter
of 1926–27.

Thereafter von Fritsch regarded himself as the chosen guardian
of the 'Seeckt Tradition', both in peace and war, and it was in
pursuit of this heritage that in 1928 he prepared plans for a sudden
descent upon Poland, which, *mutatis mutandis*, formed the basis for
the ultimate invasion in September 1939. By 1930, when he went
for a short period to command a cavalry division at Frankfurt-an-
der-Oder, he had become the leading figure in General Staff circles,
and his ideas dominated the thinking of almost all his colleagues.
His work and worth received simultaneous recognition from von
Schleicher in July 1932 when his promotion to Lieutenant-General
was coupled with the personal assignment of carrying out, under the
general direction of von Rundstedt, the operation of evicting the
Prussian Government. [2]

In the critical months which followed, von Fritsch continued to
keep himself free from the complications and entanglements which
attended the downfall of the Schleicher régime and rendered impossible the retention of von Hammerstein as Commander of the
Reichswehr. At a time when Hitler was still prepared to make

[1] Niessel, p. 70.   [2] See above, p. 253.

concessions to the Army, it was von Fritsch, the Prussian, rather than von Hammerstein, the Hanoverian, to whom the *Führer* felt that these concessions could be made with safety. And indeed the Army thought so too. If the Nazi promises of rearmament were to be implemented on the scale envisaged, it required a man of greater energy and initiative than the easy-going von Hammerstein to carry them out. For if Hitler was prepared to make concessions to the Army in return for their 'toleration', the Army was prepared to 'tolerate' him in return for rearmament.

Von Fritsch, therefore, was appointed to the Command of the *Reichswehr* in February 1934, for a variety of reasons. Hitler approved of him because he had never been an outspoken critic of the National Socialist movement, and, although perhaps contemptuous of its methods, was not unimpressed by its achievements. Von Blomberg, though he would personally have preferred von Reichenau, was compelled to recognize in von Fritsch the technical expert whose resourcefulness and ability could achieve the most for the Army from the fulsome rearmament pledges of the Nazis, while yet keeping intact and unsullied the ancient military traditions of Prussia. And there were many in the upper ranks of the military hierarchy — and indeed outside the Army also — who looked upon von Fritsch as the one General who could be depended upon, if and when the time came, to sweep out the Nazi régime with its murders and its terror — to which at the moment they were prepared to close their eyes and ears — and to replace it by a 'respectable' form of government, either a monarchy or a military dictatorship.

That von Fritsch himself entertained certain illusions at this moment is very clear, but it is equally remarkable that he was able to do so. For, on the date when he assumed command of the *Reichswehr*, the Nazi régime was celebrating its first anniversary of power. A year's record lay spread before him. Twelve months in which the civil liberties of Germany had been strangled, the structure of the Reich remodelled to identify it inextricably with the organization of the Nazi Party, and the German people handed over to the grip of a calculated and ever-increasing police terror.

All this von Fritsch must have known when he assumed command, and with most of it he would not have quarrelled. Ten years before, von Seeckt had discovered that it was method not aims which separated him from Hitler,[1] and his able successor was certainly of a similar mind. It was only the lawlessness of the Nazi régime which shocked the military mind in Germany — and not the

[1] See above, p. 118, footnote 2.

military mind alone — and there was much in the Nazi programme which, could it have been achieved decently and in an orderly manner, commended it warmly to the German Army, who were, however, determined to avoid the mistake, committed by both Ludendorff and von Schleicher, of becoming so deeply involved in the business of government as to be held responsible for everything. Thus von Fritsch himself was quite unmoved by the destruction of the Trade Unions, the dragooning of the Catholic Church and the elimination of the Jews. As achievements in themselves he viewed these steps with approval, though he might deprecate the methods employed to attain them. What worried him considerably more than the atrocities of the Brown Terror was the indication that Nazi foreign policy was about to abandon the 'distant friendliness' which the Weimar régime had preserved toward Russia and to embark upon an unexpected line of *rapprochement* toward Poland, a policy wholly distasteful to the *Reichswehr* and one which, unless it were a purely tactical expedient, must eventually lead to war with the Soviet Union.

For the moment, however, von Fritsch was prepared to ascribe the more fantastic excesses of the *Führer* to 'youthful exuberance' and even to view them with sympathy, since, after all, 'only the man who attempts the impossible gets anything done'.[1] Convinced that Germany's recovery depended upon the limitation of German aims, he was averse to any incentive, be it caused by success or opportunities or hopes or dreams, which should accelerate the tempo of events beyond the point of safety. He believed that he and the Army were the braking-force which, standing above and immune from the Nazi 'experiment', could prevent this dangerous acceleration, and, for the moment, he was prepared to limit his immediate objectives to securing a political framework for the rearmament of Germany while at the same time building up a nucleus of power, round which a new order could be formed at the appropriate time. So much for von Blomberg's dictum that it was the duty of the German officer to be crafty.

(iv)

The year which had made the Nazis unchallenged masters of Germany had brought, by reason of its very record of success, fresh problems for Adolf Hitler. The tide of revolution, though it had borne him to victory and power undreamed of and unprece-

---

[1] Hermann Rauschning, *Makers of Destruction* (London, 1942), pp. 36-8.

dented, had developed a perilous under-tow which threatened to sweep him away from the eminence achieved.

By the close of its first year the National Revolution had entered upon a period of crisis which was only terminated six months later in bloody murder. It was the only moment at which Hitler's authority was seriously threatened ; the only time before its final collapse in May 1945, at which the Nazi régime may have been said to have tottered momentarily upon its foundations. The danger, moreover, came not from resistance in the country as a whole, where all opposition had been either crushed, cowed or cajoled into submission, but from dissension within the ranks of the National Revolution itself, where the Marriage of Potsdam had already disclosed itself as a misalliance.

In January 1934 both the Right and the Left wings of the National Coalition were in a state of disgruntled apprehension and frustration. The Nationalists were clearly frightened, and the chief artificers of the coalition, Hugenberg and von Papen, the one evicted from the Cabinet altogether, the other relegated to the position of a gilded flunkey, stood in appalled contemplation of the spirits which their irresponsible action had conjured. The course of events which they had initiated a year before had carried them altogether too far to the Left for their liking, comfort or safety, and already Goebbels was talking, with disturbing reiteration, of a second and more radical Revolution to follow closely upon Hindenburg's death, an event which, all knew, could not long be delayed. If, therefore, the Nationalists were to regain some of their ground and apply the brake to the Nazi Revolutionary movement, there was no time to be lost. The President, though virtually in his dotage, still retained the unswerving loyalty of the Army, and by this means alone could the Revolution be brought under control. In January 1934, and for the next six months, the *Reichswehr*, despite its appreciation and approval of certain aspects of the régime, would have marched and fired upon the Nazis if it had received the order to do so from the Field-Marshal. But Hitler saw to it that the order never came.

The threat to the solidarity of the Revolution was even greater from the Left, where the careerists, such as Goebbels and Darré, joined with the thugs of the régime, such as Röhm and Heines, in clamouring for a second and more radical wave of attack which should sweep away the privileged and the socially secure. Of these radicals Röhm was by far the most dangerous, both in his personality, which was now a combination of the German *Landsknecht* with the South American military-politico, and by reason of the fact that he stood at the head of two and a half million dissatisfied Storm Troopers. For, if the Nationalists were alarmed at the progress of the Revolution towards the Left, these brown-shirted paladins, who, from their youth in the Party, had imbibed its pre-revolutionary propaganda, regarded the Revolution as not having gone far enough. Indeed, they were sadly disillusioned. The first six months or so of the Revolution had offered their elemental ferocity a channel of expression, but the period of open lawlessness was over now; the Brown Terror had changed from hot to cold.

Röhm and his followers recalled the pledges which had been made by Hitler in the days before the seizure of power. They had been promised National Socialism 'in our time' and they had seen the great industrialists and landowners become apparently still more firmly entrenched behind their ramparts of wealth and privilege; they had been promised the return of the Polish Corridor and they had witnessed the beginnings of a *rapprochement* with Poland which was to blossom into a ten-year pact of non-aggression; above all, they had been promised honour and glory as the soldiers of the Revolution, and that from their untrained bands should spring battalions and regiments and divisions which should lift the old cockade from the mire and set the old banners waving once more in the breeze,[1] and in fulfilment of these glorious prospects they found themselves fobbed off with the *Stahlhelm*.

Moreover, their allegiance was divided. Hitler still remained their spiritual *Führer*, to whom their ultimate loyalty was pledged, but he was separated from them by affairs of State and set apart by a congeries of factors. He was no longer their intimate comrade, whereas Röhm, their Chief of Staff and virtual commander, had never lost touch with them and openly shared and voiced their sense of disillusionment and frustration. The SA were indeed rapidly establishing within the Party the position of an *imperium in imperio* not dissimilar from the status which the *Reichswehr* had achieved for itself within the Weimar Republic, with the same potential menace to the central authority.

Amid these dangers Adolf Hitler saw clearly that his sole chance of survival depended upon his ability to keep the Army on his side. Only by means of the Army could the Right subdue him, only with the tacit approval of the Army could he subdue the Left, should it come to a show-down between himself and Röhm. Moreover, in the devious course which he had set himself in foreign affairs he needed the support of the Army; and, above all, he too did not

[1] Cf. Hitler's concluding speech at the Munich trial in 1924. (See above, p. 179.)

lose sight of the fact that the grains were rapidly running out in the Field-Marshal's glass of life, knowing full well that the success or failure of his 'experiment' would depend upon the attitude of the armed forces of the State at that crucial moment when the glass should be empty.

On all counts, therefore, it behoved the *Führer* to walk warily and keep well on the right side of the Army, the only force which could bring him down and the only force which could sustain him, and both directly and indirectly he pandered to their wishes. By the promulgation of the Army Act of July 20, 1933, he had gone far to restoring the traditional military privileges and prestige, but Hitler also went out of his way to reiterate and re-emphasize what he had consistently maintained from the earliest days of the Nazi movement, namely, that in the National Socialist State there was but one bearer of arms, the *Reichswehr*, for which the SA were neither a complement nor a substitute. 'This army of the political soldiers of the German Revolution has no wish to take the place of our army or to enter into competition with it', he told the Storm Troop leaders in July, and again a month later, 'The relation of the SA to the Army must be the same as that of the political leadership to the Army'.[1]

No views could have been more divorced from those of Ernst Röhm, Chief of Staff of the Brown Army, who had persistently held a contrary thesis as to the rôle of the Storm Troops, and whose divergent heresy had led to an open breach with Hitler in 1925 and again in 1930. Röhm had observed with interest the example of the Fascist Party, who had forced the Italian Army to incorporate as militia entire Black Shirt formations. He had, however, a different and more daring plan. Röhm was, in effect, the first of the German revolutionary Generals, and he was a revolutionary before he was an officer. Taking the historical precedent of the French Revolution, he argued that all successful revolutions based upon ideological claims must have their own revolutionary armies which should be the vital expression of their new *Weltanschauung* and the chief weapon of their propaganda. Revolutionary wars cannot be waged with reactionary troops, and Röhm, with dazzling visions of the *verve* and *élan* of the popular armies of Carnot and Bonaparte, dreamed for himself a vision of military ambition such as the world had never seen. There was to be in Germany a select Praetorian Guard, a professional mercenary army, hand-picked purely from the

[1] Speech at the SA and *Stahlhelm Führertagung* at Bad Reichenhall, July 1, 1933, and speech at Bad Godesberg, August 19, 1933 (*Völkischer Beobachter*, July 3 and August 22, 1933 ; Baynes, i, 554).

Party standpoint. Alongside this force there was to be a mass militia based on conscription.

This had been the general idea which Röhm had discussed with von Schleicher in 1930, and it was as an outcome of these discussions that the Chief of Staff of the SA had reorganized his formations on lines parallel with those of the *Reichswehr*. But what Röhm had not told to von Schleicher, or indeed to any but the most intimate members of his own *Umgebung*, was that, though his immediate objective was the amalgamation of the SA with the *Reichswehr*, the secret aim of his ambition was ultimately to reverse their rôles and to make the Storm Troops the select volunteer Praetorian Guard of the Revolution, while the *Reichswehr* was to be relegated to the status of a mass conscript army.[1]

That the Chiefs of the *Reichswehr* were completely unaware of the full extent of Röhm's ambitious planning is certain, but it is unknown how far Hitler may have been cognizant of these schemes. That he would have been hostile to them is very sure, partly because they ran counter to his own consistent thesis and partly because they would have precipitated an immediate breach between the Army and the Party, and this he could not afford. But neither could he afford a breach with Röhm at the moment, since it was essential, after Germany's abrupt departure from Geneva in October, to present abroad an impression of a Germany united, with shields locked, about her *Führer*.[2]

For this purpose, therefore, Hitler walked upon the razor edge of uncertainty between the Brown Shirts and the Field Greys, now offering a sop to one, now making a concession to the other. On December 1 he admitted Röhm to the Reich Cabinet, together with Hess, as Minister without portfolio. At the same time, he still further degraded the *Stahlhelm*, which had been incorporated with the Storm Troops in July, by creating its members 'SA Reserve No. 1'.[3]

---

[1] Rauschning, *Germany's Revolution of Destruction*, pp. 171-2 ; Rosinski, p. 221.

[2] In protest against the refusal of the Great Powers to give satisfaction to the German claims to equality in armament, Hitler withdrew from the Disarmament Conference on October 14, 1933, and also gave notice of the termination of Germany's membership of the League of Nations.

[3] The youth organizations of the *Stahlhelm*, the *Jungstahlhelm* and the *Scharnhorst Jugend* were forcibly incorporated into the Hitler Youth Movement on July 25, 1933. On December 1 a decree proclaimed that those members of the *Stahlhelm*, of between thirty-five and forty-five years of age (*i.e.* the age at which they would have entered the *Landwehr* in Imperial Germany), would henceforth constitute SA Reserve No. 1. Those over forty-five (*i.e.* the age of the former *Landsturm*), together with other ex-Servicemen's and military organizations such as the *Kyffhäuserbund*, were to comprise SA Reserve No. 2. Early

The appointment of Röhm to the Cabinet was anything but congenial to von Blomberg, who suffered a further rebuff when the High Command of the *Reichswehr* refused point-blank to accept the Defence Minister's nomination of von Reichenau as Commander-in-Chief and, on referring to the ultimate jurisdiction of the Field-Marshal, carried their point in obtaining the appointment of von Fritsch.

Any rift which may have developed within the military hierarchy over this affair was, however, speedily healed as a result of the immediately subsequent events. Scarcely had the new Commander-in-Chief installed himself in the Bendlerstrasse than he was called upon to meet the first of a series of attempts on the part of Röhm to invade the sacred preserves of the Army. In the middle of February 1934 the Chief of Staff of the Storm Troops produced in Cabinet a memorandum designed to give effect to the first stages of that grandiose dream which had for so long dazzled his 'inner eye, which is the bliss of solitude'. What he proposed was no less than the co-ordination under one Ministry, of which it was tacitly implied that he should be the head, of the armed forces of the State, together with the para-military formations of the Party (SA and SS) and the war veterans' organizations (*Stahlhelm*, *Kyffhäuserbund*, etc.) which had now been incorporated as the SA reserves. This was the first step which Röhm urged in his memorandum, and the second was the inevitable corollary that the SA, now nearly three million strong, should be used as a skeleton corps for the expansion of the *Reichswehr*.

The immediate effect of this *démarche* was to fan into flame the conflict which had been for so long smouldering beneath the surface. Here was the clash of concepts and ideologies ; on the one hand, Röhm's dream of great revolutionary armies, bearing with them not only the palms of German victory but also the tenets of National Socialism ; on the other, the carefully matured plans of the *Reichswehr* for the elaborate development, on the lines laid down by von Seeckt, of the existing Army into a military force, of which the professional excellence should be unexcelled, but which should be devoid of any extraneous doctrine, dogma or creed, save that of military orthodoxy.

The Army leaders manifested a complete unity of front in opposition to this threat both to their sacred privileges and to the

in the New Year (February 17, 1934) the *Stahlhelm* lost even its semblance of independence, being renamed the 'National Socialist League of Ex-Servicemen'. Its leader, Herr Seldte, remained a member of the Reich Cabinet, and so continued until 1945 (Theodor Duesterberg, *Der Stahlhelm und Hitler* (Hanover, 1949), pp. 67-8).

success of the essential business in hand. Von Blomberg in the Cabinet, von Fritsch and the *Heeresleitung* in the Bendlerstrasse and the Generals commanding the seven *Wehrkreise*, were unanimous in rejecting any thought of concession to Röhm's proposals. They were not averse to using the SA as a source of man-power in the course of their expansion, but they had not the slightest intention of tolerating the 'playing at soldiers' of the Storm Troops or of allowing the wild fantasies of the Chief of Staff of that body to complicate or jeopardize the carefully prepared plans for rearmament.

Moreover, the moral record of the SA was a stench in the nostrils of all decent Germans. Corruption, debauchery and perversion were so openly practised as to be impossible of concealment. The erotic orgies of Röhm himself had long been common knowledge, but it was now established that Edmund Heines, Police President of Breslau, and Röhm's deputy in Silesia, possessed a highly efficient organization throughout the Reich for the explicit recruiting of his male harem. That these conditions existed could not be — and indeed was not — denied, and it was also openly stated in Berlin — and with every justification — that the greater part of the *Winterhilfe* [1] went into the pockets of the Storm Troop leaders to defray the expenses of the luxurious establishments which many of them had set up.

These scandals were grist to the mill of the Army's opposition. Apart from the unsavoury company which they were now called upon to keep by virtue of Röhm's proposals for the amalgamation of the 'Officer Corps' of the SA with that of the *Reichswehr*, it was an added argument that men whose private lives were lived with such obscene publicity were not to be entrusted with the vital business of the Reich's defences. 'Rearmament', as General von Brauchitsch later remarked, 'was too serious and difficult a business to permit the participation of peculators, drunkards and homosexuals.'

In this contest of strength with the armed forces Adolf Hitler made no attempt to support the claims of his trusted lieutenant, the only one of his followers with whom he was on *Du-fuss*, and whose private record was certainly known to him since 1925. [2] This opening engagement must have provided the *Führer* with some valuable material for contemplation. Though he had every intention of ultimately bending the Army to his will, the time for this was not

---

[1] The *Winterhilfe* was a fund established by the Nazis for the relief of the unemployed, to which all were exhorted to contribute generously. Apart from cheques, sent as a result of blackmail or as 'insurance', public collections were made at street corners and from door to door, only too frequently with threats and menaces.   [2] See above, p. 203.

yet, nor would it be until after he had bought their allegiance to him personally on the death of Hindenburg, a date which all knew could not be far removed. He was not therefore prepared to have his good relations with the Army impaired by Röhm's ambitious schemes, which, backed by his unruly Brown Praetorians, were becoming a menace not only to the position and privileges of the *Reichswehr* but to the disciplinary authority of the *Führer*.

When, therefore, the Generals carried their case to the Field-Marshal and obtained once again his unqualified support for their contention, Hitler made no effort to gainsay them. Indeed he came down very forcefully on the side of the Army. For when Mr. Anthony Eden visited Berlin on February 21 in the course of his pertinacious but fruitless efforts to discover some solution for the insoluble problem of German re- or disarmament, he was met by Hitler with an offer of the reduction of the SA by two-thirds and the institution of a system of supervision which should verify and ensure that the remainder should neither possess arms nor receive any military training. Thus Hitler planned to rid himself of an incubus by sacrificing the SA for the double purpose of buying the support of the *Reichswehr* and of deceiving the Western Powers, a policy to which the Army was certainly not inimical.

On February 28 an important meeting was held in the Bendler-strasse. Army and SA leaders, including Röhm, were there, as well as Himmler and Göring. Hitler addressed the company on the future military development of Germany, and made it clear that the *Reichswehr* was to be the basis of an expanded and powerful German army. The SA must remain a political organization, and he urged its leaders not to make difficulties for him at that critical moment.[1] The *Reichswehr* officers present were well satisfied with Hitler's speech, especially because Röhm signed an agreement afterwards apparently confirming the *Reichswehr*'s supremacy in military matters.

The check to Röhm was, however, but temporary. Though his offending memorandum was officially withdrawn, he returned to the charge again and again in the cabinet, where the sessions became more turbulent and the scenes between Röhm and von Blomberg more and more heated. It was in the course of one of these exchanges that Röhm interjected the bitter assertion that the Minister of Defence understood the real rôle of the SA in the new Germany even less than did his predecessor von Schleicher — a remark which did not pass unnoted. The patience of the Army, even of the compliant von Blomberg, was beginning to wear thin, and hints were

[1] Wolfgang Sauer in *Die Nationalsozialistische Machtergreifung* (Cologne, 1960), pp. 943 *et seq.*

dropped that the *Führer* must assert his authority in the matter of
the SA or suffer the consequences of the withdrawal of the confidence
of the Army in the régime.

As spring drew on it became increasingly apparent that the aged
Field-Marshal's death might be expected in a few months' time.
He grew weaker and less *compos mentis* and there came a day
early in April when both Hitler and von Blomberg were officially
but secretly informed of a perceptible break in the President's health.
This occurred on the eve of the spring manœuvres in the course of
which Hitler was to go from Kiel to Königsberg on board the pocket-
battleship *Deutschland*. Von Fritsch and Raeder, the chief executive
officers of the Army and the Navy, were present on this voyage,
which began on April 11. It does not seem unreasonable to suppose
that Hindenburg's condition and the succession to the Presidency
were among the topics discussed aboard the *Deutschland*. In any
event, there seems little doubt that once Hitler had learned of the
President's imminent death he had made up his mind to break with
Röhm, and it is clear that von Blomberg was ready to accept a consoli-
dation of Hitler's political power so long as the SA was neutralized.[1]

On April 16, in a note to the British Government, Hitler reaffirmed
his offer of February to Mr. Eden for the reduction of the SA to
some 700,000-800,000 men and a week later Joachim von Ribbentrop,
the newly appointed Ambassador-at-Large for Disarmament, reiterated the same proposal to M. Barthou in Paris (April 23). So
far the *Führer* had not been backward in giving assurance of good
faith. On April 27 the German public and the world at large were
allowed to receive the first *communiqué* on the deterioration in the
President's health, and on May Day the armed services, on the
instigation of von Blomberg, made their first important concession
of assuming upon their caps and tunics the eagle and the swastika
of the Party insignia.

In making this gesture it was von Blomberg's intention to
demonstrate the solidarity of the armed forces with the Party, but
in effect it was much more than this. For Hitler to have imposed,
on their own volition, the Party insignia upon the uniform of the
Army and Navy was a far more effective victory for National
Socialism than the grandiose dreams of Röhm. The Röhm plans
had merely antagonized the Army, but Hitler had both retained their
support and at the same time achieved the first of a series of psychological victories which, by their insidious subtlety, were to undermine

---

[1] In the *Weissbuch über die Erschiessungen des 30. Juni* (Paris, 1935), pp. 52-3,
it is claimed that Hitler and von Blomberg forged a definite pact on the *Deutschland*
whereby the former agreed to support Hitler's claims to the Presidency if the SA
were to be curbed. This account is unsubstantiated but not implausible.

the seemingly impregnable position of the Army. For the effect of this act upon the officers from the rank of colonel downwards, upon the rank and file, and also upon the civilian population of Germany, was more far-reaching than von Blomberg could have dreamed. To the soldiers it meant one more obstacle in the way of overthrowing a régime whose insignia they now wore as a part of their own. In the hearts of those in Germany who had placed their trust in the Army as the last defence of decency in the country, the mounting of the swastika struck a shudder of apprehension and disillusionment.

But von Blomberg was determined to march in step with Hitler in the confident belief that by so doing he was working not only for the advantage of Hitler but also of the Army as a whole. For, if the *Führer* owed his elevation to the Presidency to the support of the Army — and he could gain it by no other means — it would make him doubly reliant upon the Army to keep him there. The disciplining and restraint of the SA were as necessary to the security and prestige of the Party as of the Army, and their continued co-operation would therefore be mutually beneficial.

The opportunity for clinching the bargain was not far distant. The *communiqué* on Hindenburg's health was issued on April 27, and some two and a half weeks later (May 16) a gathering of the senior officers of the Ministry of Defence and of the Inspectorates of the Army, presided over by von Fritsch, met at Bad Nauheim to discuss the question of the succession. It was not, in effect, the new President of the Reich whom they were considering but their own Supreme Commander, and never had the choice been more vital for the Army, even when Hindenburg had himself been selected as a candidate for the Presidency in 1925.

The possible choices were three in number : General Ritter von Epp, an ardent Nazi and *Reichsstatthalter* of Bavaria, but at the same time a member of the caste and warmly devoted to the cause of rearmament ; the German Crown Prince, who, if the Army determined upon a restoration of the Monarchy, might well be declared Regent if he were already President ; and Hitler himself. Von Blomberg was not present when the meeting began, and on his arrival found that his candidate, Hitler, was well behind the other two in general favour. He at once told his colleagues that an understanding had been reached with Hitler, by which, in return for the Presidency, he would sacrifice the SA. The effect of his disclosure was magical. With perfect unanimity the Generals voted to accept Hitler on these conditions,[1] and, as an outward and visible sign of their

---

[1] Benoist-Méchin, ii, 553-4.

acceptance, von Fritsch, on May 25, issued a new version of 'The Duties of the German Soldier'. This 'Bible of the Army' had been first produced in 1920, when von Seeckt had written : 'The German soldier must have no political activity'; ten years later, in May 1930, Heye had reinterpreted this wording as : 'The *Reichswehr* serves the State but not the Parties'; *autre temps autre mœurs*: in the passage of four years a new interpretation had become necessary, and in May 1934 thé words of von Blomberg and von Fritsch were : 'Military service is a service of honour toward the German *Volk*'.

No better epitome of the decline and fall of the German Army in politics exists than a comparison of these three general orders, which contain the transition from the Olympian *Überparteilichkeit* of von Seeckt to the ultimate and irrevocable identification of the Army with the Nazi régime.

Meantime the months of April and May had witnessed a heightening of the tension within the Reich. On the Left, the Radicals became more importunate in their clamour for a Second Revolution; while on the Right the Conservatives, realizing that their hold upon political life would virtually come to an end with the death of the President, besought their representative, Franz von Papen, to take action before it was too late. 'Fränzchen', as usual, had a plan. He prepared for Hindenburg a draft political testament which, though laudatory in its tribute to Hitler for the achievement of the regime in the realm of *Volksgemeinschaft*, made a firm recommendation for the restoration of the Monarchy. This draft was accepted by Hindenburg and signed without major alterations, on May 11.[1] Von Papen essayed, by means of this somewhat feeble effort, to ensure that Hitler would not become the Head of the State on the death of Hindenburg, and that the régime should revert to the character which he and his fellow Conservatives had originally intended it to have, namely that of a coalition of the forces of the Right and not the rule of a single Party. What 'Fränzchen' had never learned was

---

[1] The story of Hindenburg's last will and testament, its preparation by von Papen and Meissner, its alleged 'loss' after Hindenburg's death, its sudden 'recovery' and publication in an emasculated form on the eve of the national referendum of August 19, 1934, is among the many fascinating byways of history which have yet to be followed to the end. The full story may never be known, but certain details emerged from the interrogation of von Papen at Nuremberg on October 12, 1945, and from the record of the de-nazification proceedings against him at Nuremberg in January–February 1947 and against Oskar von Hindenburg at Ülzen, near Hanover, on March 14-17, 1949, in the course of which von Papen also gave evidence and Meissner contributed an affidavit. From these sources it would appear that the final text of the document signed by Hindenburg on May 11, 1934, was actually prepared by Count von der Schulenburg, the adjutant to the President, at Neudeck.

that in politics one cannot put the clock back, and that the changes effected by the Nazis in the political structure of the Reich during the first eighteen months of their rule would only be undone when the Nazis themselves fell from power.

Within the Party conclave also the strife was mounting. The relations between Hitler and Röhm had become gravely embittered. The Chief of Staff of the SA had come out in April with a further, more detailed and more determined demand that the armed forces and the para-military formations should be united and placed under his control as Minister of Defence, and Hitler, according to his own story later given to the *Reichstag*, had been categorical in his refusal of a policy which would have entailed the disavowal of a view which he had held consistently for the fourteen years of his political career. Under no circumstances would he abandon his emphatic ruling that 'the fighting organizations of the Party are political institutions and have nothing to do with the Army'.[1]

Röhm withdrew to his tents and sought solace with his young men and with the hierarchs of the SA. He was bitter and disgruntled, but, so far as any evidence has yet been produced, he was not disloyal to Hitler personally. In this mood it was not unnatural that he should be prepared for a reconciliation with von Schleicher, the one man who, though they had ultimately quarrelled, had in the past given him real encouragement and support from the Bendlerstrasse.

The dissension within the Party and the general feeling of crisis in the air had the, perhaps almost inevitable, result of drawing Kurt von Schleicher from his retirement. He now emerged and, with an irresponsible disregard for discretion, indulged in trenchant criticism of the Government. He had failed to realize that what was merely treachery before the establishment of the Totalitarian State, was now regarded as high treason. He could not reconcile himself to decent obscurity, and, although he no longer controlled the secret forces of espionage and the Generals were steadfastly against him, he yielded to the lure of possible intrigue and began to engage in his favourite pastime of 'Shadow Cabinet' making.

Before long it was rumoured that a tentative agreement had been reached between the General and Röhm. In return for the Vice-Chancellorship under Hitler, von Schleicher was said to have agreed to the appointment of Röhm as Minister of Defence and to the amalgamation of the SA with the *Reichswehr*. Von Papen, Göring and von Neurath were to be removed from the Government, the

---

[1] Hitler's speech to the *Reichstag* on July 13, 1934 (*Frankfurter Zeitung*, July 15, 1934; Baynes, i, 311-12).

whisper went, Brüning was to be offered the Ministry of Foreign Affairs, and Gregor Strasser that of National Economy. The approval of France for the change in the régime was alleged to have been obtained in advance by von Schleicher from the French Ambassador.[1]

It is true that these stories were in circulation in Berlin at the time and that typewritten lists of the new Cabinet were passed from hand to hand with a lack of discretion which was terrifying to at least one foreign observer.[2] But that these accounts were in many respects both unreliable and irresponsible may be judged from the actual facts. For example, the last occasion on which von Schleicher saw the French Ambassador was on Easter Monday (April 2), when they spent a day together in the country, and though the General was no more guarded in his remarks than usual, he gave no hint of being involved in a plot, and, according to the Ambassador, 'whenever he mentioned Röhm's name it was with contempt and disgust'.[3] Again, no communication had passed between Brüning and von Schleicher since their quasi-reconciliation after the latter's fall as Chancellor, and the inclusion of Brüning's name in the 'Shadow Cabinet' was without his knowledge or consent.[4] In so far as von Schleicher was concerned, the affair was little more than one of building castles in Spain, for he no longer had access to the President, and was discredited and without influence. The preparation of the lists was in all probability the work of his more devoted though irresponsible followers, such as General von Bredow or Werner von Alvensleben, whose indiscreet utterance on the night of January 29, 1933, had already had epoch-making results.[5]

But in the hands of Göring and of Himmler the story took on gigantic proportions. These two worthies had ranged themselves on the side of the Army and against Röhm, each for his own good reasons. Göring had always traded on his war record, his *Pour le mérite* cross, and the fact that his family belonged to the military caste, to ingratiate himself with the Army. He liked to regard himself as 'one of them' and to pose as the representative of monarchical and reactionary sympathies among the Nazi leaders. Moreover, he cordially disliked Röhm and could never forget that he, Göring, had been the original leader of the SA.

Himmler, on the other hand, was actuated by a desire to destroy

---

[1] Hitler's speech of July 13, 1934 (Baynes, i, 311-13, 318).
[2] The present writer was in Berlin at this time and was shown one of the lists of the Shadow Cabinet in the course of a conversation in a certain famous bar, where it was a well-known fact that the barmen and waiters were in the employment of the Gestapo.   [3] François-Poncet, p. 192.
[4] Wheeler-Bennett, p. 455.   [5] See above, p. 284.

the SA as a political weapon within the Party and to substitute for its influence the more compact *élite* corps of his own SS. The views of Himmler and Röhm in regard to the Army and its future rôle in the Third Reich were not widely separated. Both aimed at the subjection of the professional soldiers to the revolutionary armies of the Party, and indeed Himmler was destined to succeed where Röhm had failed. The establishment of the *Waffen*-SS, the position which it subsequently enjoyed and the appointment of Himmler to the command of the Home Army in July 1944 were in many respects the realization of those dazzling visions which had stirred Röhm's imagination.[1] For the moment, however, Himmler was content with the elimination of Röhm and the SA and of the elements which he regarded as fundamentally dangerous to the régime. The conquest of the Army could await its appropriate hour.

Both Göring and Himmler were agreed, therefore, that such an opportunity for the rapid removal of their enemies and rivals by drastic methods might never occur again. The *Führer* must be persuaded to seize the chance, and to this end they proceeded to develop the idea of a counter-revolution nearly ripe for action.

Through the evil fertility of their minds the stories current in Berlin and elsewhere in Germany were built up into a nightmare of horrific appearance. It was no longer a meeting together of disgruntled persons, it was a plot, a conspiracy to murder, to be met and fought with its own weapons. Plans were laid for a drastic purge of the Party, which should include within its scope all the enemies of the régime, both past and present, to the Right and to the Left. Lists of those to be 'liquidated' were prepared and a certain bargaining went on whereby the friends of one were to be removed from the list of the other in return for reciprocal treatment. The date was fixed for mid-June, and all that was lacking was the *Führer's* final consent for action.[2]

This consent had not been obtained when Hitler departed on June 15 for his first meeting with Mussolini in Venice. He would not commit himself to the final order. He still hoped for reconciliation with certain of the old comrades from whom he had recently

---

[1] See below, p. 678.

[2] At the end of May both Brüning and von Schleicher received warnings that they were among those marked for murder. Brüning prudently left the country in disguise and began a fifteen-year exile in Britain and the United States, which only ended when he revisited Germany in the summer of 1949. Von Schleicher, with characteristic lack of judgment, assessed the affair as a passing storm which would soon blow over. He merely went into retreat on the shores of the Starnbergersee and later took his wife for a motor tour, from which he returned to Berlin toward the end of June.

become estranged,[1] and that the restraint of the SA could be carried out without the use of force. In the course of the Venice meeting, however, a new factor emerged. Ulrich von Hassell, the German Ambassador, had been prompted by von Neurath and Meissner, on the part of the President, to persuade the Duce to indicate delicately to his visitor the necessity of removing from office certain persons such as Röhm and Heines, whose infamous notoriety blackened the name of Germany at home and abroad. This Mussolini is believed to have done, drawing for good measure upon his own experience in the case of the Matteotti murder for an example of the embarrassment which extremists in the movement could afford their leader.[2]

Still Hitler hesitated. On his return to Germany he summoned a council of the chiefs of the Party at the little town of Gera, in Thuringia, on June 17, to discuss with them the results of his conference with the Duce. But this midsummer Sunday was fated to become important in German history for other reasons than the meeting at Gera.

Franz von Papen had not been idle. He was alarmed beyond measure at the turn events were taking, and more particularly at the corruption and arrogance of the SA, whose constant bickerings with the *Stahlhelm*, bickerings which frequently ended in fisticuffs and bloodshed, constituted a direct threat to the internal peace of Germany, apart from the reign of terror which these brown-shirted bravoes imposed upon all who might be regarded as remotely inimical to the régime. The Second Revolution seemed to be 'just around the corner', and von Papen was now aware that events would not wait for the precautionary measures which he had designed to take place after Hindenburg's death. What was necessary now was immediate action, and 'Fränzchen' determined to make a reasoned and public protest against the excesses and extremism of the Nazi régime. By so doing he hoped to prevail upon Hitler to make a last-minute change of course, but if this public appeal to the

---

[1] According to Otto Strasser, a not unprejudiced source, Hitler, on the eve of his departure for Venice, sent for Gregor Strasser, whom he had not met since the breach of December 1932 (see above, p. 269), and offered him the Ministry of National Economy. Gregor Strasser replied that he would accept, provided that Göring and Goebbels were removed from the Cabinet, but to these terms the *Führer* was not prepared to agree (Otto Strasser, *Hitler and I* (London, 1940), pp. 189-90).

[2] On June 11, 1924, Giacomo Matteotti, the Italian Socialist leader and an outspoken critic of the Mussolini régime, was kidnapped and murdered by Fascist killers, after a particularly trenchant attack in the Chamber. How far this act was carried out on the personal order of Mussolini has never been established, but as a result of the mounting rage which followed it both at home and abroad the Fascist régime was shaken to its foundations, and the Duce sat more uneasily in power at that time than at any other before his downfall in 1943.

CH. I SEIZURE OF POWER TO DEATH OF HINDENBURG 319

Führer's conscience failed, the Vice-Chancellor would resign from the Cabinet with such repercussions as that might entail. Such was von Papen's plan, but, being 'Fränzchen', he said as much in the diplomatic circles of Berlin and his listeners waited breathlessly for the approaching day.

Von Papen's speech was made at the University of Marburg on Sunday, June 17, the day on which the Nazi chieftains were gathered at Gera, and, perhaps because it owed much in authorship to the genius of his assistant, Edgar Jung, it was a masterpiece in style and content. Courageous and dignified in tone, it conveyed both a warning of the danger of a second radical wave of revolution and a very thinly disguised attack upon Goebbels personally.[1] It was received with favour in the world at large and with unfeigned joy and relief by many thousands in Germany.

But in the little town of Gera, there was tumult and afright. Panic spread among the Nazi chieftains as the news of the Marburg speech beat in upon their counsels, and with it the rumour that von Papen had hoisted the standard of counter-revolution and had behind him not only the President but the *Reichswehr*. It was patent that a decision of the *Führer* as between the reactionary and radical wings of his Party was now inescapable. The Marburg speech had dragged out into the light of day too many skeletons for their rattling bones to be crammed back into the cupboard. The issue must be faced — and faced squarely.

Hitler hurried to Berlin, to find that Röhm had departed for Munich and von Blomberg to Neudeck. The rival clans were gathering in their respective strongholds. Goebbels, meanwhile, was spewing forth a torrent of venomous invective against von Papen personally and the Right in general, as a result of which the Vice-Chancellor, accompanied by von Neurath and Schwerin von Krosigk, called upon Hitler on June 20 and tendered their resignations. It was clear to the Führer that the Right were not to be intimidated and, though he refused to accept these resignations, it was with considerable concern and apprehension that he flew to Neudeck on the following morning to report to the President on the Venice Conference.

The Chancellor was met on the steps of the Schloss by General von Blomberg in full uniform ; a von Blomberg no longer the affable 'Rubber Lion' or the adoring 'Hitler-Junge Quex', but embodying all the stern ruthlessness of the Prussian military caste. He had been instructed, said the General, to consult with the Chancellor,

---

[1] *Rede des Vizekanzlers von Papen vor dem Universitätsbund, Marburg, am 17. Juni 1934* (Germania-Verlag, Berlin).

on behalf of the President, for the necessary measures to be taken to ensure the maintenance of internal peace throughout Germany. If the Government of the Reich could not of itself bring about a complete relaxation of the present state of tension, the President would declare martial law and hand over the control of affairs to the Army. In the course of a four-minute interview, in von Blomberg's presence, Hindenburg reiterated what the Minister of Defence had already stated, and in less than half an hour after his arrival Hitler found himself on the front steps again in the brilliant pitiless glare of the June sunlight.[1]

It is probable that Hitler's final decision to suppress the SA by force was taken in the course of his flight back to the Tempelhof on June 21. He could no longer deceive himself. The promise given to the Army with regard to Röhm's legions must be implemented at all costs if the Army was in its turn to honour its share of the bargain. The new tone adopted by von Blomberg, the cold relentless tone of the Prussian officer under direct orders, could have only one meaning — that the support of the Army for Hitler's accession as Chief of State would only be forthcoming if and when the price of that support had been paid in full.

The next ten days were filled with the final planning for the *coup* against Röhm, but Göring and Himmler had broadened their field of action and now included within their lists of the proscribed the names of such as those who had opposed the Nazi Movement in its early days and those whose knowledge of certain events was too detailed or too great for safety.[2] Hitler, too, was busily engaged in building up the alibi which he would later proclaim to the Reich and to the world, of the gigantic murder-plot — 'The Night of the Long Knives' — from which he was about to save Germany.

How much, it may be asked, did the *Reichswehr* know of the extent and nature of these preparations for mass-murder? Did the Generals, indeed, know anything? By their attitude at the Bad Neuheim meeting and their acceptance of Nazi insignia they had demonstrated their willingness to give their support for Hitler's

[1] Certain accounts of this interview (*e.g.* Otto Strasser, pp. 195-6) state that von Blomberg was accompanied by Göring, and Hitler by Goebbels, so that the meeting on the steps at Neudeck symbolized the clash between reaction and revolution, for it was not till after Hitler's return to Berlin that Goebbels forsook the radicals and rallied to the side of reaction. Others, however (*e.g.* Jean François, *L'Affaire Röhm-Hitler* (Paris, 1939), pp. 107-8), deny the presence of either Göring or Goebbels, but give details of a subsequent three-sided conversation between Hitler, von Blomberg and Meissner, during which the General made the position of the Army abundantly clear.

[2] It was claimed that those SA leaders thought to have been implicated in the *Reichstag* fire had been singled out for liquidation, including Karl Ernst, the SA chief of Berlin-Brandenburg.

succession to Hindenburg in return for an undertaking that the SA would be disciplined and rendered for ever harmless as a rival to the Army. This, however, does not necessarily mean that the culpability of the Generals was any greater (or less) than that of Henry II, whose petulant remark about a 'turbulent priest' led to 'Murder in the Cathedral'. Certainly the Army as a whole had no idea of the extent of the plans prepared by Göring and Himmler, and approved by Hitler. The stories that certain Generals personally supervised the issue of rifles and machine-guns from the *Reichswehr* stores to the SS, during those last breathless June days, and that certain others, notably von Rundstedt and von Witzleben, sat on the drum-head courts-martial held at the Lichter-felde Cadet School on the Berlin SA leaders, are completely lacking of confirmation and should be treated with great reserve.[1]

Nevertheless, the burden of responsibility and shame which is inescapable on the part of the *Reichswehr* for the events preceding the Blood Purge lies in the fact that they did not choose to enquire sufficiently closely into the means to be employed for implementing the pledge which Hitler had given them. It may be that they were shown the evidence of the Röhm conspiracy for an *émeute* by the SA, which Göring and Himmler, and now Goebbels also, were busily supplying to the *Führer*, and it may be that they unquestioningly believed it. It may be that they shrank, as they had shrunk once before, from the task of firing upon the Storm Troops and condoned with relief the rôle allotted to the SS in this 'disciplining operation'. Whatever the excuses, the *Generalität* cannot plead complete ignorance of what was in the wind. A mere recital of facts and events reduces their pleas of innocence to an indecent rag of covering.

On June 25 a general order was issued by von Fritsch placing the *Reichswehr* all over the country in a state of alert ; all leave was cancelled and all troops confined to barracks. Three days later the entire SS formation was put through an operation of secret mobiliza-tion and held in readiness for immediate action. On this same day (June 28) Röhm was formally expelled from membership of the German Officers' League and from all other veterans' organizations — a measure which smacked of the handing over of a victim by the Holy Office to the civil arm for execution [2] — and in the issue of the

---

[1] Cf. Serge Lang and Ernst von Schenck, *Portraät eines Menschheitsverbrechers nach den hinterlassenen Memoiren des ehemaligen Reichsministers Alfred Rosenberg* (St. Gallen, 1947), p. 254 ; Curt Riess, *The Self-betrayed: Glory and Doom of the German Generals* (New York, 1942), p. 149.

[2] The object of Röhm's expulsion was that, when, after the Blood Purge had been carried out, he would be publicly branded as a traitor and conspirator, the honour of the German Officers' League would not be besmirched by carrying his

Völkischer Beobachter of the day following (June 29) there appeared a signed article by General von Blomberg proclaiming that the Army stood resolutely behind the *Führer*. At dawn on June 30 the blow fell and for the next forty-eight hours bloody murder stalked nakedly through the Reich.

If the Generals were not at least partially informed of what was about to happen, why were the *Reichswehr* alerted ? Why was Röhm, whose conduct had richly merited such action long before, rapidly removed from the rolls of the Officers' League, and why did the Minister of Defence find it necessary to pledge anew the solidarity of the Army with the *Führer* ? The conclusion is inescapable that the upper ranks of the military hierarchy were well aware of what was to take place on June 30, and that, by consenting to the use of the SS as a'disciplinary force, they tacitly condoned the planning of mass murder and, like Pilate, washed their hands of direct responsibility. By so much were they accessories *before* the event.

The scope of the Blood Purge was wide and catholic.[1] The High Command of the SA, convened in special conference at Munich by a circular telegram signed 'Adolf Hitler', were butchered like steers in their own headquarters by SS murder squads. Röhm and Heines were arrested in the early hours of June 30, under circumstances which, though disreputable, precluded any idea that they were about to launch a *Putsch* in the immediate future.[2] Both were killed, dying unhonoured and unsung. So much for the Party feuds ; but the arm of fate stretched far back into the past. That aged reactionary, Gustav Ritter von Kahr, whom Hitler had never forgiven for his part in the fiasco of November 1923, was brutally murdered outside Munich, and a similar fate was intended for the royalist political agent,

name upon its rolls. The Army was always careful that no member of the Officer Corps was ever tried for the crime of high treason, even if he had to be precipitately expelled from the Corps before the opening of the legal proceedings. It was in accordance with this tradition that the Court of Honour, presided over by Field-Marshal von Rundstedt, declared the military conspirators of the *Putsch* of July 20, 1944, to be guilty of conspiracy and expelled them from the Army before their trial before the People's Court.

[1] For details of the Blood Purge of June 30, 1934, see Jean François, *L'Affaire Röhm-Hitler* ; Otto Strasser, *Hitler and I*, and Otto Strasser, *Die deutsche Bartholomäusnacht* (Zurich, 1935) ; Klaus Bredow, *Hitler Rast. Der 30. Juni, Ablauf, Vorgeschichte und Hintergründe* (Saarbrücken, 1934) ; Kurt G. W. Ludecke, pp. 759-80 ; Hitler's speech to the Reichstag, July 13, 1934, Baynes 1, 290-328 ; Hans Berno Gisevius, *Bis zum bittern Ende* (Zürich, 1946), i, 207-300 ; Wheeler-Bennett, pp. 454-64. The *Weissbuch über die Erschiessungen des 30. Juni 1934* (Paris, 1935) should be treated with caution. For a more recent discussion of the Purge, see Helmut Krausnick, 'Der 30. Juni 1934' in *Aus Politik und Zeitgeschichte, Beilage zur Wochenzeitung 'Das Parlament'*, 30. Juni 1954.

[2] Röhm was arrested at an inn at Wiessee and taken to Munich, where, after a persistent refusal to commit suicide, he was executed.

Freiherr zu Guttenberg, who had sought, unsuccessfully, to intrigue with von Schleicher for a Wittelsbach restoration in December 1932.[1]

While Hitler and Goebbels led the attack in Bavaria, Göring and Himmler had not been idle in Berlin. Here the story was the same. The leaders of the North German SA were rounded up and, after a perfunctory and farcical court martial, were executed by black-uniformed SS *peletons* on the parade ground of the old Lichterfelde Cadet School. But many other old scores were also settled. Gregor Strasser was kidnapped and murdered. The Vice-Chancellor, Franz von Papen himself, was arrested and removed from his office under guard; while two of his adjutants were shot down across their desks, and Edgar Jung, part author of the Marburg speech, was hunted down and killed. Treviranus escaped over the garden wall as two car-loads of SS hatchet-men drew up to his house, and later contrived to make his way to England.

The slaughter continued throughout the week-end, while fearsome rumours spread on wings of horror through the capital. The first official intimation was made by Göring late on Saturday afternoon (June 30), when, to a gathering of bewildered and horrified foreign journalists hastily called to the Chancellery, he gave a brief and brutal account of the events of the last twelve hours. The name of von Schleicher was mentioned in connection with the Röhm-Strasser 'conspiracy'.

'And what's happened to him?' someone asked.

Göring paused and looked around his audience with a wolfish smile.

'Ah yes,' he remarked, 'you journalists always like a special "headline" story; well, here it is. General von Schleicher had plotted against the régime. I ordered his arrest. He was foolish enough to resist. He is dead.' And he left the room.

It was between nine and ten in the golden morning of June 30 when the telephone rang in von Schleicher's villa in Neu-Babelsberg. An old friend, a former fellow-officer, wished to welcome the General back from his recent travels and to congratulate him on his escape from a serious motor accident. They chatted together for a while, when von Schleicher said that there was someone at the door. He must have turned from the telephone, for his friend heard his voice, distant but distinct, saying: '*Jawohl, ich bin General von Schleicher*'. Then, with piercing clarity, came the sound of shots: then silence.[2]

---

[1] See above, p. 277.

[2] The present writer received this account of von Schleicher's death from the friend in question.

The General's murderers had forced their way into the house and, apparently not recognizing him, had sought to establish his identity. This done, they emptied their pistols into his body and shot down his wife as she ran forward. The corpses remained untouched until discovered by the General's sixteen-year-old step-daughter on her return to luncheon.

Such was the end of Kurt von Schleicher, the Field-Grey Eminence of the *Reichswehr*, who in his time did more harm to the reputation, prestige and authority of the German Army than any other man in the inter-war period. He had been its true master for years. He had served it with a passionate, if misguided, devotion. Yet he had few friends within its ranks. His predilection for intrigue, his ruses, his cynicism, his proclivity for playing both ends against the middle, had cost him the regard of many, and there were many more who considered his rapid promotion as being altogether dis-proportionate with his military abilities.

Yet two devoted friends he had, von Bredow and von Hammer-stein. One of them was to share his fate and the other to labour untiringly for the vindication of both of them. Kurt von Bredow learned of von Schleicher's murder as he sat at tea that same afternoon in the lounge of the Adlon Hotel. 'I am surprised that the swine have not killed me also before now', was his comment. One of those present, a foreign military attaché, immediately invited him to his house to dine and sleep, but von Bredow refused with gratitude this thinly veiled means for his protection. 'I am going home', he said in a raised voice so that the waiters, whose reputation as Gestapo agents was well known, might hear. 'They have killed my Chief. What is there left for me?' And with a gesture of farewell to his friends he passed through the revolving glass doors into Unter den Linden. None of those present saw him again. Late that evening he himself answered a prolonged ringing of his front-door bell. A burst of revolver fire greeted him as the door opened and in a moment he had joined his Chief.

(v)

Dark was the stain of dishonour which overspread the escutcheon of the German Army on this day of June 30; heavy the burden of guilt which they assumed before the bar of history. To their shame be it said that, in conflict with their declared and acknowledged duty to maintain law and order within the Reich, they condoned the use of gangster methods in the settlement, to their own advantage, of a Party dispute. To some extent certainly they were accessories before the fact, but their culpability was the greater in that they allowed the murder and butchery to continue for two days without protest, when they alone could have stopped it by the raising of a finger. Not only did they not protest, they congratulated, and in the most sycophantic terms : 'The *Führer* has personally attacked and wiped out the mutineers and traitors with soldierly decision and exemplary courage', von Blomberg informed the Army in an Order of the Day on July 1, in which he raised the 'state of emergency' throughout the Reich. 'The *Wehrmacht* as the sole bearer of arms within the Reich, remains aloof from internal political conflict but pledges anew its devotion and its fidelity. The *Führer* asks us to establish cordial relations with the new SA. This we shall joyfully endeavour to do in the belief that we serve a common ideal.'[1]

Never was there a more damning document than this, for it adds pusillanimity and casuistry to the charges against the Army. If indeed the Government of the Reich had been menaced by 'mutineers and traitors', then it was the indisputable duty of the *Reichswehr* to take action against them. But they had not done this. In order to rid themselves of their brown-shirted rivals they had made a temporary abdication of their proud position as the sole bearer of arms within the Reich, and had permitted an operation, which was clearly more than a police action, to be undertaken by an *élite* and fanatical force, the SS, which, though now in its infancy, was to challenge and humiliate the Army in its own field. And, finally, when massacre had removed their enemies, the Army declared their willingness to enter 'joyfully' into friendly relations with the survivors. Could cynical cowardice sink lower than this public adoption by the *Reichswehr* of the moral standards of the Third Reich ?

Yet the story did not end there. Incriminated as they were, blood-brothers of the Nazis as they had now become, it was essential for the Army that the acts of the *Führer* should receive the official blessing of the Supreme Commander and the legal assent of the constitutional authorities. Forthwith von Blomberg saw to it that the proper information reached Neudeck — for Hindenburg was ever jealous of the 'honour of the German Army' — with the result that on July 2 the Field-Marshal telegraphed to the Bohemian Corporal whom he had raised to the office of Chancellor of the Reich: 'From the reports placed before me, I learn that you, by your determined action and gallant personal intervention, have nipped treason in the bud (*im Keime erstickt*). You have saved the German nation from serious danger. For this I express to you my most

[1] Benoist-Méchin, ii, 578.

profound thanks and sincere appreciation.' [1]

It was von Blomberg, moreover, as representing the armed forces of the State, who expressed the congratulations of the Cabinet to the *Führer* on the occasion of the special session called on July 3, and it was von Blomberg, as a member of the Cabinet, who gave the approval of the *Reichswehr* for the promulgation of the decree (*Staatsnotwehrgesetz*) declaring the actions of June 30 and the days following to be legal measures which had been rendered necessary 'by the right of the legitimate defence of the State'. 'In this hour I was responsible for the fate of the German people', Hitler later told the *Reichstag*, 'and I thereby became the supreme Justiciar (*oberster Gerichtsherr*) of the German people.' [2] With this view von Blomberg whole-heartedly concurred, since it publicly removed any taint of responsibility from the Army.

And yet the taint had not been fully removed; indeed, it could not be washed away except in blood, the blood of German Generals shed, futilely but not ungallantly, after the failure of their own *Putsch* just ten years later. Until that time, amongst those in Germany who were opposed to the régime, there was a gradual lessening of faith in the civil courage and military honour of the leaders of the German Army.

At first there was almost universal satisfaction at the lifting of the tyranny of the Storm Troops, but slowly the bloody details of the massacres found their way throughout Germany, and honest men stood appalled at the realization that they had but exchanged one tyranny for another, and that the brutality and corruption of the SA had but been replaced by the brutality and corruption of the SS and the Gestapo. That the Army had condoned this thing shocked many; that they tamely accepted the fact that their former Minister of Defence and Chancellor, General of Infantry Kurt von Schleicher, the man who had virtually controlled the destinies of the *Reichswehr* for at least ten years, could be shot down in his own home and publicly branded as a traitor, did not enhance their prestige within the ranks of those who had hitherto looked to the Army as the ultimate source of salvation, and was hailed as a further sign of weakness by their more astute opponents.

[1] Benoist-Méchin, ii, 579; Wheeler-Bennett, p. 454. The President also telegraphed to Göring on the same day, addressing him not only as Minister-President of Prussia, but also as General of Infantry, and therefore as one officer to another: 'For your energetic and successful proceeding of the smashing (*die Niederschlagung*) of high treason I express to you my thanks and recognition. With comradely thanks and regards, von Hindenburg' (Erich Gritzbach, *Hermann Göring, Werk und Mensch* (Munich, 1941), p. 255).
[2] Hitler's speech to the *Reichstag*, July 13, 1934 (Baynes, i, 321).

There was no more eloquent example of the loss of mental balance, of moral values and political independence, on the part of the Officer Corps as a whole, than its attitude to the murders of von Schleicher and von Bredow. The German officer had become a professional in the sense that any technician is a professional. He was no longer an Olympian figure, god-like in his aloofness ; he had become caught up in the scramble for promotion and preferment. The 'careerist', instead of being the exception, had now become the accepted rule, and, as a result, instead of leaders like von Seeckt or Gröner or von Hammerstein, who were men of character and courage, not caring whether they were in favour or not, they had come down to men such as von Blomberg and von Fritsch, who could barter away the honour of the Army for the illusion of power.

Hitler had gone about his business of the denigration of von Schleicher and von Bredow in a manner best calculated to have its favourable repercussions in the military hierarchy. In his speech to the *Reichstag* on July 13 he twice accused them of high treason in that they had got into touch with a foreign Power, namely France, with a view to obtaining support, either tacit or overt, for the projected Röhm-Strasser-Schleicher *coup d'état*.[1] It was a well-known fact that von Schleicher was on terms of personal friendship with the French Ambassador ; it was also known that von Bredow was in equally close relations with the French military attaché. Given the personalities of the two men, their passion for intrigue, their unguarded criticism of the régime, it was conceivable that, had they been contemplating a *Putsch*, they would have had no formal objection to introducing a foreign Power into an internal German political conflict. In effect, neither von Schleicher nor von Bredow was contemplating anything of the sort, but their fellow Generals, even if they did not believe them guilty, believed them capable of such action under certain circumstances, and this was sufficient to account

---

[1] Hitler's speech to the *Reichstag*, July 13, 1934 (Baynes, i, 315, 318). It should be noted, however, that, less than a year later (May 22, 1935), Hitler told M. Joseph Lipski, the Polish Ambassador in Berlin, that von Schleicher 'was rightfully murdered, if only because he had sought to maintain the Rapallo Treaty'. Göring, during his visit to Warsaw in January 1935, had already informed Count Szembek that when von Schleicher had handed over the seals of office to Hitler in January 1933 he had urged upon the *Führer* the desirability of reaching an understanding with France and Russia, and with the assistance of the latter, of eliminating Poland, but that Hitler had recoiled in horror from such a proposal (Polish White Book, *Official Documents concerning Polish-German and Polish-Soviet Relations, 1933-1939* (London, 1939), pp. 25, 29 and 216). Von Schleicher's murderers were thus not alone in exploiting this assassination to the greater duplicity of the Third Reich. However, see below, pp. 331, 337 and footnote.

for the passive acceptance by the Officer Corps of their murder. The same sense of 'correctness', which, on the one hand, made it impossible for the Corps to accept the choice as a Commander-in-Chief, of a General, such as von Reichenau, who disregarded military taboo, made it equally impossible to resent or protest against the murder of a General, such as von Schleicher, who could, perhaps, have been capable under certain circumstances of enlisting foreign aid against the Nazis.

Yet not all were silent. It is one of the redeeming features of an episode of otherwise unrelieved sordid brutality, that all von Schleicher's personal friends acted with the utmost bravery and loyalty. Von Hammerstein, apprised on the night of June 30 by Frau von Bredow of her husband's murder, went into temporary seclusion in the country, from which he returned to Berlin a few days later to attend the funeral of Kurt von Schleicher and his wife. Denied access to the cemetery by SS guards, who even confiscated the wreaths which the mourners had brought with them, von Hammerstein dedicated himself thenceforward to the task of rehabilitating his two friends. He found an indefatigable and gallant ally in the veteran Field-Marshal von Mackensen, who, but two years younger than Hindenburg, represented with him all that was venerated and admired in the pre-war Imperial Army.[1] With no little courage the old man had repeatedly tried to reach the President by telephone during that ghastly week-end of June 30, to inform him of what was happening and to request a Presidential order to the *Reichswehr* to stop the slaughter. Though he succeeded in making contact with the Schloss at Neudeck, he was each time informed that the President was too unwell to speak to him. The *Reichswehr* were quite determined that no such order should reach them, for had they received it they must have obeyed. The Marshal-

---

[1] Field-Marshal August von Mackensen, born in November 1849, was the epitome of the old world cavalryman. He rose to regimental distinction as commander of the famous 'Death's Head Hussars', in which uniform he appeared on every public occasion during his lifetime, making it his proud boast that his waist-line had not changed from subaltern to field-marshal. His reputation as a General was established on the Eastern and Balkan fronts during the First World War, though he owed much of his success to the genius of his Chief of Staff, Hans von Seeckt. Twice married, von Mackensen celebrated two silver weddings and finally died in Hanover in 1948, aged ninety-nine. One of his sons, Hans-Georg, who married von Neurath's daughter, became Ambassador in Rome and State Secretary in the Ministry of Foreign Affairs; another, Eberhard, who followed his father's profession of arms, commanded the 14th Army in Italy during the Second World War and was later indicted as a War Criminal before a British military tribunal in connection with the massacre of Italian hostages in the Ardeatine Caves. Condemned to death on November 30, 1945, his sentence was later commuted to one of imprisonment for life.

President was, therefore, kept well insulated from any shocks from the outside world.

Now, however, von Mackensen and von Hammerstein returned to the charge. Together they composed a memorandum to Hindenburg, of which the purpose was threefold.[1] In the first place, it set out, in terms of simple, straightforward narration, the circumstances of von Schleicher's assassination, to which were added the notification of von Bredow's murder and the statement that Hindenburg's own favourite 'Fränzchen' had only escaped a similar fate through the intervention of the *Reichswehr*, who had placed him under their protection. The memorandum went on to demand the punishment of those guilty of these atrocious acts, and the public withdrawal of the charges made against von Schleicher and von Bredow. It stated explicitly that the signatories could neither comprehend nor approve the attitude of General von Blomberg, who, as Minister of Defence, had condoned deeds which were, in fact, injurious to the honour of the German Army. The Marshal was urged to reconstruct the Reich Cabinet by dropping Göring, Goebbels, Darré, Ley, von Neurath and von Blomberg, and to reorientate the foreign policy of the Reich. The whole control of the affairs of the State should be placed in the hands of a small directorate. The name of Hitler does not appear in the document, and it is to be presumed that the writers either did not care, or were not prepared, to demand his elimination from the leadership of the State. Whatever the cause, the fact remains that the proposed directorate was to consist of the Chancellor (unnamed, but presumably Hitler); the Vice-Chancellor, General von Fritsch; the Minister for War, General von Hammerstein; the Minister for National Economy (unnamed) and the Minister for Foreign Affairs, Rudolf Nadolny.

The inclusion of Nadolny gave the clue to changes which the signatories of the memorandum desired to see in the conduct of German foreign policy. They clearly feared that Hitler's policy of *rapprochement* with Poland could bring no advantage to the Reich — since the hatred of the two peoples was not to be abated — and must sooner or later bring Germany into conflict with Russia. The *Führer's* policy was inevitably driving the Soviet Union into conjunction with the Western Powers and the United States and thus potentially committing Germany again to a two-front war. The President was therefore urged to command a reversion of Reich policy to the 'distant friendliness' with Russia which had obtained during the Weimar period, at the risk of creating tension with Poland. To this end the appointment of Nadolny was proposed

[1] For text of this document see *Weissbuch*, pp. 147-52.

as Foreign Minister, for the reason that, as a disciple of Brockdorff-Rantzau and von Maltzan, he was an ardent advocate of German-Russian understanding.[1]

It is perhaps ironical, though not inappropriate, that this document, designed primarily to procure the rehabilitation of Kurt von Schleicher, should have become, in effect, an attempt to persuade the President to replace the Nazi régime by a military dictatorship, which, in structure and policy, closely resembled that which von Schleicher himself had unsuccessfully endeavoured to achieve in those final hectic January days of 1933. The objective of the signatories was clearly to follow the Schleicher line of making Hitler the prisoner of the Army, and the reorientating of the German attitude toward Russia and Poland was no more than a return to the Seeckt-Schleicher policy which had been in effect since 1922.

Thus the Generals were no more averse than the Nazis to exploiting the murder of von Schleicher to the furtherance of the ideas which he had advocated.

The memorandum concluded with an appeal to the Marshal: 'Excellency, the gravity of the moment has compelled us to appeal to you as our Supreme Commander. The destiny of our country is at stake. Your Excellency has thrice before saved Germany from foundering, at Tannenberg, at the end of the War and at the moment of your election as President of the Reich. Excellency, save Germany for the fourth time! The undersigned Generals and senior officers swear to preserve to the last breath their loyalty to you and to the Fatherland.'

Some thirty Generals and senior officers of the General Staff, many of them members of the Third Regiment of Foot Guards, to which both the President and von Schleicher had belonged, signed the memorandum, in addition to von Mackensen and von Hammerstein. It was dated July 18, 1934, and it reached Neudeck two days later. But there is no reason to believe that Hindenburg ever

---

[1] Rudolf Nadolny (1873–1953) was a professional diplomat, who at the conclusion of the First World War placed himself at once at the disposal of the Provisional Government and became in 1919 the first State Secretary to the President of the Reich, a position in which he was succeeded after the Kapp *Putsch* by Otto Meissner. Later, as Ambassador in Ankara and leader of the German delegation to the Disarmament Conference at Geneva, he pursued a policy calculated to improve and strengthen relations between Berlin and Moscow, and on Germany's withdrawal from Geneva he was appointed to the Moscow Embassy in November 1933, where he remained until October 1934, when he was succeeded by Count von der Schulenburg. As a result of a disagreement with the Foreign Ministry, Nadolny received no further appointment, and remained in retirement until after the conclusion of the Second World War when he emerged as a protagonist of an understanding between the Western Allies, the Soviet Union and Germany, on the basis of a united and neutralized German Reich.

received it. He was completely isolated by this time, and Meissner maintained a watch of Cerberus. In any case the shades of death were already drawing about him, and he was beyond the taking of any sort of action. In a few days' time he was to lay down his last command and Hitler would claim from the Army his reward for the elimination of Röhm.[1]

But before the Generals were called upon to take this step, they were to have a further example of the gangster methods of their present allies and future masters. On July 25, Nazi gunmen shot down the Federal Chancellor of Austria, Engelbert Dollfuss, and allowed him to bleed to death without the services of a doctor or a priest. This barbarous act, which horrified a world already deeply shocked by the events of June 30, appears to have provided no deterrent to General von Blomberg in the honouring of his pledged word. Twice in a month the Nazi régime, the leader of which von Blomberg and his fellow Generals had secretly promised to accept as their Supreme Commander, had resorted to murder as an instrument of national policy. The events of June 30 in Germany and of July 25 in Austria removed any vestige of excuse on the part of the leaders of the German Army that they knew not what they did. Even if they had been too vain, too blind, or too proud to take warning from what had happened within the Reich during the first eighteen months of Nazi rule, it might have been supposed that as officers and gentlemen they were too honourable to make common cause with self-disclosed gangsters and killers. But it was not so.

Field-Marshal Paul von Hindenburg, twice President of the German Reich, died at Neudeck on August 1, 1934. Though it had been clear beyond doubt for the last six months that the President's long life was drawing to its close, the final event caught the Right opponents of the Nazi régime without any concerted plan of action. All were agreed in not wishing Hitler to succeed as Head of the State, but whereas some favoured the immediate restoration of the Monarchy, others favoured an intermediary stage in which von Blomberg should be appointed *Reichsverweser*, as a sort of joint

---

[1] Because the copy of the memorandum was sent to Neudeck in a blue file, it became known as the 'Blue Book of the *Reichswehr*'. What became of the original is unknown, though it is not impossible that Meissner, who undoubtedly received it, ultimately handed it to Hitler. If this were so, the arguments contained therein would provide added support for the line followed by Hitler and Göring in conversation with Polish statesmen in 1935 (see above, p. 327.) Von Hammerstein had kept a duplicate of the memorandum and, after Hindenburg's death, copies were circulated in Berlin among von Schleicher's friends. As will be seen, he finally succeeded in his endeavour to rehabilitate von Schleicher and von Bredow (see below, pp. 335-7).

M

trustee of the *Reichswehr* and the Nazi Party, with a view to an ultimate restoration.

These plans, nebulous and undefined as they were, were not such as to cause the *Führer* a moment's anxiety. Secure in his confidence of the support of the chiefs of the *Heeresleitung* and of his allies at Neudeck, Hitler proceeded, on August 1, to proclaim by decree the amalgamation of the functions of President of the Reich with those of Chancellor, and the assumption of both by himself as '*Führer und Reichskanzler*'.[1] On the following day Hitler received the oath of allegiance from General von Blomberg, General von Fritsch and Admiral Raeder, as the Leaders of the Armed Forces of the State, and throughout the Reich the troops of the garrisons were paraded in the courtyards of their barracks to take a similar oath in the presence of their officers.[2]

On August 6, in the Kroll Opera House in the first stage of the funeral ceremonies for Hindenburg, there occurred a reaffirmation of the 'Marriage of Potsdam'. Now, as on March 21, 1933, the Field-Marshal dominated the event. The alliance, originally concluded in his honour, was now re-dedicated to his memory. To the strains of the funeral march from *Götterdämmerung*, the Marshal's coffin was borne between serried ranks, the field grey of the *Reichswehr* opposite the brown and black of the SA and SS, just as at Potsdam he had passed between two guards of honour in the forecourt of the Palace. But there was a difference. Now there was no longer a 'President's Army' and a 'Chancellor's Army'; to-day they were united in the sacrament of the same oath of allegiance sworn to the same Supreme Commander. To-day they were all 'Hitler's Army'.

[1] *Reichsgesetzblatt*, 1934, i, 477. This fusion of the two chief offices of the State in the person of Hitler was later ratified by a referendum on August 19 by the affirmative votes of 88·9 per cent of the electorate.

[2] General Friedrich Hossbach, who was at once appointed 'Adjutant of the *Wehrmacht* with the *Führer*', gives in his book, *Zwischen Wehrmacht und Hitler* (Hanover, 1949, p. 10, footnote), a factual statement of the prosaic manner in which the oath was taken by the Chiefs of the Armed Services and administered by them to their subordinates, thus disposing of the more dramatic, if less accurate, account given by Gisevius of the Berlin garrison being suddenly paraded in the Königsplatz at midnight on August 1, and taking the oath by torchlight (Gisevius, ii, 18-19).

CHAPTER 2

FROM THE DEATH OF HINDENBURG
TO THE FRITSCH CRISIS

(August 1934–February 1938)

(i)

QUEM Deus vult perdere, prius dementat, and verily it seemed that the German *Generalität* had been stricken with both blindness and insanity. That they could actually have believed that, having elevated Hitler, as it were upon their shields, to the first position in the State, they would be able to retain and enjoy their ancient privileges as a Praetorian *imperium in imperio*, would be inconceivable were it not a fact. That they could imagine that with the liquidation of the SA their last rivals within the Nazi Party were disposed of, is equally amazing. But perhaps most extraordinary of all is that they should have ignored the rude and ruthless warnings of the events of June 30 and July 25, 1934, that they were dealing with a type of criminal mentality which did not play the game according to the accepted rules, but made up its own rules as it went along. Later — much later — the Generals were forced to the conclusion that only by the way of assassination could they eliminate the assassins, but in such a contest they were hampered by their amateur status as against the professional experience of Himmler, Kaltenbrunner and 'Gestapo' Müller.

But in August 1934, from their ivory tower, which they believed to be so invulnerable, the Generals looked out upon a sunlit world which seemed to offer the fruits of victory ripe for the picking. If they considered at all the gangster aspect of the Nazi régime, it was to dismiss the consideration with a supercilious shrug and the comforting thought : 'It can't happen here'. Here in their fortress of caste and privilege, they deemed themselves not only secure from all menace, but still holding the keys of power.

And indeed it suited Hitler's book, at the moment, that the Army should be well satisfied. For the *Führer* and Chancellor realized that, despite the fact that he had attained supreme personal power within the Reich, he had much to do before that position was

333

consolidated into one of impregnable security.

The murders and brutalities in Berlin and Munich and Vienna had shocked the civilized world, and the revelations of vice, corruption and disunity, which had followed the Blood Purge, had shaken the prestige and authority of the *Führer* and his régime both at home and abroad. It behoved Hitler, therefore, to be upon his best behaviour, at any rate until after that day in January 1935 on which the population of the Saar Basin Territory were to decide by plebiscite whether they wished to return to Germany, to be annexed to France, or to remain under the government of the League of Nations.[1] It was essential to the military and industrial planning of the *Führer* that the rich coal mines of the Saar should be reunited to the Reich, and he was as yet too weak militarily to seize them by force. German propaganda must therefore win the day in ensuring a plebiscitory victory, and to achieve this victory the memory of the murders of June 30 and July 25 and their attendant horrors must be diminished as much as possible. For similar reasons the home morale must needs be re-established, and the *Führer* counted upon the *Reichswehr* to reinforce his authority should the need and occasion arise.

Though Hitler did not actually whiten his face to produce an appearance of sanctity — as did Kaiser Wilhelm II when preaching sermons to the crew of the Imperial Yacht — he did make a considerable parade of the new morality of the Third Reich, and moral austerity became the watchword alike of the subdued and reorganized SA and of the exultant and expanding SS.

In his relations with the Army, the *Führer* could not have been more placatory or more amenable. He had reaffirmed before the *Reichstag* on July 13 that the Army was the sole bearer of arms within the Reich,[2] and a month later, at Hamburg, he had proclaimed — with the multiple purpose of reassuring the world, the Army and the German people — that 'there is no one in whose eyes the German Army needs to rehabilitate their fame in arms'; adding that 'the German Government has no need to seek successes in war, for

[1] The Saar Basin, the rich coal-mining area lying north of Lorraine and forming part of Prussia, was detached from Germany under Articles 45-50 of the Treaty of Versailles, and the rights of exploitation granted to France for a period of fifteen years in compensation for the destruction of her northern coal-mines by the German Army in the course of its final retreat. For this period the administration of the Saar Basin Territory was vested in a Governing Commission appointed by the Council of the League of Nations. At the close of the period the population were to decide their future status. On January 13, 1935, 90·8 per cent of the votes cast were in favour of reunion with Germany; 97·9 per cent of the electorate went to the polls.

[2] Hitler's speech to the *Reichstag*, July 13, 1934 (Baynes, i, 313).

its régime is based on a foundation which nothing can shake and it is supported by the confidence of the whole people'.[1]

Moreover, he had made it explicit, on assuming the dual office of *Führer* and Chancellor, that in all matters involving the Army he would delegate his authority to the Minister of Defence, who would act as his deputy in military affairs, even as Rudolf Hess was his vice-regent with the Party. The Army had in fact been told that, provided they kept clear of politics, they had a free hand in their own field, and Hitler had pledged himself that the work of their rearmament should not be menaced or embarrassed by political adventures in the realm of foreign policy.

And the Army, in company with the other armed services, made full use of its time. Von Fritsch and Beck pushed forward the last stage of the *Reichswehr*'s rearmament *in petto*, for with the re-organization of the SA in July there began the incorporation of the physically and morally more desirable elements within the ranks of the Army. This sudden expansion was inevitably accompanied by problems of supply and equipment, and of a scarcity in the cadres of subalterns required for training and instruction. Meantime Admiral Raeder and Vice-Admiral Foerster were vigorously engaged in feats of clandestine naval construction, while the febrile haste with which Göring was 'secretly' building up an air-force was, both at home and abroad, a *secret de polichinelle*.

And yet, all was not entirely well between the *Führer* and the Army. The ghosts of von Schleicher and von Bredow would not be laid to rest; they walked and haunted the slumbers of the Bendlerstrasse and the Chancellor's Palace, despite the efforts of both parties to ignore them. With the pertinacity of the Importunate Widow, Kurt von Hammerstein, backed by the aged von Mackensen, persisted in his campaign for rehabilitation. For six months his importunities nagged like an aching tooth at the conscience of the *Heeresleitung*. He refused to be put off by the supine von Blomberg or the enigmatic von Fritsch, and gradually he gained a following. The 'Blue Book of the *Reichswehr*', though it had failed in its primary purpose of disillusioning Hindenburg, had been circulated to advantage since his death, and many general officers now realized that the accusation of treason heaped upon their brother generals by Hitler and Göring had been but calumnies. Forthwith there arose a clamour for the official clearing of their names, even among those who had had neither liking nor respect for von Schleicher in

[1] Hitler's radio address at Hamburg on August 17, 1934, in the course of the referendum campaign for the ratification of the fusion of offices (*Berliner Tageblatt*, August 19, 1934; Baynes, i, 557).

the past. The honour of the Army, the prized and cherished heritage of centuries, was at stake, and when even such sedulous pro-Nazis as General Count von der Schulenburg, the former Chief of Staff of the German Crown Prince, who had held high rank in the SA, and immediately after June 30 had applied for admission to the SS, joined in the demand, it became evident that some measure of satisfaction must be forthcoming.

The Minister of Defence and the Commander-in-Chief of the *Reichswehr* conferred together, and their joint counsel to Hitler was to yield to the request of the Officer Corps for the formal rehabilitation of the two murdered Generals. Unless this were done, von Blomberg and von Fritsch told the *Führer* that they feared a serious schism within the Army. Such an eventuality Hitler wished to avoid at all costs at this juncture. He was preparing to take an action which, though it would in itself delight the Army, would also demand a united front at home to confront the opposition and protest which it would inevitably cause abroad.

German rearmament had reached a point where it was no longer necessary or possible to keep it a secret. All Germans, and most foreigners in Germany, were aware of it to some degree, and it had already become the subject of comment in the political cabarets of Berlin and Munich.[1] In so far as the Powers were concerned, however, the polite fiction had been maintained, even after Germany had flounced out of the Disarmament Conference in October 1933, that the restrictions imposed by Part V of the Treaty of Versailles were still in operation — or, at any rate, had not been formally denounced. The moment for this final step was now approaching, but Hitler was biding his time for the appropriate moment which should give him at least a modicum of excuse for the sudden disclosure of Germany as a fully armed State. He had not consulted the Army leaders, other than von Blomberg, on this point, but kept his own counsel, watching and waiting for the moment which, he was confident, would arrive in due course.

Such a gesture as he contemplated would restore the *Wehrhoheit* of Germany and would thus discharge one of Hitler's most important pledges to the Army, but the *Führer* was well aware that in so doing

---

[1] A current joke at this time was of two men, of whom one, whose wife had just had a baby, complained to the other that he could not afford to buy a perambulator. The friend, who worked in a perambulator factory, offered to bring back the parts, piece by piece, so that the father could assemble it himself at home. Some months passed before they met again, but when they did the father was still carrying the baby. The friend, who had completed the delivery of the perambulator parts, asked the reason. 'Well, you see', the father replied, 'I know I'm very dense and don't understand much about mechanics, but I've put that thing together three times and each time it turns out to be a machine-gun !'

he was placing additional power in the hands of the *Wehrmacht* and that it was necessary that this power should be used in accordance with, and not contrary to, his designs. For this among other reasons he listened to von Blomberg and von Fritsch and conceded the wisdom of their advice.

The occasion selected by Hitler and Göring for the rendering of 'redress' to the memory of von Schleicher and von Bredow was a secret conclave of the Party, political, and military leaders summoned at the Berlin State Opera on January 3, 1935, as a demonstration of their unity with the *Führer* before the Saar Plebiscite to be held ten days later.[1] Expressions of loyalty and solidarity were offered by Hess and Göring, the former saluting Hitler with the words : 'The heads of the Party and State — your paladins, your Generals, your Ministers — greet you as Germany's *Führer* in gratitude and veneration'. The *Führer*'s speech, as reported, was devoted largely to foreign policy, but at its close he made an off-the-record statement to the effect that the murder of von Schleicher and von Bredow on June 30 had been 'in error', that the later statements by himself and Göring had been made on the basis of information which had subsequently proved to be invalid and that the names of the two innocent officers should be restored to the honour rolls of their regiments.[2] This statement, though never published, was formally announced by von Mackensen to a gathering of officers of the General Staff Corps on February 28, the annual celebration of the birthday of the great von Schlieffen. The Field-Grey ghosts were laid at last, in so far as the Army were concerned, but the whole affair was the purest play-acting on the part of the *Führer*, who, as has been seen, did not hesitate to traduce von Schleicher in his negotiations with the Poles.[3]

The matter had been thus satisfactorily settled only just in time for Hitler. In the first week of March the French Cabinet approved the text of a law extending the period of national service with the

[1] Because of the secret character of the meeting and the fact that Hitler arrived at it with his right hand bandaged, using his left hand to acknowledge greetings and salutes, stories became current of an attempted assassination. These are believed to be completely without foundation.

[2] The account of these remarks of the *Führer*, of which no official record was ever made, was given to the writer by an officer of the *Reichswehr* who was present at the meeting. Von Hammerstein, his task completed, returned to retirement and made no further public appearance until May 1939 when he attended the funeral of Gröner, whom he and von Schleicher had treated so scurvily in the affair of the SA in April 1932. It was typical of von Hammerstein's essential honesty of character that he should make this public expiation for an act which he always regretted and for which he had sought and secured Gröner's personal forgiveness.   [3] See above, p. 327, footnote.

colours from eighteen months to two years. The ensuing debate in the Chamber was prolonged and acrimonious. The canker of disunity already at work within France was clearly displayed, but it soon became evident that the Government could command a majority for the bill's passage. This was the opportunity for which Hitler had been waiting. Timing his announcement to coincide with the date on which the French bill should become law, he promulgated, on March 16, a brief decree, which, in open defiance of the Western Powers, swept away the last remaining rags of illusion from the naked truth of German rearmament. The text of the decree is as follows:

    I. Service in the *Wehrmacht* is based on compulsory military service.
    II. The German Army, in time of peace, will comprise 12 army corps and 36 divisions.
    III. The complementary legislation, regulating the introduction and operation of compulsory military service, will be submitted to the Cabinet as soon as possible by the Minister of Defence.[1]

In these terse terms was written the epitaph of German disarmament. The days of equivocation and deception were over for good and all. Germany's Military Sovereignty (*Deutsche Wehrhoheit*) had been restored to her and from now forward it was no longer her 'equality' but only her 'superiority' which could be held in question.

The Armed Services of the Reich were suitably grateful. They were ready to make public demonstration of their gratitude. On March 17, the German Heroes' Remembrance Day (*Heldengedenktag*), the *Führer* appeared at the ceremonies with Field-Marshal von Mackensen on his right hand and the German Crown Prince on his left, while General von Blomberg proclaimed aloud : ' It was the Army, removed from the political conflict, which laid the foundations on which a God-sent architect could build. Then this man came, the man who, with his strength of will and spiritual power, prepared for our dissensions the end that they deserved, and made all good where a whole generation had failed.'

(ii)

To all outward appearances it would seem that, with Hitler's declaration of rearmament — to which the answer of the Powers

---

[1] *Reichsgesetzblatt*, 1935, i, 375. There is sufficient evidence available to assume that Hitler issued this decree without any preliminary consultation with the *Heeresleitung*, or the *Wehrkreis* commanders. The Commander of *Wehrkreis III* (Berlin-Brandenburg), General von Witzleben, and his Chief of Staff, Colonel von Manstein, first heard of the decision over the radio on March 16. According

had been but the empty gesture of the Stresa Front — the Armed Forces of the Reich stood upon the threshold of a new epoch of power and contentment. Hitler had given them all that he had promised. He had kept scrupulously to the letter of his bond. The status and privileges of the Army had been re-established ; its position as sole bearer of arms within the Reich had been bloodily assured ; and, finally, the *Wehrhoheit* of Germany had been restored to her. The Army would seem to have got all they had covenanted for, and even more — and so they themselves believed at this moment.

But slowly and sadly the Generals were to learn that the price which they had paid for all their illusory grandeur was too high. While Hindenburg lived the power which they had enjoyed, though less apparent, was infinitely greater because of their independence of the Party and the *Führer*. Once they had implemented their blood-pact with Hitler ; once they had raised him to be Chief of State and had acknowledged him, as such, as their Supreme Commander, they had abandoned the substance for the shadow. Till August 1934 the Army could have overthrown the Nazi régime at a nod from their commanders, for they owed no allegiance to the Chancellor ; but, with the acceptance of Hitler's succession, the Generals had added one more fetter, perhaps the strongest of all, to those psychological bonds which chained them ever more inescapably to a régime which they had thought to exploit and dominate.

For the oath which the Armed Forces had taken on August 2, 1934, and which was reaffirmed by law in the following year,[1] was not the mere repetition of the oath to the Constitution which had been sworn under the Republic. It was an oath of personal fealty to Adolf Hitler :

I swear before God to give my unconditional obedience to Adolf Hitler, *Führer* of the Reich and of the German People, Supreme Commander of the *Wehrmacht*, and I pledge my word as a brave soldier to observe this oath always, even at peril of my life.

This was the allegiance which von Blomberg and von Fritsch and Beck and Raeder had sworn on August 2, 1934 ; this was the

to von Manstein's evidence at Nuremberg, on August 9, 1946, the General Staff, had its views been asked for, would have proposed 21 divisions as the practical limit of the Army's expansion. The figure of 36 divisions was a spontaneous decision on the part of the *Führer* (*Nuremberg Record*, xx, 603).

[1] Law of the Oath of the *Wehrmacht* of August 20, 1934 (*Reichsgesetzblatt*, 1934, i, 785), modified by the Law of July 20, 1935 (*ibid.*, 1935, i, 1035). It is, however, important to remember that the old oath prescribed under the Constitution for the members of the Armed Forces of the State was never repealed, and the *Wehrmacht* was technically, therefore, under a double allegiance.

M 2

oath which they had administered to their inferiors and which had
been taken by every armed servant of the State within the seven
Wehrkreise of Germany. It was unequivocal and did not permit
of ambiguity. At the moment when the Army believed that all
opportunities lay open to them, they had made a capitulation infinitely more complete than their surrender to the Allies in the
railway compartment in the Forest of Compiègne. Henceforth such
opposition as the Army wished to offer to the Nazi régime was no
longer in the nature of a struggle with an unscrupulous partner, but
of a conspiracy against legitimate and constituted authority, a fact
which was to sow the seeds of a harvest of doubt and moral conflict
at all levels of the military hierarchy.

And what had been pledged and conceded in August 1934 was
confirmed in the legislation which, in accordance with the decree of
March 16, 1935, von Blomberg duly presented to the Cabinet. 'The
Supreme Commander of the *Wehrmacht*' — so runs paragraph 3
of the *Wehrmacht* Law of May 21, 1935 — 'is the *Führer* and
Chancellor of the Reich. Under the order of the *Führer*, the Reich
Minister of War exercises command over the *Wehrmacht*, of which
he is the Commander-in-Chief.' [1]

Nor were the Army as free as they imagined from para-military
competition within the Party. They had, it is true, eliminated their
immediate rivals, the SA, but they were now, had they known it,

---

[1] Under the legislation of May 21, 1935, the High Command of the *Wehrmacht*
was established as follows : Hitler, as *Führer* and Chancellor, was Supreme
Chief of the Armed Forces of the State, who were pledged to him by personal
oath. Von Blomberg, who was now designated Minister of War, and no longer
of Defence, was the active Commander-in-Chief, under the orders of the *Führer*.
Each of the three Services had its own Commander-in-Chief, respectively, General
von Fritsch, Admiral Raeder and Col.-General Göring of the newly created
Luftwaffe, and its own General Staff, of which, in the case of the Army, General
Ludwig Beck, the head of the *Truppenamt*, became the first Chief. Unity of
command was thus achieved in a far greater degree than had ever existed in the
Imperial Army. Before 1918 the Chief Command of the German Armies, under
the Kaiser as War Lord, had been exercised by the Chief of the General Staff,
who was entirely independent of the Prussian Minister of War. Now the High
Command over all the services was centred in von Blomberg, in addition to the
office of Minister of War, and over him was the *Führer* alone.

Secret legislation of the same date (May 21) enacted the Reich Defence Law
under which the *Führer* and Chancellor was empowered to declare a state
of defence in the whole, or any part, of the Reich, in case of danger of war. In
this event the entire executive powers of the State devolved upon the *Führer*, but
were exercised, under his authority, by the Minister of War, to whom all other
Ministers were subordinated and who was empowered to issue legislation by
decree and to set up special courts (*IMT Document*, PS-2261). Amendments
were also made on this day to the existing Reich Cabinet decisions of April 4, 1933,
and December 13, 1934, relative to the Reich Defence Council, strengthening its
authority and more clearly defining the scope and aims of its functions.

confronted by a far greater menace. Revolting though the erotic rule of Röhm and his fellow-perverts had been, it had not constituted as great a threat to the Army as did the cold and systematically ruthless régime of Himmler and his fellow sadists, which succeeded it.

The very fact that the Army had, with gratitude and relief, held aloof from the 'disciplinary action' of June 30, 1934, yielding a free hand to the SS, played directly into Himmler's hands. If the Army were not prepared to take action of this sort, then some force must be created which would do any dirty work which it was ordered to do. So argued Himmler to his *Führer*. And Hitler approved. To von Blomberg he pointed out that the Army could not be expected to carry out police operations, and that it was very natural that they should resent being asked to do so. Nevertheless, events might arise in which such action might need to be taken again, and it was therefore necessary to maintain a certain number of regiments — not more than three in all — of SS General Service troops (*SS-Verfügungstruppen*) who could be called upon for such special and unsavoury service.

Either the Generals did not see the danger which lay in this proposal, or they ignored it. At any rate, well content to be freed from direct contact with possible future murders, they acquiesced in the formation of these regiments of what they laughingly and contemptuously described as 'asphalt soldiers', who could at best put on a good parade performance but were worthless as real troops. The Generals little knew their Heinrich Himmler. These 'asphalt soldiers', whose existence they thus scornfully conceded, were in reality but a Trojan Horse breaching the walls of their defences. For, from these formations were to come in due course the *Waffen-SS* officered from Himmler's own training schools, with which the Army was later to fight a battle for equality. Himmler did not at this moment aspire to the control of the Army. That would come later when he had finally closed his grip upon the Reich and reduced it by terror and blackmail to cringing subservience. This he had not yet succeeded in doing, nor did he win success until in 1936 he persuaded Hitler to concentrate all police-power in his hands. But in the meantime he gave the Army a taste of his potential strength when SS microphones were discovered in the sacred precincts of the offices of Admiral Canaris and the *Abwehr*.[1]

---

[1] It was, moreover, from Himmler that the Army received the first inkling of the price which they would be expected to pay for rearmament. In February 1935 the Chief of the SS addressed some officers of the Hamburg garrison in secret session at the Hotel Vier Jahreszeiten. On this occasion he explained the necessity for increasing the number of his SS General Service Troops on the grounds that in the event of war they would be required at home to reinforce the police and to

In this, however, Himmler over-played his hand, and suffered a temporary rebuff in consequence. The representations made by von Blomberg and von Fritsch to Hitler resulted in a reaffirmation of the immunity of the Army from all such forms of Party interference. The authority of the Gestapo stopped at the doors of the Bendler-strasse. The field-grey of the Army was a protection against the grosser tyrannies and the petty persecutions to which ordinary citizens of the Reich were subjected. Where a member of the Army was suspected of 'political unreliability', the case had to be sub-mitted to the military authorities before an investigation could be made, and, in nine cases out of ten, it was never made. Even the racial laws — the Nuremberg Decrees — were only enforced with the consent of the *Heeresleitung* and then so leniently, and with so many loopholes, that their observance was practically non-existent. Certain outstandingly non-Aryan officers were advised to transfer to the Air Force where the powerful influence of Hermann Göring, who never took his anti-Semitism seriously when a case of technical ability was involved, afforded an even safer protection than the Army.[1]

As a result, many ex-officers rejoined the Army for no other reason than to take advantage of the special 'protected status' which such membership conferred. These 'supplementary officers' (*Ergänzungs-Offiziere*) bought their immunity dearly in many cases. Some took as much as a 50 per cent cut in income, with very poor hopes of promotion. All realized that in making 'an escape from the Party by way of the decent form of emigration' they were sacrificing their independence of action, but, as compensation, they hoped that, by taking refuge in the Army, they would at least preserve their independence of thought and expression, and also of worship, since the Army chaplains were protected by the shield of military privilege from Party ideological interference.

In effect the rearmament decree of March 16, 1935, and the subsequent legislation of May 21, marked the beginning of the decline of the Army's paramount influence. The new Army was as different

prevent a repetition of the situation during the First World War when the Home Front had collapsed through lack of discipline and morale. This was the first time that active preparation for war had been mentioned at a conference of officers and by a civilian ! It made a profound impression and caused some of those present to question just where rearmament was leading them.

[1] A significant illustration of Göring's policy in such cases is shown in respect of Field-Marshal Erhard Milch, Inspector-General of the *Luftwaffe* and State Secretary. Milch's mother, an Aryan married to a Jew, was made to sign an affidavit that her son was born out of wedlock, his real father being allegedly an Aryan. (See Field-Marshal Milch's evidence on March 11, 1946. *Nuremberg Record*, ix, pp. 93-4.)

from the *Reichswehr* as that body had been from the old Imperial Army. Quality gave place to quantity. The meticulous standards of careful selection for both officers and men gave place to the '*omnium gatherum*' of conscription, and sweeping changes resulted both in the Officer Corps and among the 'other ranks'. There was a planned infiltration of SS men into all military peripheries, and this had a marked effect on the younger officers; whereas the troops now comprised many who had served with both the SA and the SS and had previously been rejected as undesirable.

Moreover the Army, as such, was no longer the unchallenged superior among the armed services. The newly formed and arrogant Air Force, under the ebullient leadership of Hermann Göring, whose allegiance was always torn between his loyalty to the military caste and the claims of his own *Luftwaffe*, made no secret of its claims to parity of status with the Army. Intensely Nazi in its composition, the Air Force despised the conservative traditions of the Army with a scorn only excelled by the contempt with which the Army regarded these brash and bumptious *epigoni*.

The *Luftwaffe* enjoyed one great advantage over the Army in the person and personality of their Commander-in-Chief. Though in theory equal with von Fritsch and Raeder, Göring, because of the many other State and Party offices which he held, was in effect able to exercise a considerably greater degree of influence on events and decisions than either of his fellow Commanders-in-Chief, or indeed than the War Minister himself. Von Blomberg, despite his very positive attitude towards Hitler, did not enjoy a close or personal relationship with the *Führer*. As *Fachminister* he saw the Chancellor and Supreme Commander only in the way of business, and the Army as such had no direct contact with Hitler whatever, save through the official channel of their 'Adjutant with the *Führer*', Colonel Hossbach. There was no General in Hitler's immediate *Umgebung*, though for a brief moment von Reichenau was in favour.

Göring, on the other hand, was in no way thus inhibited. As one of the inner council of the Party, as a member of the Reich Cabinet, as Minister-President of Prussia, later as Plenipotentiary of the Four-Year Plan, he had many other and more frequent means of access to Hitler than that of Commander-in-Chief of the Air Force, and he was often able to push the interests of his Service with the *Führer* over the head and behind the back of the Minister of War.[1]

---

[1] Goring's influence was additionally strengthened later when he was officially designated as the *Führer's* successor with effect from September 1, 1939, and appointed the *Führer's* deputy by decree of June 29, 1941.

Yet there was one who had an even more intimate contact than Göring. Himmler, with the gradual accretion of power, established himself more and more firmly in the counsels 'of the *Führer*. He it was who could keep the same eccentric hours of life as Hitler and who, later, with Martin Bormann and other intimate cronies and dependents, formed that clique in the Chancellor's Palace which became known in Berlin as the 'Fire-side Circle' or the 'Midnight Club'. Here the vital and fundamental decisions of the Third Reich were taken and orders often issued on little scraps of paper above an all but illegible scrawl of 'A. Hitler', appended at three o'clock in the morning. Here it was that Himmler pursued his calculated and patiently systematic struggle against the Army, seeing to it that Hitler was kept more and more isolated from all but the most official military contacts.

Thus, while the Army occupied themselves with the tasks and problems of rearmament and expansion; while, in the illusory security of their ivory tower, they felt themselves free from interference and as still retaining power and influence in the direction of affairs outside their immediate military sphere; their days of authority were passing imperceptibly from them. From the proud position of arbiters of the destinies of the Reich, they passed to the rôle of an active participant in politics, then to an ill-concealed parity of partnership with the Party — a partnership which could be disrupted at their own volition — and later to an uncertain status of *primus inter pares* among the armed services and of an even more uncertain relationship with the Party. The days of their first humiliation were fast approaching, and from thenceforward such independence of action as remained to them could be exercised not as of right but as conspirators against a Supreme Commander to whom they had willingly, if disingenuously, given their oath of loyalty.

(iii)

The thirty-six divisions with which the *Führer* had somewhat embarrassingly presented the Army on March 16, 1935, would have kept them fully satisfied and occupied for a considerable period of time. As the result of this *embarras de richesse* the military position of Germany was at its weakest from 1935–7 and the *Generalität* were profoundly desirous of a period of peace and quiet to enable them to absorb this boa-constrictor meal of man-power and organization which they had been forced to consume. They were extremely grateful for what they had received, and when they had completed the processes of digestion they would be ready to fight, but until that time they were weak and torpid, unwilling to engage in active or aggressive exercise.

Not so the *Führer*. With him the great and evil dream of a Thousand-Year Reich which should stretch from Strasbourg to Riga and from Rostock to Trieste, holding the rest of the European continent in fee, was ever before his eyes. Under the relentless pressure of the urge to realize this dream the vaulting ambition of Adolf Hitler was never at rest. Even when outwardly quiescent that strange perverted genius was scheming and planning on a dozen different stratagems which should ultimately assist the final attainment of the vision. It must not be thought that Adolf Hitler operated to a carefully prepared time-table. Only the general scheme of things to come was clear in his mind. Neither the time, nor the detail, nor even the sequence of events, was defined long beforehand. For Hitler was a master opportunist and both his strength and weakness lay in his ability to gauge the psychological moment for his acts of aggression and his inability, on certain occasions, to resist the temptation to seize it.

The *Führer* had come a long way in the first three years of his régime and already the first stage of his dream of power, namely the rehabilitation of Germany herself, was all but completed. The withdrawal from Geneva in October 1933 had severed the links which bound Germany to the European family of nations, links which Stresemann had been at such pains to forge ; the rearmament declaration of March 1935 had been a warning to the West that Germany, outside the family, was preparing to make her demands for concessions, not as heretofore from weakness but from strength. But the full sovereignty of Germany could not be restored while one stone of the structure of the Versailles Treaty remained upon another. Reparation had gone ; disarmament was ended ; the relations with the League of Nations had been ruptured ; there remained only that zone of the Rhineland whose demilitarization had been accepted by Germany under Articles 42-44 of the Peace Treaty and voluntarily confirmed by the Pact of Locarno. Once this last link of 'the shackles of Versailles' had been shattered, the *Führer* could turn his attention to planning his next moves in the south and east. But for psychological reasons the restoration of Germany's *Wehrhoheit* must be completed first, and he awaited the moment when this new *coup* could be safely sprung upon an apathetic Europe.

The story of the operation for the reoccupation of the demilitarized Rhineland is a text-book example of Nazi planning, both from the point of view of the policy of the *Führer* and of the relation of the Army chiefs to that policy. It is a story which may be clearly understood from the mere recital of events.

It was an essential factor in the Hitlerian technique that each step on the road to aggression must be carefully camouflaged as a defensive measure. The object of this procedure was to convince the German people . that their peace-loving *Führer* was being deflected from his avowed aims of pacific settlement by the intransigence and the intrigue of the Western Powers, against whose constant machinations he was ever defending the interests of the Reich. Thus the excuse for the withdrawal from Geneva had been the alleged refusal of Britain and France to implement the agreement on equality of armaments negotiated with the Schleicher Government in December 1932. Similarly the extension of the French term of national service had been seized upon by the *Führer* as the pretext for the announcement of German rearmament. Both these steps had been decided upon by Hitler in principle some time before, but the moment for actually taking them was left to his 'intuition'.

So now in the summer of 1935 he began his long-range planning for the destruction of the Locarno Treaties, using as his motive the development' of the *rapprochement* between France and Czechoslovakia with Russia and making each step coincide with the progress of French diplomacy towards the point at which a declaration of policy in Paris might once again become the signal for action in Berlin.

Alarmed at the situation occasioned by the German rearmament announcement of March 16, 1935, the French Government sought to strengthen its position in Europe by entering into closer and more friendly relations with the Soviet Union. These negotiations resulted in the signing of a Franco-Soviet pact of mutual assistance on May 2 and 14 in Paris and Moscow respectively, supplemented on May 16 by a similar agreement between the Soviet Union and Czechoslovakia. On the first of these dates (May 2) the first planning directive was issued by von Blomberg to the High Commands of the Army, Navy and Air Force.

Three weeks later, Hitler, still presenting himself as a peacemaker, spoke to the *Reichstag* on May 21, and after expressing qualified mistrust of the treaties recently signed by Russia, France and Czechoslovakia, solemnly reaffirmed the provisions of Versailles

---

[1] For a discussion of Hitler's diplomatic technique — the so-called *Schlummerlied* — see Wheeler-Bennett, *Munich : Prologue to Tragedy* (London, 1948), pp. 215-28.

and Locarno in regard to the Rhineland, and declared that Germany would respect these obligations 'so long as the other partners are on their side ready to stand by that pact'.[1] By these words he provided himself with the means to declare the Locarno Treaty null and void at the opportune moment, simply by declaring that the other signatories (*e.g.* France) had violated its provisions. The Government of the Reich went even further when, on June 17, it assured the French *Chargé d'affaires* in Berlin that no preparations were being made within the demilitarized zone for any kind of activity for the event of war or in readiness therefor.

Both Hitler's assurance and the avowals to the French Embassy figured in the discussions of the Working Committee of the Reich Defence Council presided over by von Reichenau on June 26. They were referred to by a lieutenant-colonel in his middle forties, one Alfred Jodl, who had just become head of the Home Defence Department (*Landesverteidigung*) of the *Wehrmacht* Ministry. In view of these statements, Jodl told his hearers, the preparatory activities, which were in effect being carried on in the zone, must be kept in strictest secrecy, not only in the zone itself, but in the rest of the Reich. He went on to give some idea of what these preliminaries were, and concluded by further affirming the security measures which must be observed in dealing with the directives concerned, which, in any case, must be as few as possible so that the barest minimum was committed to paper.[2]

Thus, though the Bendlerstrasse was fully aware of the *ultimate* intention of the *Führer*'s mind and was openly conniving at the mendacious misleading of the French authorities, they had little or no idea that matters had got beyond the planning stage, and it is to be believed that they had no preconceived ideas of their own for aggressive action. They were not expecting any action which might entail armed resistance on the part of the French and were far from ready to undertake anything in the nature of a major operation.

Summer gave place to autumn, and an uneasy calm settled over Europe, a calm of which the unreality had been enhanced rather than lessened by the signing of the Anglo-German Naval Pact on June 18. On October 15, the building of the *Kriegsakademie*, closed since 1920, was solemnly rededicated by Hitler on the 125th anniversary

---

[1] Hitler's speech to the *Reichstag*, May 21, 1935, *Frankfurter Zeitung*, May 22, 1935 ; authorized English translation, Baynes, ii, 1241.

[2] Minutes of the tenth meeting of the Working Committee of the Reich Defence Council, June 26, 1935 (*IMT Document*, EC-405).

348   HITLER AND THE ARMY   PT. III

of its foundation,[1] but on the following day, the tenth anniversary of the initialing of the Locarno Pacts, the German Press remained unanimously and significantly silent.

With the New Year and the approach of the debate in the French Chamber on the ratification of the Franco-Soviet Pact, the diplomatic tension increased and the determination of the Nazis to regard it as a breach of the spirit of Locarno became more and more apparent. Moreover, despite the fact that Hitler went out of his way at his reception to the Diplomatic Corps on New Year's Day to reassure the French Ambassador that he had no intention of reopening the Locarno question, it became increasingly clear that his resentment of the pact with Moscow was to be used for something more than a mere display of diplomatic protest and annoyance on the part of Germany. These signs and portents were apparently not lost upon M. François-Poncet, who took the opportunity of telling the German Foreign Office exactly what he suspected. 'You are behaving exactly as though you wished to establish juridical justification for a future act already planned', he disconcertingly informed State Secretary von Bülow on January 10. 'This act is, of course, the occupation of the demilitarized zone.'[2]

The debate in the Chamber opened on February 11, and the spirit of discord which it disclosed in French political thought was exacerbated at every opportunity from Berlin. On February 20 M. Herriot spoke warmly in support of ratification. The following morning brought an official German *communiqué* reaffirming in terms of grave severity the thesis that the pacts which France and Czechoslovakia had concluded with the Soviet Union were incompatible with the Locarno Treaties. Forthwith the French Foreign Minister, M. Flandin, while denying the German contention, offered to submit the whole question to the jurisdiction of the Permanent Court of International Justice at The Hague, an offer which was studiously ignored by the German Press and Foreign Office. The debate continued, both among the deputies in the Chamber and at long range between Paris and Berlin, and on February 27 the bill of ratification was passed by 353 to 164.

We do not know at which exact point in the chain of events Hitler decided to march into the Rhineland. Certainly the decision was not taken as suddenly as in the case of the declaration on rearmament of a year before. If the French Ambassador had been

[1] It was on this occasion that von Blomberg, in speaking of the relations between the Party and the Army, stated that, though the Officer Corps had nothing to do with politics, 'they must recognize where the sources of the nation's strength lay, and this created an obligation to political thinking, leading to willing acknowledgement of the Nazi *Weltanschauung*'.   [2] François-Poncet, p. 240.

sufficiently aware of the potentiality to speak of it to von Bülow in mid-January, the intention was most certainly known in the higher military and diplomatic strata in Berlin from the beginning of the debate in the Chamber. As the intention became a certainty, a lively apprehension was evinced among the diplomats and an even more acute anxiety among the Generals.

Now for the first time they realized the lengths to which their earlier acts of acquiescence and concession had led them. They had accepted at their face-value the *Führer*'s public declarations that Germany had no aggressive intention towards her neighbours and his private undertakings that the process of German rearmament should progress unmenaced by alarums and excursions due to foreign policy. A year had been altogether too short a time to complete the vast task of organization and expansion which the precipitate declaration of March 16, 1935, had imposed upon them. The thirty-six divisions which Hitler had proclaimed on that date were very far from completion. It was not to be until October 1936 that even twenty-eight were organized, with a few others in embryonic existence, and even at that date the last two of the twelve army corps had just completed the formation of their headquarters staffs. The first conscripts under the new national service law had not made their appearance until November 7, and these men, born in 1914, had at once been absorbed into the skeleton organization which had been hastily improvised during the first year of conscription. Innumerable difficulties still existed — supplies and equipment were short and there was a great lack of such vital factors as the provision of artillery, support of infantry, etc. — and with the solution of these problems the energies of Ludwig Beck and the General Staff, which had come into active existence only in October 1935, were fully absorbed.

It was the weakest point in the execution of any programme of rearmament. That period of transition when the old and the new have not yet mingled harmoniously ; when organization, although efficient, has not yet begun to produce results ; when inexperience has not yet given place to assured command. The long-matured planning of von Seeckt was in fact justified in the final analysis. It had presupposed a considerably longer period of expansion, but in essentials it stood up under the rigorous demands which were made upon its efficacy. The difference between the autumn manœuvres of 1935 and 1936 showed clearly that German military genius and efficiency had overcome if not all, at least very many, of the initial difficulties and had effectively broken the back of those which remained.

But in the early months of 1936 the very thought of being called upon for active service filled the hearts of the German Generals with despondent forebodings. If the reoccupation of the demilitarized zone of the Rhineland were seriously envisaged, it was an act which, in their estimation, could only result in sanctions by Britain and France. It was inconceivable, according to the rules of the military game, that either of these two Powers should submit to the political humiliation of acquiescing in one more act of unilateral treaty revision on the part of Germany, an act this time affecting not only the Treaty of Versailles but the Pact of Locarno, which, with its ancillary agreements, was regarded as the keystone of French security. Nor was it any more conceivable that the French should condone an act which should place Germany once more as a military power upon their frontier. How could they leave Strasbourg exposed to the fire of German guns ? The withdrawal of Germany from Geneva might have been accepted, her rearmament connived at, but the tearing up of the whole legal basis of Western European security was something — thought the Generals — which could only end in war.

They were considering the matter not from a moral point of view, not as politicians or jurists, but as sober and highly skilled technicians in the art of war. With the ethical rights and wrongs of the case they did not concern themselves. For them war had been defined a hundred years before by their great predecessor Clausewitz as 'an act of violence intended to compel our opponent to fulfil our will'. This act of violence they were perfectly prepared to commit, and with the purpose avowed, provided they had the means to do it. They required the 51 per cent chance of success, and to them it seemed that the odds were all the other way. Had not the French Ambassador warned them that the occupation of the demilitarized zone would create 'a very serious situation' ? Had not his warnings been re-echoed by the German military attachés from Paris and from London ? Did not France, Poland and Czechoslovakia together possess 90 divisions in time of peace and could they not mobilize 190 divisions in the event of war, to say nothing of the Red Army now allied with those of the Locarno Powers ?

These and other spectres stood beside the pillows of the German military leaders in those hours of uncertainty which followed the announcement on February 27 that the Chamber had ratified the treaty. The Generals spoke with von Blomberg, the diplomats with von Neurath ; both Ministers voiced the apprehension of their subordinates to the *Führer*, though, it may be believed, with no great enthusiasm, since both had long qualified as supine 'Yes-men'.

In any event the *Führer* was unimpressed by these expressions of faint-heartedness. He himself was confident of the division and infirmity of purpose prevalent among his political opponents in London and in Paris. What he was about to do could be done with impunity and would provide no greater reaction than a spirited display of finger-shaking. This he knew of his own remarkable intuition, and he regarded with an arrogant scorn those humbler mortals not so eccentrically blessed with such strange prevision.

This was the first head-on clash between the conflicting theories of the German Army and their Supreme Commander. The Army had viewed their expansion and their rearmament in the light of a measure of defence, and a restoration of Germany to a position in world affairs whence she could speak from strength and not from weakness. They only envisaged initiating war under ideal circumstances with a more than 51 per cent chance of success and the full capacity 'to compel their opponent to fulfil their will'. Not so the *Führer*. He had made his position clear some half-dozen years before when he had written that 'armies for the preservation of peace do not exist'.[1] For him war still remained an instrument of national policy and, though he was confident that in this case it would not come, he would not have allowed its possibility to deter him from the business in hand. Hitler was not one who counted in 51 per cent chances. He had watched von Lossow do that in 1923 and he discounted the value of such calculations.[2]

There was yet another contrast with that November day thirteen years before. Then it had been Ludendorff, when Hitler hung back in an agony of indecision, who gave the order to march and insisted upon obedience. Now, when the Generals hesitated and counselled delay and compromise, it was Hitler who swept aside their warnings with an arrogant and contemptuous : '*Vorwärts*'.

The *Führer* reached his final decision on March 1, having taken two clear days to consider the matter after the ratification of the Franco-Soviet Pact on February 27. The preliminary orders to the three senior Commanders-in-Chief were issued by von Blomberg on March 2,[3] in which the object of the operation was stated and all preparations defined except the actual date of Z-day. The order radiated the spirit of the *Führer*'s optimism. It was clearly assumed that the re-entry of German troops into the Rhineland would not

---

[1] See above, p. 290. [2] See above, p. 172.
[3] Order from the War Minister and Commander-in-Chief of the Armed Forces to the Commanders-in-Chief of the Army, Navy and Air Force for 'a surprise move into garrisons of the demilitarized zone', signed by von Blomberg and dated March 2, 1936 (*IMT Document*, C-159).

meet with physical opposition ; however, wrote von Blomberg : 'If the other Powers who have signed the Locarno Treaty reply to the transfer of German troops into the demilitarized zone with military preparations, I reserve the right to decide on any military counter-measures'.

The receipt of these orders by von Fritsch and their subsequent transmission to the senior officers concerned called forth a further flood of protests. On his own initiative Beck proposed to Hitler that the reoccupation should be accompanied by a declaration that Germany would not fortify the area west of the Rhine. He was bluntly and brutally snubbed for his pains and a similar fate awaited von Blomberg when he put forward, on behalf of the General Staff, the suggestion that the battalions sent across the Rhine should be withdrawn on condition that the French would agree to withdraw four to five times as many men from their borders.

All that Hitler would concede to his uneasy Generals was his contemptuous assent to the withdrawal of the German troops sent across the Rhine in the event of serious military opposition being offered by the French.

At dawn on March 7 advance units of the German Army entered the Rhineland for the first time since 1918. At eleven o'clock Freiherr von Neurath handed to the British, French and Italian Ambassadors Germany's formal abrogation of the Treaty of Locarno. At noon the German battalions assigned to Aachen, Trier and Saarbrücken, the 'token force' which was to cross the river, arrived in the Rhine Valley and at the same moment Adolf Hitler mounted the tribune of the *Reichstag* to enunciate, not for the first or last time, a fantastic amalgam of defiance and concession, offering future pledges of peace while the torn fragments of past promises still floated in the air.

After consulting with the British the French Government finally did nothing, despite an offer of support from Poland. True, they concentrated thirteen divisions in the East, but they only manned the Maginot Line and stood on the defensive. But even this was too much for the nerves of the German General Staff. In view of this concentration, von Blomberg, at the instance of von Fritsch and Beck, urged the *Führer* to withdraw the three battalions which had been pushed across the Rhine.[1]

Scornfully Hitler refused. He had won and he knew it ; and

---

[1] Affidavit sworn by the Foreign Office interpreter, Paul Otto Schmidt, at Nuremberg, dated November 28, 1945 (*IMT Document*, PS-3308) ; evidence of Jodl, June 4, 1946 (*Nuremberg Record*, xv, 351-2) ; evidence of von Manstein, August 9, 1946 (*Nuremberg Record*, xx, 603-4) ; evidence of von Rundstedt, August 12, 1946 (*Nuremberg Record*, xxi, 22).

COLONEL-GENERAL FREIHERR WERNER
VON FRITSCH

FIELD-MARSHAL WERNER VON BLOMBERG

he knew, moreover, that his victory extended further than his defiance and humiliation of the Locarno Powers.[1] Britain and France had been defeated in the diplomatic field, but at home he had won a signal and almost as important a victory over his hesitant Generals. He had forced them to march against their will, he had taunted them with defeatism and lack of confidence, and now he was proved abundantly right in his judgment and the Generals returned to their quarters humbled and puzzled and considering themselves betrayed by their fellow military trade unionists on the other side who had not made the proper gambits and who had refused to take advantage of their undoubted superiority. Thereafter, though they did not cease to express their professional forebodings against the wild ebullitions of the *Führer's* 'intuition', they made their protest with an increased lack of assurance and with the growing and sickening fear that he was right and they were wrong.

(iv)

The occupation and remilitarization of the Rhineland in March 1936 and the corollarative abrogation of the Locarno Treaties, constituted a climacteric not only in the course of Nazi foreign policy but also in the relationship of Hitler with the Army. The failure of the Western Powers to oppose this flagrant breach of international agreements, freely and voluntarily entered into by Germany, confirmed the *Führer* in his belief that France and Britain could be bluffed and blackmailed into further acquiescence by the threat of war, provided that the threat remained no empty gesture. This belief was still further substantiated in the course of 1936 by the amazing propaganda success achieved by the Berlin Olympic Games, for which entrants and representatives from all countries flocked to the German capital to partake of Nazi official hospitality.

The tide of appeasement was steadily rising in 1936 and 1937; it was to reach its peak in the autumn of 1938 and thereafter to decline sharply. But for the moment it suited both the aggressor and the appeaser to wander together in a wonderland of mendacity

---

[1] According to Paul Otto Schmidt, however, Hitler was not without qualms at this time, though he kept them sternly secret. 'The forty-eight hours after the march into the Rhineland were the most nerve-wracking (*aufregendste*) in my whole life', Schmidt reports him as frequently repeating. 'If the French had marched into the Rhineland then we should have had to retreat with ignominy, for we had not the military resources at our disposal for even a feeble resistance' (Paul Schmidt, *Statist auf diplomatischer Bühne, 1923-1945* (Bonn, 1949), p. 320). See also *Hitler's Table Talk* (London, 1953), pp. 258-9.

and chicanery, of self-delusion and wishful-thinking, and to emerge finally into a temporary paradise of false security. The years 1936 and 1937 were comparable to the most halcyon period of the Weimar régime, the years 1924–9. The Nazi 'experiment', having begun with a burst of disconcerting bravura, now showed signs, at least outwardly, of settling down into an efficient form of government, with which other governments could live and let live, so long as its principles of totalitarian ideology were practised at home and not destined for export. Getting rid of the Treaty of Versailles came as a measure of relief to many in Britain and America who had suffered acutely from the guilt complex of the victors and had long before adopted the policy of 'Don't let's be beastly to the Germans', and, though this attitude found little echo of enthusiasm in France, its effect upon the foreign policies of London and Washington produced in Paris a tragic and fatalistic defeatism which was among the major causes of appeasement.

The two years from March 1936 to March 1938 were the 'respectable years' of the Nazi Revolution, and Hitler took full advantage of them. He indulged in no more outbursts of international violence but confined himself to activities of diplomacy. In this field he achieved the marked successes of the Rome-Berlin Axis and the Anti-Comintern Pact, thereby creating a new orientation of political alignment in both Europe and Asia.

The old Adam of Nazi evil, however, was not dead but sleeping. Hitler had not for a moment abandoned the general dream of expansion which he had outlined in *Mein Kampf*, but he was following his technique of allowing situations to mature and then seizing the opportunities presented. His strokes of policy, apparently carefully prepared and calculated, were in reality the results of the genius of German organization wrestling desperately to translate into practical application a sudden decision of the *Führer*, taken in accordance with his 'intuition', in realization of some part of a long-cherished dream and in exploitation of a sudden turn of events.

The weak spot in this technique was the relations of Hitler with his Army. After the complete refutation by events of the Generals' objection to the march into the Rhineland, the last remnant of respect vanished from his attitude towards his military leaders. Their inability to grasp the political nuances, as distinct from the purely military aspects, of an international situation, their lack of confidence and of initiative, and, indeed, their apparent pusillanimity, created in the mind of the *Führer* an ineradicable impression of suspicion and contempt, to which he not infrequently gave expression.[1] Where was this fierce and savage mastiff which he had doubted his ability to control when he first assumed power ? Instead of tugging him willy-nilly into war, before he was ready for it, as he had feared might happen, it was he who had to overcome the anxieties of his Generals on every occasion on which he called for their support. The withdrawal from Geneva, the declaration of rearmament, the remilitarization of the Rhineland had all been carried out over the strenuous opposition of the *Heeresleitung*, on grounds not of morality but of expediency and lack of preparation. It was not for this that Hitler had created the armed might of Germany and restored the *Wehrhoheit* of the Reich. For him armies existed 'for triumphant exertion in war', and, though he believed that he could go a long way towards the realization of his ambitions merely by threatening force as the final argument, he was not to be deterred from his ultimate aims by the fear of involving Europe in war, and he wished for an Army which was ready to fight at the drop of a hat — and not their hat but his.

Moreover, it was now a fact that the value of the Army to Hitler in the internal position of Germany had greatly diminished. They had raised him to the supreme position of power in the Reich, and, though it was still within their power to cast down what they had raised up, they were psychologically almost incapable of doing so. Hitler's admiration for the German fighting man, his sense of comradeship with the rank and file, and even with the junior officers, had not lessened, but that complex about Generals, which had developed during the thorny journey of his rise to power, had now intensified in terms of contempt. He conceived himself as now being infinitely superior in every way to these shaven-headed, bemonocled, enigmatical buddhas, who ran, as it were, 'in blinkers' and whose tongue was not even a sharp sword.

Thus, while he derived a certain perverted satisfaction in creating von Blomberg a Field-Marshal and in promoting von Fritsch to be Colonel-General in recognition of their services to German rearmament,[2] he tended more and more to exclude the Army from his counsels and his calculations. They were no longer a political factor in the Reich but were to be called out, like the police force and the fire-brigade, when occasion demanded.

It was this exclusion, this relegation to a sort of technicians' quarantine, that was most bitterly resented by certain of the leading Generals of the Army. They could not forget the position of

---

[1] See evidence of Field-Marshals von Manstein and von Rundstedt at Nuremberg on August 9 and 12, 1946 (*Nuremberg Record*, xx, 603-4 ; xxi, 22).

[2] These appointments were made on April 1, 1936.

influence which the Army had enjoyed under the Empire and the
Republic. They recalled the part which a Chief of the General
Staff, von Waldersee, had played in the affairs of State ; the memoranda on high policy which Ludendorff had addressed with effect
to both Kaiser and Chancellor ; the threatening directives which
von Lüttwitz had issued to Noske ; the tolerant, half-contemptuous
respect of von Seeckt for Ebert ; and the subtle counsels which von
Schleicher had offered to successive Chancellors and to Hindenburg.
They could not make a voluntary abdication of their claim to
be the arbiters of the destiny of the State, and they refused to
accept a situation in which this act of abnegation had been made
for them. If, with a skeleton *Reichswehr* of 100,000 men, they
had succeeded in dominating the Reich, how much more must
they stand pre-eminent with an army fully restored and steadily
expanding ?

More particularly did they take exception to the fundamentals
of Nazi foreign policy. Their own concepts, founded on the teaching
of Bismarck as interpreted by von Seeckt, were based upon friendship
with Russia and China, suspicion of Japan, contempt for Italy, a
policy of watchful neutrality toward Britain and France, and an
undying hatred for Poland. All this was directly contrary to Nazi
policy as the Army saw it. The periodic political adventures in
which the *Führer* indulged must, sooner or later, provoke Britain
and France to retaliation, if common sense and normal calculation
still stood for anything. The policy of *rapprochement* with Poland,
the new alignment with Japan, the recent intervention with Italy
in Spain, all headed inevitably away from the established orthodoxy
of foreign policy as seen from the Bendlerstrasse and towards an
ultimate conflict with the Soviet Union. Not only was this contrary
to all reason in foreign affairs, but from a military standpoint it
revived the age-old horror of the two-front war, since the U.S.S.R.
was now in alliance with France, and both were linked to Czechoslovakia.

Others among the Generals took seriously the inner condition
of the Reich ; the continued persecution of the Jews, the repressive
measures against the Christian Churches ; the disappearance of the
last poor remnants of civic freedom. The arrest of Martin Niemöller
on July 1, 1937, profoundly shocked the many in Germany who
had come to look upon him as a symbol of the Christian resistance
against Anti-Christ, and among these there were many of the Officer
Corps. But the Corps did not give battle on this issue, but upon
another which touched its own vested interests more profoundly.
The Party leaders had not abandoned their efforts to gain ideological

control over the Army, but, because they were forbidden by the *Führer*'s orders to interfere with either troops or officers whilst serving, they had devised a method of indoctrination after service. Plans were laid in 1936 for the formation of a 'National Socialist Soldiers' Ring', which both officers and men were to be encouraged to join after their release from the *Wehrmacht* and where they would become imbued with the proper spirit of National Socialism. At once the Corps was on the alert against this palpable threat to their prerogatives. Both von Blomberg and von Fritsch made earnest representations to the *Führer*, who was graciously pleased to listen to them, for he was ever conscious of the importance of the Officer Corps as a whole, though becoming less and less convinced of the efficiency of its senior members. The Ring never materialized. But it was the last victory of the Army over the Party, who were quick to take their revenge.

From the autumn of 1936 may be dated the concerted attack of the Party to undermine the influence of the Army with the *Führer*. The 'smear campaign', which was later destined to become an all-out offensive, began with a whisper in the dead reeds of the ancient loyalties of the reactionaries. Von Fritsch and his Generals, said Himmler and his friends to Hitler, were plotting to overthrow the Nazi régime and to restore the throne with either the ex-Kaiser or the Crown Prince, or Prince Louis-Ferdinand, the latter's second son, as monarch. Himmler and his deputy, Heydrich,[1] who, as chief security officers of the Reich, were personally responsible for the *Führer*'s safety, lost no opportunity of bringing the rumour, enriched with their own embellishments, to Hitler's attention. Not the Party nor the régime alone, but he personally was threatened by this reactionary clique of senior officers, who lorded their new-found strength and influence in the capital of the Reich and in the head-quarters of the *Wehrkreise*, and wild plots to kidnap, murder or deport the *Führer* were darkly hinted at.

---

[1] Reinhardt Heydrich (1904–42), originally a naval officer, had been dismissed the Service and expelled from the Officer Corps for 'conduct unbecoming to an officer and a gentleman' in connection with a young girl. Seething with hatred for the Corps and all that it stood for, Heydrich joined the SS, where he quickly attracted the attention of Himmler, who confided to him the task of building up the SD (*Sicherheitsdienst*) and later made him head of the Gestapo and the Security Police as well. He remained an implacable enemy of the Army throughout the remainder of his life and utilized his high position to the best purposes of hostility. There was unquestionably a strong measure of sadism about Heydrich, which became apparent when in 1941 he replaced von Neurath as Reich Protector of Bohemia and Moravia. His assassination was attempted by Czech patriots on May 27, 1942, and he died of his wounds on June 4. A week later, in revenge, the Czech village of Lidice, together with all its population, was wiped out by order of the German occupation authorities (June 10).

Ironically enough, at this particular period, no such plots or plans existed, and the SD and Gestapo were well aware of this fact. Discontent there certainly was among the senior officers of the Army and among certain of the senior officials of the Reich, a discontent amounting even to a degree of opposition. But in no quarter had Opposition yet crystallized into Resistance. Beck and von Hammerstein might fulminate in military circles against the fantastic risks attendant upon the *Führer's* foreign policy. Schacht, newly awakened to the dangers inherent in a régime which he had strained every effort to bring to power, might inveigh against Hitler's economic theories and the dangers of too rapid and too gross a measure of rearmament; civilian figures, such as Carl Goerdeler and Johannes Popitz,[1] themselves convinced that 'something must be done', might travel the Reich and canvass in secret what this 'something' should be, but in no case had discontent or opposition gone beyond the pious hope that one day Colonel-General Freiherr Werner von Fritsch would give the order to march.

There was something almost legendary in the attitude of the conservative elements towards von Fritsch at this juncture. There is the man, they thought, who says nothing but bides his time, and when he judges the psychological moment to have arrived he will strike and sweep away the evil rottenness of the régime. Further than this no one in high places had gone, though certain of the younger men were already clearer in their minds as to what should follow But the leaders of the malcontents had no plans other than cathartic, and it was even uncertain whether these purgative measures should embrace Hitler or not.

The blind faith thus reposed in von Fritsch could not have been more completely misplaced. He was no conspirator as Beck and von Hammerstein were to become; he was no warrior-statesman like von Seeckt. He was an extremely able staff officer but otherwise a person of limited intelligence and rigid outlook. At no time, even at the moment of his greatest trial, did he envisage any act which could have been described as remotely mutinous. His loyalty to his caste caused him to defend the prerogatives of the Officer Corps before Caesar's throne, but the idea of dethroning Caesar never occurred to him. When he had said that the Army was wedded to the Nazi Party for better or for worse, he meant it. And the fact

[1] Johannes Popitz (1884–1944), a Prussian civil servant and a friend of General von Schleicher. Having served in the Schleicher Cabinet as Minister without portfolio, he became Prussian Minister of State and Finance under Göring. An early convert to Opposition and later to Resistance, Popitz became one of the inner circle of the conspiracy as it took form. He was tried before the People's Court in Berlin and hanged on October 12, 1944.

that he said little and looked enigmatic merely made him a 'Sphinx without a riddle', and very far from the far-seeing, calculating character which he was reputed to be.

Himmler and Heydrich were perfectly well aware of the infirmity of purpose of von Fritsch. They knew that the High Command of the *Wehrmacht* as constituted in 1936–8 was not a major menace to the *Führer* or the régime. Yet because of the insatiable, predatory desire of the one to add control of the Army to his already widely flung empire, and of the other to be revenged upon the Officer Corps which had cast him out from among them, these two men aimed at the humiliation and political emasculation of the Army leaders and played upon the *Führer* accordingly.

Hitler, it is to be believed, was not at this time greatly impressed by these stories of alleged conspiratorial tendencies among this Generals. Though he never imagined that he retained their personal devotion, he had considerable confidence in the binding and inhibiting nature of the oath which they had taken to him. He did not like them, nor they him, but he was not afraid of them. Indeed he was far more disturbed at their disinclination to fight when he demanded it of them, for he had reached a major point in his career of power. He knew that sooner or later his policies would almost certainly lead Germany into war.

It may be asked, for what purpose? The Nazi régime had destroyed the structure of the Treaty of Versailles, and had elevated the German Reich to a position of greater power than it had ever attained under the Kaiser. But what now? The answer was simple but terrifying. Hitler had conceived of himself as the Saviour and Emancipator of the Germans, in the first instance of the Germans of the Reich, and latterly of all Germans. Where there were Germans subject to States contiguous to Germany, they must be freed and united within the Greater German Reich. But this was not all. The Germans, being rapid and fecund breeders, must have room for expansion (*Lebensraum*). Thus, while it was necessary to 'bring home' the Germans of Europe to the Reich, it was also essential, since neither autarchy nor an increased participation in world economy could provide a solution for Germany's problems, to give the inhabitants of the Greater German Reich thus created facilities for greater expansion.

Hitler had published his views on Germany's need for expansion in *Mein Kampf* over ten years earlier, but now the time was approaching when dreams might be translated into reality. The Nazi movement could not afford to stagnate. It had to present a façade of constant growth and vitality or lose its *raison d'être*. In the autumn of 1937 Hitler found his economic policy, distorted as it was by the rearmament programme, under attack in his own cabinet. At the centre of the opposition was the formidably expert figure of Schacht. Hitler decided to eliminate this internal obstruction by revealing his hopes for German foreign policy successes in the immediate future and impressing upon his military leaders the need for preparedness during the months and years ahead. On November 5, 1937, he summoned to the *Reichskanzlei* in secret session his Minister for War, his Foreign Minister and his three Commanders-in-Chief, together with his *Wehrmacht* Adjutant who kept the record.[1]

Hitler said that he wanted to explain his basic thoughts on foreign policy and impressed upon his hearers that in the event of his death his exposition was to be regarded as his political testament. In other countries such matters would be discussed before the full cabinet, but precisely because the issues were so vital he wished to restrict his remarks to a smaller group.

The discourse which followed was verbose and rambling but certain salient points emerged from it. The first was that Germany required living space — a common enough Nazi cliché now given more significance by its context. The question was where could she achieve the greatest gain at the lowest cost, and the answer was in Central Europe, where she must act against Austria and Czechoslovakia. A discussion of Germany's armaments position and references to Frederick the Great's acquisition of Silesia gave some idea of what sort of 'action' Hitler had in mind. Owing to the danger that Germany's war capacity might decline relative to other powers after five or six years the deadline for action against the Czechs and the Austrians was fixed at the period 1943–5. But events in Europe might enable Germany to act before then. The Spanish Civil War might touch off a wider Mediterranean conflict, for example, or there might be civil disturbances in France. In such a case Germany must act with lightning speed in order to prevent intervention on the part of other Powers, especially Britain, France or Poland.

Hitler made it clear that he did not expect the Western Powers

---

[1] The record of this conference of November 5, 1937, was written up by Colonel Hossbach from his notes five days later and is dated November 10. It was introduced in evidence at Nuremberg by the American Prosecution on November 24, 1945 (*Nuremberg Record*, ii, 262); the German text is to be found in the *Nuremberg Record* (xxv, 402-13) and also in *Akten zur deutchen auswärtigen Politik, 1918–1945* (Baden-Baden, 1950), Series D. i, 25-32. An English version of the document in a very indifferent translation was used at Nuremberg as PS-386, but a reliable English text appears in *Documents on German Foreign Policy, 1918–1945*, Series D. i, 29-39. For Hossbach's own account of the meeting, see *Zwischen Wehrmacht und Hitler*, pp. 186-94.

to honour obligations they had undertaken in Central Europe. He thought Britain and France had already tacitly written off the Czechs — a view which turned out to be tragically prophetic. There were of course risks in his policy, but what had ever been achieved without taking risks? The risks in the situation could only be offset by the speed of the military operations.

The reactions of Hitler's listeners, as recorded by Hossbach, are of interest. To all of them, with the possible exception of Göring, the exposition which they had just heard came as a considerable shock ; none of them was in complete agreement with the *Führer*, yet the objections of all of them, even those of von Neurath, were based on reasonings of policy rather than morality. No one of the six men — whatever may have been their private feelings — appears to have been in the least disturbed at the jeopardizing of the peace of Europe by the projected annexation of Austria and Czechoslovakia and the abrogation of the attendant international agreements. What did disturb them was, in the case of von Neurath, the wholly un-justifiable degree of confidence which Hitler seemed to repose in the extent to which France and Britain had written off Central Europe and the proximity, which he appeared to expect, of a conflict in the Mediterranean.

Von Blomberg and von Fritsch, as soldiers, deprecated any line of action which should bring Germany into hostilities with Britain and France and gave warning against underestimating the strength of the French Army and the Czech defences. It was clear from their remarks that they considered the German Army as not yet in a state of sufficient preparedness to undertake a major European war, in-volving a number of Powers. Even Göring suggested that before embarking on such an enterprise of expansion they should first liquidate their military commitments in Spain. Raeder appears to have made no contribution to the discussion, which lasted some four and a quarter hours.

Such was the immediate effect on the chiefs of the *Wehrmacht* and the Foreign Office of Hitler's presentation of a blue-print for aggression. Their subsequent reactions were also characteristic. Von Blomberg and Göring soon swallowed their objections and rallied to the support of the *Führer*'s thesis. In conversation with Raeder after the conference they succeeded in removing his doubts and queries by assuring him that the whole thing had been staged to 'ginger up' von Fritsch and the traditional reactionaries into an acceleration of the tempo of rearmament. It was not to be taken seriously. There was no question, they told the Commander-in-Chief of the Navy, of any danger of a naval conflict with Britain.

Reassured on the line of his own vested interest, Raeder returned to his office and appears never to have mentioned the meeting again.[1] Upon von Neurath the effect seems to have been one of delayed action. The moral (or immoral) aspects of the *Führer*'s statement do not appear to have revealed themselves to his Foreign Minister until forty-eight hours later, but when they did 'they shook him so severely that he suffered several severe heart attacks'.[2] He did not observe the oath of secrecy which had been imposed upon all present at the conclave but discussed the purport of the meeting with von Fritsch and Beck on November 7, seeking for some means to persuade the *Führer* to change his plans.[3] The Generals readily agreed with him, but their objections remained on purely technical grounds, namely, not that peace was desirable in preference to aggression, but that one should not embark on a war which one had not at least a 51 per cent chance of winning.[4] It was agreed that von Fritsch, who was to report to the *Führer* during the next few days, should explain to him all the military considerations which made his policy inadvisable, and that von Neurath could then put forward the political undesirabilities. Von Fritsch's interview took place on November 9, and with such ill effect that Hitler refused to see von Neurath before his departure for the Obersalzberg. It was not until the middle of January 1938 that the Foreign Minister could unburden his conscience-stricken soul, and when he did so he made no vestige of impression upon the *Führer*.

Hitler had made up his mind and had charted his course. The protests and objections of his lieutenants had no effect upon him other than to convince him still more firmly of the correctness of his own interpretation of the international situation and of their ineptitude and unsuitability for high office in the destiny which he had mapped for Germany. He did not suspect von Fritsch of disloyalty but merely of lack of intestinal fortitude — and he was right. The General lacked guts even in defending himself against an abominable charge. The time had come, in the consideration of the *Führer*, when the old wood must be pruned from the Cabinet, and the legacies which he had inherited from Hindenburg liquidated.

---

[1] Affidavit of Field-Marshal von Blomberg, sworn at Nuremberg on February 26, 1946; Grand-Admiral Raeder's evidence at Nuremberg, May 16, 1946 (*Nuremberg Record*, xiv, 34-7).

[2] Affidavit of Baroness von Ritter, sworn at Munich-Lochhausen, May 28, 1946.

[3] Evidence of Freiherr von Neurath at Nuremberg, June 4, 1946 (*Nuremberg Record*, xvi, 640-41).

[4] 'Certainly Beck was no pacifist', the General's biographer writes of this period (Major Wolfgang Foerster, *Ein General kämpft gegen den Krieg* (Munich, 1949), p. 24).

The policy which he now designed for Germany required the un-hesitating and unswerving confidence of those who would be charged with the immediate executive tasks. There was no longer room at his counsel board for the traditionalist and the doubter. He was one who made his own traditions, charted his own destiny and demanded implicit obedience from his stooges. Within two months of the conclave of November 5, three of the six composing his audience on that occasion had ceased to hold office.

(v)

'What an influence can a woman exert on the history of a country, and thereby on the world, without even knowing it', wrote Colonel Alfred Jodl in his diary on January 26, 1938. 'One has the feeling of witnessing a decisive hour for the German people.' [1] Few women, certainly, have swayed the course of German history more unwittingly, yet, at the same time, more decisively than Fräulein Erna Gruhn, whose name, in the first weeks of 1938, rang through the halls and offices of Berlin, precipitating chaos and disaster. For a flaming moment she became the agent of destiny and then passed into a more decent obscurity than that from which she had emerged.

The story is strange and unsavoury. It is a scandal of a type which could perhaps only happen in Germany. It is an epitome of the psychopathic atmosphere which permeated the era of the Third Reich, and of the Byzantine intrigue which also characterized the period.

In the weeks which followed the famous secret conclave of November 5, 1937, the relations between the War Minister and the Commander-in-Chief of the Army had perceptibly worsened. After reflection, von Blomberg tended more and more to support the *Führer* in the principles of the policy laid down, to which von Fritsch became increasingly hostile on the grounds of the funda-mental menace to the German Army which they contained. Nor was this all. In the opinion of von Fritsch the War Minister was now all too dilatory in his representation of the interests of the Army before the *Führer*. Recently there had been a recurrence of attempts by the Party to tamper with the authority of the Divisional Chaplains and to provide counter instruction for the troops in classes of Nazi indoctrination. Though these encroachments had been defeated, it had taken all the efforts of von Fritsch and Beck to screw up von Blomberg to the point of making their case to Hitler. Either the Field-Marshal was afraid of his *Führer* or he had become so com-

---

[1] Jodl's Diary, January 4, 1937–August 25, 1939 (*IMT Document*, PS-1780).

N

pletely acquiescent as to be incapable of taking an opposite view. In any event it was becoming increasingly difficult to make the 'Rubber Lion' roar, even by twisting his tail, and the High Command of the Army were contemplating an eventuality in which they should pronounce the fell sentence that the War Minister no longer enjoyed the Army's confidence.

Thus the position stood at the dawn of the New Year. The Army waited for an opportunity to get rid of its Minister. The Party, not uninformed of the situation, for Army security was not entirely Himmler-proof, watched and waited for a possible disintegration of the inner unity of its hated rival. Moreover, Göring was by no means averse to the removal of von Blomberg, since he now entertained ambitions of becoming War Minister of the Reich himself. And into this powder-keg of intrigue Fräulein Erna Gruhn threw the lighted match of scandal.[1]

Field-Marshal von Blomberg was a widower. In 1904 he had married the daughter of a retired Army officer in Hanover, who, having presented him with two sons and three daughters, had died in 1932. The Marshal's children had grown up, and in 1937 his youngest daughter had married the son of an obscure and not very promising Hanover officer, Wilhelm Keitel, whom von Blomberg had promoted to be head of the *Wehrmachtamt* of the War Ministry.

After six years of widowerhood the Field-Marshal wished to remarry. But this time the lady of his choice was not of that same military caste as before. She was, he confided to Göring, whose advice he sought, a typist-secretary in the War Ministry. Did the Minister-President of Prussia see any insurmountable obstacle in

---

[1] It has not been considered necessary for the purposes of this book to enter into details of the scandals involving von Blomberg and von Fritsch. Such accounts exist in Graf von Kielmansegg's book, *Der Fritsch Prozess*, and in General Hermann Foertsch's *Schuld und Verhängnis*; also in Gisevius, i, 383-458, and his evidence before the International Military Tribunal at Nuremberg on April 25, 1946 (*Nuremberg Record*, xii, 196-203); in Hossbach, pp. 121-45; and Foerster, pp. 67-8. The former head of the Legal Division of the OKW, Dr. Heinrich Rosenberger, who was charged by Keitel to investigate the case, has given his story in an article, 'Die Entlassung des Generalobersten Freiherrn von Fritsch' (*Deutsche Rundschau*, November 1946).

The present writer has consulted all these authorities and numerous others in the nature of interrogations of certain high-ranking German officers. He has also used the Diary of Colonel-General Alfred Jodl for the period and, in addition an invaluable Memorandum by Dr. Otto John, formerly of the legal division of the *Lufthansa* and one of the few survivors of the *Putsch* of July 20, 1944. This paper, entitled 'Some Facts and Aspects of the Plot against Hitler', is referred to hereinafter as the *John Memorandum*.

The present writer has also had access to the correspondence of Freiherr von Fritsch with his friend, Baronin Margot von Schutzbar-Milchling, over this period.

principle to such a marriage, asked the War Minister of the Reich ?

Göring apparently saw no obstacle at all, in principle or in practice, whereupon the Field-Marshal was emboldened to seek his aid in the disposal of a rival admirer, whom the Minister-President obligingly shipped off to South America. Göring did more. He approached Hitler and obtained his blessing on the affair. The prospect of his Field-Marshal and War Minister allying himself with a bride from outside the rigid limitations of the military caste was to the *Führer* a gratifying indication that at least one of his warrior leaders was identifying himself with the people in the accepted sense of the National Socialist State.

And so, on January 12, 1938, the Field-Marshal and Fräulein Erna Gruhn were married quietly in Berlin in the presence of the *Führer* and Göring. The event passed almost unnoticed in the Press.

But rumours soon were rampant in the capital. The fact that a German Field-Marshal should marry outside his caste was sufficiently succulent a morsel for the gossip-mongers, but with very little effort Fräulein Gruhn's name was connected in the minds of police officials with certain *dossiers* which, when placed before the Police-President of Berlin, Count Helldorf, disclosed with appalling clarity that the past life of the *Frau Feldmarschall* was all too incontrovertibly established in a police record.

Helldorf was frankly horrified, both at the discovery and its potential repercussions. This ardent Nazi, whose record was among the most impeccable in the Party, had already begun that deviation into heresy which was to lead him eventually to the hangman's noose.[1] Helldorf was pre-eminently a member of the military caste and of the Officer Corps. He had been the type which von Seeckt had sedulously purged from the *Reichswehr* and which had inevitably found refuge in the NSDAP, but, for all that, a certain devotion to military loyalty, tradition, and honour remained, and Helldorf knew well that if these incriminating files fell into Himmler's hands the forces in opposition to the Army would

---

[1] Graf Wolf-Heinrich Helldorf (1896–1944) served in the First World War as an officer of Hussars and immediately after the Armistice joined the *Freikorps* operations in Bavaria. As a member of the Rossbach Corps he took part in the Kapp *Putsch* and was exiled to Italy, whence he returned with the general amnesty of 1924 to be elected a member of the Prussian *Landtag*. Joining the Nazi Party in 1926, he quickly rose in prominence, becoming SA Führer of Berlin-Brandenburg, Police President of Potsdam, 1933–35, and finally Police President of Berlin, a position which he held until hanged in August 1944 for complicity in the *Putsch* of July 20.

be possessed of a powerful weapon of blackmail.

His duty was clear. The *dossier* should have gone to Himmler, but Helldorf took it instead to von Blomberg's closest collaborator, Wilhelm Keitel, with the suggestion that it be destroyed. He could not have picked a weaker vessel for such a proposition. Possessed by a curious amalgam of professional ambition, frustrated social pretensions, and a deep-seated inferiority complex, Keitel was the last man to enter into any conspiracy which might affect his future. He was genuinely attached to von Blomberg, both personally and by family ties, and he owed him everything in the way of military preferment, but the suppression of essential evidence required a greater degree of moral courage than he possessed. He therefore passed the papers on to Göring, who felt in duty bound to pass them to Hitler. And the *Führer* had a *crise de nerfs*.

Meantime, strange tidings reached the Bendlerstrasse. Generals were receiving playful telephone calls from restaurants and cafés where the Sisterhood of Joy were celebrating the social rise of their colleague to the position of *Frau Feldmarschall*.[1]

The reaction within the Officer Corps to this slur upon its honour was certainly more acute than after the murder of von Schleicher. The prestige of the Corps had been affronted, dragged in the mud. Above all, the Army had become the butt of more than one discreet dig from the Party leaders. 'What do you think of your Field-Marshal now?' Hans Frank had asked General von Adam when they met, and received the furious retort : 'He is not our Field-Marshal but yours'.

Beck spoke forcefully to his Commander-in-Chief. It was outrageous that the highest ranking officer in the Army should marry a prostitute and thereby insult the honour and tradition of the whole Officer Corps. He must be forced to resign, for he was not even fit to command a regiment. Not only that ; he must divorce his wife or be stricken off the list of officers, for it was intolerable (*untragbar*) that this woman should go about calling herself *Frau Feldmarschall*. Von Fritsch, said the Chief of the General Staff, must go to the *Führer* and demand von Blomberg's dismissal in the name of the Corps of Officers.

And to the *Führer* von Fritsch went, and found that Göring had got there before him. The Minister-President of Prussia had put it to Hitler that von Blomberg had grossly deceived them both in the matter of Fräulein Gruhn and had brought them into ridicule by allowing them to attend his wedding under false pretences. Von Fritsch added the arguments of the Officer Corps and between them

[1] Jodl's Diary, January 28, 1938.

they convinced Hitler that his first Field-Marshal of the Third Reich must go.

The question of a successor arose, and here again Fate took an odious twist, her agent being Heinrich Himmler. The normal successor to von Blomberg would be von Fritsch, by right and by qualification. But Göring had his eye on the War Ministry, and was therefore against von Fritsch's succession. Himmler, too, was opposed to von Fritsch. The Chief of the Reich Police saw an opportunity to strike a blow, which might even prove fatal, against his inveterate and hated field-grey rivals. Von Fritsch was not only the epitome of everything that Himmler hated about the Army, he was the leader of the clique most adamantly opposed to the SS and all that they implied. Now was the moment, when the united front of the Army was for the first time broken, to get under their guard and to savage them from within. Himmler did not want Göring in the War Ministry either, but for the moment he dissimulated and joined with him in a hideous cabal to block von Fritsch.

Scarcely had the *Führer* recovered from the shock of the Blomberg revelations than there appeared before him a second *dossier* of scandal. This time the subject was the Commander-in-Chief of the Army, who was accused of homosexual practices, with a record reaching back to 1935. In touching this particular chord in his attack upon von Fritsch, Himmler displayed diabolical inner knowledge, for, ever since the disclosures which had followed the Blood Purge of June 30, 1934, Hitler had been bitterly and even morbidly critical of any scandal which should impair the reputation for apparent austere morality which he sought to build up for the Nazi régime.

The immediate effect was to mitigate the *Führer's* attitude towards his fallen Field-Marshal, whom he now tried to find means of retaining. When this proved impossible, he summoned von Blomberg to him on January 26, and having broken the news of his dismissal with greater kindness than might have been expected, consulted him on the subject of his successor.[1] Ironically enough, von Blomberg suggested Göring. The Marshal had been deeply hurt at the reaction of the Officer Corps to his marriage. He resented

---

[1] Of the heated scene which is alleged by some to have taken place between the *Führer* and his Field-Marshal on this occasion, the present writer has been able to find no evidence. Von Blomberg in his affidavit makes no complaint of Hitler's conduct towards him at their final interview, and Jodl, who had the account third hand from Keitel, writes in his diary, perhaps a trifle fulsomely, of the *Führer's* 'superhuman kindness' and of his promise that 'as soon as Germany's hour comes, you shall be at my side' — a promise which was certainly not fulfilled but which might well have been made at the time (Jodl's Diary, January 26, 1938).

their attitude and regarded himself as having been let down and betrayed. It is to be believed, therefore, that a measure of revenge was not lacking in his suggestion of Göring to succeed him as War Minister. But the *Führer* remained true to his consistent principle of not putting a Nazi over the Army. As in 1934 he had refused to have Röhm as Minister of Defence, so now in 1938 he refused to consider Göring as Minister for War. He emphatically rejected von Blomberg's proposal with the remark that Göring was neither patient nor diligent enough to hold the post. On the other hand, he took notice of von Blomberg's other suggestion of Keitel as a reliable '*Chef de Bureau*' if such were wanted.[1]

He promised, however, that after absence from Germany for a year, the Blombergs might return to live in retirement until the moment came for the recall of the Field-Marshal to active service,[2] and with these words of comfort von Blomberg and his wife were sped upon their Roman honeymoon.[3]

The *Führer* now turned his attention to the case of his Commander-in-Chief of the Army. Though he had been genuinely surprised by the disclosures regarding both von Blomberg and von Fritsch, Hitler was now fully alive to the advantages which might be garnered from the situation. A golden opportunity was now presented to bring the Army under his own direct control and to humble the haughty Prussian who had commanded it for the past four years. There were other Generals in the service of the Reich — men such as von Reichenau, or even von Brauchitsch — who were perhaps as able soldiers as von Fritsch and would certainly be more

---

[1] Affidavits of von Blomberg sworn at Nuremberg on November 7, 1945, and February 26, 1946.

[2] After the prescribed year of exile, von Blomberg and his wife returned to Germany on January 25, 1939. They settled in Wiessee (Bavaria) and lived in complete retirement throughout the war. The Field-Marshal died at Nuremberg on March 13, 1946.

[3] The vendetta of the Officer Corps pursued the Field-Marshal even to Rome. His former naval adjutant, Kapitän-Leutnant von Wangenheim, took it upon himself, it was said with the approval of Raeder, to pursue von Blomberg to the Italian capital and there to offer him the alternatives of divorce or suicide. The Field-Marshal rejected both courses, because, as he later wrote to Keitel : 'It was evident that von Wangenheim had quite different views and standards of life from my own'. The reaction of the 'new officer' to the episode may be gauged from the comment of Jodl that 'the attempt made by von Wangenheim has probably been made with the best intentions, but shows an extraordinary arrogance on the part of a young officer who believes that it is his duty to be the guardian of the honour of the Officer Corps. Everything had to be done to avoid a suicide, the *Führer* succeeded in that, and the adjutant could have ruined everything.' In effect there was little chance of the attempt succeeding, for von Blomberg was not a man of that sensitivity, and the young Don Quixote returned to Berlin, having ruined his career (Jodl's Diary, January 29, February 1 and 2, 1938).

in tone with the *Zeitgeist* in Germany. Hitler's objective was to destroy the independent power and influence of the *Generalität* without alienating the loyalty of the Officer Corps as a whole, and without impairing the professional and technical efficiency of the Army. He succeeded remarkably well.

The interview with von Fritsch, at which Göring was present, took place at noon on the same day. It had been intended to spring a surprise on the General, but this was forestalled by the fact that Colonel Hossbach, whose loyalty to his caste was deeper than his fealty to his *Führer*, had given von Fritsch a guarded warning over the telephone.[1] The General therefore listened with icy contempt to the charges which Himmler and Heydrich had so lovingly prepared against him and then uttered a brief but emphatic and all-embracing denial. This the conspirators had expected. From a side door a shambling degenerate figure emerged and at once identified the General. Livid with rage, von Fritsch became inarticulate, and his visible emotions convinced Hitler of his guilt. The *Führer* demanded his resignation, in return for which the affair would be hushed up. This von Fritsch refused to give and in his turn demanded a court martial, to which Hitler would not at once consent, and the interview closed with the Commander-in-Chief of the Army being ordered on indefinite leave.

The scene in the Bendlerstrasse on the return of von Fritsch from the *Reichskanzlei* must have recalled a similar occasion just five years before, when, on January 28, 1933, von Schleicher came back from his dismissal as Chancellor.[2] Then, as now, the Generals raged furiously together, then as now they revealed their political impotence. The following day was the Kaiser's birthday (January 27), and an occasion among the Army for a reaffirmation of their deeper and more traditional loyalties. It could have become the opportunity for a *coup d'état*, at the risk of civil war. But shame and embarrassment were mixed with indignation in the Generals' minds and their capacity for action was crippled. Even Beck, who yearned to cleanse the Reich and restore the honour of the Army, was confused by Hitler's assertions. Beck himself had not yet the stature to lead a *Putsch*, and the opportunity slipped by.

---

[1] In taking this action Hossbach was aware that he had probably ruined his career as an officer, and possibly endangered his life. He was, in effect, dismissed from his post of Adjutant of the *Wehrmacht* with the *Führer*, in which he was succeeded by Colonel Rudolf Schmundt, but was retained on the General Staff of the Army (OKH) until the outbreak of war. He eventually rose to the rank of General of Infantry and to the command of the 4th Army, from which he was dismissed by telephone on January 28, 1945. The General has become a recent convert to Moral Rearmament.   [2] See above, p. 281.

Those who had looked forward to this day with secret longing now turned to von Fritsch with the profound confidence that in the defence of his own honour and that of Germany he would surely strike. Popular with the troops, liked by the majority of his fellow Generals, a pattern of a military leader, he lacked only the initiative to move. At the moment of confluence of his own Fate with that of Germany, he was found wanting. The Man of Steel, the Hero of the Army, bewildered and shocked by what had happened, at that moment of destiny resembled a cross between a puzzled virgin and a petrified rabbit. Despite the protests of Beck, he wrote out the resignation required of him.

Beck turned elsewhere for support. He urgently summoned von Rundstedt, as the senior ranking officer of the Army, from Königsberg, and together they went to Hitler, on January 31. The *Führer* was in an excitable mood. He inveighed vehemently against Generals in general, German Generals in particular, and von Blomberg and von Fritsch specifically. To von Rundstedt's request that the Field-Marshal be court-martialled for an offence against the code of honour of the Officer Corps he returned a point-blank refusal, but after much argument and caracoling he reluctantly agreed to a Court of Honour for von Fritsch.

The *Führer* then gave the Generals an inkling of what he had evolved as a solution for the problem of the armed services. He was not, he said, proposing to replace von Blomberg as Minister of War. Göring had been suggested to him for this position, but he knew that such an appointment would make too great a demand upon the Army. He would accordingly appoint Göring a Field-Marshal and he himself would assume, at least temporarily, the duties of War Minister and Supreme Commander of the Armed Forces, with Keitel as his Chief of Staff. Ultimately, he proposed to have a Generalissimo of the Armed Forces, as the French had in Gamelin.

Von Rundstedt at once acquiesced in this last idea and suggested that von Fritsch should be nominated to this rôle after he had been cleared by a Court of Honour. But this produced an interval of stony silence from the *Führer*, who later proceeded to discuss the succession in the command of the Army. Now, as in August 1933, Hitler wanted von Reichenau as Commander-in-Chief; now, as then, the Army were adamantly opposed to him, and for the same reasons.[1] Having disburdened themselves of a pro-Nazi Minister of War, they were not disposed to embarrass themselves with a pro-Nazi and unorthodox commander. Von Rundstedt proposed Beck,

[1] See above, p. 301.

but this Hitler in his turn refused; he countered with the name of Walter von Brauchitsch, and him von Rundstedt deemed acceptable to the Army.[1]

There now developed two battles, two parallel engagements which the Army fought against the Party. The first was to prevent the unification of the three armed services under one War Minister and to substitute for it three service ministries, of which that of the Army would be acknowledged as the senior. The second was that the tribunal before which the charges against von Fritsch should be tried and disproved should be the General Court Martial of the Armed Services and not in any sense a Party Court.

For more than a week the battle on both issues raged fiercely, and, despite all precaution of security, its repercussions reached the outside world. The atmosphere of Berlin was charged with tension, and many recalled with horrified foreboding the similar sense of strain which had preceded the bloody massacres of June 30, 1934. The torch of rumour flamed through the capital. The indefinite postponement of the ceremonial session of the *Reichstag* on January 30, held annually in celebration of the Seizure of Power, was attributed to fear on the part of the authorities of a *coup de main* by von Fritsch at a moment when all the Party leaders were collected under one roof.[2] The cancellation on February 2 of a dinner-party to which von Fritsch had invited a number of guests for the following evening, including the French Ambassador, brought forth the rumour that the General was held a prisoner under house arrest in his villa.[3]

In fact, however, nothing so dramatic had happened. The Generals had fired a number of volleys, but it was only with blank cartridge. They were disunited, lacking in leadership and initiative,

[1] I am indebted to Dr. Otto John for the account given to him after the War by Field-Marshal von Rundstedt of this interview with the *Führer*. There is, however, a discrepancy as to dates. According to von Rundstedt's recollection the interview took place at 2 o'clock on the afternoon of February 4. The final announcement of the reorganization of the Armed Forces was made at 11 o'clock on the evening of the 4th, and von Rundstedt says in his account that he only learned of the scandals concerning von Blomberg and von Fritsch, and indeed of the whole Army crisis, from Beck who met him at the station on his return from Königsberg. Jodl's diary, however, records an interview of von Rundstedt with the *Führer* on January 31, and there is little doubt that this is the correct date of the meeting.

[2] Dr. John in his memorandum writes that, in fact, it had been more than once suggested by impatient opponents of the régime, both military and civilian, that it would be the easiest thing in the world for the Army to cordon off the Kroll Opera and arrest all the Nazi leaders while the *Reichstag* was in session. He suggests that, since discretion was not always of the highest among the conspirators, such remarks had reached the knowledge of Himmler and Heydrich.

[3] François-Poncet, pp. 284-5.

and, though Beck did his best to hold them together, it became evident that the battle against unified command must end in a compromise, and a compromise was tantamount to a defeat for the Army. Hitler accepted von Brauchitsch instead of von Reichenau. So far, this was a satisfactory solution for the Army. But von Brauchitsch, with a willingness to appease that was to wring the hearts of the military conspirators in the days to come, had begun his career by selling the pass and accepting without conditions the unification of command, and also certain vital changes in the personnel of the High Command.[1]

The final blow fell shortly before midnight on February 4, with an announcement over the radio which disclosed the degree of the defeat which not only the Army but all the forces of reaction had sustained at the hands of the Party.

From henceforth [ran the *Führer's* decree], I exercise personally the immediate command over the whole armed forces. The former *Wehrmacht* Office in the War Ministry becomes the High Command of the Armed Forces [OKW], and comes immediately under my command as my military staff. At the head of the Staff of the High Command stands the former chief of the *Wehrmacht* Office [Keitel]. He is accorded the rank equivalent to that of Reich Minister. The High Command of the Armed Forces also takes over the functions of the War Ministry, and the Chief of the High Command exercises, as my deputy, the powers hitherto held by the Reich War Minister.

The task of preparing the unified defence of the Reich in all fields, in accordance with my instructions, is the function of the High Command in time of peace.[2]

The resignations of von Blomberg and von Fritsch were formally announced,[3] together with the appointment of von Brauchitsch as the latter's successor. Göring was promoted a Field-Marshal and the new Commander-in-Chief of the Army a Colonel-General.

The changes in personnel to which von Brauchitsch had agreed

---

[1] Jodl's Diary, January 29, 1938 : 'Brauchitsch is ready to agree to everything. The matter of the unified command of the *Wehrmacht* was explained to him by the *Führer* in a very impressive manner'; also February 2 : 'Brauchitsch agrees to nearly all of the important changes in personnel, the greater part of which he would have effected in his own interests'.

Arrangements were also made, through the accommodating offices of Göring, to facilitate the new Commander-in-Chief's divorce suit.

[2] Decree concerning the leadership of the Armed Forces, February 4, 1938 (*Reichsgesetzblatt*, 1938, 111).

[3] On the same day letters of the *Führer* to von Blomberg and von Fritsch were released to the press. Both were dated February 4. The tone of that to von Blomberg was most cordial, of that to von Fritsch, icy (for texts see Benoist-Méchin, ii, 663-4).

THE HIGH COMMAND OF THE WEHRMACHT SALUTE THEIR FÜHRER

as a part of the bargain with Hitler were severe and sweeping. Sixteen high-ranking Generals were relieved of their commands, and forty-four others, with a host of senior officers, were transferred to other duties. Among those who disappeared from the scene were von Rundstedt, Ritter von Leeb, Freiherr Kress von Kressenstein, von Küchler, von Kluge, von Weichs, and von Witzleben. All these disgruntled elements, who had supported von Fritsch in their interviews with the *Führer*, passed into retirement; some for only a period of weeks, some until the outbreak of the Second World War. But they all returned to active service when the *Führer* whistled, and, with one exception, they all became Field-Marshals.[1]

The retirement was also announced of Freiherr Constantin von Neurath as Foreign Minister, and his succession by Joachim von Ribbentrop;[2] and a second decree set up a secret Cabinet Council, of which von Neurath was appointed President, to advise the *Führer* on foreign affairs.[3]

The extent and effect of these changes was far-reaching in the extreme. By the elimination of von Blomberg and von Neurath Hitler had freed his hands of the last of the restrictions — feeble though they had always been — placed upon him by Hindenburg in 1933. By the dismissal of von Fritsch he had removed the last of the leading exponents of the Seeckt tradition. By himself assuming the function of War Minister and Supreme Commander of the Armed Forces he had translated into starkly practical terms the situation created by the fusion of the Presidency with the Chancellorship four years before, and had given a stiffer twist to the oath which he had exacted from the armed forces. From now on his deputies in the fields of the armed forces and of Foreign Affairs would be men who were not merely subservient to his orders but who thought as he did. For there was no doubt that both Ribbentrop and Keitel were convinced and devoted Nazis at heart.

Above all, the *Führer* had outmanœuvred, defeated, humiliated, and dragooned the German Army. The armed forces, of which they were but a part, now assumed their position as the third pillar in the structure of the Thousand Year Reich, ranking parallel with, but not above, the Reich Government and the Nazi Party. From

---

[1] The exception was von Kressenstein, the nephew of the hero of the Suez Canal campaign and the man who had reintroduced discipline into the Bavarian *Reichswehr* in 1923 after the political antics of von Lossow.

[2] At the same time the recall was announced of the Ambassadors to Vienna (Franz von Papen), Rome (Ulrich von Hassell), and Tokyo (Herbert von Dirksen).

[3] Decree establishing a secret Cabinet Council, February 4, 1938 (*Reichsgesetzblatt*, 1938, i, 112).

now on Keitel, as head of OKW, was to be equal, but certainly not superior, in rank to Hans Lammers, the Head of the Reich Chancery, and to Rudolf Hess — and later to Martin Bormann — as Head of the Party Chancery.

The Olympian position of the Army as a 'State within a State' was shattered for ever. To such a pass had the intrigues of von Schleicher brought them, to such a pass the enigmatic supineness of von Fritsch. Too great a display of cleverness in the first case and of arrogance in the second had caused the Nazis first to seize power and then to retain it. Power the Army had held, and power they had cast away. Now they were to reap the harvest of their errors, a harvest of bitter Dead Sea Fruit ; for the season of their Nemesis had begun.

(vi)

Having suffered substantial defeat in the first of their parallel engagements with the Party, the military opponents of the Nazi régime concentrated all their efforts on the second — the court martial of von Fritsch. Though they had lost in the matter of the unified command, the Army did not yet realize the magnitude of their defeat. They still believed that a 'show-down' with the Party was possible, and they conceived the idea of making the successful outcome of the Fritsch Case the occasion for such action.

Perhaps the only beneficial outcome of the Fritsch-Blomberg Crisis was the concentration which now took place for the first time of the various groups and personalities opposed to Hitler. The Generals — the striving and indignant Beck, the cynical if indolent von Hammerstein — now met and talked with the civilians — the egregious Schacht, the irrepressibly optimistic Goerdeler, the shrewd Popitz. These elder statesmen of the opposition made closer contact with their more shadowy allies, Admiral Canaris and Colonel Hans Oster, of the Counter-espionage Intelligence (*Abwehr*), and their even stranger associates, Artur Nebe and Bernd Gisevius, of the Criminal Police.

A younger group now also met their seniors, a group consisting almost entirely of lawyers employed in the Ministries and Government offices — Hans von Dohnanyi, Otto John, Fabian von Schlabrendorff, and the brothers Bonhoeffer, Dietrich, the eminent Lutheran pastor and theologian, and Klaus, the head of the legal division of the *Lufthansa*. In these days of the Fritsch Crisis was forged from these elements the first weak and unwieldy weapon of resistance.

Though uncorrelated in their activities and bound together only by ties of personal friendship and a common hatred of the Nazi régime, these individuals had in mind two objectives, clarified and defined by Beck. First to secure a fair and thorough investigation into the charges preferred against von Fritsch, and then to use his acquittal — of which all were assured, provided that the court was not packed — for a joint *démarche* to Hitler of all the Commanding Generals to demand the reinstatement of the former Commander-in-Chief and the punishment of his traducers. In Beck's mind this step must be taken in the hope, or, at least, at the risk, of a final 'show-down' between the Army and the Party, even if this entailed civil war and the removal of Hitler.

Throughout the month of February the tide of battle swung back and forth, the Party playing desperately for time, the Army pressing, with equal desperation, for action. Committed to a Court of Honour in some form or other, Hitler at first essayed to hold it under the aegis of Himmler, and von Fritsch was submitted to an interrogation by the SS of so disgusting a nature that — in the opinion of at least one general officer — had the facts been allowed to reach the troops they would have risen in mutiny.[1] But apparently even Beck stopped short at direct tampering with the loyalty and discipline of the 'other ranks', and this opportunity was allowed to pass.

The Party now fell back upon Fabian tactics. If the General Court Martial could be delayed indefinitely and the time thus bought used for an intensified 'smear campaign' against the accused, the Army might be forced to let the matter drop.

Already the Minister of Justice, Franz Gürtner, who had proved so valuable an ally to Adolf Hitler in 1923, at Munich, was reporting to his *Führer* that the nature of the evidence against von Fritsch was of such a nature that in the case of any ordinary person he would have ordered his arrest, and Admiral Raeder was expressing his conviction that the General was no mere victim of an intrigue.[2] On the principle that if enough mud is thrown sufficient will stick to the victim to blacken him, the Party delayed action on the proceedings and heightened the vigour of their slander.

But tension was rising outside the Reich as well as within it. Events in Austria were playing into Hitler's hands in order to enable him, by two spectacular *coups*, to remove the spotlight from the *Wehrmacht* and to provide a counter-irritant for the Generals. At the same time, however, in order to have a united Army behind him, he was compelled to make certain concessions.

It has been suggested in some quarters that Hitler deliberately

---

[1] Jodl's Diary, February 26, 1938.   [2] *Ibid.*, February 2, 1938.

precipitated the Austrian crisis of February-March 1938 in order to find a way of escape from an otherwise insoluble internal situation. This is held to be untenable. Though Hitler had always aimed at the annexation of Austria and had so stated his aim at the secret conclave of November 5, 1937, there is no indication that the tempo of the subversive operations, which had been *en train* ever since 1934, was accelerated during the first quarter of 1938. In fact the contrary is the case. Both the German Ambassador in Vienna, von Papen, and the *Führer's* special commissioner for Austrian Affairs, Wilhelm Keppler, were in constant complaint during this period that the independent and irresponsible intrigues of the Austrian Nazi leader, Captain Leopold, to overthrow the Federal Government by force, were endangering their own elaborate machinations with Seyss-Inquart and Glaise-Horstenau to achieve the same end by the way of evolution.

It was indeed the discovery on January 27 by the federal authorities of an Austrian Nazi plot, which caused the Chancellor, Dr. von Schuschnigg, to take disciplinary action against the Party and to consent to the meeting with Hitler at Berchtesgaden on February 11. That Hitler welcomed this eventuality there can be no doubt, but that he deliberately provoked it there is no evidence.[1]

Meantime the situation in Berlin was turning against the Party. The preliminary investigations of the charges against von Fritsch, prior to the convening of the Court Martial, were conducted by Dr. Carl Sack, the Judge Advocate-General of the Army, and Graf von der Goltz, the son of the old General, assisted by Colonel Oster and by Hans von Dohnanyi, for the Minister of Justice, and began on March 3. It revealed astounding things. Blackmail, bribery, forgery, and threats of every kind, including death, had been employed by Göring, Himmler, and Heydrich in the fabrication of the *dossier* against the General. As the proof of his innocence mounted, his friends began to hope that even a court martial would be unnecessary. Let von Brauchitsch, as Commander-in-Chief of the Army, take this incontrovertible evidence of mendacious chicanery to the *Führer* and confront him with the perfidy of his lieutenants.

Beck, Schacht, and Goerdeler urged von Brauchitsch to act in this sense. But that General was no man for precipitate action. Let the court martial take its course, he answered, and let it acquit von Fritsch with acclaim. Then, if the evidence were such as to explode and destroy the Hitler Myth before the German people and before

---

[1] See *Documents on German Foreign Policy 1918–1945*, Series D, i, 464-562.

the world, he would take action, but only on that condition.[1]

With this slight degree of encouragement, the Chief of the General Staff and his confederates pressed forward with their demands, and Hitler at length consented to the appointment of the Court. It was to be on the highest level. Göring, as the only Field-Marshal now on the active list, was designated President, and with him were the Commander-in-Chief of the Army, von Brauchitsch, the Commander-in-Chief of the Navy, Raeder, together with Dr. Sack and another senior member of the Judge Advocate-General's Department. With some trepidation, for rumours of a military *coup* were again rife in Berlin, the *Führer* set the morning of March 11 as the date for the opening of the proceedings.

The supporters of von Fritsch were jubilant. They were winning. Victory was almost in sight. The evidence which they had amassed, the witnesses whom they had collected, and whom they kept under an armed guard for protection against the SS, would not only prove their principal's innocence but would shake the Nazi edifice to its evil and corrupt foundations. After the revelations which would now come forth, von Brauchitsch and his fellow-waverers could not fail to march.

But alas for their high hopes, the loaded dice of the gods were against the Generals. The *Führer's* luck was running high and, unlike his opponents, he was not a man to let opportunities slip by him. The court martial which was due to open on March 11 might well have resulted in all that was hoped from it, but Fate once again came to the aid of Adolf Hitler. On the night of March 9 the Austrian Chancellor announced a plebiscite for Sunday the 13th, on terms which were certainly disadvantageous to the Nazis and which had the appearance of favouring a restoration of the Habsburg Monarchy. Hitler promptly sent an ultimatum to the Austrian Government. He issued orders for the invasion of Austria should this prove necessary.

When the court martial convened on the morning of March 11, the crisis was at its height. The President and the two Commanders-in-Chief were urgently required elsewhere and a week's adjournment was hastily moved. Within that week history was made. The German Army achieved its second bloodless victory. The entry into Austria was a 'campaign of flowers', unopposed by the Austrians themselves and unchallenged by the Powers who had guaranteed Austria's independence. The Generals returned from their *Blumen-*

---

[1] Evidence of Gisevius before the International Military Tribunal, April 25, 1946 (*Nuremberg Record*, xii, 203). Other of the Commanding Generals who had survived the purge of February 4, such as List, von Bock, and Blaskowitz, also held to this reserved course of action.

korso with their confidence in their *Führer* fully restored and their belief in his 'intuition' involuntarily confirmed.

When the court martial met again on March 17, all went according to plan. But the atmosphere was very different. The Party had no longer anything to fear and they knew it. Göring, as President of the Court, could not have been a more helpful ally to the accused, and it was he who eventually succeeded in bringing about a confession by the chief witness for the Prosecution that his previous testimony had been a tissue of lies. Von Fritsch himself told von Rundstedt that Göring 'had behaved very decently', and to his friend Baronin Margot von Schutzbar he wrote: 'Finally, which was rather miraculous, they managed to find the fellow who had been dragged out to testify against me . . . as a climax, at the very end, the star witness on whose testimony everything turned, admitted that all his statements were given under duress and were pure lies'.[1] In view of the evidence the verdict was inevitable. It was delivered on March 18: 'Proven not guilty as charged, and acquitted'.

But what an empty victory had been achieved. The verdict of the Court was almost contemptuous. It had already lost interest in the case. The whole thing was anti-climactic. Von Brauchitsch hastened to inform Beck and Goerdeler and Schacht that, owing to the changed conditions, he could no longer take responsibility for action which could have no possibility of success. The bombshell which was to have shattered the Nazi régime proved to be nothing more formidable than a damp squib.

From Hitler on March 25 came a telegram to von Fritsch congratulating him on his 'recovery of health', but conveying no word of apology, no message of regret.

Beck now played his last card. Something might yet be saved from the shambles of what had been the glittering structure of their hopes. With infinite difficulty he persuaded von Fritsch to agree to fight a pistol-duel with Himmler. This it was hoped might at least result in a settling of accounts between the Army and the SS. The challenge was carefully drafted in accordance with the traditional military *code de l'honneur*. Von Fritsch signed it and handed it to von Rundstedt as senior ranking officer of the Army for delivery to Himmler. With the anxiety of despair the conspirators waited day after day for an answer. But Himmler made no move. He neither accepted nor refused the challenge, he apparently ignored it — and for the very good reason that he never received it. Here again was

[1] Letter from Colonel-General von Fritsch to Baronin von Schutzbar, dated March 23, 1938.

anticlimax. Von Rundstedt could not bring himself to deliver the challenge. As he confessed to Otto John after the war, he carried it about with him for weeks and then persuaded von Fritsch privately to let the matter drop.[1]

And thus the so-called Fritsch Crisis came to an end and the Iron Man of the Army proved to have feet of clay. But the Army remained faithful to their fallen idol. They presented him with a charming manor house at Achterburg, near Soltau, in Hanover, and there, on the Lüneburger Heide, he found solace among his beloved *Feldgrauen*. Here, too, he wrote the remarkable series of letters to Baronin von Schutzbar which reveal the strange ambivalence of his later attitudes.

On August 11 came the formal announcement of von Fritsch's rehabilitation, his reinstatement in the rank of Colonel-General and his appointment as Colonel-in-Chief of his old unit, the 12th Regiment of Artillery. But for him this was no *amende honorable*. He had denied the charges made against him on the word of an officer and a gentleman, and his word had been disregarded. The bitterness of the treatment which he had received had seemingly eaten deep into his soul, leaving unhealing scars. 'Herr Hitler has lightly turned aside the word of honour of the then Commander-in-Chief of his Army, in favour of the word of an honourless scoundrel', he wrote to the Baronin. 'Nor has he found a single word of apology for me. It is this, above all, that I cannot countenance.' [2]

It would appear that he did, at one time, contemplate a more positive association with the groups of active resistance, for in November 1938 he was enquiring through British contacts in Berlin whether His Majesty's Government would be willing to grant asylum in Britain to persons involved in an unsuccessful military *coup*.[3] Though the response was not encouraging, it is doubtful whether the approach itself was very enthusiastic, for there is no evidence that von Fritsch was ever counted among the dissidents in any but a purely academic association.

Indeed he appears to have drifted into a state of mind in which involuntary and grudging admiration for the success of the Nazi policies was in constant conflict with a desire to evict the régime from power while reaping the benefits of this success, and with the endless frustration of fatalistic inertia. 'It is very strange', he wrote to Baronin von Schutzbar in December, 'that so many people should regard the future with growing apprehension, in spite of the

[1] *John Memorandum.*
[2] Letter to Baronin von Schutzbar, dated September 4, 1938.
[3] Private information in possession of the author.

Führer's indisputable successes in the past. . . . Soon after the War I came to the conclusion that we should have to be victorious in three battles, if Germany was again to be powerful :

(1) The battle against the working class, Hitler has won this ;
(2) Against the Catholic Church, perhaps better expressed Ultramontanism ; and
(3) Against the Jews.

We are in the midst of these battles, and the one against the Jews is the most difficult. I hope everyone realizes the intricacies of this campaign.' [1]

The interest of this letter, with its anti-Semitic sentiments, lies in the fact that it was written within a month of the Jewish pogroms of November 8-9, which followed the murder of Freiherr vom Rath, Third Secretary of the German Embassy in Paris, by a refugee of Polish-Jewish origin. It is perhaps remarkable that within less than a year after his own slander and mistreatment at the hands of the *Führer*, General von Fritsch could find it thus possible to write in commendation of the *Führer's* conduct of the campaign against the Jews.

His attitude was more negative, and certainly more fatalistic, when he received Ulrich von Hassell a week later and told him, in fine, that Hitler was Germany's destiny for good or evil and that if he went down into the abyss — which was more than probable — he would take them all down with him. But there was nothing to be done about it, especially by the Army. Gradually the mists of frustration and despondent tragedy closed about him. The inevitability of Germany's destruction obsessed him, but he was not

---

[1] Letter to Baronin von Schutzbar, dated December 11, 1938. A certain degree of mystery attaches to this letter. It was quoted by Mr. Justice Jackson in making his opening speech for the Prosecution before the International Military Tribunal at Nuremberg on November 21, 1945, and the immediately following portion of his speech was based on the categories of conflict itemized by General von Fritsch (*Nuremberg Record*, ii, 112-13). Subsequently the Prosecution gave the letter a documentary number — PS-1947 — but it was never submitted as evidence. It does not therefore appear in the *Nuremberg Record*, but is printed in *Nazi Conspiracy and Aggression* (Government Printing Office, Washington, 1946), iv, 585. Later in the proceedings (August 21, 1946) the Defence Counsel for the General Staff and the Army High Command, Dr. Hans Laternser, who succeeded in obtaining an acquittal for his clients, produced an affidavit sworn by Baronin von Schutzbar-Milchling to the effect that she had never received this letter from von Fritsch. In view of this statement, together with the fact that the document had never been communicated to him or submitted in evidence, Dr. Laternser moved that the references to it in Mr. Justice Jackson's remarks and that part of the speech subsequently based upon it be stricken from the record. This the Tribunal refused to order, but the President, Lord Justice Lawrence, stated that as the document had not been submitted in evidence, the

CH. II DEATH OF HINDENBURG TO FRITSCH CRISIS 381

among those who at least contemplated the overthrow of the *Führer* and his régime as a desperate measure to rescue Germany from this otherwise inevitable destiny.[1]

Instead von Fritsch chose other palliatives. In the spring of 1939 he envisaged going to live permanently abroad and even considered the possibility of serving with General Franco in a position similar to that which von Seeckt had occupied with Chiang Kai-shek.[2] This idea was, however, abandoned with the apparent change in the orientation of Nazi foreign policy *vis-à-vis* the Soviet Union and its tendency to revert to the Seeckt Tradition, and we find him in Berlin urgently advocating a *rapprochement*, military and political, with Russia as the only means of preventing war. But when this course failed and he faced at last the inevitability of war, the fog of hopelessness enclosed him altogether. There was nothing to live for — and apparently nothing to die for either ; suicide he would not contemplate but death on the battlefield he courted. 'For me there is, neither in peace or war, any part in Herr Hitler's Germany', he wrote on the eve of war, 'I shall accompany my regiment only as a target, because I cannot stay at home.'[3] Shortly thereafter there arrived the first and only letter written from Poland ; it was also his last. Dated from rest billets in a farmhouse south-east of Warsaw after the intervention of Russia, von Fritsch wrote of 'the very favourable conclusion' of the Polish operation — an operation to the early planning of which he had devoted much of his military career. The agony and uncertainty of soul which now afflicted him is vividly depicted : 'That I personally cannot rejoice over these successes is due to the practically unbearable situation in which I find myself. But to be at home would be more unbearable still.'[4]

A few days later, on September 22, Polish gunners found the target which Colonel-General von Fritsch offered with cold and hopeless gallantry, and brought to his troubled and unhappy spirit a welcome quietus. His *Führer* ordered him a State military funeral with full honours and was represented at it by Göring, who had

Tribunal would take no notice of it (*Nuremberg Record*, xxi, 381). A photostat of the original manuscript of item P.S.-1947 does not appear in the Nuremberg documentation, but the author has seen and read the original of this letter, a copy of which is now in the Foreign Office Library in London.

[1] Von Hassell's Diary entry for December 18, 1938, p. 39. A few weeks later on Fritsch wrote in the same vein to the Baronin von Schutzbar : 'I hear nothing these days about political affairs. It is perhaps just as well, for I can do nothing to change them. Things are taking their course, whether for better or worse only the future can tell' (letter dated January 28, 1939).
[2] Letter to Baronin von Schutzbar, dated April 29, 1939.
[3] Letter to Baronin von Schutzbar, dated August 7, 1939.
[4] Letter to Baronin von Schutzbar, dated September 18, 1939.

presided over the General Court Martial in March 1938. On the rain-swept square of the Berlin Lustgarten, the Field-Marshal raised his diamond-studded baton in a last cynical salute to the *preux chevalier manqué* of the German Army. The date engraved upon the base of the baton was February 4, 1938, the date on which the *Generalität* had died.

CHAPTER 3

FROM THE FRITSCH CRISIS TO THE OUTBREAK OF WAR

(February 1938–September 1939)

(i)

'BEFORE 1938–9 the German Generals were not opposed to Hitler', Field-Marshal von Blomberg stated some ten years later. 'There was no reason to oppose him since he produced the results which they desired. After this time some Generals began to condemn his methods and lost confidence in the power of his judgment. However, they failed as a group to take any definite stand against him, although a few of them tried to do so and, as a result, had to pay for this with their lives or their positions.' [1]

This statement, made a short while before the Marshal's death, may well be taken as a succinct summary of 'Opposition' and 'Resistance' in Germany toward the Nazi régime. When Hitler came to power in 1933 he had the unequivocal opposition only of his fellow authoritarians, the Communists. The Conservatives were his allies; the Army tolerated him; the Centre, whatever its mental reservations, condoned his Government by voting for him; and the Social Democrats sought to gain the best of all possible worlds by condemning his internal programme and supporting his foreign policy, and thereby gained 'an ignoble truce' which profited them nothing.

The majority of the German people, for one reason or another, whether from despair or ambition, from revenge or frustration, were in favour of the *Führer*, and the minority, large though it might have been and sincere in its opposition, was soon either crushed or cowed into submission or driven abroad, there to eat the bitter bread of exile and to eke out the between-worlds existence of the *émigré*. By the summer of 1934 the last spark of anything resembling organized opposition inside Germany had been practically extinguished, and, though it flared up again momentarily in the following

[1] Sworn statement of Field-Marshal von Blomberg, made at Nuremberg November 7, 1945.

year, the wave of arrests and the mass condemnation to concentration camps which resulted from this recrudescence effectually quenched it for some considerable time.

Outside Germany, the political emigration, hopelessly disunited, failed to produce a leader or a policy. Its press and pamphlets, clandestinely smuggled across the frontier from London and Paris, Prague, Amsterdam and Zürich, may have stimulated hope and confidence within the Reich, but it is doubtful whether this was really so.[1] While, within Germany, the so-called '*Innere Emigration*' was equally unsuccessful in developing any effective resistance to the enemy. Not that it did not produce its individual heroes and martyrs. There were such men as Ewald von Kleist-Schmenzin, the editor of the *Mitteilungsblatt der konservativen Vereinigung*, and Ernst Niekisch, the editor of *Widerstand*, who, having staunchly and publicly opposed the Nazis before their coming to power, never thereafter bowed the knee in the house of Rimmon. Both contrived to remain at liberty for some years to carry on secret propaganda against the régime.[2]

And there were those also who showed courage and were fortunate enough to survive, among them Rudolf Pechel, the editor of the *Deutsche Rundschau*, whose articles came as near defiance as those of any German journalist and who took an active part in the later plottings against Hitler, of which he became the first historian.[3]

[1] Examples of this literature were the Social-Democratic *Deutschland-Berichte*, and the Communist *Deutschland-Information*, both published in Prague, and after 1938 in London ; the Nazi 'deviationist' publications of Otto Strasser, such as the *Schwarze Front*, which appeared first in Prague and later in Mexico ; *Das wahre Deutschland*, the monthly organ of the *émigré* German Freedom Party in London ; the *Neu Beginnen* publications of Paul Hagen, issued in London and New York ; and such *émigré* reviews as *Die neue Weltbühne* and Leopold Schwarzschild's *Das neue Tagebuch* in Paris. See also an article, 'Press in exile, German anti-Nazi periodicals, 1933-45', in *The Wiener Library Bulletin* (September–November 1949, January 1950), and *Dokumente des Widerstandes*, a series of articles published in the *Hamburger Volkszeitung*, July–December 1946, and later in book form.

[2] Though widely separated in social and political background, these two men, von Kleist, a gentleman farmer of East Elbia and a descendant of the poet, and Niekisch, the ex-Social Democrat, who had negotiated with Radek on behalf of von Seeckt, became close friends and together successfully weathered many dangers. Both were authors of bitter pamphlet attacks upon Hitler, Niekisch in *Hitler, ein deutsches Verhängnis*, and von Kleist in *Der Nationalsozialismus — eine Gefahr*. Niekisch was arrested on a charge of high treason in 1938 and condemned to a concentration camp ; von Kleist was hanged after the *Putsch* of July 20, 1944, had failed.

[3] Rudolf Pechel's articles in the *Deutsche Rundschau* from 1932 until 1942, at which time he was arrested and confined for the next three years in concentration camps, have been collected under the title of *Zwischen den Zeiten* (Munich, 1948). His record of German opposition and resistance, *Deutscher Widerstand*, was published in Zürich in 1947.

Of outstanding integrity also was Ernst Wiechert, once a rabid nationalist, who in an address to 'The Youth of Germany' at the University of Munich on April 16, 1935, implored his audience 'never to keep silence when conscience commands you to speak out', because nothing in the world 'corrodes the marrow of a man and his people as does cowardice'.[1]

Nor were these isolated cases. There was from the beginning much sincere *Opposition* within the Third Reich to Hitler and the Nazis, but the measure of active *Resistance* was negligible until 1938 and thereafter woefully ineffective.[2]

The reason is not hard to find. The days of armed revolts by an enraged populace against a tyrant are well behind us. The tank, the flame-thrower, the hand-grenade, the Bren gun, have changed the nature of street fighting and rendered the barricade as archaic as the bow and arrow. Moreover, the highly organized system of terror and espionage under the Nazi police state, with its hideous penalties, not only of death, which would be welcomed, but of torture and the living hell of concentration camps, acted as a powerful deterrent upon all but the most gallant hearted.[3] These were understandably few in number, and — until the Nazis were firmly established in power and had openly shown their hand — they lacked organization and leadership. 'We had to realize', writes one of them, 'as time went on, that the German people could be divided into three groups — the Nazis, the non-Nazis and the anti-Nazis. The non-Nazis were almost worse than the Nazis. Their lack of backbone caused us more trouble than the wanton brutality of the Nazis. Many who started as adversaries of National Socialism believed that they must swallow successive draughts of the new *Weltanschauung* in the hope of escaping the necessity of draining

[1] The text of Wiechert's address is to be found in Karl Paetel's *Innere Emigration* (New York, 1946), pp. 51-8, and, in English, in *The Poet and his Time* (Hinsdale, Ill., 1948). Wiechert was also sentenced to Buchenwald and has given an account of his experiences in *Der Totenwald: ein Bericht* (Zürich, 1946); translation, *The Forest of the Dead* (New York, 1947).

[2] For studies of the German Opposition within the Reich, see Jan B. Jansen and Stefan Wahl, *The Silent War* (New York, 1943); Heinrich Fraenkel, *The German People versus Hitler* (London, 1940); Fritz Max Cahen, *Men Against Hitler* (New York, 1939); and Evelyn Lend, *Underground Struggle in Germany* (London, 1938); also *Materiale zu einem Weissbuch der deutschen Opposition* (S.P.D., London, 1946) and *Wege und Formen des Widerstandes im Dritten Reich*, an inaugural lecture by Dr. Philipp Auerbach, at the Friedrich-Alexander University.

[3] See E. K. Bramstedt, *Dictatorship and Political Police: The Technique of Control by Fear* (London, 1945), and also Eugen Kogon, *Der SS-Staat — das System des deutschen Konzentrationslagers* (Munich, 1946); translation, *The Theory and Practice of Hell* (London, 1950).

the cup to its final dregs. For many this was the beginning of the end. Scorning the ancient Roman maxim of *Principiis obsta* (resist at the outset), they were finally overwhelmed by the avalanche of National Socialism.'[1]

This was true of very many Germans. A few, however, who had embarked upon this downward path managed to pull back from the edge of the abyss, and from these few came the principal civilian leaders of the opposition, Goerdeler, Schacht, and Popitz. All had served Hitler in high office — Goerdeler as Price Controller, Schacht as Reich Minister of Economics and President of the Reichsbank, and Popitz as Prussian Minister of State and of Finance — and two of them, Schacht and Popitz, had received the Golden Badge of the Party·for their services. Of these three, Goerdeler was the first to take action. He had resigned the post of Price Controller in 1935 and had resumed his old office of *Oberbürgermeister* of Leipzig. But he resigned this too in the following year as a protest against the barbarous attitude of the city councillors in respect of anti-semitism. The firm of Krupp at once offered to make him head of their financial side, but this Hitler would not permit, and, instead, Goerdeler became the principal contact man abroad of Bosch. With this 'cover' he travelled widely and often, both inside and outside the Reich, and used his associations in Europe and America in an endeavour to awaken men of influence to the menace which was confronting them in Germany. 'Hitler means war' was the tenor of his warning to many startled hearers in London and Paris and New York — but, though startled, they were still unwilling to believe.[2]

The conversion of Schacht and Popitz was of a later date. Both men had been enthusiastic advocates of the assumption of power by the Nazis and, this having been achieved, both worked diligently for the rearmament of Germany. Popitz supported Schacht in his economic policies to bring the Reich to a war-footing — policies which, incidentally, Goerdeler vehemently opposed and which materially contributed to his decision to resign as Price Controller. Like Goerdeler, both Schacht and Popitz appear to have suffered certain qualms at the time of the massacre of June 30, 1934 —

[1] Schlabrendorff, p. 16.
[2] The present writer was acquainted with Dr. Goerdeler when Price Controller under the Brüning Administration. During Goerdeler's visit to the United States in October 1937 he visited the writer in Virginia and in the course of several conversations made him familiar with the general ideas at that time current among the conspirators for an alternative government in Germany. At that moment the views of Goerdeler tended strongly toward a restoration of a monarchy on a constitutional basis.

Popitz particularly, since he had been a friend and Minister of von Schleicher's — but they did not become unduly alarmed until it became apparent that Hitler's policies, which they had once warmly endorsed, might involve Germany in war. Even this was not in itself so appalling to them ; but what was horrifying was the prospect of a war *which Germany might not win*, and from the moment when this nightmare seized upon them — some time early in 1937 — they became numbered among the most vigorous of the opponents to the régime. Of the two, Schacht had the greater shrewdness and Popitz the greater integrity. As time went on, however, and the conspiracy against Hitler developed upon more definite lines, both men were regarded as suspect by their fellow plotters because of the enthusiasm of their early Nazi sentiments.

Other leading civilians in political opposition were Dr. Sigismund Lauter, the head of the great Catholic hospital of St. Gertrauden, and an ardent anti-Nazi from the beginning, and Professor Jens Jessen, an eminent economist who had also been an early recruit to the NSDAP and had later repented. With Popitz and von Hassell [1] he belonged to the 'Wednesday Club', a group of civil servants and university professors who met weekly in Berlin for the reading of papers and exchange of views. These gatherings offered a valuable opportunity for those of the members who were in opposition to the régime to meet each other, and so far as is known the 'Wednesday Club', though regarded as a reactionary and defeatist body, was never actually infiltrated by the Gestapo.[2]

Little by little the character of the active opposition changed. At first it was composed, such as it was, of figures who had been prominent in public life during the Weimar régime, in politics or trades union circles or in the universities or in journalism. Later, however, younger men in the professions, especially in the law and

---

[1] Christian Albrecht Ulrich von Hassell (1881–1944), a career diplomat and a member of the Hanoverian nobility, married to the daughter of Grand-Admiral von Tirpitz, was Ambassador in Rome when Hitler came to power. He was in marked opposition to the policy which resulted in the conclusion of the Rome-Berlin Axis and the Anti-Comintern Pact and thus earned the hostility of Ribbentrop. When the latter became Foreign Minister in February 1938, von Hassell was at once recalled and never held another diplomatic post. He became an early recruit to the Beck-Goerdeler group in Resistance in which he took a leading part. As a candidate for the post of Foreign Minister in the Provisional Government which was to follow the overthrow of Hitler, von Hassell was tried before the People's Court and hanged on September 8, 1944. His diary of the years 1938–44, posthumously published as *Vom andern Deutschland*, and in English as *The von Hassell Diaries*, forms one of the most important sources on Resistance during this period.

[2] For an interesting description of *Die Mittwochsgesellschaft* (The Wednesday Club) see Paul Fechter, *Menschen und Zeiten* (Gütersloh, 1949), **pp.** 365 *et seq.*

the church, began to make their appearance, until by 1937 they were the tiny core of steadily burning embers around which the flame of resistance leapt and flickered. Converts came and fell away, the leaders bickered and were reconciled, but the little group of friends, bound by ties of comradeship and a genuine desire to right a great wrong, kept their shields locked and their courage high. Unlike the conspirator in Carl Zuckmayer's play, they did not suddenly feel that they were ashamed to be Germans.[1] They were proud of their race and nation, but ashamed to sit by and watch the forces of evil corrupt and destroy their heritage. In the words of Dietrich Bonhoeffer : 'If we claim to be Christians, there is no room for expediency. Hitler is Anti-Christ. Therefore we must go on with our work and eliminate him whether he be successful or not' ; words which, uttered in 1940 at the peak of success of Nazi military fortunes, found an echo in very few German hearts.

Of this group the most prominent members were Fabian von Schlabrendorff, the friend of von Kleist and Niekisch and the descendant of Queen Victoria's mentor, Baron Stockmar ; Dietrich Bonhoeffer, the eldest son of a family which had been distinguished on both sides for its eminent divines of independent and courageous thought ;[2] his brother Klaus, who with Otto John, a young Wiesbaden lawyer, headed the legal department of the *Lufthansa* ; Otto's brother Hans, an assistant at the University, shared enthusiastically in the planning of Resistance and was one of the last victims of the Nazi terror ; and Hans von Dohnanyi and Rüdiger Schleicher, who had both married sisters of the Bonhoeffers. All these men could honestly boast that never in thought or deed had they compromised with the evil of National Socialism ; that not only had they never become members of the Party — showing that such abstention was possible — but that they had engaged in

[1] Carl Zuckmayer, *Des Teufels General* (Berlin and Frankfurt-am-Main, 1949), p. 133.
[2] Dietrich Bonhoeffer's maternal great-grandfather, Carl von Hase, and paternal grandfather, both pastors, had been imprisoned in the eighteen-thirties for their 'subversive' liberal views ; his grandfather von Hase had been chaplain to the young Emperor Wilhelm II, whose ire he had incurred when he was bold enough to differ from his imperial master's political views, a difference which led to his resignation. Dietrich Bonhoeffer himself was pastor of the Lutheran Church in London from 1933 to 1935, when he returned to Germany to take part in the struggle of the Confessional Church against the Nazis. See a Memoir by Professor G. Leibholz, printed in the English edition of Bonhoeffer's work, *The Cost of Discipleship* (S.C.M. Press, 1948) ; the original German edition, entitled *Nachfolge*, was published in Munich in 1937. Arrested on April 5, 1943, Bonhoeffer was not executed until two years later. His letters and writings over this period have now been collected under the title of *Widerstand und Ergebung* (Munich, 1951) and provide a vivid illumination of a great and gallant spirit.

Opposition, and latterly in Resistance, from the earliest opportunity presented. It is also to be recorded that of this group all but two paid the price for their devotion after the failure of their final effort on July 20, 1944.[1]

It must, however, be emphasized and reiterated that 'those who held their heads above the crowd' were pitifully few. Even when one adds to those of whom mention has been made, the group which centred around Colonel Hans Oster, of the *Abwehr*; the idealistic planners of Count Helmuth von Moltke's 'Kreisau Circle'; the equivocal shadowy figures of the renegade Gestapo officials, Artur Nebe and Bernd Gisevius; the Trade Union leaders, Jakob Kaiser, Julius Leber and Wilhelm Leuschner; the remnants of the Centre and People's Conservative Parties, Joseph Wirmer and Paul Lejeune-Jung; and such gallant individuals as Count von Bernstorff [2] and Freiherr von Guttenberg: [3] even when all these are taken together and full due is paid to them for their courage, the number is small beyond belief in a nation of eighty millions.

Among the courageous few, however, Opposition ripened into Resistance, and Resistance into Conspiracy. Very soon it was realized that a conspiracy which consisted only of planners was of little practical worth. The *Führer* and his régime were clearly not to be conjured away by moral influence. If the Nazis were to be destroyed it could only be by the action of the Army, but until the Fritsch crisis had shattered the illusions of at least some Generals,

[1] Dietrich Bonhoeffer was executed at Flossenbürg on April 9, 1945, at the age of thirty-eight. Two weeks later, April 23, his brother Klaus and his brother-in-law Rüdiger Schleicher met their death in Berlin, together with Hans John. Of the two survivors, Fabian von Schlabrendorff, having been tortured and interrogated mercilessly, was liberated from Nazi custody at Niederdorf, in South Tyrol, by the advance of the U.S. troops on May 4, 1945. He returned to the practice of law in Germany, and his book, *Offiziere gegen Hitler*, is one of the most important sources of information of the period. Otto John escaped by the simple expedient of taking the regular *Lufthansa* service to Madrid. From thence he was brought to England via Lisbon. In December 1950 he was appointed head of the office charged with the defence of the Federal Constitution of the West German Republic (*Präsident des Bundesamts für Verfassungsschutz*).

[2] Count Albrecht von Bernstorff, a nephew of the German Ambassador in Washington during the First World War, was for some years Counsellor at the Embassy in London where he had many friends. He resigned in 1935 and became a banker. With indiscreet courage, he never ceased to oppose the Nazi régime. Arrested after July 20, 1944, he was murdered on the night of April 24, 1945. See a privately printed memorial volume, *Albrecht Bernstorff zum Gedächtnis* (Berlin, 1951).

[3] Freiherr Karl Ludwig von Guttenberg, whose brother, as chief political agent of the Bavarian royalists, had been arrested on June 30, 1934, was the editor of the Catholic monthly, *Weisse Blätter*, of which he boasted that it had never printed one word in favour of National Socialism. He was arrested and executed without trial on the night of April 24, 1945.

the Army, in the words of the first Field-Marshal of the Third Reich, 'was not opposed to Hitler'.

(ii)

Prior to the Fritsch Crisis there had been some vain effort on the part of the civilian malcontents to make contact with the Army, but there was no desire on the part of the Generals to have any dealings with the politicians. With the exception of von Hammerstein, who was in retirement, and with whom Goerdeler kept in close touch, no General ever lifted his voice against the *Führer* until the despoiling hand of the SS had fallen upon the Army itself — and then it was too late.[1]

For in February 1938 there was completed that gigantic process of *Gleichschaltung* which had begun just five years before. The Army, that last stronghold of privilege, independent thought and freedom of action, had capitulated. It had now become merely the third panel in the Nazi triptych, in equality with the Party and the Government, and from this moment such privileges and immunities as it continued to enjoy were granted as a concession by the *Führer* and not as of right.

The Army, moreover, though they did not at first realize the fact, had yielded up, among the general terms of surrender, their immemorial prerogative to decide the vital issues of peace and war. The Generals had condoned the advent of Hitler to power ; they had welcomed his policy of rearmament and the rehabilitation of the armed forces of the State, but in their calculations they had never taken into consideration the possibility that anyone but themselves would decide how, when, and where this re-equipped Army was to be used.

Now they had lost control of this, their most priceless possession, and with it had gone the source of their strength. For after February 1938 Hitler ceased to fear his Generals. They had ceased to be roaring lions about the way, or even 'ravening mastiffs' ; his only anxiety about them now was — would they fight ? For he was determined not to shrink from war if it should prove a necessary instrument of policy in the realization of his ambitious dreams.

The fact that the *Führer* meant war, and, moreover, that any war meant a world war, in which Germany must certainly be overwhelmed, was revealed to few of the Generals at this time. They

---

[1] Gisevius, in his book (i, 361 *et seq.*), claims for Schacht the initiative for an unsuccessful attempt to get into touch with General von Kluge as early as February 1937. The only supporting evidence of this is that of Schacht himself.

resented the dishonour inflicted upon them by the Fritsch scandal and the Blomberg marriage, but they did not yet appreciate that they had been playing with gunpowder for the last five years and that now someone else was in possession of the box of matches. There was indeed but one exception, Ludwig Beck, Chief of the General Staff of the Army.

Beck's record is of great interest. As the military leader of the unsuccessful *Putsch* of July 20, 1944, he has become something of a legend, and whereas he was certainly a hero and a martyr, the legend must be examined dispassionately. Beck, though he was of the military caste, was no Prussian and no Junker. He came of a middle-class family in the Rhineland and his intellectual background combined liberal traditions with a tendency towards scientific development. He was a sincere Christian, an able soldier, and a gentleman of wide reading and cultivated mind. To Meinecke he appeared as 'one of the true heirs of Scharnhorst',[1] and all who knew him testify to the nobility of his character.

That he was genuine in his opposition to Hitler is beyond a doubt, and it is very certain that from an early date he felt an increasing revulsion from the *Führer*'s excesses at home and abroad and a growing fear as to what they would mean for Germany. But his reasoning and his *ethos* were those of the Prussian Army. The original basis of his apprehension was not one of morality — though he subsequently resisted on moral as well as political grounds — but of his accurate knowledge of Germany's weakness and his inaccurate computation of the strength and fortitude of her political opponents. Beck was deeply and sincerely horrified at the sinister fantasies conjured up in Hitler's dreaming ; he deprecated the gangster methods of the Nazi régime, the ruthless oppression, the crass animal brutality, the vicious sadistic propensities. But would he, one wonders, have been so disturbed if the policy of aggression had been pursued in a politer guise ? Would he have denounced the deeds of Frederick the Great, or disavowed the policies of Bismarck ? What exactly was it that he found *unsittlich* in the Nazi mentality ? Was it the repudiation of pledged words and plighted pacts ? Was it the refusal to employ negotiation as the sole means of changing peace treaties ? Or was it, in effect, the dread possibility of a premature war, a war to which Germany would be committed through Hitler's machinations before her rearmament had reached the level necessary for a successful outcome, and in which she would surely be destroyed ?

It must be remembered that in September 1930, both at the

[1] Meinecke, p. 146.

court martial at Ulm and before the Supreme Court of the Reich, Beck had given evidence in spirited defence of his subalterns, Scheringer and Ludin, charged with high treason for the propagation of Nazi doctrines within the Army, and, moreover, that Beck's evidence at Leipzig was given *after* Hitler's appearance before the Supreme Court had signified to the world that when he came to power 'heads should roll'.[1]

When on October 1, 1933, Beck succeeded Adam as Head of the *Truppenamt* he at once expressed his fear that Germany might be 'drawn into a war before we are in a position to count on a successful defensive'. In May 1934 he warned von Fritsch against too rapid an expansion of the German military establishment lest France should be provoked to act.[2] There is good reason to believe that Beck was deeply shocked at the events of June 30, 1934, and at the subsequent murder of Engelbert Dollfuss, but the only reaction quoted by his biographer is : 'Our entire international position is hopeless. Everything is in danger, especially our entire rearmament. All that has been achieved in that respect is lost. All the Powers that matter are against us.'[3] The inaccuracy of this prophecy apart, there does not appear to be any denunciation of the mass killings as *unsittlich*.

The same was true of Beck's reaction to Hitler's enunciation of policy at the secret conclave of November 5, 1937.[4] When reading Hossbach's minute, he was horrified at the lack of responsibility rather than the lack of morality in the *Führer's* proposals, and at once minuted to von Fritsch that 'while it is not disputed that, if opportunity offers, it would be advisable to settle matters with Czechoslovakia (and also perhaps with Austria), the problem must be examined and preparation made within the limits of what is feasible', and 'a far more thorough and comprehensive examination' is required.[5]

Thus, up to the close of 1937, Beck's objections to the Nazi régime had been largely professional, prompted by fear of the ultimate disaster which must, in his opinion, inevitably overtake an under-prepared Germany. The attack upon von Fritsch, however, had, as has been seen, the effect of arousing him to a pitch of active opposition and the desire for a 'show-down' with the SS. That he failed to galvanize either the chief victim or his successor, von Brauchitsch, into action was certainly not Beck's fault, and thenceforward he had the dual purpose of keeping Germany out of a war which he believed she must surely lose, and of restoring the honour

---

[1] See above, p. 220.   [2] Foerster, pp. 22-3.   [3] *Ibid.* p. 27.
[4] See above, p. 359 *et seq.*   [5] Foerster, p. 64.

and *Sittlichkeit* of the German Army. It is doubtful, however, whether he, like Dietrich Bonhoeffer, recognized Hitler as 'the Anti-Christ', or whether, like him, he would have prayed for the defeat of Germany, because 'only in defeat can we atone for the terrible crimes we have committed against Europe and the world'.[1]

Himself a man of scrupulous personal honour, Beck could not conceive that the Officer Corps would allow the Fritsch Crisis to pass without protest. Even when the inconceivable occurred he was still convinced that the affair had 'opened up a chasm between Hitler and the Officer Corps . . . which can never be closed again'.[2] In this prognostication Beck was as gravely in error as in his computation of the forces opposed to Germany. For the Officer Corps the unsavoury business of the Fritsch affair was forgotten in the satisfactory outcome of the Austrian *Anschluss*. The Generals, or the great majority of them, looked forward to a series of similar *Blumenkorsos* and, at the most, a small isolated campaign against Czechoslovakia or Poland, for which the existing state of Germany's rearmament would be perfectly adequate. The failure of the Western Powers to take action at the time of the annexation of Austria had done much to remove the fears of the more enlightened Generals that any war must necessarily become a general war. This many of them now no longer believed and their disbelief was materially strengthened by subsequent events at Munich and Prague. In the spring of 1938, when Hitler, on his return from Vienna, announced that he was in no hurry to solve the Czech question, 'as Austria has to be digested first',[3] his Generals were confident that he meant what he said. Most of them were already accustoming themselves to their new master's harsh word of command, his pat on the head or the crack of his whip. Soon they would reach that state of degradation in which von Hassell could write of them : 'The majority are out to make careers in the lowest sense. Gifts and field-marshals' batons are more important to them than the great historical issues and moral values at stake'.[4]

This was not the only difficulty which Beck encountered in his attempts to stir up his fellow Generals to resistance. The question of the Oath to the *Führer*, the *Fahneneid*, which the Armed Forces of the Reich had taken on August 2, 1934,[5] proved for all a grave, and for many an insuperable obstacle to their participation in any

---

[1] Dietrich Bonhoeffer uttered this prayer at a secret church meeting at Geneva in 1941. Allen W. Dulles, *Germany's Underground* (New York, 1947), p. 116; Hans Rothfels, *The German Opposition to Hitler* (Hinsdale, Ill., 1948), p. 141.

[2] Foerster, p. 78.

[3] Undated entry in Jodl's Diary, from context presumably made in the middle of March 1938.   [4] Hassell, p. 309.   [5] See above, p. 339.

conspiracy against Hitler. The binding qualities of the Oath to the Sovereign, sworn upon the Colours, had survived in all their mediaeval mysticism far longer in Germany than elsewhere in Europe. It was an oath which bound him who swore it not merely during his period of service as a soldier, but for the term of his natural life. This originated from the Feudal Oath (*Lehnseid*) which the knightly nobility swore to their Liege Lord (*Lehnsherr*) who led or went before them (*herzog*) and which was valid for life. This was the attitude adopted towards the *Fahneneid* by the Officer Corps, so long as it consisted exclusively of the Prussian nobility.

The collapse of Jena, followed by the defection of such distinguished officers as Yorck von Wartenburg, von Clausewitz and von Schill, who openly rejected the policies of their King and placed their Fatherland above their personal loyalty to the Sovereign, destroyed the unwavering attitude of the Corps towards the Oath, and Scharnhorst's 'democratization' of the Officer Corps in the years following the War of Liberation introduced new factors and new aspects. In the course of time, however, the new men of the nineteenth century became steeped in the traditions of the Corps, and for most officers the question of the Oath did not become a live issue until the debacle of November 1918.

Then it became very live indeed. They were released by their Sovereign Lord from their formal ties of loyalty, but many believed that this action had only been taken in deference to *force majeure*. The moral confusion which ensued was as complete as the military and political chaos. Those, like von Seeckt, who took the Emperor's release *au pied de la lettre*, after consideration, gave their allegiance to the Republic and the Constitution; others only did so after having first sought the personal sanction of Wilhelm II at Doorn, and then only with much mental reservation; others again, like von Lüttwitz, regarded themselves as still bound to their Kaiser, while many of the members of the Free Corps reverted completely to the *Lehnseid* and took a personal oath of loyalty to their individual Commanders.

Under the dominant influence of von Seeckt these differences found solution in an equivocal attitude of loyalty by the Officer Corps to the Republic, a loyalty which became at once stronger and weaker with the election of Hindenburg as Reich President. But on the death of the Marshal and the assumption by Hitler of supreme authority in the State, the issue of the Oath again revived. For the pledge which he exacted on August 2, 1934, was one of personal and binding loyalty and, at least in his interpretation of blind and unreasoning obedience.

To many, including Beck himself,[1] the undertaking of this obligation had at the time caused grave searching of heart. But by the constant process of self-examination they arrived at the conclusion, as Yorck and von Clausewitz and von Schill had done nearly a century and a half before, that there were certain fealties to Germany, and even to humanity, which transcended any oath of loyalty exacted by monarch or *Führer*. 'No Caesar and no King, no Dictator and no terror, can force me not to give to God the things which are God's', wrote one of them. 'A conscience founded on Christian ethics and morals will enable one to decide for oneself where the line between God's demands and those of secular authority must be drawn.'

But there were few among the Generals who either cared or dared to make this self-examination. Rather did they prefer to use the fact that they had taken the oath as a means of stifling conscience, refusing even to recognize the existence of the still small voice. Others again, who had been fervent Nazis, suffered 'death-bed repentance' and the snivelling reconciliation of the recanting atheist, at the moment when it became apparent to them that Hitler was losing, or had lost, the war.

A few, a very few, of the senior officers, saw this division of loyalties clearly from 1938 onwards. Ludwig Beck, Kurt von Hammerstein, Erwin von Witzleben, Karl-Heinrich von Stülpnagel, Erich Hoepner, Georg Thomas and Wilhem Adam — these names may be remembered. But, in general, the clarity of thought, and the initiative and decision of action, were infinitely greater among the junior officers and the younger civilians in the ranks of the conspirators.

(iii)

It was indeed among these younger elements that Beck's appeals for action found the greatest response. Though he had failed to persuade the Army to act at the time of the Fritsch crisis and was signally unsuccessful in convincing his fellow Generals that Hitler was leading them willy-nilly down the road to destruction, he certainly succeeded in reviving enthusiasm among the younger men, where it had lain dormant, and in arousing it where before it had been non-existent. Men such as Colonel Hans Oster, von Dohnanyi and the Bonhoeffers, who had looked in vain for constructive leadership to Goerdeler and to Popitz, now found in the Chief of the General

---

[1] '*Dies ist einer der verhängnisvollsten Augenblicke meines Lebens*', Beck is said to have remarked at the conclusion of the ceremony (cf. Gisevius, ii, 19).

O

Staff a leader whom they could follow and admire. Definite plans for a *coup d'état* were first prepared by Oster and von Dohnanyi in the spring of 1938 under Beck's instructions, and joint planning for the future was now set in motion between this group and the growing civilian opposition around Goerdeler and Popitz.

But in the final analysis all planning came down to the use of force, and force meant the co-operation of the Army. A general without troops is as useless in a *coup d'état* as a cowboy without his horse on the range. Von Hammerstein warmly supported Beck, but he was in retirement, and the authority of Beck himself did not extend to the troops direct, who would obey only their local district commander or the Commander-in-Chief. It became imperative, therefore, that either von Brauchitsch or one of the *Wehrkreis* commanders must be won over before any progress could be made.

It was here to some extent that events played into the hands of the conspirators. It was the generally accepted opinion in OKH (*Oberkommando des Heeres*) — High Command of the Army — that while Germany was, militarily speaking, in a position to crush any of her Eastern neighbours — as it might be Czechoslovakia or Poland — she was not equipped or prepared to engage in war with the Western Powers, let alone a general conflict on two fronts involving Russia. It had therefore been with relief that the General Staff had welcomed their *Führer's* dictum that the Czechoslovakian issue was not one for immediate consideration, and it was hoped that it would not become so until the process of German rearmament had been completed and OKH had secured that 51 per cent chance of success without which, very understandably, they never cared to go to war.

It is to be believed that Hitler was indeed anxious to avoid a general conflict and had, for that reason, abandoned the idea of a sudden surprise attack upon Czechoslovakia '*aus heiterem Himmel*'. But he had not abandoned the idea of reducing the Czechs by war, and his plans envisaged much earlier action than that contemplated or desired by the General Staff. At a secret meeting with General Keitel on April 21, 1938, the *Führer* had laid down the political principles which must be followed as a preliminary for the attack upon Czechoslovakia. To avoid a 'hostile world opinion which might lead to a critical situation', action was only to be taken after a series of diplomatic clashes which would gradually develop into a crisis. Then, after some such 'incident' as the assassination of the German Minister in Prague — an eventuality calmly contemplated by the *Führer* and the head of the OKW (*Oberkommando der Wehr-*

COLONEL-GENERAL LUDWIG BECK

macht) when considering the 'expendable factors' in preparation for war — the attack could be made with lightning speed.[1]

The gist of these conclusions, which became the basis for the famous 'Operation Green', were conveyed to OKH, and Beck at once indited a warning memorandum to von Brauchitsch condemning the plans of OKW as rendering a general war inevitable.[2] France, he warned, had drawn closer to Britain and would undoubtedly stand by her engagements to Czechoslovakia, while Russia, also pledged to the French and Czechs by pacts of mutual assistance, 'must more and more be considered a certain enemy of Germany'. He also considered it probable that 'on the first day [of war] Britain will come out on the side of France'. The military force of Germany was not equal to such a combination.

Much of Beck's argument was based, as we now know, on wishful thinking — both his own and of others — but his conclusions were the right and proper ones to be placed before any commander-in-chief by any chief of the general staff. They were conceived in accordance with the 'rules of the game', by which an eventuality such as the capitulation of Munich was unthinkable and impossible. But his warning had no effect at all. The planning staff of OKW, under the direction of Jodl, went steadily forward, and by the third week of May the first general directive for 'Operation Green' was ready for the *Führer*'s signature.[3]

It was now that Fate took a hand in the game. The 'May Crisis' in Czechoslovakia, caused by an alarming report received in Prague of German troop concentrations in Saxony and Silesia, resulted in a severe diplomatic humiliation for the *Führer*, who found himself confronted with an altogether unexpected display of unity among Britain, France and Russia.[4] Though, in the light of present evidence, the 'May Crisis' was in all probability a false alarm reacting upon the acute state of nervous tension existing in Prague as a result of German policy, it was only separated from truth and fact by a narrow margin of time. The British, French, Soviet and Czechoslovak Governments had acted on the belief that, despite vehement denials, the German Government were about to

---

[1] Summary of discussion between the *Führer* and General Keitel, April 21, 1938 (*IMT Document*, PS-388, item 2).

[2] For text of Beck's memorandum of May 5, 1938, see Foerster, pp. 82-7.

[3] Draft of Directive for 'Operation Green', dated May 20, 1938 (*IMT Document*, PS-388, item 5). It is of interest that the officer in charge of the preparation of this document, Lieut.-Colonel Kurt Zeitzler, of the OKW planning staff, himself became Chief of the General Staff of OKH, in September 1942, in succession to Halder.

[4] For an account of the Crisis of May 20-22, 1938, see Wheeler-Bennett, *Munich : Prologue to Tragedy*, pp. 54-9.

commit a further act of aggression, comparable to that made against Austria two months earlier, before which similar vehement denials had been made. Germany was, in effect, planning just such an attack at the appropriate moment, and Hitler's rage was the more violent since he had been prematurely accused of a crime which he had indeed every intention of committing but had not as yet had the opportunity to carry out. And to his intense surprise and annoyance the Powers had shown a marked disinclination to accept his word.

For a week the *Führer* brooded in solitude, indulging in alternate bouts of *Weltschmerz* and dreams of revenge. Then, on May 28, as he subsequently admitted,[1] he took a momentous decision. The Czech issue must be settled in that year of grace 1938 — even if this involved a general European war. 'The intention of the *Führer* not to touch the Czech problem as yet is changed because of the Czech strategic troop concentration of May 21, which occurred without any German threat and without the slightest cause for it', wrote Jodl virtuously in his diary. 'Because of Germany's restraint, it consequently has led to a loss of prestige for the *Führer*, which he is not willing to suffer again.'

Forthwith Keitel and Jodl were summoned to the presence of Hitler, who decreed that the draft directive for 'Operation Green' should be recast. It now opened with the words : 'It is my unalterable will to smash (*zerschlagen*) Czechoslovakia by military action in the near future'. This decision was made known to the leaders of the *Wehrmacht* at a secret meeting convened at the artillery school of Jüterbog on May 30, and it was accompanied by a general order fixing October 1, 1938, as the dead-line for putting 'Operation Green' into effect.[2]

This was the moment for which Beck had waited. The events of the May Crisis had produced the apparent unanimity and determination among Germany's opponents which he had foreseen in his memorandum to von Brauchitsch of May 5.[3] It was now clearly apparent that an attack upon Czechoslovakia meant a general war with Britain, France and Russia, an eventuality which could only spell utter disaster for Germany. This danger must be avoided at all costs, even at that of 'saving' the *Führer* from himself.

[1] In his speech before the Congress of the Nazi Party at Nuremberg on September 12, 1938. (See *Völkischer Beobachter*, September 14, 1938 ; Baynes, ii, 1496).

[2] For text of the revised Directive and the General Order, see *IMT Document*, PS-388, item 11.

[3] On May 30 Beck had sent a further memorandum to von Brauchitsch before attending the Jüterbog meeting. (For text see Foerster, pp. 90-5.)

Beck's reasoning was the rigid logic of the Prussian General Staff. He was no more enamoured of the Czechs than was Hitler — 'It is true that Czechoslovakia in the form imposed by the *Diktat* of Versailles is unbearable for Germany', he had written to von Brauchitsch on May 30 — but, according to orthodox reasoning, the moment to rectify this situation had not yet arrived. However much one might wish to enforce one's will by weight of arms, one waited to do so until one was at least reasonably certain of success. To a mind thus circumscribed the febrile flittings of the *Führer's* 'intuition' were incomprehensible, if not actual insanity. Hitler was virtually certain that he could bluff or bludgeon the leaders in Britain and France into acquiescence with his intentions. But, if he was unsuccessful in so doing, he was not afraid of war. Beck was equally convinced that there was no chance within measurable time of smashing Czechoslovakia by military action without immediately provoking counter-action by France, Britain and Russia; and of such a war he was very much afraid.

His views were widely shared in the High Command of the Army, and were at once made clear to OKW. 'The whole contrast becomes acute once more between the *Führer's* intuition that we *must* do it this year and the opinion in the Army that we cannot do it as yet, as most certainly the Western Powers will interfere and we are not yet equal to them', Jodl recorded somewhat lugubriously after the Jüterbog meeting.[1]

Beck's first act after the Jüterbog meeting was to send his adjutant to von Brauchitsch with the request for an immediate interview, for the purpose of establishing once and for all the exact position of the Commander-in-Chief of the Army in regard to this momentous decision which had been sprung upon the General Staff without previous notification or consultation. But von Brauchitsch was too slippery a fish to allow himself to be thus pinned down by his turbulent Chief of Staff. He sent word that he was about to take a short but immediate spell of leave and would be at Beck's disposal on his return.

Beck then turned to Schacht and Goerdeler with whom he consulted repeatedly during the month of June as to how best the situation could be exploited for the advancement of the aims of the conspirators. He himself had determined upon resignation, but, as a modest man, he did not believe that his isolated departure would have sufficient repercussions at home or abroad to deal any staggering blow to the régime. He therefore decided to force the issue with his military colleagues and if possible provoke a mass resignation of

[1] Jodl's Diary, May 30, 1938.

the senior commanding Generals, which should be accompanied by similar demands for demission by the conservative members of the Reich Government, Schacht, von Neurath, Schwerin von Krosigk and Gürtner. It mattered very little whether the three last went or stayed, but Schacht had prestige both inside and outside Germany.

The continued problem of resistance was thus clearly posed : to resign or not to resign ? To remain in office meant the retention of privilege, position and power which could be used as cover to the advantage of the cause, while to resign simply meant that one more key position passed into avowedly Nazi hands. On the other hand, particularly in the pre-war period, resignation was still possible within the Reich and, if achieved with sufficient resonance, might well strike an echoing chord at home or a warning note abroad.

Beck was bent upon resigning. Schacht elected to remain in office.

The Chief of the General Staff determined to make a last effort to carry his fellow Generals with him in a forceful demonstration against the *Führer*'s policy, apparently so fraught with disaster. He began with his Commander-in-Chief. On the return of von Brauchitsch from leave Beck sought him out and a stormy scene took place between them. Beck held that a soldier in a high position who, at a time of national danger, simply said : 'I serve', without being conscious of his supreme responsibility toward the nation, not only showed a lack of greatness and responsibility, but was guilty of a grave dereliction of duty. The duty of the Army was to 'protect' the *Führer* from himself, to 'rescue' him from the evil elements which were clearly influencing and distorting his judgment, and to 'persuade' him to rescind his orders. Von Brauchitsch felt very differently. He had no desire to place himself at the head of any movement or *fronde* to restrain the *Führer*, for he was convinced that Hitler retained the strong support of the overwhelming majority of the German people. This he plainly indicated to the infuriated Beck. 'Why, in heaven's name', von Brauchitsch demanded of Otto John after the war, 'should I, of all men in the world, have taken action against Hitler ? The German people had elected him, and the workers, like all other Germans, were perfectly satisfied with his successful policy.' [1] The Commander-in-Chief would not move.

But Beck, though discouraged, was not to be deterred from his course. He canvassed the views of OKH and on July 16 he sent to von Brauchitsch the last of his famous series of memoranda representing the logical argument of the Prussian General Staff *Mentalität* as against the 'intuition' of the Führer. The memorandum recapitu-

[1] *John Memorandum.*

Keystone

FIELD-MARSHAL WALTHER VON REICHENAU

Keystone

FIELD-MARSHAL WALTHER VON BRAUCHITSCH

lated at some length the bases of the case to which Beck had consistently adhered ever since he became Chief of the General Staff in 1935. In a word, it said once again that he and his colleagues were opposed to any policy which would lead, or cause, Germany to be involved in aggressive war against either France or Czechoslovakia, for the basic reason that Germany was unprepared for war with a combination of Great Powers.

On the basis of the above data [Beck concluded], I now feel in duty bound . . . to ask insistently that the Supreme Commander of the *Wehrmacht* [Hitler] should be compelled to abandon the preparations he has ordered for war, and to postpone his intention of solving the Czech problem by force until the military situation is basically changed. For the present I consider it hopeless, and this view is shared by all my Quartermasters-General and departmental chiefs of the General Staff who would have to deal with the preparation and execution of a war against Czechoslovakia.[1]

Together with his memorandum, the Chief of the Staff made a formal proposal to von Brauchitsch that the leading Generals should make a joint *démarche* to Hitler, and that, if they were unsuccessful in persuading him to halt his preparation for war, they should all resign their commands. His plans went even further. The Generals were not to confine themselves to mere strategical reasoning. They were to take the opportunity not only to protest against a war which they were confident they could not win, but also against the abuses of the régime — the rule of terror, the persecution of the Churches, the suppression of free speech and expression, the corruption and extravagance among the *Bonzokratie*. They must demand from the *Führer* a return to the rule of law (*Rechtsstaat*) in the Reich and to the principle of 'Prussian cleanliness and simplicity' (*preussische Sauberkeit und Einfachkeit*).[2]

One can imagine the agony of conscience through which von Brauchitsch passed at this time. Without doubt he shared the professional and technical opinions of the General Staff. He had no more confidence than had Beck in the *Führer*'s 'intuition' that France would allow the keystone of her security system in Eastern Europe to be shattered without a battle ; and, like Beck, he believed that Germany was unequal to a major war. But, on the other hand, he was a man of little moral courage and no strength of character ; *par excellence*, a careerist and, moreover, standing in no little awe

---

[1] This memorandum, which was frequently referred to in evidence, but never produced, during the proceedings of the International Military Tribunal at Nuremberg, is printed for the first time in Foerster, pp. 98-101.
[2] Foerster, pp. 105-6.

of his *Führer*. Finally, he was ruled in political matters by the opinions of his second wife, and she was an ardent and fanatical admirer of Adolf Hitler.

Torn, therefore, between the importunings of Beck, the nagging of his own conscience and the persistence of domestic influences, the Commander-in-Chief essayed to adopt Fabian tactics. Throughout the latter part of July he temporized and gave but equivocal answers, hoping, perhaps, that Hitler himself might suffer one of those lightning changes of mind and abandon the Czech enterprise, or that Beck might weary in his pertinacity. No such avenue of escape opened before him. Hitler held on his course and Beck grew desperate.

On July 29 Beck again pressed von Brauchitsch to tell Hitler that Germany was in no way prepared for war and that the leading Generals could not accept responsibility for it,[1] and when the Commander-in-Chief testily refused this office, Beck demanded, as was his right, that his views as Chief of the General Staff should be placed before the High Command of the Army at a full conference. This von Brauchitsch could not refuse, and in preparation for it Beck made his final bid to rouse his fellow Generals to a pitch of action. That they shared his strategical opinion he had little doubt ; would they act as he wanted them to act ?

With infinite care he planned the programme of the meeting. The Commander-in-Chief would preside and would call on Beck to state his views ; then the opinions of those present would be asked for, and Beck had no anxiety on that score ; finally von Brauchitsch would sum up in a speech which Beck had drafted for him. This was in effect the Chief of Staff's 'military testament' ; a clear-cut exposition of his views — views which were unfortunately becoming more and more fallacious as the process of appeasement by the Western Powers increased apace. In the mouth of the Commander-in-Chief they would have added weight and Beck had written the following peroration : 'I therefore demand from you, gentlemen, that, come what may, you must support me and follow me unconditionally along the path which I must tread for the welfare of our German Fatherland'.[2] Von Brauchitsch would then lead them to Hitler.

The meeting, long delayed, was eventually convened in great secrecy at the end of the first week of August, and to the assembled Generals Beck read his memorandum of July 16. The arguments were less cogent than when he had originally produced them in May, for the arrival in Prague on August 4 of the Runciman Mission,

---

[1] Foerster, p. 107.   [2] *Ibid.*, pp. 109-18.

on the initiative of the British Government and with the approval of the French, was already an eloquent testimony that the judgment of the Fates was more inclined to the *Führer*'s 'intuition' than to the logic of the Chief of the General Staff.

Nevertheless, Beck's deep-seated conviction that the forthcoming war would inevitably result in military disaster for Germany and must therefore be prevented, was strongly endorsed by all present — with the significant exceptions of Walter von Reichenau and Ernst Busch. General Adam, the Commander-designate of the Western Wall, an old friend of von Schleicher and an anti-Nazi of long standing, stated categorically that the fortifications of the Siegfried Line were wholly insufficient to meet a French attack in force, and offered there and then to go to Hitler and tell him so.

Beck looked to von Brauchitsch. Would the Commander-in-Chief make the speech prepared for him? Would he make the appeal to the Generals which would lead them in a body to place their ultimatum before Hitler? Would he use upon Hitler that magic formula with which the Army had in the past removed outstanding public figures from Wilhelm II to von Papen, namely that he no longer enjoyed their confidence?

Alas, even if the potency of this formula still remained, von Brauchitsch was not the man to attempt such an exorcism. Courage, character, foresight and wisdom are not attributes which can be transmitted from one who has them to one who has not. The brave words which Beck had written for him stuck in the Commander-in-Chief's throat. He would not force the issue. In his summing-up he stated the fact that, with two exceptions, all present were opposed to war, but he made no appeal for action.

He did, however, submit Beck's memorandum of July 16 to Hitler, with the result that on August 10 the Army Chiefs and the head of the *Luftwaffe* groups, together with Jodl and certain others of the OKW, found themselves summoned to the Berghof, where the *Führer* made them an after-dinner speech of three hours on the subject of his political theories. At the close of this ordeal certain of the Generals present had the temerity to speak of their apprehensions at the prospect of war and their anxiety at the inadequacy of German military preparedness. Hitler grew more and more indignant and when General von Wietersheim quoted General Adam, who was not present, to the effect that the West Wall could not be held for longer than three weeks, the *Führer*'s anger blazed up into one of his characteristic explosions of insensate rage.

'That position', he screamed, 'can be held not only for three

O 2

weeks, but for three months and for three years; the man who does not hold this fortification is a scoundrel', and he proceeded to give them an allocution on defeatism and morale, accusing them of a lack of 'vigour of the soul' because at bottom they did not believe in the genius of their *Führer*.[1]

The Generals were overborne. Their courage ebbed before the fury of the *Führer*'s fire. They did not protest or march or make a *Putsch* — they simply left the presence.

Forthwith, a week later (August 18), there occurred the last of the stormy scenes between Beck and von Brauchitsch. The Commander-in-Chief transmitted an order from Hitler that from henceforth interference by the Army in political affairs was categorically forbidden and a demand for 'unconditional obedience' from all commanding Generals and from the Chief of the General Staff. With this final bending of the neck Beck refused to comply, and he, in his turn, demanded that von Brauchitsch should join him in resignation.[2] But in the end it was Beck who resigned alone, indignant and unbending. 'Von Brauchitsch hitched his collar a notch higher and said: "I am a soldier; it is my duty to obey".'[3]

(iv)

The resignation of Beck, his transition from Chief of the General Staff to leader of a military conspiracy, was an important event in the progress of German Resistance. To be sure, Beck's resignation failed signally to make the resounding clangour which had originally been hoped for it, and this was largely his own fault. He had intended to put an end to the steady retreat which had been beaten by Ministers and Generals in the face of Hitler's policies. He had expected, perhaps naïvely, that other Generals would accompany him in a gesture of resignation. He was even prepared for a bloody counter-attack by Hitler through Himmler and the SS, but he regarded that as a legitimate risk. Above all, he aspired to alarm the nations abroad into some sense of the danger which confronted them.

Alas for these hopes and intentions; Beck's resignation achieved none of its objectives. When he found that he was acting alone and unsupported, he seemed to retire into an impenetrable cloud of

---

[1] Jodl's Diary, August 10, 1938; von Manstein's evidence before the IMT, August 9, 1946 (*Nuremberg Record*, xx, 606). According to von Manstein this was the last occasion on which Hitler permitted questions and discussion after any address of his to his Generals.

[2] *John Memorandum*.   [3] Hassell (September 27, 1938), pp. 21-2.

glacial aloofness. He said good-bye only to his intimates and that with difficulty. He made no public statement; indeed he allowed himself to be persuaded by von Brauchitsch into agreeing that the announcement of his departure should be delayed until the end of October, although his successor, Franz Halder, had in effect been in office since the first day of September.[1] Thus Beck's resignation was robbed of all its significance and was indeed withheld as an event from the knowledge of both of the German public and the world at large. Only after the signature of the Munich Agreement had given the green light for another successful and bloodless 'Blumenkorso' was it casually announced that Halder had been appointed Chief of the General Staff.[2]

But if it failed in its wider ambitions, Beck's resignation put new life and heart into the various groups now crystallizing from Opposition into Resistance. Here was a man whom all could respect and admire; a General with all the good qualities of von Hammerstein plus that of energetic initiative; a leader who was above the suspicion which attached to the past records of Schacht and Popitz, who did not inspire that lack of confidence engendered by Goerdeler's over-optimism and want of discretion. Goerdeler himself was fully prepared to co-operate with Beck, as was von

[1] The actual circumstances of Beck's resignation are most unusual. He gave notification of his resignation on August 18 to von Brauchitsch, who at first refused to accept it. But Beck simply refused to do any further service and left his office in the Bendlerstrasse. His farewell address to his colleagues on the General Staff was made on August 27 (John Memorandum). Halder took over on September 1, but neither Beck's formal resignation nor Halder's appointment was made public till after the Munich Conference. In a letter to Hossbach, dated October 20, 1938, Beck writes : 'I tendered my resignation yesterday' (Hossbach, p. 221), but the announcement of the change in the Chief of the General Staff was not made public until October 31.

The only comparable parallel is that of the crisis at Imperial Headquarters in the autumn of 1914 after the defeats of the Marne and the Aisne. The then Chief of the General Staff, Count von Moltke — Gröner's Feldherr wider Willen — resigned on September 12 and was succeeded two days later by the Prussian Minister of War, Erich von Falkenhayn. In the interests of morale, however, both at home and among the troops, von Falkenhayn's appointment was not made public until November 3, 1914, and as late as October 10 the Kaiser, at a banquet at G.H.Q. at Charleville, publicly toasted the success of von Moltke ! (Wheeler-Bennett, Hindenburg, pp. 34-5).

[2] Franz Halder, born 1884, came of a professional military family in Bavaria. His father was a distinguished General and he himself, though trained as a gunner, soon gravitated to Staff work. He served on the Staff of the Crown Prince Rupprecht of Bavaria and returned to Munich after the First World War, where he became friendly with Röhm (see above, p. 226). Transferred to the Truppenamt in 1926, he remained there until 1931 ; later he was Chief of Staff to a division and a corps, and subsequently commanded the 7th Division until 1937, when he became deputy to Beck in the General Staff of the Army.

Hammerstein — though Schacht and Popitz held somewhat aloof — and his personality commanded the devotion of the group around Hans Oster in the *Abwehr*, and of the younger of the conspirators.

By the end of August 1938 it had become patent that Hitler was bent upon the destruction of Czechoslovakia, if need be by force and at the risk of a general European war. By that time it was clear that the Runciman Mission could achieve nothing in Prague, and that the moment of crisis might well be the occasion of Hitler's speech at the Nazi Party Congress at Nuremberg on September 12. Beck believed war to be inevitable unless some action were taken to forestall it. He was still labouring under the illusion that France, in the direct interests of her own security, would stand by her alliance with Czechoslovakia, that Britain and Russia would stand by France, and that Germany would be overwhelmed by such a powerful combination.

He, and with him Oster and the *Abwehr* group, and also Goerdeler, held the view that the German people did not want war ; and that, once the sinister motives of Hitler's foreign policy could be unmasked, the glamour of his former successes in rearmament, in the Rhineland and in Austria would disappear and that this same German people, who had been the willing victims of his hypnotic influences, would awake from the thralldom of the last five years.

The threat to peace, therefore, was to be the occasion for the enlisting of popular support for a revolt against Hitler. The German people must be made aware of the danger of war ; the war itself must be forestalled ; and to the German Army, plus its civilian satellites, would accrue the merit and kudos for the preservation of peace.

Forthwith preparations were set afoot, under the inspiration of Canaris and the direction of Oster. And this occasion of the summer of 1938 is important for the fact that it did mark the beginning of definite concrete planning for a *coup d'état*.[1] The vital new factor in this phase of planning was the discovery of Generals commanding

---

[1] It is claimed by a biographer of Canaris that, in drawing up their initial plans, he and Hans Oster were influenced to a considerable extent by their study of a book by Curzio Malaparte, published in Paris in 1931, and subsequently banned in Germany, entitled *La Technique du Coup d'État*, in which the author made a penetrating study of the causes of failure of the Kapp-Lüttwitz *Putsch* and the Munich *Putsch* of 1923. (See Karl-Heinrich Abshagen, *Canaris* (Stuttgart, 1949), p. 173.) It is not without interest, therefore, to find that Erich Kordt makes the definite statement that, in the planning of the conspirators, 'No attention was paid to the weak or the strong points of the régime to be attacked, which were no secret, to say nothing of the "surveying and practical application" of the "scientific" side of the technique of a *Staatsstreich* which was dealt with in Malaparte's *La Technique du Coup d'État*, a book widely read at the time' (Kordt, *Nicht aus den Akten* (Stuttgart, 1950), p. 335).

troops who, in deference to the leadership of Beck, were prepared to enter the conspiracy. These were Erwin von Witzleben, Commander of *Wehrkreis III* (Berlin-Brandenburg), and Count Erich von Brockdorff-Ahlefeld, the Commander of the Potsdam Garrison, who, with the co-operation of Count Helldorf, the Berlin Police-President, who had already given evidence of his 'deviation' at the time of the Blomberg scandal,[1] and his second in command, another disaffected Nazi veteran, Count Fritz von der Schulenburg, son of the Crown Prince's former Chief of Staff, were prepared to seize the Government quarter of Berlin and hold the *Führer* prisoner, together with as many of his leading henchmen as could be gathered in. Meantime General Erich Hoepner, commanding an armoured division in Thuringia, was to stand ready to intercept the Munich SS, should they attempt a relief of Berlin.[2]

The plan of the plotters was to seize the person of Hitler in Berlin as soon as he gave the final order for 'Operation Green' to go into force against Czechoslovakia. At this time it was not the intention of the conspirators to assassinate the *Führer*. On the contrary, it was an essential part of their plan to take him alive and put him on trial before the People's Court which he had himself constituted for the protection of the German people. The procedure of the trial and the preparation of the prosecution's case against Hitler had been assigned some time previously to Hans von Dohnanyi and to Dr. Sack of the Judge Advocate-General's Department, and a panel of psychiatrists, under the chairmanship of the eminent Professor Dr. Karl Bonhoeffer, the father of Dietrich and Klaus, and father-in-law of Dohnanyi, had been engaged in a secret enquiry into the *Führer's* mental condition, beginning from his case history at the military hospital at Pasewalk, of which a copy had been surreptitiously provided by Hans Oster's office. This report had suggested that the patient should be certified insane. It was considered as good evidence and a strong reason for removing Hitler from office and immuring him in a lunatic asylum.

---

[1] See above, p. 365.

[2] Pechel, p. 151 ; Rothfels, p. 59 ; Franklin L. Ford, 'The Twentieth of July in the History of German Resistance', *The American Historical Review*, July 1946.

Colonel-General von Hammerstein was also closely connected with the planning of the *coup*, but at that moment he held no active command ; also associated was General Karl-Heinrich von Stülpnagel, the *Oberquartiermeister I* in OKH.

Although the planning was largely carried out by his lieutenant, Hans Oster, Admiral Canaris was personally opposed to the idea of a military *putsch* against the Chancellery by the Potsdam garrison. He favoured the kidnapping of the *Führer* by a small group of determined young officers as being easier and less cumbersome a procedure. Hitler would be held *incommunicado* until after the revolt had succeeded and would then be placed on trial (Abshagen, pp. 174-5).

Thus the conspirators had two strings to their bow. Even if the doctors could not agree upon declaring the *Führer* to be lunatic — though it was taken for granted that they would — the lawyers would reveal his plans for aggression and have him certified by the tribunal as criminally irresponsible and unfit to continue in office as *Führer* and Chancellor of the Reich.[1]

The ultimate intention of the conspirators — inasmuch as their planning had gone ahead thus far — was to have a provisional government, headed by a civilian of prominence and respectability, which should consult the country on the form of government it desired for the future. The names of von Neurath, Gessler and even Noske had been considered as candidates for provisional chief of state, but it was an essential part of the plan that during the immediate period between the arrest and trial of Hitler and the establishment of a provisional régime, the government of the country should be in the hands of the Army, under circumstances similar to those in which von Seeckt had exercised the executive power in 1923–4.[2] To ensure this it was intended that once Hitler was successfully in custody, a proclamation would be issued in the name of von Brauchitsch as Commander-in-Chief of the Army, arrogating to himself as a temporary measure the supreme authority in the Reich. But because Beck and his fellow Generals had had bitter experience of von Brauchitsch's infirmity of purpose in the past, it was agreed that he should only be brought into the picture at the last possible moment.[3]

Two other major factors were necessary for the success of the conspirators' plans ; first, that they should be kept in the closest touch with the actual progress of events so as to be prepared to strike at the exact psychological moment, and, secondly, that the fundamental basis of Beck's thesis, namely that an attack by Germany upon Czechoslovakia would precipitate a general European war, should remain extant.

For the fulfilment of the first of these conditions the conspirators were dependent upon the new Chief of the General Staff, Franz Halder, of whom Beck spoke with enthusiasm.[4] For three days after Beck's departure from his office on August 27 no candidate was forthcoming as his successor. Then von Brauchitsch persuaded Halder to allow his name to go forward to Hitler, because, though a supporter of Beck's general thesis, he was a much less active opponent of the *Führer's* policies and would therefore spare the Commander-

---

[1] *John Memorandum.*   [2] See above, pp. 110-11.
[3] Interrogation of Franz Halder at Nuremberg, February 26, 1946.
[4] Gisevius, ii, 23.

in-Chief the soul-disturbing interviews which he had suffered from Beck. Halder had accepted the appointment with Beck's approval and on the understanding that he would pursue the policy of his predecessor; but here there was a weakness. If Halder assumed office in good faith as an opponent of Hitler's policy of aggression, he was certainly not a strong enough character to carry out his intentions. No sooner was he installed in Beck's place in the Bendlerstrasse than he became painfully and patently torn between his loyalty to the conspiracy and his loyalty to the orders which he received from his *Führer* and Supreme Commander. His first orders were to expedite the tempo of the preparations for 'Operation Green', whereas Beck had followed a policy of 'go-slow'.[1]

Since the actual moment for the *coup* was to be that brief period between the issuing of the final order to invade Czechoslovakia and the first exchange of shots, it was essential that the conspirators should be exactly informed as to the orders for attack. Halder assured them that he had arranged with OKW to have from five to two clear days' notice, and that in any case the final order must reach the Army through him and must therefore reach OKH at least twenty-four hours beforehand.[2] Instead of issuing the orders to the Army to invade, he would give the signal to von Witzleben to put the *Putsch* into operation. Such at any rate was the intention.[3]

The second major factor vital for success — the attitude of the Western Powers — provided a strange anomaly. Beck's whole thesis of strategic opposition to the *Führer* had been founded upon his certain conviction that France and Britain would intervene in the event of a German attack upon Czechoslovakia. His arguments had been based upon similar illusions of Franco-British forcefulness in respect of the crisis precipitated by German rearmament, the Rhineland, and Austria, and each time he had been proved wrong. But Czechoslovakia appeared even more outstandingly a case of vital self-interest to France and Britain, and Beck had 'gone nap' on his logical conclusion as against the *Führer's* 'intuition'.

As the summer of 1938 ripened into autumn, it became more and more apparent that the united front which Great Britain, France and the Soviet Union had shown at the time of the May Crisis had

[1] *John Memorandum.*
[2] Gisevius (ii, 44) states that Halder claimed to have arranged to have *three* clear days' warning; this was agreed to by the *Führer* and OKW on August 30 (see PS-388, item 17), but Jodl records in his diary for September 8 that General von Stülpnagel requested, on behalf of OKH, to have *five* days' notice. To this Jodl agreed, but warned him that it might be cut to *two* days because of the difficulty in estimating the overall meteorological situation.
[3] Halder Interrogation, February 25, 1946.

grown small by degrees and 'unbeautifully' less. France and Britain, by no means at one in their respective policies — the one now veering toward intervention, the other tacking toward greater appeasement, and vice versa — were at least consistently unanimous in their fear of Germany and their suspicion of Russia. The chances of their intervention became less and less likely, and to the conspirators in Berlin, who were basing their plans on the inevitability of such intervention, the prospect seemed appalling. They were playing with fire in every sense of the term, for it was necessary to the success of their plans to bring Europe to the very brink of the precipice of war and then to snatch her back at the latest conceivable moment. No balancing feat, no trick of prestidigitation, demanded a greater control of nerve, timing and equilibrium — or of effrontery to fate — and in view of the increasing uncertainty in the West it behoved the conspirators to take some action which should persuade London and Paris to 'screw their courage to the sticking place' and maintain a firm and united front to Hitler's threats and menaces.

This had been the tenor of the appeals and warnings which Beck himself had secretly sounded during his official visit to Paris in 1937 and which Goerdeler had uttered in London and Washington in 1937 and 1938. But some more direct approach was now necessary, and a series of emissaries were despatched to London, since the leaders of the conspiracy rightly believed that the key to the situation lay with Britain. If she gave her public and unequivocal promise of support to France, the French Government would be compelled to honour their pledges to Czechoslovakia. Unfortunately there were never two nations less eager to offer or to receive such a promise than Britain and France at this moment.

The first approaches to London were made before Beck had actually staged his one-man 'walk-out' strike on August 27. Immediately after the conference of Generals at the beginning of August, at which the Chief of the General Staff had secured an almost unanimous endorsement of his apprehensions in the event of war,[1] Hans Oster had advised the despatch of an envoy to London to bring this news directly to the attention of certain persons in British political life who might influence the formulation of policy.

The choice of personality was wise and all important. Ewald von Kleist-Schmenzin was ideally suited for this delicate mission. He was pre-eminently a 'gentleman'; he was a member of the old Conservative Party of Germany; he had been an unwavering opponent of Hitler; and he had charm of manner, honesty of bearing and, above all, a deep sincerity.

[1] See above, pp. 402-403.

Von Kleist arrived in London on August 18,[1] and at once got into touch with Sir Robert Vansittart, the Chief Diplomatic Adviser to the Government. To him he spoke 'with the utmost frankness and gravity', saying that Hitler was determined upon war ; that the Generals alone knew the full purport of his planning and the date of the attack, and that they were unanimously against it — 'all without exception, and I include even General von Reichenau, who has hitherto passed for being the most extreme and forward of them all'.[2] But though the Generals were against war, said Herr von Kleist, they would have no power to stop it unless they received encouragement and help from outside. If this were not forthcoming, they could not refuse to march against Czechoslovakia on the date they already knew.

Von Kleist spoke, as he said, as a man who had 'come out of Germany with a rope round his neck to stake his last chance of life' in order to warn Britain that she stood not any longer in the mere danger of war but in the presence of the certainty of it by the end of September. He urged that, in addition to the unspecific statements which had already been made of Britain's intention to stand by France, some leading statesman should make a speech directed to the German Army and to other disgruntled elements within the Reich emphasizing the horror of war and the inevitable catastrophe to which it would lead. This, together with a reaffirmation by the two Western Powers of their determination to intervene in the event of German aggression against Czechoslovakia, would give the Generals that sufficient degree of encouragement to make it possible for them to act.

To Mr. Churchill von Kleist repeated much of what he had already said to Sir Robert Vansittart,[3] save that he held out the

[1] The documents concerning the visit of Herr von Kleist-Schmenzin are printed in Woodward and Butler, Third Series, ii, 683-9. The Foreign Office were apprised of his coming by the British Ambassador in Berlin, Sir N. Henderson, who characteristically advised that 'it would be unwise for him to be received in official quarters'. Lord Halifax, however, decided that, though no initiative should be taken in official quarters to see him, if he asked to be received in such quarters 'he should not be rebuffed'. He saw Sir Robert Vansittart on the afternoon of August 18, Lord Lloyd that same evening, and Mr. Winston Churchill on the following day. He returned to Germany on August 23.

[2] Whether von Kleist was deliberately over-playing his hand or whether he had been imperfectly briefed by Oster, it is now impossible to say, but he was certainly at fault in his statement concerning von Reichenau's attitude (see above, p. 403).

[3] The warnings to the British Government were reiterated simultaneously in Berlin, where another of Oster's agents informed the Military Attaché on August 21 of Hitler's avowed intention to attack Czechoslovakia at the end of September and of his conviction that France and Britain would not intervene. 'If by firm action abroad Herr Hitler can be forced at the eleventh hour to renounce his present intentions, he will be unable to survive the blow. Similarly, if it comes to

additional bait that 'in the event of the Generals deciding to insist on peace, there would be a new system of government within forty-eight hours ; such a government, probably of a monarchist character, could guarantee stability and end the fear of war for ever'. Mr. Churchill's reply, embodied in a letter dated August 19, gave as a personal opinion the conviction that 'I am as certain as I was at the end of July 1914 that England will march with France and certainly the United States is now strongly anti-Nazi. It is difficult for democracies to make precise declarations, but the spectacle of an armed attack by Germany upon a small neighbour and the bloody fighting that will follow will rouse the whole British Empire and compel the gravest decisions. Do not, I pray you, be misled upon this point. Such a war, once started, would be fought out like the last to the bitter end, and one must consider not what might happen in the first few months, but where we should all be at the end of the third or fourth year.'

Mr. Churchill then added that he had the authority of the Foreign Secretary, Lord Halifax, to say that the Prime Minister's statement in the House of Commons of March 24, 1938, in which he had stated that 'where peace and war are concerned, legal obligations are not alone involved, and if war broke out, it would be unlikely to be confined to those who have assumed such obligation', still represented the policy of His Majesty's Government,[1] a statement which was publicly reaffirmed by Sir John Simon at Lanark on August 27.[2]

This was the only concrete achievement which Herr von Kleist could carry back to Berlin as a result of his mission. But there were certain other repercussions. Sir Robert Vansittart's account of his conversation had been forwarded both to the Prime Minister and to the Foreign Secretary, and, though it reminded Mr. Chamberlain 'of the Jacobites at the Court of France in King William's time' and that consequently 'we must discount a good deal of what he [von Kleist] says', yet the minute had aroused within the withered breast of the Prime Minister some feeling of uneasiness, as he confessed to Lord Halifax, 'I don't feel sure that we ought not to do something'.[3] To go beyond his statement of March 24, or to be

war the immediate intervention by France and England will bring about the downfall of the régime.' In reporting this conversation to the Foreign Office, Sir N. Henderson characterized it as 'clearly biased and largely propaganda' (Woodward and Butler, Third Series, ii, 125-6).

[1] For the full text of the passage of the Prime Minister's speech quoted by Mr. Churchill, see *House of Commons Parliamentary Reports*, March 24, 1938, cols. 1405-6.   [2] *The Times*, August 29, 1938.

[3] Letter from Mr. Neville Chamberlain to Lord Halifax, dated August 19, 1938 (Woodward and Butler, Third Series, ii, 686-7).

more explicit than His Majesty's Government had been on May 21, he rejected out of hand, but he was disposed to summon the British Ambassador in Berlin for consultation on the serious situation which had arisen, letting the purpose of his journey be known as widely as possible in going.

Sir N. Henderson accordingly arrived on August 28. He received two important instructions : first, to convey a serious warning to the *Führer*, and, secondly, very secretly to prepare for a 'personal contact' between the Prime Minister and Herr Hitler. The first of these instructions Sir Nevile succeeded in having withdrawn 'on his own earnest insistence'.[1] The second bore fruit in the Munich Agreement.[2] Von Kleist's visit was not without its results, but not quite the results he desired.

Von Kleist returned to Berlin on August 23, bearing with him Mr. Churchill's letter which he showed to Beck, von Hammerstein, Halder and others.[3] Not entirely satisfied with results of this first dove of peace, Halder determined to send his own. His choice was a retired officer, Lieutenant-Colonel Hans Böhm-Tettelbach, a friend of Oster, who, as a director of a small industrial concern in the Ruhr, had had business connections with England. The object of his mission was to make direct contact with the War Office and with the British Military Intelligence. Herr Böhm-Tettelbach journeyed to London on September 2, and on arrival made contact with Mr. Julian Piggott, who, in 1920, had been British Representative in Cologne of the Inter-Allied Rhineland High Commission. Through him, according to Böhm-Tettelbach's own story, it was made possible for him to see the people whom he desired to see.

[1] Sir Nevile Henderson, *Failure of a Mission* (New York, 1940), pp. 147, 150.

[2] It is not without irony that after the departure of the Prime Minister and his advisers for Munich for the Four Power Conference, Lord Halifax sent the following telegram to the British Delegation on September 29 : 'Information has reached me from moderate circles in Germany that the firm attitude taken by His Majesty's Government during the last few days, especially the mobilization of the fleet and the fact that this attitude had become known to wide circles in Germany by means of broadcasts in German from this country and from Luxemburg and Strasbourg, have had considerable effect on German public opinion. This may, if true, assist you in negotiations' (Woodward and Butler, Third Series, ii, 620).

[3] On his return to Berlin von Kleist delivered Mr. Churchill's letter to Canaris and Oster. It was given to Fabian von Schlabrendorff to copy. Two copies were made, one for Beck and one for Canaris. The original was returned to von Kleist, who deposited it in his country house at Schmenzin in Pomerania. There it was discovered by the Gestapo after his arrest subsequent to the failure of the attempt of July 20, 1944. Used against him by the prosecution at his trial before the People's Court, it contributed to the sentence of death which was passed upon him and carried out on April 16, 1945. (Information given to the present writer by Fabian von Schlabrendorff in London in June 1949.)

His views were also sent to Sir Robert Vansittart, who thought very little of them, and also to the head of the Press Department of the Foreign Office.[1] In these quarters he repeated much of the warnings which von Kleist had uttered a week or two earlier and gave certain broad hints as to the action meditated by the conspirators. His powers of producing conviction seem to have been very considerably less than those of his precursor, for whereas von Kleist left a vivid impression with whomever he talked, no one can remember the substance of their conversation with Böhm-Tettelbach.

The fatal month of September had now opened. At its close, the Generals knew, there stood a scarlet cross — X-day for 'Operation Green' and, as they believed, '*Finis Germaniae*'. If Hitler were to be stopped by forces from without, it must be before the close of the Party Congress at Nuremberg. Otherwise, it was thought, things might have gone too far. Preferably, however, they desired some indication of action from Britain and from France before the speech which the *Führer* was to make on September 12 and which, it was feared, in many less well-informed quarters, might ignite the train to the powder-barrel. Desperately, therefore, they watched for a sign, not knowing that Mr. Chamberlain and M. Bonnet had already decided which group of Germans they were prepared to appease.

One must, however, consider the views of the leaders in London and Paris. Totally unprepared for war, reaping the bitter fruit of five years' neglect of national defences and armaments and of blindly and wilfully ignoring the storm signals so blatantly displayed across the Rhine, the French and British Governments were bent upon the preservation of peace at any price, even at the sacrifice of their own vital interests and, in the case of France, of her bounden duty and plighted word. Culpable they may have been on many charges, but that of neglecting the advances of the Berlin conspirators is not among the most serious. They looked at the past record of the German Army and of the German Conservatives in their relation to the Nazi Party. They re-read the reports of their Ambassadors in Berlin over the past ten years. Why indeed should they give confidence or credence to the idea of an attempt to overthrow Hitler by a conspiracy headed, so it seemed, by disgruntled Generals and former members of the Nationalist Party? The personalities of Goerdeler and von Kleist were in themselves sufficient to convince

---

[1] Herr Böhm-Tettelbach gave his account of his visit to London in an article published in the Mainz *Allgemeine Zeitung*, and was subsequently interviewed by the *Rheinische Post*, July 10, 1948. See also Peter Bor, *Gespräche mit Halder* (Wiesbaden, 1950), p. 121.

of their personal sincerity and honesty, but what of their ability to fulfil their intentions ? To Mr. Chamberlain and Lord Halifax, to M. Daladier and M. Georges Bonnet, it seemed as if they were being asked to gamble with the fate of their countries on the very uneven chance of a successful *coup d'état* in Germany. They were being asked to adopt a threatening attitude to Hitler on the assurance of the conspirators that this would not lead to war, but that Hitler would be overthrown at the moment at which his finger curled upon the trigger. This was the fantastic demand made to the political leaders of Britain and France by men in Germany who themselves, in most cases, had been enthusiastic in their support of Hitler and whose conversion had been brought about — again, in most cases — by their conviction that Hitler could gain no more for Germany without endangering her safety. To men who were as deeply committed to a policy of appeasement as were the Prime Minister of Great Britain and the Foreign Minister of France this was no deterrent argument. Supposing, as was more than likely, the *Putsch* failed and they were left confronting a belligerent Hitler with their fists doubled ?

These considerations undoubtedly played a part in the formulation of policy in London and in Paris, and, without abating the gravity of the charges made against the men of Munich, we may at least forgive their failure to take seriously either the good intentions of the conspirators or their ability to fulfil that which they claimed to be able to do.

Indeed, one may well ask, what would have happened in the very improbable event of such a *Putsch* succeeding ? Was there any indication that a junta of Generals, followed by a reactionary provisional government, followed by a restoration of the Monarchy, would be prepared to forgo anything which Hitler had gained for Germany by blackmail and menace ? Would the Germans not continue to rearm ? Would they not persist in the remilitarization of the Rhineland ? Would they not hold that Austria was an inalienable part of the German Reich ? And for the future, would they abate the territorial claims which Germany was then making upon Czechoslovakia and would make upon Poland, one day longer than the moment at which they felt strong enough to take these territories by force if they were not surrendered, even as Hitler was then demanding their surrender ?

The conspirators, however, continued their attempts to persuade Britain and France to remain firm. Their final effort, made after the return of Böhm-Tettelbach to Berlin, involved, somewhat unusually, the machinery of the German Foreign Ministry.

Within the *Auswärtiges Amt* there existed a small group of career diplomats, who belonged to that mild and ineffective Opposition within the German Civil Service whose members remained in the service of the Third Reich, did the work of their Nazi masters, and to-day, having survived untouched to tell the tale and deeply regretting their lack of initiative in the past, now vividly remember their objections to the excesses of Nazi foreign policy and even their conspiracies to restrain it. These men, some of whom are to-day once again active in the service of the Western German Republic, rely upon the pretext that things are not always what they seem to be ; that in continuing to the bitter end in the diplomatic service of the Third Reich they were merely giving lip-service and were secretly engaged in rendering even this service ineffective ; that, in short, when over a period of thirteen years they consistently said 'Yes', they as consistently meant 'No'. Such a defence plea is no novelty in courts of criminal law, especially upon charges of conspiracy. It must, of necessity, be regarded with suspicion and accepted with caution, and then only when fully corroborated.

Of this group the first was the person of Ernst von Weizsäcker,[1] the senior State Secretary in the German Foreign Ministry, whose father, a trusted friend of King William of Württemberg, had served that monarch for many years as a liberal Conservative Prime Minister. The son had come to terms with Hitler, as a fellow Swabian once wrote of him, 'in a way of which old Weizsäcker would never have approved'.[2]

Though von Weizsäcker was in touch with Beck and Schacht

---

[1] Ernst, Freiherr von Weizsäcker (1882–1951), entered the Imperial German Navy in 1900. During the First World War he saw some action, but was later transferred to the Staff of the Naval Delegation at Imperial General Headquarters at Spa, where he finished the War with the rank of Commander. In 1920 he entered the diplomatic service of the Republic, where he served as Minister to Norway 1931–3 and to Switzerland 1933–6. From Berne he was summoned to Berlin to become head of the Political Department of the Foreign Ministry, and when Hans-Georg von Mackensen, the son of the old Field-Marshal, was sent to succeed von Hassell as Ambassador in Rome in April 1938, von Weizsäcker was appointed to the vacant post of State Secretary. There he remained until 1943, when he became Ambassador to the Holy See. Arrested by Allied Military Authorities as a War Criminal, von Weizsäcker was placed on trial with other high Nazi officials on November 5, 1947, at Nuremberg in 'The Ministries Case'. On April 14, 1949, he was condemned to seven years' imprisonment to run from the date of his arrest in June 1947. This was subsequently commuted to five years, and he was actually released under amnesty in 1950. He published his Memoirs in the same year. This work should be read with great reserve and compared for its accuracy with *Documents on German Foreign Policy, 1918–1945*, Series D, ii, 'Germany and Czechoslovakia 1937–1938'. Von Weizsäcker died at Lindau am Bodensee on August 4, 1951.

[2] Ernst Jäckh, *The War for Man's Soul* (New York, 1943), p. 271.

and Goerdeler, and to some degree with Halder, he never, during his secret interrogations after his arrest by Allied Military Authorities, claimed to be a member of the Resistance Movement.[1] It was only in the course of his trial that he advanced such glowing claims for his own virtuous opposition to the aggressive policies of Hitler and Ribbentrop. In fact, he was informed of everything that went on in the field of military and political activity, for what he did not know as of right as State Secretary he learned from the conspirators in OKH. Von Weizsäcker was genuinely opposed to the policy of aggression, but for the reason that many other high-ranking German officers, military and political, were opposed to it — because of the risks involved. He wrote a minute of his views as, according to him, he expressed them to Ribbentrop on August 19 : 'I again opposed the whole theory (of an attack upon Czechoslovakia) and observed that we should have to wait political development until the English lost interest in the Czech matter and would tolerate our action, before we could tackle the affair without risk'. But there is no further evidence that he even went this far in protest, for the paper, unsigned and with the date added in pencil, was kept in a sealed envelope in his desk.[2]

Around the State Secretary in the German Foreign Ministry there was a small group of 'Resisters' who must be distinguished from those other representatives of German diplomacy, such as Adam von Trott zu Solz, Otto Kiep, Hans-Bernd von Haeften, Eduard Brücklmeier, and Albrecht von Bernstorff, who risked all, and died. Chief among the disciples of von Weizsäcker were the brothers Kordt, Erich and Theodor, two Rhinelanders who had entered the diplomatic service after the First World War.[3] Both were in key positions, Erich as *Chef de Cabinet* to the Foreign

---

[1] See Judgment of U.S. Military Tribunal IV, delivered in Case No. 11, 'Ernst von Weizsäcker and others', on April 14, 1949.

[2] Compare Weizsäcker, *Erinnerungen* (Munich, 1950), pp. 167-8, with *Documents on German Foreign Policy, 1918–1945*, Series D, ii, 593-4 and footnote. Other discrepancies of fact in von Weizsäcker's memoirs are disclosed in Sir Lewis Namier's *In the Nazi Era* (London, 1952), pp. 63-83.

[3] Erich Kordt, born 1903, was attached by the Foreign Office to the *Büro Ribbentrop* in 1934. He accompanied his chief to the Embassy in London and returned with him to Berlin in 1938 to be his *Chef de Cabinet*, a post in which he continued until 1941, when he became successively Minister in the Embassies in Japan and China until 1945. His elder brother, Theodor, born in 1893, having served in various posts abroad, was appointed Counsellor of Embassy in London in 1938 and there continued until the outbreak of war in September 1939, frequently acting as Chargé d'Affaires. From 1939-45 he was Counsellor of Legation at Berne. Both brothers were exonerated in their de-Nazification processes on their return to Germany and both testified by affidavit in favour of von Weizsäcker, in whose defence at Nuremberg both were most active.

Minister, Theodor as Counsellor of the Embassy in London ; and both shared the opinion of their mentor that an act of aggression against Czechoslovakia was to be deprecated — and if possible prevented — if only because it would inevitably precipitate a war which in the long run would be disastrous to Germany.

The brothers Kordt, with von Weizsäcker's tacit approval, had endeavoured to acquaint people of influence in London, notably Sir Robert Vansittart, of the rising tide of danger in Central Europe,[1] and after consultation with Beck and Goerdeler, and with Halder, it was agreed to make use of this channel in a last attempt to persuade the British Government to remain firm.

On the evening of September 5, Theodor Kordt, acting on the instructions and briefing of his brother, was brought by Philip Conwell-Evans to Sir Horace Wilson, the Chief Industrial Adviser to the Government and Mr. Chamberlain's *fidus Achates*, with more explicit information than had hitherto been vouchsafed of the conspirators' plans. So vital did this information appear to Sir Horace that he hurried the messenger away to the rear entrance of No. 10 Downing Street on the Horse Guards Parade and, spiriting him through the little garden door, brought him into the presence of the British Foreign Secretary. To Lord Halifax Kordt repeated what he had already said and added more. Hitler was expected to order a general mobilization on September 16, he said, with the object of attacking Czechoslovakia not later than October 1. The conspirators were prepared to strike on the day that mobilization was announced. All that was required of Britain and France was to remain firm and not to give ground before the fury of Hitler's forthcoming diatribes at the Nuremberg Party Congress.[2]

This, of course, was exactly what the Western Powers were not prepared to do, and, indeed, the decision had already been taken in London that at the appropriate moment a meeting between the Prime Minister and the *Führer* should take place. Lord Halifax, therefore, could only take note of the information which Theodor Kordt brought him, and his reply, one may be certain, was noncommittal.[3] On the following morning there appeared the famous

---

[1] They also made use of Dr. Philip Conwell-Evans, an English scholar who, having accepted a Chair at the University of Königsberg, became impressed with both the strength and the virtue of the Nazi régime. On his return to England he exercised some influence in the formulation of policy in Downing Street.

[2] For a detailed account of this conversation as retailed by Theodor Kordt to his brother Erich, see *Nicht aus den Akten*, pp. 279-81.

[3] According to Theodor Kordt, Lord Halifax said to him a few days after the Munich Conference : 'We were not able to be as frank with you as you were with us. At the time that you gave us your message we were already considering sending Chamberlain to Germany' (Rothfels, p. 62).

editorial in *The Times*, advocating the cession by Czechoslovakia 'of that fringe of alien population who are contiguous to the nation with which they are united by race'.[1]

And in Germany the preparatory machinery for 'Operation Green' was rolling relentlessly toward X-day. The very Generals in charge of the operation, von Rundstedt and von Reichenau, were now apprehensive for its success in the event of outside intervention, and urged the Commander-in-Chief of the Army to make representations to the *Führer*. At a conference with Hitler and Keitel at the Berghof on September 3, and at another on the 9th, which, with Halder present, lasted from ten o'clock at night till three-thirty the next morning, von Brauchitsch pointed out to the Supreme Commander and the Chief of OKW some of the essential difficulties with which they were confronted in invading Bohemia and Moravia. He urged that, if there was the least danger of intervention by Britain and France, the operation should be abandoned. The result was an outbreak on the part of the *Führer* and a reiteration of his accusations of faint-heartedness and lack of confidence, followed by a passionate tirade by Keitel, who declared that he would not tolerate 'criticism, scruples, and defeatism' on the part of OKH. The reason for the Generals' lack of confidence, he declared, was basically one of jealousy ; they still saw in Hitler the Corporal of the World War and not the greatest politician since Bismarck.[2]

But the gloomy forebodings of OKH were not abated. The anxiety of the Commander-in-Chief of the Army was now aroused, and he is believed to have made further representations to the *Führer*. These jeremiads, however, had not the slightest effect upon Hitler, though he later bore tribute to their justification.[3]

---

[1] *The Times*, September 6, 1938. See also Wheeler-Bennett, *Munich*, pp. 97-8

[2] The stormy nature of these discussions does not appear in the sedately discreet records of the meetings kept by Colonel Schmundt (see PS-388, items 18 and 19), but in Jodl's Diary entry for September 13, in which he quotes Keitel's account of what occurred.

[3] 'When after Munich we were in a position to examine Czechoslovak military strength from within', Hitler told Dr. Carl Burckhardt, then League of Nations High Commissioner in the Free City of Danzig, on August 11, 1939, 'what we saw of it greatly disturbed us : we had seen a serious danger. The plan prepared by the Czech Generals was formidable. So I understood why my own Generals had urged restraint' (reported by Burckhardt to M. Édouard Herriot. See Pertinax, *Les Fossoyeurs* (New York, 1943), i, 13-14).

At Nuremberg, Keitel, under direct examination on April 4, 1946, testified to the relief of OKW that a peaceful solution to the Czechoslovak affair had been reached at Munich. 'Throughout the time of preparation we had always been of the opinion that our means of attack against the frontier fortifications of Czechoslovakia were insufficient. From a purely technical point of view we lacked the means for an attack which involved the piercing of these fortifications'

In Berlin during these fateful weeks of September the leaders of the conspiracy waited eagerly for the moment to strike. Unfortunately they do not appear to have been able to recognize the moment when it arrived. The full time-table of 'Operation Green' had been known to Beck before his departure from office, and any subsequent minor details and changes were certainly within the knowledge of Halder. They knew therefore that September 30 was the last possible day of peace, that they must strike before that time. The fact remains that they did not strike, and for this failure various reasons — in some cases incompatible and inconsistent reasons — have been advanced.

Of those prominent in the conspiracy at this time only one, Franz Halder, remains alive, and he, bolstered, buttressed and bastioned on every point by the ever ready Gisevius, has left upon record a remarkable story of those latter days before the Munich Conference.[1]

Halder and his friends would have us believe that the conspiracy was prepared 'to the last gaiter button'; that von Brockdorff in Potsdam, von Helldorf and von der Schulenburg in Berlin, and Hoepner in Thuringia were but awaiting the code word to take action; that von Witzleben waited only for the order from Halder to give that code word; that behind them Goerdeler, Schacht, Beck, Popitz and von Hammerstein were ready to take over the government of the Reich; that even von Brauchitsch had been brought up to scratch. Schacht has written that of all the *Putsches* conceived against Hitler this was the most carefully planned. He is probably right.

But, if so, why did it fail?

As one man, Halder, Gisevius, Schacht and Kordt have their answer: first, the fact that Hitler remained at the Berghof, and the *Putsch* was planned to take place in Berlin; and, secondly, the action of the British Prime Minister. The conspirators watched the progress of Mr. Chamberlain's visits to Germany with mixed emotions. They fancied that the first flight to Berchtesgaden had been prompted by their warnings and had been undertaken with the intention of giving the *Führer* a last firm statement on Britain's determination to stand by France in the event of German aggression against Czechoslovakia. This was, of course, what Halder and Beck and Goerdeler and Schacht had been urging Mr. Chamberlain to do

(*Nuremberg Record*, x, 509). If Keitel had really shared the hesitancy of OKH on this occasion, his lickspittle adulation of the *Führer* and his denunciation of his fellow Generals is all the more contemptible.

[1] Halder Interrogation, February 26, 1946; Gisevius, ii, 66-76; and Evidence at Nuremberg, April 24, 1946 (*Nuremberg Record*, xii, 218-19); see also Schacht, pp. 121-5, and Kordt, pp. 277-8.

and to say, and hence it was to be welcomed, but the fact that this interview removed the person of the *Führer* from Berlin caused them dismay, as they feared that he might suddenly order mobilization from the Eagle's Eyrie without returning to the capital and, in that event, their plans would be all for nothing.

At last, however, when the second interview at Godesberg had failed, Hitler returned to Berlin, and, on September 27, after his stormy interview with Sir Horace Wilson,[1] he watched from the window of the Chancellery the icy and silent reception accorded by the burghers of Berlin to the parade of armoured troops down the Wilhelmstrasse.[2] That evening he sent the famous letter to Mr. Chamberlain which was delivered at No. 10 Downing Street at ten o'clock the same night.

According to Halder and Gisevius they became possessed of a copy of this letter on the morning of September 28, and its contents were considered so insulting and intransigent that von Witzleben, on reading it, at once asked Halder to give him the order to revolt ; and Halder was so shocked that he urgently besought von Brauchitsch to take action ; and von Brauchitsch was so outraged that he could say neither yes or no, but went to the Chancellery. Halder thereupon agreed with von Witzleben that action should be taken on the following day — the X-day minus 1 for 'Operation Green — pending the approval of von Brauchitsch. But while all these military gentlemen were in such transports of indignation that none of them could issue an executive order, the news was announced that Mr. Chamberlain was flying to Munich to negotiate with Hitler and to preserve peace. Since the conspirators had the same primary purpose, all further action was abandoned.[3]

Among the many legends which constitute the mythology of the German Resistance Movement — legends as dangerous to the future peace of the world as was that of the 'Stab-in-the-Back' after the First World War — there has grown up this story that the only attempt to remove Hitler, which might have been remotely successful, was frustrated and sabotaged by Mr. Chamberlain's announcement of his intention to go to Munich. But, it is submitted, this apology for failure, circulated by interested parties, does not hold water for a moment.

---

[1] Schmidt, pp. 407-9 ; Wheeler-Bennett, *Munich*, pp. 150-51.

[2] For eye-witness accounts of this event see Ruth Andreas-Friedrich, *Berlin Underground, 1939-1945* (London, 1948), p. 12 ; Constantin Silens, *Irrweg und Umkehr* (Basel, 1946), p. 184 ; William Shirer, *Berlin Diary* (New York, 1941), pp. 142-3 ; Henderson, pp. 165-6.

[3] Halder Interrogation of February 25, 1946 ; Gisevius, ii, 74-6 ; and Evidence at Nuremberg on April 25, 1946 (*Nuremberg Record*, xii, 219).

What are the facts ?   Halder and Gisevius allege that they,
together with von Witzleben and others, were wrought up into a
passion of indignation on reading a letter sent by Hitler to Mr.
Chamberlain by the hand of Sir Horace Wilson, with the contents
of which they became acquainted on September 28.   In the first
place, Sir Horace took back from Berlin no written communication
to the Prime Minister.   The letter was written after his departure
on the 27th, and was delivered at Downing Street by a special
messenger from the German Embassy about ten o'clock that night,
after Mr. Chamberlain had made his famous broadcast.[1]

Now, remarkably enough, it was this 'defiant' and 'insulting'
letter which gave the heart-torn Mr. Chamberlain the idea that the
door to peace had not been irrevocably barred.   Sir Nevile Henderson even found the letter 'indicative of a certain nervousness', but
whether this was justified or not, its tone was neither 'defiant' nor
'insulting', for it had been phrased in as shrewd a wording as can
be conceived to appeal to a man of Mr. Chamberlain's psychology.
It was moderate and flattering and calculated to pique the British
Prime Minister on his two weak spots — the obstinacy of the Czechs
and the 'war-mongers' in Britain.   It was an appeal from one man
of the world to another in an attempt to come to a reasonable
agreement by brushing aside unnecessary details and obstacles.   It
was an extremely subtle piece of psychological warfare and it had
precisely the effect for which it was designed, but by no stretch of
imagination could it be construed to constitute an excuse to move
armies to revolt.[2]

So much for this last straw which had broken the tolerance and
destroyed the patience of the conspirators.

That plans existed for a *Putsch* is undoubtedly true, but that they
were abandoned on September 28 on the eve of being put into
execution is equally without doubt untrue.   There is evidence,
indeed, that any plans which had existed for a *Putsch* had been
abandoned at least a fortnight before, at the time of Mr. Chamberlain's first flight to Germany.[3]   The causes of failure were that
ineptitude in planning and that fatal hesitancy in execution inherent

[1] Wheeler-Bennett, *Munich*, p. 160
[2] For text of letter see British White Paper, Cmd. 5487, No. 10 ; see also
Wheeler-Bennett, *Munich*, p. 162 *et seq.*
[3] Mr. Vernon Bartlett, who, with other newspaper correspondents, accompanied
Mr. Chamberlain on September 15, on his return to London informed Mr. Harold
Nicolson (who noted it in his diary on September 20) that while at Berchtesgaden
he had been approached by a former acquaintance on the General Staff who said
that Mr. Chamberlain's decision to meet the *Führer* had forestalled a plot by the
Army to arrest Göring and Himmler and even Hitler himself, if he persisted in
his policy of war.

in the political conspiracies of the Generals from the Kapp *Putsch* onwards. Just as von Schleicher and von Hammerstein had hesitated on the night of January 29, 1933, just as von Fritsch and von Rundstedt would not act at the moment of crisis in February 1938, so now in September 1938 von Witzleben and Halder and von Brauchitsch passed the ball from one to another and finally allowed the opportunity to escape them.

Speaking in retrospect, Halder later stated that the three essential requisites for a successful *Putsch* were, first, a clear and resolute leadership ; secondly, a willingness on the part of the masses to follow ; and, thirdly, the choice of the psychological moment to strike.[1] It is clear beyond peradventure that, among the leaders of the conspiracy of September 1938, the first of these prerequisites was lacking. The second, it may be believed, existed in a great measure. The German people were appalled at the prospect of war. Those spontaneous demonstrations which greeted Mr. Chamberlain on his arrival at the Munich airport on September 15, that sullen silence with which the Berliners watched the armoured column pass with clank and clangour down the Wilhelmstrasse on September 27, were not moods of sudden emotion. On Halder's own showing, during the days of the Party Congress at Nuremberg (September 6-12) when the *Führer* was making the air hideous with the dripping hatred of his speeches, there was a deep-seated fear of a war not only among non-members of the Party but within the group of veterans around General Ritter von Epp, who doubted the ability of Germany to emerge victorious from a major war.

If this second prerequisite was as clearly demonstrable as Halder claims — and there is no reason to doubt that it was — the third, the choice of the moment to strike, was not so difficult. In point of fact, had the conspirators been as well prepared and as resolute as it has been claimed that they were, they could have struck at any moment during the last week of August or the first weeks of September that Hitler happened to have been in Berlin, and he was in the capital on several occasions.

The truth would seem to be that, in reality, the preparations for a *Putsch* had either not progressed as far as has later been stated or were planned on such rigid lines as to be impossible of adjustment to the necessity of events. The conspirators hesitated to strike, as von Lossow had hesitated in November 1923, looking vainly for that 51 per cent chance of success without which a General Staff will not operate, but on which revolutionaries can so rarely count at the outset. They hesitated until the visitation of Mr. Chamberlain to

[1] Halder Interrogation of February 25, 1946.

Germany cut the ground from under their feet. But there is no evidence but the flimsiest assertion that, had Mr. Chamberlain never gone to Berchtesgaden or to Godesberg or to Munich, the conspirators would have been sufficiently prepared or resolute to strike, and the rapidity with which they snatched at this excuse for inaction is at least an indication of their unreadiness.[1]

The so-called *Putsch* of September 1938 has owed much to the literary genius of Franz Halder, who, having set out to prove that the German Army could have prevented the Second World War had it not been for the interference of Mr. Chamberlain, has latterly asserted that they could also have won it had it not been for the interference of the *Führer*.[2]

(v)

However nearly the conspirators came, or did not come, to making a *Putsch* in September 1938, it was manifestly evident that conditions for such an enterprise were vastly less favourable after the signing of the Munich Agreement. The wholesale surrender of the Western Democracies to the Dictators had its disastrous effects inside as well as outside Germany. Not only had France abandoned her system of continental security, not only was Britain a consenting party to a German hegemony in Eastern and Central Europe, not only was Russia excluded and Poland isolated, but the repercussions within the Reich were equally detrimental to the peace of the world.

The German people now regarded their *Führer* as a harbinger of peace. Their demonstrations in September had been genuine enough, not because they did not wish to go to war with the Czechs, whom they despised, but because they had believed that, in so doing, they would find themselves also at war with Britain, France, and Russia, and a general European war they had reason to remember

---

[1] According to another member of the conspiracy, General Georg Thomas : 'The execution of this enterprise was unfortunately frustrated, because, according to the view of the Commanding General appointed for the task (von Witzleben), the younger officers were found to be unreliable for a political action of this kind'. (See a memorandum prepared by General Thomas at his home at Falkenstein, dated July 20, 1945, entitled '*Gedanken und Ereignisse*', and subsequently published in the *Schweizerische Monatshefte* for December 1945.)

[2] Franz Halder, *Hitler als Feldherr* (Munich, 1949), translation, *Hitler as Warlord* (London, 1950). Schacht also claims almost sole credit for the organization, but no responsibility for the failure, of the abortive *Putsch* of September 1938 : ' I had made preparations for a *coup d'état* in good time, and I had brought them to within an ace of success. History had decided against me. The intervention of foreign statesmen was something I could not possibly have taken into account'. (*Account Settled*, p. 125.)

with sorrow and dismay. Now, however, their great and wonderful Adolf Hitler had obtained everything without the shedding of a drop of blood — not German blood, at any rate. His victories were peaceful victories ; his triumphs, galas, battles of flowers, and military parades. In support of such policies the German people were enthusiastically behind him and would even follow him into a 'limited war', provided it remained 'limited'.

Similarly with the Generals ; once those formidable Bohemian fortifications had been peacefully penetrated and their full strength disclosed to the satisfaction of those who had counselled caution in developing the assault against them,[1] the Generals rallied again in admiring deference to the superior judgment of their *Führer*. They had marched into the Sudetenland — as they had marched into the Rhineland and into Austria — flower-decked and with unfleshed swords ; and although he had not led them to Prague, there were few who did not believe that he would do so eventually and with as little opposition. Britain and France had retired behind the Maginot Line, and so far as any indications could be relied upon, Germany had a free hand for the peaceful penetration of Central, Eastern and South-Eastern Europe. There was no apparent reason why this occidental lethargy should not continue indefinitely, or at least until the rearmament of Germany had been completed to that point at which the General Staff believed they could engage in war with the full hope of victory. 'The genius of the *Führer* and his determination not to shun even a world war have again achieved victory without the use of force', wrote Jodl jubilantly in his diary. 'One hopes that the incredulous, the weak and the doubters have been converted, and will remain so.'[2] In the majority of cases this was true.

The vitally important point about the whole period of negotiations preceding the Munich conference was that Hitler had not been bluffing. He would unhesitatingly have gone to war had his demands not been complied with. In this he had fooled the conspirators, but not the leaders of Britain and France. Mr. Chamberlain and Lord Halifax, M. Daladier and M. Georges Bonnet, had been fully aware of this intention and it had dictated their own attitude at Munich. But the leaders of the conspiracy were still blundering in their fools' paradise of illusion and frustration. 'A magnificent opportunity has been missed. The German people did not want war ; the Army would have done anything to prevent it. . . . If England and France had taken the risk of declaring war, Hitler would never

---

[1] For the reactions of the German commanders to the strength of the Czech fortifications, see Wheeler-Bennett, *Munich*, p. 333.
[2] Jodl's Diary, September 29, 1938.

have used force, then he would have made a fool of himself. . . .
By refusing to take a small risk, Chamberlain has made a war
inevitable.' So wrote Goerdeler with all his characteristic over-
optimism to an American friend within a fortnight of the Munich
Agreement.[1]

But the risk was not small, and, if this be the standard of the
intelligence and the accuracy of the conspirators' political intuition,
the Western Powers had been very right in disregarding their
approaches. Humiliating and shameful though the terms of the
Munich Agreement were, they were yet entered into by the Western
Powers with a greater sense of reality of the immediate danger than
was displayed by Goerdeler, Beck and Schacht. Mr. Chamberlain
and M. Daladier recognized that danger and, in their wisdom,
decided that they dared not meet the challenge ; but the leaders of
the conspiracy, who were urging the British and French leaders to a
policy which would inevitably have involved their countries in war,
would not even admit that the danger existed.

Equally fallacious was Goerdeler's picture of the situation within
Germany. 'You can hardly conceive', he wrote to this same correspondent, 'the despair that both people and Army feel about the
brutal, insane, and terroristic dictator and his henchmen.' Never
was wishful thinking more eloquently expressed, never a less accurate
picture portrayed for foreign consumption. Contentment, satisfaction and relief were the salient factors of German thought at this
moment, both among the people at large and among the Army. Their
Führer had saved them from war and had given them additional
honour, glory, and security.[2]

Indeed the only discontented party to the Munich Agreement —
apart from the Czechs — was Adolf Hitler himself. Notwithstanding
the fact that he had received all that he had asked for,[3] he had not
asked for enough. Moreover, the surrender of the Western Powers
had been so unexpectedly overwhelming that the *Führer* had been
deprived not only of his 'restricted war', and his intention to

[1] For text of this letter to 'an American Politician', dated October 11, 1938,
see *Goerdelers Politisches Testament. Dokumente des Anderen Deutschland* (New
York, 1945), pp. 57-64.
[2] That Hitler accurately appreciated the popular support which his policies
enjoyed at this time may be seen from his remark to Frau Bruckmann (*née* Princess
Cantacuzène and wife of the Munich publisher) on October 14 : 'Only the "upper
ten thousand" has any doubts ; the people stand solidly behind me' (Hassell,
p. 27).
[3] Speaking at Leeds on January 20, 1940, Lord Halifax frankly admitted : 'The
Munich settlement gave Germany all she immediately wanted. In applying the
Agreement, every contentious point was decided in Germany's favour' (Viscount
Halifax, *Speeches on Foreign Policy* (Oxford, 1940), p. 347).

'smash' Czechoslovakia by military force, but also of inflicting upon the loathed and contemptible Czechs the crowning humiliation of occupying their capital. 'That fellow has spoiled my entry into Prague', he said to Schacht of Mr. Chamberlain on his return to Berlin,[1] and forthwith set about preparing to take the second bite at his cherry.[2]

But he did not hesitate to exploit his triumph over his own Generals. He had now no possible reason to respect, or indeed to give any consideration at all to, their political judgment or their political conjurations. The announcement of Beck's resignation and his replacement by Halder as Chief of the General Staff, which had been held up until after it was known whether peace or war would result from the execution of 'Operation Green', was now issued without apprehension and indeed was received without comment, just as the court martial of von Fritsch was confidently continued after the peaceful acquisition of Austria.

More surprising was the apparently complete absence of resentment which greeted the relegation of the senior ranking officer of the German Army, Gerd von Rundstedt, to the retired list on October 31, and the removal from active command of General Wilhelm Adam, the doubting defender of the Western Wall, which followed shortly thereafter (November 27). Meantime Hitler promoted Keitel to the rank of Colonel-General, and on December 17 issued his first planning directive to Halder and OKH for the occupation of 'Czechia'.[3]

The leaders of the conspiracy were discouraged and, what was even worse, they were dispersed. For example, in the military reshuffle which followed Munich, von Witzleben was promoted Colonel-General and transferred to the command of *Heeresgruppen-kdo 2*, with headquarters at Kassel. His successor as Commander of *Wehrkreis III* in Berlin was General Haase, who was not considered *verschwörungsfähig* by Halder.[4] The *Generalität* as a whole

[1] Schacht's evidence under cross-examination on May 2, 1946 (*Nuremberg Record*, xii, 531).

[2] Within a week of the Munich Conference Hitler had addressed a *questionnaire* to Keitel which is indicative of his intention to occupy Bohemia and Moravia at the first possible opportunity. The exact date of the *questionnaire* cannot be established, but Keitel's reply is dated October 11, 1938 (PS-388, item 48). As a result of these preliminary enquiries and of a later conference between Hitler and Keitel, a general directive to the *Wehrmacht* to stand ready at all times for the 'liquidation of the remainder of Czechoslovakia and the occupation of Memelland' was issued on October 21 (*IMT Document*, C-136).

[3] *IMT Document*, C-138.

[4] Halder Interrogation of February 26, 1946. This General Haase should not be confused with Lieutenant-General Paul von Hase, who, as Commandant of Berlin, participated in the *Putsch* of July 20, and was hanged on August 8, 1944.

had become either subservient or bewildered, and in neither condition were they prepared to move. A few, a very few, remained in clandestine contact with Beck, but the vast majority followed the lead of their Commander-in-Chief and their Chief of the General Staff, and maintained a masterly inactivity.

The attitude of both von Brauchitsch and Halder at this time was, to put it charitably, lukewarm towards any active conspiracy, though, to do him justice, Halder was a shade 'lukewarmer' than his superior. Von Brauchitsch was torn between two fierce fires, professional and domestic. As a soldier his instincts and training placed him inevitably in agreement with the reasoning of Beck, namely that a premature war would spell disaster for Germany and must therefore be prevented even at the risk of precipitating a civil conflict within the Reich. But the wife of his bosom was a firm supporter of the régime,[1] and so firmly had she established her hold upon him that when the moment of testing came he could not say 'boo' to a Brown Shirt. From thenceforth von Brauchitsch, though he figures intermittently in the plans and operations of the conspirators, could never again be counted on as an active force.

With Halder the position was somewhat different. Like von Brauchitsch, and like his predecessor Beck,[2] the Chief of the General Staff was no rigid, hide-bound, *borné* General, though he came of a family who had given soldiers to Bavaria and to Germany for 300 years. There was nothing of the 'blimp' about Halder; his Bavarian intelligence was quick, shrewd and witty. He could assess a situation, whether political or military, with swiftness and accuracy, but his ability, both as a soldier and as a politician, was marred by a certain inability to act, to take essential risks, to follow the path which he saw all too clearly to be the right one. In this he, like Jodl, to some extent justified Bismarck's withering remark that 'a Bavarian is a cross between a man and an Austrian'.

After Munich Halder virtually withdrew from the ranks of the conspirators, on the grounds that nothing could be done to remove

---

[1] General von Brauchitsch was divorced in the summer of 1938. On September 24 he married Frau Charlotte Schmidt, daughter of a retired high court judge named Rueffer, at Bad Salzbrunn in Silesia ; thereafter he was described as having 'become heavily involved with the Nazis, largely through the influence of his 200 per cent rabid wife' (Hassell, p. 80).

[2] Both Beck and von Brauchitsch were exceptionally well-read in fields of interest outside their profession. Beck, at the meetings of the Wednesday Club, greatly impressed his fellow members with the breadth of his views and interests and the ability of the papers which he occasionally read. Von Brauchitsch had once shocked his fellow Generals by entering 'Study of the economic and political questions of the day' among his hobbies in '*Wer Ist's*'.

Hitler and to overthrow the Nazi régime until they had suffered some outstanding reverse, either diplomatic or military, which would destroy their prestige with the people and with the troops. This, in effect, could only come about when these two powerful factors of public opinion had been disabused of their now confident belief that Hitler could achieve all his designs by miraculous and peaceful methods.

Such was the attitude of OKH. In contrast to it was the curious dichotomy of OKW, in the Bendlerstrasse, where, though the upper stratum was 200 per cent *führertreu*, the lower brackets were riddled with Resistance.

At the head stood three men, Keitel, Jodl, and Warlimont, of whose unwavering loyalty Hitler could never have been for a moment in doubt. None of the three was a Prussian; all entertained that subconscious inferiority complex and consequent hostility toward the Prussian military tradition and the Corps of Officers in which no non-Prussian could ever be accepted by the elect on terms of complete parity; all had commended themselves to the *Führer*, partly because of a personal devotion to the 'top man', partly because of a desire for gain, and partly because he, like them, was a non-Prussian, and therefore, at heart, desirous of seeing the Prussian grip upon the military forces of the Reich broken.

Wilhelm Keitel, a Hanoverian of markedly third-rate ability, in every sense justified the play which the Berliners made upon his name on the morning of his appointment : 'So Hitler has got his *Lakaitel*', they said. From the date of his appointment, February 4, 1938, to the final farewell in the Berlin bunker on April 23, 1945, he never left the *Führer*'s side. At Vienna, at Berchtesgaden and Godesberg and Munich, in the Sudetenland, at Prague and Warsaw, at Compiègne and Paris, at Montoire and at Hendaye, at the Brenner and at Feltre, and at countless conferences at the *Führerhauptquartier* the recording camera man shows Keitel ever at his master's elbow, ever ready, like a running footman, to do his will at the slightest whim. In all these years there is no evidence that Keitel ever uttered the remotest query to a single decision of the *Führer*. Rather is there reason to believe that he enjoyed an unblemished record of complete acquiescence and subservient adulation.[1] He had ambition but no talent, loyalty but no character, a certain native shrewdness and charm but neither intelligence nor personality.

---

[1] As an example of Keitel's gross flattery there is the incident at the *Führer*'s Headquarters in June 1940 when, on the capture of Abbeville, Hitler paid tribute to OKH for its training and leadership before a large gathering of Generals, Keitel immediately replied : 'No, no, my *Führer*, to you alone are due these magnificent achievements' (Erich Kordt, *Wahn und Wirklichkeit* (Stuttgart, 1947), p. 249).

Under von Seeckt it is doubtful whether he would have gone beyond his majority. Under Hitler he achieved the rank of Field-Marshal, received the highest orders and decorations of the Third Reich and ultimately attained the gallows. He served well and was well served.

Alfred Jodl was of a different pattern. No less a willing tool than Keitel, no less ambitious for personal gain, he had not the same excuses as his chief. Jodl, the Bavarian, was a man of brilliant ability. He came of a Munich family of intellectuals which had in the past produced more philosophers, priests and lawyers than soldiers. Where Keitel was merely a spineless nonentity, Jodl had a high intelligence and a strong personality which for seven years he deliberately subordinated to Hitler's evil whims and caprices. Imbued from his earliest cadet days with a Napoleonic worship, he saw in Adolf Hitler a military and political saviour for Germany in the same gigantic mould as the Emperor. He was not unaware that those who attached themselves to the young General Bonaparte in his early struggle won thrones and coronets and batons in the golden days of the Empire, and, though his efforts were not crowned in quite this same manner, he yet saw himself in history a rival to Berthier as the *Führer's* Director of Operations.

The third in this triumvirate, Walther Warlimont, was by far the most vivid personality of the three. With the ease and grace of manner of a Rhinelander, he complemented the drab mediocrity of Keitel and the academic reserve of Jodl. Warlimont was in fact the window-display element of OKW. While Keitel toadied and Jodl toiled, Warlimont was the social asset, going among the foreign diplomats in Berlin and rivalling General von Tippelskirch, the Director of Military Intelligence of OKH, as the host of the military attachés. But Warlimont was no simple play-boy ; his social facility masked an acute and vibrant mind well attuned to the main chance. He it was who, as early as 1937, when but a colonel in the *Wehrmachtamt* of the War Ministry, had submitted directly to Hitler, without the consent or knowledge of von Blomberg or von Fritsch, a memorandum prepared by himself and a colleague, a certain Colonel Müller-Lübnitz, containing a scheme for the reorganization of the Armed Forces of the Reich under one Staff unit and one Supreme Commander. The means thus offered of clipping the wings of the Army were not lost upon the *Führer*, and it was on the basis of this memorandum that he developed his plan for OKW. It was not, therefore, surprising that Warlimont should find a place in this new organization — he even found one for his more industrious if less enterprising friend, Müller-Lübnitz — and in the course of the next six years he served first as deputy then as successor, and again as deputy, to Jodl in the Operations Branch.[1]

Such were the major planets in the constellation of OKW, as firm a body of *Führer*-worshippers as one might meet, all hanging together in the certain knowledge that, if they did not, the alternative was to hang separately — and two of them did not, in effect, escape this fate.[2]

But among the satellite luminaries, the attitude was very different. At the head of the Military Intelligence Branch (*Abwehr*), 'the little Admiral', Wilhelm Canaris, though he had served successive masters well since those days in 1919 when he had been concerned in the escape of Rosa Luxemburg's murderer,[3] had now become a convinced, if detached, opponent of the Nazi régime, on the familiar grounds that its policies of aggression would inevitably end in cataclysmic disaster for Germany. Canaris was a strange amalgam of cynic and fatalist, and his sense of realism prevented him from entering with convinced enthusiasm into the more intricate planning of the conspirators. His contribution was to provide cover for many of their number who utilized the *Abwehr* as a means of movement and underground communication, and to close his eyes to the more energetically dissident activities of his immediate lieutenants, Hans Oster and Erwin Lahousen,[4] who were among the very few who kept the conspiracy alive during the intervals of depression.

Nevertheless, if the 'Little Admiral' bore no active part, he was recognized as the instigator and spiritual leader of the conspiracy

---

[1] In the reorganization of February 1938, Jodl retained his position as Chief of the National Defence Section of OKW and so continued until after the completion of 'Operation Green', when in October 1938 he took over the 44th Artillery Command, with headquarters at Brünn. Warlimont took his place as head of the National Defence Section, and, when Jodl returned in August 1939 to become Chief of the Operations Branch of OKW, Warlimont was appointed his deputy, while still retaining his other post. He retired owing to ill-health in September 1944.

[2] Both Keitel and Jodl were hanged at Nuremberg as major War Criminals on October 16, 1946. Warlimont, as a lesser War Criminal, was sentenced by a United States Military Tribunal, on October 27, 1949, to life imprisonment in Landsberg Jail; this was later commuted to a sentence of eighteen years.

[3] See above, p. 36, footnote.

[4] Erwin Lahousen, Deputy Chief of the Intelligence Division of the Austrian General Staff in 1938, was taken over by Admiral Canaris after the *Anschluss* and became head of the Second Division of the *Abwehr*. He was called before the International Military Tribunal at Nuremberg as a witness for the Prosecution and his evidence, given on November 30 and December 1, 1945 (*Nuremberg Record*, ii, 440-78; iii, 1-31), was highly damaging to the defendants. On the appearance of Lahousen in the witness-box Göring, leaning across Hess in the dock, made the clearly audible comment to Ribbentrop: 'That's one we missed after July 20th'.

within OKW.[1] Yet because of his highly individual and complicated nature, Canaris could be no more than this ; inspiration he could offer, action must be taken by others.

In a similar category was General Georg Thomas, the head of the Economic and Armaments Branch (*Wi Rü Amt*) of OKW. An admitted genius in military economics, Thomas adhered strictly to the well-founded principles of the Seeckt School. He was anti-Polish and pro-Russian, pro-Chinese and anti-Japanese. Since the *Führer* and his Party advisers on foreign affairs were set upon a *rapprochement* in Europe with Poland and as close an understanding as possible with Japan in Asia, it is not surprising that early clashes had occurred between Thomas and von Blomberg, who was in the invidious position of being compelled by his supine turn of mind to execute the military aspects of a policy in which he himself did not believe and to which many of his ablest lieutenants were fervently opposed. Nevertheless, Thomas had enthusiastically carried out his orders to restore Germany's military economy and had not found grounds for profound moral disagreement with the Nazi régime until after the murder of von Schleicher on June 30, 1934. A certain process of disillusionment then set in, and the General's 'complete inner breach with the system' ('*meinen völligen inneren Bruch mit diesem System*') was brought about by the Fritsch affair.[2] The General's conversion from National Socialism had therefore been brought about by the attacks of the system upon the privileged position and vested interests of the Army and the Officer Corps, but once his enmity had been aroused he was implacable and unrelenting — though this did not prevent him from organizing, with that extreme efficiency of which the German General Staff is capable, the economic exploitation of the Nazi invasion of Russia.

Such was the position of men and events in OKW and OKH immediately after the Munich Conference. The prospect of an opportunity to overthrow Hitler seemed exceedingly remote, since this was now only possible in the event of a general war, and such an eventuality appeared not to be destined for the immediate future.

The pogroms of November 9, in which hundreds of Jews were despoiled and rendered homeless, and every synagogue in the Reich was destroyed, only evoked a qualified degree of reprobation among the German people, and this was occasioned more by the lawless looting and damage to property which accompanied the riots than

---

[1] Halder's Interrogation of February 25, 1946; Lahousen's evidence, November 30, 1945 (*Nuremberg Record*, ii, 443).
[2] General Thomas, *Gedanken und Ereignisse*.

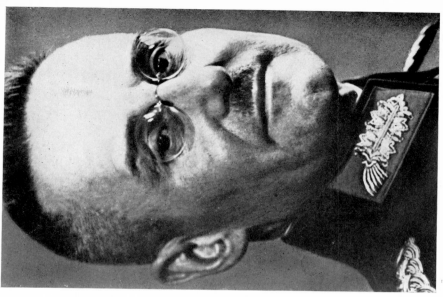

COLONEL-GENERAL FRANZ HALDER

FIELD-MARSHAL WILHELM KEITEL

by the actual persecution of the Jews.[1] It was their sense of law and order, not their humanity, that was outraged. Though von Hassell could write under the weight of 'crushing emotions'; though Popitz could offer his resignation to Göring — and withdraw it when it was refused; though Schacht could address the office boys of the *Reichsbank* at Christmas in disapproval of the pogroms and eventually attain his dismissal by Hitler in January, these were indeed isolated reactions. Von Neurath and Schwerin von Krosigk, when urged to resign in protest, failed or refused to do so. While among the Generals there was scarcely a voice raised in protestation. 'Of course the battle with international Jewry has now officially begun, and as a natural consequence that will lead to war with England and the United States, the political bastions of the Jews', von Fritsch could write pettishly at this time.[2]

Clearly this was no issue upon which to rally the *Generalität*, but very shortly thereafter an issue was provided which caused further alarms and despondency among the plotters.

On December 17 the directive was issued by OKW which clearly demonstrated the *Führer*'s intentions to complete his dismemberment of Czechoslovakia at the first available opportunity. 'The preparations for this eventuality', so ran the order, 'are to continue on the assumption that no resistance worth mentioning is to be expected. To the outside world it must clearly appear that it is merely an act of pacification and not a hostile operation.' Because of this condition the operation was to be undertaken with the existing forces of the Army and Air Force.[3] There was to be no general mobilization and the conspirators were therefore at once deprived of the circumstances on which they had previously counted to arouse public support for a *Putsch*.

As soon as these facts were known to the Intelligence Branch they were communicated to the leaders of the conspiracy, and once

---

[1] On November 7, in Paris, a seventeen-year-old Polish Jew, Herschel Grynszpan, shot and fatally wounded Freiherr vom Rath, a young Third Secretary in the German Embassy, who died two days later. His death was the signal for a fifteen-hours' pogrom throughout Germany, which, as was subsequently proved at Nuremberg from a memorandum by Julius Streicher, dated April 14, 1939 (*IMT Document*, PS-406), had been planned and organized in advance to coincide with the fifteenth anniversary of the Bürgerbräu *Putsch* of November 9, 1923. Not content with physical violence, the Nazis imposed, on November 12, a fine of a milliard marks (approximately £80 million) upon the German Jewish community, who were forced to repair, at their own expense, all the damage they had suffered, which in Berlin alone amounted to some 13 milliard marks, while, from January 1, 1939, Jews were declared to be excluded from the economic life of the Reich.

[2] Letter from Colonel-General Freiherr von Fritsch to the Baronin Schutzbar-Milchling, dated November 22, 1938.   [3] *IMT Document*, C-138.

again a frenzied activity seized upon the plotters. Goerdeler and Beck besought Halder to act. Canaris, too, counselled action, Oster assembled an array of documents and arguments to show that this time Britain and France, who had entered into a guarantee of the rump of Czechoslovakia at Munich, must resist any attempt by Germany to annex this miserable remnant. Schacht advocated the immediate arrest of Hitler or a *coup d'état* to save the peace. Erwin Planck, who had been von Schleicher's tool and Brüning's secretary,[1] added his word, and von Hassell sought to influence policy through von Weizsäcker, who informed him, as late as the fourth week of January, that 'the barometer indicated peace even in the east'.[2]

It was all in vain. Halder, still under the powerful influence of the Allied surrender at Munich, was disposed to be more than usually careful. He would enter into no preliminary conferences and would undertake no action until after British and French intervention had actually taken place. He promised to lead a *Putsch* if war was declared, but it was his personal belief that Hitler was proceeding on the basis of a secret understanding reached in advance with Paris and London.[3]

Though this was not the case, it came nearer to reality in result than the fevered wishful thinking of the conspirators. Halder's cynical disbelief in Allied action was fully justified by the event. The march into Prague on March 14 elicited no more than pious disapprobation from Paris and London, where, taken — incredibly enough — by surprise, the leaders jettisoned their guarantee to Czechoslovakia as being impossible of fulfilment. Once again the *Führer's* intuition had triumphed over the logical reasonings of his political and military advisers. Once again the German people greeted with enthusiasm a bloodless victory, and once again the German Army entered a foreign capital without a shot fired or a blow of resistance. Nothing, it seemed, could withstand the diabolical, dynamic cunning of Adolf Hitler, and the German man in the street said with evident approval : 'Hitler is lucky'.

[1] Erwin Planck (1893–1944), son of the great mathematical physicist, *Geheimrat* Professor Max Planck (1858–1947) of the University of Berlin, had, after serving as a young officer in the First World War, entered the Civil Service, whence he was selected by Brüning to be his Principal Private Secretary at the Chancellery. Planck had, however, come under the influence of Kurt von Schleicher, and became the General's *homme de confiance* within the *Reichskanzlei*, where he certainly abused his loyalty to Brüning. On Brüning's dismissal Planck became State Secretary successively to von Papen and von Schleicher as Chancellors, remaining throughout loyal only to the General. Identified with the conspiracy against Hitler from 1938 onwards, he was arrested and executed on January 23, 1945.   [2] Hassell (January 26, 1939), p. 49.
[3] Gisevius's evidence, April 25, 1946 (*Nuremberg Record*, xii, 221).

(vi)

Hitler's pacific triumphs against 'Czechia' and Memelland seemed, both to his supporters and to his opponents in Germany, a crowning and transcendent proof that he could do what he liked in Europe with no one to say him nay. After his final dismemberment of the Czechoslovak Republic, without exciting more than a pious protest from those Powers who but six months earlier had joined with Germany in guaranteeing the inviolable integrity of that State, it appeared inconceivable that any State would offer resistance to Nazi aggression or would henceforth put the least dependence upon the word of the Western Powers. Nazi enthusiasts, as well as those who groaned beneath the Nazi yoke, could look forward along an indefinite vista of 'Blumenkorsos' and 'peaceful' conquests achieved under the threat of force.

But what neither Hitler, nor his paladins, nor his enemies within the Reich, could fathom was the effect which the Führer's policies of perjured faith had had in England. It seemed as if the fell sentence: 'Czechoslovakia has ceased to exist', uttered in the very halls of the Hradschin Castle, to the accompaniment of the clank and rattle of German armoured columns through the streets of Prague,[1] had awakened the soul of Britain from that spell of inertia and malaise in whose thrall she had lain so long. The process of awakening was completed when, within a week, Nazi hegemony was extended still further with the weighted tramp of the Feldgrauen into Memel.[2] Thenceforward Britain groped stumblingly towards the light, though not without errors and omissions, and not without hesitation and uncertainties. Nevertheless, though many in Europe did not realize the fact at once, Britain had laid aside, as it were overnight, the counsels of expediency and had assumed a 'moral grandeur which yielded nothing to fear, nothing to despondency'. On March 15 a tocsin had been sounded in England of which the echoes were not to die away until the man who had driven in triumph through the streets of Prague lay dead and buried in the backyard of the Reichskanzlei in Berlin.

All this, however, was unknown to those in Germany, who, in

---

[1] On March 15, 1939, Hitler from Prague issued a proclamation to the German people in which these words occur. (See Völkischer Beobachter, March 16, 1939; Baynes, ii, 1585.)

[2] On March 22, 1939, the Lithuanian Government signed the Agreement (for text see Second German White Book, No. 342) which restored Memelland to Germany in abrogation of Article 99 of the Treaty of Versailles whereby Germany had renounced it in favour of the Allied and Associated Powers. After a military coup by the Lithuanian Government the Conference of Ambassadors accepted a fait accompli and formally bestowed the territory upon Lithuania on February 16, 1923.

the spring of 1939, saw all hopes of removing Hitler and destroying the Nazi régime seemingly in ashes around them. Some considered the question of permanent emigration; some, like Halder, merely closed their eyes and ears and withdrew from the scene. The younger members of the conspiracy were less cast down than their leaders, of whom Goerdeler and Schacht alone retained a certain optimism.

These two appear to have determined upon a fresh attempt to enlighten the Western Powers in respect of Hitler's intentions. Accompanied by the apparently omnipresent Gisevius, they journeyed to Switzerland in the latter part of March 1939 and there at Ouchy met with a mysterious individual who is severally described by Gisevius as 'a person with considerable influence in London and Paris political circles' and of having 'excellent connection with the British and French Governments'.[1] To him Goerdeler and Schacht unburdened themselves of their hopes and fears. Though the conspiracy could promise nothing comparable to the planned revolt of September 1938 — that carefully organized uprising which had withered at the first touch of reality — something, however, might still be achieved. But here the chronicler of this secret conclave becomes confused. In his evidence at Nuremberg he asserted that the object of this warning was to persuade the British and French Governments to maintain a firm stand and to reiterate, both privately to Hitler and publicly to the German people, that any further step towards aggression would mean war. 'It appeared to us that the only possibility was to warn the Generals and to get them to revolt.' So much for Gisevius before the International Military Tribunal; but in his book he gives a somewhat different picture. 'We could no longer promise that a firm stand by the Western Powers would set off a revolt of the Generals. That chance had been lost. The prime task now was not to force a revolt but to prevent a war.' Amid these contradictions it is only possible to conjecture at the truth, but it would seem that what Goerdeler and Schacht wished to convey to London and Paris was that Hitler was certainly determined to go eastwards to Danzig and to Warsaw, and to the rich black soil of the Ukraine and the rich black oil of the Caucasus and of Rumania. It is possible that they might still have laboured under the illusion that a determined opposition by Britain and France might deter the *Führer* from such a course or equally that it might incite the Generals to remove him in order to prevent

---

[1] Gisevius, ii, 99-100; Evidence before the International Military Tribunal on April 25, 1946 (*Nuremberg Record*, xii, 221-2). The record of this meeting at Ouchy rests entirely on Gisevius' accounts, which are in some respects conflicting. Schacht does not mention the meeting either in his evidence at Nuremberg or in *Account Settled*.

a two-front war. If they still believed either of these things, or, indeed, if they believed as Goerdeler is said to have stated, that Nazi economy could not much longer sustain the staggering burden of Germany's intensified rearmament, they were woefully mistaken and they must have shockingly misled those in London and Paris whom they wished to influence.[1] The sole value of this talk was to re-emphasize and confirm the view already held in the West that Hitler was planning to bring about a solution of the Danzig and Corridor issues with Poland in the summer and that London and Paris should be prepared for such an eventuality.

Beck and Oster also sought to warn London, but in a more practical vein, and, on the advice of Ewald von Kleist-Schmenzin, they conveyed their warnings to Mr. Ian Colvin, correspondent in Berlin of the *News Chronicle*, who was in close touch with some of the farther-seeing officials of the British Embassy. Mr. Colvin arrived in London on March 29, and, as a result of his initial contact with the head of the Press Department of the Foreign Office, he found himself closeted first with Sir Alexander Cadogan, the Permanent Under Secretary, then with Lord Halifax, and finally, in the company of these two, with Mr. Neville Chamberlain in the Prime Minister's room at the House of Commons. So well had Mr. Colvin been briefed by his friends in Berlin and also in Warsaw, and so cogent was his evidence of Germany's intended aggression against Poland, that it is to be believed that his arrival carried that last ounce of weight needed to influence the Cabinet in favour of taking the revolutionary decision to make a direct gesture of support to Poland. Before Mr. Colvin's conversation had ended on March 29 it had been suggested to him that Britain might offer a unilateral guarantee of support to Poland in the event of Nazi aggression, an offer which was given formal expression in the Prime Minister's declaration in the House of Commons two days later.[2]

The timeliness of the warnings from Berlin and their subsequent reactions may be judged from the fact that on April 3 and 11 Hitler

---

[1] Evidence that the mysterious unknown at Ouchy reported carefully and in detail to the French Premier on his conversation with Schacht and Goerdeler was apparently forthcoming in the discovery of this report among the papers of M. Daladier after the occupation of Paris in June 1940. The local Paris branch of the *Abwehr* suppressed the file (Gisevius's evidence, *Nuremberg Record*, xii, 222).

[2] *House of Commons Debates*, March 31, 1939, col. 2415.

Mr. Colvin published his own vivid account of these conversations with Halifax and Chamberlain in an article in the *Sunday Express* of November 8, 1953. See also *Documents on British Foreign Policy*, series III, Vol. 4, Document No. 566.

The British unilateral guarantee to Poland of March 31 was transformed into a reciprocal bi-lateral agreement on the occasion of Colonel Beck's visit to London on April 3-6, 1939.

issued his first general directives for 'Operation White', the attack on Poland.[1] His whole attitude was completely contrary to that suggested by Schacht and Goerdeler at Ouchy, and very much more in consonance with the advices of Beck and Oster. The *Führer* was not bluffing. Though he may at first have believed that a repetition of Munich was possible, he soon abandoned this idea and drove forward along his self-destined path of aggression in disregard and contempt for the clearly enunciated guarantees which Britain and France had given to Poland. But though Hitler believed that London and Paris might mean business at the moment, he was confident that they could be shocked into acquiescence with his plans by means of a diplomatic weapon which he was forging secretly.

By May 23 the military leaders could no longer be in doubt as to what was in the *Führer*'s mind. On that date he summoned to his study in the *Reichskanzlei* Göring and Raeder, Halder and von Brauchitsch, Keitel and Warlimont, and Milch, Bodenschatz and Jeschonnek of the *Luftwaffe*. To them he said frankly that he had decided 'to attack Poland at the first suitable opportunity', a decision which might well result in a war with Britain and France. In such a war, declared Adolf Hitler, 'declarations of neutrality must be ignored'. The Dutch and Belgian air-bases must be occupied with lightning speed. It would be a life-and-death struggle. 'The idea that we can get off cheaply is dangerous ; there is no such possibility. We must burn our boats ; it is no longer a question of justice or injustice, but of life or death for eighty million people.'

Lest his Generals might be appalled, as they had been in the previous September, at the prospect of a two-front war, the *Führer* gave them a gleam of encouragement from his dark lantern. Should Russia side with the Western Powers, he 'would be constrained to attack Britain and France with a few annihilating blows', but, he added meaningly : 'It is not impossible that Russia will show herself to be disinterested in the destruction of Poland (*an der Zertrümmerung Polens desinteressiert zeigt*).'[2]

This was the first inkling to be given outside the *Führer*'s most intimate circle of that new course of events which had been set in motion a month before[3] when, in the course of a momentous inter-

---

[1] *IMT Document*, C-120.

[2] Minutes of a Conference held on May 23, 1939, in the *Führer*'s study in the New Reich Chancellery, Berlin, kept by Colonel Schmundt (*IMT Document*, L-79) ; also evidence of Field-Marshal Milch before U.S. Military Tribunal IV on October 13 and 15, 1948 (German transcript, p. 25201 *et seq.*).

[3] To von Brauchitsch Hitler is alleged to have remarked jocularly some time toward the end of April : 'Do you know what my next step will be ? You had better hold on to your chair while I tell you : A state visit to Moscow' (Kordt, p. 306).

view with von Weizsäcker on April 17, the Soviet Ambassador had uttered the fateful words that 'there exists for Russia no reason why she should not live with us [Germany] on a normal footing, and from normal the relations might become better and better'.¹ From this somewhat vague *détente* in Russo-German relations there was to emerge, not however without hesitations and set-backs, that Nazi-Soviet Pact with which Hitler proposed not only to safeguard his operations against Poland but also to overwhelm with menace the statesmen of Britain and France.²

From the date of this conference in the *Führer*'s study there is no shadow of excuse that the leaders of the Armed Forces of the Reich did not know fully and entirely what was expected of them by their Supreme Commander. Since April 11, with the issue of the special order for 'Operation White',³ they had known that the attack on Poland, when it came, was to be made in such a manner as to constitute a violation not only of the Hague Convention governing such proceedings but also those provisions of the Weimar Constitution, to which they were bound by oath, which ordained that a declaration of war could only be made with the consent of the *Reichstag*.⁴ Now they had also been informed that, in the event of Britain and France honouring their commitments to Poland — an eventuality which the *Führer* at the time thought highly probable — the German Army and Air Force were to attack and occupy the Low Countries in defiance of general international law and of specific undertakings to the contrary. Thenceforth the Generals could not plead ignorance of what was in the *Führer*'s mind, the planning directives for the attack upon Poland, and upon Belgium, Holland and Luxembourg, stem from this stark declaration of May 23. The blueprint for aggression had been unrolled before their eyes.

But as the summer months drew on towards early autumn a new influence of immense importance occurred in the calculations of OKW and OKH. That which the *Führer* had softly hinted at in his

¹ Memorandum by the State Secretary in the German Foreign Office, Freiherr von Weizsäcker, dated April 17, 1939 (*Nazi-Soviet Relations 1939–1941* (U.S. Department of State, Washington, 1948), pp. 1-2).

² Apart from the documentary record of the negotiations preceding the Nazi-Soviet Pact of August 23, 1939, which is given in *Nazi-Soviet Relations*, see L. B. Namier, *Diplomatic Prelude* (London, 1948) and *Europe in Decay* (1950); A. Rossi, *Deux Ans d'alliance germano-soviétique 1939–1941* (Paris, 1949); translation, *The Russian-German Alliance 1939–1941* (London, 1950); Bernard Newman, *The Captured Archives* (London, 1948); Wheeler-Bennett, *Munich*, pp. 388-413.

³ See particularly the 'Legal Basis' in special order for 'Operation White', issued on April 11, 1939 (*IMT Document*, C-120, F).

⁴ Article 45, Section 2, of the Weimar Constitution; 'Declaration of war and conclusion of peace are effected by *Reich* law'; Article 68, Section 2: '*Reich* laws are enacted by the *Reichstag*'.

discourse of May 23 was clearly manifesting itself as a probability. The British and the French negotiators in Moscow were being fooled and hoodwinked by the parallel negotiations in process between Moscow and Berlin. To those of the *Generalität* who had been nurtured in the belief of the Seeckt School, the idea of a *rapprochement* with Russia heralded a return to sanity and the opening up of vistas of opportunities which had been closed to them since 1935. An agreement with Russia would mean that they could prosecute their war against Poland, which on the later showing of von Blomberg and Blaskowitz, they had regarded as 'a sacred duty though a sad necessity' long before Hitler had come to power,[1] not only without let or hindrance from Russia but positively with her approval and perhaps with her participation. An agreement with Russia would mean that Britain and France would either not venture to come to the support of Poland or, if they did so, that they could be dealt with without the danger of a rear-attack from the Red Army.[2] An agreement with Russia would make possible the post-war division of spoils on an amicable basis both in Eastern Europe and in Asia, where a Russo-German *rapprochement* must bring with it a resumption of those good relations with China to which von Seeckt had always attached such importance and which had been sacrificed to the politico-ideological predilection of Ribbentrop's *Dienststelle* for a Japanese alignment. In short, the happy prospect of an agreement with Russia, and consequently of 'a quick war and a quick peace' with Poland, transcended all other influences in the thinking of the *Generalität* as a whole, and gravely weakened any chances of success which might have existed for the undermining by the conspirators of their confidence in the *Führer* and of their allegiance to him.

Yet the conspirators were not idle. The shock of Prague had passed off and once again they were engaged in the old game of maintaining contact with the outside world and seeking to seduce the Generals. These activities were stimulated after Oster was able to give his fellow-plotters definite information concerning the planned aggression against Poland and the progress of the negotiations with Moscow. During the summer weeks a number of those engaged in the conspiracy left Germany on some pretext or another. Pechel conferred in London with Brüning, then visiting England from

[1] See above, p. 228.
[2] So great was the confidence in OKW and OKH that the war with Poland would be untrammelled by intervention from either East or West that when Jodl returned from Vienna on August 23 to take over the post of Chief of the Operation Branch, he found that nothing had been prepared except the plans for the attack on Poland (evidence given on June 5, 1946, *Nuremberg Record*, xv, 372).

Harvard University, who told him that von Hammerstein — 'a man without nerves' — was the only man who could remove Hitler.[1] Goerdeler was also in London in the course of May, as were also Adam von Trott zu Solz, Helmuth von Moltke and Fabian von Schlabrendorff. While the two former capitalized on their Oxford contacts to bring them into touch with the Prime Minister and Lord Halifax, von Schlabrendorff concentrated on the more dissident Conservative elements, and in talks with Mr. Churchill and Lord Lloyd gave them detailed reasoning why war with Poland was imminent and why an attempt at mediation by Britain would be doomed to failure because a pact with Russia had already been virtually concluded.[2]

It is difficult to ascertain exactly what the conspirators wanted to achieve at this moment, or what they desired to gain from Britain and France. They knew that war with Poland was now inevitable and they plainly recognized that in Britain, at any rate, a new spirit was abroad which would stomach no return to the policy of appeasement and which was sufficiently strong to carry France with it, even into war. All that had been asked from the Western Powers in 1938, therefore, was forthcoming in 1939. But in Germany itself the situation had changed and certain elements, essential for the successful formula for removing the Nazis, were lacking.

In the first place, whereas the idea of a war with Czechoslovakia had been unpopular because it had been believed that it would develop into a general war, the traditional and mutual hatred between German and Pole rendered the idea of a war with Poland not entirely unpalatable to the German people, especially in view of the fact that they now believed it impossible that the Western Powers would take any action hostile to the *Führer*. In addition, the Generals, who had doubted the ability of the German Army to conquer Czechoslovakia if backed by Britain, France, and Russia, were confident of victory over a Poland deserted and alone. The rumour of a pact with Russia confirmed the view that at least one member of the military combination which might have confronted them in September 1938 would soon be persuaded to change sides, and the elimination of Russia as an active opponent would, in all probability, carry with it at least the neutralization of Britain and France. The Generals, therefore, saw almost within the realm of realization their eternal ambition of a more than 51 per cent chance of victory in 'a quick war and a quick peace'. Why, under such circumstances, should

---

[1] Pechel, p. 153. '*Gebt mir eine Truppe, dann wird's an mir nicht fehlen*', was the fiercely smiling comment of von Hammerstein when Pechel retailed Brüning's remark. [2] Schlabrendorff, pp. 28-9.

HITLER AND THE ARMY

they overthrow the man or the régime who had brought this wonder
to pass ?

What was then actually in the minds of those men who came to
London in the summer of 1939 ? They knew that under the circumstances a military revolt for the purpose of stopping Hitler from
going to war was impossible ; that the loyalty of the Generals could
only be tampered with after some disaster had been sustained by
German arms, or at best, in order to stave off some such disaster.
They were anxious, therefore, to obviate any possible risk of a
repetition of Munich — though neither Hitler, nor Chamberlain,
nor Daladier were under any illusion that this gambit could or
should be repeated — and to ensure that Britain and France should
insist upon their intention of opposing Nazi aggression even by force
of arms. If the Generals could really be persuaded that this was
true they might conceivably act to restrain Hitler, but, on the other
hand, if they did not — and this was Goerdeler's thesis with which
Schacht disagreed — German war economy was so over-strained
and ineffective that the Reich could not possibly support a prolonged war.

But did the emissaries from Berlin really speak their full minds ?
Was there not already some idea in the hearts of at least some of
them that it might be possible to eat their cake and have it too ; to
drive a sort of *Kuhhandel* with the Western Powers and make a
price with them for overthrowing Hitler ? Certainly this aspect
developed at a later stage in the proceedings,[1] but it is not impossible
that even at this early date it was thought of.

There is no reason to suppose that it should be otherwise. What
bound many of the conspirators together was not only their bitter
opposition to the Nazi tyranny, but also a strong sense of patriotic
nationalism. What they plotted to do was no mere fanatical, nihilistic
attempt upon a ruler, or even a tyrant, but an act of salvation for
Germany, an attempt to save her from future disasters and, as a
corollary, to conserve as much as possible of what she already held,
and perhaps a little more. 'I am a good patriot', were the words with
which von Schlabrendorff began his conversation with Mr. Churchill,
and certainly Adam von Trott and Helmuth von Moltke in their
conversations with the present writer at that time gave no reason to
believe that they were less so.[2] Von Trott, in particular, had about

---

[1] See below, pp. 444 *et seq.*

[2] Adam von Trott zu Solz (1909–44) was the second son of a former Royal
Prussian *Kultusminister*, and came of a Hessian family of liberal conservative traditions. Educated at Kurt Hahn's school at Schloss Salem, he came to Mansfield
College, Oxford, in 1931 and later entered Balliol as a Rhodes Scholar. Returning
to Germany in 1934 he practised law in Cassel, and in 1937 and 1938 was employed

him a certain confused political mysticism, a vague Hegelianism, which induced in him, not, to be sure, the worship of the *Führerprinzip*, but a deep veneration for German military and political traditions and what he believed to be the innate integrity of the German soul. There was also not lacking a false sense of realism, and a belief in power politics and his own part in them. Von Moltke, on the other hand, had a wider sense of the meaning of things, a greater spiritual integrity and a more realistic appreciation of the vital issues at stake. Both were strong Nationalists and both, for example, though they deplored the spirit of the Munich Agreement and the subsequent dismemberment of Czechoslovakia, expressed strong anti-Czech sentiments, and from neither was there forthcoming any indication that a 'de-nazified' Germany would be prepared to forgo Hitler's annexation of Austria and the Sudetenland. Indeed it was hinted that Britain and France might well reward the conspirators, if successful, with the return of Germany's former colonial possessions.

Such being the case, the possibility cannot be entirely disregarded that, in the case of at least some of the plotters, the urgent anxiety that Britain and France should stand fast in their resistance to German aggression, even to the point of war, was not directed further than the removal of Hitler and the Nazi régime. In any hostilities which took place it was fairly certain that the Germans would defeat the Poles, and once Polish military resistance had been crushed, and Danzig and the Corridor were in German hands, a successful revolt against Hitler would put the new régime in the strong position of having all they desired in the East and of offering terms to the West, not on the basis of the *status quo ante* but on that of the existing situation. Since there were many in France — and even some in England — who were unenthusiastic about 'dying for Danzig', and since many in both countries had long doubted the wisdom of the German-Polish territorial settlement of 1919, and

on a research project in China by the Institute of Pacific Relations. A friend of Albrecht von Bernstorff and a protégé of von Weizsäcker, von Trott was taken into the German Foreign Office at the outbreak of war, where he became identified with the inner councils of the conspiracy.

Helmuth von Moltke (1907–45), great-great-nephew of the Field Marshal, was born of German-South African parents, both of whom were convinced Christian Scientists. Determined to follow a legal career, he practised first as an international lawyer in Berlin and was later called to the English Bar. In London he became an intimate friend of Mr. Lionel Curtis, whose frequent guest he was at All Souls, Oxford. On the outbreak of war von Moltke was attached to the *Amt Ausland* of OKW. Later he became the leader of a group of 'planners for the German future' known as the 'Kreisau Circle', to which Adam von Trott also belonged (see below, pp. 545 *et seq.*). Both were executed after the failure of the *Putsch* of July 20, 1944.

were still prepared to accept German claims to the incorporation of Austria and the Sudetenland within the Greater German Reich, the chances of success for such a claim might not have been negligible.

There came a time, however, when certain of the conspiracy in Berlin, and particularly the Weizsäcker circle, stood aghast at the forces which had been aroused in Britain as a result of German perfidy. They could not comprehend nor gauge that 'Fury of Patient Men' which had whipped the phlegmatic Britons — usually so prone to follow the apostolic injunction to be 'slow to speak, slow to wrath' [1] — into a stolid and unrelenting determination to withstand aggression whencesoever it might come. The unconditional promise of support to Poland, and the opening of negotiations with Moscow which had followed it, were characterized as over-hasty and irresponsible by the pundits of 'resistance' in the Wilhelmstrasse. The subsequent extension of the Anglo-French system of guarantees to virtually every state which might be menaced by German aggression was deprecated by von Weizsäcker and his clever young men because it was immediately represented to the German people as an attempt by Britain to encircle Germany.[2] Such indeed it was, and the only weakness in British policy was that, instead of proclaiming its objective as a 'peace bloc', which nobody believed, it did not openly declare that it aimed at nothing less than encircling Germany with a view to restraining her from further convulsive outbreaks of the *Furor Teutonicus*.

In June von Weizsäcker despatched Erich Kordt to London to reinforce the arguments of his brother Theo with the British Foreign Office that the policy of guarantees against aggression upon which the British Government had embarked in March, far from acting as a deterrent to Hitler, was more calculated to provoke the *Führer* to take precipitate action.[3]

Here again one is forced to consider whether this criticism by the Weizsäcker group of the British policy of the 'blank cheque' to Poland was not, consciously or subconsciously, motivated by a desire to see that country forced by some 'Munich Settlement' to surrender the Corridor and Danzig to Germany. It might well be to a non-Hitler Germany that the surrender should be made, in fact it might well figure as a part of the *Kuhhandel*, but that Germany should aggrandize herself at the expense of Poland was surely within their minds. There is more than a suspicion of casuistry in the argument that the British guarantee might be taken by irresponsible

[1] The Epistle General of St. James, i, 19.
[2] Von Weizsäcker, pp. 236-7 ; Kordt, pp. 311-12.   [3] Kordt, pp. 313-19.

elements in Poland as an authorization for provocative action.[1] What, it seems, the Weizsäcker group were really aiming at was an undertaking by Britain that she would bring pressure to bear upon Poland to make territorial concessions to a Germany which had eliminated Hitler and expunged the record of the Nazi régime. In other words, the fundamental principles of German foreign policy remain the same whatever the régime in power.

And, in Berlin, as the days drew fatefully toward that September 1, which had been set as the latest deadline for 'Operation White', the leaders of the conspiracy renewed their efforts to persuade the *Führer* to forgo a war and, alternatively, the Generals to prevent his making one. In an attempt to influence Keitel and, through him, Hitler, General Thomas drew up a memorandum, which after careful discussion with Goerdeler, Beck, Schacht and others, he submitted to the Chief of OKW in the middle of August. This paper said in effect that the idea of a 'quick war and a quick peace' was a complete illusion. World conditions were such that Hitler's projected attack upon Poland, far from being 'an isolated war', would unleash a world conflict which would inevitably develop into a long-drawn-out war of attrition, and for which, without powerful allies, Germany lacked the necessary raw-material and food supplies.

As Thomas read his threnody, Keitel interrupted him with the petulant remark that all his conjectures were purely academic, as the danger of a world war did not exist. France was too degenerate, Britain too decadent, America too uninterested to fight for Poland; and when Thomas begged leave to disagree on grounds of better information, he was sharply reproved for becoming infected with defeatist pacifism. The *Führer*'s greatness and superior intelligence, said Keitel, would solve the whole problem to the advantage of Germany.[2]

As a soldier and a general staff officer Keitel must have recognized the ring of truth in Thomas's warnings, but his soldierly qualities had long ago been transmuted into pliant sycophancy and his better judgment blunted and subdued in the odious flattery of the lick-spittle. His replies to Thomas were the reflection of the views which Hitler had expressed within his immediate circle with

---

[1] It is not without interest that there is to-day in circulation in Bonn the thesis that the real responsibility for the Second World War lies with Britain, who by giving her *Blankoscheck* to Poland afforded such encouragement to the irresponsible and extreme elements of Polish Nationalism that they pursued so provocative a policy that Hitler, despite his declared preference for peace, was forced to go to war. It is added that, though, of course, the Nazi foreign policy was highly reprehensible, every one was agreed that Poland should have been made to disgorge Danzig and the Corridor.   [2] Thomas, *Gedanken und Ereignisse*.

increasing confidence throughout the months of July and August. The *Führer*'s self-confidence had become overweening and un-bounded, and had infected the members of his immediate entourage with a similar sense of elated optimism.

At last the moment had come to spring his great diplomatic *coup* upon the world, that *coup* which should with one stroke of genius neutralize the East and petrify the West. Serene and confident, Hitler, on the morning of August 22, bade farewell to Ribbentrop on his departure for Moscow to sign the Nazi-Soviet Pact of Non-Aggression, and himself flew to the Berghof, where in the morning and afternoon he delivered two allocutions to his military and naval and air-force commanders, reflecting his mood of the moment, which was one of unrelieved optimism and fulsome self-congratulation.

'There will probably never again be a man with such authority or who has the confidence of the whole German people as I have', he told his listeners. 'My existence is therefore a factor of great value. But I can be eliminated at any moment by a criminal or a lunatic. There is no time to lose. War must come in my lifetime.'

Whereas to a similar gathering on May 23 he had expressed the almost complete certainty that war with Poland would entail war with Britain and France,[1] he was now equally positive to the contrary because of the conclusion of the Pact with Moscow. 'The likelihood of an intervention by the Western Powers in a conflict was not great. It seemed impossible to him that any responsible British statesman would take the risk of a long war for England in this situation. As for France, she could not afford a long and bloody war; she had been dragged along, against her will, by England. 'I have struck this instrument [assistance of Russia] from the hands of the Western Powers', declared the *Führer*. 'Now we can strike at the heart of Poland. To the best of our knowledge the military road is free.'

Nor did he let slip the opportunity to abuse those among his Generals who had previously doubted the wisdom of his 'intuition'. He reminded them that a year before they had said : 'England will intervene in favour of Czechoslovakia even with her armed forces'. When this had not happened, the majority of the doubters had admitted their error. 'We admit that we were wrong and the *Führer* was right', they said. 'He won because he had better nerves to stick it out than we had.' But this had created the impression that he had been bluffing and that, if only Britain and France had accepted his challenge of a threat to war, he would have given in.

---

[1] See above, p. 438.

This impression was now detrimental to his policies, for it was essential that the attack on Poland should be unencumbered by a simultaneous war in the West, and because of the idea that he had been, and was perhaps still, bluffing, there had been an added determination in the British and French attitudes which had been lacking a year before. But this would disappear when the news from Moscow was published; still, if they wanted war, they should have it. 'Our enemies', said Hitler, 'are men below average, not men of action, not masters. They are little worms. I saw them at Munich.' 'My only fear', he told his Generals, 'is that at the last moment some *Schweinehund* will make a proposal for mediation.' [1]

And then at the close of the second conference, the *Führer* had given the order to put 'Operation White' into effect. X-Day was to be August 26; Y-time 04.30 hours; the object of the operation, 'The elimination of the existing forces in Poland'.[2]

Hitler need not have been apprehensive of a second Munich. Such an eventuality was as far beyond the realm of possibility as some lunar or Martian intervention. The British reply to the Nazi-Soviet Pact was contained in Mr. Chamberlain's letter to the *Führer* of August 23, and the conclusion of the Anglo-Polish Treaty of Mutual Assistance two days later. While anxious as ever to avoid war, if this were compatible with honour, Britain was no longer to be intimidated by threats and menaces. She too was not bluffing.

This was apparent to the leaders of the conspiracy, whose contacts with London were of the best, but not to Hitler, who was still under the influence of Ribbentrop's disastrous opinions and his own auto-intoxication of assurance, and it was certainly not apparent to OKW in the Bendlerstrasse and to OKH now established at Zossen, eighteen miles to the south of Berlin, where the *Führer*'s speeches of August 22 had created an atmosphere of almost sublime confidence and satisfaction. Those who desired war now felt assured of it under the most favourable conditions, while those who preferred a bloodless victory still clung to the belief that Poland would at the

[1] Though no other record of these meetings on August 22, 1939, was supposed to have been taken besides the official minutes kept by Colonel Schmundt (*IMT Document*, PS-1014), several of those present made an account of one or both of the *Führer's* speeches immediately afterwards. Two of these which have survived are anonymous (*IMT Documents*, L-3 and PS-798) and in one of them the marginal note occurs that after the conclusion of the first speech Göring leapt on the table and, after offering 'bloodthirsty thanks and bloody promises', danced around 'like a savage'. There also exist the notes made by General-Admiral Hermann Boehm on the evening of August 22 after his return to the Vier Jahreszeiten Hotel in Munich (*Raeder Defence Document Book No. 2*, Document 27, p. 144) and a further account in Halder's Diary for August 22.

[2] Halder's and Jodl's Diaries for August 23, 1939.

last moment capitulate under the menaces of German military might and the desertion of her allies.[1]

The Generals had heard Hitler say clearly and plainly that his intention in entering Poland was nothing less than extermination — 'I have ordered to the East my "Death Head Units" with the order to kill without pity or mercy all men, women and children of Polish race or language' — but this had apparently not dismayed them, since the killing was to be done by the SS and SD and not by the Army. They had also heard their Supreme Commander boast that he would dress others of these Party bravoes in Polish uniforms and have them stage attacks in the Protectorate and in Upper Silesia, thereby creating a faked *raison d'être* for counter-measures.[2] But neither did this ingenious 'propaganda device' shock the sensibilities of the Army, for this too would be carried out by Party organizations. Those Generals who were subsequently appalled at what they saw in Poland and in Russia — and there were those who were appalled — could not plead that they had not had fair warning of the *Führer's* intentions, and, furthermore, of his declared purpose to attack the Soviet Union as soon as the occasion presented itself — 'My pact with Poland [in 1934] was only meant to stall for time, and, gentlemen, to Russia will happen just what I have practised with Poland. After Stalin's death (he is seriously ill) we will crush the Soviet Union.'

No man who participated in the *Führer* Conferences of August 22, 1939, and there were present the highest ranking officers of the three services, could thereafter plead ignorance of the fact that Hitler had laid bare his every depth of infamy before them, and they had raised no voice in protest either then or later. 'A few doubtful ones remained silent', says one of the records. In silent condonation they had accepted complicity in crimes which were later adjudged to constitute 'a disgrace to the honourable profession of arms'.[3]

[1] Halder Interrogation of February 26, 1946.

[2] This device was actually carried out as a result of collaborations between OKW, the *Abwehr* and the SD. The seizure of the wireless station of Gleiwitz, the incident alleged by Berlin to have actually caused the beginning of hostilities with Poland, was accomplished by these means. (See memorandum of a conversation between Keitel and Canaris on August 17, 1939 (*IMT Document*, PS-795) and affidavit sworn by General Lahousen at Nuremberg on January 21, 1946.)

[3] In acquitting the German General Staff and High Command of the charge of being a criminal organization, the International Military Tribunal in its Judgment delivered at Nuremberg on September 30, 1946, had this to say: 'They have been responsible in large measure for the miseries and suffering that have fallen upon millions of men, women and children. They have been a disgrace to the honourable profession of arms. Without their military guidance the aggressive ambitions of Hitler and his fellow Nazis would have been academic and sterile. Although they were not a group falling within the words of the Charter, they were

Those who acquiesced in silence were perhaps more contemptible than those who actively participated.

In this frame of mind the Generals were certainly in no mood to respond to overtures from disaffected elements within the Reich. When Schacht endeavoured to go to Zossen to remind von Brauchitsch and Halder of their oath to the Constitution which did not permit of a declaration of war without the previous consent of the *Reichstag*, the Commander-in-Chief of the Army sent word that if Schacht set foot in OKH he would have him arrested,[1] while to a written appeal from Beck, the last letter to pass between them, begging him to reconsider before it was too late, von Brauchitsch did not even vouchsafe a reply.[2] He had promised his *Führer* that the war with Poland would be a triumph of the technique of *Blitzkrieg* [3] — a promise which he was destined to keep most scrupulously — and no power on earth should prevent his sending the field-grey legions and squadrons across the Polish border at dawn on August 26. Or so he thought.

It was, however, into this 'unpassioned beauty of a great machine' that Hitler himself threw a monkey-wrench. On the evening of August 25 there came to Keitel and Jodl in the Bendlerstrasse and to von Brauchitsch and Halder at Zossen the imperative command to postpone the final and irrevocable stages of 'Operation White'. The *Führer*'s 'intuition' had counselled a postponement.

In effect, Hitler had been gravely disappointed in the effect of his Muscovy blitz upon Britain and France. He had barely credited

certainly a ruthless military caste. The contemporary German militarism flourished briefly with its recent ally, National Socialism, as well or better than it had in the generations of the past. . . . This must be said' (*Nuremberg Record*, xxii, 522). Five years later, on January 22, 1951, General Eisenhower, newly appointed Commander-in-Chief of SHAPE, announced in a public statement at Bad Homburg that he did not consider German military honour to have been sullied.

[1] Schacht, pp. 139-40.

[2] Gisevius, ii, 116. According to the same source, Beck also wrote to Halder and succeeded in arranging an interview at which, though agreement was reached in principle, Beck failed to convince his successor, who was anxious to acquire Danzig and the Corridor before discarding Hitler, that the psychological moment to strike was before, rather than after, the beginning of hostilities. At the close of the interview the two men shook hands for the last time. Halder had been weighed in the balance and found wanting in will-power ('*Ihm fehlte der Wille*', Gisevius, ii, 117). Thenceforth Beck never placed complete reliance upon him as a colleague in the conspiracy, despite Halder's many protestations of sympathy and willingness to co-operate.

[3] 'Colonel-General von Brauchitsch has promised me to bring the war against Poland to a conclusion within a few weeks. If he would have told me that it would take me two years, or even one year only, I would not have given the order to march and would have temporarily entered into an alliance with England instead of Russia.' (Hitler to his Generals, August 22, 1939 (*IMT Document*, L-3).)

the calm reaffirmation of Britain's attitude contained in Mr. Chamberlain's letter, the purport of which had been conveyed to him at the Berghof by the British Ambassador on August 23. On the following evening he returned to Berlin, and throughout the morning of August 25 he looked confidently for news of the fall of the Chamberlain and Daladier Governments at the hands of the 'friends of peace' in London and in Paris; when this did not materialize he fell into a frenzy of rage and gave the final order that the invasion of Poland should begin at dawn the next morning. But at last it had begun to be borne in on him that Britain and France were undeterred by the conclusion of the Nazi-Soviet Pact, that this attempt of Hitler to petrify them had failed, and that calmly, courageously, and illogically they were prepared to be constant after their fashion. If Germany attacked Poland, Britain and France would declare war.

Forthwith the *Führer* began a series of anxious conversations with the British and French Ambassadors in an effort to persuade their Governments not to interfere in matters which were clearly the affairs solely of the Germans and the Poles, and which further Anglo-French intervention could only exacerbate to a point of danger. He also condoned a wild and musical-comedy appeal to Britain by Göring through the oblique agency of Hr. Birger Dahlerus.[1] To no avail; at five-thirty that same afternoon (August 25) there was signed at the Foreign Office in London a formal treaty of Anglo-Polish Alliance, news of which reached Berlin some twenty minutes later. Almost simultaneously came tidings from Rome that in the event of a major war involving the Western Powers Italy would not be able to bear her part as a partner in the Pact of Steel without substantial subsidies in military supplies and war materials.[2]

If the *Führer* still wanted to have his 'little war' against Poland, or even an uninterrupted 'bloodless victory', all depended upon his ability to weaken the British attitude, for if he could accomplish this he knew that he would have no difficulty with the French, who were manifestly less and less desirous of being called upon to honour their Polish obligation. Hitler had offered an alliance to Britain and a guarantee of her empire, on condition that his own colonial claims were met in a generous spirit. Until the result of this gambit was

---

[1] For the story of this fantastic and ludicrous episode see the evidence of Göring and of Dahlerus at Nuremberg on March 19 and 21, 1946 (*Nuremberg Record*, ix, 475-91, 495-601); also Dahlerus's book, *Sista Försöket, London-Berlin, Sommaren 1939* (Stockholm, 1945); translation, *The Last Attempt* (London, 1947), together with Professor Sir Lewis Namier's essay, 'An Interloper in Diplomacy' (*Diplomatic Prelude*, pp. 417-33).

[2] Namier, pp. 303-81; Wheeler-Bennett, *Munich*, pp. 416-25.

known he must mark time. A temporary postponement of his plans
was inescapable, but it was only to be temporary. 'I must see
whether we can eliminate British intervention',[1] he telephoned to
Göring, and to Keitel and von Brauchitsch he issued orders cancelling
the dawn attack on the following day.[2]

To the conspirators the order to postpone 'Operation White'
brought varying reactions. In the main the civilians were cautious
and suspicious of the real motives behind so dramatic and drastic a
decision, but among the *Abwehr* there was the greatest jubilation.
A man who claimed to be a military leader and who issued orders
to attack at 2.30 P.M. and cancelled them five hours later could no
longer be taken seriously by the Army — or indeed by anyone else.
There was no longer any necessity for a *Putsch*, for Hitler would
now fall by his own weight. 'The *Führer* is finished' ('*Der Führer
ist fertig*') was Oster's verdict on the evening of August 25, and his
view was shared by Canaris, who on the following morning delivered
himself of the opinion that : 'Peace has been saved for the next
twenty years'.[3]

And indeed it appears that this rosy wishful-thinking prevailed
widely throughout Germany. The general expectation was for a
week of negotiations followed by the withdrawal of British and
French opposition and the capitulation of Poland. The conspirators,
or at least some of them, considered that the crisis had subsided,
since Hitler was about to make concessions to Britain and France in
the sense that he would not attack Poland, and that, if his prestige
ever recovered from the blow, he would certainly be less bellicose
than before and might even change his entourage. So high did the
barometer of optimism rise that Goerdeler left for Sweden on
August 26 ; Hitler addressed the *Reichstag* in moderate terms on

---

[1] Göring's testimony taken at Nuremberg, August 29, 1945 (*IMT Document*,
TC-90, pp. 7-8).

[2] Halder, in his diary, gives three different times for the issuing of the order
of postponement for 'Operation White'. On August 25 he records that he received
news of the Anglo-Polish Treaty and of the postponement at 19.30 hours, and that
Keitel confirmed the latter at 20.35. In a reconstruction of the position written
on the following day (August 26) he says that the *Führer* gave the order at 15.02,
which must clearly be an error since the Anglo-Polish Treaty was not signed until
17.40. In a long chronological table entered in the diary on August 28 Halder
gives the time of the announcement of the Treaty as 13.40 (!) and of the issuing
of the order as 20.00 hours. Jodl's Diary contains no mention of the matter. The
OKM (*Oberkommando der Marine*) War Diary (extracts from which were quoted
at Nuremberg as *IMT Document*, C-170) gives the time of the receipt of the order
as 20.30 hours.

[3] Gisevius, ii, 135-6 ; Kordt, p. 329. In his evidence before the International Military Tribunal on April 25, 1946, Gisevius gave Canaris's estimate of
the period for which the peace of Europe had been saved as *fifty* years ! (*Nuremberg
Record*, xii, 225).

August 27 ; and as late as August 30 the Ministry of Economics informed the Foreign Office that there would be no war — to which von Weizsäcker replied over the telephone that they must be drunk ! [1]

Almost alone among the Generals the indefatigable Georg Thomas clung persistently to his inveterate pessimism. On the 27th (Sunday) he sought out Keitel and recapitulated the arguments which he and Schacht had embodied in their memorandum of a week earlier,[2] now reinforcing them with graphically illustrated and statistical evidence of the military-economic impossibility for Germany to win a war against the Western Powers. As before, Keitel laughed at his fears, and on the following morning brought him the reassurance of the *Führer* that he by no means shared Thomas's anxiety over the risk of a world war.[3] The General remained unconvinced.

Whatever impression Hitler may have wished to convey to Thomas, there is no doubt that by August 28 he had decided upon war with Poland, whatever the cost. He had dithered somewhat at the outset, partly through chagrin at the failure of his *coup* with Moscow to terrify the British and partly on account of that strange ambivalence of love and hate which he entertained for Britain ; that same complex which prompted him to try to avoid war with her now and to conclude a — to his way of thinking — generous peace with her after the glorious disaster of Dunkirk. But by August 28 the 'love element' in the complex had begun to wane and 'hatred of Britain', coupled with the inherent blood-lust of German toward Pole, was now in the ascendant. 'If I am pushed to it, I shall wage even a two-front war', he said to von Brauchitsch, and authorized his Commander-in-Chief to regard September 1 as X-Day, the exact hour of attack to be determined later.[4]

On the day following, Hitler had progressed still further along the road urged by the calamitous Ribbentrop and the noxious Himmler, who were by now his only advisers. He had now determined upon the diplomatic strategy to be employed before the attack. The British had offered mediation and the settlement of the Danzig and Corridor issues by means of free negotiation ; they had urged the Polish Government to send a plenipotentiary to Berlin for this purpose, and Hitler had demanded his presence by August 30. If the Poles surrendered, well and good, but he had now no intention of allowing the issue to be settled peacefully. After a briefing from von Brauchitsch, Halder could enter in his diary : 'The Poles will come to Berlin on August 30 ; on August 31 the

---

[1] Hassell, pp. 77-81.   [2] See above, p. 445.
[3] Thomas, *Gedanken und Ereignisse*.   [4] Halder's Diary, August 28, 1939.

negotiations will blow up. On September 1 we start to use force.'[1]
But even this schedule of perfidy was not destined to be adhered
to. On the night of August 30 the British Ambassador, Sir Nevile
Henderson, had his stormy interview with Ribbentrop. The Poles,
wary of the fate of Schuschnigg and Hacha, would not send their
plenipotentiary to Berlin without certain guarantees in advance.
Hitler saw fit to descry in this a breach of faith, and Ribbentrop's
behaviour to Sir Nevile Henderson on the night of August 30, when
he gabbled through a list of terms to be offered to Poland and refused
to transmit a copy, was merely a rôle in a farce designed to show
that Poland and her allies had clearly put themselves in the wrong,
and that the *Führer* now considered himself to have regained his
full freedom of action.

Very early the next morning (August 31) von Hassell was
urgently summoned to the Foreign Office by the State Secretary,
who, in a state of great distress, explained what had happened on
the previous evening and begged von Hassell to see both Sir Nevile
Henderson and Göring as soon as possible in a final effort for peace.
Henderson should persuade the Polish Ambassador, Lipski, and also
the British Government, to put pressure on Warsaw to send an
envoy to Berlin immediately, or at least to announce their firm
intention of doing so. Göring should be made to understand that
Ribbentrop and Himmler were digging the graves of the Reich and
that, if they succeeded in their policy, Karinhall would go up in flames.[2]

Von Hassell undertook both missions, and history is a witness of
his failure. It would have taken a greater man than either von
Hassell or von Weizsäcker to stem the forces of fate at that moment.
But nevertheless they tried.[3] Göring promised his support for

---

[1] Halder's Diary, August 29, 1939.
[2] Hassell (August 31, 1939), pp. 81-5 ; Weizsäcker, pp. 259-60.
[3] What exactly it was that these diplomatic 'oppositionists' were trying to do
in Berlin and London — for, simultaneously with the efforts of von Hassell and
von Weizsäcker, Theodor Kordt was secretly meeting Sir Robert Vansittart in
the home of Conwell-Evans (Kordt, pp. 377-8) — is not entirely clear. Admittedly
they were working to preserve peace, but to what specific purpose ? The only
alternatives to war were a capitulation either by Hitler or by Poland. Neither
von Weizsäcker nor any of his colleagues can have had any doubt at this period
as to the *Führer*'s intention of going to war unless his demands upon Poland were
met *in toto*, and that he would even prefer a recourse to arms to a peaceful settlement. There remained only the capitulation of Poland. Is it possible that the
Weizsäcker group of 'Resistance' in the Foreign Office, who had always regarded
the British guarantee to Poland as a provocative action, were in reality working
for a 'respectable' Munich settlement which should give Germany all that she had
ever demanded from Poland — by peaceful means ? It must never be forgotten
that these men, though genuine in their hostility to Hitler and in their desire to
preserve peace, were also good German patriots.

moderation, and Lipski was persuaded, under instructions from Warsaw, pressure from London and as a result of the joint efforts of Henderson and von Hassell, to apply for an interview with Ribbentrop. His application was made at 1 P.M.; he was not summoned until 6.10 P.M. and was then informed that as he had not appeared as a fully empowered plenipotentiary, but only as an Ambassador armed with a declaration from his Government, the position was 'unsatisfactory', despite the fact that the declaration in question made it clear that the Polish Government were 'favourably considering' a British proposal for direct negotiations between Berlin and Warsaw.[1]

To a Government anxious to preserve the peace of the world such a proposal would have presented a chance of settlement which, however slim, should not be lost. Such, however, was not the Government of Adolf Hitler. 'We want war', Ribbentrop had told Ciano as early as August 11, and war they were determined to have.[2] Scarcely had the interview with Lipski terminated than any further efforts for peace were rendered impossible. It was announced over the radio and by DNB that the *Führer* had wanted to make a generous offer to Poland, but that it had now lapsed because the Polish plenipotentiary had not appeared within the time-limit laid down on the previous day. Later in that evening of August 31 the terms of the offer — the same which had been gabbled to the British Ambassador — were made public.[3] Later still the final and definite orders to open hostilities against Poland next morning (September 1) at four-forty-five were issued to the High Commands of the armed services, although the decision to do so had been taken the previous night and therefore well before the Lipski interview.[4]

---

[1] For M. Lipski's account of this interview see his final report to his Government after the outbreak of hostilities (*Polish White Book*, No. 147). The *German White Book* makes no mention of the interview at all, but see evidence of Paul Otto Schmidt, who acted as interpreter at the interview, before the IMT on March 28, 1946 (*Nuremberg Record*, x, 198-9) and also *Statist auf diplomatischer Bühne*, p. 460.

[2] *Ciano Diaries*, p. 582. Count Ciano recorded it as his private opinion that, even if the Germans were given more than they asked for, they would attack just the same, 'because they are possessed by the demon of destruction' (*Diaries*, p. 119).

[3] *German White Book*, Nos. 466 and 468, Annex II.

[4] The War Diary of OKM for August 31 registers the receipt of the order at 12.40 hours, but Halder, who with von Brauchitsch, was making a tour of inspection of both the Eastern and Western Fronts — 'Brauchitsch and Halder are flying about over the West Wall', von Hassell recorded bitterly on August 31 (p. 84) — received word from the Reich Chancellery at 6.30 on the morning of August 31 at the Rangsdorf air-field, where he was about to take off for Frankfurt-am-Main,, that 'the jump-off order for September 1 has been given' (Halder's *Diary*, August 31, 1939).

It is clear from the record that, although they were fully cognizant of every step in the progress of events during these last fateful days, neither the Commander-in-Chief of the Army nor the Chief of the General Staff had the remotest idea of opposing the manifest intention of the *Führer* to go to war. Von Brauchitsch had ever been, and remained, a half-hearted condoner of the conspiracy, but Halder, who had been so lavish of promises in the past and was to be so generous with advice in the future, had little or no excuse. Subsequently he reasoned that it was necessary to have a war in order to bring down Hitler and his régime of evil immediately after their first defeat. Unfortunately the first defeat was a long time coming — the calculation of OKH was even at fault on this vital issue ; they computed correctly neither their own strength nor the weakness of their adversaries — and in the meantime their excuse for inactivity grew stronger and stronger.

To those of the conspirators who had persisted in living in a fools' paradise since August 25, the final and definite order to attack on September 1 came as a shock, the greater because they had purposely deluded themselves that it could not come. Canaris, who on August 25 had declared that Hitler was finished and peace assured for the next twenty years,[1] now faced the future with a shattered spirit. Across the years to come he saw in prospect the defeat and dissolution of all that he and many of his co-conspirators held dear — the Reich, the existence of the armed forces, the Officer Corps ; power, privilege, position — all would go. 'This means the end of Germany', said the Admiral in a voice choked with tears.[2]

[1] See above, p. 451.

[2] Gisevius, ii, 139. Twenty-two years before, on January 9, 1917, when at a Crown Council the Chief of German Naval Staff had persuaded the Kaiser to approve the declaration of unrestricted U-boat warfare against neutrals, with the words : 'I pledge my word as a naval officer that no American will set foot on Continental soil', the Chief of the Imperial Civil Cabinet, von Valentini, had written '*Finis Germaniae*' in his diary (Valentini, p. 149 ; Freiherr Hugo von Reischach, *Unter drei Kaisern* (Berlin, 1925), pp. 282-3).

CHAPTER 4

VICTORY IN THE EAST AND *
'PHONEY WAR'
(September 1939-June 1940)

(i)

How differently Germany went to war in 1914 and in 1939. In the First World War, after the somewhat *opéra-bouffe* ceremonies of 'party unity' in the White Salon of the Berlin Schloss and the popular demonstrations of wild enthusiasm, the Kaiser left for Imperial Headquarters, where he rapidly became a cipher. The Chief of the Great General Staff, as the executive head of OHL (*Oberste Heeresleitung*), became automatically the most powerful official of the State and, though the Emperor and the Imperial Chancellor spent long periods at Headquarters, it was increasingly apparent that their influence and authority were being more and more freely subordinated to that of the military ; a process which, under the condominium of Hindenburg and Ludendorff, achieved the extent of direct usurpation. In the four years of 1914-18 the High Command became the ruling power in Germany.

It was quite otherwise in the Second World War. There was little enthusiasm and there were no demonstrations. Though many Germans hated the Poles, and would have given their warm support to a purely German-Polish War, they were still stunned and giddy from the *volte face* of the pact with Stalin, and deeply depressed at the prospect of a general conflict, since few now doubted that Britain and France would make good their promises to Poland. In the *Reichstag* on September 1 the *Führer*'s speech was received, even by his disciplined voting-robots, with much less cheering than on previous and less important occasions,[1] and there was none of that spontaneous outburst of patriotic enthusiasm which characterized a similar occasion on August 4, 1914.

The position of the Army, moreover, was very different. Hitler began the war not only as Supreme Commander of the Armed Forces — a position analogous to that of Supreme War Lord which

[1] Shirer, p. 197.

the Kaiser had held — but as Minister of War also, having OKW under his direct authority. By 1942 he had assumed direct command of the German Army, and two years later was attempting the impossible feat of directing operations on the Western Front by telephone from East Prussia, and there was not a field commander who dared to question the *Führer*'s orders or to proceed on his own initiative. The position, prestige, and authority of the German High Command dwindled as steadily during the Second World War as it had waxed in greatness during the First, and though the courage of the German soldier and his ability as a fighting man remained undiminished to the last, it was clear beyond mistake that military genius and initiative on the highest level had become atrophied through fear, despair or frustration.

There was also the unusual and altogether extraordinary situation within OKW, in which departmental chiefs — for example Canaris and Thomas — were frankly disloyal to the régime to the extent of plotting its downfall, and in OKH, where both the Commander-in-Chief and the Chief of the General Staff were cognizant of, if not participant in, subversive conversations and activities, which grew in volume and intent as the war progressed, and never reported them to security authority. It is impossible to conceive of a situation in terms of 1914–18, in which the Chief of Military Intelligence, Colonel Nicolai, in confederation with Hindenburg, could conspire from the very beginning of the war to bring down the Empire! Though the High Command did not hesitate to manœuvre the Kaiser into abdication and flight when the war was over and lost, this did not happen until the very last moment, and even then without a deviation of personal loyalty. Whereas the last messages which the British Embassy Staff received in September 1939 were to the effect that attempts would be made to remove Hitler as soon as possible.[1]

The outbreak of war, when it finally came on September 1, 1939, brought with it conditions which both favoured and hindered the progress of the conspiracy against Hitler. On the one hand, it provided greater opportunities and wider 'cover' for those who sought action, but on the other it afforded those whose desire for action was less insistent a stronger excuse for procrastination and inertia. The exigencies of the services enabled Canaris and Oster to take men such as von Dohnanyi, Otto Kiep and Karl Spitzy under the protection of Intelligence, while, similarly, von Witzleben could bring young Count Peter Yorck von Wartenburg, a cousin of Helmuth von Moltke, on to his staff and use him as a liaison officer

[1] See below, p. 458.

with Beck.[1]   At the same time an 'Action Group' of senior officers was formed in OKH itself, including Karl-Heinrich von Stülpnagel, the Deputy Chief of Staff, and also Lieut.-Colonel Groscurth and General Eduard Wagner,[2] through whom it was hoped to maintain direct contact with field commanders and with the actual troops themselves.   Meantime liaison between OKH and the Beck-Goerdeler-Popitz group was carried on by the agency of younger members of the conspiracy such as Otto John, Klaus Bonhoeffer, von Hammerstein's younger son Ludwig, Count Ulrich von Schwerin-Schwanenfeld and others.

The civilian Resistance Movement had thus established contact with senior Generals in the German Army and had thereby stretched out its hand to the only instrument capable of giving the *coup de grâce* to National Socialism.

It was characteristic of the man that the first General to plan independent action after the outbreak of hostilities was Kurt von Hammerstein.   The general mobilization had recalled him to the active list and had given him the troops, of the lack of which he had complained to Pechel earlier in the summer.[3]   Unfortunately, however, he was far removed from the *Führer*.   His appointment was to the command of the '*Armee Abteilung A*', an *ad hoc* force formed to assist in the defence of the West Wall in the event of an Allied attack through Belgium, while the greater part of the German Army was engaged in Poland.

Von Hammerstein's first act on assuming his new command was to look for an excuse to attract Hitler to his Army H.Q. at Cologne, where he might seize him.   Sir George Ogilvie Forbes, the British Chargé d'affaires, was informed of this intention by von Schlabrendorff, who, with considerable courage, sought him out in the Hotel Adlon after the British ultimatum had expired on September 3, 1939.[4] This was among the last communications the Embassy staff received before their departure, and it was already too late for anything to be done about it.[5]

---

[1] Kordt, pp. 340-41.   It is also stated here that members of the conspiracy were attached to the staffs of General Blaskowitz and General von Muff.

[2] Halder Interrogation, February 26, 1946.   [3] See above, p. 441, footnote.

[4] Schlabrendorff, p. 33-4.   The present writer has confirmed this account in correspondence with Sir George Ogilvie Forbes in April–May 1951.

[5] This was not the only plot to dispose of Hitler of which the British were made aware at the last moment.   An officer in the Foreign Armies section of the General Staff, who subsequently became a distinguished Panzer Commander, frankly informed the Assistant Military Attaché, Major K. W. D. Strong, of the willingness of a small group of officers in the Ministry of War to assassinate Hitler in order to prevent a general war which he was confident that Germany could not win.   The officer insisted, however, that the Polish campaign must go forward.

But the *Führer* refused to play the rôle of fly to von Hammerstein's spider. Despite every artifice employed by the General, who harped upon the necessity of emphasizing the military might of Germany by an inspection of the defences of the West by the *Führer* while the campaign in the East was pursuing its victorious course, Hitler never came within many miles of the Rhineland until well after the Polish war was over. And by then von Hammerstein's opportunity had vanished. For back came the victors of Poland to active commands in the West and von Hammerstein was transferred temporarily to the deputy command of *Wehrkreis VIII* (Silesia) and very shortly thereafter was permanently retired. The only words of farewell which he addressed to his Staff at Cologne were terse and bitter. 'I have fallen a victim to the inflation in high-ranking Army commanders, gentlemen', he said to them casually, as they sipped their coffee one evening after dinner.

Lazy von Hammerstein may have been, but he was not lacking in resolution and courage in his hatred of Hitler. 'I would have rendered him harmless once and for all — and even without judicial proceedings',[1] he said later to Otto John, and of all the boasts made in connection with the German Resistance, this one may certainly be believed. Had the *Führer* but come within his reach, there is little doubt but that '*Der rote General*', 'The Man with Iron Nerves', would have dealt faithfully and adequately with him. As it was, however, the Devil's hand protected the *Führer* now, as in the future, against all attempts of others to destroy him, and von Hammerstein was condemned to a lingering exile of inactivity, during which the pusillanimous failure of his fellow Generals to respond to the pleading of the conspirators for action caused him to exclaim in contemptuous despair : 'These fellows make of me, an old soldier, an anti-militarist'.[2]

To the last Kurt von Hammerstein warned the leaders of the conspiracy, from the bitter wealth of his past experience : 'Above all, don't make a Kapp *Putsch*'[3] — and yet this, in effect, was exactly what they did. His death in April 1943 deprived the forces of Resistance of one of their most valuable assets. For not only had he courage and daring, and clear vision in military affairs, but he was also a very wise man and one of indisputable integrity and patriotism. Two outstanding weaknesses he certainly had : a

---

[1] *John Memorandum.*

[2] *Doktor Pechel, mich alten Soldaten haben diese Leute zum Anti-militäristen gemacht*' (Pechel, p. 154). This remark is wrongly attributed to Beck by Dulles (p. 66).

[3] Hassell (March 28, 1943), p. 304.

Q

pronounced tendency to indolence and too fervent a faith in Kurt von Schleicher. It was this latter excess of loyalty which caused him to behave in so unseemly a manner toward Gröner — a fact which he never ceased to regret afterwards and which Gröner magnanimously forgave — but it was also his devotion to von Schleicher which figured so prominently among the motives for his implacable hatred of the Nazis. He died honoured and regretted by all who knew him — and to have known him is something to remember. As Brüning once said of him to the present writer : 'He is decent through and through'.

(ii)

Back came the *Wehrmacht* from their Polish conquests ; their cheeks blooded, their swords fleshed, the laurel of the victor on their brows. It had been a 'quick war', 'right out of the book', and the Polish resistance had been just sufficient to add that welcome degree of danger and adventure which differentiates a blood-sport from a *Blumenkorso*.

Now the Generals looked for that 'quick peace' which was the pendant in the traditional formula for complete success. They had embarked upon hostilities on September 1, assured by Hitler that Britain and France would not declare war, and though both they and he himself sustained something of a shock when this event actually occurred on September 3,[1] the *Führer* had at·once rallied their confidence with the further assurance that the Western Powers were making but a token gesture of solidarity with Poland. Once she had been overwhelmed Britain and France would soon come to their senses and a negotiated peace would be concluded before the winter. All, therefore, depended upon the ability of the Generals to effect a lightning victory over the Poles.

This they had now accomplished, and the fact that Britain and France had elected to sit passively behind the Maginot Line during the entire campaign on the Eastern Front had added a verisimilitude to the *Führer*'s prophecy and had greatly enhanced the confidence of the Generals in his intuition. This expressed preference of the Allies for the technique of the *Sitzkrieg* must surely betoken that

---

[1] That this was genuinely the case is borne out by the records of Paul Otto Schmidt to whom it fell to receive the British ultimatum on September 3, 1939, and to present it to Hitler. '*Was gibt es denn Neues?*' was the *Führer*'s petulant and bewildered comment, but Göring's reaction was even more significant and prophetic : '*Wenn wir diesen Krieg verlieren, dann möge uns der Himmel gnädig sein*' ('If we lose this war, then God help us'). (Schmidt, p. 464, and Evidence before the International Military Tribunal on March 28, 1946, *Nuremberg Record*, x, 200-201.)

they would welcome an avenue of escape from the necessity of adopting a more active line of strategy.[1]

But some there were among the *Generalität* who returned from Poland shocked in their souls at what they had seen. They were conditioned to the normal horrors of war, but not to the abomination of the Nazi ideological concomitants. When, on August 22 at the Obersalzberg, they had heard their *Führer* talk in terms of 'extermination', extolling Genghis Khan, who 'had millions of women and children killed by his own will and with a gay heart', they had supposed him to be revelling in elated hyperbole. When he had told them that 'our strength is in our ruthlessness and our brutality' and had spoken of killing 'without mercy all men, women and children of Polish race or language',[2] they had not thought they were expected to take his words *au pied de la lettre*, forgetting that, except in cases where he had pledged his word, Hitler always meant what he said.

They were to be speedily and shockingly undeceived. With the Polish war not two weeks old, yet clearly won, Ribbentrop conveyed to Keitel in the Headquarters train on September 12 the *Führer's* instructions for the solution of the Polish problem. These included the mass execution of the intelligentsia, the nobility and the clergy — of all elements, in fact, who might be regarded as leaders of a potential subsequent resistance movement — and a wholesale massacre of the Jews, the *raison d'être* for which was to be a faked uprising in the Galician Ukraine.

Keitel passed these instructions on to Canaris, and the 'little Admiral' was aghast. He protested that the military honour of Germany would be indelibly sullied if it condoned such crimes. But Keitel replied imperturbably that the *Führer* had commanded these things to be done and had added, moreover, that if the Army should express disagreement with them, they would have to accept the presence as equals of units from the SS and the SIPO (Security Police), who would not scruple to do the *Führer's* commands and who would operate independently of military government.[3] Under

---

[1] 'A French attack during the Polish campaign would have encountered only a German military screen, not a real defence', Keitel told the International Military Tribunal on April 4, 1946. 'Since nothing of this sort happened, we soldiers thought, of course, that the Western Powers had no serious intentions. . . . This also strengthened our views as to what the attitude of the Western Powers would probably be in the future' (*Nuremberg Record*, x, 519).

[2] *IMT Document*, L-3.

[3] This, in effect, occurred a month later, when as a result of a conference between Hitler and Keitel on October 17, the record of which was kept by Warlimont (*IMT Document*, PS-864), the Army washed its hands of administrative questions in Poland. In each military district there were both military and

such circumstances the Armed Forces of the Reich had no choice
but to concur in the commands of their Supreme Commander.
'The day will come', said Canaris to Keitel with unerring prophecy,
'when the world will hold the *Wehrmacht*, under whose eyes these
events occurred, responsible for such measures.' [1]

For one reason and another the conclusion of hostilities in
Poland brought with it a wide degree of hope among the Generals
that a 'quick peace' would follow a 'quick war'. Some desired this
as a breathing-space to complete Germany's rearmament so that she
should never again be gainsaid. Others looked forward to a fruitful
co-operation with the Russians. But a few hoped for peace in the
dread thought that the extension to Western Europe of the conduct
of war as they had seen it in Poland could only precipitate a struggle
which, though long and bloody and having varying success, could
not but terminate in the destruction of Germany.[2]

It was therefore with hope mixed with trepidation that von
Brauchitsch and Halder found themselves summoned to the presence
of the *Führer* in the *Reichskanzlei* one afternoon in late September.
They knew that the besieged city of Warsaw was about to fall.
The High Command were uncertain whether they were to be
congratulated on the conclusion of a brilliant campaign or to be

civil governors, of whom the latter were responsible for the 'extermination of
the people' (*völkische Ausrottung*) and the 'political house-cleaning' (*politische
Flurbereinigung*). The note for the policy of German occupation was struck by
Hitler when, in the presence of Keitel, he invested Hans Frank as Governor-
General of Poland : 'The task which I give to you is a devilish one. . . . Other
people to whom such territories are entrusted would be asked, "What will you
construct ?" I shall ask the opposite' (Halder Interrogation, February 26, 1946).

[1] The account of this interview is given by General Erwin Lahousen, who
was present at it and who kept Canaris's travel reports (*Reiseberichte*) during the
Polish campaign, in evidence before the International Military Tribunal on November 30, 1945 (*Nuremberg Record*, ii, 447), and his affidavit sworn at Nuremberg on
January 21, 1946.

[2] The effect of these events was clearly apparent after the return of OKW and
OKH to Berlin, for Goerdeler told von Hassell on October 11, 1939, that both
Halder and Canaris were suffering from nervous complaints as a result of 'our
brutal conduct of the war' (Hassell, p. 88). The Commander-in-Chief of the Army
of Occupation in Poland, Colonel-General Johannes Blaskowitz (1893–1948), prepared a memorandum in protest against the conduct and depredations of the
SS. Urged to send it direct to Hitler, he hesitated and finally forwarded it to
von Brauchitsch through 'the proper channels', where it was soon lost sight of
(Hassell, pp. 112, 122 ; Halder's Interrogation, February 26, 1946). Blaskowitz
was indicted as a minor war criminal in Case No. 12 ('Wilhelm von Leeb *et al.*')
before a United States Military Tribunal. A few hours before the opening of the
trial on February 5, 1948, he committed suicide in the Nuremberg jail. Later a
story of very doubtful authority became current that he had been murdered by
former members of the SS who had succeeded in being taken on as prison
'trusties'.

afforded a glimpse of the *Führer*'s future plans.[1] Hitler immediately asked what plans had been made for the continuation of the war in the West. Halder replied that these were based on a defensive deployment ; no preparation had been made for an attack. The *Führer* pondered this answer and then abruptly dismissed the Generals, saying that he was too tired to continue the conversation.

Exactly what occurred in Hitler's mind between that day and October 6 is still one of the lacunae in our knowledge of the period. It is very unlikely, however, that the 'Peace Offer' which he was about to publish reflected his innermost thoughts. Probably he was waiting for a final agreement with Russia over the division of Poland. Von Ribbentrop was duly given full powers to sign this on September 28. Talk of peace was also important for home consumption and as a form of bluff played as much against his own Generals as against the Western Powers.[2]

The fact remains that, when on September 30 von Brauchitsch and Halder submitted a memorandum in elaboration of their thesis for a defensive war in the West, Hitler received them graciously, thanked them for their labour and stated that he was prepared for peace.[3] A week later, in a speech to the *Reichstag* on October 6, he made a definite offer of peace on the basis of the recognition by the Western Powers of his Polish conquests ; satisfaction to be given to German colonial claims by Britain, but no further demands to be made upon France. 'I have refused even to mention the problem of Alsace-Lorraine.'[4]

M. Daladier replied on October 10. France, he said, would never lay down her arms until guarantees for a real peace and

---

[1] In his affidavit of February 26, 1946, Halder stated that neither he nor von Brauchitsch had any advance idea on what the *Führer* wished to consult with them at this meeting. It is clear, however, that Keitel and Warlimont knew of Hitler's intentions before the *Führer* saw von Brauchitsch and Halder. There was a second meeting with Hitler on September 27, at which the *Führer* ordered von Brauchitsch to make preparations for a possible attack in the West. These preparations were to be completed by November 12. (*Nuremberg Record*, xx, 573.) The final decision to fix X-day for November 12 was not, however, taken until later on (see below, p. 466). For detailed information about the planned assault on the Western Powers see Hans Adolf Jacobsen, *Fall Gelb* (Wiesbaden, 1957) ; Sir James Butler, *Grand Strategy*, Volume II, Chapter VIII (London, 1957), and Ellis, *The War in France and Flanders, 1939–1940*, the supplement (London, 1953).

[2] For a discussion of Hitler's peace offensive of October 1939 see Maxime Mourin, *Les Tentatives de paix dans la seconde guerre mondiale, 1939–1945* (Paris, 1949), pp. 9-27 ; also *Ciano's Diary* (London, 1947), pp. 162-5 ; Schmidt, pp. 473-474, and Bullock, pp. 554-9.

[3] Halder's Diary, September 30, 1939.

[4] For text see *Völkischer Beobachter*, October 7, 1939 ; Count Raoul de Roussv de Sales, *My New Order* (New York, 1941), pp. 722-37.

general security had been obtained.   But it was not in M. Daladier's reactions that Hitler was interested.   He knew that once again the key to any decision of the Western Allies lay, in the last instance, in the hands of Britain.   It was for Mr. Chamberlain's reply that the *Führer* seemed to be waiting, and he took the opportunity of a second speech in the Sportpalast on October 10 to re-emphasize his readiness for peace : 'Germany has no cause for war against the Western Powers'.[1]

Mr. Chamberlain's reply came two days later and, while it contained something of moment for the leaders of the conspiracy,[2] it gave no satisfaction to Hitler himself, since it dismissed his proposals as 'vague and uncertain' and offering no suggestion for righting the wrongs done to Czechoslovakia and to Poland.

But — and herein is one of the most baffling aspects of the case — Hitler appears either to have lost interest or confidence in his peace offensive almost as soon as it had been launched, or else to have decided to drop the mask and make clear to his Generals that which he expected of them.   Whatever the cause, the *Führer* chose to summon to the Chancellery at eleven o'clock in the morning of October 10 the Commanders-in-Chief of his three Armed Services, together with the Chiefs of OKW, and the Chief of the General Staff of OKH.[3]   He then read to them a memorandum, which bore the date of the previous day,[4] in which he gave, with remarkably clear perception of the military strategic considerations, his reasons and his decision to strike a swift and shattering blow in the West should Britain and France fail to respond to his peace overtures.

The Allies, Hitler explained, could only be disposed of, if hostilities were to continue by attack, never by defence.   It was useless to sit behind the Siegfried Line and await an Anglo-French offensive.   On the contrary, if the Allies wanted war they should have it — and, moreover, have it brought home to them.   By means of a lightning stroke of staggering strength the German troops must pass through Holland and Belgium and attack on so wide a front that the British and French forces would not be able to build up a solid front of opposition, and would consequently be annihilated.   'Any offensive which does not aim at the destruction of the enemy forces

---

[1] *Völkischer Beobachter*, October 11, 1939.   De Sales, pp. 757-9.

[2] See below, p. 467 *et seq.*

[3] Halder's Diary, October 10, 1939 ; Halder's affidavit sworn at Nuremberg, November 22, 1945 ; Halder Interrogation of February 26, 1946 ; an account of the meeting was also written by Warlimont in *Interim*, the BAOR Intelligence Review.

[4] *Führer* Memorandum and Directive for Conduct of the War in the West, dated October 9, 1939 (*IMT Documents*, L-52 and C-62).

from the start is senseless and leads to useless waste of human life.' And, having thus directed his Commanders-in-Chief, the *Führer*, despite the receipt of Daladier's rejection, chose that same evening at the Sportpalast, to renew his overtures of peace.[1]

Hitler's select audience of seven on October 10, Keitel, Jodl and Warlimont, von Brauchitsch, Göring, Raeder and Halder, left the presence with mixed emotions. The OKW representatives, whatever their inner feelings may have been, were dutifully enthusiastic in their support of the *Führer's* policy, and in this they were joined to some degree by Raeder, who, in a memorandum sent to the *Führer* five days later, accepted the necessity for 'the utmost ruthlessness' and called for an intensification of economic warfare in 'the siege by sea' of Britain.[2]

But the Chiefs of the Army and of the Air Force heard the words of the *Führer* with some perturbation, and their apprehension was reflected in the attitude of their subordinates. The tank experts, Guderian and Hoepner, and even von Reichenau, were all of the same mind, namely that a mechanized attack in the autumn would bog down on account of ground conditions ;[3] and Göring voiced the objections of his *Luftwaffe* paladins, Kesselring, Student and Sperrle, that the November fogs would gravely hamper the air cover necessary for the success of so great an enterprise.

These objections found expression in bitter arguments within OKH and between OKH and OKW. The unfortunate von Brauchitsch was again caught between two fires. He undoubtedly shared the professional fears of his subordinates,[4] and yet it was he and not they who had to encounter the cold eye of the *Führer* and the fanatical unreason of Keitel. In addition he was being harried by his Chief of Staff, who, both in things military and things political, was fundamentally a defeatist, and von Brauchitsch found himself

[1] Ironically enough on the following day, Wednesday, October 11, the Berlin radio put out a story in the early morning that the Chamberlain Government had been overthrown and that there would be an immediate armistice. The news was received with wild rejoicing, only to be officially denied in the afternoon (Shirer, p. 236).

[2] Memorandum regarding the intensified naval warfare against England, prepared by OKM, dated October 15, and forwarded by Raeder to the *Führer*, November 3, 1939 (*IMT Document*, UK-65).

[3] 'The conduct of a man like von Reichenau is significant', von Hassell wrote in his Diary on October 30, 1939. 'He always hears the grass grow' (Hassell, p. 97).

[4] 'Field-Marshal von Brauchitsch was dead against it', his personal assistant, General Siewert, stated after the war, '. . . (he) did not think that the German forces were strong enough to conquer France and argued that if they invaded France they would draw Britain's full weight into the War' (B. H. Liddell Hart, *The Other Side of the Hill* (London, 1948), pp. 114, 115).

bedevilled by the Bavarian gloom of Halder, on the one hand, and the Bavarian zeal of Jodl on the other.[1]

Finally Hitler lost patience, both with the Western Powers and with his Generals. On October 27 he summoned them to a further meeting at the Chancellery, where, after an investiture of decorations, he informed them that they must make final preparations for the Western Offensive. November 12 was mentioned as the probable X-day and the order confirming this was issued on November 5.[2]

This was the moment which the leaders of the conspiracy, Beck, Goerdeler, Popitz and von Hassell, had been awaiting with trepidation mingled with elation. Ever since the declaration of war upon Germany by Britain and France, plans had been afoot for the localization of the conflict and the conclusion of a negotiated peace. In other words, having failed to prevent the outbreak of war with Poland, the leaders of the conspiracy were now concentrating upon halting it before it engulfed Western Europe. It was agreed that this could only be brought about by the elimination of Hitler — though at this moment it was considered possible that Göring might be considered a satisfactory substitute by the Western Powers! But again the question was: how? And again the answer was : a general and some troops.

Halder was sounded but was not forthcoming, and there was little hope of von Brauchitsch. Others, though sympathetic, were 'playing safe'. Others again were frankly uninterested. The field narrowed once more to von Hammerstein and von Witzleben, but here again arose the same old problem of getting the lobster into the pot.

There were new difficulties also, which, though they had in reality always existed, had been less apparent in time of peace. The mystic qualities of 'the oath sworn to the living Hitler' (in Oster's phrase) [3] loomed larger and more potently to the average General when he found himself actually at war. The implication was that if confronted with the *fait accompli* of a dead Hitler the *Generalität* would feel themselves, with relief, freed from their allegiance. But how to break the vicious circle?

The further consideration which arose in the minds of all the leaders of the conspiracy, both military and political, was the vital question, 'If we bring about a revolution in Germany and overthrow

---

[1] 'We shall win this war even though it may be a hundred times contrary to the doctrines of the General Staff (OKH)', Jodl recorded after one of these bouts with von Brauchitsch and Halder. 'We shall have superior troops, superior equipment, superior armies, and a united and methodical leadership' (Jodl's Diary, October 15, 1939).

[2] Halder's Diary, October 27, 1939, *Nuremberg Record*, xx, p. 575.

[3] Kordt, p. 369.

Hitler, will not the Allies at once take advantage of our inevitable weakness as a result of this upheaval ? Will they resist the temptation, after all that has happened and with Germany at their mercy, to wreak their vengeance upon the German people even though they have got rid of Hitler ?'

Though Mr. Chamberlain had closed his famous broadcast of September 4 with the words : 'In this war we are not fighting against you, the German people, for whom we have no bitter feeling, but against a tyrannous and forsworn régime which has betrayed not only its own people but the whole of Western civilization and all that you and we hold dear',[1] this was not considered sufficiently definite. A more binding declaration was desired, specifically pledging Britain and France not to seize the opportunity presented by a revolution in Germany to launch an offensive on the West Wall.

To achieve this aim several channels of approach were utilized. In Rome Dr. Joseph Müller, an eminent Munich lawyer who had been attached by Oster to the *Abwehr*, was in touch with certain Vatican sources,[2] and the lanes of communication between the conspirators and London had been kept open by a curious arrangement clandestinely condoned by both Berlin and London. Von Weizsäcker had appointed Theo Kordt to the Legation in Berne, and there he was visited periodically by Philip Conwell-Evans.

One of these visits occurred in the latter part of October, when it was already known to the conspirators through Oster that the date of attack had been fixed for November 12. On this occasion Conwell-Evans brought with him from London what he described as a solemn obligation on the part of Mr. Chamberlain which would be scrupulously observed towards any German Government worthy of trust which should take the place of Nazi rule.[3]

In effect this 'solemn obligation' amounted to no more than textual excerpts from the Prime Minister's speech of October 12 in which he had rejected Hitler's peace proposals.

It is no part of our policy to exclude from her rightful place in Europe a Germany which will live in amity and confidence with other nations,

Mr. Chamberlain had said on that occasion,

On the contrary, we believe that no effective remedy can be found for the world's ills that does not take account of the just claims and needs of all countries, and whenever the time may come to draw the lines of a new

---

[1] *British Blue Book*, No. 144.
[2] For an account of these Vatican negotiations, see below, pp. 490 *et seq.*
[3] Kordt, p. 368.

peace settlement, His Majesty's Government would feel that the future would hold little hope unless such a settlement could be reached through the method of negotiation and agreement.

It was not, therefore, with any vindictive purpose that we embarked on war, but simply in defence of freedom. . . .

We seek no material advantage for ourselves ; we desire nothing from the German people which should offend their self-respect. We are not aiming only at victory but rather look beyond it to the laying of a foundation of a better international system which will mean that war is not to be the inevitable lot of every succeeding generation.

I am certain that all the peoples of Europe, including the people of Germany, long for peace, a peace which will enable them to live their lives without fear, and to devote their energies and their gifts to the development of their culture, the pursuit of their ideals and the improvement of their material prosperity.[1]

Though these words had originally been addressed, *inter alia*, by Mr. Chamberlain to the House of Commons, his statement had been reported over the German Service of the B.B.C. and must therefore have been heard by the many Germans who, regardless of pains and penalties, listened in regularly to these broadcasts. In addition, the text of Mr. Chamberlain's remarks would have been available to the leaders of the conspiracy through the daily reports of the Monitoring Service, and they were doubtless already familiar with them. Yet because these unconsecutive extracts from the Prime Minister's speech, taken out of their original contexts and strung together in the form of a statement, reached Berlin from London through the circuitous and illicit route of Berne and by the safe hand of Philip Conwell-Evans, they were considered to have become endowed with a special and almost mystic significance. They constituted, Conwell-Evans had said, 'a solemn obligation' which would be 'unconditionally observed', and as such they were regarded as a powerful trump card for removing the inhibitions of the General Staff.

Not only Erich Kordt but Beck and Oster regarded them as such, though in reality they were no more of a solemn obligation than any other public statement by a political leader in war-time. 'Surely now we can make some progress', Beck said, as he read the statement and listened to the report of Conwell-Evans's verbal assurances. 'We are facing a grave decision. Of course the Army must not go to pieces, for as soon as we become weak we should have to reckon with "those people from the East". . . . Early action must be taken because, if we commit another violation of neutrality, they [the

---

[1] *House of Commons Debates*, October 12, 1939, cols. 565-6.

British] will not want to make "peace without revenge" even with us.' [1]

Indeed, if the offensive against the Western Allies and the invasion of Luxembourg and the Low Countries, previously scheduled for November 12, were to be forestalled and prevented there was not a moment to lose. Beck and the civilian leaders stood ready to take over the reins of government as soon as the military could wrest them from the hands of the Nazis. But would the military take action ? Was it possible so to exploit their professional apprehension and objection to Hitler's plans, which they seriously believed were doomed to failure, to the point at which they would resort to extreme measures in order to dissuade the *Führer* from pursuing their execution ?

Halder was again considered the key-man, but he was suffering a peculiar *crise de conscience*. His Oath was troubling him again. He could not now bring himself to condone a *coup d'état* in time of war, but he was prepared to make the hideous compromise of countenancing Hitler's assassination because one could not be expected to remain loyal to a dead *Führer*.[2] 'If von Brauchitsch hasn't enough guts to make a decision, you must make it for him, and confront him with a *fait accompli*', Beck had said to Halder at their last meeting in September,[3] perhaps forgetting that he himself had failed signally to do this when occupying Halder's office in similar circumstances. But Halder was the last man to act alone. He had every desire to be well 'covered', if mutiny he must, it should be on the receipt of orders from above.

These orders, however, were, remarkably enough, almost forthcoming. Stung at last to desperation by Hitler's intransigent determination to commit the German Army to what its leaders believed to be an impossible, and therefore a disastrous, operation, von Brauchitsch was prepared to make a final effort with the *Führer*.[4]

---

[1] Kordt, p. 369.
[2] It was in order to meet this objection that Erich Kordt seems to have volunteered personally to blow up Hitler with a bomb in the Chancellery on November 11, the day before the offensive was to be launched. The reason for his failure to do so is given as being the impossibility of procuring the explosive, due to the precautions and restrictions imposed after the Bürgerbräu Keller attempt on November 8, 1939 (Kordt, pp. 371-4 ; Gisevius, ii, 215). See below, pp. 479 *et seq.*   [3] Quoted by Dulles, p. 54.
[4] It is improbable that von Brauchitsch's reasoning at that time was such as he later stated to the International Military Tribunal : 'I considered it madness that Europe would once more have to tear herself in pieces instead of progressing by peacefully working at a common task. . . . German soldiers of every rank had been trained to defend and protect their homeland. They did not think about wars of conquest, or the expansion of German domination over other peoples' (*Nuremberg Record*, xx, 574). The truth was that 'German soldiers of every

Basing his arguments on the technical reasoning of his subordinates and on the political considerations of Oster and Hasso von Etzdorff, the liaison officer of the Foreign Ministry with OKH, the Commander-in-Chief briefed himself for an audience with Hitler on November 5. If this failed he would come down on the side of the conspirators.

Halder at once changed course, and tacked into the wind. Under the arguments of Thomas and Oster he allowed himself to be persuaded into agreement with the idea of a *Putsch*, for which plans were immediately placed *en train*.[1] The Generals who had opposed the *Führer*'s decision on technical and professional grounds were now sounded as to their willingness to translate this opposition into resistance. On the understanding that they would receive a direct order from the Commander-in-Chief, they agreed to hamstring the offensive by the simple means of not transmitting to their subordinates the essential order to attack. These arrangements were finally confirmed by von Brauchitsch and Halder personally in the course of a tour of the Western Defences on November 3 and 4, and word was sent to Beck and Goerdeler by the safe hand of Helmuth Groscurth.

Breathlessly the conspirators waited for the outcome of the fatal day : Sunday, November 5. Goerdeler, as ever, was already well ahead of events — 'He often reminds me of Kapp', wrote von Hassell apprehensively.[2] For him the *Putsch* had already taken place and succeeded, and he was full of plans for the future.[3] Beck, better balanced and with greater cynicism, was more restrained, but Popitz, Planck, and von Hassell were almost as optimistic as Goerdeler. Only Schacht remained thoroughly sceptical : 'Mark my words', he said, 'Hitler will smell a rat' ('*Hitler riecht den Braten*').[4]

But as it turned out there was very little rat to smell. Von Brauchitsch arrived at the duly appointed time at the Chancellery

rank' considered it 'madness' to undertake a military operation in the West which they believed to be well beyond their competence to carry to a successful conclusion. It is even more unlikely that von Brauchitsch would have assumed this high moral tone could he have foreseen the shockingly easy victory which lay before him.

[1] Thomas, *Gedanken und Ereignisse*.

[2] Hassell, p. 104.

[3] Goerdeler had just returned from Stockholm, whither he had gone for consultations with Marcus Wallenberg, Senior, and Gustav Cassell. On November 3 he had had a three-hours' talk with that inveterate Germanophil, Dr. Sven Hedin, who records that 'he [Goerdeler] believed in Göring and thought that a speedy peace was the only thing to save Germany, but that peace was unthinkable so long as Hitler remained at the head of affairs' (Sven Hedin, *German Diary 1935-1942* (Dublin, 1951), p. 37).

[4] Gisevius, ii, 152-6.

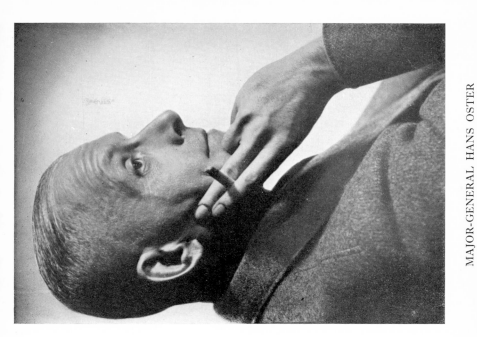

MAJOR-GENERAL HANS OSTER

MAJOR-GENERAL HENNING VON TRESCKOW

and presented his memorandum to Hitler.[1] Then he endeavoured to elaborate certain points of outstanding importance. It was impossible to mount an offensive of this magnitude in the rains of autumn and winter. 'It rains on the enemy too', interjected Hitler grimly. With some temerity the Commander-in-Chief touched upon the vexed question of the *Führer's* interference with the direction of military operations during the Polish war. OKH would be grateful for an understanding that they and they alone would be responsible for the conduct of any future campaign — a suggestion which the *Führer* received in icy silence.

With the courage of despair von Brauchitsch played his last card. The Polish campaign, he said, had shown that the aggressive spirit of German infantry was sadly below the standard of the First World War, and, with perhaps calculated exaggeration, he added that there had actually been certain symptoms of insubordination similar to those of 1917–18. This was sufficient to kindle the *Führer's* rising wrath into a white-hot flame of fury. His pride in the National Socialist training of German youth had been flicked on the raw, and from the appalled von Brauchitsch he demanded immediate proof of this monstrous assertion. What units had shown signs of disaffection? And what action had been taken? How many death penalties had been inflicted in the East and in the West? The *Führer* would soon settle that for himself. He would fly to the front to-morrow and see that the proper steps were taken.

And then Hitler turned upon von Brauchitsch the full fury of his vitriolic spleen. The Army had never been loyal; it had never had confidence in his genius. It had consistently sabotaged the rearmament effort by deliberate 'go-slow' methods. It was afraid to fight. 'The Spirit of Zossen' had become synonymous with defeatism and cowardice. Every insult, every accusation, every manifestation of the hatred and contempt which Hitler cherished for the *Generalität*, he now spewed forth upon von Brauchitsch, who quailed before the torrent. When, at the end of what Halder, with consummate restraint, describes as 'a most ugly and disagreeable scene', the *Führer* abruptly terminated his own tirade by leaving the room, the Commander-in-Chief tottered to his car and fled back the eighteen miles to Zossen, where he arrived in such poor shape that, at first, he could only give a somewhat incoherent account of the proceedings.[2]

[1] The contents of this memorandum are summarized in Halder's Diary entry for November 4, 1939.
[2] Von Brauchitsch's evidence, August 9, 1946 (*Nuremberg Record*, xx, 575). Halder's Diary, November 5, 1939; Halder's Interrogation, February 26, 1946; Warlimont in *Interim*.

Schacht had very nearly been right after all; Hitler had not given a decision as to the final order for X-day, but it had been because he had forgotten to do so in the stress of his emotions. Reminded of this deficiency by Keitel and Warlimont, he emphatically confirmed November 12 as the date, setting the time at 7.15 A.M. and ordered that this be communicated to OKH at once by telephone. When Halder requested a written confirmation, this too was immediately forthcoming.

OKH had now the definite proof of what they had clearly stated would be the legitimate *raison d'être* for a revolt. The Commander-in-Chief had tried and failed — failed how signally ! — to bring about a change in the *Führer*'s views. The *Führer* had confirmed that he would launch his offensive on the West, carrying death and destruction into three neutral countries, on November 12, and had, moreover, put it in writing. All the evidence necessary was in their hands.

But no signal of revolt came from Zossen ; no tocsin sounded ; no armoured column moved upon Berlin. Hitler had achieved a shattering moral victory over the Army. In a pitched battle with the Commander-in-Chief he had routed and overwhelmed him, and driven him in ignominy from the field. Moreover, he had seemingly paralysed any future manœuvres from this quarter. Von Brauchitsch had scarcely the character to resent the insults which had been heaped upon him. All desire to oppose, let alone resist, the *Führer* had been knocked out of him in this fateful encounter, and in future, though he later regained a little of his courage, he was never again anything but a passive sympathizer with the plans of the conspirators.

Of all the conspirators it was again Hans Oster — of whom Fabian von Schlabrendorff wrote that he was a man 'such as God meant men to be' (*'ein Mann nach dem Herzen Gottes'*) [1] — who alone took action. In despair at the irresolution of OKH, he sent to the Belgian and Netherlands Legations a guarded warning through Albrecht von Bernstorff that the attack must be expected at dawn on November 12.[2]

Anticlimax followed, for two days later (November 7) the Western Offensive was postponed, due to meteorological reasons, and thence kept on almost a day-to-day basis till the middle of January.[3] Moreover, on November 8/9, there occurred that strange con-

---

[1] Schlabrendorff, p. 21.   Also von Schlabrendorff's evidence on March 10, 1952, at the trial of Ernst Remer.   [2] Rothfels, pp. 81-2.

[3] There were in all fourteen postponements of the execution of 'Operation Yellow', between November 7, 1939, and May 9, 1940. (See a collection of General Staff reports and orders, *IMT Document*, C-72.)

catenation of phenomena, the kidnapping of two British Intelligence officers on the Dutch border and the attempt on Hitler's life in the Bürgerbräu Cellar in Munich.[1] Both of these events, as will be seen later, contributed to the increased prestige of the *Führer*, and they correspondingly diminished the chances of success for the conspirators, who, incredibly enough, were concerned with neither of them.

Hitler was quick to take the advantage to drive home his victory over the Generals. Summoning them once more to his presence in the Reich Chancellery, he addressed to them at noon on November 23 an allocution on the spirit of victory and the will to conquer and destroy. Chafing at the enforced delay in putting his plans for a Western Offensive into operation, he assured his hearers that it would take place as soon as possible and that it would culminate in victory — if they would but *believe* in victory.

'My decision is unchangeable', announced the *Führer*. 'I shall attack France and Britain at the most favourable and soonest moment. The breach of Belgian and Dutch neutrality is of no importance. No one will question that when we have won, and we shall not make the breach as idiotically as it was done in 1914.'

'No one has ever achieved what I have achieved', said Hitler to his Generals. 'My life is of no importance in all this. I am entering upon a gigantic gamble. I have to choose between victory or destruction. I choose victory. . . . A prerequisite of victory, however, is that the leadership must set an example of fanatical unity from above. There would be no failures if the leaders always had the courage of the rifleman, but when, as in 1914, commanders-in-chief have nervous breakdowns, what can one expect from the ordinary *Feldgrau*?[2] . . . I ask you to pass on this spirit of determination to your subordinates and to the lower ranks. Fate demands no more from us than from the great men of German history. I will shrink from nothing and will destroy everyone who opposes me. . . . I will destroy the enemy. . . . In this struggle I will stand or fall. I will not survive the defeat of my people. . . . But there will be no defeat. We shall emerge victorious. Our age will merge into the history of our people.'[3]

The *Führer*, well knowing the sentiments and emotions of his

---

[1] See below, p. 479 *et seq.*

[2] The reference is to the nervous prostration suffered by the German Commander-in-Chief on the Eastern Front, General von Prittwitz, and his Chief of Staff, Count von Waldersee, in face of the Russian advance in August 1914, and the collapse of Colonel-General Count von Moltke, Chief of the Great General Staff, on the Western Front in the following month.

[3] Speech of the *Führer* to Commanders-in-Chief, Army Group Commanders and the General Staff, November 23, 1939 (*IMT Document*, PS-789).

hearers, had worked himself and them into a frenzy of enthusiasm. He spoke with the wild persuasiveness of a shyster lawyer. At last he gave his final exhortation : 'No capitulation to our enemies without ; no revolution from our enemies within'. The effect was electrical. In response to this taunt of the white feather, the Generals rallied to a man in favour of the *Führer*'s views, even those who had been most strenuously opposed to them for the best of technical and professional reasons. Not a voice was raised in criticism or even in comment. Whereas the more perceptive among his listeners got the impression of a raging Genghis Khan, the majority were deeply moved.[1] A wave of enthusiasm swept the gathering. 'The reproach of cowardice turned the brave into cowards', was Oster's summing-up of the scene,[2] and if it had this effect on the brave, its effect on the not-so-brave was even more devastating.

The *Führer* had kept von Brauchitsch behind after the others had dispersed and had given him a further and personal lecture upon the 'Spirit of Zossen',[3] but on the whole this was unnecessary. For the time being both the Commander-in-Chief and his Chief of the General Staff had become, *malgré eux*, at least outwardly, enthusiastic supporters of 'Operation Yellow', and when on November 27 Halder received a visit from General Thomas, on the instigation of Popitz and Schacht, begging him to resume his importuning of von Brauchitsch to take action in a *coup d'état*, the response of the Chief of the General Staff was evasive and showed clearly that he proposed to do nothing of the sort.[4]

And thus the 'Zossen *Putsch*' of November 1939 petered out as ingloriously as the 'Berlin *Putsch*' of September 1938. The Generals could not free themselves from that stubborn mentality 'which thinks with its hands on its trouser-seams'.[5]

---

[1] Hassell, p. 106.   [2] Kordt, p. 377.
[3] Footnote to Halder's Diary for November 23, 1939 ; Jodl's Diary, November 23, 1939.
[4] Halder's Diary, November 27, 1939 ; Halder's Interrogation, February 26, 1946 ; Thomas, *Gedanken und Ereignisse*.
Halder later gave to Goerdeler his reasons for abandoning his plans to arrest Hitler after the address of November 23. They were that Ludendorff had made his great and disastrous effort in March 1918 and had not damaged his historical reputation ; that there was no great man who could take Hitler's place and that opposition had not matured sufficiently, particularly among the younger officers ; that Hitler ought to be given a last chance to deliver the German people from the slavery of English capitalism' ; and finally that 'one does not rebel when face to face with the enemy' — a consideration which appears to have come to the General rather late, considering all that had gone before! (Hassell, December 5, 1939, pp. 105-6) ; a record of Halder's reasons for abandoning the *Putsch* also appears to have been made by Thomas, *q.v.*).   [5] Hassell, p. 178.

(iii)

How far the security authorities of the Reich, the SD and the SIPO, were aware of the ramifications and intermittent ebullitions of the conspiracy against Hitler it is almost impossible to say, and in view of the wholesale destruction of Gestapo archives it is improbable that this knowledge will ever be forthcoming. That the authorities were aware of serious 'defeatism' is certain, but it is doubtful whether they suspected anyone of outright treason. The visits of Goerdeler and others to Britain and America and France and Switzerland were treated as suspicious only in that they fostered ill-feeling abroad against Germany and not that they were thought to be occasions for actual plotting with the enemies of the Reich.

Similarly, at home, it was an acknowledged fact that Beck and von Hammerstein were disgruntled Generals, that Goerdeler was an indiscreet critic, that Schacht and Popitz had expressed opposition to certain of the *Führer*'s acts and policies, and that considerable elements within the General Staff and the Foreign Office were frankly defeatist, critical, and unsympathetic to the régime. None of these deficiencies, however, measured up to a charge of high treason, and it is improbable that any of the persons named were kept under a greater degree of police surveillance than any other individual in Germany who was not a proven 100 per cent Nazi. Moreover, even within so complete a police state as the Third Reich — or the Soviet Union — it is not possible to keep watch over 'all of the people all of the time', though the terror-basis of a police state lies in its ability to convince people that this can be done.

There is little evidence to support the claim made after the war by former members of the SD that Himmler was aware of the various conspiracies in advance and allowed them to proceed, partly in order that the plotters might further incriminate themselves and partly because he did not consider them as serious.[1] It was not before the end of 1942 that the SD got on the trail and even then their information was surprisingly imperfect. An examination of what remains of the records of the 'post-mortem' investigation conducted by Kaltenbrunner, at Himmler's orders, into the circumstances of the *Putsch* of July 20, 1944, shows clearly the defective pre-knowledge of the secret police and their inability, because of their lack of background, to make full use of the information wrung in confession from their prisoners.

Nevertheless, the SD were sufficiently alive to what was going on to play a very pretty trick on the British. In England there were

[1] Cf. Walter Hagen, *Die geheime Front* (Linz/Wien, 1950), pp. 94-7.

a not inconsiderable number of persons who, with a knowledge of Germany perhaps not the most accurate or the most recent, confidently hoped for and believed in the overthrow of Hitler by the German Army at any moment after the outbreak of hostilities. These hopes and beliefs they expressed, both in England and America, in some cases with a degree of publicity which, had there been any likelihood of a military revolt, would certainly have sent the conspirators to the gallows; and the SD were not slow to see in these statements possibilities of considerable advantage to themselves.

Early in September 1939, very shortly after the outbreak of war, representatives of the British Intelligence Service at The Hague received word from a German refugee resident in Holland that certain German officers representing a military conspiracy desired to make contact with British military authorities. After preliminary consultations with London, Captain S. Payne Best and Major R. H. Stevens were authorized to meet the Germans. They did so, in company with an officer of Netherlands Military Intelligence, Lieutenant Klop, at Zutphen on October 21, but speedily found that the officers whom they met were at too low a level in the conspiracy — and also far too nervous — to be of any value. A further meeting was arranged at The Hague for October 30, and it was understood that on this occasion an officer of greater seniority and of some standing in the plot would be forthcoming.

These hopes were not disappointed. On the 30th, as arranged, Best and Stevens, with Klop, met a certain Major Schaemel, with two other officers. Schaemel spoke with frankness and decision. The German High Command, he said, had been appalled at the losses suffered in men and material during the Polish campaign and were of the opinion that German economy could not sustain the burden of a prolonged war. A quick peace was highly desirable, but it was impossible to convince Hitler of this since he was determined upon further aggression. He must, therefore, be eliminated, but not by assassination, as this would only produce chaos in the Reich. The plan was to seize him and force him to hand over the executive authority of the country to the Army, who would at once open negotiations for peace. What his superiors in the conspiracy wanted to know before they took action, said Schaemel, was what terms were Britain and France prepared to grant them in the event of a successful *Putsch*? 'We are Germans and must think of the interests of our country first', he explained.

When transmitted to London this news elicited instructions to follow up the matter 'with energy'; to convey a reply to the Germans at once sufficiently sympathetic to promote further confidences, and sufficiently non-committal not to embarrass His Majesty's Government in the event of failure. Such a reply was made to Schaemel at the little frontier town of Venlo on November 7, and arrangements were made for a further meeting next day at the same place, at which it was hoped that the General heading the conspiracy — no name was mentioned — would himself make an appearance. A special radio transmitter was given to the Germans to facilitate communication.

On the 6th of November King Leopold III of the Belgians, apprised from Berlin by his military attaché, who had received word from Oster through Albrecht von Bernstorff that an attack upon the Low Countries was imminent,[1] had motored through the night to The Hague to confer with Queen Wilhelmina, and together, on November 7, they launched an appeal for peace to all belligerents.[2] It was against the background of these events that Best and Stevens arrived at Venlo on the 8th, where they found Schaemel alone. The General — again unnamed — had been summoned to Munich by Hitler to attend a Staff conference at which the peace plea of the two Sovereigns would be considered. He hoped to be back on the following day. Could the British officers return then? It was vitally important that they should meet the General as the plot was scheduled to be carried out in three days' time, on Saturday, November 11.

Best and Stevens agreed, but that same evening there occurred the *Attentat* on the *Führer* at the Bürgerbräu Keller at Munich, and it was with the first tidings of this event that they set out from The Hague, with Lieut. Klop, on the following day (November 9). They arrived at Venlo at four o'clock, and were promptly kidnapped by a posse of armed Germans from across the frontier, after a gun-fight in which the unfortunate Klop was mortally wounded. Arrived eventually in Berlin the British Intelligence officers found to their intense surprise that the 'Major Schaemel' in whose treasonable honesty they had placed such faith was none other than Major Walter Schellenberg, head of the counter-espionage division of the Gestapo,[3] that the German refugee with whom they had originally

---

[1] See above, p. 472.

[2] See the report of the Netherlands Government Commission of Enquiry, Regeringsbeleid 1940–45 ; Teil 1. A en B : Algemene Inleïdung Militair Beleid, 1939-1940 ; Jonkheer Elko van Kleffens, Netherlands Foreign Minister 1939–45, *The Rape of the Netherlands* (London, 1940), pp. 85-8 ; *Belgium: The Official Account of What Happened 1939–1940*, published for the Belgian Ministry of Foreign Affairs (New York, 1941), pp. 12-14.

[3] For this brilliant *coup* Walter Schellenberg was decorated personally by Hitler with the Iron Cross and was launched, at the age of twenty-nine, upon a career which was to raise him by November 1944 to the rank of Major-General in the SS with control over all intelligence operations at home and abroad together

been in contact at The Hague had been an agent of German military intelligence and that the military conspiracy, at any rate in so far as he and they were concerned, was no more than a tissue of lies to entice them into captivity.[1]

Superficially it would seem that Schellenberg must have been in possession of actual detailed information about the thoughts and plans of the genuine conspirators, and yet there is no reason to believe that this was so. In planning his deception of Best and Stevens Schellenberg had plenty of 'open sources' on which to draw. It was no secret that certain Generals had returned from Poland appalled at what they had seen and genuinely shocked at the profligate expenditure of lives and equipment. It was no secret that Thomas had warned Keitel that the economy of the Reich could not support the burden of a prolonged and general war. The possibility of a *coup* by the Army had been within the realm of calculation ever since the Fritsch-Blomberg crisis, and Schellenberg was quite intelligent enough to know the working of the military mind and the kind of approach they would make to London and Paris in the event of a projected *Putsch*. He had but to think himself into the mentality of a German General and act accordingly. He need not have had — and it is believed that he did not have — any inner knowledge of the preparations for a revolt which were actually in being at that very moment — for example, that Erich Kordt had considered a bomb attempt on November 11.[2] The whole thing was a fantastic coincidence, built up on the basis of deduction and without cognizance of parallel events.

But it had its decided advantages for the Germans, for, as a

with the functions of the military intelligence department of the *Abwehr*. Having begun his career with fake peace negotiations, he closed it in April 1945 with a genuine attempt to bring about a negotiated surrender to the Western Powers on behalf of Himmler through the agency of Count Folke Bernadotte (Count Bernadotte, *The Curtain Falls* (New York, 1945), pp. 105-29, 136-55 ; Walter Schellenberg's affidavit sworn at Nuremberg on January 23, 1946 ; Hugh Trevor-Roper, *The Last Days of Hitler* (2nd edition, London, 1950), pp. 117, 128-9, 139). At the close of hostilities Schellenberg escaped from Flensburg into Sweden, but later returned to Germany and surrendered to SHAEF. He appeared as a witness for the Prosecution before the International Military Tribunal on January 4, 1946, and was himself sentenced as a lesser war criminal in Case No. 11 ('Weizsäcker *et al.*') to six years' imprisonment on April 14, 1949. His own account of the Venlo Incident, given under direct and cross examination on May 11 and 13, 1948, is to be found in the Transcript of the Trial, pp. 5058-86 ; 5269-99. He was released from custody on clemency at Christmas 1951 and died in Rome in June 1952.

[1] Captain S. Payne Best has given an excellent account of these proceedings on pp. 7-17 of his *Venlo Incident* (London, 1950). He and Major Stevens remained in German custody until the end of the war when they were liberated by the American forces at Niederdorf in northern Italy in April 1945.

[2] See above, p. 469, footnote 2.

result of Schellenberg's investigations, it was possible to establish that a close connection existed between the British and Dutch Military Intelligence, and this was embodied in a very remarkable report which was submitted by Frick and Himmler to Hitler on March 29, 1940. The *Führer* turned it to his own account, for a copy was presented to the Dutch Minister in Berlin on the morning of May 10, together with the German declaration of war, in justification of the German accusation that the Netherlands had violated their own neutrality.[1]

On the other hand, it is easy to see how the Foreign Office in London was misled by the approaches of 'Major Schaemel' as relayed by Best and Stevens. Their information reached London on October 21, that is to say a few days after Philip Conwell-Evans had delivered to Theodor Kordt at Berne the repetition of Mr. Chamberlain's speech of October 12, with the statement that it was to be considered a solemn obligation to be unconditionally observed towards any German régime who ousted Hitler.[2] What, then, could be more natural than this quick response to Mr. Chamberlain's gesture; this anxiety on the part of the conspirators to know in greater detail what was in the Prime Minister's mind? It might indeed well have been genuine and the British authorities may be exonerated from all but perhaps a little impetuosity and *naïveté*. Was not the 'Zossen *Putsch*' in process of being planned at that very time? And was it not tentatively scheduled for November 11?

The whole circumstances of the Venlo Incident were fantastic, but their fantasy pales beside that of the Bürgerbräu Keller *Attentat* of November 8, which still remains one of the unsolved mysteries of the war.

On this sixteenth anniversary of his abortive *Putsch* of 1923, Hitler, as was his annual wont, had summoned the 'Old Guard' of the Party to the scene of their notorious exploit. He there delivered an address consisting mostly of an attack upon Britain, who had, it seemed, wantonly sabotaged the *Führer*'s designs for peace both before and after the outbreak of the war.[3] He had apparently only this one theme to develop, and the speech was therefore rather shorter than usual. He had finished by nine o'clock and left the Hall immediately afterwards. Twenty minutes later a bomb which had been planted in one of the pillars in the rear of the platform exploded with tremendous force and brought down the

---

[1] For text of this report see Prosecution Document Book No. 71, Document 4672, in the case against Schellenberg in the 'Ministries Trial'; see also van Kleffens, pp. 130-34.   [2] See above, p. 467.

[3] *Völkischer Beobachter*, November 9, 1939; Roussy de Sales, pp. 761-6.

roof on the audience, who were still in their places. Seven people were killed and sixty-three injured, all of them veteran members of the Party.

On the following day a man named Georg Elser, a carpenter of Munich with a Communist past, was arrested as he attempted to cross the Swiss frontier near Bregenz. On him was found a considerable sum of money in German and Swiss currency and a picture postcard of the Bürgerbräu Keller with the pillar, in which the bomb had been installed, marked with a cross.

At once chaos reigned in the Reich, for no one seemed to know for certain who was responsible for the attempt. The military conspirators, who were themselves innocent of such initiative, though it occurred at a moment when their hopes for the 'Zossen *Putsch*' were collapsing about their ears, suspected from the first that Himmler and Heydrich had organized the whole affair to provide a fillip for the *Führer's* popularity, to whip up popular enthusiasm for the attack on the West, which was still in a state of day-to-day postponement, and, incidentally, to increase their own power.[1] It was remarked that for the first time in sixteen years both Göring and Himmler had been absent from the November 8 celebration.

Himmler himself utilized the incident to throw forty Bavarian monarchists into gaol, and then offered a personal reward of 300,000 RM. payable in foreign currency, in addition to the official reward of 600,000 RM. which had been promised for any information which would lead to the arrest of the miscreants. It was, however, during the night of November 8-9 that he telephoned to Schellenberg that Best and Stevens were to be kidnapped at their next meeting at Venlo and that an SS 'strong-arm' squad under *Sturmbannführer* Naujocks had been detailed for this purpose. It was the obvious intention to place the blame for the *Attentat* on the British Secret Service.

Heydrich's vengeance at once centred upon his bitter enemies in OKH and the Officer Corps, and Artur Nebe, the head of the criminal investigation department of the Gestapo, was instructed to enquire into the affair. Nebe, who, as a colleague of Gisevius, was already an active member of the Opposition, successfully — and truthfully — diverted suspicion from the military conspirators and their civilian confederates, and reported, as a result of his investigation, that, incredible as it might seem, Georg Elser had committed the crime on his own initiative, without external prompting and entirely as a result of his own careful planning.[2]

The official story put out for domestic consumption in Germany

[1] Kordt, pp. 373-4.   [2] Gisevius, ii, 181-3.

was a splendid hotch-potch of fact and fiction, which disclosed Elser to be a Communist 'deviationist' [1] who had been contaminated by the Nazi 'deviationist' Otto Strasser and had become the tool of the British Secret Service, who had instigated the whole affair, of which the ramifications and preparations dated back to August.[2] The fact that Elser had been arrested in the act of attempting to enter Switzerland, where Strasser was at the time operating, and that two members of the British Intelligence Service had been kidnapped on the afternoon of November 9, added verisimilitude to this story,[3] and the photographs of Elser, Best and Stevens were juxtaposed in the German Press.

Whether designed or not as a fillip to public morale and the *Führer*'s popularity, the attempted assassination was certainly exploited for this purpose and for the stimulation of an intensified hatred of Britain. At the funeral of the victims on November 11, at which Hitler appeared but did not speak, Hess declared that: 'the instigators of this crime have at last taught the German people how to hate and have awakened the devotion of the German nation to this war forced on us'. He added that just as this crime had been turned to the advantage of the *Führer*, so the greater crime of war would be converted to the gain of the *Führer*, of Germany and of the whole world, 'for Germany's victory will prevent the instigators from repeating their criminal war-mongering.[4]

Hitler's victory over his Generals on November 23[5] was therefore made easier by reason of the facts that his escape from death had once more restored and enhanced his reputation, and that those

---

[1] Communist opposition to the Nazi régime had been 'officially' called off from Moscow subsequent to the Nazi-Soviet Pact of August 23, 1939.

[2] This version was put out to the German people and to neutrals not only by the radio and by articles in the press but also by means of pamphlets such as that written by three persons, Walther Koeber, Dr. Hermann Wandescheck and Dr. Hans Zugschwert, under the alluring title of *Mord! Spionage!! Attentat!!! Die Blutspur des englischen Geheimdienstes bis zum Münchener Bombenanschlag* (Berlin, 1940), in which all political murders and mysterious deaths, including those of Count Witte, Lord Kitchener, the Archduke Franz-Ferdinand, Jean Jaurès, King Alexander of Jugoslavia and M. Louis Barthou, and the Rumanian Premier Calinescu, were laid at the door of the British Secret Service, in addition to the Munich attempt of November 8, 1939.

[3] Further gratuitous confirmation of the 'official' German story was provided by the 'German Freedom Station' which, anxious to claim credit for the plot, broadcast on November 10 that 'our illegal Front Group, which knew how to enter the Munich beer-cellar, will also push open the door of Germany's future'.

[4] On the following day, November 12, Goebbels announced on the German radio 'that there can be no justice left in the world, and that the history of the world must have been turned topsy-turvy, if we Germans . . . are to be prevented from reaching our aim by a bomb from the hand of a criminal'.

[5] See above, pp. 473-4.

among his hearers on that occasion who had entertained thoughts and hopes for his elimination, and even his assassination, were discouraged, and perhaps a little shaken, at the attempt and failure of some unknown competitor. In addition, the Elser *Attentat* provided a valid reason for the abandonment of the similar attempt which Erich Kordt was allegedly contemplating on November 11. Immediately after the explosion at Munich the security precautions on all chemical laboratories in which explosives could be compounded were intensified. Even the *Abwehr*, who dealt in these things, were temporarily included in the ban on supplies, and since it was from this source that Kordt had expected to receive his bomb, he felt justified in abandoning the project.[1]

If indeed the attempt of November 8, 1939, was engineered by Himmler and Heydrich, with or without the previous cognizance of Hitler, it would render all the more clear their motives in arranging to kidnap Best and Stevens at that particular juncture. The two exploits could well have been part of the same operation.

Unfortunately for the purposes of history, of the German participants in the drama none survives : Himmler met death by his own hand while a prisoner of the British ; Heydrich was assassinated by Czech patriots as an act of tyrannicide ; Schellenberg has died recently in Rome ; Georg Elser, who had been confined in Sachsenhausen, was removed at the beginning of 1945, when the British and American air operations over Bavaria were becoming severe, and was transferred to Dachau.[2] An SS order is alleged to exist, a personal order from Himmler, to the effect that Elser should be secretly 'liquidated' on the occasion of the next raid on Munich.[3] It is certainly true that his death was announced on April 16, 1945, as having occurred as a result of mortal injuries received during the previous day's 'terrorist attack' on Munich.

Before his transfer to Dachau, however, Elser had secretly communicated in writing, and by word of mouth, to Captain Payne Best, who was a co-inmate of Sachsenhausen, his own strange story of the attempt of November 8.[4] According to this, Elser, who had been vaguely in sympathy with Communism from his youth, was seized in Munich and sent to Dachau during the summer of 1939 for a periodic course of 'political re-education'. He was still there in October when he was called to the office of the camp commandant to be interviewed by two unknown characters who interrogated him as to his antecedents and past record. In the course of several sub-

---

[1] Kordt, p. 374.　　　　　　　　　　　　　　　[2] Best, p. 163.
[3] Maxime Mourin, *Les Complots contre Hitler* (Paris, 1948), p. 101.
[4] Best, pp. 127-36.

sequent meetings with the same persons, he was gradually initiated into a plot within a plot which must have completely bewildered one of his evidently limited intelligence. An attempt was to be made upon the life of the *Führer*, he was told, by certain scoundrelly traitors on the occasion of his speech to the Party veterans in the Bürgerbräu Keller on November 8. Although the names of these miscreants were known to the Gestapo it was considered in the interests of the Reich to avoid a scandal in war-time, since certain high personages were involved, and it had therefore been decided to exterminate them lock, stock and barrel by means of a bomb to be exploded immediately after Hitler had left the Hall, which he would do as soon as he had finished his speech. Elser, as an accomplished cabinet-maker and electrician, was to install the bomb in a pillar by the platform. In return for this he was promised his liberty, his escape into Switzerland and financial remuneration. He accepted the conditions, and as an earnest of good-will his treatment in the camp at once improved ; he was allowed better food, civilian clothes, all the cigarettes he wanted — and he was a chain smoker — and a carpenter's bench with which to pass the time.

In the first week of November he was taken to the Keller at night, where, in accordance with his instructions, he installed the bomb in the pillar with a fuse which could be operated by a push button in an alcove near the entrance of the street level, connected with the pillar by an electric lead.

His work completed, Elser was taken on the night of November 9-10 to a point not very far from the Swiss frontier, where he was given a sum of money in Swiss and German currency, and a picture postcard of the Bürgerbräu Keller with the pillar marked with a cross. This he was told to show the frontier guards, who would let him through. Not unnaturally, nothing of the sort happened, and Elser very soon found himself under close arrest in the Gestapo Berlin prison in the Albrechtstrasse, where he was again briefed for another dramatic performance.

England, he was now told, would very soon be defeated, even as Poland had been defeated, and when this had been accomplished Elser would have to testify at the trial of the Chiefs of the British Secret Service, whom all knew to be murderers and gangsters. With infinite care he was schooled in his part, which was, in fact, the official German story of the *Attentat* of November 8, with its fantastic linking of Elser, Best and Stevens, and Otto Strasser, and with certain circumstantial details added for good measure. He became word perfect, passing with acclaim the various examinations by his coaches. And then suddenly no more was heard of the trial and

HITLER AND THE ARMY

he was left to the constant vigil of his guards.

Such was Elser's own story as given to Payne Best in the prison shades of Sachsenhausen,[1] and it has much to recommend it to our credence. He was not the type of man to invent so amazing a fantasy — from Payne Best's account he was of limited intelligence but considerable sincerity — and he seemed himself to have been bewildered by the permutation of events and circumstances of which he was a victim.

If his story is true — and it is the unsupported testimony of one witness — it is still not proven that Himmler and Heydrich arranged the affair, though it is more than probable that they did so. All that is certain is that it was in no way connected either with the British Intelligence Service or with the Beck-Goerdeler group of conspirators, who, in the course of their plotting progression, had not yet reached the point of reconciling themselves to murder but only to deposition.

There is, however, a certain piquancy in the possibility that, of all the plots to remove Hitler between the years 1938–44, the only one to achieve the semblance of practical effectiveness was that concocted by Hitler's own henchmen, with his personal approval, for the greater deception of the German people.

(iv)

From early November 1939 to the beginning of the third week of January 1940 both the military planners and the military conspirators in Germany were kept on an almost continuous day-to-day *qui vive* by the *Führer*'s determination to launch his assault upon the West at the earliest possible moment permitted by meteorological conditions. However, the untoward forced landing at Mechelen in Belgium on January 10 of a *Luftwaffe* plane carrying two staff officers with important 'top secret' papers concerning the proposed attack caused a *crise de nerfs* in the *Führer*'s own headquarters which is reflected in Jodl's terse diary entry : 'If the enemy is in possession of all the files the situation is catastrophic'.[2] Partly as a result of

---

[1] When transferred to Dachau Elser repeated his story to Pastor Niemöller, who later confirmed it to Payne Best when they were subsequently confined together. On January 12, 1946, Niemöller, in an address to twelve hundred students at Erlangen, spoke to them of his talks with Elser at Dachau, and of his (Niemöller's) personal conviction that the attempt of November 8, 1939, had been sanctioned by Hitler to augment his own popularity and to stimulate the war-fever in the German people.

[2] Jodl's Diary, January 12, 1940. It was of this incident that, with reference to the carelessness of the OKL staff officers, Hitler remarked to Mussolini on April 23, 1944, at Salzburg, 'Sometimes human inefficiency passes all bounds of

this event, partly because of persistently inclement weather, and partly on account of the *Führer's* growing preoccupation with plans for the invasion of Denmark and Norway, the Western offensive was finally postponed indefinitely on January 20, and the tension eased momentarily throughout the Reich.

The conspirators utilized this breathing space for developing their plans both for the *Putsch* itself and for what should come after.[1] All were agreed that the final order for the attack must be the signal for revolt, but beyond that there had been very little clear thinking.

The primary necessity was to establish contact with the belligerent powers and with the United States, and to work out in some degree of detail the terms on which a peace with a non-Nazi Germany might be negotiated. The basic ideas for such a peace had been broadly formulated by Goerdeler as early as October 1939.[2] In return for 'the restitution of the reign of law' (*Rechtsstaat*) the new régime in Germany should receive the German-Polish frontiers of 1914, Austria and the Sudetenland. Independence was to be restored to the remainder of Poland — that is to say, the remainder of the Polish territory occupied by *German* troops, for, of course, it was not suggested that Germany and the Western Powers should embark on a crusade against the Soviet Union for the liberation of Poland's eastern provinces — and to the rump of Czechoslovakia, and there were certain nebulous ideas about general disarmament and the restoration of world commerce.

Thus the conspirators were aiming at this stage at a European settlement based on the Munich Agreement and the re-establishment of a Polish State up to the Curzon Line, or, in other words, at the retention by a non-Nazi Germany of the greater part of Hitler's conquests. It was their anxiety to obtain for such terms the

---

possibility'. The documents which were captured by the Belgian authorities on this occasion were communicated to the British, French and Netherlands Governments (*Belgium*, p. 15 ; for texts of documents, see *IMT Document*, TC-058a). The Belgian Government took the matter seriously and increased their watchfulness.

[1] A half-hearted attempt to revive plans for a *Putsch* was apparently made by Oster in December 1939. A number of divisions, in transit from west to east, were to be halted in Berlin where von Witzleben would appear and take command of them, and dissolve the SS. Beck would then go to Zossen and wrest the Supreme Command of the Army from von Brauchitsch. Hitler would be arrested and declared incapable of continuing in office on mental and medical grounds, and would be replaced temporarily by Göring, pending a constitutional decision after the termination of hostilities. The plan, which does not appear to have gone beyond somewhat loose discussion, failed to materialize since the concentration of troops in Berlin, which von Witzleben demanded as an essential prerequisite, could not be arranged without arousing suspicion (Hassell, pp. 113, 120).

[2] Hassell, pp. 89-90.

'guarantee' of some great neutral figure, such as the President of the United States or the Pope, a 'guarantee' which, it was fondly but mistakenly believed, if taken in conjunction with the 'binding obligation' which Philip Conwell-Evans had brought from London, would eventually provide the clinching argument which should goad von Brauchitsch and Halder into effective action.

The attempts of the conspirators to 'break out' of Germany for the purpose of securing this 'guarantee' also dated from October after the clandestine transaction between Theodor Kordt and Philip Conwell-Evans in the German Legation at Berne.[1] Schacht had taken the initiative in a letter to the American banker Leon Fraser, a former President of the Bank of International Settlements — upon the board of which Schacht had served when President of the *Reichsbank* — with the despatch of which in Switzerland he entrusted Gisevius. In it Schacht desired Fraser to urge upon President Roosevelt the necessity of initiating as soon as possible discussions for a just and lasting peace. 'My feeling', he wrote, 'is that the earlier discussions be opened, the easier it will be to influence the development of certain existing conditions in Germany', and he suggested that he should be invited to America on a lecture tour as a pretext for discussions on the subject of peace.[2] The State Department viewed this idea of a visit from Schacht with some suspicion and refused to give any but the most frigidly formal acquiescence. It was made clear to the American Chargé d'affaires in Berlin that under no circumstances would Schacht be officially received in Washington.[3]

Thus rebuffed, Schacht 'retired hurt', but the conspirators were more fortunate in their second choice of an envoy to the United States. Adam von Trott zu Solz had found favour with von Weizsäcker and, by virtue of a common interest in Oriental subjects, had also attracted the attention of General von Falkenhausen.[4] As a result of their joint patronage he had obtained permission to do a

[1] See above, p. 467.

[2] Letter from Dr. Hjalmar Schacht to Mr. Leon Fraser, dated October 16, 1939 (*Nuremberg Record*, xli, 256-9). See also Gisevius, ii, 148-50 ; Schacht, p. 142 ; Gisevius's evidence on April 25, 1946, and Schacht's evidence on May 2, 1946, before the International Military Tribunal (*Nuremberg Record* xii, 227-9 ; 547).

[3] *The Memoirs of Cordell Hull* (New York, 1948), i, 712. Hassell also recorded the opinion on January 25, 1940, that 'the trouble with him [Schacht] is that he is conceited and self-centred, and hence is liable to act precipitately — in the process his principles fall by the wayside' (p. 121).

[4] General of Infantry Freiherr Alexander von Falkenhausen (b. 1878) after a distinguished military careeer, in the course of which he gained the coveted *Pour le Mérite* Cross, became in 1934 the last in that succession of German Military advisers to the Chinese Nationalist Government which had begun with Colonel Bauer and among whom von Seeckt himself had been a distinguished figure.

piece of research work on some Far Eastern subject under the auspices of the Institute of Pacific Relations, and in the autumn of 1939 he received an invitation from the United States to attend a Conference of that organization at Virginia Beach. This· less illustrious envoy reached America in November, having successfully baffled the scrutiny of the British Security officials at Gibraltar by wearing a Balliol tie.

At Virginia Beach von Trott met a number of distinguished representatives of the academic and business worlds of Canada and the United States. In the plenary sessions and committees of the Conference von Trott observed a very 'correct' attitude. He did not openly defend the Nazi principles, but confined himself to several recapitulations of the German case on the usual well-known lines, which might well be employed by Germans of nearly any political complexion. In private conversation, however, he used a very different tone, frankly declaring himself an anti-Nazi, yet maintaining that Germany must keep much of what she had taken in Poland. He stressed the readiness of the Army for a 'quick peace' on the basis of the *status quo* less Congress Poland, indicated the preparations already on foot for the restoration of the *Rechtsstaat* in Germany, and urged the Western Allies to reiterate and re-define their peace terms on the lines of Mr. Chamberlain's speeches of September 4 and October 12, 1939. To the suggestion that a non-Nazi Germany might, as an earnest of good faith, restore some of the territorial acquisitions of Adolf Hitler, von Trott returned an uncompromising negative.

Von Trott's proposals reached the British Embassy in Washington, the United States Department of State, and the Department of External Affairs in Ottawa, and in all three quarters they were regarded with profound suspicion. Nor was the envoy of the conspirators received with any greater degree of confidence by the German political refugees in America, many of whom regarded him as a Gestapo agent engaged in finding out which of the *émigrés* were politically active in propaganda against the Nazis. He did, however, succeed in persuading some among them, including Kurt

---

After the signature of the Anti-Comintern Pact in 1936 and the consequent drawing together of Germany and Japan in closer union, the presence of a mission of German military advisers in Nanking became an anomaly, particularly after the Japanese attack upon Shanghai in August 1937. Hitler ordered von Falkenhausen and his staff to return to Germany in May 1938, despite the latter's protest that the withdrawal of the Mission constituted a breach of contract with Marshal Chiang Kai-shek and would involve the financial ruin of many of the advisers who had been engaged by the Chinese Government as private individuals (*Documents on German Foreign Policy, 1918–1945*, Series D, i, 826-64).

Riezler, the former secretary of Chancellor Bethmann Hollweg and Otto Meissner's predecessor as State Secretary to President Ebert, and Hans Simons, a former leader of the SPD in Prussia,[1] to prepare a memorandum on war aims and peace terms dealing not so much with their content as with the importance and desirability of their speedy publication and the significant effect which such publication would have upon 'the internal situation in Germany'. This paper reached the White House and is believed to have been read by Mr. Sumner Welles before embarking upon his strange odyssey in February 1940. This was the only concrete result of von Trott's mission.

Meanwhile in Europe the conspirators' efforts to persuade the Allies to commit themselves to a 'soft peace' with a non-Nazi Germany were being pursued with vigour, and through a variety of channels. Ulrich von Hassell had taken up the running and, through the agency of his daughter Fey's Italian husband, Detalmo Biroli, an arrangement was made whereby he should be met, while on a visit to Switzerland, by a certain Mr. J. Lonsdale Bryans, who was described as 'an English associate of Lord Halifax'. This person, who was well known in certain circles of Roman society, had taken it upon himself to endeavour to effect a liaison between the conspirators and the British Government. After some forty conversations with Signor Biroli, and a meeting with Lord Halifax at the Foreign Office in January 1940, it was arranged that he should carry a written message from von Hassell to Lord Halifax and bring back an immediate answer, which, it was hoped, would be in the form of one of those additional 'assurances' for which the German Generals panted, that the Allies would be generous to a non-Nazi Germany, and that they would not seize the opportunity provided by a revolt in the Reich to launch an attack in the West.

The meeting accordingly took place at Arosa on February 22, 1940. Von Hassell refused to name his principals in Berlin, but assured Bryans that any statement which Lord Halifax might make would reach 'the right people'. He added that the chief obstacle to a change of régime in Germany was the recollection by many, especially among the Generals, of what had happened in 1918 after the Kaiser had been sacrificed at the behest of President Wilson.[2] For this reason two things were essential if a revolution against Hitler were to be accomplished; first, it must not be demanded from without, but must be an exclusively German affair, and secondly, there must be an 'assurance' from the British as to the

---

[1] Dr. Brüning, though approached, refused to take part in this enterprise.
[2] See above, pp. 15 et seq.

treatment which a non-Nazi Germany might expect to have meted out to her in the future.

He then gave to Bryans a written statement in English on the kind of peace which would be acceptable to the German Generals, emphasizing that it only remained valid provided that it was put into effect before any further major military operations were undertaken. Once this took place the chances of a negotiated peace would diminish virtually to vanishing point.

Von Hassell's aim as expressed in his memorandum was to lay the foundation for the 'permanent pacification and re-establishment of Europe on a solid basis and a security against a renewal of war-like tendencies'. To achieve this end he laid it down as a necessity that Germany should retain both Austria and the Sudetenland and that the German-Polish border should be 'more or less identical with the German frontier of 1914'. Apart from this Poland and Czecho-slovakia should be restored to independence and there should be no discussion of Germany's western frontiers. There followed certain general aphorisms on human rights, Christian ethics, and social welfare as the *Leitmotiv* of the new Europe. And with this document Bryans left for London.[1]

Though time was recognized by both parties to be the essence of the contract, it was nearly two months before he returned to Arosa. He met von Hassell again there on April 14 and by that time the military and political situation had very greatly changed. For, five days before (April 9), Hitler had launched his surprise Scandinavian offensive and, by the time the two secret emissaries came together once more in the peace of Switzerland, British and French forces were at grips with the German invader in Norway.

In this atmosphere the discussion of a negotiated peace was purely academic and, in any case, what Bryans brought back from London was neither of value nor comfort to von Hassell. Though he had shown the memorandum to Mr. Chamberlain, Lord Halifax and Sir Alexander Cadogan, the Permanent Under-Secretary, and general agreement and symphathy had been expressed with its contents,[2] the Foreign Secretary had not been able to send an

---

[1] Hassell (February 22, 1940), pp. 127-33.

[2] It should be remembered that the counsels of Britain remained divided upon the post-war future of Austria and Czechoslovakia well into the war. The mentality of appeasement died hard ; the ghost of Munich still walked. There were still those in 1940 and 1941 who thought that Austria and the Sudetenland could and should remain a part of Germany, and though Mr. Churchill stated on September 30, 1940, that the Munich Agreement had been destroyed by the Germans, it was not until the Moscow Declaration of December 1941 that the independence of Austria was officially included among Allied war aims, and a further eight months

'assurance' by the hand of Mr. Bryans, as he had already sent one through 'another channel' a week before. What this 'other channel' might be Bryans did not know — though von Hassell did — but it had been made clear to him with that suave severity of manner, in the use of which the British Civil Servant is a master, that it was now time that his unofficial and amateur activities should cease and that such weighty matters should properly be left to the handling of experts.[1]

The 'other channel' to which Lord Halifax had referred, to the discomfiture of Mr. Bryans, had been opened up at a very early date after the beginning of the war. It consisted primarily of Dr. Josef Müller, a Munich lawyer and former member of the Bavarian People's Party, a devout Catholic and a confidant of Cardinal Faulhaber. Dr. Müller is a man of tremendous physique, indomitable courage and endurance, inexhaustible energy and unflagging zeal and still rejoices in his schoolboy nickname of 'Ochsensepp'.[2] As one of those who had never paid lip-service to the régime, Müller had been early marked by Oster for future use and at the outbreak of war he was mustered on to the strength of the Abwehr at Munich, whence he travelled to Rome in October 1939 for the purpose of establishing contact with the Vatican.[3] This he successfully accomplished with the assistance of, amongst others, Father Leiber, the Private Secretary to the Pope, and of Msgr. Kaas, the former Chairman of the German Centre Party, who, after registering the vote of his Party in favour of the Enabling Act on March 21, 1933, had retired to Rome, where he had been placed in charge of the fabric of St. Peter's, and where, with von Papen, he had negotiated the German Concordat of July 20, 1933.

Müller's object was that of all the conspiratorial envoys at this time, namely to gain an 'assurance' from Britain which would provide the Generals with sufficient justification to turn their swords against the 'living Hitler'. His task was to ascertain on what conditions Britain was prepared to end the war, it being understood

were to elapse before Mr. Eden's statement in the House of Commons on August 5, 1942, and the exchange of notes between the British and Czechoslovak Governments, marked the formal abrogation of the Munich Agreement.

[1] Hassell (April 15, 1940), pp. 147-9. Mr. Lonsdale Bryans has given his account of this affair, as well as of other of his exploits during the war, in his book, Blind Victory (London, 1951).

[2] 'Joe the Ox.' Arrested on April 5, 1943, Dr. Müller was interrogated but made no confession which could implicate his fellow conspirators. Liberated in April 1945 he later became Minister of Justice in the Bavarian Government.

[3] An account of Dr. Müller's conversations in Rome is to be found in the papers of Lieutenant-Colonel Groscurth (Vol. II, Section IV) which are now in the Federal German Archives at Coblenz.

that the Holy Father would stand surety for the execution of any agreement arrived at.

The first tentative feelers put out by Msgr. Kaas and Father Leiber to the British Minister to the Holy See, Mr. D'Arcy Osborne, were apparently sufficiently encouraging as to establish the fact that all doors to a negotiated peace with a Germany which had eliminated Hitler were not irrevocably barred, and that there were still those in London with whom it was possible to talk.

By the end of October these Papal soundings had disclosed a very evident willingness in London to make a 'soft peace' with a non-Nazi Germany. According to what Müller reported from Rome to his principals in Berlin, the Pope was apparently prepared to go to surprising lengths in his understanding of German interests, whereas Lord Halifax, while accepting the general principles of the German formula, had cagily touched upon such points as the 'decentralization' of Germany and the possibility of 'a referendum in Austria'. These points, the Pope strongly emphasized to Müller, should not constitute barriers to peace if agreement were reached on all other aspects.

The results of Müller's activities were now summarized by Dohnanyi in a memorandum, known as the 'X-Report'. This document was submitted to Beck and von Hassell in the last week of October. It stated that the Holy Father was prepared to act as intermediary for an understanding with Britain on the following terms:

1. The removal of the Nazi Régime.
2. The formation of a new German Government and the restoration of the *Rechtsstaat* in Germany.
3. No attack in the West by either side.
4. The settlement of the Eastern question in favour of Germany.

The report also purported to show that the British Government were actually ready for an understanding on these conditions.[1]

The leaders of the conspiracy were not very hopeful of the success of even this new weapon in winning over OKH. Von Brauchitsch was virtually despaired of, for though there was growing resentment within the Army at the increasing influence and independence of the *Waffen*-SS and the usurpation of authority by the 'Jodl-Army', as OKW was now called, the Commander-in-

---

[1] The above account is taken from the records of General Thomas (*Gedanken und Ereignisse*) and von Hassell (March 18, 1940), p. 140, and from the evidence of Dr. Müller at the second Huppenkothen Trial at Munich on October 14, 1952. How far the German account tallies with that of the official British record cannot be seen until the publication of the relevant documents.

R

Chief was still the prisoner of his Oath of Allegiance. Popitz had recently obtained access to von Brauchitsch and had besought him to take action 'for the honour of the Army' in rescuing Germany 'from the talons of the Black *Landsknechte*' (SS), but his appeal had struck no answering chord. Von Brauchitsch had remained virtually silent throughout the interview, but his one contribution was held to be significant. He had asked if there was still a chance of securing a decent peace for Germany,[1] and it was on the basis of this enquiry that the conspirators planned to exploit the X-Report.[2]

It was agreed, therefore, that in order to intensify von Brauchitsch's growing desire to prevent an offensive on the Western Front, General Thomas should persuade Halder to send the report to the Commander-in-Chief. In other words, the X-Report was designed to play its part in the preliminaries of the 'Zossen *Putsch*'.[3]

Thomas duly performed his task, and the result was one of monumental failure. The Commander-in-Chief not only refused even to contemplate seditious action on the basis of the Report, but declared roundly that if Thomas insisted upon seeing him in this connection he would place him under arrest. 'The whole thing was plain high treason', he complained somewhat naïvely to Otto John after the war. 'Still, I did not take action against your friends. I read that Report, but I could do nothing with it. I could have had Hitler arrested, easily. I had enough officers devoted to me to carry out his arrest. But that was not the problem. Why should I have taken such action? It would have been an action against the German people. Let us be honest. I had sounded out the *Stimmung* of the German people. I was well informed, through my son and others. The German people were all for Hitler. And they had good reason to be, particularly the working man. Nobody had ever done so much to raise their standards of living as Hitler.'[4] Von Brauchitsch was being very correct at this moment. The basis of the protest which he was already contemplating making to the *Führer* was on quite other grounds than traffic with the enemy.

Undeterred by this initial failure and by the rout of von Brauchitsch by the *Führer* on November 5,[5] the conspirators decided in April to make one more attempt to persuade Halder to take action independently of von Brauchitsch in a last effort to

---

[1] Hassell, pp. 138-9.
[2] Instructions were given by Beck to his fellow conspirators to destroy all copies of the X-Report. One was, however, found by the SD in the headquarters of OKH at Zossen in the course of the investigations after the failure of the July 20 *Putsch*.
[3] Gisevius, ii, 148.
[4] *John Memorandum*.   [5] See above, pp. 470-1.

prevent the attack on Scandinavia which all knew to be imminent. Again General Thomas was the chosen emissary, and again his approaches proved in vain.[1] Halder's first reaction to the proposal was favourable, but on consideration he found that his conscience would not permit him to act. After an affecting meeting with Goerdeler, during which the Chief of the General Staff was moved to tears when taxed with the question of his responsibility, Halder later wrote that : 'The military situation of Germany, particularly on account of the pact of non-aggression with Russia, is such that a breach of my oath to the *Führer* could not possibly be justified'. He added that a peace of compromise was senseless and that 'only in the greatest emergency could one take the action desired by Goerdeler' — '*Also doch!*' was von Hassell's comment.[2]

And thus the Generals lost the last chance — if chance there ever was — of obtaining a negotiated peace favourable to themselves. Within a week of their final rejection of the X-Report as a basis for action, Germany had swept into Denmark and Norway and a new phase of the war had opened, the curtain-raiser to the greater drama of May 10. Thereafter the question of peace terms did not enter very strongly into the calculations of the conspirators. For, by the time that it again became possible to consider a revolt, that is to say when the tide of war had turned against Germany, it was clear beyond all doubt that circumstances had changed materially and that whatever régime might succeed in ousting Hitler could expect but cold comfort at the hand of the victorious Allies — to whom by that time had been added the Soviet Union and the United States of America.

(v)

Though von Brauchitsch and Halder refused to take action against Hitler on the basis of the X-Report and, *malgré eux*,

---

[1] The actual date on which the X-Report was presented to Halder is unknown. Gisevius (ii, 232-3) says it occurred 'toward the end of March', whereas Thomas himself (*q.v.*) puts it 'at the beginning of April'. The latter is more likely to be correct since von Hassell (p. 146), writing on April 6, says that 'Thomas was to have taken the matter to Halder the day before yesterday' (*i.e.* April 4).

[2] Hassell (April 6, 1940), pp. 144-5; *John Memorandum*, p. 30. After Thomas's failure with Halder, it was agreed to send Lieutenant-Colonel Groscurth on a canvassing tour of the various Army commanders, von Falkenhausen, von Leeb, List, von Witzleben, von Kluge, for the purpose of acquainting them with the contents of the X-Report and of persuading them to make a joint *démarche* to von Brauchitsch demanding that he either take action himself or permit them to take it. Whether due to Groscurth's lack of persuasiveness or the adamant refusal of the Generals to be persuaded, or a combination of both, the mission was a signal failure (Hassell, pp. 146, 151).

proceeded with the preparations for the Western Offensive, they displayed a certain degree of courage and independence of thought in steadfastly refusing to have anything to do with the occupation of Denmark and Norway. This adventure did not originate with Hitler. It was the brain-child of the joint genius of Grand-Admiral Raeder and Alfred Rosenberg, the one for strategic, the other for ideological reasons. Hitler had, in fact, been very difficult to interest in the idea, but once he had grasped its possibilities he became enthusiastic.

Not so his General Staff; OKH were appalled at the risks and dangers inherent in the expedition, and, braving their *Führer*'s wrath, they flatly refused to participate in the preliminary preparations. The Scandinavian operation was planned entirely by OKW, and the commander of the expedition, General Nikolaus von Falkenhorst,[1] was selected personally by Hitler.

The opposition of OKH was occasioned by their confident belief that the operation would fail. Its failure might be sufficiently great to provide that much-talked-of 'catastrophe' which Halder had held to be a prerequisite for action by the Army. Once the *Führer*'s military prestige had suffered a substantial reverse, certain Generals might be prevailed upon to forget their oath to the 'living Hitler' in deference to the greater call of duty to the German Reich and the German Army. In such an eventuality the position of OKH would be the more enhanced if they could say that, from the first, they had regarded the Scandinavian adventure as a lunatic idea and had refused, despite the *Führer*'s anger and contempt, to have anything to do with it.

Lunatic in conception the Scandinavian expedition may have been from a rigidly military professional point of view, but it did not fail. It succeeded beyond even the hopes of its progenitors. Within three weeks Denmark and Norway were in German hands, despite the gallant resistance of British, French and Norwegian forces.[2]

---

[1] Colonel-General Nikolaus von Falkenhorst (b. 1888) remained in Norway as Military Commander, after the successful conclusion of the operation with which he had been entrusted by the *Führer*, until 1945. Tried as a War Criminal before a mixed British and Norwegian Military Court at Brunswick in the summer of 1946, he was sentenced to death on August 2 on charges of having handed over captured Commandos to the SS for execution. The sentence was commuted to one of life imprisonment (*United Nations Law Reports of Trials of War Criminals* (London, 1947–9), xi, 18–29).

[2] The invasion of Denmark and Norway by German troops occurred on April 9, 1940, and the first Allied landings took place on April 16. The decision to withdraw British and French troops was taken on April 27, and the operation was completed with skill, speed and success. A month later, May 27, Narvik was recaptured by a composite Allied force which drove the Germans up the railway

The *Führer*'s 'intuition', now military as well as political, had once again triumphed over the cautious professionalism of his experts. The effect was disastrous all over the world. The military prestige of the Allies sank to a hitherto unprecedented level and that of Germany was correspondingly exalted. Moreover, the infallibility of the *Führer*'s judgment was now seemingly established beyond all doubt or error. The believers became the more fanatical; the doubters wavered and rallied to their pledged allegiance; those few who still genuinely opposed retired in bewildered despair at the persistent disasters which doomed the realization of their hopes.

The leaders of the conspiracy knew that after this phenomenal success no possible hope could be entertained for support from the Army. They were now resigned to the inevitability of the Western Offensive, but they clung to the belief that, at least here, the Allies would not be taken by surprise. Again it was Hans Oster who took such precautions as were possible to ensure against this.

Oster had an intimate friend in the Netherlands Military Attaché, Colonel J. G. Sas, who visited him not infrequently after dark at his home in the Berlin suburb of Zehlendorf. To Sas, Oster talked with a freedom and confidence which he gave to few, even within the ranks of his fellow conspirators, giving him every possible warning both for his own country and for others,[1] and Sas faithfully relayed his information to a Government torn between the desire to remain neutral and at peace, and the growing realization that they were not fated to do so much longer.

A restless anxiety settled upon Berlin. Unless the Western Offensive was launched soon it seemed impossible that the secret could be kept longer, and the operation would therefore be robbed of its essential element of surprise. Surely the weather must improve. At last, late in April, just as the Norwegian campaign was brought to its successful conclusion, the meteorologists gave promise of more clement conditions, and by May 4 Sas was reporting to The Hague that an invasion of the Low Countries was but a matter of days.[2] Forthwith the Dutch awoke to a feverish activity. 'Alarming news from Holland', Jodl noted in his diary, 'cancellation of furloughs,

towards the Swedish frontier, where they were faced with the alternatives of surrender or internment. They were, however, saved by the news from France which necessitated the second Allied withdrawal.

[1] On April 1 Oster sent a warning through Sas to the Danish naval attaché warning him of the invasion plans. The information was transmitted to Copenhagen, where it was received with incredulity (Dulles, p. 59). See also Swedish White Book, *Förspelet till det tyska angrippet på Danmark och Norge den 9 April 1940* (Stockholm 1947). [2] Van Kleffens, p. 102.

evacuations, road-blocks and other mobilization manœuvres'.[1]

On Thursday, May 9, the tension reached its penultimate point. That afternoon Hitler took his great decision. He confirmed the following day, May 10, as the date for the attack upon Belgium and Holland, and, having empowered Keitel to issue the final orders, departed at 5 P.M. with Jodl from Finkenkrug, for the Eagle's Nest at the Berghof, where he arrived at dawn the next morning.[2] At 9 P.M. Keitel had issued the order in the *Führer's* name : 'A-Day, May 10 ; X-hour — 05.35'.[3]

In The Hague it was a clear spring evening. The Foreign Minister, Dr. van Kleffens, after a day full of event and tension, had sought relaxation in a short walk with his wife. He returned at 9.30, and as he entered the house the telephone rang. The head of the Dutch Intelligence Service reported the receipt of a laconic message from Berlin ; deciphered, it contained just five words : 'To-morrow at dawn ; hold tight'.[4]

Six hours later the first bombs fell on Dutch and Belgian targets.

There followed a six-weeks war of such startling speed and surpassing success as had never entered into the most sanguine calculations of OKH. Up to the last they had been, at bottom, sceptical of victory, and in this even Göring had shared their point of view to some extent,[5] but they had never even conceived of such a

---

[1] Jodl's Diary, May 8, 1940. It was on this same day that Sas had informed the head of the Foreign Armies Section of OKH, whose duty it was to maintain liaison with foreign military attachés, that, despite all rumours of a British descent upon the Dutch coast, the Netherlands Government felt itself perfectly able to maintain its own neutrality, for which it had taken full precautions, and felt in no need of 'protection'. The German officer replied that he considered the Dutch precautions as being completely in accordance with strict neutrality (van Kleffens, pp. 110-11). This statement conflicts strongly with the accusations of non-neutrality showered upon the Netherlands Government two days later by the German Foreign Office and Ministry of Propaganda.

[2] Jodl's Diary, May 9 and 10, 1940. Halder left Zossen by special train for Godesberg at six o'clock on the evening of May 9, arriving at five in the morning (Halder's Diary, May 10).

[3] 'Top Secret' Order, signed by Keitel, dated May 9, 1940 (*IMT Document,* C-72).

[4] Van Kleffens, p. 112. See also Report of Netherlands Commission of Enquiry, Parts 1 and 2.

[5] According to von Hassell, certain of the Generals had grown confident of the success of the Western Offensive during the late winter and early spring months. Von Reichenau, who always 'heard the grass grow', expressed himself in this vein as early as January 1940, and on April 25 General Fritz Fromm, the Commander of the Reserve Army, made the remarkable prophecy that 'we shall push through Holland and Belgium at one stroke, and finish off France in fourteen days'. He added that the French would run like the Poles and would then capitulate, while England would fight on for a while alone and then give up. 'Then the *Führer* will make a very moderate and statesmanlike peace' (Hassell, pp. 121,

HITLER AND HIS MARSHALS IN THE REICH CHANCELLERY, 1940

From left: Keitel, von Rundstedt, von Bock, Göring, Hitler, von Brauchitsch, Ritter von Leeb, List, von Kluge, von Witzleben, von Reichenau

progress of events as now developed before their astonished eyes.

On May 15, five days after the launching of the offensive, the Dutch Army capitulated, to be followed on the night of May 27-28 by the surrender of the Belgian Army. By June 3 the British Army, though with the added glory of Dunkirk among its battle honours, had nevertheless withdrawn from the Continent. Paris was occupied by German troops on June 14, and a week later (June 21) German plenipotentiaries, Hitler among them, had their revenge for the defeat of November 1918, when they dictated armistice terms to the French in the same historic railway carriage at Réthondes.

The evil good-fortune which had attended Hitler's exploits from the day of the Seizure of Power, through the withdrawal from Geneva, the rearmament of Germany, the remilitarization of the Rhineland, the annexation of Austria and the Sudetenland, the dismemberment of Czechoslovakia, the destruction of Poland, the aggression against Denmark, Norway, Luxembourg, Belgium and the Netherlands, had culminated in the defeat of France, the resounding collapse of the legend of French military strength. When on July 19 the *Führer*, in the flush of victory, created twelve Field-Marshals,[1] he stood at the peak of his military and political 'intuitional' success. He was never to climb higher, though he was to hold the peak for nearly a year and a half. But on that day his Generals looked upon him as a military genius and also as a 'fount of honour'. There were no doubts in 1940.

151-2). Von Brauchitsch and Halder continued, however, to doubt the chances of complete success and favoured further postponement, and Göring actually dissuaded Hitler from attacking on May 8, though the *Führer* would not brook a longer delay than May 10 (Jodl's Diary, May 8, 1940).

[1] The twelve Field-Marshals created on July 19, 1940, were : von Brauchitsch, Keitel, von Rundstedt, von Reichenau, von Bock, Ritter von Leeb, List, von Kluge, von Witzleben, and the *Luftwaffe* Generals Milch, Kesselring and Sperrle. On the same date Göring was appointed Reich Marshal.

CHAPTER 5

FROM THE *BLITZKRIEG* TO STALINGRAD

(July 1940–February 1943)

(i)

ONCE again the 'quick peace' after a 'quick war' eluded Adolf Hitler. In July 1940 he stood in dominant victory as the autocratic arbiter of an area stretching from the North Cape to the Brenner and from the English Channel to the River Bug. Italy was his ally, and the Soviet Union, to all intents and purposes, his 'neutral friend'; while, though the United States was explicitly a hostile neutral, there was no apparent danger that she would permit her hostility to get the better of her neutrality.

Had Hitler been able to achieve that reshaping of the Peace of Westphalia of which he dreamed and planned, there might indeed have been a chance for his 'New Order' and his 'Thousand-Year Reich' to attain some degree of permanent stability, with an unchallenged hegemony over continental Europe. Had Britain concurred in the terms offered by the *Führer* in his *Reichstag* speech of July 19, and agreed to recognize such a hegemony in return for a German guarantee of her imperial and colonial possessions, the *Pax Germanica* might have lasted for an indefinite period. America might well have withdrawn into isolationism; collaborationist governments might have been established in the several capitals of Europe and in London; but behind them would have lurked the disgruntled elements in all countries waiting in fierce impatience to spring upon the back of the conqueror, at the moment when he should become engaged in his inevitable clash with Russia.

All these things might have happened had it not been for the indomitable leadership of one man and the grim and courageous determination of one people. In July 1940 there stood between Adolf Hitler and the realization of his grandiose ambitions only the defiance of Mr. Winston Churchill, backed by the obstinate and traditional refusal of the British people to recognize, let alone acknowledge, defeat.

According to all the rules of logical argument Britain should have taken the opportunity of extricating herself from a disastrous predicament and of making the most advantageous peace possible under the circumstances. She had seen her allies fall one by one in battle at her side. Her own troops had been defeated, even if gloriously, and had returned to her shores minus all their equipment. Her sea and air-power made it possible for her to remain in a position where she need not accept the dictation of humiliating conditions of peace, and in any case Hitler was disposed to be magnanimous. All that he demanded of Britain was the jettisoning of Mr. Churchill, the recognition of his own status as conqueror and arbiter of Europe and the return of Germany's colonial possessions. As an alternative he offered destruction and annihilation.[1] It was, perhaps, the most outstanding example of the 'Love-hate' complex toward Britain which so many Germans through the ages have shared with Wilhelm II and Adolf Hitler.

A hundred and forty years before, a similar alternative had been placed before Britain by Napoleon and a similar reply had been tendered. In 1940 as in 1804, without hesitation or doubtings, without hysteria or histrionics, the British people set themselves to continue a struggle which they had neither sought nor desired but which, having begun, they intended to finish. Confident in their leadership and with an unshakable, if illogical, belief in ultimate victory, they sustained, withstood and defeated all the onslaughts of the enemy. Their gallant and stubborn resistance gained in each case a similar reward; for Hitler, like Napoleon, baffled by the phlegmatic refusal of the British to know when they were beaten, became stricken with that same madness which led him to attack Russia.

(ii)

For a year the Second World War stood at a deadlock. The position of the belligerents after the fall of France was that of two giant wrestlers of whom one, considerably the weaker, makes desperate efforts to prevent himself from being finally pinned down on the mat.

Not that the War seemed at a standstill to those airmen who defeated the *Luftwaffe* in the Battle of Britain, nor to those civilians who suffered the full force of Hitler's bombing, nor to those of the Royal Navy and the merchant marine who kept their long and ceaseless watch and maintained the traffic on Britain's sea approaches. But on the continent of Europe there was no military activity — if

---

[1] Speech of the *Führer* in the *Reichstag* on July 19, 1940. (*Völkischer Beobachter*, July 20, 1940 ; Roussy de Sales, pp. 809-40.)

R 2

one excludes the Italian invasion of Greece and the four-weeks German campaign in the Balkans — between the signature of the Armistice with France on June 22, 1940, and the invasion of the Soviet Union exactly a year later.

This interval was not entirely wasted by the conspirators. Once they had recovered from their immediate despondency at the phenomenal magnitude of Hitler's swift victories ; once it became apparent that the war was not at an end, that Britain had no intention of making peace ; once the defeat of the Battle of Britain had led to the abandonment of 'Operation Sea-Lion' (the plan for the invasion of England), those who had entertained hopes for the overthrow of Hitler felt these hopes rekindle.

The position was clearly very different from that before May 10, 1940. If there had ever been any possibility of a negotiated peace between the Allies and a non-Nazi Germany it had vanished into thin air when the first German bombs fell upon Belgium and the Netherlands. The Britain which had manifested itself under Mr. Churchill's inspired leadership and which was now engaged — and successfully — in keeping the grip of the enemy from her throat was in no mood, either then or later, to grant a 'soft peace' to any Germany, and the same was true of that ragged and gallant band of Frenchmen who, having rallied to General de Gaulle, were keeping alive the spirit of a fighting France beneath the banner of the Cross of Lorraine.

Mutatis mutandis, also, the same applied to the German Generals on whom the conspirators had heretofore built their hopes of revolt. The almost uncannily fantastic victory in the West had removed the last vestige of possibility that von Brauchitsch and Halder — let alone any field commander — would lift a hand against the *Führer*. The *Generalität* had ceased to exist as an independent thinking force. It had voluntarily and cheerfully bartered its honour and its critical powers in exchange for batons and decorations and swift promotion. Keitel — *Lakaitel* — was no longer the exception but the rule, the symbol of the parasitic sycophancy which the Generals had chosen to assume *vis-à-vis* Hitler.

From June 1940 until the first defeats in Russia 'the German Army in Politics' had ceased to have meaning. If ever there was a non-political Army in Germany it was at this time, when, in the full golden tide of glory and conquest, the Generals were more than content to leave politics to the *Führer* who had brought them to such heights of victory, and to accept his decisions uncomplainingly.

All that was left 'in politics' were a few — a very few — officers in OKW and OKH who had not lost heart and who, with the elder statesmen of the Army, Beck and von Hammerstein — names half-forgotten in the new flood of honours — and a handful of civilians, kept alive the embers of Resistance. It is for this reason that from now on the story centres round the conspirators and only incidentally concerns the Commanding Generals. For these had, for the most part, become merged in the dominant personality of their *Führer*.

The conspirators knew, therefore, that a long war was ahead of them ; yet, even in that heyday of Germany's military success, they realized that, with her failure to subjugate Britain, the ultimate prize of complete victory had eluded Hitler as it had eluded Philip II and Louis XIV and Napoleon and Wilhelm II before him. The decision of Britain to remain in the field at whatever the cost had in itself robbed Germany of the full measure of her conquest of Europe ; the subsequent revelation of Britain's capacity to assume the offensive with ever-increasing strength made it inevitable that sooner or later that conquest would be changed into disaster for Germany, and that that disaster would be the more cataclysmic in proportion to the hatred engendered before it occurred.

The ultimate objective of the conspirators, therefore, was clear, namely to bring the war to an end as soon as possible on the basis of the least unbearable peace terms for Germany. What the conspirators envisaged at that time was the gradual undermining by the Allies of the strength of Germany, either by starvation or bombing. At some point, they believed, the German people would become so desperate that they would be ready to abandon the struggle and that at that time, with an army intact to be used as a bargaining factor, the Generals, after a successful *Putsch*, could negotiate a cessation of hostilities with the Allies, to whom, it was already believed, America would be added in due course. What the conspirators had never conceived was a *Wehrmacht* completely shattered and in flight. That did not enter into their calculations until many months were passed. The magnitude of their ultimate disaster was to become apparent to them only with the passage of time.

Yet though this objective of shortening the war was accepted as the guiding principle for action as early as the autumn of 1940, it was also recognized that this action could not be taken until the war had taken a new turn and until Hitler's military fortunes had begun to wane. The glittering prizes of decorations and marshals' batons had temporarily dazzled the eyes of even the least avaricious among the leading Generals, and until the wells of the *Führer*'s 'intuition' and the springs of the 'fount of honour' dried up simultaneously, they would not permit themselves to entertain doubts as to the future.

The interval therefore had to be occupied in planning, not so much for the immediate preparations of a *Putsch* — that had perforce to be left very largely to *ad hoc* arrangement as the situation demanded — but for the Germany which was to come after Hitler; the Germany which was to emerge from the ashes and rubble of the Third Reich.

It is not without interest that, in these discussions for 'the shape of things to come', all were in favour of the re-establishment of the Monarchy as the most desirable and stable form of government for Germany. It is not surprising that this view should have been held by the purely military elements of the conspiracy, whose tradition and background were, after all, bound up with the throne; nor was it strange that it should be favoured by those young scions of German nobility who were joining the ranks of the conspiracy in increasing numbers; nor certainly was it singular in those time-hardened 'democrats' such as Gessler and Goerdeler, or, for that matter, Schacht and Popitz, since in Germany bourgeois capitalism had ever been allied with the Army and the nobility as pillars and bulwarks of the throne. What was of interest was that the Social Democrats and former Trade Union leaders, who had been brought into the conspiracy as its basis widened with necessity — men such as Julius Leber, Carlo Mierendorff, Wilhelm Leuschner and Jakob Kaiser — all accepted the restoration of a Monarchy, at any rate in principle. After fifteen years of the Weimar Republic and eight years of Hitler, the leaders of the Left had come to the realization of the wisdom of their predecessors Ebert and Scheidemann, who in October and November 1918 had sought so zealously to bring about the abdication of the Kaiser in order to preserve the Monarchy.

It is not to be thought that, in thus giving their support to the idea of a Monarchist restoration, the Left were prepared to accept the re-establishment of a reactionary régime. As in 1931, when Brüning had first mooted it, their idea was that of a constitutional Monarchy, based upon the support of the masses, and with clear guarantees and safeguards for the fundamental rights of the citizen. Much, therefore, depended upon the selection and personality of the candidate for the throne.

This issue had been the subject of earnest and anxious discussion among certain circles of the conspiracy even before the outbreak of the War. Goerdeler was as starry-eyed as Stresemann when it came to royalty, and readily accepted the views of Beck and von Hassell and von Witzleben in this regard. But whom should they establish on the throne? All were agreed that the former

Kaiser, both by reason of age and temperament, must be excluded, and there was neither respect nor regard, among many fervent monarchists, for the personality of the German Crown Prince, who would in any case have been anathema to the Left.[1] Another inevitable exclusion was the notorious 'Auwi', Prince August Wilhelm, the Kaiser's fourth son, who had been an early convert to National Socialism.[2]

It is perhaps characteristic of Goerdeler that his candidate was Prince Oskar of Prussia, the youngest surviving son of Wilhelm II,[3] who, though a staunch opponent of National Socialism and a man of impeccable character, was also the most unyielding legitimist of his family, who could only have been, at the very best, an 'Henri Quint'.[4] Schacht favoured the oldest son of the Crown Prince, Prince Wilhelm, whose disastrous appearance at the autumn manœuvres of 1926 had brought about the removal of von Seeckt; [5] but this was regarded as having too many complications for the more thorough-going legitimists.[6] Gessler, and possibly Halder, as Bavarians and Roman Catholics, were less enthusiastic about a Hohenzollern restoration, and certainly the former, subtle old democrat that he was, desired at one time to see the Crown Prince Rupprecht recalled to the Bavarian throne, if not to that of a unified Germany.[7]

[1] The German Crown Prince (1882–1951) had been notorious in the days before the First World War for his whole-hearted support of nationalist and military extremist elements in Germany, notably in connection with the *Reichstag* debate on the colonial settlement with France in 1911, the Zabern Incident in 1913 and the publication of Colonel Frobenius's book, *The German Empire's Hour of Destiny*, in 1914. His incursions into politics during the war had been followed by his open approval of Adolf Hitler as a candidate for the Presidency of the Reich in 1932. Nevertheless, in December 1941 Popitz is described by von Hassell as being favourably impressed with the Crown Prince as a possible candidate. Friedrich-Wilhelm had expressed himself as 'ready to step into the breach and assume all sacrifices and dangers' (Hassell, p. 216).

[2] Prince August Wilhelm (1887–1949) sat as a Nazi deputy in both the *Reichstag* and the Prussian *Landtag*, and was also a member of Göring's Prussian Council of State. He held the rank of SA-*Gruppenführer*.

[3] Hassell, p. 95.

[4] Prince Oskar (b. 1888) had been a member of the *Stahlhelm* before 1933, but resigned in protest against its support of Hitler. He retired to Potsdam, where he remained quiescent until the outbreak of the war, when he served as a battalion commander in the Polish and French campaigns.   [5] See above, p. 52.

[6] Prince Wilhelm (1906–40) had married in 1933 the Countess Dorothea von Salviati, sister of the famous horseman, Count Hans-Viktor von Salviati, who later joined the conspiracy and was shot after the failure of the July 20 *Putsch*. Because of this morganatic marriage the Kaiser had insisted upon his eldest grandson renouncing all claims and rights of succession to the Crown of Prussia, but Prince Wilhelm did not appear to take this renunciation very seriously (Hassell, p. 95).

[7] Hassell, p. 143.

These were the possible candidates before the beginning of the *Blitzkrieg*, but by the time the Battle of France had ended the circumstances governing a restoration had undergone a change like everything else. In the first place, the behaviour of the Kaiser had occasioned his loyal followers a certain despondency and mystification. Wilhelm II had conducted himself throughout his exile with great dignity and discretion. No pronouncements from Doorn had embarrassed the Weimar Republic, which in its turn had treated the former Emperor with unusual generosity in the matter of the financial settlement. With the advent of Hitler to power the same relations existed, and though the Kaiser never endorsed the Nazi régime, neither did he criticize it, or indeed mention it at all exccept in veiled and guarded terms.[1]

When war came to Holland the Kaiser behaved with courage. He refused all offers from abroad that he should leave the country and all proposals from Berlin that he should return to Germany. He had, he said, been accused of running away once before and, whatever happened now, he would stay where he was.[2] The tides of war eddied around the little Schloss at Doorn, and, despite the strict orders of the SS to the contrary, hundreds of officers found occasion to pass by the gates in the hope of catching a glimpse of the former War Lord as he walked the gravelled paths between the gate-house and the moat. So great was the attraction that a *Wehrmacht* guard was quartered in the gate-house and kept away all visitors. To this unit there was attached an SS officer who, within a very short time, had succumbed to the local atmosphere and was clicking his heels and bowing before the former sovereign with the fervour and precision of a Prussian Guards officer ![3]

---

[1] In the course of a visit by the present writer to Doorn late in August 1939, of which some account has been given by Sir Robert Bruce Lockhart in his *Comes the Reckoning* (London, 1947), pp. 35-40, the Kaiser's sole comment on immediately current affairs was : 'The machine is running away with *him* as it ran away with *me*'.

[2] Hassell, p. 157. A message from the British Government was conveyed to the Kaiser in May 1940 informing him that suitable asylum would be afforded him in England should he wish to go there. This Wilhelm II courteously declined, saying that he had received much kindness from the Dutch people and did not now propose to desert them in their misfortune. In announcing the death of the Kaiser on June 5, 1941, *The Times* printed a message from one of its correspondents repeating a story, which had been current previously, that on receipt of the British invitation, Wilhelm II had told the British Minister that he would not go to England until he accompanied Hitler's victorious troops on their entry into London. In the interests of historical accuracy, the British Minister, Sir Nevile Bland, in a letter published in *The Times* on June 12, 1941, categorically denied that this statement had ever been made to him or to any member of his staff.

[3] Information given to the present writer at Haus Doorn in March 1947 ; see also an article entitled 'A Footnote to History', by A. M. G., *Blackwood's Magazine*, October 1945.

So far, the Kaiser had retained his dignity and his reputation for impartial objectivity, but, whether or not under the influence of the gentlemen of his *Umgebung* it is impossible to say, he sent to Hitler a telegram of congratulation on the occupation of Paris, the text of which was published.

This was highly damaging to the cause of Monarchy within Germany, where it caused both bewilderment and indignation. But the detrimental effect was offset by the death of Prince Wilhelm, in a field-hospital at Nivelles on May 26, 1940.[1] This demise, at one and the same time removed a potentially controversial candidate for the throne and contributed 'a helpful factor' (as von Hassell called it) to the cause of Monarchy.[2] The funeral at Potsdam early in June 1940 was made the occasion for so enthusiastic and fervent a monarchist demonstration — some fifty thousand people attended — that, as a result, Hitler forbade any member of the former German ruling houses to serve in the armed forces of the Reich, compelling them to resign their commissions, or leave the ranks, and to serve in civilian capacities for the remainder of the War.

Thus, when the conspirators began to reconstruct their plans in the latter half of 1940, the field of possible candidates for the throne had been narrowed, and a further complication was removed on June 4, 1941, by the death of Wilhelm II himself. Under the new circumstances there was no opposition among the monarchists to the new candidate now put forward by Popitz, Prince Louis-Ferdinand of Prussia, the second and now eldest surviving son of the German Crown Prince. In face of his manifest claims and qualities Goerdeler renounced his nostalgic legitimist preference for Prince Oskar and Gessler his regional and particularist loyalties to Prince Rupprecht.

Louis-Ferdinand, then a young man of thirty-three, was a close friend of Otto John and Klaus Bonhoeffer, whose colleague he was in the *Lufthansa* and by whom he had been initiated into the general idea of the conspiracy as early as August 1939. At that time he had been regarded as a useful collaborator, there being other and senior candidates for the possible restoration, but gradually his worth had been proved and he had earned the high respect of his fellow-plotters. In fact Louis-Ferdinand combined in a unique manner many of the most valuable qualities of a modern monarch. He had grace, charm and dignity, and possessed an admirable sense of humour. Five years' experience as an employee of Henry Ford at Detroit had given him an invaluable insight into the workings —

---

[1] From wounds received in battle three days before, near Valenciennes.
[2] Hassell, p. 157.

good and bad — of a modern democracy, and had developed that sense of 'common touch' which is given to few princes. He could assume several personalities : the dignified — but never 'stuffy' — Prince of Prussia ; the hail-fellow-well-met, beloved of Americans ; the gay companion, or the more serious listener ; and all with equal sincerity.

He possessed two other great advantages : the sterling personality of his wife, formerly the Grand Duchess Kira of Russia,[1] to whose sound common sense and good judgment more than one survivor of the Plot has paid tribute in conversation with me ; and, secondly, the fact that he was on terms of personal friendship with President Franklin Roosevelt, who had invited the newly married couple to stay at the White House during their honeymoon in 1938 ; and he was also known and well liked in Britain.

Louis-Ferdinand, therefore, appealed alike to the traditionalists, such as Beck, von Hammerstein and Popitz ; [2] to the *snobbismus* of those former devotees of democracy, Schacht, Goerdeler and Gessler ; to the young and stable group within the conspiracy, Otto John, Dietrich and Klaus Bonhoeffer, Hans von Dohnanyi and Fabian von Schlabrendorff ; and also to Social Democrats and Trade Unionists, Leber, Jakob Kaiser and Leuschner. In fact, as the conspiracy again developed, it was increasingly the Prince's task to weld together the conflicting groups within the Opposition and, by his tact, good humour and practical common sense, to patch up those quarrels and schisms which inevitably occur in any group of individuals who are held together only by a common negative force — in this case the hatred of Hitler and the Nazi régime — and have little or no positive or constructive thought in common.[3]

There was indeed little common ground among many of the conspirators, and an example of its lack arose in the days immediately preceding the launching of the Western Offensive. In refusing to take action on the basis of the X-Report von Brauchitsch had repeated the argument which he had used more than once before in discussions with General Thomas, namely that action against the

[1] Princess Kira is the daughter of the late Grand Duke Cyril (a cousin of the Emperor Nicholas II), whose son, the Grand Duke Vladimir, is the present Romanov claimant to the throne of all the Russias.

[2] Von Hassell, however, was not favourably impressed with the Prince, whom he described as 'lacking many qualities he cannot get along without'. He himself, surprisingly enough, favoured the German Crown Prince as a more suitable candidate (pp. 243-4).

[3] I am indebted for much of this information to conversations with Dr. Otto John and other surviviors of the conspiracy, and with Prince Louis-Ferdinand and Princess Kira. See also interviews with Prince Louis-Ferdinand in the Berlin *Tagesspiegel* of May 1, 1947, and the *Westdeutsches Tageblatt* of May 5, 1947.

Führer would be unpopular in Germany because the majority of the workers and the men-in-the-street were all for Hitler as having done more for them than any other German leader.

In order to prove the fallacy of this view an interview was arranged between Hans von Dohnanyi, as representing the military wing of the conspiracy, and Wilhelm Leuschner. Von Dohnanyi proposed that the workers should give the lie to von Brauchitsch by taking the initiative and declaring a general strike, to be followed by similar action on the part of the Army. Leuschner's suspicions were immediately aroused. He recalled how the workers had been first beguiled and then betrayed by von Schleicher at the moment of the Rape of Prussia eight years before (July 20, 1932).[1] Then the SPD had wanted to call a general strike and a General had prevented it with promises and fair words. Now another General urged a general strike with further promises — this time of support. How could the workers trust the Generals? All this was reflected in Leuschner's disgusted reply to von Dohnanyi : 'Tell the officers that this proposal of theirs proves that there is really no common course and no basis for co-operation between them and us. If our workers rise we are very sure that they will be shot down by the Army.'[2]

And there was very little in common in these early days in the future planning of the conspirators. All were agreed on the one salient aim of eliminating Hitler, but here unanimity broke down ; for, at various times in the course of the conspiracy, there were those among the leading plotters — notably Popitz — who considered the possibility of replacing the *Führer* by Göring and even, at one wild moment, by Himmler.[3] All, however, were in enthusiastic accord that Ribbentrop must share the fate of the master whom he had so malignantly influenced and so sycophantically followed for so long.

Planning, such as it was, consisted of two phases : the immediate action to be taken after a successful *Putsch* and the long-term issue of the future political and constitutional structure of Germany, and her moral and spiritual regeneration. As always in such activities, there were clashes at every point, between progressives and reactionaries, between practical reformers and idealistic wishful thinkers, between those who yearned for Germany to continue as a *Machtstaat* and those who were dominated by the cult of German constitutional mysticism.

Goerdeler made contact with various groups in the legal, economic,

---

[1] See above, p. 255.   [2] *John Memorandum.*
                        [3] See below, pp. 574. *et seq.*

and educational spheres and set them planning in secret.[1] He himself developed his own plans for the Germany of to-morrow [2] and came into conflict at once with Popitz, whose views, as a lifelong civil servant, on constitutional development were less progressive than those of the former *Bürgermeister* of Leipzig.[3]

From this welter of ideas there emerged in January and February 1940 the first definite documentary statement of intentions. It was written by von Hassell in co-operation with Beck, Goerdeler and Popitz, and though primarily intended for use in the event of a *Putsch* to forestall the Western Offensive, it remained the basic statement of principles until after the compromise reached with the ideas of the Kreisau Circle after the fall of Stalingrad in February 1943.[4]

The Hassell draft, after some preliminary paragraphs, provided for the establishment, immediately after the overthrow of Hitler, of a council of regency of three persons which should hold supreme power in Germany 'until it is possible to re-establish a constitutional way of life'. It was here that the first clashes between the planners arose. Goerdeler considered Prince Oskar the most suitable President of the Council of Regency, Popitz stuck out for Prince Wilhelm; von Hassell himself favoured Beck. Again, Goerdeler desired an immediate plebiscite, so that the interior government could be based at once on popular support.[5] This to Popitz seemed sheer lunacy, and he urged the continuation of authoritarian government at least

---

[1] Pechel drafted an appeal to the German people and Hermann Kaiser prepared another. Well-known jurists such as Rudolf Smend and Goetze worked on legal questions. Under the leadership of Dietrich Bonhoeffer a group of political scientists, economists and historians, including Erich Wolf, Adolf Lampe, Constantin von Dietze, Walther Eucken and Gerhardt Ritter, all members of the Confessional Church, was formed at the University of Freiburg and with them Goerdeler established contact. Others consulted were Professor Albrecht of Marburg on economics and Professor Litt of Leipzig on educational affairs (Rothfels, p. 101 ; Dulles, p. 122 ; Pechel, pp. 105-106).

[2] For Goerdeler's views, see Dr. Gerhard Ritter, 'Goerdelers Verfassungspläne', *Nordwestdeutsche Hefte I*, December 1946 ; also *Carl Goerdeler und die deutsche Widerstandsbewegung* (Stuttgart, 1954), pp. 266 *et seq.*

[3] Popitz's ideas are contained in his *Gesetz über die Wiederherstellung geordneter Verhältnisse im Staats- und Rechtsleben.* For text see Appendix. Albrecht Haushofer, the son of the General and founder of the Geopolitical Institute at Munich, was also identified with Popitz in this planning ; see Rainer Hildebrandt, *Wir sind die letzten* (Berlin, 1950).

[4] For an outline of the work and personalities of the Kreisau Circle, see below, pp. 544 *et seq.* An interesting analytical comparison of the constitutional planning of the various groups and individuals in the conspiracy is to be found in an article in *Europa Archiv* for July 20, 1950, by Werner Münchheimer, entitled 'Die Verfassungs- und Verwaltungsreformpläne der deutschen Opposition gegen Hitler zum 20. Juli, 1944'.   [5] Hassell, p. 121.

for a time.¹ Though both Goerdeler and Popitz were agreed, at any rate at the outset, on the desirability of a monarchy, or of 'a monarchical regent', on whom the highest authority should rest as 'a firm central pillar', there is evidence that Popitz envisaged the restoration of the Prussian Monarchy with many of its old powers and prerogatives, whereas Goerdeler's conception was of something much more on the English model of a monarchical presidency within a parliamentary system.   As he saw it, the President, whether monarch or regent, 'is not meant to govern but to watch over the Constitution and to represent the State'.²

With these and other somewhat academic discussions and disputations did the conspirators occupy themselves in the latter half of 1940, until they were recalled to more active considerations by the premonitory symptoms of the *Führer*'s intention once again to widen the scope of the theatre of hostilities.

(iii)

In the minds of those high-ranking officers of the Army, Navy and Air Force who had constituted Hitler's audience at the Berghof on November 23, 1939, there should have been no doubt as to the *Führer*'s established intention to attack Russia at the first opportunity.   Then Hitler had told them clearly that he would proceed against the Soviet Union once Germany was free in the West, and if in the ensuing months the Generals forgot this flaming portent, the *Führer* did not forget.   It is not known at which precise moment the *Führer* took his momentous decision to attack in the East, but there is some evidence that even at the height of his victory over the Western Powers, when mechanized columns were racing at will to the shores of the Channel and the military grandeur of France lay humbled and bloody in the dust, he was thinking ahead to the day when he might turn his field-grey legions towards the East. But his mind was still busy with the problem of defeating Britain and he did not issue firm orders that preparations should be made against Russia until the end of July 1940.⁴

¹ See text of the indictment of Popitz and Langbehn at their trial before the People's Court in Berlin in September 1944, reprinted in Dulles, pp. 151-62.
² Ritter, *GoerdelersVerfassungspläne*.   ³ *IMT Document*, PS-789.
⁴ Halder noted in his diary on July 13, that 'The *Führer* is most strongly preoccupied with the question why England does not wish to follow the road to peace. He sees the answer, like us, in Britain's hope in Russia.' (Halder's Diary, July 13, also Butler, p. 536.)   The Russian issue was not finally resolved until the 'Barbarossa' edict of December 18, although Hitler's inclinations were always bent towards the eventual destruction of the Soviet Union.

It is characteristic that a glowing encomium by the *Führer*, in his speech to the *Reichstag* on July 19, of the friendly relations with Russia which had resulted from the Nazi-Soviet Pact,[1] was followed ten days later by a 'top-secret' conference of planners at Bad Reichenhall which had been called for the purpose of communicating Hitler's intention of attacking the Soviet Union in the spring of 1941.[2] Little by little the circle of those in the great secret was widened,[3] and late in August the first directive — heavily camouflaged and without even mentioning the name of Russia — was issued under the code name of '*Operation Aufbau Ost*'.[4]

In mid-November Molotov paid his famous visit to Berlin [5] and, lest this should confuse the German military planners, Hitler wrote on November 12, the day of the Soviet Foreign Minister's arrival : 'Political discussions have been initiated with the aim of clarifying Russia's attitude for the time being. Irrespective of the results of these discussions, all preparations for the East which have been verbally ordered will be continued. Instructions on this will follow as soon as the general outlines of the Army's operational plans have been submitted to me and received my approval.' [6]

These plans were duly placed before the *Führer* by Halder on December 5,[7] and forthwith there appeared on December 18 Hitler's now famous 'General Directive No. 21' in which he delineated for

[1] 'This clear definition of their several spheres of interest was followed by a new basis for German-Russian relations. All hope that the completion of this might give rise to fresh tension between Germany and Russia is futile. Germany has undertaken no steps which would have led her to exceed the limits of her sphere of interest, nor has Russia done anything of the kind' (Roussy de Sales, pp. 834-5).

[2] Affidavits sworn by General Walter Warlimont at Nuremberg on November 21, 1945 (*IMT Documents*, PS-3031, PS-3032).

[3] For example, General Thomas was informed by Göring on August 14 that the *Führer* desired the punctual delivery of war materials to Russia to continue only until the spring of 1941 (Thomas, *Basic Facts for a History of the German War and Armaments Economy*, pp. 313-15. *IMT Document*, PS-2353). Similarly, General Paulus, on assuming office as Quartermaster I of OKH on September 8, 1940, found among his files 'a still incomplete operational plan dealing with an attack on the Soviet Union' (Evidence given by Paulus before the IMT on February 11, 1945 ; *Nuremberg Record*, vii, 254).

[4] Warlimont Affidavits.

[5] Molotov's visit to Berlin took place from November 12–14, 1940. For records of his conversations with Hitler and Ribbentrop during this period, during which it was suggested that the Soviet Union might adhere to the Four Power 'Pact of Steel', see *Nazi-Soviet Relations 1939-1941*, pp. 217-54 ; also Schmidt, pp. 514-24 ; Weizsäcker, pp. 304-306.

[6] General Directive No. 18, signed by Hitler, November 12, 1940 (*IMT Document*, PS-444).

[7] Halder's Diary, December 5, 1940 ; Report of the Chief of the General Staff of the Army to the *Führer*, December 5, 1940 (*IMT Document*, PS-1796).

the benefit of the Chiefs of the *Wehrmacht* the strategic objectives of 'Operation Barbarossa' — to crush Soviet Russia in a quick campaign which was to begin not later than March 15, 1941, and before the end of the war with England.[1]

The reaction of OKH to this new project of the *Führer*'s was, as might be expected, varied in essence. The division of opinion was largely on the lines of the Seeckt school versus the Pan-Germans. Those who favoured an attack upon Russia based their arguments on those which Ludendorff had used with such effect at the famous Crown Council at Kreuznach of December 18, 1917, before the departure of the German delegates to the peace conference of Brest-Litovsk. On that occasion the Supreme Command had demanded from a reluctant Foreign Minister, Richard von Kühlmann, the annexation of the Baltic Provinces and the opening up to Germany of the rich black soil of the Ukraine.[2] Now, in 1941, though the General Staff of the Army were in no position to demand anything, they justified the *Führer*'s plans to themselves and to others on the basis of the same reasoning. Germany would never be safe with the Baltic littoral in the hands of Soviet Russia, and the necessity for occupying the Ukraine as a source of supplies to meet the rapidly developing food crisis within the Reich was an even stronger argument.

Those senior officers of OKH who opposed the Russian venture did so partly from a confident belief that the Soviet Union was more valuable to Germany as a dubious ally than as an active opponent, and that, in any case, the campaign in the East should not be undertaken while Britain remained 'bloody but unbowed' in the West; and partly because they regarded the forthcoming battles as placing an unendurable additional burden upon the resources of the Reich, already strained almost to breaking-point. The argument about the additional supplies from the Ukraine seemed to this school of thought completely illusory, since the existing imports from Russia would be immediately cut off and the territory of the Ukraine so ravaged by battle and by deliberate devastation that nothing in the way of supplies could be expected from it for a long time. Meanwhile the food crisis within the Reich would continue to develop. Finally, there was a deep fear of the complete isolation which would result

---

[1] General Directive No. 21, 'Operation Barbarossa', signed by Hitler, December 18, 1940 (*IMT Document*, PS-446).

[2] Wheeler-Bennett, *Brest-Litovsk: the Forgotten Peace* (London, 1938), pp. 107-11. It was at this Council that Hindenburg, when pressed by Kühlmann for his exact reasons for demanding so adamantly this annexation of the Baltic Provinces by Germany, made his historic remark: 'I need them for the manœuvring of my left wing in the next war'.

from an attack upon Russia, for, with Britain holding the sea approaches to continental Europe, the only contact which Germany could maintain with her ally Japan, and indeed with America, was through Moscow ; this channel of communication and supply would now inevitably be closed.

The chiefs of the conspiracy shared these views and were also appalled at the thought of the indefinite prolongation of the war with its mounting losses in casualties and its economic hardships. An attack upon Russia would transform the war into a world conflict, a maelstrom into which the United States must sooner or later also be drawn. For Germany the ultimate outcome of such a struggle could not be in doubt. However successful she might be at first, inescapable defeat and destruction faced her at the end of the road.

The weary business of attempting to win over OKH to action began once again, with its inevitable sequel of frustration. Both von Falkenhausen, now Military Governor of Belgium, and von Rabenau, Chief of the Army Archives at Potsdam and von Seeckt's biographer, took a hand at attempting to win over the Commander-in-Chief and the Chief of the General Staff, but with complete lack of success. Von Brauchitsch and Halder had lost all capacity for independent thought or action. Mentally and hierarchically, they had become mere understrappers to their *Führer*.[1]

However, as the time drew on for the launching of the Eastern Offensive there was one incident which excited the hopes of those who longed for that final act or order of the *Führer* which should goad his Generals into open opposition. On March 17, 1941, Hitler summoned the heads of the Armed Forces and the Generals commanding in the East to a conference at the Reich Chancellery, and stated to them his intentions for the conduct of the campaign.[2] The object of the operation was, as it had been in 1918, the complete elimination of Russia as a political and military force in Europe.[3] But whereas Ludendorff was content to do this by annexation and

[1] Hassell, pp. 187-8.

[2] Affidavit sworn by Halder at Nuremberg on November 22, 1945 ; evidence of Jodl and von Brauchitsch before the International Military Tribunal on June 5 and August 9, 1946, respectively (*Nuremberg Record*, xv, 410 ; xx, 581-2). At Nuremberg neither Halder nor von Brauchitsch nor Jodl could recall the date of this meeting, but it is established as March 17 from Halder's Diary entry for that date.

[3] The similarity of the political designs of Ludendorff and Hitler upon Russia may be judged from a comparison of the memorandum sent by the First Quarter-master-General to the Imperial Chancellor, on June 9, 1918 (Ludendorff, *The General Staff and its Problems* (London, 1920), pp. 571-5 ; Wheeler-Bennett, *Brest-Litovsk*, p. 326), with the account of the Conference at the *Führer's* Headquarters on July 16, 1941 (*IMT Document*, L-221).

partition, Hitler had also in mind an ideological house-cleaning. 'The war against Russia', he told his hearers, 'will be such that it cannot be conducted in a knightly fashion. This struggle is a struggle of ideologies and racial differences and will have to be waged with unprecedented, unmerciful and unrelenting harshness. All officers must rid themselves of old-fashioned and obsolete theories. I know that the necessity for making war in such a manner is beyond the comprehension of you Generals, but I cannot and will not change my orders and I insist that they be carried out with unquestioning and unconditional obedience.' He then issued the order for the liquidation of Commissars attached to the Soviet Armies. Since this was recognized as a breach of international law the *Führer* formally absolved members of the *Wehrmacht* from guilt, 'provided that the breaking of civil law, such as murder, rape or robbery was not involved'. In other words, the killing of Commissars was no murder. They were ideological vermin and as such must be exterminated, and along with them all Partisans.

This new indication of increased savagery appears to have had a considerable effect upon those present at the meeting. Though no voice was raised in protest in the *Führer*'s presence, after he had withdrawn, the Generals crowded around von Brauchitsch in outraged remonstration.[1] The Commander-in-Chief assured them that he shared their sentiments and would do all that was possible to prevent this order from being carried out. But his opposition was as pusillanimous as usual, and before many weeks had elapsed it was known that the orders had been issued by Keitel and that von Brauchitsch and Halder had subscribed to them.[2]

When the nature of the orders became known, via Canaris and Oster, to the conspirators, there was horror and dismay. 'Von Brauchitsch has sacrificed the honour of the German Army', was von Hassell's comment; 'this kind of thing turns the German into a "Boche", a type of being which had existed only in enemy propaganda'.[3] By accepting these orders the Army had assumed the onus of actions of murder, brutality, and depravity which had hitherto been confined to the SS, and this was doubtless among

---

[1] Von Brauchitsch in his evidence particularly mentions that protests were made by the Field-Marshals designated to command the three Army Groups for the invasion, von Rundstedt, von Bock and von Leeb.

[2] The orders were issued by Keitel in the name of the *Führer* on May 13, on the basis of a memorandum by Warlimont dated May 12, 1941 (*IMT Document*, PS-884), to be followed by an imperative instruction on July 27 that all copies of the original order should be destroyed, though 'the validity of the decree is not affected by the destruction of the copies' (*IMT Documents*, PS-886 ; C-50 and C-51).   [3] Hassell, p. 202.

Hitler's objectives when he issued the decree. Just as during the hideous week-end of June 30, 1934, the firing-squads on the execution grounds had been composed as far as possible of SS men who were also members of good family, in order to involve the nobility and landed gentry in the bloody work, so now the Army, with all their age-old traditions of 'chivalrous warfare', were to become the butchers of the Party in blotting out the ideological opponents of National Socialism.

When the invasion took place on June 22, 1941, and the mechanized columns rolled with irresistible force towards Moscow, it was not every commander who carried out the orders. Von Bock, commanding Army Group Centre, actually refused to issue it [1] and certain of the Army Commanders followed suit. Encouraged by this attitude — and perhaps partly in response to a formal letter of protest from Beck [2] — von Brauchitsch issued a General Order to the Army on the maintenance of discipline which, he later told the International Military Tribunal at Nuremberg, was designed to circumvent the *Führer*'s decrees on the treatment of Soviet Commissars and civilians.[3] If this were indeed his intention, it proved lamentably ineffective ; yet this was, in effect, the sum total of his protest.

The invasion of Russia had one advantage from the point of view of the conspirators. The renewal of active warfare provided better opportunities and greater facilities for a *coup* than could be found in periods of military quiescence. The hopes of the conspirators were still at this time set upon using front-line troops to make the *Putsch*, and it was only when these hopes had been blasted by continuous and persistent failure that they fell back upon the expedient of using the Home (or Reserve) Army.

The immediate centre of active operational conspiracy was located in the Headquarters of Field-Marshal Fedor von Bock, Commander-in-Chief of the Army Group Centre. Here indeed was a nest of intrigue and treason. The ring of plotters was headed by von Bock's G.S.O. I, Major-General Henning von Tresckow, who had Fabian von Schlabrendorff as his A.D.C.,[4] and together

---

[1] Schlabrendorff, pp. 44-5. As against this it should be noted that on October 10, 1941, and November 20, 1941, respectively, both von Reichenau and von Manstein issued orders calling for the 'complete annihilation of the false bolshevist doctrine of the Soviet State and its armed forces and the pitiless extermination of foreign treachery and cruelty' (*IMT Documents*, D-411 and PS-4064).

[2] Hassell, p. 215.   [3] *Nuremberg Record*, xx, 582.

[4] Von Schlabrendorff was not the brother-in-law (*Schwager*) of von Tresckow, as stated by Gisevius (ii, 252) nor even the son-in-law, as this word has been misrendered on p. 462 of the English translation. He was, in fact, no relation at all: His wife is the daughter of the former Under-State-Secretary Herbert von Bismarck. Von Tresckow was a very typical example of the *Reichswehr* officers who at

they succeeded in surrounding the Field-Marshal with a web of conspiracy. His two personal aides-de-camp, Graf Hans von Hardenberg, a descendant of the great Chancellor, and Graf Heinrich von
Lehndorff, a grandson of William I's military favourite, were active
members of the plot,[1] and many of his 'military family' had also
been initiated.[2]

The attitude of these officers was that the invasion of Russia
was futile, unnecessary and, despite its early successes, doomed to
inevitable disaster. In the words of one of their number, Colonel
Bernd von Kleist : 'The German Army in fighting Russia is like
an elephant attacking a host of ants. The elephant will kill thousands,
perhaps even millions, of ants, but in the end their numbers will
overcome him, and he will be eaten to the bone.' Their object,
therefore, was to persuade von Bock to authorize the arrest of Hitler
during one of his periodic visits to Army Group Centre H.Q., thus
igniting the fuse which would eliminate the Nazi régime.

But von Bock was not the stuff of which the leaders of a military
conspiracy are made. As one of von Seeckt's young men he had
been early destined for a brilliant career, and he was determined
that nothing should stand in the way of his attaining its fullest
achievement. Twenty years before, as a colonel, he had dealt
clandestinely with Buchrucker and the 'Black Reichswehr' in a back
room in the Bendlerstrasse ;[3] to-day as a Field-Marshal and an
Army Group Commander he had reached the zenith of his ambition,
and he was not the man to sacrifice his personal success to any other
incentive. Though he despised National Socialism and found
repellent its increasing blood-lust, he was consumed with vanity
and egotism, and the insignificance of his character prevented him

the outset embraced National Socialism enthusiastically, but who — some more
quickly than others — saw the error of their ways and passed into Opposition and
even into Resistance. A Pomeranian gentleman-farmer, with a Prussian upbringing of the old school, von Tresckow had only seen in National Socialism a
corrective for the abuses and corruption of the Weimar system and a means of
liberating Germany from the shackles of Versailles. Of the grosser forms of
brutality and dishonesty inherent in the Third Reich he was either genuinely or
purposely unaware, and he only received his full awakening to the horrors of the
régime which he had aided and abetted with the atrocities which accompanied the
Polish campaign. To his credit, however, be it said, that of the many who suffered
a similar sense of moral outrage he was one of the few who was prepared to translate
it into terms of action. After the failure of the *Putsch* of July 20, 1944, von Tresckow
committed suicide.

[1] Schlabrendorff, p. 43. Of these two, von Lehndorff was executed after the
failure of the *Putsch* of July 20, 1944.

[2] These included Colonel Freiherr von Gersdorff, Colonel Schultze-Brettger,
Lieut.-Colonel Alexander von Voss, a son-in-law of General Heinrich von
Stülpnagel, Major Ulrich von Oertzen, Captain Eggert and Lieut. Hans Albrecht
von Boddien.   [3] See above, p. 92.

from lifting a finger to overthrow a system for which he felt nothing but contempt. He was among those many whose response to the approaches of the conspirators was : 'If it succeeds, I'll support you, but I won't take the consequences of failure'.

By the middle of July 1941 the initial German thrust had penetrated 400 miles into Soviet territory. Moscow lay but 200 miles ahead. The military counsellors of the *Führer* were divided as to the development of the invasion. Von Brauchitsch, Halder and von Bock favoured a concentrated drive on Moscow ; von Rundstedt advised the immediate capture of Leningrad and a linking up with the Finns. Hitler himself inclined towards a vast enveloping movement which, having captured Leningrad and conquered the Ukraine, would turn inwards and converge upon Moscow, outflanking and surrounding the city, which would then fall like a ripe plum into his hands. This plan involved the division of von Bock's mobile forces between von Rundstedt in the southern thrust toward Kiev, and von Leeb's northern attack on Leningrad, leaving von Bock with only infantry to continue the frontal advance on Moscow.

In vain did OKH and Army Group Centre protest against this decision. The more vehement their counter-arguments, the more adamant the *Führer* became in his resistance. Finally he decided to visit von Bock at Borisow, hard by the Beresina, to give the final orders for his super-Cannae.

This was the moment for which von Tresckow and von Schlabrendorff had been waiting, to get Hitler into their own terrain and then seize him. But, in their amateurish efforts, they had reckoned without the unbelievable security precautions with which the *Führer* was hedged about. His movements were enveloped in mystery. He was coming to-day ; to-morrow. He was coming now by car, now by plane. Overnight arrangements would be cancelled, to be re-formulated next day. At last the arrival at Borisow of a fleet of cars from the *Führerhauptquartier* in East Prussia heralded his imminent approach ; it was made known that he would travel by air, but would not entrust his person to any staff car belonging to Army Group Centre for the brief journey of three miles from the airfield to headquarters. And finally he came on August 4,[1] so compassed about with bodyguards and entourage that the dilettanti plotters on the Army Group Staff could not get near him. Nor could they persuade von Bock or Guderian to stand their ground on the strategical issue, with the result that the advance on Moscow was held up for the crucial months of August and September. The

---

[1] Halder's Diary, August 4, 1941.

Führer's visit marked a signal defeat for the conspirators, who had to listen to their Field-Marshal sustain without a murmur the insults which Hitler heaped upon his General Staff.[1]

Thus, though the conditions for which von Hammerstein had striven at Cologne in September 1939[2] had been achieved at Borisow, it was clear that something more than unskilled plotters, strong intentions and the confederate season were necessary for the elimination of Hitler. It was now, in the autumn of 1941, that the original objective of seizing the *Führer* and putting him on trial was abandoned in favour of an openly declared determination to render 'the living Hitler' dead.

(iv)

But, while Hitler's legions moved to encircle Leningrad and struck deep into the heart of the Ukraine; while the local conspirators on the Eastern front were plotting earnestly and ineptly, an event of far greater importance took place upon the broad bosom of the Atlantic Ocean. Mr. Churchill and President Roosevelt held their first historic conference on August 19, 1941.

The scope and significance of the Atlantic Charter go far beyond the confines of this present study, but to the military and civilian conspirators in Germany the Charter constituted the beginning of involuntary disillusionment for many and the confirmation of the worst fears of a few. From the terms of the Churchill-Roosevelt pronouncement it was clear, first, that, though the United States was still technically non-belligerent, her President was determined to support Britain and Russia with American resources and production to the limit of his power;[3] and, secondly, that if they had ever existed, all hopes of a peace of compromise with a non-Nazi Germany were blasted and without root. What Britain had suffered at the hands of the *Luftwaffe*, what Russia was even now suffering at the hands of the *Wehrmacht*, what defeated but unconquered Europe continued to suffer under a *feldgrau* occupation, rendered impossible any desire for any settlement with Germany other than one which should make her incapable of again disturbing the peace of the world by the practice of aggression. It did not matter what régime ruled

---

[1] Schlabrendorff, pp. 47-8.   [2] See above, pp. 458 *et seq.*

[3] Further evidence of this determination of President Roosevelt's was forthcoming a few weeks later when, at the Three-Power Conference at Moscow on September 29, his representative, Mr. Averell Harriman, joined with Lord Beaverbrook in pledging to Stalin the fulfilment of nearly every Russian demand for food and war material.

in Germany. To the embattled victims of Nazi aggression and deception all Germans seemed to be alike.

And who shall blame them for this lack of discrimination at this juncture ?

There were those in Britain and the United States who still urged that offers of a 'soft peace' should be made to the 'decent elements' within Germany, forgetting, perhaps, that these same 'decent elements', though they undoubtedly existed, had shown themselves impotent to prevent Hitler from coming to power, incapable of controlling him once he had seized power, and equally incompetent to remove him from power. There was little at this moment in Germany's history — there is indeed woefully little to-day — to indicate that any widespread change of heart had taken place, or that the basic roots of the *Furor Teutonicus* had been, even partly, eradicated. Some there were in Germany who deeply and sincerely deplored the policies of the Third Reich — a few, a very few, had done so from its very foundation — but these were by no means representative of Germany as a whole. Some there were also who perceived the writing on the wall and read its message of destruction, even through the ephemeral clouds of military success, and these, prompted by fear rather than shame, by regret rather than remorse, sought to shorten the war which should bring down their world about them in rubble and ruin and destruction. But the heart and soul of Germany still beat and waxed great at the command and under the spell of Adolf Hitler. The German people forsook him — as the French forsook Napoleon — only when he had failed. There was not at this time any foundation of conversion upon which any structure of a new Germany could be builded with confidence. Nor was there any sense of mass guilt on the part of the German people, and only relatively little among the leaders of the conspiracy themselves.

That this was in the minds of the framers of the Atlantic Charter was evident from the phrasing of Point 8, in which the Signatories declared that :

They believe all of the nations of the world, for realistic as well as spiritual reasons, must come to the abandonment of the use of force. Since no future peace can be maintained if land, sea or air armaments continue to be employed by nations which threaten, or may threaten, aggression outside of their frontiers, they believe, pending the establishment of a wider and permanent system of general security, that the disarmament of such nations is essential. . . .[1]

---

[1] *British White Paper*, Cmd. 6321.

Here for the conspirators was the knell of many of their hopes and dreams. Here was no trace of Mr. Chamberlain's distinction between the 'German people' and 'a tyrannous and forsworn régime'.[1] Mr. Churchill understood the German people rather better than his predecessor in office. Here was an identification of the German people with Hitler and an indication that, even if a *coup d'état* should remove the Nazi régime, the Government of Germany which should follow must submit to precautionary measures of restraint against the further practice of aggression. And these measures were none other than disarmament ; a disarmament, it might well be imagined, which would far exceed in severity and degree the military clauses of the Treaty of Versailles and which would this time spell the complete destruction of the military caste of Germany — the very element to whom the conspirators must appeal for the requisite force to carry out their *coup d'état*.

It is not, therefore, surprising to find that Beck and Goerdeler, von Hassell, Popitz, and Langbehn, and others of the leaders of the conspiracy, were filled with despondency at the terms of the Charter.[2] The retention of a German Army *in esse* had been an essential pre-requisite in the mind of Beck for any post-war settlement,[3] and the terms of Article 8 seemed clearly directed against such a possibility. Moreover, it was held that the identification of Hitlerism with *Deutschtum*, the refusal to make any distinction between the Nazi régime and the German people, cut the ground from under the feet of those who wished to overthrow the régime. To these men it seemed that, on the one hand, the Allies blamed the German people for not rising against the Nazi tyranny, while on the other, they made it impossible, by the tone and nature of their propaganda, for such an uprising to take place.

Yet, at the same time, the conspirators deprecated any public demands made by the Allies for a change of régime in Germany as defeating their own ends. It had from the first been a fundamental principle of the plotters that the elimination of National Socialism must be represented to the German people — whose mind had been impregnated with post-war propaganda of the betrayal of Germany by the Allies after her surrender on the basis of Wilson's 14 Points — as a purely internal affair, not as the result of a *Kuhhandel* with the Allies, and least of all as something carried out at the behest of Britain and America.

The effects of the publication of the Atlantic Charter would seem to have been to have intensified the anxious desire of the conspirators

---

[1] See above, p. 467.   [2] Hassell, pp. 221-2.   [3] Cf. Kordt, p. 369.

to take action *as soon as possible* to eliminate Hitler and overthrow the Nazi régime while Germany was still in possession of certain bargaining factors. As a result of conversations between von Hassell, Popitz, Oster, von Dohnanyi and General Friedrich Olbricht, Chief of Staff of the Home Army, at the end of August it was agreed that the terms which the conspirators demanded from the Allies were very moderate and represented an irreducible minimum for Germany. It was also recognized by all that the moment would soon pass when a new Germany could insist on these terms. 'When our chances for victory are obviously gone, or only very slim, there will be nothing more to be done.' [1]

Thus, whereas before the Western Offensive the conspirators had sought to retain all that Hitler's conquests had gained for Germany as the price of overthrowing him, they were now prepared to utilize his further military successes for a similar purpose.

But again they failed to convince or carry the Generals with them. And why, indeed, should they have expected to do so? What General would, in all sanity, desert his leader in the heyday of victory? The offensive on which Hitler had determined at Borisow on August 4 had reached the gates of Leningrad in the north, and in the south had resulted in the cornering of Budyenny's armies by von Bock and von Rundstedt in the Kiev salient. Kiev itself fell to the Germans on September 19, and it is estimated that the Russian losses were not less than half a million men.[2] The elephant was trampling on the ants with a vengeance, but in the autumn of 1941 it seemed as if the latter part of Bernd von Kleist's prophecy was far from realization.[3]

Yet Moscow remained uncaptured, and on October 2 Hitler ordered a frontal attack upon the Soviet capital in what he described as 'the last great battle of the year'.[4] The offensive swept forward with seemingly irresistible force. Starting from a line 200 miles from Moscow, the armoured columns of Guderian and Hoth and Hoepner had by October 20 reduced this distance to less than 70 miles, and in the south a supporting offensive had overrun the Crimea, with the exception of beleaguered Sebastopol. Moscow was in a state of siege. The foreign embassies and many Government

---

[1] Hassell, p. 222.

[2] Cyril Falls, *The Second World War* (London, 1948), p. 113.

[3] All was not in complete harmony, however, since Halder records in his diary for August 22, 1941, that, as a result of a memorandum by the *Führer*, castigatingly critical of the field commanders as well as of OKH, he, Halder, suggested to von Brauchitsch that they should both resign.

[4] Hitler's Order of the Day, dated October 2, 1941 (not made public until October 10).

COLONEL-GENERAL HEINZ GUDERIAN

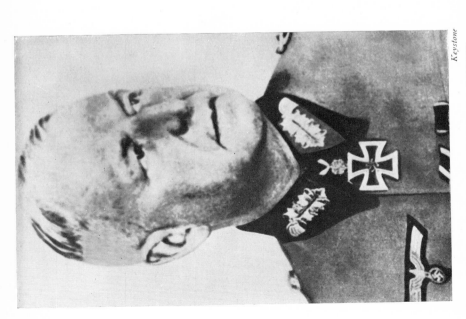

FIELD-MARSHAL ERICH VON MANSTEIN

offices were evacuated to Kuibyshev, 500 miles to the eastward. But Stalin remained within the Kremlin, and between Moscow and the invaders stood the flower of the Soviet Army under a new commander, Grigori Zhukov.

Winter was coming, Russia's most puissant ally ; the first snow had fallen ; the October offensive lost its impetus almost within sight of Moscow ; by the 30th it had ground to a halt. Now was the moment of the great decision. It would seem that at the outset Hitler was disposed to call off the attack and terminate the winter campaign. In this view he was supported by von Leeb and von Rundstedt, the Commanders in the North and the South, who feared both the effect and the outcome of prolonged winter fighting. But von Bock had set his eyes upon Moscow. Von Rundstedt and von Leeb had won their victories and he, von Bock, had been deprived of his armour to enable them to do so. Now his very human ambition to capture Moscow made him insistent upon a resumed offensive. Where both sides were so exhausted, he argued, it was the extra will-power that won the victory. One last effort and Moscow would be theirs.

Von Brauchitsch and Halder supported von Bock and their views served to win over the *Führer*, perhaps against his military 'intuition' but certainly not against his political 'inclination'. Before the final order was given, Halder summoned to his special train at Orsha on November 13 the Chiefs of Staff of the three Army Groups and seven Army Commanders, including Field-Marshal von Kluge, who was destined to command the attack on Moscow under von Bock's direction. With the exception of General von Greiffenberg, von Bock's Chief of Staff (who was in a difficult position and confined himself to purely technical details of discussion), all were in favour of breaking off and waiting until spring to renew the attack. Halder then announced that it was the *Führer*'s will that the offensive be resumed forthwith, and three days later (November 16) the advance began.[1]

The *Führer*'s strategy was to by-pass Moscow to the north and capture the railway junctions behind it. Von Kluge's columns fought their way against fierce resistance step by step nearer to the capital. They reached Dimitrou — 40 miles away ; Yakhroma — 35 miles ; Gorki — 29 miles ; Kabyushki — 22 miles. But by November 22 the offensive was beginning to flag. In a frenzy of relentless energy and ambition von Bock took over personal direction of the operations from an advanced command post.[2] He ordered a

---

[1] Halder's Diary, November 13, 1941 ; Liddell Hart, pp. 286-7.
[2] Halder's Diary, November 22, 1941.

further attack on the 24th, though heavy snow had fallen on the previous night. This, too, fell short of its objective and on December 2 von Bock ordered a third and last effort. It carried the attackers at the farthest point to within the very suburbs of the city. The towers and eagles of the Kremlin gleamed against the leaden sky before the eyes of the weary, battling German *Feldgrauen*. But the Russian workers poured out of their factories and fought in defence of the Holy City of the Revolution with sledge-hammers and even with bare fists. The tide turned back upon itself. Von Kluge, overcoming the energetic opposition of von Bock, gave the order to disengage. The Battle of Moscow had been fought and lost, the field-grey columns turned sullenly westwards, never again as free men to come within sight of the Kremlin towers.

December 7-8, 1941, was a climacteric in the history of the Second World War and of the German Army. On that day Japanese attacks on British and American possessions in the Far East and the Pacific caused the United States to pass from the status of friendly neutral to active ally, and thereby added resources of American man-power, in addition to the resources of American production, to the forces ranged against Germany. On that day Hitler announced that operations on the Eastern Front would close down for the winter, and almost at the moment that the German radio was broadcasting this statement the Soviet armies launched their first full-scale counter-offensive.

And now were felt the hideous effects of the strain under which the German armies had been battling almost without cessation since June 22. Von Bock reported that his Army Group was 'nowhere in a position to check a concentrated attack',[1] to which Guderian added that the condition of his panzer divisions 'was so critical that he did not know how to fend off the enemy'.[2]

The German Army was faced with the possibility of collapse and disintegration such as had terribly overwhelmed the *Grand' Armée* in 1812. The Generals, almost to a man, counselled a retreat to partially prepared positions between Kaluga and Vyasma. Hitler countered with the order of 'No Withdrawal'. He turned upon his defeated Generals like an angry tiger. Now at last he had them beneath the flaming lash of his contempt and ridicule. Hitherto he had merely been right and they wrong, and victory had resulted, with the consequent fawning of the Generals upon their triumphant *Führer*. Now, when faced in defeat with the rigours of a Russian winter, for which little or no preparation had been made, in addition to the advancing Red Army, their professional training counselled

[1] Halder's Diary, December 6, 1941.   [2] *Ibid.*, December 9, 1941.

retreat, and the *Führer*, with the valour of ignorance and the zeal of a fanatic, withered their hesitation with the fierce blaze of his fury.

There can be little doubt that Hitler's insistence upon 'No Withdrawal' averted a near-panic at this moment, but at the cost of very heavy losses in men and material. Moreover, in so doing he displayed a ruthlessness and a brutality towards his Generals which even they had never witnessed in him before. Ignoring OKH altogether, he maintained direct touch with the Army Group Commanders and reduced von Brauchitsch to the status of messenger boy.[1] Where commanders ordered withdrawals in defiance of his orders they were treated with implacable severity, being sentenced in some cases to death, in others to public degradation.[2]

This drastic and Draconian policy had its effect. Not only was the rot stayed and the danger averted, but, under the daemonic impulse of the *Führer*, the front was solidified and was even found to be favourable for an offensive in the spring or summer. Once again Hitler's decisive judgment had triumphed over the indecision of his Generals. Once again he had challenged them on their own ground — this time in dire circumstances — and his determination had been justified — at a price.

But the price was not only in terms of men and material, it consisted also in the sacrifice of the last shred of respect on the part of Hitler for his Generals. Having turned defeat, if not into victory, at least into success, his strategic arrogance knew no bounds. It was now patently clear to him that there was nothing in this *mystique* of generalship that anyone might not comprehend and execute as successfully as the initiated *cognoscenti*. Anyone, in fact, could be a General, and the dignity and reputation with which they had been hedged and enhanced were no more than the vapid mutterings of the priesthood — of which the *Führer* was equally contemptuous. Henceforth he treated his military leaders with such disdainful insolence that it is a matter for amazement that they did not turn and rend him. But they did not do so. They kissed the rod and licked the hand that lashed them, accepting the lashes as

---

[1] Hadler's Diary, December 7, 1941.

[2] General Graf Sponeck, for example, was sentenced to death by a court martial presided over by Göring on Hitler's orders. His sentence was later commuted to life imprisonment, but after the failure of the July 20 *Putsch* he was executed in Germersheim jail without further trial (Hassell, p. 255). General Hoepner was dismissed the service without even a court martial, his 'degradation' being publicly announced in an Order of the Day, in which he was referred to as the 'former' (*ehemaligen*) colonel-general (Hassell, p. 248). Hoepner was also executed after the July 20 *Putsch*, in which he took an active part.

S

part of the price to be paid for the batons and the decorations.[1]

It was now, however, that von Brauchitsch reached the end of his seemingly inexhaustible tether. Four years as Commander-in-Chief of the Army had taken their toll on his health. To the strain of complying, against his better judgment, with Hitler's caprices had been added the additional pressure from Beck and his fellow conspirators inside and outside OKH and OKW. Torn between duty and honour ; between his oath to the *Führer* and his integrity as a member of the Officer Corps ; between his manifest duty to report what he knew of the plots and conspiracies going on about him and his fundamental sympathy with the aims of these conspirators, von Brauchitsch had reached a point where he could go no further. Equivocation, pusillanimity, and sycophancy had carried him just so far, but now even he could no longer blind himself to the true nature of his position as a messenger-boy at headquarters. And he knew, moreover, for he had raised the question on more than one occasion since the beginning of the war against Russia, that virtually no preparation had been made for the armies under his nominal command to meet the merciless rigours of a Russian winter.

All these considerations, plus a sense of failure and a knowledge of guilt for the atrocities which had been committed in Russia by German troops, in accordance with the *Führer*'s orders but without further protest from the Commander-in-Chief of the Army, prompted von Brauchitsch to ask early in December to be relieved of his command. He was a genuinely sick man. At the moment of the vital decision in November he had suffered a heart attack which had disclosed him as the probably incurable victim of a malignant cardiac disease.[2] He now made his health the reason for his request for retirement.

His first request was made on December 7, and Hitler's response was that he was busy at the moment with more important matters. Von Brauchitsch was summoned, however, ten days later, to be given the momentous news that Hitler had decided to take over the command of the Army himself. Von Brauchitsch was sworn to secrecy, but two days later (December 19) his retirement was

---

[1] Hitler was apparently impartially contemptuous of both the real 'army Generals' and of the servile characters in OKW. Von Hassell was told by Goerdeler of a meeting of Nazi chiefs at which Goebbels had suggested that Keitel be sent for in connection with some military problem. Hitler at once replied that a man with the brain of a cinema attendant (*ein Kinoportier*) would not be of much use (Hassell, p. 249). Shortly after, Olbricht asked Keitel how matters stood between OKW and the *Führer*. 'I don't know ; he tells me nothing ; he only spits at me', was the reply (Hassell, p. 285).   [2] Halder's Diary, November 10, 1941.

announced without further preface, and on the following day he left headquarters for ever, never to see Hitler again.[1]

On the evening of the 19th Hitler announced to OKW and OKH his assumption of the active command of the Army.[2] This was the final consummation of his military triumph over his own Generals and over the Officer Corps. In August 1934 he had exacted from them their oath of loyalty to him as Supreme Commander of the Armed Forces of the Reich. In February 1938 he had added to himself the office and duties of the Minister of War. Now in December 1941 he assumed the additional power and authority of Commander-in-Chief of the Army. The Corporal had become War Lord in fact as well as in name.

Nor did he appear greatly impressed with the magnitude of the new burdens which he had shouldered. According to Franz Halder — a not entirely unprejudiced source — Hitler announced the change of command to him on December 19 in these words : 'This little affair of operational command is something that anybody can do. The task of the Commander-in-Chief is to educate the Army in the idea of National Socialism, and I know of no General who could do this in the way I want it done. So I have decided to take over the command of the Army myself.'[3]

For all the concern which General Halder says now that he felt then, and which he has subsequently described with no little style and feeling, he saw no reason to follow his former colleague and Commander-in-Chief into obscurity. He remained as Chief of the General Staff of OKH and waited for a further nine months to elapse before receiving his own quittance.[4]

(v)

The assumption by Hitler of the position of Commander-in-Chief of the Army was followed by a devastating purge of Army Groups and Army Commanders. Between December 1941 and April 1942 Field-Marshals Ritter von Leeb and von Witzleben had been retired, von Bock had been removed from command and reinstated, and von

---

[1] Evidence of von Brauchitsch before the International Military Tribunal, August 9, 1946 (*Nuremberg Record*, xx, 586-7).
[2] Halder's Diary, December 19, 1941.
[3] Franz Halder, *Hitler als Feldherr* (Munich, 1949), p. 45.
[4] Halder was to become an even greater victim of his own self-delusion. A report from Etzdorf to von Hassell, dated February 27, 1942, recorded Halder as saying that he was able to talk quite freely and informally with the *Führer* for hours on end, even with his hands in his trouser-pockets ! (Hassell, p. 256). He was dismissed on September 24, 1942.

Reichenau had died ; of the leading panzer Army Commanders, Colonel-General Guderian (who, with General de Gaulle and General J. F. C. Fuller, may be regarded as the creators of mechanized warfare) had been removed from active command, and appointed Inspector-General of training armoured units, and Colonel-General Hoepner had been publicly cashiered ; while more than thirty-five Divisional and Corps Commanders had been sent home in varying degrees of disgrace ; and this was to be but a preliminary to a consistent policy of *harassement* and humiliation.[1] Gone were the days of privilege and security enjoyed by Generals ; gone the respect which was automatically rendered to those who wore the claret-coloured trouser stripes of the General Staff. The wages of prostitution, which are so often power without responsibility, were for them degradation, helpless servility, and the disdain of their master.

Conversely, this abasement of the Generals raised the hopes of the conspirators anew. Surely the honour of the military caste, the pride of the Officer Corps, would respond to the treatment of Army Commanders like common criminals. Now at last they would be stirred to action, if not on moral grounds at least in defence of vested interest and 'trade union' privileges. At once the optimism of Goerdeler revived and even the confidence of the more sober Beck rekindled.

Plans were laid for what was known as 'isolated action'. The Marshals on the Eastern Front were, at some prearranged moment, to declare their refusal to accept orders from Hitler as Commander-in-Chief of the Army, an initiative which would at once be followed by similar action from the commanders on the Western Front. The plan was designed to overcome the inhibition still felt by some Marshals in respect of their Oath. Under the scheme envisaged they would not be violating their Oath to Hitler as Supreme Commander of the Armed Forces but would merely refuse to recognize him as Commander-in-Chief of the Army ; a fine distinction at which lesser casuists may stand amazed. The real object of the operation, however, was to create confusion, in the course of which Beck — who had no such squeamishness about an oath of loyalty which he regarded in the nature of a contract already broken by Hitler — with the support of the Home Army would seize control, proclaim the

---

[1] In his evidence before the International Military Tribunal on August 10, 1946, von Manstein asserted that 'of 17 Field-Marshals who were members of the Army, 10 were sent home during the war, and three lost their lives as a result of July 20, 1944. Only one Field-Marshal managed to get through the war and keep his position as Field-Marshal. Of 36 Colonel-Generals, 18 were sent home and 5 died as a result of July 20 or were dishonourably discharged. Only 3 Colonel-Generals survived the war in their positions' (*Nuremberg Record*, xx, 625).

dissolution of the Nazi State, the deposition of Hitler and the restoration of the independence and authority of the Army. Once this had been done, the military leaders in the East and West would regard themselves as released from their pledge of allegiance and would rally to the support of the new régime.[1]

Such was the plan conceived by Beck and Goerdeler and Popitz and von Hassell in the first weeks of 1942. Its successful execution depended upon a number of factors. First, it necessitated the acceptance by all of Ludwig Beck as the supreme head of the conspiracy, holding all the strings of the plot in his hands and being recognized as the Regent-designate of any new German régime which might evolve in the event of success. This was achieved without much difficulty since it was generally acknowledged that Beck, alone among the leaders of the conspiracy, could command equal respect and confidence at home and abroad at the moment of crisis.[2]

The second — and the most vital — prerequisite was to secure the support of the Marshals. The task of sounding out and winning over the Western commanders was entrusted to von Hassell, who in the course of a lecture tour to headquarters' staffs — a 'cover' provided by the Foreign Office — was enabled to visit both Brussels and Paris in the latter part of January 1942.[3] He found a greater measure of support than he had anticipated. General von Falkenhausen, military governor of Belgium, and General von Stülpnagel, the military governor of occupied France, were both sympathetic with the idea of any move which should free them from Hitler without the violation of their Oath. They were, in fact, prepared to share in eating the chestnuts, however indigestible, provided somebody else pulled them out of the fire !

The Field-Marshal commanding-in-chief in the West, Erwin von Witzleben, was an old initiate of the conspiracy. He was less troubled than the others by the 'oath-mystique', and with his adjutant, Graf Wilhelm zu Lynar, and his personal A.D.C., Graf Ulrich von Schwerin-Schwanenfeld, gave von Hassell encouragement, though with little confidence in the idea of 'isolated action', which both he and von Falkenhausen regarded as Utopian.

Von Witzleben was, however, prepared to take action in the West, apparently with or without the preliminary initiative of the East Front Marshals, of whom he was somewhat contemptuous. It was tentatively felt that the summer months, when the next German offensive in Russia was to be launched, would be the psychological moment to strike, and for this moment the Field-Marshal, with true

---

[1] Gisevius, ii, 257.   [2] Hassell, p. 259.   [3] *Ibid.*, pp. 248-53.

Prussian thoroughness, decided that he must be in a state of perfect physical fitness. Unfortunately von Witzleben suffered from haemorrhoids, and, like Frederick the Great, he found that this painful complaint impaired the clarity of his judgment.[1] For the work in hand it was essential that his power of decision should be untrammelled, and he therefore arranged to be operated on during the month of March.

With disastrous results; for Hitler seized upon his temporary absence to retire him from active service and to replace him by von Rundstedt, who, though he was cognizant of the plans of the conspirators, and in his heart of hearts may even have sympathized with them, was far too downy a bird to be caught on any such limed twig of incrimination. So that when von Witzleben emerged from hospital, it was to find himself one of the growing number of Field-Marshals and Generals *ausser Dienst* who, though individually they may all have been, like Beck, von Witzleben, von Hammerstein, and Hoepner, heart and soul with the conspiracy, were yet really only useful as individuals because they had no troops to command — and it was troops which were required. The conspirators were therefore left without a dependable confederate in the West.

And in the East they were not much more fortunate. The new commanders of the Army Groups on the Russian Front were von Küchler (North); von Kluge (Centre); and von Bock, and later von Manstein (South). Of these, Gunther von Kluge was adjudged by the conspirators to be the weakest vessel and therefore the most suitable for their purposes. Von Tresckow and von Schlabrendorff had remained upon the personal staff of the Commander-in-Chief of Army Group Centre and they applied to von Kluge the same methods of persuasive pressure that they had used without success upon von Bock.

Von Kluge proved in effect to be too malleable. He was *non*-Nazi rather than *anti*-Nazi, and by nature he was a man of indecision. For two and a half years Henning von Tresckow battled for von Kluge's soul, waging an intensive, clever and wearisome campaign against the Field-Marshal's vacillation. He succeeded in establishing a degree of personal ascendancy over his quarry, but it was only personal. Once removed for a moment from von Tresckow's direct influence von Kluge lapsed again into compliant obedience to Hitler.

---

[1] The memoirs of that strange individual Henri de Katt, Reader to the King of Prussia from 1758–60 (London, 1916, 2 vols.), contain frequent references to the sufferings of Frederick the Great from this malady and the degree to which it enervated and hampered his mental faculties.

Time and again von Tresckow thought he had won him over to a definite plan of action ; time and again the elusive soldier backed out at the most critical moment. Of him might it be written as of Reuben : 'Unstable as water, thou shalt not excel'.[1]

Nor did von Tresckow and von Schlabrendorff scruple to use the weapon of blackmail against the Field-Marshal. Hitler was sufficiently acute not to bludgeon his Generals beyond the point of insensibility. He pandered to their natural vanity in the matter of batons and *Ritterkreuze* and to their less natural avaricious snobbery in respect of money and landed estates. The annual pay of a General Field-Marshal was 36,000 RM. with allowances ; a sufficiently large sum, but not so large after all when compared with the corrupt fortunes put cosily away by the Party leaders. Hitler, having placed his Generals in fetters, saw to it that they were fetters of gold. Payments, which were really in the nature of large tips or bribes for good conduct and loyalty, were made to general officers above the rank of Army Commander from the *Führer*'s privy purse, and were not subject to income tax.[2]

Von Kluge was not forgotten in this distribution of largesse. On his sixtieth birthday (October 30, 1942) he received a letter of good wishes signed by the *Führer* and enclosing a cheque for a substantial amount together with a permit to spend a further large sum on improvements to his estate. Speer, the Minister who, among other activities, controlled building operations throughout the Reich, had been instructed accordingly.

Not only did von Kluge not resent this insult to his personal honesty and to his honour as a German officer, but he accepted the cheque, cashed it and also utilized his building permit. Both the letter and the details of the transaction came into von Schlabrendorff's hands, who passed them to von Tresckow, who used them

---

[1] Genesis xliv, 4. According to Allen Dulles (pp. 66-7), von Tresckow, at one moment during the summer of 1942, had persuaded von Kluge to repeat the manœuvre, which von Hammerstein had unsuccessfully tried to bring about in September 1939 and which had failed at Borisow in August 1941, namely to lure Hitler to the H.Q. of Army Group Centre at Smolensk and then arrest him. With the tacit assent of the Field-Marshal the invitation was issued and accepted by the *Führer* and all preparations made to arrest him and his Staff with the assistance of a regiment of cavalry commanded by Colonel von Boeselager. But at the last moment, as so frequently happened, the visit was cancelled.

[2] In a somewhat idealized study of Rommel, entitled *Erwin Rommel: die Wandlung eines grossen Soldaten* (Stuttgart, 1950), the author, Lutz Koch, a Rhenish journalist, includes in a chapter, with the melodramatic title of 'Der Fluch des Goldes', certain other information about these gifts from the *Führer* (pp. 246-9). Apparently Field-Marshal List refused a gift of half a million marks and Rommel declined the offer of an estate.

to effect. Within a month the Field-Marshal had agreed to a secret meeting with Goerdeler.[1]

The meeting took place in the month of November in the depths of the forest of Smolensk. Goerdeler, whose presence on any military front was highly illicit and was accomplished only with forged papers provided by Canaris and Oster, came alone ; von Kluge was accompanied by von Tresckow. They talked long and frankly. Goerdeler made a deep impression on von Tresckow and apparently upon the Field-Marshal, who agreed to take action once the word was given from Berlin. Goerdeler returned in high spirits to Beck, but already von Kluge's hesitation had overcome him. Before Goerdeler could arrive in Berlin, Beck had received a letter from the Field-Marshal which showed clearly that he had reconsidered the position.[2]

Nor were the conspirators much more fortunate in their approaches to the other 'Eastern' Field-Marshals. Popitz managed to obtain an interview with von Küchler during the autumn of 1942 of which the outcome was inconclusive. The greatest measure of success was achieved with von Manstein who, when first approached in the spring of 1942, indicated that he was not averse to joining a 'Generals' Strike' against Hitler, provided he could capture Sebastopol first. The military problem involved intrigued him, he said, and might bring him another decoration.[3] Sebastopol fell on July 1, 1942, after a siege of 250 days, and thereafter von Manstein considered himself tentatively at the disposal of Beck and the conspirators.

The events of the closing weeks of 1942 seemed to the plotters in Berlin to herald the sure approach of that psychological moment at which the plan for 'isolated action' could be put into effect. On the night of November 7-8 with the success of 'Operation Torch' — Allied landings in North Africa — the tide of war turned finally and relentlessly against Hitler. Once the German-Italian forces of Field-Marshal Rommel had been caught between the Anglo-American pincers they were lost beyond hope, and the mass surrender at Cape Bon, which occurred ultimately on May 13, 1943,

[1] Schlabrendorff, pp. 57-8 ; Hassell, p. 298.
That Hitler regarded this gift as binding von Kluge to personal loyalty is shown from his remarks at the *Führerkonferenz* of August 31, 1944, after the failure of the Generals' *Putsch* in which von Kluge had been sufficiently incriminated to commit suicide (see below, p. 674). 'I personally promoted him twice', the *Führer* complained, 'I gave him the highest decorations, gave him a large estate so that he could have a permanent home and gave him a large supplement to his pay as Field-Marshal. Therefore I am as bitterly disappointed as I could possibly be' (Felix Gilbert, *Hitler Directs His War* (New York, 1950), p. 102).
[2] Schlabrendorff, pp. 61-2 ; Hassell, pp. 285-6 ; Gisevius, ii, 252-4.
[3] Dulles, p. 66.

was a foregone conclusion. The 'soft under-belly of Europe' now lay exposed to the invaders and the *Festung Europa* became not only invested but assaulted on the first of a series of new fronts.[1]

Nor was this all. The month of November also saw the beginning of the sequel to Hitler's pitiless persistence in attempting to force through two gigantic military operations simultaneously — the conquest of the Caucasus and the capture of Stalingrad. The *Führer* had ordered the latter objective in September 1942, when, after a series of recriminatory conferences, he had eventually dismissed Franz Halder from the post of Chief of Staff of the Army, and had replaced him by Kurt Zeitzler, an officer of OKW, who in the summer of 1938 had been responsible for drawing up the plans for 'Operation Green' against Czechoslovakia.[2]

Hitler attached a mystic significance to the capture of Leningrad and Stalingrad.[3] To him they were not only military but also psychological objectives, and he was convinced that, once these two cities, named after the twin heroes of revolutionary Russia, had fallen into his hands, the political régime of the Soviet Union would crumble and collapse. Although less influenced by mystic consideration than his co-authoritarian adversary, there is evidence that, for obvious reasons, Stalin had almost equally strong views upon the holding of Stalingrad as a matter of personal prestige.

The Battle of Stalingrad became therefore a personal contest between the two dictators, both of whom had attached such value to the city that it was obvious that defeat and victory would have a vitally important moral effect upon whichever side sustained them.

With the capture of Sebastopol by von Manstein on July 1, Hitler despatched the Field-Marshal, together with his siege train, to effect the reduction of Leningrad, while the bulk of his Eleventh Army was transferred from the Crimea to the support of General Friedrich Paulus, to whose Sixth Army had been entrusted the frontal attack upon Stalingrad. An army of a million and a half men was launched against Stalingrad and the Don, and as the battle progressed, further troops were detached from the Army of

---

[1] Rommel had been withdrawn from the command of the German-Italian forces in North Africa in the middle of March 1943. The final capitulation at Cape Bon was carried out by the Italian Commander, Marshal Giovanni Messe. The main German force had been surrendered by General Sixt von Arnim on the previous day (May 12). [2] See above, p. 397, footnote.

[3] The Ukrainian town of Tsaritzin had been the scene of a signal victory by the Red Army under the direct command of Stalin over the White forces of General Denikin in September 1918, and was renamed Stalingrad in 1923 in commemoration of the event.

the Caucasus, thereby depleting its strength and hampering the success of its operations.

It was against this dissipation of man-power that Halder had protested, and the consequent conflict had resulted in his dismissal. For Halder did not resign; not even when, as he says, 'it required no gift of prophecy' to foresee the outcome of the Stalingrad operation. He waited until his *Führer* ignominiously kicked him out with bitter and insulting reproaches for his lack of ardour for the National Socialist creed, and the reminder that 'the secret of Moltke's success had been the ardour of his belief in the monarchy'.[1] So passed from the scene Franz Halder — the man who could have been a Yorck or a Lafayette, and had not the courage to be either.

The German offensive launched in September was destined never to achieve its ultimate objective. It swept eastwards, far beyond the farthest point of advance of the German armies in 1918 ; but before Stalingrad it ground to a halt. Despite assault after assault, in which city blocks were contested, at first house by house, then floor by floor and ultimately room by room, with desperate, savage courage, the city never passed into German hands.

Suddenly on November 19 the Russian counter-offensive under Marshal Zhukov, the saviour of Moscow, fell upon the Stalingrad salient. Hustled by simultaneous blows from north and south, and cut off from the Don, Paulus was gradually completely surrounded, and the defenders of the city turned upon him with fresh heart. In mid-December von Manstein, now again in command of the Eleventh Army, moved up the Katelnikov railway in relief of the beleaguered Sixth. Paulus was still sufficiently strong numerically to break through the circle of steel in one direction or another at the price of sacrificing the whole of his heavy material. But the *Führer* persisted in his order of 'No Withdrawal', which had had so magical results a year before. Paulus was to stand firm and await the arrival of von Manstein's relief force, communication being maintained with him by transport planes.

This time, however, the spell had vanished from Hitler's magic formula. Paulus perforce made 'No Withdrawal', but von Manstein was unable to effect a relief sufficiently speedily. By the last day of 1942 there were no German troops within a hundred miles of the doomed Sixth Army, and the conclusion of the story could only be one of prolonged agony.

When the inevitability of the Stalingrad *débâcle* became realized, the leaders of the conspiracy determined to turn it to good effect. The defeats of the German Army in Russia and in North Africa

---

[1] Halder, *Hitler als Feldherr*, pp. 52-3.

must, they thought, have made it clear both to the Generals and to the German people that the war was now lost and that the duty of all German patriots was to salvage what was possible from the wreck at the expense of the top hamper and supercargo. The overthrow of Hitler and the dissolution of the Nazi régime must be accomplished while a German Army still remained intact as a fighting force and as a bargaining factor, and it was with this end in mind that the conspirators planned action in the East.

Their object was to make the catastrophe which had befallen the Sixth Army in Stalingrad a beacon light to the German nation. It was feared that in the extremity of his defeat Paulus might commit suicide after his surrender, and this, it was considered, should be avoided at all costs, or at any rate, until he had issued a manifesto to the German Army and the German people calling upon them to overthrow a Leader and a régime which had wantonly sacrificed a hundred thousand German soldiers.

Communication to this effect was established with Paulus in the form of a personal appeal from Beck, flown into the besieged city by a *Luftwaffe* officer who was also a member of the conspiracy. All depended upon this final gesture from Paulus, since both von Kluge and von Manstein had agreed to fly to the *Führer*'s headquarters as soon as Stalingrad had fallen and demand that the Supreme Command on the Eastern Front be confided to them; and from this would follow the action in Berlin and in the West already planned.[1]

Slowly the moment for the final agony of Stalingrad drew near. On January 20 Paulus reported by radio the conditions within the city, the measure of misery and suffering effected by cold, hunger and epidemics, in addition to wounds received in action. These he described as 'unbearable', and added that further resistance was useless and beyond human possibility. He requested permission to accept a Russian summons to surrender. 'Capitulation is impossible', was the *Führer*'s answer. 'The Sixth Army will do its historic duty by fighting to the utmost, in order to make the reconstruction of the Eastern Front possible.'[2]

For a further ten days the doomed garrison maintained its heroic defence. And in Berlin the conspirators waited anxiously for the end in which was to be their beginning. Would Paulus give the desired signal? He sent a series of telegrams of devotion to the *Führer* which were duly communicated to the plotters by one of their number, General Fellgiebel, the chief of OKW Signals

---

[1] See above, pp. 526-7.
[2] Evidence of Paulus before the IMT, February 12, 1946 (*Nuremberg Record*, vii, 288).

at F.H.Q. These were followed by several orders of the day in which the garrison was exhorted to hold out to the last man. Was this, the conspirators asked themselves, the conduct of a man who was about to give the signal for revolt, perhaps as the last act of his life ?

On January 31 came the announcement of the promotion of Paulus to the rank of General Field-Marshal, and then the silence of utter and complete despair settled over Stalingrad.

The end came suddenly and almost as an anticlimax. Paulus did not commit suicide ; nor did he give the signal to revolt. In silence and without further consultation with F.H.Q. he and his whole Staff, together with other general officers, surrendered to the Soviet forces on the night of January 31-February 1, and thereby brought to a useless conclusion perhaps the most monumental isolated example in military history of deliberate and wasteful sacrifice of human life.[1]

The defection of Paulus came as a bitter disappointment to the conspirators, but to their surprise the news of the surrender was followed almost immediately by word that von Kluge and von Manstein had flown to the F.H.Q. at Rastenburg. Breathlessly the outcome was awaited in Berlin. Were the Field-Marshals at last about to give the signal themselves ?

But again the fates were loading the dice in Hitler's favour. Word came from Fellgiebel that von Manstein, disgusted with Paulus's ignominious finish, had reaffirmed his allegiance to Hitler, while von Kluge, flattered and fascinated by the attention paid him by the *Führer*, fell again beneath the fatal charm and followed suit. 'We are deserted', was Beck's dejected comment.

And so the Stalingrad *Putsch* failed, as the Potsdam *Putsch* had failed in January 1933 and the Berlin *Putsch* in September 1938 and the Zossen *Putsch* in November 1939, and for the same reasons — infirmity of purpose on the part of the Generals and the capacity of the *Führer* to out-think and outwit his opponents.

---

[1] A small part of the German forces, under the command of General Streicher, of the XI Corps, held out until February 2.

[2] This cannot have come as a complete surprise to Beck since, in answer to a recent letter of his to von Manstein urging action in recognition of the fact that the war was irretrievably lost, the Field-Marshal had returned the cliché : 'A war is not lost until one considers it as lost' (Evidence of Gisevius and von Manstein before the IMT on April 25 and August 10, 1946, respectively, *Nuremberg Record*, xii, 240-41 ; xx, 625 ; Gisevius, ii, 260). Von Manstein's evasiveness may have been occasioned by the fact that his previously planned joint action with von Kluge had become known to Göring (*Goebbels Diaries*, p. 199).

CHAPTER 6

FROM STALINGRAD TO NORMANDY

(February 1943–July 1944)

(i)

THE tragic epic of Stalingrad had far-reaching repercussions on Hitler, on his Generals, on the German people and on the conspirators. For the *Führer* it meant an intensification of all his complexes in respect of the Generals. He was deeply chagrined and incensed at this first failure of his hitherto magical formula of 'No Withdrawal'. To him it was inconceivable that Paulus should have behaved as he did, calmly surrendering without the gesture of suicide. There are indications that he even expected a form of mass immolation by the garrison. 'I have no respect for a man who is afraid of that [suicide] and prefers to go into captivity', he told Zeitzler on February 1 ; and again : 'They should have closed ranks, formed a hedgehog, and shot themselves with their last bullet'.[1]

He apostrophized Paulus as a 'characterless weakling', and von Seydlitz, the commander of the LI Corps, who had surrendered with him, as 'fit to be shot', and he and his Chief of the General Staff joined in a general anathema of the professional Staff officer, agreeing that, in preference to 'intellectual acrobats and spiritual athletes', one had to choose men of character, 'brave daring people who are willing to sacrifice their lives'.[2]

Finally, Hitler's bitter hatred and contempt for the Generals came out in a gush of petty spite : 'That is the last Field-Marshal I shall appoint in this war. You must not count your chickens

[1] Record of the Conference at the *Führer*'s Headquarters on February 1, 1943 (Gilbert, pp. 17-22).

[2] That Zeitzler stood high with Hitler at this moment is attested by Goebbels, who records in his Diary for March 9, 1943, that 'the *Führer* continues to be very well satisfied with Zeitzler' ; that 'Keitel plays only a very subordinate rôle. But the *Führer* keeps him . . . because he has nobody to put in his place' ; and that 'The lack of real leaders in the *Wehrmacht* is truly terrifying. That is no doubt chiefly because the selection process has been entirely wrong, in that social position, wealth and education counted for more than natural endowment and good character' (*Goebbels Diaries*, p. 212).

before they are hatched.'[1]   His suspicion of his Generals grew in equal measure with his disdain.[2]

The Generals, themselves, were at the outset shocked and horrified at the Stalingrad *débâcle*. Even those, like Fromm, who had been among the most ardent believers in the *Führer*'s 'intuition', now expressed doubts and criticisms of the conduct of the War under Hitler's active exercise of the office of Commander-in-Chief ; while those who had always lacked faith waxed warmer and more convinced in their unbelief. At no time had Hitler been potentially in greater danger from the Army. For, whereas heretofore the Generals had protested and been proved wrong, they had now protested and been proved right. Defeat — even lack of success — was the one thing that the *Führer* had to fear, and now it had come. Only a spark was needed in the days which immediately followed Stalingrad to ignite a blaze of revolt.

But the spark was lacking, and an unexpected turn of good fortune on the extreme southern flank of the eastern front soon restored the confidence and the lap-dog devotion of the Generals. Technically able and physically courageous, they yet lacked moral courage and, in the main, were wholly wanting in spiritual resistance and intellectual independence. The majority were out to make their professional and social careers in the most material sense. Marshals' batons and Knights' crosses, gifts, estates and building permits, silenced such pangs of conscience as may, from time to time, have assailed them. They were· not disposed to overthrow their *Führer* while he still had these honours within his gift.[3]

One thing, however, is very certain. The Allied formula of 'Unconditional Surrender' played no part in the hesitancy of the German Generals to remove Hitler. To this fact such otherwise

---

[1] Ironically enough the appointments of Busch, von Kleist and Freiherr von Weichs to the rank of General Field-Marshal were dated on this same day, February 1, 1943. Hitler, however, did not adhere strictly to his ruling of 'no more Field-Marshals'. He created four more after this date, two from the Army, Walter Model (March 1, 1944) and Ferdinand Schörner (April 5, 1945) ; and two from the Air Force, Freiherr Wolfram von Richthofen (February 17, 1943), and the tragi-comedy incident of the unfortunate Ritter Robert von Greim, who was appointed General Field-Marshal and Commander-in-Chief of the *Luftwaffe* on April 26, 1945, and committed suicide a month later.

[2] It should be noted that Hitler's dissatisfaction extended also to the High Command of the Navy. On January 30 Grand-Admiral Raeder was retired with the rank of Admiral-Inspector, to be succeeded as Commander-in-Chief by Karl Dönitz.

[3] That this transparent insincerity of allegiance did not, at any rate, deceive the astute Joseph Goebbels may be seen from his Diary entry for March 2, 1943 : 'We must certainly be on our guard about the old *Wehrmacht* and *Reichswehr* Generals. We have very few real friends among them. They are trying to play us off one against the other' (*Goebbels Diaries*, pp. 199-200).

conflicting authorities as Bernd Gisevius and Otto John are united in their testimony. The formula issued from the Casablanca Conference on January 24, 1943,[1] was not widely publicized until the very last days of the month, and Goebbels had not yet turned the full force of his evil genius on to exploiting this utterance as a propaganda factor.[2] Moreover, it had been proved conclusively and pragmatically that German Generals as such were not averse in principle or in practice to the formula of 'Unconditional Surrender' once they had recognized the futility of further resistance, since numbers of them had, in fact, just surrendered to the Russians on these terms.

It was not till much later that the Casablanca formula was seized upon by the Generals as a means of shifting the responsibility for their lack of initiative from their own shoulders to those of the Allies, and this process did not reach its epitome of refinement until many of the Generals had had ample opportunity for rationalization as prisoners of war in British and American hands.

To the German people, also, the name 'Stalingrad' became a symbol of the first real crisis of the War. Hitherto they had followed their *Führer* blindly with boundless confidence in his genius and his 'intuition'. Victory after victory, triumph after triumph, had been the reward of their steadfast faith. Even the failure to capture Moscow in December 1941 had not shaken them, for Hitler had

---

[1] It is no part of the purpose of the present writer to enter the controversy which has surrounded the 'pre-natal' circumstances of the formula of 'Unconditional Surrender'. Those interested in this aspect of an exceedingly important event will find it fully debated in Mr. Churchill's fourth volume of war memoirs, *The Hinge of Fate* (London, 1951), pp. 613-18 ; in Mr. Hull's *Memoirs* (ii, 1570-82) ; in Robert Sherwood's *Roosevelt and Hopkins* (New York, 1948), pp. 1695-97 ; and in the statement of the then Foreign Secretary, Mr. Ernest Bevin, in the House of Commons (*House of Commons Debates*, July 21, 1949, Cols. 1593 *et seq.*).

The statement was issued at Casablanca by President Roosevelt at a joint press conference with Mr. Churchill on Sunday, January 24, 1943. It declared that peace could only come to the world by the unconditional surrender of the Axis Powers and the total elimination of their war-power. This did not mean the destruction of the German, Italian and Japanese peoples, but the destruction of the philosophies in those countries based on fear and hate and subjugation of other peoples. The President suggested that the meeting should be called the 'Unconditional Surrender' Meeting. The effect of this statement on the thinking and reasoning of the conspirators and others in Germany will be seen in the following pages.

[2] Unfortunately the entries in Goebbels' Diary for the first ten weeks of 1943 are missing from the published edition, and the student is therefore deprived of the recorded reactions of that shrewd and perverted intellect to such events as the Fall of Stalingrad and the Casablanca formula. Subsequent entries, however, do not indicate that the Nazi leaders were either deeply impressed or greatly concerned with the issue of 'Unconditional Surrender'.

immediately proclaimed that the Russian Army had been destroyed, and, incredibly enough, many had believed him.

The first dim stirrings of uncertainty had come with Hitler's claim, in his speech to the *Reichstag* of April 26, 1942, to be above all laws, to intervene immediately, and to act on his own responsibility and initiative as circumstances dictated. In response to their *Führer's* demand 'for an explicit endorsement that I possess the legal right to compel everyone to do his duty . . . and to dismiss him irrespective of who he is or what acquired rights he may possess', the *Reichstag* had promptly voted a decree naming him *Oberster Gerichtsherr* (Supreme Law-Lord) with power to overrule all courts of justice.[1]

It was this final contemptuous relegation and destruction of the German judiciary to a position of complete and farcical impotence which disclosed to many what had hitherto been realized by comparatively few, namely the complete anarchy of the Nazi régime.[2]

Nine months later there followed Stalingrad, with its hundred thousand German dead and its ninety thousand German soldiers in Russian hands, whose names and addresses the Soviet radio carried

[1] It was this office, it will be remembered, that Hitler claimed to have exercised, as a temporary and emergency measure, during the week-end of June 30, 1934 (see above, p. 326).

[2] It was shortly after this that, much to Göring's chagrin, a minor conspiracy of an entirely Communist character and inspired on purely ideological lines was discovered within the very precincts of the Air Ministry. This group, known as the *Rote Kapelle*, was not affiliated with any other of the resistance movements, and existed specifically to assist the Red Army with intelligence communicated by means of a secret radio service. Its leaders, Lieutenant Harold Schulze-Boysen, of the *Luftwaffe*, Dolf von Schelia, of the Foreign Office, and Arvid Harnack, of the Ministry of Economics, were in fact Soviet agents within the Reich and were only discovered when one of the Russian agents with whom they were in contact, having been captured after being parachuted into Germany, either sold out to the Gestapo or betrayed them under torture. Schulze-Boysen, Arvid Harnack and the latter's American-born wife, *née* Mildred Fish, were hanged on December 22, 1942, and subsequently many other members of the *Rote Kapelle* — the alleged number varies from 78 to 400 — were also executed. Schulze-Boysen comported himself with such courage that even 'The Bloodhound', *Oberkriegsgerichtsrat* Dr. Roeder, said that 'he died like a man'. Since the war the Soviet authorities in the Eastern Zone of Germany have endeavoured to make him into a posthumously legendary figure as the Nazis did with Schlageter. (See above, p. 104 n.) A play entitled *Rote Kapelle* by one of the survivors of the group had a considerable vogue in Eastern Berlin. (See W. Flicke, *Rote Kapelle* (Düsseldorf-Hilden, 1949, 2nd edn.); Klaus Lehmann, *Widerstandsgruppen Schulze-Boysen Harnack* (Berlin, 1948); Maxim Mourin, *Les Complots contre Hitler* (Paris, 1948), pp. 123-4; Pechel, pp. 86-8; Dulles, pp. 100-101.)

More recently the issue of the *Rote Kapelle* was revived with the appearance of Dr. Roeder as a leading supporter of General Remer's 'Socialist Reich Party' (SRP), when survivors of the Schulze-Boysen group at once began an agitation for his arrest and trial. (See an article by Franz Ballhorn in *Das freie Wort*, May 1951; *Frankfurter Allgemeine Zeitung*, April 27, May 4, May 15; *Der Stern*, May 6-July 1, 1951.)

into many a listening home in Germany.[1] Now, for the first time, there was doubt and despondency among the civilian population, as well as in high military and official circles. Now, for the first time, Hitler was not able to free himself from the responsibility. For the first time the critical rumours were aimed directly at him, and to many he now was revealed not as 'the most brilliant strategist of all time' — a remark of Fromm's — but as a megalomaniac corporal, whose lucky gambles had hitherto been justified by a few intuitive master-strokes and the incompetence and unpreparedness of his opponents.

Deep depression settled upon the Reich, coupled with grumblings and complaints, which, if they had no greater significance, at least disclosed a frailty of morale and an absence of that *Vernichtungswille* which the *Führer* demanded so unreservedly from his *Herrenmenschen*. The reply of the régime was a 'demonstration of fanatical will' organized by Goebbels in the Berlin Sportpalast — in the course of which he adjured his listeners that 'only the supreme effort, the most total war, can and will meet this peril' — and a wave of arrests of Jews and suspected dissidents. Day after day the SS trucks rumbled through the streets of Berlin — and of other German cities — stopping at factory gates, in front of blocks of flats, at the doors of private houses, loading on a human freight destined for the human stockyards, the concentration and extermination camps.[2]

But, beyond the spiritual opposition of many, there was no sign of resistance, even of the few. 'Are we to go and confront the SS — attack their trucks and drag our friends out ?' wrote one perplexed German at this time. 'The SS are armed ; we aren't. No one is going to give us weapons either ; and if anyone did, we wouldn't know how to use them. We aren't just "killers". We revere life. That is our strength — and our weakness.'[3] Of such stuff are tyrannicides not made.

Yet there were some more valiant souls among the welter of mounting bitterness and discontent. The revolt of the students at Munich is a refreshing example of deliberate — if futile — gallantry on the part of a little group of young people who felt impelled to testify to their faith even at the sacrifice of their lives.

Within the student body of the University of Munich there had

---

[1] Reliable data in regard to the German losses at Stalingrad is difficult to obtain. According to one German source, of the 235,000 men who took part in the defence of Stalingrad, 40,000 wounded had been flown out before the surrender, 105,000 were killed and 90,000 taken prisoner.

[2] Andreas-Friedrich, pp. 78-81 ; Hassell, pp. 295-6.

[3] Andreas-Friedrich, p. 82.

existed a small unit of resistance from the early days of the régime
which carried on an illicit pamphlet campaign against the Hitler
Youth Organization by means of the 'White Rose Letters', main-
taining contact with other universities, and, through the Catholic
periodical *Hochland*, with the leaders of the conspiracy in Berlin.
The group, of which the student leaders were a brother and sister,
Hans and Sophie Scholl, Christoph Probst, Alexander Schmorell,
Willi Graf and Hans Leipelt, received the sponsorship of Professor
Kurt Huber, a member of the philosophy faculty of the University.[1]

The fall of Stalingrad made a deep impression upon the student
bodies in all universities. Whereas they had been the original hot-
beds of National Socialism, they now became the first forcing grounds
of active resistance. Many of the men — there were few able-bodied
youths studying in Germany at that time — had served and been
wounded on the Russian front. All had friends in the Army, of
some of whom the Russian wireless announced the names as prisoners
of war.

There came a day, February 16, 1943, when the Gauleiter of
Bavaria, Paul Giesler, on to whose table the 'White Rose Letters'
had found their way, decided to take action. He addressed the
assembled student body on the subject of their national and patriotic
duty. The men, he said, would be combed out lest there should be
found, even among these physical weaklings, military cripples, and
effete intellectuals, some who might be more usefully employed in
shouldering a gun in the defence of the Fatherland. As for the
girls, continued Gauleiter Giesler with a leer, 'They have healthy
bodies, let them bear children. That is an automatic process which,
once started, continues without requiring the least attention. There
is no reason why every girl student should not for each of her years
at the University present an annual testimonial in the form of a son.
I realize that a certain amount of co-operation is required and, if
some of the girls lack sufficient charm to find a mate, I will assign
to each of them one of my adjutants, whose antecedents I can vouch
for, and I can promise her a thoroughly enjoyable experience.'

Before the conclusion of the Gauleiter's speech, which continued
in this vein, the almost incredible had happened. His audience had
howled him down and, overpowering the SS and Gestapo men who
guarded the exits, poured from the building to continue their
demonstrations in the streets of Munich. Though unpremeditated
and unorganized the incident touched off a chain of incidents in
Bavaria which, while they did not seriously jeopardize the régime in

---

[1] Dulles speaks of Kurt Huber as a 'venerable' professor. Since he was born
in 1892 he was only fifty-one at the time of these events.

any degree, were yet considered of sufficient importance for a state of extreme emergency to be declared in the Bavarian capital. There were a number of serious acts of sabotage in the marshalling yards. The Munich telephone exchange ceased to function for three days and the Munich radio station did not broadcast for seven, though this is more likely to have been by order of the authorities, who were anxious to keep the incident from becoming widely known. Nevertheless, the news did penetrate to many distant points and demonstrations occurred in such widely dispersed centres as Vienna, Mannheim, Stuttgart, Frankfurt and the Ruhr, in some of which the SS are alleged to have fired on the demonstrators, inflicting casualties.

Encouraged by the initial success of their act of defiance, and perhaps believing, in their youthful ardour, that they had given the signal for revolt throughout the Reich, Hans and Sophie Scholl and their friends became more daring. On February 18 they publicly distributed, and threw copies from a balcony in the University, a manifesto which urged such mass action as 'Resign from the Party Organizations' and 'Fight the Party'. 'The dead of Stalingrad are calling you', the leaflet continued. 'The German name is dishonoured for all time if German youth does not rise now to take its revenge.' [1]

The sequel was swift, savage, and inevitable. Betrayed and arrested, the Scholls were placed on trial before a specially convened Senate of the People's Court in Munich, over which the dread judge, Roland Freisler, whose name will occur again in these pages, flew specially from Berlin to preside. Sophie Scholl had been so brutally treated during the preliminary interrogations that she appeared in court with a broken leg. Yet her courage was undimmed. 'You know as well as we do', she answered Freisler's brutal examination, 'that the war is lost. Why are you so cowardly that you won't admit it?' Arrested on February 18, 1943, brother and sister (twenty-four and twenty-one years old) were hanged four days later. Sophie Scholl limped to the scaffold on her crutches with a smile. That evening there appeared on the walls of many houses in Munich the inscription: '*Ihr Geist lebt weiter*'.[2] ('Their spirit lives on.')

---

[1] For text of the manifesto see *Deutsche innere Immigration*, pp. 48-50.

[2] Professor Huber and the four other student leaders of the revolt were also later arrested, tried and hanged. For details of the Munich Students' Revolt and its participants see Inge Scholl, *Die weisse Rose* (Frankfurt a. M., 1952); Karl Vossler, *Gedenkrede für die Opfer an der Universität München* (Munich, 1947); 'Der 18. February: Umriss einer deutschen Widerstandsbewegung', *Die Gegenwart*, October 30, 1946; William Bayles, *Seven were Hanged; an Authentic Account of the Student Revolt in Munich University* (London, 1945); Ricarda Huch, 'Die Aktion der Münchner Studenten gegen Hitler', *Neue Schweizer Rundschau* (Zürich), September-October, 1948; Huch, 'Alexander Schmorell',

(ii)

Thus it will be seen that of the three prerequisite conditions laid down in retrospect by Halder for a successful *coup d'état*,[1] the second and third — namely the willingness of the masses to follow the idea of a revolution and the choice of time — were to a considerable measure fulfilled in the first months of 1943. Only the first condition — a clear and resolute leadership — was lacking.

For, despite the planning and the hopeful preparation which had preceded the abortive 'Stalingrad *Putsch*', the conspirators did not find themselves in a position to exploit and profit by the deterioration of German morale which followed the Stalingrad *débâcle*. That a situation of grave discontent existed is manifest by much evidence, more particularly the reaction of the masses to the Sauckel decrees of total mobilization which were announced on February 1. With considerable astuteness Goebbels utilized the Stalingrad saga of heroism to render more acceptable the increased demands for production and man-power. This he combined with an attack upon the grumblers and waverers for their betrayal of the Legend of Stalingrad. Thus total hero-worship and almost total fear of Bolshevism were made the spring-board for insistence upon total war effort.[2]

But, though the situation produced by Stalingrad found the conspirators unprepared for 'total action', it had, nevertheless, the effect of intensifying their whole process of thought and planning. Certain important decisions which had long hung fire, or had achieved only partial acceptance, were at last taken with despatch and firmness. It was now generally agreed, for example, that the original plan for arresting Hitler and putting him on trial must be abandoned as Utopian and impractical. Even Beck, and Goerdeler, who had long opposed it, came down on the side of assassination as the only efficacious means of achieving their high aim.[3]

But this decision was not arrived at without grave searchings of heart. There were many who shrank from the moral responsiblity of murder, even when it was cloaked under the dignity of 'tyrannicide'.[4] Good Christians among the conspirators — and there were

Akademische Rundschau (Hamburg), Heft 3, 1948/49; 'Ihr Geist lebt weiter', *VVN-Nachrichten*, February 16, 1949; Dulles, pp. 120-2; Pechel, pp. 96-104; also a fictionalized study of the revolt by Alfred Neumann, entitled *Six of Them* (London, 1945).

[1] See above, p. 423.
[2] Ernst Kriss and Hans Speier, *German Radio Propaganda* (New York, 1944). p. 437.
[3] Gisevius, ii, 259.
[4] Evidence of this spiritual conflict was disclosed in the film of the trial of the conspirators before the People's Court, which is now in Allied hands. A certain

many such, both Lutheran and Roman Catholic — fought with their consciences, and in their hearts wrestled with the thought that, though primarily the guilt for the misery and death and destruction which had been loosed upon them would lie with Hitler and the Nazi régime, the German people as a whole, because of their active connivance — or at best their passive condonation and acceptance — of National Socialism and all that it had brought to Germany, must bear a heavy burden of responsibility.[1]   Thus the action of the conspirators in killing Hitler must be in the nature not so much of revenge as of expiation.   'Our action must be understood as an act of repentance', was Dietrich Bonhoeffer's expression of this feeling. But how many, even among his fellow conspirators, could follow him when he added : 'We do not want to escape repentance' ? [2]

Having thus determined upon the death sentence for the *Führer*, it was the more incumbent upon the plotters to have ready an immediate short-term scheme of action in addition to their more long-term plans for constitutional reorganization.   Among the seniors it was agreed that, while they reaffirmed their recognition of Beck as the leader and future acting chief of state, the time had come when, for practical purposes, a small directorate should be appointed to assist him in the actual running of the revolt and without prejudice to the formation of any subsequent Reich Cabinet.[3]

But who should form this inner ring ?   The original suggestion was Beck, Goerdeler, von Hassell, Popitz, Schacht and a General. But here there intervened the strong dissension which had grown up among the conspirators themselves.   Goerdeler and Popitz were suspicious of each other, and though von Hassell worked for both, he had confidence in neither, and was even critical of Beck for his too lenient leadership.   All joined in distrusting Schacht.

Nor was the choice of a General any easier.   Von Witzleben was incapacitated, and the only other active commander who was in definite sympathy with the conspiracy, von Falkenhausen, was

---

officer involved in the plot, Major Freiherr Ludwig von Leonrod, stated in his evidence that he had asked his confessor, Father Hermann Wehrle, an Army chaplain, if tyrannicide were a sin, and received the answer 'No'.   The Presiding Judge at once ordered the priest to be called as a witness, and on his testifying that he had given a hypothetical answer to a hypothetical question he was at once removed from the witness-box, arrested, placed on trial for his life and hanged with his penitent.

[1] For a bitter indictment of the German people on this score, written by a young German historian serving with the *Luftwaffe*, see Elizabeth and Albert Hoemberg, *Thy People, My People* (London, 1950), pp. 32-4.

[2] Dr. George Bell, Bishop of Chichester, *The Church and Humanity* (London, 1946), p. 172.

[3] Hassell, pp. 292-4, 297.

rejected by many as having authorized the taking and shooting of hostages in Belgium.[1]

To some extent this deficiency was met in the personality of General of Infantry Friedrich Olbricht, who had recently become an active member of the conspiracy. A deeply religious man, who had reached his decision to oppose National Socialism by assassination only after grave inner debate, Olbricht, as Chief of the General Army Office (*Allgemeines Heeresamt*), was the personal deputy at OKW of the Commander-in-Chief of the Reserve Army, Fritz Fromm, and by virtue of this office had direct authority over all troops stationed within the Reich for garrison and replacement purposes. In February 1943 Olbricht agreed to co-operate with Oster in building up a military organization in Vienna, Berlin, Cologne, and Munich which should be ready to take over control when the spark should be struck. He was an admirable Adjutant-General for the conspiracy, but he was neither the man to assassinate Hitler nor the General to take over the command of the *Wehrmacht*.[2]

If these differences of opinion existed among the seniors, there was also a serious lack of co-ordination and planning between them and those younger members of the conspiracy who, under the leadership of Helmuth von Moltke,[3] had become known as the Kreisau Circle.

For various reasons this group has become perhaps the most widely publicized and certainly the most 'glamourized' facet of the whole anti-Hitler resistance movement. This was due partly to those with whom von Moltke and certain other of his comrades had formed friendships in Britain and the United States, and by whom the Kreisau Group was extolled mightily at the expense of others for the superior purity of their motives ;[4] and partly to the

---

[1] Arrested by the Gestapo after the *Putsch* of July 20, 1944, General von Falkenhausen was confined in company with Halder, Schacht, Best, Stevens, von Schuschnigg and others at Dachau. All were subsequently liberated by U.S. forces at Niederdorf, South Tyrol, on April 28, 1945. Von Falkenhausen was rearrested by U.S. military authorities as a war criminal, and in 1947 was handed over to the Belgian authorities and placed on trial before a Belgian Military Tribunal, together with Generals Reeder, the former head of civil administration in Belgium, von Claer and Bertram, former military governors of Liége, on charges of the execution of hostages, and the deportation or Jews and Belgian workers. On March 9, 1951, von Falkenhausen and Reeder were sentenced to 12 years' penal servitude, Bertram to 10 years and von Claer acquitted. On March 27 all three were released by the Belgian Government and returned to Germany.

[2] Schlabrendorff, p. 62 ; Gisevius, ii, 254.   [3] See above, p. 443, footnote.

[4] After his death Helmuth von Moltke's letters from prison to his wife were published, together with a memoir, originally in the June number of *Round Table* for 1946, later as a pamphlet, by the Oxford University Press, and later still, in 1948, in book form, entitled *A German of the Resistance*. Both the editorial matter

fact that, when placed on trial before the People's Court after the failure of the *Putsch* of July 20, 1944, the members of the Kreisau Circle were accorded a particularly glowing encomium of invective by Roland Freisler, the notorious President of the Court, who roundly declared that 'the motive power behind July 20 really lay in these young men and not in Herr Goerdeler at all',[1] a statement which was very largely based on the faulty evidence produced by Kaltenbrunner's subsequent investigation of the conspiracy.

No word of criticism should be levelled against Helmuth von Moltke, nor is there the slightest reason to doubt the strength of character of himself or his comrades, the purity of their deeply religious motives, nor their gallantry of conduct in the face of insult and death.[2] These men were as sincere and courageous in their beliefs as any other of the original conspirators and considerably more sincere than many of the *epigoni*. Yet the majority of them were opposed to violence, and, though they might have shared in Dietrich Bonhoeffer's denunciation of Hitler as Anti-Christ, unlike Bonhoeffer, they — and particularly von Moltke — were not prepared to take part in removing him by force or death. They were, indeed, the 'conscientious objectors' of the Resistance, deeply genuine in their Christianity yet failing to take cognizance of Christ militant, and, while one may honour the distinction of their principles and the high merit of their virtue, it is perhaps too much to say of them, as the anonymous editor of the Moltke letters claims, that 'they did many things which required just as much coolness of nerve and resource as planting a bomb'.[3]

The Kreisau Circle had its beginnings in the friendship formed between Helmuth von Moltke and Peter Yorck von Wartenburg at the beginning of the war, when both found themselves unwillingly mobilized and attached, the one to OKW, the other to OKH. The two young men were in many ways complementary in character, for though they both came of the East Elbian aristocracy, von Moltke, by reason of his birth and upbringing, had a wide international outlook, while Peter Yorck was rooted in the German traditions in which he had been reared. As the war progressed both young men

and the translation of the letters vary in the two editions and it is in the introduction to the pamphlet (p. 13) that the invidious comparison of von Moltke with others of the conspirators occurs. It has been dropped from the book.

[1] *A German of the Resistance*, p. 33 (Letter from von Moltke to his wife, dated January 10, 1945).

[2] 'I stood before Freisler not as a Protestant, not as a great land-owner, not as a noble, not as a Prussian, not as a German even. . . . No, I stood there as a Christian and nothing else', wrote von Moltke in his last letter to his wife on January 11, 1945 (*A German of the Resistance*, p. 49).

[3] *A German of the Resistance*, p. 25.

became more and more deeply convinced of the hideous evil of National Socialism, of the inevitability of the defeat which awaited Germany at the end of the road, and of the necessity for planning ahead to meet the emergency when that defeat resulted, as they knew it would result, in the collapse of all constituted authority.

Yet both von Moltke and Yorck felt it more important to prepare for the sequel than to hasten the catastrophe. To them the conflict was not against a régime so much as against the perversion of the human spirit and of the dignity of man, which would not necessarily be eradicated by defeat. Their remedy, however, was little more than an amalgam of Prussian mysticism and Prussian Christian Socialism.

Gradually the Circle widened until it became a new and strange combination of conservative and socialist ideology, with many contacts throughout the country, particularly with the Roman Catholic and Lutheran Churches. These were represented in the Circle by the Provincial of the Bavarian Jesuits, Father Roesch, and Father Alfred Delp, a Munich Jesuit, and by Dr. Eugen Gerstenmaier, the Berlin representative of the Protestant Bishop of Württemberg, and Dr. Harald Poelchau, the Lutheran chaplain of Tegel prison. The elements of the Left were Carlo Mierendorff, one of the ablest survivors of the leadership of the SPD and, after his death in an air-raid on December 4, 1943, Julius Leber, Theodor Haubach and Adolf Reichwein. Administrative ability was contributed by Theodor Steltzer, a Protestant and a former *Landrat* in Schleswig-Holstein until 1933, and Hans Lukaschek, a Roman Catholic and formerly Provincial President of Upper Silesia until 1933. The jurist, Professor Hans Peters, of Berlin University, the economist, Dr. Horst von Einsiedel, of the *Wirtschaftsministerium*, and Dr. Paulus von Helsen, an expert in international law, were all members of the Circle, as were Adam von Trott zu Solz and Hans Bernd von Haeften, of the Foreign Office; while direct contact with the Beck-Goerdeler group was maintained by Count Friedrich von der Schulenburg, the *Regierungspräsident*, and Count Ulrich von Schwerin-Schwanenfeld, who had been von Witzleben's A.D.C.[1]

[1] Of this group von Moltke, Yorck von Wartenburg, Father Delp, Haubach, Reichwein, Leber, Adam von Trott zu Solz and von Haeften were all executed at various times after July 20, 1944. Of the survivors, Theodor Steltzer, whose record of illicit co-operation with the Norwegian Underground Movement resulted in their direct intervention, through Dr. Kersten, Himmler's Finnish physician, to obtain first the deferment and finally the annulment of his execution (see Dulles, pp. 91-2 ; Pechel, p. 207 ; *The Memoirs of Dr. Felix Kersten* (New York, 1947), pp. 210-11), was appointed the administrative head of the province of Schleswig-Holstein under British military government and has recently become Director of the *Institut für Foerderungen Oeffentlicher Angelegenheiten* at Frankfurt a. Main. Eugen Gerstenmaier, who was sentenced to eight years' imprisonment by the People's

The remarkable achievement of the Kreisau Circle was that it was able to reconcile, on the basis of compromise, the views of so apparently divergent a congeries of interests. This was undoubtedly due in part to the personality of von Moltke, and also to the fact that, unlike the Beck-Goerdeler group, they were planning in a vacuum, without any direct contact with day-to-day reality. Systematic discussions on specific aspects of post-war reorganization were carried on by small groups meeting in Berlin, Munich, Fulda and elsewhere, but on three occasions, in May and October 1942 and June 1943, all the leaders of the group gathered at Kreisau near Schweidnitz in Silesia on the estate which had been purchased by Helmuth von Moltke's great-great-uncle, the Field-Marshal, with the money grant voted him by a grateful *Reichstag* in 1871.

The results of these conclaves were a series of drafts constituting a basic principle for the new order in Germany — an order which turned for its fundamentals to Christianity 'for the moral and religious revival of its people, for the overcoming of hatred and falsehood and for the reconstruction of the European community of peoples' — and also certain programmes for action in, for example, the appointment of special Commissioners (*Landesverweser*) for each area of the Reich, who, nominated by agreement between all the elements of the Circle, were to possess plenary powers for the *ad interim* period. Special emphasis was also laid on the freeing of worship and education from the control of the State, and a novel proposal provided for the trial and punishment of war criminals by the Permanent Court of International Justice at The Hague.[1]

It was, however, upon the all-important point of violence that dissension arose within the Kreisau Circle. Certain of the members were for active co-operation with the Goerdeler-Beck group, and this involved acceptance of the principle of assassination. Against this von Moltke revolted with every fibre of his being. Though not a physical, and certainly not a moral, coward, he yet abhorred the idea of violence, seeing in it no solution but only a palliative. To him the immediate stage of eliminating Hitler and the régime was less important than that which was to follow, and he believed that those who were involved in post-Nazi planning should be uncontaminated by contact with the tyrannicides.

Court, miraculously survived to become the head of the Protestant Relief Society in Germany.

[1] These drafts survived the efforts of the Gestapo and SD to discover their whereabouts and have been preserved by the Countesses von Moltke and Yorck von Wartenburg, in typescript, under the title of *Der Nachlass von Kreisau*, a photostat copy of which is in the possession of the present writer.

This was a source of no little bewilderment and annoyance to certain of von Moltke's friends and admirers outside Germany. Dorothy Thompson, the eminent American columnist and broadcaster, for example, addressed her weekly radio talks to him as 'Hans'.[1] Again and again she besought him and his friends to come out fearlessly in opposition to the régime. 'Whether we would make a difference between Hitlerism and the Germans as a nation', she told him on March 27, 1942, recalling a pre-war conversation, 'would, I told you, depend on what you, Hans, and your friends would do, not only what you would say. I said that one day you would have to demonstrate by deeds, drastic deeds, where you stood, if the salvation of Germany depended on the answer to that question. And I remember that I asked you whether you and your friends would ever have the courage to act.'[2] Again, five months later, on August 28, 1942, Miss Thompson again besought 'Hans' to act before it was too late, inveighing particularly against the tendency of most Germans to refuse any measure of blame for what the Nazi régime had done. 'This could not happen in my country, Hans, without thousands of people risking their lives to cry "Stop it!" . . . I would not be a party to it. And I should not be alone either. Where are *you*, Hans?'[3]

But resisting all temptation to be lured from his ivory tower of contemplative intellectual activity — 'We merely thought . . . we are to be hanged for thinking together'[4] — Helmuth von Moltke held upon his self-appointed course, refusing, in his great humanity, to become tainted with the abhorrent doctrine of violence. Had he not been actually in jail at the moment of the July 20 *Putsch*, he would undoubtedly have used all his not inconsiderable influence to prevent it, though had it succeeded he would have supported the régime which followed.[5] But in his heart of hearts he was contemptuous of those whose intellectual progression had not developed beyond the use of violence, though he did not impugn their integrity. There is a ring of conscious and proud superiority in his statement: 'This trial sets us poles apart from the Goerdeler muck' ('*Wir sind nach dieser Verhandlung aus dem Goerdeler Mist raus*').[6]

---

[1] Dulles, p. 86.

[2] Dorothy Thompson, *Listen, Hans* (Boston, 1942), p. 138.   [3] *Ibid.*, p. 284.

[4] Letter from Helmuth von Moltke to his wife, January 10, 1945 (*A German of the Resistance*, pp. 39–40).

[5] *Ibid.*, p. 23. This view, expressed by the editor of the Moltke letters, and shared by the present writer, is characterized as 'highly questionable' by Rothfels (p. 126).

[6] Letter from Helmuth von Moltke to his wife, January 10, 1945 (*ibid.* pp. 39, 59).
The word *Mist* has been variously rendered in the English versions of the letter

As it was, in the last hours before his final ordeal, he gave thanks that he had been permitted to remain thus untainted. 'How wonderfully God has moulded this, his unworthy vessel', he wrote to his wife shortly before his execution. 'At the very moment, when the danger became acute that I might be drawn into active preparation for a rising . . . I was removed [he was arrested in January 1944], so that I was, and still am, innocent of all connection with the use of violence.' [1]

Not all the members of the Kreisau Circle, however, were as firmly wedded to passive resistance as their leader. There were contacts between the Circle and the Goerdeler-Beck group, in some of which von Moltke himself participated with what von Hassell called 'his Anglo-Saxon and pacifist inclinations',[2] and, both before and after Stalingrad, these contacts had provoked, if not disagreement, at least warm discussion between what may be termed the 'senior' and 'junior' members of the Resistance.

A preliminary meeting between von Hassell and 'the Young Turks of Kreisau' at the house of Count zu Dohna-Tolksdorf shortly before Christmas 1942,[3] resulted in a round-table conference a month later (January 22, 1943) at the home of Peter Yorck, at which both groups were very fully represented.[4] There was sharp contrast in the views expressed, though this did not run directly between 'old' and 'young' but between the younger men and Goerdeler on the subject of the social and economic policy to be followed by the post-Hitler régime. Beck presided, listening attentively but contributing little to the discussion. Goerdeler — a cross between a pedagogue, an alderman and a civil servant — hectored and lectured the younger men to an extent which provoked Gerstenmaier to a

in the pamphlet edition (p. 21) it is translated as the Goerdeler 'faction', which it manifestly does not mean. When the material was reissued in book form the translations were prepared by Professor Norman Baynes, who chose the word 'stuff' as the best English equivalent (p. 39). But even this, it is submitted, is too weak a rendering in this particular context. The primary meaning of the word *Mist* is, after all, 'dung'; the secondary, 'trash', 'bosh', or 'rubbish'. In view of the evidence the present writer believes that 'muck' comes more nearly to the meaning intended.

[1] Letter from Helmuth von Moltke to his wife, January 11, 1945 (*A German of the Resistance*, p. 48).

[2] Hassell, p. 295.   [3] *Ibid.*, p. 289.

[4] Those present included Beck, Goerdeler, von Hassell, Popitz and Jessen for the Senior Group, and von Moltke, Peter Yorck, Gerstenmaier, Fritz von der Schulenburg and von Trott for the Kreisau Circle. Accounts of the meeting are to be found in von Hassell's Diary for January 22, 1943 (p. 295) and in a letter from Eugen Gerstenmaier to von Hassell's son, Wolf-Ulrich, dated June 25, 1946, which is printed as an appendix to the German edition (pp. 379-80) but is omitted from the English.

brilliant and scintillating *riposte*, developing the more progressive tenets of the Kreisau programme in contrast to the more reactionary views of the former *Oberbürgermeister* of Leipzig. This was not well received by Goerdeler. Neither were the loud and vehement objections of von Moltke. Nevertheless, after von Hassell, for the 'seniors', and Fritz von der Schulenburg, for the 'juniors', had acted as peacemakers, a certain measure of agreement was reached, though it was by no means complete and there do not appear to have been any further plenary meetings of the two groups. This was certainly just as well, since the degree of security among the conspirators was none too high, and it is a fact that a very complete record of these discussions of January 22, 1943, was produced by the Gestapo at the trials of the conspirators before the People's Court.

Later meetings occurred, however, generally between von Hassell and Popitz on the one hand and von Trott, von Haeften and von der Schulenburg on the other, which resulted in a certain compromise of programmes,[1] and when Goerdeler came to make up his shadow Cabinet — which with criminal stupidity he committed to paper in numerous copies — he included in its composition two of the Social Democrat members of the Kreisau Circle, Julius Leber as Minister of the Interior, and Theodor Haubach as Minister of Information.[2]

(iii)

The revival of activity among the conspirators which followed the *débâcle* of Stalingrad brought with it a renewed desire to resume those contacts with the Western Allies which had waned and languished since November 1939 when von Brauchitsch had incontinently consigned the X Report to the 'confidential waste' of OKH.[3]

In the three years' interval which had elapsed there had been at

---

[1] Hassell, p. 329.

[2] For the Kreisau Circle, see Pechel, pp. 114-32 ; Rothfels, pp. 112-29 ; Dulles, pp. 81-96 ; Theodor Steltzer, *Von deutscher Politik* (Frankfurt a.M., 1949), pp. 71-80, 154-69 ; Dr. Eugen Gerstenmaier, 'Zur Geschichte des Umsturzversuchs vom 20. Juli, 1944', *Neue Zürcher Zeitung*, June 23/24, 1945 ; Dr. Wilhelm Wengler, 'Helmuth James, Graf von Moltke (1906-45)', *Die Friedens-Warte* (Zürich), 1948, No. 6 ; Stephan Hermlin, *Der Leutnant Yorck von Wartenburg* (Singen, n.d.) ; *In Memoriam Carlo Mierendorff, 1897-1943* (Darmstadt, 1947) ; Annedore Leber's pamphlet, *Den toten, immer lebendigen Freunden* (Berlin, 1946) ; 'Ein Brief des Bundespräsidenten an die Witwe des Sozialdemokratischen Widerstandskämpfers Julius Leber', *Zeitung ohne Namen*, March 16, 1950. The present writer is also indebted to Dr. Otto John for two unpublished studies of Helmuth von Moltke and Carlo Mierendorff.

Father Delp, while awaiting execution, wrote *In Angesicht des Todes* (Frankfurt a. M., 1948), the last volume of his trilogy, of which the collective title is *Christ und Gegenwart*.   [3] See above, pp. 491 *et seq.*

least two serious attempts on the part of the Beck-Goerdeler Group to 'break out' from the *Festung Europa* and to reach a basis of understanding with Germany's Western enemies. In November 1941 Mr. Louis Lochner, the Berlin correspondent of the Associated Press, whose long residence in Germany had resulted in his becoming one of the best-informed newspaper men in the country, was selected as a possible channel of communication with President Roosevelt, partly on the basis of Mr. Lochner's own record, and partly on that of a common friendship with Prince Louis-Ferdinand.

Lochner had intended to go on leave to America toward the end of 1941 and in November, after the German defeat before Moscow, he was invited by Joseph Wirmer, a former *Reichstag* deputy of the Centre Party,[1] to meet a representative group of the Resistance Movement, including officers of the Army, both active and retired, members of the old political parties and of the Trade Union movements, and representatives of the Christian Churches.

Jakob Kaiser, the Christian Trade Unionist leader,[2] presided at this meeting, at which, since all present realized that, whether the United States became an active belligerent or not, the President would inevitably have a decisive voice in the settlement which would decide the destinies of Germany, Louis Lochner was desired to bring before Mr. Roosevelt all the information at his disposal regarding the wish of those identified with Resistance to remove Hitler and eliminate the Nazi régime, and the efforts which had been made, and would continue to be made, to bring about the realization of this desire. The emissary was also urged to seek guidance from the President as to the form of government — whether monarchical or republican — which would be most acceptable

[1] Joseph Wirmer (1907-1944), a man of many gifts, unflagging energy, hope and aspiration, and of great kindness, is described by Pechel (p. 222) as being obsessed with a bitter hatred of Hitler and of National Socialism. He was Minister of Justice designate in Goerdeler's 'shadow Cabinet' and to him had been assigned the task of purging the German judiciary of the iniquities and corruption with which it had become riddled under the direction of Gürtner, Schlegelberger and Otto Thierack. Placed on trial before the People's Court after the failure of the July 20 *Putsch*, Wirmer was hanged on August 10, 1944.

[2] Jakob Kaiser (b. 1888) had been a member of the executive committee of the Christian Trade Union Movements before 1933, since which time he had been closely identified with Opposition and Resistance, as a friend of Colonel-General von Hammerstein   With Bernard Letterhaus, another Christian Trade Union leader, Kaiser was to have been charged with labour and reconstruction problems in the Goerdeler Cabinet. Fortunately, however, his name did not appear on the list and he miraculously escaped arrest after July 20, 1944. He lived an under-ground existence until the collapse of Germany, when he took a leading part in founding the CDU Party of which he was leader in the Russian Zone   On the formation of the Adenauer Cabinet in Bonn in September 1949, he was appointed Minister of All-German Affairs.

to American susceptibilities after the overthrow of the existing régime, and he was provided with a secret radio code so that direct communication could be maintained between Washington and Berlin.

Alas for these plans. Within a week of this meeting the situation resulting from the Japanese attack on Pearl Harbour and the subsequent German declaration of war on the United States on December 11, 1941, had placed Louis Lochner in internment, and it was not until June 1942 that he returned to America. Whatever may have been the chances of success of his mission when he had at first undertaken it — and they could never have been very great — they were negligible six months later. Mr. Lochner's efforts to gain access to the President were completely without success, and a written application accompanied by an explanatory memorandum, was also refused because of the 'highly embarrassing' nature of the request.[1] Neither the President nor the Department of State was disposed at this moment to have any traffic with any Germans — whatever their political complexion might be.

According to existing sources, no actual 'peace terms' were communicated to Louis Lochner for transmission to the President, and indeed it appears that, with the progressive extension of the war first to Western Europe, then to Russia and finally to Asia and to Africa, the conspirators realized the futility of attempting to bargain with the Allies in respect of anything beyond the frontiers of pre-Nazi Germany. The dream which they had entertained before the Western Blitz of 1940 of a non-Nazi Germany embodying Austria, the Sudetenland and the Polish frontiers of 1914 had undergone radical revision by the close of 1941. Plans for the future now centred upon the conservation rather than the aggrandizement of the German Reich, and to some the realization began to dawn that, unless they carried out their purpose of eliminating Hitler in the near future, they would not even be able to preserve the Reich from partition.

Faced with this growing dread the conspirators made still further efforts in the spring of the New Year. Goerdeler had excellent relations with the great Swedish banking brothers, Marcus and Jacob Wallenberg, whom he had met before the Nazi Revolution through the agency of Heinrich Brüning. To the Wallenbergs Goerdeler had frequently turned for guidance before the outbreak of war and even since September 1939 he had contrived to pay

---

[1] Professor Rothfels (pp. 139-40) has given an account of this incident which has been checked and approved by Mr. Lochner. See also Louis Lochner, *What about Germany?* (New York, 1942), chap. xvii, 'Is there another Germany?' pp. 216-37.

several visits to Sweden, while Jacob, the younger brother, had also been to Germany on more than one occasion.

April 1942 found Goerdeler once more in Stockholm with the specific request that the Wallenbergs should undertake to obtain from Mr. Churchill an assurance that the Allies would make peace with Germany in the event of Goerdeler and his friends succeeding in arresting Hitler and overthrowing the Nazi régime. Jacob Wallenberg was in no two minds as to his answer. The ambition of Goerdeler and his fellow conspirators was laudable in the extreme, but it was quite out of the question that the Allies could be expected to make promises in advance which would bind them in their future policy *vis-à-vis* Germany. This view was supported and confirmed by Marcus Wallenberg, who had recently returned from London. If the conspirators could overthrow Hitler, well and good ; but this action must be judged by the Allies on its own merits. For their memories, no less than the Germans', stretched back to October and November 1918, and the irreparable harm which had been done by the alleged 'Pre-armistice agreement' between President Wilson and the Government of Prince Max of Baden.[1] This time there was to be nothing of this sort, the Wallenbergs told Goerdeler, and before the Allies disclosed their intentions towards a non-Nazi Germany they were determined to be certain of its non-Nazi character. Both the brothers, however, assured Goerdeler that, once he and his friends had achieved a successful *Putsch* in Berlin, they would at once get into touch with Mr. Churchill on his behalf.[2]

Despite these set-backs the conspirators remained undeterred in their efforts to elicit advance assurances from London and Washington, and a few weeks later Stockholm was again the scene of a meeting, not this time between conspirators and journalists or bankers, but between churchmen. In May 1942 the Bishop of Chichester, Dr. George Bell, was requested by His Majesty's Government to visit Stockholm for the purpose of renewing contacts between the Anglican and Swedish Churches. As President of the Universal Christian Council for Life and Work and an outstanding leader in the Œcumenical Movement, Dr. Bell had become widely known and revered in Europe, with warm friendships among German churchmen — Dietrich Bonhoeffer among them — and it

---

[1] See above, pp. 15 *et seq.*

[2] M. Jacob Wallenberg wrote a memorandum summarizing his contacts with Goerdeler between 1940–44, for Allen Dulles, which is reprinted in the latter's book (pp. 142-6). M. Wallenberg later gave an interview to *Svenska Dagbladet* (September 4, 1947) in which he confirmed the accuracy of his original memorandum.

was not surprising, therefore, once his presence in Stockholm had become known in Germany, via the Swedish press, that the Lutheran leaders among the conspirators should devise a meeting with him.

On May 26 there arrived in Stockholm Dr. Hans Schönfeld of the foreign relations bureau of the German Evangelical Church.[1] The head of this bureau was Bishop Heckel, a Nazi and a nominee of the notorious Reich Bishop Ludwig Müller,[2] yet it is characteristic of the fantastic conditions which prevailed in Berlin that among Heckel's closest collaborators were Eugen Gerstenmaier and Hans Schönfeld, who were not only sympathizers with the (non-Nazi) Confessional Church but were also active members of the conspiracy.

For three days the Bishop and the Pastor conferred in the company of Swedish friends, and Dr. Schönfeld, who had been well briefed before his departure, spoke strongly and earnestly of the hopes and fears and plans of the Resistance in Berlin. Much of the information which he gave the Bishop is now known in greater detail, but it was all new and strange and almost incredible at that time. He told of the emphatic protests which had been made in the previous year by the Roman Catholic Bishop of Berlin, Count von Preysing, and the Protestant Bishop Wurm of Württemberg against the Nazi depredations upon law and liberty, and then passed to a remarkably detailed survey — without actually giving names — of the composition of the conspiracy and of what the conspirators proposed to do in the event of their success.

With Hitler eliminated and the Nazi tyranny dissolved, the new German government was prepared to pledge itself to the renunciation of aggression ; the immediate repeal of the Nuremberg Laws and co-operation in international settlement of the Jewish problem ; the progressive withdrawal of the German armies from occupied and invaded countries ; the abandonment of the Japanese alliance and the offer of assistance to the Allies in bringing the War to an end in the Far East ; and the co-operation of Germany with the Allies in the rebuilding of areas destroyed and damaged by the War.[3]

What the conspirators in Berlin wanted to know — and what Dr. Schönfeld urged the Bishop of Chichester to find out — was whether the Allies, on the assumption that the whole Hitler régime had been

---

[1] Dr. Schönfeld was one of the 'foreign correspondents' of this bureau and was resident in Switzerland (where, incidentally, he collaborated with Allen Dulles and his European outpost of the OSS). He was therefore permitted in his official capacity to visit the branches of the bureau in other countries.

[2] See above, p. 296.

[3] It must be remembered that in April 1942 the great Allied air offensive against Germany had barely got under way and the 'areas destroyed and damaged by the war' were therefore almost entirely the responsibility of the Germans.

destroyed, would be willing to negotiate a peace with such a new German government on the basis of the setting up of a system of law and social justice inside Germany, combined with a large degree of devolution in the provincial administrations; the establishment of economic interdependence within Europe, 'as the strongest possible guarantee against militarism'; the creation of a representative Federation of Free Nations, including a free Poland and a free Czechoslovakia; and the organization of a European Army for the control of Europe, of which the German Army would form a part, under a central authority.

If the Allies were prepared to consider negotiations on such a basis, they were asked to do one of two things: either to send a *private* message to this effect to the leaders of the conspiracy in Berlin through a representative of the Resistance Movement in a neutral country — Adam von Trott was named for this rôle; or to announce *publicly* that once the Nazi régime had been replaced by a new German government, they (the Allies) would be prepared to treat with this government.

The terms now offered by the conspirators as a *quid pro quo* for the overthrow of Hitler constituted in two respects a considerable departure from those previously put forward. In the first place they represented a renunciation in advance by the new German government of the Nazi acquisitions of territory and therefore of the Greater German Reich. This, according to Dr. Schönfeld, was even true with regard to Soviet Russia, since he specifically stated that the leaders of the conspiracy and those whom they represented entertained no annexationist designs upon the Soviet Union for colonial development, even though at that moment German armies held a line extending over a thousand miles of Russian territory. He added, with perhaps unconscious significance, that high-ranking officers of the German Supreme Command had been greatly impressed with the Soviet military *élite* and believed in the possibility of reaching an understanding with them.

Secondly, the suggestion that the Allied Governments should make *public* demand for the overthrow of Hitler and of the Nazi régime as the price for peace negotiations was a direct negation of the principle upon which Beck and Goerdeler and von Hassell had insisted so strongly, namely that any revolt against the *Führer* and his paladins must be represented to the German people as a purely German and spontaneous affair and in no way due to pressure from without.[1] There had, of course, been persistent efforts from the first to secure *private* assurances from London and Paris, and

---

[1] See above, p. 488.

T

latterly from London and Washington, that the Allies would be prepared to treat with a non-Nazi régime in Germany, but hitherto it had been considered that any public statement to this effect would smack too much of the Wilsonian manœuvres of October and November 1918.

Some indication, however, was given by Dr. Schönfeld that the conspirators were prepared to go forward with their plans even if no previous assurances from the Allies were forthcoming, and he stated with some definiteness that, in the event of a *Putsch* against Hitler being successful and of the refusal of the Allies to treat with the new régime, the conspirators had full confidence in the strength and capacity of the German Army to continue the War and that it would do so to the bitter end rather than accept humiliating conditions of peace, even though they were of the belief that a fight to the finish would be suicidal for Europe.

Scarcely had the Bishop of Chichester concluded his talks with Dr. Schönfeld when, to the surprise of both of them, Dietrich Bonhoeffer suddenly appeared on May 31 at Sigtuna, whither the Bishop had withdrawn for the observance of Whitsunday. Travelling secretly and on forged papers provided by the inimitable Hans Oster, Bonhoeffer's journey had been undertaken without any knowledge of the presence in Sweden of Dr. Schönfeld, but was prompted by a desire to see again the Bishop, whose friendship he cherished, and to communicate certain facts concerning the conspiracy.

Dietrich Bonhoeffer reinforced Schönfeld's appeal for public or private assurances by the Allies, but he went much further in his confidences than had Schönfeld. By the end of their talks the Bishop was in possession of the names of the leaders and even of their consideration of Prince Louis-Ferdinand as a possible candidate for the Head of the State.

But Bonhoeffer was troubled in his spirit. He was deeply disturbed at the lengths to which he had been driven by force of circumstances. He was not by nature a man of violence, let alone an assassin, but a Man of God, devoutly and nobly dedicated to his calling. It was not that he was weakening — no man was firmer in purpose or performance than Dietrich Bonhoeffer — he was ready to go on to the end with the ruthless work which he regarded as having been delegated to the conspirators by Divine grace. To him, as he had plainly stated two years before, 'Hitler is Anti-Christ. Therefore we must go on with our work and eliminate him whether he be successful or not.' [1] What disquieted his conscience was that the German people, and even the conspirators, by their earlier

[1] See above, p. 338.

toleration and tacit condonment of the Hitler régime, had rendered themselves unworthy to be the agents of God to eliminate 'Anti-Christ'. Their action in removing Hitler must not, therefore, be prompted by motives of revenge, or even of punishment, but of repentance. 'There must be punishment by God. We should not be worthy of such a solution. We do not wish to escape repentance. Our action must be considered as an act of repentance.'

After further talks with both Pastors and consultations with the British Minister in Stockholm, Mr. Victor Mallet,[1] Dr. Bell consented to acquaint the Foreign Office on his return to London with the full purport of the message of the conspirators. But he warned his German friends that no very favourable reception might be expected from the British Government and that Washington and Moscow would certainly have to be brought in.

The Bishop was true to his word. He saw the Foreign Secretary on June 30 and placed in his hands a full report of his conversations in Stockholm and also a memorandum prepared by Dr. Schönfeld.[2] Mr. Eden listened attentively and said that the Bishop's story confirmed and complemented information already in the possession of the Foreign Office, who had also received such 'peace-feelers' at other times and through other channels. He must, he said, be scrupulously careful not to appear to be entering into negotiations independently of Washington and Moscow. He would, however, consider the papers and write later. On July 17 he wrote to say that His Majesty's Government had decided that no action should be taken.

Thus ended in failure the most ambitious 'peace offensive' to be conducted by the conspirators since the Roman activity of Dr. Joseph Müller in the spring of 1940.[3] That it failed was very understandably a source of great disappointment to its initiators and to the Bishop of Chichester, who had worked so earnestly in its behalf. But it should not occasion surprise that the reaction of the British Government was what it was. In the summer of 1942 the Allies were on the defensive, hard pressed on all fronts — though, at the very moment that the Bishop of Chichester and Dietrich Bonhoeffer were talking together in the rural peace of Sigtuna on Whitsunday (May 31) the R.A.F. launched its first

---

[1] Now Sir Victor Mallett, K.C.M.G., Ambassador to Italy since 1947.

[2] Copies of the memoranda were also given to the American Ambassador, Mr. John Winant, by the Bishop of Chichester, to whom I am deeply indebted for his kindness in permitting me to read and make use of these two documents. I have also used Dr. Bell's own account of his Stockholm conversations published first in the *Contemporary Review* for October 1945 and later in his book *The Church and Humanity* (pp. 165-76).   [3] See above, pp. 490 *et seq.*

1000-plane raid on Germany, dropping nearly 1500 tons of bombs upon Cologne.

To have made a *public* announcement of the kind required at this moment would inevitably have been interpreted as a sign of weakness by the enemy and would, at best, have been dismissed by the German people as a further example of our somewhat inept 'psychological warfare'. A *private* message would, it is submitted, have been equally unjustifiable. His Majesty's Government had been in receipt of alerts regarding a military revolt in Germany ever since the summer of 1938, and none of them had resulted in a shot being fired or a sword turned against the *Führer*. Why indeed should an attempt made in the summer or autumn of 1942, when German arms were successful on all fronts and the *Führer's* military prestige — despite the failure before Moscow — was still unchallenged, have any greater chances of success than in 1938 or 1939 or 1940 ? The attitude of His Majesty's Government was entirely sound and justified. If the Generals could overthrow Hitler, well and good ; the Allies would then judge the situation thus presented on its own merits. But they could not consent to tie their own hands by the granting of preliminary assurances under circumstances which might, for all they knew, be a trap, as had been the case at Venlo, when they had found themselves negotiating with the Gestapo !

Six months later the situation had radically changed. The British and American Armies in North Africa were hustling their German and Italian opponents towards mass surrender at Cape Bon. The German Sixth Army, trapped in Stalingrad, was entering upon the final stage of its ghastly ordeal. The Anglo-American Air Forces had begun that operation of 'scourging the Reich from end to end', which was to lay Germany city by city in rubble and ruin. It was against a background of strength rather than of weakness that the announcement of 'Unconditional Surrender' was made from Casablanca on January 24, 1943.[1]

In concept the policy announced was as correct and proper as had been the attitude of reserve which the Allied Governments had maintained *vis-à-vis* peace-feelers in the days of their weakness. The policy of 'Unconditional Surrender' did not preclude the possibility of a more lenient treatment of a non-Nazi Government in Germany than that meted out to a régime still headed by Hitler and his fellow Nazis, but it did preclude the giving of preliminary assurances of such leniency. That Germany should free herself — if she could — from Nazi tyranny was considered a perfectly laud-

---

[1] See above, p. 537, footnote 1.

able ambition for her conspiratorial elements to cherish and pursue, but it was also something that Germany must do for herself without bribes or promises from outside. And having done so, she must not, in Dietrich Bonhoeffer's great phrase, 'want to escape repentance' — and, if necessary, chastisement.

The policy of 'Unconditional Surrender' meant that whatever government or régime was in power in Germany at the moment of capitulation must not seek terms or bargain for concessions, but must cast itself unreservedly upon the mercy of the victors. It was necessary for the Nazi régime and/or the German Generals to surrender unconditionally in order to bring home to the German people that they had lost the War of themselves; so that their defeat should not be attributed to a 'stab in the back', nor their subsequent treatment to the betrayal of a *pactum de contrahendo* entered into in a pre-Armistice agreement. The policy of 'Unconditional Surrender' was intended to obviate the repetition of the errors of 1918, when the German General Staff, after a moment of rocking insecurity, was enabled to seize the reins of power once more, never to let them go until wrested from their grasp by Adolf Hitler.

The purpose of 'Unconditional Surrender' was to give the Allies a clean blank slate upon which to delineate the future of Germany. It did just this. As one of its chief detractors has said: 'It left us with a Germany without law, without a constitution, without a single person with whom we could deal, without a single institution to grapple with the situation, and we have had to build from the bottom with nothing at all. . . .'[1] This was exactly what it was intended to do. No greater opportunity was ever presented to a conqueror to give a defeated country a new lease of life and a new order. If the Western Powers have failed to grasp that opportunity, if they have written the wrong thing, or nothing at all, upon the blank slate, the blame lies with those who have directed policy since 1945 and not with those who in 1942 envisaged the opportunity and made it possible.

The important thing is that, as has already been said,[2] the Casablanca Declaration constituted for the conspirators a very small embarrassment, if any at all. When Jacob Wallenberg met Goerdeler again in Berlin in mid-February 1943, the ebullient ex-*Bürgermeister* was, as usual, full of optimism. For though he admitted that in certain military circles the announcement of 'Unconditional Surrender' had made his work somewhat more difficult — since some Generals were now more disposed to allow Hitler to bear the

---

[1] Mr. Ernest Bevin. *House of Commons Debates*, July 21, 1949, Col. 1593.
[2] See above, pp. 536-7.

responsibilities and consequences of capitulation [1] — the disaster of Stalingrad, on the other hand, had more than offset this effect, since more and more of the Generals were coming to the conclusion that 'something must be done'. Something was about to be done, Goerdeler told Wallenberg. They had plans for a *coup* in March, whether they received assurance from the Allies or no, and he reminded his Swedish friend of his promise given in the previous April, that in the event of success the brothers Wallenberg would seek mediation with Mr. Churchill.[2]

(iv)

That which Goerdeler had whispered to Jacob Wallenberg was indeed no less than the truth. Once the plotters had taken their momentous decision to eliminate the *Führer* by assassination rather than by legal processes they moved with precision and despatch.

At the end of February 1943 Olbricht and Oster reported that the preparations for 'Operation Flash' — so-called because the 'flash' of Hitler's death would ignite the whole revolt — were completed. These plans included the seizure of power by the military authorities in Berlin, Cologne, Munich and Vienna.[3] For want of a more dependable figure, Beck and Goerdeler were still counting upon von Kluge to assume command of the Eastern Front as soon as Hitler's death had been confirmed and the Field-Marshal could therefore regard himself as freed from the encumbering obligation of his Oath. It was hoped and believed that other field commanders on both the Eastern and Western fronts would follow von Kluge's lead once the inhibiting force of the 'living *Führer*' had been removed.

'We are ready; it is time for the flash', was the memorable message which Olbricht and Oster sent to Henning von Tresckow at Smolensk by the word of Fabian von Schlabrendorff. For the scene of the *Attentat* was to be von Kluge's own headquarters of Army Group Centre and the master-brain of the assassination that of the Field-Marshal's own G.S.O. III. To complete the final

---

[1] There were some also, like General Georg Thomas, who considered that since the war was clearly lost and that no alternative German Government could hope for anything better than Unconditional Surrender, to assassinate Hitler would be interpreted merely as an act of ambitious Generals and would only result in the *Führer* becoming a martyr in German eyes (Dulles, p. 68).

[2] Dulles, p. 144; *Svenska Dagbladet*, September 4, 1947.

[3] Very little is known of the actual details of the plans for 'Operation Flash'. Since they were never put into force they were destroyed immediately after the failure of attempted assassinations of March 1943 and gave place to the more elaborate planning which took shape in 'Operation Valkyrie'.

FIELD-MARSHAL FEDOR VON BOCK

FIELD-MARSHAL EWALD VON KLUGE

operational planning and to provide the materials for the attempt, Admiral Canaris summoned a conference of intelligence officers at Smolensk early in March, and himself arrived there accompanied by Hans von Dohnanyi and General Erwin Lahousen, of his personal staff, the latter of whom brought with him a package of plastic bombs and time-fuses. The final touches were put to the plans ; only the psychological moment remained wanting.

It had been agreed that to have Hitler and his immediate entourage on to the unfamiliar ground of the Smolensk headquarters would give the plotters an additional advantage which they would not enjoy if the attempt were made at the *Führer*'s East Prussian headquarters at Rastenburg. In February 1943 Hitler visited the Ukraine, where he had his *Wehrwolf* headquarters at Winnitza. Despite serious difficulties [1] it was arranged that he should visit Smolensk on his way back to Rastenburg. This was done on what might be called the 'old boy' basis, between von Tresckow and Schmundt, Hitler's *Wehrmacht* adjutant, who, though devoted to the *Führer*, had a long-standing friendship with von Tresckow, of whom he was entirely unsuspicious.

As before, on the occasion of Hitler's visit to von Bock's headquarters at Borisow in 1941,[2] the date of the arrival at Smolensk was fixed and cancelled many times. Finally he announced his projected advent by air on March 13, 1943. Von Tresckow at once proposed to von Kluge that the assassination should be carried out by the officers of the cavalry unit attached to headquarters and commanded by Lieutenant-Colonel Freiherr von Boeselager. The personal loyalty of the officers to their commander and the efficiency and audacity of von Boeselager himself were well known. Both he and they were willing to 'take care of' the *Führer* and his bodyguard, but their participation in this affair necessitated an order from von Kluge — and this was not forthcoming. The Field-Marshal, true to form, was preparing to 'run out' as usual at the last moment — not for nothing was he known contemptuously as '*kluger Hans*' among the conspirators. He could not bring himself to condone by previous knowledge the assassination of his Supreme Commander, and he had more than suspected what was afoot when Canaris had arrived suddenly and unheralded at his headquarters — '*Unsere Generale kriegen kalte Füsse*', the Admiral had remarked prophetically to Lahousen and von Dohnanyi on this occasion.[3]

---

[1] Hitler, now very suspicious, left his headquarters only when heavily guarded. 'He is surrounded by a bodyguard of 3000 people', Goerdeler had gloomily — but exaggeratedly — informed Jacob Wallenberg in February. He had also had his military cap lined with more than three pounds of steel plating!

[2] See above, p. 516.   [3] Abshagen, p. 314.

So von Kluge would have nothing to do with a prepared *coup*, and von Tresckow and von Schlabrendorff were driven back upon their own devices. They determined to act themselves. It would have been possible to use a time-bomb so set as to explode while Hitler was in the midst of his conference — the technique which was ultimately employed by Claus von Stauffenberg — but this would have involved killing von Kluge also — or at least risking his death. But the conspirators needed von Kluge, together with his Army Commanders who would also be present, to put their *Putsch* into effect after the elimination of the *Führer*. The plan determined upon, therefore, was to blow up Hitler, by means of a delayed action time-bomb concealed in his airplane, during the return flight from Smolensk to Rastenburg.

On the morning of March 13 the Field-Marshal and von Tresckow drove to the airfield to await the arrival of the *Führer's* air cavalcade. In their absence von Schlabrendorff telephoned to Berlin the code word which should put Olbricht and Oster on the alert that an attempt to assassinate the *Führer* was imminent. The conference and the luncheon which followed it passed off without incident, and in the early afternoon the *Führer*, escorted by von Kluge and von Tresckow, drove back to the airfield. Von Schlabrendorff followed in his own car carrying a carefully wrapped package.

During lunch von Tresckow had asked one of the officers accompanying Hitler, Colonel Heinz Brandt,[1] the G.S.O. to General Heusinger, Chief of Operations Branch at OKH, if he would take a couple of bottles of brandy to von Tresckow's old friend General Helmuth Stieff, Chief of the Organization Branch in OKH. Brandt had agreed, and now the parcel, in which two explosive bodies had been carefully packed to represent the bottles, rested upon the knees of von Schlabrendorff.

The *Führer* boarded his plane. Colonel Brandt prepared to follow him. Von Schlabrendorff started the time fuse and handed him the parcel. The door closed. The two great planes took off and circled into the blue, accompanied by their fighter escort. The bomb was timed to explode within half an hour.

With swiftly beating hearts the two would-be assassins and the reluctant Field-Marshal returned to Headquarters. In Berlin the leaders of the conspiracy waited impatiently for the signal from Smolensk, where von Tresckow and von Schlabrendorff were in an agony of suspense. If the bomb exploded to time the *Führer's* plane

---

[1] This was that same Heinz Brandt who, as a young officer, gained a great reputation in the late 1920s and early 1930s as a consummate and intrepid horseman and the outstanding member of the German Army Olympic Team.

should be just short of Minsk and radio messages might therefore be expected from army area command there or from one of the fighter escort. Half an hour passed ; an hour ; an hour and a half. After two and a half hours the routine message arrived from Rastenburg that Hitler and his escort had arrived safely. For the waiting conspirators the hideous truth could no longer be avoided. Their attempt had failed. Once again Hitler had escaped death by a miracle.

With amazing coolness von Schlabrendorff at once set off to repossess himself of the faulty bomb. He arrived at Rastenburg by air on March 14, bringing with him a package containing two genuine bottles of brandy which he handed to Colonel Brandt, to whom von Tresckow had in the meanwhile telephoned asking him to hold up the presentation to Stieff as there had been some mistake in the date, and retrieved from him the original package. That same night, in the jolting privacy of a railway sleeping compartment, he dismantled the bomb between Korschen and Berlin and on the following morning, March 15, reported to Oster and von Dohnanyi on the defects of their detonator.[1]

A few nights later (March 16) a few friends, among them von Schlabrendorff, met at the home of Otto John to celebrate his birthday — or perhaps, more accurately, to celebrate the fact that the plot had not been discovered — and to make plans for the next attempt, which all confidently believed would succeed.[2]

The date selected was that of the *Heldengedenktag*, March 21, the day on which the annual commemoration of the dead of the First World War was to be held, at the Zeughaus on Unter den Linden. On this occasion there was also to be an exhibition of weapons captured from the Russians. Hitler, as was his yearly custom, was to be present, with Göring, Himmler, Keitel and a number of others.

For this attempt von Tresckow, who was still regarded as the operational chief of the conspiracy, selected his colleague, Major-General Freiherr Rudolf-Christoph von Gersdorff, von Kluge's G.S.O. II, who had been ordered to represent Army Group Centre at the ceremony.[3] Von Schlabrendorff and Oster provided him with another bomb, but the success of the operation depended upon the

---

[1] Fabian von Schlabrendorff's own account of the March 13, 1943 attempt, on which all others are based, is contained in *Offiziere gegen Hitler*, pp. 67-82.

[2] *John Memorandum.*

[3] There is some divergence of opinion as to when von Gersdorff actually joined the conspiracy. Von Schlabrendorff (p. 82) states that von Tresckow only recruited him in March 1943, but in his own account, published in *Die Welt* of July 31, 1947, and as recounted to Pechel (pp. 162-4), von Gersdorff maintains that he belonged to the 'Tresckow group' at Smolensk as early as the beginning of 1942.

T 2

564 HITLER AND THE ARMY PT. III

provision of a ten-minute fuse. This, in the short space of time available, it proved impossible to procure, and the attempt had reluctantly to be abandoned.[1]

Thus the month of March 1943, which was to have had such momentous results for Germany, passed by with only the continued defeats of the German armies in Russia and in Africa, and the ever-increasing fury of the Anglo-American air offensive upon the Reich. It was not entirely, however, without benefit for the conspirators. On consideration, Olbricht and Oster decided that their preparations for the subsequent exploitation of 'Operation Flash' in Berlin and the provinces were inadequate and that a further period of elaboration and perfection was necessary before the next attempt on the *Führer*'s life should be made.[2]

(v)

The months which followed the abortive attempts upon Hitler's life in March 1943 were fraught with danger and depression for the conspirators. Though they had always known that they carried their lives in their hands and that at any moment fate might strike them down with the double-knock of the Gestapo upon their doors, yet they had not been conscious of imminently impending danger. They were certainly indiscreet, yet every man charged his neighbour with indiscretion and few kept a watch upon themselves. Goerdeler was a prize offender. The wide-flung contacts of the Kreisau Circle were a cause of constant anxiety to many,[3] and the allegedly outspoken conversations of von Hassell and his wife had caused the apprehensive von Weizsäcker to break off all relations with his former friend and colleague.[4]

---

[1] According to Freiherr von Gersdorff, with whom the present writer has personally checked the account, he carried two bombs in his pocket, each with a delayed action fuse set to explode in twenty minutes. Unfortunately Hitler only remained eight minutes at the ceremony.

[2] Gisevius, ii, 221.   [3] *John Memorandum.*

[4] On April 29, 1942, von Weizsäcker, who had clearly lost his nerve, abruptly broke off his connection with von Hassell on the grounds of the lack of discretion of the latter and his wife, and also instructed the Foreign Office Staff to have no further contact with him. The consequent break was never healed, but others of von Weizsäcker's staff also told von Hassell that they had been warned against him and that Hitler regarded him and Frau von Hassell, the daughter of Grand-Admiral von Tirpitz, as 'peculiarly impossible people' (*besonders unmögliche Typen*). Von Weizsäcker, whose superior discretion — exemplified in his exhortation to the German diplomats returning in May 1942 from internment in the United States : 'We do nothing without the *Führer* ; his will is our will' — gave him the advantage of surviving to write his memoirs, in which he pointed to the existence of the Hassell Diaries as a justification for his action (Hassell, pp. 268-70 ; Weizsäcker, p. 343). Once safely ensconced in the Vatican Embassy von Weizsäcker began to press for action by the conspirators with the utmost vigour (December

But, so far, their escapes had been as miraculous as Hitler's, and the blow which fell upon them in April 1943 was due less to the pertinacious vigilance of the Gestapo on possible conspirators against the State than to the persistent professional jealousy between the two competing intelligence organizations — the RSHA and the *Abwehr*.[1] For, not content with controlling the whole police forces of the Reich, Kaltenbrunner and Schellenberg had long entertained an itching ambition to unify the German intelligence service under their control also, and it was in their efforts to provide themselves with ammunition against their rivals, Canaris and Oster, that they stumbled upon the first clues to the conspiracy.

A certain industrialist, an *Abwehr* agent, who had insinuated himself into the confidence of von Dohnanyi and had learned something, but by no means all, of the conspiratorial activities, was arrested in October 1942 on a charge of smuggling foreign currency across the frontiers of the Reich. In an effort to gain the protection of Canaris, he had attempted blackmail by threatening to disclose what he knew, and, when the Admiral indignantly refused, the arrested man carried out his threat. He did not know much, but the threads which he was able to place in the hands of the Gestapo and the SD led them to the very gate of that secret fortress of the *Abwehr*, to which Himmler and his henchmen had laid siege for so long.

Slowly before their delighted eyes there was pieced together by the skilful investigation of the Gestapo the story, not quite exact in all its details, of Joseph Müller's activities in Rome and of Dietrich Bonhoeffer's visit to Stockholm. This discovery brought to Himmler an unexpected ally. Göring was still smarting under the humiliation of the discovery of the Communist *Rote Kapelle* conspiracy within the very precincts of the Air Ministry.[2] He at once seized upon the opportunity of using a 'Christian Plot' to remove the memory of a 'Communist Plot', and persuaded Himmler to appoint the notorious 'Bloodhound Roeder', who had unearthed the *Rote Kapelle*, to investigate the *Abwehr*.

The blow fell in April 1943, when Dietrich Bonhoeffer, Joseph

---

1943). 'This is easy to do from the Vatican' was von Hassell's comment. 'He certainly took care not to get very involved before he went there' (Hassell, p. 343).

[1] The *Reichssicherheitshauptamt* (RSHA) was the main Security Office through which Himmler, with first Heydrich and then Kaltenbrunner as his deputy, controlled the criminal police (*Kripo*) under Nebe, the Foreign Political Intelligence (SD) under Schellenberg, and the Gestapo under Heinrich Müller. The uniformed police (*Ordnungspolizei*) were also under Himmler but in his capacity of Reich Minister of Interior, in which he had succeeded Frick in 1943.

[2] See above, p. 538, footnote.

Müller and Hans von Dohnanyi were all arrested. Oster retained sufficient authority to enable him to destroy virtually all the incriminating material concerning the accused, but he himself was placed on the retired list. Through the intervention of two high judges of the *Wehrmacht* the arrested men were kept in the custody of an Army prison and beyond the jurisdiction of the Gestapo, thereby delaying their interrogation by torture for more than a year. But Oster's own position was so shaken that Canaris, who was fighting with every weapon in his mysterious armoury to keep the *Abwehr* from the clutches of Himmler, was forced to let him go in the interests of the wider issue. In December 1943 Oster was transferred from the active list to the Reserve.[1]

Thus, at one stroke, the conspiracy had been deprived of many of its most valuable treasures : the high integrity of Dietrich Bonhoeffer, the noble character and intellectual ability of Hans von Dohnanyi, the tireless courage and indomitable energy of Joseph Müller and the fearless ingenuity of Hans Oster. It was the end of the original conspiracy against Hitler, which had begun at the time of the Fritsch Crisis and had been based entirely on Oster's activities and his co-operation with von Dohnanyi. Their work continued, but in other and different hands. With their disappearance from the scene the conspiracy took on a new complexion. Something departed with them ; something intangible ; something, it must be confessed, that was never really replaced, even by the fanatical zeal of Claus von Stauffenberg.

The loss of Bonhoeffer and von Dohnanyi — for, though they lived for nearly a year and a half the grey twilit half-life of the prison house, they were lost to the conspiracy from the day of their arrest — was perhaps among the most serious of the casualties which Germany sustained as a result of the conspiracy. Many there were in the ranks of the plotters whose virtue and sincerity may be measured from the date of their adherence ; some there were, even among the original leaders, who would have been but passengers in the German Ship of State had it ever been launched under non-Nazi colours. But that core of gallant and devoted spirits—who, because they were young and zealous and, even in the perils of their conspiratorial double life, maintained their sense of humour, and would, had the plot succeeded, have held in their hands the shaping of the destinies of the new Reich—was very small and could ill afford the loss of its two leaders. There were still some young recruits to come who would have played their part in a new Germany, and for whom the

---

[1] Gisevius, ii, 265-71 ; Abshagen, pp. 352-65 ; Ian Colvin, pp. 188-89 ; *John Memorandum*.

Bonn Government would be the richer to-day, but they, too, for the most part died upon the scaffold, leaving irreparable gaps for the welfare of their country.

The spring and early summer of 1943 was indeed a season of trial and loss for the conspirators. For, at the end of March, Beck underwent a serious operation for cancer at the hands of the great Ernst Sauerbruch,[1] which, though it was successful, incapacitated him for many weeks ; and on April 24 Kurt von Hammerstein-Equord died at the age of sixty-five.

Thus deprived of the advice of his two senior military colleagues, Goerdeler, ever anxious for action, chafed at the repeated technical reasons which were persistently advanced by Olbricht for the delay of a renewed attempt upon Hitler's life. To the ex-*Bürgermeister* the minutiae of detail required in planning a successful *coup d'état* were irritating and incomprehensible ; to the Staff officer, with his precise training, they were the essential prerequisites to action.

Goaded at length beyond endurance by his own impatience, Goerdeler wrote a letter to Olbricht on May 17 in which all his passionate desire for action was mingled with his heightening anxiety to bring the war to an end before the Allied air offensive had laid all the cities and treasures of the Reich in heaps of wreckage. The devastating effect of the heavy bombing both in damage and lives had deeply impressed him with a horror which could only be allayed by the cessation of hostilities. Delay he could brook no longer. He must, he would, have action.

My DEAR GENERAL [he wrote to Olbricht],
    I have again and again considered the view that we must wait for the psychologically right moment.[2]

---

[1] Ernst Ferdinand Sauerbruch (1875–1951) achieved eminence as one of the greatest surgeons of his day. He attended Hindenburg in his last illness and in 1940 he removed a growth upon Hitler's glottal ligaments. For this he was branded as a Nazi sympathizer. Nothing was farther from the truth. Sauerbruch persistently and undauntedly stood up for his non-Aryan colleagues and used his great professional prestige and his position as Professor of Surgery at the Berlin University and Director of the Charité Hospital to aid many Jewish doctors. He had been complicit in the conspiracy from its early stages and, after operating on Beck, did not hesitate to take him to his own home in the country near Dresden to recuperate — an act which resulted in a domiciliary visit from the Gestapo and an interrogation. A de-nazification court cleared Sauerbruch after the war of any complicity in National Socialism, but the East German Government dismissed him from all his posts in 1949, and he retired to the Western sector of Berlin, where he died on July 2, 1951. His memoirs, *Das war mein Leben* (Bad Wörishofen, 1951), appeared after his death.

[2] The text of the letter, which in the original was handwritten on Goerdeler's headed note-paper from his address in Leipzig, was printed in *Die Wandlung*, 1945–46, Heft 2.

If by this we mean the moment at which events cause us to take action then it will coincide with the beginning of the collapse ; action would then be too late to be exploited politically. In the meantime irreplaceable cultural monuments and the most important industrial centres would be heaps of ruins and the responsibility for precious lives would fall on the military leaders. Therefore we must not wait for the 'psychologically right' moment to come, *we must bring it about*. For we are certainly agreed that leadership without far-sighted correct action is impossible.

For the sake of the future of our fatherland I would not like to see the intelligentsia which has grown up throughout the centuries excluded from this leadership ; for the same reason the experienced leaders among our soldiers should not be excluded either.

Stalingrad and Tunis are defeats unparalleled in German history since Jena and Auerstädt. In both cases the German people were told that for decisive reasons armies had to be sacrificed. We know how false this is ; for soldiers and politicians can only describe such sacrifices as necessary when they are justified by successes in other fields which outweigh the sacrifice. The truth is that our leadership is incapable and unscrupulous ; if it had been true leadership both tragic sacrifices would have been avoided and a favourable military and political situation would have been established.

The number of civilians, men, women and children of all nations and of Russian prisoners of war ordered to be put to death before and during this war far exceeds one million. The manner of their deaths is monstrous and is far removed from chivalry, humanity and even from the most primitive ideas of decency among savage tribes. But the German people are falsely led to believe that it is the Russian Bolshevists who are constantly committing monstrous crimes against innocent victims.

The list of such things can be extended at will. I chose these two examples, because they are obvious examples of the poisoning of people's minds and, taken in conjunction with a corruption never before known in German history and with the suppression of law, they offer every opportunity of *creating* the 'psychologically right' moment. The vast majority of the German people, almost the whole working class, knows to-day that this war cannot be brought to a successful conclusion.

In face of this the patience of the people is inexplicable. But this perversity is based only on the fact that terror fosters secrecy, lies and crime. It will disappear as soon as the people realize that terror is being attacked, corruption removed and that sincerity and truth are taking the place of secrecy and falsehood. At that time every German will pull himself together again, both the decent and the corrupt, each will reject and condemn the action which he tolerated yesterday or to which he took no exception, because it was secret, because the decent German will again see decency and the others will be faced with responsibility.

If we can find no other way I am ready to do everything to talk personally to Hitler. I would tell him what he must be told, namely that in the vital interests of the people, his resignation is essential. If such a personal talk can be brought about, there is no reason why it should end badly. Surprises are possible, not probable, but the risk must be taken. Only it is not unreasonable on my part to demand that action must be taken immediately.

The political conditions for this exist.

I urgently entreat you, my dear General, to consider again whether the difficulties standing in the way of the technical measures cannot also be overcome. I also ask you to think over the method I have suggested and to give me an opportunity on my return to discuss the situation and the possibilities calmly.

With best wishes

Yours sincerely

GOERDELER

Goerdeler's proposition of an interview with Hitler, in which the latter might become converted to the views of the conspiracy, is so extraordinary that one wonders whether it was intended seriously at all. It may have been a combined emanation of his irrepressible optimism and his not inconsiderable vanity, or it may even have been an indication to Olbricht that he, Goerdeler himself, would be prepared to seek an interview with Hitler for the purpose of assassinating him — though this is an improbability. In any case nothing came of it.

The reference, however, in the final paragraph of the letter to a journey was to a visit which Goerdeler paid to the Wallenbergs in Stockholm in the third week of May. Having heard that Marcus Wallenberg was in London, he at once urged Jacob to transmit through his brother, to Mr. Churchill, a memorandum setting forth the views and intentions of a new German Government on such matters as war criminals, reparations, the actual form of government, etc., in very much the same terms as those conveyed by Dr. Schönfeld and Dietrich Bonhoeffer to the Bishop of Chichester a year before.[1] Coupled with the memorandum was the request that, should the conspirators succeed in bringing off their *coup*, the British and American Governments should call off their heavy bombing of German cities, especially of Berlin and of Goerdeler's own home town of Leipzig, partly because the nerve-centres of the conspiracy were situate in these two places and a complete disruption of communication would render the success of the *coup* the more difficult to attain, and partly to give the German people an indication that the Western Allies were favourably disposed towards the new régime. This information was passed on by Jacob Wallenberg to

[1] See above pp. 553 *et seq.*

his brother in London 'without prejudice'.[1]

On his return to Berlin, Goerdeler apparently found little improvement in the situation. Olbricht and Oster were still immersed in the details of their planning, and from neither the Eastern nor the Western Front was there the least indication that the Generals would move. Meanwhile the Allied landings in Sicily on July 9 and the rapid and brilliant outcome of that campaign made it clearly apparent that the invasion of Europe from the south was but a matter of weeks and, moreover, that the Rome-Berlin axis was in a process of rapid disintegration.

The Axis defeats in North Africa and Sicily, coupled with those in Russia, had encouraged Goerdeler to believe that the final military collapse was imminent. His sense of appalled horror at the effects of Allied bombings in Germany had been increased and stimulated by a visit paid to the West early in July, as a result of which he indited to von Kluge, who, despite his vacillation and hesitancy, was still regarded as the potential ally of the conspirators on the Eastern Front, a rebuke stinging and bitter in its language, calculated, it might well be thought, to excite the recipient either to suicide or to a challenge.[2]

The idea fostered by the high military authorities that the devastation in the west was not so bad and that after a few days, during which they 'gathered up their chattels from among the ruins', the workers return to work, induced me to look at the devastation for myself. You would be as shocked as I was. The work of a thousand years is nothing but rubble. There is no point in describing my feelings when I looked down from the Trolleturm on the ruins of the town of Barmen and on Elberfeld, half of which is destroyed. In Essen it is almost impossible to find one's way through the streets because all the familiar landmarks are lost in the rubble. Sixty per cent of Krupps is destroyed and it is working to only about 30 per cent of capacity. It is untrue to say that the contrary is the case. The damaged sections have not even been rebuilt in other parts of Germany; the process of the shifting of industry is only in its initial stages. Whoever has the courage to think must realize even without special technical knowledge that buildings must first be found, then adapted, then machinery must be procured, most of it new, and then coal and labour must be obtained. In Elberfeld even undamaged factories in the Vohwinkel area are only working to 30 per cent of their capacity, because the workers have left. In Essen and Wuppertal about two-thirds of the population have disappeared and in Cologne about four-fifths. That is how it is with the people who in three days gather up their chattels from the rubble. The coal output of the Ruhr has now dropped from 420,000

---

[1] Dulles, p. 144 ; *Svenska Dagbladet*, September 4, 1947.
[2] The text of this letter was published in *Die Wandlung*, 1945-46, Heft 5.

to 300,000 tons a day and is decreasing daily.   In June the output of the
South German armaments industry declined sharply for the first time,
because the drop in supplies from the Ruhr is making itself felt.   Furthermore, nothing can be done with these ruins.   They are heaps of debris,
concrete and iron.   Reconstruction will take generations.   The debris
cannot be disposed of on German soil, it would ruin too much land.   It
must therefore be dumped in the sea.   The removal of debris from Essen
alone will take about 3 years, using 100 waggons a day.

One hundred milliard marks would not be too high an estimate for
the damage sustained so far.   At present our national debt is 250 milliards,
in 3 months our debts will be as high as our total assets.

You, Field-Marshal, know that all theories which maintain that this
means nothing and that the pernicious economy based on debt can go on
unpunished are sheer nonsense.   No, the German people is faced with
the decision either to declare itself bankrupt ; then we have all lost everything and industry has no capital.   As this is an impossible situation
because it would mean revolution on the largest scale, those whose money
is invested in real estate must part with some of this, in order to finance
the firms which must be kept going in order to maintain economy and
avert revolution.   Thus everyone will be poor.   Or the German people
can again disguise the truth and start on the road to inflation by incurring
further debts and by letting things go on as they are doing now.   In the
end this would come to the same as the other.   For the chances of 1923
will not occur a second time.

Even now the difficulties of maintaining the life of the German people
for war and peace are tremendous.   For the whole of Europe has been
thoroughly ruined by Hitler's madness.   In 1918 Norway, Denmark, and
Holland at least were intact.   To-day every European country is to a great
extent laid waste, robbed of its supplies and its gold and its currency
ruined.   One can be seized with holy rage when one hears how frivolously
even well-educated people talk of reconstruction after the war.   It fills
one with horror that cultured people are simply living from day to day
at the expense of a universe which is collapsing and content themselves
with the thought that we have not yet collapsed, fondly imagining that
this can go on.

The transition to peace-time conditions when millions of soldiers who
have lost the habit of work are looking for homes and jobs and finding
only ruins can only come about if we have as the basis of our action a
moral, idealist conception which will seize men's minds and lift them above
the material difficulties and if we can win people over to this.

To-day the bonds of morality have been torn away ; what is left is
merely convention.   Anyone who travels as I do almost constantly sees
what is going on, for example in the big hotels.   He can see officers who
have nothing in common with our good officer class ; he can see young
louts with a party badge who talk victory but never think of doing their
duty as soldiers.   Even in the *Wehrmacht* the bases of morality must be

shattered, because the religious background has been forsaken and comrade can denounce comrade behind his back without himself being treated as a scoundrel. The introduction of the special court into the military tribunal, the penetration of the army with secret agents, speak volumes. A week ago I heard a report by an SS soldier aged 18½, who had previously been a decent lad but who now said calmly that 'it wouldn't exactly be very pleasant to machine gun trenches filled with thousands of Jews and then to throw earth on the still quivering bodies'. What has become of the proud army of the Wars of Liberation and of the Emperor William the First ? But the people know and feel this with a certainty which is admirable and instinctive and which, thank God, still exists. For God's sake, Field-Marshal, do not be deceived when you are told the people believe the lies which are forced down their throats. The people despise these lies and hate those who spread them abroad. That is the truth. It will break forth with all the greater force the longer people try to suppress it. But it will go hard with all those who share in the responsibility.

Hitler has made his fifth military blunder in the South. He is pouring German soldiers and valuable arms into Sicily, whereas reason must tell him that Italy can no longer be saved, because she does not want to save herself. The squandering of German strength, the useless sacrifice of German soldiers is a crime ; for even the time gained by defending Sicily means nothing. The secret hints of new powerful weapons are, according to my enquiries, mere irresponsible chatter, for even if these new weapons are really ready one day, they will not alter the decision which has been reached already in our minds — quite apart from the fact that the enemy has just as effective weapons. Thus from the military angle the same mistake is being made as in 1918 — only more senselessly ; one has not the courage to face the inevitable facts in time. But in 1943 that is a great deal more fateful than in 1918, for then our leaders were mentally and morally sound, whereas to-day they are insane and morally corrupt.

If there is still anyone who wants proof of this insanity, he will no longer require it when he hears that Hitler has told his entourage that his aim is the partition of Italy ! In the end Mussolini would be forced to ask him for help, he says, then he would perhaps appoint him Governor of Northern Italy and make the Apennines the German frontier ! Hitler is also prepared to accord Russia — provided she makes peace — frontiers which a decent German Government would not have to grant even to-day ; he is dreaming of another victory nearer home. In view of this national disaster which is now becoming obvious and into which we have been led by an insane and godless leadership which disregards human rights, I take the liberty of making a last appeal to you, Field-Marshal. You may be sure that it will be the last. The hour has now come at which we must take the final decision on our personal fate. On the one hand there is the way clearly indicated by conscience, on the other a different, easier way. The former may have its dangers, but it is the honourable way ; the latter will lead to a disastrous end and to terrible remorse. In face of the terrible and increasing destruction of German cities, do you, my dear Field-Marshal, know of yet another way to achieve a victory which will (1) make it possible to hold Russia off from Europe for good, (2) force the U.S.A. and the British Empire to give up these attacks and finally to make peace ? That, from the political and military point of view, is the question with which we are faced. If such a victory exists, then the chances of it must be made clear to the German people not with lies, but with the truth, which by then must be a reality. But if there is no such victory, then it is a sheer crime to continue the war, because there is never a heroic ending for the people, but simply the necessity to go on living.

I have again ascertained, and I accept the responsibility for this, that there is still the possibility to conclude a favourable peace, if we Germans again make ourselves capable of taking action. It is self-evident that no statesman in this world can negotiate with criminals and fools because he cannot lightly place the fate of his people in the hands of fools. Our own conscience too tells us that. Naturally, the possibilities are less easy to realize than a year ago. They can only be exploited if the politician still has a certain time for freedom of action, that is, if he is not, as in 1918, faced overnight by the military *Diktat* 'we can do no more' ! If this second condition, which depends on the military authorities, is fulfilled we can calmly and by reasonable action slow down the tempo of the war, at once in the case of the war in the a. and gradually in the land fighting. Anyone who to-day can tell the German people that the war in the air is over will have the people behind him, and no one will dare say a word or lift a finger against him. That and none other is the state of affairs.

I am at your service, no matter what the risk, for any such action which simply calls things by their proper name and deals with the criminals. For this purpose I could become an officer again if only I knew that this would ensure organized quick action. I can tell you to-day, that I can win over to you, Field-Marshal, and to any other General resolved to take the necessary action, the overwhelming majority of the German working class, the German Civil Service and the German business world. I can also, if you so desire, make Herr Goebbels or Herr Himmler your ally ; for even these two men have long realized that with Hitler they are doomed. Therefore, all that is required is really decision, bold thinking, and right action. What is most dangerous and in the end unbearable is to shut one's ears day after day to the voice of conscience. In this I am sure that you, my dear Field-Marshal, will agree with me.

You must, however, know that my opportunities for action are limited in time. For many years I have been looked upon as a militarist, an admirer of the military, as a promoter of militarism and as the friend of many Generals. I have had many an unpleasant moment in my life because of that, both after the first war and in recent years ; for many in Germany expected nothing of the Generals from the start. But I always took their part, saying that one could rely on their character and their sense of responsibility. Now it has come to this that I myself feel ridiculed and in South Germany, where I have many excellent friends, I am told that Prussian militarism is to blame for everything. They are not fools, the men who say this ; they are men who love Germany and the German soldier, but who despair because with our eyes open, our minds working and our hearts feeling we are letting our fatherland be led into the abyss by criminals and fools and are letting German youth and German manhood be driven unresisting to death and mutilation.

We must put an end to a state of affairs in which we allow fools to force their delusions and lies on the German people, we must make the war of conquest, started from a spirit of domination, into a war of necessary defence. We have absolutely no cause to fear Bolshevism or the Anglo-Saxons. People in these countries are the same as we are and we have much to throw into the balance. They too depend on our strength and our knowledge. But German interests must once again be represented with force and reason by decent Germans.

I will not trespass any further on your time, my dear Field-Marshal ; I only ask one more answer from you, and I know what it means if you do not give me this answer. One thing I ask you ; not to refuse to answer because you are afraid. I have learned to be silent and I shall not forget the lesson. I know what I owe to the men whom I trust. Unless at least three or four men in Germany have more confidence in each other, then we can go out of business.

With best wishes

Yours sincerely

GOERDELER

That so outspoken an indictment of the *Generalität* could pass without even acknowledgment is almost unbelievable except in the case of Field-Marshal von Kluge. But not even the savage eloquence of Goerdeler could move *kluger Hans* to action until the battle had been won — by somebody else. By devious means he sent back word to Berlin that he was 'not interested'.

(vi)

Nor was Goerdeler the only prominent leader in the conspiracy who touched the nadir of depression and frustration in the summer of 1943   Johannes Popitz was also travelling the same road but in a more 'deviationist' direction. He, like Goerdeler, had begun to despair of the Generals — 'they think only of their medals' he had once remarked bitterly — but, unlike Goerdeler, he had hit upon an alternative course of action.

The idea of a 'palace revolution' had always been in the minds of the conspirators. On the principle of 'Set a thief to catch a thief', they had, in the earlier stages of the war, considered the idea of enlisting the support of Göring and substituting him for Hitler, on the grounds that he would be acceptable as '*unser Hermann*' to the German people and that he had attained some reputation abroad as a 'moderate'. There had apparently been some difference of opinion as to whether Göring should continue as Head of the State or himself be removed as soon as the Nazi system had been liquidated, but there had been a considerable measure of agreement as to the feasibility of using him in the initial stages.

It was to this idea of 'divide and conquer' that Popitz now returned, but with a different principle. Since the devastating raids of the British and American air-forces and the manifest inability of the *Luftwaffe* either to counter-attack or to defend the Reich, Göring's prestige had waned perceptibly. 'If a single enemy bomber reaches the Ruhr, you may call me Meier', he had boasted in 1939, and now, in 1943, with the cities of the Ruhr in heaps of rubble, not only all Germany but even the *Führer* was referring to him as 'Herr Meier', and the Hermann Göring *Panzer* Division was even called the 'Meier Division'.[1]

In 1943 there was but one Nazi leader whose defection could have dethroned Adolf Hitler. As Hermann Göring's star waned in influence so the sinister planet of Heinrich Himmler blazed effulgent in the Nazi firmament. He was all-powerful. As head of the SS and of all the police of Germany, the Gestapo, the Kripo, the SD, and the Schupo, he controlled a force, if not numerically equivalent to the Army, at least its equal in influence. In 1943 his power was at its peak. He saw himself the potential successor to the *Führer*, for he had already eliminated Göring, the heir-designate, in his calculations. One rival only he acknowledged, the Head of the Party Chancery, Martin Bormann, in whom Hitler reposed, if possible, a greater measure of confidence than in the *Reichsführer*-SS.

It was Himmler, therefore, if anyone in the Nazi inner circle, who must be won over, and the thought had evidently been considered among the conspirators[2]. It had also been considered by

---

[1] Willi Frischauer, *Göring* (London, 1951), pp. 173, 227.

[2] It had figured in the talks of Dr. Schönfeld with the Bishop of Chichester and was mentioned by Goerdeler in his letter to von Kluge, wherein he stated that he could offer the Field-Marshal either Goebbels or Himmler as an ally at any time. (See above, p. 573.) Goerdeler had also told Jacob Wallenberg that 'advances had also been made to them (the conspirators) on behalf of Himmler', but that they placed no reliance upon them (Dulles, p. 145). It is clear, therefore, that though Goerdeler may not have known directly of Popitz's approach to Himmler, he could not have been as completely ignorant of the proposed SS liaison as Professor Rothfels (p. 94) would have us believe.

the Generals — or at least by one Field-Marshal. Fedor von Bock categorically informed Popitz in July that a *Putsch* by the Field Army, even with the support of the Reserve Army — of whose commander, Fritz Fromm, he expressed grave suspicions — would fail unless supported by the *Waffen*-SS, and that he himself would have nothing to do with any plot in which Himmler did not participate.[1]

This may well have been an attempt by von Bock to create an impossible condition for his own participation. For, though he had been cognizant of the conspiracy since 1941, he was among those whose vision of duty was obscured by the mystic qualities of their Oath. His remark, nevertheless, had a decisive effect upon ‹ Popitz, who now turned finally to the chief protagonist among the conspirators of a liaison with Himmler, Dr. Carl Langbehn.[2]

Langbehn, a Berlin lawyer, had earned distinction by offering to defend the Communist leader, Ernst Torgler, in the *Reichstag* Fire Trial [3] and by his spirited, if unsuccessful, defence of Dr. Günther Gereke, the former Reich Commissar for Employment in the Papen Government and an inveterate opponent of National Socialism, whom the Nazis successfully silenced in the early days of their administration with a charge of peculation, bribery, and misappropriation of public funds, which though unfounded was made to stick. Langbehn's standing as a political lawyer was thus established, but he achieved the somewhat odd reputation of both accepting briefs against the Nazis and at the same time being Himmler's confidential lawyer and adviser. He kept his actual political position a close secret, but it is certain that he was on intimate terms with Himmler — they lived next door to one another on the Walchensee and their daughters were school friends — and that

---

[1] According to the Indictment (Dulles, p. 158), the views expressed by von Bock were reiterated to Popitz by von Tresckow, who insisted that an attempt to seize the *Führer* either in his Headquarters or in Berlin was impossible by military action alone, since not the slightest troop concentration could be ordered without Hitler's knowledge. The participation of the SS was therefore an essential.

[2] The present writer has used as sources for the 'Popitz-Langbehn affair' the statement made by Fräulein Marie-Louise Sarre, a friend of both men, to Allen Dulles (pp. 149-50) ; the text of the indictment of Popitz and Langbehn prepared by the Prosecution before the People's Court in October 1944 (Dulles, pp. 151-2) ; an article on the trial appearing in *Der Morgen* on July 20, 1946 ; and an unpublished study of the affair by Dr. Otto John.

[3] The Communist Party offered to pay Torgler's defence expenses with a cheque drawn on an Amsterdam bank and payable in guilders. Langbehn, thinking that this implied that he would not dare to remain in Germany after the trial and had taken the case only for money, threw up the brief.

he used his relationship for both political and humanitarian purposes.¹

There had been a moment, at the time of the threatened military collapse after the failure before Moscow in November 1941, when Himmler, sensing defeat, had toyed with the idea of an SS *coup d'état* on his own, with the object of reaching a negotiated peace with the Allies before Germany sustained a major military disaster. However, Hitler's ruthless and daemonic energy in meeting the imminent calamity restored the situation before the idea could do more than take form in the mind of the *Reichsführer-SS*. Yet Langbehn had known of it and of subsequent doubtings of heart on the part of Himmler. In December 1942 Langbehn had held conversations, with the cognizance and approval of the SD, with a British official in Zürich and with Professor Bruce Hopper, the representative of OSS in Stockholm, with the idea of sounding out British and American reactions to the possibilities of peace under the now familiar conditions — a change of régime in Germany.² Nothing definite had emerged from these contacts, but they had still further sustained Langbehn's dual conviction that, under certain given circumstances, Himmler would 'play ball' with the conspirators and that by this means alone could the elimination of Hitler and the Nazi régime be achieved.

As a result of the situation in the late summer of 1943, which had been further complicated for the conspirators by the overthrow of Mussolini by Marshal Badoglio on July 25 — the date, significantly enough, of Goerdeler's letter to von Kluge — and the reaction thereto of both the *Führer* and the Allies, Langbehn persuaded Popitz to meet Himmler and to sound him, the ultimate intention being to use the SS for the initial seizure of power and then to provide the Army with the ineffable pleasure of liquidating them.

The interview, which was arranged with the assistance of SS-*Obergruppenführer* and General of the *Waffen-SS*, Karl Wolff, Himmler's personal Chief of Staff,³ took place, 'under four eyes',

---

¹ Dr. John, who knew Langbehn well, writes that he 'was definitely not a Nazi'. Mr. Dulles (p. 148) alleges that he was a Nazi until 1938 when his old law teacher, Professor Fritz Pringsheim, was sent to a concentration camp as a non-Aryan. On this occasion Langbehn used his influence with Himmler not only to obtain the order for Pringsheim's release but also his permit to leave the country.

² Hassell, p. 290.

³ Karl Wolff was later in a large measure responsible for the negotiations which resulted in the unconditional surrender by Colonel-General Heinrich von Vietinghoff of the German Armies in Northern Italy on April 30, 1945. For an entertaining account of this incident see Eitel Friedrich Moeblhausen, *Die gebrochene Achse* (Alfeld/Leine, 1949); also Appendix E, 'Negotiations for the German Capitulation', to Field-Marshal Viscount Alexander's Report on the Italian Campaign, December 12, 1944–May 2, 1945 (H M. Stationery Office, 1951).

at the Reich Ministry of the Interior on August 26. Popitz was very circumspect. He approached the subject from the angle of the critical military and political situation which had arisen for Germany. Was it not possible that things had perhaps got a little beyond the *Führer*'s control ? Should he not be relieved of some of the many burdens of responsibility which he bore ? Should he not be, perhaps, reduced somewhat in cares and in power, with, of course, a resulting devolution of authority upon some strong personality — Himmler himself, perhaps ; who better ? — who should take action to save the Reich ?

Himmler, too, was cautious — so cautious that no record is left as to what he actually said, for the Indictment by the Prosecution gives ‹only the contribution of Popitz to the conversation — but Popitz later reported that he had the impression that Himmler was 'not averse in principle' to what had been tentatively put forward, and he certainly authorized Langbehn to proceed to Switzerland to feel out once again the reactions of the Allies to a change of régime.

Langbehn thereupon departed for Berne with the double blessing of both Popitz and Himmler, there to indulge in the highly dangerous and complex pursuit of attempting to incriminate and double-cross the ablest crook in Europe. He succeeded in the first but not the second. The double-crossing was done by the *Reichsführer*-SS.

In the course of his conversations in Berne, Langbehn met British, American, and other Allied Intelligence officers. He may or may not have been sufficiently discreet, but the fact remains that a telegram in cipher sent by some allied agency — Mr. Dulles assures us that it was neither British nor American [1] — announced that 'Himmler's lawyer confirms the hopelessness of Germany's military and political situation and has arrived to put out peace-feelers'. The message was intercepted and decoded simultaneously by the *Abwehr* and the SD ; the latter at once passed the material to Schellenberg, who, with a full knowledge of what this information might mean for his chief, enlisted the support of 'Gestapo Müller' and arrested Langbehn immediately on his return to Germany, together with his wife and Fräulein Sarre, who were held in secret custody at the Kaiserhof Hotel.

Müller certainly was not anxious to shield Himmler, whom he had the ambition to succeed ; it was not therefore surprising that the contents of the telegram reached Bormann and Hitler in quick succession. Yet so great was the authority of the *Reichsführer*-SS

[1] Dulles, p. 162.

that he was able to disembarrass himself of this snare without apparently impairing his standing with the *Führer*. Langbehn languished in a concentration camp — it was clearly not in Himmler's interests that he should be brought to trial — and Popitz, though he failed to gain access to Himmler in his efforts to procure Langbehn's release, remained at liberty. Both, however, were marked for future elimination at the earliest opportunity.[1]

Thus ended a curious and isolated episode in the history of the conspiracy, a courageous, if ill-judged and foolhardy, attempt to overcome the supine hesitancy and infirmity of purpose on the part of the Generals by providing them with unsavoury allies, who would do the dirty work for them and whom they might subsequently remove. It redounds little to the credit of the Army that they demanded a working association with the SS as the price of action and still less to the intelligence of Popitz and Langbehn that they thought they could outwit Himmler.

The immediate effect of the affair in the leadership of the conspiracy was to complete the process of estrangement already current between Goerdeler and Popitz. Goerdeler, though he certainly knew of the proposed Himmler connection — as witness his letter to von Kluge — resented the independent action of Popitz in sending Langbehn to Switzerland without informing him, Goerdeler. For his part, Popitz had long been out of sympathy with Goerdeler's tendency to widen the basis of the conspiracy toward the Left, and, conversely, Leber and Leuschner, the SPD leaders with whom contact had been established, would have none of Popitz.[2] This original antagonism of the Left was partly due to his earlier record of sympathy with the Nazis ; partly to his advocacy of von Falkenhausen as the new Commander-in-chief in the event of a successful *Putsch*, whereas the Left regarded that General as having been to some major degree incriminated in the shooting of hostages in Belgium.[3] To these causes was now added his flirtation with Himmler. By the close of the year the estrangement was so complete that Goerdeler had dropped Popitz from his shadow cabinet.

[1] Langbehn was not ill-treated until after July 20, 1944, but was then tortured in the most barbarous and horrible manner, and, since it was not until after his own death sentence had been pronounced, not even for the purpose of eliciting information. Himmler was revenging himself on the man who had pitted his wits against him and had nearly succeeded in embarrassing the *Reichsführer*-SS with his enemies. Popitz was also arrested after July 20. Langbehn was hanged in Berlin on October 12, 1944, Popitz not until February 2, 1945.

[2] Hassell, pp. 332-3.

[3] This advocacy of von Falkenhausen also brought Popitz into conflict with Beck, who, in agreement with Goerdeler and other of the chief conspirators, had decided upon von Witzleben as the C.-in-C. designate of the *Wehrmacht*.

(vii)

But, even at this darkest of moments — when Goerdeler was writing in despair and commination to Olbricht and von Kluge, when Sauerbruch was fighting for Beck's life in the Charité Hospital, and Popitz and Langbehn were embarking upon their fantastic and forlorn hope — within the nerve-centre of the conspiracy itself there were signs and portents of a new virility, the stirrings of a new-born strength.

The failure of the attempts of March 1943 had depressed, but had not daunted, the younger conspirators, and they had at once set about reviewing their plans in the light of past failures. There were meetings, at a junior level, in Berlin and in Smolensk which resulted in general agreement that a successful *Putsch* depended upon four things : the assassination of Hitler, a complete and comprehensive plan for taking over the control of the country after this had taken place, the clarification of the political aims of the conspiracy, and a closer liaison between the 'front-line echelon' of the conspiracy on the Eastern Front and their colleagues in the Home Army.

The break-up of the *Abwehr* group and the consequent loss of Oster as an operational chief in Berlin caused Henning von Tresckow to apply for extended sick-leave necessitated by the strain of the Russian campaign. It is to be believed that von Kluge was far from unwilling to be temporarily relieved from this persistent troubler of his conscience and von Tresckow was granted a furlough of several months' duration at the end of May, with the admonition from the Field-Marshal not to return to duty until quite recovered.

Thus relieved from all official duties, von Tresckow settled down in his sister's house at Neu-Babelsberg, between Berlin and Potsdam, to devote himself to the completion of the planning, and to finding someone who could replace Oster as 'general manager' of the plot. It was in the selection of the latter individual that a choice was made which was to reshape the whole form and conspectus of the conspiracy.

The name suggested to von Tresckow by Olbricht was that of Count Claus Schenck von Stauffenberg. Thirty-seven years old, Claus von Stauffenberg came of a family which had long been devoted in service to the Royal Houses of Württemberg and of Bavaria. His father had been Privy Chamberlain to the last Bavarian monarch, and his mother, the Countess von Üxküll-Gyllenbrand, was a granddaughter of Gneisenau.

Born in 1907 in the Castle of Greiffenstein, in Oberfranken, the boy Claus was of great beauty and splendid physique. Combining a love of riding and games with wide and omnivorous reading, he grew up in an atmosphere of native Catholic piety and extreme monarchist conservatism. From the latter he reacted somewhat abruptly, but his religious fervour led him to the romantic mysticism of Stefan George from whom, and from whose thought and verse, he derived much of his formative philosophy of life.

Not that he was content to be a dreamer, a seeker of cold intellectual sensationalism, a spinner of words and fantasies ; Claus von Stauffenberg was essentially a man of action, a man whose contact with the world was real and warm and vibrant. As an officer of the crack Bavarian cavalry regiment, the *Bamberger Reiter*, he had served with gallantry and distinction in Poland, in France and later in Africa, where he achieved a reputation not only for courage but as an outstanding organizer. His career as an active officer was cut short in 1942 when, as a result of driving into a minefield in the desert, he sustained wounds so serious that a lesser man would have considered himself completely incapacitated. However, thanks in a major degree to the surgical genius of Sauerbruch,[1] the loss of his right forearm, his left eye and two fingers of his left hand, in addition to injuries to his left ear and knee, did not prevent him from reporting back for service as soon as his wounds were healed, and his administrative ability was recognized by promotion and appointment to the General Staff. In the summer of 1943, with the rank of Lieutenant-Colonel, he was Chief of Staff to Olbricht in the *Allgemeines Heeresamt*.

Nor had von Stauffenberg waited until now to make clear his position in respect of the régime. During a visit to the Eastern Front in the summer of 1941, before his departure for Africa, he had encountered von Schlabrendorff and von Tresckow at the headquarters of Army Group Centre at Borisow and had made it clear to them that he regarded Hitler and National Socialism as a menace.[2] Later, in the desert campaigns he became well known for his frank and outspoken criticism of the Nazi régime and exercised considerable influence over certain of his brother officers who later joined the conspiracy and who testified at their trials to his dynamic personality.[3]

Von Stauffenberg, therefore, was not, as some writers have averred, shocked into opposition by the impact of defeat, nor by

---

[1] Sauerbruch, p. 55.   [2] Schlabrendorff, p. 86.
[3] In particular, Major-General Helmuth Stieff and his assistant, *Oberleutnant* Albrecht von Hagen, testified to this effect at their trial. Both were hanged on August 9, 1944. (See *IMT Document, PS*-3881. Stenographic Report of the trial before the German People's Court on August 7 and 8, 1944, of Field-Marshal von Witzleben and seven other officers.)

HITLER AND THE ARMY

an inferiority complex brought about by his physical incapacity resulting from his wounds.[1] His resentment of any form of totalitarianism, and of National Socialism in particular, had a spiritual basis, emanating from his Christian background, his Catholic upbringing and the teachings he had imbibed from his intimate association with Stefan George, and he had given evidence of it long before wounds or defeat could have influenced his motives.

Not for nothing was 'Anti-Christ' his favourite among George's poems. He would recite it with fervour, his great frame striding up and down the room and his maimed claw of a left hand gesticulating fiercely; his one remaining eye gleaming a vivid blue, a black patch covering the empty socket of the other. The final verses would excite him to particular elation, since, in their fire and venom, they expressed with surpassing eloquence the hate which burned within him and the contempt which he could barely contain for those who would not act :

> *Der Fürst des Geziefers verbreitet sein reich.*
> *Kein schatz der ihm mangelt ; kein glück das ihm weicht.*
> *Zu grund mit dem rest der empörer !*

> *Ihr jauchzet, entzückt von dem teuflischen schein,*
> *Verprasset was blieb von dem früheren seim*
> *Und fühlt erst die not vor dem ende.*

> *Dann hängt ihr die zunge am trocknenden trog,*
> *Irrt ratlos wie vieh durch den brennenden hof . . .*
> *Und schrecklich erschallt die posaune.*[2]

[1] Cf. Gisevius, ii, 276, 307. Pechel (pp. 181-2) takes grave issue with this attempt of Gisevius to belittle von Stauffenberg : 'The picture which Gisevius draws of Stauffenberg is distorted ; distorted out of resentment because Stauffenberg rejected him completely . . . mistrusted him deeply and kept him out of the inner circle'. This view is shared by Professor Rothfels, who writes (p. 128, footnote 168) : 'To anyone who reads Gisevius's memoirs with a modicum of historical criticism, it is obvious that the inferiority complex and the feelings of resentment are on his side'. With these views the present writer warmly concurs.

[2]   'The Master of Vermin far stretches his realm ;
> No treasure that fails him, no luck that forsakes. . . .
> Destruction take all other rebels !

> You clamour, enticed by the devilish show,
> Lay waste what remains of the sap from the spring
> And feel your need first when the end comes.

> Then you hang out your tongues o'er the emptying trough,
> Stray like herds without aim through the courtyard in flames,
> And fearfully rings out the trumpet.'

No published translation of this great poem exists in English and I am deeply indebted to the kindness of the Warden of Wadham College, Sir Maurice Bowra, for the above masterly rendering.

Such was the man whom Olbricht now proposed, and von Tresckow promptly accepted, as Oster's successor. But they knew not what they did, for though as genuine an anti-Nazi as any of them, Claus von Stauffenberg had very definite ideas as to the sort of Germany which he desired to see emerge from the blood and murk of the Third Reich, and his ideas were far from being compatible with those of the bourgeois conservatism of Carl Goerdeler and the selfless 'State Service' of Ludwig Beck.

His first task, however, was one for which he was peculiarly well suited. Under the general direction of von Tresckow, and with the assistance of Major Ulrich von Oertzen, von Stauffenberg was set down to work out a 'staff study'— down to the last detail — for the military occupation of Berlin, and to condense this plan, once formulated, into written orders which should convey to any commanding officer exactly what he must do, on receipt of a code word, without exciting his suspicions should he be a Nazi sympathizer. At a later stage the planning was to be extended to embrace similar action in the principal cities of the Reich and on the Eastern and Western Fronts.

The official pretext and cover adopted for the planning of the *Putsch* was preparation for action by the Home Army in the dual eventuality of a mutiny by the SS — which the Army always considered a possibility — or of risings and riots by the several million foreign workers transported to Germany as slave-labour from the occupied countries, or against widespread parachute landings.[1] In all cases it was assumed that the SS would be in opposition — there was no question in the minds of the planners of any alliance, of however ephemeral a nature, with Himmler — and the real problem confronting von Stauffenberg and von Oertzen was how to contain the Berlin SS until Army reinforcements could arrive from other parts of the Reich.

For in the capital itself the SS outnumbered the forces upon which the Army could count — even supposing that they succeeded in winning over all the units available [2] — and, moreover, the SS barracks in Berlin had been strategically placed in the neighbourhood

---

[1] Schlabrendorff, p. 93 ; *John Memorandum.*

[2] The troops upon whom the conspirators felt they could count in Berlin were the Guard Battalion (*Wachbataillon*) which had been so strengthened as to possess the fire-power of a regiment, the Army Fire Brigade Training School, the Army Ordnance School, and two territorial battalions. Outside the city, there were certain units in training and also the complements of the various permanent establishments, the Infantry Training School at Döberitz, similar schools for cavalry at Krampnitz and artillery at Jüterbog, and the Panzer Training School at Wünsdorf.

of such key positions as the government buildings, the radio and power stations, the newspaper offices, the gas and water works, the central railway station, etc., many of which — and in particular the ministries and the radio station — should be seized by the rebels if their *Putsch* was to be successful. They believed, though they did not know — for by this time no one knew how far troops had been infiltrated by the pernicious basic doctrines of National Socialism and how far, in consequence, they would obey their officers under certain conditions — that they could count on the support of about 75 per cent of the troops available, and, in addition to this, they could reckon on the '*Schupos*' of Berlin — the so-called 'Blue Police', whom Count von Helldorf had promised to their side. However, plan as they would, they could not change the fact that all turned upon the events of the first twenty-four hours and the ability of the rebel Army units to hold their own against the SS during that period. Once this critical time was passed the Army could draft in sufficient troops to Berlin to relieve their hard-pressed comrades and to liquidate such SS as remained.[1]

Much, very much, depended also upon the reliability — from the point of view of the conspirators — of the men in the key military positions in Berlin. The City Commandant, Lieutenant-General Paul von Hase, was uncompromisingly on their side, as were most of his staff; but the General commanding the all-important *Wehrkreis III* (Berlin-Brandenburg), General von Kortzfleisch, and von Hase's superior officer, was known to be an enthusiastic Nazi. The conspirators, however, had succeeded in reaching an understanding with his Chief of Staff, Major-General Rost, and one of their own number, Lieutenant-General Freiherr von Thüngen, the Deputy *Gerichtsherr* of the Central Military Court, was detailed to take over the command as soon as the *Putsch* was made.[2]

The unknown quantity was Fritz Fromm, the Commander-in-Chief of the Home Army, a character whose record in the conspiracy was altogether despicable. Fromm was no fool. Like von Reichenau he 'always heard the grass grow' and he had long ago recognized the inevitability of defeat, just as he had been well ahead of his colleagues in his belief in a lightning victory in the West in 1940.[3] He had even minuted Keitel on the deplorable military situation of the Reich and had urged that spineless character — whom, incidentally, he detested — to do something about it. But he was not one to do something about it himself, and, though he was well aware of

---

[1] Schlabrendorff, pp. 88-91.
[2] Von Hase and von Thüngen were both hanged after the failure of July 20, 1944.   [3] See above, p. 496, footnote.

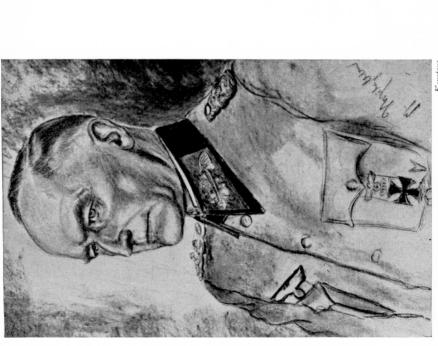

COLONEL-GENERAL FRIEDRICH FROMM

FIELD-MARSHAL ERWIN VON WITZLEBEN

much of what went on under his nose in the office of his subordinate Olbricht, and kept silence, he would not commit himself completely to the cause of the conspiracy, beyond a sinister and cryptic remark on one occasion : 'For my sake, don't forget Keitel when you make your *Putsch*'.

The impression of the conspirators was that, once Hitler was dead and the *Putsch* in operation, Fromm would play along with them. But they could not be sure and, in case of emergency, General Hoepner, who had been identified with the conspiracy since 1938,[1] had been selected to take over the command of the Home Army, though later designated as Commander-in-Chief of the whole Army. In the first stages of planning, however, it was assumed that Fromm would participate and, to give an added weight to the draft orders which were being drawn up, they were composed over his name— though without his knowledge.

The orders prepared by von Tresckow, von Stauffenberg and von Oertzen in these summer months of 1943 were in three categories. The first set were in general terms and were to be sent to all district commanders, instructing them what action to take in the event of a mutiny, riot or sudden attack. The second set, to be issued over Fromm's name, were directed specifically toward the situation within the Reich and particularly in Berlin. They asserted that an SS *Putsch* had been attempted and called upon the Army to occupy the SS barracks in the city, to disarm the inmates and not to hesitate to kill them if they resisted. The third set of orders, which were signed by Field-Marshal Erwin von Witzleben as 'Commander-in-Chief of the *Wehrmacht*',[2] announced that Hitler was dead, proclaimed a state of emergency and delegated all executive powers to the hands of the armed forces. They also included instructions for the immediate dissolution of the Nazi Party control in the country.

The whole operation was given the code name of 'Valkyrie', which was also the code word to be flashed from Berlin to the Army Commanders on X-Day. On receipt of it, local commanders would

---

[1] See above, p. 407.

[2] The chain of command of the Armed Forces of the State to be established after the success of the *Putsch* was as follows : Beck, as *Reichsverweser*, would have become automatically Supreme Commander, with von Witzleben as the actual Commander-in-Chief of the Armed Forces (*Oberbefehlshaber der Wehrmacht*) and Hoepner as Commander-in-Chief of the Army. This would have meant a return to the military hierarchical position before the Blomberg-Fritsch Crisis, with the difference that a Minister of War (or Defence) was contemplated in addition to the position held by von Witzleben, thereby separating the offices previously held by von Blomberg. There is no indication of the persons considered by the conspirators as possible Commanders-in-Chief of the Navy and Air Force.

at once put into execution the orders which they already held and would immediately receive supplementary instructions under the authority of the new régime. In the meantime, these papers had been secretly and faithfully copied by two ladies of the conspiracy, Henning von Tresckow's wife, Erika, and Margarete von Oven, the daughter of the General who had been one of von Lüttwitz's supporters and who herself had served as confidential secretary to both von Hammerstein and von Fritsch, when successively Commanders-in-Chief of the *Reichswehr*. When typed, the documents were confided to the safe keeping of Olbricht until the day came for their use.

The planning for the immediate *coup* in Berlin and elsewhere in the Reich had progressed so satisfactorily by August that Goerdeler, as ever, over-optimistic, begged Jacob Wallenberg to pay him another visit in Berlin. Here he confided to his Swedish friend that they hoped at last to bring off a *Putsch* in September, and that, as soon as this had taken place, Fabian von Schlabrendorff would be sent post-haste to Stockholm. Could the Wallenbergs persuade the British Government to send someone to meet him there to make contact on behalf of the Western Allies ? Perhaps some member of Mr. Churchill's staff would be a suitable representative ? Wallenberg accepted this assignment on condition that the proposed meeting in Stockholm should be in no way for the purpose of negotiation but merely to enable the new government in Berlin to discover how best they could set about obtaining peace terms.[1] Anxiously the Wallenberg brothers watched for the great events which were to happen in September. But the month passed without significant happenings in Berlin, though elsewhere fate was drawing together the net about the Nazi forces.

The early part of the summer of 1943 passed in an almost complete lull on the Eastern Front, where the line lay from Leningrad, through Orel and Kharkov, to the German-held Caucasian bridgehead beyond the Kerch Straits, which unite the Sea of Azov with the Black Sea. Here the last fighting had died down in the first days of June and sinister silence settled upon the whole front until, on July 5, the Germans attacked on the Kursk salient, between Kharkov and Orel, making the most powerful armoured assault

---

[1] Dulles, pp. 144-5 ; *Svenska Dagbladet*, September 4, 1947. M. Wallenberg makes no mention of the result of his approaches to London in this respect, but von Hassell records (pp. 331, 340) that, after a further visit from Jacob Wallenberg in November, Goerdeler stated that 'Mr. Churchill had made an authentic statement, by way of Sweden', that he could make no binding arrangements before the Nazi Government was overthrown in Germany, but that if the revolt succeeded and proved itself to have sufficient authority, 'he would look with benevolent interest upon a new régime'. Schacht was extremely sceptical of this statement, a view to which von Hassell himself also inclined.

they had ever launched.[1] But powerful as it was, it achieved only minor success, and on the 12th the Red Army delivered its long-prepared counter-offensive against the Orel positions and began an advance which by the end of the year had liberated Kiev, the Caucasus and the Crimea, forced the passage of the Dnieper and established a line from Narva and Lake Peipus in the North, through the Pripet Marshes, to a point to the east of Odessa.

The abandonment of Kiev by the German armies and the withdrawal on a wide front to the Dnieper, although a carefully planned and strategically correct operation, was not in the main successful. Though the retreating armies were able to effect extreme demolitions of industrial plants and to lay waste cities, towns and villages ; to carry off vast stores of grain and destroy what they could not carry, and to shorten their line to some extent, they did not succeed, by this stratagem of 'scorched earth', in stemming the Russian advance, which, contrary to the calculation of the *Führer* and his military advisers, kept up its pressure in the south and in the north throughout the autumn.

It was this ever-advancing spectre from the East which, together with the steady rain of bombs which now fell daily and nightly upon the cities of the Reich, had spurred the conspirators to an acceleration of their planning, and had, to some degree, augmented their ranks with valuable recruits. For, now that the signals of approaching disaster had become clear beyond peradventure, there were not lacking those who were genuinely, if belatedly, converted to the view that the prestige, the authority, if not indeed the very existence, of the German Army and of the Officer Corps could only be safe-guarded by the elimination of the *Führer*.

OKH became well infiltrated at this time, the more outstanding recruits to the conspiracy being the Head of the 'Foreign Armies' Department (*fremde Heere*), Colonel Freiherr Alexis von Roenne, with his Chief of Staff, Count von Matuschka ; the Head of the Ordnance Department, General Fritz Lindemann ; the First Quartermaster-General, General Eduard Wagner ; and the Head of the Organization Department, the youthful hump-backed Major-General Helmuth Stieff, whose bitter tongue had earned him the nickname of the 'Poisoned Dwarf'.[2]

But they still lacked a Field-Marshal in active command. For

---

[1] The Germans in their attack of July 5 mounted 30 divisions ; 6 armoured, 1 motor and 7 infantry divisions against the northern flank of the salient, and 9 armoured and 7 infantry divisions on the southern.

[2] With the exception of General Wagner, who committed suicide on July 26, 1944, all these officers were executed by hanging, after the failure of the *Putsch* of July 20.

U

though von Witzleben was now recognized as the military leader, he had no troops at his disposal. In the West, von Rundstedt knew all but would do nothing, though the Military Governors in France and Belgium, von Stülpnagel and von Falkenhausen, were not only initiates but active sympathizers. In the East, in the absence of von Tresckow, the wavering vacillations of von Kluge had been proof against the efforts of von Gersdorff to keep him in line. Had von Tresckow been at Army Group Centre Headquarters when Goerdeler's letter had arrived in July, the Field-Marshal's response might have been very different, for he exercised an uncanny influence over von Kluge, and, moreover, both he and von Schlabren-dorff knew of the *Führer*'s munificent birthday present.[1] It so happened, however, that von Kluge came to Berlin on leave in the autumn of 1943 and there von Tresckow was enabled to re-establish his ascendancy. At a meeting with Beck, Goerdeler, Olbricht, and von Tresckow, in Olbricht's home, the Field-Marshal categorically declared himself, at long last, to be ready to take the initiative as soon as Hitler was dead.

It was a substantial success and was justly celebrated as such by the conspirators. But Fate once more was against them. Scarcely had von Kluge returned to his headquarters than he was involved in a serious motor-accident while driving from Orscha to Minsk, the results of which incapacitated him for many months.[2] His successor, Field-Marshal Busch, was far from being '*verschwörungs-fähig*' (plot-worthy).

Nor was von Tresckow more fortunate in his efforts to bring Erich von Manstein again up to scratch. That Field-Marshal had been prepared at the time of Stalingrad to join with von Kluge in wresting the active command of the Army from Hitler, but the somewhat pitiful performance of Paulus in surrendering without a demonstration had so piqued his contempt that he scornfully with-drew from the plot.[3] Now von Tresckow tried desperately to win him back, but von Manstein would not be wooed. He was not unimpressed by the eloquence of von Tresckow, however, nor would he trust his own determination in a prolonged contest on intimate terms. When, at the end of 1943, von Tresckow suggested, through General Schmundt, that he should become von Manstein's Chief of Staff, the Field-Marshal would have none of it. As a Staff officer, he wrote to the Head of the Personnel Department of the Army, von Tresckow had no peer, but his attitude towards National

---

[1] See above, p. 529.
[2] Schlabrendorff, pp. 113, 124-5 ; Gisevius, ii, 263.
[3] See above, p. 534.

Socialism was known to be negative. It was the death-knell to Henning von Tresckow's career as a Staff officer and in great measure of his value to the conspiracy.[1] Such an indictment from such a quarter might well have meant an actual death sentence ; in effect it meant his return to an Army headquarters and his elimination from active participation in the conspiracy. On the ever-retreating Eastern Front he watched in heart-aching suspense for the signal which should proclaim the death of Hitler, and when it came, only to herald a false dawn, he took his own life rather than meet the inevitable consequences of failure at the hands of his remorseless enemies.[2]

But though the Field-Marshals were lacking, the planning was held to be complete, and it was determined to go forward with the *Putsch* as soon as the crucial factor — the assassination of Hitler — had been accomplished. 'In September', Goerdeler had said confidently to Jacob Wallenberg, and he had meant what he said. But the *Führer*'s evil guardian angel was working overtime. Again and again the *Attentat* was brought to the very threshold of consummation ; again and again some act of pure chance prevented it from accomplishment. In all, between September and December 1943 there were at least six carefully planned attempts to murder Hitler, and on each occasion Fate baulked the plotters of their prey.

Helmuth Stieff, the gay, vitriolic little hunchback, had undertaken to make the attempt at the *Führer*'s headquarters. To him was consigned a supply of explosives from the stores of the *Abwehr*, who were still sufficiently independent to be able to perform this service. After various experiments it had been decided to discard the German-made fuse, which burned with a slight hissing sound, for the superior British-manufactured article, which was completely silent, and this could only be obtained through the *Abwehr*.[3] Colonel Freiherr Wessel von Freytag-Loringhoven, of Canaris's Staff, secured the required supplies, which were flown to East Prussia accompanied by two of Stieff's Staff officers. There the explosives were secretly buried under a wooden tower in the compound of the *Führerhauptquartier*, and there they incontinently and spontaneously exploded, to the surprise and alarm of all concerned. Only the fact that the subsequent investigation was entrusted to a Colonel Werner Schrader, of the *Abwehr*, who happened to be a member of the conspiracy, saved Stieff and his officers from detection. As it was, under the masterly handling of Schrader, the

---

[1] Schlabrendorff, pp. 113-14.   [2] *Ibid.*, pp. 153-4.
[3] Among the papers of the SD investigation which Kaltenbrunner instituted into the antecedents of the *Putsch* of July 20, 1944, is a remarkable diagram showing the channels by which the conspirators acquired their English fuses.

enquiry was sabotaged and petered out without a conclusive report being made.[1] But a further supply of English material had to be procured and this inevitably delayed activities on this particular sector.

On another occasion a young member of the conspiracy, whose name is unknown, managed to obtain access to the conference room in the Berghof at Berchtesgaden in which Hitler was to address a gathering of senior officers. It was the would-be assassin's intention to employ the simple and direct method of the pistol, and although officers were required to remove their holsters before entering the presence, he succeeded in concealing a weapon in the pocket of his breeches. The conspirator's rank, however, was not sufficiently eminent to bring him within the rows of seats provided for the more distinguished members of Hitler's audience, and as a junior Staff officer he had to stand at the back of the hall under the scrutiny of the *Führer's* fanatical SS Life Guards, to whose lynx eyes the perfectly innocent extraction of a handkerchief was a signal for drawing their revolvers. Chagrined and baffled, the young Staff officer was unable to effect even a gesture.

Yet another and more ingenious attempt was made in November 1943. A new uniform greatcoat was to be introduced into the Army, and Hitler, ever careful of these details, had ordered that it should be exhibited for his inspection before being officially adopted. Here was an opportunity for courage, daring and self-sacrifice of the highest order. A young officer, Freiherr Axel von dem Bussche, volunteered to 'model' the overcoat before the *Führer*. He agreed to carry one or more bombs in his pocket, which he would ignite, and then, grappling with the *Führer*, they would perish together.

There is not a doubt as to the sincerity of the young man's intentions. But it was a nerve-racking business, for on each occasion that the demonstration was to take place the *Führer* cancelled it, as if through some premonition of disaster. At last, in November, the day and hour were fixed for an inspection at Zossen. Von dem Bussche made his final preparations, and stood ready for his immolation. But neither he nor the *Führer* was to die on that day. A sudden Allied air-raid not only completely disrupted the arrangements for the inspection, but also destroyed the models of the overcoats which were to be demonstrated. The idea was dropped; the *Führer* lived; and the young man returned to his regiment on the Eastern Front.[2]

---

[1] Schrader, like von Tresckow, committed suicide after the failure of the 20th July, rather than face the consequences of arrest.

[2] The present writer has discussed and checked this incident with Freiherr von dem Bussche, who on his return to the Front was badly wounded in the leg.

The failure of 'Operation Overcoat' brought Claus von Stauffenberg to the fore as a potential assassin. Hitherto he had not been considered, since a man with one eye, one arm and only three fingers was hardly thought suitable as a potentially successful murderer. But on consideration these actual defects were found to be veritable assets. The very fact that von Stauffenberg had been so badly maimed rendered it all the more improbable that he could ever be suspected of attempting to kill the *Führer*. His wounds were his passport of security. No three-fingered man could use a pistol with accuracy, nor was it probable that he could manipulate the intricate mechanism of a time-fuse. Consequently, he could navigate with comparative ease the ever-tightening system of security and precaution with which Adolf Hitler was surrounded.

In point of fact the latter difficulty, that of setting the fuse, had presented a real obstacle to von Stauffenberg, until he had hit upon the device of a small instrument, not unlike a pair of sugar tongs, with which, after sedulous practice, he became proficient in accuracy and manipulation.

This problem having been disposed of, the conspirators found themselves once more waiting upon the event. The perfect opportunity seemed to have arrived. A conference on man-power was called at the *Fuhrer*'s headquarters for December 26, 1943. Olbricht was among those summoned to attend, but on a plea of ill-health he arranged for his Chief of Staff, von Stauffenberg, to represent him. With the bomb in his brief-case, von Stauffenberg actually flew to Rastenburg; with the bomb in his brief-case he actually penetrated to the ante-room of the conference. But there the operation finished before it had well begun, for, in company with all those also summoned to the meeting, Olbricht's representative was informed that it would not take place. The *Führer* had changed his mind.

This was the last attempt of which we have any record until July 1944. In the intervening months the conspiracy more than once narrowly escaped shipwreck — and the *Führer* became steadily more suspicious and more inaccessible.

(viii)

Thus the conspirators entered the year 1944 in a mood of deep depression. There was much indeed to depress them. The steady Russian advance in the East, the successful Allied invasion of Italy, the devastating effect of the Anglo-American heavy bombing of Germany and the increasing imminence of an invasion in the West all betokened the utter hopelessness of continuing the struggle, the disappearance of the last hopes of victory, and the manifest and inescapable catastrophe.

There were, moreover, other causes for despondency. The failure of the Badoglio *coup* in Italy — of which the conspirators had been warned in advance [1] — to bring about a clear-cut decision *vis-à-vis* the Allies, the ruthless and effective action of Hitler in meeting the Italian crisis, and finally, the spectacular rescue of Mussolini and his reappearance as the leader of the Neo-Fascist Republic,[2] had caused a sharp decline in the morale of the plotters. This decline was in no way arrested by their inability to find an active commander in the field on whom they could rely, or to achieve their own primary objective of killing the *Führer*.

'For us the situation is simply this', wrote Ulrich von Hassell in his Diary on December 27, 1943. 'With Hitler the war will certainly be lost because it will be fought to a catastrophic end by both sides. It does not lie in Hitler's nature to yield, nor can he hope to bring about a decision favourable to us. . . . The one definite point upon which the other side is united is that Hitler must first of all be laid low.' And there follows the significant entry : 'Only after this goal has been reached can (and will) their differences come to the surface'.[3]

The essentially patriotic motives of the conspirators are, therefore, patent. They were no squalid band of traitors in the pay of the enemy, plotting to destroy their country from motives of gain or pique or jealousy. Nor were they, in the main, inspired by any higher motives than the destruction of a Leader and a régime whom they had followed and tolerated as long as he brought them advantage

----

[1] Allen Dulles maintains (pp. 69, 130), largely on the authority of Gisevius, that the conspirators in Berlin were in direct touch with the anti-German clique in Rome, which included Grandi and Ciano within the Fascist Grand Council, and Badoglio outside it. He also states that, as a result of the breaking of one of the American codes by the German Intelligence, a message to Washington, giving a fairly accurate picture of the dissension within the Fascist hierarchy, was deciphered, sent to the *Führer* and transmitted, with his compliments, to Mussolini. This was early in February 1943 ; a few days later (February 5) Ciano was removed from his post as Foreign Minister and appointed Ambassador to the Vatican.

[2] Having been overthrown by the Grand Council on July 25, 1943, and, after various vicissitudes, confined in the mountain resort of the Gran Sasso, Mussolini was kidnapped to freedom on September 12, 1943, in the most dramatic commando operation of the war, by an expedition under the *Luftwaffe* General Student and SS *Sturmbannführer* Otto Skorzeny, who had been specially charged by Hitler with this mission. Mussolini's record of this event is found in his *Memoirs 1942–43* (London, 1949), pp. 133-6 ; Student's in the *Daily Express* of May 20, 1951 ; and Skorzeny's on pp. 135-51 of *Geheimkommando Skorzeny* (Hamburg, 1950).

[3] Hassell, p. 342.

but concerning whom, at various stages along the way, they had been disillusioned. These men were patriotic Germans who sought to save Germany by the only means in their power from the cataclysmic fate that was rapidly overtaking her under the leadership of Adolf Hitler. Their action in attempting to eliminate the *Führer* was not merely symbolic — and in very few cases did it partake of Dietrich Bonhoeffer's great concept of an 'Act of Repentance' — but it was sternly practical also. By so doing they hoped to unite Germany and divide the Allies, and, as a result, to obtain terms of peace from one side or the other, which, however harsh, would nevertheless be less Draconian than Unconditional Surrender.

Treason, as Talleyrand once said, is a matter of timing (*une question de date*) — and, he might well have added, particularly treason to a régime. Judged by this standard the conspirators cannot be arraigned on a charge of lack of patriotism, but neither can they be canonized as pure idealists. Their avowed and indisputable aim was the salvation of Germany. Their greatest crime was failure.

The premonitions of failure were very manifest in the spring and early summer of 1944. Not only could the conspirators see no hope of assassinating Hitler, but it became increasingly clear that their own Nemesis was hot upon them. The Gestapo were closing in. Ever since the arrests of von Dohnanyi and Bonhoeffer in April, and of Langbehn in September 1943, Schellenberg had been actively concerned in following certain clues and indications. They led him to some startling discoveries.

Schellenberg's first success was to penetrate a peripheral group of the conspiracy known as the *Solf Kreis*, and somewhat contemptuously referred to by the SD and the Gestapo as the 'Salon Fronde'. This group was led and inspired by the widow of Dr. Wilhelm Solf, for many years Colonial Minister under Wilhelm II, and the last Foreign Minister of Imperial Germany in the Cabinet of Prince Max of Baden. Dr. Solf had served the Republic with conspicuous success as Ambassador to Japan and had, from the earliest days of its manifestation, warned against the growth, the danger and the inherent evil of National Socialism. From the Seizure of Power in January 1933 to his own death three years later, Solf opposed the régime with courage and resource, and it is believed by many that it was at his prompting and instigation that Goerdeler became actively engaged in opposition.[1]

---

[1] The present writer was often a visitor at Dr. Solf's home in the Alsenstrasse before and immediately after the Nazi revolution and can testify to the consistent, if Cassandra-like, forebodings which he gave to those leaders of all political parties who came frequently to see him.

After the death of her husband, Frau Solf and her daughter, the Countess Ballestrem, continued in the way of opposition by such means as were open to them. Frau Solf had considerable influence abroad, where her husband's reputation was known and revered by many. Mother and daughter were courageously, if unwisely, outspoken and did much to assist the victims of Nazi persecution, Jews as well as Christians, with food and money and the means of leaving the country. · The coming of war made little difference to their activities.[1]

Joined with her in this work were a group of friends, Countess Hanna von Bredow, the granddaughter of Bismarck; Otto Kiep, the former Consul-General in New York; Count Albrecht von Bernstorff, and Richard Künzer, also of the Foreign Office; Maximilian von Hagen, the historian; Father Erxleben, a Jesuit of some standing; and Fräulein Elisabeth von Thadden, the headmistress of a famous girls' school in Weiblingen, near Heidelberg. Fräulein von Thadden was well known both for her anti-Nazi sentiments and for her tea-parties, which were much frequented by intellectuals and by those Army officers who were intellectually inclined.

It was at one of these gatherings in September 1943, at which were Otto Kiep, Frau Solf and her daughter, State-Secretary Zarden and others, that there appeared, no one quite seemed to know from where, a certain young medico from the Charité Hospital, a Dr. Reckzeh, who in the brief space of an hour appears to have provoked Otto Kiep into a series of indiscreet remarks and to have invited Frau Solf to confide to him any letter which she might wish to send — as it were, 'by safe hand' — to Switzerland, an offer which she accepted. Later Reckzeh suggested a meeting with General Halder, but this the lady declined.

The letters which Frau Solf gave to Reckzeh were harmless, but in Germany of the Third Reich, and at that day and age, to have sent the most innocuous material by the illicit hand of an unknown was as culpably stupid as to have allowed oneself to have been drawn into indiscreet controversy with a stranger. It was impossible, of course, to conceive of a spy in Fräulein von Thadden's comfortable and civilized drawing-room. Yet that was exactly what Dr. Reckzeh was.

---

[1] Among many other acts of courage and kindness performed by Frau Solf and her daughter during the war was their generosity to two interned British diplomats, Sir Lancelot Oliphant, the British Ambassador in Brussels, and Mr. Peter Scarlett, who had been caught 'off base' during the retreat of May 1940, and were in detention at the Spa of Bad Eilsen. Having learnt that they were present in the same hotel as herself, Frau Solf persuaded the SS Guards to allow her to visit them, bringing with her certain of the comforts and luxuries which they had long been denied in captivity.

The Gestapo waited four months before they struck. Then in January 1944 they suddenly arrested Elisabeth von Thadden and all those who had been her guests on that fatal afternoon, and, in addition, Albrecht von Bernstorff and Helmuth von Moltke, who had also known Reckzeh and had warned Frau Solf against him. With the exception of Hanna Solf and her daughter, all were executed save Dr. Zarden, who committed suicide in an interval of interrogation by the Gestapo.[1]

One disaster led to another. The repercussions of Elisabeth von Thadden's tea-party on September 10, 1943, reached as far as Istanbul. Here were two *Abwehr* agents, Erich Vermehren and his beautiful wife, who had been Countess Elisabeth von Plettenberg. Young Vermehren had been nominated before the war as a candidate for a Rhodes Scholarship at Oxford, but had been turned down by the Selection Committee on the ground that his attitude towards National Socialism was 'negative'. Elisabeth Vermehren, a woman of strong religious views and of a redoubtable intelligence and energy, also entertained sentiments similar to those of her husband, and, like many others of the same persuasion, both sought refuge at the outbreak of war in the *Innere Emigration* of the *Abwehr*.

In due course they were sent to Istanbul, where, in January 1944, there came the news of the arrest of their friend Otto Kiep, who had unsuccessfully nominated Vermehren for one of these Scholarships. Kiep had left the Foreign Office and had been serving in the Army as a Reserve officer. His arrest by the Gestapo, therefore, held a special significance. It was the first time that an officer of the Army had been so detained, and it betokened the end of the immunity which the Army had enjoyed, ever since 1934, from the attentions of the Gestapo.

Hard upon the news of Kiep's arrest came the order for Erich Vermehren to return to Berlin. To him it meant only one thing. His 'negative' attitude toward the Nazi régime was already known to the Gestapo. He felt that, in some way, his name must have been connected with that of Otto Kiep. The arrest of himself and his wife on arrival in Germany seemed a foregone conclusion. Or,

---

[1] Frau Solf and her daughter were confined in the concentration camp at Ravensbrück. Their trial was delayed at the instance of the Japanese Ambassador until February 8, 1945. However, on February 3, Roland Freisler, the President of the People's Court, was killed by a bomb which fell during a plenary session of a trial, not only putting an end to an infamous career but also destroying the whole dossier in the Solf case. A fresh hearing was fixed for April 27, but never took place, owing to the entry of the Russians into Berlin. Frau Solf and her daughter were released by an oversight of the authorities at the Moabit Prison on April 23, and miraculously survived (Pechel, pp. 88-93 ; *John Memorandum*).

at any rate, so he thought. Rather than court death he placed
himself in contact with the British Intelligence Service in Istanbul
with a view to finding refuge with the Allies. In February, therefore, the Vermehrens went over openly to the British. They were
secretly removed to England, where unfortunately their story became
known to the press, with a consequent flourish of satisfaction, and
a corresponding flutter of scandal in Berlin, where the story was
soon being told that the pious Countess Elisabeth had been warned
in a dream, by no less a personage than a member of the Trinity,
that she and her husband should not return to Germany, which was
damned as surely as Sodom and Gomorrah. 'But', concluded the
Warning Voice, suddenly giving a practical turn to the conversation,
'don't forget to take the code books with you.'

This, in actual fact, the Vermehrens did not do. They brought
nothing in their hand to the British, and their subsequent services
do not concern the subject of this book. The important fact about
them is that they fled and that their defection coincided quite
fortuitously with the flight of two other *Abwehr* agents from
Istanbul to Cairo.[1]

The situation thus created, the circumstances of scandal and
suspicion, were exactly what Kaltenbrunner and Schellenberg had
been waiting for. Now at last they were in possession of sufficient
dynamite to blast the Canaris empire sky-high and to build their
own upon its wrecked foundations. Briefed by his lieutenants,
Himmler opened up a psychological barrage on Hitler, using every
opportunity to emphasize the inefficiency of the *Abwehr* and their
failure to keep him, the *Führer*, accurately informed of military
developments. This finally had its effect. On February 18, 1944,
Hitler signed a decree creating a unified German Intelligence Service,
of which, though Himmler was its titular chief, the actual control
was in the hands of Kaltenbrunner. Canaris ceased to be Chief of
Military Intelligence, and this office, truncated and restricted almost
beyond recognition, devolved upon Colonel Georg Hansen, who,
fortunately for the conspirators, had been nourished in the Canaris-
Oster tradition. The other activities of the *Abwehr* were divided as
spoils of war, between Schellenberg (SD) and Müller (Gestapo).[2]

[1] Abshagen, pp. 365-70 ; Colvin, pp. 181-5, 194-5.
[2] Interrogation of Ernst Kaltenbrunner at Nuremberg on October 18, 1945.
Kaltenbrunner's capacity for evasion and denial reached a point, during his trial
before the International Military Tribunal, when he even refused to acknowledge
his own signature. A certain reserve is therefore necessary in considering the
veracity of his statements on matters touching his own personal responsibility on
any occasion. His account, however, of the absorption of the *Abwehr* into the
RSHA is confirmed from other independent sources.

Thus ended the fantastic story of the *Abwehr*, over which Canaris had presided for nine years, like a grey fox, from his lair in the Tirpitz-Ufer. It had failed conspicuously as a secret intelligence service, partly because too much was demanded of it, partly because its Chief, 'the little Admiral', was himself a personal spy rather than a bureaucrat and had no sense or capacity of delegating responsibility. The *Abwehr* was patently and incontestably inefficient. The facts are known too well by all concerned to be disputed. There is a tendency, however, in certain circles to explain away this inefficiency by over-emphasizing the services rendered to the Resistance by the *Abwehr*. It is virtually alleged that the *Abwehr* was so busy resisting that it had no time for its primary professional activities.

This is simply not so. To deny that Canaris and Oster constituted the intellect and the sword-arm of the conspiracy in its early stages would be to deny truth. To underestimate the work done by many of the conspirators who were merely operating under *Abwehr* 'cover', such as Josef Müller, Dietrich Bonhoeffer, and Count von Marogna-Rednitz, the head of the office in Vienna, would be equally unjust. But to assume, as there is a certain proneness to suggest, that the *Abwehr* were 'really on the Allied side all the time' would be equally wide of the mark and equally unjust to men who, however inefficient they may have been as intelligence officers, were assuredly German patriots. That they gave warning in advance to the victims of Nazi aggression, as in the case of Denmark and Norway, Belgium and the Netherlands, is established. But this in no way excludes the equally incontestable fact that they tried to provide accurate information for the German High Command from behind the enemy lines — and failed. They were completely surprised, for example, by the Allied landings in North Africa, and this was no treasonable plan to aid the Allies but a complete breakdown in intelligence technique. Though they knew that a vast armada had assembled at Gibraltar, they genuinely could not establish its destination. This was but one outstanding example of how, time and time again, they were outwitted by the superior intelligence services of the British and the Americans.

The truth of the matter is that, though sincere and courageous in both their fields of endeavour, the *Abwehr* displayed no very great efficiency either as intelligence officers or as conspirators, and the attempt of the apologists for Canaris to depict him as 'both a brilliant head of the Secret Service, who yet continued to serve Hitler's ambition, and a brilliant anti-Nazi conspirator, who yet neither wanted nor furthered German defeat', falls to the ground on examination.

In fact, the 'little Admiral' was devious rather than brilliant, and darkly mystical rather than shrewd and cunning. 'A despairing conservative, a fatalist without faith in the future . . . Canaris might perhaps have echoed Talleyrand's observation that only those who had lived under the *ancien régime* could know the meaning of *douceur de vivre* ; but it is difficult to imagine the *ci-devant* Bishop of Autun wandering disconsolately through dusty baroque cathedrals in mental search for the vanished elixir. No — the predicament, like the temperament, of Canaris, was far more serious. His parallel is not in history but in literature. He was the Hamlet of conservative Germany.'[1]

It is, moreover, not without interest that the downfall of the *Abwehr* was brought about not on a charge of treason, but on one of technical and professional inefficiency. Kaltenbrunner and Schellenberg were not deeply moved by the treasonable activities of the Canaris machine, of which, by this time, they were undoubtedly aware or had at least their strong suspicions. They were much more strongly actuated by a desire to destroy a powerful rival, to strike another blow at the influence and prestige of the armed forces and to establish the ascendancy of the Party machine in one more sphere of the life of Germany. The assault of the RSHA on the *Abwehr* corresponds, in microcosm, to the struggle between the SS as a whole and the Army. The aim of both was to destroy the last remnants of the proud and independent position which the Army had enjoyed before 1934, and in both conflicts Fate decided the issue in favour of the Party. The final humiliation — the appointment of the *Reichsführer*-SS Heinrich Himmler to the command of an Army in the field and the enforcement of the Hitler salute upon the Armed Forces of the Reich — was yet to come.[2]

The final negotiations for the transfer of power continued into the summer. Himmler and Canaris maintained the façade of pro-fessional 'correctness' (*Richtigkeit*) and to all appearances the Admiral was granted the honours of war. But at their last meeting Himmler dropped the mask. Quite bluntly he told Canaris that he knew very well of the plots and plans which were being hatched for the overthrow of the régime, and he warned the Admiral that they would not succeed, because at the appropriate moment the Gestapo would intervene to frustrate them. He had only been waiting to know the identity of those who stood behind the conspiracy. Now

---

[1] Hugh Trevor-Roper, 'Admiral Canaris', *The Cornhill Magazine*, Summer 1950. Students of the Admiral and the *Abwehr* will find this brilliant and caustic analysis of great value and accuracy.
[2] See below, p. 678.

he knew.   And he knew also how to deal effectively with such malcontents as Beck and Goerdeler.[1]

That the *Reichsführer*-SS was not fishing for information but
knew of what he spoke is evident from the course of events.   The
conversation with Canaris took place in June, and on July 17 the
order for Goerdeler's arrest was issued.[2]   But just how much did
the Gestapo know ?   Their records indicate that their knowledge
was far from complete, and at best they could only have been aware
of the general plan for the overthrow of the régime and not of the
definitive plots for the assassination of Hitler.

Or did Himmler know ?   In view of what is known of his tentative
talks with Popitz and Langbehn and of his subsequent efforts through
Schellenberg to achieve a separate peace, is it possible that the
Reichsführer-SS was prepared to allow an attempt upon Hitler to
succeed and even to countenance a revolt which might raise him,
Himmler, to the chief power in the State ?   That he would find
Goerdeler and Beck unacceptable as allies is understandable and
their removal might be taken for granted, but did some hope lurk
at the back of that twisted, devious mind that a change of régime
might be effected to his own advantage ?   That he might use the
conspirators and then destroy them, even as, at one moment, they
had thought to use and then destroy him ?   If this is so, it would
account for the remarkable dalliance of the Gestapo in waiting to
take action against the conspirators in general until after their
attempted *Putsch* had been made and had failed.   They had much
information in their possession, derived under torture, which, though
giving an incomplete picture of the conspiracy as a whole, would
have justified a number of arrests.   Why, then, did they not act ?

On the other hand, if Himmler indeed knew as much as he
claimed in his conversation with Canaris and still, in all loyalty to
Hitler, held his hand, he was taking a long chance on the life of his
Führer, a chance which calls in question his efficiency as a secret
police chief — and, in the final analysis, his sincerity.

These unanswerable questions are a part of the general enigma
of the personality of Heinrich Himmler, to which the solution might
have been found had he not been allowed to commit suicide while
in British custody.[3]   The effect, however, of his grim warning to

---

[1] Schlabrendorff, p. 126.   [2] Gisevius, ii, 348.

[3] In the last sordid, murky days of the Third Reich, Himmler, deserted by gods
and men, dismissed by Hitler in Berlin and rejected by Doenitz in Flensburg, in
the uniform of a common soldier and with a patch over one eye by way of disguise,
wandered in aimless pursuit of he knew not what among the shattered remnants
of the German Army, which he, of all men, had done the most to destroy.   Finally
on May 23, 1945, he walked into a British control post on the Lüneburger Heide,

Canaris was to confirm the belief of the conspirators that they must act quickly if only to forestall their own destruction.

(ix)

The first six months of 1944 were marked by certain cleavages of opinion within the leadership of the conspiracy, which, though they threatened at one moment to become unbridgeable, were nevertheless resolved amicably, partly through compromise, and partly by the quirks and turns of Fate.

Up to this time there had been little dispute as to the future leadership of the New Germany. The material to hand was limited — conspiracy was unpopular in the heyday of German victory — and most of those available consisted of former civil servants and retired General officers. Had it been necessary to draw up a 'shadow Cabinet' in, say, 1942, the task would have been a difficult one, and though there was much good and healthy growth among the younger elements, the older men, though distinguished by their sincerity and devotion, were, with the exception of Beck, unimpressive.

After the catastrophe of Stalingrad and the defeats of North Africa, however, the position changed radically, and for two reasons — first, the recognition by many intelligent soldiers of the inevitability of defeat, and their consequent conversion to the idea of the elimination, if not always the assassination, of Hitler ; and secondly, the personality of Claus von Stauffenberg.

The introduction of von Stauffenberg into the circle of the conspirators ushered in a new era. Before, there had been courage and determination, a patriotic purpose and a certain grim ruthlessness. Now, however, there came new factors. Claus von Stauffenberg contributed to the general pool a strange amalgam of gifts and talents. In him were blended the intellectual clarity of the General Staff Officer, the romantic mysticism of Stefan George, and a certain strange purity of Christian thought. Added to this, he was strongminded and self-willed ; a dynamic personality within a body which, though scarred and mutilated, still retained a certain arresting beauty. He was the first natural leader to emerge from within the ranks of the plotters, a leader who could command at once the devotion of both soldiers and civilians to an extent to which neither

where his identity was either not recognized or not appreciated. There, stripped and covered only in a blanket, he felt the searching fingers of the examining doctor approaching his last precious possession. On being ordered to open his mouth, he took the last decision of his life and bit heavily on the poison capsule concealed behind his teeth. In a few seconds the German Army's bitterest enemy was dead.

'THE BAMBERGER REITER'

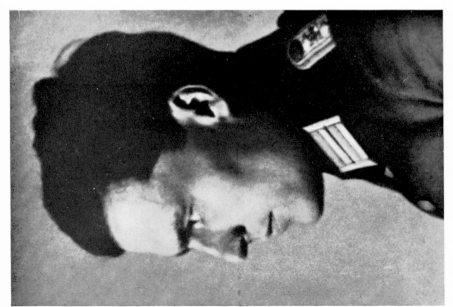

COLONEL GRAF CLAUS SCHENCK

Beck nor Goerdeler, with all the respect which they very properly enjoyed, could ever have attained. Not for nothing was he nick-named the 'Bamberger Reiter' from his remarkable resemblance to the famous thirteenth-century statue in the Cathedral of that city.

Though originally intended merely to replace Oster in the capacity of the 'business manager', von Stauffenberg soon established a marked ascendancy in the councils of the conspiracy. He, the Catholic nobleman, was considerably further to the Left in political thought and outlook than the bourgeois democracy of Carl Goerdeler, and yet it was to von Stauffenberg that the military converts to the conspiracy looked for leadership and inspiration. He was also a natural link with the Kreisau Circle — now somewhat lacking in direction since the arrest of Helmuth von Moltke in January 1944 — through his cousin and devoted admirer, Peter Yorck von Wartenburg.

It is unfortunate that we know so little of what von Stauffenberg had actually planned for the shape of things to come in Germany.[1] Certain it is that he rejected absolutely every form of rule by force and all manifestations of totalitarianism. He dreamed, and had actually taken some steps towards the practical realization of his dream [2] that the overthrow òf authoritarian tyranny in Germany should coincide with, or at least should closely precede, a similar liberation of thought and civil liberty in Russia.

To von Stauffenberg the parliamentarianism of Weimar, to which Goerdeler sought to return, was as outmoded and distasteful as were the more reactionary views of Popitz and Schacht. To him the natural leader of the New Germany which should succeed Hitler's Reich was Julius Leber, the greatest power among the surviving Socialist leaders,[3] whose personality, like his own, radiated the will to action and the readiness to shoulder the highest responsibility.

Leber had occupied an uneasy position within the Kreisau Circle, with whose ideas and aims he was in sympathy but whose preference for 'conscientious objection' found no responding chord within his fiery nature. He reserved for himself, therefore, complete

---

[1] A properly documented biographical study of Claus von Stauffenberg, for which it is believed a reasonable amount of material is in existence, would provide both a valuable contribution to history and a most repaying undertaking. The existing work by Karl Michel, *Ost und West; der Ruf Stauffenbergs* (Zürich, 1947), is marred by over-emotionalism and mental obfuscation.

[2] See below, pp. 618-19.

[3] How high the Nazis themselves rated the standing of Leber among the Socialists may be judged by the fact that at his trial before the People's Court on October 20, 1944, the President, Roland Freisler, described him as 'the Lenin of the German Workers' Movement'.

freedom of political action, and had sought — albeit completely unsuccessfully — since 1942 to find a common formula with the Goerdeler-Beck group. Now, however, in the early months of 1944, through Peter Yorck, he met von Stauffenberg, and between the two men there swiftly developed a deep human and political friendship. Despite the divergence of their background, upbringing and religious convictions, each found within the other a common spark of intellectual integrity and nobility of character. To Leber, von Stauffenberg was no ordinary Colonel on the General Staff, but a national leader in the struggle against the dark forces of their age, and as such he was prepared to follow his lead in any *coup d'état*. To von Stauffenberg, Leber represented not the time-worn shibboleths of pre-war Social Democracy, but the dynamic force of a new democracy forged in the common struggle against the dehumanization of existence by totalitarianism. He, von Stauffenberg, would lead the revolt, but Leber must be Chancellor of the new Government.[1]

It was natural, therefore, that, in holding these views, von Stauffenberg should come, if not into open conflict, at any rate into a marked degree of disagreement with Goerdeler, and it may well have been due to the tolerant wisdom of Ludwig Beck that an open breach was averted. Von Stauffenberg demanded that the Socialist leaders, Leber and Leuschner, should be included in any Cabinet which might be prepared for the morrow of the revolt. Beck agreed to the broadening of the political basis of the conspiracy and welcomed the advent of the Socialists, but, out of loyalty to Goerdeler, insisted that he remain Chancellor-designate.[2]

Beck did, however, succeed in persuading Goerdeler to accept Leber and Leuschner as fellow conspirators and future ministerial colleagues. But this at once brought about a further complication in that the Socialist leaders refused to have anything to do with any plot or conspiracy of which Popitz was a member.[3] For them there was no common ground with one who had been a friend and colleague of Kurt von Schleicher, who had so sadly beguiled and betrayed German Social Democracy, nor with a subsequent recipient of the Golden Badge of the Nazi Party. Goerdeler, however, who had had his own differences with Popitz over policy, and had in any case been estranged from him ever since the unfortunate adventure of Carl Langbehn, recognized that the co-operation of

---

[1] Countess Freya von Moltke and Countess Marion Yorck von Wartenburg, *Der Nachlass von Kreisau* ; Annedore Leber, *Den toten, immer lebendigen Freunden* (Berlin, 1946), p. 11.
[2] Leber, p. 11.   [3] See above, p. 579.

the Socialists in any future German State was infinitely more important than that of those elements of reaction which Popitz represented. He therefore accepted the conditions of Leber and Leuschner and finally jettisoned Popitz.[1]

This, however, did not satisfy von Stauffenberg. Greatly as he respected Beck, as did all who came in contact with him at this time, he saw in him a tired and disappointed man, weakened by illness, and above all, without any clear conception of politics, and completely in Goerdeler's hands — and the Generals, as von Stauffenberg told Popitz and von Hassell in March, were no longer prepared to receive Goerdeler.[2]

Thus, as the spring of 1944 drew toward summer, the situation of the conspirators was paradoxically perverse. At the very moment when high-ranking officers of the Army were displaying an inclination towards active participation in a plot to eliminate Hitler, the leaders of the conspiracy appeared to be mesmerized by the recollection of past failures, incapable of further action and acutely divided amongst themselves. It was this strange state of affairs which produced that most meretricious incident of the whole conspiracy — *l'affaire Rommel*.

At this time Erwin Rommel was still the darling of the German military-minded public, and though he had come under censure from the *Führer* after El Alamein, he still retained more of Hitler's confidence than did most of his fellow Marshals. Rommel had escaped the blame for the defeat of Alamein and the stigma of the mass surrender of Cape Bon, for which the taciturn, correct and able von Arnim was left to suffer the reproach. To the average civilian and to many soldiers he was still the *beau idéal* of a Nazi General, and his public appeal was recognized alike by Hitler and by those in opposition to the *Führer*.

Returning to Germany in March 1943, Rommel later held the post of Commander-in-Chief of the German forces in Northern Italy, with headquarters near Lake Garda. He remained in Italy until November, when he was given the special assignment by

---

[1] Unpublished MS by Dr. Otto John, entitled 'The Popitz-Langbehn Affair'. Dr. John endeavoured to bring about a meeting in March 1944 between Goerdeler, Popitz and Leber with a view to reconciliation, but Leber's refusal was so pronounced that there was clearly no chance of success. Later, Dr. John's brother, Hans, succeeded in arranging an interview between Dr. Günther Gereke, the former Reich Minister and a friend of Popitz, and Field-Marshal von Witzleben. As this interview only took place on July 18, 1944 (*i.e.* two days before the *Putsch*), it was without results. Meanwhile, in February, von Hassell had attempted a compromise between the views of Popitz and von Stauffenberg, but this had been equally unsuccessful (Hassell, p. 347).   [2] Hassell, pp. 347, 350.

Hitler of inspecting and reporting on the Western Defences of Europe from the Skagerrak to the Spanish frontier, with a view to assessing their capacity of resisting an Anglo-American invasion. Finally, in January 1944, he was given the command of Army Group B, which extended from the Netherlands to the Loire, and which, with Blaskowitz's Army Group G, was under the supreme command of Field-Marshal von Rundstedt, C.-in-C. West.

The impressions gained during the nine months thus spent in Germany and in occupied Europe had had a profound effect upon Rommel. After the fall of Tunis he had been convinced that a complete victory was now irretrievably beyond Germany's grasp and that only a swiftly negotiated peace could forestall the inevitability of military disaster. According to his somewhat partial biographer, Brigadier Desmond Young, he had had the temerity to tell this to Hitler at the *Führerhauptquartier* at Rastenburg in May 1943, and had received the surprisingly frank answer: 'Yes, I know it is necessary to make peace with one side or the other, but no one will make peace with me'.[1]

The impending disaster became the more clearly apparent to Rommel as the months sped on and as he encountered more directly, and at every turn, the obstructionist activities of OKW and the staggering demands for an unwavering confidence in the military 'intuition' of the *Führer*. It did not require a military genius or the gift of second sight to recognize the portents of catastrophe at the close of 1943, and at the time of his appointment as C.-in-C. Army Group B he was considered ripe for initiation into the conspiracy.

On taking over his command Rommel found among his immediate subordinates two friends of long standing in the Military Governors of Belgium and France, von Falkenhausen and von Stülpnagel. All three had been associated together at the School of Infantry at Dresden, where von Falkenhausen had been Commandant and von Stülpnagel and Rommel had served under him as instructors. From them, and from the First Quartermaster-General Eduard Wagner, Rommel learned of the existence of a Resistance Movement, and also something of its general plans and of the unsuccessful attempts which had already been made upon Hitler's life.

It is to be believed that from the first Rommel was emphatically opposed to the idea of assassination and that he favoured the use of reliable Panzer units to seize the person of the *Führer*, who should then be compelled to announce his own abdication, preparatory to being placed on trial before a German court for crimes against

---

[1] Desmond Young, *Rommel* (London, 1950), p. 185.

humanity and against the German people. Rommel, it should be understood, had no moral scruples as to assassination. His objection was purely psychological in that he did not wish to make a martyr of Hitler, preferring that the nation which had elected him to supreme power should also try and condemn him.

It was late in February 1944, nearly two months after he had taken over the command of Army Group B, that Rommel received his first direct approach from the conspirators. Their emissary was Dr. Karl Strölin, a fellow Württemberger and *Oberbürgermeister* of Stuttgart. Strölin had served with Rommel as an infantry captain in the First World War and had kept up the association afterwards. Both had, in their separate spheres, warmly embraced the tenets of National Socialism in its early stages, though Strölin claims that he renounced it when Hitler entered Prague in March 1939, on which occasion his friend Rommel was commanding the *Führer*'s escort.

Between Strölin and Goerdeler there was also a friendship of long standing, and in his lesser sphere the Lord Mayor of Stuttgart had endeavoured to follow the lead given by the Lord Mayor of Leipzig in resistance. In August 1943 they had jointly sponsored a memorandum, which, with no little courage, they submitted to the Reich Ministry of Interior, whose chief was Himmler, calling for the cessation of the persecution of the Jews and of the Christian Churches, the restoration of civil rights and the re-establishment of a judicature independent of the Party. Both the authors of this document had received a severe — and what was described as a 'final' — warning from the Gestapo that, should they persist in their jeremiads, they would be summarily dealt with.

Through Frau Rommel, Strölin conveyed a copy of this memorandum to the Field-Marshal in November, and then, after consultation with Goerdeler, he decided to make the first direct approach. The meeting took place in Rommel's house at Herrlingen, near Ulm, at the end of February. The conversation, which was held *à deux*, lasted between five and six hours. Strölin did most of the talking. Rommel, who had little or no understanding of politics, but much shrewd Swabian *Bauernschlauheit*, listened attentively. He no longer entertained any personal illusion about victory. To his military understanding and his ordinary common sense the war was lost beyond redeeming. All that remained was to bring it to an end as soon as possible, before the final catastrophe overwhelmed the *Wehrmacht*.

Strölin is insistent that he at no time apprised Rommel of any forthcoming plot to kill Hitler, and it may well be that he knew nothing of it himself, for he was not in the inner councils of the conspiracy. The plot, as he outlined it, was the old pre-Stalingrad plan to seize Hitler on the Eastern Front and compel him to announce his own abdication over the radio. This might well result in a civil war, unless some figure of outstanding eminence appeared immediately to dominate the situation.

'You are our most popular General', said Strölin to Rommel, 'and you are more respected abroad than any other of our commanders. You are the only one who can prevent civil war in Germany. You must lend your name to the movement.'

Rommel thought deeply for some time and then said slowly: 'I believe it my duty to come to the rescue of Germany'.[1]

Strölin returned to Berlin and reported to Goerdeler on his success with the new recruit, and together they apparently agreed that Rommel was pre-eminently the first choice for either the post of Commander-in-Chief of the *Wehrmacht* or as interim Head of the State immediately after a *Putsch* had been successfully achieved. Goerdeler urged Strölin to seek a further meeting with the Field-Marshal and to reinforce his own arguments by taking with him yet another Swabian, Freiherr Constantin von Neurath, former Foreign Minister of the Reich and more recently Protector of Bohemia and Moravia.

In the meantime circumstances seemed to be forcing Rommel along the path of destiny. His Chief of Staff, General Gause, had been forced to retire as a result of wounds received in Africa, and as his replacement Rommel had asked for an old front-line comrade and a further fellow Württemberger, General Hans Speidel, at that time Chief of Staff to the Eighth Army on the Eastern Front. His request was granted. Speidel reported to him on April 15 at La Roche Guyon, and from that moment the headquarters of Army Group B became a nerve centre of conspiracy similar to that which Henning von Tresckow and Fabian von Schlabrendorff had created at von Kluge's headquarters of Army Group Centre on the Eastern Front.

For Speidel was considerably more of an initiate in the plans of the conspiracy than was Strölin, with whom, however, he was well acquainted. He was also an intimate friend of von Stülpnagel, and

---

[1] Young, pp. 222-3. There exist three versions of Strölin's interview with Rommel, all of which tally in the essentials. In addition to the account given by Strölin to Brigadier Young, there are his evidence before the International Military Tribunal on March 25, 1946 (*Nuremberg Record*, x, 56-7), and the version given in his book, *Stuttgart im Endstadium des Krieges* (Stuttgart, 1950), pp. 35-6. See also Strölin, *Verräter oder Patrioten?* (Stuttgart, 1952) and a series of articles entitled 'Tragödie General Rommels', which appeared in the *Schwarzwälder Post* on October 22, 25, 27 and 29, 1948 ; and Lutz Koch, pp. 187-90.

together they continued to keep Rommel alive to his responsibility of saving the German people from destruction. And the German people themselves took a hand in this. Rommel was the hero both of the militarists and also of those who sought desperately to bring the war to an end. It is probable that no commander since Hindenburg in the First World War had achieved the degree of personal popularity and confidence among the German people as had Rommel in 1944. Not only those of his fellow officers who shared his gloom as to the outcome of the war frequented his headquarters, but also disgruntled Nazi hierarchs, such as the *Gauleiter* and *Reichsstatthalter* of Hamburg, Karl Kaufmann, and frightened collaborators of the régime, such as Julius Dorpmüller, the Reich Minister of Transport, begging him to deliver Germany from her desperate straits. Nor were the voices of the men and women in the street silent. The post-bag at La Roche Guyon was augmented daily by many letters from humble and unknown writers bearing testimony to their trust in the Field-Marshal as their potential saviour.

Such great pressure could not but have its effect, but, to do Rommel justice, it does not appear that he ever sought personally for any supreme position of leadership in the conspiracy. His statement to Strölin, 'I believe it my duty to come to the rescue of Germany', was highly ambiguous. Strölin had interpreted it as a pledge of support and had proceeded accordingly, but it is more than likely that Rommel himself had intended no more than a declared intention that he would take action to bring about a cessation of hostilities with the Western Powers *before* the launching of an invasion of the Continent should necessarily commit him and his armies to further resistance.

For this is exactly what Rommel planned to do, with or without the approval of Hitler and whether the conspirators in Berlin made a successful *Putsch* or not. His motive was purely and simply the saving of the German Army and the German Reich. He had reverted to the fundamental duty of the German officer ; the duty that transcended all loyalty to any political régime ; the motive which had prompted the Army to get rid of the Kaiser, to betray the Republic, and now to eliminate Hitler.

In company with von Stülpnagel and Speidel, he believed that the Western Allies would jump at the possibility of ending the war without the cost to themselves in men and material of invading the Continent. It would then almost certainly be possible to enlist their aid against the Russians, and together they would hurl the Slavonic hordes back from the frontiers of the Reich which they were now so rapidly approaching. From the moment of Speidel's arrival on

April 15, with the gloomy account of his conference *en route* at the Berghof with Hitler, Keitel and Jodl, until the very eve of D-Day, Rommel and his intimate subordinates were actively engaged in preparing an offer of armistice terms to be made to General Eisenhower by the middle of June.

These preparations were in their penultimate stage at the time when it was possible to arrange the meeting with Strölin and von Neurath for which Goerdeler had asked in February. It was considered inexpedient for Rommel to be present, both from the point of view of security and also because he had neither the mental equipment nor the personal inclination to take part in a political discussion. He was represented by the more subtle mind of General Speidel, in whose flat at Freudenstadt the meeting took place on May 27.

The three Swabians were agreed that their fellow Württemberger should be urged to place himself at the disposal of the conspiracy either as Head of the State or as Commander-in-Chief of the *Wehrmacht*, but Speidel was forced to tell his friends that the Field-Marshal would have nothing to do with an assassination, whereas Strölin reiterated the insistence of Beck and Goerdeler that the only way to eliminate Hitler satisfactorily was to kill him. No definite agreement was reached, but Strölin and von Neurath furnished Speidel with memoranda for Rommel's perusal and, after a meeting next day, at which a system of communication signals was worked out between La Roche Guyon and the headquarters of the conspiracy in Berlin, Speidel and von Stülpnagel that night (May 28) put the final touches to the draft armistice agreement.[1]

In this memorandum Rommel's position was made perfectly clear. Hitler was to be arrested by the High Command of the Army and brought before a German Court. The Field-Marshal's views against assassination were definitely stated, as was his disinclination to claim for himself the leadership of the Reich, but his readiness to assume, if asked, the command of the whole *Wehrmacht* or of the Army. Indeed, specific mention was made that the leadership under which the forces of the opposition would take over executive power in Germany would be that of Beck, Goerdeler and Leuschner. The German people were to be informed by radio from Berlin, and from all the stations under the control of the Western Command, concerning the military situation, the criminal rule of the Nazi régime, and the consequent necessity for direct action.

[1] General Hans Speidel, *Invasion 1944: ein Beitrag zu Rommels und des Reiches Schicksal* (Stuttgart, 1949), pp. 85-7 ; Strölin, pp. 36-7 ; Young, pp. 223-4.

On the Western Front an armistice, *not* unconditional surrender, was to precede peace negotiations. The Allied bombing of Germany would be suspended and the German Armies would retire to the Reich frontiers, handing over the administration of the occupied areas to the Allies. On the Eastern Front fighting would continue, but on a shortened line from the mouths of the Danube to the Carpathians, Lwow, the Vistula and Memel. Lithuania and other 'fortress areas' (*Festungen*) would be evacuated.[1]

Thus matters stood on the eve of the Invasion.

Such is the first part of the Rommel Saga of the Resistance,[2] and it is full of problems for the historian. In the first place, there is no evidence that Strölin discussed his plan for making Rommel the virtual leader of the new post-Hitler régime with anyone but Goerdeler, whom he found in March 1944 in a highly nervous and depressed condition and in constant danger of arrest.[3]   There is no doubt that to the German people Rommel would have presented a much more glamorous and appealing figure than Goerdeler or Beck or von Witzleben, though he had none of their moral fibre and was but a very newcomer to Resistance. Did Goerdeler waver for a moment in his loyalty to Beck and von Witzleben under the eloquent pleadings of Strölin ? It was true that Beck was weakened by frustration and illness and that von Witzleben lacked perhaps the drive and initiative desirable in a Commander-in-Chief, yet was Goerdeler prepared to sacrifice either or both of his co-leaders in the conspiracy upon the altar of expediency ?   And, if so, to what purpose ? For, though he may have been the darling of the German people as a whole, Rommel was anathema to the majority of the veterans of Resistance, who saw in him the very epitome of that military opportunism and irresponsible casuistry which had nourished and supported National Socialism up to the very moment of its downfall. It is greatly to be doubted, for example, whether von Stauffenberg and his followers among the plotters, or those surviving friends of Dietrich Bonhoeffer, such as Otto and Hans John, would have continued in Resistance in such a contingency. To have placed Rommel at the head of the new régime, or even in command of its armed forces, would have been to disintegrate almost irreparably the whole moral fabric of the conspiracy, and it is almost inconceivable that it was ever seriously considered except by the little ring of Württembergers, who would, perhaps, have been not

---

[1] Speidel, pp. 91-3.

[2] For the remainder of the story see below, pp. 686 *et seq.*

[3] ' He [Goerdeler] keeps very much in the background, after warnings from all sides', wrote von Hassell in his Diary on March 8, 1944 (p. 351).

averse to establishing a Swabian ascendancy in the new Reich and the new Army.

That Rommel neither took it seriously nor thought seriously of it is clear, and one of the more redeeming aspects of the story is his declaration of loyalty to Beck, Goerdeler and Leuschner, though he would apparently have been prepared either to supplant von Witzleben as Commander-in-Chief of the *Wehrmacht* or to serve under him as Commander-in-Chief of the Army.[1]

The whole episode is symptomatic of the lack of co-ordination and of the disunited leadership prevalent in the 'upper brackets' of the conspiracy, which touched its nadir of despondency at this time.

(x)

The attitude of Rommel and his subordinates towards the forestalling of an invasion in the West and the prosecution of hostilities in the East was but one facet of a wider and deeper cause of dissension within the ranks of the conspiracy. It was the same rock of contention against which the German ship of State had frequently run in the past, generally with disastrous results; the age-old German problem of whether to orientate Reich policy toward the East or the West.

Traditionally in the past the Monarchy and the landed nobility of Prussia had gravitated towards the autocratic theories of Tsardom, while the German Liberals had looked toward the West for inspiration and comradeship. Bismarck had astutely alternated his policy between the two, but had always counselled friendship with Russia — in which view he was supported by Moltke, who regarded a war on two fronts as potentially disastrous for Germany. With the rise of the rich industrial bourgeois aristocracy had come the theories and doctrines of Pan-Germanism, and that dream of the acquisition of *Lebensraum* at the expense of Russia, which ultimately infiltrated both the Foreign Office and the Great German General Staff. Bismarck opposed these heresies while he remained in office; they succeeded in achieving an ascendancy as soon as he fell from power.[2]

The advent of Bolshevism in Russia, and of Communism as a militant force abroad, complicated rather than simplified the position.

---

[1] That Rommel knew of the proposal to make him Head of the State is beyond doubt. According to Brigadier Young (p. 222), Strölin told him that 'I don't think that he [Rommel] ever heard of it until the last day of his life'. This is clearly not so, as Speidel states categorically (p. 87) that 'the Field-Marshal approved of the conversations [of May 27/28] and wished to make no claims for himself', a fact which was later specifically incorporated in the memorandum of armistice terms.   [2] See above, p. 120.

While the 'Westerners' in the Wilhelmstrasse and the Bendlerstrasse became the more intensified in their distrust of Russia, the 'Easterners' were no less anxious to remain on good terms with the Soviet Union on account of the manifest advantages accruing to Germany from such a policy. Von Maltzan, von Brockdorff-Rantzau (after his conversion) [1] and von Dirksen, in the Foreign Office, and von Seeckt, von Schleicher, von Niedermayer and Köstring in the headquarters of the *Reichswehr*, all bent their energies to the maintenance of a firm liaison with Russia to the greater glory of Germany.

Not even Hitler's ideological detestation of Communism was proof against the traditional oscillation of German policy *vis-à-vis* Russia. He condoned the military liaison until 1935, when the success of his own policies had placed Germany beyond the need of such clandestine arrangements and, with the conclusion of the anti-Comintern Pact, emerged into open hostility in 1936. This gave way three years later to the strange alliance of 1939, which in its turn was succeeded by the Nazi invasion of 1941. Up to the very eve of the final *débâcle* the *Führer* cherished the belief that dissension would disunite the Western and the Eastern Allies —'and we will join one side or the other, I don't care which',[2] and this ambivalence of attitude was reflected all along the line, as much within the plottings of the conspirators as among the policy-makers of the Third Reich.

When Hitler invaded the Soviet Union on June 22, 1941, he took what was perhaps the most controversial step of his whole career. Amongst the military circles there was a profound divergence of reaction. There were those followers of von Seeckt who strongly deprecated any breach of good relations with Russia ; there were those who were generally opposed to the extension of the theatre of operations, at any rate until British resistance had been subdued, recalling Moltke's warnings against a two-front war ; there were those adherents of Ludendorff who looked forward to annexations of *Lebensraum* in the Baltic littoral, the Ukraine and the Crimea and the Caucasus, and there were those genuine pro-Russians and anti-

---

[1] See above, p. 132.

[2] According to SS General Karl Wolff, who retailed it to Allen Dulles, this remark was made to him by Hitler ten days before his suicide on April 30, 1945 (Dulles, p. 166).

There is no doubt that in the minds of certain of the high-ranking Nazi hierarchs — if not in that of Hitler himself — the sudden death of President Roosevelt on April 12, 1945, recalled the miraculous salvation of Frederick the Great from defeat in 1762, when the accession of Peter III to the throne of Russia on the sudden death of the Tsarina Elizabeth Petrovna resulted in the disruption of the alliance against Prussia in the Seven Years' War (Schwerin von Krosigk's Diary, April 15, 1945).

Communists who hoped that, as a result of the invasion, the Bolshevik fabric would collapse and in its place would be substituted a régime with which Germany could co-operate on a basis of reciprocal alliance and security.

There seems to be no doubt that this last opinion was not entirely founded upon illusion. A considerable amount of fraternization did exist between the German troops and the populations of the Baltic, White Russia, the Ukraine and the Caucasus during the interval between the departure of the Communist Commissars and the arrival of the Gestapo, the SS, and the SD, and it is not at all impossible that an appreciable degree of co-operation could have been achieved had a more enlightened policy been pursued by the Germans. But instead of an appeal to fight for national liberation came Göring's 'colonial statute'; instead of a reasoned approach calculated to promote understanding and friendship, based on expertise and a knowledge of the peoples concerned, came the primordial confusion of Rosenberg's *Ost-Ministerium*, soon to be known throughout Germany as the '*Chaos-Ministerium*'. Instead of Red Commissars came Brown ones, as brutal and overbearing as their predecessors. Instead of political sense came the bludgeon and the whip of Erich Koch, Gauleiter of East Prussia and *Reichskommissar* for the Ukraine.

The failure of the Nazi planners to take account of the potential advantages to be derived from the pursuit of a 'separatist' policy in occupied Russia and their rigid adherence to the racial doctrines of the régime, which proclaimed all non-Germanic peoples to be *Untermenschen*, cost Germany, without exaggeration, millions of allies, a fact which may be illustrated from the experience of the one field commander who adopted an independent line of action. Colonel-General (later Field-Marshal) Erwin von Kleist, whose Army Group operated in the Caucasus area, had the foresight to attach to his staff two former military attachés at the Moscow Embassy, General Ritter von Niedermayer and General Köstring,[1]

---

[1] General Ritter Oskar von Niedermayer had been primarily responsible for the operational functions of the military liaison between the German and Russian General Staffs (see above, p. 128). Appointed to Moscow in 1933, he functioned as military attaché in all but name until that post again became 'legal' with the unilateral abrogation of Part V of the Treaty of Versailles in March 1935. On his return from Moscow in 1935, he became Professor of Geopolitics at the University of Berlin until recalled to active service. In 1943 he commanded a mixed division of Transcaucasian legions 25,000 strong. An outspoken Bavarian, von Niedermayer did not hesitate to criticize the criminal folly of the German policy in Russia and after July 20, 1944, was denounced, arrested and condemned to death. His execution was averted by the capture of Berlin, but he was transported to the Soviet Union as a prisoner of war and has not since been heard of. (Herbert von Dirksen,

whose knowledge of the peoples of the Caucasus was unrivalled among non-Russians. As a result, thousands of Karachoevs, Kabardines, Ossetes, Ingushts, Azerbaijans and Kalmucks formed legions to fight with the German armies against Communism. In all, these forces together with those Cossacks, Uzbeks and other Russian prisoners of war who formed General Vlassov's 'Army of National Liberation', are said to have numbered some eight hundred thousand, to whose courage as soldiers tribute has been paid by those German officers associated with them, and by other writers.[1]

The conduct of the war in the East, its savagery and inhuman brutality, its lost opportunities and finally its cataclysmic defeats, had been responsible for driving numerous recruits into the camp of the conspirators, but here they found discord piled upon discord, as Pelion upon Ossa. In the early stages there had, of course, been but one party with whom the plotters could hope to make peace, but, with the invasion of the Soviet Union, the traditional alternative was presented and at once found its adherents.

The Western Allies, it was pointed out by the 'Easterners', had not only failed to respond to the various overtures made to them by the conspirators but had, by the Casablanca formula, pledged themselves to accept nothing less than the unconditional surrender of Germany as the price of cessation of hostilities, whereas for some time the Soviet Government had kept its hands free. Even after the formal Russian adherence to the Casablanca formula at the Moscow Conference of October 1943, it was believed by the 'Easterners' that Stalin would be less rigid in his observance of its strict application than would the British and American Governments, who, as Adam von Trott complained to von Hassell in December 1943, persisted in their suspicions 'lest a change of régime [in Germany] should turn out to be only a cloak, hiding a continuation of militaristic Nazi methods under another label'.[2]

Moscow — Tokyo — London (London, 1951), p. 133). Von Niedermayer was succeeded as military attaché in Moscow by Major-General Ernst Köstring, born of German parents in Moscow, who continued in office until June 1941. At the outset of the invasion of Russia he had warned against the capacity of the Red Army to take punishment and recover from it, and had fallen into disgrace as a result. He remained inactive in Berlin-Grunewald until recalled to service as Inspector-General of Russian Volunteers.

[1] Dirksen, pp. 256-7 (the chapter on 'War and Catastrophe' appears in the English but not the German edition of the memoirs), gives the figure at a million, but General Köstring, in a letter to the present writer, sets it at approximately 825,000. For a particularly interesting, if highly tendentious, account of the reaction of an Austrian *Waffen*-SS man to the failure of the German policy in Russia, see Erich Kern's *Der grosse Rauch* (Zürich, 1948), of which an English translation appeared in 1951 entitled *The Dance of Death*.

[2] Hassell, pp. 343-4.

There were at least some superficial grounds for holding this belief. While British and American propaganda adhered unswervingly to the thesis of Unconditional Surrender and associated Nazi tyranny with Prussian militarism as their ideological objectives of destruction, the Moscow Radio in its German services consistently emphasized that the Soviet Union was engaged in fighting only against 'Hitlerite Germany' and not against the German people and the German Army. Even Stalin had given some public endorsement to this line of propaganda.[1]

And then, in the midsummer of 1943 — with the German Army reeling from the impact of the disaster of Stalingrad, the surrender of North Africa, the invasion of Sicily and the Anglo-American landings on the mainland of Italy, the intensive bombing of German cities and the failure of the summer offensive on the Eastern Front — there emerged what later became known throughout Germany as the 'Spectre of Tauroggen'.[2] On July 20, 1943, new voices were to be heard on the radio from Russia. German voices ; not the tones of the Russian radio 'stooges' who regularly broadcast to Germany, but fresh voices, and to them were attached names of distinction and authority.

On July 12 a conference had been called at Moscow of delegates from all German prisoner of war camps in Russia, and from this meeting there emerged the 'Free German Movement' of which the components, who comprised all classes and shades of political opinion from former Communist deputies in the *Reichstag* to officers of the German General Staff,[3] were united in their opposition to Hitler and the Nazi régime. Their initial broadcast to Germany on July 20 was the occasion for a manifesto calling upon the German people and Army, in view of the fact that the war was already lost, to overthrow Hitler and form 'a real National German Government with a strong democratic order which will have nothing in common with the impotence of the Weimar régime, a democracy which will

---

[1] For example, in his report as Chairman of the State Committee for Defence at a ceremonial session of the Moscow Soviet on November 6, 1942, to mark the twenty-fifth anniversary of the Bolshevik Revolution in 1917, Stalin had said that, although it was their aim to destroy Hitler and his army and its leaders, 'it is not our aim to destroy all organized military force in Germany, for every literate person will understand that this is not only impossible in regard to Germany, as it is in regard to Russia, but it is also inexpedient from the point of view of the victor' (*Soviet Foreign Policy during the Patriotic War — Documents and Materials* (London, 1945), i, 49).   [2] See above, p. 7, footnote.

[3] At this meeting Erich Weinert, a well-known German Communist writer, was elected chairman, with Major Karl Hertz and Lieutenant Graf Heinrich von Einsiedel, a descendant of the great Bismarck and a relative of Henning von Tresckow, as vice-presidents.

mercilessly repress any attempt at any new conspiracies against the rights of a free people or against the peace of Europe'.¹

Two months later, on September 11, 1943, the formation of a 'Union of German Officers' (*Bund Deutscher Offiziere*) was announced from Moscow under the chairmanship of General Walther von Seydlitz-Kurzbach, formerly commander of the LI Corps, with others who had also surrendered at Stalingrad, including Lieutenant-General Freiherr Alexander von Daniels, Major-General Martin Lattmann and Major-General Otto Korfes as vice-presidents. This body, speaking as the survivors of the Sixth Army and 'in the name of all the victims of Stalingrad', appealed to the German Army to follow the traditional policy of Bismarck and Seeckt and establish friendship with Russia by abandoning the struggle against the Red Army, and demanding the immediate resignation of Hitler and his Government.²

Though purely the tool of Soviet psychological warfare, the constant propaganda of the 'Free German Movement' and the 'Union of German Officers' impressed many Germans with its promises. A weekly newspaper, the *Freies Deutschland*, issued for the use of prisoners of war and to be dropped in leaflet form over Germany, and daily broadcast transmissions, assured the German people, in the name of Erich Weinert and Walther von Seydlitz, that the Soviet Union did not identify them with Hitler and 'the Fascist-beasts', and promised them a restoration of their freedom of speech, assembly, action, and worship once they had taken the initiative in making peace by eliminating Hitler.³

Later a new name began to be heard, at first but faintly, then with increasing force and vehemence, a name which to the German people personified the fate of hundreds of thousands of prisoners taken at Stalingrad, a voice which thrilled and shook the hearts of every man and woman with relatives among those unhappy captives. As a final *coup de théâtre*, Friedrich Paulus gave his public

---

¹ For text of the Manifesto of July 20, 1943, see Appendix B, p. 716.

² For text of the Appeal of September 14, 1943, see Appendix B, p. 718. With an almost uncanny intuition Hitler had foreseen just this eventuality. In talking over the Stalingrad disaster with Jodl on February 1, 1943, the *Führer* had predicted : 'You will see, it won't be a week before Seydlitz and Schmidt and even Paulus are talking over the radio' (Gilbert, p. 21). His prophecy was inaccurate only in the matter of timing ; Seydlitz spoke not a week but seven months after his surrender.

³ It is significant of the slant which the Russians gave to this new line of propaganda to Germany that the weekly issues of *Freies Deutschland* bore the old 'Black-White-Red' colours of the Imperial German Army, while the signature tune of the radio programmes was that of the patriotic song of the War of Liberation : '*Der Gott, der Eisen wachsen liess . . .*'.

approval of the programme of the National Committee for Free Germany and thereby added the prestige and authority of a German Field-Marshal — an honour which had been conferred upon him for his loyalty to the *Führer*'s military leadership at Stalingrad — to a movement which owed much to the bitter aftermath of that battle.[1]

The effect of this verbal barrage upon the conspirators was to encourage those who had always entertained a desire to make an approach to Russia, at any rate in the first instance, in order either to make peace with Stalin or to exercise pressure on the Western Powers through fear of such a separate peace. The chief protagonist of this policy was the former Ambassador in Moscow, Count Werner von der Schulenburg, who, trained in the traditional policy of Bismarck, Maltzan and Brockdorff-Rantzau, had hailed the German-Russian *rapprochement* of 1939 as a return to sanity in the conduct of German foreign policy. He had carried on his part of the negotiations with Stalin and Molotov in all sincerity, and the betrayal of the Nazi-Soviet pact on June 22, 1941, had come to him as a profound and appalling shock.

Von der Schulenburg had placed himself at the disposal of the conspirators after the defeat of Stalingrad and had assured both Goerdeler and von Hassell that, could he but reach Stalin, he was confident that he could reach the basis of an agreement which would lead in its turn to the conclusion of a general peace. Throughout the summer and autumn of 1943 plans were actually under discussion to smuggle the ex-Ambassador — now nearly seventy years old — into Soviet territory by parachuting him behind the Russian lines.[2] But there is no evidence that von der Schulenburg himself was a party to this wholly fantastic proposition.[3]

The activities of the Free German National Committee had other repercussions inside Germany. Its broadcasts were listened to extensively and its existence gave a fresh impetus to the Central Committee of the German Communist Party, now stirring into new life. Saefkow, Jacob and others began an intensive campaign of

---

[1] Paulus himself did not actually broadcast until August 8, 1944, but his name was used prior to that date with increasing frequency by other members of the National Committee. For first-hand accounts of the activities of the National Committee see Jesco von Puttkamer, *Irrtum und Schuld; Geschichte des National Komitees Freies Deutschland* (Berlin, 1948) and Graf Heinrich von Einsiedel, *Tagebuch der Versuchung* (Berlin, 1950).

[2] Dulles, pp. 169-70; Hassell, pp. 333-4.

[3] In a letter to the present writer Dr. Gustav Hilger, who had been von der Schulenburg's Counsellor of Embassy at Moscow and remained his close collaborator throughout the war, expresses his disbelief that the Ambassador ever seriously entertained this idea.

propaganda both among their German comrades and also the hundreds of thousands of Russian prisoners of war and labourers who had been carried away from the Soviet Union to slavery in Germany. As a result 'the drift to the East' and the increase in the influence of the extreme Left among the German workers gained steadily in momentum. It assumed such proportions, indeed, that the Social Democrat leaders in the conspiracy became acutely alarmed and, through their 'parlour-pink' associate, Adam von Trott zu Solz, they communicated their fears to the Western Allies.

Von Trott explained to his British and American friends in Switzerland — whither his official Foreign Office duties permitted him to go in April 1944 — that the temptation to turn East was very great. The juxtaposition of the provisions of the Atlantic Charter and the Casablanca Formula had convinced many in Germany that 'the Anglo-Saxon countries are filled with bourgeois prejudice and pharisaic theorizing'. In contrast to this attitude, the Russians were continually offering 'constructive ideas and plans for the rebuilding of post-war Germany', and these were sedulously disseminated among the workers by German Communists. Moreover, this was not the only danger. The German soldier had respect, not hatred, for the Russian, and there was little doubt that many of the officer class had been caught by the promises made from Moscow that the Soviet Government, unlike the Western Powers, made a clear distinction between the German Army as such and the clique of military lackeys and lickspittles who controlled it at the behest of Hitler.[1] Thus within Russia, among the German prisoners of war, and within Germany, among the German workers and Russian labourers, Red propaganda was actively engaged in creating suitable conditions for the formation of a Soviet-dominated Germany as soon as victory had been attained.

These warnings were conveyed not in justification of the Eastern solution but with the intention of persuading the Western Allies to utter some promises of hope to the German workers — and to the German people as a whole — which should act as a counterpoise to the succession of rosy visions evoked by Moscow. What von Trott was endeavouring to do, in fact, was to induce London and Washington to engage in a bidding-match with Moscow from the result of which Germany could not but benefit, but he certainly did not favour a Bolshevik solution.

For von Trott, to do him justice, was no Red sympathizer. He represented the somewhat confused thought of the Kreisau Circle,

[1] Dulles, pp. 131-2 ; 137-8.

who, whatever else they may have been, were not Communists and did not seek to substitute one form of authoritarian tyranny for another. Their thinking, it is true, turned to the East rather than the West because, in their idealistic impractical illusions, they looked for an upheaval both in Russia and in Germany. If this were to occur, the two states would have many problems in common, problems which could not be solved by the established bourgeois standards of the West but which called for a radically new treatment which should be neither authoritarian nor democratic, but which should be guided by a return to 'the spiritual (but not the ecclesiastical) traditions of Christianity'.

To this end they approved the fraternization between Germans and the imported Russian labour, seeing in this the basis of 'a brotherhood of the oppressed' which should one day assist in the liberation of both Germany and Russia; and in at least one aspect of this idea they had the support of Claus von Stauffenberg, who more than anyone else bridged the gap between the visionaries of Kreisau and the activists of Berlin.

One of von Stauffenberg's earliest activities after his appointment to Olbricht's staff in the *Allgemeines Heeresamt* in 1943 had been to interest himself in the organization and welfare of that strange body, the Free Russian Army, formed by Lieutenant-General Alexander Vlassov, himself a prisoner of war. Von Stauffenberg endeavoured to protect these 'volunteers' from being used as mere cannon-fodder or as the helpless tools of German or Soviet nationalism. He had, apparently, a different destiny in store for this force, regarding it as the nucleus of a potential national Russian army which, after the success of an anti-Hitler *Putsch* in Germany, should mete out a similar fate to Stalin.[1]

For though far from sympathizing with Communism or with an authoritarian Russia, von Stauffenberg was essentially an 'Easterner' by orientation and before him there shone in all its glistering enticement the vision of a Germany and a Russia liberated from despotism, free and united . . . but for what purpose? For what other purpose than to dominate Europe, if not militarily, at least by an economic hegemony? And thus the ·dream of German-Russian

---

[1] For a romanticized account of von Stauffenberg's association with Vlassov's army see Karl Michel's *Ost und West*. Very little reliable material at present exists on this curious force, but certain details and documents appear in Peter Kleist's *Zwischen Hitler und Stalin, 1939–1945* (Bonn, 1950), pp. 199-220, 318-38. The 'memoirs' of General Vlassov, entitled *J'ai choisi la potence* (Paris, 1947), in which it is claimed that he and his legions were closely connected with the conspiracy and were at one time actually requested to undertake the kidnapping of Hitler, should be read with all reserve. See also George Fischer, *Soviet Opposition to Stalin* (Harvard, 1952).

collaboration transcends alike the policies of Kaiser, *Führer* and conspirators in Germany.

In contrast to these dreamers of an Eastern solution — whether in the practical terms of von der Schulenburg's *Kuhhandel* or in the more illusory fantasies of the Kreisau Circle and of von Stauffenberg — there were many to whom the idea of any deal with Russia was not only fraught with danger and deception but would be undesirable even under the most favourable conditions. Von Hassell, for example, who had come to be looked upon as the leader of the Western School, strongly deprecated the policy urged by von der Schulenburg, not, as he said, because he was opposed to playing with both sides, which was, of course, the only opportunity for a new régime, but because what his co-conspirator suggested savoured of double-dealing, and von Hassell was of the opinion that 'the manifestation of fairness toward England is vital, [though] this must be supplemented by keeping open the possibility of an understanding with the East'.[1]

The majority of the Generals in the West, moreover, who were now induced to throw in their lot with the conspirators, were mainly influenced to do so by a desire to avoid an Allied invasion in the West which would inevitably weaken the resistance of the German armies to the Russian advance.

Beck and Goerdeler, though they endeavoured to hold the balance between the two schools, were themselves convinced 'Westerners', considering Communism no better than Nazism. Their views were always in incredulous dissidence from those of von der Schulenburg and of von Stauffenberg, and as the spring of 1944 drew on to summer they received support from an unexpected quarter. With the approach of the Red armies to the frontiers of the Reich, the Soviet line of propaganda suddenly underwent a pronounced change. An ominous silence fell upon the broadcasts of the National Free German Committee. In place of the promises of a rosy future for the German Army and people who overthrew Hitler, there was heard the stark demand that the entire *Wehrmacht* should be employed as slave labour by the victorious Allies,[2] and this effectively silenced the 'Easterners'.

In contrast to this Soviet line of approach, Mr. Churchill took the opportunity to elucidate the formula of Unconditional Surrender before the House of Commons on February 22, 1944:

The term 'Unconditional Surrender' does not mean that the German people will be enslaved or destroyed. It means, however, that the Allies

---

[1] Hassell, p. 338.   [2] *Ibid.*, p. 354.

X

will not be bound to them at the moment of surrender by any pact or obligation. . . . Unconditional Surrender means that the victors have a free hand. It does not mean that they are entitled to behave in a barbarous manner, nor that they wish to blot Germans from among the nations of Europe. If we are bound, we are bound by our own consciences to civilization. We are not bound to the Germans as a result of a bargain struck. That is the meaning of Unconditional Surrender.[1]

Somewhat encouraged by this negative interpretation, the conspirators now made a further attempt to break the united front of the Allies. Early in May 1944 Beck sent to Dulles, by the hand of Gisevius, a detailed offer for simultaneous action by Anglo-American forces and the conspirators, with the object of facilitating the occupation of Germany and at the same time holding the Russians on the Eastern front. Under this plan the centre of the *Putsch* was to be transferred from Berlin to Munich, whence reliable German troops were to be despatched to isolate the Obersalzberg and to seize the persons of Hitler and other leading Nazis in the Berghof. This operation was to coincide with the descent of three air-borne Anglo-American divisions in the Berlin area, where local military commanders, who were members of the conspiracy, would neutralize resistance. At the same time large-scale landings were to be made on the French coast and on the German coast, around Bremen and Hamburg, in all of which areas the German military commanders in the West would be instructed to give full co-operation.[2]

This remarkable offer, the last to be made before the Allied invasion, was duly forwarded from Berne to the Governments in London and Washington, who were unimpressed and unreceptive. In the first place, it was considered a *sine qua non* of Unconditional Surrender that it should be undertaken to *all* the Allies acting in conjunction, and, secondly, there was a complete disbelief in the ability, or, in the final analysis, the courage and determination of the German Generals to make good their promises in terms of performance. No answer was returned save the already well-known and reiterated formula that any German Government, no matter what its political complexion, which wished to bring about a termination of hostilities, must submit itself to the unquestioned authority of the Allied Powers, trusting in their interpretation of a peace of justice and retribution.

---

[1] *House of Commons Debates*, February 22, 1944, cols. 698-9.

[2] Dulles, p. 139. It is not known who was the author of this plan, though it is said that it was the joint product of Beck and of von Witzleben, nor whether it was in any way related to that other plan which von Stülpnagel and Speidel were maturing for Rommel at this same moment. (See above, p. 608.)

Such was the position of deadlock on the East-West controversy on the eve of the Anglo-American landings in Normandy.

(xi)

On May 24, 1944, shortly after the conclusion of the Conference of the Dominion Premiers in London, Mr. Churchill gave to Parliament a survey of the international position as of that date. In the course of a wide *tour d'horizon*, he said :

A few things have already become quite clear and very prominent at the conference which has just concluded. The first is that we shall all fight on together until Germany is forced to capitulate and until Nazism is extirpated and the Nazi Party are stripped of all continuing power of doing evil. . . . The principle of unconditional surrender . . . will be adhered to as far as Germany and Japan are concerned, and that principle itself wipes away the danger of anything like Mr. Wilson's fourteen points being brought up by the Germans after their defeat, claiming that they surrendered in consideration of them.

I have repeatedly said that unconditional surrender gives the enemy no rights but relieves us of no duties. Justice will have to be done and retribution will fall upon the wicked and the cruel. The miscreants who set out to subjugate first Europe and then the world must be punished, and so must their agents who, in so many countries, have perpetrated horrible crimes. . . .[1]

It is not immediately apparent how this passage could conceivably have been interpreted by the conspirators in a sense encouraging to their projects, but, nevertheless, such was the degree of wishful thinking to which they had attained that this was so. The references to unconditional surrender, which, to the normal reader, would seem to be clear and unequivocal, were considered, if taken in conjunction with the allusions to Nazism and the Nazi Party, to give hope that a non-Nazi régime in Germany would even now obtain preferential treatment from the Allies. Were they not all together in their common aim to extirpate Nazism and were the conspirators not ready to co-operate with the Allies in bringing war criminals to justice — though opinions might differ as to what constituted a war criminal ? In any case Mr. Churchill's remarks of May 24 were held to be a marked advance upon those of February 22, which in themselves had also caused a certain upward fluctuation of the conspiratorial morale, and when these were followed within a few weeks by a considerably more encouraging statement by the

[1] *House of Commons Debates*, May 24, 1944, cols. 783-4.

Deputy Prime Minister, Mr. Attlee, the conspirators persuaded themselves that their position was at last understood by the Allies :

So far as His Majesty's Government are concerned, it has repeatedly been made clear in public statements that we shall fight on until Germany has been forced to capitulate and until Nazism is extirpated. It is for the German people to draw the logical conclusion. If any section of them really wants to see a return to a régime based on respect for international law and for the rights of the individual, they must understand that no one will believe them until they have themselves taken active steps to rid themselves of their present régime. The longer they continue to support and to tolerate their present rulers, the heavier grows their own direct responsibility for the destruction that is being wrought throughout the world, and not least in their own country.[1]

These statements by the leaders of Britain's Conservative and Labour Parties — who certainly were not addressing themselves formally to the plotters in Berlin — gave an immediate fillip to that inveterate optimist Carl Goerdeler and others of his colleagues, including Ludwig Beck. But this optimism found no reflection among those more disillusioned and realistic members of the conspiracy, such as Otto John, who had realized for some considerable time that the Allies meant what they said about Unconditional Surrender and that the attempts made to break the united front of the Grand Alliance, however attractive the achievement of that object might be, were but wasted effort and vain hoping.

The fact remains, however, that there was a perceptible change of tempo in the activities of the conspirators after Mr. Churchill's speech. All were agreed that the attempt upon Hitler's life, which was still considered *conditio sine qua non* of a *Putsch*, must be carried out *before* the Allied invasion of France, though the military pundits were divided as to the imminence of this event.

Preparations were, therefore, pressed forward in all spheres. Perhaps most important of all, agreement was reached, at any rate in principle, between Goerdeler, von Stauffenberg and the Kreisau Circle as to the composition of the leadership of the Reich once Hitler had been satisfactorily disposed of and executive power was in the hands of the Army.

The Provisional Government, as it was finally agreed in June 1944, was as follows :

Regent (*Reichsverweser*) : Colonel-General Ludwig Beck.
State-Secretary to the Regent : Count Ulrich Schwerin-Schwanenfeld.
Chancellor : Dr. Carl Goerdeler.

[1] *House of Commons Debates*, July 6, 1944, col. 1308.

State-Secretary to the Chancellor : [1] Count Peter Yorck von Warten-
burg.
Vice-Chancellor : Wilhelm Leuschner (SPD).
Deputy Vice-Chancellor : Jacob Kaiser (Christian Trade Unions).
Minister for War : General of Infantry Friedrich Olbricht.
State-Secretary for War : Colonel Count Claus Schenk von Stauffen-
berg.
C.-in-C. Armed Forces : Field-Marshal Erwin von Witzleben.
C.-in-C. Army : Colonel-General Erich Hoepner.
Minister of Interior : Julius Leber (SPD).
State-Secretary for War : Colonel Count Claus Schenck von Stauffen-
berg.
Minister of Economics : Dr. Paul Lejeune-Jung (Lawyer and Economist).
Minister of Finance : Ewald Loeser (Nationalist).
Minister of Justice : Joseph Wirmer (Centre Party).
Minister of Education and Religious Affairs : Eugen Bolz (Centre Party,
and formerly State President of Württemberg).
Minister of Agriculture : Andreas Hermes (Centre Party, formerly Reich
Minister of Food and Finance).
Minister of Reconstruction : Bernhard Letterhaus (Christian Trade
Unions).
Minister of Information : Theodor Haubach (SPD).[2]

Notable aspects of this list of ministers and military leaders are,
first, the omission of the name of Johannes Popitz, who had been
finally dropped as a result partly of his differences of opinion with
Goerdeler and partly on the insistence of the Social Democrats
and Christian Trade Unionists ; and secondly, the inability to agree
upon an incumbent of the Ministry of Foreign Affairs. To the last
the schism between the adherents of the Eastern and Western
schools of thought had persisted, and in desperation Beck and
Goerdeler had been forced to agree that von der Schulenburg and
von Hassell should both be regarded as potential Foreign Ministers,

---

[1] Gisevius asserts (ii, 304-305) that Goerdeler wished him to be his State
Secretary in the Reich Chancellery with special charge of the office whose task it
was to be to effect the political purge and to restore public order (*Reichskommis-
sariat zur Säuberung und Wiederherstellung der öffentlichen Ordnung*). This statement is unsupported by any other authority.

[2] With the exception of Kaiser, Loeser and Hermes, all those whose names
appear on this list lost their lives, either by execution or suicide, after the failure
of the *Putsch* of July 20, 1944. Of the exceptions, Loeser, who had been financial
adviser to Krupps, was sentenced on June 30, 1948, to seven years' imprisonment
by a U.S. Military Tribunal as a defendant in the case of 'Krupp and eleven
others' (*UN War Crimes Commission Law Reports*, x, 158). Hermes, having
been condemned to death by the People's Court and escaped execution by a
miracle, became a leader of the CDU, and, having served as Food Administrator
of Berlin in May 1945, became Chairman of the German Agricultural Co-operative
Societies.

depending upon which expediency dictated the course of policy at the last moment.[1]

The composition of the Provisional Government constituted a good cross-section of German political life as it was represented in the conspiracy. With the elimination of Popitz, who had been by far the most reactionary of the plotters, there was nothing further to the Right than the bourgeois Nationalist-Democracy of Goerdeler, while it is probable that, in thought and ideology, the scion of Bavarian Catholic nobility, Claus von Stauffenberg, was more advanced to the Left than the representatives of Social-Democracy and the Trade Unions. Between these extremes were the survivors of the Centre Party, of whom Josef Wirmer, with his massive physique and implacable hatred of the Nazis, was the most outstanding; the moderate Nationalism of Loeser, and the determined and gallant personality of Andreas Hermes, who, though his name recalls the dark distant past of the pre-Stresemann era, when he had served in the Cabinets of Wirth and Cuno, had, nevertheless, since 1943, been the recognized leader of the conspiracy in the Rhineland.[2]

A further preparation for the 'after-care' of the Reich — and also a definite indication of the extent to which the thinking of the Kreisau Circle had influenced the final formulation of the planning of the *Putsch* — was the agreement to appoint Political Commissioners, and deputy commissioners, and also military liaison officers for each of the Military Districts (*Wehrkreise*) of the Reich and for the Protectorate of Bohemia and Moravia, who should immediately become responsible for the conduct of government under the supreme emergency authority of the Army. In the selection of these key men great care had been taken to obtain as representative a list as possible and to choose men whose names would inspire confidence for their ability to maintain law and order and to administer justice. Among those designated as Commissioners or deputies were the two former Defence Ministers, Noske and Gessler; the former Social Democrat *Oberbürgermeister* of Hamburg and Vienna, Gustav Dahrendorff and Karl Seitz; and Ewald von Kleist-Schmenzin and Count zu Dohna-Tolksdorf; while

---

[1] It later appeared that even these two persons were not the only candidates for the Foreign Ministry, for there was a happy moment during the proceedings before the International Military Tribunal at Nuremberg, when Schacht and von Papen, each to the obvious chagrin of the other, produced affidavits to the effect that both of them had been assured by different members of the conspiracy that he was considered as highly desirable for this post (*Schacht Defence Document*, No. 39; *Papen Defence Documents*, Nos. 89 and 90). Moreover, Dr. von Dirksen in the English edition of his memoirs (p. 251) states that he too was sounded out as a potential Foreign Minister for the plotters but that he refused.

[2] Pechel, p. 207.

the military liaison officers included Major-General Oster and Colonel Count Marogna-Redwitz, both formerly of the *Abwehr*; Lieutenant-Colonel Freiherr von Sell, who had been private secretary to the Kaiser at Doorn until his death in 1941, and Lieutenant-Colonel Count Nikolaus von Üxküll, another of von Stauffenberg's innumerable cousins.

Yet another stroke of good fortune was in store for the plotters. In the first week of June, Claus von Stauffenberg was promoted full Colonel and appointed Chief of Staff to General Fromm, Commander-in-Chief of the Home Army. Though this was a key position from the technical point of view of the conspirators, since they were dependent upon the troops of the Home Army for support against the SS, von Stauffenberg hesitated before accepting the appointment. Fromm had the reputation of being one of the 100 per cent Nazi Generals and von Stauffenberg feared that the close connection which must necessarily exist between a Commanding General and his Chief of Staff would in practice prove a liability rather than an asset.

With characteristic candour he put the position before Fromm. 'I do not think', he said, 'that I should make you a good Chief of Staff as, quite frankly, my views on the military and political situation may differ from yours.' But the wily Fromm was 'listening to the grass grow'. He knew as well as anyone else that the war was lost and he was not unaware of what was in progress at his own head-quarters. If a *Putsch* was going to be successful he was going to be in on it — but only after the resulting success had become abundantly clear. He therefore assured von Stauffenberg smoothly that he too had had to revise his opinions recently and begged him to accept the appointment; and this von Stauffenberg did, with added alacrity when he realized that it would gain him direct access to the *Führer's* conferences at the Supreme Headquarters.[1] As his successor as Olbricht's Chief of Staff, he succeeded in obtaining the appointment of Colonel Ritter Albrecht Mertz von Quirnheim, an enthusiastic, if lately converted, member of the conspiracy.

All activity was now centred on effecting the *Putsch* before the Allied invasion, in order to prevent the rise of a legend that Hitler had been eliminated only under pressure of an obvious military defeat in the West. So much was agreed, but there was complete disagreement between von Stauffenberg, who considered it highly unlikely that the British and Americans would risk a landing on the

---

[1] *John Memorandum*; Schlabrendorff, pp. 136-7. Von Schlabrendorff errone-ously gives the date of von Stauffenberg's appointment as July 1. It was in fact a month earlier.

shores of France before 1945, and Colonel Georg Hansen, the successor of Canaris in the emasculated Office of Military Intelligence, who was convinced, on the basis of reports available to him, that it was imminent.

At a meeting at Leber's house to celebrate over a bottle of wine von Stauffenberg's promotion and appointment, Otto John produced Hansen's latest information, which pointed to an almost immediate landing in force in Normandy and gave the gloomiest prognostications of the results. As against this, von Stauffenberg quoted an Intelligence report from Ankara giving an intercepted conversation between the Soviet military attaché and a high-ranking officer of the Turkish General Staff, in which the Russian complained bitterly of the failure of the British and Americans to open up a 'Second Front' and declared that in Moscow they did not seriously expect an invasion at all in 1944. Even were it to happen, von Stauffenberg argued, there was at least a fifty-fifty chance of it proving a failure, in which case 'the British, who have so far not suffered any losses of importance during this war, will become ready to negotiate with us'. Nor would he give way in the argument which followed, though he was entirely in agreement with the idea of Otto John's flying to Madrid and Lisbon, as he was able to do in the execution of his *Lufthansa* duties, there to warn the British and American authorities, with whom he had long been in intimate contact, that an attempt upon Hitler's life, followed by a *Putsch* against the whole Nazi régime, was imminent at any moment.[1]

Less than a week later the events of D-Day had conclusively decided the argument in favour of Hansen and against von Stauffenberg, and had also imposed a further crucial decision upon the conspirators. For the Allied invasion of June 6 created a situation which it had long been the anxiety of the conspiracy to avoid. By their dalliance and disbelief in the reports of their own Intelligence Service they had allowed to slip by them the great advantage of striking *before* the invasion — the premise upon which their whole course of action had been based.[2] They had now to make up their

---

[1] *John Memorandum.*

[2] The conspirators were not the only persons who were divided in their views as to the proximity of the invasion. The High Command in the West was equally undecided, and as a result were taken tactically by surprise. Though the Fifteenth Army had received a code warning on June 5 that invasion was imminent — on the strength of which it alerted its own formations and passed the word on to the armies on either side of it and to the C.-in-C. West — von Rundstedt decided not to alert the whole front. Meanwhile Rommel, who had secured a personal audience with Hitler for June 6, had gone secretly to celebrate his wife's birthday at Herrlingen *en route* to Berchtesgaden. Speidel recalled him by telephone at six in the morning of June 6, but the Commander-in-Chief of Army Group B did not

minds whether or no to proceed with the plans as prepared, despite the psychological handicap of appearing to raise the standard of revolt under pressure of a new defeat.

At this moment, with Goerdeler forced into the background by reasons of caution and security, with Beck displaying more and more the characteristics of 'a pure "Clausewitz", without a spark of "Blücher" or "Yorck",'[1] and with von Witzleben in retirement on the Lynar estate at Seesen, some miles from Potsdam, waiting for the word for action but incapable of giving it, it was to von Stauffenberg that his fellow plotters looked for a lead. Those who were in or near Berlin he canvassed personally, and to the Eastern front he sent a trusted emissary, Count Heinrich von Lehndorff-Steinort, who had earlier tried hard but vainly to win over Field-Marshal von Bock.[2]

The question posed by von Stauffenberg was clear and direct. Was it worth proceeding with the plot now that they had lost the initial and psychological advantage? There was no real dissension of opinion. The answer which von Lehndorff brought back from Henning von Tresckow might have been given by any of the leading members of the conspiracy at this moment, though there were many of the peripheral hangers-on who would neither have understood nor approved it. 'The assassination must be attempted at any cost', was von Tresckow's answer. 'Even should that fail, the attempt to seize power in the capital must be undertaken. We must prove to the world and to future generations that the men of the German resistance movement dared to take the decisive step and to hazard their lives upon it. Compared with this object, nothing else matters.'[3]

This attitude of mind was further strengthened by the success of the invasion and the evident fact that there was no longer any hope of repelling it at the outset. The new crisis not only drew the conspirators closer together as the moment for action approached, it also caused them to bury their ideological differences in the need for a united front, and this, ironically enough, brought disaster in its train.

reach his headquarters at La Roche Guyon until between four and five o'clock in the afternoon. At the *Führerhauptquartier* at Berchtesgaden, Jodl was not informed of the Allied landings before nine o'clock in the morning and it was an hour later that he informed Keitel. Neither of these officers had the temerity to awake the *Führer* before his usual time, so that Hitler did not receive the news until his regular Staff conference at noon (Speidel, pp. 97-8 ; Schlabrendorff, p. 130, also the record of the interrogation of Walter Schellenberg at Nuremberg on November 13, 1945).

[1] Hassell's Diary entry for June 12, 1944 (pp. 357-8).
[2] See above, p. 515.   [3] Schlabrendorff, p. 129.

Von Stauffenberg had urged for the past year that contact be established with the Communists, not from ideological reasons, but from a desire to broaden the basis of the conspiracy as much as possible and thereby tap all possible sources of strength. In his opinion, since the Communists had their own very active organization, they were less dangerous inside the general framework of the plot than outside in competition or possible opposition. 'In order to achieve an overthrow I would make a pact with the Devil' ('*Um zum Umsturz zu kommen, würde ich mit dem Teufel paktieren*') was his motto. Hitherto there had been opposition alike from the conservative elements and from the Socialists in the conspiracy, if for no other reason than that it was known, or at least suspected very strongly, that the Communists' organization had been infiltrated by the Gestapo, and the Communists, for their part, had shown no desire to enter what they regarded as a reactionary *fronde*.[1]

By mid-June, however, these scruples, like many others, had disappeared and a first meeting was arranged between Julius Leber and Adolf Reichwein for the SPD with the Communist leaders, Franz Jacob and Anton Saefkow, in the house of a medical man, Dr. Schmidt, in East Berlin. Unfortunately a third, and unnamed, Communist was present, who proved to be a Gestapo spy. The result was a wholesale and widespread sweep by the Gestapo of members of the former Social Democrat and Communist Parties. Reichwein was arrested on July 4, Leber the following day, and both of them, together with Jacob and Saefkow, were subsequently hanged.

Von Stauffenberg was deeply moved by Leber's arrest, which was indeed a great blow to the conspiracy. 'We are aware of our duty' was his immediate message to Frau Leber, and in the days that followed he was heard to repeat frequently, 'We need Leber, we'll get him out'.

It is more than probable that the fate of his friend decided him to make the attempt upon Hitler's life himself and in the immediate future. But it would seem to be unjust to accuse him, as some have done, of precipitate action and to attribute the failure of the *Putsch* to this precipitancy.[2] The arrest of Leber, which more than justified

---

[1] The Communists approached the idea of a *rapprochement* very much in the same attitude of *faute de mieux* as did von Stauffenberg. 'The time has come when we must make a pact with the devil himself (the Generals) and undertake a *Putsch* in common', was Jacob's remark to Frau Pechel on June 29 (Pechel, p. 70).

[2] Emil Henk, *Die Tragödie des 20. Juli, 1944* (Heidelberg, 1946), pp. 53-5; Leber, pp. 11-13. Henk states that von Stauffenberg was driven to over-hasty action because Leber had disclosed his (Stauffenberg's) name to Jacob in the course of their meeting and that Jacob had divulged it under torture. Frau Leber

the grim warning which Himmler had given to Canaris but a few weeks earlier,[1] had convinced the conspirators of the extreme peril in which they stood. They were now engaged in a race with Fate and Time as to who should strike first, they or Hitler. For it was now an openly declared 'war to the death'. Moreover, though the original time-table of the Allied invasion had been somewhat delayed by shortage of supplies,[2] its initial success, coupled with the renewed Russian offensive which was now menacing East Prussia, had been sufficient to force upon the conspirators a realization that if they wished to get rid of Hitler and the Nazi régime and to establish a decent alternative Government in Germany, they had only a few weeks left in which to do it. All these factors increased the urgency of speed upon the plotters; they could hesitate no longer, and if their final preparations were not ready now they never would be.

The natural anxiety of the conspirators to save as much as possible of the territory of the Reich from Soviet occupation led them to revive for the last time the idea of an independent surrender to the British and the Americans in the West. In this Fate appeared to give them a final flicker of hope. On July 2 the *Führer*, in outraged fury at the failure of his armies to halt and turn back the Anglo-American invasion, abruptly dismissed von Rundstedt from his position as Commander-in-Chief in the West and replaced him by Field-Marshal von Kluge, now fully recovered from the injuries sustained in the motor accident which had incapacitated him in the winter of 1943.[3]

This was a definite improvement from the point of view of the conspirators. Von Rundstedt, though he had been made fully cognizant of the circumstances of conspiracy, and though very far from being a Nazi, had always refused to commit himself even conditionally. 'You are young and popular with the people; you must do it', he had once said to Rommel during a frank discussion on the need for eliminating Hitler.[4] But he himself, though galled

---

in an article in *Telegraf* (June 16, 1946) entitled 'Dr. Leber und Stauffenberg: führte Stauffenberg das Attentat auf Hitler aus, um den Freund zu retten?' declares categorically that this is a false statement. (See also Pechel, pp. 178-9.)

  [1] See above, p. 599.

  [2] The accumulation of supplies and material on the Normandy beaches got behind schedule as a result of stormy weather which delayed landings. Consequently, for a brief period, only a limited offensive could be attempted, its primary objectives being Cherbourg and Caen. Field-Marshal Montgomery, who had originally hoped to make his break-out by July 3, was unable to launch his great attack east of Caen until July 18, and the break-out did not actually begin until the 25th (*i.e.* five days after the *Putsch* had failed); (cf. Cyril Falls, *The Second World War* (London, 1948), pp. 223-4).

  [3] See above, p. 588.   [4] Speidel, p. 90.

and furious at his dismissal and vowing that he would never again accept a command from Hitler, still remained faithful to the *Führer* after his fashion.

Von Kluge, on the other hand, though no more stable a character now than he had ever been, found himself so beset with cares, burdens and disasters upon taking up his command that he sent a member of von Stülpnagel's staff, Lieutenant-Colonel Caesar von Hofacker, a cousin of von Stauffenberg's and a tried member of the conspiracy, to Beck with the word that the military situation was so hopeless for Germany that he would support a *Putsch* once he was convinced that the *Führer* was dead.   It was the old promise that he had made times without number before — and to which perhaps he remained true, since he was never called upon to implement it — but he would have no personal connection with an assassination, nor would he agree to take the initiative in giving the order for a voluntary withdrawal before the Allies, saying sardonically that this was unnecessary since they would very shortly break through of themselves anyway.[1]

This, however, did not greatly disturb the leaders of the con- spiracy, who were, by this time, under the repeated assurances of Speidel and von Stülpnagel, pinning their faith to the determination of Rommel to bring the war in the West to an end as soon as possible and to concentrate all defence efforts against the Russians.   It was even believed that, as a last resort, Rommel would either force von Kluge's hand in this respect or simply take action without him.[2]

In anticipation of this von Stauffenberg sent word to von Tresckow in the first week of July to expect an assassination almost any day,[3] and he and Hansen despatched Otto John to Madrid, thence to warn London and Washington that the long-postponed day had at last all-but-arrived and to prepare a direct line of approach to SHAEF.   'If we can talk with General Eisenhower as soldier to soldier we shall be able to reach an understanding quickly', said Hansen to John.   'The politicians must be kept out of all armistice proceedings.   You establish the contact and send me word.   Once the blow has been struck here, I will come to Madrid with full powers.   It won't be long now.'

---

[1] Schlabrendorff, p. 132 ; Dulles, p. 176.

[2] Speidel (pp. 131-2) gives an account of a fiery encounter between von Kluge and Rommel on July 5 at La Roche Guyon, in which the new Commander-in- Chief, West, who had recently spent a fortnight at Berchtesgaden, repeated the *Führer*'s criticisms of the conduct of the High Command in the organization of the German defence hitherto and accused Rommel of acting independently of orders. The tension between the two Field-Marshals became so acute that Speidel was ordered to leave the room.   [3] Schlabrendorff, p. 136.

LIEUTENANT-GENERAL HANS SPEIDEL

FIELD-MARSHAL ERWIN ROMMEL

Associated Press

Otto John succeeded in doing this with great efficiency. That is to say, he received an assurance from the U.S. military attaché in Madrid that anything which he chose to communicate would be laid with all possible speed before General Eisenhower. But, as he had regretfully expected — for though among the most gallant he was also among the most 'unillusioned' members of the con-spiracy — he was left in no doubt that the terms of a cessation of hostilities would be Unconditional Surrender to *all* the Allies. The final blow was delivered by· one of his Allied friends who, speaking with kindly brutality, and giving it as a 'personal' opinion, told him : 'I do not think that the British and the Americans will make any effort to reach Berlin before the Russians are there. Some people hold that Germany needs a punishment. This will be gladly left to the Russians.' [1]

Again there appears to have been a grave lack of co-ordination between the various circles of the conspiracy. While the 'official' policy of Beck and Goerdeler and von Stauffenberg was to let the approach to the Allies wait upon the conclusion of a successful *Putsch*, which in its turn must be preceded by the assassination of Hitler, only the purest chance prevented an independent action being taken by Rommel.

That Field-Marshal was obsessed by one thought only — to bring hostilities on the Western Front to an end as soon as possible ; and this he proposed to do with or without the consent, approval or, if need be, the knowledge of Beck or Hitler or von Kluge. Though von Stülpnagel and Speidel were in contact with the centre of the conspiracy in Berlin, they were also aiding and abetting Rommel in his independent action, of which, apparently, they had not apprised the others.

Rommel had perfected his plans by the middle of July, and had even made an experimental effort to test the technical possibility of a local suspension of hostilities. He succeeded, through the action of General Freiherr von Lüttwitz, son of the 'Little General' who had collaborated with Kapp a quarter of a century before, in making radio contact with the Allies and in bringing about a two hours' armistice in order to arrange an exchange of German female personnel captured at Cherbourg for severely wounded Allied soldiers. With the knowledge that such an arrangement was now

---

[1] *John Memorandum*. Simultaneously with the despatch of Otto John to Madrid, Beck sent word to Allen Dulles in Berne of the approaching *coup d'état* and Goerdeler telegraphed to Jacob Wallenberg asking him to receive Erwin Planck, von Schleicher's former State Secretary, who would be arriving in Stockholm not later than July 20 (Dulles, pp. 140, 146, *Svenska Dagbladet*, September 4, 1947).

possible, Rommel spent July 13, 14 and 15 in inspecting his front-line positions and in discussing the position with his subordinate commanders. The outcome of his observations was embodied in a report to the *Führer*, dated July 15, and couched in the terms of an ultimatum. In brief, terse words, he sketched for Hitler the dire position of the troops under his command. 'The troops are fighting heroically everywhere, but the unequal struggle is nearing its end', he concluded. 'It is in my opinion necessary to draw the appropriate conclusions from this situation without delay. I feel it my duty as the Commander-in-Chief of the Army Group to express this clearly.'

This report was made in the first instance to von Kluge, who forwarded it to Hitler with a covering note to the effect that he was in agreement with its content.

'I have given him the last chance', said Rommel to his Chief of Staff on the night of July 15. 'If he does not take it, we will act.' [1]

What exactly would have happened when Rommel had been informed of Hitler's rejection of his ultimatum will never be known, for on the afternoon of July 17 his Staff car was shot up by British fighter aircraft. The driver was killed, the car wrecked and the Field-Marshal so severely injured that he was at first thought to be dead.

The elimination of Rommel removed all chance of any further attempt to make an independent deal with the Allies, for there was little thought of von Kluge's doing such a thing and the other local commanders were too junior. In tense expectation, therefore, they waited for news from Berlin.

And what, meanwhile, of Claus von Stauffenberg?

Having arrogated to himself the exclusive right of the timing and execution of the *Attentat*, he had sought diligently for a propitious moment. Adolf Hitler spent the first two weeks of July 1944 at the Obersalzberg, and there on July 3 a meeting of the leading conspirators in the *Führer's* Headquarters was held in the office of General Eduard Wagner, the First Quartermaster-General. Stieff was there and Fellgiebel as well as Wagner, and the final preparations were made for the action to be taken immediately after Hitler had been killed.[2] Von Stauffenberg was summoned, as Fromm's deputy, to attend a military conference on Wednesday, July 11. On this day he determined to carry out the assassination, and bore with him in his aeroplane to Berchtesgaden a bomb of British material concealed in his brief-case. The fuse of this he proposed to touch-off

    [1] Speidel, pp. 137-9.
    [2] Stieff's evidence before the People's Court, August 7, 1944 (*IMT Document*, PS-3881).

as soon as he had completed his report and then leave the case in the conference room.

At first all went according to plan. With his A.D.C. and friend, Lieutenant Werner von Haeften, von Stauffenberg drove from the airfield to the Berghof. Von Haeften remained in the car to ensure a rapid escape, but to his dismay, when von Stauffenberg reappeared he was still carrying his brief-case. When the conference opened he had noticed that neither Himmler, whom von Stauffenberg considered second only to Hitler in degree of evil, nor Göring was present, and this he thought so grave a drawback that he had abandoned the attempt. Sadly the conspirators returned to Berlin with their mission unfulfilled.

The *Führerhauptquartier* returned on July 14 to the *Wolfsschanze*, near Rastenburg in East Prussia, whither the Soviet Armies were daily drawing nearer. The next conference to which von Stauffenberg was summoned was for the following day, Saturday, July 15, and once again he and von Haeften set forth armed with their infernal machine and in high hopes of achievement, leaving behind them the 'General Staff' of the conspiracy to await a telephone call which should give the all-clear for 'Operation Valkyrie'.

Beck and Goerdeler waited together in the General's home in Lichterfelde — and it is significant that the civilian was more composed than the soldier. Though in danger of arrest at any moment, Goerdeler retained his optimism and his *bonhomie* to the end. But Beck was deeply troubled, not as to the essential rightness of what they planned to do, but at the very magnitude of their task. He was a prey to nerves and his sleep deserted him; each morning when he rose his bed was drenched with sweat from his nightly agonies of spirit.[1]

Hoepner, who, though he had been discharged from the Army with ignominy, still frequented the fashionable Union Club of Berlin,[2] and was admitted to the Ministry of War, reported with others of the military staff to the Bendlerstrasse, where in Olbricht's room they sat and waited, while Olbricht took from his safe the orders which must be signed and issued as soon as the prearranged telephone call came through. All the afternoon they waited. The conference was due to begin at Rastenburg at one o'clock. Von Stauffenberg had planned to set the fuse to explode as nearly to that time as possible, but two and three o'clock passed and there

---

[1] In the course of the trial of 'von Witzleben and seven others' before the People's Court in August 1944, Beck's housekeeper gave evidence that for a fortnight before the attempt she had had to change his wringing bedclothes every morning (*IMT Document*, PS-3881); see also Sauerbruch, pp. 582-6.

[2] Dirksen (English edition), p. 251.

was still no word. Finally there came a disconsolate call from von
Haeften which conveyed, in the concealed double-talk of the con-
spirators, that though both Göring and Himmler had been present
at the conference and the whole circumstance had seemed favourable,
Hitler had been called from the room at the very moment that von
Stauffenberg with his maimed left hand was fumbling with the fuse.
He had not returned ; again an evil Providence had protected him.
Once more the attempt was abandoned.

By now the margin between the two contestants in the race
for death had narrowed to a mere hand's breadth. Too many of the
members of the conspiracy were under arrest, and therefore subject
to ruthless interrogation and perhaps torture, for the final blow
against the Nazi leaders to be delayed much longer. On July 16
Beck and von Stauffenberg held a final and crucial discussion. It
was agreed that at the next conference, whenever that might be,
the bomb should explode, come what might, and that the *Putsch*
should be put into effect in Berlin even if the operation at Rastenburg
was not wholly successful. Next day came the news that a warrant
had been issued for the arrest of Goerdeler.

To Otto John, waiting in impatience and anxiety in Madrid,
there came a message from Hansen urging him to fly back to Berlin
immediately. Early in the afternoon of July 19 his brother met the
plane as it landed at Tempelhof.

'It's to-morrow', said Hans softly, as they drove away from the
airport.

CHAPTER 7

JULY 20, 1944

Or who . . .
Steps, with five other Generals
That simultaneously take snuff,
For each to have pretext enough
To kerchiefwise unfold his sash
Which, softness' self, is yet the stuff
To hold fast where a steel chain snaps,
And leave the grand white neck no gash?
ROBERT BROWNING, *Waring*.

(i) AT THE *WOLFSSCHANZE*

VERY early on the morning of July 20, 1944, Claus von Stauffenberg and Werner von Haeften motored to the Rangsdorf airfield, to the south of Berlin.[1] Fromm's Chief of Staff had been summoned to F.H.Q. to give a detailed report on the progress made in creating the new front-line divisions from the man-power of the Home Army in order to stem the tide of the Red Army's advance, which was then but fifty miles distant from the *Führerhauptquartier*. With the two officers was Werner's brother, Bernd, a lieutenant of the Naval Reserve, who, having been warned of the mighty things which were to come to pass that day, had secured leave of absence to be in Berlin for the occasion and had come to see his brother off on the first lap.

~ At the airport they were joined by Helmuth Stieff and his A.D.C., Major Roll. 'The Poison Dwarf', whose task it was to supply the explosives, had the night before produced a two-pound bomb with a time fuse for delayed action. The explosion was effected by

---

[1] Of the first-hand accounts of the happenings at the *Führer*'s Headquarters on July 20, 1944, von Stauffenberg's was given to Otto John that same afternoon on his return to the Bendlerstrasse and is recorded in Dr. John's *Memorandum*. Other accounts of survivors of the explosion are to be found in Kapitän zur See Kurt Assmann's *Deutsche Schicksalsjahre* (Wiesbaden, 1950), pp. 453-60; Lieutenant-General Adolf Heusinger's *Befehl im Widerstreit* (Stuttgart, 1950), pp. 352-55; and an article by Colonel Nikolaus von Below in *Echo der Woche* for July 15, 1949. See also the collection of reports made for the *Führer* by OKW contained in *IMT Document*, PS-1808 (G.B. Exhibit No. 493), and also Dulles, pp. 6-8.

causing a glass capsule containing acid to break in a chamber in which a taut wire was so fixed as to hold back the firing pin from the percussion cap, and the thickness of the wire determined the time required for the acid to eat through it and release the pin. This ingenious piece of destructive mechanism, wrapped in a shirt which also hid the little pair of tongs which were necessary for the crippled fingers to break the capsule, was concealed in von Stauffenberg's brief-case, together with his official papers. For though, because of his injuries, he was entitled to have the services of an A.D.C. wherever he went, he knew well that the security regulations would never permit him to take Werner von Haeften into the conference room with him, and that he must be entirely independent of all assistance.

The special plane supplied by the First Quartermaster-General, Eduard Wagner, touched down at the airfield nearest Rastenburg at 10.15 A.M. and the remaining nine miles of the journey were completed by car. As they neared F.H.Q. they passed from the sunny expanses of the East Prussian countryside into the gloomy confines of a forest, so deep and dark that sunlight rarely penetrated the leafy fastness. Here, remote from other human habitation and surrounded only by those who would either tell him what he wished to know or else keep silent, Adolf Hitler directed his war in macabre seclusion.[1]

Fear, hate and suspicion predominated here. No one from the outside world was trusted and not all those within this evil orbit of abnormality. Master and minions were held prisoner for weeks and months within the great and darksome wood, prisoners as much as anything of their own fears. Numerous electric fences and much barbed wire obstructed the approach. There were blockhouses and check-points on all the roads and in the middle was Security Ring Number 1, 'the Wolf's Lair' (*Wolfsschanze*), to which holy of holies there were no personal passes, not even for Keitel or Jodl, and guards checked the coming and going of all officers at the entrances. 'It was a cross between a monastery and a concentration camp', was Jodl's description later at Nuremberg.[2]

Having the necessary passwords and counter-signs, von Stauffenberg and his companions passed through the outer compound and

---

[1] Only on his return to Berlin at the end of November 1944 did Hitler receive any impression of war as it was waged in the Reich. As his train passed through the suburbs of his bomb-shattered capital he was completely overcome by the extent of the devastation. He had not had the slightest idea that bombing wrought such havoc, he said to those about him (Gerhardt Boldt, *Die letzten Tage der Reichskanzlei* (Hamburg, 1947), p. 32).

[2] Jodl's evidence before the International Military Tribunal on June 2, 1946 (*Nuremberg Record*, xv, 295); also Schmidt, pp. 543-4.

then separated, they going to the huts provided for Army officers and he to the *Wolfsschanze*, where, by arrangement, he was to breakfast with the Headquarters Commandant, Lieutenant-Colonel Streve, a member of the conspiracy. There followed at 11.30 a short conference with General Buhle, the Chief of the Army Staff at F.H.Q., and with General von Thadden, Chief of Staff to the G.O.C. of the Königsberg district, at which von Stauffenberg gave a preliminary report on the defence preparations by the Home Army. At noon Buhle took him to Keitel and here he received the first check to his plans.

The *Führer's* morning conference, Keitel told them, which was normally held at 1 P.M., had been put forward to 12.30 P.M. as Hitler was expecting Mussolini to arrive at the secret railway station of 'Görlitz' at three o'clock. The location of the conference was also to have a material effect on later events. Since the Headquarters had only recently been moved back to the East, work was still in progress on the underground bunker already used by the *Führer* when there was danger of air attack. So the meeting was held in the conference barracks (*Lagebaracke*) on the surface.

Before leaving Keitel's office to walk the short distance across to the *Lagebaracke*, von Stauffenberg made an excuse and went with his brief-case, from which he was never parted, to an adjoining room where, with the assistance of the little tongs, he broke the acid capsule which in time should set the fuse. Brief though his absence was, it was long enough for Keitel to remark it. A few minutes later they all walked out into the gloomy twilight of the forest and Keitel made a gesture of offering to carry the brief-case, a gesture which was at once repeated by one of his adjutants, Lieutenant-Colonel von John; but von Stauffenberg insisted that, despite his disability, he needed no help.

The *Lagebaracke* was a large wooden hut which had walls reinforced with concrete and a tarred roof. There were three windows and at each end a small table, one bearing writing materials, the other a radio-phonograph. In the centre of the room, which was some 12·5 by 5 metres, was a large table covered with situation maps.

When Keitel and von Stauffenberg entered the conference room at about 12.40 there were a score of persons standing around the table. Only the stenographer and Berger, who took notes for Hitler's personal war diary, were seated. Neither Himmler nor Göring nor Ribbentrop was present. (See diagram and key on pp. 638-9.)

General Heusinger, the Director of the Military Operations

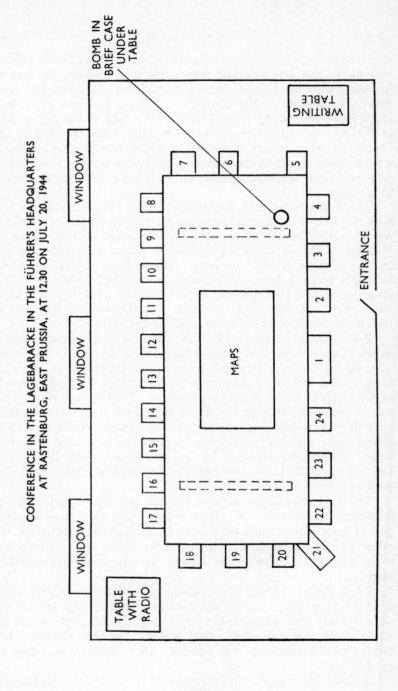

CONFERENCE IN THE LAGEBARACKE IN THE FÜHRER'S HEADQUARTERS AT RASTENBURG, EAST PRUSSIA, AT 12.30 ON JULY 20, 1944

BOMB IN BRIEF CASE UNDER TABLE

KEY TO DIAGRAM

1. Adolf Hitler.

2. Lieut.-General Adolf Heusinger, Chief of Operations Branch OKH and Deputy Chief of Staff of the Army, wounded on July 20.

3. Air Force General Gunther Korten, Chief of the General Staff of the Air Force, died of wounds received on July 20.

4. Colonel Heinz Brandt, G.S.O.1 to General Heusinger, died of wounds received on July 20.

5. Air Force General Karl Bodenschatz, Personal Chief of Staff to Commander-in-Chief of the Air Force, badly wounded in the legs on July 20.

6. Lieut.-General Rudolf Schmundt, Chief Adjutant to the *Führer* and Chief of the Army Personnel Branch, died of wounds received on July 20.

7. Colonel Borgmann, General Staff OKH, and Adjutant to the *Führer*, badly wounded on July 20.

8. Vice-Admiral Jesco von Puttkamer, Naval Adjutant to the *Führer*, slightly wounded on July 20.

9. Stenographer Berger, killed immediately on July 20.

10. Captain Heinz Assmann, Naval Operational Staff Officer in the Wehrmachtführungsstab, and Naval Adjutant to the *Führer*.

11. Major-General Walther Scherff, Chief of Historical Section of OKW, slightly wounded on July 20.

12. Lieut.-General Walther Buhle, General Staff OKH, and Chief of Army Staff OKW at F.H.Q., slightly wounded on July 20.

13. Vice-Admiral Hans Voss, Deputy for Commander-in-Chief of the Navy, and Naval Liaison Officer at F.H.Q.

14. SS *Brigadier* Hermann Fegelein, representative of the *Waffen*-SS at the *Führer's* Headquarters.

15. Colonel Nikolaus von Below, General Staff OKL, Air Force Adjutant to the *Führer*.

16. *Sturmbannführer* Otto Günsche, Adjutant to the *Führer*.

17. Stenographer. (Name unknown.)

18. Lieut.-Colonel von John, Adjutant to Field-Marshal Keitel.

19. Major Herbert Büchs, Adjutant to Colonel-General Jodl.

20. Lieut.-Colonel Waizenegger, Adjutant to Field-Marshal Keitel.

21. Counsellor von Sonnleithner, representative of the Ministry of Foreign Affairs.

22. General Walther Warlimont, Deputy to Colonel-General Jodl in Operations Branch of OKW.

23. Colonel-General Alfred Jodl, Chief of Operations Branch OKW, slightly wounded on July 20.

24. Field-Marshal Wilhelm Keitel, Chief of the High Command of the Armed Forces.

Branch and Deputy Chief of the General Staff of the Army, had already begun his report on the situation on the Eastern Front, and Hitler, standing with Jodl on his left and Heusinger on his right, his back to the entrance, was following attentively on the maps spread upon the table before him. Keitel interrupted the proceedings to present von Stauffenberg, who, he said, would give them details of the formation of the *Sperrdivisionen* which Fromm was building up, as it seemed, with painful slowness. Hitler greeted the tall young Colonel, glanced significantly at his mutilations and the black patch which covered the empty eye-socket, said that they would take his report next, and turned back to the table. Keitel took up his position on Jodl's right, next to the *Führer*.

Von Stauffenberg moved to the right-hand corner of the table and saying : 'I will leave this here for the moment, I have to make a telephone call', he placed his brief-case with its lethal contents to the right of the officer sitting there and left the room. Ironically enough, this officer was none other than that Colonel Heinz Brandt, Heusinger's G.S.O.1, into whose unsuspecting hands von Tresckow had put the brandy-bottle bomb which was intended to destroy Hitler in his aircraft as he returned to Rastenburg from von Kluge's headquarters at Smolensk on March 13, 1943.[1] Now, equally unsuspicious, Brandt found himself left in charge of a brief-case, which, as it seemed to be in his way, he pushed away from his chair farther under the map-table, so that it rested against the heavy upright support on the side farthest from Hitler.

Heusinger showed signs of concluding his report and Keitel turned to look for the man who should take up the next item on the conference agenda. 'Where's Stauffenberg?' he said to Buhle. 'It is his turn now.' Buhle rose and went to look in the ante-room, then he returned. 'I can't find him', he reported. 'He went to make a telephone call.'

A shadow of suspicion as to that unaccounted-for moment of absence before they had left his office mingled in Keitel's mind with the anger occasioned by an unanticipated hitch in the proceedings of the conference, on the smooth running of which he prided himself. The *Führer* was always annoyed if there was an interval between the reports. Where *was* Stauffenberg?

Heusinger had reached the final phase of his gloomy and discouraging report : '*Der Russe dreht mit starken Kräften westlich der Duna nach Norden ein. Seine Spitzen stehen bereits südwestlich Dunaburg. Wenn jetzt nicht endlich die Heeresgruppe vom Peipussee zurückgenommen wird, dann werden wir eine Katastrophe. . . .*'

[1] See above, p. 562.

THE GÄSTEBARACKE, RASTENBURG, JULY 20, 1944

It was at this moment (12.50 P.M.) that the bomb exploded. 'It was as if a great chandelier were coming down on your head', said Jodl later. A roar as of thunder shook the room, blew out the windows, wrecked the ceiling and shattered the central table. There were three detonations, and then thick clouds of smoke, shot with yellow flame, belched from the ruined hut. Shouts of alarm mingled with the groans of the wounded and the cries of the dying.[1] Colonel von John was the first outside. Standing at the corner diagonally opposite to Brandt and near a window, he was literally blown through it by the force of the explosion and, escaping unhurt, ran toward the guard-house, shouting : '*Attentat! Attentat!*'

Within the hut Keitel was the first to recover himself. '*Wo ist der Führer?*' he called, as reeling through the smoke, he turned to where he had last seen Hitler.

And Hitler was, miraculously enough, alive.

Colonel Brandt's unconscious action in pushing the brief-case away from his chair and farther under the table had undoubtedly saved the *Führer's* life. When the explosion occurred Hitler was leaning over the table with his right arm resting on it and his left extended over the map as he followed the details of Heusinger's report, which concerned at that moment the movements of Army Group North, whose positions were shown at the far end to the left of the map. The brief-case was propped against the right side of the heavy partition which ran across the long table as a support, and thus Hitler's body, and to some extent his legs also, were protected from the full blast of the explosion. His hair was set on fire, his right arm was partially and temporarily paralysed, his right leg was badly burned. Both ear drums were damaged and his hearing affected. His trouser-legs were blown off at the belt, and a heavy object from the roof had fallen across his back and buttocks, tearing a great piece of cloth from his tunic and so bruising him that, as he later announced, he had 'a backside like a baboon'.

Hitler's first impression was that they had been bombed from the air, then that the bomb had been thrown from outside through the window or that it had been planted under the floor. According to all accounts, he behaved with calmness. Having extricated himself

---

[1] Of the twenty-four people present in the room when the bomb exploded, one, Berger the official stenographer, was killed outright and three others, General Schmundt, General Korten and Colonel Brandt, died subsequently from the injuries which they received. Of the remainder, two, General Bodenschatz and Colonel Borgmann, were severely wounded and a number of others, including Hitler, Colonel-General Jodl, and Generals Buhle, Scherff and Heusinger, received lesser injuries. The wounded later received a decoration specially instituted by the *Führer* for the occasion, bearing the inscription : 'Hitler — 20. Juli, 1944'.

from the debris of the table and put out the flames in his hair and clothing, he allowed himself to be led by Keitel from the shattered hut to his own quarters, his right arm hanging slack at his side, his hair singed and a livid scarlet burn upon the sallow pallor of his face.[1]

In the meantime the would-be assassin and his accomplice had escaped. As soon as von Stauffenberg had entered Keitel's office, von Haeften had betaken himself to the quarters of General Erich Fellgiebel, head of the Communications Branch of F.H.Q., in Bunker 88, there to arrange for a car to be in waiting for their departure, and together he and Fellgiebel watched the little group of Keitel, von Stauffenberg and von John enter the *Lagebaracke*.

Fellgiebel himself had a vitally important rôle in the plot. His task was to telephone to Olbricht in the Bendlerstrasse in Berlin as soon as the bomb had exploded and then to put out of action the whole communication system of the *Führerhauptquartier* so that, even if the assassination were not a hundred per cent successful, F.H.Q. would be isolated for a period from all contact with the outside world, thereby giving the conspirators in Berlin a start in getting their activities under way and in securing the co-operation of the field and district commanders.

Von Stauffenberg and von Haeften drove off immediately after the explosion of the bomb. They had seen the conference hut go up in smoke and flame. They had heard the shouts and cries of the occupants. It was their conviction that Hitler was dead at the moment that their car moved off. They were challenged both at the inner and the outer barricades, for the alarm had been flashed at once to all posts and extreme security measures were supposed to be in force. On each occasion von Stauffenberg bluffed his way through by saying that he had an urgent order from the *Führer* to fly to Berlin at once, and, such was the confusion, that this statement appears to have been taken very largely at its face value. The *Feldwebel* at the outer barricade did check the statement with the Deputy Commandant, Rittmeister von Möllendorf, who, being a member of the conspiracy, at once ordered that von Stauffenberg and his A.D.C. should be allowed to proceed without further let or

---

[1] It may or may not be true that, as is reported by Rudolf Semmler, Hitler's first coherent remark on being found by Keitel was : 'Oh my best new trousers ! I only put them on yesterday' (*Goebbels — the Man Next to Hitler, being the Diary of Rudolf Semmler* (London, 1947), p. 141). But it is certain that he regarded the remnants of his ruined uniform with an almost mystic reverence as symbolic of his persistent escapes and of his future destiny. He showed them to Mussolini that afternoon (Schmidt, p. 582) and then directed his private secretary to pack them up and send them to Eva Braun at Berchtesgaden with instructions that she should carefully guard these relics (Albert Zoller, *Hitler privat: Erlebnisbericht seiner Geheimsekretärin* (Düsseldorf, 1949), p. 184).

hindrance. Their plane took off from the Rastenburg airport at 1.15, three hours after their arrival there that morning, and less than half an hour after the bomb had exploded. They arrived at Rangsdorf airfield in Berlin about 3.15, with a conscious sense of pride in 'mission accomplished'.

But this was far from being the case. In the first place, Adolf Hitler had miraculously survived, and, in the second, General Fellgiebel had not succeeded in the execution of his task. Whether indeed he lost his nerve when, from his office window in Bunker 88, he saw that little procession of injured, blackened and bleeding men, headed by Hitler and Keitel, emerge from the shattered *Lagœbaracke*, or whether in his excitement he failed in some technical respect, will never be known, for he himself was executed for treason shortly thereafter; but the fact remains that no telephone call reached the Bendlerstrasse in Berlin from the *Wolfsschanze* and that the communication centre remained intact. That Fellgiebel failed to destroy it was a major disaster for the conspirators, for unrestricted and undamaged communications were a vital factor in quelling the revolt.

Had the conference been held in an enclosed bomb-proof dugout, the effects of the explosion would have been such that none could possibly have survived; but the initial disadvantage to the conspirators of the survival of the *Führer* might well have been overcome had it been impossible for Hitler, Keitel, Himmler and others to communicate direct with Berlin. The failure of Fellgiebel to carry out his assignment was therefore as disastrous for the success of the revolt as the survival of Hitler.

Almost at the moment at which von Stauffenberg's plane touched down at Rangsdorf, the *Führer* was standing, enveloped in a great cloak despite the heat of the day, upon the platform at 'Görlitz' to receive Mussolini. Pale he was, and visibly shaken, his right arm in a sling and his hair trimmed to hide the traces of the fire. But his greeting to the Duce was warm and his smile as unfrozen as it ever was in those frost-bitten days of his life. In all the ten years of their relations there could have been no stranger meeting than this between the two Dictators. The Axis which they had forged was already broken. Mussolini, a dethroned tyrant rescued from the hands of his enemies by Hitler's desperadoes, had become no more than the *Gauleiter* of Lombardy. His sallow, shrunken face and close-cropped skull bore little resemblance to the dashing figure of the 'thirties who had dazzled multitudes and kept all Europe in a whirl. Hitler had changed perhaps the less of the two, for he had never had personal glamour or dignity to lose. But, nevertheless,

644   HITLER AND THE ARMY   PT. III

he had retained something which Mussolini, perhaps, had never possessed, a power to dominate circumstances and men even in defeat. Now they met for the last time, under the shadow of tragedy and impending disaster. Hitler at once took his guest to the scene of his escape and, standing amid the ruins, delivered himself of an outburst of rhetorical eulogy and self-laudation rarely surpassed in even his experience. 'Having now escaped death so miraculously', he concluded, 'I am more than ever sure that the great destiny which I serve will transcend its present perils and that all will be brought to a triumphant conclusion.'

Mussolini was deeply moved. He had obviously been appalled at the fact that an attempt of this kind could be made within the sacred precincts of a Dictator's Headquarters. Perhaps for the first time, his egregious self-confidence deserted him and he realized that within that shattered room wherein he stood were entombed alike the hopes and glories of the New Roman Empire and of the Thousand-Year Reich. But he rallied somewhat under the tonic of the *Führer's* elation and conceded that, though the position was bad, he might almost say desperate, after the miracle which had occurred there that day it was inconceivable that their cause should meet with misfortune.[1]

On this note, for it was now five o'clock, the two Dictators adjourned for a cup of tea, and there followed one of the most remarkable of scenes. By this time it was known that the attempt on the *Führer's* life was no isolated incident but that revolt and mutiny had occurred in Berlin and perhaps elsewhere. A stream of telephone calls poured in upon the *Wolfsschanze* giving graphic indication of the chaos which prevailed in the Reich without. Hitler had at once despatched Himmler to Berlin to take charge of the suppression of these outbreaks and was awaiting a report from him with nervous anxiety. His paladins, meanwhile, had rushed to his side, as much to establish their innocence of complicity as to express their congratulations on their *Führer's* escape. Bormann was already with him. Doenitz had flown from Berlin; Ribbentrop had driven post-haste from Schloss Steinort where he had established his headquarters, and Göring, whose relations with the *Führer* were now far from good, was lurking in his special train, the '*Kurfürst*', at the near-by station of Goldap, in the hope of being summoned to Rastenburg. When the news reached him he seized the opportunity and went uninvited. All now met for tea with Hitler, Mussolini and Graziani.

[1] Schmidt, p. 582.

It was not a gay party.[1] The *Führer*, exhausted by his burst of elation, sat silent and abstracted, sucking from time to time the brightly coloured lozenges which his medical adviser, Dr. Theo Morell, prescribed for him. Mussolini too had relapsed into depressed forebodings, and though Marshal Graziani did his best to relieve the general gloom by regaling them with stories of his African exploits, he can have had but an unresponsive audience. By contrast, the remainder of the party was a riot. The conversation quickly turned from expressions of grateful satisfaction, in varying degrees of sincerity, on the escape of the *Führer*, to mutual recrimination. Ribbentrop and Doenitz accused the Army of betraying Germany to England, and, while Keitel sought to defend the Officer Corps against these attacks, Göring, launching an offensive of his own against Ribbentrop, came under fire from the Grand Admiral for the failure of the *Luftwaffe*.

In the course of the ensuing verbal fracas someone mentioned the Blood Purge of June 30, 1934, with sudden and hideous effect. The calm with which Hitler had described his escape to Mussolini, the rhetorical spate in which he had extolled his own destiny, now gave way to the outburst of hatred and revenge and fury which had been simmering since the moment of the explosion. He leapt to his feet and paced the room in a screaming, raging frenzy ; foam flecked his lips and gathered at the corners of his mouth. He was a man possessed with a passion for rancorous vengeance. He would root out all these traitors and utterly destroy them — their women and children with them. None should be spared who raised their hand against that divine Providence which had demonstrated once again that he, Adolf Hitler, was chosen to shape the world's destiny. Not one should escape him — not one ! It was an eye for an eye and a tooth for a tooth.

The flood of imprecation was interrupted, but by no means checked, by a telephone call from Berlin to the effect that order had not yet been restored. In a further fury Hitler seized the receiver and screamed his orders over the wire, orders to the SS to shoot everyone and anyone who might be remotely suspected of complicity. Where was Himmler ? Why had he not arrived ?

Slowly the storm subsided. Sheer physical exhaustion supervened, and with it came that maniacal change from denunciation to self-pity. 'The German people', said Adolf Hitler, 'are unworthy

---

[1] An account of this scene has been left by one of the participants, *Sturmbann-führer* Eugen Dollmann, Himmler's personal representative in Italy and the official SS liaison officer with Mussolini both under interrogation and in his *Roma Nazista* (Milan, 1951), pp. 393-400. See also Dulles, pp. 9-11, and Trevor-Roper, *Last Days of Hitler*, pp. 35-7.

of my greatness. No one appreciates what I have done for them.'
At once the *Umgebung* of Nazi hierarchs, who had sat mutely with the
appalled Italians through the preceding tirade, broke into an anti-
phony of loyal protest. Göring extolled his own exploits for the
Nazi cause and the *Luftwaffe*. Doenitz expatiated on the glories of
the German Navy. Keitel, not to be outdone, spoke in terms of
unusual warmth of the achievements of the Army. Almost at once
Göring began a fierce quarrel with Ribbentrop, and in the general
hubbub the Foreign Minister's high voice could be heard shouting :
'My name is *von* Ribbentrop !' [1] When Göring was seen to threaten
him with his Marshal's baton, Dollmann felt it time to take his
shocked and bewildered Italian visitors away. No one noticed their
departure.

Yet while this Mad Hatter's tea-party was in progress in the
gloomy heart of an East Prussian forest, the conspiracy was afoot
in broad daylight in Berlin, though it was rapidly approaching its
final conclusion.

(ii) In Berlin

As Thursday, July 20, dawned over bomb-scarred Berlin, a
sweltering night gave place to a sweltering day. The sun climbed,
slow and golden, through a pearly haze into an azure sky, which
quickly became a brazen arc reflecting greater heat upon the stifling
city.

Few of the leading conspirators had rested peacefully. For one
reason or another sleep had stood away from most that night and
the nervous tension was as acute among them as in the oppressive
atmosphere. For the better part of ten days they had rested upon
the razor edge of uncertainty. They had been first alerted on
July 11, and again on the 15th, and now they knew that, come what
might, the deed and the thing for which they had planned and
prepared so long must happen to-day, this 20th of July, or not at
all, for it was impossible to maintain the secret longer.

These thoughts were in their minds early on this sultry summer
morning as they went about their duties, and later, when, primed
for the great event, they gathered in the Bendlerstrasse. Had any
one of them recalled Hitler's remark on the night of the Bürgerbräu
Putsch over twenty years before — 'To-morrow will either see a new

[1] Ribbentrop's *von*, which was rarely recognized by his Nazi colleagues, came
to him not by birth but by virtue of his adoption — as late in his life as May 15,
1925, in the thirty-second year of his age ! — by his aunt, Fräulein Gertrud von
Ribbentrop, whose father had been ennobled (*geadelt*) in 1884. A certificate to
this effect was provided by Ribbentrop on his promotion to the rank of SS-
Gruppenführer (Lieutenant-General) in 1938 (*IMT Document*, D-636).

GENERAL OF INFANTRY
FRIEDRICH OLBRICHT

COLONEL RITTER ALBRECHT MERTZ
VON QUIRNHEIM

Government in Germany or it will see us dead' [1] — he might have descried a certain appositeness to the present situation.

All the preliminary steps towards putting 'Operation Valkyrie' into execution had been set *en train* by Olbricht, his Chief of Staff, Mertz von Quirnheim, and his adjutant, Fritz von der Lancken; and all three had been in touch with Colonel-General von Hase, the Commandant of Berlin. The unit commanders of the Home Army and the Commandants of the training camps at Döberitz, Jüterbog, Krampnitz and Wünsdorf had been warned that a 'Valkyrie Exercise' was due on the 20th, and, though only a few of the officers concerned realized the full significance of this warning, it was generally believed that they would all fall into line once things got under way. By a stroke of good fortune Colonel-General Guderian, Inspector-General of Armoured Forces, had been prevailed upon by his Chief of Staff, General Thomale, a peripheral member of the conspiracy, reluctantly to postpone from July 19 to July 21 the despatch of certain panzer units from the Berlin area to Lötzen, in East Prussia, where they were urgently required as reinforcements, and these it was intended to use against the SS.[2] Arrangements had also been made to 'neutralize' the pronouncedly pro-Nazi Commander of *Wehrkreis III* (Berlin-Brandenburg), General von Kortzfleisch, and to replace him by a conspirator, General Freiherr von Thüngen.

What they could do the conspirators had done; but there were certain vital lacunae in their planning. For example, it was absolutely essential that Beck and von Witzleben should make their respective broadcasts to the German people and to the armed forces as soon as possible after the *Putsch* had been put into operation. Yet no provision had been made in advance for wiring the headquarters of the conspirators for broadcasting, a feat which was surely not impossible to achieve with the co-operation of the Signal Corps under some pretext in connection with the carrying out of 'Operation

[1] See above, p. 117.

[2] Colonel-General Heinz Guderian, *Erinnerungen eines Soldaten* (Heidelberg, 1951), p. 306. Various attempts had been made to win over Guderian to the conspiracy but all had failed. Goerdeler, von Tresckow, Friedrich von Rabenau, and Ernst von Harnack, had all tried without success. But in their negotiations with him the conspirators had had to divulge more than they could comfortably have done with security and they feared that he would betray them. To stop his mouth von Rabenau bade him remember that he was deeply involved even without having committed himself, and that 'in the Third Reich it is not only he who lights the fire that is punished but also he who first reports its outbreak' (Schlabrendorff, p. 114; Leber, p. 5). Guderian himself makes no mention of these earlier approaches and only admits to being informed on July 18 of a possible independent action on the part of von Kluge to bring hostilities to an end on the Western Front (p. 305).

Valkyrie', and this all-important factor was made dependent upon the success of the unit entrusted with the capture of the Berlin Radio Station.

As on a previous occasion, Olbricht and Hoepner lunched together on July 20, preparatory to going to the rendezvous of the conspirators at the Bendlerstrasse.[1] Olbricht was in a confident mood and they drank a private toast to the success of the *Putsch*. Hoepner had brought his uniform — which Hitler had expressly forbidden him to wear after he had been cashiered — in a suitcase, and he changed into it in the lavatory adjoining Olbricht's office. One by one the leaders of the conspiracy assembled. Beck came with his adjutant and potential State-Secretary, Count Ulrich von Schwerin-Schwanenfeld, and his A.D.C. of the day, the young Lieutenant Freiherr Ludwig von Hammerstein, the second son of the old Colonel-General, who had so determinedly combated Hitler. Few German Generals appear to advantage in civilian clothes, which seem to remove from them both dignity and distinction, and in his brown lounge suit Beck looked more like a kind old bourgeois making a social call than the man who hoped before sundown to replace Hitler as head of the German Reich; his drawn face bore witness to the agonies of his nightly vigils.

By contrast, Field-Marshal von Witzleben, who arrived in field uniform by car with his adjutant, Count zu Lynar, from the latter's estate at Seesen, looked eminently suited for the rôle he was expected to play. He saluted Beck jauntily with his marshal's *Staffel* and received with evident appreciation Otto John's report that he had arranged for a fast plane to be held in readiness to take the Field-Marshal to East Prussia to assume command of the *Wehrmacht*.

With the exception of Gerstenmaier, Gisevius and Otto John, there were no civilians in the Bendlerstrasse that day. Though various essentially non-military figures were present, as, for example, Peter Yorck, Bernd von Haeften and Berthold von Stauffenberg, they were all in uniform.[2] None of the civilian leaders of the first flight had even been warned that the assassination was to take place on that day. For reasons of expediency and of security the Army

---

[1] The present writer has used the first-hand accounts of the events in Berlin on July 20 to be found in the evidence of von Witzleben, Hoepner, Yorck von Wartenburg, and von Hase before the People's Court (*IMT Document*, PS-3881); in the *John Memorandum*; in articles by Ludwig von Hammerstein in *Die Welt*, July 19, 1947, by Eugen Gerstenmaier in *Neue Zürcher Zeitung*, June 28, 1945; by Bodo von der Heyde in *Die Welt*, July 31, 1947; in Gisevius, ii, 358-418; Semmler, pp. 132-40; in the reports of Major Otto Remer, dated July 22, 1944, and of Lieutenant Hans Hagen, dated July 25, 1944, and in numerous other sources.

[2] The uncertainty is Count Helldorf; no one afterwards remembered what he wore.

had ordained that this was to be their day and that the politicians should take over only when the success of the *Putsch* had been assured.

In Olbricht's room and outer office the conspirators sat and stood in varying degrees of nervous expectation. Von Quirnheim brought out the vital papers from Olbricht's safe and laid them on the table before him. With snatches of brittle conversation and long periods of tense silence they waited for Fellgiebel's call from the *Wolfsschanze*. One o'clock passed, and two o'clock, and still no call. Anxiety gave way to apprehension. Could von Stauffenberg have abandoned the attempt again? Could he have bungled it and been detected? Had he been too successful and himself fallen a victim to the explosion of his own bomb? Someone recalled an enigmatic remark of Beck's the previous day: 'A horse that refuses a jump twice is not likely to go over a third time', and at once there arose criticism of the ability and even the reliability of Claus von Stauffenberg, to which his brother, Berthold, supported by Peter Yorck and Bernd von Haeften, replied in his defence.

Three o'clock came and still no call from Fellgiebel; but shortly thereafter General Fritz Thiele, of Olbricht's staff, reported the ominous news that he had been able to get through to Rastenburg on the telephone and had been informed that an explosion had occurred and that a number of persons had been killed and wounded. There appeared to be great confusion at the *Wolfsschanze*.[1] Clearly, therefore, some part of the plan had miscarried since the communications centre of F.H.Q. was still operating. It was just possible that, if the majority of those in the conference room, including Hitler, had been killed or incapacitated, the situation at F.H.Q. seemed so satisfactory that Fellgiebel had felt justified in not carrying out his instructions. But in any case, where were Claus von Stauffenberg and Werner von Haeften?

Eventually, between three-thirty and three-forty-five, an irritated von Haeften telephoned from Rangsdorf to ask why no car had been sent to the airport for himself and von Stauffenberg. To Mertz von Quirnheim, who took the call, he added tersely: 'Hitler's dead'. Thus, and thus only, did the conspirators learn of the 'success' of the first stage of the *Putsch*.

But though the tempo of events had hitherto been sluggish, it

---

[1] According to Semmler (p. 132) Goebbels had received this information by telephone from Rastenburg 'at one o'clock or shortly afterwards'. There were no details and no mention of the *Führer*. If this is so, the *Gauleiter* of Berlin had a two-hours' start of the conspirators in the knowledge of what had occurred at Rastenburg, but he apparently did nothing about it, until about four o'clock, when he heard that the Home Army had been alerted for emergency.

now rose at once to the highest point of speed. By four o'clock von Hase had received his instructions as Commandant of Berlin, to put 'Valkyrie' into operation, and Mertz von Quirnheim had given out the orders to be sent over the teleprinter to local commanders.

Olbricht, in the meantime, had been making a final attempt to bring Fromm into line. This was desirable from every point of view, but more especially since the initial orders to the units of the Home Army had been issued over Fromm's name, which von Stauffenberg had thoughtfully appended above his own.

At about four o'clock (or approximately the same time that von Quirnheim had telephoned to von Hase) Olbricht informed his chief that Hitler was dead. He had, he said, just been informed of this fact by General Fellgiebel over the telephone. This prevarication was an error in tactics. The canny Fromm, who knew his Olbricht well, was not going to allow himself to be stampeded into precipitate action. Band-wagon jumping was second nature to him, but a long career had taught him never to mistake a stationary for a moving vehicle. Now he at once sought confirmation of Olbricht's story, and to the latter's suggestion that the general orders for 'Operation Valkyrie' be put into effect, he replied that he must first consult Field-Marshal Keitel before taking so weighty a decision. He therefore asked for, and, with disturbing ease and speed, received a personal connection with the *Wolfsschanze*. In a few minutes Keitel was on the telephone and, in answer to Fromm's enquiry about Hitler's death, he answered bluntly : 'That's all nonsense. An attempt was made on the *Führer*'s life but it failed. He was only slightly injured and is now with the Duce. Marshal Graziani is with me . . . and where', he added ominously, 'is your Chief of Staff, Colonel von Stauffenberg?' Fromm replied that he had not yet returned and, turning to Olbricht, gave precise orders that 'Operation Valkyrie' was not to be put into effect.

Astonished and incredulous, Olbricht returned to his own room, where he found Mertz von Quirnheim in full action. To his chief's statement that Fromm had ordered that nothing was to be done about 'Operation Valkyrie', he replied that the orders had already gone out over the teleprinter. This proved, however, to be an overstatement, for even as he spoke the young officer whom he had despatched to the communications room returned with the orders still in his hand. In his anxiety to get them out, von Quirnheim had failed to indicate the grades of priority and security to be accorded them in despatch, and the meticulous signals officers had returned them for these additions. With his pencil von Quirnheim wrote the words : 'Top Secret' and 'First Priority' on the top of the papers and gave them back to the orderly officer.[1]

It was now about four-thirty. Much had happened in the three-quarters of an hour since von Haeften's call from Rangsdorf, but he and von Stauffenberg had not yet arrived and meanwhile the situation had become more and more confused. Olbricht was with Beck when the pair from Rastenburg appeared shortly before five. To the chief of the conspiracy von Stauffenberg asserted categorically that Hitler was indeed dead. 'I saw it myself', he reiterated. 'I was standing with Fellgiebel in Bunker 88 when the explosion occurred. It was as though a fifteen-centimetre shell had hit the *Baracke*. It is impossible that anyone could have survived.'

Fortified with this reassurance Olbricht and Mertz von Quirnheim took von Stauffenberg to Fromm's office, which was on the floor above. The Commander of the Home Army received them coldly and with suspicion. 'Keitel says that the *Führer* was only slightly injured', he said at the end of his Chief of Staff's report. 'Keitel is lying, as usual', was von Stauffenberg's retort, adding for good measure, 'I myself set off the bomb and I myself saw the *Führer*'s body carried out of the hut'. To which Olbricht added the information that, despite Fromm's orders to the contrary, 'Operation Valkyrie' was now in full blast.

Fromm was dumbfounded and then livid with rage. 'You', he said to von Stauffenberg, 'must shoot yourself, for your attempt has failed. And you [to Olbricht] consider yourself under arrest.' 'I shall do nothing of the kind', replied von Stauffenberg, and Olbricht added, 'On the contrary, *Herr General-Oberst*, it is *we* who are arresting *you*'.

Leaping from his chair, Fromm reached for his pistol; but Olbricht and von Quirnheim had anticipated his action and at once grappled with him. Fromm was overpowered. Panting and furious, his arms pinioned, he was thrust back into his chair and disarmed. He was placed under guard in his A.D.C.'s office next door and von Witzleben's first act as Commander-in-Chief of the *Wehrmacht* was to appoint Colonel-General Erich Hoepner to the temporary command of the Home Army.[2]

Thus at the same moment that Hitler's paladins were indulging in violent quarrels at the Mad Hatter's tea-party at Rastenburg, his

[1] This young officer, the twenty-four-year-old Lieutenant Friedrich Karl Klausing, who had accompanied von Stauffenberg and von Haeften on their journey to Berchtesgaden on July 11, was placed on trial with von Witzleben, Hoepner and others and hanged on August 8, 1944 (*IMT Document*, PS-3881).

[2] It was characteristic of Hoepner that even in the midst of this emergency he insisted upon having his appointment put formally in writing and signed by von Witzleben.

Y

Generals were involved in a rough-and-tumble in the Bendlerstrasse. Further afield the Russians and the Anglo-American armies continued their advance.

Scarcely had Fromm been disposed of than another crisis broke upon the conspirators' headquarters. General von Kortzfleisch, commanding *Wehrkreis III*, arrived at the Bendlerstrasse in perplexity and annoyance. There were, he said, the most extraordinary rumours afloat that the *Führer* had been assassinated. No one seemed to know the truth and under the circumstances he demanded an immediate interview with Fromm. He was taken instead to Beck, who at once placed him under arrest and committed him to the custody of the same officers who were guarding Fromm, while von Witzleben issued a further order appointing General von Thüngen to succeed him.[1]

Nor was this all. To the astonishment of all there suddenly appeared in their midst SS-*Oberführer* Piffräder, the Gestapo successor to Oster as head of the *Abwehr*. Instructed by telephone from Rastenburg by Himmler to arrest von Stauffenberg as unostentatiously as possible, Piffräder had driven to the Bendlerstrasse, not knowing what was afoot there, and was promptly himself arrested.

It was of course the height of folly to permit three such dangerous opponents as Fromm, von Kortzfleisch and Piffräder to remain under honourable detention. More ruthless conspirators would have shot them out of hand, but without going to these lengths it would have been perfectly possible to have put them in the cells attached to the guardroom of the Bendlerstrasse, together with the little group of officers of the headquarters staff of the Home Army, notably Lieutenant-Colonels Bodo von der Heyde and von Pridun, who had remained loyal to Fromm. The error of judgment which Beck made in this respect is comparable with that of Ludendorff in releasing the members of the Triumvirate, von Kahr, von Lossow and von Seisser, on parole on the night of November 8, 1923.[2] In both cases the chivalrous impulse was misplaced and abused. When one is playing with one's head it rarely pays to be generous.

By six o'clock it was clear to those in the Bendlerstrasse that their initial hope had failed. Hitler was not dead and the F.H.Q. had not been isolated. They had in fact counter-attacked and field commanders in the Reich and in the occupied areas — who had already been bewildered by receiving orders issued first by von Witzleben and

---

[1] According to some sources von Kortzfleisch was summoned by telephone to the Bendlerstrasse by the conspirators ostensibly to a conference with Fromm, but actually to get him out of the way and leave the coast clear for von Thüngen to take over the command of *Wehrkreis III*.   [2] See above, p. 174.

Fromm, and later with the latter name replaced by that of Hoepner
— were now completely mystified by an order from Keitel declaring
that Hitler was alive and virtually unhurt and that no orders were
valid save those countersigned by himself or Himmler, whom the
Führer had placed in control of the security of the Reich.[1]

The result of these orders and counter-orders was, inevitably,
disorder. A flood of telephone calls poured in both upon the *Führer*'s
Headquarters at Rastenburg and on the centre of the conspiracy at
the Bendlerstrasse. What had really happened? What were the
outlying members of the conspiracy to do? Were the people in
Berlin going through with it anyway?

This was the momentous decision of policy taken by Beck. The
last he was to take in his life. There were waverers among the
leaders of the conspiracy at this moment. Hoepner bewailed the
absence of the 51 per cent chance of success.[2] Olbricht wondered
if the moment had really passed when they could call the whole
thing off. Others stood waiting in uncertainty. But Beck was never
uncertain. Though in his inner heart he may have known already
that all was lost and may even have derived some degree of relief to
feel that the agony would soon now be finished one way or the other,
he never hesitated. 'We must go forward now whatever happens',
he said; 'let us be firm at this moment. Let us be strong for
Germany.'[3]

Von Stauffenberg supported him warmly. This man with his
mutilated body and his uncrippled spirit was a tower of strength at
this moment of crisis. Though his judgment in many things may be
justly questioned, there can be no doubt about his physical or his
moral courage, nor the ferocious and indomitable energy which he
now displayed in holding the frail barque of the conspiracy together
till the last moment. It was von Stauffenberg who passed from room
to room, encouraging his fellow-plotters, laughing at their fears,
assuring them of ultimate success, rallying their spirits. It was he,
too, who throughout the afternoon and evening spoke tirelessly over
the telephone with the field and district commanders who sought
guidance for both immediate and future action, and in many cases he
was successful in the first instance in keeping them in line. 'Yes —
all orders from the C.-in-C. Home Army are to be obeyed', those

[1] For text of Keitel's order, see *Führer Conferences on Naval Affairs, 1944*
(issued by the British Admiralty in July 1947), p. 51.
[2] This may be compared with General von Lossow's attitude toward a *Putsch*
in Munich in 1923. (See above, p. 172.)
[3] Here again there is a parallel with Ludendorff's determination to go forward
on November 9, 1923, even though the practical chances of success for the *Putsch*
were virtually nil. (See above, p. 175.)

around him heard von Stauffenberg repeat to one General after another. 'You must seize all wireless stations and information centres. All SS opposition must be broken. . . . Yes, it is very likely that the *Führer*'s Headquarters will issue counter-orders, they may already have done so . . . these are not to be obeyed. They are not authentic. . . . Field-Marshal von Witzleben and the *Wehrmacht* have taken over all executive power. The Reich is in danger and, as always in its greatest need, the Army takes over the control. Do you understand? You are only to obey orders from von Witzleben or Hoepner.' Only in the case of von Kluge did he refer to Beck.

Having taken his great decision, Beck sat calm and outwardly unruffled among the mounting confusion which surrounded him. 'A good General knows how to be patient', he repeated more than once that day and he seemed to be the very pattern of his own precept. But when he was told that von Kluge was on the line he took the call personally and urged his hesitant colleague to take action. At La Roche Guyon the Commander-in-Chief West was, as may be imagined, in an agony of uncertainty. To Beck's compelling appeal that he take the initiative and raise the standard of revolt in the West, he was at first evasive. The orders were so confusing, first von Witzleben, then Keitel; he did not know what to believe. He had always promised to support a *Putsch* once the *Führer* was really dead, but was he? The reports were so contradictory. To this querulous outburst Beck replied with a direct question, was von Kluge prepared to place himself under his (Beck's) orders or was he not? There was silence at the other end of the telephone line and then the Field-Marshal said hastily that he would call back in half an hour. He did not do so.[1]

It was now seven o'clock in the evening and the sands of the conspiracy were fast running out. An announcement on the radio that the *Führer* had been only slightly wounded in an attempted assassination and would himself broadcast to the German people later in the evening was the first intimation the plotters had received that they were not in possession of the Berlin *Rundfunk*. It was now impossible for Beck to forestall Hitler in his announcement to the German people and to the world of a change of régime, and it underlined the lamentable lack of foresight in the original planning which had failed to take into consideration the necessity of providing an alternative form of radio medium.[2]

---

[1] For the events of July 20, 1944, in Paris, see section (iii) of this chapter, pp. 662 *et seq.*

[2] According to the testimony of the officer charged with seizing the *Rundfunk*, Major Jacob, an instructor at the Infantry School at Döberitz, he succeeded in

But by now it was clear that much had gone sadly awry with the plans for the *Putsch*. The conspirators' maps of the SS dispositions in Berlin had proved faulty and the panzer units on which so much reliance had been placed had not made an appearance;[1] as a result, though certain of the vital points had been occupied by the troops from the training camps, the Gestapo headquarters in the Prinz Albrechtstrasse and the Propaganda Ministry were still in the hands of the enemy. And for a very good reason.

The unit which had been entrusted with the vitally important assignment of seizing the Government quarter of Berlin was the '*Wachbataillon Grossdeutschland*', a crack regiment of guards commanded by Major Otto Ernst Remer, an officer whose military record and eight wounds had earned him the *Ritterkreuz* with oak leaves. The battalion was quartered at Döberitz, and at ten minutes past four Remer received a telephone message from the Berlin Commandant, General von Hase, to place his troops in a state of immediate alert and to report himself at once to the *Kommandatur* in Berlin. Arrived there, Remer received from von Hase his assignment in accordance with the over-all plan of 'Operation Valkyrie'. He was to cordon off the Ministries of the Reich and, having isolated them, report back for further orders ; no one, not even a Minister or a General, was to leave the area.

On his return to Döberitz Remer assembled his officers and repeated to them his instructions, giving orders for the immediate departure of the troops. One of those present was a certain Lieutenant Hans Hagen, a reserve officer of the *Wachbataillon* and a devout Nazi who, having been wounded on the Eastern Front, had been retained by Bormann on the task of compiling a history of German literature for the Nazi Party. On his way to Döberitz, Hagen told Remer, he had seen a General Staff car pass him in which was Field-Marshal von Brauchitsch in full uniform. His suspicions were aroused.

making a surprise attack on the *Funkhaus* and expelled the SS Guard before they knew what was happening. He occupied the building for some hours, despite the threatened action of the SS Commander, and only evacuated it because he had no further orders from Olbricht, to whom he had reported his success, and because he received a personal telephone call from Goebbels, giving him the official and accurate account of the position. Major Jacob at that point returned with his troops to Döberitz. He subsequently stated to his divisional commander, Major-General Brühl, that the conspirators could have kept up the entire broadcasting service if only he had received later orders from Olbricht.

[1] On receiving information about the *Putsch* by telephone from his Chief of Staff in Berlin, General Thomale, Guderian, who was inspecting troops in East Prussia on July 20, gave orders for the panzer units in Berlin to remain in their quarters at Krampnitz.

Remer should bear in mind the possibility of a military *Putsch*.[1] He suggested that a check be made with the headquarters of Joseph Goebbels, the *Gauleiter* of Berlin. Remer, who though at that time not essentially a Nazi supporter, was yet very conscious of the necessity of being on the winning side in any military revolt, at once provided Hagen with a motor-cycle and ordered him to reconnoitre the position, to visit the Gestapo headquarters and the Ministry of Propaganda and to meet him, Remer, at a given place and time.

In the meanwhile the troops of the Guard Battalion were loaded on to their vehicles which proceeded into Berlin. The cordoning-off of the Government quarter was completed by six-thirty and Remer reported back personally to von Hase in the *Kommandatur*. He was told to maintain his position. On leaving von Hase's office he received a message from Hagen, who had meantime seen Goebbels, saying that he could not keep their rendezvous for fear of being arrested but that Remer must report at once to Goebbels at the Propaganda Ministry in the Wilhelmsplatz.

Here at about seven o'clock there occurred the historic interview.[2] To Remer Goebbels gave a full and pretty accurate statement of the situation. The *Führer* was far from dead. He was only slightly injured, and would broadcast to the nation later in the evening. However, in the meantime would Remer care to speak to him personally, to satisfy himself of the truth of what the *Gauleiter* of Berlin was now telling him?

Remer, who had recently received his *Ritterkreuz* from the *Führer*, agreed and Goebbels put through a call to the *Wolfsschanze*. Hitler consented to speak to the officer. He was 'quite unhurt', the *Führer* said; did Remer recognize his voice? There was certainly no mistaking or counterfeiting that harsh metallic sound and Remer at once confirmed its genuineness. Then, said the Voice, place yourself under the orders of *Reichsminister* Himmler, whom I have appointed Commander-in-Chief of the Home Army (the third G.O.C. which this bewildered command had had in less than twelve hours!) and suppress all resistance with ruthless energy.

[1] Here again was one of those fortuitous pieces of ill-luck which beset the conspirators on this day. The general officer whom Hagen saw in the car was *not* von Brauchitsch, who was not even in Berlin on that day. But it was this case of 'mistaken identity' which touched off the train of suspicion in Hagen's mind and caused him to warn Remer.

[2] Semmler (p. 134) gives the time of this interview as 'five o'clock', but this is impossible as the orders for 'Operation Valkyrie' did not go out to von Hase until four o'clock and Remer had made two journeys from Döberitz to Berlin and had completed his assignment before he saw Goebbels. He himself, in his report, gives the time of the completion of the cordoning off of the Government quarter as six-thirty.

COLONEL-GENERAL ERICH HOEPNER

Remer then came out whole-heartedly on the side of the Nazi régime. He paraded his five hundred men in the garden of Goebbels' official residence in the Hermann Göringstrasse, where the 'Little Doctor' made them a fiery speech, and brought up reinforcements from Rangsdorf and Döberitz. Goebbels had meanwhile reported Remer's zeal to the *Führer*, with the result that he was promptly and telephonically appointed to the rank of Colonel and charged with the capture of the conspirators' headquarters in the Bendlerstrasse.[1]

To this task Remer assigned a detachment under *Oberleutnant* Schlee, telling him to reconnoitre the position and to make his assault with caution. Schlee and his men surrounded the War Ministry building from the Bendlerstrasse and the Tirpitzufer along the Landwehr Canal, and approached with care.

It was now ten o'clock at night. The light was still good, and the black-out had not yet descended upon Berlin. The War Ministry loomed grey and forbidding before them. It was strangely quiet. Were they being led into a trap, to be mown down by machine-guns masked in the building? The approaching troops reached the main entrance without challenge or resistance. There were no guards. The doors stood open, and they entered almost with a sense of awe.

With the evident defection of the miserable von Kluge the net of despair and disaster seemed to close about the feet of the conspirators in the Bendlerstrasse. By seven o'clock the First Quartermaster-General, Eduard Wagner, one of the most fervid of the plotters, would no longer answer his telephone in Zossen.[2] By eight o'clock General Freiherr von Esebeck, the Commander of *Wehrkreis XVII* (Vienna), who had previously detained in custody the deputy *Gauleiter* and certain high Austrian SS and Gestapo personalities, telephoned to say that Keitel had countermanded Hoepner's orders for 'Operation Valkyrie' and that in view of the evident confusion of authority he had called off all action. Similar messages arrived very soon thereafter from the headquarters of *Wehrkreis II* (Stettin) and from General Schaal in Prague, where Keitel's rescinding order had also been obeyed. It was clear that too many officers had shown their hand on the receipt of the news of the *Führer*'s death and were now desperately trying to exculpate themselves from their implied complicity.

Had Fellgiebel but carried out his task in destroying the com-

---

[1] Remer was awarded the *Ritterkreuz* with brilliants for his part in suppressing the *Putsch* and was subsequently promoted Major-General.

[2] General Wagner committed suicide on July 26.

munications centre a. the *Wolfsschanze*, thereby isolating F.H.Q., it is more than a strong probability that the conspirators would have succeeded in seizing power and in accomplishing some kind of *Putsch*, even though Hitler were still alive. But, because Fromm could talk to Keitel; because Keitel could send out his counter-manding orders; because Hitler could speak with Goebbels and, more particularly, with Remer, the conspiracy — which was essen-tially a conspiracy of the switchboard — was doomed almost before it could translate its plans into action. As Goebbels said later: 'It was a revolution on the telephone which we crushed with a few rifle-shots. But just a little more skill behind it and the rifle shots would not have done the trick.' [1]

About nine o'clock Field-Marshal von Witzleben, muttering, 'This is a fine mess', climbed into his car and drove back to the Lynar estate at Seesen, and almost at the same time it became known that the commander of *Wehrkreis III* (von Thüngen) and the military Commandant of Berlin (von Hase) had accepted the order of General Reinecke, a notorious Nazi who had also been on the telephone to Hitler, to withdraw their troops, surrender their authority and con-sider themselves under arrest.

Olbricht thereupon assembled in his room those officers who were privy to the conspiracy and begged them to resist the assault which was now inevitably imminent and to fight it out to the end. This they agreed to do and orders were given to put the building into some state of defence. With Beck and Hoepner, von Quirnheim, von Stauffen-berg and Werner von Haeften, Olbricht then retired to Fromm's old room (now Hoepner's) on the floor above to hold a last council of war.

Scarcely had they assembled than shots were heard on the stairs and in the corridors outside, and a group of officers, headed by Colonel Bodo von der Heyde, all armed with tommy guns and grenades, forced their way into the room and at pistol point demanded that Fromm should be released and handed over to them. It was the counter-*Putsch* and the nemesis of misplaced mercy. It was an error of judgment — equal almost in catastrophic consequences to Fell-giebel's failure and the omission to provide an alternative method of radio transmission — to have allowed Fromm and von Kortzfleisch and their fellow-prisoners to have remained in open custody in the same building with the conspirators. If they had not been shot out of hand — a fate which most of them richly deserved and which they did not hesitate to mete out when their turn came — they should at

---

[1] Semmler, p. 138. 'To think that these revolutionaries weren't even smart enough to cut the telephone wires — my little daughter would have thought of that' (Curt Riess, *Joseph Goebbels* (New York, 1948), p. 280).

least have been closely confined. Instead, they had been accorded the honours of war and food and wine had been provided for them ; in the confusion they had eluded their guards and found arms.

Olbricht showed fight and was overpowered. Von Stauffenberg was shot in the back as he was retreating into his own room next door. The others remained rooted where they stood. Then Fromm appeared.

This wretched man had been all things to all men for many years. An ardent Nazi when the fortunes of the *Führer* and the Nazi régime were in the ascendant, he had been privy to and compliant with the conspiracy which was being hatched in his own office, and, had the attempt upon Hitler's life succeeded, would have been among the first to hail the new régime in Germany. There were many who were aware of how much he knew and his conduct in the early afternoon had been anything but unequivocal. Now at the last moment he sought to rehabilitate himself in the eyes of the winning side by eliminating the chief conspirators, ostensibly as a proof of his undying loyalty to the *Führer* but actually to destroy the incriminating evidence against himself. It is of some satisfaction to know that, though he succeeded in carrying out this weasel plan, it profited him nothing.[1]

Urged on by the knowledge that retribution was hard on his track if he did not act at once, Fromm proceeded with ruthless and indecent haste. He ordered the prisoners to be disarmed and constituted himself and his recently released fellow-prisoners a drum-head court-martial of summary procedure. Beck, who had sat as if stunned throughout this last swift passage of events, asked to keep his pistol as he wished to use it for 'private purposes'. 'You would not deprive an old comrade of this privilege', he said to Fromm with quiet dignity.

So this was the end. He, Ludwig Beck, had seen it coming for a long time. In his deepest heart he had never believed in success for the *Putsch* but he had been convinced that it must be attempted as an act and gesture of expiation. 'There is no use. There is no deliverance', he had said to a friend only a few weeks before. 'We must now drain little by little the bitter cup to the bitterest end.'[2] And

---

[1] Fromm was arrested by Himmler on the following day and held for investigation. No direct proof of his complicity in the *Putsch* could be produced, but he was brought before the People's Court in February 1945 on a charge of 'cowardice' in that he had been afraid to divulge his previous knowledge of the conspiracy. Condemned to death, he was shot in the Brandenburg Prison on March 19, 1945, but not before he had experienced in his own person the worst cruelties and indignities of which the system which he had helped to create, had served, and had helped to save, was capable.

[2] Meinecke, p. 149.

why ? Because men of high character such as himself had once allowed themselves to be beguiled by the enticements and seductions of National Socialism. Beck had not scrupled to defend his subalterns, Scheringer and Ludin, when charged with the propagation of what was then (1931) the subversive doctrine of the Nazi Party. He had not been shaken in his belief that there was something good for Germany in all that Hitler promised until the first exhibition of bestial gangsterism in the Blood Bath of June 30, 1934. Yet a few weeks later he had taken the Oath of Allegiance, albeit with grave and heart-searching reservations, to the man who had ordered this massacre. Not till the defiling hand of the Party was laid upon the sacrosanct privileges of the Army itself, four years later, was Beck roused to open opposition, but it must be stated that once he had been thus aroused he never looked back. From 1938 until now, on the sultry night of July 20, 1944, when he stood at the end of the road, he had fought and struggled to free Germany and the German Army from the fetters of National Socialism which he and many of his comrades had helped to rivet upon their wrists. He symbolized the best in German military resistance, the man who saw the error of his ways and did what he could, however futile and ineffective, to undo the harm which he had done. Beck was no band-wagon jumper, as had been Fromm and von Kluge and Rommel ; he had watched inactive the Nazi circus go past him when all his world was following admiring in its train, but the years since 1938 had been a hell upon earth for him.

Something of all this must have been in his mind as he stood now, pistol in hand, confronting Fromm, with his fellow conspirators, now his fellow prisoners, about him. 'I recall the old days . . .' he began, but Fromm interrupted him with crude brutality, increased by his own guilty anxiety for speed, and ordered him to get on with the business in hand. Beck gave him one contemptuous glance, and looked once in farewell to his friends. Then he put the pistol to his grey head and pulled the trigger.

His intention was better than his aim. The bullet grazed his temple, giving him a slight flesh wound, and buried itself in the ceiling. Beck staggered to a chair and collapsed into it, his head in his hands. 'You'd better give the old man a hand', said Fromm callously, and left the room.

It was at this moment, shortly after ten o'clock, that Lieutenant Schlee and his detachment of the *Wachbataillon* made their unmolested entrance into the War Ministry. As they made their way up the deserted stairs and along the empty corridors, proceeding with caution lest a trap awaited them, they heard a single shot. There was silence for a moment, then a burst of voices and a general officer, whom Schlee recognized as Fromm, came into the passage. Schlee reported himself and placed his detachment under the General's orders. Fromm then went back to his office.

The scene was macabre. In a chair, supported by two officers, sat Beck, his face ashen and blood from his flesh wound running unchecked down his cheek. Half lying in another chair, attended by his brother and Werner von Haeften, was Claus von Stauffenberg, wounded from Bodo von der Heyde's bullet in the back. At the central table Olbricht and Hoepner were writing farewell letters to their families. Fromm looked evilly portentous : 'In the name of the *Führer*, a summary court-martial called by myself, has reached the following verdict: Colonel of the General Staff Mertz von Quirnheim, General Olbricht, the Colonel — I cannot bring myself to name him [von Stauffenberg] — and Lieutenant von Haeften are condemned to death'.

They were taken immediately to the courtyard below, von Haeften supporting the staggering von Stauffenberg. The headlights of the military trucks shone in their eyes, all but blinding them. The men of Schlee's detachment formed the firing-party. There was only one volley.[1]

Left alone with Beck and Hoepner, Fromm offered the latter a pistol but Hoepner was not prepared for this. He refused the way of suicide and allowed himself to be arrested. 'I am not a swine', he said, 'that I should have to condemn myself.' It was a decision which he was doubtless later to repent.

'Now how about you ?' Fromm asked Beck roughly, shaking him by the shoulder. Beck asked in a weak and weary voice for another pistol and it was given him. This time he was successful.[2]

The remaining prisoners who had been arrested in Olbricht's

[1] As soon as the execution had been carried out Fromm sent the following signal to all concerned : 'The *Putsch* attempted by irresponsible Generals has been ruthlessly subdued. All the leaders have been shot. Orders issued by General Field-Marshal von Witzleben, Colonel-General Hoepner, General Beck and General Olbricht are not to be obeyed. I have again assumed command after my temporary arrest by force of arms' (see *Führer Conferences on Naval Affairs, 1944*, p. 32).

[2] According to some sources Beck's second attempt at suicide was also unsuccessful and the *coup de grâce* was eventually administered by Fromm himself. Hoepner's evidence before the People's Court on August 7, is, however, quite explicit on this point. Hoepner saw the second pistol given to Beck and heard the shot as he left the room *with* Fromm, with whom he remained until taken away in custody.

room, including Peter Yorck, Fritz von der Schulenburg, Eugen Gerstenmaier, Ulrich von Schwerin-Schwanenfeld, von Stauffenberg's brother Berthold and von Haeften's brother Bernd, were now herded down into the courtyard where, under Fromm's orders, a second firing-party had been ordered.[1] But here Fate again intervened.

Before the second batch of executions could be carried out, thereby removing virtually the last traces of Fromm's complicity, there arrived at the Bendlerstrasse a group of Gestapo officials, escorting Kaltenbrunner and Skorzeny, with explicit orders that no further summary justice should take place.[2] It was the first indication of the policy which *Reichsführer*-SS Heinrich Himmler, Minister of Interior and now Commander-in-Chief of the Home Army, was to pursue. The mere slaughter of the *Führer*'s enemies was of no importance to him. They should die, certainly, but not before torture, indignity and interrogation had drained from them that last shred and scintilla of evidence which should lead to the arrest of others. Then, and only then, should the blessed release of death be granted them.

And thus the day, which was to have heralded the downfall of the Nazi tyranny, closed with the opening of a new era of hideous and sadistic persecution.

(iii) IN PARIS

It is surely ironic that the German military conspiracy achieved its highest — and indeed, its only — point of success, not in Germany at all, but in the heart of an occupied and hostile country. For in Paris the events of the 20th of July demonstrated what efficiency and resolution could achieve. The machinery of revolt moved with a well-ordered precision which betokened careful and tireless preparation and a certain genius of direction. Whereas in Berlin the military forces of the conspirators failed signally throughout the whole afternoon and evening in their initial task of eliminating the power of the SS and SD, in Paris the heavily armed force of these two organiza-

[1] In the general confusion which followed Eugen Gerstenmaier managed to elude his guards and escape. Ludwig von Hammerstein had been sent away by Beck when all seemed irredeemably lost and Otto John had left the Bendlerstrasse about 9.30 to go and see Popitz, with Werner von Haeften's last words ringing in his ears : ' Call me at eight ɔ'clock to-morrow morning, by that time we shall either have succeeded or we shall hang'. Within an hour the speaker was dead. John went home and did not actually learn of the final collapse of the *Putsch* until, turning on the radio at midnight, he heard the voice of the *Führer* addressing the German people.

[2] Skorzeny, p. 209.

tions, amounting to over 2000 men, was rendered harmless within the space of thirty minutes by means of an operation carried out without the slightest hitch, and only the infirmity of purpose displayed by the key-figure at the top — Field-Marshal Gunther von Kluge — prevented the revolt, which had failed in Berlin, from being continued successfully from Paris.[1]

The king-pin of the conspiracy in Paris was the Military Governor, Colonel-General Heinrich von Stülpnagel, ably seconded by the Chief of Staff of Army Group B, General Hans Speidel. Within the broad framework of the general directive of 'Operation Valkyrie' the conspirators on the Western Front exercised a wide degree of autonomy, and that which was organized, planned and directed from von Stülpnagel's headquarters in the Hôtel Raphael, in the Avenue Kléber, was in effect a self-contained revolt in microcosm, which could operate either as a part or independently of the central conspiracy in Berlin.

The positions of von Stülpnagel and Speidel were in themselves strong sources of influence and protection, but they were fortunate in the ability and devotion of their subordinates. These consisted primarily of the Commandant of Greater Paris, Lieutenant-General Freiherr Hans von Boineburg-Langsfeld, and Colonel Hans Otfried von Linstow, von Stülpnagel's Chief of Staff,[2] who were largely responsible for the over-all planning, and various subordinate members of von Stülpnagel's Staff, such as Lieutenant-Colonel Friedrich von Teuchert, Lieutenant-Colonel Freiherr von Bargotzky, and Freiherr von Falkenhausen, a nephew of the Military Governor of Belgium, all of whom seem to have been retained in the Hôtel Raphael in supernumerary positions for the sole purpose of planning and preparing for the revolt. Contact with Beck and von Witzleben was maintained through Lieutenant-Colonel Caesar von Hofacker, an industrialist in uniform, and through von Stauffenberg's confidential agent Dr. Reinhard Brinck, attached to the Staff of the

---

[1] The present writer has consulted the first-hand accounts of the events of July 20 in Paris by General Blumentritt in Liddell Hart, pp. 432-9 ; Speidel, pp. 142-8 ; Friedrich von Teuchert in the *Neue Zürcher Zeitung*, November 13, 1946, and *Die Welt*, July 19, 1947 ; Lieutenant-General Hans von Boineburg-Langsfeld in the *Frankfurter Rundschau*, July 20, 1948 ; the War Diary of Vice-Admiral Krancke, in *Führer Conferences on Naval Affairs 1944* ; and Otto Abetz, *Das offene Problem* (Köln, 1951), pp. 286-95. A full-length study of this episode entitled *Die Ereignisse am 20. Juli 1944 in Frankreich,* by Dr. Wilhelm von Schramme, is announced among the forthcoming publications of the *Institut für Geschichte der Nationalsozialistischen Zeit* in Munich.

[2] According to von Teuchert, Colonel von Linstow, who was suffering from heart trouble, was not informed of the final plans until the last moment, in order to spare him the additional strain and anxiety.

Commander-in-Chief, West, whose Deputy Chief of Staff, Colonel Eberhard Finckh, was also in the plot.

The position of the Paris conspirators was considerably complicated by the fact that they were under constant hostile surveillance and jealous suspicion from the SS and SD under General Karl-Albrecht Oberg, from the German Embassy personnel under Otto Abetz, from the staff of the Naval Commander-in-Chief in the West, Admiral Krancke, and from the personnel of the *Luftwaffe* headquarters of Field-Marshal Sperrle. Of these the most dangerous opponent was the Admiral, for, not only did he cherish an exaggerated professional jealousy and dislike of the military, but he was also a '200 per cent' Nazi, and of undoubted loyalty to the *Führer*. Of Oberg the conspirators stood in little awe or danger ; he was an old friend of von Stauffenberg and, though not in any way privy to the plot, was certainly not over-zealous in stimulating the zeal of his subordinates, who were, none the less, inquisitive enough without stimulus.

Otto Abetz was by this time as anxious as anyone to insure against the oncoming disaster whose approach drew daily nearer Paris. He was no longer the rampant Nazi propagandist of the 'thirties, nor the truculent representative of a conquering power in which rôle he had entered Paris in 1940. He was now a spectre-ridden fugitive from Nemesis, anxious only to appease the fury of the Fates. It was in recognition of this state of mind that von Stülpnagel had asked him to dine at the Hôtel Raphael on July 18. The Military Governor had received private advices from Berlin that the Great Day could no longer be postponed and that the next twenty-four hours would see, for better for worse, the signal for the operation of 'Valkyrie'. He wished to know where the Ambassador stood in a moment of emergency, and the Ambassador made no bones about telling him.

It is possible that Abetz may have cherished some idea of establishing some understanding or *rapprochement* between France and Germany — certainly he asserted this with some vehemence throughout his trial before a French Court in 1949 [1] — but these hopes, if they ever existed, had been blighted and destroyed by the policy dictated from the *Führer*'s headquarters, which Abetz had followed, either willingly or unwillingly. He now told the General that in his opinion the only salvation for Germany lay in the intervention at

[1] Otto Abetz has expounded the case in his defence in *Pétain et les Allemands* (Paris, 1948) ; *D'une prison* (Paris, 1949), and in *Das offene Problem* (Köln, 1951). He was sentenced by a French military court on July 22, 1949, to twenty years' hard labour.

F.H.Q. by responsible men, both military and civilian, in order to urge Hitler to resign the practical leadership of governmental affairs and the direction of strategical operations for reasons of health, and then to make peace with the Western Allies with all speed. The Military Governor did not explain that the sort of intervention which was likely to take place at the *Führerhauptquartier* would be of a more violent nature than Abetz seemed to envisage, but he was satisfied that, once Hitler was dead, they could expect no opposition from his Ambassador in Paris.

The main problem, the great imponderable, of the Paris conspiracy was, of course, von Kluge. Shortly after his assumption of command in the West on July 6, in succession to von Rundstedt, hê had sent word to Beck by Caesar von Hofacker that once Hitler was dead he would support a *Putsch*, and this intelligence had been conveyed to Rommel by Speidel. Rommel, however, was suspicious of his superior and, again through Speidel, had informed von Stülpnagel that he was prepared to take independent action against the régime if von Kluge refused to do so.[1] This step was followed by the joint representation of von Kluge and Rommel to Hitler on July 15, and two days later Rommel was incapacitated.[2]

Von Kluge took over personal command of Army Group B on July 18, moving his headquarters to La Roche Guyon and retaining Speidel as his Chief of Staff. He left the headquarters of the Commander-in-Chief, West, at St.-Germain, in charge of his own Chief of Staff, General Gunther Blumentritt.

This concentration of the two commands in the hands of von Kluge should have proved an asset to the conspirators, provided that they could count upon the Field-Marshal's living up to his promises, but this, of course, was what they could not do.[3]

Such was the position in the West on the eve of July 20.

The conspirators in Paris passed the morning of the fateful day in much the same circumstances of repressed anxiety as their fellow-plotters in Berlin. Here too the weather was sultry and oppressive, and to the Parisians, with the forces of liberation little more than a hundred miles away, the compelling question was : 'What will the Boches do with Paris ?' This, however, was not the question which

---

[1] Speidel, p. 135.   [2] See above, p. 632.

[3] The news of the intention to conclude a separate armistice agreement on the Western Front must have leaked in Berlin, for Guderian claims (p. 305) that he learned of it from a *Luftwaffe* General on the afternoon of July 18, and was greatly disturbed thereby. If this is so it is the more remarkable that his suspicions were not aroused by the request of Olbricht, telephoned by Guderian's Chief of Staff to him at Allenstein on the following morning, that the departure of certain panzer units for East Prussia should be delayed till after the 20th. (See above, p. 647.)

was concerning the German headquarters at that moment. It was known that the attempt was to be made between midday and one o'clock and the tension became increasingly severe as three o'clock came and there was no word from Berlin. At last when five o'clock had come and gone von Hofacker was called personally by his cousin von Stauffenberg on the telephone. Hitler, he said, was dead. The revolt was in full operation; the Government quarter was just about to be taken over. A few moments later the first orders signed by von Witzleben as Commander-in-Chief of the *Wehrmacht* came in over the teleprinter. They were clear and explicit: 'The elimination of SS and SD resistance is to be undertaken ruthlessly'.

Never were orders more welcome nor so long anticipated. For weeks General von Boineburg-Langsfeld and his deputy commandant, Colonel von Brehmer, had been purging the ranks of the 1st Motorized Rifle Regiment, the crack guard unit of Paris, of all elements remotely suspected of Nazi loyalties and had filled the gaps with those who could be vouched for as opponents of the régime. They therefore had at their disposal something which the Berlin conspirators could never really count upon, a picked unit of whose fealty there could be no question. Brehmer took personal charge of the battalion and awaited von Stülpnagel's final orders to go into action.

But before these could be issued there came at six o'clock over the Berlin Radio the first stunning news that Hitler was not dead after all. The hopes which only an hour before had waxed so strong now were shattered about the heads of the conspirators. Von Stülpnagel summoned von Boineburg, von Hofacker and von Linstow to a hurried council of war. It was agreed that even if the *Führer* were still alive and even if the revolt should fail in Berlin, the position could still be saved by determined action in the West. Von Stülpnagel expressed himself in favour of going ahead in any case, and, as if to give point to his decision, a telephone message arrived from von Kluge asking him to come out to La Roche Guyon to dinner. Could this mean that the Field-Marshal had at last decided to act? Von Stülpnagel had tried to get into touch with him earlier in the afternoon but without avail; now, before leaving for La Roche Guyon, he gave orders for 'Operation Valkyrie' to be put into execution forthwith.

Von Kluge had left early that morning for a conference of Army and Corps Commanders at the headquarters of the 5th Panzer Army, and did not get back to his own headquarters until six o'clock in the afternoon. On his arrival at La Roche Guyon he found two messages awaiting him: the first, telephoned by Blumentritt about five o'clock, saying that Hitler was dead and that a revolt had taken place in Berlin ; the second, received only a few minutes before his return, an extract from the German Radio to the effect that an attempt on the life of the *Führer* had failed and that he would himself broadcast later in the evening. It was at this moment that Beck telephoned from Berlin telling von Kluge that he must make a decision and requiring him to place himself under his, Beck's, authority as *Reichsverweser*.[1] Von Kluge had made his miserable evasion by promising to call back in half an hour, and in the meantime had spoken to Keitel and Warlimont at Rastenburg, from whom he had learned the true state of affairs.

In the meanwhile he had summoned von Stülpnagel from Paris and by the time the Military Governor had arrived at about half-past seven, the Field-Marshal had made up his mind. He now knew that Hitler had not been even seriously wounded by the bomb and that the position of the rebels in the Bendlerstrasse was precarious ; he knew also that they had now gone too far to draw back. The circumstances under which he had promised his allegiance to the new régime were not forthcoming and von Kluge was not the man to run risks unnecessarily. There was no trace of the spirit of Yorck von Wartenburg about '*kluger Hans*'.

But von Stülpnagel was not prepared to give up so easily. He had already burned his bridges and now he attempted once again to pull the Field-Marshal in with him. With von Hofacker he reminded von Kluge of his promise to Beck that he would support him in the event of Hitler's death. 'But he's alive', answered von Kluge. Again the Military Governor recapitulated his arguments. This was the last chance to save the German Army and the German Reich. The Allies would not make peace with Hitler but they might with someone else. 'But the attempt has failed. Everything is over,' von Kluge repeated. Von Stülpnagel made a final effort. 'Field-Marshal, everything is *not* over. It is still possible to take independent action in the West. You have pledged yourself to act, your word and honour are at stake. Something must be *done*.' Von Kluge rose to his feet with an air of finality and a forced vivacity, saying, almost gaily, 'Gentlemen, nothing can be done. The *Führer* is still alive. Now let us go in to dinner.'

It was a strange dinner-party. The windows stood open, but the sultry air scarcely stirred the candle flames upon the table. The host, von Kluge, persisted in his manifestly simulated frivolity, which certainly struck no answering chord among his guests. Of these, the hideous *Luftwaffe* Field-Marshal Sperrle came and went, finding

[1] See above, p. 654.

the atmosphere too uncertain for his liking, but von Stülpnagel and Speidel and von Hofacker sat in gloomy silence, and even the loquacious Blumentritt, who had arrived from St.-Germain, was hushed. To Heinrich von Stülpnagel it was now evident that he had burned his bridges to no purpose. However successful the operation against the Paris Gestapo might be, it could establish nothing lasting unless supported by the Commander-in-Chief, West. Such support was clearly not forthcoming, and to the Military Governor of France there remained only the satisfaction of telling the Field-Marshal that, like Fromm, he had been confronted with a *fait accompli*.

Drawing von Kluge through the long windows on to the terrace, he told him of the action which he had taken before leaving the Hôtel Raphael. 'But you can't do this without my orders', said the Field-Marshal. 'I tried to telephone to you but you were not available', was von Stülpnagel's answer. 'What is done now cannot be undone.' Von Kluge waited a moment. Should he or should he not throw in his lot with the revolt which had evidently begun in Paris ? The armies under his command could act independently of Berlin and almost with a gesture of his hand he could bring hostilities to a close, and perhaps save the German Army, or at least a large segment of it, from destruction. Should he do it ?

The indecision was but momentary. Von Kluge descended on the side of a continued 'faith unfaithful'. 'You must shoulder your own responsibility', he said to von Stülpnagel, 'but I should advise you to change into civilian clothes and go into hiding.' And with this advice he despatched him back to Paris.

Meanwhile the *Putsch* was on, but it had come into operation later than was expected. Because of the uncertain political attitude of the naval and air-force units, and in order to avoid giving to Frenchmen the satisfying spectacle of Germans fighting Germans, General von Boineburg had, on his own authority, delayed matters until after eleven o'clock. At that moment, however, his picked units of the 1st Motorized Rifle Regiment went into action with admirable discipline and effect. The SS headquarters in the Avenue Foch was taken completely by surprise and occupied without a shot being fired. Oberg was arrested personally by Colonel von Brehmer, at his apartment in the Rue de Cannes, and was escorted in custody to the Hôtel Continental. His bewildered staff were disposed of in the military prison at Fresnes, and the SS rank-and-file, who were being rounded up all over Paris, were confined in the Fort de l'Est. There were no casualties at all. The element of surprise had been so complete that resistance was never attempted. On the other hand, the conduct of the troops, though restrained in its demonstration, indicated clearly their strong aversion to Himmler's army.

By half-past eleven on the night of July 20 the SS and the SD had been eliminated as a power in Paris. The dragon had lost its head and the body was paralysed. Complete authority lay in the hands of the Army. But to what purpose ? At this same moment in Berlin the volley of Fromm's execution-squad was echoing in the courtyard of the Bendlerstrasse, and Beck's second attempt at suicide had been crowned with success. Elsewhere Commanding General after Commanding General was making the wires ring with grovelling reaffirmation of loyalty to Hitler. At La Roche Guyon, von Kluge had despatched von Stülpnagel to his doom and was drafting his own message of unswerving loyalty and that General Order of the Day which he was to issue to his armies on the morrow : 'The *Führer* lives. The war effort at home and the fighting on the fronts go on. . . . For us there will be no repetition of 1918, nor of the example of Italy.'

The Military Governor of France returned to the Hôtel Raphael shortly after midnight to find an empty triumph awaiting him. The Army was in control of Paris, the SS and SD had been bloodlessly routed, but, over the radio, Ley, Göring and later Hitler himself were giving the final lie to all claims for ultimate success. The revolt had collapsed ingloriously, leaving the conspirators in Paris isolated upon a peak of splendid if precarious victory.

When von Stülpnagel told his fellow conspirators of von Kluge's reaction, there was great dismay. A few considered the possibility of placing the Field-Marshal under arrest and proceeding without him, or of forcing his hand by the immediate execution of Oberg and other of the SS leaders. But these counsels of desperation were rejected. 'If only we had had a little more revolutionary blood in our veins', von Boineburg lamented later. 'But we were too much soldiers and too little revolutionaries.'

The final factor in determining the signal for retreat was the intervention of Admiral Krancke, who had been busily engaged throughout the night in sabotaging the revolt. The Admiral had been in communication with both Doenitz and Keitel at Rastenburg and was satisfied at an early stage that the revolt had failed. His first attempts to contact von Kluge had been evaded, but when about midnight he learned of the arrest of Oberg and the surrender of the SS and SD, he became more truculent, demanding counter-action by the Field-Marshal Commanding-in-Chief, and threatening, in default of such action by the military, to take it himself with his naval units. This threat was repeated to von Boineburg and von Stülpnagel, and with it came the news that Blumentritt was on his way from St.-Germain to assume the duties of Military Governor. It was no longer possible to do anything but retreat. Orders were given for the release of the SS.

Here came sinister anti-climax. Many of the SS officers at Fresnes refused to leave their cells, knowing full well the technique which they themselves had so frequently practised of 'Shot while attempting to escape'. They knew too the hatred and contempt with which they were regarded by the Army and they only consented to resume their freedom after receiving the most positive and explicit assurances of their safety.

The formalities of release took place at a ghostly gathering in the foyer of the Hôtel Raphael as the dawn of July 21 was breaking. Abetz was there and Blumentritt, who arrived half-way through the proceedings, and Admiral Krancke, who did not hesitate to insult von Stülpnagel to his face, but failed to break the General's impenetrable and icy restraint. By contrast, the conduct of Oberg and his Staff was remarkably co-operative. They had not yet recovered from the shock they had sustained at the ease with which they had been rendered powerless, and were clearly anxious to exculpate themselves from any possible charges either of complicity or inefficiency. Moreover they also knew that in the greater issue at stake, the result of the battles in France, the decision would inevitably be against Germany. Defeat was hot-foot upon the way and defeat meant the collapse of the Nazi Power and the liquidation of the Police State. Whereas the Army had more than once proved its resilience and capacity for survival in defeat.

All things considered, therefore, and perhaps because of his old friendship with von Stülpnagel, Oberg judged it expedient to be magnanimous. A face-saving formula was agreed upon by both sides to the effect that the arrests had been carried out as a part of an elaborate sham fight, and this version was duly published in the German official organ, the *Pariser Zeitung*. Champagne was opened ; toasts exchanged. Honour was satisfied.

But this was not the end. At nine o'clock that morning (July 21) the voice of doom called Heinrich von Stülpnagel to Berlin. He left by road, telling his driver to go by way of Verdun. There, in the neighbourhood of 'Morthomme' — where he had commanded a battalion in the First World War — he stopped the car and got out to inspect the old battlefield. He passed out of sight of his driver and of the armed guard, whose presence was necessitated by the frequent ambushes of the French Partisans, and then a shot was heard. They found him floating in the canal, unconscious. But, here again, intention had been better than aim. The shot had passed through one eye and destroyed the sight of the other. But though blind, he lived.

Carried unconscious to the Military Hospital at Verdun, the surgeons operated on him immediately. As he came out of the anaesthetic he cried out the name 'Rommel', a fact which was recorded by a Gestapo officer in attendance beside the bed. He was nursed back to health and, blind and helpless, was placed on trial before the People's Court, whence there was but one sentence. Von Stülpnagel was hanged on August 30.

And what of 'kluger Hans'? His Nemesis was not long delayed. Though his perfervid reaffirmation of loyalty to the Führer gained him a respite, Gunther von Kluge — like Fritz Fromm — had run with the hare and hunted with the hounds too long to merit or achieve survival. He was initially suspect to Hitler, who had long regarded him as 'politically unreliable', despite the many honours showered upon him by his Führer.[1] Also Guderian, who was now acting Chief of the General Staff of the Army, could not forget the rumours which he had heard on July 18 that von Kluge, whom he hated, intended to negotiate a separate armistice agreement on the Western Front, and had presumably passed this information to Hitler.[2] An investigation of von Kluge's conduct in the period immediately preceding the revolt was ordered, but such had been his circumspection that he was completely exonerated — save in the mind of the Führer.

But von Kluge himself knew how deeply he had been implicated, and he knew that many others knew it also. Each day brought evil tidings of the Paris conspirators. Von Stülpnagel in the hospital at Verdun, von Hofacker, von Linstow, of his Staff, and Dr. Horst, Speidel's brother-in-law, were all under arrest and all in a position to inculpate von Kluge if they so desired or even against their will.[3] No wonder the Commander-in-Chief, West, spent sleepless nights; no wonder that, when the time of professional testing came, his nerve and his resilience were unequal to the strain.

[1] See above, p. 530, footnote.

[2] In his evidence before the International Military Tribunal on June 20, 1946, Albert Speer testified that 'as the investigation after July 20 proved, at that time, in his capacity of Commander-in-Chief, West, von Kluge was already planning negotiations with the Western enemies for a capitulation and probably he made his initial attempts at that time' (Nuremberg Record, xvi, 470). There appears, therefore, to have been some doubt or confusion in the minds of the Nazi leaders as to whether von Kluge had been implicated in the actual Putsch of July 20, or whether he was merely guilty of planning 'independent action' to bring about an end of hostilities in the West.

[3] It is said that von Hofacker did, under torture, confess the complicity of von Kluge, Rommel and Speidel, and this, together with von Stülpnagel's mention of Rommel's name in his delirium, caused suspicion to fall on both Field-Marshals. Von Hofacker was hanged on December 20, 1944.

For on July 25, with General Patton's break-through at St.-Lô, came the beginning of that irresistible wave of advance which was to carry the Allied armies into Paris within a month. The gloomy prognostications which von Kluge and Rommel had made to Hitler were now fulfilled, but this was of little satisfaction, consolation or salvation to the wretched Field-Marshal. Out-generalled by the enemy, he was also under continual criticism, direction, and commination from F.H.Q., where to the suspicion of treason in Hitler's mind there was added a brutal contempt for his military incompetence.[1]

Von Kluge was tortured with indecision. He could not make up his mind to the great choice which confronted him. Either he could remain loyal to the ideals of the conspirators and attempt to conclude an armistice agreement in the field with Patton ; or he could remain loyal to the *Führer* and accept unquestioningly the conflicting orders which issued almost hourly from the *Wolfsschanze* ; or he could remain loyal to the professional traditions of the German Army and, disregarding the fulminations of F.H.Q., have adopted an independent strategy within the compass of his depleted forces, which might, according to his Chief of Staff, have extricated at least a part of his army from the catastrophe which later overwhelmed them in the Falaise pocket.[2]   In this conflict of loyalties von Kluge was found wanting. He could not make up his mind to do any of these things.

The end came for him at the very moment when he had reached the point at which he could no longer avoid taking a decision. On August 15 Hitler had forbidden Army Group B to break out of the

[1] This manifestation of suspicion and contempt was demonstrated in the famous occurrence of August 12 when for some hours F.H.Q. were unable to make contact with von Kluge, who had gone forward to confer with Army and Corps Commanders.   The signals unit which accompanied him for communication purposes was knocked out by a direct hit and a radio silence ensued for some hours between the Commander-in-Chief and his own headquarters.   During this period Jodl, on Hitler's instructions, rang up Speidel some thirty times to ask him if there were any possibility of von Kluge having gone over to the enemy.   On his return to La Roche Guyon, the Commander-in-Chief found an order from the *Führer* that he was in future to direct the Normandy battle from the headquarters of the 5th Panzer Army (Speidel, p. 156).   Though Dulles (p. 118, footnote) states categorically that von Kluge made ' a futile attempt to surrender to General Patton's Army Commanders in the Falaise Gap ' and varying versions of this story later appeared in the American press (cf. *Time* Magazine, June 25, 1945), there is no evidence to substantiate it, and subsequent interrogations at Nuremberg and elsewhere indicate that von Kluge's dismissal was not primarily on account of the events of August 12 but because of his failure in preventing his army from being surrounded in the Falaise Gap.   Hitler himself, however, came later to believe this story, for on August 31, when discussing von Kluge's conduct with Keitel, Krebs and Westphal, he stated that he (von Kluge) was actually waiting for an English patrol, but that they missed each other (Gilbert, p. 102).

[2] Speidel, p. 156.

Falaise pocket and that night von Kluge decided to order the retreat himself. But before the necessary orders could be issued, there arrived, unheralded, at La Roche Guyon, a new Commander-in-Chief of the Western Front and of Army Group B, in the person of Field-Marshal Walter Model, who presented to the astounded von Kluge his dismissal and the fatal summons to report himself to Berlin.

This, then, was the end. By this time the fate designed by Hitler for the leaders of the conspiracy had become a matter of history.[1] The alternative before von Kluge was either suicide or slow strangulation. But before he made even this decision he indited a letter to the *Führer*, which was at once an apologia for his failure at Avranches, an assessment of the impossibility of the tasks confronting him, and a reiteration of the advice which he and Rommel had given a month earlier, namely, to make peace as soon as possible :

My *Führer* [the letter concluded], I think I may claim for myself that I did everything within my power to be equal to the situation. In my covering letter to Field-Marshal Rommel's memorandum which I sent you, I already pointed out the possible outcome of the situation. Both Rommel and I, and probably all the commanders here in the West with experience of battle against the Anglo-Americans with their preponderance of material, foresaw the present development. We were not listened to. Our appreciations were NOT dictated by pessimism but from the sole knowledge of the facts. I do not know whether Field-Marshal Model, who has been proved in every sphere, will still master the situation. From my heart I hope so. Should it not be so, however, and your new, greatly desired weapons, especially of the Air Force, not succeed, then, my *Führer*, make up your mind to end the war. The German people have borne such untold suffering that it is time to put an end to this frightfulness.

There must be ways to attain this end and above all prevent the Reich from falling under the Bolshevist heel. The actions of some of the officers taken prisoner in the East have always been an enigma to me. My *Führer*, I have always admired your greatness, your conduct in the gigantic struggle, and your iron will to maintain yourself and National Socialism. If Fate is stronger than your will and your genius, so is Providence. You have fought an honourable and great fight. History will prove that for you. Show yourself now also great enough to put an end to a hopeless struggle when necessary.

I depart from you, my *Führer*, as one who stood nearer to you than you perhaps realized, in the consciousness that I did my duty to the utmost.[2]

[1] See below, pp. 680 *et seq.*
[2] According to Jodl, who was standing next to Hitler when he received von Kluge's letter, he read it in silence and passed it to him without comment (*Nuremberg Record*, xv, 403). Nor was mention of it made at the *Führer* Conference of

Having written this highly characteristic letter and handed it to SS-General Sepp Dietrich for delivery, Field-Marshal von Kluge entered his car and directed his driver to proceed to Metz, *en route* for Berlin. He travelled alone — without even an A.D.C. — and when they reached Metz he was dead. Poison was found in the body. An unworthy career was ended.

(iv) SEQUEL IN IGNOMINY

Adolf Hitler's first reaction on recovering his full senses after the explosion of the bomb in the *Lagebaracke* at Rastenburg was to order a thorough investigation of the circumstances of the *Attentat*. Himmler undertook this in person and it did not require many hours of sleuthing to trace the culpability to Claus von Stauffenberg.

The explosion had clearly not been caused from without or from underneath the hut, as some had first believed. It must, therefore, have come from inside. Keitel remembered the moment of absence before they went across to the *Lagebaracke*; from his death-bed Colonel Heinz Brandt testified that von Stauffenberg had placed the brief-case beside his chair and that he had pushed it farther under the table; Buhle recalled going to look for him in the ante-room just before the explosion; Fellgiebel and Stieff, his fellow-conspirators, admitted that he had tried to put through a telephone call to Berlin immediately after the explosion but had left before the connection could be made; and the guards on the inner and outer barriers gave their stories of his earnest insistence that he must fly at once to Berlin on the orders of the *Führer* and must thus leave F.H.Q., even in defiance of the strict emergency injunction that no one was to do so.

It was on the basis of this overwhelming volume of circumstantial evidence that Himmler telephoned his orders to SS-*Oberführer* Piffräder to proceed to the Bendlerstrasse and effect the arrest of the Chief of Staff of the Home Army as unostentatiously as possible in order to avoid an open scandal with the military. Neither Himmler in Rastenburg nor his subordinates in Berlin were as yet aware that what had occurred in the *Wolfsschanze* was the signal for a full-scale revolt in Berlin. Piffräder was still in ignorance of the fact when he drove up to the War Ministry at half-past five,[1] though by that time it had been in progress for about an hour and a half.

It is not known at what exact hour news of the revolt in Berlin

August 31, 1944, at which Hitler merely stated that 'there are strong reasons to suspect that, had he not committed suicide, he would have been arrested anyway' (Gilbert, p. 101). The *Führer* gave instructions that von Kluge should be buried without military honours.   [1] See above, p. 652.

reached Rastenburg. It is probable that it came from Goebbels, but whatever the source, Hitler at once despatched Himmler by fast plane to the capital with plenary powers to crush the *Putsch* with ruthless severity. It was the subsequent reports, which continued to indicate that the mutiny was on such a small scale, that touched off the *Führer*'s never lightly slumbering hysteria and produced the scene at the tea-party which had so appalled the Italians.[1]

Himmler did not actually reach Berlin much before eight o'clock in the evening of July 20, and when he did arrive he found, somewhat to his chagrin — for there was no love lost between them — that the suppression of the revolt was in full swing under the direction of Goebbels, and it was in the home of the *Gauleiter* of Berlin, in the Hermann Göringstrasse, that Himmler set up the headquarters of his enquiry, sharing perforce some of the authority with his host. He at once delegated to Ernst Kaltenbrunner, the Chief Security Officer of the Reich, the task of rounding up the conspirators and conducting the investigation, and Kaltenbrunner deputed Skorzeny to make the actual arrests.[2]

The guiding principle of these operations was that there was to be no more summary justice. The conspirators were wanted alive, not dead, and, wherever possible, suicides were to be prevented. It was in accordance with these instructions that the second of Fromm's execution squads was halted in the courtyard of the Bendlerstrasse.[3]

All night the interrogations went on in Goebbels' house. Fromm, von Hase, von Helldorf, Hoepner and others were gathered in by Skorzeny and deposited in the Hermann Göringstrasse. Here they were questioned ceaselessly by Himmler and Kaltenbrunner and confined in different rooms in the house, which had become both court-house and prison.[4] By dawn the picture had become clearer, partly as a result of these interrogations but also because of the wealth of documentary material which Skorzeny had seized in the offices of Olbricht and von Stauffenberg. This treasure trove had yielded up not only a list of the proposed members of the provisional government but also the names of those designated as political commissioners and deputy commissioners and as military liaison officers, who were to

---

[1] See above, p. 644.

[2] The investigation soon became so complex that it had to be co-ordinated into a 'Special Commission for July 20, 1944', presided over by SS *Gruppenführer* Müller, the head of the Gestapo, and comprising some 400 officials, divided into eleven groups which in their turn formed two departments. One of these two departmental chiefs, Dr. Georg Kiesel, has left an interesting report — the so-called '*SS-Bericht*' — which was published in the *Nordwestdeutsches Heft*, 1/2, 1947. The reports compiled by this Commission, and submitted by Himmler to Hitler, are the 'RSHA Reports' to which reference has already been made.

[3] See above, p. 662.   [4] Semmler, pp. 137-8.

take over control in the *Wehrkreise* as soon as the *Putsch* had become an established fact.[1]

These discoveries added to the ever-lengthening list of those whose arrests were accomplished within the next twenty-four hours, and enabled the inquisitors to beat down with comparative ease the initial denials and prevarications of their original prisoners. The dimensions of the plot began to be apparent. Previous surveillance of individuals by the Gestapo had not established anything like the extent of the actual ramifications. The number of civilians involved and their positions of authority came in many cases as a surprise to the investigators, as did the degree to which members of the Officer Corps were implicated.

This last factor was the source of considerable complication and difficulty. The *Führer* continued to reiterate a steady scream of demands for the extermination, root and branch, of all those even remotely inculpated in the *Putsch*. They and their families were to be liquidated ; they were to perish as though they had never been born, and their children after them. Such was the savage decree of Adolf Hitler. Now at last he had the royalists [2] and the aristocrats and military caste in the hollow of his hand. He would destroy them utterly, and when that Victory, which had recently eluded him, but in which he still madly and fanatically believed, had crowned his arms with laurel, he would create for the Thousand-Year Reich a new aristocracy and a new military caste devoted to his person and well inculcated with the doctrines of National Socialism.

But it was soon apparent to other and more balanced minds that the moment to choose for this monumental slaughter was not one at which the military fortunes of the Reich were in eclipse. The

---

[1] When the Gestapo searched Goerdeler's rooms in his hotel near the Anhalter Bahnhof they found a variety of incriminating documents, including the draft of his radio address to the German people as Chancellor of the Reich and alternative memoranda to the Western Allies and to the Russians (Kiesel, ' *SS-Bericht* ').

[2] Hitler persisted to the end in believing that the German Crown Prince had been implicated in the plot and that the monarchists were a strong element in the conspiracy (cf. Zoller, p. 186). The fact that among the civilians arrested were the Kaiser's former private secretary Freiherr von Sell, and also Freiherr Kurt von Plettenberg, a member of the Crown Prince's household, strengthened this belief still further. There is, however, no evidence that the Crown Prince was in any way involved in the *Putsch* or that he even knew of the existence of the conspiracy. He had long ceased to be considered as a possible candidate for the throne, for which his son, Prince Louis-Ferdinand, had generally been accepted in principle. As a matter of interest it is possible to establish at least one of the activities of the Crown Prince on the fateful day from the pages of Burke's *Peerage* (London, 1949, p. cclix), wherein it is stated that on July 20, 1944, he granted to the wife of his nephew Prince Wilhelm Viktor of Prussia (son of the Kaiser's third son, Prince Adalbert) the right and title to call herself a Princess of Prussia, she having been born a Countess Hoyos.

Führer required the Army to continue fighting and he required the Officer Corps to lead the troops. Even if mass slaughter were out of the question, the general denigration and consequent alienation of any large part of this still highly influential body of German opinion was to be avoided at all costs. The position and the prestige of the Officer Corps must be safeguarded if the Army was to remain in the field. Certain curbs might indeed be applied. The military must abandon the last vestige of their independence and accept unhesitatingly the Party dogma, but, at least outwardly, the Army, as a part of the *Wehrmacht*, must remain on a footing of equality with the Party and the State in the structure of the Reich, no one of which was subordinate to the other.

Those who realized this fact had to trim their sails between the *Führer*'s savage importunity and the current exigencies of expediency. Certain concessions would have to be made by the Army, and the Officer Corps would have to sustain some pretty severe shocks, but as far as possible a face-saving formula must be found to cover the Honour of the German Officer. It was on this basis that agreement was struck between Martin Bormann, the *Führer*'s deputy in the leadership of the Party, and Colonel-General Heinz Guderian, whom Hitler had recalled from disfavour to become Chief of the General Staff of the Army in succession to Zeitzler.

Directives were issued by Bormann by teleprinter on July 24, to all *Reichsleiter*, *Gauleiter* and *Kreisleiter*, that there was to be no general denigration of the Officer Corps and the military caste as a whole, whose loyalty to the *Führer* was to be assumed as unwavering :

It is the *Führer*'s wish that in the treatment of the events of July 20, 1944, no one should allow himself to attack the Officer Corps, the Generals, the nobility or the Armed Forces as a body or to offer them insults. On the contrary, it must always be emphasized that those who took part in the *Putsch* were a definite and relatively small officers' clique. The investigation ordered by the *Reichsführer*-SS is taking its normal course, a report on the findings will be issued in due course.

It is typical of the impeccable attitude of the German Army that in every *Gau* the *Wehrmacht* commanders did not carry out the orders of the traitors to arrest the *Gauleiter* or *Kreisleiter*. On the contrary, they consulted with the *Gauleiter*, etc., and emphasized the necessity for the closest co-operation between the NSDAP and the *Wehrmacht*.

In any discussion on the attitude of the traitors' clique, the impeccable attitude of the Army and of the *Wehrmacht* as a whole is to be stressed at the same time.

The *Führer* has emphasized meantime and has stated clearly that in particularly critical times executive power within the *Gau* cannot be transferred to the *Wehrmacht* or to any individual General, but in special emergencies, in critical times for our nation, it must remain more firmly than ever in the hands of the *Gauleiter*. Heil Hitler.

M. BORMANN.

For his part, Guderian, in an Order of the Day issued to the Army on July 23, described the conspirators as 'a few officers, some of them on the retired list, who had lost courage and, out of cowardice and weakness, preferred the road of disgrace to the only road open to an honest soldier — the road of duty and honour'. He thereupon pledged to the *Führer* and the German people 'the unity of the Generals, of the Officer Corps and of the men of the Army'.

Thus did the honour of the Officer Corps emerge unsullied from the events of July 20, 1944. Too vital a factor for even Hitler to destroy, it was found necessary to keep them in line by the application of balm to their lacerated feelings. But at what a price ! The Army were required to accept Himmler, whose name stank in the nostrils of every decent officer, as Commander-in-Chief of the Home Army ; they were also required to accept the *Waffen*-SS as equal partners with the Navy and the *Luftwaffe*. On July 24, F.H.Q. announced that *Reichsmarschall* Göring, as the senior officer of the *Wehrmacht*, and in the name of all branches of the armed services, had requested the *Führer* to introduce the Nazi salute into the Army in place of the military salute, 'as a sign of their unshakable allegiance to the *Führer* and of the closest unity between the Army and the Party' ; the *Führer* had been graciously pleased to consent.

In May 1934, as a part of their Pact of Blood with the Nazi Party, the Army had, of their own free-will, agreed to mount the National Socialist insignia upon their uniforms.[1] A month later they had sworn allegiance to Hitler as their Supreme Commander. Now ten years later, in almost cringing subservience, they were compelled to give the Nazi salute. [2]

Five days later the General Staff Corps received its final humiliation :

Every General Staff Officer must be a National Socialist officer-leader (*Nationalsozialistischer Führungsoffizier*), that is not only by his knowledge of tactics and strategy, but also by his attitude to political questions and by actively co-operating in the political indoctrination of younger commanders in accordance with the tenets of the *Führer*,

— so ran a General Order from Guderian, dated July 29.

[1] See above, p. 312.
[2] One of the few important decisions made by Doenitz during his brief tenure of power as Chief of State after the death of Hitler was to restore to the *Wehrmacht* the right to use the old military salute (General Order of May 2, 1945).

In judging and selecting General Staff Officers, superiors should place traits of character and spirit above the mind. A rascal may be ever so cunning but in the hour of need he will nevertheless fail because he is a rascal. I expect every General Staff Officer immediately to declare himself a convert or adherent to my views and to make an announcement to that effect in public. Anybody unable to do so should apply for his removal from the General Staff.

To such a nadir of supine degradation had come the child of Scharnhorst and Gneisenau and Moltke. To such a measure of abasement had attained that corps of whose independence of thought and action Ludendorff, in victory, and von Seeckt, in defeat, had been so justly proud. The Nemesis of power, the destiny which its own ambition and lack of intellectual integrity had shaped, had at last overtaken it. And in how base a guise. There was no longer a man to withstand National Socialism. Their resistance was broken, their first concern was now to save their 'honour' and at the price of their honour they achieved it. Submissively they accepted the status of a puppet and the mission to preach National Socialism. None resigned, none resisted. The futile failure of a few of their number to carry out what all had known to be necessary had left the Corps fawning and frightened; fearful and unwilling to exercise any further claims to mental freedom. So had the mighty fallen. They had tried, in their time, to play God, and had discovered to their cost that God is not mocked.

But the final farce of casuistry was yet to come. On August 4, the Army, 'in order to vindicate its honour', requested its *Führer* and Supreme Commander to carry out as soon as possible a ruthless purge to cleanse it of all criminals who had taken part in the *Putsch* and to hand over the culprits to the people's justice. Hitler accordingly appointed a Court of Honour, consisting of Field-Marshals von Rundstedt (President) and Keitel, Colonel-Generals Guderian, Schroth and Specht, to investigate the conduct of those officers who had been arrested, and who, if found guilty of the charges brought against them, would be expelled from the Army and tried before a People's Court. Immediate expulsion was decreed for those who had subsequently 'acknowledged their guilt themselves by committing suicide',[1] and for those who had 'deserted to the Bolshevists'.[2]

Here indeed was cynical sophistry. In order that their 'honour' should be vindicated the escutcheon of the now incomparably

---

[1] These included Beck, Wagner, von Tresckow, Freiherr von Freytag-Loringhoven and Schrader.

[2] Major Kuhn, of Stieff's staff, and two other members of the conspiracy, had gone over to the Russians.

Führertreu Officer Corps must be cleansed in the blood of their comrades, who, once adjudged guilty of the impious crime of attempting the life of their *Führer*, must be cast out from the body corporate of the Army. The very act of their expulsion was supposed to remove all possible taint of complicity and association from their former colleagues. So, in times past, had the Holy Office of the Inquisition handed over recalcitrant heretics.to the civil authorities for execution, so that the Church might not have blood upon its hands.

The sentence of the Court of Honour transferred the accused to the authority and jurisdiction of the People's Court. It deprived them of the right to wear uniform and exposed them to the bestial cruelties inflicted by the Gestapo upon its victims. It condemned them to the confiscation of braces, belts, neck-ties and false teeth, and to the consequent humiliation of constantly clutching at their trousers in court and of impaired articulation in answering the examination of the judge. Above all, it subjected them, helpless and defenceless, to the pitiless tongue of Roland Freisler, President of the People's Court.

The first batch of offenders, of whose guilt the Army thus Pilate-like washed their hands through the medium of the Court of Honour, included von Witzleben, von Hase, Stieff, Fellgiebel, Hansen, Fritz von der Schulenburg and Peter Yorck von Wartenburg. Of these, von Witzleben, von Hase, Yorck and Stieff, together with Hoepner, who had already been cashiered from the Army in 1942, and three junior officers, Bernardis, von Hagen and Klausing, who had been arrested in the Bendlerstrasse on the night of July 20, appeared before the First Senate of the People's Court on August 7.[1]

The trial took place in the great plenary chamber of the Provincial Court in Berlin,[2] and was 'stage-managed' by the Ministry of Propaganda, who made arrangements for copious newspaper and radio reporting, phonograph recordings and a complete film record of the proceedings.[3]

---

[1] So far as can be ascertained, the records of the Court of Honour (*Ehrenhof*) have not yet been discovered. The proceedings were *in camera* and were considered highly secret, though a few of the members of the Court and their substitutes have broken silence. In the same way, only the stenographic record of the trial of the first group of conspirators before the People's Court has survived (*IMT Document*, PS-3881). The subsequent trials were held *in camera* and no public announcement was made concerning them, except for the sentences passed upon the accused.

[2] After the occupation of Berlin by the Allies and the establishment of quadripartite authority over Germany, the Control Council held its formal monthly sessions in this same chamber.

[3] A complete film record, amounting to hundreds of thousands of feet, was kept of all the trials of the conspirators before the People's Court. This was later captured by the British and American forces and a selection from it was prepared

The chamber itself was a long rectangular room whose only decoration was two busts, one of Hitler, the other of Frederick the Great, and three great swastika banners. Along one side, five tall windows, giving on to the balcony, were slightly open owing to the great heat. A breath of scented air came in from the magnolia trees below, striking a note of sharp contrast to the sordid drama being played within. Across one end of the hall and below the banners sat the judges : Roland Freisler, in his wine-red robe, presiding, flanked on his right by General of Infantry Hermann Reinecke,[1] the Chief of the National Socialist Guidance Staff of OKW, in field-grey uniform, and on his left Councillor Lemmle, of the People's Court, in full scarlet.[2]

By contrast with this magnificence the remaining occupants of the Court appeared drab. In the body of the hall sat about 200 privileged spectators, Party hierarchs, representatives of the *Wehrmacht* and the SS and others. At right angles to the right of the tribunal, opposite the long windows, were the eight defence counsel, assigned by law and in mockery to the accused, in their black gowns and bands, and behind them, each separated from the other by two policemen, the eight accused themselves.

Unshaven, collarless and shabby, they looked what they were, men physically and spiritually broken (had they not suffered the attentions of Walther Huppenkothen ?), men who knew that their doom was sealed, who felt themselves to be upon the threshold of death and whose only prayer was for the boon of a swift ending. At the head of the row, von Witzleben, who seemed to have aged ten years in the last two weeks, sat gazing vacantly into space ; beside him the heavily built Hoepner, in breeches, shirt and cardigan, stared dully around him, his face every now and again twitching nervously. Stiffly erect and tight-lipped, von Hase seemed graven in stone ; while Helmuth Stieff, the hunchbacked 'Poison Dwarf', glanced timidly about the room, from time to time touching his throat and neck, as if in anticipation of the rope.

The proceedings of the trial were, from first to last, a farce ; a mere mockery of justice, designed and exploited to bring the defend-

by OSS, and shown during the course of the proceedings of the International Military Tribunal at Nuremberg. A copy of this film is in the possession of the Foreign Office Library in London, to whose courtesy and kindness the present writer is indebted for seeing it.

[1] Reinecke was later tried before a U.S. Military Tribunal in the case of 'Wilhelm von Leeb *et al.*', and was sentenced to life imprisonment on October 28, 1948.

[2] The other members of the Court were Town Councillor Hans Kaiser and Georg Seuberth, a merchant, with a baker and an engineer as deputy judges.

ants into the lowest depths of humiliation and ignominy. Little evidence was offered and few witnesses called, for all the accused had been taken red-handed in treasonable revolt. The occasion was, however, seized upon by Roland Freisler for a display of the most flagrant intimidation. Hurling cheap and vulgar insults at the accused, taunting them with the indignities of their position, he overwhelmed them with the sheer venomous clangour of his voice, which bore down before it all their half-hearted attempts to rebut the charges.

'You dirty old man, why do you keep fiddling with your trousers ?' the Presiding Judge screamed at von Witzleben as, toothless and mumbling, the ex-Field-Marshal desperately clutched at his waist, his braces having been taken from him ; and when Hoepner objected to being called a *Schweinehund*, Freisler asked if he could suggest a more suitable animal. 'You are a filthy rascal', he shouted at another of the accused. 'You are merely a little pile of filth which has lost all self-respect.'

In face of this storm of abuse, which cut off, almost before it had begun, any connected comment from the dock, it was exceedingly difficult for the accused to make any contribution to the proceedings. And yet it must be admitted that they did not present even that degree of courageous *riposte* which was permitted to them. In addition, their very pliancy played into Freisler's hands. When called upon as the first defendant, von Witzleben attempted to raise his arm in the Hitler salute, which gave the Presiding Judge the chance to yell at him that : 'The Hitler salute is only given by citizens whose honoui is still unimpaired'.

These eight men could have had no illusions as to their position or their future. They knew when they entered the court-room that they were already men condemned to death and that the proceedings of the trial were but play-acting preliminaries to the final grim horror of execution. They were soldiers, all of them, whose physical courage had been tried and proven in battle and who had faced death, even the youngest of them, more than once. Only a fortnight earlier they had been ready to risk all in an attempt to overthrow the Nazi régime, and yet now not one of them could muster up the strength of will to interrupt the flow of Freisler's obscene rhetoric and to make it clear to Germany and to the world — or, if this proved impossible, at least to leave on record — the reasons why they stood in the dock and why they would shortly die.

In his farewell to Fabian von Schlabrendorff on July 21, Henning von Tresckow had said : 'Now everyone will turn upon us and cover us with abuse. But my conviction remains unshaken — we have done the right thing. Hitler is not only the arch-enemy of Germany, he is the arch-enemy of the whole world. In a few hours' time I shall stand before God, answering for my actions and for my omissions. I think I shall be able to uphold with a clear conscience all that I have done in the fight against Hitler. . . . The worth of a man is certain only if he is prepared to sacrifice his life for his convictions.' ('*Der sittliche Wert eines Menschen beginnt erst dort, wo er bereit ist, für seine Überzeugung sein Leben hinzugeben.*')[1] Admittedly this was said immediately before a self-inflicted death, and was not subject to interruption, but had the accused made final pleas half as long or half as vehement, they would have achieved more than by their pitiable attempts to excuse themselves, which merely gave Freisler the opportunity for a series of passionate outbursts on the unassailability of Hitler and of National Socialism.[2]

In this there vied with him not only the Prosecution but also the Defence! Von Witzleben's counsel, for example, a certain Dr. Weissmann, praised to high heaven the *Führer*, the Nazi régime, Freisler himself, and the fairness (*sic*) of the trial, and heaped upon his client a hysterical stream of accusations and cynical insults.

Only the physical fact of conducting a case against eight defendants prolonged the trial into the second day, for the outcome was known from the first. All were condemned to death by hanging, and the pleas of those who sought the bullet rather than the rope were sneeringly rejected.

The end was neither swift nor merciful. Later that same day (August 8) in a small room in the Plötzensee Prison all eight of the condemned men were hanged under circumstances which, though revolting, should nevertheless be remembered.[3] There were two small windows in the room, which had no other lighting. Immediately in front of them eight hooks, similar to those used in butchers'

[1] Schlabrendorff, p. 157.

[2] The civilians who appeared in the subsequent trials were not much more distinguished for their outspokenness. There were, however, outstanding exceptions. Julius Leber, for example, spoke back to Freisler and refused to be intimidated. Count Ulrich Schwerin-Schwanenfeld stung the Presiding Judge into a frenzy of anger by denouncing the murders of which he had been aware 'in Germany and elsewhere', and the little Jesuit priest, the Army chaplain, Father Hermann Wehrle, who had been Freiherr von Leonrod's confessor, sealed his own doom when he fearlessly admitted that he had given the advice that tyrannicide was no crime in the eyes of the Church under certain circumstances.

[3] The following account of the execution is based on that of Hans Hoffmann, the warder in charge of von Witzleben in the Plötzensee Prison, supported by the testimony of another warder and of the camera-man in charge of the film unit, all of whom were eye-witnesses.

Z

shops for hanging up sides of meat, had been screwed into the ceiling. 'It is my wish that they be hanged like cattle', Hitler had said.

Present in the room, in the middle of which stood a table with a bottle of brandy and glasses, were officials of the Court, prison officers, some representatives (it is alleged) of the *Wehrmacht*, the executioner and his assistants, and camera-men from the Reich Film Corporation, for the *Führer* had decreed that the film of the execution was to be shown at the *Reichskanzlei* that same evening. There was no chaplain present.

The prisoners were hanged separately. The first to enter was the sixty-four-year-old Erwin von Witzleben, clad in prison garb and wooden clogs. His bearing throughout was courageous, despite the unnecessarily callous conduct of his guards, who pushed and hurried him into the room. Placed under the first of the meat-hooks, his handcuffs were removed and he was stripped to the waist. A short thin string was placed about his neck with a running noose, the other end of the halter being thrown over the hook and made fast. The old man was lifted up by the executioner's assistants and allowed to fall with the whole weight of his body. Then they took off his trousers and he hung naked and twisting, struggling fiercely and in agony, for the fine cord did not break the neck but only strangled slowly. Yet he did not scream, but only fought with ever weakening strength. It took him nearly five minutes to die.[1]

Within the next half-hour the other seven had displayed the same courage and had been executed with equal brutality. The camera worked without interruption and by the evening Adolf Hitler could see and hear how his enemies had died.[2]

This was but the beginning of a series of similar acts of barbaric horror which continued until the very eve of the collapse of the Third

---

[1] Because of an imperfect knowledge of the circumstances a legend grew up that the accused had been 'hanged on a meat hook', meaning that the hook itself had been inserted beneath the chin of the victim. The present evidence proves conclusively that this was not so, though there is little which can mitigate the horror of the actual proceedings.

[2] The film of the execution has been diligently sought for by British and American Intelligence Officers but without avail. Several copies of it were made and it was intended to show it to select *Wehrmacht* audiences '*pour encourager les autres*'. When it was tried out at one of the Cadet Schools in Berlin, however, the immediate effect on morale was so devastating that this line of propaganda was abandoned. Strict orders were given by both Hitler and Goebbels that all copies of the film should be destroyed lest they should fall into Allied hands and it would appear that these were meticulously obeyed.

Reich.[1] Hitler pursued his relentless policy of revenge as, day by day, the agents of Kaltenbrunner and Skorzeny brought in fresh victims. Fortunate indeed were those men who fell before the impetuosity of Fromm's guilty fear on the night of July 20. Their end was at least merciful, swift and honourable. Those of their comrades who survived were hanged in agony but only after they had been subjected to torture for which a parallel must be sought in the Middle Ages — and at Nuremberg.[2]

One by one nearly all of the leading conspirators were gathered in. Goerdeler, betrayed by a woman for the price of the reward placed upon his head, was hanged with Popitz in the Prinz Albrechtstrasse Prison on February 2, 1945 ; Canaris and Oster were executed in the concentration camp at Flossenbürg a few weeks later (April 9). Von Tresckow had already committed suicide.[3]

Nor was the hatred of the *Führer* directed only against the immediate culprits. In his outburst on the afternoon of July 20, he had said that he would destroy the traitors root and branch, their women and children with them, and only the sheer force of circumstances prevented him from carrying out his threat. The iniquitous system of *Sippenhaft* (arrest because of kinship) was extended mercilessly so that all should be destroyed. At one moment in Buchenwald there were ten members of the von Stauffenberg family, eight Goerdelers, the widow of General von Hammerstein and her daughter, the widow of Caesar von Hofacker and her children, General Hoepner's brother, the sister of Kurt Vermehren and his wife's brother, Count Walther von Plettenberg, and many others, all of whom were marked for death had the tempo of events not been too swift to prevent the massacre.[4]

---

[1] Particularly tragic was the mass execution carried out during the night of April 22/23, 1945, when the Russians were already in the suburbs of Berlin. Some twenty prisoners were being conveyed on foot from the Lehrterstrasse prison to the Gestapo prison in the Prinz Albrechtstrasse. As they passed along the In-validenstrasse they were halted, turned with their faces to the wall and shot in the back of the head. One member of the party escaped in the confusion, but among those who died were Klaus Bonhoeffer, Albrecht Haushofer, Hans John, Franz Kempner, Richard Künzer, Franz Leuninger, Karl Marcks, Wilhelm zur Nieden, Friedrich Perels, Rüdiger Schleicher, and Hans-Ludwig Sierks.

[2] It is of interest that the Gestapo had re-equipped the ancient torture chamber in the Burg at Nuremberg with modern appliances.

[3] The full number of the victims of the purge which followed July 20, 1944, has never been established. According to one estimate it amounted to nearly 5000, of whom over 2000 were officers. This, however, may be considered as considerably exaggerated. A careful search of existing sources has resulted in the list of names to be found in Appendix D. (See below, pp. 744 *et seq.*)

[4] Isa Vermehren, *Reise durch den letzten Akt* (Hamburg, 1947), pp. 152-3 ; Payne Best, pp. 259-60. This group of *Sippenhäftlinge* was transferred from point

686   HITLER AND THE ARMY   PT. III

There was, however, one disclosure in connection with the conspiracy which shook the confidence of even that self-deluded, purblind egotist, Adolf Hitler. The complicity of von Witzleben he had regarded as the frustrated ambition of a military aristocrat ; the defection of von Kluge had caused him to dwell, with the pathos of self-pity, upon the ingratitude of those whose loyalty he had a right to consider as having been 'bought' ; but the case of Erwin Rommel came to him as a distinct shock.[1]

Gradually it emerged from the investigations, the admissions and confessions, amassed by the Gestapo, that Rommel, though he may not have been directly implicated in the responsibility of the events of July 20, had at least given his approval to the general idea of an overthrow of the Nazi régime and had been prepared to take an active part in negotiating a cessation of hostilities in the West, both before and after the Allied invasion. The dossier of evidence, which began with the word 'Rommel', thrown out by von Stülpnagel's subconscious mind as he lay on the operating table at Verdun, had been augmented by the disclosures under torture of Caesar von Hofacker, who in his agony had told in detail of his meetings with Rommel, von Kluge and Speidel, and of his comings and goings between the Hôtel Raphael and the Bendlerstrasse. 'Tell the people in Berlin that they can count on me', he had reported Rommel as saying, and this he had confirmed in his testimony when tried before the People's Court on August 30.

This revelation was reported in all secrecy to Keitel, who at once realized its full importance and its danger. For Rommel was still the popular hero of the German people. His name and his face were known to all, down to the youngest boy and girl. To them — and indeed to the *Führer* — the Field-Marshal had seemed the *beau idéal* of a Nazi General. He had been Hitler's pet soldier and the *Führer* had even forgiven the pessimistic report on the military situation which he had made on July 15, preferring to vent his wrath upon the unfortunate von Kluge, who had merely forwarded the report with a covering letter of approval. Hitler was, in fact, anxiously awaiting the day when Rommel should be sufficiently recovered from

to point as the area of the Reich contracted between the converging battle-fronts. They were eventually liberated by U.S. forces at Niederdorf, in the South Tyrol, on April 28, 1945.

[1] For the following account of Rommel's death the present writer has consulted the Interrogation of Field-Marshal Keitel taken at Nuremberg on September 28, 1945 ; the proceedings against Lieutenant-General Ernst Maisel, before German Courts at Berchtesgaden on November 19, 1948, and at Rosenheim on July 4, 1949 ; and Manfred Rommel's statement on his father's death in the *War Office Intelligence Review* of August 1945 (quoted by Milton Shulman, *Defeat in the West* (London, 1947), pp. 138-9).

his injuries to resume an active command, and Keitel had already written this fact to the Field-Marshal. If then, this *beau sabreur* and military paladin of the Third Reich were now to be haled before the People's Court on a charge of high treason the scandal would indeed shake the foundations of the Nazi edifice, which were already sufficiently assailed by the calamities which had overtaken German arms.

In trepidation Keitel reported the facts of the situation to Hitler, who was at once alive to its dangers. Yet he would not, or could not, forgo his almost oriental blood-lust for revenge and destruction. No man who had lifted his hand against the *Führer* — even to the limited extent to which Rommel had gone — could remain alive. They must be very sure before they acted, said Hitler, but, if the case were proven, Rommel must be made to commit suicide and the real circumstances of his death must be kept secret — even from the highest authorities in the Nazi hierarchy and in the *Wehrmacht*. Keitel acted accordingly. As a preliminary, on September 5, he ordered the removal of General Speidel from the position of Chief of Staff to Army Group B, and his interrogation by the Gestapo. But that wily soldier was the equal in guile and intelligence of even Kaltenbrunner and his colleagues. He admitted nothing and betrayed nothing, and so convincing were his denials that, when his case came before the Court of Honour on October 4, he was acquitted of guilt despite the fact that Keitel informed the Court, just before it was due to deliver its verdict, that in the *Führer*'s opinion the accused was guilty and should be handed over to the People's Court.

Hitler and Keitel, however, were compelled to believe in Rommel's complicity, despite the vindication of Speidel, and on October 12, Keitel summoned General Wilhelm Burgdorff, the Head of Personnel Department of OKW, and entrusted him with a very secret mission. The General was to go to Rommel's house at Herrlingen, near Ulm, and there present him with a letter from Keitel in which was set out the testimony of von Hofacker in so far as it concerned him. If the statements therein were false, wrote Keitel, the Field-Marshal would have nothing to fear from an investigation in Berlin; if, on the other hand, they were true, he would know as an officer and a gentleman what course to pursue.

Keitel also gave to Burgdorff a box of poison ampules and charged him to give Rommel verbal assurance that, should he elect to use them, the *Führer* would promise him a State funeral with full military honours, and that no reprisals would be taken on his family.

Burgdorff, taking his deputy, Lieutenant-General Ernst Maisel, with him, left Berlin by car that afternoon and arrived at Herrlingen two days later.[1] At noon on October 14, having surrounded the house with SS men, they confronted Rommel with the evidence and conveyed to him Keitel's message. He was not long in deliberating his choice. An hour after the arrival of the emissaries he bade farewell to his wife and son and entered one of the waiting cars, followed by Burgdorff and Maisel. They drove for five minutes or so and then stopped; the two Generals got out and discreetly withdrew. A quarter of an hour later Frau Rommel received word from the Wagner-Schale Hospital at Ulm that her husband had been brought in dead, having suffered a sudden cerebral embolism evidently as a result of his original head injuries.[2]

And Hitler kept his word — because it was manifestly in his interest to do so. Frau Rommel and her son Manfred continued unmolested. A glowing order of the day was issued to the troops of Army Group B, in which Model informed them that their former beloved commander had 'died of injuries received on July 17'. And on October 17 the promised State funeral took place at Ulm, at which Field-Marshal von Rundstedt, representing the *Führer*, pronounced the final eulogium.

In later years, when a prisoner of war in England and at Nuremberg, von Rundstedt vehemently asserted that when he delivered this address he was entirely ignorant of the true circumstances of Rommel's death. 'I did not hear these rumours', he declared with emotion before the International Military Tribunal, 'otherwise I would have refused to act as representative of the *Führer*; that would have been an infamy beyond words.'[3] If this were so, his conduct after the State ceremony, when he refused to take any part in the cremation or to return to the house at Herrlingen with the

---

[1] General Burgdorff, who had succeeded as head of the Personnel Department and Chief Adjutant of the *Wehrmacht* to the *Führer* after the death of General Schmundt from wounds received from the bomb explosion of July 20, was with Hitler throughout the fantastic episode of the Chancellery Bunker, where he remained with General Krebs, the last acting Chief of the General Staff, after Hitler's suicide and after all else had fled. It is presumed that he either shot himself or is a prisoner of war in Russia. General Maisel was twice tried by German Courts, and on July 4, 1949, was classified in denazification proceedings as Category II, 'an offender' (as distinct from Category I, 'a major offender', and Categories III, IV and V, 'minor offender', 'follower' and 'exonerated', respectively) and condemned to two years' hard labour.

[2] It is possible that the doctors spoke in good faith, for Burgdorff forbade them to make an autopsy (Speidel, pp. 178-9). Keitel, in his interrogation at Nuremberg, testified that on Hitler's orders he even adhered to the fiction of an embolism in informing Jodl, Göring and Doenitz of Rommel's death.

[3] Von Rundstedt's evidence given on August 12, 1946 (*Nuremberg Record*, xxi, 47). Keitel, in his interrogation of September 25, 1945, confirmed that von Rundstedt did not know of the true circumstances of Rommel's death when he made the funeral oration, and still did not know them to that very day.

other mourners, is the more remarkable. If, on the other hand, he
did know and yet kept up the false mockery of dissimulation when
he might have seized the opportunity for a Mark Antony oration, he
may well have been hag-ridden by remorse and shame. This could
have accounted for the appearance which he gave to the onlookers
of a broken and distracted man.[1]

(v) RETROSPECT

From the evidence now available it is clear that the abortive
Putsch of July 20, 1944, and all that it stood for, was more than a
mere military revolt or a gesture of frustrated ambition. Mr.
Churchill did less than justice to it when he told the House of
Commons that 'the highest personalities in the German Reich are
murdering one another, or trying to, while the avenging armies of
the Allies close upon the doomed and ever-narrowing circle of their
power'.[2] Nor can it be dismissed, as Hitler endeavoured to dismiss
it, as the act of 'a very small clique of ambitious, irresponsible and,
at the same time, criminally stupid officers', who, at the moment of
the nation's direst need had 'emerged in Germany, as in Italy, in
the belief that they could repeat the 1918 stab in the back'.[3] It
was a considerably wider and more complex affair than either of
these statements would imply. It was not a hot-bed of militarist
reaction, but neither was it made up entirely — as some have since
sought to show — of *preux chevaliers, sans peur et sans reproche*.
There were certainly elements of democracy about it — as much to
be found among its aristocratic members as among the Socialist and
Trade Union representatives — but it was certainly not an essentially
democratic movement. The one motive which was common to all
within the conspiracy was a deep desire to save their country from
a catastrophe of cataclysmic proportions and in this, whatever else
they may have been, they were patriots.

While the statements of both Mr. Churchill and Hitler fell short
of the full truth, Mr. Churchill came nearer to it than did the
Führer. It was indeed the closing in of the avenging armies upon
the doomed Reich which had made the revolt possible. For, although
a number of the original leaders of the movement had early realized
the danger to Germany, both moral and physical, from the corroding
evil of the Nazi régime, it was not until fell disaster stared the field
and home commanders in the face that they could be brought to

---

[1] Speidel, p. 180.
[2] *House of Commons Debates*, August 2, 1944, col. 1487.
[3] Hitler's radio speech to the German People on the night of July 20/21, 1944.

share this point of view and to agree to take action — and that only if and when Hitler had been eliminated.

Those who led, and those who participated in, the revolt were prompted by a higher loyalty than fealty to a régime or even to a Leader. In the case of the Generals, their motive was that same almost mystic faith in the Fatherland and the Army which had led Yorck von Wartenburg and Clausewitz to flout Frederick William III in 1813 at Tauroggen, and Hindenburg and Gröner to make their alliance with the Republic in 1918. Beck and von Witzleben were neither more nor less of traitors than these men who, each in their own event, perceived Germany (or Prussia) to be in dire peril and sought to avert it by extraordinary means.

The inevitable defeat of Germany was patent and manifest by 1943. Peace was therefore essential, but there could be no peace while Hitler remained at the head of the State. Hence the continuation of the Nazi régime could but betoken fathomless misfortune for the Fatherland. But it did not seem inconceivable to the leaders of the conspiracy that a new government of the Reich, backed by an army which, though unable to achieve victory, could still mitigate the gravity of defeat by inspiring respect among its adversaries, might achieve some other and more favourable terms for Germany than Unconditional Surrender, even at the risk of incurring the odium for having initiated another 'stab in the back' legend. This was an entirely 'correct' political concept — if a mistaken one, and was certainly inspired by a higher patriotism. There was nothing base about it, nothing dishonourable. It must be said of these men that, though they were by no means all democrats, nor all free from responsibility for the Nazi régime, 'they were the only Germans in all that time who, without prompting from abroad and by their own decision, rebelled against a Government which they had come to recognize as both evil and ruinous. For this, even more than for their courage and self-sacrifice, they deserve honour.' [1]

But, having said this, one is justified in asking what would have happened had they succeeded, and would it have been a 'good thing'?

Success is, of course, a relative term. The *Putsch* of July 20 would have been far from complete success, even had Hitler perished in the explosion in the *Wolfsschanze*. The result would almost certainly have been chaotic. For, though Göring had been officially nominated as the *Führer*'s successor, he had powerful and venomous rivals in Himmler and Bormann, who were also mutually antagonistic. A bitter inner struggle would inevitably have ensued for the leadership of the Party and the Reich.

[1] *The Times* leading article, October 4, 1951.

And even had the *Putsch* succeeded in Berlin, the extension of the authority of the New Government to the Reich as a whole is problematic. There was no guarantee that the *fronde* of Generals who had momentarily seized power could command the obedience and allegiance of the rest of the Army. The nazification of the *Wehrmacht* had gone very far, especially among the junior officers ; how would they have reacted if some fanatical Nazi General had rallied to the standard of the swastika — would they not have brought their swords and their troops to his support ? Moreover, the incorporation of the *Waffen*-SS into the Army, which was an essential prerequisite of the new military organization, would almost certainly have encountered open and violent opposition.

The chances of civil war resulting from the 'success' of the *Putsch* were therefore very great, and, to do the conspirators justice, they had taken these chances into consideration and had decided that the horrors of an internecine struggle were less great than the continued tragedy of war and Nazi oppression. They took their decision to act with their eyes wide open, well knowing what they did.

But, even had all these obstacles been overcome, the chances of survival for the Beck-Goerdeler régime, on the basis of its announced programme and with its existing composition, could only have been very slim. The conspiracy was united by one element only — the desire to overthrow Hitler. They also had in common the desire to save Germany, but here would have arisen one of the first causes of disintegration. For it is almost impossible to imagine a coalition of persons more fundamentally incompatible than those included in the Provisional Government.

The note was predominantly conservative ; for Leber, Leuschner and Kaiser were in reality not far divorced from Goerdeler in their political concepts. But there was little basic common ground between them and the soldiers, who, if the Army had been able to represent itself to the German people as their saviours and liberators, would have exercised increasing influence. There were certain items in the Goerdeler-Beck programme, as for example, the partition of Prussia, which, with memories of the bitter debates in the Weimar National Assembly of 1919, would certainly have encountered fierce opposition from the Army and the Right.

And, moreover, there would have been the personality of Claus von Stauffenberg to be reckoned with. His fascination, his charm, his overwhelming and fierce energy would have played a predominant rôle in moulding the future of the New Germany. And in which direction would he have guided her ? For von Stauffenberg was a many-sided character . the 'white-haired boy' of the General Staff,

who referred to him fondly as 'the future Schlieffen'; the link
between the idealism of the Kreisau Circle and the more practical
considerations of government; the *Bamberger Reiter*, who sought to
combine ethical Socialism with Christian principles and aristocratic
traditions; he was all of these. And in addition, he was free from all
taint of personal ambition or self-seeking pride.

But he was nearer to the fanatic than the statesman. His 'univer-
salism' was that of a firebrand, and his spiritual, mental and physical
make-up that of a revolutionary. He thought and acted as a revolutionary, and, had he succeeded in his revolutionary accomplishment,
there is no reason to believe that he would not have continued in
the same strain. Whatever the results, they would in all probability
have been very different from those which Beck and Goerdeler had
anticipated or hoped for in their preliminary planning for the
Putsch, and there seems to be little doubt that, for better or worse,
Claus von Stauffenberg, and not they, would have been the dominant
force in the New Germany.

It has been frequently deplored in certain circles that the *Putsch*
of July 20 did not succeed and that the Allies were not enabled to
make peace with a 'new Germany'. Certainly pressure would have
been brought to bear on the British and American Governments to
do this had the *Putsch* been successful. The most cogent arguments
in favour of such a possibility are that a conclusion of hostilities in the
summer of 1944 would have resulted in the saving of many thousands
of lives on all fronts and that Germany herself would not have sustained the loss of many of her political leaders, men of probity and
tradition, of ability and strength of character, who perished in the
purge which followed the failure of the *Putsch*.

This is undoubtedly true, but one must not allow a sense of
humanity, nor of historical hindsight, to obfuscate political vision.
To have negotiated a peace with any German Government — and
particularly one which had come into existence as a result of a
military revolt — would have been to abandon our declared aim of
destroying German militarism. It must not be forgotten that this
was the purpose for which the Allies were fighting at that time, as
it had been the purpose for which they had fought and won the
First World War. It could not then have been foreseen that, having
twice defeated Germany in a global war in order to destroy her
military potential, they should later — under the irresistible pressure
of events — be forced, *malgré eux*, to rebuild that same war potential,
to a great extent at their own expense.

Had the Allies succumbed to the temptation to reach a negotiated
peace with a 'new Germany' there would have been no Uncon-

ditional Surrender at Rheims and no formal recognition by the German Army of its Unconditional Defeat. The objectives for which the youth of the world had been sacrificed would not have been fulfilled ; nor would the Allies have provided themselves with the opportunity to draw upon a clean page the blue-print of what they believed should be the future Germany. As has been said before in this book, the fact that the Allies have written what may be adjudged in the future as something woefully wrong upon the blank page — that, as a result of the Soviet menace, it has been found necessary to rearm Germany — cannot be blamed upon those who took the vital decisions in 1944 and 1945.

Then it was necessary to make pragmatically clear to the German people that the disaster which was overwhelming them had been caused by their own blind, abject, unreasoning devotion to Adolf Hitler and the Nazi régime, and the defeat, complete and absolute, of German arms. Had Hitler been assassinated, had the Allies temporized with an anti-Nazi régime, had the German Army remained in being as a combatant force, these objectives would not have been achieved. The squalid suicide in the Chancellery bunker, the stark reality of the ceremony in the schoolhouse at Rheims, were the fit and necessary conclusion to the evil glory of the Third Reich. Martyrdom and immolation would not have achieved the Allies' purpose.

This, however, should not detract from the respect due to those few, who, from an early date, had striven, albeit vainly, against the Nazi tyranny. They gave proof to the world, at any rate, that, among the German people and within the German Army, there still survived men who were not willing to live and die like dumb dogs, but who had the courage to risk their lives in a desperate attempt to free Germany and the world from a régime accursed and perjured.

EPILOGUE

(i)

THE collapse of the revolt of July 20, 1944, marked the end of any form of military resistance in Germany. It marked also the end of a period which had begun with the *Wehrmacht* Crisis of February 1938. Up to that time the Army, as represented by the Officer Corps, had been consistently in the ascendant in politics, reaching the peak of their power in the 'non-political' period of von Seeckt, and thereafter declining in influence when, in the eras of von Schleicher and Hitler, they sought to play politics rather than to dominate them. The Army dominated the Weimar Republic from the very moment of its birth and of their own apparent eclipse in November 1918, to the fantastic circumstances of their contribution to the obsequies of the Republic in January 1933. They sought to dominate the Third Reich in the same manner, and were blindly and confidently under the impression that they were doing so, until the crisis of 1938 humbled their pride and hobbled their power.

Up to 1938 the Army had been the final arbiter of the political destinies of the Reich. They had first supported, and then condoned the overthrow of, the Republic and had made a major contribution to Hitler's coming to power. They had entered into a pact with the Party in order to preserve their privileged status and influence and had, as a result, been guilty of complicity in the Blood Purge of June 30, 1934. Well knowing what they did, they had accepted Hitler as Chief of State and had pledged their loyalty to him personally as their supreme Commander, always with the reservation that at their own good pleasure they could unmake the Caesar they had made.

The Fritsch-Blomberg Crisis had awakened many to the realization of their true position, but of that many there were all too few who were prepared to take action in the cause of their own emancipation. The majority — some because of ambition, some because of the fatal mystic spell of their oath of loyalty, some through fear — elected to continue to support the *Führer*, to submit to the dictates of his 'intuition' and to follow in his train.

From 1938 onwards, however, there was a definite movement

within certain military circles, in conjunction with certain groups of civilians, most of whom had been in opposition far longer, to avoid a war in which it was felt that Germany could not be successful, and later to limit the extent of a war which Germany could not win. The phenomenal successes of Hitler's policies against the force of all professional argument and objection, culminating in the Allied collapse of June 1940, caused all Opposition in Germany to call a halt. The flame of Resistance was but just kept alive by the efforts of a devoted few until a wider interest was rekindled by the fears aroused at Hitler's intention to attack the Soviet Union in 1941, and, later, by the heavy losses sustained as a result of the failure of the German armies to effect a *blitz* victory over the Red forces in the first summer and autumn campaigns.

With the Allied landings in North Africa and the disaster of Stalingrad the number of converts to Opposition became positively embarrassing. Generals who had been foremost in their devotion to Hitler when triumph and success had crowned his criminal efforts now sought to justify their defection by reverting to the primary tradition of the German Army, which had transcended all other loyalties throughout history, that of self-preservation. Fromm and von Kluge and a host of lesser luminaries promised their support for the overthrow of the Nazi régime once someone else had taken the initial step of removing 'the living Hitler'. Rommel was not even interested in this but was mainly concerned in bringing hostilities to an end on the Western Front, so that British, American and German troops could join hands against the Russians.

But neither Fromm nor von Kluge was sufficiently imbued with the true spirit of Resistance to take a risk at the moment of crisis — they never went further than Opposition. Determined action on the part of either or both of these men on July 20 might well have given the conspiracy just that additional lease of life that it needed for success, but instead, the two Commanders-in-Chief blew hot and cold, vacillated to and fro, and finally, and most deservedly, reaped the traditional reward of such Laodicean conduct.[1]

There was no such behaviour after July 20. There was no courage of Opposition left, let alone the courage of Resistance. All that remained was a numbed sense of continuing duty, a duty which all now saw with nightmare clarity was leading swiftly and inevitably to disaster. Yet of all those who realized this truth, so great was the impact of the aftermath of July 20, with its trials and its hangings and its general horror, that none could be found even to raise a voice in respectful criticism of the *Führer*'s genius. Indeed the

[1] Cf. Revelation iii, 14-16.

reverse was true.   All who could do so vied with one another in reaffirming their loyalty and allegiance, grovelling, blind and abject, before their *Führer*.   The Commander-in-Chief, West (France), Field-Marshal Model, sent a glowing message in this vein, and in addition, ordered that Rommel's old command, Army Group B, should have a Nazi political commissar attached to it, and himself requested an SS officer as his personal aide-de-camp.[1]

Under the lash of enforced loyalty which played about their backs, even those who had been thrown into the discard in deference to the *Führer*'s whim now reappeared from their retirement with desperate protestations of devotion.   Field-Marshal von Brauchitsch issued a published statement condemning the *Putsch* of July 20 and welcoming the appointment of Himmler as C.-in-C. Home Army as a sign of the closer co-operation between the Army and the SS ;[2] while Grand-Admiral Raeder posted off to Rastenburg to give his assurances to Hitler in person, and found satisfaction in dressing down the SS officer responsible for the security of the *Wolfsschanze*, because only two days after the attempted assassination, he (Raeder) had been allowed to lunch with the *Führer* alone, with a loaded revolver in his pocket ![3]

It was not until Raeder discovered that his old chief and colleague, Otto Gessler, had been brutally tortured in a concentration camp near Fürstenberg — not indeed until he had visited the former Defence Minister in hospital after his release in March 1945, and had himself seen his scars and his maimed fingers — that he allowed himself to be convinced of the infamy of the Nazi régime.   Some gesture of protest, he felt, was called for from him, and he made it — very secretly he took off his Golden Party Badge.   Such was the honour of the Officer Corps.[4]

Slowly, implacably, relentlessly, the Allied ring tightened about the doomed Reich.   Von Rundstedt's last gamble of the Ardennes offensive (December 1944) was played and countered.   By the end of January 1945 the Russian armies had swept past East Prussia and entered Pomerania and two months later (March 23/24) British and American troops crossed the Rhine.   The German Army had therefore failed in their primary duty ; they had failed to protect the frontiers of the Reich.   For the first time since the Napoleonic era foreign troops fought their way into Germany and spread within the Fatherland that devastation and destruction which German arms had so often caused within the borders of others.

---

[1] Speidel, pp. 170-71.
[2] *Völkischer Beobachter*, August 19, 1944.
[3] Raeder, *My Relationship to Adolf Hitler and to the Party*.   [4] *Ibid.*

Now was the moment when, in accordance with tradition, the German High Command should have compelled a cessation of hostilities in order to preserve the Reich from the horrors of invasion, and indeed it does appear that Guderian made two half-hearted attempts in January and in March, to convince not Hitler but Ribbentrop, Göring and Himmler of the urgent necessity of an immediate armistice in the West. But in vain ; none of these persons, and certainly not Guderian himself, was prepared to make this proposal to the *Führer*, though both Göring and Himmler were now convinced of the inescapable doom which must result from further resistance.[1]

But Hitler, now cloistered in the Chancellery bunker as he had been secluded in the *Wolfsschanze*, was beyond the appeal of mortal man. His mentality had lifted him above normality into a world in which he disposed of the fate of imaginary forces to whom he looked with obdurate faith to raise the siege of Berlin. He 'persisted in behaving as though he was at the head of a vast army, spoke of skeleton formations of disorganized survivors as though they were army corps in full strength, and stormed at his Marshals when, with hopelessly attenuated forces, they failed to carry positions that only the vanished legions of his imagination could have taken. He cared nothing for peace ; he was only concerned with recovering his former empire. The question whether it was arithmetically possible to do so interested him no more than whether it was morally desirable.'[2]

This description, written of Napoleon in the spring of 1814 after the collapse of the peace negotiations at Châtillon-sur-Seine, is equally true of Adolf Hitler a hundred and thirty-one years later in the spring of 1945. His mania for military control had achieved for him the abject and unquestioning obedience of his Generals, but there were no more armies left with which to fight. The abasement of the German Army and their Officer Corps in their otiose and spineless submission to Hitler was now complete. Utter surrender of soul and mind and body had been consummated in utter defeat.

There followed that fantastic episode in the bunker of which so vivid and brilliant an account has been reconstructed by Mr. Trevor-Roper, culminating in the mock Viking's funeral in the shell-swept garden of the Chancellery.

The end thereafter was speedy. Grand-Admiral Doenitz, named as *Führer* by Hitler, at once initiated negotiations with General

---

[1] Boldt, pp. 32-4 ; Guderian, pp. 363-9, 382-5. It was after these conversations with Guderian that Himmler decided to take action himself and, through the agency of Schellenberg, initiated tentative negotiations with Count Folke Bernadotte.

[2] Arthur Bryant, *The Age of Elegance* (London, 1950), p. 89.

Eisenhower for an armistice on the Western Front. The reply was a demand for Unconditional Surrender to all the Allies, and on May 7, at half-past two in the morning, the instrument of Unconditional Surrender was signed at Rheims by a weeping Jodl.[1]

It was the end. There was no negotiation ; there was no haggling. There was no repetition of the conditions of November 1918 when the German High Command was able to disclaim responsibility for the acceptance of the Armistice Conditions. This time there was no doubt that the Nemesis of Power had overtaken the German Army. There was no equivocation about this instrument :

> We, the undersigned, acting by authority of the German High Command, hereby surrender unconditionally to the Supreme Commander, Allied Expeditionary Forces, and simultaneously to the Soviet High Command, all forces on land, sea and in the air, who are at this date under German control.

The proportions of the German defeat were gigantic. For the first time in modern history the entire armed forces of a State, officers, non-commissioned officers and men, became prisoners of war, and for the first time in modern history the national sovereignty of a State ceased to be exercised by its citizens and was thrown into commission under the authority of the Occupying Powers. The position of the German military was, moreover, infinitely more precarious than at the close of the First World War, since President Roosevelt, Mr. Churchill and Marshal Stalin had repeatedly emphasized that it was among the most salient of their war aims that Prussian militarism should be destroyed along with the iniquities of National Socialism, and they were now in a position to make good these statements.

It would be readily understood, therefore, that the Officer Corps, standing on the threshold of extinction, might well await some word of final guidance and farewell from their Supreme Commander. Nor were they disappointed. From his headquarters in Flensburg, the last tenuous capital of the Thousand-Year Reich, Grand-Admiral Doenitz indited his farewell address to the Officer Corps. In it he set out before them the events and circumstances which had necessitated their final humiliation. It was an *apologia pro vita sua*, but it was a great deal more than that.

> Comrades [the Admiral concluded], it must be clear to all of us that we are now fully in the enemy's hands. Our fate before us is dark. What

[1] The Rheims Agreement, signed in the early hours of May 7, 1945, came into force as from 23·01 hours on the following day. This agreement was confirmed and ratified in the final act of capitulation signed by Keitel, Admiral von Friedeburg and Colonel-General Stumpf of the *Luftwaffe* in Berlin on May 9.

they will do with us we do not know, but what we have to do we know very well. We have been set back for a thousand years in our history. Land that was German for a thousand years has now fallen into Russian hands. Therefore the political line we must follow is very plain. It is clear that we have to go along with the Western Powers and work with them in the occupied territories in the West, for it is only through working with them that we can have hopes of later retrieving our land from the Russians. . . .

The most important thing is that we must keep a zealous watch over the greatest boon that has been given us by National Socialism — our unity. Despite to-day's complete military breakdown, our people are unlike the Germany of 1918. They have not yet been split asunder. Whether we want to create another form of National Socialism, or whether we conform to the life imposed upon us by the enemy, we should make sure that the unity given to us by National Socialism is maintained under all circumstances.

The personal fate of each of us is uncertain. That, however, is un-important. What is important is that we maintain at the highest level the comradeship amongst us that was created through the bombing attacks on our country. Only through this unity will it be possible for us to master the coming difficult times and only in this manner can we be sure that the German people will not die.

We must all do our duty and above all we must not resign ourselves. That would be the worst that we could do because nothing could be accomplished thereby — only injury would result. Let us use all our strength for Germany.[1]

Here was a message full of that spirit of vibrant resilience which had sustained the Officer Corps in past defeats. This was the spirit which had carried them through the bitter aftermath of Kolin and Jena and Auerstadt and the *Zusammenbruch* of 1918. The counsel which Doenitz gave them now was similar to that proffered by von Schleicher in December 1918, when, after the fiasco of von Lequis before the *Marstall*, he advised the members of the Corps to return to their homes and wait upon the order of events — but not to resign themselves to acceptance of the prevailing reversal of their fortunes.[2]

But though the spirit of continuing life was the same in 1945 as in 1918, in all other respects the situation was very different. After the First World War Germany still had an Army in being, after the Second it was but the shattered wreck of a once proud host. In 1918

---

[1] The text of this farewell address by Doenitz was found in his desk at Flensburg after the capitulation, and forms part of the captured German documents made available by the Admiralty, to whom the present writer is indebted for its use. There is no evidence that the address was ever delivered publicly, but it is known that the Grand-Admiral did give instructions to the Officer Corps along the lines quoted above, which were scrupulously adhered to.

[2] See above, p. 34.

the Officer Corps still retained a legal as well as an actual existence, but in 1945 all combatants, officers as well as men, became automatically prisoners of war, and the dissolution of the Great General Staff and the Officer Corps had been agreed upon at Potsdam and was subsequently decreed by the Allied Control Council. Nor was the immediate season confederate to the resurgence of these formations. In 1918 the Government of the Reich, precariously held together by Ebert's skill and energy, found itself dependent upon the Officer Corps for its continued existence, and the formation of the Free Corps, composed very largely of officers, was therefore only a matter of time. But in 1945 there was no German Government. The sovereignty of the Reich was exercised by the four Occupying Powers, and it was their armies which kept the peace within its frontiers.

Thus the message conveyed by Doenitz to the Corps must have sounded, despite its note of hope, a note of depressing futurity for the realization of that hope. There could have been no more barren outlook than that of the German officer in 1945, who, with but few exceptions, had mortgaged everything, including his mind and soul, through his unyielding devotion to the Nazi régime. All — even honour — must have seemed lost.

(ii)

And yet within a few years the resurgence of the military tradition was in full flood. By 1949 General Halder was already publicly advancing the theory that, but for being hamstrung by Hitler's interference, the German High Command would, if not have won the war, at least have avoided the magnitude and completeness of the defeat sustained by German arms. The 'stab in the back' had on this occasion been delivered, not by the 'treason' of the Social Democrats but by the 'intuition' of the *Führer* and the inefficiency and corruption of the Nazi régime.

A very little while later and a rival *Dolchstoss* legend had emerged, this time from sources engaged in keeping alive the Hitler myth. According to this it was the dissident elements within the Army, the elements which had promoted and carried out the abortive *Putsch* of July 20, who had stabbed the *Führer* in the back and had, by their persistent defeatism and obstruction, prevented him from carrying his great genius to a triumphant conclusion.[1]

[1] This danger had already been foreseen and warned against by one of the survivors of the conspiracy, a Major Wolfgang Müller, in a pamphlet entitled *Gegen eine neue Dolchstosslüge* (Hanover, 1947).

MAJOR-GENERAL ERNST REMER

It was this lie which was incorporated into the propaganda of the Socialist Reich Party (SRP), a neo-Nazi group founded in 1950 under the leadership of Major-General Ernst Remer, the 'Hero' of July 20, 1944, and Count Westarp, a nephew of the veteran conservative politician. The venomous attacks of this Party on the 'criminals of July 1944' were highly reminiscent of Hitler's early campaign of hate against the 'criminals of November 1918'. Similar also was the intensified and calculated denigration by the SRP of the Bonn régime.[1]

Events played into the hands of the guardians of militarism. The ever-increasing menace of Soviet aggression compelled the Allied Governments, against their will and, perhaps, against their better judgment, to consider the rearmament of Germany as an integral part of the defence of Western Europe.

In so doing they were justified by the gravity of events, and the consequent necessity of taking first things first. Just as in 1939 it was necessary to resist and destroy the immediate threat of Nazi aggression, even at the risk of having to face a similar threat later from Russia, so in 1950 it was necessary to meet the immediate threat of Soviet aggression, even at the risk of incurring a recrudescence of German militarism. There were few who delighted in the prospect of Russia as an ally, though all were grateful for her contribution to the ultimate victory. There are perhaps correspondingly few who view with equanimity the re-creation of German military power, in however limited a degree, but all will welcome the participation of Germany in a system of Western security if by this means the system can be effectively strengthened. In such matters Man is but the prisoner and the plaything of Fate.

But the decisions of the Western Powers in New York and in Brussels in September and December 1950 had their inevitable effect upon those returned warriors in Germany who longed for association, expression — and vindication. Within a year a score or more of ex-servicemen's organizations had made their appearance. By

---

[1] The views of the SRP on general policy have been set forth in a pamphlet by Remer, in which he also stated categorically that he would unhesitatingly repeat his action in putting down the *Putsch* of July 20 if called upon to do so (Otto Ernst Remer, *20. Juli 1944*, Hamburg, 1951). On March 15, 1952, the German High Court at Brunswick sentenced Remer to 3 months' imprisonment for slandering the participants in the *Putsch* of July 20, 1944 as 'traitors'. The SRP was later the subject of an appeal by the Federal Government to the Constitutional Court at Karlsruhe to declare the Party unconstitutional. The Court granted an interim injunction on July 15, 1952, restraining the SRP from propaganda activity pending the rendering of a judgment. Without waiting for the Court's judgment, however, the SRP formally dissolved itself on September 12, 1952. The order for dissolution was issued by the Court on October 23, 1952.

September 1951 it was found necessary by the survivors of the *Generalität* to combine as many of these groups as possible into one federation — presumably on the general principle of *l'union fait la force* — and forthwith there was born the German Soldiers' League — the *Deutscher Soldaten Bund* (DSB) — with which the majority of groups became affiliated.

Much depends upon the development of this re-emergence in the political arena of the field-grey shadow of the German Army, the importance of which has certainly not lessened with the signature of the Bonn Agreement and the EDC Treaty. Questions spring to the mind, and with them memories. What will be the relationship, for instance, of the DSB (or of any other similar body which may succeed it) to the German Defence Force and contribution to the EDC, when that force becomes an accomplished fact? Will it attempt to become a political lobby for the demands of the military upon the Bonn Government? Or will it confine its activities to the care of those ex-service men and their dependants who are not absorbed into the new *Wehrmacht*? Within the answers to these questions lies the solution to the mystery which is the source of much of the apprehension attendant upon even partial German rearmament. *Is* there a new spirit abroad in Germany or is this merely 'where we came in' in the repetitive history of the German Army in politics?

APPENDICES

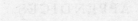

APPENDIX A

TEXT OF DRAFT BASIC LAW PROPOSED BY POPITZ, JESSEN AND VON HASSELL IN 1942

(i) TEMPORARY BASIC STATUTE

[This 'Temporary Basic Statute' and 'Principles for the Execution of the Law regarding the State of Siege'[1] were drawn up by Dr. Popitz, Dr. Langbehn and Professor Jens Jessen, in 1941, as a result of discussions between themselves and with Ambassador von Hassell, State-Secretary Planck and Colonel-General Beck, which took place at frequent intervals from 1939 onwards.]

THE present administration has brought about a state of affairs in which neither constitution nor law exists. The basic principles of the everyday life of Germans, already shaken at the end of the world war, have been completely destroyed contrary to oath and duty. Even the simplest laws of humanity have been disregarded. In order to remove this state of misery and to restore to the German people a state of order befitting its character and history, I, as the holder of executive power and with the agreement of those men who have signified their willingness to form a Government, decree the following law. Its purpose is to unite the Government and the people until such time as, with the co-operation of all sections of the people, the German Reich can be given a final constitution.

Article 1

The following principles are to be put into effect in the relations of all Germans one with another and in the measures taken by the Government and its authorities:

(1) In all human relationships the laws of decency and good morality are to be the supreme law of conduct.

(2) The inviolability of the law, independent administration of justice, security of personal freedom, of the family and of property are to be restored.

(3) As they have done for centuries Christianity and Christian morality shall form the real basis of German life. The undisturbed practice of

---

[1] *Vom andern Deutschland*, pp. 385-96. This document was not included in the English edition of the Hassell Diaries. It is reproduced here in translation by kind permission of Dr. Wolff-Ulrich von Hassell and the Atlantis Verlag of Zürich.

religion will be guaranteed. The recognized Christian religious societies will be corporations within the meaning of public law.

(4) It is the duty of every German to defend the German people and the Reich against interference from outside and against destruction from within. Every German must conduct himself in such a way that the common good is not prejudiced nor the honour of the German name violated.

(5) All sections of the people shall share in the material and spiritual things of life according to their efforts. The community shall be responsible for ensuring a decent standard of living for all those who fulfil their duty to the people and to the State. This includes care of the aged, assistance in sickness and unemployment, and the provision of homes which make possible healthy family life.

(6) In the economic field the responsibility of the private entrepreneur is to be restored. It is the duty of the State to direct Germany's economy as a whole in such a way as to guarantee the people's food supplies and the raising of the standard of living of all classes.

(7) In agriculture, the people's most important source of strength, the aim is to be a distribution of property which will ensure the highest possible production of food required for the national economy. The flight from the land is to be counteracted by raising the general standard of rural life, in particular, by suitable recompense for the work of the rural population and by the improvement of housing conditions.

(8) Schools and educational institutions of all grades are required to give those training for the Civil Service, the Church, the learned professions, art and economy the basis of a scientific and physical training as well as a background of character and morals. Their purpose is the development of a true German culture. In principle education is to be given in institutions of the State or of its provincial authorities. In schools giving a general education religious instruction is an essential part of the curriculum.

(9) The free practice of research, science and art is to be restricted only in so far as is demanded by security at home and abroad and by the reverence due to the spiritual and moral riches of the nation.

(10) The German Army will be based on compulsory military service ; those called upon to be its leaders will be men possessing the qualities of character, mind and morals of the great soldiers of German history. The Army is not only the essential safeguard of peace for the Reich, considering Germany's geographical position, but also a training ground for the spiritual and moral rebirth of the nation.

(11) In accordance with historical development the State requires in the exercise of its functions of authority a Civil Service trained to carry out its tasks. The position of confidence of the latter among the people must be restored. Only such persons as are prepared to give their whole

energy to the service of the State and the people and to devote themselves to their tasks with true patriotism, unselfishness and loyalty may become Civil Servants ; in return the State will guarantee their livelihood and will recognize true merit. Civil Servants will not be appointed to carry out functions which by their nature cannot be distinguished from functions of general economic life.

Article 2

(1) Within the territory of the Reich there shall be only one State power ; that of the Reich.

(2) The inequality of the former *Länder* as regards area, economic and financial resources and also the incompatibility of the constitutional structure of the various provinces of the Reich make a reorganization of the Reich essential. Prussia completes her mission as the architect of the Reich by renouncing the political integration of her provinces.

(3) The Reich will be divided into *Länder* which will at the same time be administrative areas of the Reich and self-governing regional corporative bodies. The division is given in the Appendix.

(4) Under the supervision of the Reich tasks will be transferred to the *Länder* in the exercise of self-administration and self-responsibility which will bring them into active co-operation in the fostering of economy and culture in the areas of the Reich allotted to them. In this they will be the guardians of the precious traditions of the German races and of the former German territories. An equalization of finance and financial burdens for the whole area of the Reich will ensure that in all parts of the Reich self-government capable of fulfilling the allotted tasks can develop.

(5) The head of the *Land* as an administrative area of the Reich will be the *Statthalter* ; at the same time, as Commissioner of the Reich Government he will exercise the supervision of the State over the *Land* as a regional corporative body. The supreme self-governing authority of the *Land* will be the *Landeshauptmann*. The *Statthalter* and the *Landeshauptmann* will each have a *Landrat* as an adviser. In each *Land* there will be a Chamber of Agriculture and a Labour Office.

Each *Land* will form a defence unit under the Commander of the military area ; a military area may include several *Länder*.

(6) The *Länder* will be divided into Government administrative areas, which will be administrative areas of the Reich ; these again will be subdivided into rural and urban areas which will be both administrative areas and regional corporative bodies with self-government.

(7) The Reich Government will fix by decree the time at which the reorganization is to be considered as carried out ; the decision can also be made for parts of the Reich. Until then the present divisions and regulations as to competency are to continue. The budget of the former *Länder*, in particular with regard to the contributions of the former

Länder to the regional corporative bodies incorporated in them will be wound up in the case of Prussia by the Reich Finance Minister direct and by the other competent Ministers, in the case of the other *Länder* by the authorities designated by the Reich Government. The Reich is the legal successor of the former *Länder*. It will transfer appropriate sums from the finances of the former *Länder* to the newly formed *Länder*. The same applies to the provinces of Prussia and to the former *Reichsgaue*.

(8) The provisions of paragraph 1 apply exactly to the three Reich cities.

Article 3

(1) The administration will be carried out either directly by the State authorities or by the authorities of the regional corporative bodies. It is to be carried out in close contact with the people. The business of administration will, under the direction of the central authorities of the Reich, be handed over to a large extent to the authorities of the *Länder*, *Bezirke* and *Kreise* for independent action.

(2) In order to ensure uniformity of administration there will be, besides the Army Commands, the general administrative authorities and the law courts, special State authorities whose sole function will be to administer taxes and customs, the railways and the postal system.

(3) Administrative action which infringes personal freedom or limits the disposal of possessions shall, in so far as the ordinary courts are not competent to deal with it, be subject to review by independent administrative courts.

Article 4

(1) Executive power will be exercised in the name of the Reich by the Head of the State and the Government of the Reich.

(2) The Head of the State and the Government of the Reich will be supported by a Council of State.

Article 5

(1) The Head of the State is the guardian of the principles on which the re-won order in Germany is based.

(2) The Head of the State is the Regent of the German Reich. In his responsibility to God and to the German name he is equally close to Germans of all tribes as the protector of all works of peace and as the first servant of the State.

Article 6

(1) The Reich Government consists of the Reich Chancellor as President and the Reich Ministers.

(2) The Reich Ministers are :

(1) Reich Minister and Minister for Foreign Affairs.
(2)   ,,   ,,   of War.
(3)   ,,   ,,   ,, Interior.
(4)   ,,   ,,   ,, Finance.
(5)   ,,   ,,   ,, Justice.
(6)   ,,   ,,   ,, Agriculture.
(7)   ,,   ,,   ,, Economy and Labour.
(8)   ,,   ,,   ,, Education.
(9)   ,,   ,,   ,, Transport.

(3) On the proposal of the Reich Chancellor the Head of the State can appoint other Reich Ministers with special functions and Reich Ministers without portfolio.

(4) With the agreement of the Reich Government the Reich Chancellor will decree the standing orders of the Reich Government.

Article 7

The duties of the Head of the State are :

(1) To represent the Reich in international affairs.
(2) To exercise supreme command of the Army.
(3) To appoint and dismiss the Reich Chancellor and, at the latter's suggestion, the other Ministers. Before dismissing the Reich Chancellor the Head of the State will seek the advice of the Reich Government which will meet for this purpose under his presidency.
(4) To appoint and dismiss Reich officials and officers ; by an order issued by the Head of the State with the agreement of the Reich Chancellor the task of appointing officers and Reich officials can be transferred to the competent Reich Ministers or other departments of the Army or to the administrative authorities.
(5) The right of pardon.
(6) The conferring of titles, orders and honours.

Article 8

To become valid, all orders and decrees by the Head of the State must be countersigned by the Reich Minister of the department concerned. This counter-signature is not required in the exercise of supreme command over the Army in cases involving purely secret affairs ; this does not include the appointment and dismissal of officers, which must have the counter-signature of the Reich Minister of War.

Article 9

(1) The Reich Government passes laws with the agreement of the Head of State, who draws them up and announces them. Before a law is passed the Reich Government must submit it to the Council of State except in cases where the law cannot be delayed.

(2) The budget will be fixed by law before the beginning of each financial year. The taking up of loans and credits also requires a bill. The proposal for the discharge of the yearly accounts will be made by the Reich Government through the Head of the State after the budget has been examined by the court of auditors and after hearing the views of the Council of State.

Article 10

(1) A Council of State will be formed. It will consist of men who are worthy of the confidence of the people by reason of their achievements, their ability and character. The Reich Ministers and the *Statthalter* are *ex-officio* members of the Council of State. The other members will be appointed by the Head of the State on the advice of the Reich Government for a period of 5 years. In so far as it is not presided over by the Head of the State, the Council of State will be presided over by the Reich Chancellor or a Minister delegated by him.

(2) The Council of State will represent the people as a whole until more stable general conditions of the German people permit of forming a representative Government on a broader basis.

(3) The functions of the Council of State can be seen from Article 9. In addition the Council of State must be consulted before important administrative measures are passed.

Article 11

(1) Reich Ministers, members of provincial Governments, State Secretaries, *Reichsstatthalter* and *Oberpräsident*, Presidents of the Supreme Reich authorities, the Chief of the German police, the chiefs of the ordinary police and security police who were in office before this law came into force will be relieved of their office. The same applies to the Reich Protector of Bohemia and Moravia, the Governor-General of Poland and the Reich Commissioners in the occupied territories. The Reich Defence Council and the offices of Reich Defence Commissioners and supreme Police Chiefs and of the Commissioner for the Four Year Plan will be abolished.

(2) The removal from the Civil Service of unsuitable persons will take place in exact accordance with the Reich Law of April 7, 1933 (*Reichsgesetzblatt* 1933, 1, page 175). Only those whose former performance of

their work shows lack of suitable qualities or who have abused their office will be removed from office. Former membership of the Party is no reason for removal from office. The dismissed Civil Servants will receive a pension in accordance with the Civil Service law of the Reich, if their dismissal was not on disciplinary grounds.

Article 12

There will be no acts of reprisal against officials of the former Government. Sentence will be passed on guilty persons either through criminal proceedings or by disciplinary action.

Article 13

(1) The Party and its organizations will be dissolved. The officials must refrain from any activity forthwith. Uniforms and badges of the Party or its organizations may no longer be worn.

(2) The funds of the Party and its organizations are forfeit to the State, which in suitable cases can hand them over to the regional corporative bodies. Buildings which are the property of the Party can, if suitable, be used to relieve the housing shortage among the population.

(3) The formation of new political associations is forbidden.

Article 14

(1) The Secret Police will be dissolved. Those functions exercised by it which cannot be dispensed with in securing public order will, under the law, be carried out by the authorities of the general administration.

(2) The concentration camps will be abolished. Their inmates will be released. Special provisions will be made regarding the time of the release of the inmates and their re-incorporation into ordinary life.

Article 15

(1) The laws and decrees passed by reason of the laws will remain in force and are to be observed until they are withdrawn or amended. This shall apply with the following provisions :

1. In so far as the laws refer to National Socialist ideology they are to be dealt with according to the principles set forth in Article 1.
2. Powers granted through laws to the Reich Government or to individual Reich Ministers allowing them to supplement the laws generally or to amend them may no longer be exercised.
3. Powers coming within the competence of the *Führer* and Reich

Chancellor by laws and decrees will pass accordingly to the Head of the State or to the Government of the Reich.

4. Provisions for the sterilization or castration of individuals are not to be put into practice until this matter has been finally settled.

5. Section 1, para. 2; Section 1, sentence 4 and para. 2 ; Section 4, para. 1 ; Section 7, para. 4 and Section 71 of the Reich Civil Service Law become void.

6 In so far as the laws and decrees make special provisions for Jews, these provisions are to be suspended until a final settlement is reached. This also applies to the provisions of Section 25 of the Reich Civil Service Law and Section 15 of the Defence Law.

The Reich Government will ensure that over and above the regulations laid down in paragraph 1 German law in all its branches will be brought into agreement with the principles set forth in Article 1.

Article 16

(1) The complete chaos in public life makes it essential to declare a state of emergency until further notice and to hand over executive power to the military authorities. Every German is expected to behave in such a way as to contribute to the restoration of security and order and so to facilitate the early ending of the state of emergency.

(2) During the state of emergency the provisions of the law regarding the state of emergency will apply. This law comes into force simultaneously with the present law.

(ii) PRINCIPLES FOR THE EXECUTION OF THE LAW REGARDING THE STATE OF SIEGE

I

(1) During the state of siege the local military commander is authorized to issue orders to all authorities in his *Bezirk*. As far as circumstances permit he will consult the head of the authority in question before giving orders.

(2) The local military commander will appoint as his adviser a leading official of the general and internal administration. If such a person is not recommended to him by the central authority (the Minister of War, who will obtain the agreement of the Minister of the Interior) he will choose one himself. The former head of the general and internal administration of his *Bezirk* (the *Reichsstatthalter*, the *Oberpräsident*, the Minister of the Interior in the *Länder* with the exception of Prussia and Bavaria) are in general not eligible for this (see II), but in their stead according to their

suitability and political reliability the representative of the aforementioned supreme Head (President of the Government in the case of a *Reichsstatthalter* or *Oberpräsident*) or the President or Vice-President of the Government in the case of a Government. The adviser appointed will be responsible for the whole area of the local military commander whatever his previous sphere of competence. The Reich Minister of War is to be notified of the appointment at once.

(3) The relationship of the local military commander to the legal authorities can be seen from the law relating to the state of siege.

(4) The functions of the former Reich Defence Commissioners pass directly to the local military commander.

(5) As far as is required, the local military commander will appoint a liaison officer to each authority in his *Bezirk* or will depute a representative (an officer or a civil servant) to take charge of the authority; the latter applies in particular to police presidents.

II

(1) The *Gauleiter* of the *Bezirke* are to be forbidden to exercise their functions; this includes cases where the *Gauleiter* is at the same time *Reichsstatthalter*, *Oberpräsident* or a Minister of the *Land*; they are to be denied access to their offices. As a general rule it will be necessary either to place them under house arrest or to take them into protective custody. The same treatment will apply to *Reichsstatthalter*, *Oberpräsident* and to Ministers in *Länder* other than Prussia who are not at the same time *Gauleiter*, if their character does not guarantee a loyal attitude. According to the circumstances of the case this would also apply to other leading officials (Presidents of Governments, Police Presidents, *Landräte* and *Oberbürgermeister*).

(2) *Kreisleiter* are to be dealt with in the same way as *Gauleiter*.

III

(1) The higher leaders of the SS and police will be taken into protective custody at once; their offices will be closed.

(2) Inspectors of the security police are to be debarred from carrying out their duty. This also applies to the leaders of the Secret Police.

IV

The leaders of the propaganda departments will be removed from office. If necessary they will be taken into protective custody to ensure that they do not engage in any activity. It will be expedient to place their offices for the time being under the care of the leading authorities of the general and internal administration.

V

Acts of reprisal by the population against officials of the Party or officials of the former régime are to be suppressed. Persons so threatened are to be taken into protective custody.

VI

Radio stations in the *Bezirk* are to be occupied.

VII

Public utility works in the *Bezirk* (electricity, gas and water works) are to be safeguarded.

VIII

It is not advisable to close down completely postal, telegraph and telephone communications. Nor will there be a general ban on railway travel. Suitable measures (placing agents in the offices) can be taken to supervise the use of postal, telegraph and telephone services by such persons as are likely to cause disturbances, and in particular such persons may be threatened with a ban on the use of postal and telephone services.

IX

(1) The Party and its formations are forbidden to wear badges and uniforms.

(2) Vehicles and petrol in the premises of the Party and its organizations are to be removed.

(3) Officials of the Party and members of its organizations will be required to surrender their arms and jack-boots at once.

(4) Certificates of indispensability of Party officials are to be cancelled.

X

Offices of the SS are to be occupied and if necessary their chiefs taken into protective custody.

XI

Offices of the NSV are to be instructed to carry on their duties for the time being. They will be under the supervision of the *Oberbürgermeister* or the *Landrat*.

XII

(1) To prevent any interruption in the distribution of ration cards, persons who previously carried out this work or co-operated on a voluntary

basis are requested to continue to do so. If necessary they will do so under compulsion.

(2) The same applies to Air Raid Precautions organizations.

XIII

(1) Persons held in custody on political grounds are to be released at once, if there are no special reasons against this. If necessary they will be handed over to the office of the public prosecutor.

(2) Concentration camps are to be occupied, and the guards disarmed. Releases are to be carried out with caution and at first limited to cases in which it can be shown beyond doubt that imprisonment took place contrary to law and reason. In all circumstances prisoners are to be treated humanely. Those released are to be provided with travelling expenses and a living allowance.

XIV

(1) Meetings and demonstrations are to be forbidden ; strikes to be suppressed and persons who incite to strike to be taken into custody and punished.

(2) Care will be taken to see that prisoners of war and foreign workers remain at their places of work for the time being.

XV

(1) In cases where the local military commander's *Bezirk* is adjacent to a foreign country or to a frontier of occupied territory care must be taken to see that the frontiers remain closed, that refugees do not escape into other countries and that no one from outside crosses the frontier into Germany. Exceptions will only be allowed with the approval of the Central authority (Reich Minister of War).

(2) If frontier control officials (frontier police) appear to be unreliable, they are to be replaced by others, if necessary by officers. It may be expedient to transfer their functions, either wholly or in part, to the customs authorities of the Reich Finance administration.

XVI

In all measures, in spite of the severe procedure according to the circumstances of the case, the action taken must be such that the people realize the contrast to the arbitrary methods of the former rulers. Persons taken into protective custody are to be treated humanely ; they are to be released when the purpose of the protective custody has been achieved.

2 A

APPENDIX B

DOCUMENTS OF THE 'FREE GERMANY' COMMITTEE IN MOSCOW, 1943

(i) MANIFESTO TO THE GERMAN ARMY AND GERMAN PEOPLE [1]

EVENTS demand of us Germans immediate decisions. In this hour of greatest danger to Germany's existence and future, the 'Free Germany' National Committee has been formed. It consists of workers and writers, soldiers and officers, Trade Unionists and politicians, men of all political and ideological views, who only a year ago would have thought such a union impossible. The National Committee expresses the thoughts and hopes of millions of Germans at the front and at home, who have the fate of their Fatherland at heart. The National Committee believes that at this fateful hour it is entitled and obliged to speak in the name of the German people, clearly and without reserve, as the situation demands.

Hitler is leading Germany to disaster. At the fronts the defeats of the last seven months are unprecedented in German history; Stalingrad, the Don, the Caucasus, Libya, Tunis. Hitler alone is responsible for these defeats. He is still at the head of the *Wehrmacht* and the Reich. Dispersed over the thousands of kilometres of the front, the German armies stand far from their homes, counting on allies whose fighting value and reliability are always questionable, and exposed to the powerful blows of a coalition which grows stronger week by week. The armies of England and America stand at the gates of Europe. Soon Germany will have to fight on all fronts simultaneously. The weakened German Army, ever more closely encircled by superior enemies, will not be able to hold out long. The day of catastrophe is approaching.

At home, Germany herself has become a theatre of war. Towns, industrial centres and dockyards are being destroyed. Our mothers, our women and children are losing their homes and property. The peasantry is deprived of all rights. The total mobilization is ruining the craftsman and tradesman and robbing the working people of its last sound strength. For years Hitler prepared this war of conquest without asking what was the will of the people. Hitler has isolated Germany politically. He has unscrupulously challenged the three greatest Powers of the world and has united them in relentless struggle against Hitler domination. He has

[1] *Freies Deutschland*, No. 1, of July 19, 1943.

made the whole of Europe the enemy of Germany and has dishonoured her. He is responsible for the hatred which surrounds Germany to-day. No foreign enemy has ever brought us Germans so much misery as Hitler. Facts prove it : the war is lost. Germany can only prolong it at the cost of tremendous sacrifices and hardships. The continuation of this hopeless war would mean the end of the nation. But Germany must not die. For our Fatherland the question is : to be or not to be.

If the German people allows itself to be led further into ruin, without a will of its own and without resistance, then it will become, with every day of the war, not only weaker, but also more guilty. Then Hitler will only be overthrown by the arms of the coalition. That would be the end of our national liberty, of our State. It would mean the dismemberment of our Fatherland and we could not blame anyone for it but ourselves. But if the German people takes heart before it is too late and proves by deeds that it wants to be a free people and is determined to free Germany from Hitler, then it wins the right to decide its fate itself and to be listened to by the world. This is the only way to save the existence, the liberty and honour of the German nation. The German people needs and wants immediate peace. But no one will conclude peace with Hitler. No one will even negotiate with him. Therefore the formation of a truly German Government is the most urgent task of our people.

The formation of a real National German Government is the urgent task of our people. Only such a Government will have the confidence of the people and of its former adversaries. It alone can bring peace. Such a Government must be strong and have the necessary power to render harmless the enemies of the people — Hitler, his patrons and favourites — resolutely to end terror and corruption, to establish firm order and to represent Germany with dignity in the outside world. Such a Government can only be formed as a result of the fighting for liberation by all sections of the German people. It must be based on the fighting groups who are uniting to overthrow Hitler. Those in the Army who are true to the Fatherland and people must play an important part in this. Such a Government will at once stop military operations, recall the German troops to the borders of the Reich, and open peace negotiations, renouncing all conquests. Thus it will achieve peace and bring Germany back into the ranks of the peoples, with equal rights. It alone will make it possible for the German people to express its national will freely and in peace and to work out its state system in sovereignty.

The aim is a free Germany. This means : a strong democratic order which will have nothing in common with the impotence of the Weimar régime, a democracy which will mercilessly suppress any attempt at any new conspiracies against the rights of a free people or against European peace. Full abolition of all laws based on national or racial hatred, of all institutions of the Hitler régime which degrade our people and all measures of the Hitlerite period directed against liberty and human dignity.

Restoration and expansion of the political rights and social achievements of the working people ; freedom of speech, of the Press, of organizations, of conscience and religion ; of economic life, of commerce and trade. The guarantee of the right to work and the right to own lawfully acquired property ; the restoration of property looted by the Fascists to its legal owners ; the confiscation of the property of those guilty of war crimes and of war profiteers ; the exchange of goods with other countries to safeguard a stable national prosperity ; the immediate liberation of victims of the Hitler terror and material compensation for damage caused to them ; the just and merciless trial of war criminals and their accomplices ; an amnesty for all followers of Hitler who by their deeds renounce Hitler in time and join the movement for a free Germany.

Forward, Germans, to the fight for a Free Germany ! We know that sacrifices are inevitable, but the more resolutely the struggle against Hitler is fought, the fewer they will be. The victims in the struggle for Germany's liberation will be a thousand times fewer than the senseless victims of a prolonged war.

(ii) Appeal by the Union of German Officers to the German People and to the Army

(September 14, 1943)

We, Generals, Officers and Soldiers of the Sixth Stalingrad Army who remain alive, address you at the beginning of the fifth year of the war, to point out to our Motherland and our people the way of salvation. All Germany knows what Stalingrad means. We have gone through all the tortures of Hell. They have buried us alive in Germany, but we have risen to a new life. We cannot remain silent. More than anybody else we are entitled to speak, not only in our name, but in the name of our fallen comrades as well, in the name of all the victims of Stalingrad. This is our right and our duty. The painful military and political misfortunes which began this year, and the constantly deteriorating state of German economy force us to admit the hopelessness of the present situation for Germany. Stalingrad was the turning point. It was followed by the Caucasus and the Kuban, by Africa and Sicily, by the breakdown of Italy, one blow following the other. The summer offensive of the German Army fell through ; the Red Army reconquered Orel and Byelgorod, Kharkov, Taganrog, and the Donetz Basin, and is advancing towards the Dnieper. Our Motherland is shaken by the cruellest air raids. A war on two fronts is inevitably approaching. The fall of Mussolini, the dissolution of the Fascist Party, the withdrawal of Italy from the war, the falling out of

Finland, Hungary and Rumania, which can be safely expected : all these are milestones on the way to complete isolation of Germany, an isolation which will be even more ominous than that of 1918. Every thinking German officer understands that Germany has lost the war. The whole of our nation feels that, and it is also understood by the ruling circles, those responsible for all the disasters. Hitler and his régime bear the complete and undivided responsibility before history for the fatal mistakes and miscalculations which will drive Germany to destruction if the people and the Army do not force a complete reversal before it is too late. Hitler as a politician has brought about an invincible coalition of the most powerful States in the world against Germany. Hitler as a strategist has brought the German Army to the most cruel defeats. He threw the German soldier into the 1941–1942 winter campaign without the necessary equipment. With the obstinacy of an ignoramus unable to learn anything, he invented and carried out the adventurous campaign against Stalingrad and the Caucasus. At Stalingrad and in Africa he sacrificed picked German Armies to his prestige. Now the whole of Germany must be saved from the same fate. The war is being continued exclusively in the interests of Hitler and his régime, against the interests of the people and the Motherland. The continuation of the senseless and hopeless war can bring about a national catastrophe any day. It is the moral and patriotic duty of every German who is conscious of the full measure of his responsibility to avert this catastrophe now. We Generals and Officers of the Sixth Army are fully determined to invest with profound meaning the death of our fallen comrades, which was senseless until now. They cannot have died in vain. The bitter lesson of Stalingrad must be transformed into an act of salvation. Therefore we appeal to the people and to the Army. We speak in the first place to the Army chiefs, the Generals and officers of our armed forces ; it depends upon you to take a great decision. Germany expects of you that you will find courage to look truth in the face, and act in accordance, daringly and without delay. Do the thing which is necessary, otherwise it will be done without you, or perhaps even against you. The National Socialist régime can never embark on the only way which can lead to peace. The recognition of this fact orders you to declare war on this disastrous régime and to create a Government founded on the confidence of the people. Only such a Government can create the conditions for an honourable withdrawal of our Motherland from the war, and for a peace which will not be unhappy for Germany and will not carry the germs of other wars. Do not repudiate your historic task. Take the initiative into your hands, the Army and the people will support you. Demand the immediate resignation of Hitler and his Government. Fight shoulder to shoulder with the people to remove Hitler and his régime and to save Germany from chaos and catastrophe. The men of the Sixth German Army, the Stalingrad Army, and all German soldiers and officers who are prisoners of war in Russia, are raising their voices, conscious that by this they are fulfilling their sacred duty to the nation. Long live free, peaceful and independent Germany.

(iii) APPEAL BY 16 CAPTURED GERMAN GENERALS
(*July* 22, 1944)

Generals and Officers of the German Armed Forces, we, generals and commanders of what was up till now the Army Group Centre, united by long common service and participants in two great wars, appeal to you, in an hour fateful for the German people ; the recent fighting and especially the defeat of the Army Group Centre, which has finally determined the outcome of the war, have firmly convinced us of the hopelessness of any further fighting, and, therefore, caused us to send out this appeal.

The truth about the situation on the Eastern Front : Following Bismarck's proven policy, the German people felt relieved when, at the end of August and beginning of September 1939, the non-aggression and friendship pact with the Soviet Union was concluded. To justify the German attack in the summer of 1941, the threat from the Red Army was given as the chief cause. This interpretation is contradicted by the very fact that the Soviet Union only concluded its total mobilization by the winter of 1941. It was even further invalidated by statements made by German propaganda in the spring of 1942, when our successes were supposed to have reached their climax. It was stated openly that the German Eastern Campaign was being waged for economic aims ; the moment when our leaders started the war with Soviet Russia was also the beginning of our decline. We had had only bluff successes — the annexation of Austria and the Sudetenland, the entry into Czech territory (Tschechei) ; with rapid victories we occupied Poland, Denmark, Norway, Holland, Belgium and France. It was only in Russia that we came to know the full gravity of war. Even the summer and autumn victories of 1941, which entailed heavy losses, were mere illusory successes against the border troops and the foremost wave of the Red Army which had to cover the mobilization of the manpower and material forces of the Soviet Union. With our advances, the vast space of Russia also became our enemy.

Then began the visible decline, from the winter of 1941–42. The progress of this deterioration was marked in mounting sequence by the following battles and defeats : (A) Winter of 1941–42, Rostov, Moscow, Tichvin ; reason for these defeats : only now were the first considerable reserves resulting from Russia's total mobilization thrown into battle. However, during the Spring of 1942 we were told that the Red Army had been bled white in these winter battles. (B) Winter 1942–43, the disaster of Stalingrad and the collapse of the whole Caucasus and Don Front; reasons : despite the further increase in the Red Army strength, which was only to be expected, the German High Command launched a concentric attack in the direction of the Caucasian oil-fields and the Lower Volga. It thus split up its forces. The defence of the deep and threatened flank on the Don was mainly entrusted to allied troops without reserves of any importance, these troops being known for their lesser fighting strength and inferior armament. (C) Summer of 1943, the collapse of the German attack on the Kursk-Orel bulge, with heavy losses, followed by a decisive Russian offensive to the Dnieper; reasons : the German attack was launched against the Russian forces massed and assembled for their own offensive. Our best divisions, important for our defence against that offensive, were thus totally smashed. (D) Winter of 1943–44, the destruction of the German Southern Front, loss of the Dnieper line, the Cherkassy encirclement, Kirovograd, Nikopol, Uman, Tarnopol, loss of the Crimea; reasons : our front was no longer firmly anchored. The German forces were continually being outflanked in individual groups and almost smashed. (E) The Russian summer offensive of 1944 against our Army Group Centre, involving the destruction of 30 divisions, in other words almost the whole of the Army Group : the whole of the Fourth Army, the bulk of the Ninth Army and the Third Panzer Army. In these unequal battles 21 generals, including ourselves, were taken prisoner and more than 10 others were killed. Reasons for this renewed defeat : a wrong interpretation of the enemy's strategic possibilities and intentions ; our flank positions threatened ever since the winter ; lack of reserves and *Luftwaffe* support. To put it briefly, the Army Group Centre was sacrificed in a game of chance.

While this is being written, the Russian Armies are approaching the Reich frontier through a gap over 500 km. wide. They stand before Dvinsk and Kaunas, in Grodno, before Brest. They have also launched an attack further south, have crossed the Polish Bug on a wide front, and having encircled several divisions, are close to Lvov. This is the beginning of the inevitable collapse of the Southern Sector. The Army Group North, as far as it has not been affected by the Russian attack on Dvinsk, is static in its positions and runs the risk of being cut off. The German Command has not as yet told the German people about the annihilation of the Army Group Centre. The German *communiqués* and other reports have so far only referred to individual places given up — which are getting closer to the Reich frontier — to shortening of the front line, and systematic disengagement of troops which fight their way to the west to contact our troops. As a matter of fact these troops, as far as they belonged to the Army Group Centre, have long since been encircled, annihilated, or taken prisoner. The *Führer* and German propaganda, however, are trying to conceal the true position on the Eastern Front from the German people, in order to keep it obedient to their attempts to continue the war. The latest radio reports on the attempts on Hitler's life show that the military threat has already developed into a political crisis and that Germany possesses men both able and willing to remove Hitler from command.

'The causes of the defeat': this situation is mainly due to Hitler's mad political and strategic conduct of the war. (A) Hitler failed to recognize the Soviet Union's might from the very beginning. His errors were based on his prejudices. In consequence he declared in 1941 and again in 1942 that victory in the East had already been won. Later he imagined that the Red Army's offensive strength had been finally broken. This mistaken view constituted a repeated betrayal of the people and the Army. (B) The failure of the expected quick success to mature and later the increasing German defeats allowed the Allies so much time that the Second Front has now come into being in France and Italy, in addition to the air war on Germany. Hitler has thus dragged Germany into a war on two fronts, which must lead the Reich to inevitable final defeat. (C) Since 1942, the Red Army had finally robbed the German Command of the initiative. From then on the German Command limited itself to defence and attempts to defend every foot of ground, without reserves worth the name, to delay disaster. Experienced and able generals who found it impossible to reconcile this mistaken and rigid method of warfare with their conscience were dismissed. (D) The best German forces were irrecoverably squandered by such methods. They were neither relieved nor granted rest periods.

Thus Germany, as a result of the political and military policy of Hitler and his immediate followers, realizes, horror-struck, that she is on the edge of the abyss. Over and over again they promised certain victory. They are deceiving the German people by withholding the truths in order to veil their crimes and mistakes. What way out is there? First: Hitler and his immediate followers intend to continue the war, following the slogan: 'Victory or Disaster' (*Sieg oder Untergang*). This slogan proves that they themselves no longer believe in victory. The real situation on the Eastern Front and its final collapse in the immediate future can no longer be ignored. This will not be without effect on the fighting in the West, where the English and Americans will throw in ever fresh forces and weapons. To continue the war in these circumstances means further useless losses and sacrifices; it means that the war will be concluded on German soil and that the German people and their means of existence will be destroyed. Second: the generals and officers aware of their responsibility towards the people can only find a way out by ending the war soon. The soldiers captured with the Army Group Centre are of the same opinion. In his speech on 20th July, after the attempt on his life, Hitler spoke of a 'stab in the back' in 1918. To recall 1918, however, is not foolproof. Then Germany's back was free in the East. The Western Powers were on the verge of exhaustion themselves. To-day our position is much worse. Superior forces are assaulting us on all fronts. Even 1918 left us a chance to rise again, which was only finally spoiled by the increasing immoderation of National Socialist policy. At the moment, there is still a prospect of ending the war before it spreads to the whole of Germany and destroys it. The German people were stabbed in the back long ago, through the political and military policy of Hitler and his close collaborators. It was they who got us into this disastrous situation and thus betrayed us. The whole German people must not be sacrificed to the illusion of an 'end with honour' under the leadership of the men on top. Loyalty to the eternal people must be valued higher than duty to a bankrupt form of Government and its representatives. The duty of the German generals and officers is, therefore: determined separation from Hitler and his circle; refusal to obey orders given by Hitler and his representatives; immediate cessation of hostilities and senseless bloodshed.

These tasks must be explained courageously to the soldiers. The gallant German front-line soldiers have had to bear bravely, with their officers, the results of this impudent leadership. They will remain faithful to the German people. Hitler has now strengthened even further the position of Himmler, his SS and the Gestapo. For the German people's sake, this must not prevent anybody from pursuing unfalteringly the aims mentioned. The possibility that the present leaders would not leave their posts of their own free will had always to be reckoned with. The further course of the war will, however, make Germany's internal position even more acute. All generals and officers who realize their responsibility are faced with an alternative: either to wait until Hitler ruins himself and the German Armed Forces, thus dragging the entire German people with him to the grave, or else to use force against force, to resist Hitler, not to fulfil his orders, to finish Hitler's régime and the war with it. Do not wait until Hitler ruins you. To act against Hitler is to act for Germany.

APPENDIX C

DOCUMENTS OF THE *PUTSCH* OF JULY 20, 1944

(i) GENERAL ORDER TO THE ARMED FORCES OF THE STATE [1]

THE Führer Adolf Hitler is dead.

An irresponsible clique of party leaders, strangers to the front, have tried to exploit this situation and to stab the hard-struggling army in the back in order to snatch power for their own selfish ends. In this hour of supreme danger the Reich Government, for the sake of preserving law and order, has proclaimed a state of military emergency and has entrusted to me both the supreme command of the armed forces and the executive power in the Reich.

In this capacity I issue these orders:

(1) I transfer the executive power, with the right of delegation, to the territorial commanders: in the home territory, to the Commander-in-Chief of the home army, who has been promoted to Commander-in-Chief of the home front; in occupied territories, to the Commanders-in-Chief.

(2) To the holders of executive power are subordinated:

    (*a*) all army units within their districts, and army officers, including the *Waffen*-SS, the Reich Labour Service and the Todt Organization;

    (*b*) the entire civil service of the Reich, the whole security and public order police and police administration;

    (*c*) all officials of branches (*Gliederungen*) of the NSDAP (National Socialist Workers' Party) and associations belonging to it;

    (*d*) lines of communication and supply.

(3) The whole of the *Waffen*-SS is to be incorporated immediately in the army.

(4) The holders of executive power are responsible for the maintenance of order and public security. Any resistance to the military executive power is to be relentlessly suppressed.

(5) In this hour of great peril to our country, close unity in the armed

---

[1] *Revolt against Hitler* (English translation of *Offiziere gegen Hitler*), pp. 96-9. Reprinted by kind permission of Mr. Ian Colvin and Dr. Fabian von Schlabrendorff.

forces and the maintenance of discipline is a paramount necessity. I therefore charge all commanding officers in the army, the navy, and the air force, to give full support to the holders of executive power in the fulfilment of their important duties, and to secure compliance to their orders from all subordinates. To the German soldier a historic task is entrusted. Whether Germany is to be saved will depend upon his energy and morale.

(Signed) VON WITZLEBEN, Field-Marshal
The Commander-in-Chief of the *Wehrmacht*

(ii) GENERAL ORDER TO *WEHRKREIS* COMMANDERS

In virtue of the authority given me by the Commander-in-Chief of the armed forces, I invest the Commanding General with executive power in all military districts. The following immediate measures are to be taken :

(a) Occupation of all transport and communication centres ; all radio amplifiers and broadcasting stations ; all gasworks, power stations and water-works.

(b) To be relieved of office forthwith and placed in secure military confinement : all *Gauleiters*, *Reichstatthalters*, Ministers, Provincial Governors, Police Presidents, all senior SS and Police Chiefs, Heads of the Gestapo, of the SS Administration, and of the Propaganda Bureau, and all Nazi District Leaders. Exceptions only by my command.

(c) The concentration camps are to be seized at once, the camp commandants are to be arrested, the guards to be disarmed and confined to barracks. The political prisoners are to be instructed that they should, pending their liberation, abstain from demonstration or independent action.

(d) If compliance by leaders of the *Waffen*-SS appears doubtful, or if they appear unsuitable, they are to be taken into protective custody, and replaced by officers of the Army.

(e) To deal with all political questions arising from the state of emergency, I attach a political officer to every military district commander.

(f) The executive power must tolerate no arbitrary or revengeful acts. The people must be made aware of the difference from the wanton methods of their former rulers.

(Signed) FROMM, Colonel-General
COUNT STAUFFENBERG

(iii) Appeal to the *Wehrmacht* [1]

German soldiers !

More than four years of the most courageous struggle lie behind you. Millions of your comrades have died on the battlefields of Europe and Asia, in the air and at sea. Hitler's unscrupulous leadership has sacrificed whole armies made up of the flower of our youth in Russia and in the Mediterranean for his fantastic plans of boundless conquest. The wanton use of the Sixth Army at Stalingrad and the senseless sacrifice throw a harsh light on the grim truth. Capable officers who opposed this insane act were removed, the General Staff pushed aside. In spite of your heroism Hitler's self-imagined military genius is driving us to a fatal end.

At home more and more centres of family life and places of work are being destroyed. Already six million Germans are homeless. In the rear corruption and crime, tolerated from the outset and even ordered by Hitler, are assuming tremendous proportions.

In this hour of extreme trouble and danger German men have done their duty before God and the people ; they have taken action and given Germany a leadership of experienced and responsible men.

The man who gave a timely warning, who as [Chief of the General Staff] [2] resolutely opposed this war and for that reason was dismissed by Hitler is [Colonel-General Beck]. For the present he has taken over the leadership of the German Reich and the Supreme Command of the *Wehrmacht*. The Government is composed of tried men from all classes of the nation, from all parts of our Fatherland. It has begun its work.

I have been entrusted with the command (*Oberbefehl*) of the whole *Wehrmacht*. The Commanders-in-Chief on all fronts have put themselves under my orders. The German *Wehrmacht* now obeys my command.

Soldiers ! We must secure a just peace which will make possible for the German people a life of freedom and honour, and for the nations voluntary and fruitful co-operation. I pledge you my word that from now on you will be called upon to make only those sacrifices necessary to achieve this end. All the strength of the nation will now be thrown in only for this task. The senseless squandering of strength, the half measures and tardy decisions which have cost so much human life are at an end.

Wherever you may be, at the front or in the occupied territories I call upon you to observe the laws of unconditional obedience, soldierly discipline and honourable, chivalrous conduct. Whoever has not observed these laws in the past or offends against them in the future will be severely called to account. At home too we are fighting for right and freedom, for decency and purity.

---

[1] *Deutscher Widerstand*, pp. 304-305. Reproduced in translation by kind permission of Dr. Rudolf Pechel and the Eugen Rentsch Verlag of Zürich.
[2] The words in square brackets are inserted.

I expect each one of you to continue to do your duty loyally and bravely. On that depends the fate of our Fatherland, our own and our children's future.

Soldiers ! What is at stake is the continued existence and the honour of our Fatherland, a true community within our own people and with the nations of the world.

[This appeal was to be signed by Field-Marshal von Witzleben.]

(iv) APPEAL TO THE GERMAN PEOPLE [1]

Germans !

In recent years terrible things have taken place before our very eyes. Against the advice of experts Hitler has ruthlessly sacrificed whole armies for *his* passion for glory, *his* megalomania, *his* blasphemous delusion that he was the chosen and favoured instrument of 'Providence'.

Not called to power by the German people, but becoming the Head of the Government by intrigues of the worst kind, he has spread confusion by his devilish arts and lies and by tremendous extravagance which on the surface seemed to bring prosperity to all, but which in reality plunged the German people into terrible debt. In order to remain in power, he added to this an unbridled reign of terror, destroyed law, outlawed decency, scorned the divine commands of pure humanity and destroyed the happiness of millions of human beings.

His insane disregard for all mankind could not fail to bring our nation to misfortune with deadly certainty ; his self-imagined supremacy could not but bring ruin to our brave sons, fathers, husbands and brothers, and his bloody terror against the defenceless could not but bring shame to the German name. He enthroned lawlessness, oppression of conscience, crime and corruption in our Fatherland which had always been proud of its integrity and honesty. Truthfulness and veracity, virtues which even the simplest people think it their duty to inculcate in their children, are punished and persecuted. Thus public activity and private life are threatened by a deadly poison.

This must not be, this cannot go on. The lives and deaths of our men, women and children must no longer be abused for this purpose. We would not be worthy of our fathers, we would be despised by our children if we had not the courage to do everything, I repeat everything, to ward off this danger from ourselves and to achieve self-respect again.

It is for this purpose that, after searching our conscience, we have taken over power. Our brave *Wehrmacht* is a pledge of security and order. The police will do their duty.

[1] *Deutscher Widerstand*, pp. 305-309.

Each civil servant shall carry out his duties according to his technical knowledge, following only the law and his own conscience. Let each of you help by discipline and confidence. Carry out your daily work with new hope. Help one another ! Your tortured souls shall again find peace and comfort.

Far from all hatred we will strive for inward reconciliation and with dignity for outward reconciliation. Our first task will be to cleanse the war from its degeneration and end the devastating destruction of human life, of cultural and economic values behind the fronts. We all know that we are not masters of peace and war. Firmly relying on our incomparable *Wehrmacht* and in confident belief in the tasks assigned to man by God we will sacrifice everything to defend the Fatherland and to restore a lawful solemn state of order, to live once more for honour and peace with respect for the divine commandments, in purity and truth !

Germans !

Hitler's despotism has been broken.

In recent years terrible things have taken place before our very eyes. Not called to power by the German people, but becoming the head of the Government by intrigues of the worst kind, Hitler has confused the minds and souls of the people by his devilish arts and lies and by his tremendous extravagance, which seemed to bring prosperity to all, but which in reality plunged us into debt and want, and has caused fatal disappointment even outside Germany. In order to remain in power, he set up a reign of terror. There was a time when our people could be proud of its honesty and integrity. But Hitler scorned the divine commandments, destroyed the law, outlawed decency and ruined the happiness of millions. He disregarded honour and dignity, and the freedom and lives of other men. Countless Germans, as well as members of other nations, have for years been languishing in concentration camps, submitted to the most terrible torments and often to frightful torture. Many of them have perished. Our good name has been sullied by cruel mass murders. With bloodstained hands Hitler has pursued his madman's course, leaving tears, sorrow and misery in his train.

With deadly certainty his lunatic disregard for all human impulses has brought misfortune to our people, and his self-imagined military genius has brought ruin to our brave soldiers.

In this war the intoxication of power, overweening presumption and the delusion of conquest have reached their epitome. The bravery and devotion of our soldiers have been disgracefully abused. The enormous sacrifices of the whole nation have been senselessly wasted. Against the advice of experts Hitler has sacrificed whole armies to his passion for glory, his megalomania, his blasphemous delusion that he was the chosen and favoured instrument of Providence.

We shall openly state the proofs of the terrible betrayal of the German people and of its soul, of the total suppression of law, of the insult to the noble demand that the good of the community shall come before that of the individual, and the shameless corruption. If anyone still doubts these terrible truths because, as a decent human being, he thinks it impossible that such infamy could be cloaked by high sounding words, the facts will convert him.

This must not go on! We would not be worthy of our fathers, we would be despised by our children if we had not the courage to do everything, I repeat everything, to ward off this frightful danger from ourselves and to regain our self-respect.

Times without number Hitler has broken the oath made to the people ten years ago by violating divine and human law. Therefore no soldier, no civil servant, in fact no citizen is any longer bound to him by oath.

At this time of grave emergency I have taken action along with men from all classes of the people and from all parts of the Fatherland. For the time being I have taken over the leadership of the German Reich and have ordered the formation of a Government under the leadership of the Reich Chancellor. It has begun its work. [Field-Marshal von Witzleben] is in supreme command of the *Wehrmacht* and the commanders-in-chief on all fronts have placed themselves under his orders. These men have joined with me to prevent collapse.

We come before you at a grave moment. We are constrained by our responsibility to God, to our people and its history, by the costly sacrifices of two world wars, by the ever increasing misery at home and by the suffering of other nations, by anxiety for the future of our young people.

The principles and aims of the Government will be announced. They will be binding until the opportunity arises of allowing the German people to make its own decision on this. Our aim is the true community of the people, founded on respect, willingness to help and social justice. We wish to replace self-idolatry by the fear of God, force and terror by law and freedom, lies and self-interest by truth and purity. We wish to restore our honour and with it our standing in the community of nations. With the best of our strength we wish to help to heal the wounds which this war has caused to all nations, and to restore confidence among them.

The guilty ones, who have brought disgrace to our good name and have caused so much misery to us and other nations will be punished.

We wish to end the feeling of hopelessness that this war will go on for ever. We are striving for a just peace which will replace the self-laceration and annihilation of nations by peaceful co-operation. Such a peace can only be based on the respect for the freedom and equal rights of all peoples.

I appeal to all decent Germans, men and women of all families and classes and to the youth of Germany. I rely on the joyous co-operation of the Christian Churches.

Have courage and confidence ! The task is a very heavy one. I cannot and I will not make you empty promises. By hard work we will have to struggle in order once more to make our way forwards and upwards. But we will go this way in decency as free men and again find peace of conscience.

Let each one of you do his duty ! Let each help to save the Fatherland ! [The appeal was to be signed by Colonel-General Beck.]

(v) STATEMENT TO THE PRESS [1]

Germans !

Since this morning, you know what is at stake, you know what our motives and intentions are. The law of extreme self-defence and the duty of self-preservation point the way both to you and to us. Our lot has been not the promised state, firmly and wisely led, but a terrible despotism. The bravery, the courage in dying and the skill of our soldiers have been shamefully abused ; and our homeland has been unscrupulously exposed to misery and destruction.

As the final link in an unnecessary chain of oppression and violation of the law, Hitler in his *Reichstag* speech of April 24, 1942, described all Germans as being as free as the birds, while he claimed for himself the right to overturn every judgment according as he saw fit. Thus he called into being a depth of lawlessness such as was never before known among civilized peoples and which cannot be surpassed. From the proud Germany of equal rights for all he made a powerless community of slaves, in which the citizen had no longer the opportunity to defend himself against injustice.

The holders of the highest honours, even Adolf Hitler himself, have committed, ordered and tolerated countless crimes against the person and against life, against property and honour. Men in high positions have shamelessly enriched themselves from public funds or from money extorted from others, and chief among these is Field-Marshal Göring ! We do not wish to see German honour sullied by such parasites. We do not wish to be led by scroundrels who cannot distinguish between mine and thine, who abuse their positions to lead a sumptuous life in magnificent rooms even in war-time, when the people are suffering, while abroad sons, husbands and sweethearts are fighting and dying and at home the mad destruction of total war rages.

An adventurous foreign policy, thirsting for power, has brought our people to a situation the seriousness of which can no longer be overlooked. Considerations of war prevent us from calling things by their proper

[1] *Deutscher Widerstand*, pp. 309-14.

names. But you know or feel to what pitch we have been brought by unscrupulousness and madness. As soon as the situation allows, we will call upon good men from all classes and from all districts and we will tell you their names ; they will carefully examine everything that has happened and will give you a detailed report on the situation as we found it.

One thing we can tell you now : the structure of the State which was built up on injustice, tyranny, crimes of all kinds, self-interest and lies will be torn down. The corner-stone of the new State will be the sure principles of human life, right and justice, truth, decency, purity, reason, mutual consideration and respect for the nations created by God and their vital interests.

If we do not want a repetition of November 1918, this is the last moment at which we can put this plan into action. In the next few days we shall publicly call to account, irrespective of their position, those who are responsible for the ruin of the State and the people.

Hard work in all walks of life lies ahead. There is no magic formula for stopping the frivolous destruction of all the basic principles of life and gradually restoring them. Together we want to save the Fatherland and restore the fabric of duty and community. We cannot promise any alleviation in ordinary life during the war and during the period of reconstruction. Think what is at stake ! For what do you want to live and die ? What are our soldiers to fight and die for ? For justice, freedom, honour and decency, or for crime, terror, shame and disgrace ? If you answer these questions rightly, there is hope of ending this war, which has developed into a wretched Second World War, in such a way that Germany's vital interests can be preserved.

But this aim is not the only decisive one. The decisive factor for us is that we will no longer tolerate the dishonouring of our people and the sullying of our good name by insolent criminals and liars. For if they carry on their dirty work, then not even our children and our children's children would be able to restore the Fatherland on a healthy basis.

You shall learn of the criminals and the crimes as soon as possible. You yourselves will be in a position to see that terrible things have happened. But we shall also see to it that only just punishment in accordance with the laws is administered. None of you must allow himself to take precipitate action ; for above all feelings of vengeance is the necessity to restore the state of equal rights for all under a just leadership.

Anyone who has an accusation to make on account of some wrong suffered, should make it either himself or through someone he trusts to any authority he thinks fit. It will be the duty of all these agencies to pass on accusations made to them to the new Ministry of Justice, which will see to it that they are dealt with immediately. Each will receive an answer. Only those accusations will be dealt with in which the accuser states his name. All others will go unexamined where they belong : into the wastepaper basket. If the complaint is justified, the proper legal proceedings will be taken ; but in the same way anyone who makes an accusation against his better knowledge will be held responsible ; for we want the honour of our fellow-men and our own moral sense to be taken seriously again.

No one whose conscience is clear need be afraid or worry. The question is not : Party member or not Party member. Away with these distinctions, which have been artificially grafted on to the German way of life ! The question is not : SS, SA or any other organization. The question is : decent or corrupt !

Each must continue to do his duty where he is, obeying only the laws and decrees of the new administration. The fate of our soldiers who are fighting a hard battle depends on each one at home giving of his best. We owe everything to them and to our beloved dead. They, the soldiers and the wounded, must come before all other cares.

It is understandable that you must feel extremely excited at what has at long last taken place. From now on, as far as considerations of war allow, you are again free to give unhampered expression to your thoughts and feelings and to follow the dictates of your own conscience. You yourselves will be responsible that our beloved Fatherland does not suffer by this, for the state of war still imposes restrictions on all of us. We will ensure that everything proceeds in a legal and orderly manner, as demanded by the well-being of the Fatherland.

The inner cleansing of Germany from corruption and crime, the restoration of law and decency regardless of the person, but at the same time without prejudice to those who hold other views can be achieved very quickly and very easily in accordance with the proud traditions of our people, if each makes his contribution. That we can expect from all right thinking men and women, for their personal happiness depends on the restoration of these benefits. Even those who previously thought they could or ought to deny this, are aware of this.

In war-time no one can loosen the fetters of State control of economy. For the present we can only introduce simplifications and attack dishonesty for which State control has prepared the ground. But as soon as possible we will restore freedom and self-administration in economy and in family life, in the small community and in the State.

The most serious aspect is that of foreign policy. Here we must take account of the interests and the wishes of other nations. We do not yet know what will be the attitude of the outside world to us. We have had to act as our conscience told us. But we will tell you the aims we envisage in foreign policy.

We Germans are no more alone in this world than any other nation. We must therefore reconcile ourselves to the best of our ability with the presence, the qualities and the interests of other nations. We are convinced that this reconciliation will not be achieved by force of arms. The more

God has allowed us, through the mental gifts which we owe to him, to make technical developments, the more destructive has war become. It destroys everything which those mental gifts are intended to build up. In the end it consumes itself.

Therefore we desire a peaceful, just settlement of the conflicting interests in the world at present, conflicting interests which are determined not so much by men as by their environment. We are convinced that such a settlement is possible, because, considered calmly, it is in the interests of all nations. It can take place provided the nations respect each other and grant each nation the right to form and administer a State independently. Nations can best advance their physical and spiritual welfare when they work together and thus bring their various forces into a great harmonious whole, which benefits everyone. Such co-operation will lead to trade which will be as untrammelled as possible. With such trade the large and small States have flourished and thriven since the beginning of the nineteenth century. We must restore it as soon as possible. Every thinking person will realize that this restoration cannot take place overnight or without great disturbance. Thinking men of all nations must study how the surest and shortest way can be found which will allow each to attain his vital interests in the best possible way, in so far as he has the firm intention to work hard and to consider the interests of others.

We therefore think it essential to end as quickly as possible further devastation and the further squandering of the national forces of each nation for the work of destruction. Each nation, whether involved in the war or not, will have a multitude of difficulties to overcome to repair the material losses caused by the war.

Such co-operation is possible only if it is built up on a stable system of acknowledged legal principles. Even a simple game cannot be ended without dispute unless each player observes definite rules of the game. How much more impossible is it if nations, living under the most widely differing conditions, will not co-operate in the greatest task of all, namely, the harmonious fusion of all forces. We believe that God wishes this. We therefore regard as the best bulwark to ensure these rules of the game in the life of nations purity of mind ; that moral sense which springs only from religious conviction. We do not forget that these rules need to be formulated and that man's imperfection makes it necessary to entrust them in addition to a protecting power. Recognizing the independence of all States as it has developed in the course of history we are prepared to co-operate in this way in small as well as in big matters.

The quickest possible restoration of an ordered public economy in all countries is essential ; for, without this, stable currencies cannot exist and without them the orderly and regular exchange of goods and services is impossible.

We shall not hesitate to transform these necessities into reality. In doing so we must take into account the facts of this terrible war. But we will see to it that, where foreign territory must still remain occupied, it will be made possible for the countries affected to be self-governing, and the presence of German troops as little of a burden as possible. We know from painful experience how deeply it enters into the soul of every nation to see the soldiers of another power on the sacred soil of their country.

So, not knowing what the attitude of the outside world towards us will be, we must continue the struggle. All of us have bitter experiences behind us. We are men who were accustomed to do our duty even in the most repugnant circumstances. We are men who took over an evil inheritance without complaining about the previous faithless arbiters of our fate. We do not want to lessen our own responsibility or to put ourselves in a better light by putting the blame on others and by slandering them. We wish to return to the language of civilized decency such as was the custom in every self-respecting German family.

We call upon you to practise active self-searching and confidence and to be ready to make sacrifices. Do not hate, help rather! Accomplish the highest good : find the soul of our nation again. Thus you will gain strength to achieve more and to help even more effectively our brave soldiers on land, at sea and in the air. Let us unite with you, knowing in our hearts that no more German blood will be sacrificed to the thirst for power of an incompetent leadership, but only for the defence of our vital interests.

With God for right and freedom and the security of peaceful work!

[This appeal was to be signed by Goerdeler as Chancellor on behalf of the Reich Government.]

(vi) Radio Governmental Statement No. 2 (3rd Version) [1]

The principles on which the Government will be conducted and the aims which we are pursuing have been announced. We make the following statement on this :

(1) The first task is the restoration of the full majesty of the law. The Government itself must be careful to avoid any arbitrary action, it must therefore submit itself to orderly control by the people. During the war this control can only be organized provisionally. For the time being upright and experienced men from all classes and from every *Gau* will be called to form a Reich Council ; we will be accountable to this Reich Council and will seek its advice.

There was a time when we were proud of the integrity and honesty of

[1] *Deutscher Widerstand*, pp. 314-25.

our people, of the security and excellence of German administration of justice. Our grief at seeing it destroyed must be all the greater.

No human society can exist without law, no one, not even those who think they can despise it, can live without it. For each man there comes the moment when he calls upon the law. In His ordering of the universe, in His creation and in His commandments God has given us the need for the law. He gave us insight and power to ensure human institutions within the framework of the law. Therefore the independence, irremovability and security of office of the judges must be restored. We know quite well that many of them acted as they did only under the pressure of extreme terrorization ; but apart from that a strict investigation will take place to find out whether judges committed the crime of misapplying the law. Those guilty will be removed. In order to restore public confidence in the administration of the law, laymen will take part in passing sentence in penal cases. This will also apply to the courts-martial which have been established temporarily.

Justice will be restored. It is not the business of the judge to make new laws. His duty is to apply the law and to do so in the most scrupulous manner. The law shall not be a rigid written code, but it must be definite and clear. It was a crime against the people and against the judge to give the latter vague ideas and so-called ideology as a guiding principle. It is intolerable that men should be condemned when they could not know that what they had done was punishable. In cases where the State has by law declared actions of its own bodies to be exempt from punishment, when in fact these actions were punishable, these exemptions will be cancelled as being incompatible with the nature of the law and those responsible will be called to account.

The law will be applied to all those who have offended against it. The punishment deserved will be meted out to the offenders.

Security of person and property will again be protected against arbitrary action. According to the law only the judge can interfere in these personal rights of the individual which are essential for the existence of the State and for the happiness of men and women.

The concentration camps will be abolished as soon as possible, the innocent released and the guilty brought to justice.

But in the same way we do not expect anyone to carry out lynch justice. If we are to restore the majesty of the law we must energetically oppose personal vengeance, which, in view of the injustices suffered and the wounding of the souls of men, is only understandable. If anyone has a grudge, let him lodge an accusation with whatever public authority he likes. His accusation will be forwarded to the proper quarter. The guilty will be pitilessly punished. But the accusation must be genuine. False accusations will be punished, anonymous accusations will find their way into the wastepaper basket.

(2) We wish to restore the principles of morality in all spheres of private and public life.

Among our people who were once so upright, corruption has been practised by high, and even by the highest, officials of the Nazi Party to an extent never known before. While our soldiers were fighting, bleeding and dying on the battlefields, men like Göring, Goebbels, Ley and company were leading a life of luxury, plundering, filling their cellars and attics, urging the people to endure, and, cowards as they were, avoiding the sacrifice going on around them, both they and their entourage. All evil-doers will be called to account before the full severity of the law, their ill-gotten gains will be taken from them and restored to those from whom they were stolen. But the chief culprits shall pay with their lives and property. All their property and that which they have assigned to their relatives will be taken from them.

The reserved occupations established for political pretexts are abolished. Every man who is fit to fight can prove his worth and his will to endure at the front. We will tolerate no more fireside heroes.

An essential part of the safeguarding of law and decency is decent treatment of all human beings. The persecution of Jews which has been carried out by the most inhuman, merciless and degrading methods and for which there can be no compensation is to cease forthwith. Anyone who thought that he could enrich himself with the assets of a Jew will learn that it is a disgrace for any German to strive for such ill-gotten possessions. The German people truly wants to have nothing more to do with pillagers and hyenas among the creatures made by God.

We feel it as a deep dishonour to the German name that crimes of all kinds have been committed in the occupied countries behind the backs of the fighting soldiers and abusing their protection. The honour of our dead is thereby sullied. There, too, we will see that restitution is made.

Anyone who has taken advantage of the war in these countries to fill his pockets or has departed from the rules of honour will be severely punished.

One of our noblest tasks is to restore the family as the nucleus of the community. For this we need the influence of the home, the power of religion, the co-operation of the Churches. Pure and healthy family life can only be built up on a serious and responsible conception of marriage. Immorality must be attacked if our children are not to be demoralized; for how can parents expect their children to be pure if they themselves do not exercise self-control and show their children the best example? The life of our nation will only recover when there is once more healthy family life.

We want no split in the nation. We know that many entered the Party out of idealism, out of bitterness against the Versailles dictate and its effects and against many national degradations, and others from economic or other pressure. The nation must not be divided according to this. All Germans, who feel and act as Germans, belong together. The only distinction which is to be made is between crime and unscrupulousness on the one hand and decency and integrity on the other. On this basis we will strive with all our might for the inner reconciliation of the people. For only if we remain united on the basis of justice and decency can we survive the fateful struggle into which God has placed our nation.

(3) We declare war on falsehood. The sun of truth shall dispel the thick fog of untruth. Our nation has been most shamelessly deceived about its economic and financial position and about military and political events. The facts will be ascertained and made public, so that everyone can examine them. It is a great mistake to assume that it is permissible for a Government to win over the people for its own purposes by lies. In His order of things God admits no double morality. Even the lies of Governments are short-lived and are always born of cowardice. Success in asserting the position of the nation, the happiness of the people, and the peace of mind of the individual can only be founded on integrity. The truth is often hard ; but a people which cannot bear the truth is lost in any case. The individual can only summon up true strength if he sees things as they are. The climber who underestimates the height of the peak to be scaled, the swimmer who misjudges the distance to be covered, will exhaust his energy too soon. All untrue propaganda shall therefore stop ; that applies first and foremost to the Reich Ministry of Propaganda. The abuse of the propaganda agencies of the *Wehrmacht* must also cease. The living and dying of our soldiers needs no propaganda. It is deeply engraven in the heart of every German wife and mother, in the heart of every German at home.

(4) The freedom of mind, conscience and faith which has been destroyed will be restored.

The Churches will again have the right freely to work for their faith. In future they will be completely separated from the State, because only by being independent and by remaining aloof from all political activity can they fulfil their task. The life of the State will be inspired by Christian thinking in word and deed. For we owe to Christianity the rise of the white races, and also the ability to combat the evil impulses within us. No community either of race or of State can renounce this combat. But true Christianity also demands tolerance towards those of other faiths or free-thinkers. The State will again give the Churches the opportunity to engage in truly Christian activities, particularly in the sphere of welfare and education.

The press will again be free. In war-time it must accept the restrictions necessary for a country in any war. Everyone who reads a newspaper shall know who is behind that paper. The press will not again be allowed to publish lies either deliberately or through carelessness.

By strict jurisdiction the editors will ensure that the rules of decency and of duty towards the welfare of the Fatherland are also observed in the press.

(5) It is, above all, German youth which calls out for truth. If proof of the divine nature of man is needed, here it is. Even the children with their instinctive knowledge of what is true and what is false turn away ashamed and angry from the falseness of the thoughts and words expected of them. It was probably the greatest crime of all to disregard and abuse this sense of truth and with it the idealism of our young people. We will therefore protect it and strengthen it.

Youth and the education of youth is one of our main cares. First and foremost this education will be placed in the hands of the parents and the schools. All schools must implant elementary principles simply, clearly and firmly in the child. Training must again be general, embracing the emotions and the understanding. It must have its roots in the people, and there must be no gulf between educated and uneducated.

Education must again be placed deliberately on the Christian-religious basis, and the Christian laws of the utmost tolerance towards those of other faiths must not be broken. On this basis the educational and training system must again be conducted calmly and steadfastly, and must be protected against constant changes and disturbances.

(6) The administration must be reorganized. Nothing which has proved its value will be abolished. But it is essential to restore at once clear responsibility and the freedom to make independent decisions. Our once so proud administration has become a pile of machines and little machines working to no purpose. No one dares to make an independent and true decision. We will demand just the opposite from the civil servants. They will do right with the greatest simplicity and with little red tape.

The civil servant must again become an example in his whole way of life, official and private ; for the people have entrusted him with public sovereign power. This power may only be exercised by those who are upright, who have acquired the technical knowledge, steeled their character and proved their ability. We will put an end to the civil servants who followed the Party rules. The civil servant shall once again obey only the law and his conscience. He must show himself conscious and worthy of the distinction of being assured of a secure livelihood by the community, while others must struggle for the barest necessities. Secure in his authority and in his rights he must proceed in the ideal endeavour to be worthy of his special position by special devotion to duty.

In order to make it possible for the civil servant to carry out his duties in this loyal way, and to spare the people from having public power exercised by unworthy persons, all appointments and promotions made since

January 1, 1933, are declared to be temporary. Every individual civil servant will in the very near future be examined to find out whether he has offended against the law, against discipline or against the behaviour expected of every civil servant. If this is found to be the case the proper measures will be taken, either by punishment, dismissal or transfer. The Civil Service tribunals will co-operate in this. Temporary civil servants, whose performance does not fulfil the demands of their office, will be transferred to positions for which they are fitted, or if this is not possible, they will be dismissed.

Luxury is out of place in Government offices, but there must be comfort in the home of the individual. Heads of departments are instructed to take the necessary measures at once. Superfluous articles of furniture will be handed over to those who have suffered damage by bombing.

(7) The arrangement of the administration, the proper distribution and fulfilment of public duties are only possible on the basis of a Constitution. A final Constitution can only be drawn up with the agreement of the people after the end of the war. For the front-line soldiers have the right to have a special say in this. So for the time being we must all content ourselves with a temporary Constitution, which will be announced at the same time. We too are bound by this.

Prussia will be dissolved. The Prussian provinces, as well as the other German *Länder*, will be amalgamated into new *Reichsgaue*. The *Reichsgau* will in law again be given a life of its own. To a large extent they will be self-governing. Public duties which are in any way compatible with the unity of the Reich and the systematic conduct of the Reich will be handed over to the self-administration of these *Reichsgaue*, *Kreise* and *Gemeinden*.

In all *Reichsgaue* authority will be exercised on behalf of the Reich by *Reichsstatthalter*, who are to be appointed at once. As far as possible they will grant freedom of activity to the organs of self-government, but at the same time will preserve the unity of the Reich. Elected corporations in the self-governing body will guarantee liaison with the people.

(8) In war-time economy can only be conducted in the form of State control and of control of prices. As long as there is a shortage of essential goods, a freer economy is, as everyone will realize, impossible, unless we want to pass over cold-bloodedly the vital interests of those with smaller incomes. We know quite well how distasteful this economy is, the abuses it fosters and that it does not, as is so often maintained, serve the true interests of the small consumer. For the time being, we can only simplify it, and free it from obscurities and from the confusion of different authorities and from the lack of a sense of responsibility. We will cancel all measures which have interfered too much with the freedom of the individual and which have destroyed livelihood in trade, handicraft, business

industry and agriculture without due consideration or where this was not absolutely necessary.

Furthermore, economy may not be unnecessarily disturbed by State interference nor may the joy of production or the possibilities of creation be stifled (economic freedom shall only be held in check by law, by the safeguarding of the integrity of competition and by decent intentions). In view of our country's poverty in raw materials and the fact that we cannot grow enough to feed ourselves, autarchy is a cowardly denial of the possibility of participating in the goods and services of the whole world by an exchange of services.

The aim of our conduct of economy is that every worker, every employee and every employer shall have a share in the benefits of our economy. It is not a question of establishing free enterprise for the employer and forcing him to struggle in competition. No, the German worker too must and will have the opportunity to take part in a creative capacity in the responsibility of economy, only we cannot free him from the effect of the natural laws governing economy.

Property is the basis of all economic and cultural progress ; otherwise man gradually sinks to the level of the animal. It will therefore be protected not only in the hands of the large, but also in the hands of the small, property owner, who can only call his household goods his own. The abuse of property will be combated just as will the accumulation of capital, which is unhealthy and only increases men's dependence.

The organization of economy will be based on self-administration. The system so far employed of administration from above must cease. What must be done is to restore the beneficial functioning of independent decision and thus the responsibility of the individual. As far as possible the confidence of all, including the workers, in the justice of the organization of economy must be restored.

(9) From this arises the essence of the State policy directed towards equality — social policy. Those who through no fault of their own have fallen upon evil days or who are weak must be protected and given the opportunity of securing themselves against the accidents of this life. The State must also intervene where the interest in acquiring savings (capital) conflicts with the interest of assuring work for those now living. (Such conflicts of interests can arise in times of great political and economic tension. It would be very foolish to overcome them in such a way that only capital, *i.e.* savings, was destroyed. It would please the small saver just as little as it would serve the interests of the people as a whole if, for example, all farms and factories were suddenly without machinery. On the other hand, all these capital goods have no value unless they can be made to serve men living now.) Thus conscientiously and with a sense of responsibility we must find a just compromise, in which each individual knows from the outset that sacrifices must be made by him as well as by others.

In cases where the powers and responsibility of the individual branches of business and industry are not sufficient to make such compromises, all those citizens engaged in business must co-operate and in the last resort a just compromise, laid on the shoulders of the people as a whole, must be assured by the State. In so far as social institutions affect the worker, they will have right to full self-administration.

But we must realize that the State does not have inexhaustible means. Even the State can only exist on what its citizens do and give to it. It cannot give to the individual citizens more than it receives from the efforts of its citizens. We therefore clearly and definitely refuse to make promises of economic well-being. Each of us knows that those who have wasted their savings must work specially hard to regain their accustomed standard of life. Thus it is in the family, in every company and also in the State. Any other idea is foolish. Cheap promises that the State can do everything are irresponsible demagogy. You with your resources are the State. We and the organs of the State are only your trustees. Each of you must stir up his resources. It is obvious that after the enormous devastation of this war we must all make special efforts to work hard to create replacements for clothing, for bombed homes and factories and for destroyed household goods. And finally we want to give our children the possibility of a better life. But we are convinced that we are all capable of doing this if we can again work in justice, decency and freedom.

(10) The basic condition for a sound economy is the organization of public funds. Expenditure must be kept within the real income which the State, the *Gau*, the *Kreis* and the *Gemeinde* can draw from their citizens. Effort, character, renunciation and struggle will be required to restore this order ; but it is the most important and essential basis of an assured currency and of all economic life. The value of all savings depends on it. Without it, foreign trade, on which we have depended for more than a hundred years, is impossible.

Taxes will be considerable ; but we will watch over their careful use all the more strictly. It is more important that the citizen should have the necessities of life than that the administration should provide itself with magnificent establishments and take upon itself duties which are in contradiction to the simple way of life of the individual.

We will also demand the same care from economy, which must again realize that expenditure in the administration only serves the comfort and the needs of the individual but must be borne by all in the shape of higher prices and by workers in the form of lower wages. The cessation of the enormous expenditure of the Party is a beginning of the remedy.

Since 1933 the principle of orderly State economy was forsaken by constant and unscrupulous wasting of funds by increasing debts. It was inconvenient to pretend to the people that the general welfare had been successfully increased by extravagance. This method was in reality contemptible, for it consisted in piling up debts. Therefore, even in war-time when each State is forced to spend enormous sums, we will restore the utmost simplicity and economy in all public services. A real levelling out generally can only take place when this war is over.

We regard the mounting debts of all belligerent and neutral States as an extremely great danger. They threaten currency. After this war every State will be faced with an extremely difficult task. We hope to be able to find ways of paying off the debts if we succeed in restoring confidence and co-operation between the nations.

(11) But we are still at war. We owe all our work, sacrifice and love to the men who are defending our country at the front. We must give them all the moral and material resources which we can summon. We are with them in rank and file, but now we know that only those sacrifices will be demanded which are necessary for the defence of the Fatherland and the well-being of the people, and not those which served the lust for conquest and the need for prestige of a madman; we know too that we will carry on this war until we obtain a just peace, fighting with clean hands, in decency and with that honour which distinguishes every brave soldier. We must all give our care to those who have already suffered in this war.

In our anxiety about the front we must reconcile the necessities with clarity and simplicity. There must be an end of the welter of bombastic orders which are incapable of fulfilment and which to-day demand from industry impossible numbers of tanks, to-morrow aircraft and the next day weapons and equipment. We shall only demand what is necessary and expedient. In contrast to the former despotic tyranny we expect from each who is called upon to carry out an order that he will on his own account point out mistakes and discrepancies.

(12) We gave a warning against this war which has brought so much misery to mankind, and therefore we can speak boldly. If national dignity at present prevents us from making bitter accusations, we will call those responsible to account. Necessary as this is, it is more important to strive for an early peace. We know that we alone are not masters of peace or war; in this we depend on other nations. We must stand firm. But at last we will raise the voice of the true Germany.

We are deeply conscious of the fact that the world is faced with one of the most vital decisions which have ever confronted the peoples and their leaders. God himself puts the question to us whether we wish to live in accordance with the order of justice imposed by Him and whether we wish to follow His commandments to respect freedom and human dignity and help each other or not. We know that this order and these commandments have been gravely violated ever since, in 1914, the nations forsook the blessed path of peace. Now we are faced with the question whether we are willing to turn to good use the bitter experiences we have had to undergo and to turn to reconciliation, the just settlement of interests and the healing of the terrible wounds by working together.

In this hour we must tell our people that it is our highest duty bravely and patiently to cleanse the much dishonoured German name. Only we Germans can and will fulfil this task. Our future, no matter what material form it takes, depends on our doing this pitilessly, seriously and honestly. For God is not there to be appealed to as Providence on each petty occasion, but He demands and ensures that His order and His commandments are not violated. It was a fatal mistake, the origins of which can be traced to the unhappy Versailles dictate, to assume that the future can be built up on the misfortune of other nations, on suppression and disregard of human dignity.

None of us wishes to malign the honour of other nations. What we demand for ourselves we must and will grant to all others. We believe that it is in the interests of all peoples that peace should be lasting. For this international confidence in the new Germany is necessary.

Confidence cannot be won by force or by talking. But whatever the future may bring, we hate the cowardly vilification of our opponents, and we are convinced that the leaders of all States want not only the victory for their own peoples but a fruitful end to this struggle, and that they are ready to alleviate at once with us the inhuman hardships, which affect all peoples, of this total war which was so thoughtlessly started.

[Here would follow an insertion depending on the situation.]

With this consciousness and relying on the inner strength of our people we shall unwaveringly take those steps which we can take towards peace without harm to our people. We know that the German people wants this.

Let us once again tread the path of justice, decency and mutual respect! In this spirit each of us will do his duty. Let us follow earnestly and in everything we do the commands of God which are engraved on our conscience even when they seem hard to us, let us do everything to heal wounded souls and to alleviate suffering. Only then can we create the basis for a sure future for our people within a family of nations filled with confidence, sound work and peaceful feelings. We owe it to our dead to do this with all our might and with sacred earnestness — those dead whose patriotism and courage in sacrifice have been criminally abused. To how many of you who have realized this did the fulfilment of your duty become the most bitter grief of conscience! How much beautiful human happiness has been destroyed in the world!

May God grant us the insight and the strength to transform these terrible sacrifices into a blessing for generations.

APPENDIX D

LIST OF VICTIMS OF JULY 20, 1944

BECK, Colonel-General Ludwig. Chief of the General Staff of the Army, 1935–38. Chief of State designate in event of successful *Putsch* on July 20, 1944. Committed suicide in Bendlerstrasse, July 20, 1944.

BERNARDIS, Lieutenant-Colonel Robert. Hanged August 8, 1944.

BERNSTORFF, Count Albrecht von. Counsellor at German Embassy, London, 1922–33. Shot in Lehrterstrasse Prison, April 24, 1945.

BLUMENTHAL, Major Count Hans Jürgen von. Military liaison officer designate for Wehrkreis II. Executed October 13, 1944.

BOEHMER, Lieutenant-Colonel Hasso. Military liaison officer designate for Wehrkreis XX (Danzig). Hanged in Oranienburg Concentration Camp, March 3, 1945.

BOESELAGER, Colonel Freiherr Georg von. Commander of 3rd Cavalry Brigade. Killed in action, summer 1944.

BOLZ, Eugen Albrecht. Formerly Minister of Justice and Interior and President of the Württemberg State. Member of the Reichstag and of the Executive Committee of the Centre Party. Minister-designate of Education and Religious Affairs in Goerdeler's Provisional Cabinet. Executed January 23, 1945.

BONHOEFFER, Pastor Dietrich. Arrested April 5, 1943. Executed at Flossenbürg Camp, April 9, 1945.

BONHOEFFER, Klaus (brother of Dietrich). Syndikus of Lufthansa. Arrested October 6, 1944. Executed April 22/23, 1945.

BÖRSIG, Ernst-August von. Member of Kreisau Circle. Died in Russian Concentration Camp, September 1945.

BREITBACH-BÜRRESHEIM, Freiherr Randolph von. Died, summer 1945.

BRÜCKLMEIER, Eduard. Counsellor of Legation in Foreign Office. Executed October 20, 1944.

CAMINECCI, Oscar. Executed March 9, 1945.

CANARIS, Admiral Wilhelm. Chief of Military Intelligence, 1934–44. Arrested July 23, 1944. Executed at Flossenbürg Camp, April 9, 1945.

CRAMER, Walter. Textile manufacturer. Director of Stohr A.G. Commissioner-designate for Wehrkreis II (Stettin). Arrested July 22, 1944. Executed November 14, 1944.

DELBRÜCK, Dr. Justus. Son of Hans Delbrück, the eminent historian. Member of the Abwehr. Died in 1945 in a Soviet concentration camp.

DELP, Father Alfred, S.J. Member of the Kreisau Circle. Hanged February 2, 1945.

DIECKMANN, Oberregierungsrat Wilhelm. Executed September 13, 1944.

DOHNA-TOLKSDORF, Major-General Count Heinrich zu. Landowner. Commissioner-designate for Wehrkreis I (Königsberg). Hanged September 14, 1944.

DOHNANYI, Hans von. Reichsgerichtsrat. Member of Abwehr. Hanged in Sachsenhausen Camp, April 9, 1945 (brother-in-law of Dietrich and Klaus Bonhoeffer).

DORSCH, Oberleutnant Hans Martin. Executed March 13, 1945.

DRECHSEL, Captain Count Max Ulrich von. Executed September 4, 1944.

ELSAS, Dr. Fritz. Deputy Bürgermeister of Berlin in 1933. Murdered by guards in Sachsenhausen, January 1945.

ENGELHORN, Lieutenant-Colonel Karl-Heinz (Abwehr). Executed in Brandenburg Prison, October 24, 1944.

ERDMANN, Colonel Hans Otto (Wehrkreis I). Executed September 4, 1944.

FELLGIEBEL, General Fritz Erich. Head of Communications Branch of OKH. Executed September 4, 1944.

FINCKH, Colonel Eberhard. Deputy Chief of Staff to Field-Marshal von Kluge as Commander-in-Chief West, July–August 1944. Hanged in Plötzensee Prison, August 30, 1944.

FLEISCHMANN, Professor Max. Executed summer of 1945.

FRANK, Dr. Reinhold, Rechtsanwalt. Deputy Commissioner-designate for Wehrkreis V (Stuttgart). Arrested July 21, 1944. Executed January 21, 1945.

FREYTAG-LORINGHOVEN, Colonel Freiherr Wessel von. Committed suicide July 26, 1944.

GEHRE, Captain Ludwig. Abwehr. Executed in Flossenbürg Concentration Camp, April 9, 1945.

GLOEDEN, Erich. Engineer-architect. Executed November 30, 1944.

GLOEDEN, Dr. Liselotte. Lawyer (wife of Erich). Executed November 30, 1944.

GOERDELER, Dr. Carl Friedrich. Formerly Oberbürgermeister of Leipzig and Price Commissioner. Chancellor-designate on July 20, 1944. Hanged in Plötzensee Prison, February 2, 1945.

GOERDELER, Dr. Fritz (brother of Carl Friedrich). City Treasurer of Königsberg. Executed March 1, 1945.

GROSCURTH, Colonel Helmuth. Died-as a prisoner in Russia in April 1943.

GROSS, Nikolaus. Formerly Catholic Trade Union Leader. Executed January 23, 1945.

GUTTENBERG, Freiherr Karl Ludwig von. Landowner. Member of the Abwehr. Executed without trial, April 24, 1945.

HABERMANN, Max. Formerly Secretary of the Deutschnationaler Handlungsgehilfenverband and a member of the Nationalist Party. Committed suicide in Gifhorn Prison, October 30, 1944.

HAEFTEN, Lieutenant (Naval Reserve) Hans Bernd von. Counsellor of Legation in the Foreign Office. Executed August 15, 1944.

HAEFTEN, Lieutenant Werner von (brother of Hans Bernd). Lawyer. ADC to Colonel Count Claus von Stauffenberg. Arrested and executed in the Bendlerstrasse, July 20, 1944.

HAGEN, Lieutenant of Reserve Albrecht von. ADC to Major-General Helmuth Stieff. Executed August 8, 1944.

HAHN, Colonel Kurt. Chief of Staff to General Fellgiebel. Executed September 4, 1944.

HALEM, Nikolaus von. Merchant. Abwehr. Executed October 8, 1944.

HAMM, Dr. Eduard. Lawyer. Formerly State Secretary at the Reich Chancellery under Cuno. Committed suicide August 1944.

HANSEN, Colonel Georg. General Staff Officer and Chief of Abwehr I. Hanged in the Plötzensee Prison, September 8, 1944.

HARNACK, Ernst von (son of famous theologian). Prominent Socialist and Regierungspräsident of Merseburg till 1933. Executed March 5, 1945.

HASE, Colonel-General Paul von. Commandant of Berlin, 1940-44. Hanged August 8, 1944.

HASSELL, Ulrich von. Career diplomat. Ambassador in Rome 1932-7. Alternate Foreign Minister-designate in Goerdeler's Provisional Government. Hanged September 8, 1944.

HAUBACH, Dr. Theodor. Socialist leader. Co-organizer of the 'Reichsbanner'. Chief Press Relations Officer, Police Praesidium of Berlin till 1932. Member of Kreisau Circle. Minister designate for Information in Provisional Government. Hanged January 23, 1945.

HAUSHOFER, Dr. Georg Albrecht (son of eminent geo-politician). Professor of Political Geography, University of Berlin, 1940-44. Shot in Lehrterstrasse Prison, April 22/23, 1945.

HAYESSEN, Major Egbert von. Liaison officer between Olbricht and von Hase. Hanged August 15, 1944.

HELLDORF, Count Wolf Heinrich von. SA Obergruppenführer. Police President of Berlin, 1935-44. Hanged August 15, 1944.

HERFURTH, Major-General Otto. Appointed Chief of Staff of Berlin General Kommando by von Witzleben on July 20, 1944. Hanged September 29, 1944.

HOEPNER, Colonel-General Erich. Appointed Commander-in-Chief, Home Army, by von Witzleben, July 20, 1944. Hanged August 8, 1944.

HOFACKER, Lieutenant-Colonel Caesar von. Industrialist. Attached to staff of Military Governor of France. Executed December 20, 1944.

HÖSSLIN, Major Roland von.   General Staff Officer.   Executed October 13, 1944.

HÜBENER, Otto.   Insurance director.   Abwehr.   Executed April 21, 1945.

JACOB, Franz.   Leading Communist.   Arrested July 4, 1944.   Committed suicide in prison.

JAEGER, Colonel Fritz.   Executed August 31, 1944.

JENNEWEIN, Max.   Mechanical Engineer.   Executed April 22/23, 1945.

JESSEN, Dr. Peter Jens.   Leading economist.   Professor of Political Science, Berlin University, 1931–33.   Formerly a member of the Economic Policy Department of the NSDAP.   Executed November 30, 1944.

JOHN, Hans.   Lawyer.   Executed April 22/23, 1945, between the Lehrter-strasse and Prinz-Albrechtstrasse Prisons.

KAISER, Captain Dr. Hermann.   Liaison officer between Beck and Goerdeler.   Executed January 23, 1945.

KEMPNER, Dr. Franz.   State-Secretary in Ministry of Reconstruction till 1933.   Executed April 22/23, 1945.

KIEP, Otto.   Career Diplomat.   OKW Amt Ausland.   Formerly Consul-General in New York.   Attempted to commit suicide but was hanged in Plötzensee prison, August 26, 1944.

KISSLING, Georg Conrad.   Estate owner.   Executed July 22, 1944.

KLAMROTH, Hans Georg.   Merchant.   Abwehr.   Executed August 26, 1944.

KLAMROTH, Lieutenant-Colonel Bernhard.   On Staff of Major-General Stieff.   Executed August 15, 1944.

KLAUSING, Captain Friedrich Karl.   Hanged August 8, 1944.

KLEIST-SCHMENZIN, Major Ewald von.   Estate owner.   Deputy-Com-missioner-designate for Wehrkreis II (Stettin).   Executed April 9, 1945.

KNAACK, Major Gerhardt.   Executed September 4, 1944.

KOCH, Hans.   Lawyer.   Executed April 24, 1945.

KÖRNER, Heinrich.   Trade Union Official.   Follower of Jacob Kaiser. Member of the Kreisau Circle.   Freed by the Russians in Berlin on April 25, 1945, only to be killed by a stray bullet from an SS barricade.

KRANZFELDER, Captain (Navy) Alfred.   Ic. in Abt. 1, Seekriegs-Leitung. Executed August 10, 1944.

KÜNZER, Richard.   Counsellor of Legation in the Foreign Office.   Executed by Gestapo near the Lehrter Station, April 22/23, 1945.

KUZNITSKYI, Frau Elise Auguste (*née* Liliencron).   Executed November 30, 1944.

LANCKEN, Lieutenant-Colonel Fritz von der, Adjutant to Olbricht. Executed September 29, 1944.

LANGBEHN, Dr. Carl.   Lawyer.   Executed October 12, 1944.

LEBER, Dr. Julius.   Social Democrat Leader.   Minister-designate of Interior in Provisional Government.   Hanged January 5, 1945.

LEHNDORFF-STEINORT, Count Heinrich von. Estate-owner and adjutant to Field-Marshal von Bock. Executed September 4, 1944.

LEJEUNE-JUNG, Dr. Paul Adam Franz. Doctor of Philosophy and Lawyer. 1924–30, German People's Party Deputy in Reichstag. Minister-designate for Economics in the Provisional Government. Executed in Plötzensee Prison, September 8, 1944.

LEONROD, Major Freiherr Ludwig von. Military liaison officer-designate for Wehrkreis VII (Munich). Executed August 26, 1944.

LETTERHAUS, Bernhard. Former Secretary-General of the Christian Trade Unions. Minister designate for Reconstruction in Provisional Government. Executed November 14, 1944.

LEUNINGER, Franz. Former Secretary-General of the Christian Metal-workers' Union. Executed March 1, 1945.

LEUSCHNER, Wilhelm. SPD leader. Minister of Interior in Hesse, 1928–33. Friend of General von Hammerstein, who introduced him to Beck. Vice-Chancellor designate in Provisional Government. Hanged September 29, 1944.

LINDEMANN, General of Artillery Fritz. Executed September 22, 1944.

LINSTOW, Colonel Hans Otfried von. Chief of Staff to Colonel-General von Stülpnagel in Paris. Executed August 30, 1944.

LÜNINCK, Freiherr Ferdinand von. Former Oberpräsident of West-phalia. Commissioner designate for Wehrkreis XX (Danzig). Executed November 14, 1944.

LYNAR, Major Count Wilhelm Friedrich zu. Landowner and Adju-tant to Field-Marshal von Witzleben. Executed September 29, 1944.

MAASS, Hermann. SPD and Trade Union leader. Executed October 20, 1944.

MARCKS, Karl. Merchant. Executed by guards during night of April 22/23, 1945.

MAROGNA-REDWITZ, Colonel Count Rudolf von. Chief of Abwehr office in Vienna. Military liaison officer designate for Wehrkreis XVII (Vienna). Executed in Vienna, October 12, 1944.

MATUSCHKA, Count Michael von. Regierungsdirektor. Executed September 14, 1944.

MEICHSSNER, Colonel Joachim. Executed September 29, 1944.

MERTZ VON QUIRNHEIM, Colonel Ritter Albrecht. General Staff. Chief of Staff to General Olbricht in succession to von Stauffenberg (June 1944). Arrested and shot in courtyard of Bendlerstrasse, July 20, 1944.

MOLTKE-KREISAU, Count Helmuth von. Lawyer. Leader of the Kreisau Circle. Executed January 23, 1945.

MÜLLER, Prelat Otto. Leader of Catholic Workers' Associations. Died in Tegel Prison, October 12, 1944.

MUMM VON SCHWARZENSTEIN, Herbert. Secretary of Legation. Executed April 1943.

MUNZINGER, Lieutenant-Colonel Ernst. OKH. Executed April 22/23, 1945.

NEBE, Artur. SS-Obergruppenführer. Head of Amt V of RSHA. Executed in Plötzensee Prison, March 3, 1945.

NIEDEN, Wilhelm zur. Industrialist. Executed by Gestapo, April 22/23, 1945.

OERTZEN, Major Ulrich von. General Staff. One of the chief planners of the *Putsch* under Olbricht. Committed suicide July 20, 1944.

OLBRICHT, General of Infantry Friedrich. Chief of Staff of the Reserve Army. Minister designate for War in Provisional Government. Arrested and shot in courtyard of Bendlerstrasse, July 20, 1944.

OSTER, Major-General Hans. Chief of Central Office of the Abwehr until 1943. Military liaison officer for Wehrkreis IV (Dresden). Executed at Flossenbürg Camp, April 9, 1945.

PERELS, Dr. Friedrich Justus. Legal adviser to the Confessional Church. Executed by prison guards, April 22/23, 1945.

PLANCK, Erwin. Son of Max Planck, eminent physicist. Secretary to Brüning, 1930–32. State Secretary in the Reichskanzlei, 1932–33. Executed January 23, 1945.

PLETTENBERG, Freiherr Kurt von. Member of the Household of the German Crown Prince. Committed suicide in the Prinz Albrecht-strasse Prison, March 10, 1945.

POPITZ, Professor Dr. Johannes. Reichsminister without portfolio, 1932–3. Prussian Minister of Finance, 1933–44. Hanged in Plötzensee Prison, February 2, 1945.

RABENAU, General of Artillery Friedrich von. Head of Heeresarchiv at Potsdam, 1935–43. Biographer of General von Seeckt. Executed in Flossenbürg Camp, April 12, 1945.

RATHGENS, Lieutenant-Colonel Karl Ernst. Executed August 30, 1944.

REICHWEIN, Professor Dr. Adolf. SPD. Socialist Youth Movement Leader. Executed October 20, 1944.

ROENNE, Colonel Freiherr Alexis von. Chief of Foreign Armies Branch of OKH. Executed October 12, 1944.

ROMMEL, Field-Marshal Erwin. Committed suicide October 14, 1944. Commander-in-Chief Army Group B (Western Front).

SACK, Carl. Chief Justice of OKH. Executed in Flossenbürg Camp, April 9, 1945.

SADROZINSKI, Lieutenant-Colonel Joachim. Executed September 29, 1944.

SAEFKOW, Anton. Member of Central Executive Committee of the Communist Party. Executed.

SALVIATI, Major Count Hans-Viktor. Brother-in-law of Prince Friedrich-

Wilhelm of Prussia. Adjutant to Field-Marshal von Rundstedt, 1941–43. Executed April 22/23, 1945.

SCHACK, Count Adolf von. Landowner. Executed January 15, 1945.

SCHLEICHER, Professor Dr. Rüdiger. Brother-in-law of Dietrich Bonhoeffer. Ministerialrat in the Air Ministry. Executed April 22/23, 1945.

SCHNEPPENHORST, Ernst. SPD and Trade Union Leader. Bavarian Minister of War, 1919–20. Member of Bavarian Diet, 1920–33. Reichstag Deputy, 1932–3. Executed near the Lehrter Station, April 24, 1945.

SCHOLZ-BABISCH, Rittmeister Friedrich. Landowner. Military liaison officer-designate for Wehrkreis VIII (Breslau). Executed October 13, 1944.

SCHÖNE, Lieutenant-Colonel Hermann. Adjutant to Colonel-General Hase. Executed January 15, 1945.

SCHRADER, Lieutenant-Colonel Werner. Liaison Officer of OKH to Abwehr. Committed suicide, July 28, 1944.

SCHULENBURG, Count Friedrich Dietlof von der. Youngest son of Chief of Staff of the German Crown Prince during First World War. Vice Police President of Berlin, 1935–39. Deputy Oberpräsident of Silesia, 1939–44. Member of Kreisau Circle. Executed August 10, 1944.

SCHULENBURG, Count Friedrich Werner von der. Ambassador in Moscow, 1935–41. Alternate Foreign Minister designate in Provisional Government. Executed November 10, 1944.

SCHULTZE-BÜTTGER, Lieutenant-Colonel Georg. G.S.O.1 to Field-Marshal von Manstein. Executed October 13, 1944.

SCHWAMB, Ludwig. SPD. Staatsrat in Hessen Ministry of Interior till 1933. Executed January 23, 1945.

SCHWERIN-SCHWANENFELD, Captain Count Ulrich Wilhelm von. Adjutant to Field-Marshal von Witzleben, 1940–42. Executed September 8, 1944.

SIERKS, Hans Ludwig. Former Councillor of State. Executed near the Lehrter Station, April 22/23, 1945.

SMEND, Lieutenant-Colonel Günther. General Staff Officer. Executed September 8, 1944.

SPERR, Franz. Bavarian Envoy to Berlin till 1934. Member of Kreisau Circle. Executed January 23, 1945.

STAEHLE, Colonel Wilhelm. Commandant of the Invalidenhaus, Berlin. Member of Abwehr. Executed in Moabit Prison, April 22/23, 1945.

STAUFFENBERG, Count Berthold Schenk von. Lawyer. Brother of Claus Schenk von Stauffenberg. Hanged August 10, 1944.

STAUFFENBERG, Colonel Count Claus Schenk von. Chief of Staff to Colonel-General Fromm, as Commander-in-Chief, Home Army.

State-Secretary designate in Ministry of War in Provisional Government. Carried out attempt on Hitler's life on July 20, 1944. Shot in Bendlerstrasse, July 20, 1944.

STIEFF, Major-General Helmut. Chief of Organization Office, OKH. Executed August 8, 1944.

STRÜNCK, Dr. Theodor. Rittmeister, Abwehr. Insurance company director in Frankfurt. Executed April 9, 1945, in Flossenbürg Camp.

STÜLPNAGEL, General of Infantry Karl-Heinrich von. Military Governor of France, 1942–4. Attempted suicide July 21, 1944. Hanged August 30, 1944.

TELLGMANN, Lieutenant-Colonel Gustav. Executed February 26, 1945.

THADDEN, Elisabeth von. Headmistress. Executed September 8, 1944.

THIELE, Lieutenant-General Fritz. Head of Signals branch of OKW. Executed September 5, 1944.

THOMA, Major Busso. Executed January 23, 1945.

THÜNGEN, Lieutenant-General Freiherr Carl von. Deputy Gerichtsherr of the Central Court of the Army. Appointed by Hoepner to succeed Kortzfleisch as G.O.C. Wehrkreis III (Berlin). Executed October 24, 1944.

TRESCKOW, Lieutenant-Colonel Gerd von. Committed suicide September 2, 1944.

TRESCKOW, Major-General Henning von. G.S.O.1, and later Chief of Staff to Field-Marshal von Kluge as Commander-in-Chief Army Group Centre. Committed suicide July 21, 1944.

TROTT ZU SOLZ, Freiherr Adam von. Counsellor of Legation in the Foreign Office. Member of Kreisau Circle. Hanged August 25, 1944.

ÜXKÜLL, Colonel Count Nikolaus von. Military liaison officer designate for the Protectorate of Bohemia and Moravia. Hanged at Plötzensee, September 14, 1944.

VOIGT, Karl. Trade Union Leader. Executed March 1, 1945.

VOSS, Lieutenant-Colonel Hans-Alexander von. Son-in-law of General von Stülpnagel. G.S.O. to Field-Marshal von Witzleben. Committed suicide November 8, 1944.

WAGNER, General of Artillery Eduard. First Quartermaster-General OKH. Committed suicide July 26, 1944.

WAGNER, Colonel Siegfried. G.S.O. to General Olbricht. Committed suicide July 22, 1944.

WEHRLE, Father Hermann. Army Chaplain and confessor to Freiherr von Leonrod. Executed September 14, 1944.

WENTZEL-TEUTSCHENTHAL, Carl. Landowner. Executed December 20, 1944.

WIERSICH, Oswald. Christian Trade Union Leader. Executed February 28, 1945.

WIRMER, Josef. Lawyer. Centre Party. Minister designate of Justice in the Provisional Government. Executed September 8, 1944.

WITZLEBEN, Field-Marshal Erwin Job von. Supreme Commander-in-Chief designate of the Wehrmacht. Hanged August 8, 1944.

YORCK VON WARTENBURG, Count Peter Hans Ludwig. Member of Kreisau Circle. State-Secretary designate to the Chancellor in the Provisional Government. Hanged August 8, 1944.

ZARDEN, Dr. Artur. State-Secretary in Reich Ministry of Finance till 1933. Arrested January 1944, committed suicide in prison, March 1944.

ZIEHLBERG, General Gustav Heistermann von. Executed February 22, 1945.

NOTE.—This list is not complete. Many more were condemned to death and executed for their complicity in the conspiracy. A complete list has, however, not so far been compiled.

APPENDIX E

TABLES TO ILLUSTRATE ORGANIZATION OF THE GERMAN HIGH COMMAND, 1919–1945

(i) HIGH COMMAND OF THE ARMED FORCES

1. PRESIDENTS OF THE GERMAN REICH AND SUPREME COMMANDERS OF THE ARMED FORCES

   Friedrich Ebert, 1919–25.
   Field-Marshal Paul von Beneckendorff und Hindenburg, 1925–34.
   Adolf Hitler (Führer and Chancellor), 1934–45.

2. MINISTERS OF DEFENCE

   Gustav Noske, 1919–20.
   Otto Gessler, 1920–28.
   Lieutenant-General Wilhelm Gröner, 1928–32.
   General of Infantry Kurt von Schleicher, 1932–3.
   Colonel-General Werner von Blomberg, 1933–5.

3. MINISTERS OF WAR

   Field-Marshal Werner von Blomberg, 1935–8.
   Adolf Hitler, 1938–45.

4. COMMANDERS-IN-CHIEF OF THE ARMY

   Major-General Walter Reinhardt, 1919–20.
   Colonel-General Hans von Seeckt, 1920–26.
   Colonel-General Wilhelm Heye, 1926–30.
   Colonel-General Freiherr Kurt von Hammerstein-Equord, 1930–1934.
   Colonel-General Freiherr Werner von Fritsch, 1934–8.
   Field-Marshal Walter von Brauchitsch, 1938–41.
   Adolf Hitler, 1941–5.

5. CHIEFS OF THE TRUPPENAMT OF THE DEFENCE MINISTRY

   Major-General von Seeckt, 1919–20.
   Major-General Heye, 1920–23.
   Major-General Otto Hasse, 1923–5.
   Major-General Wetzell, 1925–6.

Major-General von Blomberg, 1926–9.
Major-General von Hammerstein-Equord, 1929–30.
Major-General Wilhelm Adam, 1930–33.
General of Artillery Ludwig Beck, 1933–5.

6. CHIEFS OF THE GENERAL STAFF OF THE ARMY (OKH)

Colonel-General Beck, 1935–8.
Colonel-General Franz Halder, 1938–42.
Colonel-General Kurt Zeitzler, 1942–4.
Colonel-General Heinz Guderian, 1944–5.
General of Infantry Hans Krebs, May 1945.

7. HIGH COMMAND OF THE WEHRMACHT (OKW)

Field-Marshal Wilhelm Keitel, Chief of High Command, 1938–45.
Colonel-General Alfred Jodl, Chief of Operations Staff, 1938–45.

(ii) ORGANIZATION OF THE HIGH COMMAND OF THE GERMAN ARMED FORCES

1. 1920–1934

President of the Reich and
Supreme Commander
|
Chancellor of the Reich
|
Minister of Defence

Chief of the
Army High Command   Chief of the
                                     Navy High Command

2. 1934–1938

The Führer and Chancellor
Supreme Commander
|
Minister for War
Commander-in-Chief

Commander-in-Chief   Commander-in-Chief   Commander-in-Chief
Army   Navy   Air Force

3. 1938–1941

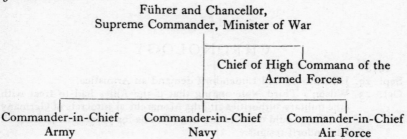

Führer and Chancellor,
Supreme Commander, Minister of War

Chief of High Command of the
Armed Forces

Commander-in-Chief   Commander-in-Chief   Commander-in-Chief
Army   Navy   Air Force

4. 1941–1945

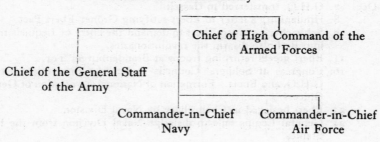

Führer and Chancellor,
Supreme Commander, Minister of War,
Commander-in-Chief Army

Chief of High Command of the
Armed Forces

Chief of the General Staff
of the Army

Commander-in-Chief   Commander-in-Chief
Navy   Air Force

CHRONOLOGY

1919
June 17. Hindenburg's letter to Ebert favouring acceptance.
     23. Noske refuses proposal of Maercker and Lüttwitz to establish a
         military dictatorship.
     24. Gröner gives final word of Supreme Command in favour of
         acceptance.
     25. Hindenburg retires.
     28. Signature of Treaty of Versailles.
July 5. Seeckt appointed head of Commission to reorganize the R/W.
Sept. 16? Adolf Hitler joins the DAP in Munich.
Oct. 1. Gröner retires.
     21. Opening of Reichstag Commission of Enquiry into responsibility
         for the War.
Nov. 18. Hindenburg and Ludendorff appear before the Commission.

1920
Jan. 10. Treaty of Versailles comes into force.
Feb. 3. Allies present their list of War Criminals for surrender by the
         German Government.
      9. Seeckt informs his departmental heads that resistance to the allied
         demands must be made at all costs, even at the risk of hostilities.
     25. NSDAP founded at Munich.
Mar. 10. Lüttwitz demands from Ebert the dissolution of the National
         Assembly, the holding of new elections, etc.
     11. Lüttwitz dismissed from command of Wehrkommando I : arrest
         ordered of Kapp, Papst, Bauer and others.
     13. Ebert and Reich Government escape from Berlin to Dresden and
         later to Stuttgart. New Government headed by Kapp and
         Lüttwitz, proclaimed in Berlin.
     17. 2 P.M. : Kapp resigns and flees to Sweden. 6 P.M. : Lüttwitz
         resigns and flees to Hungary. Seeckt resumes command of the
         R/W.
     21. Ebert and Reich Government return to Berlin.
     24. Noske resigns and is succeeded as Minister of Defence by Gessler.
     27. Bauer Government resigns. Hermann Müller Chancellor.
Sept.   Buchrucker begins formation of 'Black R/W' units with approval
         and cognizance of R/W.

1921
Mar. 23. Law governing the organization of the R/W passed by Reichstag.
May   6. German-Soviet economic agreement signed in Berlin.
Aug. 26. Assassination of Erzberger.

1922
Apr. 16. German-Soviet Agreement signed at Rapallo.
June 24. Assassination of Rathenau

1923
Jan. 10. Germany declared in default of reparation payments.

1923
Jan. 11. French and Belgian troops occupy Ruhr zone.
      12. Reich Government proclaims passive resistance.
      15. Allied troops occupy whole Ruhr territory.
Aug. 13. Cuno resigns. Stresemann Chancellor.
Sept. 2. Hitler and Ludendorff form the Kampfbund at Nuremberg.
      15. Buchrucker mobilizes Black R/W for march on Berlin.
      24. Seeckt refuses proposal from Class, President of Pan-German
          League, to establish military dictatorship.
      25. Hitler named Political Director of Kampfbund.
      26. Stresemann declares end of passive resistance. Kahr assumes full
          power as State Commissioner of Bavaria and proclaims State of
          Emergency on Separatist issue. Hitler and Ludendorff demand
          march on Berlin.
      26. Ebert, under para. 48 of Constitution, places full power in hands
          of Defence Minister Gessler and Seeckt. Kahr refuses to recog-
          nize Ebert's proclamation and appoints Lossow as independent
          Commander of Bavarian R/W.
      28. Kahr abrogates Law for the Protection of the Republic. Com-
          munists and Socialists in Saxony proclaim common front against
          Berlin.
Oct.   1. Lossow refuses to obey Seeckt's orders.
     1–3. Seeckt suppresses Black R/W revolt.
      13. Reichstag passes Enabling Act.
      17. General Müller (Wehrkreis IV) gives 24-hour ultimatum to
          Saxon Government.
      21. Rhineland Republic proclaimed at Aachen.
      25. Buchrucker condemned to 10 years fortress arrest for Black
          R/W revolt.
      29. R/W occupy Saxon Ministries. Reich Commissioner installed.
Nov.   2. SPD Minister resigns from Reich Cabinet in protest against R/W
          action in Saxony.
       4. Seeckt announces that R/W will act against all anticonstitutional
          movements.
     8–9. Hitler-Ludendorff *Putsch* in Munich defeated by R/W and police.
      11. Hitler arrested.
      23. Stresemann resigns. Marx Chancellor.

1924
Jan.   3–9. Correspondence between Prof. Quidde and Seeckt regarding
          clandestine rearmament.
       4. Thormann, of the Wicking organization and Ehrhardt Brigade,
          and Tettenbaum, of the Racial Party, plan to assassinate Seeckt on
          Jan. 12, on which day they are arrested themselves.
Feb. 13. Collapse of Rhineland Republic. Ebert proclaims end of State
          of Emergency.
Feb. 26–Apr. 1. Trial of Munich *Putsch* conspirators. Hitler condemned to
          5 years fortress arrest.
Oct.–Dec. The Magdeburg 'Stab in the Back' Trial.
Dec. 20. Hitler released under General Amnesty.

1925

Feb. 28. Death of Ebert.

Apr. 27. Hindenburg elected President of the Reich

Oct.–Nov. Munich 'Stab in the Back' Trial.

Oct. 5. Locarno agreement initialled.

Dec. 1. Locarno Agreement signed.

1926

Jan. 31. Completion of Evacuation of First Occupation Zone.

Mar. 16. Postponement of Germany's entry into League of Nations.

Apr. 24. German-Soviet Non-Aggression Pact signed in Berlin.

May 18. Preparatory Disarmament Commission opens at Geneva.

Sept. 8. Germany admitted to League of Nations and elected to permanent seat on the Council.

14. Locarno ratifications exchanged.

Oct. 9. Seeckt resigns as G.O.C. R/W, succeeded by Heye.

Dec. 16. Scheidemann's interpolation in Reichstag on clandestine rearmament.

1927

Jan. 31. Allied Commission of Control withdrawn from Germany.

1928

Jan. 30. Gessler resigns. Gröner becomes Minister of Defence.

Aug. 27. Kellogg-Briand Pact signed in Paris.

Nov. Gröner threatens to resign if construction on pocket-battleship A is delayed.

1929

Mar. 15. Hitler in a speech at Munich begins battle for the disruption of the R/W by Nazi doctrines.

June 7. Young Plan signed in Paris.

Aug. 6-31. First Hague Conference on Young Plan ; signature of Agreement for Evacuation of Second and Third Zones of Occupation.

Oct. 3. Death of Stresemann.

Sept.–Dec. Evacuation of Second Zone.

1930

Jan. 22. Gröner issues General Order to R/W recapitulating the rôle of the Army in the State, attacking National Socialism.

Mar. 6. Three junior officers (Scheringer, Ludin and Wendt) arrested for spreading National Socialist propaganda in the Army.

Mar. 30. Heinrich Brüning appointed Chancellor on instance of Gröner and Schleicher.

Sept. 14. General election results in return of 107 Nazi deputies to the Reichstag.

25. Hitler, as a witness at the Scheringer trial at Leipzig, makes a statement about the legality of the NSDAP and disavows any intention of disrupting R/W.

1930
Oct.   6. Gröner in a secret order to the Officer Corps requires an unequi-
            vocal sign of allegiance to the Republic.
       18. Hammerstein succeeds Heye as G.O.C. R/W.

1931
May 19. First pocket-battleship launched at Kiel.
Oct.   9. Brüning reconstructs Cabinet with himself as Chancellor and
            Foreign Minister and Gröner as Minister of Defence and Interior.
       11. Seeckt joins the Harzburg Front. Schleicher begins secret
            negotiations with Röhm.
       14. Hitler sends Open Letter to Brüning on 'the true task of the Army
            of the Reich'.
Nov. 25. Boxheim Incident.

1932
Jan.   7. Brüning, Gröner and Schleicher meet Hitler in negotiations for
            prolongation of Hindenburg's term of office.
       11. Gröner warns Hitler not to depart from legal methods and
            expresses disapproval of SA.
       24? Gröner and Schleicher prevail upon Hindenburg not to dismiss
            Brüning.
Feb.   2. Opening of General Disarmament Conference in Geneva.
Apr.   5. Representatives of the Länder demand from Gröner the suppres-
            sion of the SA.
       10. Hindenburg re-elected President of the Reich.
       13. Cabinet promulgates decree suppressing SA and SS.
       14. Schleicher informs Gröner that R/W is opposed to the decree.
       26. Brüning at Geneva reaches tentative disarmament formula with
            MacDonald, Stimson, Norman Davis and Grandi.
May   8. Secret meeting in Berlin between Schleicher and Hitler.
       10. Göring attacks Gröner in Reichstag. Schleicher informs Gröner
            that he no longer has the confidence of the R/W.
       13. Gröner resigns.
       20. Schleicher refuses to become Minister of Defence in Brüning's
            Cabinet.
       30. Brüning dismissed at instance of Schleicher and Oskar von
            Hindenburg. Papen appointed Chancellor, Schleicher Defence
            Minister.
June 16–July 9. Conference at Lausanne ends reparation payments.
June 17. Ban on SA and SS lifted.
July 20. Papen evicts the Prussian Government and places Prussia under
            a Reich commissar.
       31. General election results in 230 Nazis in Reichstag.
Aug.   5. Meeting between Schleicher and Hitler at Fürstenberg Barracks.
       30. Papen and Schleicher meet Hitler, who refuses to become Vice-
            Chancellor.
Sept.   2. Hitler renews pledge to R/W at speech in Sportpalast.
Nov. 17. Hindenburg, under pressure from Schleicher, accepts Papen's
            resignation.

1932
Dec.   3. Schleicher appointed Chancellor and Minister of Defence.

1933
Jan.   4. Meeting of Papen and Hitler at Cologne.
      28. Schleicher resigns.
      30. Hitler appointed Chancellor of National Coalition Government, with Blomberg as Minister of Defence. R/W ordered by Hindenburg to co-operate with new régime.
      31. Hitler addresses the troops of the Berlin Garrison.
Feb. 27. Reichstag Fire.
Mar.   5. General Elections give Nationalist Coalition 51 per cent of the seats in the Reichstag (340 out of 647) the Nazis obtaining 288 seats and more than 17¼ million votes.
      21. Ceremonial meeting of the Reichstag in Garrison Church at Potsdam.
Apr.   4. Cabinet decision to set up a Reich Defence Council.
June 22-27. Hugenberg resigns from Cabinet.
July   1. Hitler defines relationship of SA and Stahlhelm to Army in speech at Bad Reichenhall.
Sept. 23. Hitler in speech states 'that if, in the days of the Revolution, the Army had not stood on our side, we should not be standing here to-day'.
Oct. 14. Germany leaves the League of Nations and the Disarmament Conference.

1934
Jan. 26. SA disrupt celebrations for Kaiser's birthday at Kaiserhof Hotel, Berlin.
Feb.   1. Fritsch replaces Hammerstein as G.O.C. R/W.
      21. Mr. Eden in Berlin. Hitler offers to reduce the SA by two-thirds.
Apr. 12. Conference between Hitler, Blomberg and Fritsch on board the *Deutschland* during Fleet manœuvres *in re* future of SA and Army, and consequences of Hindenburg's death.
      16. Offer of reduction of SA reaffirmed in Note to British Government.
      27. First announcement of Hindenburg's illness.
May   16. Conference of Generals at Bad Nauheim, presided over by Fritsch, agrees that Röhm is unacceptable as R/W Minister and discusses Hindenburg's successor.
June   4. Publication of new version of 'Duties of a Soldier'.
       6. Announcement that SA would be sent on leave for one month as from July 1.
      14. Hitler meets Mussolini in Venice.
      16. Ribbentrop in Paris reaffirms intention to reduce SA drastically.
      17. Papen's speech at Marburg.
      20. Papen resigns as Vice-Chancellor.
      21. Hitler sees Hindenburg at Neudeck.
      25. R/W in state of alert all over Reich.
      28. SS mobilized ; Röhm expelled from German Officer League.
      29. Blomberg in article in *V.B.* announces that the Army stands behind the Führer and the Reich.

1934

June 30. Blood Purge. Röhm *et al.*, Schleicher and Bredow killed.

July 1. Blomberg issues order of the day to R/W. Hindenburg congratulates Hitler and Göring.

     3. Blomberg expresses the approval and congratulations of the Cabinet to Hitler.

     13. Hitler in the Reichstag justifies the Blood Purge.

     20. Thirty Generals and Officers of the General Staff send memorandum to Hindenburg deprecating assassination of Schleicher and demanding rehabilitation.

     25. Murder of Chancellor.Dollfuss by Austrian Nazis.

Aug. 1. Death of Hindenburg. Hitler becomes Führer and Chancellor.

     2. The Army takes the Oath to him as Supreme Commander.

     18. Hitler in speech at Hamburg announces that 'there is no one in whose eyes the German Army needs to rehabilitate its fame in arms'.

1935

Jan. 3. At a secret conclave of the Party and Army leaders at the Kroll Opera, Hitler agrees to the rehabilitation of Schleicher and Bredow.

Feb. 28. Mackensen announces the rehabilitation to a gathering of members of the General Staff.

Mar. 9. Existence of the Luftwaffe officially announced.

     16. Hitler announces reintroduction of compulsory military service.

May 2. Franco-Soviet Treaty signed in Paris.

     21. New Wehrmacht Law passed by the Reichstag. Secret Defence Law adopted by the Cabinet.

1936

Feb. 27. Franco-Soviet Treaty ratified by French Chamber.

Mar. 7. Hitler occupies the demilitarized zone of the Rhineland.

Apr. 1. Blomberg created a Field-Marshal.

June 17. Himmler appointed Chief of all police forces in the Reich.

Oct. 25. Rome-Berlin Axis Agreement signed.

Nov. 23. German-Japanese Anti-Comintern Agreement signed.

1937

Nov. 5. Secret Conclave in Berlin at which Hitler develops his plans for future policy to Blomberg, Fritsch, Raeder, Neurath and Göring.

1938

Jan. 12. Blomberg's marriage with Fräulein Erna Gruhn.

     24. Blomberg resigns as Minister of Defence. Fritsch, accused of homosexuality, is sent on leave.

Feb. 3-4. Hitler announces that he will personally assume office of Defence Minister, with von Brauchitsch as C.-in-C. of Army; also creation of OKW with Keitel as Chief of Staff. Göring appointed a Field-Marshal.

Mar. 11. A special military tribunal, composed of Göring, as President, Brauchitsch, Raeder, and two judges of the Supreme Court, open the trial of Fritsch ; the hearing hurriedly adjourned as German troops march into Austria.

  17-18. The hearings in the Fritsch case resumed. Verdict of Not Guilty returned.

  25. Hitler publicly congratulates Fritsch on his 'recovery of health'

May 28. Hitler gives to Keitel the secret directions for 'Operation Green' against Czechoslovakia.

  30. Hitler communicates his intention to his Generals at a Conference at Jüterbog.

July 16. Beck submits a memorandum to Brauchitsch protesting against a war of aggression, even a *Blitzkrieg.*

Aug. (first week). Beck at conference of Generals.

  10. Hitler at military conference at the Berghof upbraids Generals for defeatism.

  11. Fritsch formally rehabilitated, reinstated in rank of Col-Gen. and appointed Col.-in-Chief of 12th Regiment of Artillery.

  19. Winston Churchill gives letter to von Kleist.

  31. Beck removed from office as Chief of General Staff of OKH, replaced by Halder, but public announcement delayed until October 31.

Sept. 2. Halder sends Böhm-Tettelbach to London.

  5. Theodor Kordt sent to Halifax by Weizsäcker.

  9. Brauchitsch and Halder in long interview with Hitler advise him against war.

  13. Hitler admonishes departmental heads of OKW on danger of defeatism.

  28. Halder and Witzleben, convinced that Hitler means war, consider making a *Putsch* to arrest him and other Nazi leaders.

  30. Munich Agreement signed.

Nov. 4. Rundstedt removed from command ; Keitel promoted Colonel-General.

  7. Murder of Secretary of German Embassy in Paris by a German-Polish refugee.

  9. Jewish pogrom throughout Germany.

  27. Adam removed from command of West Wall defences.

1939

Mar. 14. Hitler marches into Prague.

  Schacht and Goerdeler meet at Ouchy with G.'s 'contact man' and later with Montagu Norman to warn London and Paris that Hitler would attack Poland in autumn.

May 23. Hitler announces to his Generals his intention to attack Poland.

July Schlabrendorff sees Winston Churchill and Lord Lloyd in England.

Aug. 14. Thomas presents to Keitel memoranda written by himself and Schacht opposing a second world war. Assured by Keitel that no general war possible.

1939

Aug. 22. Führer Conference in the Berghof.
23. Nazi-Soviet Pact signed in Moscow.
27. Thomas again warns Keitel, with statistics. These shown to Hitler (28), who believes general war impossible.
(last week). Beck writes to von Brauchitsch and Halder.

Sept. 1. Germany invades Poland.
3. Britain and France declare war on Germany.
Hammerstein plans to arrest Hitler during a visit to Army H.Q. on Western Front. Visit cancelled.

Oct. First attempts of Joseph Müller to contact British Government through Vatican.
10. Hitler informs Commanding Generals of his intention to attack in the West as soon as possible, probable date for X-day November 12.
15. Hammerstein relieved of command and retired.
16. Schacht sends letter to President of BIS at Basel.
(end). X-Report on Müller's activities in Rome presented to Brauchitsch, who refuses to act. Conwell-Evans visits Berne with British 'binding obligation'.

Nov. 3. Halder informs Beck, Schacht and Goerdeler that Brauchitsch and he will make a *Putsch* on November 5, when Hitler visits OKH G.H.Q. at Zossen, if Führer insists upon attack in the West.
5. Brauchitsch opposes Hitler's plans for attack in the West and reports adversely on morale of troops. Hitler, enraged, accuses OKH of defeatism. Plans for second attempt to arrest Hitler abandoned by Halder and Brauchitsch.
8. Attempt to assassinate Hitler at Bürgerbräu Cellar in Munich fails.
9. Stevens and Best kidnapped at Venlo.
23. Brauchitsch and Halder lectured by Hitler on the 'Spirit of Zossen' (defeatism).
27. Halder rebuffs Thomas.
Leuschner (SPD) and Kaiser (CTU) make contact with Beck and Goerdeler.

Nov.–Feb. Adam von Trott in U.S. attending IPR Conference.

1940

Feb. 22. Hassell has interview at Arosa with J. Lonsdale Bryans.
Mar. 1-6. Sumner Wells in Berlin.
Apr. 4. X-Report presented by Thomas to Halder, who refuses to act. Halder writes to Goerdeler that a compromise peace is now impossible.
9. German invasion of Denmark and Norway.
14-15. Hassell has second interview at Arosa with J. Lonsdale Bryans.
May 10. German invasion of Belgium, Holland, Luxemburg and France.
June 22. Franco-German Armistice signed at Compiègne.
July 19. Hitler creates 12 Field-Marshals.

1941

June 22. Germany invades Soviet Union.

1941

Aug. 4. Plans to assassinate Hitler during conference of A.G.H.Q. of Bock miscarry owing to too great security precautions.

14. Atlantic Charter signed by Churchill and Roosevelt.

Nov.–Dec. German failure to capture Moscow.

Nov. (end). Louis Lochner entrusted with Mission to Roosevelt.

Dec. 11. Germany declares war on U.S.A.

19. Brauchitsch dismissed as C.-in-C. Army. Hitler assumes active and direct command.

(end). Witzleben agrees to make a military *Putsch*, in conjunction with Beck and Goerdeler, on the Western Front. Plans abandoned owing to Witzleben's undergoing an operation in March 1942.

1942

Apr.   Goerdeler meets Wallenberg in Stockholm.

May 26–31. Bonhoeffer and Schönfeld meet Bishop of Chichester in Stockholm.

July   Meeting of Goerdeler and Kluge at Smolensk.

Aug.   Gestapo arrest many members of the 'Rote Kapelle'

Nov. 8. Allied landings in North Africa.

Wallenberg meets Goerdeler in Berlin.

1943

Jan.   Plans drafted in Berlin for military revolt to take place after assassination of Hitler. 'Operation Flash'. Trott zu Solz in Switzerland.

24. Announcement of 'Unconditional Surrender' at Casablanca Conference.

31. Surrender of Stalingrad.

Feb. 10. Student Rising in Munich. Hans and Sophie Scholl arrested, Feb. 19.

(end). Plans completed for *Putsch*.

Mar. 13. Attempt to assassinate Hitler at Conference at Smolensk fails because of faulty fuse in bomb placed in his plane.

21. Further attempt to assassinate Hitler at the Berlin War Museum fails for technical reasons.

(end). Beck operated on by Sauerbruch.

Apr. 5. Arrest of Dohnanyi and Bonhoeffer
Oster dismissed.

24. Death of Hammerstein.

May 17. Goerdeler's letter to Olbricht.

June (early). Claus von Stauffenberg introduced into the conspiracy.

July 20. Manifesto of the 'Free German Committee' broadcast from Moscow.

25. Goerdeler's letter to Kluge.

Aug.–Sept. Popitz-Langbehn Affair.

Sept. 14. Appeal of the 'Union of German Officers' broadcast from Moscow.

Nov.   Attempt to assassinate Hitler with bomb in new overcoat pocket fails because allied air-raid cancels demonstration at Berchtesgaden.

1943

Dec. 26. Attempt on Hitler by Stauffenberg fails because conference at which bomb was to have been used was cancelled.

1944

Feb.   Break-up of Abwehr group. Canaris is retired and replaced by Hansen, and Abwehr placed under control of Kaltenbrunner.

May   Gisevius brings Beck's proposal to Dulles for a surrender in the West but not in the East.

    28. Mr. Churchill's speech in House of Commons.

June   Kluge succeeds Rundstedt as C.-in-C. West.

    6. Allied landings in Normandy.

    22. Agreement reached that Communists should be included in the Beck-Goerdeler Government.

July   4-6. Wholesale arrests of ex-Communists and SPD by Gestapo.

    6. Mr. Attlee's statement in House of Commons.

    9. Rommel requests permission to withdraw his troops from Normandy ; on Hitler's refusal he agrees to support *Putsch*.

    11. Stauffenberg abandons attempt on Hitler's life at Obersalzberg owing to absence of Himmler. Gisevius proposes that Goerdeler and he make last moment attempt to win over Kluge.

        Kluge sends Hofacker to Beck agreeing to support *Putsch*.

    15. Stauffenberg abandons attempt on Hitler's life at Rastenburg as Führer leaves room just as fuse of bomb is about to be started. Rommel incapacitated as result of automobile accident.

    16. Beck and Stauffenberg have final meeting in Berlin.

    17. Warrant issued for arrest of Goerdeler.

    20. Unsuccessful attempt to blow up Hitler at Rastenburg ; *Putsch* fails in Berlin and, though successful in Paris, is abandoned.

    24. Nazi salute substituted for military salute in the Army.

Aug.   4. Court of Honour established to dismiss convicted conspirators from the Army.

    7-8. Trial of first group of conspirators before People's Court.

    8. Witzleben and seven others hanged.

    18. Kluge commits suicide.

Oct.   14. Rommel commits suicide.

Dec.   16–Jan. 16. Rundstedt's Ardennes offensive.

1945

Jan.   15. Red Armies invade East Prussia.

Mar.   7. Allied Armies cross the Rhine.

Apr.   23. Red Army reaches Berlin.

    24. Himmler offers to arrange German surrender to Western Allies alone ; refused.

    30. Hitler commits suicide in Chancellery bunker. Dönitz continues Reich Government at Flensburg.

May   1. Unconditional Surrender of German Armies in Italy.

    7. Unconditional Surrender signed by Jodl at Rheims.

    8. VE Day.

    9. Unconditional Surrender ratified by Keitel in Berlin.

BIBLIOGRAPHY

I. UNPUBLISHED SOURCES

(i) DIARIES

Diary of General Alfred Jodl, 1937–1942.
Diary of General Franz Halder, 1939–1942.
My Diary at the Peace Conference. David Hunter Miller. (Privately printed, 1928.)
'The Beginning and the End.' Diary of Count Lutz Schwerin von Krosigk, for November 5, 1932–February 6, 1933 and April 15–May 1, 1945.

(ii) LEGAL PROCEEDINGS

De-nazification Proceedings against General Ernst Franz Johann Maisel; at Berchtesgaden, November 19, 1948; Rosenheim, July 1949.
De-nazification Proceedings against General Halder at Munich, September 1948.
De-nazification Proceedings against Oskar von Hindenburg at Ulzen/Hanover, March 1949.
De-nazification Proceedings against von Papen at Nuremberg, January 1949.
Judgment in the Trials of Walter Huppenkothen before the Bavarian Landesgericht, February 1951 and October–November 1952.
Judgment in the Trial of Wolfgang Hedler before the Landesgericht of Kiel, August 6, 1951.
Judgment in the trial of Otto Ernst Remer before the Landesgericht of Brunswick, March 15, 1952.
Proceedings of the Trial of Franz von Papen before the Spruchkammer of Nuremberg, February 1947.
Proceedings of the 'Ministries Case', No. 11 ('von Weizsäcker and 20 others'), before U.S. Military Tribunal IV at Nuremberg, November 1947–April 1949.

II. OFFICIAL DOCUMENTS

Belgium, the Official Account of What Happened, 1939–1940. Published for the Belgian Ministry of Foreign Affairs. (New York, 1941.)
Die Ursachen des deutschen Zusammenbruches im Jahre 1918. (Berlin, 1928.)
Die Rückführung des Ost-Heeres. (Berlin, 1920.)
Der Waffenstillstand, 1918–1919. (Berlin, 1928.)
Deutscher Geschichtskalender, vom Waffenstillstand bis zum Frieden von Versailles. (Leipzig, 1919.)
Documents diplomatiques relatifs aux réparations. (26 décembre 1922–27 août 1923.) *Belgian Grey Book.* (Brussels, 1924.)

768 BIBLIOGRAPHY

Documents on British Foreign Policy, 1919–1939. (Woodward and Butler, London, 1947.)
Documents on German Foreign Policy, 1918–1945. (London, 1949.)
Dokumente zur Vorgeschichte des Krieges, *German White Book*, No. 2. (Berlin, 1939.)
Field-Marshal Viscount Alexander's Report on the Italian Campaign, December 12, 1944–May 2, 1945. (H.M. Stationery Office, 1951.)
Förspelet till det tyska angreppet på Danmark och Norge den 9 April 1940. *Swedish White Book*. (Stockholm, 1947.)
Führer Conferences on Naval Affairs, 1944. (The Admiralty, 1947.)
Le Procès Benoist-Méchin. (Paris, 1948.)
Nazi Conspiracy and Aggression. 8 vols. and 2 supplements. (U.S. Government Printing Office, Washington, 1946–1948.)
Nazi-Soviet Relations, 1939–1941. (U.S. Department of State, Washington 1948.)
Official Documents concerning Polish-German and Polish-Soviet Relations, 1933–1939. *Polish White Book*. (London, 1939.)
Official Record of the Trial of the Major War Criminals before the International Military Tribunal. 42 vols. (Nuremberg, 1947–1949.)
Regeringsbeleid, 1940–1945, Teil 1 A en B: Algemene Inleiding/Militair Beleid, 1939/40. Report of the Netherlands Commission of Enquiry.
The Atlantic Charter. *British White Paper*. Cmd. 6321.
United Nations Law Reports of Trials of War Criminals. (London, 1947–9.)
Urkunden zum Friedensvertrag zu Versailles vom 28. Juni 1919. (Berlin, 1920–21.)
Vorgeschichte des Waffenstillstandes. (Berlin, 1919.)

III

(i) UNOFFICIAL COLLECTIONS OF DOCUMENTS AND SPEECHES

Adolf Hitlers Reden. (Munich, 1933.)
Beckmann, Ewald. Der Dolchstoss-Prozess in München. (Munich, 1925.)
Brammer, Karl. Der Prozess des Reichspräsidenten. (Berlin, 1925.)
Dokumente des Widerstandes. (Hamburg, 1946.)
German Documents relating to the World War. Carnegie Endowment for International Peace. (New York, 1923.)
Golder, Frank Alfred. Documents of Russian History, 1914–1917. (New York, 1927.)
Halifax, Rt. Hon. the Earl of. Speeches on Foreign Policy. (Oxford, 1940.)
Materiale zu einem Weissbuch der deutschen Opposition. (SPD, London, 1946.)
My New Order. Hitler's Speeches, 1919–1941, edited by Count Raoul de Roussy de Sales. (New York, 1941.)
Preliminary History of the Armistice. Carnegie Endowment for International Peace. (New York, 1924.)
Rede des Vizekanzlers von Papen vor dem Universitätsbund, Marburg, am 17. Juni 1934. (Berlin, 1934.)

BIBLIOGRAPHY
769

Soviet Foreign Policy during the Patriotic War — Documents and Materials. (London, 1945.)
The Causes of German Collapse in 1918. Documents selected by Ralph Haswell Lutz. (Stanford University, Calif., 1934.)
The Speeches of Adolf Hitler, 1922–1939. Edited by Professor Norman Baynes. (Oxford, 1942.)
Weissbuch über die Erschiessungen des 30. Juni 1934. (Paris, 1935.)

(ii) DIARIES

Ciano's Diary, 1937–1938 (London, 1952.)
Ciano's Diary, 1939–1943. (London, 1947.)
Goebbels Diaries, January 1942–December 1943. (Louis Lochner, Ed. London, 1948.)
Goebbels, the Man next to Hitler; being the Diaries of Rudolf Semmler. (London, 1947.)
Gustav Stresemann, His Diaries, Letters, Papers. (Eric Sutton, Ed. London, 1935–40.)
My Part in Germany's Fight. Goebbels Diaries from January 1932–May 1933. (London, 1935.)
Sven Hedin's German Diary, 1935–1942. (Dublin, 1951.)
Vom andern Deutschland. (The Hassell Diaries.) Ulrich von Hassell. (Zürich, 1946.)

IV. BOOKS AND PAMPHLETS

ABETZ, OTTO. Pétain et les Allemands. (Paris, 1948.)
  D'une prison. (Paris, 1949.)
  Das offene Problem. (Köln, 1951.)
ABSHAGEN, KARL HEINZ. Canaris. (Stuttgart, 1949.)
ALMOND, GABRIEL A., and KRAUS, WOLFGANG H. 'Resistance and Repression under the Nazis'; 'The Social Composition of German Resistance'; chapters in the 'Struggle for Democracy in Germany'. (G. Almond, Ed. Chapel Hill, N.C., 1949.)
ANDREAS-FRIEDRICH, RUTH. Berlin Underground, 1939–1945. (London, 1948.)
APFEL, ALFRED. Behind the Scenes of German Justice, 1882–1933. (London, 1935.)
ASSMANN, KAPITÄN ZUR SEE KURT. Deutsche Schicksalsjahre. (Wiesbaden, 1950.)
BADEN, PRINCE MAX OF. Memoirs. (New York, 1928.)
BAGNOLD, ENID, et al. Albrecht Bernstorff zum Gedächtnis. (Altenhof, 1952. Privately printed.)
BAINVILLE, JACQUES. L'Allemagne. (Paris, 1939.)
BARTH, EMIL. Aus der Werkstatt der deutschen Revolution. (Berlin, 1919.)
BARTZ, Karl. Die Tragödie der deutschen Abwehr. (Salzburg, 1955.)
BAUMONT, PROFESSOR MAURICE. L'Abdication de Guillaume II. (Paris, 1930.)
BAVARIAN SOCIAL DEMOCRATIC PARTY. Hitler und Kahr. (Munich, 1928.)

BAYLES, WILLIAM. Seven were Hanged. (London, 1945.)

BELOFF, MAX. The Foreign Policy of Soviet Russia, 1929–1941. (Oxford, 1947–9.)

BENOIST-MÉCHIN, JACQUES. Histoire de l'armée allemande depuis l'armistice. (Paris, 1936–8.)

BERNADOTTE, COUNT FOLKE. The Curtain Falls. (London, 1945.)

BERNDORFF, H. R. General zwischen Ost und West. (Hamburg, 1951.)

BERNHARD, HENRY. Finis Germaniae. (Stuttgart, 1948.)

BEST, CAPT. S. PAYNE. The Venlo Incident. (London, 1950.)

BETHMANN HOLLWEG, THEOBALD VON. Betrachtungen zum Weltkriege (Berlin, 1919–21.)

BLÜCHER, WIPERT VON. Deutschlands Weg nach Rapallo. (Wiesbaden, 1951.)

BLÜCHER VON WAHLSTATT, COUNT CURT. Know Your Germans. (London, 1952.)

BLUMENTRITT, MAJOR-GENERAL GÜNTHER. Von Rundstedt, the Soldier and the Man. (London, 1952.)

BOLDT, CAPTAIN GERHARDT. Die letzten Tage der Reichskanzlei. (Hamburg, 1947.)

BONHOEFFER, DIETRICH. Widerstand und Ergebung. (Munich, 1951.)

BONN, MORITZ J. A Wandering Scholar. (London, 1949.)

BOR, PETER. Gespräche mit Halder. (Wiesbaden, 1950.)

BORCHMEYER, DR. JUR. (ed.). Hugenbergs Ringen in deutschen Schicksalsstunden. (Detmold, 1951.)

BRACHER, KARL DIETRICH. Die Auflösung der Weimarer Republik. Eine Studie zum Problem des Machtverfalls in der Demokratie. (3rd edition, Cologne, 1960.)

BRACHER, KARL DIETRICH, SAUER, WOLFGANG, and SCHULZ, GERHARD. Die Nationalsozialistische Machtergreifung. (2nd edition, Cologne, 1962.)

BRAMSTEDT, E. K. Dictatorship and Political Police : the Technique of Control by Fear. (London, 1945.)

BRAUN, OTTO. Von Weimar zu Hitler. (New York, 1940.)

BRAUWEILER, HEINZ. Generäle in der Deutschen Republik. (Berlin, 1932.)

BRECHT, ARNOLD. Prelude to Silence ; the end of the German Republic. (New York, 1944.)

BREDOW, KLAUS. Hitler rast. Der 30. Juni. Ablauf, Vorgeschichte und Hintergründe. (Saarbrücken, 1934.)

BRYANS, J. LONSDALE. Blind Victory. (London, 1951.)

BRYANT, ARTHUR. The Age of Elegance. (London, 1950.)

BUCHRUCKER, MAJOR. Im Schatten Seeckts, die Geschichte der Schwarzen Reichswehr. (Berlin, 1928.)

BULLOCK, ALAN. Hitler : A study in Tyranny. (Revised edition, London, 1962.)

BÜLOW, PRINCE BERNHARD VON. Imperial Germany. (New York, 1915.) Memoirs, 1849–1919. (London, 1931–2.)

BUTLER, SIR JAMES. Grand Strategy, Vol. II. (London, 1957.)

CAHEN, FRITZ MAX. Men against Hitler. (New York, 1939.)

CARO, K., and OEHME, W. Schleichers Aufstieg. (Berlin, 1933.)

CARR, EDWARD HALLETT. German-Soviet Relations between the two World Wars, 1919–1939. (Baltimore, Md., 1951.)

CARRIAS, Col. EUGÈNE. L'Armée allemande. (Paris, 1938.)
La Pensée militaire allemande. (Paris, 1948.)
CASTELLAN, G. Le Réarmement clandestin du Reich, 1933–1935. (Paris, 1954.)
CATT, HENRI DE. Frederick the Great. (London, 1916.)
CHICHESTER, BISHOP OF (Dr. GEORGE BELL). The Church and Humanity. (London, 1946.)
CHURCHILL, Rt. Hon. WINSTON S. The Hinge of Fate. (London, 1951.)
CLARK, R. T. The Fall of the German Republic. (London, 1935.)
COLVIN, IAN. Chief of Intelligence. (London, 1951.)
CRAIG, GORDON. The Politics of the Prussian Army, 1640–1945. (Oxford, 1955.)
CZERNIN, COUNT OTTOKAR. In the World War. (London, 1919.)
D'ABERNON, VISCOUNT. An Ambassador of Peace. (London, 1929–30.)
Portraits and Appreciations. (London, 1931.)
DAHLERUS, BIRGER. The Last Attempt. (London, 1947.)
DAHRENDORF, GUSTAV. Julius Leber, ein Mann geht seinen Weg. (Frankfurt a.M., 1952.)
DALLIN, ALEXANDER. German Rule in Russia, 1941–1945. (London, 1957.)
DANIELS, H. G. The Rise of the German Republic. (London, 1927.)
DARCY, PAUL. L'Allemagne toujours armée. (Paris, 1933.)
DENNIS, A. L. P. The Foreign Policies of Soviet Russia. (New York, 1926.)
DEUERLEIN, ERNST. Der Hitlerputsch. Bayerische Dokumente zum 8/9 November 1923. (Stuttgart, 1962.)
DIRKSEN, HERBERT VON. Moscow-Tokyo-London. (London, 1951.)
DOLLMANN, EUGEN. Roma Nazista. (Milan, 1951.)
DÖNHOFF, COUNTESS MARION. Den Freunden zum Gedächtnis ; in Memoriam 20. Juli 1944. (Hamburg, 1946.)
DORTEN, ADAM. La Tragédie rhénane. (Paris, 1945.)
DUESTERBERG, THEODOR. Der Stahlhelm und Hitler. (Hanover, 1949.)
DULLES, ALLEN W. Germany's Underground. (New York, 1947.)
EBELING, H. The Caste : the Political Rôle of the German General Staff between 1918 and 1938. (London, 1945.)
EBERT, FRIEDRICH. Schriften, Aufzeichnungen, Reden. (Dresden, 1926.)
EBERT, FRIEDRICH (jun.). Friedrich Ebert : Kämpfe und Ziele aus seinem Nachlasse. (Berlin, 1927.)
EDSCHMID, KASIMIR. In Memoriam Carlo Mierendorff. (Darmstadt, 1947.)
EINSIEDEL, COUNT HEINRICH VON. Tagebuch der Versuchung. (Berlin, 1950.)
ENDRES, MAJOR FRANZ CARL. Reichswehr und Demokratie. (Leipzig, 1919.)
EPSTEIN, KLAUS. Matthias Erzberger and the Dilemma of German Democracy. (Princeton, 1959.)
ERZBERGER, MATTHIAS. Erlebnisse im Weltkrieg. (Berlin, 1920.)
FALKENHAYN, LIEUT.-GENERAL ERICH VON. General Headquarters, 1914–1916, and its Critical Decisions. (London, 1919.)
FALLS, CYRIL. The Second World War. (London, 1948.)
FECHTER, PAUL. Menschen und Zeiten. (Gütersloh, 1949.)
FEILING, KEITH. The Life of Neville Chamberlain. (London, 1946.)
FISCHER, GEORGE. Soviet Opposition to Stalin. (Harvard, 1952.)

FISCHER, LOUIS. The Soviets in World Affairs. (London, 1930.)
FISCHER, RUTH. Stalin and German Communism. (Cambridge, Mass., 1948.)
FITZGIBBON, CONSTANTINE. The Shirt of Nessus. (London, 1956.)
FLICKE, W. Rote Kapelle. (Düsseldorf-Hilden, 1949.)
FOERSTER, MAJOR WOLFGANG. Ein General kämpft gegen den Krieg. (Munich, 1949.)
FOERTSCH, GENERAL HERMANN. Schuld und Verhängnis. (Stuttgart, 1951.)
FOLTMANN, JOSEF, and MOLLER, HANS. Opfergang der Generale. (Berlin, 1952.)
FRAENKEL, HEINRICH. The German People versus Hitler. (London, 1940.)
FRANÇOIS, JEAN. L'Affaire Röhm-Hitler. (Paris, 1939.)
FRANÇOIS-PONCET, ANDRÈ. Souvenirs d'une ambassade à Berlin, septembre 1931–octobre 1938. (Paris, 1946.)
FREUND, GERALD. Unholy Alliance. (London, 1957.)
FRIED, HANS ERNST. The Guilt of the German Army. (New York, 1942.)
FRIEDENSBURG, FERDINAND. Die Weimarer Republik. (Berlin, 1946.)
FRISCHAUER, WILLI. Göring. (London, 1951.)
FROBENIUS, COLONEL H. The German Empire's Hour of Destiny. (London, 1914.)
FULLER, MAJOR-GENERAL J. F. C. The Second World War. (London, 1948.)
GÄSSLER, CHRISTIAN W. Offizier und Offizierkorps der alten Armee in Deutschland als Voraussetzung einer Untersuchung über die Transformation der militärischen Hierarchie. (Mannheim, 1930.)
GATZKE, HANS W. Stresemann and the Rearmament of Germany. (Baltimore, 1954.)
GAULLE, GENERAL CHARLES DE. La Discorde chez l'ennemi. (Paris, 1944.)
GAUSS, CHRISTIAN. The German Emperor as shown in his Public Utterances. (New York, 1915.)
GENTIZON, PAUL. L'Armée allemande depuis la défaite. (Paris, 1920.)
GESSLER, OTTO. Reichswehrpolitik in der Weimarer Zeit. (Stuttgart, 1958.)
GILBERT, FELIX. Hitler directs his War. (New York, 1950.)
GILBERT, MARTIN, and GOTT, RICHARD. The Appeasers. (London, 1963.)
GISEVIUS, HANS BERND. Bis zum bittern Ende. (Zürich, 1946.)
GLOMBOWSKI, FRIEDRICH. Frontiers of Terror : The Fate of Schlageter and his Comrades. (London, 1935.)
GOLTZ, GENERAL COUNT VON DER. Als politischer General im Osten 1918 und 1919. (Berlin, 1936.)
GORDON, HAROLD J., JR. The Reichswehr and the German Republic, 1919–1926. (Princeton, 1957.)
GÖRING, HERMANN. Germany Re-born. (London, 1934.)
GÖRLITZ, WALTER. Der deutsche Generalstab. (Frankfurt-a-M., 1950.)
Der zweite Weltkrieg. (Stuttgart, 1951–1952.)
Keitel, Verbrecher oder Offizier ? Erinnerungen, Briefe und Dokumente des Chefs OKW. (Göttingen, 1961.)
GREINER, HELMUTH. Die Oberste Wehrmacht Führung, 1939–1943. (Wiesbaden, 1951.)
GRITZBACH, ERICH. Hermann Göring, Werk und Mensch. (Munich, 1941.)

GRÖNER, WILHELM. Lebenserinnerungen. Jugend, Generalstab, Weltkrieg. (Göttingen, 1957.)

GROENER-GEYER, DOROTHEA. General Gröner. Soldat und Staatsmann. (Frankfurt-a-M., 1955.)

GRÖNER, GENERAL WILHELM. Feldherr wider Willen. (Berlin, 1931.)

GRZESINSKI, ALBERT. Inside Germany. (New York, 1939.)

GUDERIAN, COLONEL-GENERAL HEINZ. Erinnerungen eines Soldaten. (Heidelberg, 1951.)

GUMBEL, E. J. Vier Jahre politischer Mord. (Berlin, 1922.)
Les Grands Crimes politiques en Allemagne. (Paris, 1931.)

HAGEN, WALTER. Die geheime Front. (Linz/Wien, 1950.)

HALDANE, VISCOUNT. Before the War. (London, 1920.)

HALDER, COLONEL-GENERAL FRANZ. Hitler als Feldherr. (Munich, 1949.)
Kriegstagebuch, Vol. I (1962), Vol. II (1963). (Edited by Hans-Adolf Jacobsen. Stuttgart.)

HALLGARTEN, GEORGE W. F. Hitler, Reichswehr und Industrie. (Frankfurt, 1955.)

HALPERIN, S. WILLIAM. Germany tried Democracy. (New York, 1946.)

HANFSTAENGEL, ERNST. Hitler, The Missing Years. (London, 1957.)

HARMS, B. (Ed.). Volk und Reich der Deutschen. (Berlin, 1929.)

HART, B. H. LIDDELL. The Other Side of the Hill. (2nd edn., London, 1948.)

HARZENDORF, FRITZ. Der 20. Juli 1944. (Constance, n.d.)

HEGEMANN, JAKOB. Entlarvte Geschichte. (Leipzig, 1933.)

HEIDEN, KONRAD. A History of National Socialism. (London, 1934.)
Der Führer, Hitler's Rise to Power. (London, 1945.)

HEINZ, HEINZ A. Germany's Hitler. (London, 1934.)

HELFFERICH, KARL THEODOR. Denkwürdigkeiten. (Berlin, 1930–31.)
Der Weltkrieg. (Berlin, 1919.)

HENDERSON, SIR NEVILE. Failure of a Mission. (New York, 1940.)

HENEMAN, HARLOW JAMES. The Growth of Executive Power in Germany. (Minneapolis, 1934.)

HENK, EMIL. Die Tragödie des 20. Juli, 1944. (Heidelberg, 1946.)

HERMLIN, STEPHAN. Der Leutnant Yorck von Wartenburg. (Singen, n.d.)

HERTLING, RITTMEISTER COUNT CARL VON. Ein Jahr in der Reichskanzlei. (Freiburg-im-Breisgau, 1919.)

HEUSINGER, LIEUT.-GENERAL ADOLF. Befehl im Widerstreit. (Stuttgart, 1950.)

HEUSS, THEODOR. Kapp-Luttwitz. Das Verbrechen gegen die Nation. (Berlin, 1920.)
Friedrich Naumann, der Mann, das Werk, die Zeit. (Stuttgart, 1949.)

HILDEBRANDT, RAINER. Wir sind die Letzten. (Berlin, 1950.)

HILGER, GUSTAV, and MEYER, ALFRED. The Incompatible Allies, German-Soviet relations, 1918–1941. (New York, 1953.)

HINSLEY, F. H. Hitler's Strategy. (Cambridge, 1951.)

HITLER, ADOLF. Mein Kampf. (Munich, 1936.)
Der Hitlerprozess vor dem Volksgericht in München. (Munich, 1924.)
Hitlers Lagebesprechungen. Die Protokolfragmente seiner militärischen Konferenzen, 1942–45. (Ed. Helmut Heiber. Stuttgart, 1962.)

HOEM, MARTIN. Halder, Schuld oder Tragik. (Munich, 1948.)
HOEMBERG, ELIZABETH and ALBERT. Thy people, my people. (London, 1950.)
HOFMANN, HANS HUBERT. Der Hitlerputsch. Krisenjahre deutscher Geschichte. (Munich, 1961.)
HOSSBACH, GENERAL FRIEDRICH. Zwischen Wehrmacht und Hitler. (Hanover, 1949.)
HULL, Hon. CORDELL. Memoirs. (New York, 1948.)
JÄCKH, ERNEST. The War for Man's Soul. (New York, 1943.)
JACOB, BERTHOLD. Das neue deutsche Heer und seine Führer. (Paris, 1936.)
JACOBSEN, HANS ADOLF. Fall Gelb. (Wiesbaden, 1957.)
  Dokumente zur Vorgeschichte des Westfeldzuges, 1939–40. (Berlin, 1956.)
JANSEN, JAN B., and WAHL, STEFAN. The Silent War. (New York, 1943.)
KABISCH, LIEUT.-GENERAL ERNST. Gröner. (Leipzig, 1932.)
KANTOROWICZ, HERMANN. Der Offiziershass im Deutschen Heer. (Freiburg im Breisgau, 1919.)
KERN, ERICH. The Dance of Death. (London, 1951.)
KESSELRING, ALBERT. Soldat bis zum letzten Tag. (Bonn, 1953.)
KIELMANSEGG, COUNT. Der Fritsch-Prozess, 1938. (Hamburg, 1949.)
KLEFFENS, JONKHEER ELKO VAN. The Rape of the Netherlands. (London, 1940.)
KLEIST, PETER. Zwischen Hitler und Stalin, 1939–1945. (Bonn, 1950.)
KNIGHT-PATTERSON, W. M. Germany from Defeat to Conquest. (London, 1945.)
KNUDSEN, HELGE. Oprøre i Hitlers Borg. (Copenhagen, 1947.)
KOCH, LUTZ. Erwin Rommel : die Wandlung eines grossen Soldaten. (Stuttgart, 1950.)
KOEBER, WALTHER (et al.). Mord ! Spionage ! ! Attentat ! ! ! Die Blutspur des englischen Geheimdienstes bis zum Münchner Bombenanschlag. (Berlin, 1940.)
KOERSTEN, FELIX. Memoirs. (New York, 1947.)
KOGON, EUGEN. Der SS-Staat ; das System des deutschen Konzentrationslagers. (Munich, 1946.)
KORDT, ERICH. Wahn und Wirklichkeit. (Stuttgart, 1947.)
  Nicht aus den Akten. (Stuttgart, 1950.)
KRAUS, FRIEDRICH (Ed.). Goerdelers Politisches Testament. (New York, 1945.)
KRAUS, HERBERT. The Crisis of German Democracy, a Study of the Spirit of the Constitution of Weimar. (Princeton, 1932.)
Kriegstagebuch des Oberkommandos der Wehrmacht. (Wehrmachtführungsstab.) (Frankfurt-a-M., 1961.)
KRISS, ERNST, and SPEIER, HANS. German Radio Propaganda. (New York, 1944.)
KROSIGK, COUNT LUTZ SCHWERIN VON. Es geschah in Deutschland. (Tübingen/Stuttgart, 1951.)
KÜHLMANN, RICHARD VON. Erinnerungen. (Heidelberg, 1948.)
LANDSBERG, OTTO. The Germans at Versailles (Ed. Viktor Schiff. London, 1930.)

LANG, SERGE, and SCHENCK, ERNST VON. Porträt eines Menschheitsverbrechers nach den hinterlassenen Memoiren des ehemaligen Reichsministers Alfred Rosenberg. (St. Gallen, 1947.)

LANGE, EITEL. Der Reichsmarschall im Kriege. (Stuttgart, 1950.)

LEBER, ANNEDORE. Den Toten, immer lebendigen Freunden. (Berlin, 1946.)

Das Gewissen steht auf. (Berlin, 1954.)

LEHMANN, KLAUS. Widerstandsgruppen Schulze-Boysen/Harnack. (Berlin, 1948.)

LEHMANN-RUSSBUELDT, OTTO. Aggression; the Origin of Germany's War Machine. (London, 1942.)

LEND, EVELYN. Underground Struggle in Germany. (London, 1938.)

LILJE, DR. HANS, BISHOP OF HANOVER. The Valley of the Shadow. (London, 1950.)

LÖBE, PAUL. Erinnerungen eines Reichstagspräsidenten. (Berlin, 1949.)

LOCHNER, LOUIS. What about Germany? (New York, 1942.)

LOCKHART, SIR ROBERT BRUCE. Comes the Reckoning. (London, 1947.)

LOMMER, HORST. Das tausendjährige Reich. (Berlin, 1947.)

LOSSBERG, MAJOR-GENERAL BERNHARD VON. Im Wehrmachtführungsstab; Bericht eines Generalstabsoffiziers. (Hamburg, 1949.)

LUCKAU, ALMA. The German Delegation at the Paris Peace Conference. (New York, 1941.)

LUDECKE, KURT. I knew Hitler. (New York, 1934.)

LUDENDORFF, GENERAL ERICH. Auf dem Weg zur Feldherrnhalle. (Munich, 1937.)

My War Memories. (London, 1919.)

The General Staff and its Problems. (London, 1920.)

LUDENDORFF, MARGARITTE. Als ich Ludendorffs Frau war. (Munich, 1929.)

LUEHR, ELMER. The New German Republic. (New York, 1929.)

LÜTTWITZ, GENERAL FREIHERR WALTHER VON. Im Kampf gegen die November-Revolution. (Leipzig, 1921.)

MAERCKER, GENERAL LUDWIG. Vom Kaiserheer zur Reichswehr. (Leipzig, 1922.)

MALAPARTE, CURZIO. La Technique du coup d'état. (Paris, 1931.)

MANSTEIN, ERICH VON. Verlorene Siege. (Bonn, 1955.)

Aus einem Soldatenleben, 1887–1939. (Bonn, 1958.)

MATTERN, JOHANNES. The Constitutional Jurisprudence of the German Republic. (Baltimore, 1928.)

MATTHIAS, ERICH, and MORSEY, R. Das ende der Parteien. (Düsseldorf, 1960.)

MAYER, J. P. Max Weber and German Politics. (London, 1944.)

MEINCK, GERHARD. Hitler und die deutsche Aufrüstung, 1933–1937. (Wiesbaden, 1959.)

MEINECKE, FRIEDRICH. Die deutsche Katastrophe. (Zürich/Wiesbaden. 1946.)

MEISSNER, Otto. Staatssekretär unter Ebert, Hindenburg und Hitler. (Hamburg, 1950.)

MELVILLE, CECIL F. The Russian Face of Germany. (London, 1932.)

MENNE, BERNHARD. Krupp, or the Lords of Essen. (London, 1939.)

MERKER, PAUL.   Deutschland, sein oder nicht sein ?   (Mexico City, 1945.)
MICHAELIS, GEORG.   Für Staat und Volk.   (Berlin, 1922.)
MICHEL, KARL.   Ost und West ;   der Ruf Stauffenbergs.   (Zürich, 1947.)
MILLER, MAX.   Eugen Bolz, Staatsmann and Bekenner.   (Stuttgart, 1951.)
MINSHALL, COLONEL T. H.   Future Germany.   (London, 1943.)
MOEBLHAUSEN, EITEL FRIEDRICH.   Die gebrochene Achse.   (Alfed/Leine, 1949.)
MOLTKE, COLONEL-GENERAL COUNT HELMUTH VON.   Erinnerungen, Briefe, und Dokumente.   (Berlin, 1922.)
MOLTKE-KREISAU, COUNT HELMUTH VON.   A German of the Resistance. (Anon. ed.   Oxford, 1948.)
MORGAN, BRIGADIER-GENERAL J. H.   Assize of Arms.   (London, 1945.)
MOURIN, MAXIME.   Les Complots contre Hitler.   (Paris, 1948.)
   Les Tentatives de paix dans la seconde guerre mondiale, 1939-1945. (Paris, 1949.)
MOWRER, EDGAR ANSELL.   Germany puts the Clock Back.   (London, 1933.)
MÜLLER, JOHANNES.   Sturz in den Abgrund ; die letzten zehn Monate, 20. Juli 1944 bis 8. Mai 1945.   (Offenbach, 1947.)
MÜLLER, MAJOR WOLFGANG.   Gegen ein neue Dolchstosslüge.   (Hanover, 1947.)
MURAWSKI, ERICH.   Der deutsche Wehrmachtbericht, 1939-1945.   (Bop-pard-a-R., 1962.)
MUSSOLINI, BENITO.   Memoirs 1942-1943.   (London, 1949.)
NAMIER, SIR LEWIS.   Diplomatic Prelude.   (London, 1948.)
   In the Nazi Era.   (London, 1952.)
NEUMANN, ALFRED.   Six of Them.   (London, 1945.)
NICHOLS, K. R., and ANSBACHER, H. L.   Selecting the Nazi Officer.   (Wash-ington, D.C., 1941.)
NIEMANN, ALFRED.   Kaiser und Heer.   (Berlin, 1929.)
   Kaiser und Revolution.   (Berlin, 1928.)
NIESSEL, GENERAL.   L'Évacuation des pays baltiques par les Allemands, contribution à l'étude de la mentalité allemande.   (Paris, 1935.)
NOLLET, GENERAL.   Une Expérience de désarmement.   (Paris, 1932.)
NOSKE, GUSTAV.   Von Kiel bis Kapp.   (Berlin, 1920.)
   Erlebtes aus Aufstieg und Niedergang einer Demokratie.   (Zürich, 1947.)
NOWAK, KARL FRIEDRICH.   Versailles.   (London, 1928.)
OERTZEN, F. W. VON.   Die deutschen Freikorps 1918-1923.   (Munich, 1936.)
   In Namen der Geschichte.   (Hamburg, 1934.)
OLDEN, RUDOLF.   Hitler.   (New York, 1936.)
   Stresemann.   (London, 1930.)
PAETEL, KARL (Ed.).   Innere Emigration.   (New York, 1946.)
PAPEN, FRANZ VON.   Memoirs.   (London, 1952.)
PECHEL, RUDOLF.   Deutscher Widerstand.   (Zürich, 1947.)
   Zwischen den Zeilen.   (Munich, 1948.)
PERTINAX.   Les Fossoyeurs.   (New York, 1943.)
PETER, K. H. (Ed.).   Spiegelbild einer Verschwörung.   Die Kaltenbrunner Berichte an Bormann u. Hitler über das Attentat von 20. Juli 1944. (Stuttgart, 1961.)

PICKER, HENRY. Hitlers Tischgespräche im Führerhauptquartier. (Bonn, 1951.)

PRUSSIA, PRINCE LOUIS-FERDINAND OF. Rebel Prince. (Hinsdale, Ill., 1952.)

PUTTKAMMER, JESCO VON. Irrtum und Schuld. Geschichte des National Komitees Freies Deutschland. (Berlin, 1948.)

RABENAU, LIEUT.-GENERAL FRIEDRICH VON. Seeckt, aus seinem Leben. (Leipzig, 1940.)

RAEDER, ERICH. Mein Leben. (Tübingen, 1956.)

RAUSCHNING, HERMANN. Germany's Revolution of Destruction. (London, 1939.)

Makers of Destruction. (London, 1942.)

REINHARD, COLONEL WILHELM. 1918–1919, die Wehen der Republik. (Berlin, 1933.)

REISCHACH, FREIHERR HUGO VON. Unter drei Kaisern. (Berlin, 1925.)

REITLINGER, GERALD. The S.S. Alibi of a Nation. (London, 1956.)

REMER, MAJOR-GENERAL OTTO ERNST. 20. Juli 1944. (Hamburg, 1951.)

REUTER, FRANZ. Der 20. Juli und seine Vorgeschichte. (Berlin, 1946.)

RIESS, CURT. Joseph Goebbels. (New York, 1948.)

The Self-Betrayed : Glory and Doom of the German Generals. (New York, 1942.)

RITTER, GERHARD. Carl Goerdeler und die deutsche Widerstandsbewegung. (Stuttgart, 1954.)

RODDIE, STEWART. Peace Patrol. (New York, 1933.)

RÖHM, ERNST. Die Memoiren des Stabschefs Röhm. (Saarbrücken, 1934.)

The Rommel Papers. (Edited by Liddell Hart. Trans. P. Findlay. London, 1953.)

ROSENBERG, ARTHUR. The Birth of the German Republic. (London, 1931.)

A History of the German Republic. (London, 1936.)

ROSINSKI, HERBERT. The German Army. (London, 1939.)

ROSSBACH, GERHARD. Mein Weg durch die Zeit. (Weilburg-Lahn, 1950.)

ROSSI, A. Deux Ans d'alliance germano-soviétique 1939–1941. (Paris, 1949.)

ROTHFELS, HANS. The German Opposition to Hitler. (London, 1961.)

SALOMON, ERNST VON. Die Geächteten. (Berlin, 1931.)

Der Fragebogen. (Hamburg, 1951.)

SAUERBRUCH, ERNST FERDINAND. Das war mein Leben. (Bad Wörishofen, 1951.)

SCHACHT, HJALMAR. Account Settled. (London, 1949.)

My first 76 Years. (London, 1955.)

SCHEELE, GODFREY. The Weimar Republic. (London, 1946.)

SCHEIDEMANN, PHILIP. Der Zusammenbruch. (Berlin, 1921.)

The Making of New Germany. (New York, 1929.)

SCHELLENBERG, WALTER. The Schellenberg Memoirs. (London, 1956.)

SCHEMANN, LUDWIG. Wolfgang Kapp und das Märzunternehmen vom Jahre 1920. (Munich/Berlin, 1937.)

SCHLABRENDORFF, FABIAN VON. Offiziere gegen Hitler. (Zürich, 1946.)

SCHLANGE-SCHÖNINGEN, HANS. Am Tage danach. (Hamburg, 1947.)

SCHMIDT, PAUL. Statist auf diplomatischer Bühne, 1923–1945. (Bonn, 1949.)

SCHMIDT-BÜCKEBURG, K. Das Militär-Kabinett. (Berlin, 1933.)

SCHMIDT-PAULI, EDGAR VON. Geschichte der Freikorps 1918–1924. (Stuttgart, 1936.)

SCHNEIDER, REINHOLD. Gedenkwort zum 20. Juli. (Freiburg, 1947.)

SCHOLL, INGE. Die Weisse Rose (Frankfurt-a-M., 1952.)

SCHOTT, GEORG. Das Volksbuch vom Hitler. (Munich, 1928.)

SCHRAMM, WILHELM VON. Rommel, Schicksal eines Deutschen ! (Munich, 1949.)

Der 20. Juli in Paris. (Bad Wörishofen, 1953.)

SCHÜDDEKOPF, OTTO ERNST. Das Heer und die Republik. Quellen zur Politik der Reichswehrführung, 1918 bis 1933. (Hanover, 1955.)

SCHUSCHNIGG, KURT VON. Farewell Austria. (London, 1938.)

SCHWEND, KARL. Bayern zwischen Monarchie und Diktatur. (Munich, 1954.)

SCHWEPPENBERG, GENERAL FREIHERR GEYR VON. Erinnerungen eines Militärattachés London 1933–1937. (Stuttgart, 1949.)

SEECKT, GENERAL HANS VON. Die Reichswehr. (Leipzig, 1933.)

The Future of the German Empire. (London, 1930.)

Thoughts of a Soldier. (London, 1930.)

SEVERING, CARL. Mein Lebensweg. (Cologne, 1950.)

SHERWOOD, ROBERT. Roosevelt and Hopkins. (New York, 1948.)

SHIRER, WILLIAM. Berlin Diary. (New York, 1941.)

The Rise and Fall of the Third Reich. (London, 1960.)

SHULMAN, MILTON. Defeat in the West. (London, 1947.)

SILENS, CONSTANTIN. Irrweg und Umkehr. (Basel, 1946.)

SKORZENY, OTTO. Geheimkommando Skorzeny. (Hamburg, 1950.)

SPEIDEL, GENERAL HANS. Invasion 1944 : ein Beitrag zu Rommels und des Reiches Schicksal. (Stuttgart, 1949.)

SPEIDEL, HANS (Ed.). Ludwig Beck. Studien. (Stuttgart, 1955.)

SPIECKER, KARL. Germany from Defeat to Defeat. (London, n.d.)

STAMPFER, FRIEDRICH. Die vierzehn Jahre der ersten Deutschen Republik. (Karlsbad, 1936.)

STELTZER, THEODOR. Von deutscher Politik. (Frankfurt-a-M., 1949.)

STOLPER, GUSTAV. This Age of Fable. (London, 1943.)

STRASSER, OTTO. Die deutsche Bartholomäusnacht. (Zürich, 1935.)

Hitler and I. (London, 1940.)

STRESEMANN, GUSTAV. Von der Revolution bis zum Frieden von Versailles. (Berlin, 1919.)

STRÖBEL, HEINRICH. The German Revolution and After. (London, n.d.)

STRÖLIN, KARL. Stuttgart im Endstadium des Krieges. (Stuttgart, 1950.)

Verräter oder Patrioten. (Stuttgart, 1952.)

TAYLOR, A. J. P. The Origins of the Second World War. (London, 1961.)

TAYLOR, TELFORD. Sword and Swastika. (New York, 1952.)

TESSIN, GEORG. Formationsgeschichte der Wehrmacht, 1933–1939. (Boppard-a-R., 1959.) Stabe und Truppenteile des Heeres und der Luftwaffe.

THIMME, ANNELISE. G. Stresemann. Eine politische Biographie. (Hanover, 1959.)

THOMÉE, MAJOR GERHARDT. Der Wiederaufstieg des deutschen Heeres 1918–1938. (Berlin, 1939.)

THOMPSON, DOROTHY. Listen Hans. (Boston, 1942.)

THYSSEN, FRITZ. I paid Hitler. (New York, 1941.)

TIPPELSKIRCH, GENERAL KURT VON. Geschichte des zweiten Weltkriegs. (Bonn, 1951.)

TIRPITZ, GRAND-ADMIRAL ALFRED VON. My Memoirs. (London, 1919.)

TOYNBEE, ARNOLD, and VERONICA. Hitler's Europe. Survey of International Affairs, 1939–1946. (London, 1954.)

TREVIRANUS, G. R. Revolutions in Russia. (New York, 1944.)

TREVOR-ROPER, HUGH. Last Days of Hitler. (Revised edition, London, 1950.)

VALENTINI, COUNT RUDOLF VON. Kaiser und Kabinettschef. (Oldenburg, 1931.)

VERMEHREN, ISA. Reise durch den letzten Akt. (Hamburg, 1947.)

VLASSOV, GENERAL A. J'ai choisi la potence. (Paris, 1947.)

VOGELSANG, THILO. Reichswehr, Staat und NSDAP. Beiträge zur deutschen Geschichte. 1930–1932. (Stuttgart, 1962.)

VOLKMANN, ERICH OTTO. Revolution über Deutschland. (Oldenburg, 1930.)

Die Vollmacht des Gewissens. (3rd edition, Frankfurt, 1960.)

VOSSLER, KARL. Gedenkrede fur die Opfer an der Universität München. (Munich, 1947.)

WAITE, ROBERT G. L. Vanguard of Nazism. (Harvard, 1952.)

WARLIMONT, WALTER. Im Hauptquartier der deutschen Wehrmacht. 1939–1945. Grundlage, Formen, Gestalten. (Frankfurt, 1962.)

WEISENBORN, GUENTHER. Der lautlose Aufstand. (Hamburg, 1953.)

WEIZSÄCKER, FREIHERR ERNST VON. Erinnerungen. (Munich, 1950.)

WESTARP, COUNT KUNO VON. Das Ende der Monarchie am 9. November 1918. (Berlin, 1952.)

WESTPHAL, GENERAL SIEGFRIED. Heer in Fesseln. (Bonn, 1950.)

WHEATLEY, RONALD. Operation Sea Lion. (London, 1958.)

20. Juli 1944. (3rd edition. Ed. Erich Zimmermann and Hans-Adolf Jacobsen. Bonn, 1960.)

WHEELER-BENNETT, JOHN W. Hindenburg : the Wooden Titan. (London, 1936.)

Brest-Litovsk : The Forgotten Peace. (London, 1938.)

Munich : Prologue to Tragedy. (London, 1948.)

WINNIG, AUGUST. Das Reich als Republik 1918–1928. (Berlin, 1929.)

WOLFF, THEODOR. Through two Decades. (London, 1936.)

WOLLENBERG, ERICH. The Red Army. (London, 1938.)

YOUNG, BRIGADIER DESMOND. Rommel. (London, 1950.)

ZARNOW, GOTTFRIED. Gefesselte Justiz. (Munich, 1931.)

ZEDLITZ-TREUTSCHLER, COUNT ROBERT VON. Zwölf Jahre am deutschen Kaiserhof. (Berlin, 1923.)

ZELLER, EBERHARD. Geist der Freiheit. Der zwanzigste Juli. (Munich, 1954.)

ZOLLER, ALBERT. Hitler Privat : Erlebnisbericht seiner Geheimsekretärin. (Düsseldorf, 1949.)

ZUCKMAYER, CARL. Des Teufels General. (Berlin/Frankfurt-a-M., 1949.)

2C

V. ARTICLES IN NEWSPAPERS AND PERIODICALS

A. M. G. 'A Footnote to History.' *Blackwood's Magazine*, October 1945.
BELOW, COLONEL NIKOLAUS VON. 'Der 20. Juli 1944.' *Echo der Woche*, July 15, 1949.
BESSON, WALDEMAR. Zur Geschichte des Nationalsozialistischen Führungsoffiziers (NSFO). *Vierteljahrshefte für Zeitgeschichte*, January 1961.
BOINEBURG-LANGSFELD, LIEUT.-GENERAL HANS VON (interview by Karl Reichert). 'Der 20. Juli in Paris.' *Frankfurter Rundschau*, July 20, 1948.
BRÜNING, HEINRICH. 'Ein Brief.' *Deutsche Rundschau*, July 1947.
CARSTEN, F. L. 'The Reichswehr and the Red Army.' *Survey*, October 1962.
CASTELLAN, G. 'Von Schleicher, von Papen et l'avènement de Hitler.' *Cahiers d'histoire de la guerre*, January 1949.
CRAIG, GORDON. 'Reichswehr and National Socialism ; the Policy of Wilhelm Gröner.' *Political Science Quarterly*, June 1948.
'Briefe Schleichers an Gröner.' *Die Welt als Geschichte*, November 1951. Heft 2.
'Die Tragödie General Rommels.' *Schwarzwälder Post*, October 22, 25, 27, and 29, 1948.
DEIST, WILHELM. 'Schleicher und die deutsche Abrustungspolitik im Juni/Juli 1932.' *Vierteljahrshefte für Zeitgeschichte*, April 1959.
DEUERLEIN, ERNST. 'Hitlers Eintritt in die Politik und die Reichswehr.' *Vierteljahrshefte für Zeitgeschichte*, April 1959.
EPSTEIN, JULIUS. 'Der Seeckt-Plan.' *Der Monat*, November 1948.
FORD, FRANKLIN L. 'The 20th of July in the History of German Resistance.' *American Historical Review*, July 1946.
GATZKE, HANS W. 'The Stresemann Papers.' *Journal of Modern History*, March 1954.
GERSTENMAIER, EUGEN. 'Zur Geschichte des Umsturzversuchs vom 20. Juli 1944.' *Neue Zürcher Zeitung*, June 23/24, 1945.
Goerdeler's Letter to Olbricht of May 17, 1943. *Die Wandlung*, 1945/46. Heft 2.
Goerdeler's Letter to von Kluge, July 25, 1943. *Die Wandlung*, 1945/46. Heft 5.
GÖRLITZ, WALTER. 'Die deutsche Militäropposition, 1939–1945.' *Frankfurter Hefte*, March 1949.
'Wallensteins Lager, 1920–1938.' *Frankfurter Hefte*, May 1948.
Gröner's Memorandum of November 1928. *Review of Reviews*, January 15, 1929.
HALE, ORON JAMES. 'Adolf Hitler as Feldherr.' *Virginia Quarterly Review*, Spring 1948.
'The Führer and the Field-Marshal.' *Virginia Quarterly Review*, Autumn 1950.
HALLGARTEN, GEORGE W. F. 'General Hans von Seeckt and Russia— 1920–1922.' *Journal of Modern History*, March 1949.
HAMMERSTEIN, FREIHERR LUDWIG VON. 'Die Gegenseite.' *Die Welt*, July 19, 1947.

HEYDE, COLONEL BODO VON DER. 'Beteiligte sagen aus . . .' *Die Welt*, July 31, 1947.

HUSEN, Dr. PAULUS VON. 'The 20th of July and the German Catholics.' *Dublin Review*, July 1946.

HUSS, PIERRE. 'The Plot against Hitler.' *Cosmopolitan Magazine*, July 1946.

KAISER, LUDWIG. 'Tagebuch.' *Die Wandlung*, 1945–1946. Heft 6.

KRAUSNICK, HELMUT. 'Aus den Personalakten von Canaris.' *Vierteljahrshefte für Zeitgeschichte*, July 1962.

'Der 30. Juni 1934.' *Aus Politik und Zeitgeschichte. Beilage zur Wochenzeitung 'Das Parlament'*, June 1954.

'Erwin Rommel und der deutsche Widerstand.' *Vierteljahrshefte für Zeitgeschichte*, January 1953.

KEMPNER, ROBERT M. W. 'Blueprint of the Nazi Underground — Past and Future Subversive Activities.' *Research Studies of the State College of Washington*. (Pullman, Washington.) June 1945.

KIESEL, GEORG. 'SS-Bericht.' *Nordwestdeutsches Heft*, 1/2, 1947.

KOCHAN, LIONEL. 'The Russian Road to Rapallo.' *Soviet Studies*, October 1950.

LUCKAU, ALMA. 'Kapp-putsch — Success or Failure ?' *Journal of Central European Affairs*, January 1948.

PARET, PETER. 'An Aftermath of the Plot against Hitler. The Lehrterstrasse Prison in Berlin, 1944–45. *Bulletin of the Institute for Historical Research*, May 1959.

PHELPS, REGINALD H. 'Aus den Gröner-Dokumenten.' *Deutsche Rundschau*. July 1950–January 1951.

'Aus den Seeckt-Dokumenten.' *Deutsche Rundschau*, September 1952 et seq.

PREISSEISEN, ERNST L. 'Prelude to Barbarossa. Germany and the Balkans, 1940–1941.' *Journal of Modern History*, December 1960.

PRUSSIA, PRINCE LOUIS-FERDINAND OF. 'Neue Aspekte zum 20. Juli, 1944.' *Der Tagesspiegel*, May 1, 1947.

'Generäle ohne Entschlusskraft.' *Westdeutsches Tageblatt*, May 7, 1947.

REITLINGER, GERALD. 'The Truth about Hitler's "Commissar Order".' *Commentary*, July 1959.

RITTER, GERHARD. 'Goerdelers Verfassungspläne.' *Nordwestdeutsches Heft*, 1, December 1946.

'The German Opposition to Hitler.' *Contemporary Review*, June 1950.

ROSENBERGER, HEINRICH. 'Die Entlassung des Generalobersten Freiherrn von Fritsch.' *Deutsche Rundschau*, November 1946.

ROTHFELS, HANS. 'Zerrspiegel des 20. Juli.' *Vierteljahrshefte für Zeitgeschichte*, January 1962.

RUGE, VICE-ADMIRAL FRIEDRICH. 'Rommel and the Invasion of Normandy.' *An Cosantóir* (Dublin), May 1950.

SCHÜTZINGER, HERMANN. 'Die "Machtergreifung".' *Deutsche Rundschau*, February 1947.

SCHWEPPENBURG, GENERAL FREIHERR GEYR VON. 'Invasion without Laurels.' *An Cosantóir* (Dublin), December 1949 and January 1950.

SPEIDEL, HELM. 'Reichswehr und Rote Armee.' *Vierteljahrshefte für Zeitgeschichte*, January 1953.

SWING, RAYMOND GRAM. 'Unconditional Surrender.' *Atlantic Monthly*, September 1947.

TEUCHERT, FRIEDRICH VON. 'Tragisches Versagen in Paris.' *Die Welt*, July 19, 1947.

'Die Verschwörung vom 20. Juli 1944 in Paris.' *Neue Zürcher Zeitung*, November 13, 1946.

THOMAS, GENERAL GEORG. 'Gedanken und Ereignisse.' *Schweizerische Monatshefte*. December 1945.

THEIMER, WALTHER. 'The Bomb in the Brief Case.' *Harper's Magazine*. October 1946.

TREVIRANUS, G. R. 'Brüning geht.' *Deutsche Rundschau*, September 1962.

TREVOR-ROPER, HUGH. 'Admiral Canaris.' *The Cornhill Magazine*. Summer 1950.

'The German Opposition 1937–1944.' *Polemic*, No. 8.

VYVYAN, MICHAL. 'The German "Opposition" and Nazi Morale.' *The Cambridge Journal*, December 1948.

WHEELER-BENNETT, JOHN W. 'Ludendorff : the Soldier and the Politician.' *Virginia Quarterly Review*, Spring 1938.

Das Parlament (Bonn). Special issue, July 20, 1952.

INDEX

Aachen, 104, 352

Abetz, Otto (1903–   ), 664 & n., 670

Abmachungen, 128, 129-30, 132

Abwehr, SS microphones in offices of, 341 ; Oster and, 374, 389, 406 ; and war in 1938, 406 ; Canaris head of, 431 ; and postponement orders for Operation White, 451 ; contacts with Britain, 467 ; Schellenberg and, 478 n. ; included in ban on chemical supplies, 482 ; Müller and, 490 ; professional jealousy between RSHA and, 565 & n. ; Himmler and, 565 ; and Langbehn's message, 578 ; break-up of conspiracy in, 580 ; and supply of fuses, 589 & n. ; agents in Istanbul, 595-6 ; dissolution of, 596-8 ; its inefficiency, 597

Adam, General Wilhelm, appointed head of *Truppenamt*, 224 ; and v. Schleicher, 265, 266 ; replaced by Beck, 298, 392 ; and v. Blomberg, 366 ; realizes division of loyalties, 395 ; and Siegfried Line, 403 ; his views quoted to Hitler, 403 ; removed from active command, 427

Adenauer, Dr. Konrad (1876–   ), 40, 551 n.

Africa, Allied campaigns in, 530, 558, 695 ; continued defeats of Germans in, 564, 570, 600, 614 ; *Abwehr* surprised by Allied landings in, 597

Alamein, Battle of El (1942), 603

Albert I, King of the Belgians (1875–1934), 230

Albrecht, Professor, 508 n.

Alexander I, Tsar of Russia (1777–1825), 7 n., 95

Alexander, King of Jugoslavia (1888–1934), 481 n.

Allemann, Fritz René, vii

Allied Control Council, xiv, 71-2, 144 & n., 145, 185-6, 187

Allies, insist on overthrow of Hitler, before giving promises, 553 ; Church leaders appeal to, for terms in return for undertakings, 554-5 ; suggestion for appeal from, for overthrow of Nazis, 555-6 ; unlikely to give favourable response to conspirators' queries, 557, 558 ; and unconditional surrender, 689, 692, 698

Altona riots, 251, 253

Alvensleben, Freiherr Werner von, 283, 284, 316

Anglo-German Naval Agreement (1935), 347

Anglo-Polish Treaty of Mutual Assistance (1939), 447, 450, 451 n.

Anschluss (1938), 165, 272 n., 375-7, 393

Anti-Comintern Pact (1936), 354, 611

Appeasement, British policy of, 353-4, 441, 489 n.

Arbeits-Kommandos (Black *Reichswehr*), formation of, 92 ; their exploits gain publicity in the Press, 93 ; v. Bock and, 93, 515 ; Gessler and, 94, 194 ; military leaders and, 94-5 ; sources on, 95 n. ; and the abortive *Putsch* of Sept. 1923, 111-12 ; dissolved, 112 ; v. Schleicher and, 152, 184 ; the *Reichswehr* budget and, 187 ; mentioned, 227 n., 515

Arco-Vally, Count, 157

Armistice Negotiations (1918), 23 & n., 27 & n., 45, 52-3, 121

Army, German :

Bundeswehr, vii and viii

Under Imperial Régime : General Staff declared dissolved, xiii ; abdication of Wilhelm II end of an epoch for, 3 ; position of, under Wilhelm II, 9, 11 ; General Staff system in 1914, 11-12, 12 n. ; General Staff rules Germany, 14, 456 ; v. Hindenburg and effort to make, saviour of country, 15-16 ; growing weariness of, 17 ; Gröner and, 22 ; lacks Commander-in-Chief, 22 ; and the revolution, 22-3 ; and armistice negotiations, 23-5, 26-7, 27 n.

Under Weimar Republic : responsibility of, for bringing Hitler to power, xvi ; and collaboration with Ebert, 25, 29-30 ; Supreme Command of, and revolutionary situation, 26 ; and the retreat into Germany, 27-8 ; Soviet Congress and, 32 ; Supreme Command becomes weakened, 33 ; fall in morale, 33 ; Supreme Commander's bluff succeeds, 33-4 ; the Socialists and the General Staff, 35 ; reorganized on a unified basis,

THE END

PRINTED OFFSET LITHO IN GREAT BRITAIN
BY R. & R. CLARK, LTD., EDINBURGH